To my wife and best friend, Veena, with love.

"A prudent wife is from the LORD."

PROVERBS 19:14

"Husbands, love your wives, even as Christ also loved the church, and gave himself for it."

EPHESIANS 5:35

Brief Contents

Contents

Foreword

Basic Marketing Research: A Decision-Making Approach, third edition, is yet another outstanding text book from Dr. Naresh K. Malhotra, a very well-known and highly successful author, researcher, and teacher. Dr. Malhotra's highly successful previous text, *Marketing Research: An Applied Orientation,* has been translated into Chinese, Spanish, Portuguese, French, Russian, Hungarian, Indonesian, and Japanese and published in several English editions including North American, International, European, Indian, and Australian editions. This text will likely follow suit.

Basic Marketing Research: A Decision-Making Approach, third edition, carries Dr. Malhotra's skills and expertise in marketing research to the next level. With its focus on contemporary issues such as international marketing research, the newer technologies, and practical ethics, the book effectively captures the current environment. The application of Web-based marketing research is integrated in a pervasive way throughout the book. That's state-of-the-art.

The book is rich in real-world examples that bring the student closer to the business world and everyday realities of the marketplace. The opening vignettes, interwoven throughout the respective chapters, further illustrate the marketing research concepts in real-life settings. The Experiential Learning exercises provide a rich hands-on experience. The research-in-action examples, case studies, and video case studies are great learning tools and further reinforce the highly applied and managerial orientation of the text. Particularly noteworthy are the additions of comprehensive critical thinking cases and several other cases that include actual questionnaires and the resulting data. There are many diagrams, figures and concept maps in each chapter that truly enhance learning. The lessons are conceptually sound, technically accurate, and communicate basic research concepts with simplicity and clarity. The book is strong in qualitative concepts and imparts the necessary quantitative knowledge and skills, with the use of SPSS, Excel, and other statistical software. The SPSS and Excel demonstration movies, screen captures, step-by-step instructions, and Study Guide and Technology Manual provide the greatest resources available anywhere for students to learn these programs.

Basic Marketing Research: A Decision-Making Approach, third edition, provides a strong foundation that I believe every student should have. This book is unsurpassed as a basis for students to become researchers and intelligent users of marketing research.

William D. Neal

Senior Partner

SDR Consulting

Preface

The Third Edition—Helping You Learn Marketing Research

Marketing research is an integral part of marketing. The task of marketing research is to assess the information needs and provide management with relevant, accurate, reliable, valid, and current information to aid marketing decision making (see Figure 1.5). Companies use marketing research to stay competitive and avoid the high costs associated with making poor decisions based on unsound information. If you are a marketing major, understanding the various customer groups (consumers, suppliers, channel partners, employees, and so on), competitors, and the environment is the foundation for developing effective marketing programs. Such an understanding is gained by conducting marketing research. This course will help you succeed in your marketing career.

If you are not a marketing major, consider all of the marketing research around you in the form of information available on the Internet, newspapers, magazines, government, commercial firms, and other sources. Any company or organization you work for will use such information for making decisions. It is important to understand how such information is generated and how it should be evaluated to assess its relevance, accuracy, and usefulness. The research process that we describe in this book is very general and can be applied to conduct research in any area of management, not just marketing. Only the context in which we illustrate the research is marketing. Therefore, this course and this book will help you to be more effective in your job, regardless of the specific area in which you work. This knowledge will also provide you with a better understanding of those involved in marketing in the organization where you will work, and it will equip you with better information to function as a consumer.

Since research is best learned by doing, this book emphasizes a hands-on, do-it-yourself approach. We created *Basic Marketing Research: A Decision-Making Approach,* in part, to help students understand and learn the importance of sound information to make marketing decisions and to see the interaction between marketing research and marketing management decisions. We provide you with several opportunities to experience these interactions through pedagogical tools such as the Opening Vignette, Be an MR!, Be a DM!, Experiential Learning, What Would *You* Do?, Research in Action, cases, video cases, and extensive review questions, applied problems, and group discussions. The data analysis chapters involve a tight integration of SPSS and Excel, illustrating each step in running these programs in detail. We provide four distinct ways in which you can learn these programs on your own. SPSS and Excel files are provided for all datasets, and outputs and screen captures are posted on the Web site (www.pearsonhighered.com/malhotra). This book provides the most extensive help available to marketing research students in learning SPSS and Excel.

We prepared this textbook and all of the additional materials in a way that will best help you to understand the fundamental principles of marketing research and their applications in real-life marketing situations. Students need opportunities to apply concepts to real-life situations. This application helps you clearly understand and retain the ideas. As a result, we have prepared a variety of end-of-chapter materials that are designed to help you practice using the concepts. These materials include review questions, applied problems, group discussion, cases, and video cases. The data analysis chapters include several datasets where the files have been provided in both SPSS and Excel.

Integrated Learning Package

We have created several devices that are designed to help you learn the materials in this text. If you take advantage of them, you might find this textbook interesting and even fun. Even those who are not marketing majors may discover marketing research and all of the involved activities are enjoyable subjects to talk about and study.

- **Opening Vignettes.** Each chapter begins with a vignette related to the presented topic. The majority of the vignettes revolve around success stories about companies and products most of you will recognize, such as Reebok, Gillette, P&G, Olympics, Sears, Spiegel, and United Airlines. The opening vignette is used as a running example throughout the chapter. After discussing the main concepts in each chapter, we revert to the Opening Vignette to summarize and illustrate the concepts in a section entitled Summary Illustration Using the Opening Vignette.

- **Stimulating Critical Thinking.** The principles for critical thinking, including Socratic questioning, critical reading and writing, and higher order thinking and assessment, have been embodied in the three comprehensive critical thinking cases, end-of-chapter review questions, applied problems, and group discussions. These materials have been designed based on the guidelines provided by the Foundation for Critical Thinking.

- **Interrelationships among Concepts.** Substantial research shows that concept maps aid in learning. One or more concept maps appear in each chapter to illustrate the interrelationships among concepts. These maps have been developed based on the principles and tools provided by the Institute for Human and Machine Cognition. These maps will help you acquire a better understanding of the various concepts. Please be sure to review them!

- **Real-Life Examples and Illustrations.** Several real-life examples, called Research in Action, are presented in each chapter. These examples describe in detail the kind of marketing research used to address specific managerial problems and the decisions that were based on the findings. Where appropriate, the sources cited have been supplemented by additional marketing research information to enhance the usefulness of these examples. In addition, there are several other examples and illustrations that are blended in the text.

- **Cases and Video Cases.** Each chapter of the book contains the Hewlett-Packard running case and a video case. Toward the end of the book, there are comprehensive cases with actual questionnaires and real-life data. The video cases have been drawn from the Prentice Hall video library and have been written from a marketing research perspective. The questions at the end of each video case are all marketing research questions. The cases and video cases relevant to each chapter have been identified toward the end of that chapter.

- **Extensive and Pervasive Internet Coverage.** The Internet has become a part of our lives. The text discusses how the Internet can be integrated in each step of the marketing research process and how it can be used to implement the concepts discussed in each chapter. The coverage of the Internet is so extensive and pervasive that it has not been singled out. Internet applications are everywhere. For example, all of the Be an MR! exercises require you to do Internet research.

- **International Focus.** Many of you have travelled to other countries. Most of you interact with students from other countries. Global/international business is all around, which makes understanding international marketing research issues important. Every chapter, except data analysis in Chapters 16, 17, and 18, has a section entitled International Marketing Research. This section discusses how the concepts of that chapter should be implemented while conducting marketing research in an international setting. Note that data analysis in international marketing research is discussed in Chapter 15.

- **Ethics Focus.** Ethical issues are pervasive in marketing research. Every chapter, except data analysis in Chapters 16, 17, and 18, has a section entitled Ethics in

Marketing Research. This section presents the salient ethical issues involved while implementing the concepts of that chapter. These ethical issues are discussed from the perspectives of the four stakeholders: the client, the marketing research firm, respondents, and the general public. Note that the ethical issues pertinent to data analysis are discussed in Chapter 15.

■ **Focus on Technology.** You may or may not be a technology buff, but you do make use of technology on a daily basis. Technological developments have shaped the way in which marketing research is conducted. Every chapter, except data analysis in Chapters 16, 17, and 18, has a section entitled Technology and Marketing Research. This section covers the role and impact of technology in implementing the concepts of that chapter while conducting marketing research. In the data analysis chapters, this section is replaced with one entitled Software Applications.

■ **Contemporary Focus.** A contemporary focus has been achieved by illustrating the applications of marketing research to current topics such as customer value, satisfaction, loyalty, customer equity, brand equity and management, innovation, entrepreneurship, return on marketing, relationship marketing, and socially responsible marketing throughout the text. These examples cover a diversity of products and companies that will interest undergraduate students.

■ **Opening Diagrams.** Each chapter, except Chapter 1, opens with a diagram that gives the focus of that chapter, its relationship to the previous chapter(s), and its relationship to the marketing research process. This diagram is an excellent way to see the linkages between chapters and to trace the entire marketing research process throughout the book. We also include a diagram that provides an overview of the chapter, showing the major topics, and linking them to figures and tables. There is also an abundance of other diagrams in each chapter.

■ **SPSS, Excel, SAS, and Minitab.** Data analysis procedures are illustrated with respect to SPSS, Excel, SAS, and Minitab, along with other popular computer programs. However, the emphasis is on SPSS and Excel. Detailed, step-by-step instructions are given for running the various statistical procedures using SPSS and Excel. SPSS and Excel files are provided for all datasets, and outputs are provided for the analyses contained in the chapters.

■ **Conducting a Live Marketing Research Project.** Toward the end of each chapter is a section entitled Live Research: Conducting a Marketing Research Project. These sections show how to implement one or more live marketing research projects in the course. The approach is flexible and can handle a variety of organizations and formats. The entire class could be working on the same project, with each team working on all aspects of the project, or each team could be assigned a specific responsibility (for example, a specific component of the problem or a specific aspect of the project like collection and analysis of secondary data). Alternatively, the class could be working on multiple projects with specific teams assigned to a specific project. If your course includes a class project, your instructor will choose the approach that is best for you!

■ **Acronyms.** Each chapter contains one or more helpful acronyms that summarize the important concepts. Acronyms are the most popular mnemonic technique used by undergraduate students. Theoretical and empirical evidence supporting the effectiveness of mnemonic techniques and their usefulness as a pedagogical tool has been discussed in a paper I published in the *Journal of the Academy of Marketing Science,* (Spring 1991: 141–150).

You Can Learn SPSS and Excel on Your Own!

Many students complain that they spend a substantial amount of time learning SPSS or Excel. We have addressed this situation. The Third Edition provides four ways in which you can learn SPSS and Excel on your own:

1. Detailed step-by-step instructions are given in the chapter.
2. You can download computerized demonstration movies illustrating these step-by-step instructions from www.pearsonhighered.com/malhotra.

3. You can download screen captures with notes illustrating these step-by-step instructions from www.pearsonhighered.com/malhotra.
4. Extensive instructions for SPSS and Excel are given in the Study Guide and Technology Manual, a supplement that accompanies this book.

Thus, we provide the most extensive help available anywhere to learn SPSS and Excel!

Tips on How to Use This Textbook

We want to offer you a few tips on how to use this book and some suggestions on how to master the material:

- **Read the Chapter.** Start by reading the chapter. Be sure to look at the opening questions and diagrams and read the overview so you will know what is in the chapter. Often this is skipped because students don't believe it is important.
- **Review the Key Terms.** It is important to read through these new terms to be sure you understand each one. Key terms are often targets of quiz and exam questions.
- **Answer the Review Questions.** Go through the review questions and see if you can answer them without looking in the chapter. When you are finished, go back and check to see if you got each one correct. For the ones you couldn't answer, go back and locate the correct information in the chapter.
- **Do the Applied Problems.** Pick several problems you believe would be interesting. Spend some time thinking about the question and the concepts being explored. You can make these problems fun to do as you analyze the concepts at a deeper level.
- **Pick One of the Cases or Video Cases.** The cases and video cases provide an excellent summary of the material presented in the chapter. Read the case or the video case and answer each of the questions at the end. Note that all the video cases have been written in a stand-alone format so you do not need to see the video to answer the case questions.
- **Have Some Fun with Critical Thinking.** Go to one of the critical thinking cases 2.1 American Idol, 2.2 Baskin-Robbins, or 2.3 Akron Children's Hospital. These cases are comprehensive and contain questions on all the chapters except the data analysis chapters. Based on the knowledge you have learned in the chapter and the case information, answer the critical thinking questions as well as the technical questions. Doing these cases will help you understand and apply the concepts in real-life situations from a critical thinking perspective.

Suggestions for Preparing for Exams

If you have followed the tips provided in the previous section, you will almost be ready for the exam. A brief review of the key terms and a scan of the chapter will be all that you need. But if you have not followed all of the tips, here is a sequence of activities you can follow that will aid in learning the material.

- Read the chapter.
- Review the concept maps.
- Review the key terms.
- Answer the review questions.
- Read the chapter overview.
- Read the chapter summary.
- Go through the chapter and locate all of the bold and italic words. Read the context for all the terms to make sure you understand them.
- Start at the beginning of the chapter and read the topic sentence—the first sentence—of each paragraph. These sentences should provide a good summary.
- Re-read the chapter summary.
- Re-review the key terms.

Congratulations! You are now ready for the exam. Relax, you will do well.

Student Supplements and Value Packs

A set of supplements can enhance your learning.

1. **A functional and useful Web site.** The book is supported by a student Web site that can be accessed at www.pearsonhighered.com/malhotra. This site contains useful materials that you can download, including:

   - Data for cases 1.1 Hewlett-Packard, 3.1 Bank of America, 3.2 McDonald's, and 3.3 Boeing, given in the book (SPSS and Excel)
   - Files for all the Experiential Learning exercises
   - Data files for all the Applied Problems (SPSS and Excel)
   - Data file for the dataset(s) used in each data analysis chapter (SPSS and Excel)
   - SPSS and Excel Computerized Demonstration Movies
   - SPSS and Excel screen captures
   - Additional materials that supplement the topic discussed in the book

2. **Student version of SPSS.** A student version of SPSS can be obtained as an optional value package with this book.

3. **Study Guide and Technology Manual.** This supplement will help deepen your learning and is available in print format.

Acknowledgments

Several people have been extremely helpful in writing this textbook. I would like to acknowledge Professor Arun K. Jain (State University of New York at Buffalo) who taught me marketing research in a way I will never forget. My students, especially former doctoral students, as well as several MBA research assistants, have been helpful in many ways. The students in my marketing research courses have provided useful feedback, as the material was class-tested for several years. William D. Neal, founder and senior executive officer of SDR Consulting, Incorporated, and Ken Athaide, Senior Vice President, Market Strategies International, have been very helpful and supportive over the years.

The reviewers have provided many constructive and valuable suggestions. Among others, the help of the following reviewers is gratefully acknowledged.

Reviewers for the First Edition

Dennis B. Arnett, University of Texas at San Antonio

Jerry Katrichis, University of Hartford

Paul L. Sauer, Canisius College

Alan G. Sawyer, University of Florida

Reviewers for the Second Edition

Ronald E. Goldsmith, Florida State University

Manish Kacker, Tulane University

John S. Kakalik, Western Connecticut State University

Alyse Lancaster, University of Miami

Tom Schmidt, Simpson College

Larry Seibert, University of Central Oklahoma

Donald E. Stem, Jr., Washington State University

R. Greg Surovick, Lehigh University

The team at Prentice Hall provided outstanding support. Special thanks are due to Sally Yagan, editorial director; Ashley Santora, product development manager; Anne Fahlgren, senior marketing manager; Kelly Warsak, production editor; Karin Williams, editorial assistant; and Teri Stratford, photo researcher. Special recognition is due to the several field representatives and sales people who have done an outstanding job.

I want to acknowledge, with great respect, my parents, the late Mr. H. N. Malhotra and Mrs. S. Malhotra. Their love, encouragement, support, and the sacrificial giving of themselves have been exemplary. My heartfelt love and gratitude go to my wife Veena, and my children Ruth and Paul, for their faith, hope, and love.

Most of all, I want to acknowledge and thank my Savior and Lord, Jesus Christ, for the abundant grace and favor He has bestowed upon me. This book is, truly, the result of His favor—"For thou, LORD, wilt bless the righteous; with favor wilt thou compass him as with a shield" (Psalms 5:12). I praise God and give Him all the glory.

Naresh K. Malhotra

About the Author

Dr. Naresh K. Malhotra is Regents' Professor (highest academic rank in the university system of Georgia), in the College of Management, Georgia Institute of Technology. He has been listed in Marquis *Who's Who in America* continuously since its fifty-first edition in 1997, and in *Who's Who in the World* since 2000. In 2005, he received the Academy of Marketing Science's Outstanding Marketing Educator Award.

In an article by Wheatley and Wilson (1987 *AMA Educators Proceedings*), Professor Malhotra was ranked number one in the country based on articles published in the *Journal of Marketing Research* during 1980 through 1985. He also holds the all-time record for the maximum number of publications in the *Journal of Health Care Marketing*. He is ranked number one based on publications in the *Journal of the Academy of Marketing Science* (JAMS) since its inception through Volume 23, 1995. He is also number one based on publications in JAMS during the 10-year period 1986 through 1995. In an editorial by Schlegelmilch (JIM 11(1), 2003), Dr. Malhotra was ranked number one based on publications in the *International Marketing Review* from 1992 to 2002. He is also ranked number one based on publications in the *International Marketing Review* since its inception (1983) to 2003 (Table V, IMR, 22(4) (2005)). He is also ranked number one based on publications in the *International Marketing Review* from 1996 to 2006 based on a study by Xu et al. published in the *Asia Pacific Journal of Management* (25 (2008): 189–207). In a landmark study by West et al. (2008) examining publications in the top four marketing journals (JMR, JM, JAMS, and JCR) over a 25-year period from 1977 to 2002, Professor Malhotra has three top-ten rankings: number three based on publications in all four journals combined; number three based on publications in JMR; and number one based on publications in JAMS.

He has published more than 100 papers in major refereed journals, including the *Journal of Marketing Research, Journal of Consumer Research, Marketing Science, Management Science, Journal of Marketing, Journal of Academy of Marketing Science, Journal of Retailing, Journal of Health Care Marketing*, and leading journals in statistics, management science, and psychology. He has received seven best-paper awards for articles published in the *Journal of Marketing Research, Journal of Retailing, Journal of the Academy of Marketing Science, International Marketing Review* (twice), *Journal of International Marketing*, and *Journal of Consumer Research* (finalist), and additional awards for best papers presented in national and international conferences.

He was chairperson of the Academy of Marketing Science Foundation, 1996 to 1998; was president of the Academy of Marketing Science, 1994 to 1996; and chairperson of the Board of Governors, 1990 to 1992. He is a distinguished fellow of the Academy and a fellow of the Decision Sciences Institute. He is the founding editor of the *Review of Marketing Research*. He has served as an associate editor of *Decision Sciences* for 18 years and has served as section editor of "Health Care Marketing Abstracts," *Journal of Health Care Marketing*. He serves or has served on the editorial boards of several journals including the *Journal of Marketing Research, Journal of Consumer Research, Journal of Marketing,* and the *Journal of the Academy of Marketing Science*.

His book entitled *Marketing Research: An Applied Orientation*, fifth edition, was published by Prentice Hall in 2007. This book has been translated into Chinese, Spanish, Portuguese, Russian, French, Hungarian, Indonesian, and Japanese. In addition to these eight translations, this book also has several English-language editions, including North

American, International, European, Indian, and Australian. The book has received widespread adoption at both the graduate and undergraduate levels, with more than 144 schools using it in the United States. His book, *Basic Marketing Research: Application to Contemporary Issues,* was first published by Prentice Hall in 2002. He is also the author of *Fundamentals of Marketing Research*, six-volume set, published by Sage, United Kingdom in 2007 and has authored other books on marketing and marketing research.

Dr. Malhotra has consulted for business, nonprofit, and government organizations in the United States and abroad, and has served as an expert witness in legal and regulatory proceedings. He has special expertise in data analysis and statistical methods. He is the winner of numerous awards and honors for research, teaching, and service to the profession, including the Academy of Marketing Science, Outstanding Marketing Teaching Excellence Award, 2003.

Dr. Malhotra is a member and deacon of First Baptist Church, Atlanta, Georgia, and is a Bible preacher and Sunday School teacher. He lives in the Atlanta area with his wife, Veena, and children, Ruth and Paul.

Company/Product Index

1

Introduction and Early Phases of Marketing Research

CHAPTER one

Introduction to Marketing Research

OPENING QUESTIONS

1. How is marketing research defined, and what are the major classifications of marketing research?
2. What are the six steps in the marketing research process?
3. What role does marketing research play in designing and implementing successful marketing programs?
4. What considerations guide the decision to conduct marketing research?
5. What is the marketing research industry, and how should a firm select a marketing research supplier?
6. What careers are available in marketing research, and what skills do you need to succeed in them?
7. How is marketing research relevant to decision support systems?
8. Why is international marketing research more complex than domestic marketing research?
9. How can technology improve marketing research?
10. What are the ethical aspects of marketing research? What responsibilities do the marketing research stakeholders have to themselves, each other, and the research project?

How Reebok Fits Shoes

"As a user of marketing research, I gain so much from a well-crafted research project. You can implement marketing programs so much more vigorously when you are confident you understand what is currently important to the customer."

Justin Stead,
VP International, Fossil, Inc.,
USA.

U.S.-based Reebok, which was acquired by the German sports lifestyle company adidas AG in 2006, designs, markets, and distributes sportswear and athletic footwear and equipment. In order to provide "complete comfort" for athletes and consumers, Reebok invests a lot of effort into its marketing research. Although the slogan belongs to Nike, when it comes to marketing research, Reebok just does it!

Reebok uses "time-use" research to determine how consumers spend their spare time. This type of information enables Reebok to identify opportunities for new products and markets and then design its marketing program to take advantage of them, as illustrated by the recently introduced line of custom-designed Ventilator shoes. The company uses a variety of methods to research time-use trends, including analysis of secondary data (data collected for other purposes, e.g., data available from publications, the Internet, and commercial sources). It also uses qualitative research, such as focus groups (interviews with 8 to 12 people as a group); survey research via telephone, in the malls, and on the Internet; and interviews at consumers' homes.

Management wanted to identify ways that Reebok could increase its market share. Analysis of secondary data showed that health club memberships in the United States had increased more than 10 percent in the early 2000s. Focus groups indicated that a new popular fitness activity was step aerobics (standard aerobics made more intense by the addition of a 3- to 7-inch platform, the "step"). Reebok then conducted a survey to determine the market potential of step aerobics and found that health club members were spending less time in the clubs by an average of 12 percent. The research also showed that the percentage of adults who exercised in the home had grown from 20 percent in 1990 to more than 30 percent in 2006. In response to these results, several research questions were framed around exercising at home.

Based on the results of this research, Reebok designed a home-step aerobics line, including home steps, videotapes, aerobic shoes, and body weights. Product research indicated a strong consumer preference for the home-step aerobics line, and the line was launched nationally. The home-step aerobics line has been very successful, and the popularity of these products has resulted in a Reebok step-workout program on the U.S. all-sports network ESPN.

Reebok's in-house marketing research specialists were actively involved in defining and designing the research. However, Reebok contracted data collection and data analysis to external suppliers, who collected and analyzed the data using appropriate statistical techniques. External suppliers can also be used in writing the report, but presentation of the results to the management and assistance in implementation is the responsibility of Reebok's in-house marketing research department. Reebok makes use of full-service suppliers who provide assistance in all the steps of the marketing research process, as well as limited-service suppliers who might handle only one or a few steps of the process. Its in-house marketing research department has helped Reebok introduce many successful products and enabled it to become a premier sportswear and athletic footwear company.[1]

Overview

Marketing research is one of the most important and fascinating aspects of marketing. As the opening vignette illustrates, marketing research provides a company with valuable information that guides all of its marketing activities. In this chapter, we define and describe the two broad forms of marketing research: (1) research designed to identify problems and (2) research designed to solve problems. We explain the six steps of the marketing research process and take a look at how marketing research fits into the entire marketing decision process. The marketing research industry consists of a variety of firms, and the field offers exciting career opportunities. We conclude by describing the contribution of marketing research to marketing information systems (MIS) and decision support systems (DSS).

Information on the use of the Internet in marketing research is interwoven into each chapter. Throughout this book, we also discuss applications to contemporary issues of importance in the current marketing and marketing research environment: international marketing research, technology, and ethics. This first chapter provides an introduction to these important application areas; an overview is presented in Figure 1.1. As can be seen in Figure 1.1, the opening vignette and Application to Contemporary Issues encompass all of the topics discussed in each chapter. We encourage a hands-on approach through the use of "Be an MR!" (Be a Marketing Researcher!) and "Be a DM!" (Be a Decision Maker!) boxes found in each chapter. These hands-on exercises use the Internet and other electronic sources to focus on the interaction between marketing research and marketing decision making. To further highlight this interaction, sometimes the "Be an MR!" box appears first, whereas at other times "Be a DM!" appears first. The research–decision-making interaction also is emphasized in each chapter by the "What Would *You* Do?" situation facing a real company. The situation is described and opportunities are provided to address the marketing research and the marketing management decisions facing the company. This hands-on orientation is further reinforced through the "Experiential Learning" exercises. Thus, we provide a better overall understanding of the key concepts and illustrate how applications can be made in other important areas that are discussed throughout the book.

Definition of Marketing Research

In this book, we emphasize the importance of research in marketing decision making. **Marketing research** is the systematic and objective identification, collection, analysis, dissemination, and use of information that is undertaken to improve decision making related to identifying and solving problems (also known as opportunities) in marketing.

This definition gives marketing research a broad scope, and several aspects of the field are noteworthy. Marketing research involves the identification, collection, analysis, and dissemination of information (Figure 1.2). Each phase of this process is important. Marketing research begins with the identification or definition of the research problem or opportunity. *Problems* often lead to *opportunities* in business, so from a research perspective, the two words often are used interchangeably. An investigation of each follows the same research process. For example, the discovery that U.S. adults were spending less time in health clubs and more time exercising at home represented a problem as well as an opportunity for Reebok. The problem was that when people were spending less time in health clubs, they also were using athletic shoes and equipment to a lesser extent, which resulted in decreased demand. The opportunity was more time spent exercising at home, which represented greater potential for shoes and home exercise equipment.

The range of data collection methods and the sources used to obtain the data vary in sophistication and complexity. The methods used depend on the specific requirements of the project, including budget and time constraints. The data are then analyzed, and the results are formally presented to the client and used in decision making.

Marketing research is systematic, which means that it follows a predictable path. A marketing research project is planned and documented. It has a scientific basis in that data are collected and analyzed to draw conclusions. The time-use research reported in the

marketing research
The systematic and objective identification, collection, analysis, dissemination, and use of information that is undertaken to improve decision making related to identifying and solving problems (also known as *opportunities*) in marketing.

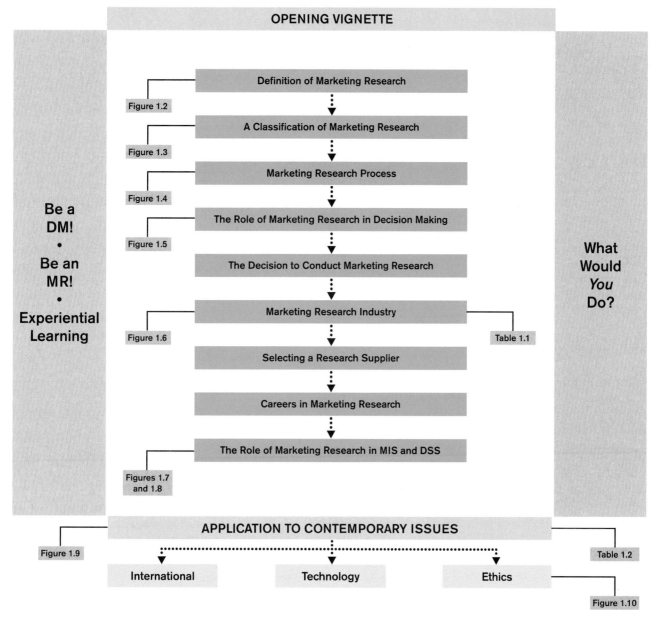

FIGURE 1.1

Introduction to Marketing Research: An Overview

Reebok vignette is an example of this. Marketing research obtains its value from its objectivity. It should be conducted impartially, free from the influence of personal or political biases. This is easier said than done, because companies sponsoring the research sometimes pressure the researcher or research firm to generate "support" for a certain desired outcome. However, bending to this sort of pressure is a breach of the ethical codes of conduct that guide the profession. The notion that it provides an unbiased "outside," or objective, opinion, gives marketing research its value. Without that objectivity, results cannot be trusted, and the entire discipline is undermined.

The Internet is fast becoming a useful tool in the identification, collection, analysis, and dissemination of information related to marketing research. Based in the United States, the Interactive Marketing Research Organization (www.imro.org), which was formed in 2000, is a worldwide association of researchers dedicated to providing an open forum for the discussion of best practices and ethical approaches to research being conducted via the Internet.

FIGURE 1.2

Defining Marketing Research

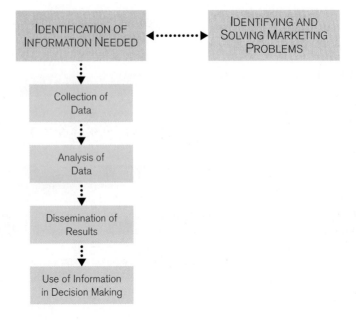

Research in Action

A CEO's View of Marketing Research

What does a time-pressed senior executive expect from in-house marketing researchers? CEO Allen Franklin of Southern Company (www.southerncompany.com), a large U.S. energy provider, offers some valuable insights on this question. Franklin described one manager-researcher exchange of which he was part as follows:

MARKETING RESEARCHER:	"What do you want?"
FRANKLIN (RESPONDING SLOWLY AND FEELING SLIGHTLY EMBARRASSED FOR NOT HAVING A READY ANSWER):	"What do you have?"
MARKETING RESEARCHER:	"I don't have anything, yet. That's why I am here."
FRANKLIN (GROWING INCREASINGLY IRRITATED):	"Well, then get out of here! You are keeping me from what I need to be doing!"

The implication of this exchange is that the researcher needs to understand the current context for decision makers.

Researchers can develop this understanding by scanning the business press, following developing stories, attending conferences within the industry, as well as conducting focused research projects. In short, the researcher needs to be curious and be one of the best learners in the firm. Franklin says it this way: "It is not data that are critical, but the people between the data and the management decision maker. Senior managers will tend to work with those who make the managers more comfortable. Comfort is not increased by 2-hour presentations that leave management saying to itself, 'What are we going to do with that?'"

Here is one way a marketing researcher should approach a senior executive like Allen Franklin:

MARKETING RESEARCHER:	"We know the firm currently has this problem. We can resolve or minimize it by doing this study and acting upon what we learn."

Fortune magazine has named Southern Company the "most admired" electric and gas utility in the United States, in no small part due to its reliance on marketing research.[2]

Be an MR!

Visit Coca-Cola's Web site at www.coca-cola.com and click on the USA button. How does this site collect marketing research information? How would you improve the Web site in order to collect more or better marketing research information?

Be a DM!

As the brand manager for Coca-Cola, how would you use information collected on the Web site to market your brand more effectively?

The next section elaborates on this definition of marketing research by classifying the types of marketing research.

A Classification of Marketing Research

Our definition states that organizations engage in marketing research for two reasons: to identify and to solve marketing problems. This distinction serves as a basis for classifying marketing research into problem-identification research and problem-solving research, as shown in Figure 1.3.

Problem-identification research involves going below the surface to identify the underlying problem that the marketing manager is facing. Often these problems are not readily apparent or they are likely to arise in the future. Problem identification research can be designed to analyze market potential, market share, brand or company image, market characteristics, and sales. It can also be used in short-range forecasting, long-range forecasting, and uncovering business trends. For example, Polo Ralph Lauren (which operates stores in the U.S., Latin America, Europe, and the Asia-Pacific region) might undertake research to determine the size of the market for men's shirts, the projected growth rate of this market, and the market share of major brands. This research might reveal a problem. Say that although Polo's sales of men's shirts have been increasing, they have not been keeping pace with industry growth. Moreover, market research might determine that Polo has been gradually losing market share to competitors, such as Tommy Hilfiger.

Problem identification is the more common of the two forms of research and is undertaken by virtually all marketing firms. This type of research is used to assess the environment and diagnose problems. Information regarding changes in the market provides an initial alert to potential opportunities or problems. A firm that is operating in a growing market but suffering from a declining market share might be dealing with company-specific problems, such as ineffective advertising or high turnover in its sales force. In other instances, problems, such as declining demand, might be common to all the firms in the industry. Considering the economic, social, cultural, or consumer behavior trends can help to identify such problems or opportunities.

Once a problem or opportunity has been identified, a firm undertakes **problem-solving research** to address the problem. Most marketing firms conduct problem-solving research as well. Problem-solving research addresses many topics, including market segmentation and product pricing, promotion, and distribution. Problem-identification

problem-identification research
Research undertaken to help identify problems that are not necessarily apparent or that are likely to arise in the future.

problem-solving research
Research undertaken to help solve specific marketing problems.

FIGURE 1.3

A Classification of Marketing Research

research and problem-solving research go hand in hand, and a given marketing research project can combine both types of research.

Research in Action

The Arch of Marketing Research at the Golden Arches

In the 1960s, McDonald's (www.mcdonalds.com) earned about $170 million in the United States; today, the company earns more than that in 2 days. Marketing research has played a vital role in fostering this growth. In 1968, McDonald's formed its marketing research department, which has grown dramatically since its creation. The most prominent aspect of its operation is that 85 percent of all McDonald's are franchises. McDonald's marketing research department actively supports these restaurants by conducting problem-identification and problem-solving research.

In 2005, problem-identification research in the form of customer satisfaction surveys (market characteristics research) revealed that in-store atmosphere and décor were becoming an increasingly important part of the customers' dining experience, even in fast-food restaurants. Based on subsequent problem-solving (segmentation and product) research, in 2006 McDonald's introduced its "Forever Young" brand by remodeling its restaurants, the first major redesign since the 1970s. This was done to keep the brand relevant and appealing to a younger generation of consumers. The new design includes the traditional McDonald's yellow and red colors, but the red is muted to terra cotta, the yellow is now golden for a more "sunny" look, and olive and sage green have been added. The concept consists of a new building design, as well as interior changes, such as recessed lighting, classical music, and new paint and wall graphics. Re-imaged restaurants attract more customers and enhance perceptions of McDonald's as a place adults, not just kids, enjoy. The company plans to eventually incorporate the new look in all of its 13,700 franchised and company-owned U.S. locations.

As of 2008, the company is the world's leading food service retailer, with more than 31,000 restaurants in 115 countries serving 54 million customers each day. McDonald's success is a direct result of the problem-identification and problem-solving research that it undertakes on an ongoing basis.[3]

Classifying marketing research into two main types is useful from a conceptual as well as a practical viewpoint. The McDonald's example illustrates that these two types of research often go hand in hand. Marketing research discovered that in-store atmosphere and décor were becoming an increasingly important part of the customers' dining experience (problem identification), and the solution was the introduction of the "Forever Young" brand by remodeling restaurants (problem solving). The Reebok vignette also illustrates this point. Problem identification involving analysis of secondary data, focus groups, and a market potential survey revealed that adults were spending less time in health clubs and more time exercising at home. Problem-solving research in the form of product research led to the development and introduction of the successful home-step aerobics line.

Be a DM!

As the marketing director of Major League Baseball (MLB), the governing body of the popular U.S. sport, what marketing strategies would you formulate to target female fans?

Be an MR!

You have been hired by the MLB to devise a marketing strategy for female fans. Visit www.mlb.com and search the Internet, as well as your library's online databases, to obtain information on women's attitudes toward the MLB. What kind of marketing research would you recommend?

Marketing Research Process

The **marketing research process** consists of six steps (Figure 1.4). This process is a general one and can be followed for conducting research in any functional area (e.g., marketing, finance, accounting, and so forth). Each of these steps is discussed in greater detail in subsequent chapters. We will provide only a brief overview here.

Step 1: Defining the Problem

The first step in any marketing research project is to define the problem. Researchers accomplish problem definition through discussions with decision makers, interviews with industry experts, analysis of secondary data, and, perhaps, some qualitative research, such as focus groups. Problem definition involves defining the management-decision problem (what should the management do) and the marketing research problem (what information is needed). In the opening vignette, the management-decision problem was: What should Reebok do to increase its market share? The marketing research problem for Reebok was assessing the market potential for home-step aerobic products. Once the problem has been defined, the research can be designed and conducted properly. (See Chapter 2.)

Step 2: Developing an Approach to the Problem

Developing an approach to the problem includes formulating an analytical framework and models, research questions, and hypotheses. This process is guided by the same tasks performed to define the problem. (See Chapter 2.) In the opening vignette, several research questions were investigated related to exercising at home.

Step 3: Formulating a Research Design

A research design is a framework or blueprint for conducting the marketing research project. It details the procedures needed to obtain the required information. A study might be designed to test hypotheses of interest or to determine possible answers to the research questions, both of which contribute to decision making. Conducting preliminary or exploratory research, defining the variables, and designing appropriate scales to measure them also are part of the research design. The issue of how the data should be obtained from the respondents (e.g., by conducting a survey or an experiment) must be addressed. In the opening vignette, the research design involved analysis of secondary data and focus groups, and a survey was conducted to assess the market potential for home-step aerobic

marketing research process A set of six steps that defines the tasks to be accomplished in conducting a marketing research study: problem definition, developing an approach to the problem, research design formulation, field work, data preparation and analysis, and report preparation and presentation.

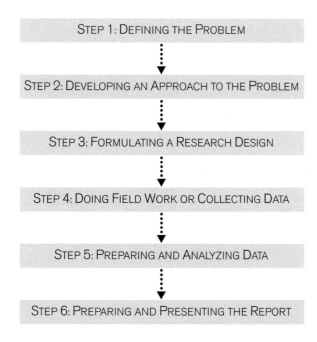

FIGURE 1.4

The Marketing Research Process

equipment. It also may involve designing a questionnaire and a sampling plan to select respondents for the study. These steps are discussed in detail in Chapters 3 to 13.

Step 4: Doing Field Work or Collecting Data

Data collection is accomplished using a staff that operates in the field. Field work involves personal, telephone, mail, or electronic interviewing. Proper selection, training, supervision, and evaluation of the field force are essential to ensure high-quality data collection. Reebok contracted field work or data collection to external suppliers, who analyzed the data using appropriate statistical techniques. (See Chapter 14.)

Step 5: Preparing and Analyzing Data

Data preparation involves data-processing steps leading up to analysis. This includes the editing, coding, and transcribing of collected data. This entire process must then be verified for accuracy. The editing process involves an initial inspection of questionnaires or observation forms for completeness and reasonableness of responses. After this initial inspection, the response to each question is coded to ensure standardized entry into the computer. The data from the questionnaires are transferred onto storage media and then analyzed using different statistical techniques. These results are then interpreted in order to find conclusions related to the marketing research problem. In the opening vignette, Reebok contracted data analysis to external suppliers, who analyzed the data using appropriate statistical techniques. (See Chapters 15 to 18.)

Step 6: Preparing and Presenting the Report

The entire project should be documented in a written report that addresses the specific research questions; describes the approach, the research design, data collection, and data analysis procedures; and presents the results and the major findings. The written report is supplemented by tables, figures, and graphs to enhance clarity and impact and is usually accompanied by a formal presentation. Reebok might use external suppliers in writing the report, but presentation of the results to the management and assistance in implementation is the primary responsibility of its in-house marketing research department. (See Chapter 19.) Reebok follows a research process that incorporates all six of these steps.

Although we have described the research process as a sequence of steps, it should be noted that these steps are interdependent and iterative. Thus, at each step the researcher should not only look back at the previous steps, but also look ahead to the following steps. As we show, the marketing research process (see Figure 1.4) is very consistent with the definition of marketing research presented earlier (see Figure 1.2).

Definition of Marketing Research (Figure 1.2)	Marketing Research Process (Figure 1.4)
Identification of information needed	Step 1: Defining the problem
Collection of data	Step 2: Developing an approach to the problem
	Step 3: Formulating a research design
	Step 4: Doing field work or collecting data
Analysis of data	Step 5: Preparing and analyzing data
Dissemination of results	Step 6: Preparing and presenting the report
Use of information	

The Internet is very useful for project management. Researchers and clients use e-mail combined with software such as Lotus Notes to communicate with each other and to coordinate the six steps of the marketing research process. The Internet also is being used to disseminate marketing research results and reports, which can be posted on the Web and made available to managers on a worldwide basis.

As the marketing chief for Fossil, a U.S.-based apparel and accessories retailer with outlets in North America, Europe, Australia, and Southeast Asia, you are considering the introduction of a fashionable wristwatch for men and women priced at $99. What kind of information do you need to help you make this decision?

You've been hired to help Fossil to determine whether to introduce its new wristwatch. Visit www.fossil.com and search the Internet, as well as your library's online databases, to obtain information on consumers' preferences for wristwatches. Describe the six steps of the marketing research process that should be followed.

The Role of Marketing Research in Marketing Decision Making

The Reebok vignette illustrates only a few applications of marketing research and its role in the marketing decision-making process. Marketing research, indeed, has a broad range of applications and plays a crucial role in the marketing decision-making process. One way to describe the role of marketing research is in light of the basic marketing paradigm given in Figure 1.5.

A major goal of marketing is to identify and then satisfy needs of various customer groups (e.g., consumers, employees, channel members, suppliers). To do this, marketing managers need information about the various customer groups, competitors, and other forces, such as environmental trends in the marketplace. In recent years, timely market information has become even more valuable. For example, the speed of new products entering the marketplace, domestic and international competition, and the increase in

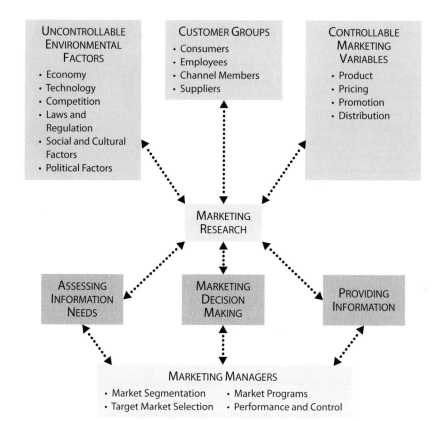

FIGURE 1.5

The Role of Marketing Research in Marketing

demanding and well-informed consumers all contribute to the importance of this type of market data.

The task of marketing research is to assess the information needs and provide management with relevant, accurate, reliable, valid, and current information to aid marketing decision making (see Figure 1.5). Companies use marketing research to stay competitive and to avoid high costs associated with making poor decisions based on unsound information. Sound decisions are not based on gut feeling, intuition, or even pure judgment; they are based on sound information. Without sound information, management cannot make sound decisions. Reebok's successful introduction of the home-step aerobics line was guided by systematic marketing research.

The following example illustrates how Sony improves its products through the use of marketing research. Sony reinforces the fact that management cannot make sound decisions without reliable information provided by marketing research.

Research in Action

Sony Gives Santa a Few Tips

The Christmas holiday season is one of the most intensely competitive in terms of gift-giving products. This is true for Sony (www.sony.com), the giant Japanese electronics firm, just as much as any other company. However, Sony gains a leg up on its competition by using marketing research to refine its gift products just in time for Christmas.

Sony asks consumers what they would like from Sony's products. It uses descriptive studies of consumer behavior, with actual product-usage information, to refine its offerings. Surveys, focus groups, interviews, tracking devices, and even syndicated data are all used to gain more knowledge on consumers' perception of Sony products. For example, Sony uses focus groups in which participants get to sample and use a product that might be released for the Christmas season. The participants let Sony know if they like the product, how much they like it, what they would change about it, and whether they would buy it. Sony also uses surveys to determine if there is a current need that could be satisfied by a product that is under development. Tracking devices are used to find out how often and when potential products are put into use by participating "test" consumers.

For instance, focus groups in the United States evaluating a preliminary design for the Sony Reader gave Sony feedback

that its electronic book reader had too many buttons and its alkaline battery design was clunky and awkward. Sony engineers modified the design based on the consumers' feedback, including replacing alkaline batteries with rechargeable ones and reducing the number of buttons to ease navigation. The Sony Reader enjoyed high demand throughout the holiday season and beyond.[4]

The Sony example illustrates the numerous strategic and tactical decisions marketing managers face and how marketing research can be helpful in improving the decision-making process. Identifying and finding solutions to customer needs (a primary goal of marketing) requires the integration of a wide range of factors, not just intuition. Figure 1.5 illustrates this range, which includes decisions about potential opportunities, target market selection, market segmentation, planning and implementing marketing programs, marketing performance, and control. These decisions often result in actions related to product, pricing, promotion, and distribution.

To make the decision process even more complicated, a manager must also consider uncontrollable external factors that influence the marketing process. In the United States, these include general economic conditions (e.g., an economic slowdown or recession), technology (e.g., the impact of new technology, such as the Internet), public policies and laws (e.g., those related to environmental pollution affect automobile companies), the political environment (e.g., Republicans are considered to be pro-business), competition (e.g., many dot-coms have not been able to survive because of competition), and social and cultural changes (e.g., changes in traditional marital roles). Another factor in this mix is the complexity of the various customer groups: consumers, employees, channel members, and suppliers. The marketing manager must attempt to monitor and incorporate all these factors. Marketing research removes some of the uncertainty and improves the quality of decision making in this highly complex environment.

The Internet can be useful to marketing researchers in many ways. Marketing research information related to the client company, its competitors, and the industry, as well as relevant marketing, economic, governmental, and environmental information, can be obtained by conducting a search using any of the following popular search engines:

- AlltheWeb (www.alltheweb.com)
- AltaVista (www.altavista.com)
- Ask (www.ask.com)
- Google (www.google.com)
- Lycos (www.lycos.com)
- Live Search (www.live.com)
- Netscape Search (search.netscape.com)
- WebCrawler (www.webcrawler.com)
- Yahoo! (www.yahoo.com)

Of particular interest is KnowThis (www.knowthis.com), a specialty search engine for a virtual marketing library.

Other important sources of marketing research information on the Internet include bulletin boards, newsgroups, and blogs. A *newsgroup* is an Internet site (e.g., groups.google.com) where people can read and post messages pertaining to a particular topic. *Blogs,* or *Web logs,* can be used to obtain information on a variety of topics and to recruit survey respondents. Although blogs can be located via most search engines, special search engines, such as Blog Search Engine (www.blogsearchengine.com), have been designed for blog searches.

Traditionally, a clear distinction existed between the responsibilities of the marketing researchers and those of the marketing manager. However, these roles are beginning to merge as marketing researchers become more involved in decision making and marketing managers become more involved with research. This trend can be attributed to better training of marketing managers, the Internet, advances in technology, and the use of research as an ongoing aspect of the marketing function.

In essence, marketing research must add value to marketing decision making, indeed, to the entire organization.[5] Note that marketing managers do not work in isolation from other functions in the organization. Rather, the marketing orientation embodies a cross-functional perspective to meet consumer needs and attain long-term profitability. Therefore, marketing research should interface with the other functions in the organization, such as manufacturing, research and development, finance, accounting, and other functional areas, as may be relevant in a given project.

Be an MR!

Visit Nokia, the Finnish mobile-communications company, at www.nokia.com and search the Internet, as well as your library's online databases, to obtain information on consumers' preferences for cellular handsets. What type of marketing research information would you obtain to help Nokia target 15- to 24-year-olds, who are heavy users of cellular handsets?

Be a DM!

As the marketing manager for Nokia, what strategies would you formulate to target 15- to 24-year-olds?

The Decision to Conduct Marketing Research

Although marketing research can be beneficial in a variety of situations, the decision to conduct research is not automatic. Rather, this decision should be guided by a number of considerations, including the costs versus the benefits, the resources available to conduct the research, the resources available to implement the research findings, and management's attitude toward research. Marketing research should be undertaken when the expected value of information it generates exceeds the costs of conducting the marketing research project. In general, the more important the decision confronting management and the greater the uncertainty or risk facing them, the greater the value of information obtained. Formal procedures are available for quantifying the expected value as well as the costs of a marketing research project. Although in most instances the value of information exceeds the costs, in some instances the reverse might be true. For example, a pie manufacturer wanted to understand the purchase of pies in convenience stores. We advised against a major marketing research project when we discovered that less than 1 percent of the sales were coming from convenience stores and that this situation was unlikely to change in the next 5 years.

Resources, especially time and money, are always limited. If either time or money is not available in adequate amounts to conduct a quality project, then that project probably should not be undertaken. It is better to forego a formal project rather than undertake one in which the integrity of the research is compromised because of lack of resources. In one instance, we advised Fisher Price, a U.S. maker of toys and children's apparel, not to undertake a formal research project because a go/no-go decision regarding the introduction of a new toy had to be made in just a few days and time was too limited to conduct quality research. Likewise, a firm might lack the resources to implement the recommendations arising from the findings of marketing research. In that case, spending the resources to conduct the research might not be warranted. If management does not have a positive attitude toward research, then it is likely that the project report will gather dust if the research is conducted. However, sometimes there are exceptions to this guideline. For example, we conducted a project for a retail chain where the chain management was hostile toward the project, but the research was commissioned and funded by the parent organization. Although the store management was opposed to the findings that reflected negatively on the store chain, the parent company did implement our recommendations.

Other circumstances also might indicate that a particular marketing research project should not be undertaken. If the required information is already available within the organization, the decision for which the research is to be conducted has already been made, or the research is going to be used for political ends, then the value of the information generated is greatly reduced and the project is generally not warranted.

Be a DM!

As the marketing director of the U.S. firm Estée Lauder, which sells cosmetics and skin-care products in more than 100 countries, would you conduct a formal marketing research project to determine consumer response to a proposed new line of cosmetics? Why or why not?

Be an MR!

Visit www.esteelauder.com and search the Internet, as well as your library's online databases, to find information on Estée Lauder's marketing strategy. What type of problem-solving research would you conduct?

An Overview of the Marketing Research Industry

marketing research industry
The marketing research industry consists of suppliers who provide marketing research services.

internal suppliers
Marketing research departments located within a firm.

The **marketing research industry** consists of suppliers who provide marketing research services. Figure 1.6 broadly categorizes research suppliers as either internal or external. An **internal supplier** is a marketing research department within the firm. Internal research departments can be found in large organizations across a wide range of industries, including automobiles (e.g., GM, Toyota, Daimler AG), consumer products (e.g., P&G, Nestlé, Coca-Cola), and banking (e.g., Citigroup, Deutsche Bank, Barcaly's). For these larger companies, the research function often is located at the corporate headquarters, and this one corporate marketing research department caters to all of the firm's research needs. For smaller or decentralized firms that operate independent divisions, the market research function is distributed among the separate divisions. In decentralized organizations, divisions can be structured around products, customers, or geographical regions, with marketing research personnel assigned across the country. Each division (or group based on product line or

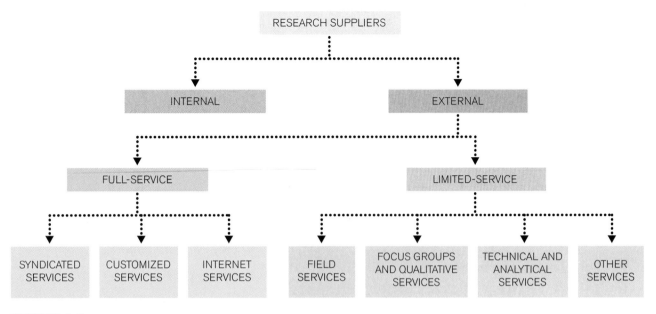

FIGURE 1.6

Marketing Research Suppliers and Services

geographical region) will have its own marketing research operation. Although companies can be found operating under a number of organizational structures, the recent trend has been toward centralization and a trimming of internal marketing research staff.

External suppliers are outside firms hired to supply marketing research services. Even large firms such as Acer, a Taiwanese computer maker, and adidas AG, a German maker of sports apparel and equipment, which maintain in-house marketing research departments make at least some use of external suppliers. External suppliers range in size from one- or two-person shops to multinational corporations. Most of the research suppliers are small operations. Table 1.1 lists the top 25 global marketing research suppliers.[6] Many external suppliers form strategic alliances with other firms in the marketing research industry. These alliances enable participating firms to access each other's expertise and resources. Such alliances are formed through mergers, acquisitions, or contractual agreements. Major marketing research companies, such as Britain's Taylor Nelson Sofres (TNS), establish partnerships with several marketing research firms in other countries. These partnerships and alliances give firms like TNS access to international markets.

External suppliers can provide either full or limited service. **Full-service suppliers** offer the entire range of marketing research services, from problem definition, approach development, questionnaire design, sampling, data collection, data analysis, and interpretation to report preparation and presentation. The services of these suppliers can be further broken down into syndicated services, customized services, and Internet services (see Figure 1.6).

Syndicated services are companies that collect and sell common pools of data designed to serve information needs that are shared by a number of clients. These data are collected primarily through surveys, purchase and media panels, scanners, and audits. In the United States, for example, the Nielsen Television Index provides information on audience size and demographic characteristics of households watching specific television programs (www.nielsenmedia.com). The ACNielsen Company (www.acnielsen.com) also provides scanner tracking data, such as that generated by electronic scanners at checkout counters in supermarkets. The NPD Group (www.npd.com), another example of a syndicated service, maintains one of the largest consumer panels in the United States. Syndicated services are discussed in more detail in Chapter 5.

Customized services offer a wide variety of marketing research services customized to suit a client's specific needs. Each marketing research project is designed to meet the client's unique needs. Some of the marketing research firms that offer customized services are Synovate, TNS, and Burke, Inc.

external suppliers
Outside marketing research companies hired to conduct a complete marketing research project or a component of it.

full-service suppliers
Companies that offer the full range of marketing research activities.

syndicated services
Companies that collect and sell common pools of data designed to serve the information needs of multiple clients.

customized services
Companies that tailor research procedures to best meet the needs of each client.

TABLE 1.1 Top 25 Global Research Organizations

Rank 2006	Rank 2005	Organization	Headquarters	Parent Country	Web Site (www.)	No. of Countries with Subsidiaries/ Branch Offices[1]	Global Research Revenue[2] (U.S. $, in millions)	Percent of Global Revenue from Outside Home Country
1	1	The Nielsen Co.	New York	U.S.	Nielsen.com	108	$3,696.0	46.7%
2	3	IMS Health Inc.	Norwalk, Conn.	U.S.	Imshealth.com	76	1,958.6	63.4
3	2	Taylor Nelson Sofres plc	London	U.K.	tns-global.com	75	1,851.1	85.0
4	5	The Kantar Group*	London & Fairfield, Conn.	U.K.	kantargroup.com	59	1,401.4	63.7
5	4	GfKAG	Nuremberg	Germany	gfk.com	57	1,397.3	75.8
6	6	Ipsos Group SA	Paris	France	ipsos.com	50	1,077.0	88.4
7	8	Synovate	London	U.K.	synovate.com	52	739.6	91.1
8	7	IRI	Chicago	U.S.	infores.com	8	665.0	35.0
9	9	Westat Inc.	Rockville, Md.	U.S.	westat.com	1	425.8	—
10	10	Arbitron Inc.	New York	U.S.	arbitron.com	2	329.3	4.0
11	11	INTAGE Inc.**	Tokyo	Japan	intage.co.jp	2	264.8	0.7
12	14	J.D. Power and Associates*	Westlake Village, Calif.	U.S.	jdpa.com	8	232.6	26.7
13	12	Harris Interactive Inc.	Rochester, N.Y.	U.S.	harrisinteractive.com	5	216.8	22.0
14	13	Maritz Research	Fenton, Mo.	U.S.	maritzresearch.com	4	216.4	17.7
15	16	The NPD Group Inc.	Port Washington, N.Y.	U.S.	npd.com	13	186.9	22.1
16	15	Video Research Ltd.**	Tokyo	Japan	videor.co.jp	3	173.7	0.1
17	17	Opinion Research Corp.	Princeton, N.J.	U.S.	opinionresearch.com	3	154.7	37.4
18	18	IBOPE Group	Sao Paulo	Brazil	ibope.com.br	16	103.9	20.4
19	19	Lieberman Research Worldwide	Los Angeles	U.S.	lrwonline.com	4	78.3	19.4
20	—	Telephia Inc.	San Francisco	U.S.	telephia.com	1	71.8	2.8
21	23	comScore Inc.	Reston, Va.	U.S.	comscore.com	5	66.3	8.6
22	20	Dentsu Research Inc.	Tokyo	Japan	dentsuresearch.co.jp	1	61.2	—
23	22	AbtAssociates Inc.	Cambridge, Mass.	U.S.	abtassociates.com	1	53.6	—
24	21	Nikkei Research Inc.	Tokyo	Japan	nikkei-r.co.jp	4	50.7	—
25	25	Burke Inc.	Cincinnati	U.S.	burke.com	1	50.0	13.0
					Total		$15,522.8	55.8%

*Estimated by Top 25
**For fiscal year ending March 2007
[1] Includes countries that have subsidiaries with an equity interest or branch offices or both.
[2] Total revenue that includes nonresearch activities for some companies are significantly higher.

Several marketing research firms, including some who have specialized in conducting marketing research on the Internet, offer **Internet services.** Among U.S. firms, for example, Greenfield Online Research Center Inc. (www.greenfieldonline.com), a subsidiary of the Greenfield Consulting Group (www.greenfieldgroup.com), offers a broad range of customized qualitative and quantitative online marketing research for consumer, business-to-business, and professional markets. Using large, proprietary databases, studies are conducted within the company's secure Web site. Jupiter Research (www.jupiterresearch.com) offers research and consulting services that focus on consumer online behavior and interactive technologies.

Limited-service suppliers specialize in one or a few steps of the marketing research process. Limited-service suppliers specialize in field services, focus groups and qualitative research, technical and analytical services, and other services. **Field services** collect data. They might use the full range of data collection methods (i.e., mail, personal, telephone, and electronic interviewing), or they might specialize in only one method. Some field service organizations maintain extensive interviewing facilities across the country for interviewing shoppers in malls. Many offer qualitative data-collection services, such as focus-group interviewing (discussed in Chapter 6). Two U.S. firms that offer field services are Field Facts, Inc. (www.fieldfacts.com) and Field Work, Inc. (www.fieldwork.com).

Focus groups and qualitative services provide facilities and recruit respondents for focus groups and other forms of qualitative research, such as one-on-one depth interviews. Some firms might provide additional services, such as moderators, and prepare focus group reports. Examples of such firms include Jackson Associates (www.jacksonassociates.com) and The Focus Group (www.thefocusgroup.co.uk).

Technical and analytical services are offered by firms that specialize in design issues and computer analysis of quantitative data, such as those obtained in large surveys. Firms such as the U.S. firm SDR (www.sdr-consulting.com) offer sophisticated data analysis using advanced statistical techniques. Sawtooth Technologies (www.sawtooth.com) provides software for research data collection and analysis. Microcomputers and statistical software packages enable firms to perform data analysis in-house. However, the specialized data-analysis expertise of outside suppliers is still in demand. Other services include branded marketing research products and services developed to address specific types of marketing research problems. For example, the U.S. research firm Survey Sampling International (www.surveysampling.com) specializes in sampling design and distribution. Some firms focus on specialized services, such as research in ethnic markets (i.e., Hispanic, African, multicultural). In the United States, Latin Facts Research (www.latinfactsresearch.com) focuses on research in ethnic markets. In New Zealand, FCB (www.draftfbc.com) conducts extensive research in "social marketing."

A firm without an internal marketing research department or specialists will be to rely on external, full-service suppliers. A firm with an internal marketing research staff will make use of both full- and limited-service suppliers. The need for external suppliers arises when the firm does not have the resources or the technical expertise to undertake certain phases of a particular project. Also, conflict-of-interest issues might necessitate that a project be conducted by an outside supplier, as in the case of Reebok in the opening vignette. At Reebok, data collection and data analysis frequently are contracted to external suppliers. Sometimes Reebok uses full-service suppliers to conduct the entire marketing research project.

Selecting a Research Supplier

When initiating a marketing research study, a firm often will need to hire external suppliers for all or part of the project. The process of selecting an outside supplier can be informal, relying primarily on word-of-mouth endorsements, or it can be very formal, involving a "request for proposal." In the latter case, research suppliers are asked to submit formal proposals for evaluation by the hiring firm. The first step involves compiling a list of prospective suppliers from trade publications, professional directories, Internet sources, and personal contacts. In the United States, for example, www.greenbook.org can be used to locate marketing research suppliers by region, specialty, and other criteria.

Internet services
Companies that specialize in conducting research on the Internet.

limited-service suppliers
Companies that specialize in one or a few phases of the marketing research project.

field services
Companies whose primary service offering is their expertise in collecting data for research projects.

focus groups and qualitative services
Services related to facilities, recruitment, and other services for focus groups and other forms of qualitative research, such as one-on-one depth interviews.

technical and analytical services
Services related to design issues and computer analysis of quantitative data, such as those obtained in large surveys.

Regardless of the formality of the process, the hiring firm must develop a checklist detailing its selection criteria for outside suppliers. That checklist should go beyond technical requirements, covering the following areas:

- What is the supplier's reputation?
- Does the firm complete projects on schedule? Is it flexible?
- Is it known for maintaining ethical standards?
- Are its research projects of high quality?
- What kind and how much experience does the supplier have?
- Has the firm had experience with projects similar to this one?
- Do the supplier's personnel have both technical and nontechnical expertise? If it's U.S. based, do its personnel have Professional Researcher Certification offered by the Marketing Research Association (www.mra-net.org)?
- Has the firm formed any strategic alliances? What resources does it have access to?

Reebok International, which subcontracts a great deal of its research to external suppliers, uses a similar checklist. You can also find checklists for qualifying marketing research suppliers at the Web sites of prominent marketing research associations (e.g., www.esomar.org). A checklist helps managers examine the working relationships as well as the project requirements. Because of the importance of most research efforts, compatible working relationships and good communication skills can become primary considerations when hiring an outside firm.

A competitive bidding process usually is used in selecting external suppliers, particularly for large jobs. Often the organization commissioning the research will issue a request for proposal (RFP), a request for information (RFI), a request for application (RFA), an invitation to bid (ITB), or a similar call, inviting suppliers to submit bids. You can locate actual RFPs on the Internet by doing a Google advanced search using "RFP" and "Marketing Research." Some marketing research firms will post RFP forms on their Web sites that prospective clients can use to issue RFPs. Note that awarding projects based on the lowest price is not a good rule of thumb. The completeness of the research proposal and the selection criteria must all be factored into the hiring decision. Moreover, long-term contracts with research suppliers are preferable to selection on a project-by-project basis.

Be an MR!	Be a DM!
As the research director for Yahoo! you are to select a marketing research firm that specializes in researching consumers who shop on the Internet. Visit www.greenbook.org and identify the marketing research firms in your area that conduct Internet-based surveys. Make a list of five such firms. Which firm will you select and why?	As the director of marketing at Yahoo!, how would you use information on consumer shopping on the Internet in redesigning the Yahoo! Web site?

Careers in Marketing Research

Promising career opportunities are available with marketing research firms (e.g., ACNielsen, TNS, Synovate, Ipsos Group SA). Equally appealing are careers in business and nonbusiness firms and agencies with in-house marketing research departments (e.g., Coca-Cola, Nestlé, Reebok, the Australian Bureau of Statistics, the U.S. Census Bureau, India's Energy Resources Institute). Advertising agencies (e.g., BBDO International, McCann Erickson, Ogilvy & Mather, J. Walter Thompson, Young & Rubicam) also conduct substantial marketing research and employ professionals in this field.

A career in research often begins with a supervisory position in field work or data analysis. With experience, the researcher moves up to project-management positions, resulting in director and, eventually, in a vice-president-level position. In the United States, the most common entry-level position in the marketing research industry for people with bachelor's degrees (e.g., a Bachelor of Business Administration [BBA]) is operational supervisor. An operational supervisor is responsible for supervising the day-to-day operations of specific aspects of the marketing research process, ranging from field work to data editing to coding for programming and data analysis. Rather than entering the discipline from the operations side, BBAs with strong organizational skills might start as assistant project managers. An assistant project manager assists in questionnaire design, reviews field instructions, and monitors timing and costs of studies. As research techniques become more sophisticated, there is a growing preference for people with master's degrees. Those with Masters of Business Administration (MBAs) or equivalent degrees are likely to be employed as project managers. In marketing research firms, such as Burke, Inc., the project manager works with the account director in managing the day-to-day operations of a marketing research project.

A researcher entering the profession on the client side would typically begin as a junior-research analyst (for BBAs) or research analyst (for MBAs). The junior analyst and the research analyst learn about the particular industry and receive training from a senior staff member, usually the marketing research manager. The junior analyst position includes a training program to prepare individuals for the responsibilities of a research analyst, including coordinating with the marketing department and sales force to develop goals for product exposure. Research analyst responsibilities include checking data for accuracy, comparing and contrasting new research with established norms, and analyzing data for the purpose of market forecasting. As these job titles indicate, careers in marketing research can be highly technical, specializing in the design and the statistical side of the industry, or they can be of a general management nature, with emphasis on client relationships. For descriptions of other marketing research positions and current salaries in the United States, visit www.marketresearchcareers.com.

Marketing research is a growing industry offering attractive employment opportunities. The 2007 Annual Survey of Market Research Professionals (see www.market researchcareers.com) revealed important trends for U.S. students interested in a career in market research:

- More than half of all research firms expect to hire additional help in the near term.
- The average raise for market research professionals in 2007 approached 6 percent.
- Demand for entry level project managers and market research managers was substantial throughout 2007.

To prepare for a career in marketing research, you should:

- Take all the marketing courses you can.
- Take courses in statistics and quantitative methods.
- Acquire computer and Internet skills.
- Take courses in psychology and consumer behavior.
- Acquire effective written and verbal communication skills.
- Think creatively. Creativity and common sense command a premium in marketing research.

It is important for marketing researchers to be liberally educated in order to better understand the problems managers face and then be able to address them from a broad perspective.[7] A career in marketing research will involve working with other bright, energetic people in a fast-paced, dynamic environment. You will get to work on diverse qualitative and quantitative projects with clients in a variety of industries, including e-commerce, travel, telecommunications, pharmaceuticals, government, and nonprofit. The benefits include ongoing training and career development, a competitive salary, comprehensive health and dental plans, a 401K, the option to wear business casual attire, and excellent advancement opportunities.

College graduates' lack of awareness of marketing research as a career and a growing demand for marketing researchers in the fields of information technology, pharmaceuticals, financial services, and other booming industries has created a shortage of professionals in the field. Marketing research organizations would like to have more incoming talent in order to have a greater presence in senior management in the future. The need for marketing researchers could not be greater. This makes it a career worth pursuing for both the short and the long term. For more information on U.S. jobs in marketing research, check out the American Marketing Association's career center at www.marketing power.com or the WorldOpinion Web site (www.worldopinion.com).

Experiential Learning

The World of Marketing Research on the Internet

The WorldOpinion Web site (www.worldopinion.com) offers up-to-date news and comprehensive information on the U.S. market research industry. Here's how to find what you're looking for and get the most out of your visit.

If you're job hunting or hiring, the classifieds section lists jobs in research, marketing, advertising, public relations, and allied professions. The site lists thousands of current job openings. Résumés and job listings can be submitted to the site at no charge.

Looking for the right research company for your project? The directory of researchers lists over 8,500 research

locations in 99 countries. Search by company name or search by company type and/or geography.

The news section, updated daily, provides company, conference, and product news from the world of market research.

If you are thinking of attending a marketing or research event or need more information on research education opportunities, check out the WorldOpinion calendar. Hundreds of events and research courses from throughout the world are listed.

There are many other ways the WorldOpinion Web site brings the world of marketing research to you. Explore it!

---

marketing information systems (MIS)
A formalized set of procedures for generating, analyzing, storing, and distributing pertinent information to marketing decision makers on an ongoing basis.

decision support systems (DSS)
An information system that enables decision makers to interact directly with both databases and analysis models. The important components of a DSS include hardware and a communication network, database, model base, software base, and the DSS user (decision maker).

The Role of Marketing Research in MIS and DSS

Earlier, we defined *marketing research* as the systematic and objective identification, collection, analysis, dissemination, and use of information for use in marketing decision making. Combining external market information with internal billing, production, and other records results in a powerful marketing information system (MIS) (Figure 1.7).

A **marketing information system (MIS)** is a formalized set of procedures for generating, analyzing, storing, and distributing information to marketing decision makers on an ongoing basis. Such systems are differentiated from marketing research in that they are continuously available. Marketing information systems are designed to complement the decision maker's responsibilities, style, and information needs. The power of a MIS is in the access it gives managers to vast amounts of information, combining production, invoice, and billing information with marketing intelligence, including marketing research, into a centralized data warehouse. MIS offer the potential of much more information than can be obtained from ad hoc marketing research projects. However, that potential often is not achieved when the information is structured so rigidly that it cannot be easily manipulated.

Developed to overcome the limitations of MIS, **decision support systems (DSS)** have built-in flexibility that allows decision makers to interact directly with databases and

---

FIGURE 1.7

The Development of MIS and DSS

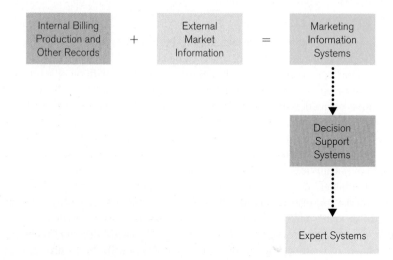

MIS	DSS
• Structured problems • Use of reports • Information displaying restricted • Can improve decision making by clarifying new data	• Unstructured problems • Use of models • Adaptability • Can improve decision making by using "what-if" analysis

FIGURE 1.8

Marketing Information Systems (MIS) Versus Decision Support Systems (DSS)

analysis models. A DSS is an integrated system that includes hardware, a communications network, a database, a model base, a software base, and the DSS user (decision maker) who collects and interprets information for decision making. Information collected by marketing research becomes a part of the DSS, as in the case of Reebok in the opening vignette. Specifically, marketing research contributes research data to the database, marketing models and analytical techniques to the model base, and specialized programs for analyzing marketing data to the software base. Many firms are building huge internal databases as part of the DSS (see database marketing in Chapter 4). The analytical techniques and the software used to analyze these data are discussed later in the text (see Chapters 15 through 18). Decision support systems differ from MIS in that they combine the models and analytic techniques of traditional marketing research with the easy access and retrieval of MIS (Figure 1.8). Well-designed DSS adapt to the decision-making needs of the user with easy interactive processes. In addition to providing easy access to data, DSS can also enhance decision-making effectiveness by using "what-if" analysis. Reebok International makes use of a sophisticated DSS that enables it to assess the impact of introducing new footwear, making a promotional offer, or opening a new facility at a specific location when these projects are still in the planning stage.

MIS and DSS can greatly improve decision making by enabling management to access a wide range of information. An advanced form of DSS, called expert systems, uses artificial intelligence procedures to incorporate expert judgment. In addition to crunching numbers and storing and retrieving information, these systems are programmed to reason and make inferences. Thus, the expert systems can actually lead to decisions recommending certain courses of action to the management. All these systems can greatly enhance the effectiveness of marketing.

Be a DM!

As the marketing manager for Sony digital cameras your objective is to switch more traditional photographers to the digital camera. What information from the company's DSS would you find helpful in achieving this goal?

Be an MR!

Visit www.sony.com and search the Internet, as well as your library's online databases, to find information on the digital camera market. What kind of marketing research would you undertake to obtain the information identified by the DM?

Summary Illustration Using the Opening Vignette

To summarize and illustrate the concepts in this chapter, let's return to the opening vignette. Marketing research involves the identification, collection, analysis, dissemination, and use of information about consumers, channel members, competitors, and changes and trends in the marketplace and other aspects of the firm's environment. In the opening vignette, the U.S.-based, German-owned firm Reebok used "time-use" research in an attempt to discover what consumers do with their spare time. Marketing research can be classified as problem-identification research or problem-solving research. Reebok used problem-identification research involving secondary data analysis, focus groups, and a market potential survey to discover that adults were spending less time in health clubs and more time exercising at home. Problem-solving research, in the form of product research, then led to the development of the successful home-step aerobics line.

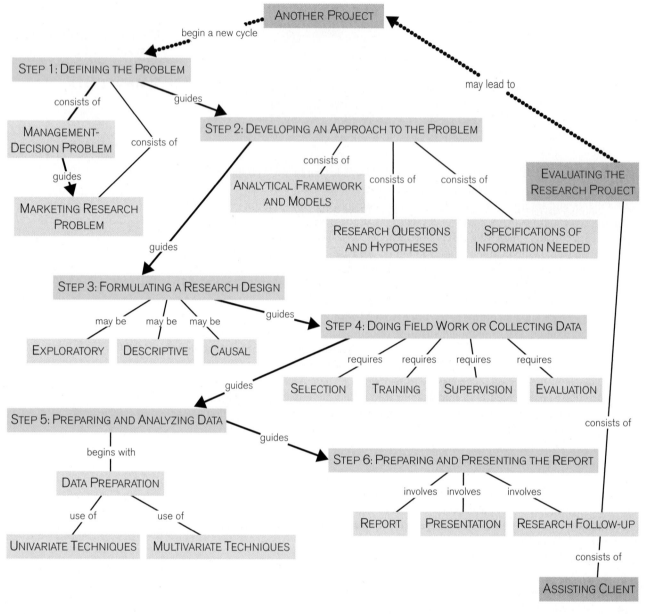

FIGURE 1.9

A Concept Map for the Marketing Research Process

The marketing research process consists of six steps. Figure 1.9 provides a concept map of these steps, which must be followed systematically. Reebok follows a very similar marketing research process, and some of these steps were illustrated in the opening vignette. Marketing research can be conducted internally or purchased from external suppliers. In the case of Reebok, in-house marketing research specialists are actively involved in defining and designing the marketing research project. The in-house specialists also have the primary responsibility for presenting the results to management and providing assistance in implementation. Reebok also makes use of full-service suppliers who provide assistance in all the steps of the marketing research process as well as limited-service suppliers who may handle only data collection and analysis and assist in report writing.

The marketing research industry offers a wide range of careers in both corporate (e.g., Reebok) and independent service organizations. Information obtained using marketing research can stand alone or be integrated into an MIS and DSS, as in the case of Reebok.

Application to Contemporary Issues

Although several contemporary issues are discussed throughout each chapter, we focus special attention on international marketing research, technology and marketing research, and ethics in marketing research. Each of these issues receives a separate section in each chapter of the text (except the data analysis chapters, Chapters 16 through 18). We show how marketing research principles can be applied when conducting research in an international setting. Because we live in a technological age, the technological developments that impact marketing research also are discussed. Ethical issues in marketing research are described.

International Marketing Research

The United States accounts for about 40 percent of worldwide marketing research expenditures; another 40 percent is attributable to Western Europe and about 10 percent to Japan. Most of the research in Europe is done in the United Kingdom, Germany, France, Italy, and Spain. Japan is the clear leader in the Asia Pacific region, followed by Australia, China, South Korea, and Taiwan. Brazil and Mexico lead the Central and South American markets in terms of marketing research expenditures.[8]

With the globalization of markets, marketing research has assumed a truly international character, a trend that is likely to continue. Several U.S.–based market research firms are equipped to conduct international marketing research. They include IMS Health, Information Resources, and Maritz Research (see Table 1.1). Foreign-based firms include the Kantar Group and TNS (United Kingdom) and the GfK Group (Germany).

International marketing research is much more complex than domestic marketing research. Research of this type should be sensitive to differences in customs, communication, and culture. The environment in the countries or international markets that are being researched influences the way the six steps of the marketing research process should be performed. These environmental factors include marketing, government, legal, economic, structural, informational and technological, and sociocultural factors. When conducted properly, international marketing research can yield high dividends, as demonstrated by the success of Procter & Gamble in China.

Research in Action

Head & Shoulders Stands Head and Shoulders Above Competition in China

As of 2008, the U.S.-based consumer-products firm Procter & Gamble (P&G) (www.pg.com) marketed about 300 products to more than 5 billion consumers in 180 countries. P&G products are the largest daily-use consumer products in China. The company has achieved this status by ignoring popular maxims, instead relying on marketing research.

P&G succeeded because it ignored the standard practices used in marketing to the Chinese audience. It did not cater to a wealthy audience, although it was told that none other could afford its expensive products. By relying on marketing research, such popular maxims were seen for what they were—misunderstandings. Additionally, by conducting proper cross-cultural research P&G was able to overcome Western biases based on erroneous beliefs about China, such as that middle-class Chinese could not afford expensive Western products.

Marketing research revealed that dandruff was a major concern, because the Chinese have dark hair, causing dandruff to readily stand out. Furthermore, Chinese shampoos were ineffective in fighting this malady. Research revealed that most Chinese were willing to pay a premium for a shampoo that addressed this problem.

P&G decided to establish its foothold in China by fighting dandruff. P&G targeted a broad segment, rather than just the wealthy. P&G introduced Head & Shoulders as a premium brand, and within 3 years it was China's leading shampoo. P&G then introduced antidandruff versions of Pert and Pantene. Using careful targeting, both brands performed extremely well. Overall, P&G commands 57 percent of the shampoo market in China, even though its products are priced over 300 percent higher than local brands. This example show that those who overcome their biases and conduct proper research can stand head and shoulders above the competition.[9]

Visit www.levis.com and search the Internet, as well as your library's online databases, to find information on consumer preferences for jeans. The U.S.-based apparel maker Levi's would like to conduct marketing research to increase its share of the jeans market in the United States and India. How would you conduct marketing research in the two countries?

As Levi's marketing chief, what information would you need to formulate strategies aimed at increasing marketing share?

Technology and Marketing Research

third wave
The third wave denotes the move away from information-based decision making to system-based decisions and involves a number of developments centered on DSS and expert systems.

The term **third wave,** coined by American futurist Alvin Toffler, has come to symbolize the transition to doing old things in new ways through the use of technology. The third wave of marketing research will shape not only the way information is used, but also our fundamental conception of the role of marketing research in assisting management decisions.

In the first wave, we progressed from seat-of-the-pants decision making to data-based decisions. The emphasis was on supporting marketing decisions with data. As more data became available, a large problem arose. Marketers were soon floating in a sea of individual facts about their products and markets with very little way of assimilating the data.

In the second wave, the progression was from data-based decisions to information-based decision making. Rather than review a multitude of individual facts, the role of marketing research became analyzing data to summarize the underlying patterns. If marketing researchers could understand the relationships and patterns in the data, so the logic went, this would lead to the insights necessary to make sound marketing decisions.

With the third wave, marketing is moving away from information-based decision making to system-based decisions. Computer technology, a major driving force behind the third wave, allows for a better fit of marketing information to the needs of the market planning process. We can create a better interface and information exchange between marketing researchers and marketing managers, resulting in a unique knowledge base that captures the expertise of each group. The third wave involves a number of developments centered on DSS and expert systems that put the power of marketing information directly into the hands of nontechnical decision makers, allowing an ever-increasing focus on specific consumers, which often results in one-to-one marketing.

A major goal of this new improved technology is to link the customer to the information superhighway through the Internet, interactive telephone, interactive TV, home shopping channels, and integrated call centers. Such a system knows who is calling based on the customer's phone number and can identify information the customer will likely need. This allows researchers to know in real time what is happening in the marketplace. In the twenty-first century, the use of cyberspace as a data collection, communication, research, and management tool will rival the importance of the telephone to marketing research. Subsequent chapters describe the profound impact of the Internet on each step of the marketing research process. As the leading edge of the third wave begins to emerge, one can imagine many intriguing ways that marketing research will be used in the future.[10]

Ethics in Marketing Research

Business activities often are discussed from the perspectives of different stakeholders, those individuals or groups who have an interest in or are directly involved in activities related to business. Marketing research activities affect four stakeholders: (1) the marketing researcher, (2) the client, (3) the respondent, and (4) the public. Ethical questions arise when conflict occurs between these stakeholders (Figure 1.10).

In the face of conflict, the behavior of the stakeholders should be guided by codes of conduct. In the United States, several organizations, including the Marketing Research Association (MRA) and the American Marketing Association (AMA), provide codes in the area of ethical research behavior. For example, see the respondent bill of rights on the Web site of the Council for Marketing and Opinion Research (www.cmor.org). Each stakeholder has responsibilities.

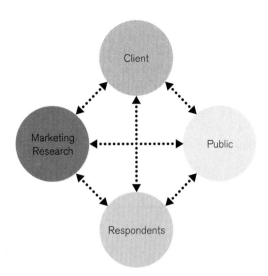

FIGURE 1.10

Stakeholders in Marketing Research: An Ethical Perspective

Neglect of these responsibilities might result in harm to another stakeholder or to the research project. It will always damage the research process and the integrity of the profession.[11]

Ethical issues can arise at each step of the marketing research process. Table 1.2 provides an overview of some of the ethical issues encountered in marketing research. These issues are discussed in more detail in subsequent chapters.

TABLE 1.2 An Overview of Ethical Issues in the Marketing Research Process

I. Problem definition
- Using surveys as a guise for selling or fundraising
- Personal agendas of the researcher or client
- Conducting unnecessary research

II. Developing an approach
- Using findings and models developed for specific clients or projects for other projects
- Soliciting proposals to gain research expertise without pay

III. Research design
- Formulating a research design more suited to the researcher's rather than the client's needs
- Using secondary data that are not applicable or that have been gathered through questionable means
- Disguising the purpose of the research
- Soliciting unfair concessions from the researcher
- Not maintaining anonymity of respondents
- Disrespecting privacy of respondents
- Misleading respondents
- Disguising observation of respondents
- Embarrassing or putting stress on respondents
- Using measurement scales of questionable reliability and validity
- Designing overly long questionnaires, overly sensitive questions, piggybacking
- Using inappropriate sampling procedures and sample size

IV. Field work
- Increasing discomfort level of respondents
- Following unacceptable field work procedures

V. Data preparation and analysis
- Identifying and discarding unsatisfactory respondents
- Using statistical techniques when the underlying assumptions are violated
- Interpreting the results and making incorrect conclusions and recommendations

VI. Report preparation and presentation
- Incomplete reporting
- Biased reporting
- Inaccurate reporting

Experiential Learning

Ethical Guidelines

Compare the ethical guidelines for conducting marketing research posted at the following Web sites:

- CASRO: The Council of American Survey Research Organizations (www.casro.org)
- CMOR: Council for Marketing and Opinion Research (www.cmor.org)
- ESOMAR: European Society for Opinion and Marketing Research (www.esomar.org)

Which organization has the most stringent set of guidelines?

Which organization's ethical guidelines are the most complete?

What is missing from the guidelines of all the three organizations?

Be a DM!

As the marketing director of the U.S. cable-TV news network CNN, how would you deal with the situation in which an Internet marketing research firm you hired to determine consumers' usage of your Web site (www.cnn.com) has violated respondents' privacy rights in the course of the project?

Be an MR!

Visit www.mra-net.org and describe the Marketing Research Association's ethical guidelines for the use of the Internet for conducting opinion and marketing research. As a researcher conducting Internet research for CNN, how would you ensure that respondents' privacy rights are not violated?

What Would *You* Do?

Samsonite. Life's a Journey

The Situation

With headquarters in the United States, Samsonite is one of the world's largest designers, manufacturers, and distributors of luggage. They sell their products using a number of quality brand names, including Samsonite® and American Tourister®. With net sales of $1.1 billion for their fiscal year ending January 31, 2007, they are a leader in the highly fragmented global luggage industry. Through aggressive product development and marketing, President and Chief Executive Officer Marcello Bottoli hoped to increase the company's market share from 35 percent in 2005 to 40 percent in 2010. Bottoli recognizes the importance of new product development and acknowledges that Samsonite must continually introduce successful new products in the marketplace.

The Marketing Research Decision

1. What type of marketing research should Samsonite undertake? (Check as many as are applicable.)
   a. Product research
   b. Pricing research
   c. Promotion research
   d. Distribution research
   e. All of the above
2. Discuss the role of the type of research you recommend in enabling Marcello Bottoli to increase the market share of Samsonite.

The Marketing Management Decision

1. Marcello Bottoli's aggressive marketing strategy should be built around (check as many as are applicable):
   a. New product development
   b. Price discounts
   c. International marketing
   d. Distribution through flagship stores
   e. All of the above
2. Discuss how the marketing management decision action that you recommend to Marcello Bottoli is influenced by the research that you suggested earlier and by the findings of that research.

What Marcello Bottoli Did

Marcello Bottoli unveiled a directional luggage collection by world-renowned designer Alexander McQueen. The collaboration brought together inspiration and ideas from McQueen's own life experience and travels. The design ethos contrasts fragility and strength, tradition and modernity, resulting in a collection of key travel pieces to appeal to the world's most discerning globe trotters. Underpinning the design features are Samsonite Black Label's contemporary style and luxury, and its values of ultimate performance, function, and durability.

The result is a totally unique collection that fuses nature and technology. Patterns and designs found in nature have been brought to life using the latest technological know-how. It is an ergonomic collection featuring natural shapes and curves that look revolutionary against the traditional hard lines of travel pieces and travel bags.

The world of travel is constantly changing, and so is Samsonite. As the brand is taken beyond luggage, Samsonite is constantly seeking opportunities to expand internationally and become present in new distribution channels, leading to the opening of flagship Samsonite Black Label stores in high-end locations in New York, London, Moscow, Berlin, Seoul, Tokyo, Hong Kong, Singapore, Taipei, and Shanghai.[12]

SPSS Windows and Excel

In this book, we feature SPSS programs, not merely as a statistical package, but as an integrative package that can be used in the various stages of the marketing research process. We illustrate the use of SPSS for defining the problem, developing an approach, formulating the research design, data collection, data preparation and analysis, and report preparation and presentation. In addition to the BASE module, we also feature other SPSS programs, such as Decision Time, What If?, Maps, Data Entry, SamplePower Missing Values, TextSmart, and SmartViewer.

The data analyses also are illustrated with three other software packages: Excel, SAS, and Minitab. Detailed, step-by-step instructions are provided for both SPSS WINDOWS and Excel. All the data files are available for both SPSS and Excel. The computerized demonstration movies and screen captures for these software programs can be downloaded from the Web site for this book.

Summary

Marketing research assesses information needs and provides relevant information in order to improve the marketing decision-making process. It is a systematic and objective process designed to identify and solve marketing problems. Thus, marketing research can be classified as problem-identification research and problem-solving research. The marketing research process consists of six steps that must be followed systematically. Marketing research provides information about consumers, channel members, competitors, changes and trends in the marketplace, and other aspects of the firm's environment. The decision to conduct marketing research should be guided by a number of considerations, including the costs versus the benefits, the resources available to conduct the research, the resources available to implement the research findings, and management's attitude toward research.

A firm can conduct its own marketing research or purchase it from external suppliers. External suppliers might provide full service or specialize in one or more aspects of the process. Full-service suppliers provide the entire range of marketing research services, from problem definition to report preparation and presentation. The services provided by these suppliers can be classified as syndicated services, customized services, or internet services. Limited-service suppliers specialize in one or a few phases of the marketing research project. These suppliers might offer field services, other services such as coding and data entry, or data analysis.

The marketing research industry offers a wide range of careers in both corporate and independent service organizations. Marketing research firms, business and nonbusiness firms, and advertising agencies all employ research professionals. Information obtained using marketing research can stand alone or be integrated into an MIS or DSS. Marketing research contributes to the DSS by providing research data to the database, marketing models and analytical techniques to the model base, and specialized marketing research programs to the software base.

International marketing research is much more complex than domestic research because researchers must consider the environment in the international markets they are researching. Technological developments are reshaping the role of marketing research, as well as the way in which it is conducted. The ethical issues in marketing research involve four stakeholders: (1) the marketing researcher, (2) the client, (3) the respondent, and (4) the public.

Key Terms and Concepts

Marketing research, 30	Marketing research process, 35	Full-service suppliers, 41
Problem-identification research, 33	Marketing research industry, 40	Syndicated services, 41
	Internal supplier, 40	Customized services, 41
Problem-solving research, 33	External suppliers, 41	Internet services, 43

Suggested Cases and Video Cases

Running Case with Real Data

1.1 Hewlett Packard

Comprehensive Critical Thinking Cases

2.1 American Idol   2.2 Baskin-Robbins   2.3 Akron Children's Hospital

Comprehensive Cases with Real Data

3.1 Bank of America   3.2 McDonald's   3.3 Boeing

Video Cases

1.1 Burke   2.1 Accenture   3.1 NFL   9.1 P&G   11.1 Dunkin' Donuts
12.1 Motorola   13.1 Subaru   14.1 Intel   19.1 Marriott

Live Research: Conducting a Marketing Research Project

1. Give a background of the client organization.
2. Discuss the client's marketing organization and operations.
3. Explain how the project's result will help the client make specific marketing decisions.
4. Organize the class. This might require the formation of project teams. The entire class could be working on the same project with each team working on all aspects of the project or each team could be assigned a specific responsibility (e.g., a specific component of the problem or a specific aspect of the project, such as collection and analysis of secondary data). Each student should participate in primary data collection. Alternatively, the class could be working on multiple projects with specific teams assigned to a specific project. The approach is flexible and can handle a variety of organizations and formats.
5. Develop a project schedule clearly specifying the deadlines for the different steps.
6. Explain how the teams will be evaluated.
7. One or a few students should be selected as project coordinators.

Acronym

The role and salient characteristics of marketing research can be described by the acronym RESEARCH:

R ecognition of information needs

E ffective decision making

S ystematic and objective

E xodus/dissemination of information

A nalysis of information

R ecommendations for action

C ollection of information

H elpful to managers

Review Questions

1. Define *marketing research.* What are some of the noteworthy aspects of this definition?
2. Describe a classification of marketing research and give examples.
3. Describe the steps in the marketing research process.
4. Describe the task of marketing research and illustrate with an example.
5. What decisions do marketing managers make? How does marketing research help them to make these decisions?
6. How would you classify marketing research suppliers?
7. What are syndicated services, and how do they help a firm conduct marketing research?
8. What is the main difference between a full-service and a limited-service supplier?
9. List five guidelines for selecting an external marketing research supplier.
10. What career opportunities are available in marketing research? Are you interested in pursuing such a career? Why or why not?
11. What is a marketing information system (MIS)?
12. How is DSS different from MIS?
13. Who are the stakeholders in marketing research?

Applied Problems

1. Visit the Web sites of one of the marketing research firms listed in Table1.1. Write a report on the types of marketing research conducted by this firm. Classify this firm based on the scheme presented in Figure 1.6.
2. Look through recent issues of newspapers and magazines to identify five examples of problem-identification research and five examples of problem-solving research.
3. Describe one marketing research project that would be useful to each of the following organizations:
   a. Your campus bookstore
   b. The public transportation authority in your city
   c. A major department store in your area
   d. A restaurant located near your campus
   e. A zoo in a major city
4. Visit www.productscan.com and click on What's New. Select one innovation on the list and research it using the Internet and your library's online databases. Write a report about the marketing research undertaken to develop this product.
5. Visit the Web sites of the following organizations: MRA (www.mra-net.org), ESOMAR (www.esomar.org), and MRSA (www.mrsa.com.au). Compare and contrast the information available at these sites. Of the three marketing research associations, which has the most useful Web site? Explain.
6. Visit the U.S. Bureau of Labor Statistics Web site at www.bls.gov and search the Internet to obtain information on the employment potential for marketing researchers.

Group Discussion

As a small group of four or five, discuss the following issues.

1. What type of institutional structure is best for a marketing research department in a large business firm?
2. What is the ideal educational background for someone seeking a career in marketing research?
3. Can ethical standards be enforced in marketing research? If so, how?

Hewlett-Packard Running Case

Review the Hewlett-Packard (HP) case, Case 1.1, and questionnaire given toward the end of the book. Answer the following questions.

1. Discuss the role that marketing research can play in helping HP maintain and build on its leadership position in the personal computers market.
2. What problem-identification research should HP undertake?
3. What problem-solving research should HP undertake?
4. Would you like to pursue a marketing research career with HP? Explain.

VIDEO CASE 1.1

BURKE: Learning and Growing Through Marketing Research

Alberta Burke, who previously worked in P&G's marketing department, founded Burke, Inc. in 1931. At that time, there were few formalized marketing research companies, not only in the United States, but also in the world. As of 2008, Burke, based in Cincinnati, Ohio, is a marketing research and decision-support company that helps its clients to understand their business practices and make them more efficient. Burke's employee owners add value to research and consulting assignments by applying superior thinking to help clients solve business problems. Burke is 100 percent employee owned. This video case traces the evolution of marketing research and how Burke implements the various phases of the marketing research process.

The Evolution of Marketing Research

The first recorded marketing research took place more than a century ago, in 1895 or 1896. By telegram, a professor sent questions to advertising agencies about the future of advertising. He got back about 10 responses and wrote a paper describing what was happening. In the first years, most of the marketing research done was a spin-off of the Bureau of Census data, and the analysis was basically limited to counting.

The next wave of marketing research came in the early 1930s, often done by ladies in white gloves who knocked on doors and asked about cake mixes. The primary methodology was door-to-door surveys; the telephone was not a very widely utilized service at that time.

Then came World War II, which saw the introduction of the psychological side of marketing research. Through the 1950s and 1960s, television became an integral part of life, and with that came television advertising. Testing of television commercials became the hot area of marketing research in the 1960s and 1970s. Another fundamental change happening at that time was when the marketing research industry made a shift from just generating and testing new ideas and sharing them with clients to working more with clients on how to use those ideas to make decisions.

In the 1980s and 1990s, Burke moved a notch higher by developing processes to provide further value. It began working with customers to identify the basic decision that needed to be made and then determine what information would be required to make that decision. The marketing research industry started developing processes that generated information to be used as input into management decision making.

The marketing research industry has come a long way from the telegrams of 1895. As of 2008, the industry is trying to find creative ways to research consumers using methods such as telephone interviews, mall intercepts, Web interviews, mobile phone surveys, and multimode methods. As Debbi Wyrick, a senior account executive at Burke, notes, when people can respond in more than one way—responding in the way that is most efficient for them—it increases the chance of getting a response.

To stay on the cutting edge, Burke conducts meta-research (research about how to do research). Recently, Burke was concerned whether the length of an online (Internet) survey has an adverse impact on the completion rate. In an effort to find out, Burke fielded two Internet surveys. One was brief (10 questions taking an average of 5 minutes to complete), and the other was longer (20 questions taking about 20 minutes to complete). The completion rate for the short survey was 35 percent, whereas it was only 10 percent for the longer survey. Burke now designs shorter Internet surveys so as to reduce the proportion of people who drop off without completing the survey.

How Burke Implements the Marketing Research Process

We briefly describe Burke's approach to defining the marketing research problem, developing an approach, research design, data collection and analysis, and report preparation and presentation.

DEFINING THE MARKETING RESEARCH PROBLEM AND DEVELOPING AN APPROACH The simplest way to find out when a company needs help is when it has to make a decision. Any time there is a go or no go, a yes or no, or a decision to be made, Burke asks what information can help reduce the risk associated with the decision. Burke then talks with the company to develop the information that might help to reduce that risk.

The first step is to define the marketing research problem, and a lot of discovery takes place at this stage. The account executive (AE) will sit down with a client and try to determine whether what the client believes is the problem really is the problem, or whether Burke needs to change or broaden the scope of the problem. Discussions with the key decision makers DMs might reveal that the company has been focusing on too narrow an issue or that it has been focusing on the wrong problem altogether.

Burke believes that defining the marketing research problem is critical to a successful research project. The company finds out what the symptoms are and works with the client to identify the underlying causes. Considerable effort is devoted to examining the background or the environmental context of the problem. In at least half the cases, when they go through the process of exploring the problem, the problem will change. It will gain a new scope or direction. This process results in a precise definition of the marketing research problem, including an identification of its specific components.

Once the problem has been defined, Burke develops a suitable approach. The problem definition is refined to generate more specific research questions and sometimes hypotheses. Because of its vast experience, Burke has developed a variety of analytical models that are customized to the identified problem. This process also results in the identification of information that will help the client solve its problem.

RESEARCH DESIGN FORMULATION In formulating the research design, Burke places special emphasis on qualitative research, survey methods, questionnaire design, and sampling design.

Qualitative Research One of the pitfalls that Burke encounters comes with qualitative research. Qualitative research is nice because it is immediate. The information generated tends to be extremely rich and in the customer's words. Burke gets to see what kinds of answers are being given and what kinds of questions and concerns customers or potential customers might have. However, one of the dangers is thinking that all customers or potential customers might view products or service offerings in the same manner; that is, generalizing the findings of qualitative research to the larger population. Burke also can conduct focus groups online.

Survey Methods Although Burke uses a variety of methods, telephone studies represent about 70 percent of its surveys. Other methods used include mall intercept, mail, and Internet or Web-based surveys. Burke carefully selects the method that is best suited to the problem. Burke predicts that telephone surveys will decrease, whereas Internet surveys will increase. If Burke is trying to interview customers around the globe, it sends an e-mail invitation to respondents to complete the survey via the Web. Burke likes the Internet's ability to show pictures of a particular product or concept to the survey respondents.

Questionnaire Design In designing the questionnaire, Burke pays particular attention to the content and wording of the questions. Some questions are well defined and can be easily framed, for other issues the exact questions to ask might not be clear. The simpler the question and the more clear it is who the target respondents are, the better the information generated.

Sampling Design Burke has a sampling department that consults with the senior account management team and account executives to determine the proper sample to use. The sampling frame is defined in terms of who the respondents are who can answer the questions that need to be addressed. The target population is defined by the marketing research problem and the research questions. Burke often buys the sampling lists from outside firms that specialize in this area. Burke is concerned about using a representative sample so that the results can be generalized to the target population (e.g., all the target consumers as opposed to only the consumers included in the sample).

DATA COLLECTION AND ANALYSIS Once the information has been collected, it will reside either in a computer-related format or a paper format that is entered into a computer format. The results are tabulated and analyzed via computers. Through the "Digital Dashboard" product, Burke not only has the ability to disseminate the results to clients when the project is finished, but also to show them the data as it is being collected. Burke breaks down the data analysis by relevant groups. You might see information by total respondents, and you might see information broken out by gender or business size. Essentially, Burke looks at different breaks in the data to try to understand what is happening, if there are differences based on different criteria, and, if so, how to make decisions based on that information. In addition, Burke likes the data to be categorized into usable units such as time, frequency, or location instead of the vague responses that respondents sometimes give.

REPORT PREPARATION AND PRESENTATION Clients need information much faster than they have in the past because decisions need to be made much more quickly. Organizing large meetings to present data analysis results is no longer practical. Most of the time Burke reports and delivers data over the Web. The report documents the entire research process. It discusses the management decision problem, the marketing research problem, the approach and research design, the information obtained to help management make the decision, and the recommendations.

The report-writing process starts from the first conversation with the client, and it is written as the research proceeds, not simply when the project is almost done. The report focuses on improving management's decision making. Burke's goal is to help clients have better decision-making abilities so that the clients are more valuable to their respective companies. Burke emphasizes this focus by reminding its clients, "Here are the management decision and marketing research problems we agreed upon. Here's the information we gathered. Here's the decision it points to." Burke might even add, "This is what we recommend you do."

Burke believes that a successful research project often leads to a subsequent research project; the research process is more of a circular process. It does not typically have a finite beginning and end. Once you solve a problem there is always another one to work on.

Conclusion

The field of marketing research has evolved in sophistication, scope, and importance over the years. Advances in technology have improved processes and methodologies, providing higher value-added services. Burke has a strong identity and a long, rich legacy in market research—since 1931—and hence it is an apt representative of the marketing research industry. This case also demonstrates key aspects of the marketing research process, from problem definition to collecting data to analyzing data and presenting the macro-analysis report. Burke is continually undertaking efforts to improve the marketing research process, and this is what helps Burke and its clients learn and grow.

Questions

1. Describe the evolution of marketing research. How has the role of marketing research changed as the field has evolved?
2. What is Burke's view of the role of marketing research?
3. Visit www.burke.com and write a report about the various marketing research services offered.
4. What is Burke's view of the importance of defining the marketing research problem?
5. What is Burke's view of the marketing research process? How does it compare with the one given in Chapter 1?
6. If Burke were to offer you a position as an account executive with the responsibility of providing marketing research services to P&G, would you accept this position? Why or why not?

Reference

1. See www.burke.com, accessed February 15, 2008.

Defining the Marketing Research Problem and Developing an Approach

OPENING QUESTIONS

1. What is a marketing research problem, and why is it important to define it correctly?

2. What tasks are involved in problem definition?

3. How do environmental factors affect the definition of the research problem, and what are these factors?

4. What is the distinction between the management-decision problem and the marketing research problem?

5. How should the marketing research problem be defined?

6. What are the various components of the approach to the problem?

7. Why are defining the problem and developing an approach more complex processes in international marketing research?

8. How can technology help in defining the problem and developing an approach?

9. What ethical issues and conflicts arise in defining the problem and developing an approach?

> "The most challenging part of any research project is defining the problem in the terms management understands and in a way that ensures the desired information is obtained."
>
> *Chet Zalesky,*
> *Founder and president of CMI,*
> *a U.S. marketing research firm.*

The World's First Sport Utility Wagon

The 2008 Outback 2.5 XT Limited Wagon was marketed as having a five-star government crash test rating and received rave reviews from automotive magazines. How was the Outback born?

In the early 1990s, Japanese-owned Subaru of America was searching for new ways to penetrate the U.S. automobile market. The marketing research firm hired by the company undertook a comprehensive examination of the marketing situation (a problem audit). The audit enabled the research firm to identify the real problem confronting management (the management-decision problem) as "What can Subaru do to expand its share of the automobile market?" The marketing research problem was defined broadly as determining the various needs of automobile users and the extent to which current product offerings were satisfying those needs. However, for marketing research to be conducted effectively and efficiently, the problem had to be defined more precisely. Subaru's management and the research firm agreed on the following specific problem components:

1. What needs do buyers of passenger cars, station wagons, and sport utility vehicles (SUVs) seek to satisfy?

2. How well do existing automobile product offerings meet these needs?

3. Is there a segment of the automobile market whose needs are not being adequately met?

4. What automobile features does the identified segment desire?

5. What is the demographic and psychographic profile of the identified segment?

The approach to the marketing research problem was developed based on the postulate, or framework, that buyers first decide on the type of car (e.g., station wagon, SUV, passenger car) they want and then select a particular brand. The research firm formulated specific research questions and possible answers (hypotheses) to be tested by collecting survey data.

The research indicated a strong market potential for a vehicle that combined the features of a station wagon and a compact SUV. The needs of a sizable male-dominated segment were not being met by either the station wagon or the SUV, and this segment wanted a hybrid product.

Based on these findings, Subaru of America introduced the 1996 Outback as "the world's first sport utility wagon." Subaru said in a press release that the Outback filled the niche between the SUV and the passenger car. The Outback has several important features that are missing from most SUVs, including an all-wheel-drive system that operates under all road conditions and vehicle speeds, four-wheel independent suspension, antilock brakes, dual air bags, and a side-intrusion protection system. It also has a low door threshold for easy passenger entry and exit and a lower center of gravity for road handling and ride comfort. Inside amenities were also upgraded, and several other features were added.

A TV campaign for Outback featured Australian actor Paul Hogan, star of the *Crocodile Dundee* movies. Viewers liked the ads, and, of course, the product. Those taking a test drive were very impressed with the vehicle's capabilities. The result? Sales were triple what Subaru originally expected. Sales of the Outback continued to be strong through the 2008 model year.[1]

Overview

This chapter examines the first two steps of the six steps of the marketing research process described in Chapter 1: defining the marketing research problem and developing an approach to the problem. Figure 2.1 briefly explains the focus of the chapter, the relation of this chapter to the previous one, and on which steps of the marketing research process this chapter concentrates.

In the opening vignette, Subaru's introduction of the Outback to exploit a new market segment demonstrates the crucial importance of correctly defining the marketing research problem. Subaru correctly defined the marketing research problem as determining the various needs of automobile users and the extent to which current product offerings were satisfying those needs. Defining the research problem is the most important aspect of the research process. Only when a problem has been clearly and accurately identified can a research project be conducted properly. This is because problem definition sets the course for the entire project. In this chapter, we will identify the tasks involved and the factors to be considered at this stage and provide guidelines to help the researcher avoid common errors.

The chapter also discusses how to develop an approach to the research problem once it has been identified. The approach lays the foundation for how to conduct the research by specifying the relevant theory and models. It further refines the specific components of the problem by asking more specific questions and formulating the hypotheses that will be tested. The approach also specifies all the information that would need to be collected in the marketing research project. The special considerations involved in defining

FIGURE 2.1

Relationship of Problem Definition and Approach to the Previous Chapter and the Marketing Research Process

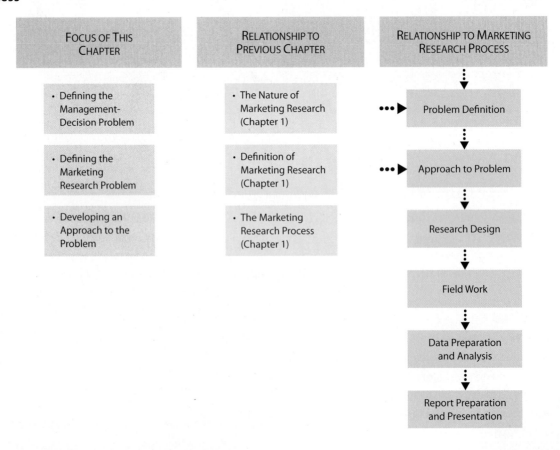

the problem and developing an approach in international marketing research are discussed. The impact of technology and several ethical issues that arise at this stage of the marketing research process also are considered. Figure 2.2 provides an overview of the topics discussed in this chapter and how they flow from one to the next.

FIGURE 2.2

Defining the Marketing Research Process and Developing an Approach: An Overview

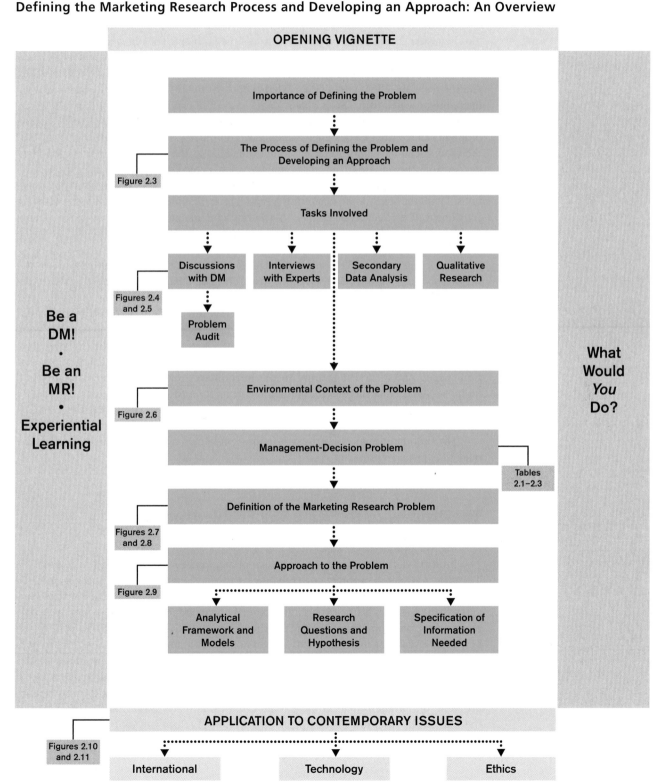

The Importance of Defining the Problem

problem definition
A broad statement of the general problem and identification of the specific components of the marketing research problem.

Although every step in a marketing research project is important, problem definition is the most important step. As mentioned in Chapter 1, marketing researchers consider problems and opportunities confronting management to be interchangeable, because the investigation of each follows the same research process. **Problem definition** involves stating the general problem and identifying the specific components of the marketing research problem, as illustrated in the opening vignette.

The opening vignette provided a broad statement of the problem confronting Subaru and identified its five specific components. The researcher and the key decision makers on the client side should agree on the definition of the problem. The *client* is the individual or organization commissioning the research. The client might be an internal person, as in the case of a research director dealing with a decision maker in her or his own organization. Alternatively, the client might be an external entity if the research is being conducted by a marketing research firm. (See Chapter 1.)

Only when both parties have clearly defined and agreed on the marketing research problem can research be designed and conducted properly. Mistakes made at this stage of the process can only mushroom into larger mistakes as the project progresses. As stated by the well-known American management expert Peter Drucker, the truly serious mistakes are made not as a result of wrong answers, but rather from asking the wrong questions. Of all the steps in the marketing research process, none is more vital to the ultimate fulfillment of a client's needs than an accurate and adequate definition of the research problem. All the effort, time, and money spent from this point on will be wasted if the problem is not defined properly.

This point is worth remembering. Inappropriate problem definition is one of the major sources of failure in marketing research. The basic message here is that clear identification and definition of the marketing research problem are critical. This was illustrated in the opening vignette. Subaru defined the problem correctly by determining the various needs of automobile users and the extent to which those needs were being satisfied by the current product offerings. The research resulted in an important finding that a substantial segment of the marketplace desired the features of both a station wagon and an SUV, leading to the introduction of a very successful product. Suppose Subaru had incorrectly defined the problem as determining the preferences of the red-hot SUV owners. In such a scenario, it is highly unlikely that the Outback would have been developed.

The problem definition process provides guidelines on how to correctly define the marketing research problem.

The Process of Defining the Problem and Developing an Approach

problem definition process
The process of defining the management-decision problem and the marketing research problem.

The problem definition and approach development process is illustrated in Figure 2.3. To define a research problem correctly, the researcher must perform a number of tasks. The researcher must discuss the problem with the decision makers in the client organization, interview industry experts and other knowledgeable individuals, analyze secondary data, and sometimes conduct qualitative research. This informal data collection helps the researcher understand the context or environment within which the problem has arisen. A clear understanding of the marketing environment also provides a framework for identifying the management-decision problem: What should the management do? The management-decision problem is then translated into a marketing research problem, the problem that the researcher must investigate. Based on the definition of the marketing research problem, the researcher develops an appropriate approach. Further explanation of the **problem-definition process** follows, with a discussion of the tasks involved.

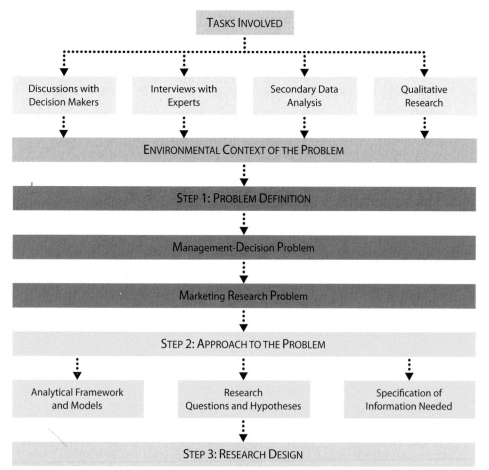

FIGURE 2.3

The Problem Definition and Approach Development Process

Tasks Involved in Problem Definition

As mentioned earlier, the tasks involved in problem definition include discussions with the decision makers, interviews with industry experts, analysis of secondary data, and qualitative research. The purpose of performing these tasks is to obtain information on the environmental factors that are relevant to the problem and to help define the management-decision problem and the corresponding marketing research problem, as well as to develop an approach. We will discuss and illustrate each of these tasks.

Discussions with Decision Makers

It is essential that the researcher understand the nature of the decision faced by the firm's managers—the management-decision problem—as well as management's expectations of the research. This discussion gives the researcher an opportunity to establish achievable expectations. The decision maker needs to understand the capabilities, as well as the limitations, of the research. Research does not provide automatic solutions to problems; rather, it serves as an additional source of information that the manager should consider in the decision-making process.

To identify the management problem, the researcher must possess considerable skill in interacting with the decision maker and maneuvering through the organization. When the ultimate decision maker is a senior executive, the researcher might have difficulty gaining access to that individual. To complicate the situation even further, several individuals might be involved in the final decision. All individuals responsible for resolving the marketing problem should be consulted in this early phase of the project. The quality of the project will be dramatically improved when the researcher is given the opportunity to interact directly with the key decision makers.

problem audit
A comprehensive examination of a marketing problem to understand its origin and nature.

Discussions with the decision maker can be structured around the **problem audit**, which helps to identify the underlying causes of the problem. The problem audit, like any other type of audit, is a comprehensive examination of a marketing problem with the purpose of understanding its origin and nature (Figure 2.4). The problem audit involves discussions with the decision maker on the following issues, which are illustrated with a problem facing the U.S. candy maker M&M/Mars.

1. *The history of the problem.* This includes an analysis of the events that have led to the decision to act. M&M/Mars, the second-leading manufacturer of candies in the United States, with a market share of 24.8 percent, would like to maintain and increase its share of the market. This problem has come into focus due to recent introductions by Hershey's, the category leader with 43.0 percent share as of 2006. Hershey's recent product spin-offs, including Hershey's Goodness and York Pink Patties, are threatening M&M/Mars market share.

2. *The alternative courses of action available to the decision maker.* The set of alternatives might be incomplete at this stage, and qualitative research might be needed to identify the more innovative courses of action. The alternatives available to the management of M&M/Mars include introducing new brands of chocolates, reducing the prices of existing brands, expanding channels of distribution, and increasing advertising expenditures.

3. *The criteria that will be used to evaluate the alternative courses of action.* For example, new product offerings might be evaluated on the basis of sales, market share, profitability, return on investment, and so forth. M&M/Mars will evaluate the alternatives based on contributions to market share and profits.

4. *The nature of potential actions that are likely to be suggested based on the research findings.* The research findings will likely call for a strategic marketing response by M&M/Mars.

5. *The information that is needed to answer the decision maker's questions.* The information needed includes a comparison of Hershey's and M&M/Mars on all the elements of the marketing mix (product, pricing, promotion, and distribution) in order to determine relative strengths and weaknesses.

6. *The manner in which the decision maker will use each item of information in making the decision.* The key decision makers will devise a strategy for M&M/Mars based on the research findings and their intuition and judgment.

FIGURE 2.4

Conducting a Problem Audit

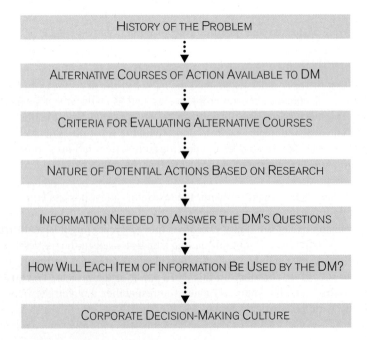

HISTORY OF THE PROBLEM

ALTERNATIVE COURSES OF ACTION AVAILABLE TO DM

CRITERIA FOR EVALUATING ALTERNATIVE COURSES

NATURE OF POTENTIAL ACTIONS BASED ON RESEARCH

INFORMATION NEEDED TO ANSWER THE DM'S QUESTIONS

HOW WILL EACH ITEM OF INFORMATION BE USED BY THE DM?

CORPORATE DECISION-MAKING CULTURE

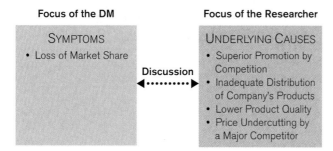

FIGURE 2.5

Discussion Between the Research and the DM

7. ***The corporate culture as it relates to decision making.*** In some firms, the decision-making process is dominant; in others, the personality of the decision maker is more important. A sensitivity to corporate culture in order to identify the individuals who are either responsible for the decision or who have a significant influence over the decision process is essential. In this case, the corporate culture at M&M/Mars calls for a committee approach in which key decision makers make the critical decisions.

Conducting a problem audit is essential in order to clarify the problem for the researcher. Not surprisingly, it may serve the same function for the decision maker. Often, the decision maker has only a vague idea of the real problem. For example, the decision maker might know that the firm is losing market share but might not know why. This is because most decision makers focus on the symptoms of a problem rather than its causes. An inability to meet sales forecasts, loss of market share, and a decline in profits are all symptoms. Research that adds value goes beyond the symptoms to address the underlying causes. For example, loss of market share might be caused by a superior promotion by the competition, inadequate distribution of the company's products, lower product quality, price undercutting by a major competitor, or any number of factors (Figure 2.5). As shown in Table 2.1, a definition of the problem based on symptoms can be misleading. Only when the underlying causes are identified can the problem be successfully addressed, as exemplified by the effort of the U.S. sports-apparel company Nike to stop the loss of market share.

Research in Action

Increased Advertising in the Video Game Industry Puts Nike Back in the Game

Nike (www.nike.com) reported revenues of $13.74 billion for the fiscal year ending May 31, 2005. Although the company was the global and U.S. leader in athletic footwear, it was losing market share. Its U.S. market share had dropped from 47 percent in 2000 to 32 percent in 2005. Clearly there was a problem. However, loss of market share was a symptom of a problem, and the underlying causes of the problem had to be identified. A problem audit revealed that a major underlying cause of the problem was the amount Nike was spending on advertising, specifically on advertising in the video game industry. German-owned competitor adidas had increased its advertising in the video game industry and was one of the top brands recalled by gamers in a study conducted by Phoenix Marketing International. Therefore, the marketing research problem was defined as whether Nike should increase its advertising budget in the video game industry.

In an effort to answer this problem an online survey of 540 video gamers was conducted. The results showed that although Nike was popular with gamers aged 8 to 17 years, it lagged behind in the 25-to-35-year segment, a segment that was growing in video game use and that also was a massive contributor to sales of athletic shoes.

Based on these findings, Nike decided to increase its advertising budget devoted to the video game industry. This effort yielded good results and revenues for the fiscal year ending May 31, 2007 increased to $16.33 billion, and Nike's U.S. market share improved to 34.5 percent.

Nike has continued its emphasis on advertising in the video game industry and has maintained its leadership in the U.S. and global athletic footwear market. Correctly identifying the underlying cause of the problem was a key in this turn-around.[2]

The Internet provides several mechanisms that can help the researcher communicate with decision makers. The first and most obvious is e-mail. Researchers can use e-mail to reach decision makers at any place or time. Chat rooms also are good forums for discussion with decision makers. For instance, a chat room discussion with multiple decision

TABLE 2.1 **Problem Definition Based on Symptoms Can Be Misleading**

| | | Problem Definition | |
Firm	Symptoms	Based on Symptoms	Underlying Causes
Manufacturer of orange soft drinks	Consumers say the sugar content is too high	Determine consumer preferences for alternative levels of sugar content	Color. The color of the drink is a dark shade of orange giving the perception that the product is too "sugary."
Manufacturer of machine tools	Customers complain prices are too high	Determine the price elasticity of demand	Channel management. Distributors do not have adequate product knowledge to communicate product benefits to customers.

makers could be developed around a problem audit. The researcher could introduce the audit issues in the chat, and then the decision makers could respond to the issues and to the each other's responses. Chat rooms can be secured with a password if there is a need to protect the discussion's contents.

Be a DM!

As the brand manager for Sprite, the Coca-Cola product that happens to be the third-largest soft drink brand in the United States, you are concerned about improving the brand's performance. Identify possible symptoms that indicate that Sprite's performance is below expectations.

Be an MR!

You are conducting marketing research for Sprite to help improve the brand's performance. Identify possible underlying causes that might be contributing to the brand's lack of performance. Visit www.cocacola.com and www.sprite.com and obtain as much information about Sprite's marketing program as you can.

Interviews with Industry Experts

In addition to discussions with decision makers, interviews with industry experts—individuals knowledgeable about the firm and the industry—can help researchers formulate the marketing research problem. Experts can be found both inside and outside the firm. If the notion of experts is broadened to include people knowledgeable about the general topic being investigated, then the interview also is referred to as an **experience survey** or as the **key-informant technique**. Another variation of this in a technological context is the **lead-user survey**, which involves obtaining information from the lead users of the technology.

Although formal questionnaires normally are not used, a prepared list of topics to be covered during the interview can be often helpful. The order in which these topics are covered and the questions to ask should not be predetermined, but rather decided as the interview progresses. This allows greater flexibility in capturing the experts' insights. The purpose of interviews with experts is to help define the marketing research problem rather than to develop a conclusive solution.

Expert interviews are more commonly used in industrial rather than consumer-research applications. In industrial or highly technical environments, the experts often are more easily identified than in consumer-research settings. This is because consumer settings are more broad and diffused than industrial or technical environments. Expert interviews also are helpful in situations where little information is available from other sources, as in the case of radically new products.

experience survey
Interviews with people knowledgeable about the general topic being investigated.

key-informant technique
Interviews with people knowledgeable about the general topic being investigated.

lead-user survey
Surveys that involve obtaining information from the lead users of the technology.

Experts can provide valuable insights in modifying or repositioning existing products, as illustrated by the repositioning of Sears. For years, sales at this giant retailer floundered, and it lost its status as America's number-one retailer to Wal-Mart in 1989. When industry experts were consulted, researchers were able to identify the real problem: lack of image. Traditionally a discount store, Sears had unsuccessfully tried to upgrade its image to a prestigious department store, thereby alienating its loyal customers. Sears finally gave up its attempt to upgrade and re-embraced the image of a discount chain store. Since then, sales and profitability have improved.

Researchers can use the Internet to enhance their ability to obtain information from experts in a specific industry. One approach to finding experts is to use newsgroups. Due to the large amount of information available, searching through the newsgroups for specific information can be an arduous task. A good place to start is www.groups.google.com, which provides categorized lists of newsgroups. Also, you may have access to newsgroups through your ISP (Internet service provider). After finding a relevant newsgroup, access the newsgroup and search for postings about the topic of interest. Surveying postings in a news-group is a good starting point for making contacts with the experts in a particular industry.

Be an MR!

Visit www.walmart.com and search the Internet, as well as your library's online databases, to identify the challenges and opportunities facing Wal-Mart, the largest retailer in the United States.

Visit www.groups.google.com and browse retailing newsgroups to identify an expert in online retailing. Interview this expert (via telephone or online) to identify the challenges and opportunities facing Wal-Mart. Alternatively, you can search for and analyze this expert's comments by searching the Internet.

Be a DM!

As the CEO of Wal-Mart, what marketing strategies would you formulate to overcome the challenges and capitalize on the opportunities identified by the marketing researcher?

Secondary Data Analysis

The information that researchers obtain from decision makers and industry experts should be supplemented with available secondary data. **Secondary data** are data collected for some purpose other than the problem at hand, including data available on the Internet, from trade organizations, or through such government agencies as the U.S. Bureau of Census (www.census.gov), the UK Statistics Authority (www.statistics.gov.uk), or the Census of India (www.censusindia.net). In contrast, **primary data** are originated by the researcher for the specific problem under study, such as survey data. Secondary data include information made available by business and government sources, commercial marketing research firms, and computerized databases. Secondary data are an economical and quick source of background information.

secondary data
Data collected for some purpose other than the problem at hand.

primary data
Data originated by the researcher to address the research problem.

Analyzing available secondary data is an essential step in the problem-definition process and should always precede primary data collection. Secondary data can provide valuable insights into the problem situation and lead to the identification of innovative courses of action. For example, the U.S. Department of Labor says that the median age of the American labor force will increase from 38.7 years in 1998 to 40.7 years by the year 2008. This is, in part, the result of the maturation of the "baby bust" generation (those born between 1965 and 1976), which will cause a decline in the number of young (ages 16 to 24) workers available to fill entry-level positions. This potential shortage of young workers has caused many marketers, particularly those in the service industries, to investigate the problem of consumer response to self-service. Some companies, such as the restaurant chain Arby's, have switched from a "high-touch" to a "high-tech" service orientation. By using high-tech equipment, consumers now perform many of the services formerly done by workers, such as placing their own orders by entering them directly into the electronic terminal. Given the tremendous importance of secondary data, this topic will be discussed in detail in Chapters 4 and 5.

Qualitative and Exploratory Research

qualitative research
An unstructured, exploratory research methodology based on small samples intended to provide insight and understanding of the problem setting.

pilot surveys
Surveys that tend to be less structured than large-scale surveys in that they generally contain more open-ended questions and the sample size is much smaller.

case studies
Involve an intensive examination of a few selected cases of the phenomenon of interest. Cases could be customers, stores, or other units.

Information obtained from decision makers, industry experts, and secondary data might not be sufficient to define the research problem. Sometimes qualitative research must be undertaken to gain a clear understanding of the factors underlying a research problem. **Qualitative research** is unstructured in that the questions asked are formulated as the research proceeds. It is exploratory in nature and based on small samples. It might involve popular qualitative techniques such as focus groups (group interviews) or in-depth interviews (one-on-one interviews that probe the respondents' thoughts in detail). Other exploratory research techniques, such as pilot surveys and case studies, can also be undertaken to gain insights into the phenomenon of interest. **Pilot surveys** tend to be less structured than large-scale surveys in that they generally contain more open-ended questions and the sample size is much smaller. **Case studies** involve an intensive examination of a few selected cases of the phenomenon of interest. The cases could be consumers, stores, firms, or a variety of other units, such as markets, Web sites, and so forth. The data are obtained from the company, external secondary sources, and by conducting lengthy unstructured interviews with people knowledgeable about the phenomenon of interest. In a project we conducted for a major department chain store, valuable insights into factors affecting store patronage were obtained in a case study comparing the five best stores with the five worst stores of that chain. The role of qualitative research in defining the marketing research problem is further illustrated by Norwegian Cruise Lines.

Once the leader in the Caribbean cruise market, U.S.-based Norwegian Cruise Lines had slipped to fourth position. To identify the underlying causes and define the problem, focus group and pilot (small-scale) surveys were conducted. This qualitative research revealed that one worry that kept people from cruising was the fear of being confined to a boat for a week or more with little to do. This concern was particularly acute among young people. This concern became a major component of the problem, and a large survey was conducted to address it. The survey verified the qualitative research findings.

In response to this information, Norwegian Cruise Line developed advertising that fought this myth, emphasizing that passengers have the flexibility to make their cruise vacation whatever they want it to be. Its provocative, award-winning print and TV campaigns featured close-ups of young people, often on land, having lots of fun. The campaign helped Norwegian attract new and younger customers and improve its market share and penetration. This success was achieved despite the fact that Norwegian was outspent in advertising two to one by Carnival Cruise Lines (which operates out of both the UK and the U.S.) and one and one-half to one by Royal Caribbean Cruises (which actually is Norwegian- as well as American-based).[3] (Exploratory research is discussed in more detail in Chapter 3, and qualitative research techniques are discussed in detail in Chapter 6.)

Although research undertaken at this stage might not be conducted in a formal way, it can provide valuable insights. These insights, together with information obtained from discussions with the decision makers, industry experts, and analysis of secondary data, guide the researcher to an appropriate definition of the problem, as illustrated by the Century City Doctors Hospital in Los Angeles.

Research in Action

Century City Doctors Hospital Moves into New Century of Health Care

At first glance, Century City Doctors Hospital (CCDH) (www.ccdoctorshospital.com), located in Los Angeles, California, looks and feels like a five-star hotel—a serene oasis of calm and luxury. The lobby sets the tone for an atmosphere that features concierge service, gourmet cuisine, and bedside Internet access.

However, CCDH has not always used luxury as a positioning tool. As most hospitals across the country were doing in the early 2000s, the hospital (then named Century City Hospital) was considering a course of action that emphasized cost cutting to improve profitability. An external marketing research firm was hired to suggest areas where costs could be cut without alienating consumers. However, the research firm realized that lower profitability was merely a symptom. Based on discussions with key decision makers and industry experts, the underlying cause of low profitability was identified as lack of a clear focus and market positioning by the hospital. Specifically, the hospital did not know who its target customers were or their unique needs.

Secondary data from the Bureau of Census indicated that nearly 50 percent of the local residents had high incomes.

Qualitative research in the form of focus groups revealed that this group valued the best in food, accommodations, privacy, and exclusiveness. These people were not price sensitive and were willing to pay for added benefits.

As an outcome of this process, the problem was redefined as to how CCDH could best meet the medical needs of its high-income residents. Based on the findings of subsequent research, CCDH opened its deluxe Century Pavilion, offering luxurious private accommodations at a premium price. Thus, CCDH was able to carve a profitable niche. Salus Surgical Group of Beverly Hills purchased the hospital with more than 170 physician investors in 2004, investing almost $100 million in refurbishment and equipment, furthering the luxury appeal of the entire hospital. As of 2008, CCDH is one of the nation's largest physician-owned and operated hospitals.[4]

Environmental Context of the Problem

The insights gained from qualitative research, along with discussions with decision makers, interviews with industry experts, and analysis of secondary data, help the researcher understand the environmental context of the problem. The researcher must have a full understanding of the client's firm and industry. Several factors that comprise the **environmental context of the problem** can play an important role in defining the marketing research problem. These factors consist of past information and forecasts pertaining to the industry and the firm, the firm's resources and constraints, decision makers' objectives, buyer behavior, the legal environment, the economic environment, and the firm's marketing and technological skills (Figure 2.6). Each of these factors is discussed briefly.

Past Information and Forecasts

Past information and forecasts of trends with respect to sales, market share, profitability, technology, population, demographics, and lifestyle are combined to provide the researcher with a fuller picture of the underlying marketing research problem. Not only should the firm's performance and projections be analyzed, but the firm's performance

environmental context of the problem
Factors that have an impact on the definition of the marketing research problem, including past information and forecasts, resources and constraints of the firm, objectives of the decision maker, buyer behavior, legal environment, economic environment, and marketing and technological skills of the firm.

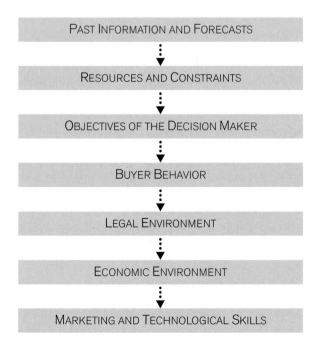

FIGURE 2.6

Factors to Be Considered in the Environmental Context of the Problem

relative to the overall industry should be examined as well. For example, if a firm's sales have decreased but industry sales have increased, the problems will be very different than if industry sales have also decreased. In the former case, the problems are likely to be specific to the firm.

Past information, forecasts, and trends can be valuable in uncovering potential opportunities and problems. In the United States, for example, pizza restaurants have sought to exploit potential opportunities in the recent trend toward takeout food and home delivery. Pizza Hut has successfully capitalized on this trend by emphasizing takeout and home-delivery services. It opened several takeout-only (with no dine-in service) outlets to better serve this market. As another illustration, in the Subaru vignette, forecasts of future sales of station wagons and SUVs indicated to management that both types of automobiles were not tapping the full market potential.

Be an MR!	Be a DM!
Obtain from secondary sources data on the sales of U.S. restaurants for the past year and sales forecasts for the next 2 to 5 years. How can you use the Internet to obtain this information?	You are the marketing manager for Houston's restaurants. You have come across information stating that more and more people are having lunch on the go and that this trend is expected to continue for the next 5 years. What problems and opportunities does this information suggest?

Past information and forecasts can be especially valuable if resources are limited and there are other constraints on the organization.

Resource Constraints and Objectives

To formulate a marketing research problem of appropriate scope, it is necessary to take into account the resources available, such as money, research skills, and operational capabilities, as well as operational and time constraints. Although adjustments in proposed research expenditure levels are common, proposing a large-scale $100,000 project when only $40,000 has been budgeted will put the research firm at a serious competitive disadvantage. Time constraints also are an important factor in many research projects. A project for Fisher-Price, a major U.S. toy manufacturer, involving mall-intercept interviews (conducted with shoppers in malls) in six major cities (Chicago, Fresno, Kansas City, New York, Philadelphia, and San Diego) had to be completed in 4 weeks. Why the rush? The results had to be presented at an upcoming board meeting where a major (go/no-go) decision was to be made about a new product introduction. The time constraint was a major factor that guided the problem definition and the approach adopted.

objectives
Goals of the organization and of the decision maker that must be considered in order to conduct successful marketing research.

In formulating the management-decision problem, the researcher must also have a clear understanding of two types of **objectives**: (1) the organizational objectives (the goals of the organization) and (2) the personal objectives of the decision makers. For the project to be successful, it must serve the objectives of the organization and of the decision makers. This may become a challenge when the two are not complementary. For example, a decision maker might wish to undertake research to postpone an awkward decision, to lend credibility to a decision that has already been made, or to get promoted.

It might take skill to get the decision maker to think in terms of objectives that management can act upon (actionable objectives). One effective technique is to confront the decision maker with a number of possible solutions to a problem and ask whether he or she would follow a particular course of action. If the answer is no, further probing might be needed to uncover deeper reasons as to why a particular solution is unsatisfactory.

buyer behavior
A body of knowledge that tries to understand and predict consumers' reactions based on an individual's specific characteristics.

Buyer Behavior

Buyer behavior is a central component of the environment. It includes the underlying motives, perceptions, attitudes, buying habits, and demographic and psychographic (psychological and lifestyle) profiles of buyers and potential buyers. Most marketing decisions involve a prediction of the buyers' response to a particular marketing action. An understanding of the underlying buyer behavior can provide valuable insights into the problem. Note that in the Subaru vignette, information on the demographic and psychographic characteristics of the automobile segment whose needs were not being met was an important component of the marketing research problem.

Be a DM!

As the marketing manager for Timberland, how would your understanding of the consumers' decision-making process affect your decision to sell outdoor shoes on the Internet?

Be an MR!

Timberland is a major American manufacturer of outdoor footwear. Visit www.timberland.com and search the Internet and your library's online database to obtain information on Timberland's marketing program for outdoor shoes. What decision-making process do consumers follow when purchasing outdoor shoes?

In another case, buyer behavior research told ConAgra Frozen Foods that more than 55 percent of Americans pack a lunch and that more and more meals are eaten on the run. However, although consumers increasingly want their food to be portable, they still demand high flavor and good nutrition. Wanting to capitalize on this aspect of buyer behavior, ConAgra further investigated the marketing research problem of consumer preferences for healthy, delicious, and portable food.

The company's answer, based on the findings of this research, was a new entry into the premium-meals category, Healthy Choice Hearty Handfuls frozen sandwiches. As an alternative to many frozen convenience foods, the product targeted an adult taste profile with bakery-style breads, lean meats, and crisp vegetables. True to the name, the sandwiches are both healthy (low in fat and calories) and hearty (at 6 ounces, they are an estimated 35 percent larger than most frozen sandwiches). According to ConAgra, the Hearty Handfuls line exceeded sales expectations, becoming the number-three frozen sandwich brand in its first 6 months.

The increased preference for portable, healthy, and hearty food could be attributed to changes in the sociocultural environment, which includes demographic trends and consumer tastes. The legal, economic, and marketing environment also has a significant impact in some industries.

Legal, Economic, Marketing, and Technological Environments

The **legal environment** includes public policies, laws, government agencies, and pressure groups that influence and regulate various organizations and individuals in society. Important areas of law include patents, trademarks, royalties, trade agreements, taxes, and tariffs. Government regulation and deregulation has had a huge impact on the marketing process in many industries, such as the airline, banking, and telecommunication industries. The legal and regulatory considerations relevant to a business must be taken into account by the researcher.

legal environment
Regulatory policies and norms within which organizations must operate.

Another important component of the environmental context is the **economic environment**, which is composed of purchasing power, gross income, disposable income, discretionary income, prices, savings, credit availability, and general economic conditions. The general state of the economy (rapid growth, slow growth, recession, or stagflation) influences the willingness of consumers and businesses to take on credit and spend on big-ticket items. Thus, the economic environment can have important implications for marketing research problems.

economic environment
It is composed of purchasing power, gross income, disposable income, discretionary income, prices, savings, credit availability, and general economic conditions.

JCPenney is one of the largest and most well-known department stores in the United States. In the 1980s, JCPenney suffered due to inconsistent sales growth and a drop in the company's image. In the early 2000s, JCPenney began a massive overhaul toward a higher-quality image to counter these problems. The company courted famous name brands such as Oshkosh B'Gosh, Levis, and Charles of the Ritz. Unfortunately, JCPenney decided to raise prices and go for high-end fashions at a bad time. Price increases coincided with the recession and the economic downturn of 2001 and 2002, and consumers did not have sufficient money to spend. Its most recent attempt in 2008 to recover its image has been to stick with good brand names, to control prices, and to market itself as the store for "middle America" (which is say, the more or less conservative American middle class). JCPenney's lost image has been found by keeping prices competitive and carrying good brand names.

A firm's marketing and technological skills greatly influence which marketing programs and strategies can be implemented. A company's expertise with each element of the marketing mix, as well as its general levels of marketing and production skills, affect the nature and scope of the marketing research project. For example, the introduction of a new product that requires retooling of a manufacturing process or that presumes sophisticated marketing skills might not be a viable alternative if the firm lacks the skills to manufacture or market such a product. However, if the company is able to capitalize on its marketing and technological skills its products and new introductions are more likely to succeed, as illustrated in the Subaru vignette.

A good understanding of the environmental context of the problem enables the researcher to appropriately define the problem, as illustrated by Gillette.

Research in Action

Satin Care for Women Provides a Satin Touch for Gillette

Analysis of past information indicated that most women pamper themselves with products for their beauty regimen and that this trend was likely to continue. Gillette, a part of P&G (www.pg.com) since 2005, was willing to devote its tremendous financial resources and marketing expertise to capturing a larger share of the women's shaving-products market.

An examination of underlying buyer behavior revealed that women had a strong preference for personal-care products that were rich in moisturizers. Economic and marketing analysis indicated that a substantial segment of this market was not price sensitive and was willing to pay a premium for such products. Accordingly, the marketing research problem was formulated as the investigation of women's preferences and purchase intentions for a shaving preparation rich in moisturizers.

The research showed that women were willing to spend more on shaving products that contained moisturizers. To capitalize on those findings, Gillette introduced Satin Care for Women (www.satincare.com). The product was an innovation in the shaving-products category, because it was the first non-soap-based shaving preparation and it was infused with seven moisturizers. The product introduction was so successful that

Satin Care for Women exceeded all expectations in the launch markets of the United States, Canada, and northern Europe. This success reinforced Gillette's understanding of the environmental factors in the shaving-products market. Gillette continued to build on the success of Satin Care for Women by extending the line. As of 2008, the Satin Care for Women line included six fragrances (Alluring Avocado, Melon Splash, Oceania, Radiant Apricot, Vanilla Dream, and Wild Berry) and catered to three different skin conditions (Dry Skin, Sensitive Skin, and Skin Soothing).[5]

Many of the factors to be considered in determining the environmental context of the problem can be researched via the Internet. Past information and trend forecasts can be found by searching for the appropriate information with the search engines. For company-specific information pertaining to the client or a competitor, the researcher can go to the company's home page.

Gaining an adequate understanding of the environmental context of the problem allows the researcher to define both the management-decision problem and the marketing research problem.

Management-Decision Problem and Marketing Research Problem

The **management-decision problem** asks what the decision maker needs to do, whereas the **marketing research problem** asks what information is needed and how it can best be obtained (Table 2.2). Research is directed at providing the information necessary to make a sound decision. The management-decision problem is action oriented, framed from the perspective of what should be done. How should the loss of market share be arrested? Should the market be segmented differently? Should a new product be introduced? Should the promotional budget be increased?

In contrast, the marketing research problem is information oriented. Research is directed at providing the information necessary to make a sound decision. The management-decision problem focuses on the symptoms, whereas the marketing research problem is concerned with the underlying causes (Table 2.2).

In the opening vignette, the management-decision problem was "What can Subaru do to expand its share of the automobile market?" The marketing research problem focused on information about the needs of the buyers of passenger cars, station wagons, and SUVs and on identifying a segment whose needs were not being met. Also, information was to be obtained on the automobile features desired by the identified segment and on the demographic and psychographic characteristics of this segment.

To further illustrate the distinction between the two orientations, consider an illustrative problem: the loss of market share for P&G's Old Spice product line (aftershave, cologne, deodorant). The decision maker is faced with the problem of how to recover this loss (the management-decision problem). Possible responses include modifying existing products, introducing new products, reducing prices, changing other elements in the marketing mix, and segmenting the market. Suppose the decision maker and the researcher believe that the problem can be traced to market segmentation, in that Old Spice should be targeted at a specific segment. They decide to conduct research to explore that issue. The marketing research problem would then become the identification and evaluation of different ways to segment or group the market. As the research process progresses, problem definition can be modified to reflect emerging information. Table 2.3 provides additional examples, including that of Subaru from the opening vignette, that further clarify the distinction between the management-decision problem and the marketing research problem.

A good way to link the broad statement of the marketing research problem with the management-decision problem is through the use of a conceptual map.[6] A **conceptual map** involves the following three components:

Management wants to (take an action).

Therefore, we should study (topic).

So that we can explain (question).

The first line states the rationale for the question and the project. This is the management-decision problem. The second line of the conceptual map declares what broader topic is being investigated. The third line implies the question being investigated—the who/how/why that needs to be explained. Thus, the second and third

management-decision problem
The problem confronting the decision maker. It asks what the decision maker needs to do.

marketing research problem
The marketing research problem asks what information is needed and how it can best be obtained.

conceptual map
A way to link the broad statement of the marketing research problem with the management-decision problem.

TABLE 2.2 Management-Decision Problem Versus the Marketing Research Problem

Management-Decision Problem	Marketing Research Problem
Asks what the decision maker needs to do	Asks what information is needed and how it should be obtained
Action oriented	Information oriented
Focuses on symptoms	Focuses on the underlying causes

TABLE 2.3 **Management-Decision Problem and the Corresponding Marketing Research Problem**

Management-Decision Problem	Marketing Research Problem
Should the advertising campaign be changed?	To determine the effectiveness of the current advertising campaign.
Should the price of the product be changed?	To determine the impact on sales and profits of various levels of price changes.
What can Subaru do to expand its automobile market?	To determine the various needs of the automobile users and the extent to which those needs were being satisfied by the current product offerings.

lines define the broad marketing research problem. Here is a conceptual map for AT&T Mobility, a division of the largest wireless firm in the United States:

> Management wants to (develop retention programs that will retain 90 percent of heavy users of wireless services and lead to 10 percent higher sales over the next 2 years).
> Therefore, we should study (heavy-user loyalty).
> So that we can explain (what will be the most important variables in retaining these customers over the next 2 years).

As can be seen, the preceding example provides valuable definitions of the management-decision problem and the broad marketing research problems that are closely linked. The problem is now focused on a segment of customers (heavy users) and one behavior of these customers (staying with the company over the next 2 years). Measurable results, such as "90 percent retention of heavy users," are included, as well as a company goal (10 percent increase in sales over the next 2 years).

Experiential Learning

P&G's Conceptual Map

In an attempt to take market share away from archrival Kimberly-Clark's Huggies, P&G's baby-care division has developed a diaper that remains wet for 2 minutes prior to drying. Called "Feel 'n Learn Advanced Trainers," these diapers prompt toddlers to try tinkling in the toilet once they partially wet the diaper. The Pampers team has a keen interest in the primary customer segment it calls "30 & Smart." This segment currently accounts for 15 percent of Pampers and 20 percent of Huggies sales. Members of this segment live primarily in metropolitan areas, are between 30 and 39 years of age, and are well educated.[7]

Visit www.pg.com and search the Internet and your library's electronic database to obtain information on P&G's and competing diaper brands. Develop a three-level conceptual map from the following elements:

a. Management wants to overtake Huggies in the diaper wars.

b. Management wants to successfully introduce a new diaper that will capture an 80 percent market share in the 30 & Smart segment within 12 months after introduction.

c. Therefore, we are studying what will make the best diaper.

d. Therefore, we are studying 30 & Smart evaluations of Feel 'n Learns in a test market.

e. So that we can explain preferences for competing brands of diapers.

f. So that we can explain the probability of switching to the Feel 'n Learn diapers within this segment.

Defining the Marketing Research Problem

A general guideline for defining the research problem is that the definition should (1) allow the researcher to obtain all the information needed to address the management-decision problem and (2) guide the researcher in proceeding with the project. Researchers often err by defining the research problem either too broadly or too narrowly (Figure 2.7). A broad definition fails to provide clear guidelines for the subsequent steps involved in the

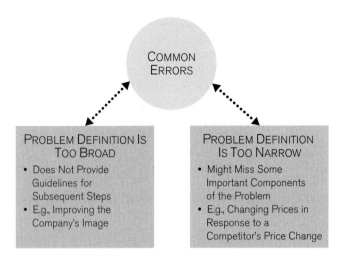

FIGURE 2.7

Errors in Defining the Market Research Problem

project. The following are examples of overly broad marketing research problem defini-tions: developing a marketing strategy for the brand, improving the competitive position of the firm, or improving the company's image. These definitions are not specific enough to suggest an approach to the problem or a research design.

Focusing the problem definition too narrowly can also be a serious flaw. A narrow focus might inhibit a full examination of plausible options, particularly innovative ones. It might also prevent the researcher from addressing important components of the management-decision problem. For example, a problem will be too narrowly defined if it is confined to how a company should adjust its pricing, given that a major competitor has initiated price changes. The narrow focus on pricing alone leaves out other possible responses (alternative courses of action), such as introducing new brands, changing adver-tising, or adding new distribution channels.

A narrow definition of the problem could also lead to restrictive sampling, resulting in erroneous conclusions. If Revlon, a leader in U.S. mass-market cosmetics, is targeting females aged 16 to 29 for its cosmetics line, that is fine for guiding media placement; however, the problem would be too narrowly defined for research measuring advertising effectiveness if the study is restricted to females aged 16 to 29. The reason is that TV advertising has a much larger reach. Suppose the advertising turns out to be really effective among women aged 34 to 54 instead of 16 to 29. Revlon might have canceled a very effective campaign because it appeared to be failing among the target audience. However, it is possible that Revlon's commercials are working among the 16-to-29 group, but driving all other age groups away. If we were sampling only the 16-to-29 segment, we would have overlooked this critical failing. Remember: Always define the problem broadly enough so as not to overlook any relevant aspects.

To minimize the possibility of a wrong decision due to an incorrect definition of the marketing research problem, the researcher should adopt a two-stage process: First, the marketing research problem is stated in broad, general terms; then, it is reduced to its spe-cific components (Figure 2.8). The **broad statement of the problem** provides perspective

broad statement of the problem
The initial statement of the marketing research problem that provides an appropriate perspective on the problem.

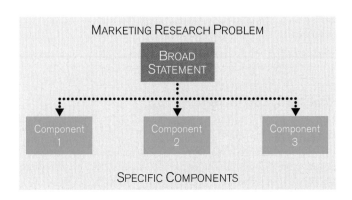

FIGURE 2.8

Proper Definition of the Marketing Research Problem

specific components of the problem
The second part of the marketing research problem definition. The specific components focus on the key aspects of the problem and provide clear guidelines on how to proceed.

on the problem and acts as a safeguard against committing the second type of error. The **specific components of the problem** focus on the key aspects and provide clear guidelines on how to proceed further, avoiding the first type of error.

This process was illustrated in the opening vignette. The broad statement of the problem was to determine the various needs of automobile users and the extent to which current product offerings were satisfying those needs. In addition, five specific components were identified. *Tennis* magazine provides another example of an appropriate marketing research problem definition.

Research in Action

Research Serves *Tennis* Magazine

Tennis magazine (www.tennis.com), a publication of the New York Times Company, wanted to obtain information about its readers. The broad marketing research problem was defined as gathering information about subscribers. The specific components of the problem were as follows:

1. ***Demographics.*** Who are the men and women who subscribe to the magazine?

2. ***Psychological characteristics and lifestyles.*** How do subscribers spend their money and their free time? The following lifestyle indicators were examined: fitness, travel, car rental, apparel, consumer electronics, credit cards, and financial investments.

3. ***Tennis activity.*** Where and how often do subscribers play tennis? What are their skill levels?

4. ***Relationship to Tennis magazine.*** How much time do subscribers spend with the issues? How long do they keep them? Do they share the magazine with other tennis players?

Because the questions were clearly defined, the information provided by this research helped management design specific features on tennis instruction, equipment, famous tennis players, and locations to play tennis to meet readers' specific needs. These changes made *Tennis* magazine more appealing to its readers and resulted in increased circulation and enhanced advertising revenues.

Once the marketing research problem has been broadly stated and its specific components identified, as in the case of *Tennis* magazine, the researcher is in a position to develop a suitable approach.

Be a DM!

A TiVo DVR is like a VCR, but without the hassles of videotapes or timers. Browse the TiVo Web site (www.tivo.com) to get a better idea of this innovative product/service.

As the marketing manager, you want to increase TiVo's market share. What information do you need in accomplishing this goal?

Be an MR!

Broadly define and identify the specific components of the marketing research problem facing TiVo.

Components of the Approach

The tasks performed earlier also help in developing an approach. An approach to a marketing research problem should include the following components: analytical framework and models, research questions and hypotheses, and a specification of the information needed (see Figure 2.3). Each of these components is discussed in the following sections.

objective evidence
Unbiased evidence that is supported by empirical findings.

theory
A conceptual scheme based on foundational statements, which are assumed to be true.

Analytical Framework and Models

In general, marketing research should be based on objective evidence and supported by theory. **Objective evidence** (evidence that is unbiased and supported by empirical findings) is gathered by compiling relevant findings from secondary sources. A **theory** guides the collection of this data. It is a conceptual framework based on foundational statements, called *axioms*, which are assumed to be true. Theory may come from academic literature contained in books, journals, and monographs. For example, according to attitude theory, attitude toward a brand, such as Nike sneakers, is determined by an evaluation of the brand on salient attributes (e.g., price, comfort, durability, and style). Relevant theory provides insight regarding which variables should be investigated and which should be treated as dependent variables (those whose values depend on the values of other variables) and which should be treated as independent variables (those whose values affect the values of other variables). Thus, attitude toward Nike will be the dependent variable; price, comfort, durability, and style will be independent variables. The approach should be based on some kind of working theory or framework. This also is helpful in developing an appropriate model.

An **analytical model** consists of a set of variables related in a specified manner to represent all or a part of some real system or process. Models can take many forms. The most common are verbal, graphical, and mathematical structures. In **verbal models**, the variables and their relationships are stated in prose form. These models often are a summary or restatement of the main points of the theory. **Graphical models** are visual and pictorially represent the theory. They are used to isolate variables and to suggest directions of relationships; however, they are not designed to provide numerical results. They are logical, preliminary steps to developing mathematical models. **Mathematical models** explicitly specify the strength and direction of relationships among variables, usually in equation form. Graphical models are particularly helpful in conceptualizing an approach to the problem, as the following jeans purchase model illustrates.

analytical model
An explicit specification of a set of variables and their interrelationships designed to represent some real system or process in whole or in part.

verbal model
Analytical models that provide a written representation of the relationships between variables.

graphical model
Analytical models that provide a visual picture of the relationships between variables.

mathematical model
Analytical models that explicitly describe the relationships between variables, usually in equation form.

Research in Action

Lee Riveted Rivets Young Consumers with "The Brand That Fits"

According to consumer decision-making theory, the consumer first decides whether to purchase jeans or other casual clothes. If jeans are to be purchased, the consumer will form selection criteria for evaluating alternative brands.

The selection criteria consist of factors such as color, price, fit, cut, comfort, and quality. The competing brands of jeans are then evaluated based on the selection criteria to purchase one or more brands. The accompanying graphical model illustrates the decision process for jeans for a consumer considering the purchase of casual clothing.

American-made Lee Riveted jeans (www.leejeans.com) are targeted at young people, who buy jeans based primarily on fit and cut. Therefore, the marketing theme of Lee Riveted with tag lines "the brand that fits" and "cut to be noticed" was based on this model. In 2007, Lee Jeans expanded its reach by introducing three new lines of fit: Lee Custom Fit, Lee Natural Fit, and Lee Relaxed Fit.[8]

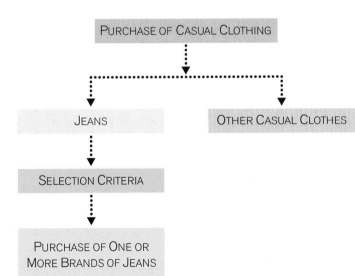

In the opening vignette, the analytical model postulated that buyers first decide on the type of car they want (e.g., station wagon, SUV, passenger car) and then select a specific brand based on their choice criteria (e.g., features, performance, price, repair and maintenance, gas mileage, and so forth). The verbal, graphical, and mathematical models complement each other and help the researcher identify relevant research questions and hypotheses, as shown in Figure 2.9.

FIGURE 2.9

Development of Research Questions and Hypothesis

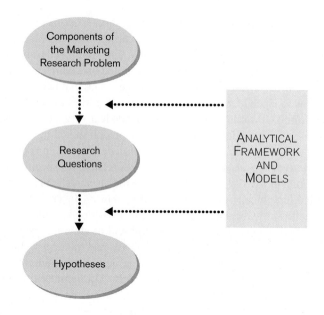

Be an MR!

Write a report about American carmaker GM's brands by visiting www.gm.com. Develop a graphical model explaining consumers' selection of an automobile brand.

Be a DM!

As the marketing chief of GM, how can a graphical model explaining consumers' selection of an automobile brand help you to position GM's various brands?

Research Questions and Hypotheses

research questions
Refined statements of the specific components of the problem.

Research questions (RQs) are refined statements of the specific components of the problem. A problem component might break into several research questions. Research questions are designed to ask the specific information required to address each problem component. Research questions that successfully address the problem components will provide valuable information for the decision maker.

The formulation of the research questions should be guided, not only by the problem definition, but also by the analytical framework and the model adopted. In the Lee Riveted jeans example, the factors that influenced consumers' selection of jean brands were postulated based on theoretical framework as color, price, fit, cut, comfort, and quality. Several research questions can be posed related to these factors: What is the relative importance of these factors in influencing consumers' selection of jeans? Which factor is the most important? Which factor is the least important? Does the relative importance of these factors vary across consumers?

hypothesis
An unproven statement or proposition about a factor or phenomenon that is of interest to the researcher.

A **hypothesis** (H) is an unproven statement or proposition about a factor or phenomenon that is of interest to the researcher. It may be a tentative statement about the relationships discussed in the theoretical framework or represented in the analytic model. The hypothesis can also be stated as a possible answer to the research question. Hypotheses are statements about proposed relationships rather than merely questions to be answered. They reflect the researchers' expectation and can be tested empirically. (See Chapter 16.) Hypotheses also play the important role of suggesting variables to be included in the research design. The relationship between the marketing research problem, research questions, and hypotheses, along with the influence of the objective/theoretical framework and analytical models, is described in Figure 2.9.

In commercial marketing research, the hypotheses are not formulated as rigorously as they are in academic research. An interesting research question and related hypotheses that could be posed about the need for a hybrid product in the Subaru vignette are as follows:

RQ: Is there an overlap between the features sought by station wagon buyers and buyers of SUVs?

H1:   The buyers of station wagons rate certain features of SUVs as important.

H2:   The buyers of SUVs rate certain features of station wagons as important.

The following example further illustrates research questions and hypotheses.

Research in Action

"Got Milk?"

Milk consumption in the United States had steadily declined for 20 years. Qualitative research indicated that people had misconceptions about milk. Hence, survey research was undertaken to address the following RQ and Hs:

RQ: Do people have misconceptions about milk?

H1:   Milk is perceived as fat-laden and unhealthy.

H2:   Milk is perceived as an old-fashioned drink.

H3:   People believe that milk is meant only for kids.

When the survey data supported these hypotheses, the Milk Processor Education Program launched the well-known "milk mustache" campaign with the "Got Milk?" slogan. This creative advertising was a real attention-getter, showing American entertainment celebrities sporting the famous white mustache. The result? Humble milk, until a few years before an also-ran in the advertising race behind soft drinks and juices, became a key beverage-industry player. The decline in milk consumption was arrested and annual milk consumption among children reached 28 gallons in 2002—the highest level in 10 years. Consumption continued to be stable through 2008 (www.gotmilk.com). In 2008, "Got

Milk?" ads were touting the health benefits of milk with tag lines such as "Stay lean with milk" and "Drink and dance your way to health."[9]

Be an MR!

Visit www.tennis.com and write a report about the current editorial content and features of the magazine. Formulate two research questions with corresponding hypotheses for the third component of the problem in the *Tennis* magazine example.

Be a DM!

As the editor of *Tennis*, how would you change the editorial content of the magazine if the formulated hypotheses were supported by data collected in a survey of readers?

Specification of Information Needed

By focusing on each component of the problem, the analytical framework and models, and the research questions and hypotheses, the researcher can determine what information should be obtained. It is helpful to carry out this exercise for each component of the problem and to make a list specifying all the information that should be collected. We illustrate this process with respect to the opening vignette.

COMPONENT 1

- Needs of buyers of passenger cars are operationalized in terms of the attributes or features desired in an automobile.
- Needs of buyers of station wagons are operationalized in terms of the attributes or features desired in an automobile.
- Needs of buyers of SUVs are operationalized in terms of the attributes or features desired in an automobile.

COMPONENT 2

- Evaluation of passenger cars on the desired attributes.
- Evaluation of station wagons on the desired attributes.
- Evaluation of SUVs on the desired attributes.

COMPONENT 3

- No new information to be collected. The segment can be identified based on information obtained for the first two components.

COMPONENT 4

- No new information to be collected. The desired features can be identified based on information obtained for the first two components.

COMPONENT 5

- Standard demographic characteristics (e.g., gender, marital status, household size, age, education, occupation, income, and type and number of automobiles owned) and psychographic characteristics. Psychographic characteristics include outdoor and recreational activities, family orientation, and attitude toward daily commuting.

Experiential Learning

Defining the Problem and Developing an Approach

Visit a local business located near your campus. Interview the business owner or manager and identify some of the marketing challenges facing this business. Also, interview an expert in this industry. Search and analyze secondary data pertaining to this business and the industry and identify the environmental context of the problem.

1. Define the management-decision problem.
2. Define the marketing research problem.
3. Develop a graphical model explaining the consumer-choice process leading to the patronage of this business or its competitors.
4. Develop an appropriate research question and hypothesis.

Summary Illustration Using the Opening Vignette

We can summarize and illustrate the major concepts discussed in this chapter by returning to the opening vignette. The Subaru vignette illustrates the importance of correctly defining the problem and showing how a problem audit can help in the process. The tasks involved in formulating the marketing research problem should lead to an understanding of the environmental context of the problem. In the case of Subaru, forecasts of future sales of station wagons and SUVs indicated that these two types of automobiles were not tapping the market potential. Subaru undertook research to understand the underlying behavior of the consumers and their needs and desires. It capitalized upon its marketing and technological skill to achieve the successful introduction of "the world's first sport utility wagon."

Analysis of the environmental context should help identify the management-decision problem, which should then be translated into a marketing research problem. The management-decision problem asks what the decision maker should do, is action oriented, and focuses on the symptoms. The marketing research problem asks what information is needed and how it should be obtained, is information oriented, and focuses on the underlying causes. In the opening vignette, the management-decision problem was "What can Subaru do to expand its share of the automobile market?" The marketing research problem focused on information about the needs of the buyers of passenger cars, station wagons, and SUVs and identification of a segment whose needs were not being met. Also, information was to be obtained on the automobile features desired by the members of this segment and on their demographic and psychographic characteristics. A broad statement of the problem was given, and specific components were identified. Figure 2.10 provides a concept map for problem definition.

Developing an approach to the problem is the second step in the marketing research process. The components of an approach consist of an analytical framework and models, research questions and hypotheses, and specification of the information needed. The analytical model postulated that buyers first decide on the type of vehicle (e.g., station wagon, SUV, passenger car) and then decide on a specific brand. Research questions and hypotheses related to the overlap between the features sought by station wagon buyers and buyers of SUVs were formulated. In specifying the information required, the researcher operationalized the needs of automobile buyers in terms of the attributes or features desired. Evaluations of passenger cars, station wagons, and SUVs on the desired attributes had to be obtained. Information on standard demographic characteristics and the identified

FIGURE 2.10

A Concept Map for Problem Definition

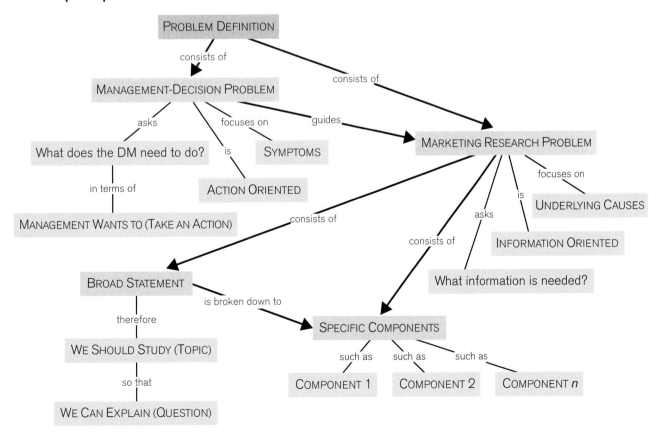

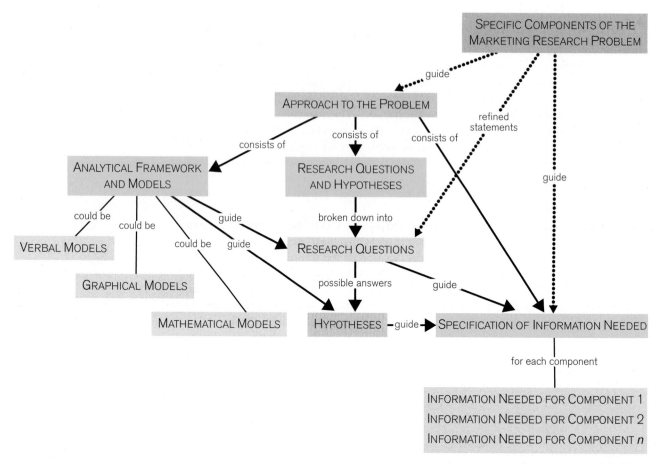

FIGURE 2.11

A Concept Map for Approach to the Problem

psychographic characteristics also was needed. Figure 2.11 provides a concept map for developing an approach.

International Marketing Research

Conducting research in international markets often means working within unfamiliar environments. This lack of familiarity with the environmental factors of the country in which the research is being conducted can greatly increase the difficulty of appropriately defining the problem, as illustrated by the experience of the U.S. food-products firm Heinz in Brazil.

Research in Action

Heinz Ketchup Couldn't Catch Up in Brazil

As of 2008, H. J. Heinz Company is one of the world's leading marketers of branded foods to retail and foodservice channels. Heinz has number-one or number-two branded businesses in more than 50 world markets. Despite good track records domestically and overseas, H. J. Heinz failed in its initial attempts to penetrate South America's biggest and most promising market. As an entry strategy into Brazil,

Heinz entered into a joint venture with Citrosuco Paulista, a giant orange juice exporter, with the future possibility of buying the profitable company. However, the sales of Heinz products, including ketchup, did not take off. Where was the problem?

A post-entry problem audit revealed that the company lacked a strong local distribution system. Heinz had attempted to duplicate a strategy that had been successful in Mexico: distribution through neighborhood shops. However, the problem audit revealed that 75 percent of grocery shopping in São Paulo, Brazil's largest city, is done in supermarkets, not small, neighborhood shops. Although Mexico and Brazil may appear to have similar cultural and demographic characteristics, consumer behavior was found to vary greatly. A problem audit and an examination of the environmental context of the problem prior to entry in Brazil could have prevented this failure.[10]

Many international marketing efforts fail because a problem audit is not conducted prior to entering the foreign market, and the relevant environmental factors are not taken into account. This leads to an incorrect definition of the marketing research problem and an inappropriate approach, as illustrated in the case of Heinz. While developing theoretical frameworks, models, research questions, and hypotheses, remember that differences in the environmental factors, especially the sociocultural environment, can lead to differences in the formation of perceptions, attitudes, preferences, and choice behavior.

For example, orientation toward time varies considerably across cultures. In Asia, Latin America, and the Middle East, people are not as time conscious as Westerners, which can influence perceptions and preferences for convenience foods, such as frozen foods and prepared dinners. In defining the problem and developing an approach, the researcher must be sensitive to the underlying factors that influence consumption and purchase behavior.

Technology and Marketing Research

Decision support and expert systems (see Chapter 1) can help in identifying alternative courses of action, defining the marketing research problem, and developing an approach. Other specialized software enables the researcher to use a systematic approach to organizing problems into components, resulting in logical problem formulation. Such programs, which include MaxThink (www.maxthink.org), can portray graphically the relationship between the many facets of a complex problem and incorporate both quantitative and qualitative information, including managerial experience and intuition. This type of software allows the researcher to structure complex problems into manageable forms and to develop suitable approaches, as illustrated by Marriott.

One of the world's largest lodging companies, Marriott International, which operates hotels and resorts in the United States and more than 60 other countries, was faced with the problem of developing an effective marketing strategy for U.S. resorts. Data obtained from in-depth interviews with potential customers were analyzed with an outline processor. The analysis revealed that different ideas are associated with different regions of the United States. West Coast cities, such as San Diego, are associated with sand, surf, sun, and palm trees. Midwest cities, such as Chicago, are considered exciting, fun, and big. East Coast cities, such as Buffalo, elicit ideas such as Niagara Falls, friendliness, and neighbors. The results indicated that a successful marketing approach would use different marketing strategies for resorts in different regions. Furthermore, decision-support systems can be used to conduct "what if" analyses and determine the demand for resorts in different regions based on assumed levels of marketing expenditures. Regions can be combined or split so that the demand potential for each region lies in a predetermined range.

Ethics in Marketing Research

The stakeholders involved in ethical conflicts during the process of defining the problem and developing an approach are likely to be the marketing researcher and the client. Personal interests or hidden agendas of either stakeholder can lead to ethical dilemmas. Ethical issues arise when the personal objectives of the decision maker (e.g., defending a decision) are at variance with the objectives of the client firm. The client should be forthright in disclosing the relevant objectives and the purpose for which the research is being undertaken. Likewise, the researcher should have the best interest of the client at heart.

Suppose that while conducting the problem-definition tasks, a researcher discovers that the problem is a lot simpler than both parties originally thought. Although the reduced scope of the problem will result in substantial savings for the client, it will also cut the revenues for the research firm. Does the researcher continue with the problem definition given in the proposal? Codes of ethics suggest that this situation should be discussed with the client.

Sometimes a client wants to conduct research that, in the opinion of the researcher, is not warranted or needed. Again, the researcher is faced with the ethical dilemma of what to do. Codes of ethics indicate that the researcher should communicate to the client that the research is not necessary. If the client is still insistent, the researcher should feel free to undertake the research.[11]

Likewise, ethical issues might also arise in developing an approach to the problem. Such issues include using models and approaches developed for specific projects for other clients. In the United States, researchers who conduct studies for different clients in related industries (e.g., banks and brokerage firms) or in similar research areas (e.g., measuring company image) might be tempted to reuse client-specific models or findings from other projects. However, unless the researcher has obtained client permission, this practice might be unethical.

What Would *You* Do?

Kellogg's: From Slumping to Thumping

The Situation

U.S.-based Kellogg's is the world's leading producer of cereal and a leading producer of convenience foods, including cookies, crackers, toaster pastries, cereal bars, frozen waffles, meat alternatives, pie crusts, and cones, with 2007 annual sales of about $11.776 billion and a market share of more than 30 percent. David Mackay, CEO of Kellogg's, takes pride in being a part of the Kellogg's company because of the consistency of the decisions that are made within the company to promote the long-term growth of the business, as well as serve the needs of their people and communities.

With such a large market share, one would think that Kellogg's is untouchable. However, Kellogg's faced a slump in the market. Its cereal sales were declining, and it had to face the challenge of getting out of its slump. Kellogg's, therefore, turned to marketing research to identify the problem and develop several solutions to increase cereal sales.

Kellogg's used several tasks to identify the problem. The researchers spoke to decision makers within the company, interviewed industry experts, conducted analysis of available data, and performed some qualitative research. Several important issues came out of this preliminary research. Current products were being targeted to the kids. Bagels and muffins were winning for favored breakfast foods. High prices were turning consumers to generic brands. Some other information also came to light during the research. Adults want quick foods that require very little or no preparation.

The Marketing Research Decision

1. What do you think is the underlying problem facing Kellogg's? Check as many of the following as are applicable:
   a. Kellogg's is targeting the wrong segment: kids.
   b. Competition from bagels and muffins is stiff.
   c. Kellogg's prices are too high.
   d. Kellogg's needs to introduce new products.
   e. Kellogg's needs to change its advertising.
2. Define an appropriate marketing research problem that Kellogg's needs to address.
3. Discuss the role of the type of marketing research problem you have identified in enabling David Mackay to increase Kellogg's sales.

The Marketing Management Decision

1. David Mackay is wondering what changes Kellogg's should make to increase market share. Should Kellogg's (check as many as are applicable):
   a. Introduce new cereals targeted at adults.
   b. Decrease prices.
   c. Increase advertising budget and launch a new campaign.
   d. Launch a sales promotion campaign.
   e. All of the above.
2. Discuss how the marketing management decision action that you recommend to David Mackay is influenced by the research that you suggested earlier and by the findings of that research.

What David Mackay Did

Kellogg's began to introduce flavors more suited to the adult palette. For example, it introduced Honey-flavored Shredded Wheat and Honey Crunch Corn Flakes, both aimed toward the adult market. It also implemented promotions featuring Microsoft software for the entire family instead of the usual toys. Then, it launched an ad campaign aimed at adults called, "Cereal. Eat It for life." These efforts were successful and not only arrested the decline in sales but also led to increased sales and profits.[12]

SPSS Windows

In defining the problem and developing an approach, the researcher can make use of Decision Time and What If? distributed by SPSS. Forecasts of industry and company sales, and other relevant variables, can be aided by the use of Decision Time. Once the data are loaded onto Decision Time, the program's interactive wizard asks you three simple questions. Based on the answers, Decision Time selects the best forecasting method and creates a forecast.

What If? uses the forecast by Decision Time to enable the researcher to explore different options to get a better understating of the problem situation. The researcher can generate answers to questions such as: How will an increase in advertising affect the sales of the product? How will a decrease/increase in price affect the demand? How will an increase in the sales force affect the sales by region?

Forecasts and what-if analyses can help the researcher to isolate the underlying causes, identify the relevant variables that should be investigated, and formulate appropriate research questions and hypotheses.

Summary

The most important step in a research project is defining the marketing research problem. This task often is made more difficult because of the tendency of managers to focus on symptoms rather than underlying causes. The researcher's role is to help management identify and isolate the problem.

The tasks involved in formulating the marketing research problem include discussions with management, including the key decision makers, interviews with industry experts, analysis of secondary data, and qualitative research. This data-gathering process should lead to an understanding of the environmental context of the problem. Within the environmental context, a number of factors should be analyzed and evaluated. These factors include past information and forecasts about the industry and the firm, the decision maker's objectives, buyer behavior, the firm's resources and constraints, the legal and economic environment, and the firm's marketing and technological skills.

Analysis of the environmental context should help identify the management-decision problem, which should then be translated into a marketing research problem. The management-decision problem asks what the decision maker should do, is action oriented, and focuses on the symptoms. The marketing research problem asks what information is needed and how it should be obtained, is information oriented, and focuses on the underlying causes. The researcher should avoid defining the marketing research problem either too broadly or too narrowly. The researcher can avoid these errors by first defining the research problem using a broad statement and then breaking it down into specific components.

The next step in the marketing research process is to develop an approach to the problem. The components of an approach are the analytical framework and models and research questions and hypotheses. In addition, all the information that needs to be obtained in the marketing research project should be specified. The approach developed should be based on objective or empirical evidence and be grounded in theory. Models are useful for portraying the relationships among variables. The most common kinds of models are verbal, graphical, and mathematical. The research questions are refined statements of the components of the problem that ask what specific information is required with respect to each component. Research questions can be further refined into hypotheses. By focusing on each component of the problem and the analytical framework and models, research questions, and hypotheses, the researcher can determine what information should be obtained.

When defining the problem and developing an approach in international marketing research, the researcher must isolate and examine the impact of cultural factors. Technological advances have produced software in the form of text or idea processors and outline processors that can process and analyze facts and ideas, restructuring them to facilitate problem definition and the development of an approach. Several ethical issues that have an impact on the client and the researcher can arise at this stage, but they can be resolved by open and honest communication.

Key Terms and Concepts

Problem definition, 62
Problem definition process, 62
Problem audit, 64
Experience survey, 66
Key-informant technique, 66
Lead-user survey, 66
Secondary data, 67
Primary data, 67
Qualitative research, 68
Pilot surveys, 68
Case studies, 68
Environmental context of the
    problem, 69

Objectives, 70
Buyer behavior, 70
Legal environment, 71
Economic environment, 71
Management-decision
    problem, 73
Marketing research problem, 73
Conceptual map, 73
Broad statement of the
    problem, 75
Specific components of the
    problem, 76
Objective evidence, 76

Theory, 76
Analytical model, 77
Verbal model, 77
Graphical model, 77
Mathematical model, 77
Research questions, 78
Hypothesis, 78

Suggested Cases and Video Cases

Running Case with Real Data

1.1 Hewlett-Packard

Comprehensive Critical Thinking Cases

2.1 American Idol	2.2 Baskin-Robbins	2.3 Akron Children's Hospital

Comprehensive Cases with Real Data

3.1 Bank of America	3.2 McDonald's	3.3 Boeing

Video Cases

2.1 Accenture	3.1 NFL	4.1 Mayo Clinic	5.1 eGO
6.1 Nike	9.1 P&G	10.1 Nivea	11.1 Dunkin' Donuts
12.1 Motorola	13.1 Subaru	14.1 Intel	19.1 Marriott

Live Research: Conducting a Marketing Research Project

1. Invite the client to discuss the project with the class.
2. Have the class (or different teams) analyze the environmental context of the problem: past information and forecasts, resources and constraints, objectives, buyer behavior, legal environment, economic environment, and marketing and technological skills.
3. Jointly with the client, the instructor should make a presentation to the class discussing the management-decision problem and the marketing research problem.

The students should come up with formal definitions of the management-decision problem and the marketing research problem. In conjunction with the client, arrive at consensual definitions.

4. Ask the class or specific teams to develop an approach (analytical framework and models, research questions, hypotheses, and identification of the information needed). Through class discussion, arrive at a consensus.

Acronym

The factors to be considered when analyzing the environmental context of the problem can be summed up by the acronym PROBLEM:

P ast information and forecasts

R esources and constraints

O bjectives of the decision maker

B uyer behavior

L egal environment

E conomic environment

M arketing and technological skills

Review Questions

1. What is the first step in conducting a marketing research project?
2. Why is it important to correctly define the marketing research problem?
3. What are some reasons that management often is not clear about the real problem?
4. What is the role of the researcher in the problem definition process?
5. What is a problem audit?
6. What is the difference between a symptom and an underlying cause? How can a skillful researcher differentiate between the two and identify the true problem?
7. What are some differences between a management-decision problem and a marketing research problem?
8. What are the common types of errors encountered in defining a marketing research problem? What can be done to reduce the incidence of such errors?
9. How are the research questions related to components of the problem?
10. What are the differences between research questions and hypotheses?
11. What are the most common forms of analytical models?

Applied Problems

1. Visit www.census.gov and obtain data relating to population trends by age groups. What are some of the marketing implications of these trends?
2. State the marketing research problems for each of the following management-decision problems.
   a. Should a new product be introduced?
   b. Should an advertising campaign, which has run for 3 years, be changed?
   c. Should the in-store promotion for an existing product line be increased?
   d. What pricing strategy should be adopted for a new product?
   e. Should the compensation package be changed to motivate the sales force better?
3. State the management-decision problems for which the following marketing research problems might provide useful information.
   a. Estimate the sales and market share of department stores in a certain metropolitan area.
   b. Determine the design features for a new product that would result in maximum market share.
   c. Evaluate the effectiveness of alternative TV commercials.
   d. Assess current and proposed sales territories with respect to their sales potential and workload.
   e. Determine the prices for each item in a product line so as to maximize total sales for the product line.
4. Identify five symptoms and a plausible cause for each one.
5. Suppose you are conducting research for American Airlines. Identify, from secondary sources, the attributes or factors passengers consider when selecting an airline.
6. You are a consultant to Coca-Cola USA working on a marketing research project for Diet Coke.
   a. Use the online databases in your library to compile a list of articles related to the Coca-Cola Company, Diet Coke, and the soft-drink industry published during the past year.

   b. Visit the Coca-Cola (www.cocacola.com) and PepsiCo (www.pepsico.com) Web sites and compare the information available at each.

   c. Based on the information you have collected, write a report on the environmental context surrounding Diet Coke.

7. Select any firm. Using secondary sources, obtain information on the annual sales of the firm and the industry for the last 5 years. Use a spreadsheet package, such as Excel, or any microcomputer or mainframe statistical package, to develop a graphical model relating the firm's sales to the industry's sales.

8. Visit the Web sites of competing sneaker brands (Nike, Reebok, and Adidas). The URLs are www.nike.com, www.reebok.com, and www.adidas.com. From an analysis of information available at these sites, determine the criteria used by consumers in selecting a sneaker brand.

Group Discussion

1. Form a group of five or six people to discuss the following statement: "Correct definition of the marketing research problem is more important to the success of a marketing research project than sophisticated research techniques." Did your group arrive at a consensus?

2. We are all aware that Coca-Cola changed its flagship brand of 99 years to New Coke and subsequently returned to the old favorite, Coca-Cola Classic. Working in a group of four, read as much material as you can on this marketing bungle. Identify the decision problem that Coke management faced. As a team, define the marketing research problem and its specific components.

Hewlett-Packard Running Case

Review the Hewlett-Packard (HP) case, Case 1.1, and the questionnaire provided toward the end of the book.

1. Conduct an Internet search on HP and briefly describe the environmental context of the problem surrounding HP.

2. Define the management-decision problem facing HP as it seeks to maintain and build on its leadership position in the personal computers market.

3. Define an appropriate marketing research problem that corresponds to your definition of the management-decision problem.

4. Present a graphical model describing consumers' selection of a personal computer brand.

5. Describe three research questions, with one or more hypotheses associated with each.

VIDEO CASE 2.1

ACCENTURE: The Accent Is in the Name

Accenture

As of 2008, Accenture (www.accenture.com) is the largest consulting firm in the world and one of the largest computer services and software companies on the *Fortune* Global 500 list. It has more than 170,000 employees in 49 countries and reported revenues of $19.70 billion in 2007. Through its network of businesses, the company enhances its consulting, technology, and outsourcing expertise through alliances, affiliated companies, venture capital, and other capabilities. Accenture delivers innovations that help clients across all industries quickly realize their visions. With over 110 offices in about 50 countries, Accenture can quickly mobilize its broad and deep global resources to accelerate results for clients. The company has extensive experience in 18 industry groups in key business areas, including customer relationship management, supply chain management, business strategy, technology, and outsourcing. Accenture's clients include 89 of the *Fortune* Global 100 and more than half of the *Fortune* Global 500.

Accenture was originally named Andersen Consulting and was created in 1989 as a part of Arthur Andersen. In 2000, Andersen Consulting won the right to divorce itself from Arthur Andersen after the parent company broke contractual agreements, moving into areas of service where Andersen Consulting was already an established leader. However, it then had to change its name. This was an extremely significant event, because Andersen Consulting had built up considerable brand equity in its name, partly by spending approximately $7 billion over 10 years on building the name. In addition, the new name would need to be trademarked in 47 countries. Thus, the name change became a top priority, and the company focused much of its time and effort on this task.

The first task was to pick a new name. The company challenged its employees to come up with suggestions for a new name by creating an internal contest, which resulted in a list of over 2,500 entries. After extensive marketing research on various names, which included surveys of target customers, it decided to go with the name Accenture. Marketing research revealed that the "Acc" in the name connotes accomplishment and accessibility, and the name sounds like "adventure." The company settled on this name because it believed this name conveyed the message that it was focused on the future. It also spent a considerable amount of time creating a new logo. The final version of the logo was the company's name accented with a greater than (>) symbol placed above the letter t, which it believed stressed its focus on the future.

Another task, which occurred simultaneously, was to get the word out and prepare the target market for the brand change. The company began running ads notifying everyone that its name would change at the beginning of 2001. Accenture has a well-defined group of companies that comprises the target market, and it had to focus its efforts on them. A teaser advertisement created by Young & Rubicam with the old signature torn through at the corner of the ad and typing in "Renamed. Redefined. Reborn 01.01.01" set the stage for the change. Marketing research revealed that 01.01.01, the launch date of the new brand, had a resonance with the computer industry, because 0 and 1 are the two digits of the binary world of computers.

Finally, on January 1, 2001, the company announced its new name to the world. The initial campaign illustrated the change by the slogan, "Renamed. Redefined. Reborn." Accenture used this opportunity not only to present the new name, but also to sell its services and help people understand what it had to offer. In the end, Accenture spent a total of $175 million to rebrand itself, but it did not stop there. In February it began a new campaign titled, "Now it gets interesting." This campaign took the perspective that despite all the incredible changes that have occurred recently due to technology, even more challenges lie ahead. The commercials showed how Accenture could help clients capitalize on these challenges. The success of this campaign was evidenced by the increased traffic on the company's Web site. This is very important to Accenture, because it believes that if it can get somebody to visit its site, it has a better opportunity to tell the whole story. Next came the "I Am Your Idea" theme. This campaign was followed by "High Performance. Delivered," which was still running in 2008. It also featured Tiger Woods with the tag line, "We know what it takes to be a Tiger."

Accenture has been successful in transferring the brand equity to its new name. Marketing research revealed that it has approximately 50 percent awareness with the public, which is essentially the same number it had under the old name. Accenture's marketing goes far beyond the name, because it is constantly challenged as the product it offers changes.

Conclusion

The case describes the marketing research conducted by Andersen Consulting to change its name, while at the same time maintain the brand equity and the goodwill of its previous name. Andersen Consulting was able to successfully transition to a new name and a new identity, reflecting the new realities of the market and Accenture's positioning in it. Finding a new name is only the beginning; repositioning a global brand today requires good marketing research, creative marketing, big budgets, and awareness of the next business trends. Such efforts will help Accenture to further strengthen the accent in its name by building brand equity.

Questions

1. Discuss the role of marketing research in helping Andersen Consulting select a new name (Accenture).
2. Define Accenture's target market. Discuss the role of marketing research in helping Accenture understand the needs of its target customers.
3. Accenture would like to increase preference and loyalty to its services. Describe the management-decision problem.
4. Define a suitable marketing research problem corresponding to the management-decision problem that you identified in question 3.
5. Develop a graphical model explaining how a *Fortune* 500 firm would select a consulting organization.
6. Develop two research questions, each with two hypotheses, based on the marketing research problem you defined in question 4.

References

1. See www.accenture.com, accessed on February 10, 2008.
2. Todd Wasserman, "Accenture Accents Idea Campaign," *Brandweek* (September 30, 2002): 4.

Research
Design
Formulation

three

CHAPTER 3

Research Design

OPENING QUESTIONS

1. What is a research design, and what are the kinds of basic research designs?

2. How can the basic research designs be compared and contrasted?

3. What are the major sources of errors in a research design?

4. How does the researcher coordinate the budgeting and scheduling aspects of a research project?

5. What elements make up the marketing research proposal?

6. What factors should the researcher consider when formulating a research design in international marketing research?

7. How can technology facilitate the research design process?

8. What ethical issues arise when selecting a research design?

> "Formulating a methodical research design is crucial in every project. It's like making a map for what you will do later in the research project when time is of the essence."
>
> **Chris Wallace,**
> *Research Director, VHA Inc.,*
> *a U.S. network of health-care systems.*

Marketing Research Helps Spiegel Redesign Its Product Lines

Spiegel (www.spiegel.com), a leading direct marketer in the United States, offers the benefits of home-based shopping via the catalog and the Internet. However, in March 2003 the company filed for Chapter 11 bankruptcy protection. Spiegel realized that a turnaround was needed to regain profits and customers. To achieve this turnaround, the company lowered expenses, reduced inventory, and concentrated on creating an improved Web site to draw in new customers and ultimately boost revenues. Spiegel also wanted to improve its products and marketing programs.

Spiegel conducted extensive marketing research. The marketing research problem was to understand the shopping behavior of potential and current consumers. Several research questions and hypotheses were formulated to examine the unique aspects of consumers' buying behavior. Spiegel used a two-phase research design. The first phase, the exploratory phase, consisted of analysis of secondary data plus 10 focus groups with Spiegel customers. Secondary data provided good background information on current and potential catalog shoppers and vital statistics, such as the

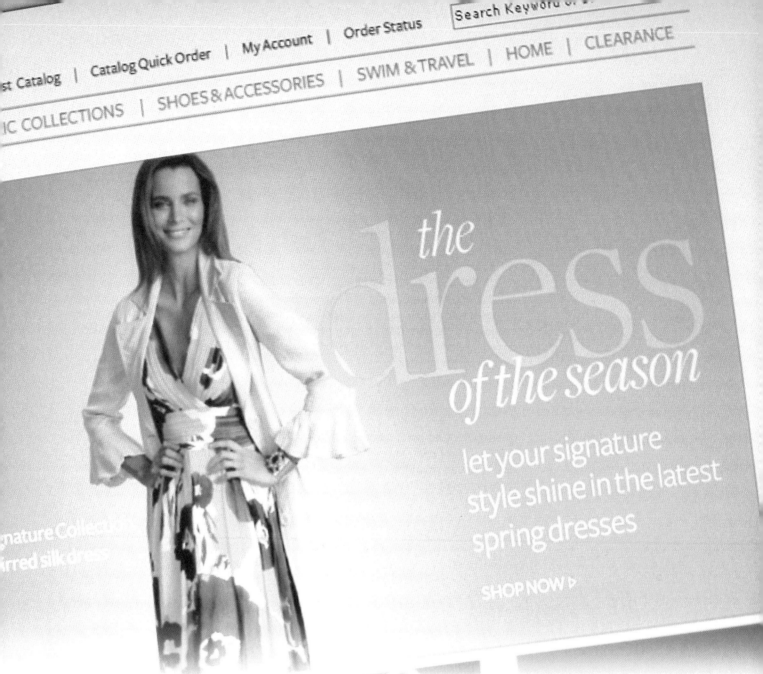

size of this segment. Focus groups helped Spiegel understand the values, attitudes, and behavior of its customers as they related to clothing, home furnishings, and shopping. The focus groups revealed that customers wanted variety and quality. They also felt appreciated when a company designed special promotions directed to them. Spiegel came up short on all of these dimensions.

In the second phase, the descriptive phase, the findings of the exploratory phase were tested with a telephone survey of a sample of 1,000 randomly selected Spiegel customers. Efforts were undertaken to control the various sources of nonsampling error. For example, the interviewers were carefully selected and thoroughly trained, and close supervision was exercised to minimize interviewing errors. The results of the survey confirmed the demand for more Spiegel product offerings, and also showed that the Spiegel lines needed more promotion. In the fall of 2003, Speigel spent millions of dollars on a print campaign aimed at revitalizing its product lines. In 2004, the company introduced the "Idea Resource," which offers consumers expert advice from designers and stylists. The research results led to increased product offerings and more promotions across the product lines in years 2005 to 2008. Since making these changes, Speigel has experienced good growth, which hopefully will lead to success.[1]

Overview

As discussed in Chapter 2, defining a marketing research problem and developing a suitable approach are critical to the success of the entire marketing research project. The next step is to formulate a detailed research design to achieve the defined goals. Figure 3.1 gives the relationship of research design to previous chapters and to the marketing research process.

This chapter classifies and describes the basic research designs. At the broad level, the two major types of research designs are exploratory and conclusive designs. Conclusive research designs can be further classified as descriptive or causal. Thus, this classification results in three basic designs: exploratory, descriptive, and causal. These three basic designs are used in different combinations and sequences.

In this chapter, we consider the value of marketing research information within the context of controlling research design errors. We discuss budgeting and scheduling of a proposed research project and present guidelines for writing research proposals. As applications, we consider research design concepts in the context of international marketing research, technology, and ethics in marketing research. Figure 3.2 presents an overview of the chapter's contents.

research design
A framework or blueprint for conducting the marketing research project that specifies the procedures necessary to obtain the information needed to structure and/or solve the marketing research problem.

What Is a Research Design?

The **research design** is a roadmap for conducting the marketing research project. It provides details of each step in the marketing research project. Implementation of the research design should result in all the information needed to structure or solve the management-decision problem. The design process begins by defining the marketing research problem.

FIGURE 3.1

Relationship of Research Design to the Previous Chapters and the Marketing Research Process

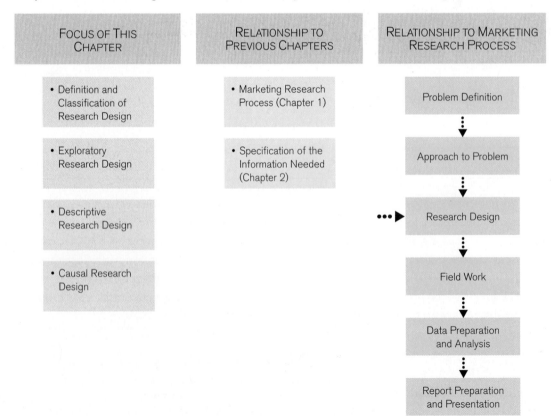

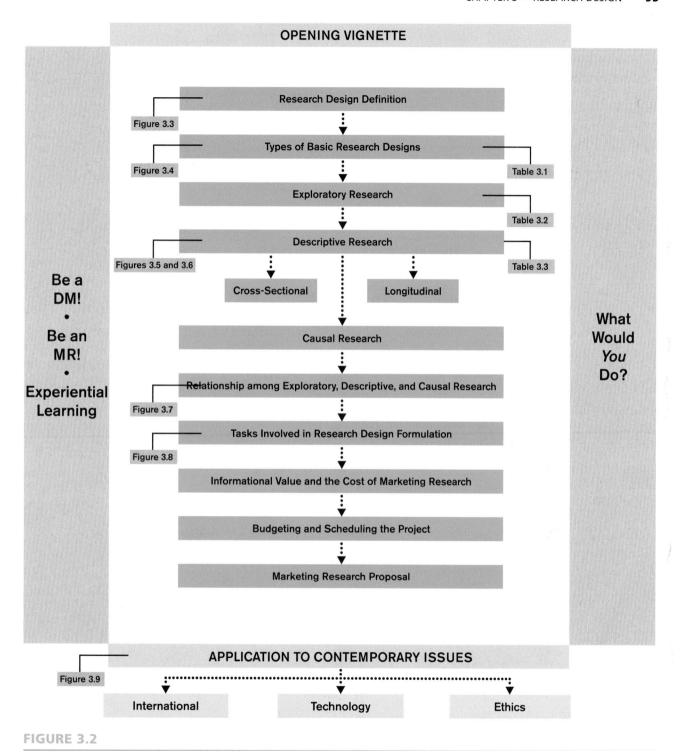

FIGURE 3.2

Research Design: An Overview

Next comes the approach: a conceptual framework, research questions, hypotheses, and the information needed (see Chapter 2). The research design is based on the results of these first two steps: the problem definition and the approach (Figure 3.3).

Many different designs might be appropriate for a given marketing research problem. A good research design ensures that the information collected will be relevant and useful to management and that all of the necessary information will be obtained. A good design should also help to ensure that the marketing research project will be conducted effectively

FIGURE 3.3

Steps Leading to the Formulation of a Research Design

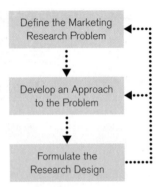

and efficiently. In this chapter, we will consider the basic types of research designs available. These basic designs can be classified in terms of the research objectives.

Basic Research Designs

Research designs are of two broad types: exploratory and conclusive. Conclusive designs are either descriptive or causal. Descriptive designs can be further categorized as either cross-sectional or longitudinal. Exploratory, descriptive, and causal are the basic research designs we examine in this chapter (see Figure 3.4).

Table 3.1 states the differences between exploratory and descriptive research. **Exploratory research** is conducted to explore the problem situation; that is, to gain ideas and insight into the problem confronting the management or the researcher. Exploratory research might be used when management realizes a problem exists but does not yet understand why. Perhaps sales are slipping in a particular region, or customer service complaints have increased sharply. As a first step, the problem must be defined and alternate courses of action identified.

Because the information needs are only loosely defined at this stage, exploratory research has to be flexible and unstructured. For example, exploratory research that investigates why some customers are dissatisfied with Procter & Gamble's Ivory bath soap might begin with an analysis of calls recorded on the consumer hotline regarding the nature of complaints. Then, depending on the nature of the findings, the researcher might decide to conduct focus groups with users of Ivory soap. Suppose six focus groups, each involving 10 respondents, reveal that users are dissatisfied with the lack of lather and moisturizing ability. Should P&G immediately change the Ivory formula?

exploratory research
A type of research design that has as its primary objective the provision of insights into and comprehension of the problem situation confronting the researcher.

FIGURE 3.4

A Classification of Market Research Designs

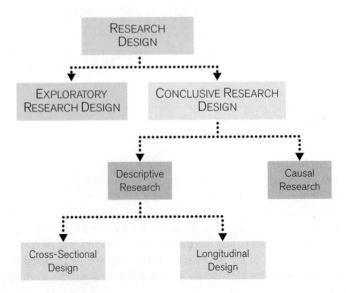

TABLE 3.1 Differences Between Exploratory and Conclusive Research

	Exploratory	Conclusive
Objective:	To provide insights and understanding	To test specific hypotheses and examine relationships
Characteristics:	Information needed is defined only loosely	Information needed is clearly defined
	Research process is flexible and unstructured	Research process is formal and structured
	Sample is small and nonrepresentative	Sample is large and representative
	Analysis of primary data is qualitative	Data analysis is quantitative
Findings/Results:	Tentative	Conclusive
Outcome:	Generally followed by further exploratory or conclusive research	Findings used as input into decision making

No! Exploratory research is conducted on a small and nonrepresentative sample, so the findings should be regarded as tentative and be used as building blocks for further research. Typically, more formally defined exploratory research or conclusive research follows. It is dangerous when exploratory research is the only step taken toward developing a solution. The tendency to overlook the limited usefulness of the information, particularly if it confirms preconceived ideas about a problem, can lead management in the wrong direction. Despite these risks, exploratory research can be valuable when researchers are faced with a problem that is not fully understood, for example, why some customers are dissatisfied with a specific brand of bath soap. Exploratory research in the form of depth interviews or focus groups could provide valuable insights.

Conclusive research is research designed to assist the decision maker in determining, evaluating, and selecting the best course of action in a given situation. Conclusive research can be used to verify the insights gained from exploratory research. As illustrated in the opening vignette, the findings from secondary data and focus groups (exploratory research) were further tested in a telephone survey (conclusive research). Conclusive research is based on the assumption that the researcher has an accurate understanding of the problem at hand. The information needed for addressing the management-decision problem has been clearly specified. The objective of conclusive research is to test specific hypotheses and examine specific relationships.

Conclusive research is typically more formal and structured than exploratory research. The researcher specifies the detailed steps in the research to be conducted prior to initiating the project. Large, representative samples are used to collect data that are then analyzed with statistical techniques. In the Ivory soap example, a large national survey involving 1,000 randomly selected respondents could be conducted to verify the findings of focus groups. The survey could be used to obtain consumer evaluations of Ivory soap and competing brands on the important attributes such as mildness, lather, shrinkage, price, fragrance, packaging, moisturizing, and cleaning power.

conclusive research
Research designed to assist the decision maker in determining, evaluating, and selecting the best course of action for a given situation.

Be an MR!

Visit InterContinental Hotels Group PLC, a U.K.-based firm that operates 4,000 hotels in nearly 100 countries, at www.ichotelsgroup.com/h/d/hi/1/en/home and write a report about the various hotel brands owned by Holiday Inn. What type of research would you conduct to determine a coherent marketing strategy for the various Holiday Inn hotel brands?

Be a DM!

As the vice president of marketing for Holiday Inn, discuss the role that exploratory and conclusive research can play in determining a coherent marketing strategy for the various hotel brands owned by Holiday Inn, such as Holiday Inn Hotels and Resorts, Holiday Inn Select, Holiday Inn SunSpree Resorts, and Holiday Inn Family Suites Resorts.

Exploratory Research

As the name implies, the objective of exploratory research is to explore or search through a problem or situation to gain insights and understanding (Tables 3.1 and 3.2). For example, the German sports apparel and equipment maker adidas AG could make use of exploratory research to understand the reasons for its lower market share in the United States as compared to that of American rival Nike. Exploratory research could be used for any of the following purposes, which are illustrated using the Adidas brand in the United States as an example.

1. *To formulate a problem or define a problem more precisely.* Exploratory research might reveal that Adidas has a lower U.S. market share because its brand image in the United States is not as strong as Nike's.
2. *To identify alternative courses of action.* Alternative courses of action to boost Adidas' image might include improving product quality, increasing the television advertising budget, distributing the product through upscale company-owned stores, increasing the prices of its athletic shoes and apparel, and so forth.
3. *To develop hypotheses.* An interesting hypothesis is that heavy users of athletic shoes are more brand conscious than light users. Another is that heavy users have a weaker image of Adidas as compared to the light users.
4. *To isolate key variables and relationships for further examination.* Celebrity endorsements can have a positive influence on the image of Adidas.
5. *To gain insights for developing an approach to the problem.* Brand image is a composite variable that is influenced by the quality of the product, the pricing strategy, the image of the outlets through which the product is distributed, and the quality and intensity of advertising and promotion.
6. *To establish priorities for further research.* Adidas might want to examine the purchase and consumption behavior of heavy users of athletic shoes.

Exploratory research often is conducted in the beginning stages of a project, as illustrated in the Spiegel vignette. Secondary data provided good background information on Spiegel's customers, whereas focus groups helped Spiegel understand the values, attitudes, and behavior of this segment with regard to clothing and shopping. The results indicated that current and potential customers wanted variety and quality and also appreciated special promotions. However, exploratory research can be used at any point in the research process when the researcher is unclear about the problem situation.

TABLE 3.2 A Comparison of Basic Research Designs

	Exploratory	Descriptive	Causal
Objective:	Discovery of ideas and insights	Describe market characteristics or functions	Determine cause-and-effect relationships
Characteristics:	Flexible Versatile	Marked by the prior formulation of specific hypotheses	Manipulation of one or more independent variables
	Often the front end of total research design	Preplanned and structured design	Control of other mediating variables
Methods:	Expert/experience surveys	Secondary data: Quantitative	Experiments
	Pilot surveys	Surveys	
	Case studies	Panels	
	Secondary data: Qualitative	Observational and other data	
	Qualitative research		

Exploratory research relies heavily on the researcher's curiosity and insight. It is more like a process of informal discovery. Yet the abilities of the researcher are not the sole determinants of good exploratory research. Although the process is highly flexible and relatively informal, exploratory research can benefit from use of the following methods (see Table 3.2):

- Survey of experts/experience surveys (discussed in Chapter 2)
- Pilot surveys (discussed in Chapter 2)
- Case studies (discussed in Chapter 2)
- Qualitative analysis of secondary data, including literature review (discussed in Chapters 4 and 5)
- Qualitative research, such as focus groups and one-on-one depth interviews (discussed in Chapter 6)

As discussed in Chapter 2, the Internet offers many resources for marketing research. Newsgroups, list servers, and other bulletin-board-type services can be very useful in the exploratory phase of research. Messages posted to newsgroups can often direct the researcher to other valid sources of information. Newsgroups can be used to set up more formal focus groups with experts or individuals representing the target audience in order to obtain initial information on a subject. In Chapter 6, we discuss the use of the Internet for conducting focus groups in more detail.

Spiegel analyzed secondary data and conducted 10 focus groups as part of its exploratory research to understand the clothing preferences and shopping behavior of its customers. The use of exploratory research in defining the problem and developing an approach was discussed in Chapter 2. The following example provides another application of exploratory research.

Research in Action

Banking on Exploratory Research

As of 2008, Bank of America (www.bankofamerica.com) is one of the world's largest financial institutions. The company serves clients in 175 countries and has relationships with 98 percent of the U.S. *Fortune* 500 and 80 percent of the *Fortune* Global 500. In order to increase its share of a very competitive market, Bank of American (BOA) conducted exploratory research using focus groups of current and potential customers to find out where new branches should be located and what new products should be introduced. Many new product ideas were generated through exploratory research. These ideas were further investigated using descriptive research in the form of customer and noncustomer surveys. The research enabled BOA to successfully introduce new products, such as innovative checking, savings, and institutional accounts, and to improve profitability.

Focus groups followed by a telephone survey revealed that a large segment of households wanted interest payments on their checking account balances but were very sensitive to any checking account fees. These consumers maintained large balances in their checking account and were therefore open to a reasonable minimum balance requirement. Accordingly, BOA introduced an interest-paying checking with no fees (monthly or per check) that had a minimum balance requirement of $2,500. Exploratory and descriptive research have helped BOA to become the largest bank in the world with a brand positioning of "Bank of Opportunity."[2]

Note that BOA, like Spiegel, did not rely exclusively on exploratory research. Once new product ideas were identified, they were further tested by descriptive research in the form of surveys.

Be an MR!

Visit www.haagendazs.com and search for additional information about the American ice cream maker on the Internet. Write a report describing the flavors and products offered by Häagen-Dazs and the company's marketing strategy.

You are conducting a project for Häagen-Dazs to understand consumers' perceptions and preferences for high-quality ice cream. Would you conduct exploratory research? If yes, which methods would you use and why?

Be a DM!

As the marketing manager for Häagen-Dazs, how would you use information on consumers' perceptions and preferences for high-quality ice cream to penetrate upper-income U.S. households?

Descriptive Research

descriptive research
A type of conclusive research that has as its major objective the description of something—usually market characteristics or functions.

Descriptive research is a type of conclusive research that has as its major objective the description of something—usually market characteristics or functions. Most commercial marketing research is descriptive in nature. Descriptive research is particularly useful when research questions seek to describe a market phenomenon, such as determining purchase frequencies, identifying relationships, or making predictions (see Table 3.2). The following are examples of descriptive research goals:

1. *To develop a profile of a target market.* American apparel maker Levi-Strauss would like to know the age, educational level, income, and media habits of heavy users of jeans in order to make advertising-placement decisions.
2. *To estimate the frequency of product use as a basis for sales forecasts.* Knowing that a "heavy" perfume user buys 1.8 bottles of perfumes per month can help U.S. cosmetics company Mary Kay predict potential sales for a new perfume brand.
3. *To determine the relationship between product use and perception of product characteristics.* In developing its marketing platform, the American electronics and communications company Motorola would like to determine if and how heavy users of cellular phones differ from nonusers in terms of the importance they attach to performance and ease of use.
4. *To determine the degree to which marketing variables are associated.* Microsoft would like to know to what extent Internet usage is related to age, income, and education level.

Descriptive research assumes that the researcher has prior knowledge about the problem situation. This is one of the major differences between descriptive and exploratory research. Descriptive research, in contrast to exploratory research, is based on a clear statement of the problem, specific hypotheses, and specification of the information needed (see Chapter 2). Data are collected in a structured fashion, typically using large, representative samples. The findings are then used to make generalizations about an entire customer group or market. Microsoft, for example, could survey a representative sample of Internet users to determine Internet usage and project the findings to the larger population of Internet users.

Descriptive studies are used to portray market variables. They describe the customer and the market and measure the frequency of behaviors, such as purchasing. Among the major types of descriptive studies are internally or externally focused sales studies, consumer perception and behavior studies, and market characteristic studies (Figure 3.5).

Sales studies include market potential studies, market share studies, and sales analysis studies. Market potential studies describe the size of the market, the buying power of consumers, and historic growth rates. Market share studies determine the proportion of total sales a company and its competitors receive. Sales analysis studies describe sales by geographic region, product line, and type and size of the account.

Consumer perception and behavior studies include image studies, product usage studies, advertising studies, and pricing studies. Image studies determine consumer perceptions of the firm and its products. Product usage studies describe consumption patterns. Advertising studies describe media consumption habits and audience profiles for specific

FIGURE 3.5

Major Types of Descriptive Studies

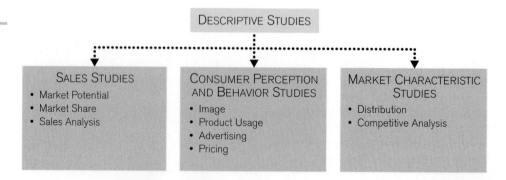

television programs and magazines. Pricing studies describe the range and frequency of price changes and the probable consumer response to proposed price changes.

Market characteristic studies include distribution studies and competitive analyses. Distribution studies determine traffic flow patterns and the number and location of distributors. Competitive analyses compare strengths and weaknesses of industry participants.

Say that Swatch AG, the Swiss maker of watches and other luxury accessories, would like to determine the size of the market for sports watches, at what rate the market is growing, and the market shares of the leading brands. It might do an analysis of its own sales of Swatch sports watches by type of outlet—jewelry stores, department stores, sporting-goods stores, specialty stores, catalog, Internet operations, and other outlets. Management might ask: How do consumers perceive Swatch? Does the image of Swatch vary between owners and nonowners? Which TV programs do people who buy premium sports watches view? How much of a premium are consumers willing to pay for a high-quality sports watch? Swatch would have to undertake consumer perception and behavior studies to provide management with answers to these questions. Market characteristic studies might examine the following questions: How many distributors does Swatch have for each type of outlet? How does this compare with other competing brands?

These examples demonstrate the range and diversity of descriptive research studies. Descriptive research also uses a variety of data-collection techniques, which we discuss in the following chapters. These techniques include:

- Quantitative analysis of secondary data (Chapters 4 and 5)
- **Surveys** (interviews with a large number of respondents using a predesigned questionnaire) (Chapter 7)
- Panels (Chapters 5 and 7)
- Observational and other data (Chapter 7)

survey
An interview with a large number of respondents using a predesigned questionnaire.

The survey Spiegel conducted in the opening vignette is an example of descriptive research. Descriptive research using these methods can be further classified into cross-sectional and longitudinal research (see Figure 3.4).

Be a DM!

As the CEO of American Airlines, how would you use information on the image of your airline versus major competitors to improve your competitive positioning?

Be an MR!

Visit www.americanairlines.com and search the Internet, as well as your library's online databases, to obtain information on the competitive positioning of American Airlines. What type of exploratory and descriptive research would you undertake to determine the image of American Airlines versus its major competitors?

Cross-Sectional Designs

A **cross-sectional design,** sometimes called a *sample survey,* can be thought of as a snapshot of the marketplace taken at a specific point in time. In this design, the selected group of respondents is measured only once. The cross-sectional survey is the most frequently used descriptive design in marketing research. Spiegel's survey of 1,000 customers is a cross-sectional design, and so is the Jergens Body Shampoo example that follows.

cross-sectional design
A type of research design involving the one-time collection of information from any given sample of population elements.

Research in Action

Jergens Body Shampoo Washes Away Consumer Gripes

Now a subsidiary of Tokyo-based Kao Corporation (www.kao.co.jp), Jergens (www.jergens.com) periodically conducts surveys to measure consumers' perceptions, attitudes, and use of soap bars and related personal-care products. A cross-sectional survey involving 600 mall-intercept interviews in six major cities showed that many consumers had complaints about the standard soap bar: They didn't like having to pick a mushy bar out of the dish. They didn't like the nasty film it left in their shower or bath. They didn't like the way it dried out their skin. These findings led to the development of an innovative new product. Jergens Body Shampoo was designed to eliminate those woes by providing what the company calls "a creamy lather that rinses away easily for a clean that never felt so good." The product met with instant success upon introduction.

The company credits the product for revolutionizing its category, noting that it has spawned more than 10 competitors. Jergens reports that the brand is the number-one seller among body shampoos in food stores and that it helped the category grow to over $500 million by 2007, almost a quarter of the soap category. Cross-sectional surveys have helped Jergens develop and introduce other successful products such as the Jergens® Natural Glow Face Daily Moisturizer, introduced in 2007.[3]

Longitudinal Designs

longitudinal design
A type of research design involving a fixed sample of population elements that is measured repeatedly. The sample remains the same over time, providing a series of pictures which, when viewed together, portray both the situation and the changes that are taking place.

panel
A panel consists of a sample of respondents, generally households that have agreed to provide information at specified intervals over an extended period.

The typical cross-sectional design offers a snapshot at a single point in time. In contrast, a **longitudinal design** provides a series of pictures, which track the changes that take place over time. In longitudinal designs, a fixed sample from the population is measured repeatedly on the same variables. In other words, two or more measurements on the same variables are obtained from a given group of respondents at different points in time (Figure 3.6). A cross-sectional design would be used to ask the question, "How did the American people rate the performance of George W. Bush immediately following the Iraq war in 2003?" A longitudinal design would be used to address the question, "How did the American people change their view of Bush's performance before and after his last State of the Union address?"

Sometimes, the term *panel* or *true panel* is used interchangeably with the term *longitudinal design*. A **panel** consists of a sample of respondents, generally households that have agreed to provide information at specified intervals over an extended period. Because of the long-term commitment needed for participation on a panel, its members are compensated with gifts, coupons, information, or cash. Panel data are typically collected by commercial research organizations known as *syndicated firms*. NPD is one such firm that tracks changes in consumer purchase patterns and then sells the data to other businesses or interested groups for a flat subscription price. The Tylenol example illustrates longitudinal design. Panels are discussed in more detail in Chapters 5 and 7.

Research in Action

Longitudinal Research Leads to Rapid Success for Tylenol Rapid Release Gels

Tylenol (www.tylenol.com), marketed by the U.S. consumer-products company Johnson & Johnson, conducts longitudinal surveys with consumer panels to determine how respondents feel about new products prior to their introduction into the marketplace. The company also uses the panel after the product has been in the market for a while to find out information about the product's performance and image in the marketplace. A recent example of the use of panels by Tylenol to ensure the success of a new product is the Rapid Release Gels line of pain relievers.

Tylenol first formed a panel of prospective consumers for the new line of pills it was introducing, making sure that the respondents not only thought well of the product, but would buy it. This panel revealed that the speed of the medicine was a key point that should be emphasized. Everyone wanted pain relief, but the quickest product to deliver the relief would definitely sell the best. Tylenol's Extra Strength Rapid Release Gels have gel caps with specially designed holes to release powerful medicine fast. Rapid release equates to rapid relief. The color of the pill was established based on feedback from the panel as blue and red, which the majority of the panelists found "soothing" and related to comfort and care. The introductory advertising campaign featured NASCAR drivers for marketing the product as a sign of the speedy recovery from illness by consuming the tablet. They even had testimonials to prove that this new Tylenol has the power to act as a fast pain reliever and yet be gentle on the stomach.

Tylenol reconvened the panel at 3, 6, and 9 months after the product launch. The same panelists were asked about the advertising, how well the product actually worked, the color scheme, how their friends felt about the product, and if it was better than the products produced by some of Tylenol's competitors. They were also asked the brand of pain reliever they purchased last and when the purchase was made.

Based on the feedback, Tylenol determined that the use of celebrities and sports stars in its ads was not beneficial in the marketing campaign. Most people wanted a simple, down-to-earth message about the new pain reliever's attributes. They wanted to know that it was one of the most preferred pain relievers on the market and that brand loyalty was high.

In response to this feedback, Tylenol changed the advertising campaign and started advertising to the common man, using common people. The new marketing campaign focused on everyday situations requiring a fast pain reliever. Tylenol revised the homepage of its Web site to show an employee who has been working in the company for 3 years, just like her grandfather did for 30 years, who promises people that she will put as much care into making Tylenol as her grandfather did. The Web site also offered links so visitors could hear more from the people who make Tylenol. This type of marketing was aimed at connecting with the people.

The use of a longitudinal design using a panel gave Tylenol valuable insight into the direction it should take with its new product line, leading to its success in the marketplace.[4]

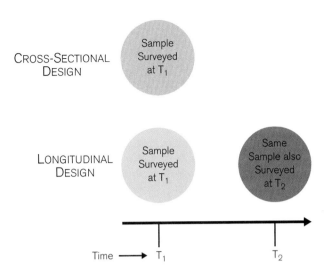

FIGURE 3.6

Cross-Sectional Versus Longitudinal Designs

Cross-Sectional Versus Longitudinal Designs

The relative advantages and disadvantages of longitudinal versus cross-sectional designs are summarized in Table 3.3. Because in most situations the researcher is interested in obtaining a picture of the marketplace at one point in time, cross-sectional designs are far more commonly used than longitudinal designs. Cross-sectional studies cost less. It is relatively simple to select a representative sample, a group of respondents whose characteristics of interest are a reflection of the entire population. Because different respondents are selected each time a survey is conducted, bias due to the same set of respondents answering multiple surveys is eliminated.

A major advantage of longitudinal designs is the ability to detect change as a result of repeated measurements of the same variables on the same respondents. This is illustrated in the Tylenol example. Because the same individuals provide data on the same variables repeatedly, it is possible to compare the brand of pain reliever an individual purchases at any given time with the brand purchased in the preceding time period. Thus, the researcher can determine whether an individual is engaging in repeat purchase or brand switching.

Panel research also has an advantage over cross-sectional research in terms of the amount of data that can be collected as well as the accuracy of that data. A typical cross-sectional survey requires recall of past purchases and behavior. Panel data, which rely on continuous recording of purchases in a diary, place less reliance on the respondent's memory. A comparison of panel and cross-sectional survey estimates of retail sales indicates that panel data give more accurate estimates.

The main disadvantage of panels is that they might not be representative of the population of interest. This might happen because of refusals to participate and high dropout rates for panel participants. Bias is introduced when participants try to give the "right" answer or become bored or fatigued and make incomplete diary or Internet entries. In addition, longitudinal designs are more expensive to implement because of the expenses

TABLE 3.3 Relative Advantages and Disadvantages of Longitudinal and Cross-Sectional Designs

Evaluation Criteria	Cross-Sectional Design	Longitudinal Design
Detecting change	−	+
Large amount of data collection	−	+
Accuracy	−	+
Representative sampling	+	−
Response bias	+	−

Note: A "+" indicates a relative advantage over the other design.
  A "−" indicates a relative disadvantage.

associated with maintaining a panel. In light of these limitations, longitudinal designs are used only when it is necessary to examine changes over time, such as in studies of repeat purchases, brand switching, and brand loyalty.

Experiential Learning

Exploratory and Descriptive Research

Visit www.gallup.com and examine some of the recent projects conducted by the Gallup organization, a U.S. consulting company best known for its public-opinion polling. Read through some of the reports posted on this Web site. What type of exploratory research was conducted in these projects? Which methods were used? What type of descriptive research was conducted in these projects? Which methods were used? In which project was the research design most appropriate? Why?

Causal Research

causal research
A type of conclusive research whose major objective is to obtain evidence regarding cause-and-effect (causal) relationships.

causal design
A design in which the causal or independent variables are manipulated in a relatively controlled environment.

Like descriptive research, **causal research** requires a planned and structured design. Although descriptive research can determine the degree of association between variables, it is generally not very appropriate for examining causal relationships. Causal relations are those that involve cause-and-effect variables.

The hypothesis that a promotional campaign will lead to (*cause*) an increase in sales is an example. To examine this hypothesis, a researcher would need a **causal design**—a design in which the causal or independent variables are manipulated in a relatively controlled environment. A relatively controlled environment is one in which the other variables that might affect the dependent variable are controlled or checked as much as possible. The effect of this manipulation on one or more dependent variables is then measured to infer causality.

The main method of causal research is an experiment. Experiments can take place either in a laboratory or in a natural setting. An experiment can be designed to test the causal relationship that promotion causes brand sales. Here, the independent variable that will be manipulated is promotion and the dependent variable is brand sales. Variables other than promotion, which also affect sales, such as product quality, price, and distribution need to be controlled. Participants in a laboratory study might be told to imagine they are on a shopping trip. Various promotional offers, as manipulated by the researcher, will be displayed, with each group of respondents seeing only one offer. The purchases of the respondents in this simulated shopping experience would be measured and compared across groups. The experimenter creates and controls the setting so that product quality, price, and distribution are held constant. In a field experiment, the same study would occur in a natural setting, such as retail stores. Various promotional offers would be displayed in stores, with each group of respondents seeing only one offer. The resulting brand sales would be monitored.

In the opening vignette, Spiegel did not make use of causal research. However, it could have, for example, in testing three alternative depictions of its product lines in its catalog. Each of the three versions of the catalog could be mailed to a distinct group of customers. The purchases of Spiegel products by each group could be monitored and compared to determine the depiction that resulted in the highest sales. Causal research is appropriate for the following purposes, illustrated in the context of examining the effect of a promotional campaign on the sales of Mercedes cars:

1. *To understand which variables are the causes (independent variables) and which are the effects (dependent variables) of a phenomenon.* In other words, if an independent variable is manipulated, a change should be detected in the dependent variable. The independent variables will be the dollar amount spent on advertising and the dollar amount spent on sales promotion during a given time period. The dependent variable will be the sales of Mercedes (measured in units and dollars).

2. *To determine the extent of the relationship between the predicted effect and the causal variables.* The relationship between sales promotion and advertising expenditures and the sales of Mercedes is likely to be nonlinear: As more and more is spent on advertising, sales of Mercedes will increase less and less due to the saturation effect.

A causal design is needed for examining the effect of a promotional campaign on the sales of Mercedes cars.

The implementation of a causal design is further illustrated by Microsoft's experiment with Windows Vista.

Research in Action

Windows Vista: A Window into the Hearts of Computer Users

The key to the success (high awareness and high sales) of Windows Vista (www.microsoft.com) was that the product was carefully designed and tested. In a controlled experiment, one group of computer users was asked to work with Windows Vista. Two other carefully matched groups worked with the previous versions of Windows: one with Windows XP and the other with Windows 2000. All three groups rated the operating system on ease of use, power, capabilities, and the ability to enhance a computer user's experience. Windows Vista was rated significantly better than the previous versions on all factors, leading to the introduction of this operating system.[5]

In the Microsoft experiment, the causal (independent) variable was the operating system, which was manipulated to have three levels: Windows Vista, Windows XP, and Windows 2000. The effect (dependent) variables were ease of use, power, capabilities, and ability to enhance a computer user's experience. The influence of the user's background was controlled by carefully matching the three groups on relevant demographic and computer-usage characteristics.

Due to its complexity and importance, the topic of causal designs and experimental research will be fully explained in a separate chapter (Chapter 8). In that chapter, we discuss the conditions for causality, validity in experimentation, and specific types of experimental designs.

Be a DM!

As the advertising manager for Taco Bell, an America restaurant chain specializing in Mexican-styled fast food, how would you determine whether the advertising budget for the next year should be increased, decreased, or remain the same as the current budget?

Be an MR!

Visit www.tacobell.com and search the Internet, as well as your library's online databases, to obtain information on Taco Bell's advertising. Write a brief report.

Design an experiment to determine whether the advertising budget for Taco Bell for the next year should be increased, decreased, or remain the same as the current budget. Identify the independent, dependent, and the control variables.

Relationships Among Exploratory, Descriptive, and Causal Research

Although the preceding example distinguished causal research from other types of research and showed the benefits of causal research, causal research should not be viewed in isolation. Rather, exploratory, descriptive, and causal designs should be used to complement each other. A given problem might lend itself to exploratory, descriptive, or causal research. Consider the loss of market share:

Exploratory Research:	Why are we losing market share?
Descriptive Research:	How do consumers evaluate our brand compared to competing brands?
Causal Research:	By how much will our sales increase if we decrease the price by 5, 10, or 15 percent?

As mentioned earlier, a given project may incorporate more than one basic research design, depending on the nature of the problem and the approach. We offer the following general guidelines for choosing research designs:

1. When little is known about the problem situation, it is desirable to begin with exploratory research. For example, exploratory research is suitable for generating alternative courses of action, research questions, or hypotheses. Exploratory research can then be followed by descriptive or causal research, as in the Spiegel vignette (Figure 3.7(a)).
2. It is not necessary to begin every research design with exploratory research. If the researcher has a good understanding of the problem situation, descriptive or causal research might be a more appropriate initial step (Figure 3.7(b)). Quarterly consumer-satisfaction surveys are an example of research that does not need to begin with or include an exploratory phase.
3. Exploratory research can be used at any point in a study. For example, when descriptive or causal research leads to results that are unexpected or difficult to interpret, the researcher may turn to exploratory research for insight (Figure 3.7(c)).

Suppose an image study is conducted for the American supermarket chain Kroger to identify its strengths and weaknesses relative to competing supermarkets. Exploratory research, including secondary data analysis and focus groups, is first conducted to define the problem and to develop a suitable approach. This is followed by a descriptive study consisting of a survey in which a questionnaire is constructed and administered by telephone interviews.

FIGURE 3.7

Some Alternative Research Designs

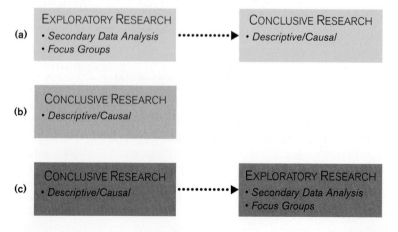

Suppose the image study is to be repeated after one year to determine if any changes had taken place. At that point, exploratory research would probably be unnecessary, and the research design could begin with the descriptive study.

Assume that the survey is repeated a year later and that some unexpected findings are obtained. Kroger management wonders why its supermarkets' ratings on in-store service have declined when the supermarket staff has increased. Exploratory research in the form of focus groups might be undertaken to probe these unexpected findings. The focus groups might reveal that although the store clerks are present, they are not very helpful. This would suggest the need for training the store clerks.

This example illustrates how exploratory and descriptive research can be integrated. Exploratory and descriptive designs are frequently used in commercial marketing research; causal research is not as popular. Another example of the use of exploratory and conclusive research is provided by Kellogg's.

Research in Action

Kellogg's: Smart and Special with Exploratory and Descriptive Research

With 2007 sales of $11.776 billion, U.S.-based Kellogg's is the world's leading producer of cereal and a leading producer of convenience foods, including cookies, crackers, toaster pastries, cereal bars, fruit snacks, frozen waffles, and veggie foods. As of 2008, its products were manufactured in 19 countries worldwide and sold in more than 180 countries.

Introducing new products, brand extensions, and making changes to existing brands has been a core element of the company's marketing strategy. By undertaking exploratory research followed by conclusive research, Kellogg's understands what new products should be developed and how existing products could be extended into a series of variants that keep the core product strong, but grow the brand as a whole.

Exploratory research in the form of focus groups revealed that consumers wanted cereals and snacks that were natural and healthy and yet tasted great. Conclusive research in the form of descriptive surveys verified demand for such products. Therefore, Kellogg's has developed numerous products that contain whole grains or provide fiber, such as the Smart Start brand, which can help to lower both high blood pressure and cholesterol. It also introduced products that can help consumers watch

their weight, such as Special K, and products that are lower in fat and sodium. Kellogg's also has introduced innovative packaging that provides the benefits of portion control. The company introduced a number of new products in 2006, including Vive and GoLean Crunch Honey Almond Flax. As a result of Kellogg's effort to create products that are natural and encourage a healthy diet, in 2006 *Business Ethics* magazine named Kellogg's one of the 100 best corporate citizens.[6]

Be an MR!

Visit www.wellsfargo.com and search the Internet, as well as your library's online databases, to obtain information on consumers' attitudes towards online banking. The large American financial-services provider Wells Fargo would like to determine consumers' attitudes toward online banking and hopes to repeat this project annually. Which type of research design would you implement and why?

Be a DM!

As the CEO of Wells Fargo, how would you use information about consumers' attitudes towards online banking to improve the competitiveness of your bank?

Tasks Involved in Formulating a Research Design

In formulating a research design, in most cases the researcher must perform the following tasks (Figure 3.8):

1. Specify the information needed (Chapter 2).
2. Design the exploratory, descriptive, and/or causal phases of the research (Chapters 4 through 8).

FIGURE 3.8

Tasks Involved in a Research Design

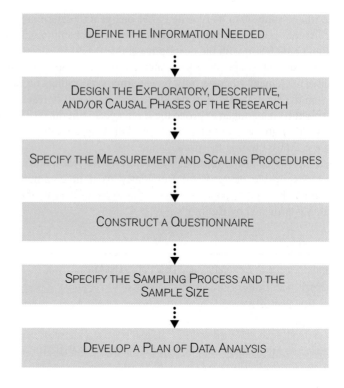

3. Specify the measurement and scaling procedures (Chapters 9 and 10).
4. Construct and pretest a questionnaire (interview form) or an appropriate form for data collection (Chapter 11).
5. Specify the sampling process and sample size (Chapters 12 and 13).
6. Develop a plan of data analysis (Chapter 15).

Chapter 2 described how to specify the necessary information. As noted, we will discuss in detail the rest of the tasks involved in a research design in subsequent chapters.

Research Design and The Value of Marketing Research

Research is conducted to help reduce management error in decision making. The key word here is *reduce*. Research is not designed to "prove" assumptions, but rather to provide management with an assessment of the degree of risk associated with making decisions based on tested assumptions. As the cost of making the wrong decision increases, typically the formality and structure of a study design increase as well. The research design has a major impact on the cost and value of the marketing research project. Ultimately, the cost of any project must be weighted against the reduced risk of making the decision with additional information.

Before committing funds to a study, management must assess, either formally or informally, the value of the additional information obtained by marketing research. For example, suppose an American brand manager for Dannon yogurt (a subsidiary of the French Groupe Danone) is faced with a proposal to spend $50,000 to conduct a causal study regarding the effect of using various promotional offers. The manager must decide whether the value of a decision based on current knowledge could be improved by more than $50,000 with the help of research. If the various promotional offers involved coupons versus free trials, the difference in expenses associated with the two approaches (not to mention the difference in consumer response) could far exceed the $50,000 cost of research. In that case, the high cost of making the wrong decision makes it easier to justify the cost of the research.

The information value of research must also be discounted by the degree of error inherent in a study. No research design, no matter how sophisticated, can eliminate all risk from a decision, because no research is completely error-free. Several potential sources of error can affect a research design. Estimating the level of error in a study is complicated by the fact that, typically, only random sampling error is quantified. A **random sampling error** is an error resulting from the particular sample selected being an imperfect representation of the population of interest. Total error is made up of both sampling and nonsampling errors. In formulating the research design, the researcher should attempt to control the total error, not just the sampling error.

Nonsampling errors, as would be expected, can be attributed to sources other than sampling. They result from a variety of causes, including errors in problem definition, approach, scales, questionnaire design, survey methods, interviewing techniques, and data preparation and analysis. These nonsampling errors can be attributed to the researcher, the interviewer, or the respondent. A good research design attempts to control the various sources of error, as illustrated in the opening vignette, where Spiegel made an effort to control the sampling and nonsampling errors. Random sampling errors were controlled by having a large sample (1,000) that was randomly selected. Spiegel also controlled various sources of nonsampling errors, including interviewer and respondent errors, by careful selection, training, and supervision of the interviewers. These errors are discussed in great detail in subsequent chapters.

random sampling error
The error due to the particular sample selected being an imperfect representation of the population of interest.

nonsampling error
Errors that can be attributed to sources other than sampling; they can be random or nonrandom.

Budgeting and Scheduling the Project

Once a research design has been specified, the researcher should prepare a detailed budget and schedule. **Budgeting and scheduling** help to ensure that the marketing research project is completed with the available resources: money, time, personnel, and others. The budget process allows the researcher and the decision maker to compare the estimated value of the information with the projected costs. Additionally, the project schedule will help to ensure that the information is obtained in time to address the management-decision problem.

budgeting and scheduling
Management tools needed to help ensure that the marketing research project is completed within the available resources.

Marketing Research Proposal

Once the research design has been formulated and the budgeting and scheduling of the project has been accomplished, the researcher should prepare a written research proposal. The **marketing research proposal** contains the essence of the project and serves as a contract between the researcher and management. The proposal covers all phases of the marketing research process, including cost and schedules. The format of a research proposal can vary considerably depending on the nature of the problem and the relationship of the client to the research supplier. Most proposals present a detailed research design and contain some or all of the following elements:

marketing research proposal
Contains the essence of the project and serves as a contract between the researcher and management.

1. *Executive summary.* The proposal should begin with an overview of the entire project, a summary of the major points from each of the other sections.
2. *Background.* The background to the problem, including the environmental context, should be described.
3. *Problem definition/research objectives.* Normally, a statement of the problem should be presented. If this statement has not been developed (as in the case of exploratory research), then the objectives of the marketing research project should be clearly specified.
4. *Approach to the problem.* A review of the relevant academic and trade literature, along with some kind of an analytical model, should be included. If research questions and hypotheses have been identified, these should be included in the proposal.
5. *Research design.* The type of research design, whether exploratory, descriptive, causal, or a combination, should be specified. Information should be provided on the

following components: (a) the kind of information to be obtained, (b) the method of administering the questionnaire (i.e., mail, telephone, personal, or electronic interviews), (c) scaling techniques, (d) the nature of the questionnaire (i.e., type of questions asked, length, average interviewing time), and (e) the sampling plan and sample size. This section often forms the heart of the proposal.

6. *Field work/data collection.* The proposal should discuss how the data will be collected and who will collect it. If the field work is to be subcontracted to another supplier, this should be stated. Control mechanisms to ensure the quality of data collected should be described.

7. *Data analysis.* The kind of data analysis that will be conducted, and how the results will be interpreted, should be described.

8. *Reporting.* The proposal should specify the nature and number of intermediate reports. The form of the final report, including whether a formal presentation of the results will be made, also should be stated. Industry professionals refer to this part of the report as the "deliverables." The proposal writer must specify what information (specifically, which documents) will be given to the client. Sometimes, the client will want a formal report that is more comprehensive and narrative than a PowerPoint presentation and discussion that might cover many projects. At the least, an executive summary of one to two single-spaced pages should be provided to explain what insights have been gained by the research and what these results mean for the client firm's managers.

9. *Cost and time.* The cost of the project and a schedule, broken down into phases, should be presented. A payment schedule should be worked out in advance, especially for large projects. Conventional industry practice is to have a project paid in three parts: the first payment is due after the proposal is accepted, the second at the project midpoint, and the third at the conclusion of the project. The schedule developed for the proposal becomes an important coordinating document between the client and the research agency as the project is conducted.

10. *Project personnel.* All personnel who will be working on the project should be identified. The job, duration, responsibility, and authority of each person should be stated.

11. *Appendices.* Any statistical or other information that is of interest to only a few people should be presented in appendices.

The research proposal represents the contract between management and the researcher. It ensures that there is agreement regarding the objectives of the project, and it helps sell the project to management. Therefore, a research proposal should always be prepared, even when repeating a project for a repeat client.

Experiential Learning

Crafting a Research Proposal

Go to the textbook's Web site, select "Chapter 3," and download the following file: Meteor Proposal.doc. Meteor Motorcycle Company is one of the U.S. industry's leading manufacturers of customized, high-performance bikes in the luxury cruiser class. It is one of the only custom motorcycle makers equipped with full-service design, engineering, manufacturing, paint and polishing, and administrative teams.

The company produces four different kinds of bikes. They are all individually branded under Meteor X, Meteor Y, Meteor Z, and the Comet Chopper brand names and represent the company's varied product offerings, ranging in price from $23,000 to $100,000 or more. The company has seen tremendous growth—from approximately 27 bikes sold in 2000 to an

impressive 4,000 in 2006. Comet Chopper, the brainchild of Jeff Branson, the creative force behind Meteor, currently accounts for nearly 55 percent of the company's annual sales of approximately $70 million.

1. Open Meteor Proposal.doc and read about an actual study done for one of the exciting heavy-weight cruiser motorcycle companies. The names have been changed here. How well does this proposal correspond to the recommendations about proposals just discussed?

2. If you were the head of the marketing team for the Meteor Motorcycle Company, what would you like to be made more clear in this proposal?

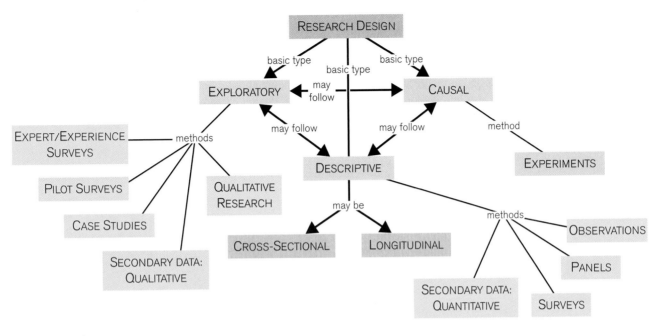

FIGURE 3.9

A Concept Map for Research Design

Summary Illustration Using the Opening Vignette

The research design in the opening vignette described how a project was conducted for Spiegel. Research designs can be broadly classified as exploratory or conclusive, whereas conclusive research can be either descriptive or causal. Typically, the project begins with exploratory research, which is followed by descriptive (or causal) research. As seen in the opening vignette, in order to understand the problem situation, Spiegel analyzed secondary data and conducted 10 focus groups. This exploratory research helped Spiegel to identify and understand the unique aspects of its customers' shopping behavior and clothing needs. The findings of exploratory research were treated as tentative and were further verified by descriptive research consisting of telephone interviews with a randomly selected sample of 1,000 customers.

Typically, as in the case of Spiegel, a research project begins with exploratory research. However, other combinations of the basic designs are possible. Exploratory research can be conducted at any point in the project or it might not be undertaken at all. A well-formulated research design will attempt to control the random sampling as well as the nonsampling errors, as demonstrated in the opening vignette. A large and randomly selected sample was used to measure and control random sampling error. Efforts also were made to control the various sources of nonsampling error. For example, the interviewers were carefully selected and thoroughly trained, and close supervision was exercised to minimize interviewing errors attributed to the interviewers and respondents. Figure 3.9 provides a concept map for research design.

International Marketing Research

The various methods associated with implementing each step of the research design discussed in this chapter must be reassessed within the context of cultural differences before they can be used internationally. Given environmental and cultural differences, a research design appropriate for one country might not be suitable for another. Consider the problem of determining household attitudes toward major appliances in the United States and Saudi

Arabia. When conducting exploratory research in the United States, it is appropriate to conduct focus groups jointly with male and female heads of household. It would not be appropriate to conduct such focus groups in Saudi Arabia. As a result of their traditional culture, wives are unlikely to participate freely in the presence of their husbands. It would be more useful to conduct one-on-one depth interviews with both male and female heads of households included in the sample. Procter & Gamble (P&G) encountered a similar situation in Japan.

Research in Action

P&G: Exploring and Wooing Japanese Women

The consumer market in Japan is one of the toughest, most competitive, fastest-moving markets in the world. Japan represents the cutting edge of worldwide technology in many product categories. When P&G started business in Japan, it conducted a detailed study of market characteristics and market profile. The target market for P&G was homemakers, who were largely responsible for the consumption of several products, such as diapers, household cleaners, soaps, and detergents. Exploratory research followed by descriptive research was undertaken for this purpose. Whereas focus groups are most popular in the United States, one-on-one, depth interviews were used because of the Japanese cultural tendency to not disagree openly in group settings. The descriptive surveys were fielded using in-home personal interviews.

Results showed that the average Japanese homemaker was uncompromising in her demands for high quality, value, and service. She was a paragon of conservation and efficiency in the management of the household. About half the adult women in Japan were employed, but they generally worked outside of the home only before marriage and after their children were raised. Child rearing was the number-one priority for Japanese mothers.

When it came to foreign versus domestic brands, Japanese women preferred foreign-name brand products that had style and status, such as fashionable clothing, French perfumes, wines, liquors, and designer bags. They did not prefer functional products made in foreign countries, because these products usually did not meet their exacting and demanding standards.

Japanese women greatly preferred commercials that conserved traditional social and family values and roles, rather than the typical Western examples. P&G initially made a few mistakes in misjudging nuances of Japanese culture before this study was conducted. For example, the introduction of Camay bath soap and Pampers diapers were supported with Western-style advertising that was not well received by Japanese women. However, based on the market profile study, the advertising was changed to stress traditional social and family values, thereby increasing its effectiveness. P&G opened an information site exclusively for mobile phones in Japan in 2007. This site features information on a variety of topics, including beauty, culture, and fashion, in addition to introducing new products. The decision to open this site was based on the heavy usage of cell phones as a shopping medium by Japanese women as determined by exploratory and descriptive research.[7]

In developing countries, consumer panels often are not available, which makes it difficult to conduct descriptive longitudinal research. In many countries, such as Sierra Leone in Africa, the marketing support infrastructure—retailing, wholesaling, advertising, and promotion development—is often lacking, which makes it difficult to implement a causal design involving a field experiment. In formulating a research design, considerable effort is required to ensure the equivalence and comparability of secondary and primary data obtained from different countries. In the context of collecting primary data, qualitative research, survey methods, scaling techniques, questionnaire design, and sampling considerations are particularly important. We discuss these topics in more detail in subsequent chapters.

Be an MR!

Visit www.unilever.com and search the Internet, as well as your library's online databases, to find information on consumer preferences for bathing soaps. Unilever PLC, the British- and Dutch-based multinational maker of food, home, and personal-care brands, would like to determine consumer preferences for Lux bath soap in the United States, the United Kingdom, and India. Discuss the similarities and differences in the research design that should be adopted in each country.

Be a DM!

As the global marketing manager for Unilever PLC how would you use information on consumer preferences for Lux in the United States, the United Kingdom, and India to formulate the marketing strategy for the brand in each of these countries?

Technology and Marketing Research

"Smart" products have been around for years. Coffeemakers and VCRs can be told when to perform their respective duties. Automobiles tell the driver when the lights have been left on or when the door is not fully closed. In the very near future, these products, and others, will become even more "intelligent." Networking subsystems, both hardware and software, will soon be embedded into numerous products, giving them the ability to "talk" and to remember.[8]

These networking subsystems could be added to the production process for new products or easily added to existing products. The necessary technology already exists; it is just a matter of applying it. When triggered by a preprogrammed event, the product would "speak" with the user and record the conversation. The conversation (or data) could then be transmitted to the producer instantly or stored and gathered in batches and transmitted at a later date. Dell Computers uses software installed at the factory to periodically run diagnostic tests on Dell PCs and inform Dell of the status of the PCs via the Internet. This feature becomes valuable during troubleshooting of equipment malfunctions and also provides useful information for product design. Such data can also be invaluable to marketing managers. Smart products could be used to collect not only exploratory data, but also cross-sectional or longitudinal descriptive data.

In some form, these subsystems are already proving very useful to companies, including software developers such as Microsoft. When added to a software application such as Microsoft Office, they are programmed to activate when the user encounters an error message. After interacting with the user, the subsystem stores all the relevant data. Then, the developer can determine what happened and what could be done to prevent that error from recurring. Any user observations or opinions can also be stored for analysis. This information assists Microsoft when producing new products or upgrading versions of Microsoft Office.

Ethics in Marketing Research

The choice of a research design has ethical overtones for both the client and the research firm. For example, if Maxwell House, a brand of American food and beverage giant Kraft Foods (www.kraftfoods.com), is interested in examining brand switching in coffee purchases, a longitudinal design is the only appropriate way to assess changes in an individual respondent's choice of coffee brands. A research firm that justifies the use of a cross-sectional design simply because it has no experience in conducting longitudinal studies is behaving unethically.

Researchers must ensure that the research design will provide the information needed to address the marketing research problem. The client should have the integrity not to misrepresent the project, should describe the constraints under which the researcher must operate, and should not make unreasonable demands. If customer contact has to be restricted, or if time is an issue, the client should make these constraints known at the start of the project. It would be unethical for a client to extract details from a proposal submitted by one research firm and pass them to another who actually would do the project for the client. A proposal is the property of the research firm that prepared it, unless the client has paid for it. The client should not take advantage of the research firm by making false promises of future research contracts in order to solicit concessions for the current project.

Research in Action

Just Business Versus Unethical Concessions

Ethical dilemmas can arise due to the strong desire of marketing research firms to become suppliers to large businesses that are heavy users of marketing research. For example, Visa, Delta Airlines, Coca-Cola, and Ford Motor Company have large marketing research budgets and regularly hire external marketing research suppliers. These large clients can manipulate the price for the current study or demand unreasonable concessions in the research design (e.g., more focus groups, a larger sample, or additional data analyses) by suggesting the potential for the marketing research firm to become a regular supplier. This might be considered just business, but it becomes unethical when there is no intention to follow up with a larger study or to use the research firm in the future. Marketing research firms should be aware of such unethical practices and must discern the intent of the client firms before offering concessions to gain future business.[9]

Equally important, responsibilities to respondents must not be overlooked. The researcher should design the study so as not to violate the respondents' right to safety, privacy, or choice. Furthermore, the client must not violate the anonymity of the respondents. (Respondent-related issues are discussed in more detail in the Chapters 4 through 7.)

What Would *You* Do?

NASCAR: Changing the Redneck Image

The Situation

The sound of roaring engines, screaming fans, and beating hearts—the excitement of NASCAR! The National Association of Stock Car Auto Racing (NASCAR) is a company unlike any other. Although NASCAR generates excitement in fans across the United States, it has been stereotyped as only appealing to low-income Southerners who work in laborer-type jobs. Brian France, chair and CEO of NASCAR, wanted to increase NASCAR's audience and makeover its stereotyped image.

NASCAR conducted exploratory research to identify ways to penetrate the nonrace market, reach younger fans, and build its brand image across the nation. Extensive focus groups revealed that: (1) NASCAR had a rural sports image, (2) this image was not necessarily negative, and (3) companies that supported sports were viewed positively.

The Marketing Research Decision

1. Do you think the research design adopted by NASCAR was appropriate? Why or why not?
2. Which of the following research designs would you recommend?
    a. Exploratory research: focus groups
    b. Exploratory research: depth interviews
    c. Exploratory research followed by a descriptive survey
    d. Exploratory research followed by causal research
    e. Descriptive survey followed by exploratory research
3. Discuss the role of the type of research design you recommend in enabling Brian France to change the image of NASCAR.

The Marketing Management Decision

1. Brian France realizes that it is crucial for NASCAR to project the right image. However, he wonders what that image is. Is it (check as many as are applicable):
    a. A rural sports image
    b. An urban sports image
    c. Southern heritage
    d. Blue-collar sports
    e. A national sport for all lifestyles

2. Discuss how the course of action you recommend to Brian France is influenced by the research that you suggested earlier and by the findings of that research.

continued

What Brian France Did

Brian France attempted to position NASCAR as a national sport for all lifestyles. He took several initiatives to involve minorities in the sport, which was expanded both by Sprint's national sponsorship and by moving races from the South to speedways across the country. NASCAR also targeted the nontraditional demographic segments, including families, children, and minorities. To further reinforce the national image, Brian France appointed non–Southerners to key positions in the company. As of 2008, NASCAR featured three major national series (NASCAR Sprint Cup Series, NASCAR Nationwide Series, and the NASCAR Craftsman Truck Series), as well as eight regional series and one local grassroots series. NASCAR sanctioned 1,500 races at over 100 tracks in 35 U.S. states, Canada, and Mexico.[10]

Summary

A research design is the roadmap for conducting the marketing research project. It specifies the details of how the project should be conducted. Research designs can be broadly classified as exploratory or conclusive. The primary purpose of exploratory research is to provide insights into the problem. Conclusive research is used to test hypotheses and examine specific relationships. Conclusive research can be either descriptive or causal and is used as input into managerial decision making.

The major objective of descriptive research is to describe market characteristics or functions. Descriptive research can be further classified into cross-sectional and longitudinal designs. Cross-sectional designs involve the collection of information from a sample drawn from a population at a single point in time. In contrast, longitudinal designs entail repeated measurements on a fixed sample at different points in time. Causal research is designed to obtain evidence about cause-and-effect (causal) relationships via an experiment.

In evaluating a research proposal, management must discount the value of the information by the level of error inherent in the study. Error can be associated with any of the six components of the research design. Managers should prepare a written marketing research proposal that includes all the elements of the marketing research process.

The various methods associated with implementing each step of the research design must be reassessed within the context of cultural differences before they can be used internationally. Technology and the Internet can facilitate the implementation of exploratory, descriptive, or causal research. In addition to ethical aspects that concern researcher and client, the rights of respondents must be respected when formulating the research design.

Key Terms and Concepts

Research design, 94	Cross-sectional design, 101	Random sampling error, 109
Exploratory research, 96	Longitudinal design, 102	Nonsampling error, 109
Conclusive research, 97	Panel, 102	Budgeting and scheduling, 109
Descriptive research, 100	Causal research, 104	Marketing research proposal, 109
Survey, 101	Causal design, 104	

Suggested Cases and Video Cases

Running Case with Real Data

1.1 Hewlett Packard

Comprehensive Critical Thinking Cases

2.1 American Idol   2.2 Baskin-Robbins   2.3 Akron Children's Hospital

Comprehensive Cases with Real Data

3.1 Bank of America   3.2 McDonald's   3.3 Boeing

Video Cases

3.1 NFL	4.1 Mayo Clinic	5.1 eGO	8.1 AFLAC	9.1 P&G
10.1 Nivea	13.1 Subaru	14.1 Intel	19.1 Marriott	

Live Research: Conducting a Marketing Research Project

1. Each team should present to the class the type of research design they think is appropriate. Normally, the teams will end up with similar research designs, unless they are working on different projects.

2. As a class, discuss and select the research design for this project.
3. It is helpful to invite the client to this session.
4. Prepare a formal proposal, as described in this chapter, and obtain client approval.

Acronym

The components of a research design may be summarized by the acronym DESIGN:

D ata analysis plan

E xploratory, descriptive, causal design

S caling and measurement

I nterviewing forms: questionnaire design

G enerating the needed information

N umber: Sample size and plan

Review Questions

1. Define *research design* in your own words.
2. How does formulating a research design differ from developing an approach to a problem?
3. Differentiate between exploratory and conclusive research.
4. What are the major purposes for which descriptive research is conducted?
5. Compare and contrast cross-sectional and longitudinal designs.
6. Discuss the advantages and disadvantages of panels.
7. What is a causal research design? What is its purpose?
8. What is the relationship among exploratory, descriptive, and causal research?
9. List the major components of a research design.

Applied Problems

1. Sweet Cookies is planning to launch a new line of cookies and wants to assess the size of the market. The cookies have a mixed chocolate-pineapple flavor and will be targeted at the premium end of the market. Discuss the type of research design that could be used.
2. Welcome, Inc. is a chain of fast-food restaurants located in major metropolitan areas in the South. Sales have been growing very slowly for the last 2 years. Management has decided to add some new items to the menu; however, first they want to know more about their customers and their preferences.
   a. List two hypotheses.
   b. What kind of research design is appropriate? Why?
3. Visit the Greenfield Online Research Center (www.greenfieldonline.com).
   a. What are the surveys currently being conducted by Greenfield?
   b. How are the respondents being recruited for these surveys?
   c. Discuss the different type of errors likely to arise given the way the respondents are being recruited.
4. Visit the Web page of three of the marketing research firms listed in Table 1.1. What types of research designs have these firms implemented recently?
5. You are conducting an image study for Carnival Cruise Lines. As part of exploratory research, analyze the messages posted to the newsgroup rec.travel.cruises to determine the factors that consumers use in evaluating cruise companies. This newsgroup can be located at http://groups.google.com.

Group Discussion

1. Discuss the following statement: "If the research budget is limited, exploratory research can be dispensed with."
2. Discuss the following statement: "The researcher should always attempt to develop an optimal design for every marketing research project."
3. "There are many potential sources of error in a research project. It is impossible to control all of them. Hence, marketing research contains many errors and we cannot be confident of the findings." Discuss these statements as a group. Did your group arrive at a consensus?

Hewlett-Packard Running Case

Review the Hewlett-Packard (HP) case, Case 1.1, and the questionnaire given toward the end of the book.

1. How can HP make use of exploratory research to understand how household consumers buy personal computers and related equipment?
2. Describe one way in which HP can make use of descriptive research.
3. Describe one way in which HP can make use of causal research.
4. HP would like to determine consumer response to a new lightweight tablet PC that it has developed. What research design would you recommend?

VIDEO CASE 3.1

NATIONAL FOOTBALL LEAGUE: The King of Professional Sports

NFL

The National Football League (www.nfl.com) is considered the king of all professional sports in the United States. It was formed by 11 teams in 1920 as the American Professional Football Association and adopted the name National Football League in 1922. The league currently consists of 32 teams from American cities and regions, divided evenly into two conferences (AFC and NFC), with four, four-team divisions. The NFL governs and promotes the game, sets and enforces rules, and regulates team ownership. It generates revenue mostly through sponsorships, licensing of merchandise, and selling national broadcasting rights. It has been extremely successful because it is advertiser-friendly. The teams operate as separate businesses but share a percentage of their revenue. NFL revenues amounted to $5.86 billion in 2006, and the average player salary was $1.4 million in the same period.

Tough, strong, and fiercely competitive on the field, but remove the players' helmets and a softer side emerges. Marketing research has documented the positive impact of cause-related marketing on corporate image. The NFL has a strong tradition of public service and is an active contributor to various social causes. Bettering communities and helping others ties into the basic team concept and is an extension of the NFL's philosophy. NFL players strongly believe and encourage others to get involved, whether it is time or money or anything else—even the smallest of gestures can make a big difference to someone else.

Focus groups and surveys have shown that community involvement is particularly important for an organization that depends on the community for support. The NFL has a rich history of giving, and each of the 32 teams has its own community relations initiatives. The fact that there are around 1,600 players in the league indicates the far-reaching capabilities of this powerful organization. According to Joe Browne, Executive Vice President of Communications and Public Affairs, the NFL views its public service activities as giving something back to its customers—the fans who attend the games and watch them on TV. The NFL has worked with a number of nonprofit and charitable organizations over the years, with each team taking on a different issue, such as the Philadelphia Eagles building community playgrounds. Each year the Eagles take time off from the world of sports and business and build a playground in the Philadelphia area. The New England Patriots help deliver Thanksgiving dinners to those in need, and the Pittsburgh Steelers visit the elderly—football players reaching out to make a difference.

Back in 1974, the league formed a partnership with the United Way, a national network of more than 1,300 locally governed organizations that work to create lasting positive changes in communities and people's lives. This partnership is still in existence today and has encouraged fans to give back to society. Consequently, fundraising for United Way has soared from $800 million to $4 billion. The relationship between United Way and the NFL has blossomed into a charitable enterprise that touches 30 million people each year by providing funds and programs to the needy. The NFL's ongoing ad campaigns remind fans that football players are regular guys who want to do good in the community where they work and live. The effectiveness of these ad campaigns is evaluated by undertaking surveys that measure people's awareness, perceptions, preferences, intentions, and behaviors toward the NFL and comparing them against benchmarks.

Based on marketing research, the NFL's marketing strategy has two pillars: football and community. Football is its product, something that NFL does best.

Community means giving back to the community in exchange for all its support and love. The support of the community is tremendous, with 18 million tickets sold each season and more than 120 million people watching NFL games on TV each week. Then, there is the huge impact of the Super Bowl—an event that has been the top-rated show each year, seen by more viewers than any other program, an exposure that has proven to be an effective messaging medium. The tremendous reach and power of TV commercials helped the NFL's "join the team" initiative get a spectacular start with thousands of eager fans calling up NFL teams across the country ready to join the team. NFL believes that charity and being a good corporate citizen are essential to achieve success in business. This makes the entire entity stronger. By giving back to its customers, the NFL shows that it cares about them.

The NFL's impact on the community extends way beyond the games played on Sundays and Monday nights, because there is a special bond that fans feel with each of the teams in the league. Consumer perception and attitudinal surveys have consistently shown that the NFL is held in high regard, and the League tries hard to maintain these positive perceptions. It realizes that at the end of the day, the NFL is an energy, a symbol that represents American tradition, which if not maintained would wither away.

Joe Browne describes people's relationship with the NFL as a love affair in which the NFL and the teams have to give this love back to the people for supporting them so well. That's what the NFL does through its various programs such as NFL charities, the NFL football fund, and the disaster relief fund that the NFL established after 9/11 to give back to the families of those killed in New York and Washington. There is charity on the field, too; each time a player is fined the money is used to help fund various causes. Fans can get into the game by going to the auctions section on the NFL Web site, because all of the proceeds go to players' charities. According to Beth Colleton, Director of Community Affairs, NFL stands for quality, tradition, and integrity—all of which come together to define Americana. The NFL captures the American energy like no other—an energy that continues to ignite goodwill with each passing season.

Conclusion

The NFL has used marketing research to foster immense goodwill and influence to make a difference to the community. The strong public service feeling at the NFL and the active involvement by NFL players in various social initiatives and programs bear testimony to how seriously the NFL takes its responsibility toward society and the immensely positive impact it has on society, all supported by marketing research. Continued reliance on marketing research can help the NFL to remain the king of professional sports.

Questions

1. Football is a male-dominated sport. Discuss the role that marketing research can play in helping the NFL more effectively market the league to women.
2. The NFL would like to increase its penetration of the women segment. Define the management-decision problem.
3. What is the main competition faced by the NFL?
4. Define an appropriate marketing research problem corresponding to the management-decision problem in question 2.
5. Develop three appropriate research questions, each with suitable hypotheses.
6. What type of research design would you recommend for investigating the marketing research problem?

References

1. Inside to NFL's Success, www.economist.com/business/displaystory.cfm?story_id=6859210, accessed January 2, 2008.
2. NFL Team values/revenues, ranked, www.forbes.com/lists/2006/30/06nfl_NFL-Team-Valuations_land.html, accessed January 2, 2008.
3. NFL Studies What Women Want, www.reuters.com/article/MediaMarketing06/idUSN2933923020061129, accessed January 2, 2008.
4. Making Sure Ads Play to Women, Too, www.boston.com/sports/football/patriots/articles/2004/01/28/making_sure_ads_play_to_women_too/?page=1, accessed January 2, 2008.
5. Why the NFL Struggles to Attract Female Fans, www.dmwmedia.com/news/2006/12/05/why-the-nfl-struggles-to-attract-female-fans, accessed January 2, 2008.

Exploratory Research Design: Secondary Data

OPENING QUESTIONS

1. How does secondary data differ from primary data?
2. What are the advantages and disadvantages of secondary data?
3. How should secondary data be evaluated to determine their usefulness?
4. What are the different sources of secondary data?
5. What is database marketing, and how does it make use of secondary data?
6. How can published secondary data be classified?
7. How can computerized databases be classified?
8. How do we identify and classify the sources of secondary data useful in international marketing research?
9. What is the impact of technology on the use of secondary data?
10. What ethical issues are involved in the use of secondary data?

THURSDAY

• • • •

April 10, 2008

Vindy.com
The Valley's Homepage

Entertainment extra

Crooked cops rule in 'Street Kings'

►**THE AIR** is thick with tough-guy talk, but there's mostly hot air at the core of "Street Kings," a tale of corruption in which the cops are the crooks. The film, which opens this weekend, stars Keanu Reeves. Review.

PAGE D7

LOCAL

KFC helps victim of robbery, attack

►**SUNDAY** is Joe Kaluza Day at KFC on South Avenue in Youngstown, with all proceeds going to the res-
tʌurʌnt mʌnʌger who

City

An Austintown tr
doesn't know a tov
resident who supp

By DAVID SK
CITY HALL RE

YOUNGSTOWN — A
ficial wants contrac
town and Boardman
to implement an ec

Nei

The eagles, ro
a home once o
the Firestone
tolerant of the

By D. A. WH
VINDICATOR SA

See video for this story at **Vindy.com**

> "Open source information—also called secondary data—is the foundation for any competitive intelligence effort and can be very significant if properly analyzed."
>
> *Paul Dishman,*
> *President (2002–2003), Society of Competitive Intelligence Professionals (SCIP), a global network serving the business-knowledge industry.*

Secondary Data Vindicate the *Vindicator*!

The *Vindicator* (or www.vindicator.com), a medium-sized newspaper in the middle-American city of Youngstown, Ohio, wanted to increase its advertising revenues. Management set forth a 1-year goal for its 14 retail and 4 classified salespeople to substantially increase the number of advertisers, and thus total ad revenue. To be able to increase ad revenues, the sales force needed to pinpoint what they could specifically do to recruit more advertisers to the newspaper or to increase the amount that existing advertisers were spending. From past experience, many on the sales force knew that recruiting advertisers required proving to these advertisers, with hard facts, that their money spent in the *Vindicator* would be an excellent investment. For this purpose, the internally available data routinely collected by the *Vindicator* on the number of customers, duration of subscription, renewals/nonrenewals, and so forth would be insufficient. Additional data would have to be obtained by conducting marketing research.

In this case, the *Vindicator* decided that it needed information on the market potential in advertising readership and how these numbers compared to the potential of other advertising media that the advertisers could use instead of the *Vindicator*. Although the sales force could commission marketing research to obtain primary data, such a project would be quite

*The*Vindicator

35¢

...ants August goal for JEDD

...ment plan, including the imposition of income taxes on those working in the townships, by August.

"It's a reachable goal," Sarah Lown, the city's development incentive director, said after a city council meeting to discuss the plan.

Austintown Trustee David Ditzler, who also attended the meeting, said Lown's goal is going to be "extremely difficult" to achieve.

City council and administrators met

publicly for the first time Wednesday to discuss the proposal known as a joint economic development district, or JEDD.

The proposal calls for the city to charge a 2-percent income tax on those who work in the portions of Boardman and Austintown that receive Youngstown water. That's about half of Boardman and almost all of Austintown.

The townships could place its own

▶ **FAST FACTS** about Joint Economic Development Districts, **A3**

0.25-percent income tax on those same people.

In exchange, the city would reduce its income tax from 2.75 percent to 2.25 percent, a move that would put more money in the pockets of those who

See JEDD on Page A3

Ditzler

...oorly eagles nest in Valley

New pact viewed as start of new era

Faculty members will get raises in each year of the new pact, which will require $4.5M in additional spending.

expensive and time-consuming. Hence, that course of action was not taken. Instead, the *Vindicator* decided to search for secondary research that could be used to obtain the answers it sought. Because the *Vindicator* is a medium-sized newspaper with limited staff resources, it turned to an outside supplier. Inland Research Corp., a small company in Erie, Pennsylvania, was commissioned to conduct a secondary research study.

Inland Research Corp. compiles data from about 40 different sources. Half of its data come from general business sources, such as the Audit Bureau of Circulations (www.accessabc.com), and the other half come from state and federal agencies, such as the U.S. Census Bureau (www.census.gov) and the Bureau of Labor Statistics (www.bls.gov). In addition to print publications, Inland Research also searches several online and Internet databases. Inland Research evaluates all secondary data by examining the methodology, accuracy, timeliness, and nature of the data. Only data from dependable sources are used.

Inland Research receives requests for data from a client who needs to solve a specific problem. It then begins an exhaustive search of its data warehouse to obtain information that is pertinent to the client's needs. In about 4 to 6 weeks, Inland Research produces a report addressing the client's problem. In the case of smaller firms like the *Vindicator*, this represents a fraction of the time it would take for the client to do the research in-house. Inland's biggest selling point is the low price it charges for its research services. Prices range from $3,595 for a newspaper with a circulation of up to 14,900 to $8,445 for a newspaper with a circulation of 60,000 or more. According to Inland Research president and CEO Jerry Szorek, "No other company produces similar reports for newspapers," which makes the information it provides to firms like the *Vindicator* extremely valuable.

For the *Vindicator*, Inland Research focused on obtaining data reports on topics such as the advertising effectiveness of and penetration for different forms of media. For example, data on the relationship between advertising frequency in different media and the resulting effectiveness were collected. Using Inland Research results and secondary data available internally within the organization, *Vindicator* sales representatives were able to persuade some current advertisers to increase the frequency at which their ads were run. They accomplished this in a number of ways utilizing the Inland reports. For instance, one Inland Research chart demonstrated that advertisement readership grows from 53.5 percent with one ad per week to 81.3 percent with five ads per week. This gave advertisers a reason to increase the frequency of their advertising.

In an attempt to wean advertisers' dollars away from radio, *Vindicator* sales representatives were able to use Inland data indicating that each of the city's seven biggest radio stations had fewer than 8,000 listeners during an average quarter hour, whereas internal secondary data showed that the *Vindicator* had a circulation of 200,000 as of 2008. To reduce advertising spending on television, the sales representatives used the following statistics on viewer activity during commercials: 33.6 percent got up and left the viewing room, 29.6 percent talked with others, 9.2 percent switched channels, and 5.9 percent muted the television. Furthermore, secondary data revealed that only 21.7 percent watched the TV commercial. Such selling tactics by the sales force were successful. *Vindicator* management discovered that using secondary research during sales calls strengthened the sales pitches with hard data that could sway advertisers toward spending more on advertising in the Vindicator.[1]

Overview

Chapter 1 discussed the Internet as a source of marketing research information. As mentioned in Chapter 2, analysis of secondary data helps to first define the marketing research problem and then to develop an approach to that problem. Also, as part of formulating the research design (Chapter 3), researchers analyze the relevant secondary data, as illustrated by the *Vindicator* vignette. The relationship of secondary data to the research issues presented in the previous chapters is shown in Figure 4.1. This chapter discusses the distinction between primary and secondary data, as well as the advantages, disadvantages, and criteria for evaluating secondary data, which can be generated both internally and

FIGURE 4.1

Relationship of Secondary Data to the Previous Chapters and the Marketing Research Process

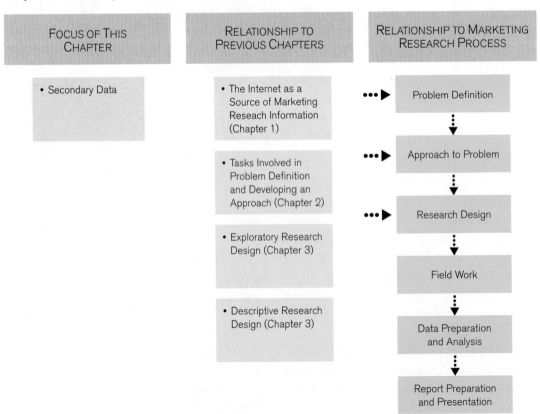

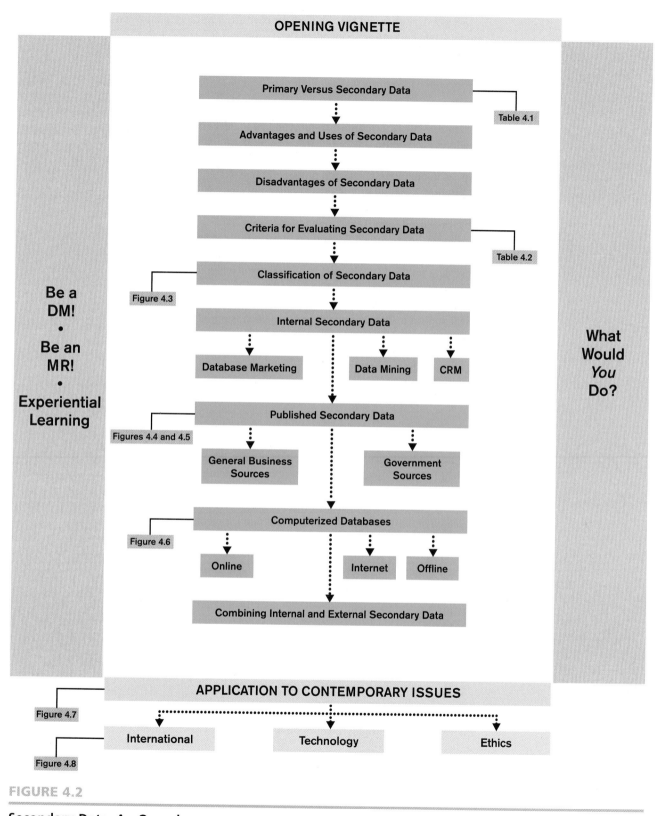

FIGURE 4.2

Secondary Data: An Overview

externally. The chapter also includes discussion of the practice of merging internal and external secondary data. Additionally, the chapter discusses the collection of international secondary data, the impact of technology, and ethical questions related to secondary data. Figure 4.2 presents an overview of this chapter.

Secondary data can best be distinguished from primary data when the purpose of the original data collection is considered.

Primary Versus Secondary Data

primary data

Data originated by the researcher for the specific purpose of addressing the research problem.

secondary data

Data collected for some purpose other than the problem at hand.

An early outcome of the research process is to define the marketing research problem and to identify specific research questions and hypotheses (Chapter 2). When data are collected to address a specific marketing research problem, they are referred to as **primary data.** Obtaining primary data can be expensive and time-consuming because it involves all six steps of the marketing research process (Figure 4.1).

Before initiating primary data collection, a researcher should remember that the problem under study might not be unique. It is possible that someone else has investigated the same or a similar marketing research problem. A search through existing data might lead to relevant information. **Secondary data** represent any data that have already been collected for purposes other than the problem at hand. Relative to primary data collection, these data can be located quickly and inexpensively, as in the case of the *Vindicator*. The differences between primary and secondary data are summarized in Table 4.1.

It is easy to overlook the many sources of secondary data when developing a formal research design. Once a secondary data search is initiated, however, the volume of existing information can be overwhelming. In order to cost-effectively browse through this mountain of information, it is important that the researcher be familiar with various sources of secondary data, including marketing research firms that specialize in secondary data, such as Inland Research in the opening vignette.

Advantages and Uses of Secondary Data

The main advantages of secondary data are the time and money they can save. This was evident from the low-cost secondary research provided by the Inland Research Corp. in the opening vignette. Additionally, the collection of some secondary data, such as those provided by the U.S. Census Bureau, would not be feasible for individual firms such as Inland Research or the *Vindicator*. Although it is rare for secondary data to provide all the answers to a nonroutine research problem, analysis of secondary data should always be the first step taken toward solving a research problem. Secondary data provided the *Vindicator* with a better understanding of advertising effectiveness and penetration for different forms of media. Such data can help the researcher to:

1. Identify the problem.
2. Better understand and define the problem.
3. Develop an approach to the problem.
4. Formulate an appropriate research design (e.g., by identifying the key variables).
5. Answer certain research questions and test some hypotheses.
6. Interpret primary data with more insight.

Additionally, secondary data also are useful for estimating demand, monitoring the environment, developing business intelligence systems, segmenting and targeting, and a variety of other applications.

TABLE 4.1 A Comparison of Primary and Secondary Data

	Primary Data	Secondary Data
Collection purpose	For the problem at hand	For other problems
Collection process	Very involved	Rapid and easy
Collection cost	High	Relatively low
Collection time	Long	Short

Given these advantages and uses of secondary data, we state a basic rule of research:

Examine available secondary data first. The research project should proceed to primary data collection only when the secondary data sources have been exhausted or yield marginal returns.

In the opening vignette, the *Vindicator* exemplifies the rich dividends obtained by following this rule. Another example involves Frost National Bank.

Research in Action

Bank "Zips" Up the Market

From its inception in 1868 as a small downtown bank in the southwest American city of San Antonio, Texas, Frost Bank (www.frostbank.com) has grown into a multibillion-dollar, full-service financial institution with more than $13.5 billion in assets in 2008. It offers a full range of banking and financial services to retail and commercial customers throughout its home state of Texas. The bank was considering modifying its Young Leaders Club (YLC) account to enhance its appeal to San Antonians between the ages of 21 and 35. The YLC offered members a checking account with enhancements such as life insurance, discount movie tickets, store coupons, tours, and social events, all for a monthly membership fee.

Extensive analysis of secondary data was conducted. Using internal secondary data on transactions and addresses, club members were evaluated by zip code and account activity. The results of zip code analysis helped attract advertising and discount coupons from merchants in areas of San Antonio where large numbers of YLC members lived. External secondary data available on this age group provided additional insights for redeveloping the YLC package. Census information related to population, age, and income allowed Frost National Bank to estimate the size of the potential market for the YLC. This secondary data analysis was followed by focus groups and survey research. After completing its market research, which began with the examination of secondary data, Frost National Bank was able to significantly increase the number of YLC accounts in the target market.[2]

This example shows that analysis of secondary data can provide valuable insights and lay the foundation for conducting more formal research, such as focus groups and surveys. The researcher should be cautious when using secondary data, however, because there are some disadvantages.

Be an MR

Search the Internet, as well as your library's online databases, to obtain information on the use of celebrity endorsements in marketing. You are conducting a marketing research project to determine the effectiveness of celebrity endorsements in advertising campaigns mounted by the American sports-apparel company Nike. What type of secondary data would you examine?

Be a DM!

As the marketing director of Nike, how would you use secondary data on celebrity endorsements to determine whether you should continue to contract celebrities to endorse the Nike brand?

Disadvantages of Secondary Data

The value of secondary data is typically limited by their degree of fit with the current research problem and by concerns regarding data accuracy. The objectives, nature, and methods used to collect secondary data might not be compatible with the present situation. Also, secondary data might be lacking in terms of accuracy, compatibility of units of measurement, or time frame. Before using secondary data, it is important to evaluate them using the criteria in Table 4.2. The Inland Research Corp. used similar criteria in the opening vignette.

Criteria for Evaluating Secondary Data

The criteria used for evaluating secondary data consist of specifications, error, currency, objective, nature, and dependability.

TABLE 4.2 Criteria for Evaluating Secondary Data

Criteria	Issues	Remarks
Specifications/Methodology	Data collection method Response rate Quality of data Sampling technique Sample size Questionnaire design Field work Data analysis	Data should be reliable, valid, and generalizable to the problem at hand.
Error/Accuracy	Examine errors in: approach, research design, sampling, data collection, data analysis, reporting	Assess accuracy by comparing data from different sources.
Currency	Time lag between collection and publication Frequency of updates	Census data are periodically updated by syndicated firms.
Objective	Why were the data collected?	The objective will determine the relevance of data.
Nature	Definition of key variables Units of measurement Categories used Relationships examined	Reconfigure the data to increase their usefulness, if possible.
Dependability	Expertise, credibility, reputation, and trustworthiness of the source	Data should be obtained from an original rather than an acquired source.

Specifications: Methodology Used to Collect the Data

The research design specifications—that is, the methodology used to collect the data—should be examined to identify possible sources of bias. Factors that are important in identifying potential error, as well as relevance of the data, include the size and nature of the sample, response rate and quality, questionnaire design and administration, procedures used for field work, and data analysis and reporting procedures. One reason it is advantageous to use data from the originating source is that a description of the research design is typically provided as a part of the original published study.

Error: Accuracy of the Data

Both secondary and primary data can have errors, stemming from the research approach, research design, sampling, data collection, analysis, and reporting stages of the project. Moreover, it is difficult to evaluate the accuracy of secondary data when the researcher has not directly participated in the research.

Secondary data can be obtained either directly from the source that originated the data or from a secondary source that secured the data from someone else. The further removed one is from the originating data source, the greater the possibility of problems with accuracy. An original source is likely to be more accurate and complete than a nonoriginating source. Always use the originating source if it is available.

One approach to controlling accuracy problems is to find multiple sources of data and compare them using standard statistical procedures. The accuracy of secondary data can also be verified by conducting field investigations, as recommended by the International Council of Shopping Centers.

As this example indicates, the accuracy of secondary data can vary, particularly if it relates to highly volatile market conditions. Moreover, data obtained from different sources might not agree. In these cases, the researcher should verify the accuracy of

Research in Action

Population Dynamics and the Accuracy of Secondary Data

A trade association with members in more than 80 countries, the International Council of Shopping Centers (www.icsc.org) conducted a study to evaluate the consistency of market profiles provided by private vendors of secondary demographic information. Several American vendors participated in the research, including CACI (www.caci.com), a specialist in security services; Claritas (www.claritas.com), a target-market data company; and Donnelley Marketing (www.donnelleymarketing.com), a data-management provider for the direct-marketing industry. Markets in three U.S. cities were analyzed: Baltimore, Detroit, and Phoenix. The vendors supplied the Council with statistics and demographic data for each market area. The Council then analyzed the differences among the vendors' reports using standard statistical procedures.

The results indicated that there was little variation in the data from different sources when the population was relatively stable. However, the vendor-supplied demographic data varied considerably in areas with rapidly changing population. In such cases, the Council recommends that users verify vendor data findings with field investigations of their own.[3]

secondary data by conducting pilot studies or by other appropriate methods. With a little creativity, this can often be accomplished with little expense and effort.

Currency: When the Data Were Collected

Secondary data might not be current. A time lag might exist between data collection and publication, as with census data. Additionally, the data might not be updated frequently enough to answer questions related to the problem at hand. Marketing research requires current data; therefore, the value of secondary data is diminished as they become dated. For instance, although the data from the 2001 U.K. census are comprehensive, they might not be applicable to a metropolitan area whose population has changed rapidly during the last few years. Thus, such data might not be current enough for demand in 2009 at a company like Pinelog Ltd., which specializes in architecturally designed leisure buildings. Fortunately, several marketing research firms update census data periodically and make the current information available for a fee.

Objective: The Purpose for the Study

Understanding why secondary data were originally collected can sensitize the researcher to the limitations of using them for the current marketing problem. Suppose *The Spectator*, a weekly magazine in the United Kingdom, surveyed its renewing subscriber base regarding readership of its articles and recall of its advertising. One objective of this study would be to use the information to sell advertising space. With that in mind, the results of the study would be made available to advertising managers, who would likely make decisions regarding advertising placement. This type of secondary information might be relevant to the question of where to place future advertising. The results of this survey would be biased, however, in that they would reflect the behavior of renewing subscribers, a group that might be more involved with the magazine than general subscribers. To accurately interpret this secondary data, the advertising manager would have to understand how closely *The Spectator's* renewing segment represents its total subscribing population.

Nature: The Content of the Data

The *nature*, or *content*, of the data should be examined with special attention to the definition of key variables, the units of measurement, the categories used, and the relationships examined. One of the most frustrating limitations of secondary data comes from differences in definition, units of measurement, in the time frame examined, or questionable assumptions regarding the relationships of key variables. If the key variables have not been defined or are defined in a manner inconsistent with the researcher's definition, then the usefulness of the data is limited.

Consider, for example, secondary data related to retail sales. As the researcher interprets the information, questions might arise regarding whether the sales are defined net of returned items or whether they represent cash and credit sales. For example, if Visa decides to investigate the sale of credit card services, this level of distinction becomes critical. Visa spends millions of dollars in marketing the card to retailers and in advertising the card to consumers. The 2008 Olympic Games marked the 22nd year of Visa's sponsorship. Visa is signed on with the Olympic Games through 2012. In order to determine the effectiveness of its Olympic advertising and sponsorships, Visa needs secondary data with relevant content.

Secondary data might be measured in units that are inappropriate for the current problem. For example, income can be measured by individual, family, household, or spending unit, and it can be reported as gross or net after taxes and deductions. If income categories reported in secondary sources are different from those required by the research, the information might not be usable. If the German carmaker Mercedes is interested in high-income American consumers with gross annual household incomes of more than $90,000, then secondary data with income categories less than $15,000, $15,001 to $35,000, $35,001 to $50,000, and more than $50,000 will not be of much use.

Finally, we must consider the variables of interest to the researcher. For example, if the researcher is interested in actual purchase behavior, then information on attitudes that only imply behavior might have limited usefulness.

Dependability: How Dependable Are the Data?

An overall indication of the dependability of the data can be obtained by examining the expertise, credibility, reputation, and trustworthiness of the source. This information can be obtained by checking with others who have used information from this source. Data published to promote sales, to advance specific interests, or to carry on propaganda should be viewed with suspicion. The same can be said of data published anonymously or in a form that attempts to hide the details of the data collection methodology and process. In contrast, secondary data published by reputable organizations, such as the U.S. Census Bureau or the U.K.'s Office for National Statistics, are very dependable and of high quality.

Be a DM!

As the CEO of Home Depot, an American home-improvement chain, you come across a Gallup poll reporting that an increasing number of women are shopping for home improvement products and services. How will you use this information to improve the competitiveness of Home Depot?

Be an MR!

Visit www.gallup.com. Examine the information on how Gallup conducts its polls. By applying the criteria we have considered, evaluate the quality of Gallup polls.

Classification of Secondary Data

internal data
Data available within the organization for which the research is being conducted.

external data
Data that originate external to the organization.

As represented in Figure 4.3 and discussed earlier in this chapter, the two primary sources of secondary data are internal and external data. **Internal data** are data generated within the organization for which the research is being conducted. **External data** are data generated by sources outside the organization. In the opening vignette, the data on circulation obtained from the *Vindicator*'s records were internal data. However, data obtained from Inland Research on advertising effectiveness and penetration for different forms of media were external data.

Internal Secondary Data

Before collecting external secondary data, it is always useful to analyze internal secondary data. Internal data are typically generated as part of the ongoing process of doing business. These data can come from accounting records, sales reports, production or operation reports, or internal experts. In the opening vignette, the *Vindicator* routinely collects data on the number of customers, the duration each customer has been a subscriber, renewals/nonrenewals, and so on. Although it is possible that internal secondary data might be available in usable form, it is more typical that considerable processing effort will be required before such data can be used. For example, cash register receipts of a department store might contain a wealth

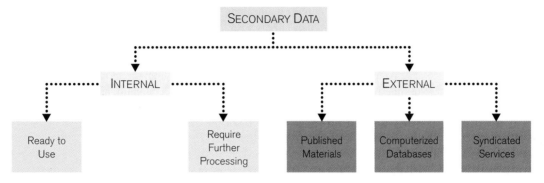

FIGURE 4.3

A Classification of Secondary Data

of information, such as sales by product line, sales by specific stores, sales by geographical region, sales by cash versus credit purchases, sales in specific time periods, sales by size of purchase, and so on. To derive this information, however, data must be transcribed from the paper-based sales receipts to a computer database and analyzed extensively. Many organizations are building sophisticated internal databases as platforms for their marketing efforts. A **data warehouse** is a centralized database that consolidates company-wide data from a variety of operational systems. Of special interest to us are customer databases.

CUSTOMER DATABASES For many companies, the first step in creating a customer database is to transfer raw sales information, such as that found on sales call reports or invoices, to a personal computer. Customer information also is obtained from other sources, such as warranty cards and loyalty programs (e.g., frequent flier programs of airlines). This is augmented with demographic and psychographic information about the customers obtained from external secondary sources. **Psychographics** refer to quantified psychological profiles of individuals. Several companies in this business, including R. R. Donnelley (www. rrdonnelley.com) and R. L. Polk (www.polk.com), in the United States and Psychographics Ltd. (www.consumersketch.co.uk) in the United Kingdom, have compiled household lists that include names, addresses, and a great deal of individual-specific data. The elements of a customer database include the following:

- A unique ID or match code
- Name and title of the individual organization
- Mailing address
- Telephone number(s)
- E-mail address
- Source of referral, inquiry, or order
- Complete transaction history by date, frequency, purchase amounts, and products
- Credit history and rating score
- Demographic and psychographic data for individuals, such as gender, marital status, age, education, occupation, number of children, income, type of residence, geodemographic information, psychographics, and lifestyle data
- Organizational data for institutions, such as North American Industry Classification System (discussed later in this chapter), sales, number of employees, length of time in business, headquarters, international operations, and other relevant data

The size of these customer databases can be staggering. The retail chain Sears, for example, has more than 75 percent of U.S. households in its customer database. The analysis of such large databases requires special skills and resources and has been termed *data mining*.

DATA MINING, CUSTOMER RELATIONSHIP MANAGEMENT SYSTEMS, AND DATABASE MARKETING **Data mining** involves the use of powerful computers with advanced statistical packages and other software to analyze large databases in order to discover hidden patterns in

data warehouse
A centralized database that consolidates company-wide data from a variety of operational systems.

psychographics
Quantified psychological profiles of individuals.

data mining
Technique involving the use of powerful computers and advanced statistical and other software to analyze large databases in order to discover hidden patterns in the data.

customer relationship management (CRM) system
A decision support system that is used for managing the interactions between an organization and its customers.

database marketing
The practice of using CRM databases to develop relationships and highly targeted marketing efforts with individuals and customer groups.

the data. The term derives its meaning from the exercise of digging through a lot of "coal" (seemingly valueless data) to discover "golden nuggets" (invaluable marketing information). It is a broad term that encompasses many different types of data analyses, including the use of artificial intelligence procedures that model the way the human brain processes information. The patterns discovered can be very useful for targeting marketing effort. For example, data mining revealed that American husbands tend to buy additional life insurance immediately after the birth of their first child. Therefore, the slogan of U.S. insurer Allstate (www.allstate.com), "You're in good hands," is particularly appropriate for targeting first-time fathers with life insurance products.

Customer databases and data mining are the building blocks for **customer relationship management (CRM) systems.** A CRM is a decision support system (see Chapter 1) that is used for managing the interactions between an organization and its customers. **Database marketing** is the practice of using CRM databases to develop relationships and highly targeted marketing efforts with individuals and customer groups. The CRM databases can be analyzed in terms of a customer's activity over the life of the business relationship. Signs of change in the usage relationships (e.g., a heavy user decreases usage) or significant "customer life cycle" events (e.g., anniversaries) can be identified and addressed. These databases provide the essential tool needed to nurture, expand, and protect the customer relationship and can also serve as a foundation for developing marketing programs.

Organizations that bill their customers for services or that provide statements of customer activities are in a particularly strong position to use their internal secondary data. Utilities, cable television systems, banks, department stores, and health care providers are all examples of organizations that use database marketing.

Research in Action

General Electric: Electrifying Marketing with a Customer Database

As of 2008, General Electric (GE; www.ge.com) operates in more than 100 countries around the world. This includes 250 manufacturing plants in 26 different nations. (In the United States, the company has built a huge customer database of more than 60 million households, which it uses effectively for target marketing. GE has combined demographic, psychographic, media consumption, and purchasing data available externally with internal customer transaction records to pinpoint a customer's appliance ownership and history.

Using this database, GE can determine, for example, which customers are typically ready to replace their washing machines: those who bought the washing machine 6 years ago and have large families. The company can then direct marketing efforts in the form of gift certificates, discounts, and special deals for washing machines at these customers. The database has electrified GE's marketing, resulting in increased market share and profitability.[4]

As the GE example illustrates, database marketing can lead to quite sophisticated and targeted marketing programs. Most large organizations have intranets, which greatly facilitate the search for and access to internal secondary data. Procter & Gamble (P&G), for example, has developed powerful intranet applications that enable its managers worldwide to search for past and current research studies and a wide variety of marketing-related information on the basis of keywords. Once located, the information can be accessed online. Sensitive information can be secured electronically with user names and passwords.

Be a DM!	Be an MR!
As the marketing director for Apple Computer, how would you use database marketing to increase the penetration of Apple computers in U.S. households?	Visit www.apple.com and search the Internet to obtain information on Apple's marketing strategy. Identify the variables available internally within Apple as well as from external sources that you would use to build a database to help Apple increase its penetration of U.S. households.

External Secondary Data: Published Sources

Secondary data sources have grown dramatically over the past 20 years. This growth has been stimulated, in part, by the introduction of personal computers into the workplace, which give employees easy access to commercial databases. The following section provides an overview of some of the sources of published external secondary data. Nonprofit organizations (e.g., chambers of commerce), trade and professional organizations, commercial publishers, investment brokerage firms, and professional marketing research firms are just a few of the nongovernmental sources available. To enable you to sort through the overwhelming amount of secondary data, we begin our discussion with a classification of published secondary data (Figure 4.4).

Published external sources can be broadly classified as general business data or government data. General business sources include guides, directories, indexes, and statistical data. Government sources can be broadly categorized as census data and other publications.

General Business Data

Businesses publish a great deal of information in the form of books, periodicals, journals, newspapers, magazines, reports, and trade literature. Audit Bureau of Circulations, cited in the opening vignette, is a general business source that provides data on audits of media. London-based Media Audits Group (now a division of Accenture, www.accenture.com) performs the same service in several European countries. Moody's (www.moodys.com) and Standard and Poor's (www.standardandpoors.com) provide information on U.S. and foreign

FIGURE 4.4

A Classification of Published Secondary Sources

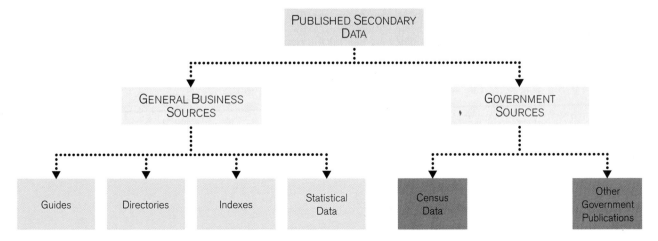

companies. A useful source for industrial brand and trade information in the United States is ThomasNet (www.thomasnet.com). In the United Kingdom, Marketing Strategies for Industry Reports provide a range of data on the industrial and business-to-business sectors. In the United States, valuable marketing and marketing research information can be obtained from SecondaryData.com (www .secondarydata.com).

A variety of business-related sites can provide sales leads, mailing lists, business profiles, and credit ratings for U.S. businesses. Many sites supply information on businesses within a specific industry. For example, you can gain access to the full text *American Demographics* and *Marketing Tools* publications at www.marketingtools.com. All of the American Marketing Association's publications can be searched by keywords at www.marketingpower.com. Encyclopedia Britannica provides free online access to its entire 32-volume set (www.britannica.com). Data on U.S. manufacturers and key decision makers can be obtained from Harris InfoSource (www.harrisinfo.com). Another good source is USAData (www.usadata.com).

Guides, indexes, and directories can help in locating information available from general business sources. Sources also are available for identifying statistical data. A brief description of each of these resource categories follows.

GUIDES   Standard or recurring information is summarized in guides. Guides provide a path to other sources of secondary data contained in directories or published by professional or trade associations. Because guides can open the door to other sources of data, they are one of the first sources a researcher should consult. In the United States, some of the most useful are *Business Information Sources, Encyclopedia of Business Information Sources,* and the *Monthly Catalog of United States Government Publications.* Guides also are available on the Internet. @BRINT (www.brint.com) is a guide to business technology management and knowledge management sites with editorial comments.

INDEXES AND BIBLIOGRAPHIES   Bibliographies, which are organized alphabetically by topic, are another good place to start external secondary research. Current or historic discussion of a particular topic of interest will be indexed in these references, leading the researcher to a number of authors.

In the United States, several indexes are available for referencing both academic and business topics. The following are some of the more useful business indexes:

- *Business Index*
- *Business Periodical Index*
- *General Business File*
- *National Newspaper Index*
- *Social Sciences Citation Index*
- *Wall Street Journal Index*

You can also find indexes on the Internet; for example, the *Librarian's Internet Index* at www.lii.org. *CI Resource Index* (www.ciseek.com) features sites for competitive intelligence information.

DIRECTORIES   Directories provide brief descriptions of companies, organizations, or individuals. They are helpful for identifying manufacturers operating in a particular market, for compiling names and addresses of associations in a sales territory, or for verifying names and addresses of prospective customers who carry a specific job title. The following are some of the more important U.S. directories:

- *Directories in Print*
- *Consultants and Consulting Organizations Directory*
- *Encyclopedia of Associations*
- *FINDEX: The Directory of Market Research Reports*
- *Fortune 500 Directory*
- *Million Dollar Directory: Leading Public and Private Companies*
- *Standard Directory of Advertisers*
- *Thomas Register of American Manufacturers*

A number of directories are on the Internet, for example, Google Directory at http://directory.google.com and Yahoo! Directory at http://dir.yahoo.com.

Business Statistical Data

Business research often involves compiling statistical data reflecting market or industry factors. A historic perspective of industry participation and growth rates can provide a context for market share analysis. Market statistics related to population demographics, purchasing levels, television viewership, and product usage are just some of the types of nongovernmental statistics available from secondary sources. The following are some important U.S. sources of nongovernmental statistical data:

- *A Guide to Consumer Markets*
- *Predicasts Basebook*
- *Predicasts Forecasts*
- *Sales and Marketing Management Survey of Buying Power*
- *Standard & Poor's Statistical Service*
- *Standard Rate and Data Service*

Several commercial firms, such as FIND/SVP (www.findsvp.com), specialize in conducting information searches over the Internet and obtaining data from other secondary sources. FIND/SVP provides customized research and analysis related to market and industry profiles, business and competitive intelligence, benchmarking, new business opportunities, and other applications.

Government Sources

The federal government is the largest source of secondary data in the United States, and in the United Kingdom, a government agency, the U.K. Statistics Authority, produces and monitors the collection of secondary data. In each case, the data that the government collects could not feasibly be collected by private industry. In the opening vignette, Inland Research obtained data from government sources such as the U.S. Census Bureau and the Bureau of Labor Statistics. Government publications can be divided into census data and other types.

CENSUS DATA   Census data are useful in a variety of marketing research projects. The demographic data collected by the U.S. Census Bureau includes information about household types, sex, age, marital status, and race. Consumption detail related to automobile ownership, housing characteristics, work status, and practices as well as occupations are just a few of the categories of information available. What makes this demographic information particularly valuable to marketers is that these data can be geographically categorized at various levels of detail. These data can be summarized at various levels: city block, block group, census tract, Metropolitan Statistical Area (MSA), Consolidated Metropolitan Statistical Area (CMSA), region (Northeast, Midwest, South, and West), or they can be aggregated for the nation as a whole. Figure 4.5 shows the geographic subdivision of an MSA. Census tracts have a population of more than 4,000 and are defined by local communities. In urban areas, MSAs have a population of at least 50,000 and comprise counties containing or surrounding a central city. In addition, census data are available by civil divisions, such as wards, cities, counties, and states.

In general, the quality of census data is quite high, and the data often are extremely detailed. To facilitate business analysis, this information is available in multiple forms. One can purchase computer tapes, diskettes, or CD-ROMs from the U.S. Census Bureau for a nominal fee and recast this information into the desired format. Important census data include Census of Housing, Census of Manufacturers, Census of Population, Census of Retail Trade, Census of Service Industries, and Census of Wholesale Trade. Claritas (www.claritas.com), a secondary research company, has created a number of research tools using census and other lifestyle data. Integrating

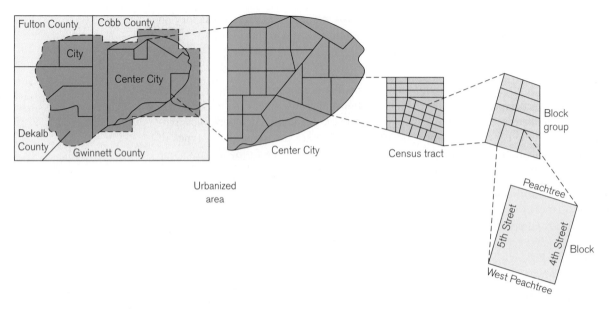

FIGURE 4.5

The Geographic Subdivision of an MSA

enhanced census data with internal company databases is a useful application of multiple secondary sources. This integration of secondary data is discussed later in the chapter.

Experiential Learning

U.S. Census Bureau

The 2000 census of the United States provides insight into the demographic profile of not only the United States in full, but also smaller U.S. regions, such as states and MSAs. Go to the homepage for the U.S. Census Bureau (www.census.gov) and do the following:

1. Find the population clocks on the U.S. Census Bureau's homepage. What is the current population estimate for the United States? For the world?

2. Find "state and county quick facts." Compare your home state's "population percentage change from 1990 to 2000" with that of the United States in full. Which grew faster?

3. Find out how many "singles without children living at home" were counted in your zip code in the 2000 census. Look on the left side of the homepage, select "American FactFinder," and follow the steps shown.

OTHER GOVERNMENT PUBLICATIONS   In addition to the census, the U.S. government collects and publishes a great deal of statistical data, much of it relevant to business. The government developed the Standard Industrial Classification Code (SIC) as the classification scheme used for its Census of Manufacturers. The SIC system classified manufacturing into 20 major groups. Each group was further classified into industry groups and then product categories. The United States, Mexico, and Canada have created a new common classification system to replace the previous classification of each country. The four-digit SIC of the United States has been replaced by a six-digit North American Industry Classification System (NAICS), which was phased in beginning in 1999.

Why was NAICS (www.naics.com) needed? According to statements from the U.S. Department of Commerce, the SIC was not keeping up with the rapid changes in the U.S. and world economies. The two extra digits in the NAICS accommodate a larger number of sectors and are more flexible in designating subsections. NAICS is organized in a hierarchical structure, much like the SIC. The new codes will be reviewed every 5 years.

Other useful government publications include *Business America, Business Conditions Digest, Business Statistics, County Business Patterns, County and City Data Book, Index to Publications, Statistical Abstract of the United States,* and *Survey of Current Business.* Several U.S. government sources can be accessed at FedWorld (www.fedworld.gov). Extensive business statistics can be obtained from FedStats (www.fedstats.gov) and Stat-USA (www.stat-usa.gov). FedStats compiles statistical information from more than 100 agencies. The U.S. Department of Commerce can be reached at www.doc.gov. Bureau of Census information can be accessed via the Department of Commerce Web site or directly at www.census.gov. The Bureau of Labor Statistics provides useful information, especially Consumer Expenditure Surveys (www.bls.gov). A wide range of economic statistics can be obtained from the Bureau of Economic Analysis (www.bea.doc.gov). Information about public companies can be obtained from the EDGAR Database of Corporate Information, which contains SEC filings (www.sec.gov/edgar.shtml). Information about small businesses can be obtained at www.sbaonline.sba.gov. Two of the most useful sources for locating government organizations are the *U.S. Government Manual* and the *Congressional Directory*; both can be located at www.gpoaccess.gov. These government sites can provide valuable information to the marketing researcher, as exemplified by the efforts of Greensboro, North Carolina, to attract young people.

Research in Action

Over the Hill for Greensboro

For years, officials in the small American city of Greensboro, North Carolina (www.greensboro-nc.gov), have been worried about the lack of young people in the community. The population of certain age groups, namely those aged 15 to 19, 20 to 24, and 25 to 34, has been shrinking. A comparison of the 2000 census data with information in the 2005 American Community Survey showed that Greensboro's average age had increased 2.8 years, from 33.0 to 35.8 years of age, drastically higher than nearby North Carolina cities that were studied for comparison purposes. Raleigh had an age increase of 1.7 years, and Durham had an age increase of 1.5 years. This either meant old people were arriving for retirement, young people were leaving, or both! A comparison of the 2005 population with that of 2000 by age group revealed that both were true.

This analysis not only confirmed officials' worries but pointed to a dwindling working population, the group that pays taxes and effectively provides revenue for the city. In business terms, Greensboro was losing sales! The growth in the active-retiree-age population (ages 55 to 59 and 60 to 64) was likely to continue: The first baby boomers had turned 60, and North Carolina, with its mountains, beaches, moderate climate, golf courses, and military bases, likely will remain among the nation's leading destinations for retirees.

Based on the analysis of secondary data, Greensboro is putting its marketing energy into attracting younger people, namely professionals aged 20 to 39. An example of this can be seen in the revitalization of and increased activity in the downtown area to give Greensboro more of an urban feel and, hopefully, to attract target "consumers."[5]

Most published information also is available in computerized databases.

Computerized Databases

Computerized databases, which are accessed online or offline or available over the Internet, have made secondary data easily available to organizations of all sizes, as demonstrated in the opening vignette. A personal computer linked to relevant telecommunication networks can connect a researcher to vast libraries of information, accessible at any time from any place. Marketing researchers no longer need to leave their offices to monitor changes in their industry, technology, or regulatory environments.

Today, thousands of databases are available. The phenomenal growth in the number of databases is a result of the advantages of electronic dissemination of data over printed data:

1. *Current information.* Because printing is no longer an essential step in information dissemination, data can be updated continuously. Publishers who use computers to edit and publish their periodicals can now electronically transfer those documents to relevant databases, making them available with remarkable speed as compared to the traditional methods of print production and physical distribution.

2. *Faster data search.* Online vendors provide increasing uniformity in the search process, enabling even a relative novice at secondary research to access data more quickly and completely.

3. *Low cost.* The relative cost of accessing computerized databases is low.

4. *Convenience.* This has become perhaps one of the greatest benefits computerized databases have delivered. Information providers now have a direct link to the end user equipped with a personal computer and modem. They are no longer forced to distribute their products through libraries or retail outlets.

Conducting secondary research via computerized databases, however, is not without limitations. A researcher who does not know how to conduct a focused keyword search or who is unsure whether a particular database provides abstracts or articles in their entirety can be buried under a mountain of irrelevant data. However, researchers can overcome these limitations as they gain experience in the computerized search process.

Knowing how computerized databases are classified can help the researcher narrow the search. Database vendors provide a wide array of public information, available to anyone who has computer access to a telecommunications network. Based on how they are distributed, computerized databases are classified as either online, Internet, or offline (Figure 4.6).

Online Databases

online databases
Databases stored in computers that require a telecommunications network to access.

Online databases provide direct, interactive access to data stored remotely on a mainframe computer. A personal computer linked to these mainframes via a telecommunication network is all that is required to initiate a data search and retrieval process. Usage fees are typically based on minutes spent searching a computer file (time online) and on the number of data requests. A flat monthly access fee might also be charged.

The online database provides an advantage in terms of its currency. Data can be updated and made available for distribution almost simultaneously.

Internet Databases

Internet databases
A specific type of online database comprising information sources available on the World Wide Web (WWW).

Internet databases are a special form of online database. All knowledge workers, and especially marketing researchers, can benefit from **Internet databases,** which are information sources available on the World Wide Web (WWW). In addition to worldwide e-mail access, the Internet can provide a variety of marketing research documents, as well as both primary and secondary research data. Document access and retrieval via keyword search are of particular interest for secondary data searches.

Numerous search engines can be launched from Internet browsers, such as Internet Explorer. Browsers are general, user-friendly, all-purpose Internet navigation tools that

FIGURE 4.6

A Classification of Computerized Databases

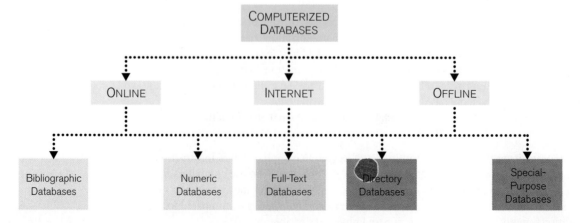

provide access to the Web, including download and document-browsing services. Popular Internet search tools in the United States include Google and Yahoo! Researchers in the United Kingdom can use GoogleUK or YahooUK or smaller local search tools such as Exalead. Likewise, Indian users can go to GoogleIndia or YahooIndia or to local search engines like ByIndia, which focuses exclusively on Indian Web sites.[6]

Offline Databases

Another way of making information available to users is via **offline databases,** which are distributed on CD-ROM disks. This type of database service transfers information from the mainframe environment to a personal computer. Access to a telecommunication network is not necessary if the researcher is using offline databases. Thus, there are typically no usage fees. However, the potential cost savings must be offset against the time lag inherent in updating offline data. Nevertheless, there is a market for offline databases. The U.S. Census Bureau makes its data files available on CD-ROM. These disks contain detailed information organized by census track or zip code. InfoUSA (www.infousa.com) offers a number of databases on CD-ROM, including BusinessUSA, HouseholdsUSA, Physicians & Surgeons, Big Businesses, Manufacturers, and Small Business Owners.

offline databases
Databases that are available on diskette or CD-ROM.

Categories of Database Types

All databases, whether online, Internet, or offline, vary in terms of their nature and content. As shown in Figure 4.6, the five major types of databases are bibliographic, numeric, full-text, directory, and special-purpose databases.

BIBLIOGRAPHIC DATABASES **Bibliographic databases** are indexes of studies and reports published in journals, magazines, and newspapers. They can be on any subject, ranging from marketing research to technical reports and government documents. Summaries of the report findings, known as *abstracts*, often are provided. An example is ABI/INFORM, a U.S.-oriented bibliographic database which contains 200-word abstracts of articles published in more than 1,000 journals and general business publications. It is distributed by ProQuest Information & Learning (www.proquest.com). Dialog (www.dialog.com), an online-based information services from Thomson Scientific, also distributes a number of databases that are very useful for marketing research.

bibliographic databases
Databases composed of citations to articles in journals, magazines, newspapers, marketing research studies, technical reports, government documents, and the like. They often provide summaries or abstracts of the material cited.

NUMERIC DATABASES **Numeric databases** disseminate statistical information, such as survey and time-series data. Economic and industry data lend themselves to time-series presentations, which are developed when the same variables are measured over time. Such data are particularly relevant for assessing market potential, making sales forecasts, or setting sales quotas. The American Statistics Index (ASI) provides abstracts and indexes of federal government statistical publications. Global Financial Data (www.globalfinancialdata.com) provides historical data on securities, dividends, and exchange rates.

numeric databases
Databases that contain numerical and statistical information.

Commercially updated census data are another example of numeric databases. Several sources provide updated, current-year and 5-year projections on population statistics collected in the latest census. A variety of geographic categorization schemes, including census tract, zip code, and ACNielsen's Designated Market Areas or Selling Areas, can be used as keys for searching these databases. Claritas, now know as Nielsen's Claritas (www.claritas.com) is one firm that provides updated demographic information annually.

FULL-TEXT DATABASES As the name implies, **full-text databases** contain the complete text of the source documents contained in the database. ABI/Inform Global (www.proquest.com) provides electronic abstracts and full-text delivery and search capabilities for several business and management journals. One of the most useful full-text business databases is LexisNexis. It provides full-text access to hundreds of business data sources, including selected newspapers, periodicals, company annual reports, and investment firm reports.

full-text databases
Databases containing the complete text of secondary source documents comprising the database.

Research in Action

Market Research Library

Customers can purchase report information online from the LexisNexis Market Research Library (www.lexisnexis.com) by subsection, eliminating the cost of buying an entire report. Users can browse the entire table of contents and study the methodology of most reports as well as view actual tables, minus the data, before purchasing the information. The subsections of the marketing research reports on the LexiNexis Market Research Product have been formatted by the market-ing research providers as complete, stand-alone units of information. The product offers research data from such sources as ACNielsen, Business Trend Analysts, Datamonitor, Euromonitor, FIND/SVP, the Freedonia Group, the Leading Edge, and Packaged Facts. For more information, call 800–227–4908 or visit the company's Web site at www.lexis-nexis.com.[7]

directory databases
Databases providing information on individuals, organizations, and services.

DIRECTORY DATABASES   **Directory databases** provide information on individuals, organizations, and services. Standard & Poor's Corporate Descriptions is an example of a directory database that provides summary data on publicly held U.S. corporations. A secondary researcher wanting to compile information on a competitor or prospective customer can obtain data related to the growth of the organization, the size of its workforce, and its financial performance.

Firmographics are the business equivalents of demographics. They include variables such as market share, corporate location, industry classification, and employment size. D&B (formerly Dun and Bradstreet; www.dnb.com) provides this type of data.

The national Electronic Yellow Pages (www.yellowpages.com) is the largest database of U.S. companies. This database contains more than 10 million records compiled from the nation's 4,800 telephone books. The names, addresses, phone numbers, and NAIC codes for manufacturers, wholesalers, retailers, professionals, and service organizations are available through this source.

special-purpose databases
Databases that contain information of a specific nature, for example, data on a specialized industry.

SPECIAL-PURPOSE DATABASES   **Special-purpose databases** are more focused in their scope, such as the Profit Impact of Market Strategies (PIMS). In the United States, the Strategic Planning Institute maintains PIMS, which reflects research and analysis of business strategies from more than 250 companies, representing more than 2,000 businesses.

Locating the database most relevant to a specific research problem might seem overwhelming at first. Fortunately, directories of databases have been developed to assist the researcher in narrowing the database search.

Directories of Databases

To avoid being buried under mountains of irrelevant data and to make the research process more efficient, a search of database directories might be a useful early step. The following are some useful database directories for American researchers:

- *Directory of Online Databases,* Cuadra Associates, Inc., Santa Monica, California
- *Encyclopedia of Information System and Services,* Gale Research Company, Detroit
- *Information Industry Marketplace,* R. R. Bowker, New York

Combining Internal and External Secondary Data

The usefulness of secondary data can be greatly enhanced when internally generated data are merged with data obtained from external sources. By using both internal and external secondary sources, marketing researchers can overlay demographic, economic, or business statistics on proprietary customer files. These data can then be used to develop market assessments or profiles of various customer groups or simply to educate the sales force. The combination of internal and external data results in inexpensive and valuable information that can be used for a variety of purposes, including database marketing, discussed earlier. The following sections describe the merging of internal and external secondary data with applications to geo-demographic coding and geo-visual mapping, as well as a discussion of the buying power index.

Geo-Demographic Coding

Geo-demographic coding involves merging internal customer data with external geographic, demographic, and lifestyle data on the same customers. Some **syndicated services,** which typically offer their information databases by subscription, have developed demographic and psychographic databases at the household level, along with many products based on these data.

Consider the U.S. cable television operator Comcast, which maintains a computerized database of its cable subscribers. This internal database contains customer information on the number of cable services subscribed to, the length of service, changes in subscribed services over time, and the billing history for the past 3 years. Imagine that the president of the cable company has ambitious plans to increase penetration and market share over the next year. He is looking for a recommendation regarding which geographic markets to target. He wants the geographic market potential, profitability of various customer segments, and current cable operating restrictions to be incorporated into this analysis.

In response to this request, the director of marketing research decides to supplement the internal customer database with external secondary data. To expand the internal customer file, the director reviews several outside sources of geographic, demographic, and lifestyle data and then selects Claritas, Inc.

Claritas (www.claritas.com) combines data from a number of sources, including the U.S. Census and commercial marketing research firms, such as Arbitron (www.arbitron.com), Simmons Marketing Research Bureau (www.smrb.com), and Mediamark (www.mediamark.com). One of its products, PRIZM (Potential Rating Index for Zip Markets), seems highly appropriate for this research problem. PRIZM is a target marketing system that describes every U.S. neighborhood in terms of 62 distinct lifestyle types called *clusters*. Geographic matching of the internal customer database with PRIZM files begins with a zip code match followed by street address.

These external data are overlaid on the customer file in a process called *geo-coding*. The researcher can use the geo-coded information to develop demographic and lifestyle profiles of customer types in terms of cable subscription levels or any other relevant variable. For example, the analysis of geo-coded data might reveal that heavy users of cable television can be described as midscale families with children at home. This group falls into the lifestyle cluster PRIZM has named "pools and patios." The PRIZM profiles provide a colorful description of customer segments in terms of income, education, and family size as well as lifestyles. Combining profiles with customer profit history helps the researcher formulate the cable company's expansion plans. Based on this information, the cable company can target direct selling efforts and direct-mail campaigns and also design an appropriate advertising campaign to reach heavy users of cable television.

geo-demographic coding
Involves merging internal customer data with external geographic, demographic, and lifestyle data on the same customers.

syndicated services
Information services offered by marketing research organizations that provide information from a common database to firms that subscribe to their services.

Be an MR!

Visit www.subway.com and search the Internet, as well as your library's online databases, to obtain information on the marketing program at Subway, an American chain of sandwich shops. Write a report about the PRIZM product and its appropriateness for determining Subway restaurant locations.

Be a DM!

As Subway's marketing chief, how will you use geo-demographic information to enhance your market share?

Geo-Visual Databases

Another factor to consider before beginning a marketing campaign for our Comcast example is the physical coverage of the cable system's wire. It is pointless to launch a full-scale effort in geographic areas where cable services are not currently available. This pitfall can be avoided by making use of geo-visual databases. **Geo-visual databases** are created by combining internal customer databases with geographic data, as from the U.S. Census Bureau, and making use of appropriate computer mapping software. **Computer mapping** generates thematic maps for solving marketing problems by electronically combining geographic and demographic information and a company's sales data or other proprietary information.

The U.S. Census Bureau has introduced a geo-visual product called TIGER (Topologically Integrated Geographic Encoding and Referencing), which provides digital street maps of the entire United States. These mapping files contain data on street locations, highways, railroads, pipeline, power lines, and airports. Overlaying the maps of current neighborhoods wired for cable with customer geo-demographic information results in a powerful targeting tool. Such information is very useful in target-market selection and in *micromarketing,* tailoring the marketing mix (the four Ps: product, price, promotion, and place/distribution) to local neighborhoods. Geo-demographic and geo-visual databases can also aid in competitive intelligence, the process of enhancing marketplace competitiveness through a greater—yet unequivocally ethical—understanding of a firm's competitors and the competitive environment.

geo-visual databases
Databases created by combining internal customer databases with geographic data, as from the U.S. Census Bureau, and making use of appropriate computer mapping software.

computer mapping
Maps that solve marketing problems are called thematic maps. They combine geography with demographic information and a company's sales data or other proprietary information and are generated by a computer.

Research in Action

Competitive Intelligence: The Broad Way to Broadband for AT&T

In its current incarnation as the largest U.S. provider of telephone and wireless services and DSL Internet access, AT&T realized that cable TV companies could become competitors in the emerging field of cable telephony and broadband service. Thus, a competitive intelligence effort called "Project Pronto" was undertaken that combined both primary research as well as both internal and external secondary data. Its mission was to understand the extent and capability of potential competition from cable TV companies.

In the primary research stage, members of Project Pronto used tips from AT&T's sales representatives and outside plant technicians to identify the network components of cable TV companies, such as fiber networks, repeaters, and fiber nodes, that could provide two-way cable services with cable modems. Actual field surveys were then used to validate these reports about cable TV network deployment. Next, the knowledge obtained in the first stage was merged with secondary data. Using geo-visual mapping software, routes of these cable TV components were overlaid onto maps with the types and locations of current AT&T customers. In this way, firm leaders were able to see the extent and capability of potential competition from cable TV companies.

These insights gained through Project Pronto shaped the strategic direction of the firm. Based on this knowledge, AT&T directed several billion dollars to the deployment of broadband services and led the way for the company to become the largest provider of broadband DSL (digital subscriber line) services. To further solidify its leadership position, in 2007 AT&T started offering satellite-based non–DSL broadband services in several rural markets for customers who cannot receive traditional high-speed Internet services.[8]

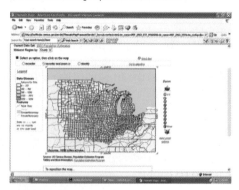

Buying Power Index

Sales & Marketing Management's annual *Survey of Buying Power* (www.mysbp.com) provides data to help in analyzing U.S. markets, whether cities, counties, metro areas, or states. It features statistics, rankings, and projections for every county and media market in the United States, with demographics broken out by age, race, city, county, and state; information on retail spending; and projections for future growth in these areas. The rankings are divided into 323 metro markets (geographic areas established by the U.S. Census Bureau) and 210 media markets (television or broadcast markets determined by Nielsen Media Research), all furnished by Claritas Inc.

A number of statistics are unique to the *Survey*. Effective buying income (EBI) is a measurement of disposable income. The buying power index (BPI), for which the *Survey* is best known, is a unique measure of spending power that takes population, EBI, and retail sales into account to determine a market's ability to buy. The higher the index, the better.

Summary Illustration Using the Opening Vignette

In this section, we summarize and illustrate secondary data by returning to the chapter's opening vignette. In contrast to primary data, which are collected for a specific research problem, secondary data have been generated for reasons other than the research problem at hand. The data on advertising effectiveness and penetration for different forms of media provided by the Inland Research Corp. and used by the *Vindicator* are an example of secondary data. The cost and speed advantages of secondary data must be weighed against their limited applicability and accuracy. In evaluating secondary data, factors such as specifications, error, currency, objectivity, nature, and dependability should be considered, as was done by Inland Research.

Internally generated information can represent a gold mine for a marketing researcher. Any department that touches the final consumer in some way might be a source of valuable market data. The *Vindicator* generates data on the number of customers, subscription duration, and renewals/nonrenewals as a normal business operation. The internally generated data can be supplemented with data available from external sources to produce a rich database that can target customers and guide marketing efforts. In the opening vignette, external data on advertising effectiveness and penetration for different forms of media were combined with internal data on circulation to stress the comparative advantages of the *Vindicator* over other media (i.e., radio and television).

External data are generated by sources outside the organization. These data exist in the form of published (printed) material; online, Internet, and offline databases; or information made available by syndicated services. Inland Research obtains secondary data from all of these sources. Figure 4.7 features a concept map for secondary data.

International Marketing Research

Secondary international data are available from both domestic government and nongovernment sources (Figure 4.8). The following are some of the most important U.S. government sources:

- Department of Commerce (www.commerce.gov)
- Agency for International Development (www.usaid.gov)
- Small Business Administration (www.sba.gov)
- Export–Import Bank of the United States (www.exim.gov)
- Department of Agriculture (www.usda.gov)
- Department of State (www.state.gov)
- Department of Labor (www.dol.gov)
- Port Authority of New York and New Jersey (www.panynj.gov)

The Department of Commerce offers a number of publications as well as a variety of other services, such as the foreign buyer program, matchmaker events, trade missions, an export contact list service, the foreign commercial service, and the custom statistical service for exporters. The National Trade Data Bank (www.stat-usa.gov) provides useful information about exporting to and importing from countries around the world. Another very useful source is the CIA World Factbook (www.cia.gov).

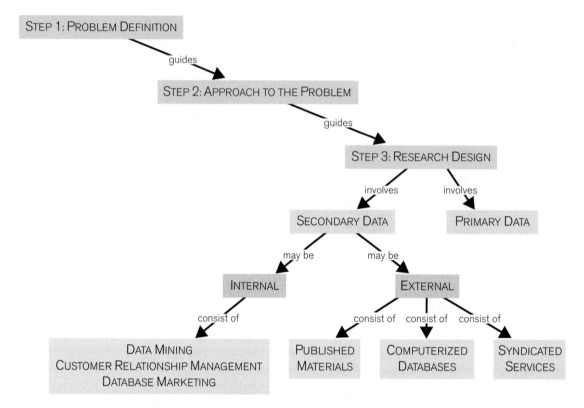

FIGURE 4.7

A Concept Map for Secondary Data

Nongovernment organizations, including international organizations located in the United States, are another source of information about international markets. These data sources include the following international organizations:

- United Nations (www.un.org)
- Organization for Economic Cooperation and Development (www.oecd.org)
- International Monetary Fund (www.imf.org)
- World Bank (www.worldbank.org)

FIGURE 4.8

Sources of Secondary Data for International Marketing Research

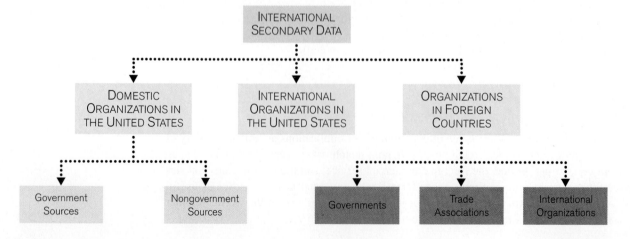

- International Chambers of Commerce (www.iccwbo.org)
- Commission of the European Union to the United States (www.eurunion.org)
- Japanese External Trade Organization (www.jetro.org)

Finally, locally sourced secondary data are available from foreign governments, international organizations located abroad, trade associations, and private services, such as syndicated firms. To illustrate, the following sites provide useful country information:

- Australia (www.nla.gov.au)
- France (www.insee.fr)
- Japan (portal.stat.go.jp)
- Norway (www.ssb.no)
- South Africa (www.statsa.gov.za)
- U.K. (www.statistics.gov.uk)

The problems with data compatibility are even more pronounced when dealing with secondary data from international sources. Differences in units of measurement for such common economic statistics as personal disposable income make comparisons between two countries difficult. The accuracy of secondary data might also vary with the level of industrialization in a country. Data from countries such as the United States are likely to be more accurate than those from developing countries. The taxation structure and the extent of tax evasion affect reported business and income statistics. The measurement frequency of population census data varies considerably. An extreme example is the comparison of the U.S. Census, conducted every 10 years, to the census conducted in the People's Republic of China, where a 29-year gap occurred between the census of 1953 and 1982. However, the situation in China has changed, and secondary data are now easily available in China and can be very useful to firms seeking to enter or establish themselves in China, as illustrated by eBay.

Research in Action

eBay Learns the China Lesson: You Gotta Be There

eBay (www.ebay.com), having successfully established itself in the U.S. e-commerce market, moved on to another big market—China. According to secondary data, in 2004 the Chinese online-auction market had about $561 million in sales. In 2005, that number jumped 200 percent, reaching $1.7 billion. In 2004, China had roughly 15 million online auction users. By the end of 2005, that number was almost 30 million—a 100-percent increase. The number of members of auction Web sites also increased by 152 percent from 2004, reaching 37.87 million. In 2006, online shopping and auctions in the Chinese market accounted for $4.37 billion in sales.

In 2005, Taobao (www.taobao.com), part of the Web portal Alibaba (www.alibaba.com), accounted for 57.74 percent of total auction transaction value, followed by eBay with 31.46 percent. 1Pai, part of Yahoo! China (but part of Taobao in 2008), had 5.75 percent of the market, and PaiPai (www.paipai.com) had 3.76 percent. How do Taobao and eBay differ? Unlike eBay, Taobao is a home-grown Chinese company, whereas eBay purchased a Chinese site called EachNet. In addition, eBay charges auctioneers a portion of the final sale amount, whereas Taobao charges nothing throughout the auctioning process and is totally free to users.

According to surveys conducted by the China Market Research Group (CMR), a marketing research firm in Shanghai, eBay's listings fees were not one of the top five reasons why consumers used Taobao over eBay. In fact, even after eBay offered free listings in early 2006 it still lost customers to Taobao. CMR found that Chinese consumers like to buy from brands and people they "trust" and that offer "over-the-top" customer service. Many consumers disliked eBay because of what they perceived to be bad service and because it did not focus on building trust.

Based on this secondary data from CMR, eBay was able to identify why it was losing market share in China. In response to this information, eBay committed to spending up to $100 million dollars in a massive marketing campaign with a focus on drastically dropping listing fees and repositioning itself in the market to cater to the desires of Chinese consumers. Because of these changes, which were made possible by secondary research, eBay might still end up as the number one online auctioning company in China.[9]

Technology and Marketing Research

New information technologies will continue to revolutionize how marketing research is undertaken. Innovations will change the way secondary and primary research are conducted. Technological advances have not only facilitated the establishment of sophisticated internal databases, they have enabled external research suppliers to collect a wide variety of consumer and business data efficiently and distribute them to clients, as exemplified by USAData.com.

Ethics in Marketing Research

Researchers sometimes overlook the disadvantages and advantages of secondary data discussed earlier, which raises ethical issues. The research firm has the ethical responsibility to use only secondary data that are relevant and appropriate to the problem. The data used should be evaluated, using the criteria described in this chapter. The researcher should discuss issues surrounding the relevance and accuracy of secondary data with the client.

After a detailed analysis of secondary data has been conducted, the researcher should reexamine the collection of primary data stipulated in the proposal to see if it is still appropriate. Any needed changes in the primary data collection methodology should be discussed with the client. In the extreme case, if primary data are no longer needed, then it is the ethical responsibility of the researcher to disclose this to the client.

In addition to evaluating their quality and completeness, researchers should also evaluate secondary data in terms of moral appropriateness. Data collection might be unethical if the data are generated without the respondents' knowledge or consent and if their use raises ethical questions. When generating secondary data, researchers and syndicate firms should not engage in any questionable or unethical practices, such as abuse of respondents' privacy. Privacy has, indeed, become a burning issue, as illustrated by the following example.

Research in Action

Privacy Goes Public

The legal environment is becoming increasingly hostile toward marketing research. In the United States, both the federal government and many states are considering legislation that will cover a host of alleged privacy abuses by marketing research. More than 500 bills that cover various privacy abuses and protections have already been introduced. The privacy issue has gone public with a wave of consumer complaints against many forms of marketing research.

Two main issues are involved. First, consumers feel they should not have to cope with the unsolicited sales pitches that flood their mailboxes, phones, and e-mail addresses. The second issue concerns the sophisticated databases that maintain enormous amounts of information about consumers, ranging from their names to specifics about their lifestyles and product consumption habits. In a privacy survey conducted by Equifax, 78 percent of the respondents said they were concerned about the personal privacy issue. A majority of the respondents said they thought it was reasonable for companies to conduct public record information checks, such as credit checks, auto insurance checks, or job checks, but that consumers should be able to opt out of all other transactions.[10]

What Would *You* Do?

Tommy Hilfiger: Keeping Abreast of the Market to Remain a High Flyer

The Situation

From the blacktop to the golf course, American designer Tommy Hilfiger has the streets covered. His namesake casual wear is worn by rap, rock, teen, and sports stars and fans. These days, many of them are women. Tommy designs, sources, makes, and markets men's and women's sportswear and denim wear, as well as athletic wear, children's wear, and accessories. Through extensive licensing deals (almost 40 product lines), Tommy also offers products such as fragrances, belts, bedding, home furnishings, and cosmetics. The company's clean-cut clothing is sold in major department and specialty stores as well as through 165 Tommy Hilfiger shops and outlets. Apax Partners bought the firm in 2006 in a deal valued at some $1.6 billion. With such a large empire, it is no wonder that Tommy Hilfiger Corp. CEO Fred Gehring is always busy making sure the company does not forget the most important aspect of its business—satisfying consumers' needs!

Selling apparel will never be an easy job. "Just when you think you've figured out exactly what your customers want, everything changes—sometimes overnight," says apparel expert Richard Romer, executive vice president for The CIT Group/Commercial Services, a New York–based credit protection and lending services provider for apparel manufacturers. "Basically, changes in apparel occur every other year: long skirts to short skirts and back to long." The apparel market's constant state of flux forces catalog retailers and other marketers to constantly reevaluate the market they are targeting and then reinvent their companies, their offerings, and their catalogs.

The Marketing Research Decisions

1. What sources of secondary data should Tommy Hilfiger consult to keep informed about apparel fashion trends? (Check all that apply.)
   a. Apparel industry trade association databases
   b. U.S. Bureau of the Census, census of population
   c. University of Michigan, consumer confidence index
   d. United Nations' International database
   e. All of the above

2. How would the type of secondary research you recommend enable Fred Gehring and Tommy Hilfiger to keep abreast of apparel trends?

continued

The Marketing Management Decision

1. In order to enhance the appeal of Tommy Hilfiger clothing to the fashion conscious consumer, Fred Gehring should (check all that apply):
   a. Introduce new lines of designer clothing.
   b. Feature supermodels in Tommy Hilfiger's advertising.
   c. Increase the distribution of Tommy Hilfiger clothing through fashion boutiques and other specialty channels.
   d. Lower the prices of Tommy Hilfiger clothing.
   e. Acquire additional brands.

2. How is your marketing management decision influenced by the information in the secondary data sources that you suggested earlier?

What Fred Gehring Did

Tommy Hilfiger Corp. announced that it would begin a search to acquire additional brands. Tommy Hilfiger now says it hopes to develop a multibrand, multichannel business strategy. According to the company, "While we continue to be focused on improving operations in our existing business, we are aggressively seeking opportunities to further diversify our revenue and earnings base."

Bold stripes and high contrast were the visual hallmarks of Tommy Hilfiger's newly designed advertising campaign. Fall fashions were mod-inspired and flaunted by a cast of young, sexy models with tousled hair and smoky eyes, all evoking the iconic imagery of the 1960s. The stripes and bold graphic lines reflect the timeless, universal appeal of the classic Hilfiger designs.[11]

SPSS Windows

SPSS Maps integrates seamlessly with SPSS base menus, enabling you to map a variety of data. The user can choose from six base thematic maps or create other maps by combining map options. Maps can be further customized using the SPSS Syntax Editor. Such maps can be used for a variety of purposes, including (1) interpreting sales and other data geographically to determine where the biggest customers are located, (2) displaying sales trends for specific geographic locations, and (3) using buying trend information to determine the ideal location for new company stores.

Summary

In contrast to primary data that are collected for a specific research problem, secondary data have been generated for reasons other than the current research problem. The cost advantage and speed with which secondary data can be obtained must be weighed against their limited fit to the current research problem and concerns regarding data accuracy. In evaluating secondary data, the researcher should consider factors such as specifications, error, currency, objectivity, nature, and dependability.

Internally generated information can represent a gold mine for a researcher. Any department that touches the final consumer in some way can be a source of valuable market data. The internally generated data can be supplemented with demographic and lifestyle data available from external sources to produce a rich database that can target customers and guide marketing efforts.

External data are generated by sources outside the organization. These data exist in the form of published (printed) material; online, Internet, and offline databases; or information made available by syndicated services. Published external sources are broadly classified as general business data or government data. General business sources comprise guides, directories, indexes, and statistical data. Government sources can be broadly categorized as census data and other data. Computerized databases can be online, Internet, or offline, and they can be further classified as bibliographic, numeric, full-text, directory, or specialized databases.

Both internal and external databases yield potentially helpful information. Conducting international research predisposes to problems of data quality, and thus these data should be carefully evaluated. Technological advances are facilitating the establishment of sophisticated internal databases. The researcher has the ethical responsibility to use only secondary data that are relevant and appropriate to the problem.

Key Terms and Concepts

Primary data, 124
Secondary data, 124
Internal data, 128
External data, 128
Data warehouse, 129
Psychographics, 129
Data mining, 129
Customer relationship management
    (CRM) system, 130

Database marketing, 130
Online databases, 136
Internet databases, 136
Offline databases, 137
Bibliographic databases, 137
Numeric databases, 137
Full-text databases, 137
Directory databases, 138
Special-purpose databases, 138

Geo-demographic coding, 139
Syndicated services, 139
Geo-visual databases, 140
Computer mapping, 140

Suggested Cases and Video Cases

Running Case with Real Data

1.1 Hewlett-Packard

Comprehensive Critical Thinking Cases

2.1 American Idol   2.2 Baskin-Robbins   2.3 Akron Children's Hospital

Comprehensive Cases with Real Data

3.1 Bank of America   3.2 McDonald's   3.3 Boeing

Video Cases

4.1 Mayo Clinic   5.1 eGO   7.1 Starbucks   8.1 AFLAC
9.1 P&G   11.1 Dunkin' Donuts   12.1 Motorola   13.1 Subaru
14.1 Intel   19.1 Marriott

Live Research: Conducting a Marketing Research Project

1. Assign one, some, or all teams the responsibility of collecting and analyzing secondary data.
2. If this work is divided, one or some teams could search the library's electronic database; others could search government sources; and yet other teams could visit the library and work with a reference librarian to identify relevant sources.

Acronym

The criteria used for evaluating secondary data can be described by the acronym SECOND:

S pecifications: methodology used to collect the data

E rror: accuracy of the data

C urrency: when the data were collected

O bjective: purpose for which data were collected

N ature: content of the data

D ependability: overall, how dependable are the data

Review Questions

1. How do primary and secondary data differ?
2. Why is it important to obtain secondary data before primary data?
3. What are the advantages of secondary data?
4. What are the disadvantages of secondary data?
5. What criteria are used to evaluate secondary data?
6. How do internal and external secondary data differ?
7. What are the various sources of published secondary data?
8. What are the different forms of computerized databases?
9. What are the advantages of computerized databases?
10. Is it useful to combine internal and external secondary data? Why or why not?
11. What is geo-coding? Give an example.
12. Describe a geo-visual database.
13. What is database marketing?

Applied Problems

1. Select an industry of your choice. Using external published sources, obtain industry sales and the sales of the major firms in that industry for the past year. Estimate the market share of each major firm. Use a computerized database to obtain information on the market shares of these same firms. Do the two estimates agree? Was it easier to obtain the information from published sources or from a computerized database?
2. Determine total e-commerce sales for the past year from each of the following sources: Forrester Research (www.forrester.com), ComScore (www.comscore.com), Nielsen/Netratings (www.netratings.com), and the U.S. Commerce Department (www.commerce.gov). Do these four estimates agree?
3. You are enhancing Dell's internal household customer data with externally available information. Visit the Equifax Web site (www.equifax.com) to determine what demographic and psychographic data are available that would be useful to Dell for targeting the household computer market.
4. Visit the NAICS Association Web site (www.naics.com). Find the NAICS codes for "Computers manufacturing" and "Hospitals, general medical and surgical." Discuss the significance and usefulness of these codes.
5. Visit www.dnb.com and write a report about the type of information on businesses available from D&B.
6. Visit the Web site of the U.S. Census Bureau (www.census.gov). Write a report about the secondary data available from the Bureau that would be useful to a fast-food firm such as McDonald's for the purpose of formulating a domestic marketing strategy.
7. Visit www.census.gov/statab. Use State Rankings and Vital Statistics to identify the top six states for marketing products to the elderly.

Group Discussion

1. Discuss the significance and limitations of U.S. Census data as a major source of secondary data.
2. Discuss the growing use of computerized databases.

Hewlett-Packard Running Case

Review the Hewlett-Packard (HP) case, Case 1.1, and questionnaire given toward the end of the book.

1. Search the Internet to find information on the latest U.S. market share of HP and other PC marketers.
2. Search the Internet to obtain information on HP's marketing strategy. Do you agree with HP's marketing strategy? Why or why not?
3. Visit the U.S. Census Bureau at www.census.gov. As HP seeks to increase its penetration of U.S. households, what information available from the U.S. Census Bureau is helpful?

VIDEO CASE 4.1

The Mayo Clinic

THE MAYO CLINIC: Staying Healthy with Marketing Research

William and Charles Mayo began practicing medicine in the 1880s in Rochester, Minnesota. They were quickly recognized as extremely talented surgeons, and they gained so many patients that they were forced to think about expanding their practice. Around the turn of the century, the Mayo brothers began inviting others to join their practice. The partnerships that the Mayos entered into created one of the first private group practices of medicine in the United States. In 1919, the Mayo brothers turned their partnership into a not-for-profit, charitable organization known as the Mayo Foundation. All proceeds beyond operating expenses were to be contributed to education, research, and patient care. The Mayo Clinic (www.mayoclinic.org) has been operating in this fashion ever since. The Mayo Clinic's primary value is, "The needs of the patient come first." Its mission is, "Mayo will provide the best care to every patient every day through integrated clinical practice, education, and research."

As of 2008, more than 3,300 physicians and scientists and more than 52,000 allied health staff worked at the original Mayo Clinic in Rochester and newer clinics in Jacksonville, Florida, and Phoenix/Scottsdale, Arizona. Collectively, the three clinics treat more than half a million people each year. Philanthropy is a big part of the Mayo Clinic. From the Mayos' donations in 1919, philanthropy has been deeply rooted in the Mayo Clinic's operations. In 2006, 87,000 donors provided $230 million in contributions, private grants, and endowments. These donations are used heavily in research and education, and Mayo's capital expansion depends on these investments. Total revenues for 2006 were $6.29 billion, up from $5.81 billion in 2005. Net income from current activities was $117.4 million, down from $195.9 million in 2005. Patient care is the largest form of revenue, bringing in $5.3 billion in 2006. The Mayo Clinic continues to donate huge amounts of money to education and research. In 2006, Mayo contributed $314 million to research and education.

The majority of its business is brought in because of the positive experiences that patients have at the Mayo Clinic. This is a result of the care the Mayo Clinic provides as well as the environment it has created. Collaboration throughout the Mayo Clinic has resulted in excellent care, better methods, and innovation, while also being mindful of the environment in which the care takes place. Marketing research revealed that the clinic environment is an important part of the patient's experience. Therefore, Mayo breaks the mold of a plain, static look with the addition of soothing music and elaborate art, believing that this adds to the patients' experience and helps them to heal faster.

Over the years, the Mayo Clinic has become a name that the public trusts despite the lack of any advertising. It has a strong reputation as a research center, a specialty care provider, and a school of medicine. Explaining the Mayo Clinic's success and how it became the top choice for people in need of care, John la Forgia, chair of the Department of Public Affairs at the Mayo Clinic, says that a key differentiator for Mayo Clinic is its ability to diagnose and treat ailments that other clinics and doctors cannot; the patient then goes home and tells others his or her story, creating immense goodwill and word-of-mouth publicity for Mayo Clinic.

What helps Mayo achieve strong brand recognition is its emphasis on marketing research. A significant portion of marketing research is devoted to brand management. Marketing research is used to continuously monitor consumer perceptions and evaluations of the Mayo Clinic. According to John la Forgia, the Mayo Clinic's Office of Brand Management serves two basic functions. The first is operating as a clearinghouse for external perceptions. The second is to provide physicians with an understanding of the brand as they branch out into new areas. A brand-equity research project found that the Mayo Clinic was considered to be the best practice in the country. It also found that 84 percent of the public is aware of the Mayo Clinic, and that they associate words such as *excellence, care,* and *compassion* with it.

The other part of its strategy is the enhancement of the brand. To accomplish this, the Mayo Clinic relies on marketing research to monitor the perceptions of its patients, the public, donors, the medical staff, and other constituencies. A recent marketing research study revealed that consumers' choice of a health care organization is determined by their evaluation of the alternative health care organizations on the following salient attributes: (1) doctors, (2) medical technology, (3) nursing care, (4) physical facilities, (5) management, and (6) ethics. Since then, the Mayo Clinic has sought to emphasize these factors.

In the service industry, the onus of maintaining a good reputation and name depends largely on the way the service is delivered. Thus, it is most important for Mayo to keep delivering the product and not lose sight of the fact that Mayo is a health care provider and all of the brand equity it has in the minds of Americans depends on its continued delivery of excellent health care. Mayo Clinic marketers say that keeping the brand strong well into the future will depend primarily upon patients' day-to-day experiences, which can be enhanced by marketing research identifying patient needs and developing medical programs to meet those needs.

Conclusion

Through an unflinching focus on patient care, cutting-edge research in medical science, and reliance on marketing research, the Mayo Clinic has been able to carve a special place for itself in the hearts and minds of people and build a strong brand.

Questions

1. The Mayo Clinic would like to further strengthen their brand image and equity. Define the management-decision problem.
2. Define the marketing research problem corresponding to the management-decision problem you have defined in question 1.
3. What type of research design should be adopted? Why?
4. Describe the sources of secondary data that would be helpful in determining consumer preferences for health care facilities.

References

1. www.mayoclinic.org, accessed on February 20, 2008.
2. www.wikipedia.org, accessed on February 20, 2008.
3. Misty Hathaway and Kent Seltman, "International Market Research at the Mayo Clinic," *Marketing Health Services* (Winter 2001): 19.
4. Daniel Fell, "Taking U.S. Health Services Overseas," *Marketing Health Services* (Summer 2002): 21.

Exploratory Research Design: Syndicated Sources of Secondary Data

OPENING QUESTIONS

1. How do syndicated data differ from other types of secondary data?
2. How are syndicated data classified?
3. What are the major methods of obtaining syndicated data from households/consumers?
4. How are syndicated data collected from institutions?
5. Why should multiple sources of secondary data be used? What is meant by *single-source data*?
6. What syndicated data are available for conducting international marketing research?
7. How does technology enhance the usefulness of syndicated data?
8. What ethical issues are involved in the use of syndicated data?

> "As competition intensifies, companies increasingly want marketplace metrics to gauge their performance relative to the competition. For many, syndicated data is what they use."
>
> *Kris Baker,*
> *Vice President, Group Client Director,*
> *ACNielsen.*

A Casual Affair

Even though clothing designers seem to be defining fashion as dressy, most Americans seem to be opting for a more casual approach to their fashion needs. Today, companies are saying goodbye to three-piece suits, wingtips, and high heels and welcoming a more casual dress style. The West Coast dot-com companies have definitely contributed to the trend in casual dress. More recently, consulting firms, law firms, and investment companies on the East Coast have joined this trend as well. A recent survey reported that a remarkable 87 percent of responding companies have a casual Friday or an everyday casual policy at their place of business. Companies such as Coca-Cola, Ford, J.P. Morgan, and Accenture have implemented full-time casual dress policies. At many companies today, when someone wears a suit to work, the question immediately asked is, "Are you going on a job interview?"

According to data from syndicated marketing research firms, the "business casual" segment is growing. As discussed in Chapter 1, syndicated data are made available for purchase by multiple clients on a subscription basis. For example, according to a recent survey by the NPD Group, a well-known source of syndicated services, almost 90 percent of U.S. workers said they were dressing down at least some of the time. The NPD study revealed that although sales in many categories of

tailored clothing, including dresses and men's suits, were down, sales of casual apparel, such as no-iron cotton slacks and sweaters, were on the rise. Several marketers of casual clothing have built their strategies based on these findings.

Haggar Clothing Co. (www.haggar.com) is out to convince its male customers that the company can do everything from tailored to casual. Based on syndicated data, Haggar realized that the trend is not in the direction of tailored suits, where for years the company has been the market leader. The company responded by introducing its "City Casuals" line. Its wrinkle-free cotton trousers have been the line's biggest success. Haggar supported all its lines, formal to casual, with the slogan, "Haggar. Stuff You Can Wear," which was developed by Goodby, Silverstein & Partners.

Haggar's internal research showed that Enron and WorldCom were not the only ones in corporate America allegedly tinkering with numbers. It seems most men do not like to admit their true waist size and end up buying pants that are too small. The product born of this realization was Comfort Fit, a cotton khaki introduced in 2002 that expands up to 3 inches through hidden elastic embedded in the waistline. The pant also appeals to more economically conservative men who, even if they have gained several pounds, hate to throw out pants that are in good condition. In keeping with this trend, Haggar adopted a new theme and in 2008 was marketing its clothing with the slogan, "Making things right," emphasizing shrink-resistant fabric, unbreakable buttons and zippers, unbustable seams, and bigger, unrippable pockets.

In an effort to capitalize on this trend toward casual clothing, Levi Strauss (www.levistrauss.com) is pushing both its Dockers and jeans lines. Although 90 percent of U.S. offices permit employees to wear jeans, some employees are still reluctant to wear them to work because they consider them to be too casual. The company has had huge success with the Dockers trouser line, which has become standard wear for the casual business dresser. The success of Haggar's Comfort Fit has not been lost on Dockers, which in 2003 introduced its own expandable version, called Individual Fit. As of 2008, in addition to Dockers, Levi Strauss &Co. was also marketing Levis and Levi Strauss Signature lines of clothing. This sort of cross-pollination is going on throughout the industry, and the time seems near when consumers will be able to purchase virtually any garment in a stain-free, wrinkle-free, expandable variant.[1]

As this vignette illustrates, even competing firms such as Haggar and Levi Strauss are able to make use of the same data available from syndicate firms such as the NPD Group to formulate their marketing strategies.

Overview

Chapters 1 and 4 introduced the concept of syndicated sources of information. In this chapter, we explain syndicated data in detail and distinguish them from other external sources of secondary data. As shown in Figure 5.1, this chapter relates to marketing research suppliers and services discussed in Chapter 1, tasks involved in problem definition and developing an approach covered in Chapter 2, exploratory and descriptive research designs described in Chapter 3, and secondary data presented in Chapter 4. Thus, this chapter is related to the first three steps of the marketing research process.

This chapter describes the three major methods of collecting syndicated data related to consumers and households: surveys, panels, and electronic scanner services. Syndicated data also are collected from institutions via retail and wholesale audits and industrial services. The chapter also includes a discussion of single-source data. As the name indicates, single-source data combine data from various sources to create a unified database that contains information on consumer purchases, demographic and psychographic variables,

FIGURE 5.1

Relationship of Syndicated Sources to the Previous Chapters and the Marketing Research Process

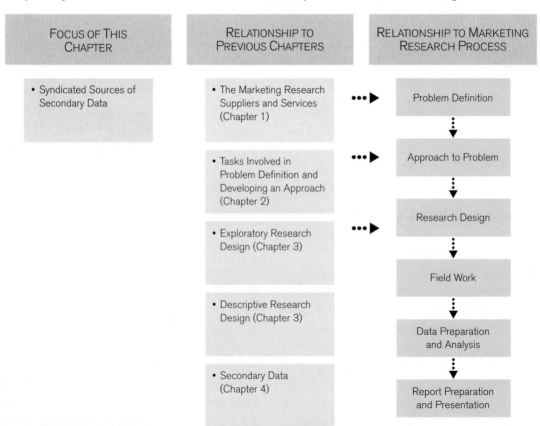

and marketing management variables. Finally, the applications of syndicated data to international marketing research, the impact of technology on syndicated data, and the ethics of collecting and using such data are presented. Figure 5.2 provides an overview of the topics discussed in this chapter and how they flow from one to the next.

FIGURE 5.2

Syndicated Sources of Secondary Data: An Overview

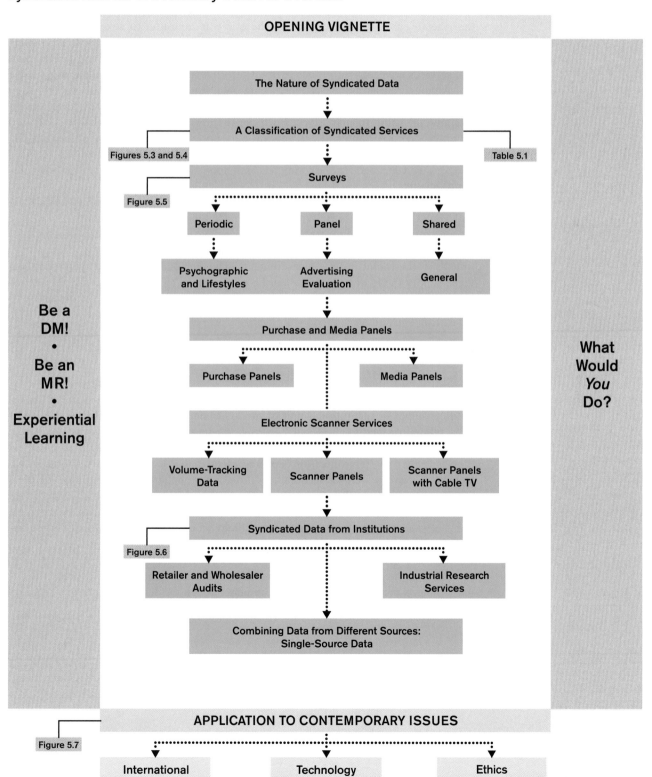

The Nature of Syndicated Data

syndicated sources
Companies that collect and sell common pools of data designed to serve information needs shared by a number of clients, including competing firms in the same industry.

In addition to published data or data available in the form of computerized databases, syndicated sources constitute the other major source of external secondary data. **Syndicated sources**, also referred to as *syndicated services*, are companies that collect and sell common pools of data of known commercial value, designed to serve information needs shared by a number of clients, including competing firms in the same industry. This was illustrated in the opening vignette. Survey data collected by the NPD Group were useful to Haggar and Levi Strauss. These data differ from primary data in that the research objective guiding the study is common to several client firms. Syndicated firms make their money by collecting data and designing research products that fit the information needs of more than one organization. Often, syndicated data and services are designed for use by multiple clients from multiple industries.

Although classified as secondary data, syndicated data differ from other sources of secondary data in that syndicated data are collected because they have known commercial value to marketers. Both census data and other externally generated secondary data (Chapter 4) are general data collected for purposes other than the client's specific research problem. In contrast, the types of data syndicated services collect have very specific marketing research applications that are of interest to a number of clients.

Any client, even two competitors in the same industry (e.g., U.S.-based Coca-Cola and PepsiCo, the U.K.'s Britvic) can purchase the same syndicated data, typically through a subscription process. This process reflects the ongoing nature of many syndicated projects. These projects provide data that enable the tracking of change over time as well as point-in-time measurements. The data and reports that syndicated services supply to client companies can be personalized to fit their specific needs. For example, reports could be organized on the basis of the client's sales territories or product lines.

A Classification of Syndicated Services

Figure 5.3 presents a classification of syndicated sources based on either a household/consumer or institutional unit of measurement. Household/consumer data typically relate to general values and lifestyles, media use, or product-purchase patterns. Data can be collected through a survey process, recorded by panel respondents in diaries (paper or electronic), or captured electronically via scanners (Figure 5.4). Consumer surveys are used to obtain information on beliefs, values, attitudes, preferences, and intentions. Panels used in consumer research emphasize information on purchases or media consumption. Electronic scanner services track purchases at the point of sale or in the home through handheld scanners. These data collection techniques can also be integrated, linking electronic scanner data with panels, survey data, or targeted television advertising through cable.

When syndicated services obtain data from institutions rather than households, the primary subjects they track are product movement through the distribution channel (retailers

FIGURE 5.3

A Classification of Syndicated Services

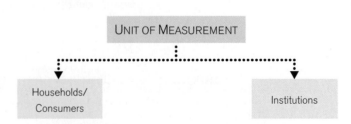

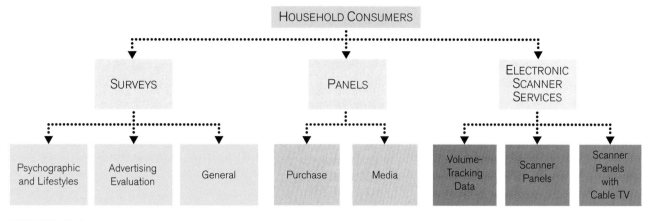

FIGURE 5.4

A Classification of Syndicated Services: Household Consumers

and wholesalers) or corporate statistics. An overview of the various syndicated sources is given in Table 5.1. These sources will be discussed in the following sections.

Surveys

We will begin our discussion with general surveys. The survey by the NPD Group discussed in the opening vignette is an example. The three types of general surveys are periodic, panel, and shared surveys (Figure 5.5).

PERIODIC SURVEYS   **Periodic surveys** collect data on the same set of variables at regular intervals, each time sampling a new group of respondents. Like longitudinal research, periodic surveys track change over time. However, the change due to variation in the respondent pool is not controlled in the way it is for true longitudinal studies. A new sample of respondents is chosen with each survey. Once analyzed, the data are made available to subscribers.

> **periodic surveys**
> Surveys that collect data on the same set of variables at regular intervals, each time sampling from a new group of respondents.

PANEL SURVEYS   Syndicated **panel surveys** measure the same group of respondents over time, but not necessarily on the same variables. A large pool of respondents is recruited to participate on the panel. From this pool, different subsamples of respondents might be drawn for different surveys. Any survey technique can be used, including telephone, personal, mail, or electronic interviewing. The content and topics of the surveys vary and cover a wide range. Also known as *omnibus panels*, these panels are used to implement different cross-sectional designs at different points in time, generally for different surveys. For example, Synovate (www.synovate.com), a marketing research firm that operates without fixed headquarters in 50 countries, offers a number of different omnibus surveys. Its eNation survey involves five weekly online surveys of a sample of 1,000 people that is nationally representative of the American adult population. Another Synovate omnibus panel is TeleNation, which involves two national telephone surveys each week that total 2,000 interviews.[2] Omnibus panels are different from panels that use longitudinal designs, which were discussed in Chapter 3. Recall that in a longitudinal design repeated measurements on the same variables are made on the same sample. Such panels are sometimes referred to as *true panels* to distinguish them from omnibus panels.

> **panel surveys**
> Surveys that measure the same group of respondents over time, but not necessarily on the same variables.

Panel surveys are used primarily because of their lower cost compared to random sampling. These savings result due to streamlining of the data collection process, enhanced response rates, and readily available sample frames, which can be precisely targeted. Comprehensive demographic, lifestyle, and product-ownership data are collected only once as each respondent is admitted into the panel. The panel is used as a respondent pool from which the research organization can draw either representative or targeted samples based on the relevant background characteristics of the panel members. Response rates to

TABLE 5.1 Overview of Syndicated Services

Type	Characteristics	Advantages	Disadvantages	Uses
Surveys	Surveys conducted at regular intervals	Most flexible way of obtaining data; information on underlying motives	Interviewer errors; respondent errors	Market segmentation; advertising theme selection, and advertising effectiveness
Purchase Panels	Households provide specific information regularly over an extended period of time; respondents asked to record specific behaviors as they occur	Recorded purchase behavior can be linked to the demographic/psychographic characteristics	Lack of representativeness; response bias; maturation	Forecasting sales, market share, and trends; establishing consumer profiles and brand loyalty and switching; evaluating test markets, advertising, and distribution
Media Panels	Electronic devices automatically record behavior, supplemented by a diary	Same as purchase panels	Same as purchase panels	Establishing advertising rates; selecting media program or air time; establishing viewer profiles
Scanner Volume-Tracking Data	Household purchases are recorded through electronic scanners in supermarkets	Data reflect actual purchases; timely data; less expensive	Data may not be representative; errors in recording purchases; difficult to link purchases to elements of marketing mix other than price	Price tracking; modeling; assessing effectiveness of in-store promotion
Scanner Panels with Cable TV	Scanner panels of households that subscribe to cable TV	Data reflect actual purchases; sample control; ability to link panel data to household characteristics	Data may not be representative; quality of data limited	Promotional-mix analyses; copy testing; new-product testing; positioning
Audit Services	Verification of product movement by examining physical records or performing inventory analysis	Relatively precise information at the retail and wholesale levels	Coverage may be incomplete; matching of data on competitive activity may be difficult	Measuring consumer sales, market share, and competitive activity; analyzing distribution patterns; tracking of new products
Firm Syndicated Services	Data banks on industrial establishments through direct inquiries of companies, clipping services, and corporate reports	Important source of information on industrial firms; particularly useful in initial phases of the marketing research process	Data is lacking in terms of content, quantity, and quality	Determining market potential by geographic area; defining sales territories; allocating advertising budget

FIGURE 5.5

Classification of Syndicated Survey Research

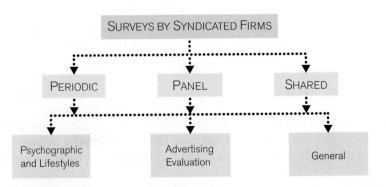

panel surveys, including mail panels, are substantially improved over the random sampling process because of the commitment panel members make to participate in surveys.

SHARED SURVEYS   As the name implies, **shared surveys** are developed and executed for multiple clients, each of whom shares the expenses. The bulk of a shared survey deals with questions of general interest to the client group. These general questions are typically supplemented with proprietary questions from each participating client. Responses to the general interest questions are available to the entire group, whereas the answers to proprietary questions are held in confidence and provided only to the appropriate client. This survey might be repeated at regular intervals, or it might be a one-time study. The sample can be drawn from an omnibus panel or randomly from the population of interest. Shared surveys are one way for syndicated research organizations to offer customized reports to their clients.

> **shared surveys**
> Surveys developed and executed for multiple clients, each of whom shares the expenses.

The primary advantage of shared surveys, as with all forms of secondary research, is lower cost. The fixed cost of research design and the variable cost of data collection are shared by the participants, making the cost per question relatively low for each client. Popular ongoing shared surveys include TeleNation and Data Gage from Synovate and GfK Roper OmniTel Telephone Survey by GfK Custom Research North America (www.gfkamerica.com). Although a number of clients share these surveys, a certain degree of customization is offered, as illustrated by GfK Custom Research North America.

Research in Action

GfK Custom Research North America: Customization via Syndication

Headquartered in Germany, GfK Roper OmniTel (www.gfkamerica.com) is a syndicated service offering customized survey reports. GfK's public opinion research service collects data on a broad range of social, economic, political, and consumer issues every 5 weeks. The organization conducts telephone interviews with a national sample of 1,000 adults aged 18 and older. In addition to the standard questions that are common across clients, clients can add customized, proprietary questions. Thus, an American firm such as Ford Motor Company can purchase the general survey results related to automobiles. Ford can also request proprietary questions about its models, such as Taurus, to determine why sales are lagging behind major competitors, such as Toyota's Camry and Honda's Accord.

According to the GfK Custom Research North America, the ability to add proprietary questions along with customized report generation offers a unique combination of frequency, speed of report delivery, quality, low cost, large sample size, and extensive demographic breaks. This ability to customize surveys and reports has been a major factor in the popularity of the OmniTel survey.

Be an MR!

Visit www.gfkamerica.com and write a brief report about the company's GfK Roper OmniTel Telephone Survey. How can you use the OmniTel Telephone Survey to obtain information that will help the Japanese electronics and entertainment company Sony increase the penetration of flat-panel television sets in the United States?

Be a DM!

What marketing strategies should Sony adopt to increase the penetration of flat-panel television sets in the United States?

Surveys can be broadly classified on the basis of their content as psychographics and lifestyles, advertising evaluation, or general surveys (Figures 5.4 and 5.5).

PSYCHOGRAPHICS AND LIFESTYLES   The term **psychographics** refers to psychological profiles of individuals and to psychologically based measures of lifestyle, such as brand loyalty and risk taking. The term **lifestyle** refers to the distinctive modes of living within a society or some of its segments, such as the DINKs (Double Income No Kids) lifestyle characterized as being money rich and time poor. Together, these measures are generally referred to as *activities, interests,* and *opinions,* or simply as AIOs. The U.S. firm Yankelovich Research and Consulting Services (www.yankelovich.com) provides the Yankelovich Monitor, a survey that contains data on lifestyles and social trends. The survey is conducted

> **psychographics**
> Quantified psychological profiles of individuals.
>
> **lifestyle**
> A distinctive pattern of living that is described by the activities people engage in, the interests they have, and the opinions they hold of themselves and the world around them (AIOs).

at the same time each year among a nationally projectable sample of 2,500 adults, aged 16 and older, including a special sample of 300 college students living on campus. The sample is based on the most recent census data updates. All interviews are conducted in person at each respondent's home and take approximately 2.5 hours to complete.

As another example, U.S.-based SRI Consulting (www.sric-bi.com), in partnership with the nonprofit research institute SRI International, conducts an annual survey of consumers that is used to classify persons into VALS (values and lifestyles) types for segmentation purposes. Information on specific aspects of consumers' lifestyles also is available. GfK Custom Research North America conducts an annual survey of 5,000 consumers who participate in leisure sports and recreational activities. In the United States, several firms conduct surveys to compile demographic and psychographic information at the household, sub-zip (e.g., 30306-3035), and zip-code level, which is then made available on a subscription basis. Such information is particularly valuable for client firms seeking to enhance internally generated customer data for database marketing.

ADVERTISING EVALUATION   The purpose of these surveys is to measure the size and profile of the advertising audience and to assess the effectiveness of advertising using print and broadcast media. A well-known survey is the U.S. Gallup and Robinson Magazine Impact Research Service (MIRS) (www.gallup-robinson.com).

Research in Action

Magazine Impact Research Service

In the Magazine Impact Research Service (MIRS) by Gallup and Robinson (www.gallup-robinson.com), ads are tested using an at-home, in-magazine context among widely dispersed samples. Interviewers screen respondents for eligibility, door-to-door, and ask them to read a current issue magazine as they normally would at home. The issue they receive contains a test ad. The following day they are recontacted and measurements are made on core variables such as intrusiveness, persuasion, brand rating and ad liking, without looking at the magazine. Next, the entire sample is asked to look at the test ad before they are administered diagnostic questions, which can be both standardized and customized. This information is very useful to companies that advertise heavily in print media, such as American Airlines, Gucci, and GM, for evaluating the effectiveness of their advertising. MIRS has become an industry standard for magazine ad testing.[3]

Evaluation of effectiveness is even more critical in the case of television advertising. Television commercials are evaluated using either the recruited-audience method or the in-home viewing method. In the recruited audience method, respondents are brought to a theater or mobile viewing laboratory. After viewing a series of advertisements, they are surveyed regarding product knowledge, attitudes, and preferences, as well as their reaction to the advertisements. With the in-home viewing method, consumers evaluate commercials in their normal viewing environment. New commercials can be pretested at the network level or in local markets. Audience reaction to the advertisements is recorded along with respondent demographics. Gallup & Robinson, Inc. offers testing of television commercials using both of these methods. These methods also are used for testing the effectiveness of advertising in other media, such as magazines, radio, newspapers, and direct mail. Simmons Media/Marketing Service (www.smrb.com) conducts four different surveys with a large sample of respondents to monitor U.S. magazine, TV, newspaper, and radio media. Mediamark Research (www.mediamark.com) is another firm that makes available information on the consumption of media, products, and services by American households.

GENERAL SURVEYS   Surveys also are conducted for a variety of other purposes, including examination of purchase and consumption behavior. Gallup (www.gallup.com) surveys a random sample of 1,000 U.S. households by telephone about a variety of topics. The weekly Harris Poll by Harris Interactive (www.harrisinteractive.com) also is based on a nationally representative telephone survey of 1,000 American adults aged 18 or over. Again, a wide range of topics is considered. Another example of general surveys is provided by BIGresearch.

Research in Action

BIGresearch Syndicated Surveys Lead to Big Decisions

BIGresearch's (www.bigresearch.com) syndicated Consumer Intentions and Actions (CIA) survey monitors the pulse of over 8,000 American consumers each month. The survey is conducted online and is based on a representative sample. It delivers fresh, demand-based information on where retail consumers are shopping and their changing behavior. In the context of automobile purchase, the survey is predictive of automotive sales at the national level 3 months in advance.

BIGresearch determines automobile market share each month by comparing the percentage of people who own a car (e.g., Chrysler, which came in at 5.0 percent for June 2006), and people who selected that vehicle as a first choice (e.g., Chrysler was 1.7 percent) and second choice (e.g., Chrysler was 2.7 percent). The first and second choices are averaged to 2.2 percent and compared to present ownership of a Chrysler (5.0 percent). Based on these numbers Chrysler's market share decreased by 2.8 percent for June 2006. In addition, BIGresearch surveys showed that Chrysler was losing market share to Toyota during 2005 to 2008.

Based on these findings, Chrysler made some strategic adjustments to build off its historic strengths, but not rely too much on them so as to be at a competitive disadvantage. Chrysler added a more robust customer and brand focus while continuing to stress product leadership. It decided to continue the product offensive through 2009, with more than 20 all-new vehicles and 13 refreshed vehicles. In addition, Chrysler will introduce its first two-mode full hybrid with the 2009 Durango HEMI Hybrid.[4]

Uses of Surveys

Surveys that are designed to collect psychographic and lifestyle data can be used for market segmentation, developing consumer profiles, or determining consumer preferences, as with casual clothing in the opening vignette. Surveys also are useful for determining product image or positioning and for conducting price-perception analysis and advertising research.

Advantages and Disadvantages of Surveys

Surveys are the primary means of obtaining information about consumers' motives, attitudes, and preferences. The flexibility of surveys is reflected in the variety of questions that can be asked and the visual aids, packages, products, or other props that can be used during the interviews. Additionally, the sampling process enables targeting of respondents with very specific characteristics.

Because survey researchers rely primarily on respondents' self-reports, data gathered in this way can have serious limitations. What people say is not always what they actually do. Errors might occur because respondents remember incorrectly or feel pressured to give the "right" answer. Furthermore, samples might be biased, questions poorly phrased, interviewers not properly instructed or supervised, and results misinterpreted.

Although surveys remain popular for both primary and secondary research, panels do a much better job of tracking consumer behavior.

Purchase and Media Panels

Purchase and media panels are composed of a group of individuals, households, or organizations that record their purchases and behavior in a diary or on the Internet over time. Households are continually being recruited and added to the panel as respondents drop out of the study or are removed in order to rotate respondents. The makeup of the panel is designed to be representative of the U.S. population in terms of demographics.

Although panels also are maintained for conducting surveys, the distinguishing feature of purchase and media panels is that the respondents record specific behaviors (e.g., product purchases or media usage) as they occur. This makes the information more accurate. Previously, behavior was recorded in a diary, and the diary was returned to the research organization every 1 to 4 weeks. Paper diaries have been gradually replaced by electronic diaries. Now, most of the panels are online, and the behavior is recorded electronically, either entered online by the respondents or recorded automatically by electronic devices. Panel members are compensated for their participation with gifts, coupons, information, or cash. Based on the type of information recorded, these panels can be classified as either purchase panels or media panels.

Purchase Panels

purchase panels
A data-gathering technique in which respondents record their purchases in a diary.

Survey data can often be complemented with data obtained from **purchase panels**, in which respondents record their purchases in a diary or on the Internet. The NPD Group (www.npd.com), which operates in more than 20 countries, is a leading provider of market information collected and delivered online for a wide range of industries and markets. The NPD Group combines information obtained via surveys with that recorded by respondents about their behaviors to generate reports on consumption behaviors, industry sales, market share, and key demographic trends. Consumer information is collected from its Online Panel on a wide range of product categories, including fashion, food, fun, house and home, technology, and automobile. Respondents provide detailed information regarding the brand and amount purchased, the price paid, whether any special deals were involved, the point of purchase, and the product's intended use. In any given country, panel composition is representative of the population as a whole. In South Korea, for example, information provided by the panel might be used by a company like Denticoen Toothpaste to determine brand loyalty and brand switching and to profile heavy users of various brands.

Another organization that maintains purchase panels is U.K.-based TNS Global (www.tnsglobal.com). TNS Global maintains a number of panels, including a large interactive one. Special panels, such as Baby Panel, provide access to highly targeted groups of consumers. Each quarter, approximately 2,000 new mothers and 2,000 expectant mothers join the TNS Baby Panel.

Media Panels

media panels
A data-gathering technique that involves samples of respondents whose television viewing behavior is automatically recorded by electronic devices, supplementing the purchase information recorded in a diary.

In **media panels**, electronic devices automatically record viewing behavior, supplementing a diary. Perhaps the most familiar media panel is the Nielsen Television Index (NTI) by Nielsen Media Research (www.nielsenmedia.com). The NTI consists of a representative sample of approximately 11,000 American households. Each of these households has an electronic device, called a *storage instantaneous peoplemeter*, attached to its television sets. The peoplemeter continuously monitors television viewing behavior, including when the set is turned on, what channels are viewed, and for how long. These data are stored in the peoplemeter and transmitted via telephone lines to a central computer. The data collected by the peoplemeter are supplemented with diary panel records, called *audilogs*. The audilog contains information on who was watching each program, so that audience size and demographic characteristics can be calculated.[5] The NTI is useful to such large American firms as AT&T, Kellogg, JCPenney, and Pillsbury, who are looking for advertising media that are reaching their target markets. Nielsen has also developed a passive peoplemeter that recognizes when a person enters or leaves the room and keeps track of the person's activities as he or she watches television. In April 2007, Nielsen Media Research introduced the new commercial-minute ratings that allow advertising agencies, advertisers, and programmers to develop individualized minute-by-minute ratings of national commercials by demographic group for all national television programs.

Other U.S. services also provide media panels. Arbitron maintains local and regional radio and TV diary panels. Arbitron's portable peoplemeter is a panel-based measure of multimedia, including TV, radio, satellite radio, and the Web. TV BehaviorGraphics, by Simmons Market Research Bureau (www.smrb.com), is a behavioral targeting system used to identify the best prospects for products and services based on consumers' viewing of broadcast and cable television programs. The system was developed through an integration process that merges the NTI with the Simmons National Consumer Survey (NCS). It consists of a multisegment cluster system that classifies consumers into distinct groups based on their television-viewing behavior. Based in the United Kingdom, GfK NOP Media (www.gfknopmedia.com) specializes in quantitative audience measurements for clients in more than 70 countries. Another U.K. company, Research Now (www.researchnow.co.uk), operates 28 separate panels, with some 2 million respondents, in Europe and Australia.

Syndicated services also track Internet usage. The U.S. firm Nielsen//NetRatings, Inc. (www.netratings.com) tracks and collects international Internet-usage data in real time from home and work users. It reports site and e-commerce activity, including the number of visits to properties, domains, and unique sites, rankings by site and by category, time and frequency statistics, traffic patterns, and e-commerce transactions. It also reports on banner advertising, including audience response to banners, creative content, frequency, and site placement. This service has been launched in collaboration with ACNielsen. Another leader in the field is ComScore Networks (www.comscore.com). It has built a massive cross-section of more than 1.5 million global Internet users who have given ComScore explicit permission to confidentially capture their Web-wide browsing, buying, and other transaction behavior, including offline purchasing.

Uses of Purchase and Media Panels

Purchase panels provide information that is useful for forecasting sales, estimating market shares, assessing brand-loyalty and brand-switching behavior, establishing profiles of specific user groups, measuring promotional effectiveness, and conducting controlled store tests. Media panels yield information helpful for establishing advertising rates by radio and TV networks, selecting appropriate programming, and profiling viewer or listener subgroups. Advertisers, media planners, and buyers find panel information to be particularly useful.

Advantages and Disadvantages of Purchase and Media Panels

The advantages of panel data over survey data relate to data accuracy and the generation of longitudinal data. Repeated measurement of the same variables from the same group of respondents classifies this as a form of longitudinal data. Longitudinal data enables manufacturers to measure changes in brand loyalty, usage, and price sensitivity over time. Involvement in a purchase panel represents a commitment on the part of the respondent. That commitment is thought to enhance the accuracy, and therefore the quality, of panel data. Purchase panels that record information at the time of purchase also eliminate recall errors. Information recorded by electronic devices is even more accurate, because the devices eliminate human errors.

The disadvantage of panel data can be traced to the fact that panel members might not be representative of the larger population and to increased response errors uniquely associated with the process of maintaining a diary. Recruiters for purchase and media panels attempt to mirror the population in the panel makeup. However, certain groups tend to be underrepresented, such as minorities and those with low education levels. The time commitment necessary to participate on panels contributes to the relatively high level of refusal and dropout rates. Additionally, response biases can occur because simply being on the panel might alter a panel member's behavior. Because some purchase or media data are entered by hand, recording errors also are possible.

Experiential Learning

Nielsen//Net Ratings

Nielsen//Net Ratings reports on nearly 70 percent of the world's Internet usage to give a broad view of the online world. Nielsen//Net Ratings focuses its research on Internet usage in the following countries: Australia, Brazil, France, Germany, Italy, Japan, Spain, Switzerland, the United Kingdom, and the United States.

Go to Nielsen//Net Ratings' homepage at www.netratings.com. On the top menu bar, select "Resources" and then select "Free Data and Rankings." Under "Internet Audience Metrics," to view results for a country, double-click on the country name. For the following exercises, choose "Home Panel" and "Monthly Web Usage Data" to view the most recent month's results for each country. (If the Web site has been restructured, follow a similar procedure.) Record your findings about each country's "PC Time Per Person" in a table.

1. Which country posts the most "PC Time Per Person"?

2. Which country posts the least "PC Time Per Person"?

Now choose "Global Index" instead of "NetView Usage Metrics" in order to view the latest month's Global Internet Index: Average Usage.

1. What is the average "PC Time Spent per Month" for the set of countries?

2. Which countries were above the average for "PC Time Spent per Month" for the latest month?

3. Which countries were below the average for "PC Time Spent per Month" for the latest month?

Electronic Scanner Services

scanner data
Data obtained by passing merchandise over a laser scanner that reads the UPC code from the packages.

Scanner data are obtained by using electronic scanners at the cash register that read the Universal Product Code (UPC) from consumer purchases. Among the largest syndicated U.S. firms specializing in this type of data collection are ACNielsen and Information Resources, Inc. (www.infores.com). These companies compile and sell data, which tell subscribers how well their products are selling relative to the competition. This analysis can be conducted for each item with a unique UPC—that is, brand, flavor, and package size. Scanner-based companies represent formidable competition for both purchase panels and physical audit services. The accuracy and speed with which product movement at the retail level can be recorded using electronic scanners have reshaped the marketing research industry.

volume-tracking data
Scanner data that provide information on purchases by brand, size, price, and flavor or formulation.

Three types of scanner data are available: volume-tracking data, scanner panels, and scanner panels with cable TV. **Volume-tracking data** are routinely collected by supermarkets and other outlets with electronic checkout counters. When the consumer's purchases are scanned, the data are automatically entered into a computer. These data provide information on purchases by brand, size, price, and flavor or formulation based on sales data collected from the checkout scanner tapes. However, this information cannot be linked to consumers' background characteristics, because their identities are not recorded when their purchases are scanned. In the United States, such information is collected nationally from a sample of supermarkets with electronic scanners. Scanner services providing volume-tracking data include SCANTRACK (ACNielsen) and InfoScan (Information Resources, Inc.). The SCANTRACK service gathers data weekly from a sample of more than 4,800 stores representing more than 800 retailers in 52 major markets. It provides basic tracking information at multiple levels, ranging from category-level total U.S. all-outlet sales volume to single-item performance in one market. The InfoScan Syndicated Store Tracking service monitors more than 34,000 supermarket, drugstore, and mass-merchandiser outlets. An example of the type of information available from Information Resources follows.

Research in Action

Supersizing the Supermarket

Information Resources' (www.infores.com) *Times & Trends*, available at the company's Web site, highlights the consumer packaged goods (CPG) industry's year-end review. *Times & Trends* is a valuable report for busy executives who need a summary insight into today's economic and general business conditions but who also need a detailed insight into CPG trends and retail marketing conditions. For example, a recent report highlighted that at 60-percent household penetration in the United States, Wal-Mart Supercenters grab 10 percent of shopper spending. Expanding Supercenter distribution enables Wal-Mart to grab a larger share of the faster growing dinner-solution market. About 25 percent of Wal-Mart Supercenters' shopper spending is for the most challenged meal occasion of the day, the dinner meal. Frozen dinners and entrees are the fifth-most purchased food-and-beverage category item by Wal-Mart Supercenter shoppers, with frozen poultry at number nine. Such information has enabled Wal-Mart to further expand its line of frozen dinners and entrees.[6]

With **scanner panels**, each household member is given an ID card that can be read by the electronic scanner at the cash register. Scanner panel members simply present the ID card at the checkout counter each time they shop. In this way, the consumer's identity is linked to product purchases as well as the time and day of the shopping trip. This enables the firm to build a shopping record for that individual. Alternatively, some firms provide handheld scanners to panel members. These members scan their purchases once they are home.

ACNielsen's Homescan consumer panel records the purchases of approximately 125,000 households throughout the world. The consumer scans the bar codes on purchases with a handheld scanner, which records the price, promotions, and quantity of each item. The information in the handheld scanner is then transmitted to ACNielsen through telephone lines. ACNielsen uses the information from the scanner and additional information gathered from the consumer to determine such things as consumer demographics, quantity and frequency of purchases, percentage of households purchasing, shopping trips and expenditures, price paid, and usage information. Manufacturers and retailers use this information to better understand consumers' purchasing habits.

scanner panels
Scanner data collected from panel members who are issued an ID card that enables their purchases to be linked to their identities.

Research in Action

At Home with Quality via Homescan

The large American food-products company Kellogg's (www.kelloggs.com) uses ACNielsen's Homescan scanner panel (www.acnielsen.com), discussed earlier in this chapter, to answer a variety of questions:

- In what areas of the country are Kellogg's cereals purchased most frequently?
- What promotions were offered at the time of purchase?
- What is the number and size of the cereal boxes the typical consumer purchases?
- What are the demographic characteristics of the heavy cereal users?

Kellogg's uses this information to better target its products to consumers. The information also is used to design sales promotions, such as coupons and point-of-sale displays, to better meet consumers' needs. For example, larger families of Hispanic origin in California tend to be heavy users of Kellogg's Cornflakes. Kellogg's has attempted to cultivate and retain the patronage of these users by directing coupons and promotional offers to them. Thus, the quality of Kellogg's marketing is greatly increased by achieving a greater focus on consumer needs through Homescan.[7]

An even more advanced use of scanning technology, **scanner panels with cable TV**, combines scanner panels with new technologies that have grown out of the cable TV industry. Households on these panels subscribe to one of the cable TV systems in their market. By means of a cable TV "split," the researcher targets various commercials into panel members' homes. For example, half the households might see test commercial A during the 6 o'clock newscast, while the other half views test commercial B. This enables marketing researchers to conduct fairly controlled experiments in a relatively natural environment. The technology also offers a way to target marketing effort. In Australia, for example, it is possible to transmit a Bush Foods Breakfast cereal commercial only to consumers who prefer Good Girls museli cereal to determine if they can be induced to switch brands. Information Resources' BehaviorScan system contains such a panel.

scanner panels with cable TV
The combination of a scanner panel with manipulations of the advertising that is being broadcast by cable TV companies.

Systems have been developed to allow transmission of advertising into participating households without the use of a cable TV system. Because these panels can be selected from all available TV households, not just those with cable TV, the bias of cable-only testing is eliminated. Using this type of system, for example, the Australian food-products firm Dick Smith Foods (www.dicksmithfoods.com.au) can determine which of four test commercials for Bush Foods Breakfast cereal results in the highest sales. Four groups of panel members are selected, and each receives a different test commercial. These households are monitored via scanner data to determine which group purchased the most Bush Foods Breakfast cereal. Scanner services incorporate advanced marketing-research technology, which results in some advantages over survey and purchase-panel data.

Uses of Scanner Data

Scanner data are useful for a variety of purposes. National volume-tracking data can be used for tracking sales, prices, and distribution and for modeling and analyzing early warning signals. Scanner panels with cable TV can be used for testing new products, repositioning products, analyzing promotional mix, and making advertising and pricing decisions. These panels provide marketing researchers with a unique controlled environment for the manipulation of marketing variables.

Advantages and Disadvantages of Scanner Data

Given that the large grocery chains have largely completed the conversion to electronic scanning, and drugstores are following suit, electronic data collection is likely to continue to grow. The prompt feedback about point-of-sale product activity enables managers to evaluate existing marketing programs as well as to formulate new ones.

Scanner data are not only available more quickly, but they are typically more accurate than data collected through either surveys or purchase panels. The response bias that plagues manual data collection is lessened, because the respondents are much less conscious of their role as members of a scanner panel. Errors due to failures in recall also are eliminated with electronic data collection. Scanners also offer the ability to study very short time periods of sales activity.

Another advantage of scanners is that in-store variables, such as pricing, promotions, and displays, also are recorded. Finally, a scanner panel with cable TV provides a highly controlled test environment for alternate promotional messages.

A major weakness of scanner data is its lack of representativeness. Only retailers equipped with scanners are included in the research. Entire retail categories, such as food warehouses and mass merchandisers, might be excluded. Likewise, the availability of scanners might be lacking in certain geographical areas.

The quality of scanner data is only as good as the scanning process itself and can be limited by several factors. All products might not be scanned. For example, a clerk might use the register to ring up a heavy item to avoid lifting it. If an item does not scan on the first try, the clerk might key in the price and ignore the bar code. Sometimes a consumer purchases many flavors of the same item, but the clerk scans only one package and then rings in the number of purchases. Thus, the transaction is recorded inaccurately.

With respect to scanner panels, the available technology permits the monitoring of only one television per household. Hence, there is a built-in bias if the household has a second or third television, because the viewing of these additional sets is not considered. Also, the system provides information only on the television in use rather than actual viewing behavior. Thus, the television might be turned on, but the people might not be paying any attention to it. Although scanner data provide behavioral and sales information, they do not provide information on underlying attitudes, preferences, and reasons for specific choices.

Be a DM!	Be an MR!
As the marketing manager for Lay's potato chips (a division of PepsiCo), how would you determine the right price?	Visit ACNielsen at www.acnielsen.com and write a brief report about its SCANTRACK service. How can you use SCANTRACK to determine the optimal price for Lay's potato chips?

Syndicated Data from Institutions

We have already discussed syndicated data collected from consumers and households. Parallel electronic and manual systems also are used to collect institutional and industrial data. As Figure 5.6 shows, syndicated data are available for retailers and wholesalers as well as industrial firms/organizations.

Retailer and Wholesaler Audits

Collecting product-movement data for wholesalers and retailers is referred to as an **audit**. These periodic audits can be a physical count of the inventory or managed through a link to the scanning process. These audits track inventory flow, current inventory levels, and the impact of both promotional and pricing programs on inventory levels.

audit
A data-collection process derived from physical records or inventory analysis. Data are collected personally by the researcher or by representatives of the researcher, and the data are based upon counts, usually of physical objects.

A physical audit is a formal examination and verification of product movement carried out by examining physical records or analyzing inventory. An example of the traditional audit is the ACNielsen Convenience Track, which is a retail audit of convenience stores in 30 local markets. Another example is the National Retail Census by GfK Audits & Surveys (www.gfkauditsandsurveys.com), which provides updated measurements of product distribution in all types of retail and service outlets. Conducted annually since its inception in 1953, it is based on a national probability sample of approximately 30,000 outlets of all kinds throughout the country in more than 500 different geographic areas. The audit is conducted by personal store visits, making GfK Audits & Surveys' Retail Census the largest annual product availability measurement in the United States. For high speed and accuracy, these in-store audits use handheld computers to capture UPC information electronically. Retail audit data can be useful to consumer product firms. For example, say that Colgate Palmolive is contemplating introducing a new toothpaste brand. A retail audit can help determine the size of the total market and distribution of sales by type of outlet and by different regions.

Wholesale audit services, the counterpart of retail audits, monitor warehouse withdrawals. Participating operators, which include supermarket chains, wholesalers, and frozen-food warehouses, typically account for more than 80 percent of the volume in this area. Audits are now being increasingly conducted by using scanner data and electronic records rather than by physical examination and verification.

USES OF AUDIT DATA Standardized as well as customized reports are available to help subscribers manage their brands. These reports provide information that can be used to (1) determine market size and share for both categories and brands by type of outlet, region, or city; (2) assess competitive activity; (3) identify distribution problems, including shelf-space allocation and inventory issues; (4) develop sales potentials and forecasts; and

FIGURE 5.6

Classification of Syndicated Services: Institutions

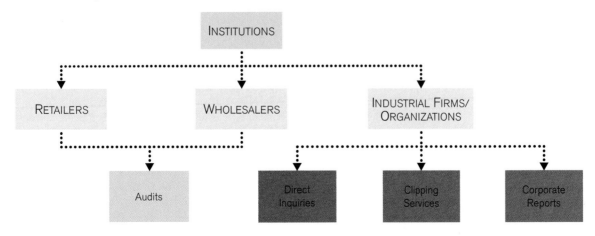

(5) develop and monitor promotional allocations based on sales volume. Scanners are now used to collect data that cross the wholesale, retail, and customer levels. The information they offer has had a profound impact on the marketing process.

ADVANTAGES AND DISADVANTAGES OF AUDIT DATA   Audits provide relatively accurate information on the movement of many products at the wholesale and retail levels. Furthermore, this information can be broken down by a number of important variables, such as brand, type of outlet, and size of market.

A major disadvantage of physical audits, however, is the limited retail coverage and delay associated with compiling and reporting inventory data. Typically, a 2-month gap exists between the completion of the audit cycle and the publication of reports. Another disadvantage of physical audits is that, unlike scanner data, audit data cannot be linked to consumer characteristics. In fact, it can be difficult to relate audit data to advertising expenditures and other marketing efforts.

Research in Action

Hispanic Small Food Store Audit

The Hispanic Small Food Store Audit is a bimonthly audit conducted by GfK Audits & Surveys (www. gfkauditsandsurveys.com). Marketers targeting the burgeoning Hispanic segment in the United States can now measure the results of their campaigns through the Hispanic Small Food Store Sales Index. A measurement of sales in a channel for which there is little sales data, this study is conducted through personal visits to over 400 stores in high-density Hispanic markets. Manual audits are conducted by trained bilingual local-market field personnel. Store participation on an ongoing basis is secured through the payment of cooperation fees to each individual outlet. Inventory measurements are taken on a bimonthly basis, six times per year (January–February, March–April, etc.); invoice and other

purchase memoranda might be recorded more frequently, as jointly determined with the store owners/managers. The audit tracks the following:

- Sales and brand shares
- Distribution
- Inventories
- Pricing
- Causal data

Marketers, such as P&G, attempting to penetrate the Hispanic market, can make use of the audit findings to determine distribution outlets, product mix, inventories, advertising campaigns, and prices.[8]

Be an MR!

Visit the GfK Audits & Surveys Web site at www. gfkauditsandsurveys.com and write a brief report about the firm's audit services. How can you make use of retail audit data to determine new store locations for Paul Stuart Custom Jewelers?

Be a DM!

As the marketing chief for Paul Stuart Custom Jewelers, how would you determine the best store locations?

Industry Services

industry services
Secondary data derived from industrial firms and organizational sources and intended for industrial or institutional use.

Industry services provide syndicated data about industrial firms, businesses, and other institutions. Financial, operating, and employment data also are collected by these syndicated research services for almost every North American Industry Classification System (NAICS) category. These data are collected by making direct inquiries from clipping services that monitor newspapers, the trade press, or broadcasts, and from corporate reports. The range and sources of syndicated data available for industrial goods firms are more limited than those available to consumer goods firms. D&B can provide reports of businesses located in the United States and abroad.

The D&B International Business Locator (www.dnb.com) provides one-click access to more than 35 million public/private companies located around the world. After locating a business, the Locator will provide key business data, including full address information, NAIC/line of business details, business size (sales, net worth, employees), names of key principals, and identification of this location's headquarters, domestic parent company, and/or global parent company.

These data are very useful in developing business-to-business sales plans and direct-marketing lists, estimating market potential and share within industries, and devising overall marketing strategies. Business statistics related to annual sales, geographic coverage, supplier relationships, and distribution channels are just a few of the categories of information available to business-to-business market planners. These secondary sources also serve as a source for sampling frames when conducting business-to-business research.

USES OF INDUSTRY SERVICES   Information provided by industrial services is useful for sales management decisions, including identifying prospects, defining territories, setting quotas, and measuring market potential by geographic areas. It can also aid in advertising decisions, such as targeting prospects, allocating advertising budgets, selecting media, and measuring advertising effectiveness. This kind of information also is useful for segmenting the market and designing custom products and services for segments in the target markets.

ADVANTAGES AND DISADVANTAGES OF INDUSTRY SERVICES   Published industrial information provides a valuable first step in business-to-business marketing. The information is typically limited to publicly traded firms, however, and dissemination of that data is typically controlled by the reporting firm itself. A researcher has to be wary of the completeness of reported data as well as the bias introduced by this form of respondent self-report. These data are limited in the nature, content, quantity, and quality of information.

Combining Information from a Variety of Sources: Single-Source Data

As discussed in Chapter 4, combining data from different sources can enhance the value of secondary data. This practice in syndicated services is referred to as *single-source research*. Single-source research tracks the full marketing process from initial advertising communication through product purchase. The process links a person's demographic and psychographic information with television, reading, and shopping habits. A combination of surveys, diaries, and electronic scanners is used to integrate such information. Manufacturer pricing and promotional activities are overlaid on this consumer data as well. Thus, **single-source data** provide integrated information on household variables, such as media consumption and purchases, and on marketing variables, such as product sales, price, advertising, promotion, and in-store marketing effort.

> **single-source data**
> An effort to combine data from different sources by gathering integrated information on household and marketing variables applicable to the same set of respondents.

Information Resources, Inc. collects consumer purchase information from a nationally representative household panel of approximately 70,000 recruited households with coverage at the regional, national, and individual market level. It is designed to supply strategic direction to marketers by focusing on the consumer dynamics that drive brand and category performance. Complete multi-outlet purchase information on these households is tracked electronically. Panel households use a simple in-home scanning device, called a ScanKey, to record their purchases from all outlets. Panelists are not required to record any causal information except for manufacturer coupons. Price reductions are recorded by scanner, and features and displays are captured by Information Resources' in-store personnel, ensuring an accurate and unbiased record of sales. In the United States, other examples of single-source data include CACI Marketing Systems (www.caci.com), MRI Cable Report by Mediamark Research (www.mediamark.com), and PRIZM by Claritas (www.claritas.com). The MRI cable report integrates information on cable television with demographic and product usage information. PRIZM, discussed in Chapter 4, combines census data, consumer surveys about shopping and lifestyles, and purchase data to identify segments. The following example illustrates Campbell Soup Company's application of single-source data.

Research in Action

Soaps Shed a "Guiding Light" on V8 Consumption

CBS's *Guiding Light* celebrated its 71st anniversary on January 25, 2008, making it the longest running American TV drama ever broadcast. In 2008, both *Guiding Light* and ABC's *General Hospital* were popular in terms of overall soap opera viewership (www. soapzone.com).

The Campbell Soup Company (www.campbell.com) used single-source data to target its advertising for V8 juice (www.v8juice.com). By obtaining single-source data on product consumption, media consumption, and demographic characteristics, Campbell found that demographically similar TV audiences consume vastly different amounts of V8. For example, on an index where 100 was the average household's V8 consumption, *General Hospital* viewers had a below-average index of 80 index, whereas *Guiding Light* viewers had an above-average index of 120. These results were surprising, because the *General Hospital* audience actually had a slightly higher percentage of women 25 to 54 years old, the demographic group most predisposed to buy V8, and so would have been expected to be a better medium to reach V8 drinkers. Using this information, Campbell rearranged its advertising schedule to raise the average index by allocating more advertising to *Guiding Light* and other TV programs that had an above-average index and reducing the allocations to TV programs with below average values of the index. As of

2008, the V8 (www.v8juice.com) line consisted of V8 100% Vegetable Juice, V8 Splash juice drinks, and V8 V-Fusion, a blend of vegetable and fruit juice.[9]

Summary Illustration Using the Opening Vignette

Syndicated research firms specialize in designing research systems that collect data of commercial interest to multiple users. This was seen in the opening vignette, where the results of the NPD survey were used by multiple firms in the same industry: Haggar and Levi Strauss.

Syndicated sources can be classified based on the unit of measurement (households/ consumers or institutions). Syndicated data from households can be obtained via surveys, purchase or media panels, or electronic scanner systems. Although a survey was used in the opening vignette, data on purchases of business casual clothing can also be collected using purchase panels and electronic scanners (or similar systems) installed in department stores. When institutions are the unit of measurement, the data can be obtained from retailers, wholesalers, or industrial firms. It is desirable to combine information obtained from different secondary sources to get a more complete picture of the marketplace. Thus, one could combine data on casual clothing obtained from American consumers with data from retailers (e.g., Macy's, Sears, etc.) and manufacturers (e.g., Haggar, Levi Strauss, etc.) to get a better understanding of the casual clothing market. Figure 5.7 offers a concept map for syndicated data.

Experiential Learning

Syndicated Firms

Identify and describe syndicated firms, other than those listed in this chapter, that offer the following services. Briefly describe each service. Cite all URLs and references.

a. Lifestyle surveys

b. Advertising evaluation surveys

c. Omnibus panels

d. Purchase panels

e. Media panels

f. Scanner data (volume tracking)

g. Scanner panels

h. Audits

i. Information on business firms

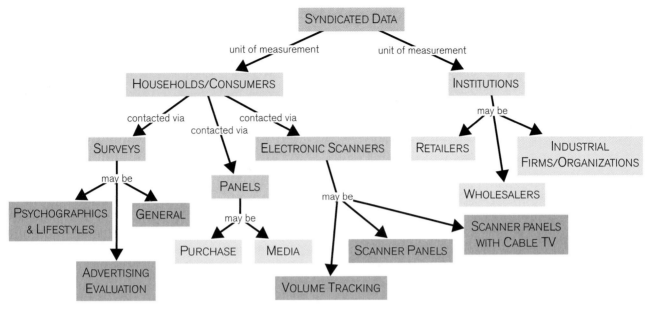

FIGURE 5.7

A Concept Map for Syndicated Data

International Market Research

U.S. syndicated research firms are an important source of information on overseas consumer and industrial markets. For companies considering expansion internationally or managing existing international ventures, one of the first steps toward understanding and monitoring these markets can be through syndicated sources. The need for relatively inexpensive, comprehensive data related to international markets, consumer and social trends, as well as existing market structures creates a built-in demand for international syndicated services. Many of the same major syndicated firms operating in the United States have invested heavily in creating data collection systems to support their internationally operating clients. Gallup International is just one of the U.S. syndicated firms that have expanded their services to include international research.

Research in Action

Euroconsumers Go for Spending Splash

Gallup (www.gallup.com), which specializes in survey research obtaining both lifestyle and psychographic data, recently conducted interviews with more than 22,500 adults across the European Union. The results point to an exploding consumer durable market, particularly for convenience items, such as remote control TVs, microwave ovens, VCRs, and cellular phones. The educational level and the standard of living among this consumer group are generally improving. Europeans also are displaying higher levels of discretionary purchasing, demonstrated in growing demand for travel packages, which continued to be strong through the year 2008. In the personal care market, the number of European women using perfume is declining, offset by growing demand for deodorants.

Such syndicated data are useful to U.S. marketers such as Motorola, GE, and AT&T, which are looking to further develop European markets. For example, when renting an apartment in Germany, the renter must install all the major appliances and lighting fixtures. GE has developed value packages offering significant savings on appliances and lighting fixtures that are carefully targeted at apartment renters.[10]

Like Gallup, ACNielsen has made huge investments in European markets over the past 30-plus years, introducing scanner and tracking services at the retail level. With international operations almost as large as those of the United States, more than 45 percent of Nielsen's business is outside the United States. Of that overseas business, 50 percent is in Europe.

Technology and Marketing Research

As technology develops, syndicated firms will establish newer types of panels using sophisticated data collection methods. One distinct possibility in the near future is panels based on two-way TV and on interactive TV and video services. In fact, such technology has been developed and is being refined and tested.

The U.S. wireless companies AT&T (www.att.com) and Verizon (www.verizon.com) have already conducted market trials of their interactive video service and made such services available to consumers. American marketers that participated in the testing and launching of these services included Lands' End, Nordstrom, J.C. Penney, Nissan Motor Cars USA, and Visa International. Verizon Video Services spokesman told marketing researchers to be prepared, because interactive TV will be here much sooner than people expect. "The leaders will establish themselves very fast," he said. "The rest will have trouble ever catching up."[11]

In addition, technology used in existing panels, such as scanner and media panels, is being continuously refined. Both Nielsen and its main competitor, Arbitron, have developed new "passive peoplemeters." With this type of system, the viewers only need to turn their televisions on or off. Using computer-image recognition technology, which is a more advanced version of the scanner technology used in supermarkets, the passive peoplemeter scans the room to identify all preprogrammed viewers. The new system also detects whether the viewers are looking at the television or at something else in the room.

The new passive systems allow researchers to monitor families at a much cheaper rate than possible with the previous technology. With the older meters, it cost thousands of dollars to monitor a single family. The new technology is expected to decrease this cost to somewhere in the hundreds of dollars. With this dramatic reduction in the average cost per household, researchers are able to increase the size of the samples, and hence the accuracy of the data, while keeping overall costs at a constant level.[12]

Ethics in Marketing Research

Ethical issues in formulating a research design, which were discussed in Chapter 3, also are relevant in collecting syndicated data. Respondents' rights, particularly their privacy, are another salient issue. In many countries, obtaining data from respondents without their full knowledge or consent is an invasion of privacy. Consider, for example, the frequent shopper cards issued by supermarkets such as Sainsbury in the United Kingdom and Kroger in the United States. These cards provide a variety of services, such as check cashing identification, special notification of sales, and cash discounts or rebates, at no apparent cost to the cardholders. Although this might sound like a good deal, many cardholders are unaware of the hidden costs involved.

When applying for a card, each shopper provides data on demographic and shopping-related variables and is assigned a UPC code. The shopper's card, which contains the UPC code, is scanned before the grocery purchases are scanned. Thus, a shopper's purchases are linked to that shopper's demographic and shopping-related data collected at the time of card application. This information results in a database that contains rich information on shoppers, including a demographic profile, when they shop, how much they spend, how they pay for purchases, and what products they buy. As discussed in Chapter 4, this database can be used to target consumers and formulate effective marketing strategies. Often, these data are sold to syndicated firms, who in turn sell them to multiple clients, resulting in much wider dissemination and use. Most consumers, however, are unaware that the supermarket has all this information about them simply because they are cardholders.

The supermarkets and other firms engaging in this practice of collecting data without the respondent's direct knowledge or consent are violating the ethical principle of informed consent. According to this principle, researchers have the ethical responsibility to avoid both uninformed and misinformed participation by respondents in market research projects. On a positive note, syndicated firms are playing a significant role in researching ethical issues and sensitizing marketing firms, the marketing research industry, and the general public about these concerns.

Research in Action

Reaching Kids but Alienating Adults: Ethical Repercussions

According to a recent survey in the United States by GfK Roper Public Affairs & Media, a syndicated marketing division of GfK Custom Research North America (www.gfkamerica.com), the general public is skeptical about advertising aimed at children. Eight of 10 adults agree that business marketing and advertising exploit children by convincing them to buy things that are bad for them or that they do not need.

Adults do not necessarily object to all advertising, only to that they perceive to be harmful to children. Eight of 10 adults say it is "all right" to advertise products such as toys, cereal, and clothing on television during children's programming. American adults are more likely to object to commercials that "sell" sex and poor nutrition, such as PG-13 movies and candy bars. Thus, marketers who engage in such practices in an attempt to reach children run the risk of alienating adults. Several syndicated firms, including GfK Roper Public Affairs & Media, are playing a significant role in addressing ethical issues in marketing research by sensitizing researchers, clients, and the general public to such issues and providing reasonable solutions.[13]

What Would *You* Do?

Boston Market: Sizing the Market

The Situation

Richard Arras, president and CEO of Boston Market (www.bostonmarket.com), a U.S. chain of casual restaurants, is well aware of the fact that according to syndicated data home meal replacement (HMR) will be the family dining business of the century. HMR is portable, high-quality food that is meant for take-out, and it is the fastest growing and most significant opportunity in the food industry today. According to ACNielsen's consumer panel data, 55 percent of respondents purchased a meal for at-home consumption several times a month. Convenience and type of food were the two most influential factors when purchasing an HMR. Also, 77 percent of these respondents preferred their meals be ready to eat.

Another recent study by the NPD Group (www.npd.com) projected that between 2005 and 2010, virtually all growth in food sales will come from food service, defined as food prepared at least partially away from home. Estimates of total HMR market size, as well as future potential, vary widely. Numbers ranging from $50 billion to $150 billion have been given for the year 2010. Sara Lee projections show HMR accounting for as much as 80 percent of food industry growth by 2010. Findings by McKinsey & Company support that premise from two perspectives: (1) the fact that virtually all foods sales growth by the year 2010 will come from food service and (2) that by 2010 many Americans will never have cooked a meal from scratch. HMR is the most important trend to hit the food industry since the advent of frozen food.

Boston Market is now the HMR leader. As of August 2008, Boston Market had about 600 locations in 28 states, with more than 13,000 employees. Richard Arras wants to capitalize on the HMR trend. Boston Market is testing new HMR products that could be introduced in 2008. The products being tested include prepackaged "take-and-go" lunch boxes, expanded catering services, enhanced drive-through operations, and call-ahead pick-up services.

The Marketing Research Decision

1. Given the wide estimates of $50 billion to $150 billion for HMR potential sales for 2010, how can Boston Market get a more reasonable estimate? What sources of syndicated data should be consulted? (Check all that apply.)
   a. Information Resources, Inc.
   b. ACNielsen
   c. McKinsey & Company
   d. NPD Group
   e. All of the above

2. How will the type of research you recommend enable Richard Arras to size the HMR market and determine what new products and services Boston Market should introduce?

The Marketing Management Decision

1. What new products and services should Richard Arras introduce? (Check all that apply.)
   a. Opening of new restaurant concepts
   b. Expanded catering services
   c. Enhanced drive-through operations
   d. Launching of a new advertising campaign
   e. All of the above

2. Discuss how the marketing management-decision action that you recommend to Richard Arras is influenced by the syndicated sources of data that you suggested earlier and by the information they provide.

What Richard Arras Did

Boston Market worked with Arnold Worldwide of Boston to produce a new advertising campaign. In an effort to energize its brand, Boston Market reminded consumers that the restaurant fulfills their need for quick, convenient, wholesome meals. Portraying real-life, recognizable situations Americans often encounter concerning dinner, the tagline was "We're Always Cooking," which was later replaced by "Time for something good."[14]

Summary

Syndicated research firms specialize in designing research systems that collect data of commercial interest to multiple users. Collecting data to serve a known commercial purpose is one of the primary differentiators when comparing syndicated services to other types of secondary data (discussed in Chapter 4). Syndicated data are timely and cost-effective. Given the need for an impartial monitor of market-wide trends, as well as consumer reactions or behaviors, syndicated researchers provide a unique and valuable service.

Syndicated sources can be classified based on the unit of measurement (households/consumers or institutions). Syndicated data from households can be obtained via surveys, purchase or media panels, or electronic scanner systems. When institutions are the unit of measurement, the data can be obtained from retailers, wholesalers, or industrial firms. It is desirable to combine information from different sources, resulting in single-source data.

U.S. syndicated research firms are an important source of information on overseas consumer and industrial markets. As technology develops, syndicated firms will establish newer types of panels that collect data from panel members using sophisticated methods. One distinct possibility in the near future is panels based on two-way television and interactive television and video services. A major ethical issue in collecting syndicated data is the invasion of privacy of the respondents by obtaining data without their full knowledge or consent.

Key Terms and Concepts

Syndicated sources, 154
Periodic surveys, 155
Panel surveys, 155
Shared surveys, 157
Psychographics, 157

Lifestyle, 157
Purchase panels, 160
Media panels, 160
Scanner data, 162
Volume-tracking data, 162

Scanner panels, 163
Scanner panels with cable TV, 163
Audit, 165
Industry services, 166
Single-source data, 167

Suggested Cases and Video Cases

Running Case with Real Data

1.1 Hewlett-Packard

Comprehensive Critical Thinking Cases

2.1 American Idol   2.2 Baskin-Robbins   2.3 Akron Children's Hospital

Comprehensive Cases with Real Data

3.1 Bank of America   3.2 McDonald's   3.3 Boeing

Video Cases

5.1 eGO   8.1 AFLAC   9.1 P&G   11.1 Dunkin' Donuts
12.1 Motorola   13.1 Subaru   19.1 Marriott

Live Research: Conducting a Marketing Research Project

1. Visit the Web sites of syndicated firms to identify the relevant information, some of which can be obtained without cost.
2. If the project is supported by a budget, then relevant information can be purchased from syndicated sources.
3. One, a few, or all the teams can be assigned the responsibility of collecting and analyzing data from the Internet.
4. Encourage the students to visit relevant Web sites of the client and its competitors as well to conduct a thorough online search using search engines.

Acronym

The salient characteristics of syndicated data may be described by the acronym SYNDICATED:

S urveys

Y ields data of known commercial value

N umber of clients use the data

D iary panels

I nstitutional services

C ost is low

A udits

T imely and current

E lectronic scanner services

D ata combined from different sources: single-source data

Review Questions

1. How do syndicated data and data available from other secondary sources differ?
2. List and describe the various syndicated sources of secondary data.
3. What is the nature of information collected by surveys?
4. How can surveys be classified?
5. Explain what a panel is. How do purchase panels and media panels differ?
6. What are the relative advantages of purchase panels over surveys?
7. What kinds of data can be gathered through electronic scanner services?
8. Describe the uses of scanner data.
9. What is an audit? Discuss the uses, advantages, and disadvantages of audits.
10. Describe the information provided by industrial services.
11. Why is it desirable to use multiple sources of secondary data?
12. Explain what is meant by single-source data.

Applied Problems

1. Visit www.npd.com and write a description of the panel maintained by NPD.
2. Visit www.acnielsen.com and write a report about the various services offered by ACNielsen.
3. Visit www.infores.com and write a report about the products and services offered by Information Resources, Inc.
4. Visit www.gallup.com and write a report about Gallup's syndicated services.
5. Visit www.arbitron.com and write a report about Arbitron's syndicated services.
6. Select an industry of your choice. Contact one of the syndicated firms to obtain industry sales and the sales of the major firms in that industry for the past year. Estimate the market shares of each major firm. From a published source, obtain information on the market shares of these same firms. Do the two estimates agree?

Group Discussion

Discuss how the Nielsen TV ratings can affect the price that advertisers pay for a commercial broadcast during a particular time.

Hewlett-Packard Running Case

Review the Hewlett-Packard (HP) case, Case 1.1, and questionnaire given toward the end of the book. Answer the following questions.

1. What information available from syndicated firms would be useful to HP as it seeks to increase its penetration of U.S. households?
2. How can HP make use of lifestyle information available from syndicated services?
3. What information is available on consumer technology usage from syndicated firms? How can HP make use of this information? Hint: Visit www.npd.com, and under "Industries" select "Consumer Technology."
4. What information available from www.netratings.com can help HP evaluate the effectiveness of its Web site?

eGO: Reinventing Wheels

eGO Vehicles (www.egovehicles.com), based in Cambridge, Massachusetts, was founded in 1999 by its current president and CEO, Andrew Kallfelz. It produces light, electric vehicles and claims to be the leading manufacturer of "fun, easy-to-ride, eco-friendly personal transportation." eGO cycles do not require gas or oil and produce zero emissions. They run entirely on electricity and have a range of 20 to 25 miles while traveling at 20 to 25 miles per hour. The company is constantly monitoring market condition to find opportunities to expand globally, for example, shifting its production site from the United States to Taiwan.

Based on marketing research in the form of focus groups, surveys, and personal observations, the eGO cycle was conceptualized to perform almost any errand one can think of. Although the concept seemed promising, taking the product from the design to the marketplace presented several challenges and hurdles. The first challenge was the design of the cycle. The team at eGO was very particular about the cycle not having a motorcycle-like look and feel. In addition, the team did not want the technology and the engine to be visible. Andrew Kallfelz described the designing goal as "Make it almost like a magic carpet." The cycles are distinctive looking. The designers sought such distinctiveness. They did not want people to think, "Oh, a motorcycle" (bad for the environment), or "Oh, a bike" (you have to pedal). The idea was to have a mode of transportation to make small trips without using three tons of steel to do it. After a year and a half of product

testing, the eGO cycle gained the approval of the National Highway and Transportation Safety Agency. With this approval, eGO was able to register the cycle in every state.

The eGO is a new and different concept and its looks should—and do—reflect that. This specific niche provides eGO with its greatest strength and its greatest challenge. Although consumers might want the product, no distribution channels were available. Bike stores did not want a nonbike product taking up floor space, and motorcycle shops did not want a bicycle in their stores.

The solution to this problem was found through marketing research. eGO needed to find how to distribute the product and with whom to distribute the

product through. Marketing research showed that customers wanted to test the cycle even though it was unavailable in many stores. eGO responded by bringing the bikes to football games, shows, and events for people to test drive. In addition, research showed that articles in trade journals and appearances on popular television shows would help customers become more familiar with the product without actually seeing it first hand. eGO's bikes have appeared in *Time* and on TV programs such as *Good Morning America* and the *Today Show*. eGO believes these appearances provide customers with the assurance they need to pay $1,400 on their credit cards to a Web site to buy a product they have never seen. A survey of existing eGO owners revealed that the vehicle is used for commuting, recreation, business, and errands. Finally, research showed these products would also be successful in markets where golf carts are already used for transportation and in resort areas for rentals.

The team at eGO found, to great pleasure, that the cycle was an instant hit, turning heads and fast becoming the topic of hot discussion—in effect marketing itself. Jim Hamman, founder and vice president of marketing and sales, recounts " . . . it (eGO cycle) would create a discussion everywhere you went. People would be talking out of their cars to you at a stop sign and ask where did you get that? How does it work? How much is it? It created such a buzz that there was certainly something there." Strong customer reaction led to strong demand, and in a short span of 2 years eGO grew its orders from zero to hundreds of products shipped globally each month.

The eGO Cycle2, already in its second version, is eGO's core product. It comes in three models; features vary based on local requirements and marketing research. For instance, three options are available in the U.S. market: the eGo Cycle 2 classic, SE, and LX. For the European marketplace, the brand name was changed to Helios and three different models are available. The price for an eGO Cycle ranges from $1,399 to $1,999. The price is determined by the model and the country of purchase by applying product and geographic price segmentation. The pricing strategy takes into account not only product costs, but also consumer price sensitivity (elasticity of demand) based on marketing research.

The eGO's energy costs do not exceed half a cent per mile. Warranties are provided for the battery (6 months), the chassis (10 years), and all other parts for up to one year. Furthermore, customers are able to individualize their eGO Cycle. Across all models one can customize the cycle and choose from four colors upon request. This customization strategy was adopted after marketing research revealed strong desire of consumers to have a role in configuring the cycle. eGO also offers additional accessories, such as eGO clothing.

With no established marketing or distribution model to follow, eGO had to develop its own model and perfect it as it went along, learning from experience and feedback. The direct marketing and direct distribution model has been the mainstay of eGO's marketing and distribution process, although it is slow and time-consuming and requires a lot of creativity. The eGO Cycle is sold by authorized dealers, and accessories can be purchased online. In cases where there is no authorized dealer available in non–U.S. markets, eGO provides shipping as an exception. In North America, distributors are only found in the United States, but plans for Canadian dealers are in the works. The expansion into the Asia-Pacific (APAC) region only covers Japan, Korea, Taiwan, and Australia. Since 2004, contract dealers have sold eGO cycles in seven European countries, including the Czech Republic, Germany, and the United Kingdom.

Referring to the Electric Bikes Worldwide Reports (2007) the eGO Vehicles Company is on the right track and is likely to succeed and cope with future challenges. This is certainly due to the company's ability to quickly adapt and sense consumer needs as determined by marketing research. First, eGO Vehicle produces a core model of electric bike that can comply with local restrictions as well as local consumer tastes. Second, the manufacturing site has been relocated to Taiwan, where industry concentration takes place. Thus, various location advantages can be exploited because the environment enforces innovation, knowledge and expertise as well as cheaper production costs.

Conclusion

The case presents an engaging example of marketing a new, innovative, and in some ways, unconventional, product. The case demonstrates how the marketing effort at eGO overcame challenges such as lack of established media to reach customers and novelty of the product to develop eGO's brand equity and establish its brand image. Strategies and initiatives such as marketing research, customer feedback, direct marketing, and online sales are exemplary for any small startup trying to establish a strong market image for its product or service.

Questions

1. eGO would like to increase its U.S. sales. Define the management-decision problem.
2. Define the marketing research problem corresponding to the management-decision problem you identified.
3. What type of research design do you think the company adopted in conducting marketing research to determine consumer preferences for eGO vehicles?
4. Can eGO make use of a panel? If so, what type of a panel for what purpose?
5. How would you use the Internet to determine men's preferences for electric vehicles?
6. What sources of syndicated data would be useful to eGO in projecting future demand for its vehicles?

References

1. www.egovehicles.com, accessed on April 8, 2007.
2. eGo Vehicles, "Consumer Purchase Criteria for Personal Electric Vehicles," http://egovehicles.com/fileadmin/user_upload/PDFs/technical_note_60.pdf, accessed on April 8, 2007.
3. F. E. Jamerson and E. Benjamin, "Electric Bikes Worldwide Reports, 8th edition," www.ebwr.com, accessed on May 8, 2007.

Exploratory Research Design: Qualitative Research

OPENING QUESTIONS

1. How is qualitative research different from quantitative research in terms of the objectives, sampling methods, data collection methods, data analysis, and outcomes?

2. What are the various forms of qualitative research?

3. How are focus groups conducted?

4. How are focus groups used, and what are their advantages and disadvantages?

5. How do depth interviews differ from focus groups?

6. What are the applications of depth interviews, what are their advantages and disadvantages?

7. What are projective techniques, and how are they used?

8. How does conducting qualitative research in an international setting differ from research conducted domestically?

9. What is the role of technology in qualitative research, and what qualitative research software is available?

10. What ethical issues are involved in conducting qualitative research?

Gillette Supports Equal Rights for Women: A Close Shave

> "I have degrees in mathematics, but have become an enthusiastic user of qualitative research because of the rich insights I have gained with well done qualitative research."
>
> *Mary Klupp,*
> *Director, Ford Credit Global*
> *Consumer Insights,*
> *Ford Motor Company.*

In 2003, Global Gillette, a division of the American consumer-products company Procter & Gamble, successfully introduced the Venus Embrace in 2008. The new product idea was inspired by the successful introduction of Sensor for Women earlier.

How was Sensor for Women developed? After being given the job of redesigning Gillette's feminine razor, Jill Shurtleff relied heavily on qualitative research. She used one-on-one or individual depth interviews with 30 women she chose based on her own judgment from different segments of the potential target market. Individual depth interviews were selected over focus groups because shaving is a rather personal experience for women. This technique allowed for extensive probing of the respondent's feelings in a more personal setting and thus provided deeper insights into the shaving experience.

The depth interviews showed that women shave very differently from men. The American woman shaves much more surface area than a man but only shaves two or three times per week. She changes the blade about once a month. Whereas men usually shave in front of a well-lit mirror, women generally prefer to shave in the shower, which is often dimly lit, and they must shave areas that they cannot see well, such as their underarms and the backs of their legs. The research indicated

that shaving was a personal experience for women that evoked feelings of anticipation and acceptance.

The research also showed that most women did not like so-called women's razors and opted instead for men's razors or cheap disposables. Women preferred razors with a firm grip and those that gave a clean, smooth shave. Typically, men's razors have a much sharper blade than women's. Although a woman was more likely to nick herself with a man's razor, the shaving quality with a man's razor was better than traditional women's razors. These findings were substantiated in a survey of women using in-home personal interviews. A representative sample of 500 women was selected for this purpose.

With information on the current state of affairs under her belt, Shurtleff began her product design. She first tossed out the T-shaped design used for men's razors, which gives men the sensitive control they need but puts women at risk due to shifting blade angles.

Shurtleff settled on a wafer-like design for the handle, white with an aqua insert in the center. The colors were different from the typical pink for women's razors and evoked a clean, watery feeling. The aqua insert was clear plastic and had wavy ridges to help prevent slippage. The razor head was nearly the same as that used by the Sensor (men's razor) and was angled at 46 degrees, a compromise between the ideal underarm and leg-shaving angles.

The finishing touch was the name. The name Lady Sensor was declined because it seemed condescending and many women did not like it. The company settled on the name Sensor for Women, because it seemed straightforward, honest, and elicited the most favorable response in a word-association test examining several possible names.

Shurtleff used qualitative research helped to develop a successful product. The Sensor for Women quickly and easily displaced the market leader, Schick's Personal Touch, and garnered 60 percent of the market share. Moreover, Sensor for Women provided a strong launching pad for the Venus line. When qualitative research in the form of focus groups and depth interviews revealed that women wanted the convenience of a shave gel and razor combined in a single system, and quantitative research estimated a definite demand for such a product, in 2007 Gillette introduced a new two-in-one razor and shave gel bars. In 2007, Gillette was marketing the New Venus Breeze as the "only razor with built-in shaving gel bars. Just wet and shave." The new system has been a tremendous success. For the fiscal fourth quarter ended June 30, 2007, the U.S. all-outlet value share for Venus razors was up more than 8 points to 27 percent for the quarter. Sales from Gillette's women's products increased to more than $1 billion dollars by the year 2008.

Overview

In Chapter 3, marketing research was classified as exploratory or conclusive. Secondary data analysis, discussed in Chapters 4 and 5, is one aspect of exploratory research. The other major exploratory technique, qualitative research, is the subject of this chapter. Figure 6.1 presents the focus of the chapter, the relation of this chapter to the previous ones, and the steps of the marketing research process on which this chapter concentrates. As demonstrated in Figure 6.1, qualitative research is part of the marketing research process presented in Chapter 1, is one of the tasks involved in problem definition and development of an approach covered in Chapter 2, and is one of the exploratory research design techniques discussed in Chapter 3.

Often, qualitative research follows a review of internal and external sources of secondary data. It is typically used to define the problem more precisely, to formulate hypotheses, or to identify or clarify key variables to be investigated in the quantitative phase. The opening vignette illustrated this. The findings of depth interviews regarding how women shaved were further investigated by conducting an in-home personal survey (quantitative research).

FIGURE 6.1

Relationship of Qualitative Research to the Previous Chapters and the Marketing Research Process

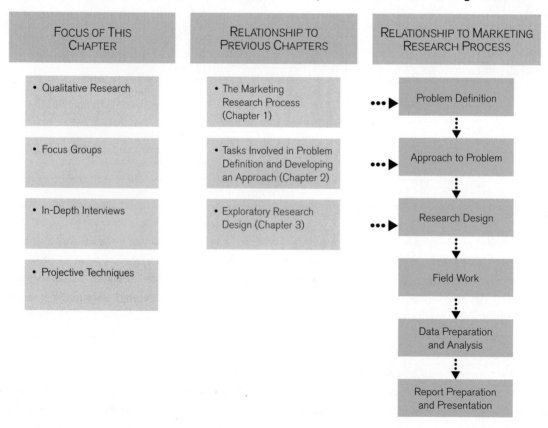

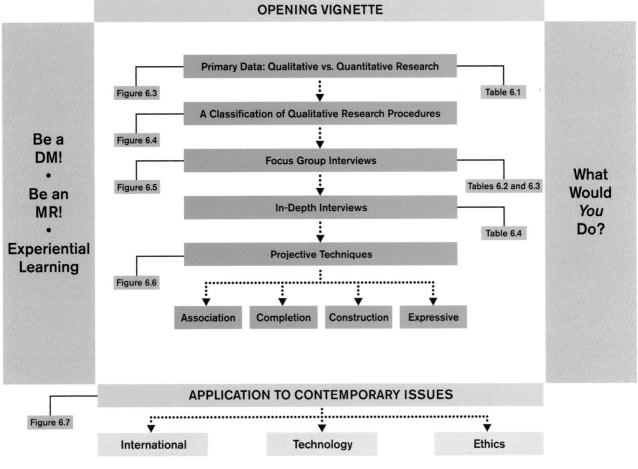

FIGURE 6.2

Qualitative Research: An Overview

Unlike secondary data, which are generated for purposes other than the specific marketing research problem at hand, qualitative research generates primary data. The definition of the marketing research problem guides qualitative data collection.

This chapter presents the differences between qualitative and quantitative research and the role of each in the marketing research project. We provide a classification of qualitative research techniques, as well as an overview of the major qualitative techniques used in the industry. These techniques include focus groups, depth interviews with individuals, and projective techniques. The chapter then moves to discussion of the application of qualitative research in international marketing research, the impact of technology, and ethical issues. Figure 6.2 offers an overview of the topics discussed in this chapter and how they flow from one to the next.

Primary Data: Qualitative Versus Quantitative Research

Even though qualitative research is exploratory in nature, it results in primary data because the research is carried out for the specific purpose of addressing the problem at hand. Therefore, both qualitative and quantitative research can generate primary data, as shown in Figure 6.3. The distinction between qualitative and quantitative research closely parallels the distinction between exploratory and conclusive research discussed in Chapter 3 (see Table 3.1). The differences between the two research methodologies are summarized in Table 6.1. Note that Table 6.1 is similar to Table 3.1.

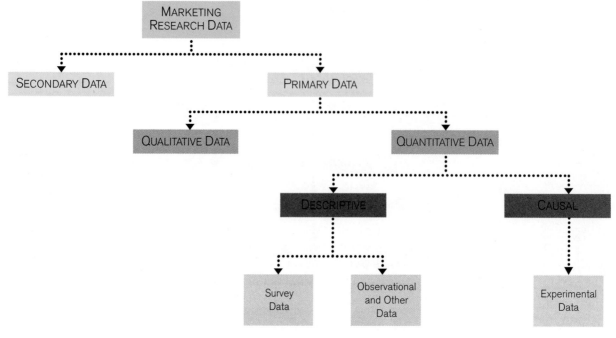

FIGURE 6.3

A Classification of Marketing Research Data

qualitative research
An unstructured, exploratory research methodology based on small samples that provides insights and understanding of the problem setting.

quantitative research
A research methodology that seeks to quantify the data and typically applies some form of statistical analysis.

Qualitative research provides insight into and understanding of the problem setting. It explores the problem with few preconceived notions about the outcome of that exploration. In addition to defining the problem and developing an approach, qualitative research also is appropriate when facing a situation of uncertainty, such as when conclusive results differ from expectations. It can provide insight before or after the fact. In the opening vignette, Gillette used qualitative research at the beginning of the project to better understand women's shaving needs. Qualitative research is based on small, nonrepresentative samples, and the data are analyzed in a nonstatistical way. For depth interviews in the Gillette vignette, the researcher chose a sample size of 30 women selected judgmentally from various segments of the target market.

In contrast, **quantitative research** seeks to quantify the data. It seeks conclusive evidence based on large, representative samples and typically involving some form of statistical analysis. In contrast to qualitative research, the findings of quantitative

TABLE 6.1 Qualitative Versus Quantitative Research

	Qualitative Research	Quantitative Research
Objective	To gain a qualitative understanding of the underlying reasons and motivations	To quantify the data and generalize the results from the sample to the population of interest
Sample	Small number of nonrepresentative cases	Large number of representative cases
Data collection	Unstructured	Structured
Data analysis	Nonstatistical	Statistical
Outcome	Develop a richer understanding	Recommend a final course of action

research can be treated as conclusive and used to recommend a final course of action. In the opening vignette, Gillette used quantitative (survey) research based on a representative sample of 500 women to substantiate the findings of qualitative research (depth interviews).

The approach to data collection can vary along a continuum from highly structured to completely unstructured. In a highly structured approach, the researcher predetermines the wording of the questions asked and the range of responses available. Thus, the researcher assumes full understanding of the range of possible response options. A multiple-choice question is an example of a highly structured question. Typically, a formal questionnaire is used. This is in contrast to an unstructured data collection approach in which neither the questions nor the possible responses are predetermined. The respondent is encouraged to talk freely about the subject of interest. Qualitative or exploratory research lies at the unstructured end of this continuum, whereas quantitative research is highly structured.

Whenever a new marketing research problem is addressed, quantitative research must be preceded by appropriate qualitative research, as Gillette did. Sometimes qualitative research is undertaken to explain the findings obtained from quantitative research. The findings of qualitative research are misused, however, when they are regarded as conclusive and are used to make generalizations to the population of interest. For example, if 20 of the 30 women in the depth interviews said they preferred men's razors to women's razors, it would not be appropriate to conclude that 66.7 percent of the women in the general population have the same preference. Quantitative data from a large, representative sample should be collected using a survey, as in the opening vignette, if the sample results are to be projected to the population. It is a sound principle of marketing research to view qualitative and quantitative research as complementary rather than competitive parts of the research process.

The danger of ignoring qualitative research when the research problem is not fully understood and directly proceeding to quantitative research is illustrated by Coca-Cola's decision to change Coke to New Coke. The decision to change the formulation of the flagship soft-drink brand was based on extensive quantitative taste tests without the benefit of appropriate qualitative research. The results clearly indicated that consumers preferred the taste of the new formulation. However, when the change was made and New Coke replaced Coke, there was a strong consumer backlash. Coke's loyal consumers reacted because their favorite soft drink had been changed. The quantitative research conducted was misguided because it asked the wrong questions. The researchers were focusing on taste rather than the emotional attachment consumers had forged with the brand, which was actually a more significant variable guiding brand preference and loyalty than taste.

These types of mistakes can be avoided by conducting qualitative research. Had the researchers first used qualitative techniques to explore why people purchased Coke, rather than assuming they knew why, the quantitative research conducted would have been different, leading management to a different decision. This classic marketing mistake also points out that the researcher must obtain an adequate understanding of the problem situation before formulating a research design. Qualitative researchers can be located through the Qualitative Research Consultants Association (www.qrca.org), a U.S.-based nonprofit organization which is the largest body of independent qualitative research consultants in the world.

Be a DM!

As the marketing manager, what marketing strategies would you formulate in helping Nine West, an American marketer of branded apparel, footwear, and accessories, increase its penetration of the women's shoe market?

Be an MR!

Visit www.ninewest.com and search the Internet, as well as your library's online databases, to obtain information on Nine West's marketing strategy. How would you use qualitative and quantitative research in helping Nine West increase its penetration of the women's shoe market?

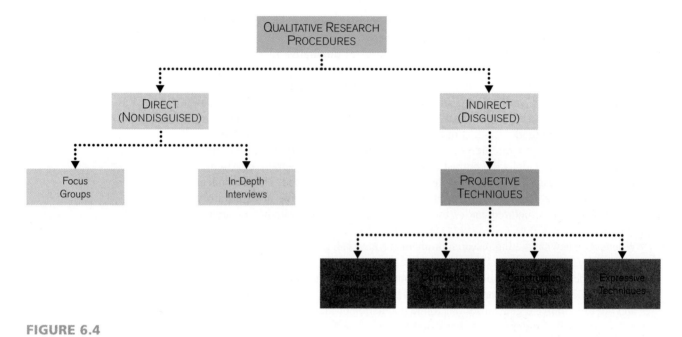

FIGURE 6.4

A Classification of Qualitative Research Procedures

A Classification of Qualitative Research Procedures

A classification of qualitative research procedures is presented in Figure 6.4. These procedures are classified as either direct or indirect, based on whether the respondents know the true purpose of the project. A **direct approach** is not disguised. The purpose of the project is disclosed to the respondents or is otherwise obvious from the questions asked. Focus groups and depth interviews are the major direct techniques. In contrast, research that takes an **indirect approach** disguises the true purpose of the project. Projective techniques are the most commonly used indirect approach. A discussion of each of these techniques follows, beginning with focus groups.

Focus-Group Interviews

A **focus group** is an interview with a small group of respondents conducted by a trained moderator who leads the discussion in a nonstructured and natural manner. The main purpose of a focus group is to gain insights on issues of interest to the researcher by listening to a group of people from the appropriate target market. The value of the technique lies in the rich findings that can be obtained from a free-flowing group discussion.

Focus groups are the most important qualitative research procedure. They are so popular that many marketing research practitioners consider this technique to be synonymous with qualitative research. Several hundred facilities around the country now conduct focus groups several times a week. The typical focus group costs the client about $4,000. Given their importance and popularity, the procedure for conducting focus groups is described in detail.

Conducting a Focus Group

The process of conducting a focus group, as with any research effort, involves careful planning. This chapter discusses considerations related to the environment for focus groups, the selection of participants, and the moderator. It also covers the development of a discussion guide, how the group interview is conducted, and the format for summarizing the results (Figure 6.5).

direct approach
A type of qualitative research in which the purposes of the project are disclosed to the respondent or are obvious given the nature of the interview.

indirect approach
A type of qualitative research in which the purposes of the project are disguised from the respondents.

focus group
An interview conducted by a trained moderator among a small group of respondents in an unstructured and natural manner.

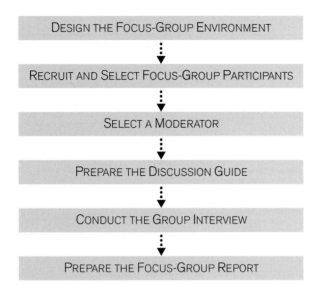

FIGURE 6.5

Procedure for Conducting a Focus Group

DESIGNING THE ENVIRONMENT Focus-group sessions typically are held in facilities specially equipped to comfortably accommodate and record a group discussion. In most instances, the setting is an informal conference room equipped with a one-way mirror and with microphones throughout the room. Behind the one-way mirror is a viewing room for management.

Most focus groups are scheduled to last 1 to 3 hours (Table 6.2). This amount of time is needed to establish rapport with the participants and to explore in depth their beliefs, feelings, ideas, attitudes, and insights regarding the topics of concern. Focus groups are either audio-recorded or videotaped to preserve the comments for analysis. Videotaping has the advantage of recording facial expressions and body movements, but it can increase the costs significantly.

Frequently, clients observe the session from an adjacent room using a one-way mirror. Clients can also use video-transmission technology to observe the focus-group session live from a remote location.

RECRUITING AND SELECTING FOCUS-GROUP PARTICIPANTS The major characteristics of a focus group are summarized in Table 6.2. A focus group usually has 8 to 12 members. The advantages that come from the group dynamics are often lost to groups larger than

Layout of the focus group room and viewing room.

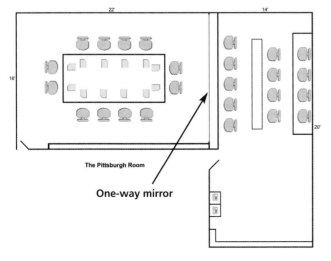

Viewing room looking into the focus group room through a one-way mirror.

TABLE 6.2 Characteristics of Focus Groups

Group size	8 to 12 participants
Group composition	Homogeneous; respondents prescreened
Physical setting	Relaxed, informal atmosphere
Time duration	1 to 3 hours
Recording	Use of audiocassettes and videotapes
Moderator	Observational, interpersonal, and communication skills of the moderator are critical

this. Smaller groups of four or five respondents might be used if the session is highly exploratory and if extensive, unstructured probing is necessary.

A focus group should be homogeneous in terms of product usage, demographics, and socioeconomic characteristics. This commonality among group members avoids interactions and conflicts on side issues. Suppose a focus group is conducted to evaluate the appeal of a line of frozen foods. It might not be desirable to include professional women and homemakers in the same group. It is clear that these two subgroups have strong differences of opinion regarding the role of women in the family. If they are included in the same group, the conversation could deviate into a discussion of the role of women in the family rather than the appeal of the frozen foods. If so, the researcher would not gain any insights relevant to the objective of assessing the product's basic appeal.

Not only should the group be homogeneous in terms of demographic and socioeconomic characteristics, group members should also have a common base of experience or involvement with the object or issue being discussed. Thus, heavy users and nonusers of the product should not be included in the same group. Finally, people who have participated in multiple focus groups become familiar with the process to the point that their responses might be biased by their exposure to the technique. These so-called professional respondents should be screened out of the group. To ensure that the focus-group respondents are homogeneous in terms of experience, demographics, and other relevant variables, potential respondents are prescreened. A questionnaire covering demographic characteristics, attitudes, product use, and experience of the respondent is typically developed and administered to potential respondents to select only those who meet the qualifications.

SELECTING A MODERATOR   The moderator plays a key role and must be well trained. General group management skills as well as a background in psychology and marketing typically suffice in most focus-group situations. The moderator must be able to establish rapport with the participants, keep the discussion moving forward, and probe the respondents to elicit insights. In addition, this individual might also play a central role in the analysis and interpretation of the data. Therefore, the moderator should possess knowledge of the discussion topic and an understanding of the nature of group dynamics in order to appropriately interpret focus-group responses. Despite the importance of the moderator, at present, no central body certifies or trains focus-group moderators. This lack of standardization in qualifications is one of the problems to be overcome in this type of research. This limitation can be minimized by preparing a detailed moderator discussion guide.

PREPARING THE DISCUSSION GUIDE   Regardless of the moderator's skills or qualifications, any focus group will flounder without an outline of the topics to be covered. The discussion guide should reflect the objectives of qualitative research. The objectives, in turn, should be derived from the definition of the marketing research problem, approach, and the research design adopted. A moderator's discussion guide can reduce some of the reliability problems inherent in focus groups, such as the lack of consistency in topics covered from group to group.

Most group discussions can be broken into three phases, the first being a preamble and introduction to establish rapport, relax the group, and describe the process. The bulk of the group session revolves around discussion of the research topic. In the closing phase, the moderator summarizes the comments and attempts to get a final read on the strength of the group's commitment to the statements made. The questions are typically kept fairly general to allow the moderator to pursue important ideas when participants mention them. To be effective, the moderator must understand the client's business, the focus-group objectives, and how the findings will be used. The following is a sample discussion guide for focus groups on purchase motivations and the buying process for pocket PCs/handheld organizers.

Research in Action

Focus-Group Discussion Guide for Pocket PCs

Preamble (5 minutes)

- Thanks and welcome
- Nature of a focus group (informal, multiway, all views acceptable, disagree)
- There are no right or wrong answers—all about finding out what people think
- Audio and video recording
- Colleagues viewing
- Help self to refreshments
- Going to be talking about pocket PCs
- Questions or concerns?

Introductions and Warm-Up (5 minutes)

I'd like to go around the room and have you introduce yourselves:

- First name
- Best thing about having a pocket PC
- Worst thing about having a pocket PC

Pocket PC Usage (15 minutes)

I'd like to understand a bit about how you typically use your pocket PC:

- How many times a day do you use it?
- What are some of the most common types of things you use it for?

Briefly Explore

- If we were to take away your pocket PC from you, what difference would that make to your life?

Briefly Explore

Past Pocket-PC Purchase (15 minutes)

Thinking now about your current pocket PC, I'd like to talk about two different things:

- How did you actually go about the process of choosing the pocket PC?
- Did you have any criteria for the pocket PC itself?

Past Pocket-PC Selection Process

- Thinking first only about *how* you went about choosing your pocket PC, *not* any features you wanted, how did you go about choosing one?

Explore Process
Past Pocket-PC Criteria

- Now tell me what you actually looked for in a pocket PC.

Explore
Usage of Pocket-PC Features (20 minutes)

- Thinking now about pocket-PC features, I'd like to start by making a list of all the features you can think of—anything the pocket PC can do, any settings you can change, etc.
- We'll talk in a minute about which features you actually use, but I want to start with a list of everything your pocket PC could do.

Flipchart

- Which features have you ever used, even if only once?

Flipchart

- Are there any settings you only changed once, but are really glad you could change?
- Why?

Explore

- Which features do you use regularly?
- Why?

Explore
Desired Features (10 minutes)

- Are there any features your pocket PC doesn't have but that you wish it did?

Explore
Motivations for Buying (20 minutes)

You've all been invited here because you own a pocket PC.

- What motivated you to buy your pocket PC?

Explore

- What do you think are some of the reasons that people would buy pocket PCs?

Explore

- What were *all* the factors involved in that decision?
- What was the single biggest reason?

Explore

Closing Exercise (10 minutes)

- Finally, I'd like your creativity for a few minutes in coming up with ideas.

- Don't worry about whether it's a good idea or a bad idea.

- The only word I'm going to ban is "free!"

- Supposing a pocket-PC manufacturer wanted to encourage you to buy tomorrow. What could they do?

- Just call out anything at all that occurs to you—obvious, profound, serious, silly, whatever.

Explore and Refine

- Thank the respondents and close the session

CONDUCTING THE GROUP INTERVIEW   During the interview, the moderator must (1) establish rapport with the group, (2) state the rules of group interaction, (3) set objectives, (4) probe the respondents and provoke intense discussion in the relevant areas, and (5) attempt to summarize the group's response to determine the extent of agreement.

The number of focus groups conducted depends on (1) the nature of the issue, (2) the number of distinct market segments, (3) the number of new ideas generated by each successive group, and (4) the time and cost. Ideally, groups should be conducted until the moderator becomes familiar enough with the range of responses and can anticipate what will be said. This usually happens after three or four groups. It is recommended that a minimum of two groups be conducted.[2]

PREPARING THE FOCUS-GROUP REPORT   Following the focus-group session, the moderator and the managers who viewed the session will often engage in an instant interpretation. This free exchange has value in that it captures the impressions of the group and might be a good source of information for additional brainstorming. The danger is that the emotional power of the group's comments can cloud important points, which may be lost unless a detailed review of the focus-group tapes is conducted. Hence, no conclusions should be drawn until either the moderator or an analyst reviews and analyzes the results and a complete report has been prepared.

Due to the small number of participants, frequencies and percentages are not usually reported in a focus-group summary. Instead, reports typically include expressions such as "most participants thought" or "participants were divided on this issue." The report should not only present the findings based on the verbal comments but should also analyze consistent responses, new ideas, and concerns suggested by facial expressions and body language. Meticulous documentation and interpretation of the session lays the groundwork for the final step, taking action. This usually means doing additional research. A topline report that gives preliminary results, usually showing responses to a few key questions, is prepared first followed by a more detailed report. We illustrate a topline report in the case involving an American shopping center called Mall of the Boondocks (the actual name has been disguised).

Research in Action

Mall of the Boondocks Focus-Group Topline

Focus-Group Objectives

The latest in a quarterly series, Mall of the Boondocks focus groups were conducted to understand shopping-mall expectations of the student segment, to determine this group's perceptions of a recent weekend visit, and to analyze the perceived brand identity of the mall based on the individual's experience.

Method and Procedures

Reactions were solicited for the Mall of the Boondocks experience from 20 student visitors (8 males and 12 females) who attended the mall on the weekend prior to the group discussion (i.e., Labor Day Weekend). Two focus groups were conducted, each with 10 respondents. A variety of ages, life stages, and previous work experience was represented within the groups. The current focus groups were conducted at Good Stuff's videoconference facility on September 17, 2007. Students were given $30 and instructed to visit the mall between September 1 and 2; however, no other instructions or explanations were given to the students. They were not aware that they would be participating in a discussion group when they visited the mall.

Summary of Findings

Mall-Visit Experience

- For entertainment, participants typically engage in movies (theater and rental), sports (spectator and participatory), drinks, or just "hanging out" with friends. They typically need only 3 or 4 hours to experience the mall and try to hold cost to under $30, except for a special occasion.

- Examples of special occasions include dinner, concerts, theater, museums, and theme malls. Most often, the theme mall is a destination like Mall of America, Universal Studios, or Sea World. Many have visited Mall of the Boondocks more than once, and a few have been Mall of the Boondocks "Crown Customers," who shop at the Mall of the Boondocks loyally.

- Visitors were pleasantly surprised and delighted with the mall's entertainment, the surprisingly short lines in the children's area, the first-class magic show, and winning a large stuffed animal.

- When asked to describe feelings surrounding the experience, most were very positive—"excited to go," "feel like a kid again," "didn't feel like I should have to go to work tomorrow," and "friendly, fun to share the experience with others in attendance." The only negatives were "tired," "hot," and "yucky."

- On the other hand, visitors were frustrated to find a lack of signage and maps, a "deserted" feeling resulting from the lack of hosts or guides, and the dry, dirty look of some areas in the mall.

- Visitors were asked to suggest necessary changes in the mall.

  - Crowds. Can be daunting, and there must be a way to make them more palatable, such as drinking fountains, benches, water misters, ceiling fans that work, or entertainment. Made comparisons to Mall of America, which respondents said had more space and better-groomed patrons.

  - Dress code. There were complaints that many people were showing a lot of skin but hardly anyone looked like Britney Spears or Ricky Martin. Who wants the bowling-alley crowd to dress this way? Several agreed there should be a "no shirt, no shoes, no service" policy.

  - Information. Booths placed in visible spots throughout the mall would be helpful. Visitors agreed that maps were very hard to find and that handing them out in line at the entrance of the mall might help.

Brand Identity Versus Mall of America
General Personality

- **Mall of the Boondocks.** Definitely male, but surprisingly, not teenaged. Middle-aged or older, a little tired, moody. Blue-collar worker, not very smart, wearing "gimme" t-shirt and cap, maybe with a beer logo (e.g., Budweiser). Drives a big old American car, may have money problems. A follower rather than a leader.

- **Mall of America.** Both female and male, perhaps that loving, indulgent aunt and uncle who shower you with experiences you don't get at home. Dressed classically in khakis and a polo shirt. Nurturing, approachable, well-rounded, and affluent. Like this person better than the Mall of the Boondocks personality because it's more fun.

Brand Value

To many, Mall of the Boondocks was described as "just a bunch of shops and rides." Other malls, such as Mall of America, encompass a complete entertainment experience. Several "long-timers" remember a time when Mall of the Boondocks included the experience of regional history and of other cultures. What made it unique in the past is gone now, as the specific areas have become less distinct and not associated with as much meaning. As a result, there was a general feeling that the value had declined.

Implications

In general, the results of this latest in the series of focus groups—focusing upon student perceptions—are similar to those from previous focus groups with nonstudents. Respondents view the Mall of the Boondocks as more of a "working person's" mall. The student respondents' perceptions of the Mall of the Boondocks were markedly more negative when compared to the Mall of the America than the perceptions of any other segment of customers included in this series of quarterly focus groups begun 2 years ago. Perhaps Mall of America's recently completed remodeling has become more salient in the minds of the Mall of the Boondocks student customers because of students' higher use of informal "buzz" (word-of-mouth). More research on this topic using a large sample survey is needed.

Advantages and Disadvantages of Focus Groups

Focus groups are popular because of their many advantages. The immediacy and the richness of the comments, which come from real customers, make this technique highly useful. The group interaction produces a wider range of information, insights, and ideas than do individual interviews. The comments of one person can trigger unexpected reactions from others, leading to snowballing with participants responding to each other's comments. The responses are generally spontaneous and candid, providing rich insights. Ideas are more likely to arise out of the blue in a group than in an individual interview and are likely to be unique and potentially creative.[3]

However, some of the qualities that make focus groups so strong also create some of their more serious limitations. The disadvantages of focus groups should not be overlooked. The clarity and conviction with which group members often speak leads to a tendency for researchers and managers to regard findings as conclusive rather than as exploratory. Focus groups also are difficult to moderate. The quality of the results depends heavily on the skills of the moderator; unfortunately, moderators who possess all of the desirable skills are rare. Further, the unstructured nature of the responses makes coding, analysis, and interpretation difficult.

Experiential Learning

Gatorade: From a Sports Drink to a Lifestyle Drink

Management at Gatorade (a division of U.S. beverage giant PepsiCo) would like to transform Gatorade from a sports drink to a lifestyle drink. Visit www.gatorade.com and search the Internet, as well as your library's online databases, to obtain information on the marketing strategy of Gatorade energy drinks.

1. Prepare a focus-group discussion guide to determine why people consume Gatorade drinks and what would lead them to consume more Gatorade.

2. Conduct a focus group of 8 to 12 students using your discussion guide.

3. Prepare a focus-group topline report for Gatorade management.

Online Focus Groups

Online focus groups are becoming increasingly popular because of their greater convenience and cost-effectiveness and faster turnaround as compared to traditional focus groups. Using Internet technologies, marketing research companies have created virtual focus-group facilities consisting of waiting rooms, focus-group rooms, and client rooms. Respondents are prerecruited, generally from an online list of people who have expressed an interest in participating. Some are recruited through e-mail lists, Web intercepts, banner ads, or traditional methods (phone or mail). A screening questionnaire is administered online to qualify the respondents. Those who qualify are invited to participate in a focus group and receive a time, a URL, a room name, and a password via e-mail. Generally, four to six people participate in the online group. An online focus group has fewer participants than a face-to-face meeting because too many respondents can cause confusion.

Before the focus group begins, participants receive information about the focus group that covers such things as how to express emotions when typing. Emotions are indicated by using keyboard characters and are standard in their use on the Internet. For example, :-) and :-(represent smiling and sad faces, respectively. The emotion indicators usually are inserted into the text at the point where the emotion is meant. Emotions can also be expressed using a different font or color. The participants can also preview information about the focus-group topic by visiting a Web site and reading information or downloading and viewing an actual TV ad on their PCs. Then, just before the focus group begins, participants visit a Web site where they log on and get some last-minute instructions.

When it is time for the group, they move into a Web-based chat room. They go to the focus-group location (a URL) and click on the "Enter Focus Room" item. To enter, they must supply the room name, user name, and password that was e-mailed to them earlier. The moderator signs on early and administers a rescreening questionnaire as the respondents enter the waiting room to verify their identities. Once in the focus-group chat room, the moderator and the participants type to each other in real time. The general practice is for the moderators to pose their questions in all capital letters, and the respondents are asked to use upper- and lowercase. The respondents also are asked to always start their response with the question number, so the moderator can quickly tie the response to the proper question. This makes it fast and easy to transcribe a focus-group session. The group interaction lasts for about 60 to 90 minutes. A raw transcript is available as soon as the group is completed, and a formatted transcript is available within 48 hours. The whole process is much faster than the traditional method. Examples of companies that provide online focus groups include SurveySite (www.surveysite.com), Harris Interactive (www.harrisinteractive.com), and Burke (www.burke.com) in the United States, The Focus Group (www.thefocusgroupuk.co.uk) in the United Kingdom, and Asean Focus Group (www.aseanfocus.com), an India-based organization that also serves Australia and several other countries in Southeast Asia.

New forms of online focus groups continue to emerge. For example, online bulletin board focus groups involve the moderator and the respondents over an extended period of time, from a few days to a few weeks. Thus, respondents can think and respond at their own convenience. An example is SurveySite's FocusSite for holding an in-depth discussion among 25 or more participants over an extended period of time. Participants enter the discussion several times over 1 to 2 days, depending on the research objectives. The extended time period allows respondents to react to and build on each other's ideas in a way that often is not possible during a typical 2-hour focus-group session. Other forms of online qualitative research also have emerged, including blogs, message boards, online media sites, and online communities. Some of the useful insights gained from these procedures are illustrated by Del Monte.

Research in Action

Del Monte: Understanding the Love of Dog Lovers

Since its inception during the California Gold Rush of 1849, Del Monte foods (www.delmonte.com), one of the largest U.S.-based marketers of branded food and pet products, has become a $3 billion company, leading the food industry in innovative marketing practices. Recently, the Pet Products Division needed to connect with dog owners in a new way in order to get closer to them, gain fresh perspectives on their attitudes and behaviors, and drive true innovation. The company used MarketTools (www.markettools.com) Insight Networks to bring together three important sources of insight:

- **Analysis.** The key topics consumers are discussing and their overall sentiment and engagement levels are discovered by identifying and analyzing relevant content from over 50 million blogs, message boards, and media sites.

- **Online community interaction.** Clients gain an online environment through online communities built by MarketTools, a U.S. research firm that maintains an extensive global panel network. Through these communities, clients can observe and interact, with a targeted audience to gain an understanding of their attitudes, behaviors, and preferences.

- **Quantitative survey research.** Clients can qualify trends and validate the potential of new concepts and ideas through MarketTools' on-demand survey platform and large consumer panel.

After identifying dog lovers as the key target segment, Del Monte Foods and MarketTools created a custom Insight Network. One of the first activities provided by the Insight Network was "Text Analysis," in which relevant content from more than 50 million blogs was collected and analyzed to evaluate current topics of discussion among the target consumers.

First, the analysis revealed that of the topics dog lovers are most interested in, doggie daycare, travel with dogs, and even pet entertainment were some of the most popular. Compared to other topics, dog care proved to be a high-involvement topic that generated repeated mentions among bloggers who were in the target group. Dog care engagement was higher, for example, than holiday cookie-baking, an online topic used to benchmark engagement level.

The text analysis also revealed that while each age group has a dog-lover segment, this segment is most prominent in the Baby Boomer demographic. Older dog owners seem to prize the companionship their dog provides at a proportionately higher level, whereas Gen X tends to be more concerned with on-the-go issues such as daycare and travel. Gen Y tends not to concern itself as much with the responsibility-oriented themes—day care, grooming, and so on. Their focus is on companionship, dog care, and apparel.

To refine these insights, MarketTools created the "I Love My Dog" online community, which gave members and Del Monte a place to interact and collaborate. This was followed by an online survey to quantify and statistically validate the qualitative insights. Based on the results, Del Monte formulated a number of targeted marketing strategies. For example, the premium brands in its product line (Kibbles 'n Bits, Gravy Train, and Nature's Recipe, as well as dog snack brands such as Milk-Bone, Snausages, and Meaty Bone) were targeted at the Baby Boomer dog lovers given their greater attachment to and love for their dogs. This effort resulted in increased sales and market share.[4]

Advantages of Online Focus Groups

People from all over the country or even the world can participate in online focus groups, and the client can observe the group from the convenience of home or office. Geographical constraints are removed, and time constraints are lessened. Unlike traditional focus groups, online groups offer the unique opportunity for recontacting group participants at a later date to either revisit issues or to introduce them to modifications in material presented in the original focus group. The Internet enables the researcher to reach segments that are usually hard to recruit, such as doctors, lawyers, other professional people, working mothers, and others who lead busy lives and are typically not interested in taking part in traditional focus groups.

Moderators might also be able to carry on side conversations with individual respondents, probing deeper into interesting areas. People are generally less inhibited in their responses and are more likely to fully express their thoughts online. A lot of online focus groups go well past their allotted time because so many responses are expressed. Finally, because there is no travel, videotaping, or facilities to arrange, the cost is much lower than for traditional focus groups. Firms are able to keep costs between one-fifth and one-half the costs of traditional focus groups. Online groups can also be conducted more quickly than traditional focus groups.

Disadvantages of Online Focus Groups

Only people that have and know how to use a computer can be interviewed online. Because the name of an individual on the Internet often is private, actually verifying that a respondent is a member of a target group is difficult. This is illustrated in a cartoon in *The New Yorker*, where two dogs are seated at a computer and one says to the other "On the Internet, nobody knows you are a dog!" To overcome this limitation, traditional methods, such as telephone calls, are used for recruitment and verification of respondents. Body language, facial expressions, and tone of voice cannot be obtained online, and electronic emotion indicators obviously do not capture as full a breadth of emotion as does videotaping.

Another factor that must be considered is the lack of general control over the respondent's environment and his or her potential exposure to distracting external stimuli. Because online focus groups could potentially have respondents scattered all over the world, the researchers and moderators have no idea what else the respondents might be doing while participating in the group. Only audio and visual stimuli can be tested. Products cannot be touched (e.g., clothing) or smelled (e.g., perfumes). It is difficult to get the clients as involved in online focus groups as they are in observing traditional focus groups. Table 6.3 presents a comparison of online and traditional focus groups.

Applications of Focus Groups

Focus groups, whether traditional or online, can be used in almost any situation that requires preliminary understanding or insight into the problem. The range of research topics relevant for focus-group investigation includes research designed to do any of the following:

1. Understand consumer perceptions, preferences, and behavior concerning a product category (e.g., how consumers select a cellular service provider and their perceptions of such providers as AT&T and Verizon in the United States, Vodacom in South Africa, or Mobiles India).
2. Obtain impressions of new product concepts (e.g., consumer response to the high-definition one-time-use cameras by Kodak or Fuji).
3. Generate new ideas about older products (e.g., new packaging and positioning for such detergent products as Cheer in the United States, Persil in Germany, or Ariel in the United Kingdom).
4. Develop creative concepts and copy material for advertisements (e.g., a new campaign for Diet Pepsi in the United States, Lemee Orange in India, or Frank Ginger Beer in New Zealand).
5. Secure price impressions (e.g., the role of price in consumer selection of luxury cars, such as Cadillac, Lexus, Mercedes, or BMW).

TABLE 6.3 Online Versus Traditional Focus Groups

Characteristic	Online Focus Groups	Traditional Focus Groups
Group size	4 to 6 participants	8 to 12 participants
Group composition	Anywhere in the world	Drawn from the local area
Time duration	1 to 1.5 hours	1 to 3 hours
Physical setting	Researcher has little control	Under the control of the researcher
Respondent identity	Difficult to verify	Easily verified
Respondent attentiveness	Respondents can engage in other tasks.	Attentiveness can be monitored.
Respondent recruiting	Easier. Can be recruited online, by e-mail, or by traditional means (telephone, mail).	Recruited by traditional means (telephone, mail).
Group dynamics	Limited	Synergistic, snowballing (bandwagon) effect
Openness of respondents	Respondents are more candid due to lack of face-to-face contact.	Respondents are candid, except for sensitive topics.
Nonverbal communication	Body language cannot be observed. Emotions expressed by using symbols.	Easy to observe body language and emotions.
Use of physical stimuli	Limited to those that can be displayed on the Internet.	A variety of stimuli (products, advertising, demonstrations, and so on) can be used.
Transcripts	Available immediately	Time-consuming and expensive to obtain
Observers' communication with moderator	Observers can communicate with the moderator on a split screen.	Observers can manually send notes to moderator in the focus-group room.
Unique moderator skills	Typing, computer usage, familiarity with chat-room slang.	Observational
Turnaround time	Can be set up and completed in a few days.	Takes many days for set up and completion.
Client travel costs	None	Can be expensive
Client involvement	Limited	High
Basic focus-group costs	Much less expensive	More expensive due to facility rental, food, audio- and videotaping, and transcript preparation.

Research in Action

Intel: Inside the Health Care Industry

Intel conducts exploratory research such as customer focus groups to find out what consumers think the future will hold. Intel became extremely interested in the health industry because focus groups showed that health professionals, including doctors, nurses, and hospital staff, are increasingly recognizing the benefits of information technology (IT). More and more doctors were interested in using IT to help organize and integrate patient records in a more efficient and modern way. In addition, increasing computational abilities of medical research platforms and devices will inevitably save costs and accelerate medical research. This is different from the traditional trend of health care being slow to adopt IT due to the high amount of person-to-person contact in the industry.

These findings led Intel to create a digital health division. This division works directly with hospitals and health care professionals to innovate new products for the industry. Through the use of exploratory research through focus groups, Intel was able to discover an industry untapped by the technological market segment. For example, the U.S. semiconductor company Intel is developing technologies that

will allow for greater and better data storage and management efficiency to deal with increasing data volumes and MPOC (mobile point of contact) technologies that will provide health care workers with greater information access and sharing at the point of decision making. This way, health care workers will be able to take more precise decisions that might save the lives or improve the health of patients.

As of 2008, the digital health division was growing and contributing significantly to Intel's revenues. A focus on customers' needs through qualitative and quantitative research has enabled Intel to become one of the top ten most valuable brands in the world.[5]

6. Obtain preliminary consumer reaction to specific marketing programs (e.g., instant coupons issued by General Mills for Cheerios in the United States or by Muir Glen for Hearty Tomato soup in Australia).
7. Interpret previously obtained quantitative results (e.g., the reasons for a sales decline of Gloria Vanderbilt perfume in the United States, Dolce & Gabbana in Australia, or Jean-Paul Gaultier in Japan).

Despite broad applicability, focus groups are only one of the personal interviewing techniques used to collect qualitative data. One-on-one depth interviews are another technique.

Depth Interviews

depth interview
An unstructured, direct personal interview in which a single respondent is probed by a highly skilled interviewer to uncover underlying motivations, beliefs, attitudes, and feelings on a topic.

Depth interviews are loosely structured conversations with individuals drawn from the target audience. Like focus groups, depth interviews are an unstructured and direct way of obtaining information. Unlike focus groups, however, depth interviews are conducted on a one-on-one basis. These interviews typically last from 30 minutes to more than an hour. They attempt to uncover underlying motives, prejudices, or attitudes toward sensitive issues.

Conducting Depth Interviews

As with focus groups, the interviewer prepares a discussion outline to guide the interview. However, the purpose of depth interviews is to uncover hidden issues that might not be shared in a group setting. Therefore, substantial probing is done to surface underlying motives, beliefs, and attitudes. This was illustrated in the opening vignette in which Gillette used depth interviews to understand the underlying motives and attitudes of women toward shaving. The depth interviews showed that women shave much more surface area than men do, that they do this only two or three times a week, that they often shave in a dimly lit shower, and that they must shave areas they cannot see well. Furthermore, shaving tends to be a personal experience for women that evokes feelings of anticipation and acceptance. Probing is necessary to understand these findings and feelings. Probing is done by asking such questions as "Why do you say that?" "That's interesting, can you tell me more?" or "Would you like to add anything else?" (Probing is discussed in detail in Chapter 14.) As the interview progresses, the type of questions asked, the probes used, and the wording of the questions depend on the answers received.

To illustrate the technique, suppose an interviewer is conducting depth interviews with working men and women who are frequent catalog shoppers. The objective is to understand how these shoppers view the catalog-shopping experience. The interview may go something like this:

INTERVIEWER: "How do you feel about shopping through catalogs?" *The interviewer then encourages the subject to talk freely about attitudes and feelings about catalog shopping. After asking the initial question, the direction of the interview is determined by the respondent's initial reply.*

RESPONDENT: "I sometimes like to relax with a cup of coffee, flipping through a catalog at the end of the day. It's fun and relaxing."

INTERVIEWER: "Why is it fun and relaxing?" *If the answer is not very revealing (e.g., "It lets my mind wander?"), the interviewer might ask further probing questions (e.g., "Why is it fun to let your mind wander?").*

RESPONDENT: "I have to think logically all day long. When I sit down with a catalog, I can fantasize about how I will look in certain clothing or how my living room will look with a piece of furniture. And, there is no pressure to do anything!"

INTERVIEWER: "Why is it important to have no pressure to do anything?"

RESPONDENT: "My whole day is pressure. In my job, I have to constantly react to pressure someone else is putting on me. Home is the one place where I can control the pressure, even eliminate it."

As this example indicates, probing is effective in uncovering underlying or hidden information. In this case, the respondent finds catalog shopping relaxing and a form of low-stress escape (the need to feel "no pressure to do anything").

As with focus groups, the success of depth interviews rests with the skill of the interviewer. The interviewer should (1) avoid appearing superior and put the respondent at ease; (2) be detached and objective, yet personable; (3) ask questions in an informative manner; (4) not accept brief "yes" or "no" answers; and (5) probe the respondent.

Depth interviews can be used to create an environment that fosters a more candid and comprehensive discussion of an issue than can be done in a group. The resulting data provide insight into motivation, beliefs, attitudes, and perceived consequences of behavior. Also, because depth interviews are conducted one-on-one, the comments can be traced directly to individual respondents. This might be particularly relevant in business-to-business research where a decision maker's comments can be evaluated within the context of that individual's personal and corporate background.

Advantages of Depth Interviews

Depth interviews can uncover deeper insights about underlying motives than focus groups can. Also, depth interviews attribute the responses directly to the respondent, unlike focus groups, where it is often difficult to determine which respondent made a particular response. Depth interviews result in a free exchange of information that might not be possible in focus groups, where there is sometimes social pressure to conform. As a result of probing, it is possible to get at real issues when the topic is complex. This was illustrated in the opening vignette in which Gillette used depth interviews to understand the shaving needs of women.

Disadvantages of Depth Interviews

The disadvantages of focus groups are magnified in individual depth interviews. Skilled interviewers capable of conducting depth interviews are expensive and difficult to find. The lack of structure makes the results susceptible to the interviewer's influence, and the quality and completeness of the results depend heavily on the interviewer's skills. The data obtained are difficult to analyze and interpret; the services of skilled psychologists are typically required for this purpose. The length of the interview combined with high costs means that only a small number of depth interviews can be conducted in a project.

Despite these disadvantages, depth interviews do have applications, particularly in business-to-business marketing where it is often difficult to assemble a group of executives for a focus-group session. They are also useful in advertising research where it is important to understand the feelings and emotions the advertisement evokes. A relative comparison of focus groups and depth interviews is given in Table 6.4.

Applications of Depth Interviews

As with focus groups, the primary use of depth interviews is for exploratory research to gain insight and understanding. Unlike focus groups, however, depth interviews are used

TABLE 6.4 Focus Groups Versus In-Depth Interviews

Characteristic	Focus Groups	In-Depth Interviews
Group synergy and dynamics	+	−
Peer pressure/group influence	−	+
Client involvement	+	−
Generation of innovative ideas	+	−
In-depth probing of individuals	−	+
Uncovering of hidden motives	−	+
Discussion of sensitive topics	−	+
Interviews with respondents who are competitors	−	+
Interviews with respondents who are professionals	−	+
Scheduling of respondents	−	+
Amount of information	+	−
Bias in moderation and interpretation	+	−
Cost per respondent	+	−

+ indicates a relative advantage over the other procedure
− indicates a relative disadvantage over the other procedure

infrequently in marketing research. Nevertheless, depth interviews can be employed effectively in special problem situations, such as those requiring the following:

1. Detailed probing of the respondent (e.g., automobile purchase)
2. Discussion of confidential, sensitive, or embarrassing topics (e.g., personal finances, loose dentures)
3. Situations where strong social norms exist and the respondent might be easily swayed by the group's response (e.g., attitude of college students toward sports)
4. Detailed understanding of complicated behavior (e.g., department-store shopping)
5. Interviews with professional people (e.g., industrial marketing research)
6. Interviews with competitors, who are unlikely to reveal the information in a group setting (e.g., travel agents' perceptions of airline package travel programs)
7. Situations where the product consumption experience is sensory in nature, affecting mood states and emotions (e.g., shaving experience, as in the opening vignette)

Research with children is an example for which depth interviews might be productive. M&M/Mars used depth interviews to uncover an effective advertising approach.

Research in Action

Mission from Mars

As of 2008, U.S. candy maker M&M/Mars (www.mmmars.com) was a global business whose products are consumed in 100 countries. Perhaps more surprisingly, and unusual for a business of this magnitude, the company is still privately owned, making it one of the largest "small family businesses" in the world.

Most children have a very active and colorful fantasy life. Recognizing this characteristic in their target audience,

M&M/Mars decided to use depth interviews to uncover childhood fantasies that might be relevant to the company's promotional efforts. Mars conducted depth interviews with schoolchildren and found that a majority of these fantasies revolves around extraterrestrial beings, wars, and exciting action. Previously, the candy manufacturer had never fully developed its extraterrestrial images, although they seemed natural given product names such as Mars and Milky Way. In response to the depth interview findings, it decided to introduce extraterrestrial characters from the planet Mars.

The company developed an imaginative story involving the Mars' Minister of Candy. He directed four Martians to bring back the "best candy in the universe" in order to eliminate the suffering Martians had endured for many years. Moreover, this advertising was linked to a promotional campaign that included back-to-school sweepstakes offering a grand prize of $100,000, 50 trips to Disney World, and other prizes. The four extraterrestrial heroes made appearances at malls and children's hospitals across the country. This successful multimillion-dollar campaign was shaped by the fantasies of children, uncovered by using depth interviews.[6]

Research with children is an example for which in-depth interviews might be productive. M&M/Mars used depth interviews to uncover an effective advertising approach. This example illustrates the value of depth interviews in uncovering the hidden responses that underlie the clichés elicited in ordinary questioning (e.g., "It's good" or I like it"). Like focus groups, depth interviews can be conducted online. A special way in which depth interviews are used is grounded theory. **Grounded theory** uses an inductive and more structured approach in which each subsequent depth interview is adjusted based on the cumulative findings from previous depth interviews with the purpose of developing general concepts or theories. Sometimes historical records also are analyzed. This approach is useful in designing new products or modifying existing products and developing advertising and promotion strategies.

grounded theory
An inductive and more structured approach in which each subsequent depth interview is adjusted based on the cumulative findings from previous depth interviews with the purpose of developing general concepts or theories.

Be an MR!

Search the Internet, as well as your library's online databases, to obtain information on why people use credit cards. Conduct two depth interviews for determining why people use credit cards.

Be a DM!

As the marketing manager for the credit-card company Visa, how would you use information about why people use credit cards to increase your market share?

Projective Techniques

Both focus groups and depth interviews are direct approaches in which the true purpose of the research is disclosed to the respondents or is otherwise obvious to them. **Projective techniques** are different from these techniques in that they attempt to disguise the purpose of the research. They are used in marketing research situations in which the respondent is unable or unwilling to answer a question directly. To get around this problem, the interviewer presents the respondent with a series of vague or incomplete pictures, statements, or scenarios. The underlying assumption is that when asked to respond to these prompts, the individual will reveal personal information that is perhaps held subconsciously.

Projective techniques are unstructured, indirect forms of questioning that require respondents to describe vague and ambiguous stimulus situations. In describing these situations, respondents indirectly project their own motivations, beliefs, attitudes, or feelings into the situation. The underlying information about respondents is uncovered by analyzing their responses. As an example, respondents might be asked to interpret the behavior of others rather than describe their own behavior. In doing so, respondents indirectly project their own

projective technique
An unstructured and indirect form of questioning that encourages respondents to project their underlying motivations, beliefs, attitudes, or feelings regarding the issues of concern.

motivations, beliefs, attitudes, or feelings into the situation. In a landmark study, the U.S. Postal Service (USPS) made use of this technique to determine why most boys aged 8 to 13 years did not collect stamps as a hobby. A sample of boys was shown a picture on a screen of a 10-year-old boy fixing stamps in his album and asked to describe the scene and characterize the boy. Most respondents described the boy in the picture as a "sissy." After these findings were confirmed with survey research, the Postal Service undertook a successful advertising campaign directed at 8- to 13-year-olds to dispel the belief that stamp collecting was for "sissies."

Projective techniques used in marketing research can be classified as association, completion, construction, or expressive techniques.

Association Techniques

association techniques
A type of projective technique in which the respondent is presented with a stimulus and asked to respond with the first thing that comes to mind.

With **association techniques**, the individual is presented with a list of words or images and asked to respond with the first thing that comes to mind. Word association is the best known of these techniques. With **word association**, respondents are presented with a list of words, one at a time, and asked to respond to each with the first word that comes to mind. The words of interest, called *test words,* are interspersed throughout the list, which also contains some neutral, or filler, words to disguise the purpose of the study. For example, in a retailing study some of the test words might be *location, parking, shopping, quality,* and *price.* The subject's response to each word is recorded verbatim, and responses are timed. Respondents who hesitate or reason out a response (defined as taking longer than 3 seconds to reply) are identified.

word association
A projective technique in which respondents are presented with a list of words, one at a time. After each word is presented, respondents are asked to give the first word that comes to mind.

In analyzing these data, the researcher looks at the frequency with which a response is given, the amount of hesitation before responding, and the number of instances when no response is given. Patterns in responses are analyzed, as are the response times. It often is possible to classify the associations as favorable, unfavorable, or neutral. The longer an individual hesitates before answering, the higher the assumed level of involvement with the subject. A nonresponse is thought to indicate the highest level of emotional involvement, because these people are too involved to be able to respond in a short time. Gillette used word association to help it name the Sensor for Women shaver (see opening vignette). A sample of women was presented with several different names for the new feminine razor, including Sensor for Women and Lady Sensor, and asked to write down the first word that came to mind. Because Sensor for Women elicited the most favorable responses, the company selected this name.

Completion Techniques

completion technique
A projective technique that requires the respondent to complete an incomplete stimulus situation.

Completion techniques are a natural extension of association techniques, generating more detail about the individual's underlying feelings and beliefs. The respondent is asked to complete a sentence, a paragraph, or a story. With **sentence completion**, respondents are given incomplete sentences and asked to finish them. Generally, they are asked to use the first word or phrase that comes to mind, as in the following example.

sentence completion
A projective technique in which respondents are presented with a number of incomplete sentences and asked to complete them.

Research in Action

Tommy Hilfiger Is a High Flyer in Men's Shirts

In order to determine men's underlying attitudes toward Tommy Hilfiger shirts, sentence completion could be used as follows:

A person who wears Tommy Hilfiger shirts is _____.

As compared to Polo, Gant, and Eddie Bauer, Tommy Hilfiger shirts are _____.

Tommy Hilfiger shirts are most liked by _____.

When I think of Tommy Hilfiger shirts, I _____.

Using such techniques, U.S.-based Tommy Hilfiger (www.tommy.com), which makes and markets casual wear and accessories, discovered that men preferred shirts that were less formal and that had a nontraditional cut. Men preferred to buy these shirts at upscale department stores, such as Macy's. These findings, after they were confirmed by survey research, formed the platform for Tommy Hilfiger's successful marketing strategy. The New York–based lifestyle brand Spring/Summer 2008 global advertising campaigns for all collections epitomized the classic, cool, American style for which the Tommy Hilfiger brand is known.

A variation of sentence completion is paragraph completion, in which the respondent finishes a paragraph that begins with the stimulus phrase. An expanded version of sentence completion and paragraph completion is **story completion**. With story completion, respondents are given part of a story, enough to direct attention to a particular topic, but not enough to hint at the ending. They are required to give the conclusion in their own words.

Construction Techniques

Construction techniques follow the same logic as other projective techniques, requiring the respondent to construct a response to a picture or cartoon. These techniques provide even less initial structure than verbally oriented association or completion techniques. With **picture-response techniques**, persons or objects are depicted in pictures, and respondents are asked to write a descriptive story, dialogue, or description. The responses are analyzed in an attempt to identify themes reflecting the individual's perceptual interpretation of the pictures. The USPS example given earlier illustrated the use of this technique. In a variation of this technique—Zaltman's Metaphor Elicitation Technique—respondents are asked to bring 12 to 15 pictures of their choice to the interview and then are asked to describe the salient content of each picture. The picture descriptions reveal respondents' underlying values, attitudes, and beliefs. In another variation, called *photo sort,* respondents are provided with a photo deck portraying different types of people. Respondents sort the photos to connect the people in the photos with the brands that they would use. A photo sort for Visa revealed that, in the United States, the credit card had a middle-of-the road, female image. Therefore, Visa renewed its relationship with the National Football League through 2010 to attract more males. Another variation of this technique requires the respondents to draw pictures or drawings to express their feelings about the brand or object being investigated.

In **cartoon tests**, highly stylized stick characters are used to eliminate references to clothing, facial expressions, and even gender. The respondents are asked to complete the conversation they would attribute to the cartoon characters. These techniques typically ask for verbal responses from the cartoon characters and for unspoken thoughts. This tends to maximize the candid nature of the response. Because cartoon tests are simpler to administer and analyze than picture-response techniques, they are the most commonly used construction technique. An example is shown in Figure 6.6.

In marketing research applications, construction techniques are used to evaluate attitudes toward the topic under study and to build psychological profiles of the respondents, as illustrated by Porsche.

story completion
A projective technique in which respondents are provided with part of a story and required to give the conclusion in their own words.

construction technique
A projective technique in which the respondent is required to construct a response in the form of a story, dialogue, or description.

picture-response technique
A projective technique in which the respondent is shown a picture and asked to tell a story describing it.

cartoon tests
Cartoon characters are shown in a specific situation related to the problem. The respondents are asked to indicate the dialogue that one cartoon character might make in response to the comment(s) of another character.

FIGURE 6.6

A Cartoon Test

Research in Action

Taxonomy of a Porsche Buyer

The well-known German automaker Porsche (www.porsche.com) sells sports cars; the lowest-priced unit costs more than $40,000. The demographics of Porsche owner are well known: male, mid-40s, college graduate, with average earnings exceeding $200,000 per year. Traditional advertising had focused on the car's performance and how good the car makes the owner look.

In an attempt to learn more about customers' motivations and their psychological profile, Porsche hired a group of researchers to find out why its buyers bought the car. Among other techniques, the researchers used picture responses. Current and potential buyers were shown pictures of Porsche owners with their cars and asked to describe the owners. The results were surprising and revealed that Porsche had been using the wrong advertising approach.

According to the results, most Porsche owners did not care if people saw them in their Porsche. To better direct advertisements to potential buyers, researchers produced five psychographic profiles:

1. **Top Guns.** Driven, ambitious types. Power and control matter to these people, and they expect to be noticed.

2. **Elitists.** Old money, blue bloods. To them, a car is just a car, not an extension of their personality;

3. **Proud Patrons.** Their car is a trophy earned for hard work, and they are not concerned with whether they are seen in it or not.

4. **Bon Vivants.** Worldly jet setters and thrill seekers. Their car adds excitement to their passionate lives.

5. **Fantasists.** Their car is a fantasy escape. They are not trying to impress anyone and, in fact, are a little embarrassed about owning a Porsche.

After survey research confirmed these findings, marketing and advertising were directed at these psychographic segments. As a result of this research and after years of poor sales, Porsche's sales in the United States increased significantly and sales continued to be strong through 2007. The 2008 Cayenne Turbo had a performance of 500hp (506kW) at 6,000 rpm, 0 to 60 mph (95.6 km/h) in 4.9 seconds, top track speed of 171 mph (275 km/h), and was priced (MSRP) $93,700 (€60,500).[7]

---

expressive techniques
Projective techniques in which the respondent is presented with a verbal or visual situation and asked to relate the feelings and attitudes of other people to the situation.

role playing
Respondents are asked to play the role or assume the behavior of someone else.

third-person technique
A projective technique in which the respondent is presented with a verbal or visual situation and asked to relate the beliefs and attitudes of a third person to the situation.

Expressive Techniques

In **expressive techniques**, respondents are presented with a verbal or visual situation and asked to relate, not their own feelings or attitudes, but those of others. The two main expressive techniques are role playing and the third-person technique. In **role playing**, respondents are asked to play the role or assume the behavior of someone else. The researcher assumes that the respondents will project their own feelings into the role.

In the **third-person technique**, the respondent is presented with a verbal or visual situation and asked to relate the beliefs and attitudes of a third person rather than directly expressing personal beliefs and attitudes. This third person might be a friend, a neighbor, a colleague, or a "typical" person. Again, the researcher assumes that the respondent will reveal personal beliefs and attitudes while describing the reactions of a third party. Asking the individual to respond in the third person reduces the social pressure to give an acceptable answer, as the following example shows.

Research in Action

What Will the Neighbors Say?

A study was performed for a commercial airline to understand why some people do not fly. When the respondents were asked, "Are you afraid to fly?" very few people said "yes." The major reasons given for not flying were cost, inconvenience, and delays caused by bad weather. It was suspected, however, that the answers were heavily influenced by the need to give socially desirable responses. Therefore, a follow-up study was done using the third-person technique. In the second study, the respondents were asked, "Do you think your neighbor is afraid to fly?" The answers indicated that most of the neighbors who traveled by some other means of transportation were afraid to fly. Thus, the third-person technique was able to uncover the true reason for not flying: fear of flying.[8]

Note that in the example asking the question in the first person ("Are you afraid to fly?") did not elicit the true response. Phrasing the same question in the third person ("Do you think your neighbor is afraid to fly?") lowered the respondents' defenses and resulted in truthful answers. In another popular version of the third-person technique, the researcher presents the respondent with a description of a shopping list and asks for a characterization of the purchaser, thus gaining data on shopping behavior.

Suppose the researcher is interested in determining attitudes toward prepared dinners. Two otherwise identical grocery shopping lists are prepared, except that one list contains prepared dinners. Respondents would be asked to characterize the purchaser identified with each list. The differences in the characteristics of the two purchasers reveal attitudes toward prepared dinners. For example, as compared to the other purchaser, the purchaser of prepared dinners may be described as lazy and disorganized. This would reveal that respondents think that lazy and disorganized people purchase prepared dinners.

We conclude our discussion of projective techniques by describing their advantages, disadvantages, and applications.

Advantages of Projective Techniques

Projective techniques have a major advantage over the unstructured direct techniques (i.e., focus groups and depth interviews): They may elicit responses that subjects would be unwilling or unable to give if they knew the purpose of the study. At times, in direct questioning, the respondent might intentionally or unintentionally misunderstand, misinterpret, or mislead the researcher. In these cases, projective techniques can increase the validity of responses by disguising the purpose. This is particularly true when the issues to be addressed are personal, sensitive, or subject to strong social norms. Projective techniques also are helpful when underlying motivations, beliefs, and attitudes are operating at a subconscious level.

Disadvantages of Projective Techniques

Projective techniques suffer from many of the disadvantages of unstructured direct techniques, but to a greater extent. These techniques generally require personal interviews with highly trained interviewers and require skilled interpreters to analyze the responses. Hence, they tend to be expensive. Furthermore, interpretation bias is a serious risk. With the exception of word association, all techniques are open-ended, making analysis and interpretation difficult and subjective.

Some projective techniques, such as role playing, require respondents to engage in unusual behavior. For example, to assess a company's image, respondents might be asked to play the role of a person that best describes the company. It is possible that respondents who agree to participate are themselves unusual in some way. Therefore, they might not be representative of the population of interest. As a result, it is desirable to compare findings generated by projective techniques with the findings of the other techniques that permit a more representative sample.

Application of Projective Techniques

With the exception of word association, projective techniques are used much less frequently than either focus groups or depth interviews. Word association is commonly used for testing brand names and, occasionally, to measure attitudes about particular products, brands, packages, or advertisements. Like focus groups, depth interviews and virtually all the projective techniques discussed can be implemented over the Internet. For example, various companies and marketing researchers are using the picture-response technique effectively. Coca-Cola can provide a picture on a Web site and ask respondents to write a story about it. The demographic data of the person coupled with the story can provide valuable insights into the respondent's psychographic profile and consumption patterns. The success of conducting qualitative research over the Internet lies in the respondents having access to and being comfortable with the Internet.

Experiential Learning

Online Qualitative Research Experiential Learning

The following Web sites illustrate the types of qualitative research that can be conducted online.

1. To experience the steps involved in designing and analyzing online bulletin board research, go to www.2020research.com, click "Online Research," and then select "QualBoard." To advance this overview, use the buttons at the bottom of the screen.

2. If you would like to join a panel of respondents who can earn prizes and other rewards for participating in online discussions, visit SurveySite's Web site (www.surveysite.com) or 20/20 Research Inc.'s Web site (www.2020research.com) and follow the instructions provided for joining a panel.

3. To experience how a sponsor of an online focus group monitors the actual focus group as if one was behind the one-way mirror in the back room of the focus-group facility, go to www.activegroup.net. Click "products," select "ActiveGroup," and then take the "Client Lounge" demo. You will have to provide an e-mail address and a one-word user name to activate the streaming video.

As the examples have shown, projective techniques can be used in a variety of situations. The usefulness of these techniques is enhanced when the following guidelines are observed:

1. Projective techniques are used when the sensitivity of the subject matter is such that respondents might not be willing or able to answer honestly to direct questions.
2. Projective techniques are used to uncover subconscious motives, beliefs, or values, providing deeper insights and understanding as part of exploratory research.
3. Projective techniques are administered and interpreted by trained interviewers who understand their advantages and limitations.

Given these guidelines, projective techniques, along with other qualitative techniques, can yield valuable information.

Be a DM!

As the brand manager for Esteé Lauder's Clinque, the world's largest brand of prestige makeup and fragrance products, how would you use information about the reasons why women use cosmetics to formulate marketing strategies that would increase your market share?

Be an MR!

Visit www.clinique.com and search the Internet, as well as your library's online databases, to obtain information on the underlying reasons why women use cosmetics. Which, if any, of the projective techniques would you use to determine why women use cosmetics?

Analysis of Qualitative Data

Sophisticated computer programs are available for processing large volumes of qualitative data and conducting complex analyses efficiently. The data are transmitted into text using a word processor and then converted into ASCII format. The ASCII format is imported into the computer program. The data are then coded. Codes are labels assigned by the researcher to data segments to facilitate organization of the data. Thus, the computer can recall and print all the material belonging to a particular code. The source of each data segment is identified so that the researcher can see from where it was extracted. The computer program can perform complex searches, such as listing data segments pertaining to code "scary rides in theme parks," as described by teenagers. The program also enables the researcher to examine relationships between data segments such as the relationship between "scary rides in theme parks" and "fun and excitement in the park." Popular software programs include XSight (www.qsr.com.au), Atlas/Ti (www.atlasti.com), HyperResearch (www.researchware.com), and NVivo 8 (www.qsrinternational.com). The analysis of qualitative data is further illustrated in the section entitled "Qualitative Research Software."

CHAPTER 6 • EXPLORATORY RESEARCH DESIGN: QUALITATIVE RESEARCH

Experiential Learning

Galaxy of Rides: A Joy Ride?

One type of qualitative research involves participation. Here, researchers actually involve themselves in the consumer behavior of interest. For example, a set of researchers was hired to better understand the experience of consumers visiting the Galaxy of Rides amusement park (a division of U.K.-based Galaxy, a maker of mechanical and interactive entertainment systems). Go to the textbook Web site, select "Chapter 6," and download "Five Narratives.doc." Read the narratives provided by the five participant observers.

1. Which participant helped you understand the consumer experience at Galaxy of Rides the best? Why?

2. Which participant helped you understand the consumer experience at Galaxy of Rides the least? Why?

These narratives could serve as the foundation for a thematic analysis.

1. What themes emerge across the narratives?

2. How do these themes help organize your insights about what could be done by the owners and managers of Galaxy of Rides to improve the consumer experience?

Summary Illustration Using the Opening Vignette

Qualitative research is appropriate when a company is faced with an uncertain situation or is presented with conclusive results that differ from expectations. This type of research can provide insight either before or after the fact. Qualitative research methods tend to be much less structured than quantitative methods and are based on small, nonrepresentative samples. In the opening vignette, Gillette used qualitative research at the beginning of the project to understand the shaving needs of women.

In contrast, quantitative research seeks conclusive evidence that is based on large, representative samples and that typically involves some form of statistical analysis. This was seen in the opening vignette in which Gillette used quantitative research involving a survey of a representative sample of 500 women to substantiate the findings of qualitative research (depth interviews).

Focus groups, the most frequently used qualitative technique, are conducted in a group setting, whereas depth interviews are conducted one-on-one. In the opening vignette, Gillette chose depth interviews over focus groups because shaving is a rather personal experience for women, and their personal feelings could be tapped much better in a one-on-one setting than in a group environment.

Projective techniques aim to project the respondent's motivations, beliefs, attitudes, and feelings onto ambiguous situations. Projective techniques can be classified as association, completion, construction, or expressive techniques. Gillette used word association to select an appropriate name for the new razor. Using word association to select names for new products is quite common. Figure 6.7 provides a concept map for qualitative research.

International Marketing Research

When a company is unfamiliar with the nuances of foreign markets, decisions that appear on the surface to be harmless and logical from a strategic business perspective might fail because the company did not fully understand the culture. This is why qualitative research is crucial in international marketing research. In the initial stages, qualitative research can provide insights into the problem and help in developing an approach by generating relevant models, research questions, and hypotheses. Thus, qualitative research might reveal the differences between foreign and domestic markets.

Focus groups can be used in many settings, particularly in industrialized countries. However, professional standards and practices might vary from those in the United States. For example, in Mexico it is considered acceptable for recruiters to invite family and friends to participate in a focus group. In some countries, such as India and Bolivia, due to lack of proper facilities, focus groups are held in hotels with closed-circuit monitoring.

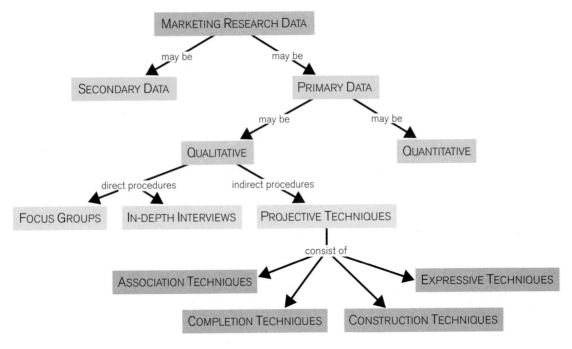

FIGURE 6.7

A Concept Map for Qualitative Research

The moderator should not only be trained in focus-group methodology, but should also be familiar with the language, culture, and patterns of social interaction prevailing in that country. The focus-group findings should be derived not only from the verbal contents, but also from nonverbal cues, such as voice intonations, inflections, expressions, and gestures. In some countries, such as those in the Middle and Far East, people are hesitant to discuss their feelings in a group setting. In these cases, depth interviews should be used. The use of projective techniques should be carefully considered, because the responses that these techniques generate can reflect deeply rooted cultural influences. When used appropriately, however, as in the following example, qualitative techniques can play a crucial role in the success of the marketing research project.

Research in Action

Spanish Expansion

The Spanish airline Iberia (www.iberia.com) was faced with the problem of expanding the number of routes from Europe to South and Central America. Amidst a multitude of airlines operating over the Atlantic, the question was how to differentiate Iberia from its many competitors. Focus groups provided some initial answers by revealing several insights: (1) International travelers saw Iberia as "the gateway to South America"; (2) providing several days' layover in Miami would attract a number of passengers, particularly tourists; and (3) the pairing of destinations, such as Miami and Cancun, in travel packages would promote more business. When subsequent survey research confirmed the focus-group findings, Iberia chose to make Miami a hub for its flights to South America. These findings also were used to design travel packages, make changes in services, and differentiate the airline. In 2008, Iberia was offering free additional services, such as hotel stays, lunches, and tours, at transfer destinations for customers using new transatlantic routes between Europe and destinations in the Americas and vice versa, further strengthening the airline's position.[9]

Technology and Marketing Research

Researchers are using remote data-collection techniques for qualitative research. The availability of videoconferencing links, remote-control cameras, and digital-transmission equipment has boosted the amount of research that can be conducted long distance. Although videoconferencing might never replace direct interaction with focus groups, it does offer time and cost savings. FocusVision (www.focusvision.com) is a U.S.-based firm offering this service. Keypads and other electronic devices are being used to gauge group opinion. When the moderator wants to poll the focus group participants on a certain issue, respondents express their opinions using the keypad on a scale of 0 to 10 or 0 to 100, and the results are instantly displayed on a large video screen. This process is also called *electronic group interviewing* (EGI).

Qualitative Research Software

The objective of qualitative research is to perform induction—to go from the specific details to the general organizing idea explaining the data. In other words, qualitative researchers must sift and resift data in order to detect important patterns in the data and make an interpretation, if possible. This is difficult mental work. The process is lengthy, and it is easy to become "lost" in the details of the project.

Once interviews begin, qualitative researchers begin to accumulate an enormous amount of textual data when transcripts of interviews are made. In today's media-rich environment, researchers can also collect photo images, vocal recordings, illustrations, drawings by respondents, as well as artifacts, such as physical prototypes of improved products created by respondents in model form. With any data that can be put in digital form, software is now available for archiving, hyperlinking, and analyzing all such data from qualitative research endeavors.

One of the new tools enabling qualitative researchers to obtain more powerful perspectives on their data is XSight software by QSR International Ltd., a global specialist in qualitative data with offices serving Europe, North America, and the Asia Pacific region. With XSight, project artifacts and transcripts can be imported and coded. Simple frequency counts can be made of words. Queries can be made about where words are located in the text and what demographic variables are associated with respondents using such focal words. For example, in an extensive qualitative research project about cell-phone usage, researchers could use XSight to query about how many times the word "security" occurs. Because XSight allows researchers to list the respondents' demographic profiles, researchers could also use XSight to query about how many of those mentioning "security" comprises teenage girls. In this way, analysis can continue so that meaningful patterns can be identified.

The accompanying screen capture is from an actual marketing research project focused on cell-phone usage. The Project Explorer in XSight comprises the far left-side of the screen. Project Explorer acts like a frame for a Web page that is always accessible to the user as subsequent navigation using hyperlinks occurs. In this way, Project Explorer offers an overview of the project structure. Such a structure is developed interactively between the user and XSight. Project Explorer offers nine frameworks for accessing the data under the heading "Analysis Frameworks." Among these frameworks are "Relationship with Cell Phones," "Core Values of NX (a brand)," and "Response to Club Ad," among others. Additionally, seven navigational buttons underneath the analysis

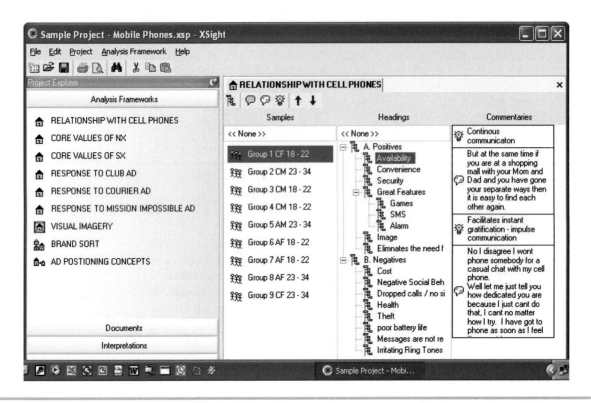

Software, such as QSR International's XSight, enable researchers to identify important patterns in qualitative data.

frameworks are hyperlinked to important parts of the investigator's notes, such as "Documents" and "Interpretations."

In this example, "Relationship with Cell Phones" is the analysis framework selected, so the details of this analysis framework are presented to the right of Project Explorer. Here, the "Group 1 CF 18-22 (Chicago Females 18-22 years old)" sample is chosen as well as the "Availability" heading. On the right side of the screen, one can see the commentaries in the data about availability for this sample. The first and third commentaries represent notes made by the investigator at an earlier stage in the analysis of the data. The rest of the commentaries are actual quotes from the respondents. In this way, the investigator is able to select different samples and make comparison of the raw data that the investigator has previously coded as being related to availability. Thus, the XSight software allows powerful movement back and forth through the hyperlinked data. This provides the investigator with the ability to make comparisons across samples in pursuit of identifying new themes (headings).

For a Web-based product tour of QSR International's XSight software, go to www.qsr.com.au/products/productoverview/XSight.htm.

Ethics in Marketing Research

Respondents' rights and privileges must be respected when conducting qualitative research. Some of the salient ethical issues relate to misleading or deceiving respondents, not maintaining their anonymity, and embarrassing or harming the respondents. An additional issue with wider ramifications is the use of research results in an unethical manner.

Some qualitative researchers allow their clients to be present at focus-group discussions by introducing them as co-researchers. Nonetheless, many participants are able to discern that the co-researcher is in fact the client. This deception raises ethical concerns and generates mistrust that has an adverse impact on the quality of the data and the integrity of marketing research.

As mentioned earlier, focus-group discussions often are recorded using hidden video cameras. Whether or not they are initially told of the hidden camera, the respondents should be informed about the recording at the end of the meeting. The purpose of the video, including who will be able to view it, should be disclosed. In particular, if the client will have access to it, this should be made known as well. Each respondent should be asked to sign a written statement granting permission to use the recording. Participants should be given the opportunity to refuse signing, in which case the tapes should be edited to completely omit the identity and comments of the respondents who refuse.

The researcher has an obligation to make the respondents feel comfortable. If a respondent is experiencing discomfort or stress, the interviewer should show restraint and should not aggressively probe any further. At the end of the interview, respondents should be allowed to reflect on all they have said and be allowed to ask questions. This helps reduce their stress and return them to their preinterview emotional state. A final issue relates to the ethics of using qualitative research results for questionable purposes, as in the presidential campaigns profiled here.

Research in Action

Focus (Groups) on Mudslinging

The ethics of negative or "attack" ads has been debated for some time. The focus, however, has shifted from the ads themselves to the ethics of employing marketing research techniques to design the ad message. Nowhere is this phenomenon more prevalent than in political "mudslinging" campaigns. The Bush campaign against Dukakis in the 1988 U.S. presidential election is one example.

Before designing negative ads about Dukakis, Bush campaign leaders tested negative information about Dukakis in focus groups. The idea was to develop some insight into how the American public would react if this negative information was released in the form of advertisements. Negative issues that elicited very negative emotions about Dukakis from the focus groups were chosen for Bush's political advertising. The result? Partly because he was painted "as an ineffectual, weak,

liberal, do-gooder lacking in common sense," Dukakis lost the election by a wide margin.

Similar misuse of qualitative research was observed in the 1992 and 1996 presidential elections that Bill Clinton won, in part, by negatively attacking the Republicans. In the 2000 presidential election, Gore unfairly attacked Bush as lacking in experience after data culled from focus groups and surveys revealed that experience was an important criterion for voters. The 2004 presidential election also was noted for negative attacks by both parties, particularly by Kerry on Bush, again based on focus-group and survey findings. Similar (mis)use of qualitative research was attributed to Clinton and Obama in the hotly contested 2008 Democratic primaries. It was also observed by both the Democrats and the Republicans in the 2008 presidential elections.[10]

What Would *You* Do?

Lotus Development Corporation: Developing Its Web Site

The Situation

Mike Rhodin is the CEO of Lotus Software (www.lotus.com), which is one of the brands of the IBM Software group. Lotus is a company that recognizes the need for individuals and businesses to work together. Therefore, it redefines the concept of conducting business through practical knowledge management, e-business, and other groundbreaking ways of connecting the world's ideas, thinkers, buyers, sellers, and communities via the Internet. As of 2008, Lotus marketed its products in more than 80 countries worldwide through direct and extensive business partner channels. The company also provides numerous professional consulting, support, and education services through the Lotus Professional Services organization. To help Lotus stay ahead of its competitors, Mike Rhodin wishes to increase the number of Web site visitors and for Lotus to maintain a Web site that is going to best meet the needs of its customers.

Lotus conducts focus groups of customers and business partners every 4 months to determine users' reactions to its Web site. This routine recognizes the fact that Web sites have very short lifecycles and need ongoing attention to keep them up-to-date.

The focus groups evaluate Lotus' Web site and those of other companies. Some objectives for the focus groups include identifying factors that lead Internet users to visit a Web site, identifying what factors entice visitors to return often to a Web site, and identifying users' technological capabilities.

The use of focus groups enables Lotus to actively collect some information that is not collected passively. Passive counters can keep track of the number of visitors to a Web site as well as the number of visitors who actually use the site. For example, Lotus can monitor the number of visitors who use its chat rooms that pertain to specific products. Just knowing that the number of visitors is changing, however, does not provide a company with insights concerning why there is a decrease or increase in visitors. Focus groups can be used to gain those insights.

From focus groups, Lotus learned that customers wanted improved navigation and a higher level of consistency. In the past, the emphasis was on making sure that information was delivered quickly to customers. Focus groups revealed that the company needed to further develop the site to make it easier for Web site visitors to navigate through all of the information.

continued

The Marketing Research Decision

1. Do you think that Lotus adopted the right research design? Which one of the following types of research designs would you recommend and why?
   a. Focus groups
   b. Depth interviews
   c. Survey research
   d. Projective techniques
   e. Focus groups followed by survey research
2. Discuss the role of the type of research you recommend in enabling Mike Rhodin to design an effective Web site.

The Marketing Management Decision

1. What should Mike Rhodin do to increase traffic to the Web site and enhance the user experience?
   a. Redesign the Web site.
   b. Upgrade the existing Web site, making only the necessary changes.
   c. Engage in aggressive banner advertising.
   d. Engage in aggressive print advertising.
   e. Offer price discounts to customers on the Web site.
2. Discuss how the marketing management decision action that you recommend to Mike Rhodin is influenced by the research design that you suggested earlier and by the findings of that research.

What Mike Rhodin Did

Mike Rhodin redesigned the Lotus Web site completely to improve navigation and enhance the efficiency with which visitors could search and download the information they wanted. He also engaged in aggressive print and banner advertising. IBM launched Lotus Workplace with print advertising in three American newspapers—the *Wall Street Journal*, the *New York Times*, and the *Boston Globe*. In addition, banner advertising was launched on a wide variety of Web sites, including eWeek, Information Week, BusinessWeek, and Forbes. These ads were all part of the "Can You See It" ad campaign that demonstrated how IBM Software enables on-demand business and invited readers to the Web site.[11]

Summary

Qualitative and quantitative research should be viewed as complementary. Qualitative research methods tend to be much less structured and are based on small, nonrepresentative samples. The various qualitative options vary in terms of how directly they ask questions of the respondent. Direct methods, such as focus groups and depth interviews, do not attempt to disguise the purpose of the research. Focus groups, the most frequently used qualitative technique, are conducted in a group setting, whereas depth interviews are done one-on-one.

Indirect techniques make a deliberate attempt to disguise the true purpose of the research. They are called projective techniques because they seek to project the respondent's motivations, beliefs, attitudes, and feelings onto ambiguous situations. Projective techniques can be classified as association, completion, construction, or expressive techniques. Projective techniques are particularly useful when respondents are unwilling or unable to provide the required information by direct methods.

In the international context, qualitative research can reveal differences between foreign and domestic markets. Technological advances, such as the availability of videoconferencing links, remote-control cameras, and digital-transmission equipment, have boosted the amount of research that can be conducted long distance. Ethical issues in qualitative research relate to respecting respondents' rights and privileges. Focus groups and other qualitative procedures can be conducted using the Internet.

Key Terms and Concepts

Qualitative research, 180	Projective techniques, 195	Picture-response techniques, 197
Quantitative research, 180	Association techniques, 196	Cartoon tests, 197
Direct approach, 182	Word association, 196	Expressive techniques, 198
Indirect approach, 182	Completion techniques, 196	Role playing, 198
Focus group, 182	Sentence completion, 196	Third-person technique, 198
Depth interviews, 192	Story completion, 197	
Grounded theory, 195	Construction techniques, 197	

Suggested Cases and Video Cases

Running Case with Real Data

1.1 Hewlett Packard

Comprehensive Critical Thinking Cases

2.1 American Idol   2.2 Baskin-Robbins   2.3 Akron Children's Hospital

Comprehensive Cases with Real Data

3.1 Bank of America   3.2 McDonald's   3.3 Boeing

Video Cases

6.1 Nike	7.1 Starbucks	9.1 P&G	10.1 Nivea	11.1 Dunkin' Donuts
12.1 Motorola	13.1 Subaru	14.1 Intel	19.1 Marriott	

Live Research: Conducting a Marketing Research Project

1. For most projects, it will be important to conduct some form of qualitative research.
2. Different teams can be assigned different responsibilities (e.g., interviewing key decision makers, interviewing industry experts, conducting depth interviews with consumers, doing a focus group, and so forth). Alternatively, all the teams can work on these tasks.
3. If possible, have at least one team use the qualitative research software discussed in this chapter and make a presentation to the class.

Acronyms

The key characteristics of a focus group may be described by the acronym FOCUS GROUPS:

F ocused on a particular topic

O utline prepared for discussion

C haracteristics of the moderator

U nstructured

S ize: 8 to 12 participants

G roup composition: homogeneous

R ecorded: audiocassettes and videotapes

O bservation: one-way mirror

U ndisguised

P hysical setting: relaxed

S everal sessions needed: One to three hours each

The main features of a depth interview may be summarized by the acronym DEPTH:

D epth of coverage

E ach respondent individually interviewed

P robe the respondent

T alented interviewer required

H idden motives may be uncovered

Review Questions

1. What are the primary differences between qualitative and quantitative research techniques?
2. What is qualitative research, and how is it conducted?
3. What are the differences between direct and indirect qualitative research? Give an example of each.
4. Why is the focus group the most popular qualitative research technique?
5. Why is the focus-group moderator so important in obtaining quality results?
6. What are some key qualifications of focus-group moderators?
7. Why should one safeguard against professional respondents?
8. What are two ways in which focus groups can be misused?
9. What is a depth interview? Under what circumstances is it preferable to focus groups?
10. What are the major advantages of depth interviews?
11. What are projective techniques? What are the four types of projective techniques?
12. What is the word-association technique? Give an example of a situation in which this technique is especially useful.
13. When should projective techniques be employed?

Applied Problems

1. Following the methods outlined in the text, develop a plan for conducting a focus group to determine consumers' attitudes toward and preferences for imported automobiles. Specify the objectives of the focus group and write a screening questionnaire.
2. Suppose Baskin-Robbins wants to know why some people do not eat ice cream regularly. Develop a cartoon test for this purpose.
3. The Coca-Cola Company has asked you to conduct Internet focus groups with heavy users of soft drinks. Explain how you would identify and recruit potential respondents.
4. Could a depth interview be conducted via the Internet? What are the advantages and disadvantages of this procedure over conventional depth interviews?
5. Visit the Web site of Qualitative Research Consultants Association (www.qrca.org). Write a report about the current state-of-the-art in qualitative research.
6. *Tennis* magazine would like to recruit participants for online focus groups. How would you make use of a newsgroup to recruit participants? Visit http://groups.google.com and then select rec.sport.tennis.

Group Discussion

1. In a group of five or six, discuss whether qualitative research is scientific.
2. Discuss the following statement in a small group: "If the focus-group findings confirm prior expectations, the client should dispense with quantitative research."
3. Discuss the following statement in a small group: "Quantitative research is more important than qualitative research because it results in statistical information and conclusive findings."

Hewlett-Packard Running Case

Review the Hewlett-Packard (HP) case, Case 1.1, and questionnaire given toward the end of the book.

1. In gaining an understanding of the consumer decision-making process for personal computer purchases, would focus groups or depth interviews be more useful? Explain.
2. Develop a focus group discussion guide for understanding the consumer decision-making process for personal computer purchases.
3. Can projective techniques be useful to HP as it seeks to increase its penetration of U.S. households? Which project technique(s) would you recommend?
4. Devise word-association techniques to measure consumer associations that might affect attitudes toward personal computer purchases.
5. Design sentence completion techniques to uncover underlying motives for personal computer purchases.

NIKE: Associating Athletes, Performance, and the Brand

Nike

Nike is the largest seller of athletic footwear, athletic apparel, and other athletic gear in the world, with about 30 percent market share worldwide. Nike markets its products under its own brand, as well as Nike Golf, Nike Pro, Air Jordan, Team Starter, and subsidiaries, including Bauer, Cole Haan, Hurley International, and Converse. As of 2008, the company sells its products through a mix of independent distributors, licensees, and subsidiaries in approximately 120 countries worldwide. Nike has grown from an $8,000 company in 1963 to a company with revenues of $16.3 billion for the year ended May 31, 2007.

In 2007, Nike spent an enormous amount of money, more than a billion dollars, on advertising, endorsements, and sales promotion. In order to make sure that this money is being spent properly, Nike relies on marketing research. It has shown a history of innovation and inspiration in its marketing and is quick to adapt to the changing consumer and the world of sports. Nike has used marketing research in understanding where the future growth lies. A recent example is Nike's shift from marketing in the more traditional sports (basketball and running) to other sports (golf and soccer), where it has not been as strong. Marketing research surveys revealed that the awareness of Nike among soccer and golf players was low, and Nike decided to work on increasing these numbers. Nike has decided that the money needed for licenses in its strong areas can be better spent in other areas where Nike does not have the brand awareness.

Today, the Nike Swoosh is recognized around the world. This is the result of more than 40 years of work and innovation. It signed the first athletes to wear its shoes in 1973. Early on, Nike realized the importance of associating athletes with its products. The partnerships help relate the excellence of the athlete with the perception of the brand. Through focus groups and surveys, Nike discovered the pyramid influence, which shows that the mass market can be influenced by the preferences of a small group of top athletes. After it realized this effect, Nike began to spend millions on celebrity endorsements. The association with the athlete also helps dimensionalize the company is and what it believes in. With Nike, this was, and remains, extremely important. It wants to convey a message that the company's goal is to bring innovation to every athlete in the world. Nike also uses the athletes to design new products by attempting to meet their individual goals.

Explaining Nike's strategy of celebrity endorsements, Trevor Edwards, Vice President of U.S. Brand Management, says that the sports figures, such as Ronaldo, Michael Jordan, and Tiger Woods, who have endorsed Nike brands all have represented excellence in some way. Nevertheless, the athletes also have a personal side, such as their drive to win or their ability to remain humble. All these qualities speak something about the Nike brand; this not only benefits the brand, but also helps to define what the Nike brand is and what it stands for.

The company also realized that in order to achieve its lofty growth goals, it must appeal to multiple market segments. Based on marketing research, Nike divided the market into three different groups: the ultimate athlete, the athletics participant, and the consumer who is influenced by sports culture. The first segment is the professional athletes. The second constituency is the participants, those who participate in sports and athletic activities but do not see themselves as athletes or as being part of the larger sport. The third segment comprises those who influence others and are influenced by the world of sports. These three different constituencies form three different consumer segments and Nike uses very different strategies for each.

Nike has always been an aggressive user of marketing research and this has been shown in its attack on the European market. It decided to concentrate on different sports in order to reach European consumers. Americans love baseball. And football. And basketball. But Europe's favorite game is soccer. Nike placed its focus on major sporting events (World Cups and Olympics) and celebrity athletes that are relevant to the European consumer. Marketing research in the form of focus groups and survey research revealed that the best positioning for Nike shoes was one that enhanced performance in the sport. Through massive advertising campaigns, it has been able to change the perception of its products from fashion to performance, and in the process increase sales dramatically.

Another technique Nike has used is to specifically design a product line for a certain market. Nike uses marketing research to determine the lifestyles and product usage characteristics of a particular market segment and then designs products for that segment. An example is the Presto line, which was designed for a certain youth lifestyle. Nike focused on the lifestyle and designed the products around this group. It also used marketing research to determine the most effective media to communicate with the target market.

Because of these methods, the Nike logo is recognized by 97 percent of U.S. citizens, and its sales have soared as a result. However, Nike faces a new concern: that it has lost its traditional image of being a smaller, innovative company. It also faces future obstacles in maintaining brand equity and brand meaning. Continued reliance on marketing research will help Nike to meet these challenges, associate its brand with top athletes and performance, and enhance its image.

Conclusion

Nike used marketing research to build its brand into one of the most well-known and easily recognized brands in the world. Nike's strategy of celebrity endorsements, its expansion into Europe, and the resulting stronger association with soccer, are some of the steps taken by Nike to grow its brand. In the coming years, as Nike expands to newer markets and capitalizes newer opportunities, it will have to continue its reliance on marketing research and continue to associate athletes, performance, and the brand.

Questions

1. Nike would like to increase its share of the athletic shoe market. Define the management decision problem.
2. Define an appropriate marketing research problem corresponding to the management decision problem you have identified.
3. Develop a graphical model explaining consumers' selection of a brand of athletic shoes.
4. How can qualitative research be used to strengthen Nike's image? Which qualitative research technique(s) should be used and why?

References

1. www.nike.com, accessed February 15, 2008.
2. Hoover's, A D&B Company, available at http://premium.hoovers.com.gate.lib.buffalo.edu/subscribe/co/factsheet.xhtml ?ID = rcthcfhfshkyjc, accessed May 31, 2007.

Descriptive Research Design: Survey and Observation

OPENING QUESTIONS

1. What survey methods are available to marketing researchers, and how can these methods be classified?

2. What are the criteria for evaluating survey methods and comparing them to determine which is best suited for a particular research project?

3. How can survey response rates be improved?

4. How does observation differ from the survey method? What procedures are available for observing people and objects?

5. What are the relative advantages and disadvantages of observational methods as compared to survey methods?

6. How can survey and observation methods be implemented in an international setting?

7. How can technology improve survey and observation methods?

8. What ethical issues are involved in conducting survey and observation research?

> "Much of the insights about consumers' future behavior are gained by simply asking consumers about their attitudes and intentions."
>
> *Surjya Roy,*
> *Senior Project Manager,*
> *Marketing Strategies, Inc.*

Procter & Gamble's New Marketing Platform: Everyday Low Pricing and Brand Extensions

As part of its ongoing marketing research, the giant U.S. consumer-products company Procter & Gamble (P&G) routinely analyzes scanner data and conducts consumer surveys. Scanner-panel data from ACNielsen (see Chapter 5), the world's leading marketing-information company, revealed that a typical, brand-loyal American family spent $725 each year on P&G products. In comparison, a family that bought similar products as private-label or low-priced brands spent less than $500. In a time when value-consciousness dominated, this premium-pricing strategy presented a problem to P&G. This led P&G to create a new marketing platform for its products.

At the base of the new platform was the concept of value. The platform was designed to recognize that P&G had been overcharging for many of its products, including Tide detergent, Crest toothpaste, Pampers disposable diapers, Vick's cough syrup, and Head & Shoulders shampoo. Focus groups and depth interviews conducted by P&G revealed that customers were no longer willing to pay for non–value-added costs. Furthermore, surveys using mail panels indicated that customers loyal to P&G preferred prices that were consistently low rather than price discounts and special deals. A computer-assisted telephone survey of a randomly selected representative sample resulted in similar findings for the general

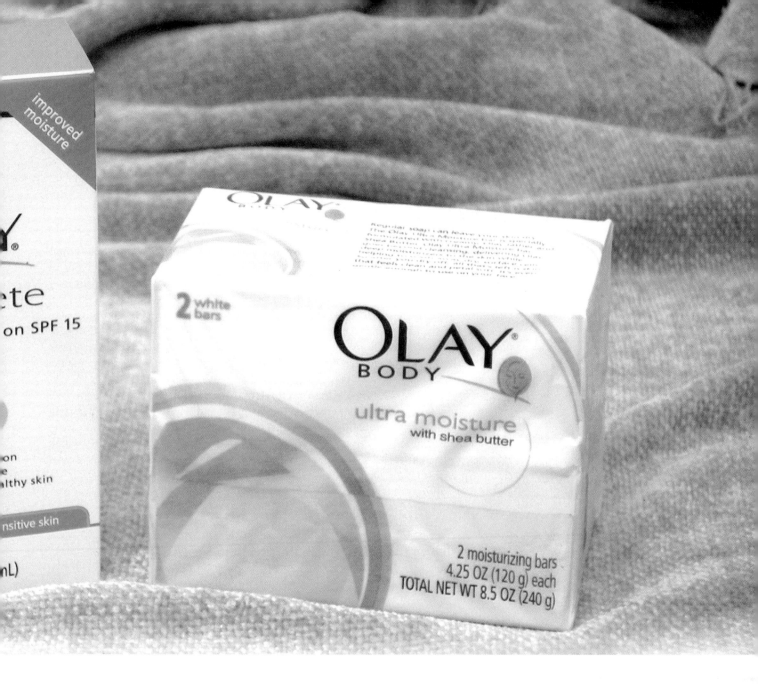

population. The concept developed from these findings is known as everyday low pricing (EDLP). This concept was the exact opposite of P&G's previous platform of maintaining high list prices offset by frequent and irregular discounts.

Another problem that led P&G to reformulate its platform had to do with new-product development. Previous research indicated that P&G brands enjoyed considerable equity in that they were well known and preferred by a large segment of the market. In 2000, P&G decided to drop the word Oil from Oil of Olay, its line of skin-care products and cosmetics, in an effort to make the line more appealing to younger women. This led to the strategy of brand extensions (BE), the practice of using a successful brand name to launch a new or modified product. An example is Olay Beauty Bar, a brand extension of Olay lotion. The beauty bar was developed as a response to the growing consumer demand for a product that would keep skin feeling soft and young, not only on the face, but all over.

The bar was specially engineered with a synthetic cleansing system and light Olay moisturizers that help the skin to hold moisture better than soap does. In addition to the special formulation, the bar was designed to stay firm during use and not melt away like most other beauty bars.

Prior to its introduction, the Olay Beauty Bar was tested in mall-intercept interviews. In these interviews, respondents actually washed their hands and face with the bar in a test area located in the mall before responding to a survey. Because the results of these mall-intercept interviews were quite positive, three types of bars were introduced: pink and white with different scents and an unscented hypoallergenic version for sensitive skin. The Olay Beauty Bar has been a great success and won one of *Marketing News'* Edison Best New Products Awards. P&G continued this strategy of brand extension, launching other extensions of the Olay line, such as the Olay Regenerist line that consists of an eye-lifting serum, a daily regenerating serum, and an anti-aging lip treatment. As of 2008, the Olay product line was being marketed with the theme, "Love the skin you're in."

P&G is gaining momentum in the U.S. market and abroad. Domestic unit volumes and market shares are once again increasing in 22 out of 32 categories. The strategies of EDLP and BE continue to pay dividends for the company. The company's sales and market share continued to improve through 2008, strengthening its position as a world leader in consumer products, with P&G brands touching the lives people around the world, 3 billion times a day.[1]

Overview

The marketing research process begins by defining the research problem and then formulating an approach and a research design. As discussed in Chapter 3, the major types of research designs are exploratory and conclusive. Exploratory designs rely primarily on secondary data analysis (Chapters 4 and 5) and qualitative research (Chapter 6). Conclusive research designs can be classified as causal or descriptive. Causal designs are explained in Chapter 8. This chapter discusses survey and observation methods, the quantitative techniques typically used to collect descriptive research data. Figure 7.1 briefly explains the focus of the chapter, the relation of this chapter to the previous ones, and the steps of the marketing research process on which this chapter concentrates.

Survey data do much more than merely report behavior. Surveys can provide insights into who the consumers are, how they behave, and why they behave in certain ways. Respondents' reports of their conscious motives, values, or beliefs provide some insight into consumer behavior. This was illustrated in the opening vignette in which P&G used different types of surveys to understand consumers' preferences for everyday low prices versus discounts and special sales.

FIGURE 7.1

Relationship of Survey and Observation to the Previous Chapters and the Marketing Research Process

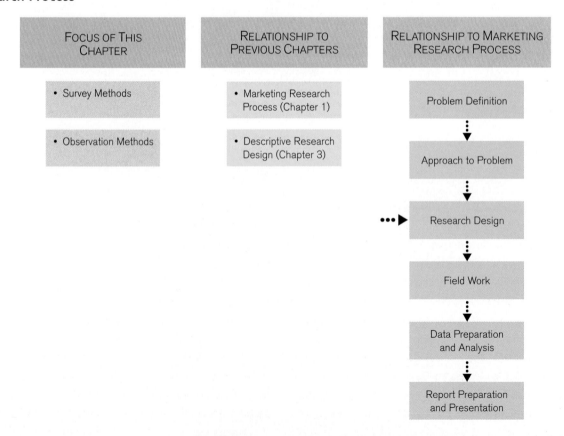

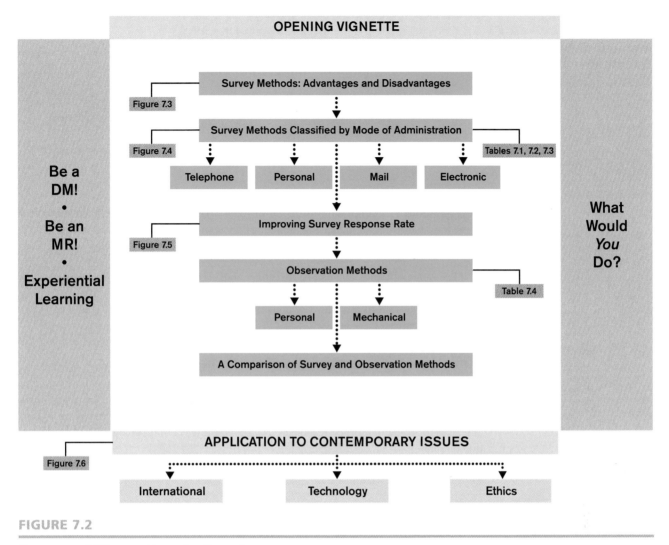

FIGURE 7.2

Survey and Observation: An Overview

Surveys can be classified in terms of how the data are collected: telephone interviews, computer-assisted telephone interviews, in-home interviews, mall-intercept interviews, computer-assisted personal interviews, mail interviews, mail panels, and electronic surveys (e-mail and Internet). In this chapter, each of these methods is described and the criteria used to select an appropriate method for a particular project are discussed.

The chapter also presents the major observational methods of personal observation and mechanical observation. It also discusses the advantages and disadvantages of observation compared to survey methods, as well as the role of survey and observation methods in international marketing research. The impact of technology and Internet applications is discussed, and several ethical issues that arise in survey research and observation methods are identified. Figure 7.2 gives an overview of the topics discussed in this chapter and how they flow from one to the next.

Survey Methods

The **survey method** of obtaining information is based on questioning respondents. Surveys are used when the research involves sampling a large number of people and asking them a series of questions (Figure 7.3). Surveys can be conducted in person, by telephone, through a mailed questionnaire, or electronically via the computer. Perhaps the biggest issue researchers must tackle is how to motivate respondents to candidly answer

survey method
A structured questionnaire given to a sample of a population and designed to elicit specific information from respondents.

FIGURE 7.3

Methods of Obtaining Quantitative Data in Descriptive Research

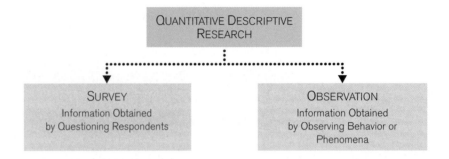

their questions. The uninvited intrusion of telemarketers and direct marketers into the home has resulted in an increasing number of consumers shutting the door to anyone trying to make contact. The challenges of controlling this nonresponse problem are discussed later in the chapter.

The range of topics that can be investigated using surveys is as varied as the research problems businesses face. Questions regarding behavior, intentions, attitudes, beliefs, awareness, motivations, and demographic and lifestyle characteristics all lend themselves to survey research.

Advantages and Disadvantages of Survey Research

The survey method has the advantages of ease, reliability, and simplicity. Questionnaires are relatively easy to administer. Using fixed-response (multiple-choice) questions reduces variability in the results, which can be caused by differences among interviewers, and enhances the reliability of the responses. It also simplifies coding, analysis, and interpretation of data.

Disadvantages of the survey method are that respondents might be unable or unwilling to provide the desired information. For example, consider questions about motivational factors. Respondents might not be consciously aware of the real reasons they prefer one brand over another. The subconscious nature of their motives might make it impossible for them to answer questions accurately. Respondents might be unwilling to respond if the information requested is sensitive or personal. For example, consider questions about religious beliefs. Some respondents might view this topic as very personal and might be unwilling to answer any questions related to it.

structured data collection
Use of a formal questionnaire that presents questions in a prearranged order.

Also, **structured data collection** involving a questionnaire with fixed-response choices can result in loss of validity for certain types of data, such as beliefs and feelings. Finally, it can be quite difficult to properly phrase questions (see Chapter 11 on questionnaire design). Yet, despite these disadvantages, the survey approach is by far the most common method of primary data collection in marketing research, particularly quantitative data.

Experiential Learning

Surveys and You

The Council of American Survey Research Organizations (CASRO) is the trade association of survey-research businesses, representing over 200 companies and research operations in the United States, Canada, and Mexico. CASRO communicates the importance of survey research in the public realm and helps educate those in the research industry about standards for ethics and performance. Go to the CASRO Web site (www.casro.org) and click "Surveys and You" under "For

the Public." Here you will find a user-friendly overview to survey research entitled "Surveys and You." Read this short overview and then answer the following questions:

1. Of the questions posed in "Surveys and You," which one helped you learn the most?

2. What did you learn as a result of this question?

3. What did you learn about the importance of surveys?

Survey Methods Classified by Mode of Administration

Figure 7.4 illustrates the various methods of collecting survey data, broadly classified as telephone, personal, mail, or electronic interviews. Telephone interviewing can be further broken down in terms of whether computers are used in the interview process. Personal interviews can be conducted in the home, as mall-intercept interviews, or as computer-assisted personal interviews (CAPI). The third major method, mail interviewing, takes the form of ordinary mail surveys or surveys conducted using mail panels. Electronic interviews are generally administered over the Internet or by using e-mail. Of these methods, telephone interviews are the most popular in the United States, followed by personal interviews. The popularity of electronic surveys is increasing quickly. Mail interviews are the least popular.

Telephone Methods

As stated earlier, telephone interviews vary in terms of the degree of computer assistance supporting the interview.

TRADITIONAL TELEPHONE INTERVIEWS Traditional telephone interviews involve phoning a sample of respondents and asking them a series of questions. The interviewer uses a paper questionnaire and records the responses with a pencil. Telephone interviews are generally conducted from centrally located research facilities. Telephone research centers are specifically equipped to accommodate large groups of interviewers. These facilities have proliferated because of the cost and control advantages they offer. The low cost of telecommunication services has made nationwide telephone interviewing from a central location practical.

Additionally, field service supervisors can closely monitor the telephone conversations. This monitoring helps to control interviewer bias that results from variation in the way in which the questions are asked and the responses are recorded. Data quality is enhanced with on-the-spot review of completed questionnaires. Finally, the research budget, both in terms of labor costs and time restrictions, can be more easily managed when the interviewers are assembled in one location.

FIGURE 7.4

Classification of Survey Methods

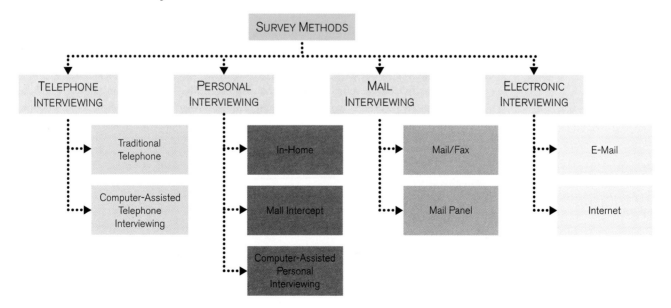

COMPUTER-ASSISTED TELEPHONE INTERVIEWING   Computer-assisted telephone interviewing (CATI) uses a computerized questionnaire administered to respondents over the telephone. The interviewer sits in front of a computer screen and wears a headset. The computer screen replaces a paper and pencil questionnaire, and the headset substitutes for a telephone. CATI from a central location is now much more popular than the traditional telephone method. More than 90 percent of all telephone interviews in the United States are conducted using a CATI system.

Upon command, the computer dials the telephone number to be called. When contact is made, the interviewer reads the questions posed on the computer screen and records the respondent's answers directly into the computer memory bank. CATI combines the interview with the editing and data-entry steps to produce a highly efficient and accurate survey process. Because the responses are entered directly into the computer, interim and update reports can be compiled instantaneously as the data are being collected.

CATI software has built-in logic, which also enhances data accuracy. The program will personalize questions and control for logically incorrect answers, such as percentage answers that do not add up to 100 percent. The software has built-in branching logic, which will skip questions that are not applicable or will probe for more detail when warranted. For example, if a respondent answered "yes" to the question, "Have you ever purchased Nike athletic shoes?" an entire series of questions related to the experience with shoes made by the American apparel maker would follow. If, however, the respondent answered "no," that line of questioning would be skipped. An application of CATI was illustrated in the opening vignette where P&G used this method to survey a randomly selected sample, asking questions related to pricing preferences.

ADVANTAGES AND DISADVANTAGES OF TELEPHONE INTERVIEWING   Telephone interviewing, in a computer-assisted format, remains one of the most popular survey methods. This popularity can be traced to several factors. Interviews can be completed quickly, because the travel time associated with personal interviews is eliminated. **Sample control**, or the ability to reach the units specified in the sample, is good when proper sampling and callback procedures are followed. Control of the field force is good, because the interviewers can be supervised from a central location. The control is even better in CATI, because these systems allow the supervisor to monitor an interview without the interviewer or the respondent being aware of it. The **response rate**, the percentage of total attempted interviews that are completed, also is good. Moreover, telephone surveys are not very expensive.

However, telephone interviews do have some inherent disadvantages (Table 7.1). The questioning is restricted to the spoken word. Interviewers cannot use physical stimuli, such as visual illustrations or product demonstrations, and they cannot ask complex questions. This limits the applicability of telephone techniques for certain types of research, such as new product or advertising research.

Personal rapport and commitment are difficult to establish due to lack of face-to-face interaction between the interviewer and the respondent. Respondents can easily escape the interview process, either by cutting the interview short or simply hanging up the phone. This results in less tolerance for lengthy interviews over the phone and limits the quantity of data that can be collected.

Personal Methods

Personal interviewing methods can be categorized as in-home, mall-intercept, or computer-assisted interviews.

PERSONAL IN-HOME INTERVIEWS   In personal in-home interviews, respondents are interviewed face-to-face in their homes. The interviewer's task is to contact the respondents, ask the questions, and record the responses. In recent years, the use of personal in-home interviews has declined. Nevertheless, they are still used, particularly by syndicated firms (see Chapter 5).

---

sample control
The ability of the survey mode to effectively and efficiently reach the units specified in the sample.

response rate
The percentage of the total attempted interviews that are completed.

TABLE 7.1 **Relative Advantages of Different Survey Methods**

Method	Advantages	Disadvantages
Telephone	Fast Good sample control Good control of field force Good response rate Moderate cost	No use of physical stimuli Limited to simple questions Low quantity of data
In-Home	Complex questions can be asked Good for physical stimuli Very good sample control High quantity of data Very good response rate Longer interviews can be done	Low control of field force High social desirability Potential for interviewer bias Most expensive Some samples (e.g., high-crime areas) may be difficult to access May take long to collect the data
Mall Intercept	Complex questions can be asked Very good for physical stimuli Very good control of environment Very good response rate	High social desirability Potential for interviewer bias Moderate quantity of data High cost
CAPI	Complex questions can be asked Very good for physical stimuli Very good control of environment Very good response rate Low potential for interviewer bias	High social desirability Moderate quantity of data High cost
Mail	No field-force problems No interviewer bias Moderate/high quantity of data Low social desirability Low cost	Limited to simple questions Low sample control for cold mail No control of environment Low response rate for cold mail Low speed
Mail Panel	No field-force problems No interviewer bias High quantity of data Low social desirability Low/moderate cost Good sample control	Limited to simple questions No control of environment Low/moderate speed
Electronic: E-mail	No interviewer bias Low cost Low social desirability High speed Contact hard-to-reach respondents	Low sample control No control of environment Low response rate Moderate quantity of data Security concerns
Electronic: Internet	No interviewer bias Low cost Low social desirability Very high speed Visual appeal and interactivity Personalized, flexible questioning Contact hard-to-reach respondents	Low sample control No control of environment Low response rate Moderate quantity of data

Research in Action

Telephone Calling Makes Pizza Hut the One to Call

As of 2008, U.S.-based Pizza Hut was the largest pizza restaurant company in the world. It had 10,000 outlets in 100 countries and territories and served more than 1.4 million pizzas every day to approximately 4 million customers worldwide. Pizza Hut, which initiated a customer satisfaction survey in January 1995, currently conducts 50,000 interviews a week. Data are collected through an outbound telephone survey (i.e., Pizza Hut initiates the telephone call). Selected customers in Pizza Hut's delivery and carryout database are called within 24 hours of their purchases. The outbound interviews are limited to 4 minutes, and customers are given a 60-day breather before they are called again.

In the United States, the company also has an interactive 800-number inbound survey of randomly selected dine-in customers (the customer initiates the call). One of every 20 to 30 dine-in customers receives a coupon at the bottom of the receipt and a toll-free number to call to participate in the interactive survey. Tracking results show that 67 percent of the surveys are completed within 1 day of the visit, fulfilling a desire by management for the inbound survey results to be fresh.

The survey focuses only on issues that unit managers can control. The questions deal with service, food, and problems during the customer's most recent visit. The survey results have been very useful. For example, customers rushed to buy the new Stuffed Crust Pizza, but there was no subsequent rise in loyalty. Survey results showed that because of service problems, new customers were not making return trips. The survey helped Pizza Hut identify problems, and it now has a better understanding of how to handle the next major product launch. Half of the unit manager's quarterly bonus is linked to the survey results. As a result, customer satisfaction is at an all-time high.[2]

Be a DM!

As the marketing manager for U.S.-based Delta Airlines, how would you use information on consumers' airline preferences for domestic travel to formulate marketing strategies that would increase your market share?

Be an MR!

Visit www.delta.com and search the Internet, as well as your library's online databases, to obtain information on consumers' preferences for selecting an airline for domestic travel.

What would be the advantages and disadvantages of using telephone interviewing to conduct a survey to obtain information on consumers' airline preferences for domestic travel? Would you recommend this method to Delta Airlines?

Advantages and Disadvantages of In-Home Interviewing   In-home interviewing offers many advantages. It enables the interviewer to provide clarifications to the respondent, allowing for complex questions. It permits the use of physical stimuli, such as visual aids, charts, and maps, and it allows the interviewer to display or demonstrate the product. It provides very good sample control as well, because homes can be selected without generating a list of all the homes in a given area. The homes can be selected by instructing the interviewer to start at a given location, travel in a certain direction, and select every nth (e.g., every eighth) home. A large quantity of data can be collected because the respondents are interviewed in their own homes, and they might be more willing to participate for a longer period of time. The response rate is very good, particularly if respondents have been prenotified.

In-home interviewing has lost favor due to social, labor, control, and cost factors. Changes in the family, particularly related to the dominance of two-income earners, leaves few people at home during the day. Interviewer supervision and control is difficult, because the interviewers are traveling door to door. Consequently, problems with the questionnaire or with the style of the interviewer become more difficult to detect and correct. **Social desirability**, the tendency of respondents to give answers that are socially desirable but incorrect, is high when there is face-to-face contact between the interviewer and the respondent. This factor also leads to a high potential for **interviewer bias**. Interviewers can influence the answers by facial expressions, intonations, or simply by the way they ask the questions. This method also is the most expensive.

social desirability
The tendency of the respondents to give answers that might not be accurate but that might be desirable from a social standpoint.

interviewer bias
The error due to the interviewer not following the correct interviewing procedures.

Despite their value, personal in-home interviews are being largely replaced by mall intercepts.

Mall-Intercept Personal Interviews

In mall-intercept personal interviews, respondents are approached and interviewed in shopping malls. The process involves stopping the shoppers, screening them for appropriateness, and either administering the survey on the spot or inviting them to a research facility located in the mall to complete the interview. For example, in a survey for a cellular phone manufacturer, a shopper is intercepted and asked about his or her age, education, and income. If these characteristics match the client's target population, the individual is then questioned on product usage. Some usage of cellular phones is a prerequisite for inclusion in the sample. Only those who have experience with cellular phones are invited to a test facility located in the mall to evaluate several new prototype designs under consideration.

Although the sample is composed only of individuals who shop in that retail mall, this is not a serious limitation. Although not representative of the population in general, shopping mall customers do constitute a major share of the market for many products.

ADVANTAGES AND DISADVANTAGES OF MALL INTERCEPTS   A major advantage of mall-intercept interviews is that it is more efficient for the respondent to come to the interviewer than for the interviewer to go to the respondent. The popularity of this method is evidenced by the several hundred permanent mall-research facilities located across the country. Complex questions can be asked when there is face-to-face contact. Mall intercepts are especially appropriate when the respondents need to see, handle, or consume the product before they can provide meaningful information. This was illustrated in the opening vignette when P&G used this technique to determine consumers' responses to Olay Beauty Bar prior to introduction. Mall-intercept interviewing was chosen because it conveniently allowed the respondents to use the beauty bar in a test area in the mall before they responded to the survey. The researcher has very good control of the environment in which the data are being collected, and the response rate is very good.

The main disadvantages are the potential for social desirability and interviewer bias due to face-to-face contact in the interviewing process. The quantity of data that can be collected is only moderate, because people are generally in a hurry while shopping. The cost of mall-intercept interviewing is high.

Research in Action

Altamonte Mall Relies on Mall Intercepts

The U.S. shopping center Altamonte Mall (www.altamontemall.com) regularly surveys its customers. In a recent mall-intercept survey, 300 consumers were surveyed regarding what changes might convince them to visit the mall more often or for a longer period of time. The results indicated that 36 percent wanted a children's play area, 60 percent a movie theater, and 50 percent a casual dining establishment. Other survey results showed that consumers preferred book superstores to small book outlets; that they wanted additional, specific retailers, such as Hollister (casual wear) and Gymboree (children's clothing); and they wanted additional parking that was easy to access.

Altamonte Mall took the survey results to heart and put $28 million into constructing new niceties for visitors. A luxurious $232,000 play space for children was constructed; an AMC 18-screen movie theater was built. An 8,500 square-foot casual dining establishment was opened, and a second parking deck was built. Furthermore, Barnes & Noble responded to the marketing research as well and removed its small B. Dalton bookstore located in Altamonte and set up a 26,000 square-foot Barnes & Noble book superstore. These moves resulted in increased patronage of the mall and enhanced customer loyalty.[3]

Computer-Assisted Personal Interviewing

In computer-assisted personal interviewing (CAPI), the third form of personal interviewing, the respondent sits in front of a computer terminal and answers a questionnaire on the screen by using the keyboard or a mouse. Several user-friendly electronic packages can aid in designing easy and understandable questions. Help screens and courteous error messages also are provided. The colorful screens and on- and off-screen stimuli add to the respondent's interest and involvement in the task. This method has been classified as a personal-interview technique, because an interviewer is usually present to serve as a host and to guide the respondent as needed.

This approach is used in shopping malls, preceded by the intercept and screening process described earlier. It also is used to conduct business-to-business research at trade shows or conventions. For example, the U.S. delivery firm UPS could measure its image and test the effectiveness of its slogan, "What can Brown do for you?" by administering a CAPI survey at the expedited package delivery trade show. The process of interacting with the computer is simplified to minimize respondent effort and stress. Thus, the use of open-ended questions that require typing is minimized.

ADVANTAGES AND DISADVANTAGES OF CAPI   CAPI seems to hold respondent interest and has several advantages. Complex questions can be asked, and the computer automatically performs skip patterns and conducts logic checks. Interviewer bias is reduced, because the computer administers the interview. Like mall intercepts, CAPI can be useful when the survey requires the use of physical stimuli. It also offers excellent control of the data collection environment and results in a very good response rate.

Its main disadvantages, which are shared with mall-intercept interviews, are the effects of high social desirability, moderate quantity of data, and high cost.

Be an MR!

Visit www.espn.com and search the Internet, as well as your library's online databases, to obtain information on consumers' perceptions of the U.S. sports-programming network. What are the advantages and disadvantages of personal interviews in conducting a survey to obtain information on consumers' perceptions of ESPN? Which, if any, method of personal interviewing would you recommend for administering the survey?

Be a DM!

As the marketing manager for ESPN, how would you use information on consumers' perceptions of ESPN to formulate marketing strategies that would increase your audience?

Mail Methods

Mail interviews, the third major form of survey administration, can be conducted with independently compiled mailing lists or by using a mail panel.

MAIL INTERVIEWS   The traditional mail interview is a "cold" mail survey that is sent to individuals who meet a specified demographic profile but who have not been precontacted to participate in the survey. A typical mail interview package consists of the outgoing envelope, cover letter, questionnaire, postage-paid return envelope, and possibly an incentive. Those individuals motivated to do so complete and return the questionnaire through the mail. There is no verbal interaction between the researcher and the respondent. Individuals are selected for cold surveys through mailing lists the client maintains internally or has purchased commercially. Commercial mailing lists typically contain some demographic and psychographic information that assists in the targeting process. Regardless of its source, a mailing list should be current and closely related to the population of interest.

The researcher must also make decisions about the various elements of the mail interview package (Table 7.2). The type of envelope, the cover letter, the length of the questionnaire, and the incentive, if one is offered, all affect response rates.

The time involved and the response rate can be improved by faxing the questionnaire instead of mailing it. In a **fax survey**, the questionnaire is transmitted by a fax machine to respondents. The respondents can then return the completed questionnaire by faxing it to a designated (toll-free) number or, sometimes, by mail. Fax surveys share many characteristics with mail surveys; however, they can provide faster, and often higher, response rates. Greater urgency is associated with fax correspondence, and people are more likely to respond and do so sooner than they would to mail correspondence. Although the image quality of the fax transmission does not match that of a mailed questionnaire, this does not

fax survey
A survey for which the questionnaire is transmitted by a fax machine to respondents. The respondents can than return the completed questionnaire by faxing it to a designated (toll-free) number or, sometimes, by mail.

TABLE 7.2 Some Decisions Related to the Mail Interview Package

Outgoing Envelope

Size, color, and return address for envelope

Postage

Method of addressing

Cover Letter

Sponsorship

Signature

Personalization

Postscript

Type of appeal

Questionnaire

Length

Layout

Content

Color

Size

Format

Reproduction

Respondent anonymity

Return Envelope

Type of envelope

Postage

Incentives

Monetary vs. Nonmonetary

Prepaid vs. Promised

reduce the quality of the data. Fax numbers can be programmed into computers and the documents (cover letter and questionnaire) sent directly by the computer to the fax machine. This not only saves paper and printing costs, but labor as well, because there is no need to type addresses, print labels, stuff envelopes, and so on. Because many households do not have fax machines, this method is not suitable for household surveys. It can be used in a variety of surveys with commercial and other institutional respondents, however.

MAIL PANELS   In contrast to a cold mail interview, a **mail panel** consists of a large and nationally representative sample of individuals who have agreed to participate in periodic survey research (see Chapters 3 and 5). Incentives in the form of cash or gifts are often offered to the individuals who agree to participate. Once the individuals have been admitted to the panel, detailed demographic and lifestyle data are collected on each household. The researcher uses this information to select targeted mailing lists within the panel based on client needs.

The U.K.-based marketing-research company TNS (www.tns-global.com) is an example of a marketing research organization that maintains mail panels. Mail panels can be used to reach a general as well as a targeted sample. In the opening vignette, P&G used mail panel surveys to target consumers loyal to P&G and determine their pricing preferences. In a longitudinal design, the purchases of these customers for P&G and competing brands were monitored over time to identify the loyal customers.

Advantages and Disadvantages of Mail Surveys   Mail surveys are an economical and efficient way to reach consumers. Cold mail surveys have a low cost, and the cost of mail panels is only moderately higher. The problems of interviewer bias and the expense of field staff management

mail panel
A large and nationally representative sample of households that have agreed to periodically participate in mail questionnaires, product tests, and survey research.

are eliminated. Social desirability is low, because there is no personal contact with the respondent during data collection. A moderate amount of data can be collected through cold mail surveys, whereas mail panels permit the collection of large quantities of data.

These clear advantages are offset, however, by problems regarding lack of control of the interviewing process. Unlike telephone and personal interviewing, there is no personal contact, and the respondent might feel less compelled to either participate or candidly complete the questionnaire. This problem is particularly acute with cold mail interviews. With cold mail interviews, the researcher has little control over who answers the questionnaire, how they answer it, and how quickly they return it. This results in low sample control, low speed, and no control over the data-collection environment. Thus, it is difficult to assess the quality and validity of the data.

Finally, response rates to cold mail surveys are low, and nonresponse introduces a serious bias in the data. Those individuals who choose not to participate in mail interviews might have very different demographic and psychographic profiles than responders, resulting in **nonresponse bias**. Individuals with higher income and educational levels, or individuals inexperienced or uninterested in the research topic, all tend to have lower response rates. Mail panels are successful in boosting response rates, and the problem of nonresponse bias also is reduced.

Despite its shortcomings, the relative ease and low cost of mail interviews continue to make this a viable research option.

nonresponse bias
Bias that arises when actual respondents differ from those who refuse to participate in ways that affect the survey results.

Research in Action

Kick the Can: Canned Soup, That Is

In a mail survey, respondents were asked to make canned or dry soups at home and then respond to a questionnaire. The findings indicated a strong desire for a fresh alternative to canned and dry soups. Guided by these results, Stockpot Soups (www.stockpot.com), a subsidiary of U.S. food-products supplier Campbell Soup, developed Stockpot Classic Soups Soup Concentrate. Packed in resealable pouches, these soups are sold in the refrigerated dairy case as an alternative to canned and dry soups. Each 10-ounce pouch makes four bowls of hearty home-style soup with ingredients such as fresh-cut vegetables, real dairy products, and premium meats and seafood. This new product has been a success, because it was born of consumer desire discovered via a mail survey. As of 2008, StockPot was the leader in fresh-refrigerated soups, and the food-service industry leader, with about 45 percent market share nationwide.[4]

Be a DM!

As the marketing manager for Outback Steakhouse, an Australian restaurant chain with outlets in some 20 countries, how would you use information on consumers' preferences for casual restaurants to formulate marketing strategies that would increase your sales and market share?

Be an MR!

Visit www.outback.com and search the Internet, as well as your library's online databases, to obtain information on consumers' preferences for casual restaurants. What are the advantages and disadvantages of using mail, a mail panel, or fax in conducting a survey to obtain information on consumers' preferences for casual restaurants? Which, if any, of these methods would you recommend for conducting a survey for Outback?

Electronic Methods

Electronic surveys can be conducted via electronic mail (e-mail), if the respondents' addresses are known, or by posting the survey to a Web site.

E-MAIL SURVEYS   E-mail surveys are questionnaires distributed through electronic mail. If the addresses are known, the survey can simply be mailed electronically to respondents included in the sample. E-mail usage in the United States is very high, particularly in business firms where virtually everyone has access to e-mail. Using batch-type e-mail, researchers send e-mail surveys to potential respondents who use e-mail. Respondents key in their answers and send an e-mail reply. Typically, a computer program is used to prepare the questionnaire and the e-mail address list and to prepare the data for analysis.

E-mail surveys are simple to prepare and can be distributed quickly. They also are convenient for the respondent, because they show up in the e-mail box and catch the respondent's attention. As compared to regular mail (snail-mail) surveys, e-mail surveys offer time and cost advantages and more flexibility. Respondents are also more willing to answer open-ended questions in e-mail surveys.

Some e-mail systems can handle color and graphics, whereas others are limited to plain text. Respondent anonymity is difficult to maintain, because a reply to an e-mail message includes the sender's address. Security and privacy issues can also be a concern.

E-mail surveys are especially suited to projects for which the e-mail lists are readily available, such as surveys of employees, institutional buyers, and consumers who frequently contact the organization via e-mail (e.g., frequent fliers of an airline). E-mail letters can also be used to ask respondents to participate in an Internet survey and provide them with a link and password to the Web site where the survey is posted.

INTERNET SURVEYS   An Internet survey is a questionnaire posted on a Web site that is self-administered by the respondent. The questions are displayed on the screen, and the respondents provide answers by clicking an icon, keying an answer, or highlighting a phrase. Web survey systems are available for constructing and posting Internet surveys. They consist of a questionnaire designer, a Web server, a database, and a data-delivery program. The questionnaire is constructed with a user-friendly editor that uses a visual interface. The Web server distributes the questionnaire and files responses in a database. At any time, the researcher can obtain survey completion statistics, descriptive statistics of the responses, and graphical display of the data. As compared to e-mail surveys, Internet surveys offer more flexibility, greater interactivity, personalization, automatic skip patterns, and visual appeal. In the United States, several Web sites, including SurveyMonkey (www.surveymonkey.com) and Zoomerang (www.zoomerang.com) allow users to design surveys online without downloading the software. The survey is administered on the design site's server. Some sites offer data tabulation services as well. The Qualtrics (www.qualtrics.com) software distributed with this book will also enable you to design electronic surveys.

Internet panels are gaining in popularity and can be an efficient source of obtaining Internet samples (as discussed in more detail in Chapter 12). In fact, many marketing research suppliers and syndicated firms have replaced their traditional mail panels with Internet panels. Internet panels take less time and cost less to build and maintain as compared to mail panels. Several American research firms offer Internet panels that can be used by other researchers—for a fee—to draw Internet samples. Such firms include Harris Interactive, Survey Sampling International, and Greenfield Online. The advantages and disadvantages of electronic surveys relative to the other methods are discussed in more detail in the next section.

ADVANTAGES AND DISADVANTAGES OF ELECTRONIC METHODS   Both e-mail and Internet methods survey thousands of potential respondents simultaneously and quickly. Of the two, Internet surveys can be conducted more quickly; the data collected can be analyzed speedily, almost in real time. The incremental cost of reaching additional respondents is marginal, and hence, much larger samples can be accommodated as compared to the other methods.

Both methods are cost-effective. The cost savings as compared to the other methods can be dramatic for large samples. Moreover, both methods are good for contacting hard-to-reach respondents, because the survey can be answered at a time and place convenient to each respondent. Thus, high-income professionals, such as doctors, lawyers, and CEOs, can be reached. These groups are well represented online.

Internet surveys, and to some extent e-mail surveys, can be readily personalized. In addition to personalizing the name, the questions themselves can be personalized based on the respondent's answers to the previous questions; for example, "If your favorite brand of toothpaste [say, P&G's Crest in the United States or China, Anchor White in India, Macleans Protect in Australia] was not available, which brand would you buy?" Internet surveys can be programmed to automatically perform skip patterns (if the answer to Question 3 is "no," go to Question 9). Internet surveys are interactive and can utilize color, sound, graphics, and animation, much like computer-assisted personal interviewing.

Callbacks are easier to make in e-mail surveys and Internet surveys that draw respondents from a panel. The computer software can automatically send e-mail reminders to respondents who have not answered the survey. The electronic method shares many of the advantages of the mail method, including the absence of field-force problems and interviewer bias. It also has low social desirability.

Both methods have some disadvantages as well. Both suffer from respondent-selection bias in that only people with access to e-mail or the Internet can be included in the sampling frame. This bias is further accentuated by the fact that heavy users of these media have a higher probability of being included in the sample. These individuals might differ from the target population in ways that might bias the results. Another potential problem is that if no controls are imposed, the same respondent can answer over and over again. In addition, some Internet users might consider e-mail surveys to be a form of spam.

The electronic methods also share many of the disadvantages of mail surveys. Only simple questions can be asked; sample control is low; the data collection environment cannot be controlled; and response rates are low. Only moderate quantities of data can be obtained. Even though these disadvantages exist, the Internet holds tremendous promise that is increasing with the increased penetration of the Internet in homes.

Some Other Survey Methods

Researchers have developed a number of variations based on the basic survey methods just described. The more popular of these other methods are presented in Table 7.3.

TABLE 7.3 Additional Survey Methods

Method	Advantages/ Disadvantages	Comment
Completely automated telephone surveys (CATS)	Same as CATI	Useful for short, in-bound surveys initiated by respondent.
Wireless phone interview (voice-based format)	Same as CATI	Useful for point-of-purchase survey if respondent cooperation is obtained.
Wireless phone interview (text-based format)	Same as e-mail	Useful for point-of-purchase survey if respondent cooperation is obtained.
In-office interview	Same as in-home interview	Useful for interviewing busy managers.
Central location interview	Same as mall-intercept interview	Examples include trade shows, conferences, exhibitions, purchase intercepts
Kiosk-based computer interview	Same as CAPI	See www.intouchsurvey.com for more information.
Fax interview	Same as mail survey, except higher response rate	Useful in some business surveys.
Drop-off survey	Same as mail survey, except higher cost and higher response rate	Useful for local-market surveys.

Experiential Learning

Internet Surveys

The following Web sites demonstrate Internet surveys for respondents as well as researchers.

1. To experience what an Internet survey is like, go to Web Online Surveys at www.web-online-surveys.com. Select "Sample," and take the short "Website Survey."

2. If you would like to join a panel of respondents who can earn prizes and other rewards for completing online surveys, sign up at Lightspeed (http://us.lightspeedpanel.com and/or www.zoomerang.com.

3. To experience how a sponsor of an Internet survey can monitor results during the field portion of the project, go to http://us.lightspeedpanel.com, read the Lightspeed mini-poll question, and select "View Results."

4. To examine actual Internet surveys (and some results) fielded by firms in their research programs, go to www.createsurvey.com and click any of the hyperlinks under "Real Life Surveys by Customers."

5. To get a feel for building your own electronic survey, access the Qualtrics (www.qualtrics.com) software made available with this book and go through the tutorials.

Criteria for Selecting a Survey Method

When evaluating the various survey methods within the context of a specific research project, one has to consider the salient factors relevant to data collection. Often, certain factors dominate, leading to a particular survey method as the natural choice. For example, if a new perishable food product has to be tested, respondents would have to taste the product before answering the questionnaire. This would involve interviewing at central locations, leading to mall intercept or CAPI as the natural choices. If no method is clearly superior, the choice must be based on an overall consideration of the advantages and disadvantages of the various methods. We offer the following guidelines:

1. If complex and diverse questions have to be asked, one of the personal methods (in-home, mall intercept, or CAPI) is preferable. Internet surveys are an option as well, but the other self-administered methods (mail, mail panels, and e-mail) might not be appropriate because it is not possible to clarify respondent questions in an interactive manner. Telephone surveys are limited, because the respondent cannot see the questionnaire and the interviewer-respondent contact is not face-to-face.

2. From the perspective of the use of physical stimuli, personal methods (in-home, mall intercept, or CAPI) are preferable.

3. If sample control is an issue, cold mail (but not mail panel), fax, and electronic methods might not be appropriate.

4. Control of the data collection environment favors the use of central location (mall intercept and CAPI) interviewing.

5. High quantity of data favors the use of in-home and mail panels and makes the use of telephone interviewing inappropriate.

6. Low response rates make the use of cold mail and electronic methods disadvantageous.

7. If social desirability is an issue, mail, mail panel, fax, and Internet surveys are best.

8. If interviewer bias is an issue, the use of mail (cold and panels), fax, and electronic interviewing (e-mail and Internet) is favored.

9. Speed favors Internet, e-mail, telephone, and fax methods.

10. Costs favor cold mail, fax, electronic (e-mail and Internet), mail panels, telephone, mall intercept, CAPI, and in-home methods, in that order (most favorable to least favorable).

Often, these methods are combined to enhance the quality of data in a cost-effective manner. This is likely when the research project is large in scope, as in the case of P&G formulating its new marketing platform in the opening vignette. Note that P&G used scanner panels to monitor household expenses of P&G and competing brands and used mail panels to target consumers loyal to P&G. It used CATI to reach a representative sample of all households and used mall intercepts to determine consumer response to P&G's Olay Beauty Bar prior to introduction. However, caution should be exercised when using different methods in the same domestic marketing research project, which is referred to as using mixed-mode surveys. The method used can affect the responses obtained, and hence responses obtained by different methods might not be comparable. The results of studies examining the effect of survey methods on respondents are not very consistent. The Microsoft examples illustrate the selection of survey modes.

Research in Action

Microsoft: Accessibility Technology in Computing

Microsoft hired the U.S. technology and market-research company Forrester Research to conduct a study to determine the market potential for a new accessibility technology. This new technology would enable people to adjust their computers to meet their particular visual, hearing, dexterity, cognitive, and speed needs. The goal of the study was to identify cognitive and physical abilities among working-age adults and current computer users in the United States and the range of impairments limiting activity.

The selection of a survey method was based on the relative advantages and disadvantages of the different methods as well as the survey's subject matter. Because physical impairments can limit computer usage, electronic survey methods, such as e-mail and Internet surveys, were not considered suitable. Given the potential for high social desirability (i.e., inhibition of admitting an impairment) and the high cost, in-home and mall-intercept interviews were not favored. Mail and telephone methods were selected. A mail survey was considered to be the best way to survey people with a hearing impairment, and telephone interviews were viewed as the best option for those with visual impairments. Therefore, the research involved a nationwide phone and mail survey of 15,000 people. The sample included 10,464 respondents who were members of a mail panel managed by the German-based firm GfK Custom Research North America (www.http://www.gfk.com/ north_america/); 5,013 respondents

were contacted by phone through random digital dial. People were asked a range of questions designed to assess a variety of difficulties and impairments experienced by individuals who use computers. The survey examined multiple types of impairments and difficulties; and people were asked about their daily tasks, impairments, and problems with employment. Additionally, they were asked demographic and lifestyle questions.

The findings showed that 27 percent of respondents had a visual difficulty or impairment, 26 percent had a dexterity difficulty or impairment, 21 percent had a hearing impairment, 20 percent had cognitive difficulty, and 4 percent had a speech impairment. Thus, the majority of working-age adults are likely to benefit from the use of an accessibility technology. The average age of computer users is rising. Difficulties and impairments increase with age, indicating a clear need for accessibility technologies that can be used by an aging population.

Microsoft has used these findings to create new products with accessibility technologies in order to meet consumers' needs. It is building accessibility options into its products as well as developing specialty hardware and software products that help individuals interact with their computers. As of 2007, 57 million people in the United States use some form of accessibility technology. By 2010, the number of users using such technologies is expected to rise to 70 million.[5]

Improving Survey Response Rates

Regardless of the survey method chosen, researchers should attempt to improve response rates. This can be done through prior notification, incentives, follow-up, and other methods (Figure 7.5).

PRIOR NOTIFICATION   Prior notification consists of sending a letter or e-mail or making a telephone call to potential respondents, notifying them of the imminent mail, telephone, personal, or electronic survey. Prior notification increases response rates for samples of the general public because it reduces surprise and uncertainty and creates a more cooperative atmosphere.

prepaid incentive
Coupons, money, or some other incentive to participate that is included with the survey or questionnaire.

promised incentive
Coupons, money, or some other incentive to participate that is sent only to those respondents who complete the survey.

INCENTIVES   Offering monetary as well as nonmonetary incentives to potential respondents can increase response rates. Monetary incentives can be prepaid or promised. A **prepaid incentive** is included with the survey or questionnaire. A **promised incentive** is sent to only those respondents who complete the survey by the specified deadline. The most commonly used nonmonetary incentives are premiums and rewards, such as pens, pencils, books, and offers of survey results.

Prepaid incentives have been shown to increase response rates to a greater extent than promised incentives. The amount of incentive can vary from $0.25 to $50.00 or more, with a dollar being the most common in consumer surveys. The amount of the incentive has a positive relationship with response rate, but the cost of large monetary incentives might outweigh the value of the additional information obtained.

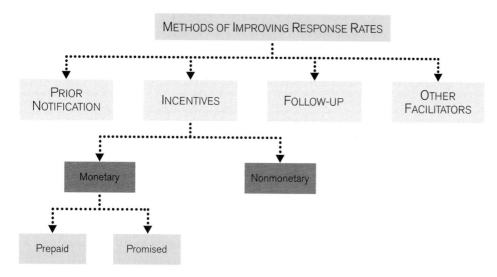

FIGURE 7.5

Improving Response Rates

FOLLOW-UP Follow-up, or contacting nonrespondents periodically after the initial contact, is particularly effective in decreasing refusals in mail surveys. The researcher might send a postcard or letter to remind nonrespondents to complete and return the questionnaire. Two or three mailings might be needed in addition to the original one. With proper follow-up, the response rate in mail surveys can be increased to 80 percent or more. Follow-up can also be done by telephone, e-mail, or personal contact.

OTHER FACILITATORS OF RESPONSE Personalization, or sending letters addressed to specific individuals, is effective in increasing response rates. The example that follows describes the procedure that *Bicycling* magazine used to increase its response rate.

Research in Action

Bicycling Magazine's Procedure for Increasing Response to Mail Surveys

As of 2008, *Bicycling* magazine (www.bicycling.com) was owned by Rodale, a U.S.-based global content company in health and wellness. Rodale reaches more than 30 million people in 57 countries each month through its category-leading media properties and integrated marketing solutions and is one of the largest direct-to-consumer businesses. *Bicycling* magazine conducts a semiannual survey of individual bicycle dealers throughout the United States. The following procedure is used to increase the response to the survey.

1. An "alert" letter is sent to advise the respondent that a questionnaire is coming.

2. A questionnaire package is mailed 5 days after the alert letter. The package contains a cover letter, a five-page questionnaire, a new $1 bill, and a stamped return envelope.

3. A second package, containing a reminder letter, a questionnaire, and a stamped return envelope, is mailed 5 days after the first package.

4. A follow-up postcard is mailed a week after the second package.

5. A second follow-up postcard is mailed a week after the first.

In a recent survey, 1,000 questionnaires were mailed to bicycle dealers, and 68 percent of these were returned after follow-up. This represents a good response rate for a mail survey.

Observation Methods

observation
The recording of behavioral patterns of people, objects, and events in a systematic manner to obtain information about the phenomenon of interest.

Observation methods are the second type of methodology used in descriptive research. **Observation** involves recording the behavioral patterns of people as well as data on objects and events in a systematic manner to obtain information about the phenomenon of interest. The observer does not question or communicate with the people being observed. Information can be recorded as the events occur or from records of past events. The major observation methods are personal observation and mechanical observation.

Personal Observation

personal observation
An observational research strategy in which human observers record the phenomenon being observed as it occurs.

In **personal observation**, a trained observer collects the data by recording behavior exactly as it occurs. The observer does not attempt to control or manipulate the phenomenon being observed, but simply records what takes place. For example, a researcher might record traffic counts and observe traffic flows in a department store. This information could aid in determining store layouts, the location of individual departments, shelf locations, and merchandise displays. **Humanistic inquiry** is a special form of personal observation in which the researcher is immersed in the system under study. This is in contrast to the traditional scientific method in which the researcher is a dispassionate observer. In yet another application, called *on-site observation*, observers are positioned in supermarkets and presented as shoppers who need advice from another shopper in making purchase decisions.

humanistic inquiry
A special form of personal observation in which the researcher is immersed in the system under study.

The main advantage of personal observation is that it is a highly flexible method, because the observer can record a wide variety of phenomena (Table 7.4). It also is highly suitable for use in natural settings. For example, the sales manager of General Motors can observe the attitudes of dealers toward a new inventory policy at one of the regular sales meetings.

The main disadvantage is that the method is unstructured in that an observation form is generally not used for recording the behavior as it occurs. Rather, the observer records the phenomenon after completing the observation in a free, unstructured format. This leads to high observation bias. Also the data and their interpretation are highly subjective, leading to high analysis bias.

TABLE 7.4 Relative Advantages and Disadvantages of Observation Methods

Method	Advantages	Disadvantages
Personal observation	Most flexible	High observation bias
	Highly suitable in natural settings	High analysis bias
Mechanical observation	Low observation bias	Can be intrusive
	Low-to-medium analysis bias	Not always suitable in natural settings

Research in Action

Identifying High-Potential Starbucks' Locations by Personal Observation

China is the most important, and potentially largest, market for Starbucks outside North America. Since the opening of the first Starbucks in Taiwan in 1998, in China in 1999, in Hong Kong in 2000, and in Macau in 2002, the growing appreciation and interest in coffee and the Starbucks experience by Chinese consumers has produced steady store expansion throughout China. To determine the location of its stores, Starbucks used a variety of methods, including a heavy reliance on personal observation.

A team of researcher observers were sent to monitor pedestrians outside a potential Starbucks store site with handheld counting devices, tallying likely customers. By doing this, they were able to tally the number of potential customers who would patronize the store. One such example was a woman in her 50s; although normally she would have been passed off as a normal pedestrian, researchers for Starbucks included her based on the fact she had looked into a nearby boutique store. This was seen as a sign of a person who loves adventure and experience.

The other method that Starbucks uses to determine where to set up stores is sending a team of "hot-spot" seekers to trace paths that link the places where potential customers live, work, and play. Starbucks can use this method to effectively locate stores in areas where its sales would definitely go up.

As of 2008, Starbucks had 500 stores in China, including mainland China, Hong Kong and Macau. In the mainland, the region with the fastest growth, Starbucks has over 230 stores in 22 cities, including Beijing, Tianjin, Shanghai, Guangzhou, and Shenzhen.[6]

Experiential Learning

Observing Customers' Movements in Retail Stores

Observation of customers' movements in retail stores can provide marketers with valuable insights about improving store layouts. In one study done by Integral GIS, an American firm specializing in software for information management, research teams followed 150 customers through four different retail stores and noted what the customers examined, rejected, and bought. At www.esri.com/mapmuseum/mapbook_gallery/volume18/business3.html, visit the Web site of ESRI, a U.S. firm that develops technology for geographic information systems (GISs), and find the case study for Mapping Movement through Retail Stores. If this URL has changed, search www.esri.com to locate "Mapping Movement through Retail Stores." Download the plug-in that will allow you to readily zoom in and zoom out on the map, as well as move the map on your screen. This will enable you to read the legends on the maps and better understand the information these maps contain.

1. Can you tell where most of the visual examinations occur that do not result in placing items in a shopper's cart?

2. In what parts of the store might shoplifting be greatest?

3. Which cash registers appear to be the most used? How would the use of other cash registers affect the flow of customers at the front of the store? How would it affect where displays could be placed to take advantage of this new movement within the store?

4. What are the ethical issues of employing such personal observations in retail stores?

5. What steps would need to be taken to collect these personal observations in an ethical manner?

Mechanical Observation

Mechanical observation, as one would expect, involves the use of a mechanical device to record behavior. These devices might or might not require respondents' direct participation. Such devices are particularly useful for recording continuous behavior, such as traffic flow in a grocery store. In the United States, ACNielsen's peoplemeter (Chapter 5) is an example of indirect observational devices in use today. Respondents do not need to change their behavior in any way to be involved in this type of observational study. The peoplemeter is attached to a television and continually records not only the channels the television is tuned to, but also who is watching. Arbitron has developed the portable peoplemeter, a wearable device that measures what television and radio programming a person watches or listens to during their waking hours. The PreTesting Company (www.pretesting.com) uses the People Reader, which unobtrusively records reading material and reader's eye movements to determine the reader's habits as well as the stopping power and the brand recall associated with different size ads.

Other common examples of indirect mechanical observation include turnstiles that record the number of people entering or leaving a building and traffic counters placed across streets to determine the number of vehicles passing certain locations. On-site cameras (still or video) are increasingly used by retailers to assess the impact of package designs, counter space, floor displays, and traffic-flow patterns. In the United States, the Universal Product Code (UPC), a barcode system for tracking trade goods, is a built-in source for mechanical observation. For those retailers equipped with optical scanners, the UPC system allows for

mechanical observation
An observational research strategy in which mechanical devices, rather than human observers, record the phenomenon being observed.

the automatic collection of consumer purchase information, classifying it by product category, brand, store type, price, and quantity (see Chapter 5).

The scanner data that P&G used in the opening vignette is an example of mechanical observation. The data revealed that a typical brand-loyal family spent $725 annually on P&G products. In comparison, a family that bought similar products as private-label or low-priced brands spent less than $500.

The Internet can be a very good source for observation and can provide valuable information. The observations can be made in a variety of ways. The primary observations can be made by the number of times the Web page is visited. The time spent on the page can also be measured through more advanced techniques, such as a timer that starts when a person visits a page and clicks on a certain icon and then stops when the person clicks the next icon. Further, various other links can be provided by the researcher on the Web page, and the research can observe which links are accessed more often. This will provide the researcher with important information about the information needs of the individuals and also the interests of the target segment. Analysis of the links that direct a person to a company's Web site provides the marketing researcher with important information regarding consumers' related interests, and an in-depth analysis of the link sites will provide information on advertising, competitors, consumers, and target market demographics and psychographics.

Web-based tracking of Internet users is an exciting and controversial electronic observation technique. Web surfers are served cookies. The cookie is a group of letters and numbers stored in a Web surfer's browser that identify the user. It is a sophisticated means by which a Web site can collect information on visitors. Often this process takes place without the Web surfer's knowledge. Companies and individuals that host Web sites use cookies to collect marketing research information on visitors. Cookies follow the traveler through the Web site and record the pages accessed by the visitor and the number of minutes spent on each page. The user's name, address, phone number, and access site can be collected by the cookie and saved into a database if the visitor enters any additional information. During a follow-up visit, the cookie accesses this information and has the ability to repeat it to the visitor. In essence, the cookie collects data on the user during every visit to the site. The online advertising company DoubleClick (www.doubleclick. com) uses information obtained from cookies to target advertising. For example, if a user visits an airline site and then a hotel site, that individual will be targeted with Delta Airlines and Marriott advertisements. Such practices are controversial because they raise issues of consumer privacy.

When it comes to developing new products, some U.S. companies, such as HP, Motorola, and Steelcase, are observing their customers rather than just listening to what they say. Traditional research, relying exclusively on questioning, can produce bland products. New Coke did well in taste tests, yet was a dismal failure. People said they wanted low-calorie burgers, but would not buy McDonald's McLean. The movie *Junior* did great in screenings, but made only $36 million. Baseball players said they loved the pump baseball glove, but would not pay the increased cost. This is why it is important to combine questioning with observation methods and why mechanical observation is gaining ground.

Research in Action

Steelcase Makes the Case for Mechanical Observation

Steelcase (www.steelcase.com), a major American furniture manufacturer, won six Best of Neocon 2007 awards. The company used mechanical observation when it designed a furniture line for work teams. It set up hidden video cameras at various companies to observe what really goes on during the workday, looking for information on behavior and routines people might not even know they exhibited.

The company found that teams function best when members can work collectively some of the time and independently at others. The results of this study led to the very successful introduction of modular office furniture. This furniture can be quickly and easily assembled or reassembled to allow office workers to work in a large team area or in individual work spaces.[7]

Although the Steelcase study did not require the direct involvement of the participants, many mechanical observation devices do. Physical responses to sights, sounds, smells, or any sensory stimuli are an important area of observational research. Advertising or other promotional changes, such as special sales, can elicit a physical response in consumers that cannot be observed by merely looking at them. Specialized equipment designed to monitor heart and breathing rates, skin temperature, and other physiological changes is used in these situations. Because these measurements cost more than verbal reports of the respondent's reaction, they are only used when it is assumed that the respondent cannot, or will not, respond accurately to questioning. All of the physiological measurement devices operate on the assumption that the cognitive and emotional responses to stimuli elicit predictable differences in physical response. This assumption has not yet been clearly demonstrated, however.

The main advantage of mechanical observation is low observation bias, because the behavior is recorded mechanically and not by an observer. Likewise, the data are analyzed according to prespecified norms and guidelines, resulting in low analysis bias. The main disadvantages are that some of these methods can be intrusive or expensive and might not be suitable in natural settings, such as the marketplace.

Be an MR!

Visit www.disney.com and search the Internet, as well as your library's online databases, to obtain information on the criteria that consumers use for selecting theme parks. If Disney World wants to determine how many people visit its theme parks on a daily basis and which are the most popular exhibits, can the observation method be used? If yes, which observation method would you use?

Be a DM!

As the marketing manager for Disney World, how would you use information on criteria that consumers use for selecting theme parks to formulate marketing strategies that would increase attendance and market share?

A Comparison of Survey and Observation Methods

With the exception of scanner data and certain types of media panels, marketing research is seldom conducted solely with observational methods. However, observational data do offer some unique advantages. When combined with survey techniques, observation can deliver excellent results.

Relative Advantages of Observation

Observational data collection methods offer several advantages. First, many of these methods do not require conscious respondent participation, which minimizes nonresponse errors. Although ethical questions surround the practice of observation without consent, even conscious participation requires less effort from the respondent than that required with other research techniques.

Interviewer bias resulting from interaction with the respondent or subjective interpretation of the questionnaire is minimized, because the observer only has to record what is occurring. Additionally, the errors inherent in self-reported behavior are eliminated given that the observer records only actual behavior; the observer does not have to ask any questions of the respondent.

Data regarding product preferences or reactions to marketing materials from children or pets can best be collected using observational techniques. Observation also is useful in situations investigating unconscious behavior patterns or behaviors that individuals might be unwilling to discuss honestly.

Observational techniques are best applied to phenomena that occur frequently or are of short duration. In these types of applications, observational methods might cost less and be faster than survey methods.

Relative Disadvantages of Observation

Observational data provide insight into what behavior is occurring, but not why. Attitudes, motivations, and values are all lost to the observational method. Additionally, highly personal behaviors related to personal hygiene or intimate family interactions are not available for observation.

Individuals have a tendency to selectively observe only what they want to, and that might cause an observer to overlook important aspects of behavior. This perceptual difference among observers threatens the integrity of the approach.

Finally, observational techniques can be adopted for only frequent behaviors of short duration. Behaviors occurring infrequently or spanning a long period of time (e.g., individual car purchases over time) are too expensive to record using this technique.

To sum up, observation can potentially provide valuable information when properly used. From a practical standpoint, it is best to view observation as a complement to survey methods rather than as being in competition with them.

Ethnographic Research

ethnographic research
The study of human behavior in its natural context that involves observation of behavior and setting along with depth interviews.

Ethnographic research is the study of human behavior in its natural context and involves observation of behavior and setting along with depth interviews. Sometimes, audio and visual recordings also are obtained. Thus, both the questioning and observation methods are combined to understand the behavior of consumers. The following example illustrates this method.

Research in Action

PortiCo Documents with Documentaries

PortiCo Research (www.porticoresearch.com), a U.S. marketing-research and consulting firm with offices in Canada and Europe, specializes in observing individuals, questioning them in depth, recording them on videos, and selling these tapes for tens of thousands of dollars to major international clients, such as Honda, Delta, Lipton, and Procter & Gamble. They have fine-tuned the method of collecting ethnographic data and turned it into a very profitable business.

PortiCo's specialty is total immersion in the lives of consumers in an effort to document how they make purchasing decisions. Research teams of anthropologists, social psychologists, and ethnographers (professionals who comparatively study people) go into the subjects' homes with videographers. The teams tape the subjects in their homes and also take shopping trips with them to watch what they buy and to get feedback on the reasons for their purchases. After filming, employees of PortiCo transcribe the findings of the videos and analyze them for their clients. The analysis is based on the research problem that the client must gather more information about or solve. For example, PortiCo did a large study for Lipton to find out about American attitudes toward tea. With the results of the study, Lipton, a division of Unilever, the giant Dutch supplier of food and personal-care products, would be able to determine whether to invest more in advertising, to develop new flavors, or to market more iced tea instead of hot tea. The findings showed that Americans do not drink very much hot tea, especially because of the presence of caffeinated coffee in the marketplace. If and when they do drink hot tea, it is normally flavored herbal tea. Most of Lipton's hot tea is not in special flavors. Lipton has recently begun to bring herbal teas to market, however. The study did find that American consumers like iced tea. As a result of the findings, Lipton has initiated a number of creative developments in the iced-tea arena. It pushed the marketing of Brisk Iced Tea in a can, which is now the number-one selling brand of ready-to-drink iced tea. Lipton also created a Cold Brew Blend tea bag in both family size to make a whole pitcher and single-glass size for one serving. This tea bag allows iced tea to be brewed with cold water instead of boiling water. Therefore, consumers can enjoy their tea faster with much less hassle. These marketing efforts, guided by the findings of PortiCo Research, have resulted in increased sales and market share for Lipton.[8]

Other Methods of Descriptive Research

In addition to ethnographic research, a variety of other methods combine the use of questioning and observation. One such method that is commonly used is mystery shopping. Trained observers pose as consumers and shop at the company's stores or those of competitors to collect data about customer–employee interaction and other marketing variables, such as prices, displays, layout, and so forth. The mystery shoppers question the store employees, mentally take note of the answers, and observe the variables of interest. IntelliShop (www.intelli-shop.com) is an American firm that specializes in mystery shopping. For more information on mystery shopping, visit www.mysteryshop.org.

Be a DM!

As marketing manager for the U.S. supermarket chain Kroger, how would you use information on consumer behavior related to supermarket shopping to formulate marketing strategies that would increase your market share?

Be an MR!

Visit www.kroger.com and search the Internet, as well as your library's online databases, to obtain information on consumer behavior related to supermarket shopping. Kroger wants to determine to what extent consumers plan their product and brand purchases before entering the store. How will you combine the survey and observation methods to obtain this information?

Summary Illustration Using the Opening Vignette

Surveys involve the administration of a questionnaire and can be classified as traditional telephone interviews, computer-assisted telephone interviews (CATI), in-home personal interviews, mall-intercept interviews, computer-assisted personal interviews (CAPI), mail surveys, mail panels, or electronic surveys administered by e-mail or Internet. These data collection methods should not be considered mutually exclusive. Often, it is possible to employ them productively in combination, as illustrated in the opening vignette. P&G used the CATI method to survey the general population, a mail panel to determine the pricing preferences of consumers loyal to P&G brands, and mall-intercept interviews to assess reaction to the Olay Beauty Bar prior to introduction.

CATI is very suitable for surveying a representative sample of households, because telephone numbers can be randomly generated using computer programs. A mail panel allows repeated measurements on the same respondents; thus brand-loyal users can be identified (respondents who purchased P&G brands repeatedly). Mall-intercept interviews are very conducive to showing a new product to respondents before questioning them. Thus, this method was appropriate for assessing consumer response to P&G's brand extension (Olay Beauty Bar). Electronic methods, especially Internet surveys, can obtain information from large samples of respondents quickly and at a low cost.

In contrast to direct questioning in surveys, observation methods simply observe people and objects. The major observational methods are personal observation and mechanical observation. Certain types of data are best obtained through observation. An example would be consumers' purchases of various brands in supermarkets. P&G used scanner-panel data (mechanical observation) to determine that a typical brand-loyal family spent $725 each year on P&G products. In comparison, a family that bought similar products as private-label or low-priced brands spent less than $500. Figure 7.6 provides a concept map for quantitative descriptive data.

FIGURE 7.6

A Concept Map for Quantitative Descriptive Data

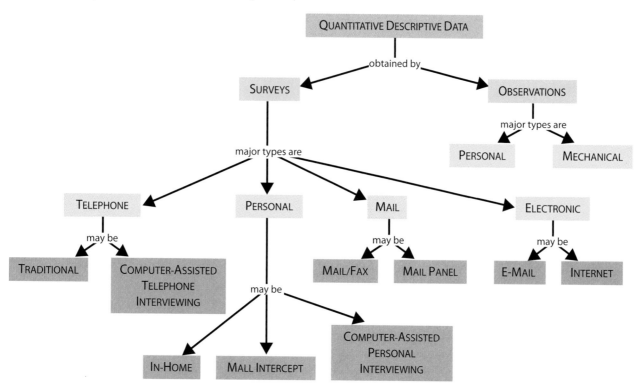

International Marketing Research

Selecting appropriate interviewing methods for international marketing research is much more difficult because of the challenges of conducting research in foreign countries. Given the differences in the economic, structural, informational, technological, and sociocultural environments, the feasibility and popularity of the different interviewing methods vary widely. Table 7.5 provides an illustration of how cultural and environmental factors can impact survey method selection. In the United States and Canada, nearly all households have telephones. As a result, telephone interviewing is the dominant mode of administering questionnaires. This is also true in some European countries, such as Sweden. In many other European countries, however, not all households have telephones. In some developing countries, only a few households have them.

In-home personal interviews are the dominant mode of collecting survey data in many European countries, such as Switzerland, and in newly industrialized countries (NICs) or developing countries. Although mall intercepts are being conducted in some European countries, such as Sweden, they are not popular in other European countries or in developing countries. In contrast, central location/street interviews constitute the dominant method of collecting survey data in France and the Netherlands.

Due to their low cost, mail interviews continue to be used in most developed countries where literacy is high and the postal system is well developed. Some examples are the United States, Canada, Denmark, Finland, Iceland, Norway, Sweden, and the Netherlands. In Africa, Asia, and South America, however, the use of mail surveys and

TABLE 7.5 The Impact of Cultural and Environmental Factors on the Selection of Survey Methods

- A survey that takes 20 minutes in the United States could take more than twice as long in Germany. The German language is not as concise as English, and Germans like to talk more than Americans do. For similar reasons, the interviewing time could be longer in other countries as well, such as in Brazil.
- Telephone directories are unreliable in some countries (e.g., some African nations, such as Sierra Leone), because they are updated infrequently.
- The incidence of unlisted telephones can vary widely across countries and across segments. For example, in Colombia, the numbers of some members of the elite and upper classes are never listed.
- In some countries, such as Japan, China, Thailand, Malaysia, and those in Southeast Asia, telephone interviews are considered rude. In contrast, in some South American countries, such as Argentina and Peru, the response rates to telephone surveys is high given the low levels of telemarketing and the element of surprise in receiving an unexpected long-distance or local call.
- Traditional personal interviewing methods remain popular in some European countries (e.g., Switzerland, Sweden, France), Asian countries (e.g., China, India, Hong Kong), African countries (e.g., Nigeria, Kenya), and South American countries (e.g., Colombia, Mexico) due to the prevalence of face-to-culture.
- Low literacy rates and/or the lack of a reliable postal system in rural areas might make mail surveys infeasible in some countries (e.g., Ghana, Ivory Coast, El Salvador, Uruguay, Paraguay).
- Mall interviews are limited due to the lack of shopping malls in many developing countries and some developed countries (e.g., Germany). In addition, domestic laws might prohibit or make it more difficult to interview people while shopping.
- Telephone penetration is low in some countries, particularly in rural areas. In some countries, such as Cambodia, multiple families might share a phone line because of high phone rates.
- In countries with high cellular/mobile phone penetration and low hard/wired-line penetration (e.g., Thailand, Malaysia), the use of traditional phone surveys is unappealing.
- Poor access to computers and the Internet make the use of electronic interviewing infeasible in some countries (e.g., rural populations in Africa, Asia, and South America).

mail panels is low because of illiteracy and the large proportion of the population living in rural areas. Mail panels are used extensively only in a few countries outside the United States, such as Canada, the United Kingdom, France, Germany, and the Netherlands. However, the use of panels might increase with the advent of new technology. Likewise, although a Web site can be accessed from anywhere in the world, access to the Web or e-mail is limited in many countries, particularly developing countries. Hence, the use of electronic surveys is not feasible, especially for interviewing households. European marketing research firms have been slower to adopt electronic interviewing, because Internet penetration in Europe has lagged that in the United States.

Different incentives are more or less effective in improving response rates in different countries. In Japan, it is more appropriate to use gifts with business surveys rather than cash as incentives. The same is true for household surveys in Mexico. Some methods are more reliable in some countries than others. When collecting data from different countries, it is desirable to use survey methods with equivalent levels of reliability rather than necessarily using the identical method, as illustrated in the Global Food, Diet & Wellbeing Monitor.

Research in Action

The Global Food, Diet & Wellbeing Monitor

The GfK NOP's Global Food, Diet & Wellbeing Monitor, a product of German-based GfK Group, is a population-based survey that samples 18 countries on 5 continents. In each country, a representative sample of 500 adults is interviewed. This sample is structured to be representative of the true population in the age range 18 to 71 (or 18 to 60 in less developed markets outside of Europe). For each country, quotas are set for age, sex, work status, presence of children, income, region, and personal values in order to ensure a representative picture of a particular country. In addition, a boost sample of mothers with children aged 3 to 16 living at home is interviewed, providing a robust base of approximately 150 mothers in each country.

The first wave of research was conducted in May–June 2005. The second wave of research was conducted in November 2005. Subsequent waves of research are conducted every 6 months. The research addresses more than 25 major topics, including eating patterns, foodstuffs being targeted/avoided, weight management, obesity, relaxation, exercise, disease concerns, and individuals' confidence in their general health and that of their children.

Interviews are conducted using a methodology that is relevant to each country. In each of the European markets except Spain, interviewing is conducted online; in Spain it is conducted face-to-face (Spain has a lower incidence of Internet usage). Online methodology also is employed in the United States, Canada, and Australia, whereas field work in countries such as China, the Philippines, Mexico,

Brazil, Russia, Egypt, and Saudi Arabia is conducted face-to-face.

The findings of these surveys reveal that health and nutrition awareness and action differ across countries. The majority of Italians and Swedes agree on the need to combine exercise and a healthy diet to stay healthy, whereas only half of the population in the United Kingdom and Spain make this connection. In France, a big focus is on reducing alcohol consumption. However, there was some commonality in limiting fat in the diet and increasing nutritious content. Based on these findings, the American food-products company Kraft Foods, a founding sponsor of the GfK NOP survey, voluntarily introduced content details on its food packages in 2006, so that consumers know the nutritional value of the food that they are consuming.[9]

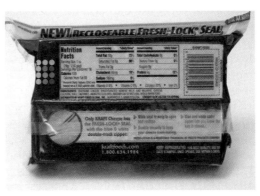

As in the case of surveys, the selection of an appropriate observation method in international marketing research should also take into account the differences in the economic, structural, informational, technological, and sociocultural environment.

Technology and Marketing Research

New information technologies will continue to revolutionize the ways in which both primary and secondary data are collected. Chapters 4 and 5 explored the role of automated databases in secondary research. Primary data collection and analysis also is changing due to advances in information technology. The researcher can use a computer to automatically dial the telephone numbers of potential respondents' fax machines and electronically send a survey. New software allows fax machines to read and store incoming text and data using optical character recognition (OCR) technology. This makes it possible to conduct and tabulate surveys on a computer. This technology could replace the traditional mail survey, especially in researching business customers, because it can gather the same type of information with much greater speed.

Field workers are gathering information in various locations with the aid of notebook computers and electronic handheld devices. These computers have built-in, wireless modems, allowing for transmission of data to and from virtually anywhere in the world. Another technological innovation is the use of interactive kiosks to collect data in central-location interviews conducted at malls and trade shows.

Marketing researchers now have access to a new form of survey data: interactive phone technology. These systems are called completely automated telephone surveys (CATS) and use the interactive voice-response (IVR) technology to circumvent the need for the human interviewer. The CATS system uses interactive voice-response technology to conduct interviews. The recorded voice of a professional interviewer asks the questions. The individual simply keys in the corresponding push button to log an answer. For surveys requiring more detailed consumer responses, individual answers can be recorded and later transcribed. This can be very beneficial, because managers not only learn what customers said, but also hear how they said it.

CATS systems can be of the outbound or inbound format. With the outbound format, a computer dials from a sample of phone numbers, the interactive voice asks questions, and the responses are automatically recorded. This method is not very successful, because it is very easy for the respondent to hang up. The inbound format has better results because the consumer initiates the call, so the likelihood of a completed call is far greater. Generally, some added incentive is attached to influence the individual to participate. Identification codes can help limit multiple call-ins (to hoard the incentives). These codes can also help to determine the characteristics of the individual who calls in (i.e., if the incentive card/letter is mailed, the code can be used as a tag for the person's location, sex, income, and so on), which aids in the examination of the data.[10]

Another technology that increasingly is being used in survey research is the use of mobile phones and devices. Realizing that an astounding 74 percent of all teens send approximately nine text messages daily, the American research firm Greenfield Online has developed Text2Express (www.text2express.com), in which members can participate in surveys anytime, anywhere, with their mobile phone. Participants no longer have to be tied down to their personal computers when doing surveys, but rather complete them on the go, carrying their "survey device" in their pocket or handbag. With the number of mobile phone subscribers expected to reach 4 billion by 2010, mobile phones become an extremely powerful device for marketing research, changing the way we think about gathering consumer feedback.

Likewise, technological developments are giving rise to new ways of observation. New tools, such as functional magnetic resonance imaging (fMRI), which originally was developed to view brain tumors, are now being used to see how a person reacts to different stimulants. A researcher can place a branded item in front of a person and use fMRI to see exactly what part of the brain the product affects and how strongly. These tools help measure the emotional and thought processes associated with decision making and highlight how the brain functions during the decision-making process. By discovering what elements trigger positive brain responses, marketers might be able to devise more appealing products or more effective advertising campaigns.

All of these innovations, as well as future advances in information technology, will continue to improve the way in which researchers collect data.

Ethics in Marketing Research

Surveys often are used as a cover for a targeted sales effort. The real purpose is not to obtain information to address a marketing research problem, but to sell a product. This practice, called "sugging" in the trade language, is unethical. A similar unethical practice is "frugging" and involves fundraising under the guise of research. To illustrate, assume you get a call from a company stating that they are conducting research on consumer attitudes. After asking a few diagnostic questions, the company tries to sell you one of its products (sugging) or asks for a donation (frugging).

Respondents' anonymity, discussed in the context of qualitative research in Chapter 6, is an important issue in both survey and observational search. Researchers have an ethical obligation to not disclose the identities of respondents to anyone outside the research organization, including the client. Only when researchers notify respondents in advance and obtain their consent prior to administering the survey can an exception be made and the respondents' identities revealed to the client. Even in such cases, prior to disclosing identification information the researcher should obtain an assurance from the client that the respondents' trust will be kept and their identities will not be used for sales effort or misused in other ways. Ethical lapses in this respect by unscrupulous researchers and marketers have resulted in a serious backlash for marketing research.

The researcher has the responsibility to use an appropriate survey method in an ethical and legal way. In the United States, for instance, legislation prohibits unsolicited faxed surveys. In many states, totally automated outgoing (initiated by the researcher) telephoning is illegal.

Researchers often observe people's behavior without their consent, arguing that informing the respondents might alter their behavior. This can be considered an invasion of the respondents' privacy. One guideline proposed to resolve this problem is that research observation should only be conducted in places where people would expect to be observed by the public. Public places such as malls or grocery aisles, places where people observe other people routinely, are fair game. Nonetheless, notices stating that these areas are under observation for marketing research purposes should be posted at the sites. After observing their behavior, the researcher is still obligated to obtain the necessary permission from the subjects.[11]

It should also be mentioned that the common practice of serving cookies on the Internet raises ethical concerns. Many users do not realize it, but they have been served a cookie or two while on the Internet. A cookie is not a culinary delight in this case. It is a sophisticated means by which a Web site can collect information on visitors. Often this process takes place without the Web surfers' knowledge and is an invasion of their privacy and right to consent.

Research in Action

Have a Cookie!

Hotwired (www.hotwired.com), a Web site devoted to technology and culture, offers dynamic online tools, such as search engines, that provide people with important information. Hotwired uses cookies to collect information about Web site traffic by tracking an individual's preference for hotel choice, airline travel, and other interests. Hotwired uses this information to target customers with advertisements by promoting discounts and specials using the individual's preferred choices. In addition, the information helps marketing personnel collect demographics on the reader. Also, the company can monitor "hits" on particular topics and gain valuable feedback on user interest. For example, using cookies, Hotwired might find out that after visiting its Web site, a particular respondent then visits Travelocity (www.travelocity.com) for flight and hotel information pertaining to Jamaica. The next time that same visitor visits Hotwired.com, a pop-up Web advertisement will alert that visitor of special airfare and hotel packages to Jamaica offered by Hotwired.

This technique enables Hotwired to monitor use patterns and to eliminate socially acceptable response bias. Information collected in this manner has been used to modify editorial content and the site's format to make the site more appealing. Although this information is helpful to Hotwired, the use of cookies in this way raises several ethical issues.[12]

What Would *You* Do?

Microsoft: Small Businesses Represent a Big Market

The Situation

Statistics from the U.S. Small Business Administration show that in 2008 small businesses generated about 50 percent of all U.S. sales and contributed about 50 percent of the private gross domestic product. Small businesses also employed about 50 percent of the U.S. workforce. Microsoft Corp. is impressed with these statistics, because they indicate that small businesses might represent a big market for its products. It wonders whether the needs of small businesses are different than those of large businesses. Steve Ballmer, Microsoft CEO, would like to develop specialized products for the small businesses. Some of these products could include the following: a Web site just for small businesses; the Microsoft Small Business Council (which provides information to help small businesses use technology); the Microsoft Small Business Technology Partnership Board (an educational resource); the BackOffice Small Business Server (for a more direct route to small businesses); and a small business edition of Microsoft Works.

The Marketing Research Decision

1. To survey small businesses' preferences for software products, which survey method would you recommend and why?
   a. CATI
   b. On-site personal interviews
   c. Mail
   d. Internet
   e. E-mail
2. Discuss the role of the type of research you recommend in enabling Steve Ballmer to determine small businesses' preferences for software products.

The Marketing Management Decision

1. Which of the following should Microsoft do to effectively meet the needs of small businesses?
   a. Develop a specific Web site for small businesses.
   b. Develop new products for small businesses.

   c. Customize existing products (e.g., Microsoft Office).
   d. Give price discounts to small businesses.
   e. Develop an advertising campaign specifically directed at small businesses.
2. Discuss how the marketing-decision action that you recommend to Steve Ballmer is influenced by the type of survey that you suggested earlier and by the findings of that survey.

What Steve Ballmer Did

Steve Ballmer decided to develop a dedicated Web site for small businesses (www.microsoft.com/smallbusiness/hub.mspx). Small businesses can use this site to access tech support, security, products, and a learning center, all designed specifically for small businesses. For example, specialized products include Office Small Business 2007, Small Business Server, Financial Management, Customer Management, and Online Services.[13]

Summary

Surveys and observations are the two primary methods of conducting quantitative, descriptive research. Surveys involve the direct questioning of respondents, whereas respondent behavior is simply recorded in observation.

Surveys involve the administration of a questionnaire and can be classified based on the method or mode of administration as traditional telephone interviews, computer-assisted telephone interviews (CATI), in-home personal interviews, mall-intercept interviews, computer-assisted personal interviews (CAPI), mail surveys, mail panels, or electronic surveys administered by e-mail or Internet. Of these methods, telephone interviews (CATI) are the most popular in the United States. However, each method has some general advantages and disadvantages. Although these data collection methods are usually thought of as distinct and competitive, they should not be considered mutually exclusive. It is possible to employ them productively in combination.

The major observational methods are personal observation and mechanical observation. As compared to surveys, the relative advantages of observational methods are (1) they permit measurement of actual behavior; (2) there is no reporting bias; and (3) there is less potential for interviewer bias. Also, certain types of data can be obtained best, or only, by observation. The relative disadvantages of observation are (1) very little can be inferred about motives, beliefs, attitudes, and preferences; (2) there is potential for observer bias; (3) most methods are time-consuming and expensive; (4) it is difficult to observe some forms of behavior; and (5) there is potential for unethical behavior. With the exception of scanner data and certain types of media panels, observation is rarely used as the sole method of obtaining primary data, but it can be usefully employed in conjunction with survey methods.

An important consideration in selecting the methods of administering surveys internationally is to ensure equivalence and comparability across countries. New technologies, such as computerized fax machines, completely automated telephone systems, and mobile phones, are revolutionizing survey administration. Misuse of surveys as a guise for selling, failing to maintain the anonymity of respondents, and observing behavior without respondents' knowledge or consent are major ethical issues in implementing survey and observation methods.

Key Terms and Concepts

Survey method, 213	Fax survey, 220	Personal observation, 228
Structured data collection, 214	Mail panel, 221	Humanistic inquiry, 228
Sample control, 216	Nonresponse bias, 222	Mechanical observation, 229
Response rate, 216	Prepaid incentive, 226	Ethnographic research, 232
Social desirability, 218	Promised incentive, 226	
Interviewer bias, 218	Observation, 228	

Suggested Cases and Video Cases

Running Case with Real Data

1.1 Hewlett Packard

Comprehensive Critical Thinking Cases

2.1 American Idol   2.2 Baskin-Robbins   2.3 Akron Children's Hospital

Comprehensive Cases with Real Data

3.1 Bank of America   3.2 McDonald's   3.3 Boeing

Video Cases

7.1 Starbucks	9.1 P&G	10.1 Nivea	11.1 Dunkin' Donuts
12.1 Motorola	13.1 Subaru	14.1 Intel	19.1 Marriott

Live Research: Conducting a Marketing Research Project

As a class, discuss the various survey methods and select one that is appropriate for the project. In addition to the criteria given in this chapter, certain practical constraints might have to be considered if the students must collect data. Examples include the following:

1. A budget for making long-distance calls should be supplied if a telephone survey is to be done beyond the local calling area.
2. If a CATI system is not available, the telephone method can be limited to traditional telephone.
3. Students will not be allowed to conduct mall-intercept interviews unless permission is obtained from the mall management. Some malls have signed exclusive contracts with marketing research firms for data collection.
4. It might not be practical to do in-home personal interviews covering a large geographic area, or even in a local region.
5. There might not be enough time for a mail survey, and a mail panel might be prohibitively expensive.
6. E-mail addresses might not be available or might be very difficult to get.
7. Mechanical observation devices can be impractical to obtain and use.

The survey/data collection method selected should be discussed and approved by the client.

Acronym

The classification of survey methods by mode of administration may be described by the acronym METHODS:

M ail panels

E lectronic interviews

T elephone interviews

H ome (in-home personal) interviewing

O n-site mall interviews

D irect-mail interviews

S oftware for CATI/CAPI

Review Questions

1. Explain briefly how the topics covered in this chapter fit into the framework of the marketing research process.
2. Name the major modes for obtaining information via a survey.
3. What are the relevant factors for evaluating which survey method is best suited to a particular research project?
4. What would be the most appropriate survey method for a project in which control of field force and cost are critical factors?
5. Name the types of mechanical observation, and explain how they work.
6. What are the relative advantages and disadvantages of observation?

Applied Problems

1. Describe a marketing research problem in which both survey and observation methods could be used for obtaining the information needed.
2. The campus food service would like to determine how many people eat in the student cafeteria. List the ways in which this information could be obtained. Which method is best?
3. Locate and answer an Internet survey for which you would qualify as a respondent. How would you evaluate this survey based on the discussion in this chapter?
4. Locate an Internet survey and examine the content of the questionnaire carefully. What are the relative advantages and disadvantages of administering the same survey using CATI or mall-intercept interviewing?
5. Design an e-mail survey to measure students' attitudes toward credit cards. E-mail the survey to 10 students. Summarize, in a qualitative way, the responses received. Are student attitudes toward credit cards positive or negative?

Group Discussion

1. As a small group, discuss the ethical issues involved in disguised observation. How can such issues be addressed?
2. "With advances in technology, observation methods are likely to become popular." Discuss this statement as a small group.

Hewlett-Packard Running Case

Review the Hewlett-Packard (HP) case, Case 1.1, and questionnaire given toward the end of the book.

1. The HP survey was administered by posting it on a Web site and sending an e-mail invitation to respondents. Evaluate the advantages and disadvantages of this method. Do you think that this was the most effective method?
2. Compare the various survey methods for conducting the HP survey.
3. Can HP make use of the observation method to determine consumers' preferences for PCs and notebook computers? If yes, which observation method would you recommend and why?
4. Visit a store selling PCs and notebooks (e.g., CompUSA, Best Buy, Circuit City, Sears, etc.). If this store wants to conduct a survey to determine consumer preferences for PCs and notebook computers, which survey method would you recommend and why?

STARBUCKS: Staying Local While Going Global Through Marketing Research

Starbucks

Named after the first mate in the novel *Moby-Dick*, Starbucks is the largest coffee-house company in the world. As of August 2007, there were 6,566 company-operated stores and 3,729 licensed stores in the United States and 1,613 company-operated stores and 2,488 joint venture and licensed stores outside the United States. The company's objective is to establish Starbucks as the most recognized and respected brand in the world. It expects to achieve this by continuing with rapid expansion of retail stores and growing its specialty sales and other operations. It will also continually pursue other opportunities to leverage the Starbucks brand through new products and new distribution channels that meet consumer needs determined by marketing research.

Over the last two decades, Starbucks has revitalized the coffee industry. The inspiration behind Starbucks was conceived when CEO Howard Schultz visited Italy. At that time, Starbucks was a coffee company, and people were very passionate about the coffee, but in Milan Howard saw the passion around the coffee-house experience. In Milan, Howard went from one espresso bar to the next and saw how people at the coffee houses knew each other. These people were getting their daily coffees, but they also were making daily connections with other people, with the baristas, and with the artistry; the folks making the drinks were connecting with their customers and knew them personally. From this experience, Howard recognized that although Starbucks was passionate about the coffee, it also had the opportunity to be equally passionate about the coffeehouse experience.

Marketing research determined four strategic pillars for expressing the Starbucks brand. The four pillars are (1) the coffee, which is Starbucks' foundation and which gives Starbucks its credibility; (2) some of the finest products that are associated with the coffee experience; (3) the warm, welcoming, and inspiring environment; and (4) community involvement. Even though the coffee and the products are important, the key to Starbucks' success has been the latter two. It has designed an environment that is warm and welcoming and provides an experience that makes the company a part of the community or local culture. It has been able to achieve this success by emphasizing the Starbucks culture.

Starbucks also draws upon customers for ideas by conducting extensive marketing research. Many of its products and services are a direct result of suggestions from patrons or local employees. Much more than most companies, consumers touch and influence the corporation. Many innovations and retail items resulted directly from customers' feedback obtained by conducting marketing research and by suggestions made to the baristas. From customized CD music collections to sales of sandwiches, gums, and chocolates—all were a result of customer recommendations. Many stores even offer wireless Internet access in response to customer demand. Through its baristas, Starbucks found that people were interested in an iced Starbucks and the blended Starbucks, and thus the Frappuccino was born—an idea that came from customers and the baristas rather than corporate headquarters.

This local connection with customers and the consequent brand building have allowed Starbucks to move into other successful venues—from coffee bean sales at grocery stores to partnership with United Airlines, Marriott, Pepsi, Kraft,

and others. Starbucks has some of the best coffee in the world, but it was missing from grocery stores, which is where most coffee is purchased. Syndicated data from ACNielsen showed that grocery stores sell two-thirds of the coffee in the United States, and Starbucks has been able to enter this lucrative market. It has also used partnerships in other industries to increase revenues.

In the past few years, Starbucks has been aggressively expanding its global footprint by entering newer markets and strengthening its position in countries in which it already has a presence. Growing a brand overseas, however, can be different from doing so in Starbucks' home market. According to Thomas Yang, former Senior VP of International Marketing, this difference in growth behavior in different countries can be attributed to Starbucks' different stages of development in the United States and different parts of the world. In international markets, Starbucks is at the brand development and establishment stage, allowing consumers to discover what the brand is about and what the Starbucks experience is about. In contrast, Starbucks has had a presence in North America since 1971. In the United States, the Starbucks experience is pretty well-known and understood, and thus it is in a different stage.

Starbucks has been extremely successful in achieving its objectives. It has been able to maintain a local feel despite massive growth around the globe. It has done this by stressing its culture and placing the focus on its employees and customers through marketing research. Starbucks hopes to continue staying local while going global through marketing research.

Conclusion

Starbucks has gone from a small local coffee startup in the 1970s to the largest coffeehouse company in the world. This success has been largely been due the strong connection it has been able to foster with its consumers and maintain a local charm and feel in its stores even as it continues to expand globally at breakneck speed. This strong connection has also enabled Starbucks to gather useful feedback and marketing research information from customers leading to the introduction of several successful new products and penetration into new global markets.

Questions

1. Use the Internet to identify secondary sources of information pertaining to coffee consumption in the United States.
2. What are consumers looking for in a coffeehouse experience? How do they view the Starbucks coffeehouse experience? How can Starbucks determine answers to these questions?
3. A survey is to be conducted to determine the image coffee drinkers have of Starbucks and other coffee chains. Which survey method should be used and why?
4. Starbucks is thinking of introducing a new gourmet coffee with a strong aroma. Can the observation method be used to determine the consumer reaction to this coffee prior to national introduction? If so, which observation method should be used?

References

1. www.starbucks.com, accessed February 15, 2008.
2. Steven Gray and Kate Kelly, "Starbucks Plans to Make Debut in Movie Business," *Wall Street Journal*, January 12, 2006, pp. A1, A8.
3. Bob Keefe, "Starbucks to Offer CD-Burning Capabilities at Stores in Future," *Knight Ridder Tribune Business News*, June 28, 2004, p. 1.

Causal Research Design: Experimentation

OPENING QUESTIONS

1. How is the concept of causality defined in marketing research, and how does one distinguish between the ordinary meaning and the scientific meaning of causality?

2. What are the conditions for causality, and can a causal relationship be demonstrated conclusively?

3. How are the two types of validity (internal and external) defined, and how do they differ?

4. What are the various types of experimental designs, and what are the differences among pre-experimental, true experimental, quasi-experimental, and statistical designs?

5. How can the use of laboratory versus field experimentation and experimental versus nonexperimental designs in marketing research be compared and contrasted?

6. What is test marketing, and how does it involve experimentation?

7. Why are the internal and external validity of field experiments conducted overseas generally lower than in the United States?

8. How does technology facilitate causal research?

9. What ethical issues are involved in conducting causal research, and how can debriefing address some of these issues?

Muzak: An Uncommon Remedy for the Common Cold

> "Marketing research—and marketing—would be much better off if researchers conducted more experiments. Well-done experiments are and have always been the 'gold standard' of evidence in science."
>
> *Larry Gibson,*
> *Senior Associate,*
> *Eric Marder and Associates.*

Once referred to as "background music," in the business world Muzak (www.muzak.com) is now referred to as "audio architecture." As of 2008, Muzak provided products to more than 350,000 businesses, and more than 100 million Americans hear its harmonic convergences each day. The company offers music, sound systems, videos and TV, and messaging at 200 sales and service locations across the United States.

Muzak has now moved into audio marketing in supermarkets. In a time of increasing competition, more store advertising at the point of purchase might be just what is needed. Research shows that few customers come to the grocery store with a specific brand in mind. Most consumers know what items they need and choose brands or sizes when they reach the store. So audio advertising, such as that provided by Muzak, seems to hold promise.

An experiment was designed to test the effectiveness of Muzak advertising. Twenty randomly selected supermarkets were assigned to one of two groups, each group containing 10 supermarkets. One group of supermarkets, randomly selected, was the experimental group and the other was the control group. Muzak ads for selected products were run in the experimental group supermarkets for a period of 10 weeks. These ads were informational, telling consumers of the

benefits of the advertised products. The price and other factors (e.g., shelf space) affecting the sale of these items were kept the same in both the experimental and control group stores. The sales of the advertised products were monitored for both the experimental and control groups. The results showed an increase in the sales of advertised items, with cold/allergy/sinus-relief products recording the highest increase of 29.8 percent (see chart). Thus, there might be an expanding market for Muzak in the near future.[1]

Product	Percent Sales Increase in Experimental Stores
Potato chips	3.5%
Condensed milk	7.1
Tea bags	13.7
Cold cereal	12.2
Juice	14.5
Laundry detergent	27.4
Toothpaste	28.9
Cold/allergy/sinus relief	29.8

Overview

Chapter 3 introduced two broad categories of conclusive research: causal and descriptive research designs. Descriptive designs were discussed in Chapter 7. This chapter concentrates on causal research designs. Figure 8.1 briefly explains the focus of the chapter, its relation to the previous ones, and the steps of the marketing research process on which this chapter concentrates. Experimentation is the primary method employed to collect data in causal research designs. The opening vignette illustrates an experiment conducted to determine the effect of in-store Muzak advertising on the sales of selected items.

This chapter presents experimentation in detail. The concept of research validity and threats to that validity are discussed. A classification of experimental designs is provided as well as consideration of specific designs, along with the relative merits of laboratory versus field experiments. The applications of experimentation in international marketing research and the impact of technology on experimentation are discussed. The chapter ends with a discussion of ethical issues in experimentation. Figure 8.2 gives an overview of the different topics discussed in this chapter and how they flow from one to the next.

The Concept of Causality

A causal inference relates to whether a change in one marketing variable produces a change in another variable. Marketing managers often are faced with decisions in which they attempt to infer causal relationships. For example, will a 10-percent price reduction in a given brand of coffee—say, Maxwell House in the United States, Madras Filter in India, or Frisco in South Africa—result in an increase in sales to a level that will at least cover the revenues lost due to the price reduction? In evaluating this question, marketing managers may draw a causal inference that price influences the sale of at least some coffee brands.

FIGURE 8.1

Relationship of Experimentation to the Previous Chapters and the Marketing Research Process

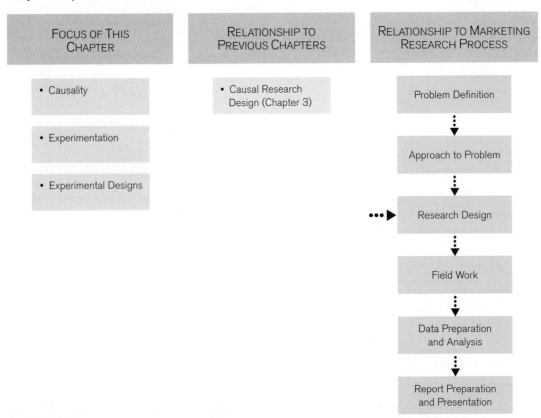

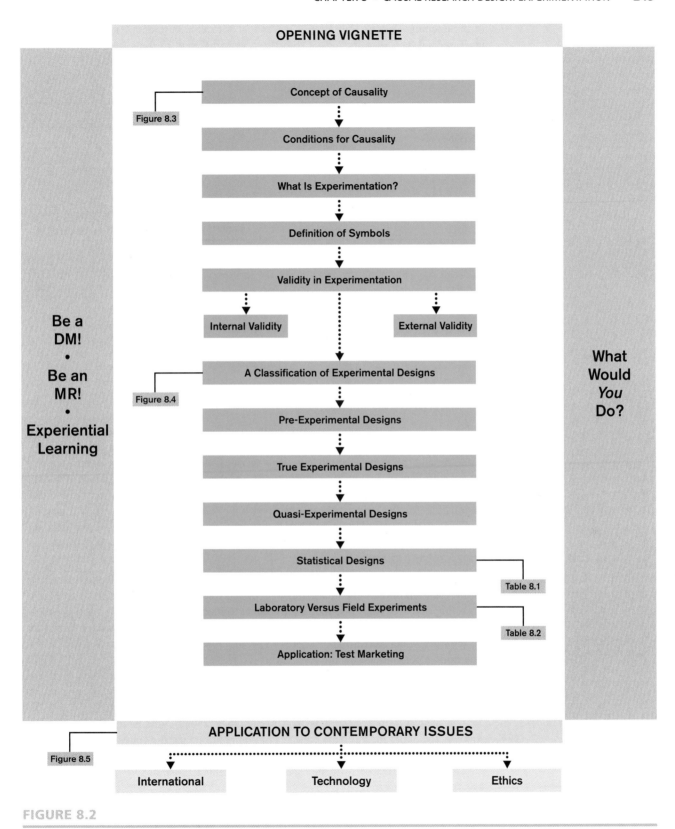

FIGURE 8.2

Experimentation: An Overview

causality
When the occurrence of X increases the probability of the occurrence of Y.

In the opening vignette, the inference was that Muzak advertising leads to (i.e., causes) increased sales. **Causality** means something very different to the average person on the street than it means to a scientist. Take, for example, the statement "X causes Y."

Ordinary Meaning	Scientific Meaning
X is the only cause of Y.	X is only one of a number of possible causes of Y.
X must always lead to Y. (X is a deterministic cause of Y.)	The occurrence of X makes the occurrence of Y more probable. (X is a probabilistic cause of Y.)
It is possible to prove that X is a cause of Y.	We can never prove that X is a cause of Y. At best, we can infer that X is a cause of Y.

The scientific meaning of causality is more appropriate to marketing research because it is sensitive to the limitations that surround the data collection process and the causal inferences that can legitimately be drawn. In the opening vignette, experimenters realized that in-store advertising was only one cause of sales. Other causes, such as prices and shelf displays, also affected sales and consequently had to be controlled.

Conditions for Causality

At least three conditions must be satisfied in order to justify the inference of a causal relationship between two variables: (1) concomitant variation, (2) time order of occurrence of variables, and (3) absence of other possible causal factors. These conditions are necessary but not sufficient to demonstrate causality; that is, they must be satisfied to justify drawing a causal inference. However, their presence does not guarantee that the true variables responsible for the effects being observed have been isolated. These conditions are explained in more detail in the following sections.

Concomitant Variation

concomitant variation
A condition for inferring causality that requires that a cause, X, and an effect, Y, occur together or vary together as predicted by the hypothesis under consideration.

Concomitant variation occurs when the presumed cause (X) and presumed effect (Y) are both present and both vary in a manner predicted by the hypothesis. Suppose a regional marketing manager for a fast-food outlet wants to identify the causes of variation in food sales across the 20 outlets in her region. After visiting all 20 sites, she has concluded that the monthly outlet performance scores (X)—which reflect factors such as average wait time during peak hours, cleanliness, and food quality—directly impact sales (Y). Given that hypothesis, outlets that are scoring high on performance measurements should be recording the highest sales levels. Her analysis indicates that this relationship does, in fact, hold. Can she conclude that high performance scores "cause" high sales?

The answer to that question is "no." Many other factors might be impacting sales. For example, the outlet location, the presence of competition, and the concentration of the surrounding residential area might all have an impact on sales, even though they are not included in the outlet performance score. This example illustrates the limitations associated with drawing causal inferences. It is not possible to conclude that the cause of fast-food-outlet sales has been identified from this research. The researcher can only say that an association exists between performance scores and sales.

Time Order of Occurrence of Variables

Another requirement in determining a causal relationship relates to when the variables occur; that is, the occurrence in time of the presumed cause relative to the presumed effect. For one variable to hypothetically cause another, it must precede or occur simultaneously with the effect; it cannot occur afterwards. This is referred to as the *time order of variables*.

Although time order of variables seems like an intuitively obvious requirement, it is not always easy to determine time order in a marketing situation. For example, customers who shop frequently at Debenhams department stores in the United Kingdom are more likely to have a Debenhams credit card. Also, customers who have a department store's charge card are likely to shop there frequently. The time order of these variables—charge card ownership and frequent shopping—is not obvious. Did charge card ownership precede frequent shopping or did frequent shopping precede charge card ownership? An understanding of the underlying phenomena associated with department store shopping might be necessary to accurately identify time order.

Absence of Other Possible Causal Factors

As can be seen in the previous examples, both time order and concurrent variation conditions might be satisfied, but the relevant cause-and-effect relationship might remain unidentified. The presence of additional or extraneous variables that impact the effect (i.e., dependent) variable must be controlled in order to draw causal inferences. To illustrate, Debenhams might be able to isolate in-store service as a cause of sales if it is possible to ensure that changes in all other factors that affect sales—such as pricing, advertising, level of distribution, product quality, competition, and so on—are held constant or otherwise controlled. Ruling out other possible causal factors is seldom an easy task. The point-of-purchase buying example shows the difficulty of establishing a causal relationship.

Research in Action

POP Buys

Recent statistical data indicate that consumers make as much as 80 percent of their buying decisions at the point-of-purchase (POP). POP buying decisions have increased concurrently with increased advertising efforts in stores. These include radio advertisements as well as ads on shopping carts, floor space, grocery bags, ceiling signs, and shelf displays. It is difficult to separate the cause from the effect of POP advertising and POP buying. It is possible that these variables might be both causes and effects in this relationship. In other words, there is more POP advertising because there is more POP buying, and there is more POP buying because there is more POP advertising.[2]

If, as the POP example indicates, it is difficult to establish cause-and-effect relationships, what is the role of evidence obtained in experimentation?

Role of Evidence

The combination of evidence of causality in the form of concomitant variation, time order of occurrence of variables, and elimination of other possible causal factors does not guarantee a causal relationship. However, an accumulation of consistent evidence increases the confidence that a causal relationship exists. Controlled experiments can provide strong evidence of all three conditions.

Be a DM!

As the head of the U.S. Federal Trade Commission, what are your concerns about the increased availability of information on the Internet?

Be an MR!

Search the Internet, as well as your library's online databases, to obtain information on Internet usage by consumers. What conditions are necessary for you to conclude that increased use of the Internet by consumers is increasing the availability of information on the Internet?

What Is Experimentation?

Experimentation is the research technique used in causal research (Figure 8.3). It is the primary method for establishing cause-and-effect relationships in marketing (see Chapter 3). Experiments can be described in terms of independent, dependent, and extraneous variables; test units; and random assignment to experimental and control groups. To conduct an **experiment**, the researcher manipulates and controls one or more independent variables and then observes the effects that those manipulated variables have on the dependent variables, while controlling the influence of outside or extraneous variables. In this section, these concepts are defined and illustrated using the example from the opening vignette.

Independent Variables

Independent variables are variables or alternatives that are manipulated (i.e., the researcher changes their levels) and whose effects are measured and compared. These variables, also known as *treatments*, might include price levels, package designs, and advertising themes. In the opening vignette, the independent variable was Muzak advertising, and the treatments consisted of Muzak advertising versus no advertising; at Debenhams, treatment of the independent variable may include the application of different procedures for in-store service.

Test Units

Test units are individuals, organizations, or other entities whose response to the independent variables or treatments is being examined. Test units might include consumers, stores, or geographic areas. Test units might be Debenhams stores or, as in the opening vignette, supermarkets.

Dependent Variables

Dependent variables are the variables that measure the effect of the independent variables on the test units. These variables might include sales, profits, and market shares. The dependent variables, in the opening vignette, were the sales of specific products.

Extraneous Variables

Extraneous variables are all variables other than the independent variables that affect the response of the test units. These variables can confound the dependent variable measures in a way that weakens or invalidates the results of the experiment. Extraneous variables include store size, store location, and competitive effort. In the opening vignette, the extraneous variables would be other variables—such as price, amount of shelf space, and so on—that would affect the sales of the selected products. At Debenhams, they might be differences in price, product quality, or level of competition.

experiment
The process of manipulating one or more independent variables and measuring their effect on one or more dependent variables, while controlling for the extraneous variables.

independent variables
Variables that are manipulated by the researcher and whose effects are measured and compared.

test units
Individuals, organizations, or other entities whose response to independent variables or treatments is being studied.

dependent variables
Variables that measure the effect of the independent variables on the test units.

extraneous variables
Variables, other than the independent variables, that influence the response of the test units.

FIGURE 8.3

Experimentation as Conclusive Research

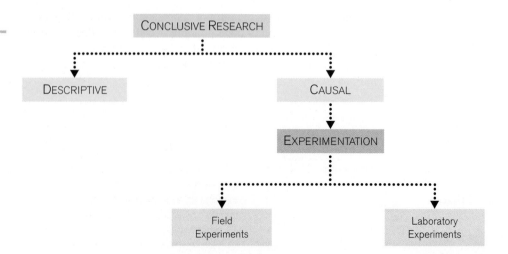

Random Assignment to Experimental and Control Groups

Random assignment involves randomly assigning test units to the experimental and control groups and is one of the most common techniques used to control for the effect of extraneous variables on the dependent variable. Random assignment to experimental and control groups attempts to minimize the influence of extraneous factors such as age, income, or brand preference by spreading them equally across the groups under study.

When an experiment is being conducted, at least one group will be exposed to the manipulated independent variable. This is called the **experimental group**. The results of this experimental group might be compared to another experimental group at a differing level of manipulation or to a control group. The **control group** is not exposed to the independent variable manipulation. It provides a point of comparison when examining the effects of these manipulations on the dependent variable. In the opening vignette, the supermarket stores were randomly assigned to the two groups. One group was randomly chosen to be the experimental group (that was exposed to Muzak advertising), and the other served as the control group (that received no advertising).

Experimental Design

An **experimental design** is a set of procedures specifying (1) the test units and how these units are to be divided into homogeneous subsamples, (2) what independent variables or treatments are to be manipulated, (3) what dependent variables are to be measured, and (4) how the extraneous variables are to be controlled.

In the opening vignette, the test units were stores that were randomly assigned to two groups. The independent variable to be manipulated was Muzak advertising versus no advertising, and the dependent variables were the sales of specific products. Extraneous variables such as price and shelf space were kept at the same levels in both the experimental and control group supermarkets by exercising managerial control.

As a further illustration of these definitions, consider the following example.

random assignment
Involves randomly assigning test units to the experimental and control groups. It is one of the most common techniques used to control for the effect of extraneous variables on the dependent variable.

experimental group
The group exposed to the manipulated independent variable.

control group
The control group is not exposed to the independent variable manipulation. It provides a point of comparison when examining the effects of these manipulations on the dependent variable.

experimental design
The set of experimental procedures specifying (1) the test units and sampling procedures, (2) independent variables, (3) dependent variables, and (4) how to control the extraneous variables.

Research in Action

Taking Coupons at Face Value

An experiment was conducted to test the effects of coupon value on redemption. Personal interviews were conducted in New York with 280 shoppers who were entering or leaving a supermarket. Two levels of the independent variable (coupon value) were used, one offering 15 cents off and the other 50 cents off. Shoppers were randomly assigned to these two coupon value levels.

Brand usage was presumed to be an extraneous variable. Four brands—Tide detergent, Kellogg's Corn Flakes, Aim toothpaste, and Joy liquid dishwashing detergent—were used. The respondents answered questions about which brands they used so that the effect of this extraneous variable could be controlled during analysis. Respondents also were asked how likely they were to cash coupons of the given face value the next time they shopped. An interesting finding was that higher face value coupons produced a greater likelihood of redemption among infrequent or nonbuyers of the promoted brand but had little effect on regular buyers.[3]

In the coupon experiment, the independent variable was the value of the coupon (15 cents versus 50 cents). The dependent variable was the likelihood of cashing the coupon. The extraneous variable that was controlled was brand usage. The experimental design required the random assignment of shoppers to two experimental groups. A control group was not used in this design.

Definition of Symbols

To help in our discussion of extraneous variables and specific experimental designs, we will use a set of symbols commonly used in marketing research.

X = the exposure of a group to an independent variable, treatment, or event, the effects of which are to be determined

O = the process of observation or measurement of the dependent variable on the test units or group of units

R = the random assignment of test units or groups to separate treatments

In addition, the following conventions are adopted:

- Movement from left to right indicates movement through time.
- Horizontal alignment of symbols implies that those symbols refer to a specific treatment group.
- Vertical alignment of symbols implies that those symbols refer to activities or events that occur simultaneously.

For example, the symbolic arrangement

$$X \quad O_1 \quad O_2$$

means that a given group of test units was exposed to the treatment variable (X), and the response was measured at two different points in time, O_1 and O_2.

Likewise, the symbolic arrangement

$$R \quad X_1 \quad O_1$$
$$R \quad X_2 \quad O_2$$

means that two groups of test units were randomly assigned (R) to two different treatment groups at the same time (X_1 and X_2), and the dependent variable was measured in the two groups simultaneously (O_1 and O_2).

Validity in Experimentation

In conducting an experiment, a researcher has two goals. The first is to draw valid conclusions about the effect of the independent variables on the dependent variables. This is referred to as *internal validity*. The second goal is to make valid generalizations from the specific experimental environment to a larger population. This goal is satisfied when external validity is achieved.

Internal Validity

internal validity
A measure of accuracy of an experiment. It measures if the manipulation of the independent variables, or treatments, actually caused the effects on the dependent variable(s).

Internal validity refers to whether the manipulation of the independent variables or treatments actually caused the observed effects on the dependent variables. Internal validity is threatened when the influences of extraneous variables are mixed with the independent variables. Without proper control of the extraneous variables, the researcher is unable to isolate the effect of the independent variable and thus cannot establish internal validity. In the opening vignette, to claim internal validity the researcher had to show that the increase in sales of the products in the experimental group supermarkets was in fact due to (i.e., caused by) Muzak advertising. Thus, the researcher had to show that price and other extraneous variables (e.g., shelf space) affecting the sale of these products were kept the same in both the experimental and control group stores.

External Validity

external validity
A determination of whether the cause–effect relationships found in the experiment can be generalized.

External validity refers to whether the cause-and-effect relationships found in the experiment remain the same when replicated in a larger population. In other words, can the results be generalized beyond the experimental situation? If so, to what populations, settings, times, independent variables, and dependent variables can the results be projected?

In the opening vignette, to claim external validity the researcher must show that the sample of 20 supermarkets was representative, no peculiar conditions were encountered, and the results are generalizable to all supermarkets.

Threats to external validity arise when the experiment is conducted in an unrealistic manner, limiting the ability to generalize. This occurs when the experimental conditions do not account for factors likely to be encountered in the real world. Experiments conducted in a laboratory environment are more likely to lack external validity than field experiments. This is because laboratory experiments are conducted in artificial, highly controlled environments.

Marketing researchers often have to make decisions to trade off one form of validity in order to gain another. However, internal validity must be protected in order to produce results that are meaningful enough to generalize. Extraneous variables threaten both the internal and external validity.

Extraneous Variables

The need to control extraneous variables in order to establish internal and external validity has already been discussed. In this section, extraneous variables are classified into the following categories: history, maturation, testing, instrumentation, statistical regression, selection bias, and mortality.

History

Contrary to what the name implies, **history** (*H*) does not refer to the occurrence of events before the experiment. Rather, *history* refers to specific events that are external to the experiment but occur at the same time as the experiment. For example, general economic conditions might decline during the experiment, thereby contaminating the posttreatment observation. The longer the time interval between observations, the greater the possibility that history will confound an experiment.

history
Specific events that are external to the experiment but that occur at the same time as the experiment.

Maturation

Maturation (*MA*) is similar to history except that it refers to changes in the test units themselves. These changes are not caused by the impact of independent variables or treatments, but occur with the passage of time. In an experiment involving people, maturation takes place as people become older, more experienced, tired, bored, or uninterested. Tracking and marketing studies that span several months are vulnerable to maturation, because it is difficult to know how respondents are changing over time.

maturation
An extraneous variable attributable to changes in the test units themselves that occur with the passage of time.

Testing Effects

Testing effects are caused by the experimentation process. Typically, these are the effects on the experiment of taking a measure on the dependent variable before and after the presentation of the treatment. For example, the respondents try to maintain consistency between their pre- and posttreatment attitudes. As a result of the testing effect, posttreatment attitudes might be influenced more by pretreatment attitudes than by the treatment itself.

Instrumentation

Instrumentation (*I*) refers to changes in the measuring instrument, in the observers, or in the scores themselves. Sometimes, measuring instruments are modified during the course of an experiment. Consider an experiment in which Debenhams measures the sales in pounds of a product before and after exposure to an in-store display (treatment). If there is a nonexperimental price change between measurements, this results in a change in instrumentation, because sales in pounds will be measured using different unit prices. Instrumentation effects are likely when interviewers make pre- and posttreatment measurements. The effectiveness of interviewers can differ at different times.

instrumentation
An extraneous variable involving changes in the measuring instrument or in the observers or scores themselves.

Statistical Regression

statistical regression
An extraneous variable that occurs when test units with extreme scores move closer to the average score during the course of the experiment.

Statistical regression (*SR*) effects occur when test units with extreme scores move closer to the average score during the course of the experiment. In the advertising experiment, suppose that some respondents had either very favorable or very unfavorable attitudes. On posttreatment measurement, their attitudes might have moved toward the average. People's attitudes change continuously. Those with extreme attitudes have more room for change, so variation is more likely. This has a confounding affect on the experimental results, because the observed effect (change in attitude) might be attributable to statistical regression rather than to the treatment (test commercial).

Selection Bias

selection bias
An extraneous variable attributable to the improper assignment of test units to treatment conditions.

Selection bias (*SB*) refers to the improper assignment of test units to treatment conditions. This bias occurs when selection or assignment of test units results in treatment groups that differ on the dependent variable before the exposure to the treatment condition. If test units self-select their own groups or are assigned to groups on the basis of the researchers' judgment, selection bias is possible. For example, consider a merchandising experiment in which Debenhams assigns two different merchandising displays (old and new) to different groups of stores. The stores in the two groups might not be equivalent to begin with. They might vary with respect to a key characteristic, such as store size. Store size is likely to affect sales regardless of which merchandising display was assigned to a store.

Mortality

mortality
An extraneous variable attributable to the loss of test units while the experiment is in progress.

Mortality (*MO*) refers to the loss of test units while the experiment is in progress. This happens for many reasons, such as test units refusing to continue in the experiment. Mortality confounds results because it is difficult to determine if the lost test units would respond to the treatments in the same manner as those that remain. Consider again the Debenhams merchandising display experiment. Suppose that during the course of the experiment three stores in the new display treatment condition drop out. The researcher could not determine whether the average sales for the new display stores would have been higher or lower if these three stores had continued in the experiment.

Controlling Extraneous Variables

Extraneous variables represent alternative explanations of experimental results. They pose a serious threat to the internal and external validity of an experiment. Unless they are controlled, they affect the dependent variable and thus confound the results. For this reason, they also are called *confounding variables*. Extraneous variables can be controlled in four ways: randomization, matching, statistical control, and design control.

Randomization

randomization
A method of controlling extraneous variables that involves randomly assigning test units to experimental and control groups by using random numbers. Treatment conditions also are randomly assigned to experimental groups.

Randomization refers to the random assignment of test units to experimental and control groups by using random numbers. Treatment conditions also are randomly assigned to experimental groups. For example, respondents are randomly assigned to one of three experimental groups. One of the three versions of a test commercial, selected at random, is administered to each group. As a result of random assignment, extraneous factors can be represented equally in each treatment condition. It is possible to check whether randomization has been effective by measuring the possible extraneous variables and comparing them across the experimental and control groups. Therefore, randomization is the preferred method for controlling extraneous variables.

Matching

matching
A method of controlling extraneous variables that involves matching test units on a set of key background variables before assigning them to the treatment conditions.

Matching involves comparing test units on a set of key background variables before assigning them to the treatment conditions. In the Debenhams merchandising display experiment, stores could be matched on the basis of annual sales, size, or location. Then one store from each matched pair would be assigned to each experimental group. Matching has two drawbacks. First, test units can be matched on only a few characteristics, so the test units might be similar on the variables selected but unequal on others. Second, if the matched characteristics are irrelevant to the dependent variable, then the matching effort has been futile.

Statistical and Design Control

Statistical control involves measuring the extraneous variables and adjusting for their effects through statistical analysis. **Design control** involves the use of experiments designed to control specific extraneous variables. A classification of experimental designs is described in the next section.

A Classification of Experimental Designs

The four broad categories of experimental designs are pre-experimental, true experimental, quasi-experimental, and statistical designs (Figure 8.4). **Pre-experimental designs** do not use randomization to control for extraneous factors. Thus, they suffer from many threats to internal and external validity. However, with a proper note of their limitations, they can add value when used in an exploratory fashion. Three examples of this design are the one-shot case study, the one-group pretest–posttest design, and the static group. These designs, along with the others that follow, are discussed in detail later.

In **true experimental designs**, the researcher can randomly assign subjects and experimental groups. Therefore, these designs provide a larger degree of control over extraneous variables. Included in this category are the pretest–posttest control group design and the post-test-only control group design.

Quasi-experimental designs result when the researcher is unable to fully manipulate the independent variables or treatments but can still apply part of the apparatus of true experimentation. These designs are typically employed in natural environments, enabling some degree of experimental control in a natural setting. Two such designs are time series and multiple time series designs.

Statistical designs are series of basic experiments that allow for statistical control and analysis of external variables. Statistical designs are classified on the basis of their characteristics and use. Statistical designs include factorial designs.

We will illustrate the various experimental designs in the context of measuring the effectiveness of PepsiCo advertising. Pepsi makes heavy use of celebrities in its advertising. To capture the teenage market, Pepsi ads have highlighted superstars Michael Jackson and Lionel Richie with the theme "Choice of a New Generation." Other "New Generation" stars featured in Pepsi ads have included, Michael J. Fox (star of *Back to the Future)* and comedian Billy Crystal. The "You've Got the Right One Baby, Uh Huh!" campaign for

statistical control
A method of controlling extraneous variables by measuring the extraneous variables and adjusting for their effects through statistical methods.

design control
A method of controlling extraneous variables that involves using specific experimental designs.

pre-experimental designs
Designs that do not control for extraneous factors by randomization.

true experimental designs
Experimental designs distinguished by the fact that the researcher can randomly assign test units to experimental and control groups and also randomly assign treatments to experimental groups.

quasi-experimental designs
Designs that apply part of the procedures of true experimentation, while lacking full experimental control.

statistical designs
Designs that allow for the statistical control and analysis of external variables.

FIGURE 8.4

A Classification of Experimental Designs

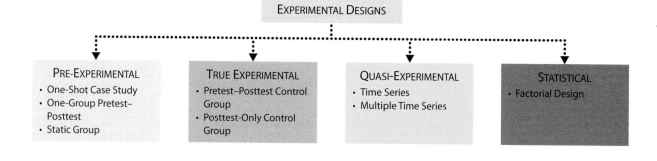

The effectiveness of Pepsi advertising that makes use of celebrities can be assessed by using appropriate experimental designs.

Diet Pepsi featured the late Ray Charles. Pepsi struck the right chord when it launched the much-lauded "Joy of Pepsi" campaign, featuring appearances by dimpled Hallie Eisenberg and the comedian Tom Green. Pepsi ads have included other stars, including Shakira, Enrique Iglesias, Britney Spears, Mariah Carey, the Spice Girls, David Beckham, and Puff Daddy. Around the world, the roster has included model Aishwariya Rai (India), singer-songwriter Kylie Minogue (Australia), actor-singer Leslie Cheung (Hong Kong), and soccer star Younus Khan (Pakistan).

Should Pepsi continue to feature celebrities in its advertising? Is this advertising effective? Experimental research that measures advertising effectiveness can provide useful information. We begin our discussion with the pre-experimental designs.

Pre-Experimental Designs

Pre-experimental designs are characterized by an absence of randomization. This section describes three specific designs: the one-shot case study, the one-group pretest–posttest design, and the static group.

One-Shot Case Study

one-shot case study
A pre-experimental design in which a single group of test units is exposed to a treatment X, and then a single measurement on the dependent variable is taken.

Also known as the *after-only design,* the **one-shot case study** can be represented symbolically as

$$X \quad O_1$$

A single group of subjects is exposed to a treatment (X), and then a single measurement on the dependent variable is taken (O_1). This type of design is constructed using a nonrandom sampling process in which the subjects are self-selected or selected arbitrarily by the researcher. Without randomization, the observed dependent variables are subject to the influences of several extraneous variables.

Additionally, the design lacks a control group. Without a control group, there is no point of comparison for the results. Due to lack of randomization and the absence of a control group, this design is clearly weak in terms of internal validity. It does not control for history, maturation, selection, or mortality. For these reasons, the one-shot case study is more appropriate for exploratory rather than conclusive research.

Research in Action

One Shot at Pepsi Advertising

To assess the effectiveness of Pepsi advertising featuring celebrities, telephone interviews would be conducted with respondents who report watching the particular TV program on which the commercial was aired the previous night (X). The dependent variables (Os) are unaided and aided recall and attitudes toward the advertisement, the brand, and the celebrity. First, unaided recall would be measured by asking the respondents whether they recall seeing a commercial for a soft drink. If they recall the Pepsi commercial, details about commercial content and execution would be solicited. Respondents who do not recall the test commercial would be asked if they saw a Pepsi commercial (aided recall). For those who have an unaided or aided recall of the commercial, attitudes toward the commercial, the brand advertised, and the celebrity featured would be measured. The results of these experimental measures can be compared with normal scores for these types of questions in order to assess the effectiveness of the advertising and the celebrity featured.

One-Group Pretest–Posttest Design

The **one-group pretest–posttest design** can be symbolized as

$$O_1 \quad X \quad O_2$$

In this design, a group of subjects is measured once before the experimental treatment (O_1) and once after (O_2). Again, this design lacks a control group for comparison. The treatment effect is computed as $O_2 - O_1$. Although this design is considered better than a case study, the validity of conclusions is questionable, because extraneous variables are largely uncontrolled due to lack of randomization and the lack of a control group. History, maturation, testing, instrumentation, selection, mortality, and regression could possibly be present. The following example shows how this design is used.

one-group pretest–posttest design
A pre-experimental design in which a group of test units is measured twice, once before and once after the treatment.

Research in Action

Can Pepsi Perform in a Theater?

Firms such as GfK Custom Research North America (www.gfkamerica.com), a division of German-based GfK Group, commonly use the one-group pretest–posttest design to measure the effectiveness of test commercials. Respondents are recruited to central theater locations in various test cities. The respondents are interviewed, and their attitudes toward Pepsi advertising, the brand, and the celebrity (O_1) are measured. Then they watch a TV program containing the Pepsi commercial (X) and other filler commercials. After viewing the TV program, the respondents are again interviewed regarding their attitudes toward Pepsi advertising, the brand, and the celebrity (O_2). The effectiveness of the test commercial is determined by the difference between O_2 and O_1.

Static Group Design

The **static group** is a two-group experimental design in which one of the groups acts as a control group (CG). Only one group, the experimental group (EG), receives the experimental treatment. The subjects are not assigned randomly, and measurements are made on both groups following the treatment (posttest). This design is expressed symbolically as:

$$\begin{aligned} \text{EG:} \quad & X \quad O_1 \\ \text{CG:} \quad & \quad O_2 \end{aligned}$$

static group
A pre-experimental design in which there are two groups: the experimental group (EG), which is exposed to the treatment, and the control group (CG). Measurements on both groups are made only after the treatment, and test units are not assigned at random.

The treatment effect would be measured as the difference between the control and experimental group ($O_1 - O_2$). The lack of randomization leaves the experiment open to some extraneous effects. The two groups might differ before the treatment, leading to selection bias. Mortality effects might be present, because more test units might withdraw from the experimental group than the control group.

In practice, the control group often is defined as the group receiving the current level of marketing activity, rather than as a group that receives no treatment at all. In many cases, it is impossible to reduce marketing input (e.g., price) to zero.

Research in Action

Is Pepsi Advertising Static?

A static group comparison to measure the effectiveness of a Pepsi commercial would be conducted as follows. Two groups of respondents would be recruited on the basis of convenience. Only the experimental group would be exposed to the TV program that contains the Pepsi commercial (X). Attitudes toward Pepsi advertising, the brand, and the celebrity would then be measured in both the experimental (O_1) and the control group (O_2). The effectiveness of the Pepsi commercial would be measured as the difference between the test and control group ($O_1 - O_2$).

Be an MR!

Visit www.foxnews.com and search the Internet, as well as your library's online databases, to obtain information on American consumers' preferences for network news channels. Fox News wants to determine which one of three new formats it should implement. Would you recommend a pre-experimental design? If so, which one would you recommend?

Be a DM!

As the marketing manager of Fox News, how would you use information on consumers' preferences for network news channels to formulate marketing strategies that would increase your audience and market share?

True Experimental Designs

True experimental designs are differentiated from pre-experimental designs by the fact that subjects are randomly assigned to groups. Treatment conditions also are randomly assigned to groups. For example, respondents are randomly assigned to one of three experimental groups. One of the three versions of a test commercial, selected at random, is administered to each group. As a result of random assignment, extraneous factors can be represented equally in each group or treatment condition. Randomization is the preferred procedure for ensuring the prior equality of experimental groups. However, randomization might not be effective when the sample size is small, because it merely produces groups that are equal on average. It is possible, though, to check whether randomization has been effective by measuring the possible extraneous variables and comparing them across the experimental groups.

True experimental designs include the pretest–posttest control group design and the posttest-only control group design.

Pretest–Posttest Control Group Design

pretest–posttest control group design
A true experimental design in which the experimental group is exposed to the treatment but the control group is not. Pretest and posttest measures are taken on both groups. Test units are randomly assigned.

In the **pretest–posttest control group design**, subjects are randomly assigned to either the experimental or the control group. A pretreatment measure is taken on each group. Thus, each group is measured prior to administering the treatment to the experimental group. This design is symbolized as:

$$\text{EG:} \quad R \quad O_1 \quad X \quad O_2$$
$$\text{CG:} \quad R \quad O_3 \qquad O_4$$

The treatment effect (TE) is measured as:

$$(O_2 - O_1) - (O_4 - O_3)$$

The use of a control group and randomization in this design controls for most extraneous variables. The extraneous effects are presumed to be represented equally in both the control and experimental groups. The difference between the control and experimental groups is thought to reflect only the treatment. With the use of a pretest measure in this design, the posttest measurement is susceptible to **interactive testing effects**, which means that a prior measurement affects the test unit's response to the independent variable.

interactive testing effect
An effect in which a prior measurement affects the test unit's response to the independent variable.

Research in Action

Pepsi Pre- and Postmortem

An experiment for measuring the effectiveness of Pepsi's advertising using a pretest–posttest control group design would be conducted as follows. A sample of respondents would be distributed randomly, half to the experimental group and half to the control group. A pretest questionnaire would be administered to the respondents in both groups to obtain a measurement on attitudes toward Pepsi advertising, the brand, and the celebrity. Only the respondents in the experimental group would be exposed to the TV program containing the Pepsi commercial. Then, a questionnaire would be administered to respondents in both groups to obtain posttest measures on attitudes toward Pepsi advertising, the brand, and the celebrity.

As this example shows, the pretest–posttest control group design involves two groups and two measurements on each group. A simpler design is the posttest-only control group design.

Posttest-Only Control Group Design

The **posttest-only control group design** does not involve any premeasurement. It can be symbolized as:

$$EG:\ R\ X\ O_1$$
$$CG:\ R\ \ \ \ O_2$$

posttest-only control group design
A true experimental design in which the experimental group is exposed to the treatment but the control group is not and no pretest measure is taken. Test units are randomly assigned.

The treatment effect is the difference between the experimental and control group measurements.

$$TE = O_1 - O_2$$

The simplicity of this design offers time, cost, and sample-size advantages. For these reasons, it is the most popular experimental design in marketing research. However, this design is not without limitations. Although randomization is used to equalize groups, without a pretest, there is no way to verify group similarity. Selection bias and mortality might be present. Without a pretest, researchers also are unable to examine changes in individual subjects over the course of the study. Note that, except for premeasurement, the implementation of this design is very similar to that of the pretest–posttest control group design. The opening vignette provided an application. The supermarket stores were randomly assigned to the experimental group and the control group. No premeasurements were taken. Only the stores in the experimental group were exposed to Muzak advertising. Measurements on the sales of advertised items were obtained in the experimental group (O_1) and control group (O_2) stores. The increase in sales due to Muzak advertising was determined as ($O_1 - O_2$).

Experiential Learning

Canon wants to determine consumers' price sensitivity for its new advanced digital camera and hires you as a consultant.

1. Visit the Web site of Best Buy, a U.S.-based consumer-electronics retailer, at www.bestbuys.com and identify the price ranges of the digital cameras by Canon and other brands.

2. Search the Internet, as well as your library's online databases, to obtain information on consumers' price sensitivity for digital cameras.

3. Canon wants to determine consumers' price sensitivity for its new advanced digital camera. Design an appropriate experiment. Would you recommend a true experimental design? If yes, which one?

4. As the marketing manager of Canon cameras, how would you use information on consumers' price sensitivity for digital cameras to formulate pricing strategies that would increase your market share?

Quasi-Experimental Designs

Quasi-experimental designs are appropriate when researchers are faced with situations where they are unable to randomize or control the scheduling of experimental treatments. The experimenters might, however, be able to control when and on whom experimental measurements are taken. Quasi-experimental designs are faster and less expensive than other experimental designs and, in some natural research settings, might be the only avenue open for data collection. However, because full experimental control is lacking researchers must take into account the specific variables that are not controlled. Popular forms of quasi-experimental designs are time series and multiple time series designs.

Time Series Design

time series design
A quasi-experimental design that involves periodic measurements on the dependent variable for a group of test units. Then, the treatment is administered by the researcher or occurs naturally. After the treatment, periodic measurements are continued in order to determine the treatment effect.

The **time series design** involves the use of periodic measurements of a group or individuals. At some point during the measurement, an experimental manipulation occurs naturally or is artificially introduced. Additional measurement follows. A time series experiment can be symbolized as:

$$O_1 \, O_2 \, O_3 \, O_4 \, O_5 \, X \, O_6 \, O_7 \, O_8 \, O_9 \, O_{10}$$

This is a quasi experiment because the researcher lacks control in terms of randomization of the subjects to treatments. Additionally, the researcher may have no control over the timing of treatment presentation, as well as which subjects are exposed to the treatment. Multiple measurements might create a testing effect, causing a change in measured behavior simply because the respondents know they are being measured. History is not controlled. Nevertheless, time series designs are useful, particularly when evaluating behavior occurring in a natural setting.

Research in Action

Time Will Tell the Effectiveness of Pepsi Advertising: Time Series Design

The effectiveness of a Pepsi commercial (*X*) could be examined by broadcasting the commercial into a series of markets a predetermined number of times. The test units or respondents are members of a panel. Although the marketer can control the scheduling of the test commercial, it is not possible to control when or if panel members are exposed to it. The marketer will examine panel members' attitudes toward Pepsi advertising, the brand, and the celebrity, as well as purchases before, during, and after the campaign to determine whether the test commercial had a short-term effect, a long-term effect, or no effect.

multiple time series design
A time series design that includes another group of test units to serve as a control group.

The **multiple time series design** is similar to time series except that it adds a control group that also is repeatedly measured. This group is not subject to the experimental treatment. If the control group is carefully selected, this design can be an improvement over the simple time series experiment.

Statistical Designs

Statistical designs consist of a series of basic experiments that allow for statistical control and analysis of external variables. In other words, several basic experiments are conducted simultaneously. Thus, statistical designs are influenced by the same sources of invalidity that affect the basic designs being used. Statistical designs offer the following advantages:

1. The effects of more than one independent variable can be measured.
2. Specific extraneous variables can be statistically controlled.
3. Economical designs can be formulated when each subject is measured more than once.

The most common statistical designs are the factorial designs.

Factorial Design

A **factorial design** is used to measure the effects of two or more independent variables at various levels. It allows for the measurement of interactions between variables. An interaction is said to take place when the simultaneous effect of two or more variables is different from the sum of their separate effects. For example, an individual's favorite drink might be coffee and her favorite temperature level might be cold, but she might not prefer cold coffee, leading to an interaction.

factorial design
A statistical experimental design used to measure the effects of two or more independent variables at various levels and to allow for interactions between variables.

A factorial design can also be thought of as a table. In a two-factor design, each level of one variable represents a row, and each level of another variable represents a column. Factorial designs involve a cell for every possible combination of treatment variables, as in the example that follows.

Research in Action

Factoring Humor and Information in Pepsi Commercials

Suppose that in the Pepsi case the researcher is interested in examining the effect of humor and the effect of various levels of brand information on advertising effectiveness. Three levels of humor (no humor, some humor, and high humor) are to be examined. Likewise, brand information is to be manipulated at three levels (low, medium, and high). The resulting table would be three rows (levels of information) by three columns (levels of humor), producing nine possible combinations or cells, as laid out in Table 8.1. The respondents would be randomly assigned to one of the nine cells. Respondents in each cell would receive a specific treatment combination. For example, respondents in the upper-left-hand corner cell would view a commercial that had no humor and low brand information. After exposure to a treatment combination, measures would be obtained on attitudes toward Pepsi advertising, the brand, and the celebrity from respondents in each cell.

Statistical procedures such as analysis of variance (discussed in Chapter 17) are used to analyze the treatment effects and interactions. The main disadvantage of a factorial design is that the number of treatment combinations increases multiplicatively with an increase in the number of variables or levels. However, this is often not a serious limitation as the researcher can control both the number of variables and the levels.

TABLE 8.1 An Example of a Factorial Design

Amount of Brand Information	Amount of Humor		
	No Humor	Medium Humor	High Humor
Low			
Medium			
High			

Selecting an Experimental Design

Selecting an experimental design often involves a trade-off in terms of control. Designs that offer the greatest degree of internal validity typically are conducted in highly artificial environments that can threaten the generalizability or external validity of the experimental results.

One solution to finding the optimum combination of internal and external validity might be to use differing experimental designs at differing points in the study. For example, designs that offer tight internal validity (i.e., laboratory experiments) could be used during the early stages of the research effort. In this way, a more reliable measure of the true treatment effect could be secured. During later stages of the study, more natural settings (i.e., field experiments) could be used to enable generalization of results.

The following section discusses the distinction between laboratory and field experimentation in more detail.

Laboratory Versus Field Experiments

laboratory environment
An artificial setting for experimentation in which the researcher constructs the desired conditions.

demand artifacts
Responses given because the respondents attempt to guess the purpose of the experiment and respond accordingly.

field environment
An experimental location set in actual market conditions.

A **laboratory environment** is an artificial one, which affords the greatest amount of control over the crucial factors involved in the study. Advertising testing and test kitchens in central-location theaters are examples of laboratory experiments used in marketing research. Because the environments are highly contrived, questions of external validity are raised. Compared to field experiments, the artificial nature of laboratory environments might cause reactive error in that the respondents react to the situation itself rather than to the independent variable. Also, laboratory environments can cause **demand artifacts**, a phenomenon in which the respondents attempt to guess the purpose of the experiment, modifying their responses accordingly. On the positive side, laboratory experiments do allow for more complex designs than field experiments. Hence, the researcher can control for more factors or variables in the laboratory setting, which increases internal validity.

A **field environment** involves measurement of behavior, attitudes, or perceptions in the environment in which they occur. The researcher has much less control over extraneous variables that might impact internal validity. However, if internal validity can be maintained, the results can be generalized more easily than those obtained in a laboratory setting. The opening vignette presents an example of a field experiment. The use of scanner panels to conduct field experiments was discussed in Chapter 5. The differences between the two environments are summarized in Table 8.2.

The Internet can provide a mechanism for controlled experimentation in a laboratory-type environment. Continuing with the example of testing the effectiveness of Pepsi's

TABLE 8.2 Laboratory Versus Field Experiments

Factor	Laboratory	Field
Environment	Artificial	Realistic
Control	High	Low
Reactive error	High	Low
Demand artifacts	High	Low
Internal validity	High	Low
External validity	Low	High
Time	Short	Long
Number of units	Small	Large
Ease of implementation	High	Low
Cost	Low	High

advertising, various Pepsi advertisements or commercials can be posted at various Web sites. Matched or randomly selected respondents can be recruited to visit these sites, with each group visiting only one site. If any pretreatment measures have to be obtained, the respondents answer a questionnaire posted on the site. They are then exposed to a particular Pepsi advertisement or a commercial at that site. After viewing the advertisement or commercial, the respondents answer additional questions providing posttreatment measures. Control groups can be implemented in a similar way. All of the experimental designs that we have considered can be implemented in this manner.

Internet experiments can also be used to test the effectiveness of alternative Web designs. Visitors are randomly exposed to different Web designs and their purchases are tracked over time, keeping the other marketing variables constant. Thus, the most effective design can be determined and implemented on the company's Web site.

Experiential Learning

Factorial Experimental Design

Let's say that Eagle Boys, Australia's largest homegrown chain of pizza makers, is considering changing its cheese from mozzarella to a provolone/mozzarella cheese mix in a 1:2 ratio or a 2:1 ratio. This pizza maker also is considering holding the price for pizza the same, increasing the price 10 percent, or reducing the price 10 percent.

1. Search the Internet, as well as your library's online databases, to obtain information on consumers' preferences for and consumption of pizza.

2. Design a marketing experiment that will determine which formulation customers prefer. Your experimental design and format should consist of the following parts:
   a. Independent variables: The things that you changed.
   b. Dependent variable(s): What changed as a result of the manipulated variables, such as rating the formulation of cheese and price.
   c. Extraneous variables: Everything else that did not change during the experiment, such as location of the test, the crust, and so forth.
   d. Control group: Did you use one? Why or why not?

3. Would it be better to use a laboratory or a field experiment to conduct your research? Explain.

4. Thirty respondents would be needed in each cell to accurately test your results. If each respondent receives $20 to participate, how much would the incentives cost in your experiment?

5. Describe how you would change your experiment to make it less costly. How might these changes affect your results?

6. How can the pizza maker use this information to increase its market share?

Limitations of Experimentation

Although experimentation is becoming increasingly important in marketing research, it does have limitations: time, cost, and administration of an experiment.

Time

Many types of field experiments become increasingly accurate with time. For example, to observe the long-term effect of a promotional campaign or a product introduction, purchase behavior must be observed over multiple purchase cycles. The accuracy of such behavioral information tends to increase with the passage of time. This added precision must be weighted against the costs of delaying a product rollout or the launch of a new advertising campaign.

Cost

New-product research in field environments can be extremely expensive. It is much more expensive than laboratory experiments, which typically occur on a small scale and use a limited number of subjects. In order to field test a new product, management must consider more than just the direct costs of data collection and analysis. Production must be initiated on a limited scale; point-of-sale promotional campaigns as well as mass advertising must be developed and introduced on a limited basis. Limited distribution channels might also have to be opened. Test market experiments can easily cost millions of dollars.

Administration

Controlling the effects of extraneous variables is an essential aspect of experimental research. Achieving the desired level of control becomes increasingly difficult as the research moves from the laboratory to the field. Field experiments often interfere with a company's ongoing operations, and obtaining cooperation from the retailers, wholesalers, and others involved can be difficult. Also, competitors might deliberately contaminate the results of a field experiment.

Application: Test Marketing

test marketing
An application of a controlled experiment done in limited, but carefully selected, test markets. It involves replicating the planned national marketing program for a product in the test markets.

test markets
Carefully selected parts of the marketplace that is particularly suitable for test marketing.

Test marketing is an example of a controlled field experiment conducted in limited but representative parts of a market. The research sites are called **test markets**. In a test market experiment, a national marketing program is replicated on a small scale. The two major objectives of test marketing are (1) to determine market acceptance of the product and (2) to test alternative levels of marketing mix variables. The independent variables being manipulated in such studies typically include elements of the marketing mix. The researcher can manipulate factors such as promotional investments, pricing, product modifications, or distribution elements. Observed consumer reactions represent the dependent variables, measured in terms of purchase behavior (i.e., sales) and/or attitudes or reactions to the marketing manipulations being studied. Test marketing is being practiced by both consumer-product and industrial-product companies.

Designing a standard market test involves deciding what criteria to use for selecting test markets, how many test markets to use, and the duration of the test.[4] Among all of the criteria considered in selecting a test market, representativeness is perhaps the most important. For example, information gathered from a new-product test can be used to predict ultimate market acceptance of that product and will govern the go/no-go decision regarding full market rollout. The test market must also be self-contained in terms of media coverage if mass-market advertising is planned to support the test. This prevents wasting promotional dollars. Additionally, the promotion of new products that are available in only a limited area can create negative consumer reaction toward future rollouts.

Test marketing runs the risk of revealing strategies, new product developments, or modified product positioning to the competition. Therefore, the strength of competition in a particular test site is another important consideration. In the United States, commonly used test markets include Charlotte, North Carolina; Indianapolis, Indiana; Kansas City, Missouri; Nashville, Tennessee; Rochester, New York; and Sacramento and Stockton, California. These cities are desirable test markets because each is considered to be fairly representative of a large segment of the U.S. population.

In general, the more test markets that can be used, the better. If resources are limited, at least two test markets should be used for each program variation to be tested. However, when external validity is important, at least four test markets should be used. Despite its limitations in terms of time demands, costs, and competitive responses, test marketing can be very beneficial to a product's successful introduction.

Summary Illustration Using the Opening Vignette

Three conditions must be satisfied before causal inferences can be made that X is a cause of Y: (1) concomitant variation, which implies that X and Y must vary together in a hypothesized way; (2) time order of occurrence of variables, which implies that X must precede or occur simultaneously with Y; and (3) elimination of other possible causal factors, which implies that competing explanations must be ruled out. Thus, for Muzak advertising to be a cause of sales, sales of advertised products must be higher in stores with Muzak than in stores without Muzak; Muzak advertising must occur before or simultaneously with an increase in sales (it cannot occur afterwards); and the sales increase must not be attributable to other factors, such as price, shelf space, and so forth.

Experiments provide the most convincing evidence of all three conditions. An experiment is formed when the researcher manipulates one or more independent variables (presence or absence of Muzak advertising) and measures their effect on one or more dependent variables (sales of advertised products), controlling for the effect of extraneous variables (price, shelf space, and so forth).

In designing an experiment, it is important to consider internal and external validity. Internal validity refers to whether the manipulation of the independent variables actually caused the effects on the dependent variables. External validity refers to the generalizability of experimental results. In the opening vignette, to claim internal validity the researcher must show that Muzak advertising was, in fact, the cause of the increase in sales of the products in the experimental group of supermarkets. Thus, the researcher must show that price and other extraneous variables (e.g., shelf space) affecting the sale of these products were kept the same in both the experimental and control group stores. To claim external validity, the researcher must show that the sample of 20 supermarkets selected was representative, that no peculiar conditions were encountered, and that the results are generalizable to all supermarkets.

Experimental designs can be classified as pre-experimental, true experimental, quasi-experimental, and statistical designs. The design selected in the opening vignette was a true experimental design, because the supermarkets were randomly selected and assigned to the two groups, and one of the groups was randomly chosen as the experimental group. The specific design adopted was the posttest-only control group. An experiment can be conducted in a laboratory environment or under actual market conditions in a real-life setting, as in the opening vignette. Figure 8.5 provides a concept map for experiments.

FIGURE 8.5

A Concept Map for Experiments

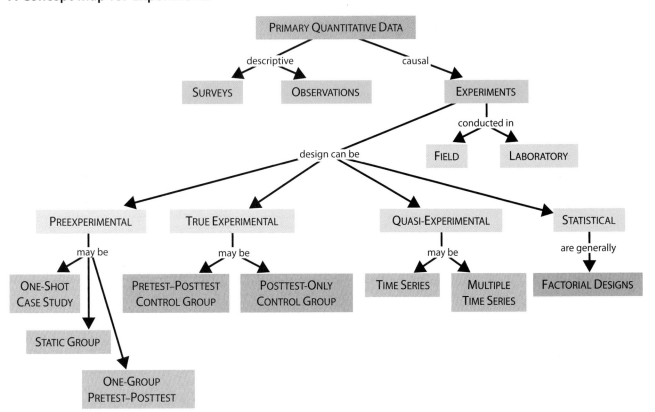

International Marketing Research

Field experiments pose even greater challenges in international markets than those faced in the United States. The researcher might be faced with market differences in terms of marketing support systems, economics, structural differences, information availability, and the technological environment. For example, in many countries, television stations are owned and operated by the government, with severe restrictions on television advertising. This makes field experiments manipulating advertising levels extremely difficult, because the researcher might lack the flexibility to vary advertising content and expenditures.

Differential levels of infrastructure development and differing practices associated with retailing also plague test market feasibility. In the Baltic States, for example, the limited availability of supermarkets makes it difficult for a U.S. consumer-products company such as Procter & Gamble to conduct experiments to determine the effect of in-store promotions on the sales of its detergents. In emerging countries in Asia, Africa, and South America, achieving adequate distribution of products to the rural populations is difficult because of the lack of basic infrastructures, such as roads, transportation, and warehouses.

Thus, the internal and external validity of field experiments conducted overseas is generally lower than in the United States. While pointing to the difficulties of conducting field experiments in other countries, we do not wish to imply that such causal research cannot or should not be conducted. To the contrary, as the following example indicates, creatively designed field experiments can result in rich findings.

Research in Action

Pepsi: Experimenting in Europe

In 2006, sales of Pepsi soda dropped. In the fourth quarter, 2006 the volume of drinks sold by PepsiCo rose by only 0.5 percent in North America, and sales of soda actually fell. However, beverage volume rose 7 percent internationally, led by markets such as Brazil, China, Argentina, and the Middle East. To boost sales, Pepsi International changed its advertising in 2007.

The new advertising strategy attempted to emphasize consumer choice and was reinforced through new television advertising. The first advertisement in the campaign featured a young man walking down a city street. The screen is split into four parts. In the first window, a soccer ball bounces into the picture. The young man juggles it, whereupon he is joined by Ronaldinho, the Brazilian soccer ace. In the second screen, the young man ignores the bouncing ball, but walks on to a record store, where he enters and joins a guitar band for a jam. In the third screen, he bypasses the ball and the record store, but instead meets a young woman. In the last screen, he ignores all the other possibilities but bumps into a lamppost as he turns his head to look at what he missed.

The new strategy was decided in favor of previous advertising focusing on celebrities, such as a Roman–gladiator-themed spot featuring American singer Britney Spears. The decision was based on experiments in which respondents were randomly assigned and asked to evaluate either the new or the previous campaign. The new campaign resulted in more favorable evaluations. The new campaign resulted in increased sales in 2007 and 2008.[5]

Technology and Marketing Research

Virtual Reality (VR) is a real-time, 3D environment made to represent a real or an imaginary environment. Such environments are created by high-powered computer systems. As with many of the technological innovations used in marketing research, VR was not developed specifically with marketing research in mind, but it is finding its way into field marketing research and holds great promise for conducting causal research. Using VR, the researcher can create an environment that represents the field (marketplace) and yet exercise a degree of control possible only in a laboratory setting.

A program called Visionary Shopper, developed by the Canadian-based marketing-research firm IFOP-CMR (www.ifop.com), allows respondents to shop in a VR store. The goal of the program is to give the user as real, or as close to real, shopping experience as possible. It does not require the "space-age" gadgetry normally associated with VR; respondents do not have to wear helmets or gloves, and they are not hooked up to a machine with an inordinate number of wires. The system uses a high-resolution, color video screen that provides 3D images. The screen shows the user a shelf filled with products, just as would be seen in the actual store. The image is complete with brand names, price tags, and special displays.

The respondents use either a track-ball or a touch-screen to go "shopping" in the VR store. They can choose the aisle and the product category. For example, the user can "walk" to the cereal aisle and see the multitude of choices that would be in any grocery store, including Cap'n Crunch, Cheerios, and Frosted Flakes. The shopper can select a specific item, which is then displayed more prominently on the screen. The shopper can turn the box and read any of the labels on the product. The item's price is displayed when the item is selected. After the shopper is done looking at the item, it can be placed back on the shelf or put in the cart to be "purchased."

Visionary Shopper allows marketing researchers to manipulate almost any variable that they would be able to change in a real-world store. They can experiment with prices, special displays, labeling, shelf location, and/or packaging. The system even allows researchers to test new product concepts. These new items can be placed near goods that researchers believe will be the main competition if and when the item is introduced. Again, the "Four Ps" of marketing—product, price, promotion, and place—can be tested to come up with the best alternative for the concept.

The system is being used at malls throughout the United States. Respondents are selected as they are in any other mall-intercept survey. Each volunteer participates in a 20-minute session. In contrast to the typical questionnaire survey, which often is quite daunting, this new method of researching consumer goods is described as enjoyable or fun. In addition, it is much more realistic.[6]

Ethics in Marketing Research

In experimentation, oftentimes the researcher deliberately attempts to disguise the purpose of the research, arguing that disguise is needed to produce valid results. Consider the earlier example of determining the effectiveness of Pepsi commercials. The respondents are recruited and brought to a central facility. They are told that they will be watching a television program on food and then will be asked some questions. Interspersed in the program is the commercial for Pepsi (test commercial) as well as commercials for some other products (filler commercials). After viewing the program and the commercials, the respondents are administered a questionnaire. The questionnaire obtains evaluations on the program content, the test commercial, and some of the filler commercials. The evaluations of the program content and the filler commercials are not of interest but are obtained to reinforce the nature of the disguise. If the respondents knew that the true purpose was to determine the effectiveness of the Pepsi commercial, their responses might be biased. However, disguising the purpose of the research does not have to, and should not, lead to deception.

debriefing
After the experiment, the process of informing test subjects what the experiment was about and how the experimental manipulations were performed.

One solution to this problem would be to tell respondents about the possible existence of deception at the start of the experiment and allow them to inquire about it at the conclusion of the experiment. Thus, at the beginning, the researcher should explain the general nature of the experiment, including that the purpose of the experiment will be disguised but will be fully explained at the end, and the role of the respondents. The respondents should know that they are free to discontinue the experiment at any time and withdraw the information they have provided.

Explaining the purpose and details at the conclusion of the experiment is called **debriefing**. Debriefing should include procedures for reducing experimental stress. In the Pepsi example, the respondents could find it discouraging that they had spent their time evaluating a soft-drink commercial. The researcher should address this issue and ease the respondents' discomfort by explaining the true purpose and importance of the experiment, as well as the experimental procedures.

It is the researcher's responsibility to use the most appropriate experimental design for the problem at hand. The researcher should disclose to the client any problems that arise during the course of the experiment, and the research firm and the client should jointly work out a solution, as in the following example.

Research in Action

Diet Pepsi Advertising: Shooting the Star

The effectiveness of Pepsi advertising featuring Brazilian soccer ace Ronaldinho is investigated using a one-group pretest–posttest design. Respondents' attitudes toward Pepsi advertising, Pepsi, and Ronaldinho are obtained prior to respondents being exposed to a food program and several commercials, including the one for Pepsi. Attitudes are again measured after respondents have viewed the program and the commercials. By observing the first few subjects, it is discovered that strongly held prior attitudes about Ronaldinho are affecting the measurement of attitudes toward Pepsi and Pepsi advertising. This problem should be disclosed immediately to the client, and corrective action should be determined jointly. For example, the client and the researcher might decide that a more sophisticated statistical design is needed that explicitly controls for attitude toward Ronaldinho. If the researcher chooses to ignore this problem and continue with the experiment, a serious ethical breach takes place. In this case, the researcher discovers that the research design adopted is inadequate, but this knowledge is withheld from the client.

What Would *You* Do?

Levi's: Fading Jeans and Market Share

The Situation

American apparel maker Levi's has a long history, with over 150 years in the clothing business. Although one might think that this long history can only result in good things, Levi's heritage has been its worst enemy. John Anderson, president and CEO for Levi Strauss & Company, had to work to revamp Levi's antique image and make the brand appealing to younger generations in efforts to boost its declining sales. In the last few years, Anderson saw worldwide sales drop 40 percent, losing market share to Gap, Calvin Klein, Tommy Hilfiger, and Diesel. Another problem for Anderson was store-brand jeans, such as J.C. Penney's Arizona brand jeans, and Gap's in-house brand, which have changed their image and launched an assault on big brand names like Levi's. These store-brand jeans, along with other store-label jeans, now target the teenage market with "cutting edge" advertising. American trade publication *Brand Strategy* estimated that the Levi's brand lost about 50 percent of the younger consumer market share worldwide in the early 2000s.

To compete with these brands and maintain leadership, Levi's, the market leader, is considering introducing its own line of private-label jeans to capture a larger

continued

portion of the teenage market. Anderson wonders how powerful a national brand like Levi's is when compared to an in-house brand such as Gap or a store brand such as J.C. Penney's Arizona jeans.

The Marketing Research Decision

1. If you were John Anderson, what type of research would you want to be conducted to help arrive at an answer? Which one of the following types of research would be most appropriate?
   a. Secondary data analysis
   b. Focus groups
   c. Descriptive cross-sectional survey
   d. Descriptive longitudinal survey
   e. Causal research

2. Explain how you would implement the type of research you have recommended.

3. Discuss the role of the type of research you recommend in enabling John Anderson to determine the power of a national brand like Levi's compared to an in-house brand like Gap or a store brand like J.C. Penney's Arizona jeans.

The Marketing Management Decision

1. What should John Anderson do to compete with in-house and store brands of jeans?
   a. Discount the price of Levi's.
   b. Introduce a new brand of lower-priced jeans.
   c. Sell Levi's through discount stores, such as Wal-Mart and Target.
   d. Increase the advertising budget for Levi's.
   e. Aggressively sell Levi's over the Internet.

2. Discuss how the marketing-management decision action that you recommend to John Anderson is influenced by the research that you suggested earlier and by the findings of that research.

What John Anderson Did

John Anderson introduced a new line of cheaper jeans and clothing to mark its first foray into the discount market. The new Signature brand was made available through Wal-Mart stores in the United States and is a key feature in Levi's drive to reverse years of declining market share.[7]

Summary

The scientific notion of causality implies that the condition where X causes Y cannot be proven. At best, it can only be inferred that X is one of the causes of Y, in that it makes the occurrence of Y probable. Three conditions must be satisfied before causal inferences can be made: (1) concomitant variation, which implies that X and Y must vary together in a hypothesized way; (2) time order of occurrence of variables, which implies that X must precede Y; and (3) elimination of other possible causal factors, which implies that competing explanations must be ruled out. Experiments provide the most convincing evidence of all three conditions. An experiment is formed when a researcher manipulates or controls one or more independent variables and measures their effect on one or more dependent variables.

In designing an experiment, it is important to consider internal and external validity. Internal validity refers to whether the manipulation of the independent variables actually caused the effects on the dependent variables. External validity refers to the generalizability of experimental results. For the experiment to be valid, the researcher must control the threats that extraneous variables pose.

Experimental designs can be classified as pre-experimental, true experimental, quasi-experimental, and statistical designs. An experiment might be conducted in a laboratory environment or under actual market conditions in a real-life setting.

Although experiments have limitations in terms of time, cost, and administration, they are becoming increasingly popular in marketing. Test marketing is an important application of experimental design. Field experiments pose even greater challenges in international markets than those faced in the United States. Using technological advances, such as virtual reality, the researcher can create an environment that represents the field (marketplace) and yet exercise the degree of control possible only in a laboratory setting. Disguising the purpose of the research should not lead to deception, and debriefing should be used to reduce experimental stress.

Key Terms and Concepts

Suggested Cases and Video Cases

Running Case with Real Data

1.1 Hewlett Packard

Comprehensive Critical Thinking Cases

2.1 American Idol   2.2 Baskin-Robbins   2.3 Akron Children's Hospital

Comprehensive Cases with Real Data

3.1 Bank of America   3.2 McDonald's   3.3 Boeing

Video Cases

8.1 AFLAC   9.1 P&G   12.1 Motorola   13.1 Subaru   19.1 Marriott

Live Research: Conducting a Marketing Research Project

If an experiment is to be conducted, an experimental design should be chosen based on class discussion. The choice of an experimental design might have to be tempered by several considerations:

1. It might not be possible to control for certain extraneous variables.
2. There might be only limited flexibility to manipulate the independent variables (e.g., advertising or sales effort cannot be reduced to the zero level).
3. Random assignment of test units to the treatment conditions might not be possible.
4. The choice of dependent variables might be limited by measurement considerations.

The experimental design selected should be discussed and approved by the client.

Acronym

The salient characteristics of experiments may be described by the acronym EXPERIMENT:

E xtraneous variables

X independent variable or treatment

P re-experimental, true experimental, quasi-experimental, and statistical designs

E ffect or dependent variable

R andom assignment

I nternal validity

M easurement or observation

E xternal validity

N eutral or control group

T est units

Review Questions

1. What are the requirements for inferring a causal relationship between two variables?
2. Differentiate between internal and external validity.
3. What key characteristic distinguishes true experimental designs from pre-experimental designs?
4. List the steps involved in implementing the posttest-only control group design. Describe the design symbolically.
5. What is a time series experiment? When is it used?
6. How does a multiple time series design differ from a basic time series design?
7. What advantages do statistical designs have over basic designs?
8. Compare laboratory and field experimentation.
9. What is test marketing?

Applied Problems

1. A prolife group wants to test the effectiveness of an anti-abortion commercial. Two random samples, each of 250 respondents, are recruited in Chicago. One group is shown the anti-abortion commercial. Then, attitudes toward abortion are measured for respondents in both groups.
   a. Identify the independent and dependent variables in this experiment.
   b. What type of design was used?
2. In the anti-abortion commercial experiment just described, suppose the respondents had been selected by convenience rather than randomly. What type of design would result?
3. Identify the type of experiment being conducted in the following situations:
   a. A major distributor of office equipment is considering a new sales presentation program for its salespeople. The largest sales territory is selected, the new program is implemented, and the effect on sales is measured.
   b. Procter & Gamble wants to determine if a new package design for Tide detergent is more effective than the current design. Twelve supermarkets are randomly selected in Denver. In six of them, randomly selected, Tide is sold in the new packaging. In the other six, the detergent is sold in the old

package. Sales for both groups of supermarkets are monitored for 3 months.
4. Describe a specific situation for which each of the following experimental designs is appropriate. Defend your reasoning.
   a. One-group pretest–posttest design
   b. Pretest–posttest control group design
   c. Posttest-only control group design
   d. Time series design
   e. Factorial design
5. Design an experiment for determining the effectiveness of online coupons based on relevant information obtained from www.coupons-online.com.
6. Coca-Cola has developed three alternative package designs for its flagship product, Coke. Design an Internet-based experiment to determine which, if any, of these new package designs is superior to the current one.
7. Microsoft has developed a new version of its Excel spreadsheet, but is not sure what the user reaction will be. Design an Internet-based experiment to determine user reaction to the new and previous versions of Excel.
8. Explain how you would implement a posttest-only control group design on the Internet to measure the effectiveness of a new print ad for Toyota Camry.

Group Discussion

1. "Because one cannot prove a causal relationship by conducting an experiment, experimentation is unscientific for examining cause-and-effect relationships." Discuss this statement as a small group.

Hewlett-Packard Running Case

Review the Hewlett-Packard (HP) case, Case 1.1, and questionnaire given toward the end of the book.

1. Is causal research necessary in this case? If so, which experimental designs would you recommend and why? If not, describe a scenario in which it would be.

2. If a mall-intercept interview is used and HP conducts causal research without randomizing respondents, which pre-experimental design would you recommend?

3. Can you think of any way in which the static group design can be randomized to increase its validity?

AFLAC: Marketing Research Quacks a Duck

AFLAC

AFLAC Incorporated (www.aflac.com) sells supplemental health and life insurance. In the United States, AFLAC is known for its policies that "pay cash" to supplement or replace a policyholder's income when an accident or sickness prevents the policyholder from working. In 1989, the Columbus, Georgia, company American Family Life Assurance Company adopted the acronym AFLAC. At that point, the company had very little brand recognition; the name AFLAC meant nothing to potential customers. To boost brand recognition, AFLAC undertook extensive marketing research and emerged with the symbol of the duck. As of 2008, AFLAC boasts 90 percent brand recognition. This is so high that it actually rivals Coke, the company with the highest brand recognition, at 95 percent. Even children (aged 8 to 13) are familiar with the AFLAC name, ranking it in the company of Pepsi, Old Navy, and M&M's. This is important, because as children grow up and start to buy insurance, the AFLAC name will be at the front of their minds.

Marketing research was at the forefront of the campaign. First, the decision was made to simply try to use ads to increase brand recognition rather than sell insurance. This decision came from focus groups and survey research that found customers would think that they did not need whatever type of insurance was being advertised, whether life, health, home, or so on. Instead, research indicated that customers would respond to insurance ads better if they simply raised the recognition of the brand. Then, salespeople would do the job of educating potential customers about the need for different types of insurance products.

After the decision was made to just raise brand awareness with ads, a specific campaign had to be created. Again, marketing research played a major role. From the start it was decided that the ads that tested the best were going to be the ads that would be used. The research said that test customers viewing the ads preferred the AFLAC duck much more than any other ad viewed. But where did the duck come from? During the ad development process, one of the ad agency (the Kaplan Thaler Group) researchers just began to say the word "AFLAC" over and over again. Eventually, it was noticed that this word, said a certain way, sounded like a quacking duck. The risk in this was that AFLAC was making fun of the fact that no one knew about the brand name, and humor in advertising does not always appeal to people who want a more serious tone from their insurance company. What if the people had seen the television commercial and thought, "How stupid!" or "A life insurance company should be more serious than that." Therefore, the duck commercials were tested against alternatives in experimental design situations. The test audiences loved the duck commercials and rated them the most memorable out of all the possibilities (AFLAC's main objective). Thus, the duck was born.

The campaign has been nothing but a success. Not only has AFLAC's brand recognition soared, but the company's sales have as well. Before the duck campaign, AFLAC's annual sales were growing in the 10 to 15 percent range. Post duck, AFLAC's sales are growing at an annual rate of 24 percent. Surprisingly, the growth is not limited to the United States. In fact, 70 percent of AFLAC's profits are from clients in Japan. The duck is now a world phenomenon, and AFLAC has marketing research to thank.

Conclusion

The case describes the crucial role of marketing research in designing the right advertising campaign and the resulting impact on brand recognition. The extraordinary growth in AFLAC's name recognition within just a few years of the launch of a new advertising campaign speaks volumes about the marketing research that was conducted to test the duck commercials.

Questions

1. If AFLAC wants to forecast the demand for supplemental health and life insurance, what type of research design should be adopted and why?
2. Identify sources of secondary data that would be useful in forecasting the demand for supplemental health and life insurance.
3. Identify sources of syndicated data that would be useful in forecasting the demand for supplemental health and life insurance.
4. AFLAC wants to test a duck commercial against a nonduck commercial to determine which ad generates more favorable attitudes toward AFLAC. What type of experimental design would you recommend? Why would you recommend this type of design?
5. If a duck commercial is to be tested against two nonduck commercials to determine which ad generates more favorable attitudes toward AFLAC, what type of experimental design would you recommend?

References

1. http://aflac.com/us/en/Default.aspx, accessed February 20, 2008.
2. www.wikipedia.org, accessed February 20, 2008.
3. Suzanne Vranica, "AFLAC Duck's Paddle to Stardom: Creativity on the Cheap," *The Wall Street Journal*, July 30, 2004, pp. B1–B2.
4. Tony Adams, "Sales in Japan Help AFLAC Raise First-Quarter Net Earning by Almost 33 Percent," *Knight Ridder Tribune Business News*, April 28, 2004, p. 1.

CHAPTER nine

Measurement and Scaling: Fundamentals and Comparative Scaling

OPENING QUESTIONS

1. What is meant by measurement and scaling, and can scaling be considered a part of measurement?

2. What are the primary scales of measurement, and how do they differ?

3. How are scaling techniques classified, and what are the various comparative scaling techniques?

4. How do measurement and scaling relate to the various steps of the marketing research process?

5. What considerations are involved in implementing the primary scales of measurement in an international setting?

6. How does technology improve measurement and scaling?

7. What ethical issues are involved in selecting scales of measurement?

> "In every survey project, researchers have to decide what type of scales will be used to measure the variables. You really have to know what these scale types can give you."
>
> *James C. Fink,*
> *CEO, Worldwide Marketing Research,*
> *Opinion Research Corporation.*

Scaling the Olympics

In 2008, tens of thousands swarmed Beijing, China, for the 2008 Olympics; the games also are very popular among teen television watchers. In fact, the Olympics are the single most popular televised sporting event (ranked number one) among teenage boys (71 percent) and girls (62 percent), according to The New World Teen Study. The BrainWaves Group, an American global consulting and trends company, conducted this survey of 6,500 teens in 26 countries. Elissa Moses, managing director of The BrainWaves Group, says, "The Olympics are young people's favorite athletic package because in the global teen culture sport is a dominant theme, with both boys and girls being active participants and spectators."

Globally, the Olympics enjoys its highest popularity rating in the Middle East, where it is the favorite televised sporting event of 85 percent of teen boys and girls. Australia, host of the 2000 Olympic Games, is third, where the games

are the favorite of 84 percent of teen males and 80 percent of teen females. The United States is lower in the ranking: Only 71 percent of teen girls and 68 percent of teen boys named the Olympics their favorite televised sports competition.

However, any similarity between the tastes of teen boys and girls ends with the Olympics. A majority of teen boys (63 percent) cite basketball as their favorite sport, followed by soccer (58 percent). Teen girls voted gymnastics their most popular sport (57 percent), followed by basketball (51 percent). Only 17 percent of the boys voted gymnastics their favorite spectator sport. In fact, on a global basis of both boys and girls, teens' favorite spectator sport is basketball. Note that each respondent could name more than one sport as his/her favorite.

The BrainWaves Group developed a complete ranking of the popularity of all sports in terms of the percentage of teenagers who indicated each sport as their favorite. Information of this type can be used by marketers of global brands, such as U.S. apparel maker Levi's, in their attempts to penetrate the teen market. For example, Levi's would do well to air its commercials on televised basketball and soccer games in order to reach teenage boys. However, to reach teenage girls, Levi's should replace soccer advertising with gymnastics.[1]

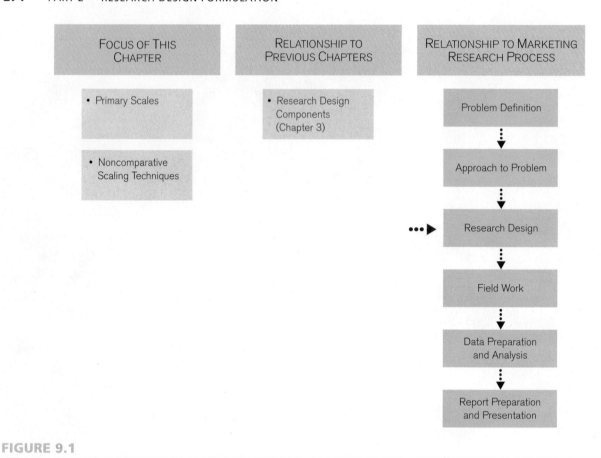

FIGURE 9.1

Relationship of Comparative Scaling to the Previous Chapters and the Marketing Research Process

Overview

After developing the research design (Chapters 3 through 8), the researcher is ready to move to the next phase of research. The researcher must decide how to measure information and which types of scales to use. In the opening vignette, scales were designed to measure the popularity of various sports and sporting events.

This chapter describes the concepts of scaling and measurement. Figure 9.1 briefly explains the focus of the chapter, the relation of this chapter to the previous ones, and the steps of the marketing research process on which this chapter concentrates. This chapter discusses the fundamental scale characteristics of description, order, distance, and origin. Four primary scales of measurement are reviewed: nominal, ordinal, interval, and ratio. Comparative and noncomparative scaling techniques are presented, and comparative techniques are explained in detail. (Noncomparative techniques are discussed in more depth in Chapter 10.) The applications of primary scales and comparative scaling in international marketing research are discussed. The impact of technology on scaling and ethical issues that arise in measurement and scaling also are presented. Figure 9.2 provides an overview of the topics discussed in this chapter and how they flow from one to the next.

Measurement and Scaling

measurement
The assignment of numbers or other symbols to characteristics of objects according to certain prespecified rules.

Measurement is assigning numbers or other symbols to characteristics of objects being measured, according to predetermined rules. Characteristics of the item are measured, rather than the item directly. Thus, this means that consumers are not measured, only their perceptions, attitudes, preferences, or other relevant characteristics. In the opening vignette, teenagers' preferences for various sports and sporting events were measured.

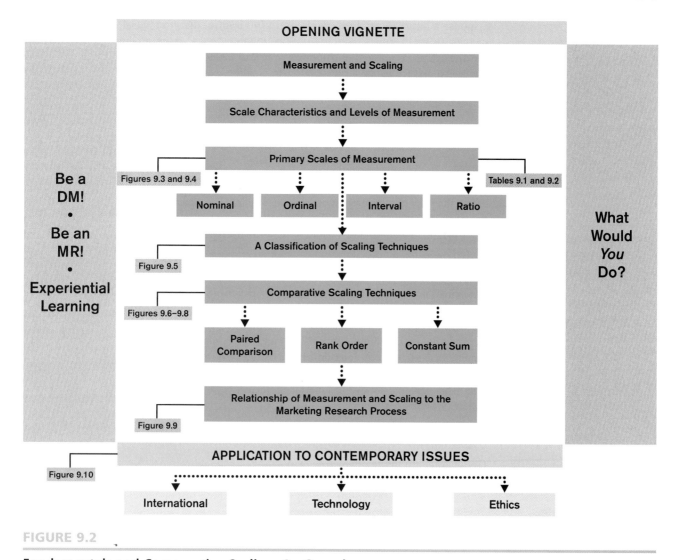

FIGURE 9.2

Fundamentals and Comparative Scaling: An Overview

In marketing research, numbers usually are assigned for one of two reasons:

- To permit statistical analysis of the generated data
- To help communicate information about the results

The most important aspect of measurement is deciding how to assign numbers to the characteristics being studied. In the opening vignette, numbers had to be assigned to measure the popularity of different sports in terms of the percentage of respondents who mentioned each sport as their favorite (most preferred). In developing the assignment process, a one-to-one correspondence must exist between the numbers and the characteristics being measured. Only then can the numbers be associated with specific characteristics of the object being measured. For example, the same dollar figures are assigned to products that are priced the same. In addition, the rules for assigning numbers should be applied in a standard way. They must not change over objects or time.

Scaling can be considered a part of measurement. Scales place the objects being measured along a continuum. To illustrate, suppose a marketer in India wanted to measure consumers in terms of their attitude toward Boomer chewing gum. Based on the response, each consumer would be assigned a number indicating an unfavorable attitude (measured as 1), a neutral attitude (measured as 2), or a favorable attitude (measured as 3). Measurement is the actual assignment of 1, 2, or 3 to each respondent using a scale that ranges from one to three. In this example, scaling is the process of placing consumer

scaling
The generation of a continuum upon which measured objects are located.

response along an attitudinal continuum from unfavorable, to neutral, to favorable. The scale is the set of values ranging from one to three. In the opening vignette, measurement was the actual assignment of a number from 0 to 100 to each sport given its preference (as favorite sport) for teenage boys and girls. Scaling was the process of placing each sport along a preference continuum from 0 to 100 percent.

Scale Characteristics and Levels of Measurement

All the scales used in marketing research can be described in terms of four basic characteristics. These characteristics are description, order, distance, and origin, and together they define the level of measurement of a scale. The level of measurement denotes what properties of an object the scale is, or is not, measuring. An understanding of the scale characteristics is fundamental to understanding the primary type of scales.

Description

description
Refers to the unique labels or descriptors that are used to designate each value of the scale. All scales possess description.

Description involves the unique labels or descriptors that are used to designate each value of the scale. Some examples of descriptors are 1 = Female, 2 = Male; 1 = Strongly disagree, 2 = Disagree, 3 = Neither agree nor disagree, 4 = Agree, and 5 = Strongly agree; and the number of dollars earned annually by a household. To amplify, Female and Male are unique descriptors used to describe values 1 and 2 of the gender scale. It is important to remember that all scales possess this characteristic of description. Thus, all scales have unique labels or descriptors that are used to define the scale values or response options.

Order

order
The relative sizes or positions of the descriptors; it is denoted by descriptors such as *greater than, less than,* and *equal to.*

Order refers to the relative sizes or positions of the descriptors. No absolute values are associated with order, only relative values. Order is denoted by descriptors such as *greater than, less than,* and *equal to.* For example, a Japanese respondent's preference for three brands of athletic shoes is expressed by the following order, with the most preferred brand being listed first and the least preferred brand last.

    Asics

    Nike

    Adidas

    For this respondent, the preference for Japanese-made Asics is greater than the preference for American-made Nike. Likewise, the preference for German-made Adidas is less than the preference for Nike. Respondents who check the same age category, say 35 to 49, are considered to be equal to each other in terms of age, and older than respondents in the 20 to 34 age group. All scales do not possess the order characteristic. In the gender scale (1 = Female, 2 = Male) considered earlier, it is not possible to determine whether a female is greater than or less than a male. Thus, the gender scale does not possess order.

Distance

distance
The absolute differences between the scale descriptors are known and can be expressed in units.

The characteristic of **distance** means that absolute differences between the scale descriptors are known and can be expressed in units. A five-person household has one person more than a four-person household, which in turn has one person more than a three-person household. Thus, the following scale possesses the distance characteristic.

    Number of persons living in your household _____

Notice that a scale that has distance also has order. We know that a five-person household is greater than the four-person household in terms of the number of persons living in the household. Likewise, a three-person household is less than a four-person household. Thus, distance implies order, but the reverse might not be true.

Origin

The **origin** characteristic means that the scale has a unique or fixed beginning or true zero point. Thus, an exact measurement of income by a scale such as:

What is the annual income of our household before taxes? $ _____

has a fixed origin or a true a zero point. An answer of zero would mean that the household has no income at all. A scale that has origin also has distance (and order and description). Many scales used in marketing research do not have a fixed origin or true zero point, as in the disagree-agree scale considered earlier. Notice that such a scale was defined as 1 = Strongly disagree, 2 = Disagree, 3 = Neither agree nor disagree, 4 = Agree, and 5 = Strongly agree. However, 1 is an arbitrary starting point. This scale could just as easily have been defined as 0 = Strongly disagree, 1 = Disagree, 2 = Neither agree nor disagree, 3 = Agree, and 4 = Strongly agree, with 0 as the origin. Alternatively, shifting the origin to -2 will result in an equivalent scale: -2 = Strongly disagree, -1 = Disagree, 0 = Neither agree nor disagree, 1 = Agree, and 2 = Strongly agree. These three forms of the agree-disagree scale, with the origin at 1, 0, or -2, are equivalent. Thus, this scale does not have a fixed origin or a true zero point and consequently does not possess the characteristic of origin.

Note that description, order, distance, and origin represent successively higher-level characteristics, with origin being the highest-level characteristic. Description is the most basic characteristic that is present in all scales. If a scale has order, it also has description. If a scale has distance, it also has order and description. Finally, a scale that has origin also has distance, order, and description. Thus, if a scale has a higher-level characteristic, it also has all the lower-level characteristics. However, the reverse might not be true; that is, if a scale has a lower-level characteristic, it might or might not have a higher-level characteristic. With an understanding of scale characteristics, let's now discuss the primary type of scales.

origin
A unique or fixed beginning or true zero point of a scale.

Primary Scales

The word *primary* means "basic" or "fundamental." The four primary scales of measurement are nominal, ordinal, interval, and ratio scales (Figure 9.3). The nominal scale is the most limited, followed by the ordinal, the interval, and the ratio scale. As the measurement level increases from nominal to ratio, scale complexity increases. For the respondents,

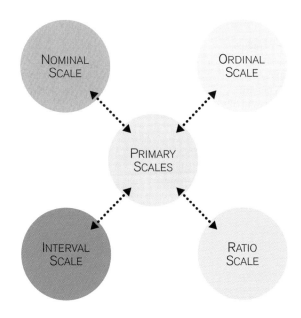

Primary Scales of Measurement

FIGURE 9.4

Primary Scales Measurement

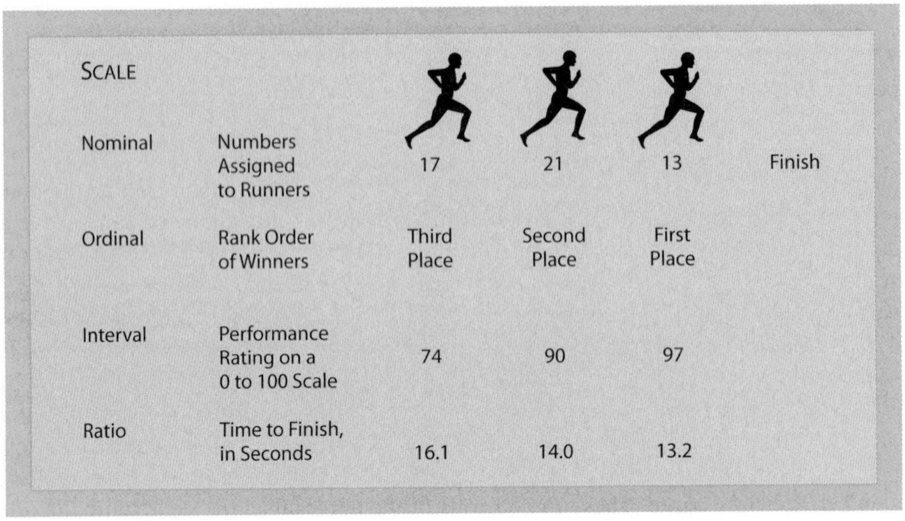

SCALE					
Nominal	Numbers Assigned to Runners	17	21	13	Finish
Ordinal	Rank Order of Winners	Third Place	Second Place	First Place	
Interval	Performance Rating on a 0 to 100 Scale	74	90	97	
Ratio	Time to Finish, in Seconds	16.1	14.0	13.2	

nominal scales are the simplest to use, whereas ratio scales are the most complex. These scales are illustrated in Figure 9.4. Their properties are summarized in Table 9.1 and are discussed in the following sections.

Nominal Scale

nominal scale
A scale whose numbers serve only as labels or tags for identifying and classifying objects. When used for identification, there is a strict one-to-one correspondence between the numbers and the objects.

A **nominal scale** uses numbers as labels or tags for identifying and classifying objects. The only characteristic possessed by these scales is description. For example, teenagers participating in the sports survey discussed in the opening vignette might each be assigned a number. This number would be a nominal scale. When a nominal scale is used for identification, a strict one-to-one correspondence exists between the numbers

TABLE 9.1 Primary Scales of Measurement

Primary Scale	Basics Characteristics	Common Examples	Marketing Examples	Permissible Statistics
Nominal	Numbers identify and classify objects	Social Security numbers, numbering of football players	Brand numbers, store types, gender classification	Percentages, mode
Ordinal	Numbers indicate the relative positions of the objects but not the magnitude of differences between them	Quality rankings, rankings of teams in a tournament	Preference rankings, market position, social class	Percentile, median
Interval	Differences between objects can be compared; zero point is arbitrary	Temperature (Fahrenheit, Celsius)	Attitudes, opinions, index numbers	Range, mean, standard deviation
Ratio	Zero point is fixed; ratios of scale values can be computed	Length, weight	Age, income, costs, sales, market shares	Geometric mean, all statistics

A common example of a nominal scale is numbers assigned to soccer players.

being assigned and the objects being measured. Each number is assigned to only one object, and each object has only one number assigned to it. Common examples include social security numbers and numbers assigned to football players and worn on their shirts. In marketing research, nominal scales are used for brands, attributes, stores, objects, and identifying participants in a study. In the opening vignette, numbers could be used to denote the various spectator sports: 1. tennis, 2. hockey, 3. football, 4. basketball, and so on, resulting in a nominal scale. Note that the numbers merely identify the sports and do not denote any characteristic of the sport. Thus, a 1 denotes tennis and a 3 denotes football; but these numbers do not tell us whether tennis is more or less popular than soccer.

Nominal scales are used for classification purposes. They serve as labels for classes or categories. The classes are mutually exclusive and collectively exhaustive. *Mutually exclusive* means that there is no overlap between classes; every object being measured falls into only one class. The objects in each class are viewed as equivalent in terms of the characteristic represented by the nominal scale. All objects in the same class have the same number, and no two classes have the same number. *Collectively exhaustive* means that all the objects fall into one of the classes. For example, the numbers 1 and 2 can be used to classify survey respondents based on gender, with 1 denoting female and 2 denoting male. Each respondent will fall into one of these two categories.

The numbers assigned in a nominal scale do not reflect relative amounts of the characteristic being measured. For example, a high social security number does not imply that the person is in some way superior to those with lower social security numbers or vice versa. The same applies to numbers assigned to classes. By assigning 1 to female and 2 to male, the researcher does not imply that either sex is superior to the other in any way. The numbers in a nominal scale can only be counted. Therefore, the only statistics that are useful when using a nominal scale are those based on frequency counts. These include percentage, mode, and chi-square (see Chapter 16). It is not meaningful to compute an average social security number or the average gender of the respondents in a survey. The following example on nominal scale illustrates this limitation.

Research in Action

Nominal Scale

In a study to measure consumer preferences for jeans, numbers 1 through 10 were assigned to the 10 American brands being considered (Table 9.2). Thus, brand number 9 referred to the store brand Old Navy. Brand number 6 was assigned to the national brand Jordache. This did not imply that Old Navy was in any way superior or inferior to Jordache. Any reassignment of the numbers, such as switching the numbers assigned to Old Navy and Jordache, would have no effect on the results. The numbers did not reflect any characteristics of the brands.

It is meaningful to make statements such as, "Thirty-five percent of the respondents had purchased Levi jeans, or brand number 8." The *mode*, defined as the number with the highest frequency, denotes the brand preferred by the largest number of respondents, for example, Guess? However, although the average of all the assigned numbers, 1 to 10, is 5.5, it is not meaningful to state that the number of the average brand of jeans is 5.5.

Ordinal Scale

ordinal scale
A ranking scale in which numbers are assigned to objects to indicate the relative extent to which some characteristic is possessed. Thus, it is possible to determine whether an object has more or less of a characteristic than some other object.

An **ordinal scale** is a ranking scale. In an ordinal scale, numbers are assigned to objects, which allows researchers to determine whether an object has more or less of a characteristic than some other object. However, we cannot determine how much more or less from this type of scale. Objects ranked first have more of the characteristic being measured than objects ranked second; however, it is not possible to determine whether the object ranked second is a close second or a distant second. Thus, ordinal scales possess description and order characteristics, but not distance (or origin). Common examples of ordinal scales include quality rankings, rankings of teams in a tournament, and educational levels (primary school, secondary school, some higher education, and so on).

In marketing research, ordinal scales are used to measure relative attitudes, opinions, perceptions, and preferences. Measurements of this type ask the respondent to make "greater than" or "less than" judgments. Asking respondents to rank order the various sports in terms of their preference, as in the opening vignette, is an example of an ordinal scale.

Ordinal scales are like nominal scales in that equivalent objects receive the same rank. Any series of numbers can be assigned as long as they preserve the ordered relationships between the objects. Because of this quality, ordinal scales can be transformed in any way as long as the basic ordering of the objects is maintained. In ordinal scales, numbers differ only in terms of their order, not in terms of their magnitude (see the following example on ordinal scale). For these reasons, in addition to the counting operation allowable for nominal scale data, ordinal scales also permit the use of statistics based on centiles. This means that it is meaningful to calculate percentile, median, or other summary statistics from ordinal data (see Chapter 16).

TABLE 9.2 Illustration of Primary Scales of Measurement

No.	Nominal Scale Jean Brand	Ordinal Scale Preference Rankings		Interval Scale Preference 1–7	Ratings 11–17	Ratio Scale Price in Dollars ($)
1.	Bugle Boy	7	79	5	15	30
2.	Calvin Klein	2	25	7	17	48
3.	Diesel	8	82	7	17	27
4.	Gap	3	30	6	16	32
5.	Guess?	1	10	7	17	34
6.	Jordache	5	53	5	15	35
7.	Lee	9	95	4	14	30
8.	Levi	6	61	5	15	33
9.	Old Navy	4	45	6	16	29
10.	Wrangler	10	115	2	12	24

Research in Action

Ordinal Scale

Table 9.2 gives one respondent's preference rankings. Respondents ranked 10 brands of jeans in order of preference by assigning a 1 to the most preferred brand, a 2 to the second most preferred brand, and so forth. Note that Guess? (ranked 1), is preferred to Calvin Klein (ranked 2). However, it is not possible to determine how much more it is preferred. Also, it is not necessary to assign numbers from 1 to 10 to obtain a preference ranking. The second ordinal scale, which assigns a number 10 to Guess?, 25 to Calvin Klein, 30 to Gap, and so on, is an equivalent scale. The two scales result in the same ordering of the brands according to preference. This illustrates an important property of ordinal scales: Any series of numbers can be assigned as long as they preserve the ordered relationships between the objects.

Note that the ordinal scale does not replace the nominal scale, but merely supplements it. One could say that brand number 5 receives the highest preference ranking—rank 1 on the first ordinal scale—and identify it as Guess?

Be a DM!

As the marketing director for U.S. retail giant Sears, what marketing strategies would you formulate to enhance satisfaction with Sears?

Be an MR!

Visit www.sears.com and search the Internet, as well as your library's online databases, to obtain information on customer satisfaction with department stores. How would you use nominal and ordinal scales to measure customer satisfaction with the major department stores, such as Sears?

Interval Scale

In an **interval scale**, numerically equal distances on the scale represent equal values in the characteristic being measured. An interval scale contains all the information of an ordinal scale. In addition, it allows you to compare the differences between objects. The difference between 1 and 2 is same as the difference between 2 and 3, which is the same as the difference between 5 and 6. The distance between descriptors is known. The interval scales possess the characteristics of description, order, and distance. In marketing research, data on attitudes (e.g., attitude toward sports) obtained from rating scales (1 = do not like at all, 7 = like very much) often are treated as interval data. In the opening vignette, interval data would be obtained if the respondents were asked to rate each sport in terms of preference using a seven-point scale with ratings of 1 = not at all preferred and 7 = greatly preferred. Note that in an interval scale two objects can be assigned the same number if they each contain the characteristic being measured to the same extent. Scales of this type are discussed further in Chapter 10.

In an interval scale, the location of the zero point is not fixed. Both the zero point and the units of measurement are arbitrary; that is, these scales do not possess the origin characteristic. This is illustrated in the measurement of temperature. The Fahrenheit scale uses different zero points and smaller units of measurement than the Celsius scale. However, both are used to measure the same characteristic: temperature. Any positive linear transformation of the form $y = a + bx$ will preserve the properties of the scale. Here, x is the original scale value, y is the transformed scale value, b is a positive constant, and a is any constant. Two interval scales that rate women's handbag brands Coach, Dooney & Burke, Vende, and Gucci as 1, 3, 3, and 5, or as 22, 26, 26, and 30 are equivalent. Note that the latter scale can be derived from the former by using $a = 20$ and $b = 2$ in the transforming equation. Their equivalence can also be seen as follows.

> **interval scale**
> A scale in which the numbers are used to rank objects such that numerically equal distances on the scale represent equal distances in the characteristic being measured.

$$\text{Poor} \quad 1 \quad 2 \quad 3 \quad 4 \quad 5 \quad \text{Excellent}$$

or

$$\text{Poor} \quad 22 \quad 24 \quad 26 \quad 28 \quad 30 \quad \text{Excellent}$$

Because the zero point is not fixed, it is not meaningful to take ratios of scale values. Thus, it is not meaningful to say that it is 2 times as hot in Havana, Cuba (temperature = 32 degrees Celsius) as it is in Toronto, Canada (temperature = 16 degrees Celsius). When the temperatures are converted to the Fahrenheit scale, the ratio (90 degrees to 61 degrees) is no longer 2 to 1. In the handbag example, the ratio of Gucci to Dooney & Burke is 5:3 using the first scale. It becomes 15:13 when the scale is transformed.

All the statistical techniques and measures of central tendency (mode and median) that apply to nominal and ordinal data can also be applied to interval scale data. In addition, the arithmetic mean, standard deviation (see Chapter 16), and other statistics commonly used in marketing research are permitted. However, certain specialized statistics, such as geometric means, are not meaningful on interval scale data. The jeans example gives a further illustration of an interval scale.

Research in Action

Interval Scale

In Table 9.2, a respondent's preferences for the 10 brands in the jeans study are expressed on a seven-point rating scale. We can see that although Gap received a preference rating of 6 and Wrangler a rating of 2, this does not mean that Gap is preferred three times as much as Wrangler. When the ratings are transformed to an equivalent 11 to 17 scale by adding 10 (next column), the ratings for these brands become 16 (6 + 10) and 12 (2 + 10), and the ratio is no longer 3 to 1. This example becomes clearer when you realize that an interval scale has an arbitrary origin or zero point.

Ratio Scale

ratio scale
This is the highest level of measurement. It allows the researcher to identify or classify objects, rank-order the objects, and compare intervals or differences. It also is meaningful to compute ratios of scale values.

A **ratio scale** possesses all the properties of the nominal, ordinal, and interval scales. In addition, a zero point is specified; that is, the origin of the scale is fixed. Thus, ratio scales possess the characteristic of origin (and distance, order, and description). When measurement is taken using ratio scales, the researcher can identify or classify objects, rank the objects, and compare intervals or differences. Unlike interval data, it is meaningful to compute ratios of scale values. Not only is the difference between 2 and 5 the same as the difference between 14 and 17, but 14 is seven times as large as 2 in an absolute sense. Common examples of ratio scales include height, weight, age, and income. In marketing, sales, costs, market share, and number of customers are variables measured on a ratio scale. In the opening vignette, ratio data would be obtained if the teenagers were asked to state the amount of time they spent watching each sport on TV during the Olympics.

Ratio scales can be transformed using proportions. The transformation formula is $y = bx$, where b is a positive constant. Note that the a of the interval-scale-transformation formula is missing here. One cannot transform a ratio scale by adding an arbitrary constant (a), as in the case of an interval scale. An example of a ratio transformation is provided by the conversion of yards to feet ($b = 3$). Comparisons between measurements are identical, whether made in yards or feet.

All statistical techniques can be applied to ratio data. These include specialized statistics, such as the geometric mean. An illustration of the use of a ratio scale in the context of the jeans example follows.

Research in Action

Ratio Scale

The ratio scale illustrated in Table 9.2 gives the prices of the 10 brands of jeans. Note that because the price of Calvin Klein is $48 and the price of Wrangler is $24, Calvin Klein costs the buyer twice as much as Wrangler. In dollar terms, the zero point is fixed. A price of zero dollars means that the item is free. Additionally, multiplying these prices by 100 to convert dollars to cents results in an equivalent scale, illustrating the fact that the ratio scale has an absolute zero or a fixed origin.

Be an MR!

Visit Coach, a leading maker of luxury handbags and accessories, at www.coach.com and search the Internet, as well as your library's online databases, to obtain information on consumer preferences for leather goods. How would you use interval and ratio scales to measure consumer preferences for leather goods?

Be a DM!

As the marketing director for Coach, how would you use information on consumer preferences for leather goods to increase your market share?

Selecting a Level of Measurement

A variable of interest can be measured using different types of primary scales. We illustrate this in the context of measuring annual household income.

Nominal Scale

In the past year, who made a contribution to your household income?

1. Male head of the household
2. Female head of the household
3. Both male and female head of the household

Ordinal Scale

In the past year, what was your annual household income before taxes?

1. Less than $20,001
2. $20,001 to $50,000
3. $50,001 to $100,000
4. $100,001 to $150,000
5. More than $150,000

Interval Scale

In the past year, what was your annual household income before taxes?

Much Below Average			Average			Much Above Average	
1	2	3	4	5	6	7

Ratio Scale

In the past year, what was your annual household income before taxes? $_____

Which type of primary scale should be selected to measure the variable of interest (i.e., income)? The amount of information obtained increases from nominal to ordinal to interval to ratio scale. However, the cognitive load imposed on the respondents while obtaining information also increases in that order. So a trade-off has to be made. The general rule is to select the lowest level of measurement that will enable the researcher to obtain the needed information and conduct the appropriate statistical analyses. Suppose the researcher is merely interested in cross-tabulating the level of income with consumer purchases to see if the level of income has an effect on the amount purchased. To meet this objective, measuring income at an ordinal level would be sufficient. More than one type of primary scale is used in a typical survey, as the following example illustrates.

Research in Action

Primary Scales in Online Surveys

A specialist in HR assessment and feedback with offices in Australia and the United States, CustomInsight (www. custominsight.com) provides Web-based survey software and tools that make creating and deploying online surveys quick and painless. CustomInsight's software guides users through the creation of surveys and allows for the use of all of the scales of measurement. Surveys can easily be designed for employee or customer satisfaction, group feedback, organizational effectiveness, and various other applications. A sample employee satisfaction survey includes questions using the following measurement scales:

1. Job function: nominal scale
2. Employee level: nominal scale
3. Years of service: ratio scale
4. Empowerment assessment: interval scale
5. Compensation assessment: interval scale
6. Ranking of management efficiency: ordinal scale

Surveys of this type have been used to develop better human resource programs to attract and retain the best employees.

A Classification of Scaling Techniques

comparative scales
Scaling techniques in which there is direct comparison of stimulus objects with one another.

The scaling techniques commonly used in marketing research can be classified into comparative and noncomparative scales (Figure 9.5). **Comparative scales** involve the direct comparison of two or more objects. For example, respondents might be asked whether they prefer Coke or Pepsi. A comparative rating scale gives the marketer data that measure relative differences. It has only ordinal or rank order properties.

Comparative scaling is sometimes referred to as nonmetric scaling. The opening vignette presented an example of comparative scaling when the different sports were ranked in terms of the percentage of respondents mentioning each sport as their favorite. The resulting scale presented a relative comparison of all the sports. As Figure 9.5 illustrates, comparative scales include paired comparisons, rank order, and constant sum scales.

The major benefit of comparative scaling is that small differences between objects under study can be detected. The comparison process forces respondents to choose between two objects. Respondents asked to perform a ranking task bring the same point of reference to the task. This makes comparative scales easy to understand and apply. They also tend to reduce halo or carryover effects in which early judgments influence later judgments. The major disadvantage of comparative scales is the limitation in terms of analyzing ordinal data. In addition, it is not possible to generalize beyond the objects under study. For instance, say a study was done to compare Coke and Pepsi. If later these brands were to be compared to RC Cola, America's third-best-selling cola brand, the researcher would have to do a new study. These disadvantages are substantially overcome by noncomparative scaling techniques.

noncomparative scales
Scaling techniques in which each stimulus object is scaled independently of the others.

In **noncomparative scales**, also referred to as *monadic* or *metric* scales, objects are scaled independently of each other. The resulting data are generally assumed to be interval

FIGURE 9.5

A Classification of Scaling Techniques

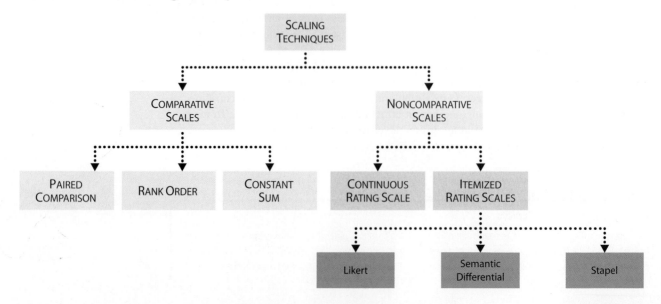

scaled. For example, respondents might be asked to evaluate Coke on a 1 to 7 preference scale (1 = not at all preferred, 7 = greatly preferred). Similar evaluations would be obtained for Pepsi and RC Cola. In the opening vignette, the use of noncomparative scaling would involve respondents rating each sport, taken by itself, on a 1-to-7 preference scale. As Figure 9.5 illustrates, noncomparative scales comprise continuous rating or itemized rating scales. The itemized rating scales can be further classified as Likert, semantic differential, or Stapel scales.

Noncomparative scaling is the most widely used scaling technique in marketing research. Chapter 10 is devoted to noncomparative scaling. The rest of this chapter focuses on comparative scaling techniques.

Comparative Scaling Techniques

We describe the main comparative scaling techniques consisting of paired comparison, rank order, and constant sum scaling (Figure 9.5).

Paired Comparison Scaling

As its name implies, in **paired comparison scaling** a respondent is presented with a pair of alternatives and asked to select one based on some criterion (Figure 9.6). Data obtained in this way are ordinal in nature. A consumer involved in a paired comparison study might state that she shops at JCPenney more often than at Sears, likes Total cereal better than Kellogg's Product 19, or likes Crest toothpaste more than Colgate. Paired comparison scales are frequently used when the research involves physical products. Coca-Cola is reported to have conducted more than 190,000 paired comparisons before introducing New Coke. Paired comparison scaling is the most widely used comparative scaling technique.

Paired comparison scaling is useful when the number of brands under consideration is limited to no more than five. When a large number of brands is involved, the number of comparisons becomes unwieldy. For example, to evaluate the 10 brands of jeans in Table 9.2, 45 paired comparisons would be involved. The order in which the alternatives are presented might bias the results. Also problematic is the fact that paired comparisons bear little resemblance to the marketplace situation, which involves selection from

paired comparison scaling
A comparative scaling technique in which a respondent is presented with two objects at a time and asked to select one object in the pair according to some criterion. The data obtained are ordinal in nature.

FIGURE 9.6

Paired Comparison Scaling

INSTRUCTIONS
We are going to present you with 10 pairs of shampoo brands. For each pair, please indicate which one of the two brands of shampoo in the pair you would prefer for personal use.

RECORDING FORM

	Jhirmack	Finesse	Vidal Sassoon	Head & Shoulders	Pert
Jhirmack		0	0	1	0
Finesse	1[a]		0	1	0
Vidal Sassoon	1	1		1	1
Head & Shoulders	0	0	0		0
Pert	1	1	0	1	
Number of times preferred	3[b]	2	0	4	1

[a] A "1" in a particular box means that the brand in that column was preferred over the brand in the corresponding row. A "0" means that the row brand was preferred over the column brand.
[b] The number of times a brand was preferred is obtained by summing the 1s in each column.

multiple alternatives. Respondents might prefer one alternative to another; however, that does not imply that they like it in an absolute sense. The GlaxoSmithKline example provides further insights into paired comparison scaling.

Research in Action

Looking Good: Dietary Supplements Versus Prescription Weight Loss Drugs

U.K.-based GlaxoSmithKline Consumer Healthcare sponsored a study to explore American consumer perceptions and experiences with dietary supplements for weight loss. The research was conducted between November 18, 2005, and January 10, 2006, using random-digit dialing that reached 12,599 households. A sample of 3,500 people completed the telephone interview (for a response rate of 27.8%). The respondents were asked a variety of questions about their beliefs and opinions about the safety and effectiveness of weight loss products. Paired comparison scaling was used to obtain respondents' opinions and attitudes about the relative safety and effectiveness of dietary supplements, prescription weight loss drugs, and over-the-counter weight loss drugs.

The research had some interesting findings. Comparative ratings between dietary supplements (for weight loss treatment) and prescription weight loss drugs found that respondents considered supplements to be safer but less effective than the prescription drugs. Also, African Americans (50%) and Hispanics (49%) were more likely than Caucasians (36%) to believe that dietary supplements were safer relative to over-the-counter weight loss drugs or relative to prescription weight loss drugs. The survey, being ordinal in nature, could not determine the magnitude of such perceptions. However, the research was revealing in that it suggests that many adults are confused about the safety and regulation of dietary supplements for weight loss. As another example, more than 60 percent of the 1,444 respondents who had made significant efforts to lose weight mistakenly said that such supplements have been tested and are proven to be safe (65%) and effective (63%); and more than half (54%) mistakenly believe that these products are approved by the U.S. Food and Drug Administration (FDA).

GlaxoSmithKline used the results of the survey to point to the importance and need of accurate information on the best programs and products to help people achieve their weight loss goals. As part of its corporate social responsibility, the company launched educational programs about the benefits and risks associated with the myriad of weight loss products available.[2]

Experiential Learning

Which Is It? Coke or Pepsi

Which cola drink would be the most popular among your friends in a taste test? Download the Kit Kat Taste Test from the Web site of this textbook and use it as a guide to develop a script for testing for preference between two cola drinks: Coke and Pepsi. Make sure the drinks are chilled to the same temperature and poured into three groups of identical cups. Each person will select a cup from the first group, taste the cola, eat a cracker, and take a swallow of water. Repeat this when tasting from the second and third groups. (The first group might be Pepsi, the second group Coke, and the third group Pepsi.) After tasting from each of the three cola sample groups, have the respondents complete the survey form you created. To avoid a biasing effect from the order of presentation of the samples, it will be important for half of the respondents to have a rotated order of presentation: The first group Coke, the second group Pepsi, and the third group Coke. Conduct the taste test on 30 respondents/students.

1. How many respondents correctly identified the two identical samples of cola?

2. Of those who correctly identified the two identical samples of cola, which cola was preferred: Coke or Pepsi?

3. Of those who correctly identified the two identical samples of cola, how many had no preference between Coke and Pepsi?

4. In sum, who would you say is the winner in your taste test: Coke or Pepsi? Or, is it too close to tell?

Rank Order Scaling

rank order scaling
A comparative scaling technique in which respondents are presented with several objects simultaneously and asked to order or rank them according to some criterion.

After paired comparisons, the most popular comparative scaling technique is rank order scaling. In **rank order scaling**, respondents are simultaneously presented with several alternatives and asked to rank them according to some criterion (Figure 9.7). For example, consumers might be asked to rank brands of jeans according to overall preference, as in Table 9.2. These rankings typically are obtained by asking the respondents to assign a rank of 1 to the most preferred brand, 2 to the second most preferred, and so on, until each alternative is ranked down to the least preferred brand. Like paired comparison, this approach is also comparative in nature. However, it is possible that even the brand ranked 1 is not liked in an absolute sense; that is, it might be the least disliked. Rank order scaling also results in ordinal data. See Table 9.2, which uses rank order data to derive an ordinal scale.

FIGURE 9.7

Rank Order Scaling

INSTRUCTIONS

Rank the various brands of toothpaste in order of preference. Begin by picking out the one brand that you like most and assign it a number "1." Then, find the second most preferred brand and assign it a number "2." Continue this procedure until you have ranked all the brands of toothpaste in order of preference. The least preferred brand should be assigned a rank of "10."

No two brands should receive the same rank number.

The criterion of preference is entirely up to you. There is no right or wrong answer. Just try to be consistent.

BRAND	RANK ORDER
1. Crest	_____
2. Colgate	_____
3. Aim	_____
4. Mentadent	_____
5. Macleans	_____
6. Ultra Brite	_____
7. Close Up	_____
8. Pepsodent	_____
9. Plus White	_____
10. Stripe	_____

Rank order scaling often is used to measure preferences among brands as well as among brand attributes. Rank order scaling forces the respondent to discriminate among alternatives. This type of scaling process comes closer to resembling the shopping environment. It also takes less time than paired comparisons. Another advantage is that it is easily understood, and the results are easy to communicate. The opening vignette showed that the Olympic games are the single most popular (ranked number one) sporting venue among teenage boys and girls, with basketball as teens' overall favorite spectator sport around the globe. These results are easy to communicate. The major disadvantage of this technique is that it produces only ordinal level data.

Research in Action

Winning Votes with Marketing Research

For years, Gallup (www.gallup.com) and many other research firms have been asking Americans what they believe is the most important problem facing this country today. These surveys are used to determine the voters' concerns and to guide politicians in developing their election platforms. According to a survey taken in 2008, the five most important issues, in order of importance, were (1) job creation and economic growth, (2) the Iraq war, (3) health care, (4) illegal immigration, and (5) terrorism. This order of importance reflects a rank order scale. These issues turned out to be crucial in the 2008 U.S. presidential election and were hotly debated by all candidates.[3]

Constant Sum Scaling

In **constant sum scaling**, respondents allocate a constant sum of units, such as points, dollars, or chips, among a set of alternatives according to some specified criterion. Respondents might be asked, for example, to allocate 100 points to eight attributes of a bath soap (Figure 9.8). The points are allocated to represent the importance attached to each attribute. If an attribute is unimportant, the respondent assigns it zero points. If an attribute is twice as important as some other attribute, the respondent assigns it twice as many points. All the points a respondent assigns must total 100. Hence, the name of the scale: constant sum. A constant sum scale also results whenever percentages are calculated, as in the opening vignette.

constant sum scaling
A comparative scaling technique in which respondents are required to allocate a constant sum of units, such as points, dollars, chits, stickers, or chips, among a set of stimulus objects with respect to some criterion.

FIGURE 9.8

Constant Sum Scaling

INSTRUCTIONS

Below are eight attributes of bathing soaps. Please allocate 100 points among the attributes so that your allocation reflects the relative importance you attach to each attribute. The more points an attribute receives, the more important the attribute is. If an attribute is not at all important, assign it zero points. If an attribute is twice as important as some other attribute, it should receive twice as many points.

FORM

AVERAGE RESPONSES OF THREE SEGMENTS

Attribute	Segment I	Segment II	Segment III
1. Mildness	8	2	4
2. Lather	2	4	17
3. Shrinkage	3	9	7
4. Price	53	17	9
5. Fragrance	9	0	19
6. Packaging	7	5	9
7. Moisturizing	5	3	20
8. Cleaning Power	13	60	15
Sum	100	100	100

Note that the constant sum scale has an absolute zero—10 points are twice as many as 5 points, and the difference between 5 and 2 points is the same as the difference between 57 and 54 points. For this reason, constant sum scale data are sometimes treated as metric. Although this might be appropriate in the limited context of the objects scaled, these results are not generalizable or applicable to other objects not included in the study. Hence, strictly speaking, the constant sum should be considered an ordinal scale.

The main advantages of the constant sum scale are that it allows for fine discrimination among alternatives and does not require too much time. However, it has one major disadvantage: Respondents can allocate more or fewer units than those specified. For example, a respondent might allocate 108 or 94 points. If this occurs, the researcher must adjust the data to sum to 100 points or eliminate that respondent from analysis.

Constant sum scales in the form of percentages often are used to present research results. In the opening vignette, the popularity of a spectator sport was measured in terms of the percentage of respondents who reported it as their favorite. As another example, consider the following.

Research in Action

The Malling of America

The number of malls and shopping centers dotting the U.S. landscape in 2008 exceeded 50,000. The state of California had the highest number of shopping centers, followed by Florida, Texas, and Illinois. According to a recent Maritz Ameri-Poll, visiting the local mall has become part of the American lifestyle. The results of this poll indicated that, on average, 23 percent of adults make less than one trip per month, while 40 percent of adults shop at a mall one or two times per month. Another 20 percent shop three or four times per month, and 10 percent make five to seven trips. "Born to shop" is the description applied to people who average eight or more trips each month. According to this poll, seven percent of the population is "born to shop."

Information conveyed as percentages is an illustration of a constant sum scale. Department store chains use this type of information in planning the number of store locations in malls. The 23 percent who shop less than once per month represent a segment that needs to be penetrated.[4]

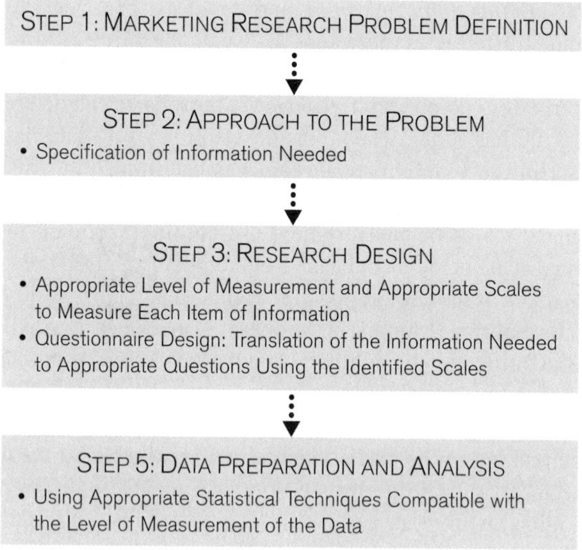

STEP 1: MARKETING RESEARCH PROBLEM DEFINITION

⋮

STEP 2: APPROACH TO THE PROBLEM
• Specification of Information Needed

⋮

STEP 3: RESEARCH DESIGN
• Appropriate Level of Measurement and Appropriate Scales to Measure Each Item of Information
• Questionnaire Design: Translation of the Information Needed to Appropriate Questions Using the Identified Scales

⋮

STEP 5: DATA PREPARATION AND ANALYSIS
• Using Appropriate Statistical Techniques Compatible with the Level of Measurement of the Data

FIGURE 9.9

Relationship of Measurement and Scaling to the Marketing Research Process

Be a DM!

As the marketing manager for Lexus, the luxury brand of Japanese automaker Toyota, how would you use information on American consumer purchase intentions for luxury cars to increase your sales?

Be an MR!

Visit the Lexus division of Toyota Motor Sales U.S.A. at www.lexus.com and search the Internet, as well as your library's online databases, to obtain information on consumer purchase intentions for luxury cars in the United States. Would you use a comparative scaling technique to measure consumer purchase intentions for luxury cars? If yes, which technique?

Relationship of Measurement and Scaling to the Marketing Research Process

The relationship of measurement and scaling to the previous and subsequent steps of the marketing research process is described in Figure 9.9. The marketing research problem is defined in Step 1. Based on this definition, an approach to the problem is developed (Step 2). An important component of the approach is specifying the information needed to address the marketing research problem. Measurement and scaling are part of the research design (Step 3). The researcher must identify an appropriate level of measurement (nominal, ordinal, interval, or ratio) for each item of information needed. If the measurement level is ordinal, the researcher generally selects one of the comparative techniques (paired comparison, rank order, or constant sum). If the data are interval, the researcher selects one of the noncomparative techniques (continuous or itemized rating scale: Likert, semantic differential, or Stapel).

Likewise, the researcher must select an appropriate scale for an information item that is to be measured on a nominal or ordinal level. When designing a questionnaire, also part of the research design, the researcher must translate the information needed to appropriate questions using the identified scales. When analyzing the data (Step 5), the researcher should only use those statistical techniques that are compatible with the measurement level of the data. For example, regression analysis, discussed in Chapter 18, assumes that the dependent variable is measured using an interval or ratio scale. Thus, regression analysis should not be used when the data have been measured on an ordinal level.

Summary Illustration Using the Opening Vignette

The fundamental scale characteristics are description, order, distance, and origin. Description means that unique labels or descriptors are used to designate each value of the scale. Order means the relative sizes or positions of the descriptors. Order is denoted by descriptors such as *greater than, less than,* and *equal to.* The characteristic of distance means that absolute differences between the scale descriptors are known and can be expressed in units. The origin characteristic means that the scale has a unique or fixed beginning or true zero point. Description is the most basic characteristic that is present in all scales. If a scale has order, it also has description. If a scale has distance, it also has order and description. Finally, a scale that has origin also has distance, order, and description.

The four primary scales of measurement are nominal, ordinal, interval, and ratio. Of these, the nominal scale is the most basic. The numbers are used only for identifying or classifying objects under study. In the opening vignette, numbers could be used to denote the various spectator sports: 1. tennis, 2. hockey, 3. soccer, 4. basketball, and so forth. Although soccer is identified by the number 3 and basketball by the number 4, this does not mean that soccer is either more or less preferred to basketball. In the ordinal scale, the numbers indicate the relative position of the objects, but not the magnitude of difference between them. The ranking of the various sports, with basketball at the top, constitutes an ordinal scale. The interval scale permits a comparison of the differences between the objects. However, it has an arbitrary zero point. Therefore, it is not meaningful to calculate ratios of scale values on an interval scale. Preference ratings for the various spectator sports on a seven-point scale (1 = Not so preferred, 7 = Greatly preferred) would be an interval scale.

Alternatively, this preference scale could go from −3 to +3. The latter scale can be derived from the former by subtracting 4 from each scale unit. The ratio scale in which the zero point is fixed represents the highest level of measurement. The researcher can compute ratios of scale values using this scale. The ratio scale incorporates all the properties of the lower-level scales: nominal, ordinal, and interval. Time or money spent watching each sport would be examples of ratio scales.

Scaling techniques can be classified as comparative or noncomparative. Comparative scaling involves a direct comparison of alternatives. The opening vignette presented an example of comparative scaling when the different sports were ranked in terms of the percentage of respondents mentioning each sport as their favorite. The resulting scale presented a relative comparison of all the sports. In noncomparative scaling, objects are evaluated individually, one at a time. In the opening vignette, the use of noncomparative scaling would involve respondents rating each sport, taken by itself, on a 1-to-7 preference scale. Comparative scales include paired comparisons, rank order, and constant sum. The data obtained by these procedures have only ordinal properties. The opening vignette illustrates the use of rank order scaling by ranking basketball at the top. Figure 9.10 gives a concept map for primary scales.

International Marketing Research

The higher levels of education and product experience of respondents in many developed countries enable them to provide responses on interval and ratio scales. In some developing countries, the respondents might have difficulty expressing their opinions in a fashion required by interval and ratio scales. Therefore, consumer preferences in these types of countries are best measured with ordinal scales. In particular, dichotomous scales (such as preferred/not preferred), the simplest type of ordinal scale, are recommended. For example, when measuring preferences for jeans in the United States, Levi Strauss could ask consumers to rate their preferences for wearing jeans on specified occasions using a seven-point interval scale. Consumers in the United States have experience with jeans, which should lead to a wide range of preference levels. However, consumers in rural Papua, New Guinea, could be shown a pair of jeans and simply asked whether they would prefer to wear it for a specific occasion (e.g., when shopping, working, relaxing on a holiday, and so on). In Japan, it is best to use a 100-point scale for measuring performance, because the Japanese commonly use this scale for such purposes. The advantage of matching the primary scales to the profile of the target respondents is well illustrated by the Japanese survey of automobile preferences in Europe.

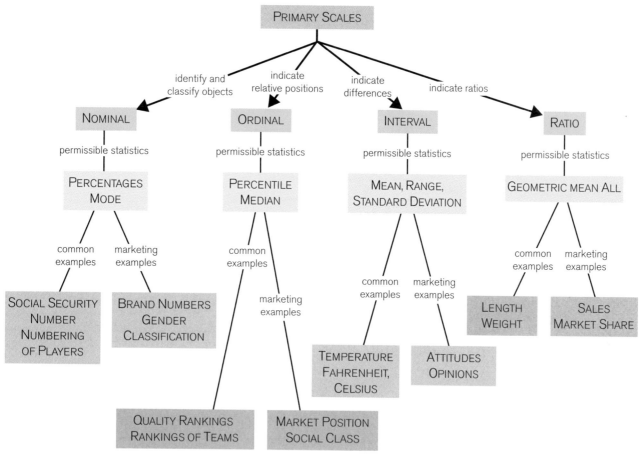

FIGURE 9.10

A Concept Map for Primary Scales

Research in Action

Car War—Japan Making a Spearhead

The Japanese carmaker Nissan (www.nissan-global.com) formed an alliance with Renault, SA, and was 44.3 percent owned by the French automaker as of 2008. Recently, European journalists gave their car-of-the-year award to Nissan's new British-made Micra, a $10,000 subcompact. This came as a blow to European automakers, who had been trying to keep the Japanese off the continent. "They will change the competitive balance," warned Bruce Blythe, Ford of Europe's head of business strategy.

How did the Japanese do it?

Nissan conducted a survey of European consumers' automobiles preferences. Nissan used interval scales to capture the range of differences in preference. For instance, consumers were asked to rate the popular automobile brands and features in terms of preference, using a seven-point scale, with 1 = not at all preferred and 7 = greatly preferred. The data derived from these interval scales enabled Nissan to compare the differences between automobile brands and features and determine which features were preferred for what brands. The findings revealed distinct consumer preferences. The cars were redesigned to meet consumer preferences and needs.

Nissan also benefited by setting up production plants in Europe to customize its cars to local styling tastes and preferences. By 2008, the Japanese were producing more than 1 million cars a year in Europe, 75 percent of them in Britain. With a strong focus on consumer preferences measured via interval scales, the Japanese are taking away market share from European manufacturers in the European markets.[5]

Be an MR!

Visit the U.S. specialty retailer Gap at www.gap.com and search the Internet, as well as your library's online databases, to obtain information on consumer preferences for casual clothing. Which comparative scaling technique(s) would you use to measure consumer preferences for casual clothing in the United States and in rural Nigeria?

Be a DM!

As the marketing manager for Gap, how would you use information on consumer preferences for casual clothing to increase your sales?

Technology and Marketing Research

Database managers allow researchers to develop and test several different scales to determine their appropriateness for a particular application. Several questionnaire design and survey programs are available to design basic types of scales and comparative and noncomparative scales. Qualtrics is an online survey-building and survey software provider. Qualtrics' online survey-building site allows one to build, enhance, and analyze surveys, forms, and databases instantly and online.

Experiential Learning

Qualtrics Question Library and Corresponding Scales

Access to Qualtrics is included with this book. Use the Qualtrics question library to electronically develop the following scales.

1. Gender measured on a nominal scale

2. Age measured on an ordinal scale

3. Age measured on a ratio scale

4. Income measured on an ordinal scale

Design your own question to measure income on an interval scale.

Ethics in Marketing Research

It is the researcher's responsibility to use the appropriate scales to obtain the necessary data to answer the research questions and test the hypotheses. Take, for example, a study that Lenovo, the worlds largest supplier of computer products and services, initiated to measure and explain consumer preferences for different brands of computers (Lenovo, HP, Acer, Gateway, NEC, Apple, Compaq, and Dell). One way to gain information on consumers' preferences would be to give each respondent several cards, each listing one computer brand. The respondent then ranks the brands (cards) in order of preference. The respondent selects the card for the most preferred brand first, followed by the card for the second most preferred brand, third most preferred brand, and so on, until, last of all, the card for the least preferred brand is selected. This results in ordinal data. Although it will provide rich insight into brand preference by allowing respondents to compare the cards, shuffle them, compare again, and reshuffle, these data cannot be analyzed using popular statistical techniques. To explain preferences for computer brands in terms of the relevant attributes, interval scale data are needed.

Knowingly using inappropriate scales raises ethical questions. It is the obligation of the researcher to obtain the data that are most appropriate given the research questions, as the following example illustrates.

Research in Action

Scaling Ethical Dilemmas

In a study designed to measure ethical judgments of male and female marketing researchers, scale items from a previously developed and tested scale were used. However, after a pretest was conducted on a convenience sample of 65 marketing professionals, it became apparent that some original scale items were worded in a way that did not reflect current usage. Therefore, these items were updated. For example, an item that was gender specific, such as, "He pointed out that . . . " was altered to read, "The project manager pointed out that . . . " Respondents were asked to show their approval or disapproval of the stated action of a marketing research director with regard to specific ethical dilemmas using the scenario approach. Realizing that a binary or dichotomous scale (disapprove/approve) would be too restrictive, approval or disapproval was indicated by having respondents supply interval level data via five-point scales with descriptive labels of 1 = Disapprove, 2 = Disapprove somewhat, 3 = Neither approve or disapprove, 4 = Approve somewhat, and 5 = Approve. The results revealed some differences, and female marketing researchers were found to be more ethical than their male counterparts. These differences probably would not have been discovered if the original dichotomous scale (approve, disapprove) had been used. However, the finer discrimination afforded by the five-point interval scale enabled the researcher to discover these differences. This example illustrates the use of appropriate scaling techniques in examining ethical issues in marketing research.[6]

What Would *You* Do?

New Balance: Attaining a Balance in Marketing Strategy

The Situation

The U.S. athletic footwear market is likely to grow slowly from 2005 to 2010, according to a recently published report from the U.K.-based marketing research firm Mintel International. This is due to factors such as overly complex manufacturer–retailer relationships that sap brand loyalty and foster excessive bargain hunting, a slow-growth economy, and competition from brown shoe manufacturers, as the previously distinct line between athletic and brown shoes becomes blurred. In addition, weak retail pricing is likely to lead to more of a two-tier market—(1) an upscale shoe market for those most dedicated to athletic shoes (young males) and those with higher levels of discretionary income and (2) a mass market for the rest of the nation. One bright spot revealed by Mintel's consumer research is that respondents overwhelmingly agree that they are willing to "spend money on good sneakers."

Jim Davis, chair of American shoe and apparel provider New Balance Athletic Shoe, Inc., is trying to appeal to those consumers identified in Mintel's research. New Balance rose quickly starting in the mid-1990s to become the third-largest seller of athletic shoes. Its strategy mirrored Nike's in launching the largest possible number of shoe styles and selling primarily through specialty athletic shoe stores and sporting goods stores. A big difference, however, was that New Balance created an upscale brand image that aimed to attract a greater number of 35- to 64-year-olds. Times are changing, however, and New Balance is learning that it must also change to keep improving its market growth and profits.

The Marketing Research Decision

1. New Balance would like to determine consumer preferences for its brand as compared to Nike, Reebok, and Adidas. Which scaling technique should be used?
   a. Paired comparison
   b. Rank order
   c. Constant sum
   d. Continuous rating scales
   e. Itemized rating scales
2. Discuss the role of the type of scaling technique you recommend in enabling Jim Davis to determine consumer preferences for New Balance as compared to Nike, Reebok, and Adidas and increase the market share of New Balance.

The Marketing Management Decision

1. In order to increase the market share of New Balance, Jim Davis should:
   a. Use celebrity endorsements.
   b. Introduce lower-priced shoes.
   c. Enhance the style and color of shoes.
   d. Increase the promotional budget.
   e. Sell New Balance shoes on the Internet.
2. Discuss how the marketing-management decision action that you recommend to Jim Davis is influenced by the scaling technique that you suggested earlier and by the findings of that research.

What Jim Davis Did

Rather than use endorsements, New Balance looked at sponsorships and promotions as a way to gain notoriety for its product. Some of the events included the Chicago Marathon, the title sponsorship for the national indoor track and field championships in New York, various walking organizations, and the U.S. modern pentathlon team. Along the promotional aspect, the company offered The Million Dollar Challenge, a seven-figure prize to the man or woman who broke existing U.S. marathon records. Also, its sponsorship of the Race For the Cure, in partnership with Susan G. Komen (www.komen.org), has raised money and awareness of New Balance among women.

To continue its success, New Balance added style and color to its already available models, but not enough to lose integrity with old customers. This helped New Balance attract new consumers while maintaining the old ones. New Balance also is planning to boost media spending. Most of the increase is allotted for television advertising of men's running and cross-training shoes. New Balance also will run print ads accenting men's and women's running shoes and women's walking shoes, focusing on the baby-boomer crowd. In addition, New Balance is looking at other market opportunities, such as lower price points, that would best be accomplished under a different brand name.[7]

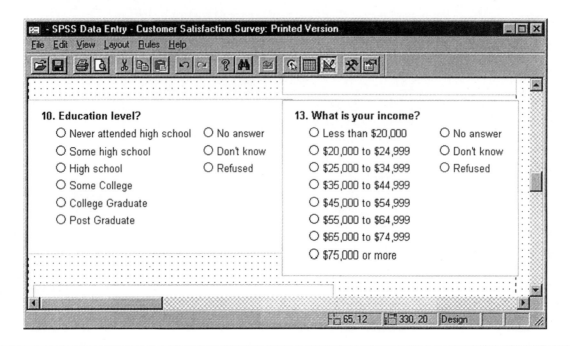

SPSS Data Entry can be used to design ordinal scales to measure education and income.

SPSS Windows

Any of the primary type of scales—nominal, ordinal, interval, or ratio—can be designed using SPSS Data Entry. Either the question library can be used or customized scales can be designed. Moreover, paired comparison, rank order, and constant sum scales can be easily implemented. We show the use of SPSS Data Entry to design ordinal scales to measure education and income. This software is not included but can be purchased separately from SPSS.

Summary

Measurement is the assignment of numbers or other symbols to characteristics of objects according to set rules. Scaling involves the generation of a continuum upon which measured objects are located. The fundamental scale characteristics are description, order, distance, and origin. Description means the unique labels or descriptors that are used to designate each value of the scale. Order means the relative sizes or positions of the descriptors. Order is denoted by descriptors such as *greater than, less than,* and *equal to.* The characteristic of distance means that absolute differences between the scale descriptors are known and can be expressed in units. The origin characteristic means that the scale has a unique or fixed beginning or true zero point. Description is the most basic characteristic that is present in every scale. If a scale has order, it also has description. If a scale has distance, it also has order and description. Finally, a scale that has origin also has distance, order, and description.

The four primary scales of measurement are nominal, ordinal, interval, and ratio. Of these, the nominal scale is the most basic and possesses only the description characteristic. The numbers are used only for identifying or classifying the objects under study. In the ordinal scale, the numbers indicate the relative position of the objects but not the magnitude of the difference between them. The ordinal scale possesses description and order characteristics. The interval scale permits a comparison of the differences between the objects and possesses the characteristics of description, order and distance. However, because it has an arbitrary zero point, it is not meaningful to calculate ratios of scale values on an interval scale. The ratio scale, in which the zero point is fixed, represents the highest level of measurement. The researcher can compute ratios of scale values using this scale. The ratio scale incorporates all the properties of the lower-level scales and possesses all the scale characteristics.

Scaling techniques can be classified as comparative or noncomparative. Comparative scaling involves a direct comparison of alternatives. Comparative scales include paired comparisons, rank order, and constant sum. The data obtained by these procedures have only ordinal properties.

In developed countries, respondents are used to providing responses on interval and ratio scales. However, in developing countries responses are best measured with simple ordinal scales. Software is available to enable researchers to construct a variety of comparative scales. Ethical considerations require that the appropriate type of scales be used in order to get the data needed to answer the research questions and test the hypotheses.

Key Terms and Concepts

Measurement,   274
Scaling,   275
Description,   276
Order,   276
Distance,   276

Origin,   277
Nominal scale,   273
Ordinal scale,   280
Interval scale,   281
Ratio scale,   282

Comparative scales,   284
Noncomparative scales,   284
Paired comparison scaling,   285
Rank order scaling,   286
Constant sum scaling,   287

Suggested Cases and Video Cases

Running Case with Real Data

1.1 Hewlett Packard

Comprehensive Critical Thinking Cases

2.1 American Idol   2.2 Baskin-Robbins   2.3 Akron Children's Hospital

Comprehensive Cases with Real Data

3.1 Bank of America   3.2 McDonald's   3.3 Boeing

Video Cases

9.1 P&G   1.1 Dunkin' Donuts   13.1 Subaru   19.1 Marriott

Live Research: Conducting a Marketing Research Project

1. As a class, discuss the level of measurement (nominal, ordinal, interval, or ratio) that is appropriate for the key variables.
2. Discuss which, if any, of the comparative techniques are appropriate.
3. Consider the practical constraints. For example, if a certain level of measurement has been used to measure a variable in the past (e.g., ordinal preference), the same level might have to be used again to compare the findings with past results.

Acronyms

The four primary types of scales can be described by the acronym FOUR:

F igurative: nominal scale

O rdinal scale

U nconstrained zero point: interval scale

R atio scale

The different comparative and noncomparative scales can be represented by the acronym SCALES:

S emantic differential scale

C onstant sum scale

A rranged in order: rank order scale

L ikert scale

E ngaged: paired comparison scale

S tapel scale

Review Questions

1. What is measurement?
2. What are the primary scales of measurement?
3. Describe the differences between a nominal and an ordinal scale.
4. What are the implications of having an arbitrary zero point in an interval scale?
5. What are the advantages of a ratio scale over an interval scale? Are these advantages significant?

6. What is a comparative rating scale?
7. What is a paired comparison?
8. What are the advantages and disadvantages of paired comparison scaling?
9. Describe the constant sum scale. How is it different from the other comparative rating scales?

Applied Problems

1. Identify the type of scale (nominal, ordinal, interval, or ratio) being used in each of the following. Please explain your reasoning.
   a. I like to solve crossword puzzles.

Disagree				Agree
1	2	3	4	5

   b. How old are you? _____
   c. Please rank the following activities in terms of your preference by assigning ranks 1 to 5, with 1 being most preferred and 5 being least preferred.
      i. Reading magazines _____
      ii. Watching television _____
      iii. Dating _____
      iv. Shopping _____
      v. Eating out _____
   d. What is your social security number?
   e. On an average week day, how much time do you spend doing your homework and class assignments?
      i. Less than 15 minutes _____
      ii. 15 to 30 minutes _____
      iii. 31 to 60 minutes _____
      iv. 61 to 120 minutes _____
      v. More than 120 minutes _____
   f. How much money did you spend last month on entertainment? _____

2. Show how intentions to purchase four brands of soft drinks (Coke, Pepsi, Dr. Pepper, and 7-Up) can be measured using ordinal, interval, and ratio scales.
3. Visit the Web sites of two marketing research firms conducting surveys. Analyze one survey from each firm to critically evaluate the primary type of scales being used.
4. Surf the Internet to find two examples of each of the four primary types of scales. Write a report describing the context in which these scales are being used.
5. Search the Internet to identify the top five selling automobile brands during the last calendar year. Rank-order these brands according to sales.
6. Target and Wal-Mart are two of the major department stores. Develop a series of paired comparison scales comparing these two stores on store image characteristics. Identify the relevant store image characteristics by visiting the Web sites of these two stores (www.target.com, www.walmart.com).

Group Discussion

1. "A brand could receive the highest median preference rank on a rank order scale of all the brands considered and still have poor sales." Discuss.

2. Select one of the readings from the notes in this chapter and lead a class discussion.

Hewlett-Packard Running Case

Review the Hewlett-Packard (HP) case, Case 1.1, and questionnaire given toward the end of the book.

1. What primary scales of measurement have been employed in the HP questionnaire? Illustrate each type.

2. Access to Qualtrics is included with this book. What primary scales are available using Qualtrics? How can HP make use of these scales?

3. Use the Qualtrics question library to illustrate the use of rank order and constant sum scales in a customer perception survey by HP.

PROCTER & GAMBLE: Using Marketing Research to Build Brands

As of 2008, Procter & Gamble (www.pg.com) delivered products under 300 brand names to nearly 5 billion consumers in more than 160 countries around the world. P&G employed about 110,000 employees in approximately 80 countries worldwide. Its revenues amounted to $76.5 billion in 2007. The company began operations in the United States in 1837 and has continued to expand its global operations. The stated purpose of the company is to "provide products and services of superior quality and value that improve the lives of the world's consumers."

Over time, P&G has proven to be an innovator in creating brands and understanding consumers by making extensive use of marketing research. Building brands has been a cornerstone of P&G's success. The marketers at P&G use marketing research to determine a brand's equity and then make sure everyone understands it, because it drives every decision made about the brand. P&G always thinks about the consumer and why a particular product is relevant to the consumer. P&G always asks "*What is in this for the consumer?*" This strategy has served the company well. It believes in catering to the consumer. With that in mind, P&G has spent a tremendous amount of money, effort, and innovation on marketing research.

A focus group talking about a product is simply not enough; the marketers at P&G dig deeper to try to really understand consumer behaviors. Leonara Polonsky, the marketing director at P&G, describes the intensity with which P&G pursues its marketing research efforts. Some of these efforts include shopping with consumers and spending several hours in consumers' homes. In fact, Polonsky describes her own experience at spending time at consumers' homes in Caracas, making coffee with them and trying to understand how these consumers think about coffee. This marketing research initiative is an innovative approach that puts the consumer at the center of everything P&G does. P&G now thinks much more holistically about the consumer's entire experience related to its brands, and so it pays much more attention, for example, to the in-store experience.

P&G's basic marketing principles have not changed, but its methods of targeting and identifying consumers have changed to meet the increasingly complicated consumer base. In the early days, P&G would mass market through television and other sources, because this was the most effective strategy at the time. P&G has changed its key strategy from mass marketing to *consumer* targeting. According to Jim Stengel, P&G's Global Marketing Director, targeting is the future of brand marketing and brand building, because the better a company understands its market the better its marketing will be.

One of the areas that P&G constantly researches is the consumers' in-store experience, viewing it as another way of connecting with consumers and making their experience better. One of the ways it does this is by partnering with retailers to develop in-store experiences to please consumers, which has become more difficult because consumers have less time and higher expectations.

P&G realizes that it is no longer possible to shout at consumers. It has to talk to them when they want to listen, and it is the consumers who choose the time and the place for this communication. That time and place, today, is increasingly becoming the Internet. An excellent example is the Pampers Web site, where caregivers can get helpful parenting information. The Pampers site is P&G's way of connecting with consumers on their terms. All parents want information about babies, and Pampers provides information about babies. The Pampers' Web site is not about selling diapers, but about helping parents understand their babies and answer questions about them. In the process, P&G also collects valuable marketing research information.

Sometimes new-product plans result from Internet marketing research. P&G has discovered that Internet research offers a more representative feel for consumer reactions, and P&G is leveraging the Internet to understand consumers. This was the case when P&G decided to launch Crest White Strips not on television, but on the Internet. The Crest White Strips product launch was one of the most successful product launches in history.

The Pampers brand also presents an example of understanding brand equity; the brand has recently been redefined from one about absorption to one about baby development. Focus groups and surveys revealed that parents are very emotionally involved in the development of their babies. This simple but deep change from a functional equity to a broad emotional one has resulted in a whole different look for Pampers diapers, a whole different look in the advertising, a different media plan, and a totally new product plan.

P&G is always conducting marketing research to discover new ways to reach out to consumers, sometimes by developing new products and introducing new product categories. P&G invented disposable diapers, home dry-cleaning, and the very popular cleaning tool the Swiffer, which was designed after extensive marketing research. P&G marketing has been innovative and pioneering over the years, and one would expect the same from it in the future.

Conclusion

The case presents P&G's strong culture of understanding its consumers by conducting marketing research and innovating to meet their needs and desires. P&G, with its long and rich legacy, has continuously evolved newer ways to connect with its consumers and gain insights into their behavior. P&G has been adept at adopting newer technologies, such as the Internet, and leveraging marketing research to enhance its understanding of its consumers. P&G is constantly using marketing research to solve the problems of today and to build brands that will continue to be leaders tomorrow.

Questions

1. Discuss the role that marketing research can play in helping P&G build its various brands.
2. P&G is considering further increasing its market share. Define the management decision problem.
3. Define an appropriate marketing research problem based on the management decision problem you have identified.
4. Formulate an appropriate research design to address the marketing research problem you have defined.
5. Use the Internet to determine the market shares of the major toothpaste brands for the last calendar year.
6. What type of syndicated data will be useful in addressing the marketing research problem?
7. Discuss the role of qualitative research in helping P&G to increase its share of the toothpaste market.
8. P&G has developed a new toothpaste that provides tooth and gum protection for 24 hours after each brushing. It would like to determine consumers' response to this new toothpaste before introducing it in the marketplace. If a survey is to be conducted to determine consumer preferences, which survey method should be used and why?

9. What role can causal research play in helping P&G increase its market share?

10. Illustrate the use of the primary type of scales in measuring consumer preferences for toothpaste brands.

11. If marketing research to determine consumer preferences for toothpaste brands were to be conducted in Latin America, how would the research process be different?

12. Discuss the ethical issues involved in researching consumer preferences for toothpaste brands.

References

1. www.pg.com, accessed on February 20, 2008.
2. Chris Isidore, "P&G to Buy Gillette for $57B," online at http://money.cnn.com/2005/01/28/news/fortune500/pg_gillette/, accessed on September 3, 2005.
3. Jack Neff, "Humble Try: P&G's Stengel Studies Tactics of Other Advertisers—and Moms—in Bid to Boost Marketing Muscle," *Advertising Age*, February 18, 2002, p. 3.

ten

CHAPTER

Measurement and Scaling: Noncomparative Scaling Techniques

OPENING QUESTIONS

1. How are noncomparative scaling techniques different from comparative scaling, and what is the distinction between continuous and itemized rating scales?
2. What are the differences among Likert, semantic-differential, and Stapel scales?
3. What decisions are involved in constructing itemized rating scales, and what options should be considered?
4. How are scales evaluated, and what is the relationship between reliability and validity?
5. What considerations are important in implementing noncomparative scales in an international setting?
6. How does technology impact noncomparative scaling?
7. What ethical issues are involved in developing noncomparative scales?

LEONARDO DiCAPRIO

> "Different cultures use scales in different ways. For example, in Mexico no one bothers to use points 1 through 4 on a 10-point scale because they learned in school that a grade of '5' on a 10-point scale means you already flunk the test."
>
> *Manuel Barbarena,*
> *President, Mexico Subsidiary,*
> *Pearson Research.*

Noncomparative Scaling Techniques Result in an Incomparable Hit Movie

The entertainment industry regularly conducts market research to determine audience response to new offerings. In the United States, for example, film studios routinely conduct prerelease screenings in order to gauge audience reaction. One method of measuring audience reaction is electronic continuous measurement. Audience members are each given a dial and are told to continuously rate their reaction to the film while watching it. They simply turn the dial from positive to negative to record their reactions. Because the recording is continuous, audience reaction to every scene can be measured. This method is particularly useful when the size of the audience is 100 or fewer; that is, when the sample size is relatively small.

When the size of the audience is large, a survey questionnaire is administered at the end of each segment of the movie. These surveys generally employ Likert-type scales that are five-point scales measuring respondents' degree of agreement or disagreement with the specified statements.

The scales are balanced so that they have an equal number of agree and disagree categories. Moreover, the scales have an odd number of categories, generally five, to allow neutral responses, such as neither agree nor disagree, because many respondents might not like or dislike specific scenes. All the scale categories are labeled to reduce ambiguity.

A "no opinion" option is not provided, because it is believed that all respondents should be able to express an opinion, having just seen the movie. Sometimes, both electronic continuous measurement and Likert scales are used to allow an assessment of the validity of the scales by comparing responses from the two methods. For example, the following is a statement designed to measure the response to ending scenes:

	Strongly disagree	Disagree	Neither agree nor disagree	Agree	Strongly agree
I like the ending of the movie.	1	2	3	4	5

Audience reaction and response to the original ending of the movie *Fatal Attraction* was the primary reason its original ending was changed. Although the audience liked the movie in general, electronic continuous measurement and survey responses indicated that the ending was poorly received. With the changes, the movie went on to become one of the blockbuster hits of the last two decades. How was the ending changed?

Released in 1987 by the U.S. production company Paramount Pictures, *Fatal Attraction* has gone down in history as a major romantic/thriller/slasher-style movie. Michael Douglas stars as a caring husband and father who has a very brief affair with his colleague, Glenn Close. Douglas thinks nothing of the affair, but Close becomes obsessed with Douglas and eventually turns into a psychotic. The original ending of this movie made Douglas out as the villain, and Close as the victim. However, test audiences despised Close's character so much that Paramount spent $1.3 million to switch the ending of the movie to make Close the villain and Douglas the victim. *The Departed* also made extensive use of continuous measurement and Likert-type scales to adapt the movie to audience reactions, and it won four U.S. Academy Awards.[1]

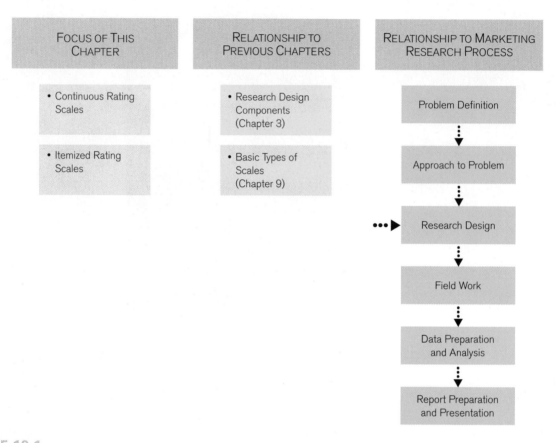

FOCUS OF THIS CHAPTER	RELATIONSHIP TO PREVIOUS CHAPTERS	RELATIONSHIP TO MARKETING RESEARCH PROCESS

- Continuous Rating Scales

- Itemized Rating Scales

- Research Design Components (Chapter 3)

- Basic Types of Scales (Chapter 9)

Problem Definition

Approach to Problem

Research Design

Field Work

Data Preparation and Analysis

Report Preparation and Presentation

FIGURE 10.1

Relationship of Noncomparative Scaling to the Previous Chapters and the Marketing Research Process

Overview

As discussed in Chapter 9, scaling techniques are classified as either comparative or non-comparative. The comparative techniques discussed in the last chapter consisted of paired comparison, rank order, and constant sum scaling. The subject of this chapter is noncomparative techniques. Figure 10.1 briefly explains the focus of the chapter, the relation of this chapter to the previous ones, and the steps in the marketing research process on which this chapter concentrates.

As discussed in Chapter 9, noncomparative scales are broadly classified as either continuous or itemized. The most popular itemized scales are Likert, semantic differential, and Stapel scales (see Figure 9.5). The opening vignette illustrated the use of both continuous and itemized rating scales to measure audience response to movies prior to release. Continuous scaling was illustrated by the use of handheld dials that the respondents turn while watching the movie. The five-point Likert scale that was used to measure response to the ending of the movie is an example of an itemized rating scale.

In this chapter, the multi-item rating scales and the importance and meaning of a scale's reliability and validity are briefly described. It also discusses the applications of these scaling techniques in international marketing research, the impact of technology, and several ethical issues that arise in rating-scale construction. Figure 10.2 provides an overview of the topics discussed in this chapter and how they flow from one to the next.

noncomparative scale
One of two types of scaling techniques in which each stimulus object is scaled independently of the other objects in the stimulus set.

Noncomparative Scaling Techniques

A **noncomparative scale** often is called a *monadic scale* because only one object is evaluated at a time. An object is not compared to another object or to some specified ideal, such as "the perfect brand." Respondents using a noncomparative scale apply their own rating

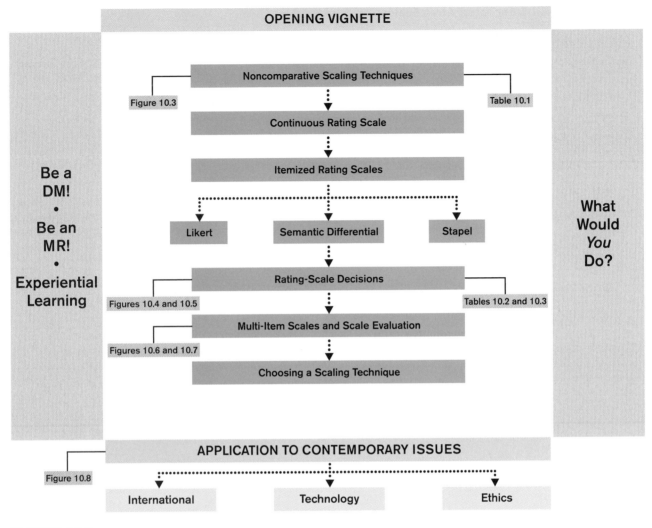

FIGURE 10.2

Noncomparative Scaling Techniques: An Overview

standard. This was illustrated in the opening vignette in which the movie *Fatal Attraction* was evaluated by itself, without comparison to any other movie. The range of noncomparative techniques and their relationship to each other is illustrated in Figure 10.3. The basic characteristics of each scale are summarized in Table 10.1 and are discussed later in this chapter.

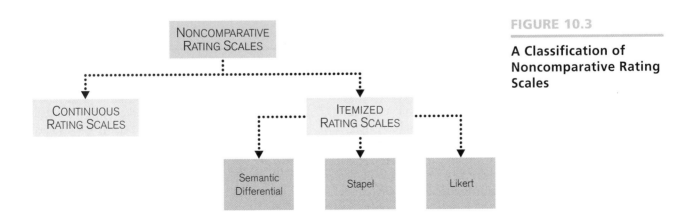

FIGURE 10.3

A Classification of Noncomparative Rating Scales

TABLE 10.1 **Basic Noncomparative Scales**

Scale	Basic Characteristics	Examples	Advantages	Disadvantages
Continuous Rating Scale	Place a mark on a continuous line	Reaction to TV commercials	Easy to construct	Scoring can be cumbersome unless computerized
Itemized Rating Scales				
Likert Scale	Degree of agreement on a 1 (strongly disagree) to 5 (strongly agree) scale	Measurement of attitudes	Easy to construct, administer, and understand	More time-consuming
Semantic Differential	Seven-point scale with bipolar labels	Brand, product, and company images	Versatile	Difficult to construct appropriate bipolar adjectives
Stapel Scale	Unipolar 10-point scale, −5 to +5, without a neutral point (zero)	Measurement of attitudes and images	Easy to construct and administered over telephone	Confusing and difficult to apply

Continuous Rating Scale

continuous rating scale
A measurement scale in which respondents rate the objects by placing a mark at the appropriate position on a line that runs from one extreme of the criterion variable to the other.

A **continuous rating scale** allows the respondent to place a mark at any point along a line running between two extreme points rather than selecting from among a set of predetermined response categories. Thus, a score on a continuous scale could be 28.637, whereas an itemized-rating scale would require the respondent to circle one of the numbers (1, 10, 20, and so on up to 100). The form of the continuous scale can be vertical or horizontal. The scale points might be brief descriptions or numbers. Continuous rating scales are sometimes referred to as *graphic rating scales*. Three versions of a continuous rating scale are illustrated here.

SURVEY QUESTION:

How would you rate Dial as compared to other brands of bath soap? The cursor/tick mark may be placed at any point along the line.

Version 1
Probably   Probably
the worst - - - - - - - | - the best

Version 2
Probably   Probably
the worst - - - - - - - | - the best
     1 10 20 30 40 50 60 70 80 90 100

Version 3
              Very bad   Neither good   Very good
                         nor bad
Probably   Probably
the worst - - - - - - - | - the best
     1 10 20 30 40 50 60 70 80 90 100

Once the respondent has provided the ratings or markings on the continuous line, the researcher divides the line into as many categories as desired and assigns scores based on the categories into which the ratings fall. Because the distance between categories is constant and the zero point is arbitrary, this type of scale would produce interval data. Thus, this scale possesses the characteristics of description, order, and distance, as discussed in Chapter 9.

Continuous scales are easy to construct. However, scoring them can be difficult and unreliable unless they are presented on a computer screen, as in computer-assisted personal interviewing or Internet surveys discussed in Chapter 7, or using computerized equipment, as in the opening vignette (Table 10.1). Continuous rating scales can be easily implemented on the Internet. The cursor can be moved on the screen in a continuous fashion to select the exact position on the scale that best describes the respondent's evaluation. The computer can automatically score the scale values, increasing the speed and accuracy of processing the data.

Continuous scales are being used more frequently as computers, the Internet, and other technologies are used more often in surveys, as illustrated by the opening vignette. Continuous scales are particularly useful for evaluating objects and things, such as movies and TV commercials, continuously over time. An example of a commercial follows.

Research in Action

Scaling Emotional Peaks

Developed by MSInteractive, a U.S. firm specializing in dial-group technology, the Perception Analyzer (www.perceptionanalyzer. com) is a computer-supported, interactive feedback system composed of wireless or wired handheld dials for each participant, a console (computer interface), and special software that edits questions, collects data, and analyzes participant responses. Members of focus groups use it to record their emotional response to television commercials, instantly and continuously. Each participant is given a dial and instructed to continuously record his or her reaction to the material being tested. As the respondents turn the dials, the information is fed to a computer. Thus, the researcher can determine the second-by-second response of the respondents as the commercial is run. Furthermore, this response can be superimposed on the commercial to see the respondents' reactions to the various frames and parts of the commercial.

Perception Analyzer was recently used to measure responses to a series of "slice of life" commercials for McDonald's. The researchers found that mothers and daughters had different responses to different aspects of the commercial. Using the emotional-response data, the researchers could determine which commercial had the greatest emotional appeal across mother–daughter segments.[2]

Be an MR!

Visit www.disney.com and search the Internet, as well as your library's online databases, to obtain information on consumer movie-viewing habits and preferences. How would you measure audience reaction to a new movie slated for release by the Walt Disney Company?

Be a DM!

As the marketing director for Disney movies, how would you develop "hit" movies?

Itemized Rating Scales

An **itemized rating scale** has a number of brief descriptions associated with each response category. The categories typically are arranged in some logical order, and the respondents are required to select the categories that best describe their reactions to whatever is being rated, as illustrated in the opening vignette. Itemized rating scales are the most widely used scales in marketing. This section presents the commonly used itemized rating scales—the Likert, semantic differential, and Stapel scales—and examines the major issues surrounding the use of itemized rating scales. All these scales possess the characteristics of description, order, and distance, as discussed in Chapter 9. The data typically are treated as interval because the origin is arbitrary.

itemized rating scale
A measurement scale that has numbers and/or brief descriptions associated with each category. The categories are ordered in terms of scale position.

Likert Scale

Likert scale

A measurement scale with five response categories ranging from "strongly disagree" to "strongly agree," which requires the respondents to indicate a degree of agreement or disagreement with each of a series of statements related to the stimulus object.

Named after its developer, American psychologist Rensis Likert, the Likert scale is one of the most widely used itemized scales. The end points of a **Likert scale** typically are "strongly disagree" and "strongly agree." The respondents are asked to indicate their degree of agreement by checking one of five response categories. The following example shows how a Likert scale was used in a retailing study.

INSTRUCTIONS

Listed below are different opinions about Macy's. Please indicate how strongly you agree or disagree with each statement by placing an X beside a number from 1 to 5, where:

1 = Strongly disagree
2 = Disagree
3 = Neither agree nor disagree
4 = Agree
5 = Strongly agree

FORM

	Strongly disagree	Disagree	Neither agree nor disagree	Agree	Strongly agree
1. Macy's sells high-quality merchandise.	1	2X	3	4	5
2. Macy's has poor in-store service.	1	2X	3	4	5
3. I like to shop at Macy's.	1	2	3X	4	5
4. Macy's does not offer a good mix of different brands within a product category.	1	2	3	4X	5
5. The credit policies at Macy's are terrible.	1	2	3	4X	5
6. Macy's is where America shops.	1X	2	3	4	5
7. I do not like the advertising done by Macy's.	1	2	3	4X	5
8. Macy's sells a wide variety of merchandise.	1	2	3	4X	5
9. Macy's charges fair prices.	1	2X	3	4	5

When using this approach to determine the total score for each respondent regarding each store, it is important to use a consistent scoring procedure so that a high (or low) score consistently reflects a favorable response. This requires that the categories assigned to the negative statements by the respondents be scored by reversing the scale. Note that for a negative statement, an agreement reflects an unfavorable response, whereas for a positive statement, agreement represents a favorable response. Accordingly, a "strongly agree" response to a favorable statement and a "strongly disagree" response to an unfavorable statement would both receive scores of five.

In the scale shown above, if a higher score is to denote a more favorable attitude, the scoring of items 2, 4, 5, and 7 will be reversed. This can be easily done by subtracting the original scale value from a number that is the highest scale value plus one. Thus, the second item will be scored as follows: $(5 + 1) - 2 = 4$. The respondent in our example has an attitude score of 22. This equals the sum of all nine item scores after scores for the negative items (2, 4, 5, and 7) are reversed. Each respondent's total score for each store is calculated. A respondent will have the most favorable attitude toward the store with the highest score.

The Likert scale has several advantages (Table 10.1). It is easy for the researcher to construct and administer, and it is easy for the respondent to understand. Therefore, it is suitable for mail, telephone, personal, or electronic interviews. Several variants of the Likert scale are commonly used in marketing which vary the number of scale points (e.g., seven or nine points) as well as the descriptors (e.g., importance, familiarity) and other characteristics discussed later. Consider, for example, a seven-point scale designed to measure the importance of attributes, where 1 = not at all important and 7 = very important.

The major disadvantage of the Likert scale is that it takes longer to complete than other itemized rating scales. Respondents have to read the entire statement rather than a short phrase. Sometimes, it might be difficult to interpret the response to a Likert item, especially if it is an unfavorable statement. In our example, the respondent disagrees with statement number 2 that the well-known American retailer Macy's has poor in-store service. By reversing the score of this item prior to summing, it is assumed that this respondent would agree with the statement that Macy's has good in-store service. This, however, might not be true; the disagreement merely indicates that the respondent would not make statement number 2. The following example shows another use of a Likert scale in marketing research.

Research in Action

Happiness Is a Lexus?

A product of the U.S. marketing-information firm J. D. Power and Associates (www.jdpa.com), the "Automotive Performance, Execution and Layout" (APEAL) survey is based on responses from more than 110,000 new-vehicle owners and measures what excites and delights them about their vehicle's features and design. It comprises eight specific areas of vehicle performance and design, including more than 110 attributes that identify what consumers like and dislike about their new vehicles during the first 90 days of ownership. These areas include the following: vehicle exterior styling; engine and transmission; comfort and convenience; ride, handling, and braking; seats; heating, ventilation, and cooling; cockpit and instrument panel; and sound system.

Carmakers use the results of the J. D. Power survey in advertisements and to check the results of their own consumer satisfaction surveys as well as those of competitors. Thus, they can benchmark their performance.

In the 2007 survey, several Lexus models attained top honors in the luxury car segments. The Lexus IS350 was in the top three most appealing entry luxury cars, the GS 450h was in the top three in the mid-luxury car segment, and the LS460 ranked in the top three among premium luxury cars. Lexus, a division of Japanese carmaker Toyota, used these results in its advertising to convince consumers that its cars are more appealing to own and operate. As of 2008, Lexus was pushing the hybrid versions of the LS, GS, and RX models.[3]

Semantic Differential Scale

The **semantic differential scale** is a seven-point rating scale on which the end points are adjectives representing opposites. When using a semantic differential, the respondent is typically asked to rate a brand, store, or some other object in terms of these bipolar adjectives, such as "cold" and "warm." This scale is illustrated here by presenting a respondent's evaluation of Macy's on five attributes.

semantic differential scale
A seven-point rating scale with end points associated with bipolar labels that have semantic meaning.

INSTRUCTIONS

This part of the study measures what certain department stores mean to you. We want you to judge the department stores in terms of the following questions. Each question is bounded by bipolar adjectives, which are opposite in meaning. Please mark (X) at the point along the scale that best describes what the store means to you.

Please be sure to mark every scale; do not omit any scale.

Form

Macy's is:

Powerful	:—:—:—:-X-:—:—:	Weak
Unreliable	:—:—:—:—:-X-:—:	Reliable
Modern	:—:—:—:—:-X-:	Old-Fashioned
Cold	:—:—:—:—:-X-:—:	Warm
Careful	:-X-:—:—:—:—:—:	Careless

The respondents mark the blanks that best indicate how they would describe the object being rated. Thus, in the Macy's example, Macy's is evaluated as somewhat weak, reliable, very old-fashioned, warm, and careful. To encourage careful consideration of each question, the negative adjective or phrase sometimes appears on the left side of the scale and sometimes on the right. This helps to control the tendency of some respondents, particularly those with very positive or very negative attitudes, to mark the right- or left-hand sides without reading the labels. For an expanded discussion of how to select labels for semantic differential scales, see the referenced work by the author describing the application of this scaling technique to the measurement of self-concepts, person concepts, and product concepts.[4] That scale is described in the following example.

Research in Action

A Semantic Differential Scale for Measuring Self-Concepts, Person Concepts, and Product Concepts

1. Rugged	:—:—:—:—:—:	Delicate	12. Orthodox	:—:—:—:—:—:	Liberal
2. Excitable	:—:—:—:—:—:	Calm	13. Complex	:—:—:—:—:—:	Simple
3. Uncomfortable	:—:—:—:—:—:	Comfortable	14. Colorless	:—:—:—:—:—:	Colorful
4. Dominating	:—:—:—:—:—:	Submissive	15. Modest	:—:—:—:—:—:	Vain
5. Thrifty	:—:—:—:—:—:	Indulgent			
6. Pleasant	:—:—:—:—:—:	Unpleasant			
7. Contemporary	:—:—:—:—:—:	Noncontemporary			
8. Organized	:—:—:—:—:—:	Unorganized			
9. Rational	:—:—:—:—:—:	Emotional			
10. Youthful	:—:—:—:—:—:	Mature			
11. Formal	:—:—:—:—:—:	Informal			

American soft-drink giant PepsiCo, for example, can make use of such a scale for measuring the self-concept of target consumers, the concept or image of selected celebrities, as well as the concept or image of the Pepsi brand (see Chapter 8 examples). This analysis will help Pepsi determine the brand image that will have the greatest appeal to target consumers. It will also help Pepsi select the right celebrities to endorse the brand so as to achieve the desired image and positioning.

Individual items on a semantic differential scale can be scored on either a -3 to $+3$ or a 1 to 7 scale. The resulting data are typically treated as interval data and analyzed using profile analysis. In profile analysis, means or median values for each item are calculated, plotted, and statistically analyzed. By plotting the results, the researcher can see overall differences and similarities among the objects measured. Differences across respondent groups also can be compared. When the researcher requires an overall comparison of objects, such as to determine store preference, the individual item scores can also be summed to arrive at a total score, as with the Likert scale.

The semantic differential is a highly popular scale in marketing research because of its versatility (Table 10.1). It is used to compare brand, product, and company images, to develop advertising and promotion strategies, and in new product development studies. The major disadvantage is the difficulty in determining the appropriate bipolar adjectives required to construct the scale. Several modifications of the basic scale have been proposed.

Stapel Scale

The **Stapel scale** was named after its developer, Dutch researcher Jan Stapel, and is typically presented vertically, with one adjective appearing at the midpoint of a scale ranging from +5 to −5. The respondent is not allowed a neutral response, because no zero point is offered. Respondents are asked to indicate how accurately or inaccurately each term describes the object by selecting the appropriate number. The higher the number, the more accurately the adjective describes the object. In the retailing study, evaluations of Macy's would be obtained as follows.

Stapel scale
A scale for measuring attitudes that consists of a single adjective in the middle of an even-numbered range of values.

INSTRUCTIONS

Please evaluate how accurately each word or phrase describes each of the department stores. Select a plus number by placing an (X) beside it for the phrases you think describe the store accurately. The more accurately you think the phrase describes the store, the larger the positive number you should choose. You should select a negative number for phrases you think do not describe the store accurately. A large negative number indicates that the phrase does not describe the store at all. You can select any number, from +5 for phrases you think are very accurate, to −5 for phrases you think are very inaccurate.

FORM

Macy's

High Quality	Poor Service	Wide Variety
+5	+5	+5
+4	+4	+4X
+3	+3	+3
+2	+2	+2
+1	+1	+1
High Quality	Poor Service	Wide Variety
−1	−1X	−1
−2X	−2	−2
−3	−3	−3
−4	−4	−4
−5	−5	−5

The data obtained from a Stapel scale are treated as interval data, analyzed in much the same way as semantic differential data. Using only one adjective in the Stapel scale has an advantage over semantic differentials, in that no pretest is needed to assure that the adjectives chosen are indeed opposites. The simplicity of the scale also lends itself to telephone interviewing. Some researchers believe the Stapel scale is confusing and difficult to apply, however. It is therefore used the least of the three itemized rating scales discussed here (Table 10.1). The advantages of this scale warrant wider applications than have been made in the past. For instance, it could be used more widely in telephone interviewing, which is currently the most popular method of administering consumer surveys in the United States.

Be a DM!	Be an MR!
As the brand manager for Diet Coke, how would you use information on consumer attitudes to segment the market?	Visit www.dietcoke.com and search the Internet, as well as your library's online databases, to obtain information on consumers' attitudes toward diet soft drinks. How would you use each of the three itemized scales to measure consumers' attitudes toward Diet Coke and other diet soft drinks? Which scale do you recommend?

Noncomparative Itemized Rating Scale Decisions

One of the advantages of using noncomparative scales is the flexibility of adapting them to a specific research project. When constructing the itemized scales discussed in this chapter, six factors can be adjusted. These factors, along with recommended guidelines, are described in Table 10.2 and briefly reviewed here.

Number of Scale Categories

sensitivity
The ability to detect subtle differences in the attitude or the characteristic being measured.

From the researcher's perspective, the larger the number of categories contained in a scale, the finer the discrimination between the brands, alternatives, or other objects under study. The **sensitivity** of a scale is the ability to detect subtle differences in the attitude or the characteristic being measured. Increasing the number of scale categories increases sensitivity. The larger the number of categories, however, the greater the information-processing demands imposed on the respondents. Thus, the desire for more information must be balanced against the demands on the respondent. There is a limit to how much information a respondent can process when answering a question. Another important factor is the mode of data collection. Telephone interviews, in which the respondent cannot see the questionnaire, can become very confusing if the number of scale categories is too large. Space limitations on the survey form itself represent another constraint.

Although there is no optimal number, the researcher should strive to balance the need for information with consideration of the demands placed on the respondent and the nature of the data-collection task. Traditional guidelines suggest that no fewer than five and no more than nine categories of information should be used. With fewer than five scale categories, not enough discrimination is generated to make the research useful. Beyond nine scale categories, the respondents become confused and fatigued, and the quality of data suffers. The opening vignette illustrated the use of five-point scales to measure reaction to new films.

TABLE 10.2 Summary of Itemized Rating Scale Decisions

Decision Factor	Guidelines
Number of categories	While there is no single optimal number, traditional guidelines suggest there should be between five and nine categories.
Balanced vs. unbalanced	In general, the scale should be balanced to obtain objective data.
Odd vs. even number of categories	If a neutral or indifferent scale response is possible for at least some of the respondents, an odd number of categories should be used.
Forced vs. nonforced	In situations where the respondents are expected to have no opinion, the accuracy of data may be improved by a nonforced scale.
Verbal description	An argument can be made for labeling all or many scale categories. The category descriptions should be located as close to the response categories as possible.
Physical form	A number of options should be tried and the best one selected.

Balanced Scale	Unbalanced Scale
SURFING THE INTERNET IS	SURFING THE INTERNET IS
_____ Extremely Good	_____ Extremely Good
_____ Very Good	_____ Very Good
_____ Good	_____ Good
_____ Bad	_____ Somewhat Good
_____ Very Bad	_____ Bad
_____ Extremely Bad	_____ Very Bad

FIGURE 10.4

Balanced and Unbalanced Scales

Balanced Versus Unbalanced Scale

In a **balanced scale**, the number of favorable and unfavorable categories or scale points is equal. In an unbalanced scale, they are unequal. Examples of balanced and unbalanced scales are given in Figure 10.4. Generally, balanced scales are desirable, ensuring the data collected are objective, as in the opening vignette. If the researcher suspects that the responses are likely to skew either negatively (i.e., most of the responses will be negative or unfavorable) or positively, an unbalanced scale might be appropriate. Under these conditions, more categories are included in the direction of the skew. For example, customer satisfaction is typically positively skewed because most of the customers are satisfied with the company and its products. Therefore, many researchers prefer to use an unbalanced scale with a larger number of satisfied categories and fewer unsatisfied categories when measuring customer satisfaction. When unbalanced scales are used, the nature and degree of unbalance in the scale should be taken into account in data analysis.

balanced scale
A scale with an equal number of favorable and unfavorable categories.

Odd or Even Numbers of Categories

When an odd number of categories are used in a scale, the midpoint typically represents a neutral category. The decision to use a neutral category and its labeling has a significant influence on the response. The Likert scale is an example of a balanced rating scale with an odd number of categories and a neutral point.

The scale should have an odd number of categories if the researcher has reason to believe that a portion of the respondent population is actually neutral on a particular subject. This was illustrated in the opening vignette in which a neutral response was allowed for measuring audience response. It was recognized that many respondents might not like or dislike specific scenes in movies. However, if the researcher wants to force a response or believes that no neutral or indifferent response exists, a rating scale with an even number of categories should be used. A related issue is whether the choice should be forced or nonforced.

Forced or Nonforced Choice

In a **forced rating scale**, the respondents are forced or required to express an opinion, because a "no opinion" option is not provided. When forced rating scales are applied to situations where a significant portion of the response population holds no opinion, the respondents will tend to select an option at the midpoint of the scale. Marking a middle position when, in fact, "no opinion" is the desired response will distort measures of central tendency and variance. In situations where the respondent holds no opinion rather than simply being reluctant to disclose that opinion, a nonforced scale that includes a "no opinion" category can improve the accuracy of data. For example, respondents might not be familiar with some of the brands in a study comparing multiple brands and, therefore, be unable to express an opinion. Otherwise, the use of a "no opinion" category should be avoided, as in the opening vignette. Although the neutral point would be the midpoint of the scale, a "no opinion" option might be better placed at the far right or left of the scale, as shown:

forced rating scale
A rating scale that forces the respondents to express an opinion because a "no opinion" option is not provided.

Strongly Disagree				Strongly Agree	
1	2	3	4	5	No opinion

Nature and Degree of Verbal Description

The way a scale category is described can have a considerable effect on the response. Scale categories can have verbal, numerical, or even pictorial descriptions. They might be provided for each category or only at the end points of the scale. Surprisingly, providing a verbal description for each category may not improve the accuracy or reliability of the data. Yet, an argument can be made for labeling all or many scale categories to reduce scale ambiguity. The category descriptions or labels should be located as close to the response categories (i.e., the scale point numbers) as possible, as illustrated by the Likert scale in the opening vignette.

The strength of the adjectives used to anchor the scale also influences the responses. Suppose respondents are asked to indicate their degree of (dis)agreement with the statement, "The moral values in Hong Kong are declining." Strong anchors (1 = completely disagree, 7 = completely agree) will result in more responses toward the midpoint of the scale because respondents are hesitant to check extreme responses (1 or 7). By contrast, weak anchors (1 = generally disagree, 7 = generally agree) produce uniform or flat distributions. In such cases, the respondents feel more comfortable in checking the scale end points (1 or 7), because these responses are not that extreme. Knowledge of the distribution of the characteristic being measured along with the objectives of the study can help the researcher select appropriate anchors.

Physical Form or Configuration

The way a scale is presented can vary quite dramatically. Scales can be presented vertically or horizontally. Categories can be expressed by boxes, discrete lines, or units on a continuum and might or might not have numbers assigned to them. If numerical values are used, they may be positive, negative, or both. Several possible configurations are presented in Figure 10.5. Before selecting a configuration, the researcher should try a

FIGURE 10.5

Rating Scale Configurations

A variety of scale configurations may be employed to measure the comfort of Nike shoes. Some examples follow:

Nike shoes are

1) PLACE AN "X" ON THE APPLICABLE BLANK SPACE:

Very Uncomfortable _____ _____ _____ _____ _____ _____ Very Comfortable

2) CIRCLE A NUMBER:

Very Uncomfortable   1   2   3   4   5   6   7   Very Comfortable

3) PLACE AN "X" ON THE APPLICABLE BLANK SPACE:

_____ Very Uncomfortable

_____

_____ Neither Uncomfortable nor Comfortable

_____

_____ Very Comfortable

4) PLACE AN "X" ON THE APPLICABLE BLANK SPACE:

Very Uncomfortable | Uncomfortable | Somewhat Uncomfortable | Neither Comfortable nor Uncomfortable | Somewhat Comfortable | Comfortable | Very Comfortable

5) CIRCLE A NUMBER:

−3   −2   −1   0   1   2   3

Very Uncomfortable   Neither Comfortable nor Uncomfortable   Very Comfortable

TABLE 10.3 Some Commonly Used Scales in Marketing

Construct	Scale Descriptors				
Attitude	Very Bad	Bad	Neither Bad nor Good	Good	Very Good
Importance	Not at All Important	Not Important	Neutral	Important	Very Important
Satisfaction	Very Dissatisfied	Dissatisfied	Neither Dissatisfied nor Satisfied	Satisfied	Very Satisfied
Purchase Intent	Definitely Will Not Buy	Probably Will Not Buy	Might or Might Not Buy	Probably Will Buy	Definitely Will Buy
Purchase Frequency	Never	Rarely	Sometimes	Often	Very Often

number of options. Table 10.3 presents some commonly used scales. Although these particular scales have five categories, the number of categories can be varied based on the researcher's judgment.

Finally, different types of itemized rating scales can be used in a single questionnaire, as the following example illustrates.

Research in Action

Unbalanced Scales Help Advanced Micro Devices Achieve Balance in Customer Satisfaction

CustomerSat (www.customersat.com) is a premier U.S. provider of Internet-survey research services. It conducted an Internet-based customer satisfaction survey for Advanced Micro Devices (AMD; www.amd.com), a leading American manufacturer of integrated circuits. Various types of itemized rating scales were employed. The importance of attributes used to evaluate AMD was measured on seven-point balanced scales (Extremely Important, Very Important, Important, Neutral, Unimportant, Very Unimportant, Extremely Unimportant). However, satisfaction was measured using five-point unbalanced scales (Excellent, Very Good, Good, Fair, Poor). The use of unbalanced scales to

measure satisfaction was justified, because satisfaction levels tend to be positively skewed.

Furthermore, a "Not Applicable (N/A)" option was also allowed when measuring satisfaction with AMD on specific attributes, because not all attributes might be relevant for a particular respondent. The results of this survey helped AMD identify customer concerns affecting satisfaction levels and to take corrective actions. For example, filling the orders accurately and in a timely manner had a very important impact on customer satisfaction. Yet, this was an area where AMD was not up to par. Accordingly, AMD reorganized this function, resulting in improved performance and increased customer satisfaction.

Be an MR!

Visit the U.S. shoemaker Rockport at www.rockport.com and search the Internet, as well as your library's online databases, to obtain information on consumers' preferences for dress shoes. Develop an itemized scale to measure American consumers' preferences for dress shoes and to justify your rating scale decisions.

Be a DM!

As the marketing manager for Rockport, how would you use information on consumers' preferences for dress shoes to increase your sales?

Multi-Item Scales

A **multi-item scale** consists of multiple items, where an item is a single question or statement to be evaluated. The Likert, semantic differential, and Stapel scales presented earlier to measure attitudes toward Macy's are examples of multi-item scales. Note that each of these scales has multiple items. Developing multi-item rating scales requires considerable technical

multi-item scale
A scale consisting of multiple items, where an item is a single question or statement to be evaluated.

FIGURE 10.6

Developing a Multi-Item Scale

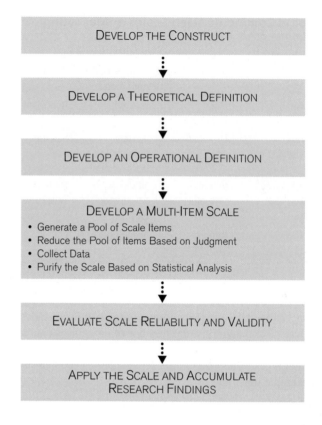

construct

A specific type of concept that exists at a higher level of abstraction than do everyday concepts.

expertise. The steps involved in constructing a multi-item scale are described in Figure 10.6. The characteristic to be measured is frequently called a *construct*. The researcher begins by developing the construct of interest. A **construct** is a specific type of concept that exists at a higher level of abstraction than do everyday concepts, such as brand loyalty, product involvement, attitude, satisfaction, and so forth. Next, the researcher must develop a theoretical definition of the construct that states the meaning of the central idea or concept of interest. For this, we need an underlying theory of the construct being measured. A theory is necessary not only for constructing the scale but also for interpreting the resulting scores. For example, brand loyalty might be defined as the consistent repurchase of a brand prompted by a favorable attitude toward the brand. The construct must be operationalized in a way that is consistent with the theoretical definition. The operational definition specifies which observable characteristics will be measured and the process of assigning value to the construct. For example, in the context of toothpaste purchases, consumers will be characterized as brand loyal if they exhibit a highly favorable attitude (top quartile) and have purchased the same brand on at least four of the last five purchase occasions. Then, the multi-item scale should be developed. The researcher generates a set of questions based on theory, analysis of secondary data, and qualitative research. This initial pool is repeatedly reduced using input from experts and the researcher's qualitative judgment. If the reduced set of items is still too large, quantitative techniques are available for further reduction and "purification." The researcher evaluates the purified scale for reliability and validity and selects a final set of scale items. The final scale is used in a variety of applications so that a wealth of research findings can accumulate.

Experiential Learning

Measuring Satisfaction Using Qualtrics Question Library

Access to Qualtrics is included with this book. Use the Qualtrics question library to electronically develop the following satisfaction scales.

1. Five-point Likert (type) balanced scale
2. Five-point Likert (type) unbalanced scale.
3. Seven-point Likert (type) balanced scale
4. Seven-point semantic differential scale
5. Five-point smiling faces scale

Scale Evaluation

A multi-item scale should be evaluated for reliability and validity, as shown in Figure 10.7. To understand these concepts, it is useful to think of total measurement error as the sum of systematic error and random error. **Systematic error** affects the measurement in a constant way, that is, in the same way each time the measurement is made. **Random error**, in contrast, arises from random changes and has a different effect each time the measurement is made. Thus,

$$\text{Total measurement error} = \text{Systematic error} + \text{Random error}$$

Reliability

Reliability refers to the extent to which a scale produces consistent results if repeated measurements are made. Therefore, reliability can be defined as the extent to which measures are free from random error.

Reliability is determined by repeatedly measuring the construct or variable of interest. The higher the degree of association between the scores derived through this repeated measurement, the more reliable the scale. Popular approaches for assessing reliability are test–retest, alternative-forms, and internal-consistency methods.

Test–Retest Reliability

In **test–retest reliability**, respondents are administered identical scales at two different times under as nearly equivalent conditions as possible. The retest typically follows the original measurement by 2 to 4 weeks. The degree of similarity between the two measurements is determined by computing a correlation coefficient (see Chapter 18). The higher the correlation coefficient, the greater the reliability.

Alternative-Forms Reliability

In order to test **alternative-forms reliability**, two equivalent forms of the scale are constructed. The same respondents are measured using alternative scale forms. Correlation between the responses to the two equivalent forms of the scale provides a measure of reliability.

Internal-Consistency Reliability

Internal-consistency reliability is used to assess the reliability of a summated scale, or subscale, where scores for several items are summed to form a total score for a construct (e.g., attitude). In a scale of this type, each item measures some aspect of the construct

systematic error
Systematic error affects the measurement in a constant way and represents stable factors that affect the observed score in the same way each time the measurement is made.

random error
Measurement error that arises from random changes that have a different effect each time the measurement is made.

reliability
The extent to which a scale produces consistent results if repeated measurements are made on the characteristic.

test–retest reliability
An approach for assessing reliability in which respondents are administered identical sets of scale items at two different times under as nearly equivalent conditions as possible.

alternative-forms reliability
An approach for assessing reliability, which requires two equivalent forms of the scale to be constructed, and then measures the same respondents at two different times using the alternate forms.

internal-consistency reliability
An approach used to assess the reliability of a summated scale and refers to the consistency with which each item represents the construct of interest.

FIGURE 10.7

Scale Evaluation

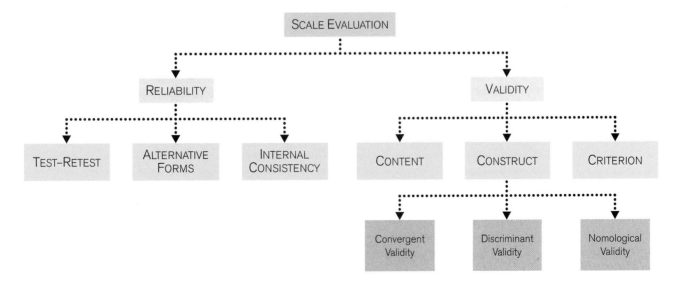

split-half reliability

A form of internal-consistency reliability in which the items constituting the scale are divided into two halves, and the resulting half scores are correlated.

coefficient alpha

A measure of internal-consistency reliability that is the average of all possible split-half coefficients resulting from different splittings of the scale items.

measured by the entire scale. The items should be consistent in what they indicate about the characteristic. This measure of reliability refers to the consistency with which each item represents the construct of interest. Consider the nine-item Likert scale used to measure attitudes toward Macy's discussed earlier in this chapter. How consistently do items such as "Macy's sells high-quality merchandise" or "I like to shop at Macy's" measure attitudes toward Macy's?

The simplest measure of internal consistency is **split-half reliability**. In applying this procedure, the scale items are randomly divided into halves, and the resulting half scores are correlated. High correlations between the halves indicate high internal consistency. The correlation between the halves will be affected by how the groups are split.

A popular approach to overcoming this problem is to use the coefficient alpha. The **coefficient alpha**, or Cronbach's alpha, is calculated by averaging the coefficients that result from all possible combinations of split halves.[5] This coefficient varies from 0 to 1, and a value of 0.6 or less generally indicates unsatisfactory internal-consistency reliability.

Experiential Learning

McCann Erickson and Ad Promises

Based in the United Kingdom, McCann Erickson Worldwide Advertising (www.mccannerickson.com) is the world's largest advertising agency network, with offices in more than 130 countries. Joe Plummer, Executive Vice President and Director of Research & Insight Development for McCann Erickson, has become concerned that viewers might be overcome with the "dazzle" of television ads at the expense of actually learning about the brands featured in them. To address the need for improved measures of viewer response to ads, researchers have developed a set of multi-item scales called Ad Promises.[6] Eight-point Likert type scales were used to measure each of the eight subscales of Ad Promises.

Go to the Web site for this book and download the following files: (10a) McCann Erickson Experiential learning (Word file); (10b) Ad promises not reversed (Excel file); (10c) Ad promises reversed (SPSS file).

1. Read the Word file (10a) to understand the context of Ad Promises.

2. Use the Excel file (10b) to perform the following operations [see detailed instructions in the Word file (10a)]:

   a. Reverse-code the original eight variables into these eight new variables.

   b. Save your Excel file as "Ad Promises Reversed Coded.xls" and then import its contents into SPSS.

3. Use the SPSS file that you have created to perform the following operations [see detailed instructions in the Word file (10a)]:

   a. Create a composite variable representing each of the eight Ad Promise constructs.

   b. Compute Cronbach's Alpha for each of these eight sets of items.

Validity

validity

The extent to which differences in observed scale scores reflect true differences among objects on the characteristic being measured, rather than systematic or random errors.

The **validity** of a scale can be defined as the extent to which differences in observed scale scores reflect true differences in what is being measured, rather than systematic or random error. A scale with perfect validity would contain no measurement error; that is, no systematic error and no random error. Researchers can assess validity in different ways: content validity, criterion validity, or construct validity.

content validity

A type of validity, sometimes called *face validity*, that consists of a subjective but systematic evaluation of the representativeness of the content of a scale for the measuring task at hand.

CONTENT VALIDITY **Content validity** involves a systematic but subjective assessment of how well a scale measures the construct or variable of interest. For a scale to be content valid, it must address all dimensions of the construct. This is a commonsense evaluation of the scale. For example, a scale designed to measure the construct store image would be considered inadequate if it omitted any of the major dimensions of image (quality, variety and assortment of merchandise, and so on). Content validity alone is not a sufficient measure of the validity of a scale. It must be supplemented with a more formal evaluation of the scale's validity, namely criterion validity and construct validity.

criterion validity

A type of validity that examines whether the measurement scale performs as expected in relation to other variables selected as meaningful criteria.

CRITERION VALIDITY **Criterion validity** reflects whether a scale performs as expected given other variables considered relevant to the construct. These variables are called *criterion variables*. They may include demographic and psychographic characteristics, attitudinal and behavioral measures, or scores obtained from other scales. For example, the researcher may measure attitudes toward cereal brands using a multi-item scale administered to members of a scanner panel. Based on attitude levels, future purchases of cereal (criterion variable) are predicted. Scanner data are used to track the actual cereal purchases of the panel members. The predicted and actual purchases are compared to assess criterion validity of the attitudinal scale.

CONSTRUCT VALIDITY **Construct validity** addresses the question of what construct or characteristic the scale is, in fact, measuring. In order to assess construct validity, the researcher must have a strong understanding of the theory that provided the basis for constructing the scale. The researcher uses theory to explain why the scale works and what deductions can be drawn from it. As Figure 10.7 shows, construct validity includes convergent, discriminant, and nomological validity. **Convergent validity** is the extent to which the scale correlates positively with other measures of the same construct. **Discriminant validity** is the extent to which a measure does not correlate with other constructs from which it is supposed to differ. **Nomological validity** is the extent to which the scale correlates in theoretically predicted ways with measures of different, but related, constructs.

In the opening vignette, construct validity is assessed by measuring audience reaction via continuous measurement using a dial and Likert scales and correlating the measures. We illustrate construct validity in the context of a multi-item scale designed to measure self-concept, the image that consumers have of themselves. This construct is of interest to marketers because consumers prefer products and brands that are consistent with and reinforce their self-concept.

construct validity
A type of validity that addresses the question of what construct or characteristic the scale is measuring. An attempt is made to answer theoretical questions of why a scale works and what deductions can be made concerning the theory underlying the scale.

convergent validity
A measure of construct validity that measures the extent to which the scale correlates positively with other measures of the same construct.

discriminant validity
A type of construct validity that assesses the extent to which a measure does not correlate with other constructs from which it is supposed to differ.

Research in Action

To Thine Own Self Be True

Following are findings that provide evidence of validity for a multi-item scale to measure self-concept:

- Three experts agree that all the items in the scale are relevant for measuring self-concept (content validity).

- High correlations exist between scales designed to measure self-concept and personality assessments of the same person by their friends (criterion validity).

- High correlations exist with other scales designed to measure self-concepts (convergent validity).

- Low correlations exist with unrelated constructs of brand loyalty and variety seeking (discriminant validity).

- Brands that are congruent with the individual's self-concept are more preferred, as postulated by the theory (nomological validity).

- There is a high level of reliability.

Notice that a high level of reliability was included as evidence of construct validity in this example. This illustrates the relationship between reliability and validity.

Relationship Between Reliability and Validity

If a measure is perfectly valid, it also is perfectly reliable. In this case, neither systematic nor random error is present. Thus, perfect validity implies perfect reliability. (No measurement error implies no random error.) If a measure is unreliable, it cannot be perfectly valid, because, at a minimum, random error is present. (If random error is present, measurement error is present.) Furthermore, systematic error might also be present. Thus, unreliability implies invalidity. If a measure is perfectly reliable, it might or might not be perfectly valid, because systematic error might still be present. (If there is no random error, measurement error might still be present due to systematic error.) Although lack of reliability constitutes negative evidence for validity, reliability does not in itself imply validity. Reliability is a necessary, but not sufficient, condition for validity.

nomological validity
A type of validity that assesses the relationship between theoretical constructs. It seeks to confirm significant correlations between the constructs as predicted by theory.

Choosing a Scaling Technique

In addition to theoretical considerations and evaluation of reliability and validity, the researcher should consider certain practical factors in selecting scaling techniques for a particular marketing research problem. These include the level of measurement desired (nominal, ordinal, interval, or ratio), the experience of the respondents with the research topic, the difficulty of administering the scales, and the context. Additionally, using multiple scale items to measure the same characteristic will improve the accuracy of results. In many situations, it is desirable to use more than one scaling technique, as illustrated in the opening vignette.

Summary Illustration Using the Opening Vignette

Noncomparative rating scales can be either continuous or itemized. Both types were illustrated in the opening vignette. Audience members viewing a movie are each given a dial and are told to continuously rate their reactions to the film from positive to negative by turning the dial in the desired direction, thus recording their response on a continuous scale. The itemized rating scales are further classified as Likert, semantic differential, or Stapel scales. The data from all these three types of scale are typically treated as interval scale data. Thus, these scales possess the characteristics of description, order, and distance, as discussed in Chapter 9.

Large-scale surveys conducted to assess respondents' reactions to movies make use of Likert scales. When using noncomparative itemized rating scales, the researcher must decide on the number of scale categories, balanced versus unbalanced scales, odd or even number of categories, forced versus nonforced scales, nature and degree of verbal description, and the physical form or configuration. The Likert scale in the opening vignette made use of five categories following the traditional guidelines and is balanced to avoid bias in any direction. A neutral response (3) is allowed as it is recognized that many respondents might not like or dislike specific scenes in movies. All the scale categories are labeled in order to reduce ambiguity. A forced scale is used, without a "no opinion" category, because people generally express opinions on movies they have seen.

Multi-item scales consist of a number of rating-scale items. These scales should be evaluated in terms of reliability and validity. Reliability refers to the extent to which a scale produces consistent results if repeated measurements are made. Approaches to assessing reliability include test–retest, alternative forms, and internal consistency. Validity, or accuracy of measurement, can be assessed by evaluating content validity, criterion validity,

FIGURE 10.8

A Concept Map for Noncomparative Scales

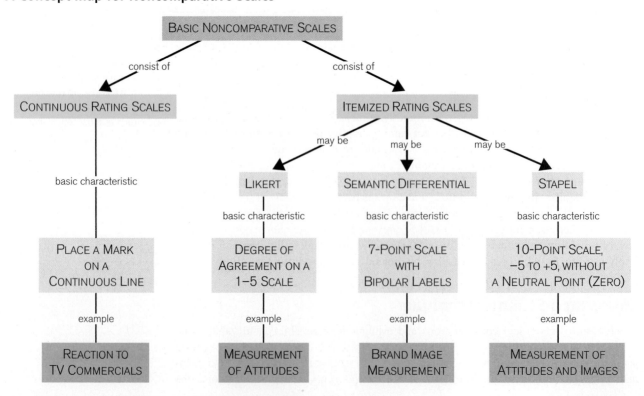

and construct validity. In the opening vignette, convergent validity is assessed by measuring audience reaction using different methods (continuous measurement using a dial and Likert scales) and then correlating the measures.

The choice of particular scaling techniques in a given situation should be based on theoretical and practical considerations. As a general rule, the scaling technique used should be the one that will yield the highest level of measurement feasible. Also, multiple measures should be obtained, as in the opening vignette. Figure 10.8 provides a concept map for noncomparative scales.

International Marketing Research

Pan-cultural scales, designed to be free of cultural biases, are used in international research. In addition to eliminating cultural biases, it also is essential to accommodate differing levels of education and experience. Of the scaling techniques considered, the semantic differential has been applied with the greatest consistency in results across countries. Rating scales also are used to construct indexes used to make global comparisons, as illustrated by the MasterCard Worldwide Centers of Commerce Index.

Research in Action

Mastering Global Commerce

Recognizing a need for cutting-edge insights into the evolving global marketplace, the MasterCard Worldwide Centers of Commerce Index, introduced in 2007, ranks the world's top cities in terms of their performance as Centers of Commerce in the global economy. The index is based on six dimensions: (1) legal and political framework, (2) economic stability, (3) ease of doing business, (4) financial flow, (5) business center, and (6) knowledge creation and information flow. Rating scales are used to rate the cities on each of these dimensions and to develop a composite score. The Commerce Index ranks the top 50 Centers of Commerce based on six measurement dimensions. In 2007, it placed London first, followed by New York, Tokyo, Chicago, and Hong Kong. Completing the top 10 were Singapore, Frankfurt, Paris, Seoul, and Los Angeles, in that order.

London beats New York by a narrow margin of only 3.99 in the overall Index value. With a flexible operating environment for business, strong global financial connections, and exceptionally high levels of international trade, travel, and conferences, London secured the top spot. The city outper-

formed New York in four of the six measurement dimensions and scored significantly higher than other European cities. To maintain its leading position, London must improve its legal and political framework and knowledge creation and information flow—the two dimensions on which New York did better. Such efforts will fortify London's number one position and strategic role in global marketplace.[7]

An alternative approach to developing pan-cultural scales is to use descriptors the respondents create themselves. For example, respondents might be asked to indicate the verbal descriptors for the extreme scale categories (anchors) before positioning an object along the scale. This approach is useful when conducting attitude research related to cultural norms (e.g., attitude towards friends). Suppose the researcher is interested in measuring the influence of friends on the purchase of personal clothing in a cross-cultural study involving students in Indonesia and India. The question asked is "To what extent should your friends influence your purchase of personal clothing?" The responses are obtained on a seven-point scale. Respondents in Indonesia might provide the anchors as 1 = little and 7 = much. Respondents in Indonesia might provide different anchors: 1 = not at all and 7 = a great deal. Such scales have proven to be universally adaptable because they are relatively insensitive to differences in educational level across countries. However, if the researchers specify the anchors, they should pay special attention to determining equivalent verbal descriptors in different languages and cultures. The end descriptors used to anchor the scale are particularly prone to different interpretations.

Additionally, the scale numbering may have different meanings. In some cultures, a score of 1 might be interpreted as best, whereas in others it might be interpreted as worst, regardless of how it is scaled (1 = best and 7 = worst or 1 = worst and 7 = best). In such cases, it might be desirable to avoid numbers and to just use boxes that respondent can check (worst ☐ ☐ ☐ ☐ ☐ ☐ best). It is important that the scale end points and the verbal descriptors be employed in a manner that is consistent with the culture. Finally, in international marketing research it is critical to establish the equivalence of scales and measures used to obtain data from different countries. This topic is complex and is discussed elsewhere by the author.[8]

Technology and Marketing Research

Software programs, such as Survent, a product of the American firm Computers for Marketing Corp. (CfMC) (www.cfmc.com), can be used to generate customized scales for printed questionnaires or for use by telephone interviewers. For each new scale, the researcher is presented a screen asking for information about the intended scale. For example, if the question is a noncomparatively scaled question, the researcher would indicate that a "number" response is sought. The researcher would then indicate the valid range of the numbers. After this, a second screen would allow formatting of the scale on the screen as interviewers would see it during data collection.

Another technological development is "smart" instruments that can monitor their own condition and the quality of the information they provide. They can also "talk" directly to the other components of the measurement process, making the integration and processing of information quick and reliable. One such instrument is Option Finder (www.optionfinder. com) from Option Technologies, a U.S. firm specializing in audience-response systems. This system allows for instantaneous feedback. It is designed for use in gathering information from groups as large as 250 persons rather than single individuals. Respondents read a question and then input their responses into the system using a keypad. Because the keypad is the method of data entry, questions are limited to fixed response, including paired comparisons, Likert-type scales, and discrete-labeled points. The feedback from Option Finder is immediate. The answers to the questions are tallied and processed into graphical form as the respondents enter them.

Ethics in Marketing Research

Because scale construction can influence scale responses, and hence the results of the study, several ethical issues are pertinent. Of particular concern is the researcher's attempt to deliberately bias the results by building that bias into noncomparative scales. This can be done, for example, by using scale descriptors that can be manipulated to bias results in a desired direction (e.g., to generate a positive view of the client's brand or a negative view of a competitor's brand). To project the client's brand favorably, the respondents can be asked to indicate their opinion of the brand on several attributes using seven-point scales anchored by the descriptors "extremely poor" to "good." Note that this scale has a strongly negative descriptor with only a mildly positive one. Respondents will be reluctant to rate the product extremely negatively by rating it as "extremely poor." In fact, respondents who believe the product to be only mediocre will end up responding favorably. Try this yourself. How would you rate Lexus automobiles on the following attributes?

Reliability:	Horrible	1	2	3	4	5	6	7	Good
Performance:	Very poor	1	2	3	4	5	6	7	Good
Quality:	One of the worst	1	2	3	4	5	6	7	Good
Prestige:	Very low	1	2	3	4	5	6	7	Good

Did you find yourself rating Lexus cars positively? The same technique can also be used to negatively bias evaluations of competitors' products by providing a mildly negative descriptor against a strongly positive descriptor.

Thus, it is clearly important to use scales with comparable positive and negative descriptors. This problem emphasizes the need to adequately establish the reliability and validity of scales so that we can be confident that the variables have been accurately measured. The researcher has a responsibility to both the client and respondents to ensure the applicability and usefulness of the scale, as illustrated by the following example.

Research in Action

An Ethical Scale for Measuring Ethics

The theory of moral philosophy was used to develop a scale for measuring ethical evaluations of marketing activities. The resulting scale had 29 seven-point bipolar items ranging from fair to unfair and efficient to inefficient. Evaluations of this scale, through its use in evaluating various ethical scenarios, indicated high internal consistency, reliability (measured via Cronbach's alpha), and a strong degree of construct (convergent, discriminant, and nomological) validity. Accordingly, this scale has been useful in a variety of contexts for investigating ethical issues in marketing. In a recent study, this scale was used to classify the firms as ethical or unethical and to examine the variables that differentiated the two groups. It was found that in ethical firms ethics are considered to be important, the leadership is committed to ethical practices, and codes of ethical conduct are enforced. Also, smaller firms tended to be more ethical than larger firms.[9]

What Would *You* Do?

Monster: The Monster of Career Networks

The Situation

When you think of the word *monster*, what do you think? Scary creatures under your bed? Elmo and Grover from the American TV show *Sesame Street*? The Walt Disney movie *Monsters, Inc.*? These days, when one hears the word *monster*, the person is apt to think of the so-named online job-search company that has connected millions of job searchers with employers. U.S.-based Monster (www.monster.com) was founded in 1994 by Jeff Taylor, and Sal Iannuzzi was appointed Chairman and CEO in 2007. It is the leading online global careers network and the world's number one hiring management resource. As of 2008, its clients included more than 90 of the *Fortune* 100 and approximately 490 of the *Fortune* 500 companies. The company had operations in 36 countries around the world. No wonder this company has added a whole new meaning to the word.

Monster makes heavy use of marketing research techniques in a unique way. Instead of companies which, like the well-known U.S. marketing-information firm ACNielsen, conduct research for different companies, Monster researches companies that are in need of employees to fill their positions and provides the service of matching job searchers to these companies. Although Monster is doing well, more and more companies have followed in the company's footsteps and have entered the arena of providing online job-search services. In the United States, Monster's competitors include HotJobs (hotjobs.yahoo.com), Kforce (www.kforce. com), eJobs (www. ejobs.com), and eCareers (www.ecareers.org). With all of these different services available, the market is becoming saturated with Internet recruiting Web sites. It is important for Monster now more than ever to differentiate itself from the competition.

The Marketing Research Decision

1. Monster's success lies in its ability to match client companies' job specifications with applicants' skills and qualifications. What scaling techniques should Monster use to measure companies' job specifications and job applicants' skills and qualifications?
   a. Ordinal
   b. Likert
   c. Semantic differential
   d. Stapel
   e. Paired comparison
2. Discuss the role of the type of scaling technique you recommend in enabling Sal Iannuzzi to match companies' job specifications and job applicants' skills and qualifications and thereby increase Monster's market share.

The Marketing Management Decision

1. What should Sal Iannuzzi do to gain market share over competitors?
   a. Offer price discounts to client companies.
   b. Aggressively recruit job applicants.
   c. Develop a more efficient system to match their client companies' job specifications with job applicants' skills and qualifications.
   d. Increase the quality of job applicants.
   e. Promote Monster more aggressively.
2. Discuss how the marketing management-decision action that you recommend to Sal Iannuzzi is influenced by the scaling technique you suggested earlier and by the findings of that research.

What Sal Iannuzzi Did

Sal Iannuzzi decided to promote Monster more aggressively. Monster planned to invest about $50 million a year into directly marketing itself to consumers. Monster earns money when employers post job openings on its site and when they hire for those openings. Monster wants to make itself a household name in cities across the country; therefore, the more resumes it has on its site, the more willing corporate human resource departments will be to spend money advertising job openings there. As part of raising awareness of Monster in locations across the country, Sal Iannuzzi said he is open to doing something extremely bold to build buzz, such as sitting on a billboard for a month.[10]

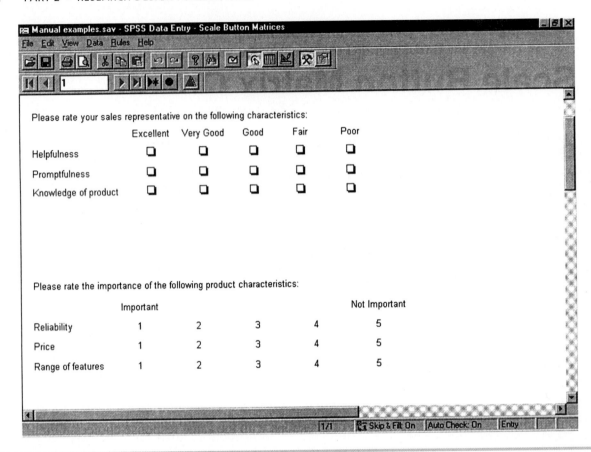

Examples of Likert-type scales designed using SPSS Data Entry.

SPSS Windows

A researcher can use SPSS data entry to design any of the three noncomparative scales: Likert, semantic differential, or Stapel. Moreover, multi-item scales can be easily accommodated. Either the question library can be used or customized scales can be designed. We show the use of SPSS data entry to design Likert-type scales for rating sales people and product characteristics.

Summary

In noncomparative scaling, each object is scaled independently of the other objects in the stimulus set. Noncomparative rating scales can be either continuous or itemized. The itemized rating scales are further classified as Likert, semantic differential, or Stapel scales. The data from these three types of scales typically are treated as interval scales. These scales possess the characteristics of description, order, and distance, as discussed in Chapter 9. When using noncomparative itemized rating scales, the researcher must decide on the number of scale categories, balanced versus unbalanced scales, odd or even number of categories, forced versus nonforced scales, nature and degree of verbal description, and the physical form or configuration.

Multi-item scales consist of a number of rating scale items. These scales should be evaluated in terms of reliability and validity. Reliability refers to the extent to which a scale produces consistent results if repeated measurements are made. Approaches to assessing reliability include test–retest, alternative-forms, and internal-consistency. Validity, or accuracy of measurement, can be assessed by evaluating content validity, criterion validity, and construct validity. The choice of particular scaling techniques for a given situation should be based on theoretical and practical considerations. As a general rule, multiple measures should be taken.

In international marketing research, special attention should be devoted to determining equivalent verbal descriptors in different languages and cultures. Software is available for developing and testing continuous and itemized rating scales, particularly multi-item scales. The misuse of scale descriptors also raises serious ethical concerns. Ethically, the researcher has the responsibility to both the client and respondents to ensure the applicability, usefulness, and honesty of the scales.

Key Terms and Concepts

Noncomparative scale, 302
Continuous rating scale, 304
Itemized rating scale, 305
Likert scale, 306
Semantic differential scale, 307
Stapel scale, 309
Sensitivity, 310
Balanced scale, 311
Forced-rating scale, 311

Multi-item scale, 313
Construct, 314
Systematic error, 315
Random error, 315
Reliability, 315
Test–retest reliability, 315
Alternative-forms reliability, 315
Internal-consistency reliability, 315
Split-half reliability, 316

Coefficient alpha, 316
Validity, 316
Content validity, 316
Criterion validity, 316
Construct validity, 317
Convergent validity, 317
Discriminant validity, 317
Nomological validity, 317

Suggested Cases and Video Cases

Running Case with Real Data

1.1 Hewlett Packard

Comprehensive Critical Thinking Cases

2.1 American Idol   2.2 Baskin-Robbins   2.3 Akron Children's Hospital

Comprehensive Cases with Real Data

3.1 Bank of America   3.2 McDonald's   3.3 Boeing

Video Cases

10.1 Nivea   13.1 Subaru   19.1 Marriott

Live Research: Conducting a Marketing Research Project

1. Continuous measures are generally more difficult to implement.

2. As a class, discuss the type of itemized rating scales (Likert, semantic differential, or Stapel) that are appropriate for the key variables.

3. Discuss multi-item scales and the issues of reliability and validity.

4. Consider the practical constraints. For example, if a certain type of scale has been used to measure a variable in the past (e.g., a 10-point Likert-type scale to measure customer satisfaction), the same scale might have to be used again to allow a comparison of the findings with past results or industry norms (e.g., the American Customer Satisfaction Index).

Acronym

The rating scale decisions may be described by the acronym RATING:

R esponse option: forced versus nonforced

A ttractive vs. unattractive number of categories: balanced versus unbalanced

T otal number of categories

I mpartial or neutral category: odd versus even number of categories

N ature and degree of verbal description

G raphics: physical form and configuration

Review Questions

1. What is a semantic differential scale? For what purposes is this scale used? Give an example.
2. Describe the Likert scale. Give an example.
3. What are the differences between the Stapel scale and the semantic differential scale? Which scale is more popular?
4. What are the major decisions involved in constructing an itemized rating scale?
5. How many scale categories should be used in an itemized rating scale? Why?
6. What is the difference between balanced and unbalanced scales? Give an example of each.
7. Should an odd or even number of categories be used in an itemized rating scale? Why? When?
8. What is the difference between forced and nonforced scales? Give an example of each.
9. How does the nature and degree of verbal description affect the response to itemized rating scales?
10. What are multi-item scales? Give an example.
11. What is reliability?
12. What are the differences between test–retest and alternative-forms reliability?
13. Describe the notion of internal-consistency reliability.
14. What is validity?
15. What is criterion validity? How is it assessed?
16. What is the relationship between reliability and validity?
17. How would you select a particular scaling technique?

Applied Problems

1. Develop a Likert, semantic differential, and a Stapel scale for measuring store loyalty.
2. Develop a multi-item scale to measure students' attitudes toward internationalization of the management curriculum. How would you assess the reliability and validity of this scale?
3. Construct a Likert scale for measuring Internet usage. Explain how the rating-scale decisions were made.
4. Design Likert scales to measure the usefulness of Ford Motor Company's Web site. Visit www.ford.com and rate it on the scales that you have developed.
5. Design semantic differential scales to measure the perception of FedEx overnight delivery service and compare it to that offered by UPS. Relevant information can be obtained by visiting the Web sites of these two companies (www.fedex.com, www.ups.com).
6. Visit the Office of Scales Research at Southern Illinois University (www.siu.edu/departments/coba/osr/). (If this URL has changed, search www.siu.edu to locate it.) Identify one application of the Likert scale and one application of the semantic differential. Write a report describing the context in which these scales have been used.
7. Visit the Web sites of two marketing research firms conducting surveys. Analyze one survey of each firm to critically evaluate the itemized rating scales being used.
8. Surf the Internet to find two examples each of Likert, semantic differential, and Stapel scales. Write a report describing the context in which these scales are being used.

Group Discussion

1. "It really does not matter which scaling technique you use. As long as your measure is reliable, you will get the right results." Discuss this statement as a small group.
2. "One need not be concerned with reliability and validity in applied marketing research." Discuss this statement as a small group.
3. As a small group or as a class, discuss one of the articles listed in the notes to this chapter.

Hewlett-Packard Running Case

Review the Hewlett-Packard (HP) case, Case 1.1, and questionnaire given toward the end of the book. Go to the Web site for this book and download the HP data file.

1. Perform the following operations:
   a. Reverse the scoring of the second and the third items under the Innovativeness scale.
   b. Sum the Market Maven items (q10_1 to q10_4) to form a Total Market Maven Score.
   c. Sum the Innovativeness items (q10_5 to q10_10) to form a Total Innovativeness Score. Note that you will have to reverse the scores for the negatively worded items (q10_6 and q10_7) before summing.
   d. Sum the Opinion Leadership items (q10_11 to q10_13) to form a Total Opinion Leadership Score.
   e. Compute Cronbach's alpha for each of these three sets of items.
2. Design Likert, semantic differential, and Stapel scales to measure consumers' preferences for HP computers.

NIVEA: Marketing Research Leads to Consistency in Marketing

Nivea (www.nivea.com), the skin care products company, is part of the German Beiersdorf conglomerate. As of 2008, Nivea's skin care product line is marketed in more than 150 countries. The product line has been around for about 10 decades, originating with a scientific breakthrough of the first skin cream that did not separate into water and oil. That, coupled with intelligent marketing based on marketing research, has led to a strong positive brand image, which accounts for much of Nivea's success.

Nivea, founded in 1911, began marketing in the 1920s when it changed its logo and began selling its product around the world. Early on, Nivea established its brand identity as a pure and gentle product that families could rely on. Early advertisements featured the Nivea Girl. In 1924, it broke from tradition and began advertising with the Nivea Boy. This helped Nivea convey the message that Nivea skin cream was for the entire family. Its brand image has transcended the decades with the help of a foundation built upon advertising that stresses family relationships and values.

In the 1970s, Nivea had to defend itself against true competition for the first time. It relied heavily on marketing research, which helped it to formulate a two-pronged response: (1) defense of its core business through a new advertising campaign—Crème de la Crème and (2) the introduction of new products, which helped keep the brand fresh and introduced new sources of sales.

In the 1980s, marketing research indicated that brand differentiation was becoming increasingly important. In response, Nivea began branding with sub-brands. These sub-brands included skin care, bath products, sun protection, baby care, facial care, hair care, and care for men. It used an umbrella strategy with the sub-brands, meaning that it used its core brand to encompass all of the sub-brands. The goal was to establish individual images that were distinct but consistent with Nivea's core image. Nivea focused on strengthening the brand name and linking the new sub-brands with the core brand's traditional values. The result was an explosion in sales.

Nivea was able to continue its success into the 1990s, and sales grew rapidly throughout the decade. The growth was due in large part to the introduction of new products, each based on extensive marketing research. The most successful products were its antiwrinkle cream and an entire line of cosmetics.

Nivea entered the new millennium as the number one skin care and cosmetics company in the world. However, Nivea, a nearly 100-year-old brand, found itself in need of a makeover to evolve its strongly entrenched brand image of being a mild, reliable family product. The company had to revamp its product portfolio and marketing and branding strategy in order to address the changing needs and aspirations of its consumers and to appeal to a younger, more modern audience. This initiative placed a great emphasis on marketing research to transform the Nivea brand to a new, youthful identity.

The launch of *Nivea Styling* is an example of the how the old Nivea image had become a handicap. Marketing research revealed that Nivea was very strongly identified with richness and creaminess, whereas in styling products consumers look for long-lasting hold and funky hairstyles. Nivea had to convince customers that it was not only about mild and caring products, but could also fulfill the needs of the category, which meant long-lasting hold.

However, Nivea, did not want to restrict itself to an exclusively young audience, but sought to extend the Nivea legacy and the Nivea line of products to more mature women. The launch of *Nivea Vital*, a line of products for mature women, was not without its share of challenges. Older women had not been given due attention by most beauty products companies, and hence there was a lack of understanding of awareness about how older women feel about beauty and aging. The company relied on marketing research to fill this gap. An unprecedented ad campaign featuring a mature woman was planned. Nivea was fearful that showing an older woman in an ad campaign could negatively impact the brand, making it appear old and less modern, thereby losing the support of its younger consumers. Marketing research was used to carefully test the choice of the model for the ad, and her beauty and self-confidence helped Nivea prevent this harmful side-effect to its brand image. The model, a 50-year-old woman, turned out to be the perfect model for the brand, and the campaign had the opposite effect of what was feared. Consumers felt that Nivea, by daring to show a mature and beautiful model, was truly a modern brand.

The company still faces many challenges. Its greatest challenge is in the U.S. market, where the brand is not as strong as it is in other parts of the world. The U.S. market poses many obstacles because it is the largest and most dynamic market in the world. Nivea hopes to overcome these obstacles through the use of extensive marketing research. This research will lead Nivea to launch more products and to develop focused marketing strategies.

Nivea seeks consistency in its marketing, which can be problematic when trying to communicate the same message across various cultures and countries. However, Nivea will do whatever it takes to maintain this consistency, because it believes it gives them an edge over competitors. It helps consumers relate all its products to its core brand and identity. Nivea will continue to rely on marketing research to retain and refine the consistency in their marketing across global markets.

Conclusion

Nivea, a large company, had to rely on marketing research to revamp its brand image to keep itself relevant and to appeal to consumers. The company's launch of *Nivea Vital* demonstrates that if researched well, a product line can significantly enhance a company's brand image, even though the product might not be targeted at the core target audience. In sum, the case shows the use of marketing research in some of the aspects of developing, sustaining, and evolving a brand.

Questions

1. Nivea would like to increase its share of the U.S. market. Define the management decision problem.
2. Define an appropriate marketing research problem based on the management decision problem identified in question 1.
3. Nivea would like to undertake research to understand the preferences of American consumers for skin care products. What type of research design should be adopted and why?
4. Discuss the role of qualitative research in understanding the preferences of American consumers for skin care products. Which qualitative research techniques should be used and why?
5. If a survey is to be conducted to understand the preferences of American consumers for skin care products, which survey method should be used and why?
6. Develop Likert, semantic differential, and Stapel scales for determining consumers' evaluation of skin care products.

References

1. www.nivea.com, accessed February 20, 2008.
2. www.wikipedia.com, accessed February 20, 2008.
3. Anonymous, "World's Top 100 Brands—Are They Fact or Fiction," *Brand Strategy*, August 21, 2002, p. 10.

Questionnaire and Form Design

OPENING QUESTIONS

1. What is the purpose of a questionnaire, and what are its objectives?
2. What is the process of designing a questionnaire, what steps are involved, and what are the guidelines for each step?
3. How are observational forms designed to most effectively observe behavior?
4. What considerations are involved in designing questionnaires for international marketing research?
5. How does technology interface with questionnaire design?
6. What ethical issues are involved in questionnaire design?

> "Pretesting a questionnaire is absolutely essential for success. All legitimate researchers understand this and won't dare waste the public's time or their own effort with a questionnaire that hasn't been pretested."
>
> *Diane Bowers,*
> *President, Council of American Survey Research Organizations (CASRO).*

World Vision Imparts Donors a Vision for Caring

World Vision (WV), one of the leading charities in 2008, is a U.S.-based Christian organization that helps relief victims and needy children in nearly 100 countries around the world, aiding 100 million people. World Vision needed at least $800,000 to continue caring for unsponsored children in developing countries. The children, who needed food, shelter, and medical care, had either never been sponsored or had lost their sponsors for various reasons. World Vision designed a questionnaire to determine donors' motivations for giving. The information obtained, and the order in which it was obtained, follows:

1. Priorities and motivations for giving
2. Awareness of the WV organization
3. Perceptions of the organization
4. Communication with donors
5. Demographic information

To increase the willingness of donors and potential donors to participate and complete the questionnaire, the researchers made the context of the survey clear, and minimized the effort required of the respondents by asking them questions that were easy to answer. Only necessary questions were asked, and combined questions were avoided. Most of the questions were structured; the respondents simply had to circle a number on the scale. However, open-ended questions were included where it was felt that the respondents needed the freedom to express underlying motivations for giving.

In deciding on question wording, words with unequivocal meanings that were familiar to the donors were used. Special effort was made to be objective so as not to bias the responses in any direction. The questionnaire was kept simple and detailed, and clear instructions were given because it had to be administered by mail. The questionnaire was divided into parts, with a separate part devoted to each type of information sought. The name and address of the respondents were optional and obtained at the end of the questionnaire. The questionnaire was professionally reproduced to have a neat appearance and was thoroughly pretested.

The results of the mail survey showed that the most important factors motivating donors to sponsor a child were the feelings of warmth and contact with the child they were sponsoring. Based on these findings, the charity decided to target its in-house list of current sponsors to see if they would consider sponsoring additional children. To motivate these already generous supporters, WV designed a warm, interactive mail package to increase the donor's involvement with the organization. The package included a letter from the WV president, a sticker with the sponsored child's name on it, and a small notebook. The letter explained that in developing nations paper for schoolchildren is extremely scarce. The recipient was then asked to affix the sticker to the cover of the notebook, sign the inside cover, and mail the book back in an enclosed, postage-paid envelope. The organization would then deliver the notebook to the sponsored child, along with another rarity—a pencil.

With a total budget of $117,796, WV sent 240,893 pieces of direct mail. The response rate in terms of donations received was 46.1 percent, beating the previous campaign by 25.95 percent. The cost per response was a low amount of about a dollar. The total income exceeded the goal by $197,000. Beyond the 46.1 percent who responded by making a donation, more than 80 percent of the respondents returned their notebooks, signifying a much higher level of donor involvement than suggested by the donations. Thus, the campaign was very successful. A properly designed questionnaire that resulted in valuable findings was crucial to this success.[1]

Overview

The opening vignette illustrates the importance of questionnaires to the research process. The findings obtained by using a questionnaire can assist in the formulation of effective marketing strategies. A well-designed questionnaire enabled WV to discover donors' underlying motivation and design a successful campaign to solicit funds for children in developing countries.

The development of a questionnaire or observational form follows problem definition and approach (see Chapter 2), specification of the type of research design (see Chapters 3 through 8), and selection of the scaling procedures (see Chapters 9 and 10). Figure 11.1 briefly explains the focus of this chapter, the relation of this chapter to the previous ones, and the steps of the marketing research process on which this chapter concentrates.

This chapter describes the importance of a questionnaire and presents the process for developing questionnaires and observational forms. Guidelines are provided for each stage of the questionnaire-construction process. The chapter also discusses questionnaires in relation to international marketing, technology, and ethics. Figure 11.2 provides an overview of the topics discussed in this chapter and how they flow from one to the next.

FIGURE 11.1

Relationship of Questionnaire Design to the Previous Chapters and the Marketing Research Process

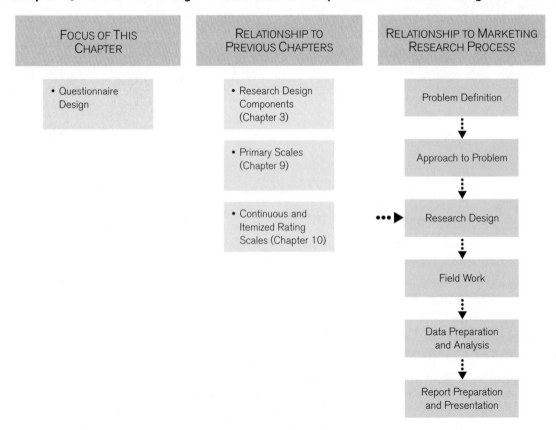

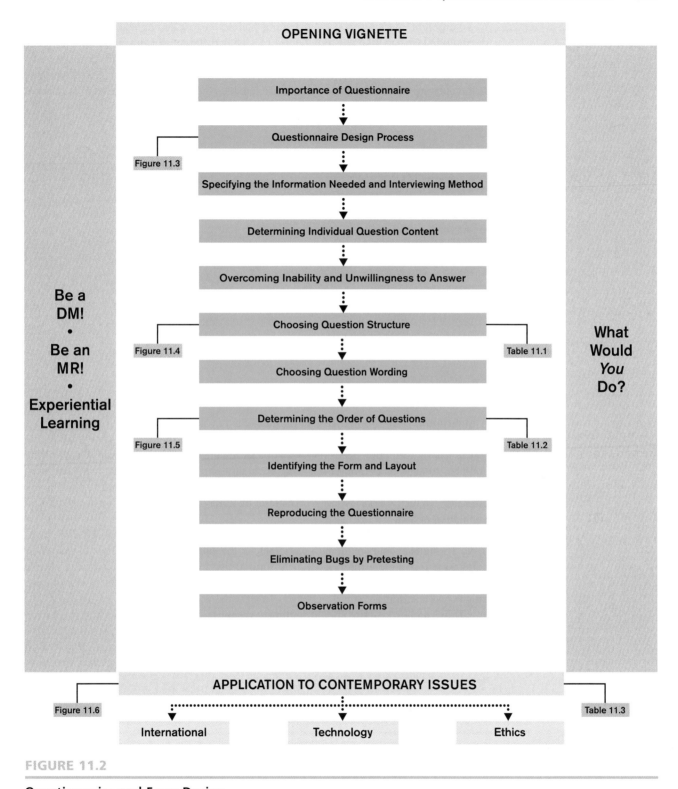

FIGURE 11.2

Questionnaire and Form Design

Importance of the Questionnaire

As discussed in Chapter 6, researchers can collect quantitative primary data for descriptive research through surveys or observation. Standardization of the data-collection process is essential to ensure internally consistent and coherent data for analysis. Imagine how difficult it would be to analyze the results of a national survey conducted by 40 different interviewers if the questions had not been asked in a standard way (i.e., if the interviewers had asked different questions using different wording and order). A questionnaire ensures standardization and comparability of the data across interviewers, increases speed and accuracy of recording, and facilitates data processing. As illustrated in the opening vignette, a questionnaire also enables the researcher to collect the relevant information necessary to address the management-decision problem.

Experiential Learning

How Important Is a Questionnaire?

Sprite, a caffeine-free lemon-lime beverage produced by Coca-Cola, is the third most popular soft drink brand in the United States, behind Coke and Pepsi. College students are heavy users of soft drinks.

1. As the brand manager for Sprite, what information do you need to target this segment?

2. Search the Internet, as well as your library's online databases, to obtain information that will assist the brand manager of Sprite in targeting the student segment.

3. You and a fellow student each interview a different respondent (another student) to determine preferences for soft drinks, without constructing a questionnaire. How comparable are the data each of you obtained? Develop a formal questionnaire jointly and each of you administer it to another respondent. Are the data you two obtained more comparable than before? What does this teach you about the importance of a questionnaire?

Questionnaire Definition

questionnaire
A structured technique for data collection that consists of a series of questions, written or verbal, that a respondent answers.

A **questionnaire** is a formalized set of questions for obtaining information from respondents. It has three specific objectives. The overriding objective is to translate the researcher's information needs into a set of specific questions that respondents are willing and able to answer. Although this may seem straightforward, questions can yield very different and unanticipated responses. For example, how would you answer the following question: "Which market is larger, Australia or Malaysia?" Would you answer based on population or area?

Second, a questionnaire should be written to minimize demands imposed on respondents. It should encourage them to participate in the entire interview, without biasing their responses. Incomplete interviews have limited usefulness, at best. In order to keep a respondent involved throughout a questionnaire, the researcher should attempt to minimize fatigue and boredom.

Third, a questionnaire should minimize response error. These errors can arise from respondents who give inaccurate answers or from researchers incorrectly recording or analyzing their answers. Minimizing the error introduced by the questionnaire itself is an important objective of questionnaire design. The following is an example of how questionnaires can be designed to achieve these objectives.

Research in Action

An Old-Fashioned Approach with Young Respondents

A U.S. research firm called Just Kid, Inc. (www.justkidinc.com) surveys two age categories of children—6- to 8-year-olds and 9- to 12-year-olds—on a quarterly basis. The objective is to record children's views on favorite snack foods, television shows, commercials, radio, magazines, buzzwords, and movies. The one-on-one interviews conducted in malls are kept short, typically lasting only 8 to 10 minutes.

Just Kid attempts to make questions as clear and meaningful as possible so that kids can understand and answer them. This is done by establishing a context for questions. For example, when asking about a child's radio-listening habits, they ask, "What about when you're in Mom's car, do you listen to the radio?" rather than, "How often do you listen to radio? More than once a day, once a day, more than once a week?" The latter queries are big questions for little children.

A trade-off is made between attempting to cover all possible areas of interest in one study and ensuring that the most important information is of high quality. Given children's limited attention span, minimizing boredom and being sensitive to fatigue becomes more important than asking all possible questions. Thus, Just Kid motivates the kids to complete the questionnaire.

Some clients attempt to meet all of their research objectives with one study. The questionnaires keep going through the approval process and people keep adding questions, "Well, let's ask this question, let's add that question, and why don't we talk about this also?" This results in keeping children 25 minutes in a central mall location, which makes them kind of "itchy." The response error increases and the quality of data suffers. By keeping the questionnaire short and clear, Just Kid also tries to reduce response error. Conducting research on children is not easy, but Just Kid has been successful in designing questionnaires that meet stated objectives.[2]

Questionnaire Design Process

No scientific principles guarantee an optimal or ideal questionnaire. Questionnaire design is as much an art as a science. The creativity, skill, and experience of the researcher play a major role in the end design. However, several guidelines are available to assist researchers in the questionnaire development process and to help them avoid major mistakes.

The guidelines to support questionnaire design are shown as a series of 10 steps (Figure 11.3): (1) specify the information needed, (2) specify the type of interviewing

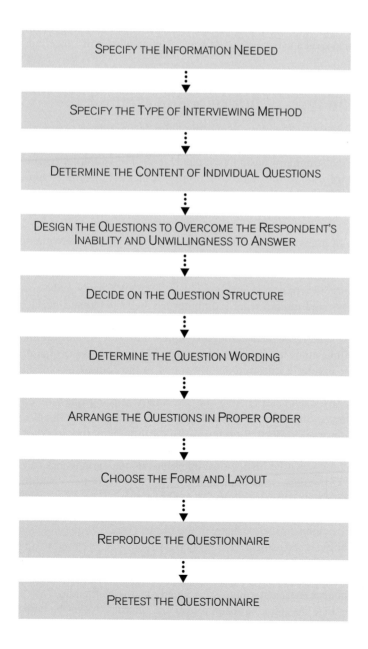

FIGURE 11.3

Questionnaire Design Process

method, (3) determine the content of individual questions, (4) design the questions to overcome the respondent's inability and unwillingness to answer, (5) decide on the question structure, (6) determine the question wording, (7) arrange the questions in proper order, (8) choose the form and layout, (9) reproduce the questionnaire, and (10) pretest the questionnaire. In practice, questionnaire design is an iterative rather than a sequential process. For example, pretesting of a question might reveal that respondents misunderstand the wording, sending the designer back to an earlier step.

Specify the Information Needed

The first step in questionnaire design is to specify the information needed. A continual review of the earlier stages of the research project—particularly the specific components of the problem, the research questions, and the hypotheses—will help keep the questionnaire focused. This was illustrated in the WV study in the opening vignette, which clearly specified the information the questionnaire was to obtain.

Questionnaires should also be designed with the target respondents in mind, taking into account their educational level and experience. The language used and the context of the questions must all be familiar to the respondents. Questions that are appropriate for college students might not be appropriate for those with only a high school education. Questionnaires that fail to keep in mind the characteristics of the respondents, particularly their educational level and experience, lead to a high incidence of "uncertain" or "no opinion" responses.

Specify the Type of Interviewing Method

Another important consideration in questionnaire design relates to how the data will be collected. An understanding of the various methods of conducting interviews provides guidance for questionnaire design (see Chapter 7). For example, personal interviews use face-to-face interaction. Due to the opportunity for feedback and clarification, questionnaires can be lengthy, complex, and incorporate visual aids. Because a respondent cannot see the questionnaire in telephone interviews, the questions must be short and simple.

Any type of interviewer-administered questionnaire should be written in a conversational style. Mail and electronic questionnaires are self-administered, involving no personal interaction between the researcher and the respondent. Therefore, both questions and instructions must be kept simple and thorough, as in the WV study in the opening vignette. In computer-assisted interviewing [computer-assisted telephone interviewing (CATI), computer-assisted personal interviewing (CAPI), or Internet surveys, see Chapter 7], the computer guides the respondent through complex skip patterns and can incorporate randomization of questions to eliminate order bias. The impact of the type of interviewing method on the nature of questions is illustrated in the context of obtaining consumer preferences for luxury cars.

In the luxury car example, you can see how a ranking question changes as the method of interviewing changes. In mail, e-mail, or Internet questionnaires, the respondent records the rank orders. Ranking seven car brands is too complex a task to be administered over the telephone. Therefore, the simpler rating task in which brands are rated one at a time was used. In personal interviewing, the ranking task can be simplified by giving the respondent cards imprinted with the car brand name, and the interviewer is provided with special instructions (in capital letters). The interviewer records the brand names.

Internet questionnaires share many of the features of CAPI questionnaires. The questionnaire can be designed using a wide variety of stimuli, such as graphics, pictures, advertisements, animations, sound clips, and full-motion video. The researcher can control the amount of time that the stimuli are available to the respondents and the number of times a respondent can access each stimulus. This greatly increases the range and complexity of questionnaires that can be administered over the Internet. As in the case of CATI and

Research in Action

Effect of Interviewing Method on Questionnaire Design

Mail, E-mail, or Internet Questionnaire

Please rank the following luxury cars in order of your preference. Begin by picking out the one car brand that you like most and assign it a number 1. Then find the second most preferred car brand and assign it a number 2. Continue this procedure until you have ranked all the cars in order of preference. The least preferred car brand should be assigned a rank of 7. No two brands should receive the same rank number. The criterion of preference is entirely up to you. There is no right or wrong answer. Just try to be consistent.

Car Brand	Rank Order
1. Acura	_____
2. Cadillac	_____
3. Lexus	_____
4. Lincoln	_____
5. Infiniti	_____
6. Mercedes	_____
7. BMW	_____

Telephone Questionnaire

I will read to you the names of some luxury cars. Please rate them in terms of your preference. Use a six-point scale, where 1 denotes not so preferred and 6 denotes greatly preferred. Numbers between 1 and 6 reflect intermediate degrees of preference. Remember that the higher the number, the greater the degree of preference. Now, please tell me your preference for (READ ONE CAR BRAND AT A TIME.)

Car Brand	Not So Preferred					Greatly Preferred
1. Acura	1	2	3	4	5	6
2. Cadillac	1	2	3	4	5	6
3. Lexus	1	2	3	4	5	6
4. Lincoln	1	2	3	4	5	6
5. Infiniti	1	2	3	4	5	6
6. Mercedes	1	2	3	4	5	6
7. BMW	1	2	3	4	5	6

Personal Questionnaire

(HAND CAR BRAND CARDS TO THE RESPONDENT.) Here is a set of luxury car names, each written on a separate card. Please examine these cards carefully. (GIVE RESPONDENT TIME.) Now, examine these cards again and pull out the card that has the name of the car brand you like the most, that is, your most preferred car. (RECORD THE CAR NAME AND KEEP THIS CARD WITH YOU.) Now, please examine the remaining six cards. Of these remaining six names, what is your most preferred car brand? (REPEAT THIS PROCEDURE SEQUENTIALLY UNTIL THE RESPONDENT HAS ONLY ONE CARD LEFT.)

	Car Rank	Name of the Car
1.	1	_____
2.	2	_____
3.	3	_____
4.	4	_____
5.	5	_____
6.	6	_____
7.	7	_____

CAPI, complicated skip patterns can be programmed into the questionnaire. The questions can be personalized, and answers to previous questions can be inserted into subsequent questions, a process called *variable piping*.

The type of interviewing method also influences the content of individual questions.

Determine the Content of Individual Questions

Once the information needed is specified and the type of interviewing method is decided, the next step is to determine question content. In other words, the researcher must determine what should be included in each question.

Is the Question Necessary?

Before including a question, the researcher should ask, "How will I use these data?" Questions that might be nice to know, but that do not directly address the research problem, should be eliminated. There are exceptions to this rule. Filler questions can be added to disguise the purpose or sponsorship of the project. For example, in brand studies a researcher might include questions about the full range of competing brands so the respondents will not know who is sponsoring the study. Early in the interviewing process when the researcher is attempting to build a relationship with respondents and capture their attention, a few easy-to-answer neutral questions can be helpful. At times, certain questions can also be repeated for the purpose of assessing reliability or validity.

Are Several Questions Needed Instead of One?

In some cases, two questions are better than one. However, asking two questions in one is not the solution. Consider the following question:

Do you think Niketown offers better variety and prices than other Nike stores?

(Incorrect)

A "yes" answer will presumably be clear; however, what if the answer is "no"? Does this mean that the respondent thinks that Niketown (a chain of shoe and sportswear outlets operated by the American apparel and equipment maker) does not offer better variety, that it does not offer better prices, or that it neither offers better variety nor better prices? Such a question is called a **double-barreled question**, because two or more questions are combined into one. To avoid confusion, these questions should be asked separately, as follows:

double-barreled question
A single question that attempts to cover two issues. Such questions can be confusing to respondents and can result in ambiguous responses.

Do you think Niketown offers better variety than other Nike stores?
Do you think Niketown offers better prices than other Nike stores?

(Correct)

Another example of multiple questions embedded in a single question is the "why" question. In marketing research, a primary question of interest to researchers concerns brand selection. This is a "why" question in actuality. In other words, the researcher might be tempted to ask the question this way: "Why did you choose the Ford Explorer?" A typical answer to this question will likely be short. Answers such as "It was the best buy," or "I liked it" do not help the researchers understand much about this brand-choice decision. Instead, a series of questions are needed. For example, "What was your main motivation in choosing the Ford Explorer?" "How does the Ford Explorer compare to other SUV brands?" "What features of the Ford Explorer appealed to you?"

More than one question is needed to measure the respondents' evaluations of Nike Town.

As the CEO of Old Navy, a chain of family clothing stores in the United States and Canada, what would you do to improve consumers' perceptions of the quality of your brand?

Visit www.oldnavy.com and search the Internet, as well as your library's online databases, to obtain information on Old Navy's marketing program. Formulate a double-barreled question to determine consumer perceptions of the quality and style of Old Navy clothing. Then reformulate this question to obtain unambiguous answers.

Design the Questions to Overcome the Respondent's Inability to Answer

Respondents might not always be able to answer the questions posed to them. Researchers can help them overcome this limitation by keeping in mind the reasons people typically cannot answer a question: They might not be informed; they might not remember; or they might be unable to articulate certain types of responses.

Is the Respondent Informed?

Respondents often are asked to answer questions they are uninformed about. A husband might not be informed about monthly expenses for groceries and department store purchases if it is the wife who makes these purchases, or vice versa. Despite the fact that they are uninformed, respondents might provide answers, as the following example shows.

Research in Action

Unknown Question Elicits Known Answers

In a study conducted in the United States, respondents were asked to express their degree of agreement or disagreement with the following statement: "The National Bureau of Consumer Complaints provides an effective means for consumers who have purchased a defective product to obtain relief." Even with a "don't know" option available, 51.9 percent of the lawyers and 75.0 percent of the general public still expressed an opinion about the National Bureau of Consumer Complaints. Why should this high response rate be problematic? Because there is no such entity as the National Bureau of Consumer Complaints![3]

When the research topic requires specialized experience or knowledge, **filter questions** that measure familiarity, product use, and past experience should be asked before questions about the topics themselves. Filter questions enable the researcher to eliminate from the analysis those respondents who are not adequately informed.

In addition to filter questions, a "don't know" option to a question is helpful. This option has been found to reduce the number of uninformed responses without reducing the overall response rate. If it is suspected that many respondents might be uninformed about the topic, "don't know" should be added to the list of response alternatives.

filter questions
Initial questions in a questionnaire that screen potential respondents to ensure they meet the requirements of the sample.

Can the Respondent Remember?

Many common experiences or practices are difficult to remember. Can you remember the brand name of the shirt you are wearing, what you had for lunch a week ago, or what you were doing a month ago today? Further, do you know how many gallons of soft drink you consumed during the past 4 weeks? When making estimates about product consumption levels, in particular, research has found that consumers dramatically overestimate usage.

People tend to remember events that are personally relevant or unusual or that occur frequently. Americans, for example, remember their wedding anniversaries and birthdays or the day that former U.S. President Ronald W. Reagan died. Likewise, the more recently the event occurred, the more readily an event will be recalled. For example, you are more likely to remember the purchases you made on your last trip to the grocery store than the purchases you made three shopping trips ago.

Questions can be designed to aid recall or they can be unaided, depending on the research objectives. For example, unaided recall of soft drink commercials could be measured by questions such as, "What brands of soft drinks do you remember being advertised last night on TV?" A question that employs aided recall attempts to stimulate the respondent's memory by providing cues related to the event of interest. The aided-recall approach would list a number of soft drink brands and then ask, "Which of these brands were advertised last night on TV?" One of the risks of presenting cues is that they can bias responses and make a respondent unduly sensitive to a topic, thus distorting their answers.

Can the Respondent Articulate?

Respondents might be unable to articulate certain types of responses. This does not mean, however, that they do not have an opinion on that topic. For example, it is difficult to describe the ideal atmosphere of a department store. However, if the respondents are provided with alternative descriptions of store atmosphere, they will be able to indicate the one they like best. When asked to provide answers that are difficult to articulate, respondents are likely to ignore that question and might refuse to complete the questionnaire. Visual aids in the form of pictures, diagrams, or maps, as well as verbal descriptions, can help respondents to articulate responses.

Be an MR!

Search the Internet, as well as your library's online databases, to obtain information on factors that influence the atmosphere of a department store. Develop four alternative descriptions of store atmosphere. Also, write a description of the ideal atmosphere of a department store.

Be a DM!

As the CEO of Nordstrom, an upscale chain of U.S. department stores, what type of atmosphere do you desire to have in your stores? Explain.

Design the Questionnaire to Overcome the Respondent's Unwillingness to Answer

Even if respondents are able to answer a particular question, they might be unwilling to do so. Respondents might refuse to answer a question due to a variety of circumstances. The respondent might feel simply too much effort is involved, that the question serves no legitimate purpose, or that the information requested is too sensitive.

Effort Required of the Respondent

Although most individuals are willing to participate in a survey, this sense of cooperation might vanish if the questions require too much effort to answer. Suppose the researcher is interested in determining from which departments in a store the respondent purchased merchandise on the most recent shopping trip. This information can be obtained in at least two ways. The researcher could ask the respondent to list all the items purchased on his or her most recent shopping trip, or the researcher could provide a list of departments and ask the respondent to check those that are applicable. Consider the following examples:

Please list all the departments from which you purchased merchandise on your most recent shopping trip to a department store.

(Incorrect)

In the list that follows, please check all the departments from which you purchased merchandise on your most recent shopping trip to a department store.

1. Women's dresses _____
2. Men's apparel _____
3. Children's apparel _____
4. Cosmetics _____
    .
    .
    .
8. Jewelry _____
9. Other (please specify) _____

(Correct)

The second option is preferable because it requires less effort from respondents. In the WV questionnaire in the opening vignette, the effort required of the respondents was reduced by asking easy questions for which the respondents merely had to check one of the response options.

Legitimate Purpose

Respondents also object to questions that do not seem to serve a legitimate purpose. In Australia, for example, why should a firm that is marketing cereal biscuits want to know a respondent's age, income, and occupation? A researcher for, say, Uncle Toby's Oatbrits should anticipate these types of objections and attempt to overcome them by explaining why the data are needed. A statement such as, "To determine how the consumption of cereal biscuits and preferences for cereal-biscuit brands vary among people of different ages, incomes, and occupations, we need information on . . ." can make the request for information seem legitimate. Moreover, the context of the survey should be clearly explained, as in the WV project.

Sensitive Information

It can be difficult to obtain information of a personal or highly sensitive nature from respondents. Examples of sensitive topics include money, family life, political and religious beliefs, and involvement in accidents or crimes. Respondents might be embarrassed to answer such questions, because accurate responses might threaten their prestige or self-image. To increase the likelihood of obtaining sensitive information, such topics should be placed at the end of the questionnaire. By then, rapport has been created and legitimacy of the project established, making respondents more willing to give information. Where appropriate, sensitive information should be obtained in the form of response categories rather than asking for specific figures. Whereas respondents might refuse to answer the question,

What is your household's exact annual income?

(Incorrect)

they might be willing to check the appropriate income category. In order to obtain information on income, for example, our Australian researchers might ask:

FIGURE 11.4

Types of Questions

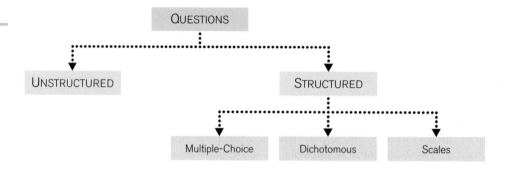

Which one of the following categories best describes your household's annual income?

_____ under A$25,001

_____ A$25,001 to A$50,000

_____ A$50,001 to A$75,000

_____ over A$75,000

(Correct)

Decide on the Question Structure

A question can be unstructured or structured. In the following sections, we define unstructured questions and discuss their advantages and limitations. This is followed by a discussion of the popular forms of structured questions: multiple-choice, dichotomous, and scales (Figure 11.4).

Unstructured Questions

unstructured questions
Open-ended questions that respondents answer in their own words.

Unstructured questions are open-ended questions that respondents answer in their own words. They are also referred to as free-response or free-answer questions. The following are examples of unstructured questions:

■ What is your favorite pastime?
■ How would you describe the typical user of Land Rover SUVs?
■ Do you intend to travel overseas within the next 6 months?

Open-ended questions are good as first questions on a topic. They enable the respondents to express general attitudes and opinions that can help the researcher interpret their responses to structured questions. Open-ended questions allow respondents to express their attitudes or opinions without the bias associated with restricting responses to predefined alternatives. Thus, they can be useful in identifying underlying motivations, beliefs, and attitudes, as in the WV vignette. Analysis of the verbatim comments provides a rich context for interpreting later questions. Unstructured questions are useful in exploratory research (Table 11.1).

The disadvantages of unstructured questions relate to recording error, data coding, and the added complexity of analysis. In personal or telephone interviews, successfully recording verbatim comments depends entirely on the recording skills of the interviewer. Interviewer bias is introduced as decisions are made regarding whether to record answers verbatim or to write down only the main points. Tape recorders should be used if verbatim reporting is important.

Categorizing the recorded comments to open-ended questions introduces the second source of bias and another major disadvantage. Implicitly, unstructured questions give extra weight to respondents who are more talkative or articulate. The process of summarizing comments into a format that can be analyzed is both time-consuming and expensive. Unstructured questions also are of limited value in self-administered questionnaires (mail, CAPI, or electronic), because respondents tend to be more brief in writing than in speaking.

TABLE 11.1 Advantages and Disadvantages of Unstructured and Structured Questions

Question Type	Advantages	Disadvantages	Comments
Unstructured	Good as first questions	Potential for interviewer bias	Useful for exploratory research
	Responses are less biased	Coding is costly and time-consuming	
	Can provide rich insights	Greater weight to articulate respondents	
		Unsuitable for self-administered questionnaires	
Multiple-Choice	Interviewer bias is reduced	Order or position bias	Responses should be mutually exclusive and collectively exhaustive
	Easy to code and analyze	Difficult to design response options	
	Improved respondent cooperation		Useful in large surveys
Dichotomous	Same as multiple-choice	Wording can bias the responses	Use split-ballot technique
Scales	Same as multiple-choice	Difficult to design multi-item scales	Scales should be evaluated for reliability, validity, and generalizability

Research in Action

Open-Ended Questions Open the Way to a New Opportunity for Nabisco

In an exploratory survey, ConAgra Foods, a large provider of branded food products in the United States and Canada, asked a series of open-ended questions related to cookies to identify any consumer needs it was not meeting. The survey included questions like: "What do you like about cookies?" "What do you dislike about cookies?" "What are the health benefits of cookies?" "What are health disadvantages of cookies?"

The findings revealed that the needs of a subset of specialty cookie consumers were not being met by existing "wellness specialty offerings," cookies offering health benefits. These consumers wanted great taste combined with health benefits, so that they could enjoy the cookies without feeling guilty. Seeing this opportunity, Nabisco and ConAgra joined to create and market Healthy Choice (www.healthychoice.com), an adult specialty cookie with an indulgent, yet healthful, profile. Healthy Choice cookies rank among the top-100 specialty cookie/cracker category. The Raspberry Tart ranks 33, the Apricot Tart 92. According to the company, both were outselling all of key competitor Pepperidge Farms' wellness cookies. This success is attributed to a focus on unsatisfied consumer needs identified through open-ended questions. As of 2008, Healthy Choice offers more than 200 products that expand to a variety of food categories, none of which compromise on taste or nutrition.[4]

In general, open-ended questions are useful in exploratory research and as opening questions. However, in a large survey, the complexity of recording, tabulation, and analysis outweighs their advantages.

Structured Questions

Structured questions specify the set of responses as well as their format. A structured question might offer multiple choices, only two choices (dichotomous question), or a scale (see Figure 11.4).

structured questions
Questions that prespecify the set of response alternatives and the response format. A structured question could be multiple-choice, dichotomous, or a scale.

MULTIPLE-CHOICE QUESTIONS In multiple-choice questions, the researcher provides a choice of answers, and respondents are asked to select one or more of the alternatives given. Consider the following question:

Do you intend to travel overseas within the next 6 months?

_____ Definitely will not travel

_____ Probably will not travel

_____ Undecided

_____ Probably will travel

_____ Definitely will travel

Many of the issues associated with constructing itemized rating scales (see Chapter 10) also apply to multiple-choice questions. Two additional concerns in designing multiple-choice questions are (1) the number of alternatives that should be included and (2) order or position bias.

Multiple-choice questions should include choices that cover the full range of possible alternatives. The alternatives should be mutually exclusive and collectively exhaustive. An "other (please specify)" category should be included where appropriate. Instructions should clearly indicate whether the respondent is to choose only one alternative or to select all that apply. (For example, "Please indicate all the brands of soft drinks that you have consumed in the past week.") As the list of choices increases, the questions become more difficult to answer. When the alternative list becomes long, the researcher should consider using more than one question to simplify the respondents' workload.

order or position bias
A respondent's tendency to choose an alternative merely because it occupies a certain position on the page or in a list.

Order or position bias is the respondents' tendency to check an alternative merely because it occupies a certain position in a list. Alternatives that appear at the beginning and, to a lesser degree, at the end of a list have a tendency to be selected most often. When questions relate to numeric values (quantities or prices), there is a tendency to select the central value on the list. Order bias can be controlled by preparing several forms of the questionnaire with changes in the order of the alternatives from form to form. Each alternative should appear once in each of the extreme positions, once in the middle, and once somewhere in between.

Multiple-choice questions are easier for respondents to answer. They also are easier to analyze and tabulate than open-ended questions. Interviewer bias also is reduced, given that these types of questions work very well in self-administered conditions. Respondent cooperation in general is improved if the majority of the questions are structured.

Multiple-choice questions are not without disadvantages. It is difficult to develop effective multiple-choice options. Often, exploratory research must be conducted using open-ended questions to identify the appropriate response options. When large numbers of respondents check the "other (please specify)" category, it indicates that the alternative list might be seriously flawed. The list of options itself also introduces bias.

dichotomous question
A structured question with only two response alternatives, such as yes and no.

DICHOTOMOUS QUESTIONS A **dichotomous question** has only two response alternatives: yes or no, agree or disagree, and so forth. Sometimes, multiple-choice questions can be dichotomous, as in the overseas travel question asked earlier:

Do you intend to travel overseas within the next 6months?

_____ Yes

_____ No

Dichotomous questions should be used when the researcher has reason to believe that the respondent thinks of the topic in yes/no terms. When the respondent is highly involved in a subject or has a great deal of knowledge related to the topic, a multiple-choice question or scale might be more appropriate.

Dichotomous questions have many of the same strengths and weaknesses of multiple-choice questions. They are among the easiest type of questions to code and analyze, as illustrated by the following American Airlines example. They have one serious flaw, however. The direction of question wording can have a significant effect on the responses given. To illustrate this directional bias, the statement, "Individuals are more to blame than social conditions for crime and lawlessness in this country," produced agreement from 59.6 percent of the respondents in a research study. However, on a matched sample that responded to the opposite statement, "Social conditions are more to blame than individuals for crime and lawlessness in this country," 43.2 percent agreed (as opposed to 40.4% expected based on agreement with the opposite statement). To overcome this directional bias, the question should be framed in one direction on one-half of the questionnaires and in the opposite direction on the other half. This is referred to as the *split-ballot technique.* Consider the use of dichotomous questions by American Airlines.

Research in Action

The Use of Dichotomous Questions Is American

American Airlines is the largest scheduled passenger airline in the world. As of 2008, American and its regional airline affiliates, American Eagle and the AmericanConnection airlines, serve 250 cities in over 40 countries with more than 4,000 daily flights. Naturally, the world's largest airline would need to implement surveys and other methods of feedback in order to continuously improve its service. American Airlines employs Key Survey (www.KeySurvey.com) to conduct customer-satisfaction tracking surveys on topics from ticket booking to in-flight meals. The surveys are conducted online. A random sample of about 25,000 people is picked every 2 weeks from American's customer database. The respondents are e-mailed a link to the survey. The survey asks them how their flight was and information about the in-flight service so that American Airlines can get an overview of how well it is performing. The survey questions are structured in such a way so as to ask "did this happen?" For example, survey questions might ask "When you checked in, were you greeted by the agent?" "Were you served a predeparture drink?" and so on. All respondents have to do is answer yes or no for 30 dichotomous questions.

As a result of these surveys, several modifications have been made. Customer insights gathered through surveys revealed that customers felt baffled and confused when trying to use the American Airlines Web site to book a flight. Therefore, the process for booking a flight has been made more transparent and easy for the end user.[5]

SCALES   Scales were discussed in detail in Chapters 9 and 10. Sometimes, multiple-choice questions can alternatively be framed as scales, as in the overseas travel question asked earlier.

Do you intend to travel overseas within the next 6 months?

Definitely will not travel	Probably will not travel	Undecided	Probably will travel	Definitely will travel
1	2	3	4	5

Questions making use of scales are easy to answer and, therefore, are popular, as in the WV opening vignette.

Be a DM!

As the marketing chief for U.S.-based Estée Lauder, which markets cosmetics, fragrances, and skin-care products in more than 135 countries, how would you instill positive consumer attitudes toward your brands?

Be an MR!

Search the Internet, as well as your library's online databases, to obtain information on consumers' attitudes toward perfumes. Obtain information on consumers' attitudes toward Estee Lauder perfumes using an unstructured, a multichotomous, a dichotomous, and a scaling question.

Determine the Question Wording

Translating the information needed into clearly worded questions that are easily under-stood is the most difficult aspect of questionnaire development. Poorly worded questions can confuse or mislead respondents, leading to nonresponse or response error. Poorly worded questions can also frustrate the respondents to the point that they refuse to answer those questions or items. This is referred to as *item nonresponse* and leads to nonresponse error. If respondents interpret questions differently than intended by the researcher, serious bias can occur, leading to response error.

To avoid problems in question wording, consider the following five guidelines: (1) define the issue, (2) use ordinary words, (3) avoid ambiguous words, (4) avoid leading questions, and (5) use positive and negative statements.

Define the Issue

Questions should always clearly define the issue being addressed. Beginning journalists are told to define the issue in terms of *who, what, when, where, why,* and *way* (the six Ws). These—particularly *who, what, when,* and *where*—can also serve as guidelines for defining the issue in a question. Consider the following question:

Which brand of toothpaste do you use?

(Incorrect)

On the surface, this might seem to be a well-defined question, but a different conclu-sion can be reached when it is examined under the microscope of *who, what, when,* and *where.*

The Ws	Defining the Question
Who	**The Respondent** It is not clear whether this question relates to the individual respondent or the respondent's total household.
What	**The Brand of Toothpaste** It is unclear how the respondent is to answer this question if more than one brand is used.
When	**Unclear** The time frame is not specified in this question. The respondent could interpret it as meaning the toothpaste used this morning, this week, or over the past year.
Where	**Not Specified** At home, at the gym, on the road?

A more clearly defined question might read:

Which brand or brands of toothpaste have you personally used at home during the past month? In case of more than one brand, please list all the brands that apply.

(Correct)

Use Simple Words

Simple, ordinary words that match the vocabulary level of the respondent should be used in a questionnaire. When choosing words, keep in mind that, in the United States, for

A well-defined question is needed to determine which brand(s) of toothpaste a person uses.

example, the average person has a high school, not a college, education. For certain respondent groups, the education level is even lower. Simplicity in wording and a conscious effort to avoid technical jargon should guide questionnaire development. As marketing professionals, it also is important to remember that most respondents do not understand marketing terminology. For example, instead of asking,

Is the distribution of snack foods adequate?

(Incorrect)

ask,

Are snack foods readily available when you want to buy them?

(Correct)

Use Unambiguous Words

When selecting words for a questionnaire, the questionnaire designer should choose words with only one meaning. This is not an easy task given that a number of words that appear unambiguous can have different meanings to different people. These include *usually, normally, frequently, often, regularly, occasionally,* and *sometimes.* Consider the following question:

In a typical month, how often do you go to a movie theater to see a movie?

_____ Never

_____ Occasionally

_____ Sometimes

_____ Often

_____ Regularly

(Incorrect)

Assessing the distribution of snack foods requires the use of words as ordinary and commonplace as snack foods themselves.

The categories of this multiple-choice question can have different meanings to different people, leading to response bias. Three respondents who go to movie theaters once a month might check three different categories: occasionally, sometimes, and often. The following is a much better worded question:

In a typical month, how often do you go to a movie theater to see a movie?

_____ Less than once

_____ 1 or 2 times

_____ 3 or 4 times

_____ More than 4 times

(Correct)

This question is less ambiguous because each respondent is answering it from a consistent frame of reference. Response categories have been objectively defined, and respondents are no longer free to interpret them in their own way. Additionally, all-inclusive or all-exclusive words are understood differently by different people. Some examples of such words are *all, always, any, anybody, ever,* and *every.* Such words should be avoided. To illustrate, *any* could mean "every," "some," or "one only" to different respondents, depending on how they look at it.

Avoid Leading or Biasing Questions

leading question
A question that gives the respondent a clue as to what the answer should be.

acquiescence bias
Bias resulting from some respondents' tendency to agree with the direction of a leading question (yea-saying).

A **leading question** is one that clues the respondent to what the answer should be. Some respondents have a tendency to agree with whatever way the question is leading them to answer. This tendency is know as *yea-saying* and results in a bias called **acquiescence bias**. Consider the following question:

Do you think that Great Britain should provide financial aid to poor foreign countries when it is not our responsibility to do so?

_____ Yes

_____ No

_____ Don't know

(Incorrect)

This question would lead respondents to a "no" answer. The answer would be unduly biased by the phrase "it is not our responsibility to do so." Therefore, this question would not help determine the preferences of Americans for providing aid to poor foreign countries. A better question would be:

Do you think that Great Britain should provide financial aid to poor foreign countries?

_____ Yes

_____ No

_____ Don't know

(Correct)

Words can lead respondents in a particular direction. Identification of the research sponsor can have the same effect. When respondents are made aware of the sponsor, they tend to answer questions about that sponsor in a positive manner. In India, for example, the question,

Is Babool your favorite toothpaste?

(Incorrect)

is likely to bias the responses in favor of Babool. A more unbiased way of obtaining this information would be to ask,

What is your favorite brand of toothpaste?

(Correct)

Likewise, the mention of a prestigious or nonprestigious name can bias the response, as in, "Do you agree with the Indian Dental Association that Babool is effective in preventing cavities?" Question wording should be objective, as in the WV opening vignette.

Balance Dual Statements

Many questions, particularly those measuring attitudes and lifestyles, are worded as statements to which respondents indicate their degree of agreement or disagreement using Likert scales. The statements in these types of questions can be worded either positively or negatively. Evidence shows that the responses obtained often depend on the direction of the wording of the questions: that is, whether they are stated positively or negatively. Questions of this type should be balanced by dual statements, some of which are positive and some negative. Two different questionnaires that reverse the direction of the questions could also be used to control for any bias introduced by the positive or negative nature of the statements. An example of dual statements was provided in the summated Likert scale in Chapter 10 that was designed to measure attitudes toward Macy's.

Arrange the Questions in Proper Order

When arranging questions in a proper order, the researcher should consider the opening questions, the type of information sought, question difficulty, and the effect on subsequent questions. Questions should be arranged in a logical order, organized around topic areas.

Opening Questions

Opening questions set the stage for the remainder of the questionnaire. They serve a variety of purposes. They can introduce the topic, attempt to gain the confidence and cooperation of respondents, or establish the legitimacy of the study. The opening questions should be interesting, simple, and nonthreatening. Questions that ask respondents for their opinions are always good openers, because most people like to express their opinions.

Sometimes opening questions might be asked to simply establish rapport. Some studies require a prescreening of the respondents to ensure that they are eligible to participate in the interview. In these cases, qualifying questions are used as opening questions.

Research in Action

Qualifying Respondents Leads to Unqualified Success for Kellogg's

Looking to expand its share of the ready-to-eat cereal category, Kellogg's, a U.S. producer of more than 20 brands, conducted a telephone survey of American users. The nonusers of ready-to-eat cereals were not relevant for this study and, thus, not part of the target population. The first question was:

How often do you have ready-to-eat cereal for breakfast?

_____ Less than twice a week
_____ Two or three times per week
_____ Four or five times per week
_____ More than five times per week

If the answer was "less than twice a week," that respondent was thanked and the interview terminated. Such respondents were operationally classified as nonusers and excluded from the study.

The results of the survey indicated that consumers were looking for a crunchy, tasty, yet low-fat and healthy cereal. Based on the survey's findings, Kellogg's introduced Honey Crunch Corn Flakes. The oven-baked flake is 20 percent thicker than other flakes, offering a crunchier texture. It is low in fat, cholesterol-free, and a source of nine essential vitamins and minerals. The bright yellow package features Cornelius the Rooster, which has been on the Kellogg's Corn Flakes box since 1957. To support the product launch, Kellogg's ran a national TV spot emphasizing the cereal's "Taste of Honey, Heart of Gold." This new brand has been a great success in a very competitive cereal market.[6]

basic information
Information that relates directly to the marketing research problem.

classification information
Socioeconomic and demographic characteristics used to classify respondents.

identification information
A type of information obtained in a questionnaire that includes name, postal address, e-mail address, and phone number.

Type of Information

Three types of information are obtained from a questionnaire: (1) basic information, (2) classification information, and (3) identification information. **Basic information** relates directly to the research problem. **Classification information** consists of socioeconomic and demographic characteristics. It is used to classify the respondents in order to analyze results across different groups. **Identification information** includes name, postal address, e-mail address, and telephone number. Identification information can be obtained for a variety of purposes, including verifying that the respondents listed were actually interviewed, remitting promised incentives, and so forth. Because basic information is the most important aspect of a study, it should be obtained first, followed by classification and then identification information. Classification and identification information is of a more personal nature. Respondents might resist answering a series of personal questions. Therefore, these types of questions should appear at the end of the questionnaire, as in the WV vignette.

Question Difficulty

Respondents can perceive questions as difficult for a variety of reasons. They might relate to sensitive issues or be embarrassing, complex, or dull. Questions that could be perceived as difficult should be placed late in the sequence, after a relationship has been established and the respondent is involved in the process. The last question of the classification section is typically income information. The respondent's telephone number is the final item in the identification section for the same reasons.

Effect on Subsequent Questions

Initial questions can influence questions asked later in a questionnaire. As a rule, a series of questions should start with a general introduction to a topic, followed by specific questions related to the topic. This prevents specific questions from biasing responses to the general questions. Consider the following sequence of questions:

Q1: What considerations are important to you in selecting a department store?
Q2: In selecting a department store, how important is convenience of location?

(Correct)

The first question is general, whereas the second is specific. If these questions were reversed, respondents would be more likely to cite convenience of location as the response to the general question. Going from general to specific is called the **funnel approach**, because it begins with broader (more general) questions and then asks narrower (more specific) questions, reflecting the shape of a funnel (Figure 11.5).[7] The funnel approach was illustrated in the opening vignette when general information about motivations for giving was obtained before measuring awareness and perceptions of World Vision. Although the funnel approach is more commonly used, sometimes an inverted funnel approach is used when the respondents do not have clearly formulated views about a topic or when they lack

funnel approach
A strategy for ordering questions in a questionnaire in which the sequence starts with the general questions, which are followed by progressively specific questions, in order to prevent specific questions from biasing responses to general questions.

BROAD OR GENERAL QUESTIONS

NARROW OR SPECIFIC QUESTIONS

FIGURE 11.5

The Funnel Approach to Ordering Questions

a common frame of reference in responding to general questions on the topic. In this approach, the specific questions are asked first, followed by more general questions.

Logical Order

Questions should be asked in a logical order, organized around topic areas. This was illustrated in the WV vignette. The order in which the questions were asked was as follows: (1) priorities and motivations for giving, (2) awareness of the organization (WV), (3) perceptions of the organization, (4) communication with donors, and (5) demographic information. When switching topics, brief transitional phrases or sentences should be used to help respondents switch their train of thought; for example, "In this section, we ask questions related to your purchase of a new car in the last 6 months."

branching questions
Questions used to guide respondents or interviewers through a survey by directing them to different spots on the questionnaire depending on the answers given.

Branching questions direct respondents or interviewers to different places in the questionnaire based on their response to the question at hand. To avoid confusion, they should be designed carefully. Here is an example of a well-designed question: "If the answer to Question 4 (Have you purchased a new car in the last 6 months?) is "no," go to Question 10; skip Questions 5 through 9 related to a new car purchase." Branches enable respondents to skip irrelevant questions or elaborate in areas of specific interest. Skip patterns can become quite complex to the point that they are best administered in computer-aided interviewing environments (CATI, CAPI, or Internet, see Chapter 7). The general order of questions is outlined in Table 11.2 and illustrated in the context of grocery shopping.

Be an MR!

Search the Internet, as well as your library's online databases, to obtain information on U.S. consumer perceptions, preferences, and purchase intentions for flat-panel television sets. Specify the information needed and the order in which you would obtain information on consumers' perceptions, preferences, and purchase intentions for Sony flat-panel television sets.

Be a DM!

As the vice president of marketing, what marketing strategies would you formulate to increase Sony's penetration of the flat-panel television market?

TABLE 11.2 The General Ordering of Questions in a Questionnaire

Question Type	Nature	Function	Example
Qualifying/Screening Questions	Focus on respondent inclusion criteria	To determine if a respondent is eligible to participate in the survey	Who in your household does most of the shopping for groceries?
Introductory Questions/ Warm-Ups	Broad, easy questions	To break the ice and put the respondent at ease	How often do you shop for groceries?
Main Questions: Easy	Related to the information needed but easy to answer	To focus on the survey topic and reassure the respondent that survey is easy	How important is each of the following factors in selecting a supermarket?
Main Questions: More Difficult	Related to the information needed but may be difficult be to answer	To obtain the rest of the information needed	How would you rank order the following eight supermarkets in terms of your preference to shop?
Psychographics/Lifestyles	Not relevant in all surveys	To obtain personality-related information	Please indicate your degree of disagreement with the following statements.
Demographics	Personal information	To classify the respondents	What was your household's total annual income last year?
Identification Information	Name, address, telephone	To identify the respondent	Name:_____

Choose the Form and Layout

The physical characteristics of a questionnaire, such as the format, spacing, and positioning, can have a significant effect on the results. This is particularly true for self-administered questionnaires. Experiments on mail questionnaires for the 2000 and earlier census revealed that questions at the top of the page received more attention than those at the bottom. Instructions printed in red made little difference, except that they made the questionnaire appear more complicated to the respondents.

Dividing a questionnaire into sections with separate topic areas for each section is a good practice, as illustrated in the WV project. Several parts might be needed for questions pertaining to the basic information. The questions in each part should be numbered, particularly when branching questions are used. Numbering also makes coding the responses easier. Preferably, the questionnaires should be precoded. In **precoding**, the codes to enter in the computer are printed on the questionnaire. Typically, the code identifies the line number and the column numbers in which a particular response will be entered. Note that when CATI or CAPI are used, the precoding is built into the software. Coding of questionnaires is explained in more detail in Chapter 15 on data preparation. An example of precoding a questionnaire is shown in the residential carpeting survey.

precoding
In questionnaire design, assigning a code to every conceivable response before data collection.

Research in Action

Precoding a Questionnaire

Residential Carpeting Survey

(1–3)

(Please ignore the numbers alongside the answers. They are only to help us in data processing.)

Please answer the following questions pertaining to household carpeting by following the specified directions.

Part A

Q1. Does your household currently own carpeting?

   1. _____ Yes   (5)
   2. _____ No

(IF YES, GO TO QUESTION Q2; IF NO, GO TO QUESTION Q7.)

Q2. Which of the following styles of carpeting do you have in your home? Please check as many as apply.

   a. _____ One Color; Traditional Style   (6)
   b. _____ Multicolor; Traditional Style   (7)
   c. _____ One Color; Contemporary Style   (8)
   d. _____ Multicolor; Contemporary Style   (9)
   e. _____ Other   (10)

Please indicate your agreement with each of the following statements (Q3 through Q6).

Q3. Carpeting is an important part of my home.

Strongly Disagree   Neutral   Strongly Agree
   1   2   3   4   5   6   7   (11)

Q4. Carpeting is a fashion item for the home.

Strongly Disagree   Neutral   Strongly Agree
   1   2   3   4   5   6   7   (12)

Q5. Carpeting is a central item in my interior design for my home.

Strongly Disagree   Neutral   Strongly Agree
   1   2   3   4   5   6   7   (13)

Q6. It is more important for a carpet to last long than look pretty.

Strongly Disagree   Neutral   Strongly Agree
   1   2   3   4   5   6   7   (14)

The next question deals with your likelihood of buying new carpeting.

Q7. How likely is your household to buy new carpeting in the next 3 months?

Not so Likely   Maybe/Maybe Not   Very Likely
   1   2   3   4   5   6   7   (15)

In the preceding example, the first precoding value (1–3) indicates that the first three columns are used for the questionnaire ID. In general, the questionnaires themselves should be numbered serially, because this enhances control of questionnaires in the field, as well as the coding and analysis. This numbering system alerts the researcher if questionnaires are misplaced or lost. A possible exception to this rule is mail questionnaires. Respondents are promised anonymity, and the presence of a questionnaire identifier might be interpreted as a breach of that promise. Some respondents might refuse to participate or answer differently if they believe the answers can be traced to them. However, recent research suggests that this loss of anonymity has little, if any, influence on the results.

Reproduce the Questionnaire

The quality of the paper and print process used for the questionnaire also influences response. For example, if the questionnaire is reproduced on poor-quality paper or is otherwise shabby in appearance, the respondents might conclude that the project is unimportant, and this perception will be reflected in the quality of the responses. Therefore, the questionnaire should be reproduced on good-quality paper and have a professional appearance, as illustrated in the WV study. Multipage questionnaires should be presented in booklet form rather than simply stapled or clipped. This format is easier for the interviewer to handle and enhances the overall appearance.

Questions should not be continued from one page to the next. In other words, researchers should avoid splitting a question, including its response categories. Respondents might be misled into thinking that a split question has ended at the bottom of a page and base their answers on the incomplete question.

The tendency to crowd questions together to make the questionnaire look shorter should be avoided. Overcrowding leaves little space for responses, which results in shorter answers. It also increases errors in data tabulation. In addition, crowded questionnaires appear more complex, resulting in lower cooperation and completion rates. Although shorter questionnaires are more desirable than longer ones, reduction in size should not be obtained at the expense of crowding.

Experiential Learning

Designing a Survey Questionnaire

Meteor Motorcycle Company is one of the U.S. industry's leading manufacturers of customized, high-performance bikes in the luxury cruiser class. Return to Chapter 3's experiential learning, "Crafting a Research Proposal," to review the proposal presented to this company. Go to the textbook Web site, select "Chapter 11," and download the following file: Meteor Survey A.doc. This is the draft version of the survey used to fulfill the research objectives listed in the research proposal for the Meteor Motorcycle Company presented in Chapter 3 as Meteor Proposal.doc. Open Meteor Survey A.doc and read the actual draft version of the survey questionnaire done after this proposal was accepted by Meteor.

1. How would you improve this draft of the questionnaire? Hints: Think about what was promised in the proposal.

Think also about the guidelines presented in this chapter.

2. Create an electronic copy of Meteor Survey A.doc entitled "Meteor Survey A2.doc. Make your proposed revisions in this new document.

3. How would you make this draft of the survey appear more appealing to the respondent? Hint: Think about the "Form and Layout" and "Reproduce the Questionnaire" sections.

4. Make your proposed revisions in this new document Meteor Survey A2.doc.

5. Using Qualtrics (access is included with this book), develop an online version of your revised survey as given in Meteor Survey A2.doc.

Pretest the Questionnaire

pretesting
The testing of the questionnaire on a small sample of respondents for the purpose of improving the questionnaire by identifying and eliminating potential problems before using it in the actual survey.

Pretesting refers to testing the questionnaire on a small sample of respondents, usually 15 to 30, to identify and eliminate potential problems. Even the best questionnaire can be improved by pretesting. As a general rule, a questionnaire should not be used in the field study without extensive pretesting, as in the WV vignette. All aspects of the questionnaire, including question content, wording, sequence, form and layout, question difficulty, and instructions should be tested. Additionally, pretesting should be conducted with a subset of the respondent group. The pretest groups should be similar to the survey respondents in terms of their background characteristics, familiarity with the topic, and attitudes and behaviors of interest.[8]

Pretests are best done by personal interviews, even if the actual survey is to be conducted by telephone, mail, or electronically, so that interviewers can observe respondent reactions and attitudes. After the necessary changes have been made, another pretest could be administered using the actual data collection approach, if it is mail, telephone, or electronic. This stage of the pretest will reveal any potential problems in the interviewing method to be used in the actual survey. The pretest should be conducted in an environment and context similar to that of the actual survey.

Based on feedback from the pretest, the questionnaire should be edited, and the identified problems corrected. After each significant revision of the questionnaire, another pretest should be conducted, using a different sample of respondents. Pretesting should be continued until no further changes are needed. As a final step, the responses obtained during the pretest should be coded and analyzed. The analysis of pretest responses can serve as a check on the adequacy of the problem definition, and provide insight into the nature of the data as well as analytic techniques that will be required. Table 11.3 outlines the questionnaire design process in the form of a checklist.

TABLE 11.3 Questionnaire Design Checklist

Step 1   Specify the Information Needed

1. Ensure that the information obtained fully addresses all the components of the problem.
2. Have a clear idea of the target population.

Step 2   Type of Interviewing Method

1. Review the type of interviewing method determined based on considerations discussed in Chapter 7.

Step 3   Individual Question Content

1. Is the question necessary?
2. Are several questions needed instead of one to obtain the required information in an unambiguous manner?
3. Do not use double-barreled questions.

Step 4   Overcoming Inability and Unwillingness to Answer

1. Is the respondent informed?
2. If respondents are not likely to be informed, filter questions that measure familiarity, product use, and past experience should be asked before questions about the topics themselves.
3. Can the respondent remember?
4. Questions that do not provide the respondent with cues can underestimate the actual occurrence of an event.
5. Can the respondent articulate?
6. Minimize the effort required by the respondents.
7. Make the request for information seem legitimate.
8. Is the information sensitive?

Step 5   Choosing Question Structure

1. Open-ended questions are useful in exploratory research and as opening questions.
2. Use structured questions whenever possible.
3. In multiple-choice questions, the response alternatives should include the set of all possible choices and should be mutually exclusive.
4. In a dichotomous question, if a substantial proportion of the respondents can be expected to be neutral, include a neutral alternative.
5. Consider the use of the split-ballot technique to reduce order bias in dichotomous and multiple-choice questions.
6. If the response alternatives are numerous, consider using more than one question.

Step 6   Choosing Question Wording

1. Define the issue in terms of *who, what, when, where, why*, and *way* (the six Ws).
2. Use ordinary words. Words should match the vocabulary level of the respondents.
3. Avoid ambiguous words: *usually, normally, frequently, often, regularly, occasionally, sometimes*, and so forth.
4. Avoid leading questions that clue the respondent to what the answer should be.
5. Use positive and negative statements.

(Continued)

TABLE 11.3 (Continued)

Step 7   Determine the Order of Questions

1. The opening questions should be interesting, simple, and nonthreatening.
2. Qualifying questions should serve as the opening questions.
3. Basic information should be obtained first, followed by classification, and, finally, identification information.
4. Difficult, sensitive, or complex questions should be placed late in the sequence.
5. General questions should precede specific questions.
6. Questions should be asked in a logical order.

Step 8   Form and Layout

1. Divide a questionnaire into several parts.
2. Number the questions in each part.
3. Precode the questionnaire.
4. Serially number the questionnaires themselves.

Step 9   Reproduction of the Questionnaire

1. The questionnaire should have a professional appearance.
2. Use a booklet format for long questionnaires.
3. Reproduce each question on a single page (or double-page spread).
4. Avoid the tendency to crowd questions to make the questionnaire look shorter. Place directions or instructions for individual questions as close as possible to the questions.

Step 10   Pretesting

1. Always pretest.
2. Test all aspects of the questionnaire, including question content, wording, sequence, form and layout, question difficulty, and instructions.
3. Use respondents in the pretest that are similar to those who will be included in the actual survey.
4. Begin the pretest by using personal interviews.
5. Conduct the pretest by mail, telephone, or electronically if those methods are to be used in the actual survey.
6. Use a variety of interviewers for pretests.
7. The pretest sample size should be small, varying from 15 to 30 respondents for the initial testing.
8. After each significant revision of the questionnaire, conduct another pretest, using a different sample of respondents.
9. Code and analyze the responses obtained from the pretest.

Observational Forms

Observational forms are designed to record respondent reaction to new products, advertising, packaging, or some other marketing stimuli. Because there is no questioning of the respondents, the researcher does not need to be concerned with the psychological impact of the questions and the way they are asked. Observational forms are designed primarily for the field work and the tabulation phase, providing a guide for recording information accurately and to simplify coding, entry, and analysis of data.

Observational forms should specify the *who*, *what*, *when*, *where*, *why*, and *way* of behavior to be observed. Refer to the discussion on descriptive research in Chapter 3 for a similar analysis. Suppose that the U.S. fast-food giant McDonald's wants to observe American consumers' reaction to the deluxe sandwiches to be introduced nationally. An observational form to record customer reaction would include space for all of the information specified in the McDonald's example.

Research in Action

Are McDonald's Deluxe Sandwiches Truly Deluxe?

Who: Purchasers, adults, parents with children, teenagers

What: Deluxe sandwiches, other sandwiches and menu items considered/purchased, influence of children or other family members

When: Day, hour, and date of observation

Where: At checkout counter, inside the store in the eating area, outside the store upon exit

Why:	Influence of promotion or family members on the purchase.	Way:	Personal observer disguised as sales clerk, undisguised personal observer, hidden camera, or obtrusive mechanical device

The same physical design considerations of layout and reproduction apply to both questionnaires and observational forms. A well-designed form guides the observer to appropriately record the details of the observation rather than merely summarize them. Finally, like questionnaires, observational forms also require adequate pretesting.

Be a DM!	Be an MR!
As the marketing director for Neiman Marcus an upscale chain of American department stores, develop marketing programs to capitalize upon consumers' Christmas retail shopping for the upcoming season.	Search the Internet, as well as your library's online databases, to obtain information on American consumers' Christmas retail shopping behavior. Specify the method and design an observation form to observe the consumers' Christmas retail shopping behavior.

Summary Illustration Using the Opening Vignette

We summarize and illustrate the questionnaire design process by returning to the opening vignette. Notice that the information obtained for WV and the order in which it was obtained were clearly specified. The questionnaire was kept simple, and detailed instructions were provided, because it had to be administered by mail. Only necessary questions were asked, and combined questions were avoided. To increase the willingness of the donors and potential donors to participate and complete the questionnaire, the context of the survey was made clear, and the effort required of the respondents was minimized. Most of the questions were structured questions, requiring the respondents to simply circle a number on the scale. However, a few open-ended questions were included where it was felt that the respondents needed the freedom to express underlying motivations for giving to charity.

Words with unequivocal meanings but that were familiar to the donors were used. Special effort was made to not bias the responses in any direction. The ordering of the questions was logical, and the funnel approach was used. General questions about priorities and motivations for giving were asked first; questions about awareness and perceptions of WV followed. The questionnaire was divided into parts, with a separate part devoted to each type of information sought. Information on name and address was optional and was obtained at the end of the questionnaire. The questionnaire was professionally reproduced and thoroughly pretested. Figure 11.6 provides a concept map for question wording

International Marketing Research

The questionnaire or research instrument should be designed to be sensitive to cultural differences encountered in international research. Differences in underlying consumer behavior, decision-making processes, psychographics, lifestyles, and demographic variables should all be considered. Questions related to marital status, education, household size, occupation, income, and dwelling unit might have to be modified to be comparable across countries, requiring rewording. For example, household definition and size vary greatly, given the extended family structure in some countries and the practice of two, or even three, families living under the same roof.

Although personal interviewing is the dominant survey method in international marketing research, different interviewing methods might be used in different countries. Therefore, the questionnaire must be adaptable to a variety of administration methods. In countries with lower levels of education or product experience, two or more simple questions rather than a single complex question should be used. The researcher should realize that respondents in some countries, for example, in some African nations, might not be as well informed about the subject matter of the survey as respondents in the United States.

FIGURE 11.6

A Concept Map for Question Wording

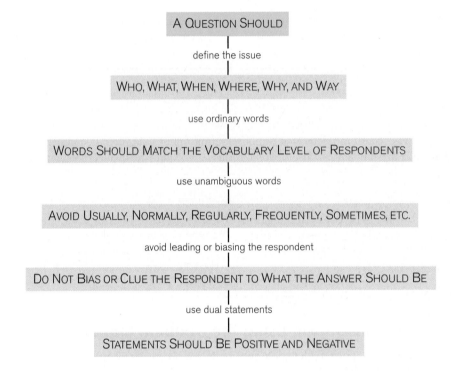

Using unstructured questions might be necessary if the researcher does not fully understand the range of alternatives associated with a response. Using unstructured questions can also minimize the risk of cultural bias. However, unstructured questions are more sensitive to differences in educational levels than are structured questions. They should be used with caution in countries with high illiteracy rates.

In addition to design considerations, the researcher must also pay close attention to translation issues. An equivalent word or phrase might not be available in some languages. For example, it is not easy to translate *self-respect* into German or *macho* into Arabic. Pretesting of the questionnaire is complicated in international research, because the linguistic equivalence must be pretested. Two sets of pretests are recommended. The translated questionnaire should be pretested on respondents who speak only their native language, as well as on bilingual subjects. Multiple languages are spoken in some countries, and a national survey in such a country can require questionnaire translation into different languages. This is true in some large countries such as India, which has 19 major languages and over 200 dialects. It also is true in some small countries such as Singapore, where the languages spoken include English, Malay, Hokkien, Tamil, Mandarin, and Cantonese. The pretest data from administering the questionnaire in different countries or cultures should be analyzed, and the pattern of responses compared, to detect any cultural biases.

Research in Action

Engaging Respondents About Engagement

A questionnaire dealing with engagement rings was administered to women in seven European countries. The first set of questions used in England was:

1. Are you married?
   If yes, in what year were you married?
   If no, are you engaged to be married?

   If married or engaged:
2. Do you own an engagement ring, or did you obtain one or more rings at the time of your engagement?

If "yes":
3. What type of ring is it/was it?
   _____ No stones
   _____ Single diamond only
   _____ Several diamonds, no other stones
   _____ Diamonds and other stones
   _____ Other stones only

This looks like a very simple list of questions, involving no difficulty of direct or literal translation. Yet, if the questionnaire were literally translated for use in some of the other countries, the results would have been meaningless. The question, "Do you own an engagement ring?" would not have worked in Germany, because many German women receive a plain gold band at the time of engagement, which they later transfer to the other hand and use as a wedding ring. Instead of a single question, a whole battery of questions was needed to obtain information from Germany that was equivalent to that of the other six countries. Thus, the researcher had to translate the meaning rather than do a literal translation (transliteration).

Another modification to ensure comparability concerned the list of precoded ring types. Although pearl rings were relatively unimportant in most countries covered, they were a high proportion of engagement rings in Spain and France. To include pearl rings as a separate category in most of the countries would have unnecessarily complicated the list. However, to exclude them in Spain or France would have resulted not only in the loss of information, but also in confusion arising from the list of type of rings being incomplete. Therefore, the pearl ring was included as a ring type in only the Spanish and French questionnaires.[9]

Technology and Marketing Research

Software is available for designing questionnaires administered over the Internet or through other modes (e.g., telephone, personal interviews, or mail). Although the following describes the use of software for constructing Internet questionnaires, the functions are essentially similar for questionnaires constructed by other modes. The software will help in the development and dissemination of the questionnaire, and, in many cases, retrieve and analyze the collected data and prepare a report. The software can automatically perform a variety of tasks, including:

- *Personalization.* The respondent's name and personal responses are automatically inserted into key questions.
- *Incorporate complex skip patterns.* The software can check many conditions and responses to determine which question should be asked next.
- *Randomize response choices.* The order of presentation of response options in multiple-choice questions can be randomized for each respondent to control for order bias.
- *Consistency checks.* Consistency checks can be programmed to identify inconsistent responses while the interview is still in progress so that corrective action can be taken, if necessary.
- *Add new response categories as the interviewing progresses.* If many respondents give a particular response to the "Other, please specify" category, that response will be automatically converted into a check-off category and added to the set of prespecified response options.

In addition, most programs have a variety of features that facilitate questionnaire construction:

- *Question list.* The user can select a variety of formats from a menu of question types, such as open ended, multiple choice, scales, dichotomous questions, and so forth.
- *Question libraries.* The user can select predefined questions or save often used questions in the question library. For example, the question library might contain predefined questions for measuring satisfaction, purchase intention, and other commonly used marketing constructs.
- *Questionnaire appearance.* The user can select the background color and graphics of the questionnaire from a range of available templates or create a customized template.
- *Preview.* The questionnaire can be viewed as it is being developed to examine the content, interactivity, type of questions, and background design and make any needed changes.
- *Publish.* This user can create the HTML questionnaire, post it to a unique Web page, create a database to collect the data on the hosting server, and obtain a unique URL to which respondents can be directed.
- *Notification.* The user can create, personalize, send, and track e-mail invitations to participate in the survey.

As each respondent completes the survey, the data are transferred over the Web to the data file on the host server. The data can be downloaded and analyzed at any time, even when the survey is running. Thus, results can be examined in real-time. In the United States, commonly used questionnaire software includes SurveyTime (www.surveytime.com), SurveyPro (www.surveypro.com), Surveyz (www.surveyz.com), and PerfectSurveys (www.perfect surveys.com). Other popular packages include EFM Feedback (www.vovici.com) and SSI Web by Sawtooth Software (www.sawtoothsoftware.com). With this book you have access to Qualtrics (www.qualtrics.com), which will enable you to electronically design questionnaires.

Several Web sites allow users to create and file their own questionnaires for free. CreateSurvey (www.createsurvey.com) allows anyone to create and administer online surveys to whomever they want. It distributes the survey, monitors participation and participants, and then collects and analyzes the data, all for free, because it is sponsored by Web advertising. However, CreateSurvey does not provide respondents. Users do this at their discretion. For instance, they can create a Web page and have the survey as a link from the Web page or send out an e-mail with the link asking people to participate in the survey. Another Web-based service is Zoomerang (www.zoomerang.com) by MarketTools (www.markettools.com).

A number of Web sites housed in universities offer valuable resources, such as scales and question libraries, for constructing questionnaires. Some helpful sites include the Interuniversity Consortium for Political and Social Research at the University of Michigan (www.icpsr.umich.edu); the Roper Center at the University of Connecticut (www.ropercenter.uconn.edu); the Survey Research Library at Florida State University (www.fsu.edu/~survey); and the Odum Institute, which houses the Louis Harris Data Center at the University of North Carolina, Chapel Hill (www.irss.unc.edu).

The following example illustrates the guidelines a marketing research firm follows in order to design good online questionnaires.

Research in Action

Designing Internet Survey Questionnaires: The DSS Research Way

DSS Research (www.dssresearch.com) is a full-service American marketing research firm specializing in research using the Internet. It has developed the following guidelines for designing good online questionnaires:

- To ensure that the questionnaire provides the necessary decision-making information for management, DSS includes the responsible managers in the design process and also requires them to sign off on the questionnaire.

- The questionnaires are specifically designed for the intended respondents. Thus, marketing jargon and business terminology that respondents might not understand are not used.

- DSS uses the multimedia capabilities of the Internet to design a questionnaire that is appealing and interesting to the respondents.

- The questionnaire is personalized for each respondent by inserting the name and answers to previous questions, as appropriate. This increases the respondent's involvement.

Ethics in Marketing Research

Administering the questionnaire is a substantial intrusion by the researcher. Therefore, several ethical concerns arise pertaining to the researcher–respondent relationship. Ethical issues pertinent to the researcher–client relationship might also have to be addressed.

In consideration of the respondents, questions that are confusing, that exceed the respondents' ability, that are difficult, or that are otherwise improperly worded should be avoided. When asking sensitive questions, researchers should attempt to minimize the respondents' discomfort. It should be made clear at the beginning of the questionnaire that respondents are not obligated to answer any question that makes them uncomfortable. Similarly, overly long questionnaires should be avoided. As a general guideline, the following are considered overly long: a personal, in-home interview lasting over 60 minutes; a telephone interview over 30 minutes; a mall-intercept interview over 30 minutes; and a mail or electronic interview over 30 minutes. Overly long questionnaires are a burden on the respondents and adversely affect the quality of responses.

The researcher has the ethical responsibility to design a questionnaire that obtains the required data in an unbiased manner. Deliberately biasing the questionnaire in a desired direction—for example, by asking leading questions—cannot be condoned. In deciding the question structure, the most appropriate, rather than the most convenient, option should be adopted, as illustrated by the next example. If the questionnaire is not thoroughly pretested, an ethical breach has occurred.

Research in Action

Questioning International Marketing Ethics

One way to avoid biased questions in the international arena is to use open-ended questions. This is particularly appropriate if the response categories are not known. In a study designed to identify ethical problems in international marketing, a series of open-ended questions were used. The objective of the survey, directed at Australian firms engaged in international marketing activities, was to find the three most frequently encountered ethical problems, in order of priority. After reviewing the results, the researcher tabulated and categorized them into 10 categories that occurred most often: traditional small-scale bribery, large-scale bribery, gifts/favors/entertainment, pricing, inappropriate products/technology, tax evasion practices, illegal/immoral activities, questionable commissions to channel members, cultural differences, and involvement in political affairs. The sheer number of categories indicates that international marketing ethics should probably be questioned more closely! The use of structured questions in this case, although more convenient, would have been inappropriate, raising ethical concerns as the researcher lacked knowledge of the set of possible response options required for multiple-choice questions.[10]

What Would *You* Do?

Does Delta Stack Up to the Competition?

The Situation

Richard Anderson has been chief executive officer of Delta Air Lines since 2007. Delta is the third-largest U.S. airline in terms of operating revenue and the world's second-largest air carrier in terms of passengers carried. The airline's innovative developments in the areas of technology and e-commerce have also been widely noted. The annual Wichita State University Airline Quality Rating study named Delta the number-one airline. In addition, *Forbes* ranked Delta number one based on five important customer-service criteria.

Since 2000, the Global Airline Performance (GAP) study teamed up with P. Robert and Partners and the London-based Aviation Information and Research unit of the International Air Transport Association (IATA) to perform a two-part syndicated survey for measuring passenger satisfaction on 22 different airlines in 30 different countries. It samples 240,000 passengers each year and is conducted in seven languages. The interviewers catch the respondents at the most opportune time: while waiting to board the plane. The first part of the survey consists of 20 questions about the airline staff and their willingness to assist; the second part, one that must be sent by mail or fax, asks questions of the boarding process, service on the plane, and comfort. Delta General Manager of Marketing Research, Paul Lai, agrees that keeping the information fresh in the respondent's mind helps get a clearer view of how the airline can increase customer satisfaction. Another benefit of the survey is that it is ongoing, so responses can be tracked over time. Lai also enjoys receiving the data for other airlines so Delta can conduct comparative analyses and identify areas in which Delta is lagging the competition. The survey revealed to Delta and other airlines that two service issues are most important. One is the operational service, such as arrival/departure times without delays. The second is more subjective and cannot be controlled as easily—airline employee and customer relations. If Richard Anderson remains in tune with the surveys conducted by GAP, Delta should be able to stay ahead of the flight competition.

The Marketing Research Decision

1. Paul Lai would like to improve the effectiveness of Part 2 of the GAP questionnaire given in Appendix 11A. This can be done best by (check as many as are applicable):
   a. Eliminating double-barreled questions
   b. Eliminating leading questions
   c. Rearranging the order of questions
   d. Using unstructured questions
   e. Reducing the length of the questionnaire

2. Discuss the role of the questionnaire you recommend in enabling Richard Anderson to determine consumer preferences for airlines and increase Delta's market share.

continued

The Marketing Management Decision

1. Richard Anderson would like to improve Delta's in-flight services. Which of the following should he improve?
   a. The cabin features
   b. The cabin crew
   c. Food and beverages
   d. Onboard amenities/entertainment
   e. All of the above

2. Discuss how the marketing-decision action that you recommend to Richard Anderson is influenced by the questionnaire that you suggested earlier and by the findings of that research.

What Richard Anderson Did

Richard Anderson stepped up the level of food and drinks and in-flight amenities Delta offers. In particular, he sought to overcome the bad connotations associated with the generally sub-par "airplane food." Delta provides "real" food from popular restaurants and bakeries. Therefore, it is now possible to purchase a quality lunch from Gate Gourmet or a favorite sandwich from the Atlanta Bread Company, not to mention the continued availability of kosher and vegetarian meals.

In order to meet the needs of the new technologically savvy business class, Delta has also added e-mail access and hopes to soon have full broadband Internet service. All BusinessElite seats now have a personal telephone and increased console space to serve as a desk. However, if a strict work ethic does not appeal while onboard the fleet's newest member, the Boeing 777, have no fear—television screens at every seat offer a choice of movies and an array of programming.[11] On April 14, 2008, Delta and Northwest airlines announced a $17.7 billion merger that will create the world's largest carrier.

Summary

To collect quantitative primary data, a researcher must design a questionnaire or an observation form. A questionnaire has three objectives. It must (1) translate the information needed into a set of specific questions, (2) motivate respondents to complete the interview, and (3) minimize response error.

Designing a questionnaire is as much an art as it is a science. Development guidelines are available, but no one optimal questionnaire design fits every research need. The process begins by specifying the information needed and the type of interviewing method. The next step is to decide on the content of individual questions.

Questions must be written to overcome the respondents' inability to answer. Respondents might be unable to answer if they are not informed, cannot remember, or cannot articulate the response. When too much effort is required or the research context seems inappropriate, respondents will be unwilling to participate. Questions that attempt to collect sensitive information might also be met with resistance. Questions can be unstructured (open ended) or structured to a varying degree. Structured questions include multiple-choice, dichotomous questions, and scales.

Determining the wording of each question involves defining the issue, using ordinary words, using unambiguous words, and using dual statements. The issue should be clearly defined in terms of *who*, *what*, *when*, and *where*. The *why* and *way* might not always be relevant. The researcher should avoid leading questions. Once the questions have been worded, the order in which they will appear in the questionnaire must be decided. Special consideration should be given to opening questions, type of information, question difficulty, and the effect on subsequent questions. The questions should be arranged in a logical order.

The stage is now set for determining the form and layout of the questions. The physical considerations in reproducing the questionnaire include appearance, use of booklets, fitting the entire question on a page, response category format, avoiding overcrowding, placement of directions, color coding, and cost. The effectiveness of all these design decisions must be assessed in a pretest.

The design of observational forms requires explicit decisions about what is to be observed and how that behavior is to be recorded. It is useful to specify the *who*, *what*, *when*, *where*, *why*, and *way* of the behavior to be observed.

The questionnaire or research instrument should be adapted to the specific cultural environment and should not be biased in terms of any one culture. Several software packages are available to facilitate questionnaire design. Several firms provide software and services for designing computer and Internet-administered questionnaires. In consideration of the respondents, overly long questionnaires or questions that exceed the respondents' willingness or ability to respond should be avoided. The questionnaire should be designed to obtain information in an unbiased manner.

Key Terms and Concepts

Questionnaire,   330
Double-barreled question,   334
Filter questions,   335
Unstructured questions,   338
Structured questions,   339
Order or position bias,   340

Dichotomous question,   340
Leading question,   344
Acquiescence bias,   344
Basic information,   346
Classification information,   346
Identification information,   346

Funnel approach,   347
Branching questions,   348
Precoding,   349
Pretesting,   350

Suggested Cases and Video Cases

Running Case with Real Data

1.1 Hewlett-Packard

Comprehensive Critical Thinking Cases

2.1 American Idol   2.2 Baskin-Robbins   2.3 Akron Children's Hospital

Comprehensive Cases with Real Data

3.1 Bank of America   3.2 McDonald's   3.3 Boeing

Video Cases

11.1 Dunkin' Donuts   12.1 Motorola   13.1 Subaru   14.1 Intel   19.1 Marriott

Live Research: Conducting a Marketing Research Project

1. Each team can develop a questionnaire following the principles discussed in the chapter. The best features of each questionnaire can be combined to develop the project questionnaire.
2. Each team should be assigned a few pretest interviews.
3. If a questionnaire has already been prepared, it should be critically evaluated in the class.
4. The resulting questionnaire should be discussed and approved by the client.

Acronyms

The objectives and steps involved in developing a questionnaire may be defined by the acronym QUESTIONNAIRE:

Objectives
    Q uestions that respondents can answer
    U plift the respondent
    E rror elimination

Steps
    S pecify the information needed
    T ype of interviewing method
    I ndividual question content
    O vercoming inability and unwillingness to answer
    N onstructured versus structured questions
    N onbiased question wording
    A rrange the questions in proper order
    I dentify form and layout
    R eproduction of the questionnaire
    E liminate bugs by pretesting

The guidelines for question wording may be summarized by the acronym WORDS:

W ho, what, when, where, why, and way

O bjective questions: Avoid leading questions

R egularly, normally, usually, etc., should be avoided

D ual statements (positive and negative)

S imple, ordinary words

The guidelines for deciding on the order of questions may be summarized by the acronym ORDER:

O pening questions: simple

R udimentary or basic information should be obtained first

D ifficult questions toward the end

E xamine the influence on subsequent questions

R eview the sequence to ensure a logical order

Review Questions

1. What is the purpose of questionnaires and observation forms?
2. Explain how the mode of administration affects questionnaire design.
3. How would you determine whether a specific question should be included in a questionnaire?
4. What is a double-barreled question?
5. What are the reasons that respondents are unable to answer the question asked?
6. Explain the concepts of aided and unaided recall.
7. What are the reasons that respondents are unwilling to answer specific questions?
8. What can a researcher do to make the request for information seem legitimate?
9. What are the advantages and disadvantages of unstructured questions?
10. What are the issues involved in designing multiple-choice questions?
11. What are the guidelines available for deciding on question wording?
12. What is a leading question? Give an example.
13. What is the proper order for questions intended to obtain basic, classification, and identification information?
14. What guidelines are available for deciding on the form and layout of a questionnaire?
15. Describe the issues involved in pretesting a questionnaire.
16. What are the major decisions involved in designing observational forms?

Applied Problems

1. Develop three double-barreled questions related to flying and passengers' airline preferences. Also, develop corrected versions of each question.
2. List at least 10 ambiguous words that should not be used in framing questions.
3. Do the following questions define the issue? Why or why not?
   a. What is your favorite brand of shampoo?
   b. How often do you go on a vacation?
   c. Do you consume orange juice? 1. Yes 2. No
4. Design an open-ended question to determine whether households engage in gardening. Also, develop a multiple-choice and a dichotomous question to obtain the same information. Which form is the most desirable?
5. Formulate three questions that exceed respondents' ability to answer. Then, reformulate these questions correctly.
6. A new graduate hired by the marketing research department of a major telephone company is asked to prepare a questionnaire to determine household preferences for telephone calling cards. The questionnaire is to be administered in mall-intercept interviews. Using the principles of questionnaire design, critically evaluate this questionnaire.

Household Telephone Calling Card Survey

1. Your name _____

2. Age _____

3. Marital status _____

4. Income _____

5. Which, if any, of the following telephone calling cards do you have?

    1. AT&T _____   2. Verizon _____   3. Sprint Nextel _____   4. Others _____

6. How frequently do you use a telephone calling card?

    Infrequently   Very Frequently

        1   2   3   4   5   6   7

7. What do you think of the telephone calling card offered by AT&T?

    _____

    _____

8. Suppose your household were to select a telephone calling card. Please rate the importance of the following factors in selecting a card.

	Not Important			Very Important	
a. Cost per call	1	2	3	4	5
b. Ease of use	1	2	3	4	5
c. Local and long distance charges included in the same bill	1	2	3	4	5
d. Rebates and discounts on calls	1	2	3	4	5
e. Quality of telephone service	1	2	3	4	5
f. Quality of customer service	1	2	3	4	5

9. How important is it for a telephone company to offer a calling card?

    Not important   Very Important

        1   2   3   4   5   6   7

10. Do you have children living at home? _____

Thank You For Your Help!

---

7. Lenovo would like to conduct an Internet survey to determine the image of Lenovo PCs and the image of its major competitors (e.g., Sony, Dell, and HP). Develop such a questionnaire. Relevant information can be obtained by visiting the Web sites of the following companies: www.lenovo.com, www.sony.com, www.dell.com, and www.hp.com.

8. Using an electronic questionnaire design package, such as Qualtrics (included with this book), design a questionnaire to measure consumer preferences for sneakers. Then, develop the same questionnaire manually. Compare your experiences in designing this questionnaire electronically and manually.

9. Visit the Web site of one of the online marketing research firms (e.g., Greenfield Online Research Center, Inc. at www.greenfieldonline.com). Locate a survey being currently administered at this site. Critically analyze the questionnaire using the principles discussed in this chapter.

Group Discussion

1. "Because questionnaire design is an art, it is useless to follow a rigid set of guidelines. Rather, the process should be left entirely to the creativity and ingenuity of the researcher." Discuss in a small group.

2. In a small group, discuss the role of questionnaire design in minimizing total research error.

3. Discuss the importance of form and layout in questionnaire construction.

Hewlett-Packard Running Case

Review the Hewlett-Packard (HP) case, Case 1.1, and questionnaire given toward the end of the book.

1. Critically evaluate the HP questionnaire using the principles discussed in this chapter.
2. Draft a questionnaire to measure students' preferences for notebook computers.
3. Evaluate the questionnaire you have developed using the principles discussed in this chapter.
4. Develop a revised questionnaire to measure students' preferences for notebook computers.
5. What did you learn in the questionnaire revision process?

Appendix 11A

Global Airline Performance Questionnaire
Part 2 – English – 211

Welcome on Board

Thank you for agreeing to complete this questionnaire.

Your opinion on today's flight performance is *essential,* because it will allow the airline to improve its performance according to your needs.

Please answer Part 2 after you have landed and collected your luggage (if any). Then mail/fax it back to us.

Thank you for your help

Unless stated otherwise, all ratings should be provided using the following scale:

Excellent
Very good
Good
Fair
Poor
Did not notice/use

1. Please rate this flight on the following items. (Please tick.)

Boarding and Departure
1 Efficiency of aircraft boarding
2 Punctuality of flight departure
3 Information given if flight delayed
Overall rating for boarding and departure

Your Comfort and the Cabin Features
4 Space to store carry-on hand luggage
5 Condition of cabin interior
6 Comfort of seat
7 Sleeping comfort
8 Amount of legroom
9 Cleanliness of your seat and table on departure
10 Cleanliness of toilets/lavatories
Overall rating for comfort and cabin features

The Cabin Crew
11 Professional appearance of cabin crew
12 Responsiveness of cabin crew in serving your needs
13 Courtesy/helpfulness of cabin crew
14 Availability of cabin crew throughout the flight
15 Ability to speak your language
16 Information provided by cabin crew and pilots
Overall rating for cabin crew

Food and Beverages
17 Quality of the meal(s) and/or snack(s)
18 Quantity/sufficiency of the meal(s) and/or snack(s)
19 Choice of beverages available on board
Overall rating for food and beverages

Onboard Amenities/Entertainment
20 Choice of newspapers and magazines
21 Telecommunications services (phone, fax, PC port)
22 Choice of movies shown

23 Choice of other video programming
24 Quality of the video system (sound, vision)
25 Choice of audio programming
26 Quality of the audio programs (sound)
Overall rating for onboard amenities/entertainment

2. **After leaving this flight, please rate the following items. (Please tick.)**
27 Punctuality of flight arrival
28 Efficiency of leaving aircraft
29 Speed of luggage delivery
30 Arrival lounge
Overall rating for postflight

3. **From the specific items you have just rated in Sections 1 and 2, could you please indicate which three items (numbered 1–30) are most in need of improvement for this airline:**
The three items in their order of need of improvement:
1 st
2 nd
3 rd

4. **Your overall judgment of today's flight:**
31 Value for money you received from this flight
32 Your overall rating of this airline's performance today, taking everything into account
33 The airline's performance compared with your expectations
Much better
Little better
Much as expected
Little worse
Much worse

5. **Based on your experience of today's flight, would you select this airline for your next trip on this route?**
Definitely would
Probably would
Might/might not
Probably not
Definitely not

6. **Based on your experience of today's flight, how likely would you be to recommend this airline to a friend or colleague?**
Extremely likely
Very likely
Somewhat likely
Not very likely
Not at all likely

7. **Approximately how many of the seats were occupied in your section of the aircraft?**
Up to half full
Half to three-quarters full
Over three-quarters to nearly full
Full
Completely full

8. **In which class did you sit on this flight?**
First
Business
Economy/coach
Special economy (which)

9. Flight Date: DD MM YY Airline:
Flight No.: LETTERS NUMBERS Name: Mr./Ms.:

Dunkin' Donuts

DUNKIN' DONUTS: Dunking the Competition

In 1950, Bill Rosenberg founded the Dunkin' Donuts chain (www.dunkindonuts.com) by opening the first location in Quincy, Massachusetts. By 1975, 1,000 locations nationwide were grossing a collective $300 million in sales. At the beginning of 2008, there were 7,988 Dunkin' Donuts stores worldwide, including 5,769 franchised restaurants in the U.S. and 2,219 internationally. The company clocked worldwide sales of $5.3 billion during fiscal year 2007.

This impressive growth would not have been possible without extensive marketing research and a commitment to quality. Bill Rosenberg began the culture within the company of listening to what the customer wanted and then providing it, and that tradition continues today. Marketing research in the form of focus groups and survey research revealed that customers select a coffee and donut shop based on five factors: accessibility, quality, variety, image, and affordability. The company's business is built around these factors. From research, Dunkin' Donuts found that its customers wanted a coffee and donut shop that was very accessible—close to work or home and easy to get to. To accompany its stand-alone locations, Dunkin' Donuts has opened locations in Home Depot, Wal-Mart, 7–11, and Stop & Shop stores to add to the convenience that customers desire. Every location is strategically placed and designed with these customers' preferences in mind. Because these purchases are so convenience driven, the locations can be placed close together without cannibalizing business.

Marketing research further revealed that quality translates to freshness in the donut business. Therefore, Dunkin' Donuts makes donuts at least four times a day. Upon conducting research with survey questionnaires and taste testing in many different markets, Dunkin' Donuts found the blend of coffee that customers favor the most. This coffee is brewed and then allowed to sit for no longer than 18 minutes. After the 18-minute window, the coffee is poured out, and a fresh pot is brewed. This commitment to quality was made as a result of researching what the customer desired in a cup of coffee.

The company also offers variety—52 flavors of donuts. Recently, Dunkin' Donuts has expanded its coffee line (again, due to research and taste testing) to include iced coffees, cappuccinos, lattes, espressos, and flavored coffees, such as hazelnut coffee.

Marketing research showed that customers preferred an image that related to the common person. They did not want a coffee shop that was flashy with lots of bells and whistles; they just wanted a common shop that made a great cup of coffee. Therefore, Dunkin' Donuts appeals to just about everyone. During the late 1970s and the 1980s, the ad campaign of "Fred the Baker" brought this image to life. With commercials showing him waking up in the middle of the night with a commitment to quality, he appealed to the common person. The Mercedes and the pickup truck come together in an egalitarian Dunkin' Donuts parking lot. In addition, Dunkin' Donuts is affordable. Just about any consumer can afford the Dunkin' Donuts experience. Dunkin' Donuts is much less expensive compared to Starbucks and other upscale coffee shops.

Dunkin' Donuts realizes that first and foremost its donuts and coffee need to be up to par to customers' expectations. Already the retail market leader in donuts and bagels, Dunkin' Donuts knows that it takes a commitment to marketing research to stay there. Bob Pitts, the current Technology Product Developer, demands a continuing commitment to listening to what the customers prefer. Again, this manifests itself through constant research and taste testing. The customer is a very important source of wisdom and insight at Dunkin' and customer opinion and feedback is important. Customers' preferences have not only shaped the recipes of donuts and

bagels, they have also prompted the introduction of the Dunkin' Decaf and flavored coffees such as Hazelnut and French Vanilla. The huge success of these introductions reaffirmed the importance of customers in Dunkin' Donuts and its new products. This journey of innovation has continued with the launch of indulgent coffee drinks, such as cappuccinos, lattes, and espressos. In August 2007, Dunkin' announced a partnership with Procter & Gamble. In this alliance, P&G will roast Dunkin's packaged coffee according to Dunkin's specifications and will be responsible for distribution as well as a national marketing campaign based on the coffee-shop chain's current "America runs on Dunkin'" theme. The initiative helps P&G gain entry into the premium coffee market, and Dunkin' Donuts gets P&G's distribution expertise and a new source of income. The packaged coffee will be available at Kroger, Wal-Mart, and other stores.

Speaking to customers and getting their insights is a crucial part of Dunkin' Donuts' marketing research strategy. The use of focus/consumer groups and market surveys for taste testing and feedback is an ongoing process. With a commanding presence in the market, reliance on marketing research has had obvious positive effects that are sure to continue in the future, and Dunkin' Donuts can continue dunking the competition.

Conclusion

Marketing research has kept Dunkin' Donuts relevant and appealing to people across the world throughout the years. Dunkin's positioning as an everyday, accessible store for everyone has helped it to foster a bond with its customers. This relationship of respect and humility has endured even as Dunkin' has expanded its product portfolio to include more varieties and target newer customers, all without alienating its existing customers. The emphasis that Dunkin' places on using marketing research to make the customers critical stakeholders who provide feedback and insight and help direct the innovation process has reaped rich benefits for Dunkin' Donuts.

Questions

1. Discuss the role that marketing research can play in helping a coffee shop such as Dunkin' Donuts formulate sound marketing strategies.
2. Dunkin' Donuts is considering further expansion in the United States. Define the management-decision problem.
3. Define an appropriate marketing research problem based on the management-decision problem you have identified.
4. Use the Internet to determine the market shares of the major coffee shops for the last calendar year.
5. What type of syndicate data will be useful to Dunkin' Donuts?
6. Discuss the role of qualitative research in helping Dunkin' Donuts expand further in the United States.
7. Dunkin' Donuts has developed a new line of pastries with a distinctive French taste. It would like to determine consumers' response to this new line of pastries before introducing them in the marketplace. If a survey is to be conducted to determine consumer preferences, which survey method should be used and why?
8. Design a taste test comparing Dunkin' Donuts coffees with those offered by Starbucks.
9. Develop a questionnaire for assessing consumer preferences for fast coffee shops.

References

1. www.dunkindonuts.com, accessed January 15, 2008.
2. "Dunkin' Donuts Competes With Coffee Chains with Latte Offerings in Michigan," *Knight Ridder Tribune Business News*, March 19, 2004, p. 1.

CHAPTER 12

twelve

Sampling: Design and Procedures

OPENING QUESTIONS

1. How does a sample differ from a census, and what conditions favor the use of a sample over a census?

2. What steps are involved in the sampling design process?

3. How can sampling techniques be classified, and what is the difference between nonprobability and probability sampling techniques?

4. What are the various nonprobability sampling techniques, and when are they used?

5. What are the various probability sampling techniques, and when are they used?

6. What conditions favor the use of nonprobability sampling versus probability sampling?

7. How should online samples be selected?

8. How are sampling techniques used in international marketing research?

9. How does technology interface with sampling, and what ethical issues relate to the sampling design process?

> "A good sampling design, carefully executed, is a key to obtaining high quality data. Too often this is taken for granted, and the results can be profound."
>
> **David Fruend,**
> *Director and Manager, Market Research,*
> *Progress Energy, Inc.*

Old Spice Red Zone Invisible Solid Spices Growth in the Deodorant Market

After spending millions to develop invisible solid and controlled-release scent technologies, American consumer-products giant Procter & Gamble (www.pg.com) conducted consumer research on the best way to introduce a new antiperspirant/deodorant—Old Spice Red Zone Invisible Solid—based on these technologies. The sampling procedures played a critical role in revealing important findings that guided the development of the new product and its introduction. The company defined the population of interest, the *target population*, as male heads of households. It then developed a questionnaire to measure preferences for solid deodorants versus other forms, such as sprays and roll-ons, and to compare the invisible solid to conventional solids. The questionnaire was administered via computer-assisted telephone interviewing.

Given the large size of the target population and limited time and money, it was clearly not feasible to interview the entire population, that is, to take a *census*. So a sample was taken, and a subgroup of the population was selected for participation in the research. The basic unit sampled was American households, and within the selected households the male heads of households were interviewed. Probability sampling, where each element of the population has a fixed

chance of being selected, was chosen, because the results had to be generalizable to the larger population; that is, projectable to all male heads of U.S. households. Simple random sampling was used to select 1,000 households. This sample size was selected based on qualitative considerations, such as the importance of the decision, nature of the research, statistical analyses that would be required, resource constraints, and the sample sizes used in similar studies P&G had conducted on new-product development. Simple random sampling was selected, because efficient computer programs were available to randomly generate household telephone numbers and to minimize waste due to nonexistent household telephone numbers. An initial call was made to recruit the respondents and to explain the study. Those who qualified and agreed to participate were mailed a sample of the new invisible solid deodorant with instructions to use it for 2 weeks. A follow-up telephone interview was then conducted.

The results indicated that 56 percent of men preferred solid deodorants. Moreover, invisible solids were preferred to conventional solids on a variety of attributes: gliding on without dragging, ease of application, and no white residue on the skin or clothing. Based on these findings, P&G introduced Old Spice Red Zone Invisible Solid. The launch was successful, and Old Spice Red Zone Invisible Solid accelerated the retail value growth of the entire antiperspirant/deodorant market. Sound sampling procedures adopted in this research resulted in clear-cut findings that aided in the development and launch of a successful product. As of 2008, Old Spice Red Zone Invisible Solid was being marketed in the following scents: After Hours, Aqua Reef, Glacial Falls, Pure Sport, and Showtime (www.oldspice.com).[1]

Overview

Sampling design issues are a part of the research design process. By this point in the research process, the researcher has identified the information needs of the study as well as the nature of the research design (exploratory, descriptive, or causal) (Chapters 3 through 8). Furthermore, the researcher has specified the scaling and measurement procedures (Chapters 9 and 10) and has designed the questionnaire (Chapter 11). The next step is to design suitable sampling procedures. Figure 12.1 briefly explains the focus of the chapter, the relation of this chapter to the previous ones, and the steps of the marketing research process on which this chapter concentrates.

Five basic questions are addressed in the sample design phase: (1) Should a sample be taken? (2) If so, what process should be followed? (3) What kind of sample should be taken? (4) How large should it be? (5) What can be done to adjust for incidence—the rate of occurrence of eligible respondents—and completion rates?

This chapter addresses the first three questions of the sample design phase. Chapter 13 addresses the last two questions. The chapter discusses sampling in terms of the qualitative considerations underlying the sampling design process. The question of whether or not to sample is addressed and the steps involved in sampling are described. Next, nonprobability and probability sampling techniques are presented. These issues were introduced in the opening vignette, in which P&G used a probability sampling scheme to select the respondents. Sampling techniques in international marketing research are described. The chapter also discusses the sampling technologies and identifies the relevant ethical issues and Internet applications. Figure 12.2 provides an overview of the topics discussed in this chapter and how they flow from one to the next.

FIGURE 12.1

Relationship of Sampling Design to the Previous Chapters and the Marketing Research Process

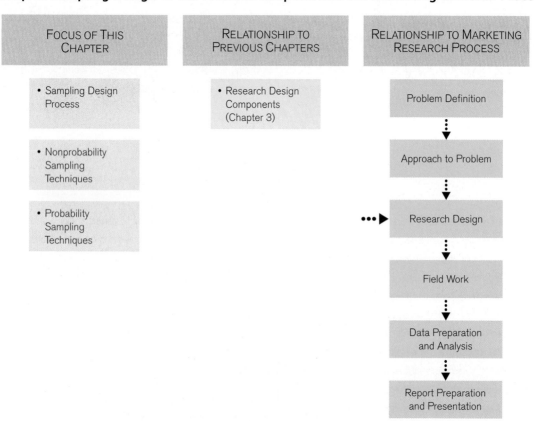

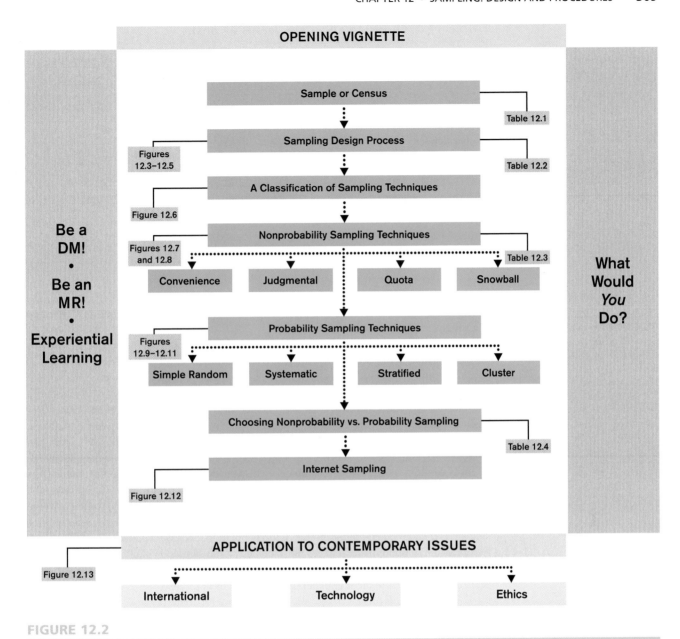

FIGURE 12.2

Sampling Design Procedures: An Overview

Sample or Census

In sampling, an **element** is the object (or person) about which or from which the information is desired. In survey research, the element is usually the respondent. A **population** is the total of all the elements that share some common set of characteristics. Each marketing research project has a uniquely defined population that is described in terms of its parameters. The objective of most marketing research projects is to obtain information about the characteristics or parameters of a population. The proportion of consumers loyal to a particular brand of toothpaste is an example of a population parameter. In the opening vignette, the percentage of male heads of household that preferred a solid deodorant was a population parameter. This parameter was estimated via sampling to be 56 percent. The researcher can obtain information about population parameters by taking either a census or

element
Objects that possess the information the researcher seeks and about which the researcher will make inferences.

population
The aggregate of all the elements, sharing some common set of characteristics, that comprise the universe for the purpose of the marketing research problem.

TABLE 12.1 Choosing a Sample Versus a Census

Factors	Conditions Favoring the Use of	
	Sample	Census
Budget	Small	Large
Time available	Short	Long
Population size	Large	Small
Variance in the characteristic	Small	Large
Cost of sampling error	Low	High
Cost of nonsampling errors	High	Low
Nature of measurement	Destructive	Nondestructive
Attention to individual cases	Yes	No

census
A complete enumeration of the elements of a population or study objects.

sample
A subgroup of the elements of the population selected for participation in the study.

a sample. A **census** involves a complete count of each element in a population. A **sample** is a subgroup of the population.

Table 12.1 summarizes the conditions favoring the use of a sample over a census. The primary considerations favoring a sample are budget and time limits. Conducting a census is costly and time-consuming. In research studies involving large populations, such as nationwide users of consumer products, it is generally not feasible to take a census, as illustrated in the opening vignette. Therefore, a sample is the only viable option. However, business-to-business research involving industrial products typically involves a much smaller population. A census becomes not only possible, but often desirable, in such situations. For example, while investigating the use of certain machine tools by European automobile manufacturers, a census would be preferable to a sample, because the population of automobile manufacturers is small. A census also becomes more attractive when there are large variations in the population. For example, large differences in machine-tool usage from Volkswagen to Volvo would suggest the need for taking a census instead of sampling. In this case, if a sample was taken, it is unlikely to be representative of the population, because the machine-tool usage of European automobile manufacturers not included in the sample is likely to be substantially different than those in the sample. Small populations, which vary widely in terms of the characteristics of interest to the researcher, lend themselves to a census.

The cost of sampling error (e.g., omitting a major manufacturer such as Mercedes Benz from the machine-tool study) must be weighed against nonsampling error (e.g., interviewer errors). In many business-to-business studies, concerns involving sampling error support the use of a census. In most other studies, however, nonsampling errors are found to be the major contributor to total error. Although a census eliminates sampling errors, the resulting nonsampling errors might increase to the point that total error in the study becomes unacceptably high. In these instances, sampling would be favored over a census. In the United States, this is one of the reasons the Bureau of the Census checks the accuracy of its census by conducting sample surveys.[2]

Sampling also is preferable if the measurement process results in the destruction or consumption of the product. In this case, a census would mean that a large quantity of the product would have to be destroyed or consumed, greatly increasing the cost. An example would be product usage tests that result in the consumption of the product, such as a new brand of cereal. Sampling might also be necessary to focus attention on individual cases, as in the case of depth interviews. Finally, other pragmatic considerations, such as the need to keep the study secret (an important consideration for firms such as Coca-Cola), might favor a sample over a census. In the opening vignette, P&G chose sampling over a census, because the size of the population of male heads of households in the United States is too large to make a census feasible, particularly given limited time and money. Also, as is generally the case in consumer research, the cost of sampling errors was small as compared to the cost of nonsampling errors. As explained in Chapter 3, sampling error is the error due to the particular sample selected being an imperfect representation of the population of interest. In contrast, nonsampling errors result from a variety of causes, including errors in problem definition, approach, scales, questionnaire design, survey methods, interviewing techniques, and data preparation and analysis. Evidence shows that in consumer research the cost of sampling error is small compared to the cost of nonsampling errors.

Be an MR!	Be a DM!
Search the Internet, as well as your library's online databases, to determine the population of all airlines operating in the United States. If a survey of airlines is to be conducted to determine their future plans to purchase/lease airplanes, would you take a sample or a census? Explain.	As the CEO of U.S. aircraft manufacturer Boeing, how would you use information about the future plans of airlines to purchase/lease airplanes to formulate your marketing strategy?

The Sampling Design Process

The sampling design process includes five steps, which are shown sequentially in Figure 12.3. Each step is closely related to all aspects of the marketing research project, from problem definition to presentation of the results. Therefore, sample design decisions should be integrated with all other decisions in a research project.

Define the Target Population

Sampling design begins by specifying the target population. The **target population** is the collection of elements or objects that possess the information the researcher is seeking. It is essential that the researcher precisely define the target population if the data generated are to address the marketing research problem. Defining the target population involves translating the research problem into a precise statement of who should and who should not be included in the sample. In the opening vignette, the target population was defined as all male heads of households in the United States.

The target population should be defined in terms of elements, sampling units, extent, and time frame. As stated earlier, an element is the object (or person) about which or from which the information is desired. The respondent is an example. A **sampling unit** might be the element itself, or it might be a more readily available entity containing the element. Suppose that U.S.-based Revlon, a world leader in cosmetics and personal-care products, wanted to assess consumer response in South Africa to a new line of lipsticks and wanted to sample women over 18 years of age. In this study, Revlon's element would be South African women over 18 years of age. It might be possible to sample them directly, in which case the sampling unit will be the same as an element. More typically, Revlon would use a sampling unit such as households, interviewing one woman over age 18 in each selected household. Here, the

target population
The collection of elements or objects that possess the information the researcher seeks and about which the researcher will make inferences.

sampling unit
The basic unit containing the elements of the population to be sampled.

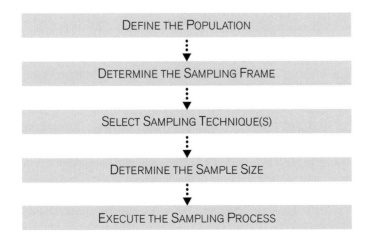

FIGURE 12.3

Sampling Design Process

FIGURE 12.4

Defining the Target Population

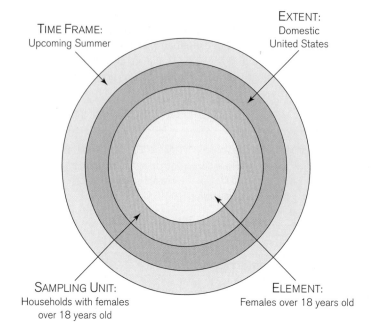

TIME FRAME:
Upcoming Summer

EXTENT:
Domestic
United States

SAMPLING UNIT:
Households with females
over 18 years old

ELEMENT:
Females over 18 years old

sampling unit and the population element are different. As another illustration, in the opening vignette, the element was male head of household, and the sampling unit was a household.

Extent refers to geographical boundaries. In our example, Revlon is interested only in the South African market. The *time frame* is the time period of interest. Revlon may be interested in studying lipstick demand for the upcoming summer market. This target population is defined in Figure 12.4.

Determine the Sampling Frame

sampling frame
A representation of the elements of the target population. It consists of a list or set of directions for identifying the target population.

A **sampling frame** is a representation of the elements of the target population. It consists of a list or set of directions for identifying the target population. A sampling frame can come from the telephone book, a computer program for generating telephone numbers, an association directory listing the firms in an industry, a mailing list purchased from a commercial organization, a city directory, or a map. If a listing is not readily available, it must be compiled. Specific instructions for identifying the target population should be developed, such as procedures for generating random telephone numbers of households mentioned in the opening vignette.

The process of compiling a list of population elements often is difficult and imperfect, leading to sampling frame error. Elements may be omitted, or the list might contain more than the desired population (Figure 12.5). For example, the telephone book often is used as a sampling frame for telephone surveys. However, at least three sources of sampling frame error are present in the telephone book: (1) it does not contain unlisted numbers; (2) it does not contain the telephone numbers of people who have moved into the area after the telephone book was published; and (3) it lists the inactive telephone numbers of people who have moved out of the area since the telephone book was published. Small differences between the sample frame and the population can be ignored. In most cases, however, the researcher should recognize and treat the sampling frame error. The researcher has three options:

1. The population can be redefined in terms of the sampling frame. When the telephone book is used as the sampling frame, the population can be defined as households with a correct listing in the telephone book in a given area. This approach is quite simple and eliminates any misinterpretation of the definition of the population under study.[3]
2. The representativeness of the research frame can be verified during the data collection process. Basic demographic, product familiarity, product usage, and other relevant information can be collected to ensure that the elements of the sampling

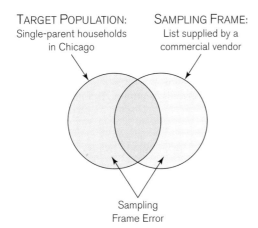

FIGURE 12.5

Sampling Frame Error

frame satisfy the criteria for the target population. Although inappropriate elements can be identified and eliminated from the sample in this way, this procedure does not correct for elements that have been omitted.

3. The data can be statistically adjusted by weighting under- or overrepresented segments to achieve a more representative sample. Although sample frame error can be minimized through this type of adjustment, it assumes the researcher has accurate knowledge of the makeup of the target population.

The researcher can adopt any combination of these adjustments. The important point is to recognize and attempt to eliminate sampling frame error, so that inappropriate population inferences can be avoided.

Select a Sampling Technique

Selecting a sampling technique involves choosing nonprobability or probability sampling (Figure 12.6). **Nonprobability sampling** relies on the personal judgment of the researcher, rather than chance, in selecting sample elements. The researcher might select the sample arbitrarily, based on convenience, or make a conscious decision about which elements to include in the sample. Examples of nonprobability sampling include interviewing people at street corners, in retail stores, or in malls. Although nonprobability sampling produces good estimates of population characteristic, these techniques are limited. It is not possible to objectively evaluate the precision of the sample results. **Precision** refers to the level of uncertainty about the characteristic being measured. Suppose the researcher wanted to determine how much an average Swedish household spends on Christmas shopping and surveyed people in such malls as Stockholm's Sturegallerian. Due to the convenience nature of the sample, there would be no way of knowing how precise the results of this survey are. The greater the precision, the smaller the sampling error. The probability of selecting one element over another is unknown. Therefore, the estimates obtained cannot be projected to the population with any specified level of confidence.

In **probability sampling**, elements are selected by chance, that is, randomly. The probability of selecting each potential sample from a population can be prespecified. Although every potential sample need not have the same probability of selection, it is possible to specify the

nonprobability sampling
Sampling techniques that do not use chance selection procedures, but that instead rely on the researcher's personal judgment and/or convenience.

precision
The level of uncertainty about the characteristic being measured. Greater precision implies smaller sampling error.

probability sampling
A sampling procedure in which each element of the population has a fixed probabilistic chance of being selected for the sample.

FIGURE 12.6

Classification of Sampling Techniques

SAMPLING
TECHNIQUES

Nonprobability
Sampling
Techniques

Probability
Sampling
Techniques

probability of selecting a particular sample of a given size. Confidence intervals can be calculated around the sample estimates, and it is meaningful to statistically project the sample results to the population; that is, to draw inferences about the target population. Because projectability of the sample results to the population of all male heads of households was important, P&G used probability rather than nonprobability sampling in the opening vignette. We will discuss the various nonprobability and probability sampling techniques later in this chapter.

Determine the Sample Size

sample size

The number of elements to be included in a study.

Sample size refers to the number of elements to be included in the study. Determining the sample size involves both qualitative and quantitative considerations. The qualitative factors are discussed in this section; the quantitative factors are discussed in Chapter 13. Important qualitative factors that the researcher should consider in determining the sample size are (1) the importance of the decision, (2) the nature of the research, (3) the number of variables, (4) the nature of the analysis, (5) sample sizes used in similar studies, and (6) resource constraints.

As a general rule, the more important the decision, the more precise the information must be. This implies the need for larger samples. The need for greater precision must be weighed against the increase in cost that comes with the collection of information from each additional element.

The nature of the research also has an impact on the sample size. Exploratory research, such as a focus group, employs qualitative techniques that are typically based on small samples. Conclusive research, such as a descriptive survey, requires large samples. As the number of variables in a study increases, the sample size must grow accordingly. For example, problem identification surveys that measure a large number of variables typically require large samples of 1,000 to 2,500 (Table 12.2).

The type of analysis planned also influences the sample size requirements. Sophisticated analysis of the data using advanced techniques or analysis at the subgroup rather than the total population level requires larger samples, as in the case of P&G in the opening vignette.

Prior studies can serve as a guide for estimating sample sizes. Table 12.2 gives an idea of sample sizes used in different marketing research studies. These sample sizes have been determined based on experience and can serve as rough guidelines, particularly when nonprobability sampling techniques are used, but they should be applied with caution. Finally, the sample-size decisions are guided by money, personnel, and time limitations. In any marketing research project, resources are limited, in turn limiting the sample size. In the opening vignette, the sample size of 1,000 was based on the following considerations: P&G would use the results to make an important decision involving the introduction of invisible solid deodorants; quantitative analysis would be conducted; and this sample size had been adequate in similar studies conducted by P&G in the past.

TABLE 12.2 **Sample Sizes Used in Marketing Research Studies**

Type of Study	Minimum Size	Typical Range
Problem-identification research (e.g., market potential)	500	1,000–2,500
Problem-solving research (e.g., pricing)	200	300–500
Product tests	200	300–500
Test-marketing studies	200	300–500
TV/radio/print advertising (per commercial or ad tested)	150	200–300
Test-market audits	10 stores	10–20 stores
Focus groups	2 groups	10–15 groups

Execute the Sampling Process

Execution of the sampling process refers to implementing the various details of the sample design. The population is defined, the sampling frame is compiled, and the sampling units are drawn using the appropriate sampling technique needed to achieve the required sample size. If households are the sampling unit, an operational definition of a household is needed. Procedures should be specified for vacant housing units and for call-backs in case no one is home.

Sometimes it is necessary to qualify the potential respondents to make sure they belong to the target population. In such a case, the criteria used to qualify the respondents should be specified, and the qualifying questions should be asked at the beginning of the interview (see Chapter 11). In a survey of heavy users of online services at home, a criterion for identifying heavy users is needed (e.g., those using online services for more than 30 hours per week at home). Detailed information must be provided for all sampling design decisions. This is illustrated by a survey done in the United States for the State of Florida Department of Tourism.

Research in Action

Tourism Department Telephones Birthday Boys and Girls

A telephone survey was conducted for the Florida Department of Tourism related to the travel behavior of in-state residents. The sampling unit was the household. Probability sampling was used. Data were collected using a stratified random sample from three regions: north, central, and south Florida. To participate in the study, respondents had to meet the following qualifying criteria:

- Age 25 years or older
- Live in Florida at least 7 months of the year
- Have lived in Florida for at least 2 years
- Have a Florida driver's license

All household members meeting these four qualifications were eligible to participate in the study. The person with the next birthday in the household was selected. Repeated call-backs were made to reach that person. The following are the components of the sampling design process:

1. Target population: Adults meeting the four qualifications (element) in a household with a working telephone number (sampling unit) in the state of Florida (extent) during the survey period (time)

2. Sampling frame: Computer program for generating random telephone numbers

3. Sampling technique: Probability sampling

4. Sample size: 868

5. Execution: Allocate the sample among the north, central, and southern strata. Use the probability sampling technique of computerized random-digit dialing. List all members in the household who meet the four qualifications. Select one member of the household using the next-birthday method.[4]

Experiential Learning

The New York Yankees is one of America's favorite baseball teams.

1. As the marketing manager of the N.Y. Yankees, what marketing programs will you design to target families?

2. Search the Internet, as well as your library's online databases, to obtain information that will assist the marketing manager of the N.Y. Yankees to target families.

3. The N.Y. Yankees want to conduct a telephone survey to determine how to attract more families to the Yankees' games. Design the sampling process.

A Classification of Sampling Techniques

Sampling techniques can be broadly classified as nonprobability or probability (Figure 12.6). Commonly used nonprobability sampling techniques include convenience sampling, judgmental sampling, quota sampling, and snowball sampling (Figure 12.7). The important probability sampling techniques are simple random sampling, systematic sampling, stratified sampling, and cluster sampling.

FIGURE 12.7

Nonprobability Sampling Techniques

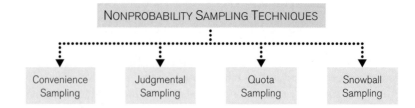

Nonprobability Sampling Techniques

Figure 12.8 presents a graphical illustration of the various nonprobability sampling techniques. The population consists of 25 elements; a sample size of 5 is needed. A, B, C, D, and E represent groups and can also be viewed as strata or clusters.

FIGURE 12.8

A Graphical Illustration of Nonprobability Sampling Techniques

1. CONVENIENCE SAMPLING

A	B	C	D	E
1	6	11	**16**	21
2	7	12	**17**	22
3	8	13	**18**	23
4	9	14	**19**	24
5	10	15	**20**	25

Group D happens to assemble at a convenient time and place. So all the elements in this group are selected. The resulting sample consists of elements 16, 17, 18, 19, and 20.
NOTE: No elements are selected from groups A, B, C, and E.

2. JUDGMENTAL SAMPLING

A	B	C	D	E
1	6	**11**	16	21
2	7	12	17	22
3	**8**	**13**	18	23
4	9	14	19	**24**
5	**10**	15	20	25

The researcher considers groups B, C, and E to be typical and convenient. Within each of these groups one or two elements are selected based on typicality and convenience. The resulting sample consists of elements 8, 10, 11, 13, and 24.
NOTE: No elements are selected from groups A and D.

3. QUOTA SAMPLING

A	B	C	D	E
1	**6**	11	16	21
2	7	12	17	**22**
3	8	**13**	18	23
4	9	14	19	24
5	10	15	**20**	25

A quota of one element from each group, A to E, is imposed. Within each group, one element is selected based on judgment or convenience. The resulting sample consists of elements 3, 6, 13, 20, and 22.
NOTE: One element is selected from each column or group.

4. SNOWBALL SAMPLING

RANDOM SELECTION   REFERRALS

A	B	C	D	E
1	6	11	16	21
2	7	**12**	17	22
3	8	**13**	**18**	23
4	**9**	14	19	24
5	10	15	20	25

Elements 2 and 9 are selected randomly from groups A and B. Element 2 refers to elements 12 and 13. Element 9 refers to element 18. The resulting sample consists of elements 2, 9, 12, 13, and 18.
NOTE: No element is from group E.

Convenience Sampling

Convenience sampling, as the name implies, involves obtaining a sample of elements based on the convenience of the researcher. The selection of sampling units is left primarily to the interviewer. Respondents often are selected because they happen to be in the right place at the right time. Examples of convenience sampling are (1) use of students, church groups, and members of social organizations; (2) mall-intercept interviews conducted without qualifying the respondents; (3) department stores using charge account lists, (4) tear-out questionnaires included in a magazine; (5) "people on the street" interviews; and (6) Internet browsers.

> **convenience sampling**
> A nonprobability sampling technique that attempts to obtain a sample of convenient elements. The selection of sampling units is left primarily to the interviewer.

Convenience sampling has the advantages of being both inexpensive and fast. Additionally, the sampling units tend to be accessible, easy to measure, and cooperative. Despite these advantages, this form of sampling has serious limitations. Primary among them is that the resulting sample is not representative of any definable target population. This sampling process suffers from selection bias, which means the individuals who participate in a convenience sample might have characteristics that are systematically different than the characteristics that define the target population. Because of these limitations, it is not theoretically meaningful to generalize to any population from a convenience sample.

Convenience samples are not appropriate for descriptive or causal research where the aim is to draw population inferences. Convenience samples are useful, however, in exploratory research where the objective is to generate ideas, gain insights, or develop hypotheses. They can be used for focus groups, pretesting questionnaires, or pilot studies. Even in these cases, caution should be exercised in interpreting the results. Despite these limitations, this technique is sometimes used even in large surveys, as in the example that follows.

Research in Action

Starbucks Bucks Up on Ice Cream

When U.S.-based Starbucks, the world's number-one coffee retailer, wanted to assess the brand equity behind its name in order to consider possible line extensions, researchers used convenience sampling to select a group of people patronizing its various coffee shops and retail outlets. Using convenience sampling in this manner was justified because the core market for the line extensions would consist of existing Starbucks customers.

A survey was administered that obtained information on the respondents' preference and loyalty for Starbucks coffee and for other products they would like to see branded with the Starbucks name. Results of this survey revealed a tremendous potential to extend the Starbucks name to ice creams. Accordingly, Starbucks leveraged the strong equity of its coffee and loyal customer base to create a line of ice cream based on its coffee. The product is a rich, creamy ice cream that delivers on the intense flavor of Starbucks coffee. According to Information Resources, Inc., data, it became the nation's number-one brand of coffee ice cream 3 months after it was introduced. As of 2008, Starbucks was selling seven coffee and noncoffee flavors of ice cream: Java Chip, Mud Pie, Coffee Almond Fudge, Coffee Fudge Brownie, Low-Fat Latte, Classic Coffee, and Caramel Cappuccino Swirl.[5]

Judgmental Sampling

Judgmental sampling is a form of convenience sampling in which the population elements are selected based on the researcher's judgment. The researcher chooses the sampling elements because she or he believes they represent the population of interest. Common examples of judgmental sampling include (1) test markets selected to determine the potential of a new product; (2) purchase engineers selected in industrial marketing

> **judgmental sampling**
> A form of convenience sampling in which the population elements are purposively selected based on the judgment of the researcher.

research, because they are considered to be representative of the company; (3) bellwether precincts selected in voting-behavior research; (4) expert witnesses used in court; and (5) department stores selected to test a new merchandising display system.

Judgment sampling has appeal because it is low cost, convenient, and quick. It is subjective, however, relying largely on the expertise and creativity of the researcher. Therefore, generalizations to a specific population cannot be made, usually because the population is not defined explicitly. This sampling technique is most appropriate in research when broad population generalizations are not required. For example, Frito-Lay, a U.S. division of PepsiCo that specializes in snackfoods, test-marketed its WOW line of Ruffles, Lays, and Doritos chips, all made with Olestra, in the midwestern city of Indianapolis. Indianapolis was selected because the researcher felt it would provide a good general indicator of initial response to the new line. Note that Frito-Lay was only looking to evaluate the initial response to WOW, not to make projections of how much WOW would sell nationally.

An extension of judgment sampling involves the use of quotas.

Quota Sampling

quota sampling

A nonprobability sampling technique that is a two-stage restricted judgmental sampling. The first stage consists of developing control categories or quotas of population elements. In the second stage, sample elements are selected based on convenience or judgment.

Quota sampling introduces two stages to the judgmental sampling process. The first stage consists of developing control categories, or *quotas*, of population elements. Using judgment to identify relevant categories such as age, sex, or race, the researcher estimates the distribution of these characteristics in the target population. For example, white women aged 18 to 35 years might be considered the relevant control category for a study involving cosmetic purchases. The researcher would then estimate the proportion of the target population falling into this category based on past experience or secondary information sources. Sampling would then be done to ensure that the proportion of white women aged 18 to 35 years in the target population would be reflected in the sample. Quotas are used to ensure that the composition of the sample is the same as the composition of the population with respect to the characteristics of interest.

Once the quotas have been assigned, the second stage of the sampling process takes place. Elements are selected using a convenience or judgment process. Considerable freedom exists in selecting the elements to be included in the sample. The only requirement is that the elements that are selected fit the control characteristics. This technique is illustrated in the following example.

Research in Action

How "Metro" is *Metropolitan Home* Magazine's Readership?

A readership study was conducted for the American magazine *Metropolitan Home* using a quota sample. One thousand adults living in a metropolitan area of 500,000 people were selected. Age, sex, and race were used to define the makeup of the sample. Based on the composition of the adult population in that community, the quotas were assigned as follows:

Control Characteristic	Population Composition Percentage	Sample Composition Percentage	Number
Sex			
Male	48	48	480
Female	52	52	520
	100	100	1,000
Age (years)			
18–30	27	27	270
31–45	39	39	390
45–60	16	16	160
Over 60	18	18	180
	100	100	1,000

Race

White	59	59	590
Black	35	35	350
Other	6	6	60
	100	100	1,000

By imposing quotas proportionate to the population distribution, the researcher was able to select a sample that reflected the composition of the metropolitan area in terms of sex, age and race.

In the preceding example, proportionate quotas were assigned so that the composition of the population in the community was reflected in the sample. In certain situations, however, it is desirable either to under- or oversample elements with certain characteristics. For example, heavy users of a product might be oversampled in order to examine their behavior in greater detail. Although this type of sample is not representative, it might nevertheless be quite relevant.

A number of potential problems are associated with this sampling technique. Relevant characteristics might be overlooked in the quota-setting process, resulting in a sample that does not mirror the population on relevant control characteristics. Because the elements within each quota are selected based on convenience or judgment, many sources of selection bias are potentially present. Interviewers might be tempted to select areas where they believe they will have success in soliciting participants. They might avoid people who look unfriendly, who are not well dressed, or who live in undesirable locations. Quota sampling also is limited in that it does not permit assessment of sampling error.

Quota sampling attempts to obtain representative samples at a relatively low cost. Quota samples are also relatively convenient to draw. With adequate controls, quota sampling obtains results close to those for conventional probability sampling.

Snowball Sampling

In **snowball sampling**, an initial group of respondents is selected, usually at random. After being interviewed, these respondents are asked to identify others who belong to the target population of interest. This process is continued, resulting in a snowball effect, as one referral is obtained from another. Thus, the referral process effectively produces the sampling frame from which respondents are selected. Although this sampling technique begins with a probability sample, it results in a nonprobability sample. This is because referred respondents tend to have demographic and psychographic characteristics that are more similar to the person referring them than would occur by chance.

Snowball sampling is used when studying characteristics that are relatively rare or difficult to identify in the population. For example, the names of users of some government or social services, such as food stamps, are kept confidential. Groups with special characteristics such as widowed men under 35 years old or members of a scattered minority population might be impossible to locate without referrals. In industrial research, snowball sampling is used to identify buyer–seller pairs.

The major advantage of snowball sampling is that it substantially increases the likelihood of locating the desired characteristic in the population. It also results in relatively low sampling variance and costs. Snowball sampling is illustrated by the following example.

snowball sampling
A nonprobability sampling technique in which an initial group of respondents is selected randomly. Subsequent respondents are selected based on the referrals or information provided by the initial respondents. This process may be carried out in waves by obtaining referrals from referrals.

Research in Action

Survey Snowball

To study the demographic profile of marketing research interviewers in the midwestern U.S. state of Ohio, a sample of interviewers was generated using a variation of snowball sampling. Interviewers were initially contacted by placing classified advertisements in the newspapers of seven major metropolitan areas. These notices asked experienced marketing research interviewers willing to answer 25 questions about their job to write to the author. These responses were increased through a referral system. Each responding interviewer was asked for the names and addresses of other interviewers. Eventually, this process identified interviewers from many communities throughout the state who had not seen the original newspaper notices. Only 27 percent of returned questionnaires resulted from the classified notices; the remainder could be traced to referrals and to referrals from referrals.[6]

In this example, the initial groups of respondents were contacted using a nonrandom selection technique, through classified advertisements. In this instance, the procedure was more efficient than random selection. In other cases, random selection of respondents through probability sampling techniques is more appropriate.

Be a DM!

As the vice president of marketing for Polo Ralph Lauren, the American clothier with more than 10,000 worldwide locations, what information would you need to determine whether the company should launch a new line of unisex shirts in the United States?

Be an MR!

Visit www.polo.com and search the Internet, as well as your library's online databases, to obtain information on Polo Ralph Lauren's marketing strategy. Polo Ralph Lauren would like to determine initial consumer reaction to a new line of unisex shirts it has developed. If nonprobability sampling is to be used, which sampling technique would you recommend and why?

Probability Sampling Techniques

The probability sampling techniques consist of simple random, systematic, stratified, and cluster sampling (Figure 12.9). Probability sampling techniques vary in terms of sampling efficiency. *Sampling efficiency* is a concept that reflects a trade-off between sampling cost and precision. Costs increase with improved precision. The trade-off comes into play as researchers balance the need for greater precision with higher sampling costs. The efficiency of a probability sampling technique can be assessed by comparing it to that of simple random sampling. Figure 12.10 presents a graphical illustration of the various probability sampling techniques. As in the case of nonprobability sampling, the population consists of 25 elements, and a sample size of 5 must be selected. A, B, C, D, and E represent groups and can also be viewed as strata or clusters.

Simple Random Sampling

simple random sampling
A probability sampling technique in which each element in the population has a known and equal probability of selection. Every element is selected independently of every other element, and the sample is drawn by a random procedure from a sampling frame.

In **simple random sampling** (SRS), each element in the population has a known and equal probability of selection. Furthermore, each possible sample of a given size *(n)* has a known and equal probability of being the sample actually selected. The implication in a random sampling procedure is that each element is selected independently of every other element. Placing the names in a container, shaking the container, and selecting the names in a lottery-style drawing is an example of a random sampling procedure. To draw a simple random sample, the research frame is compiled by assigning each element a unique

FIGURE 12.9

Probability Sampling Techniques

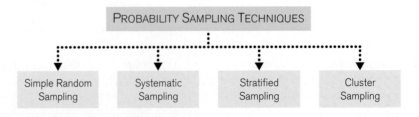

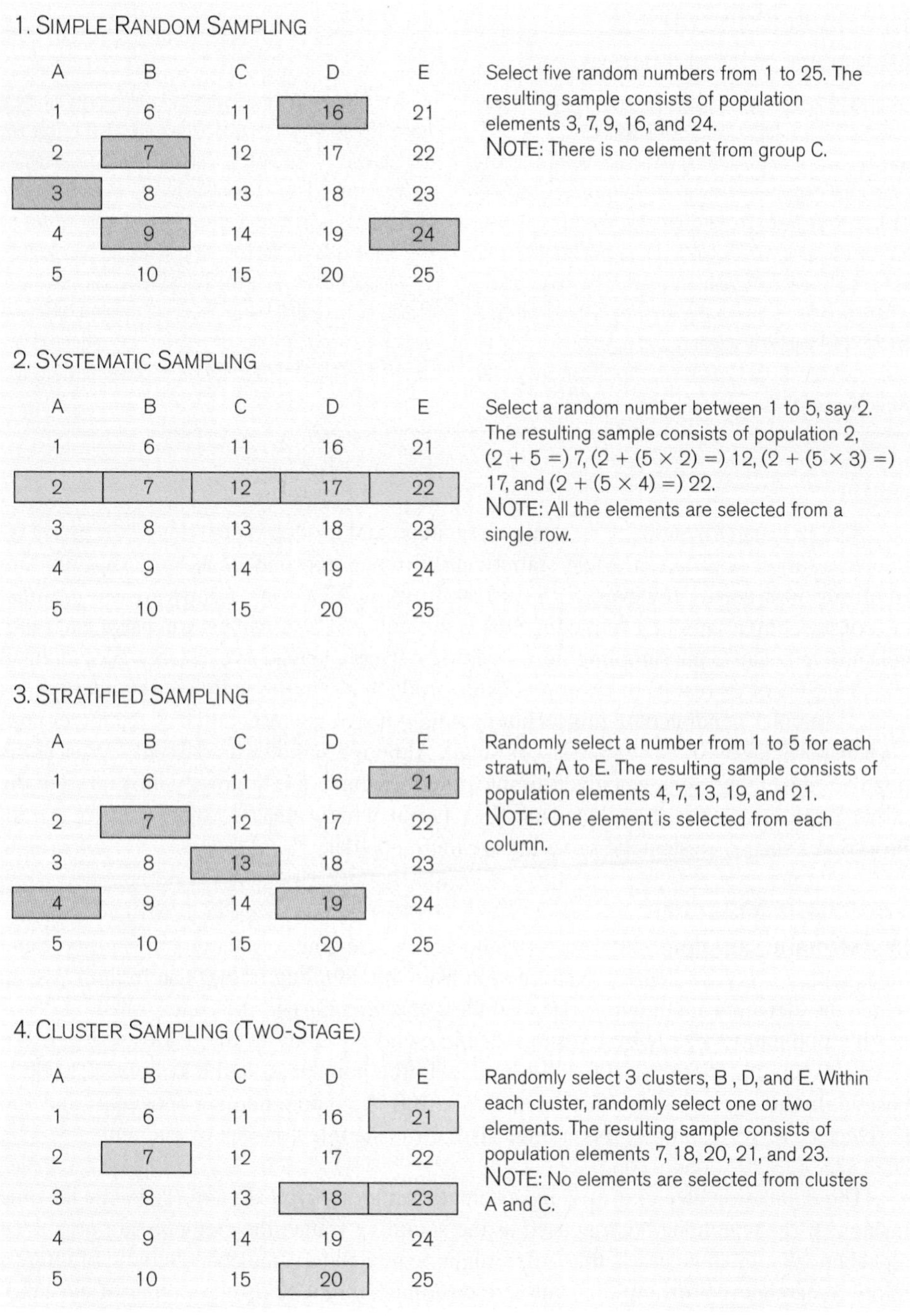

FIGURE 12.10

A Graphical Illustration of Probability Sampling Techniques

1. SIMPLE RANDOM SAMPLING

A	B	C	D	E
1	6	11	16	21
2	7	12	17	22
3	8	13	18	23
4	9	14	19	24
5	10	15	20	25

Select five random numbers from 1 to 25. The resulting sample consists of population elements 3, 7, 9, 16, and 24.
NOTE: There is no element from group C.

2. SYSTEMATIC SAMPLING

A	B	C	D	E
1	6	11	16	21
2	7	12	17	22
3	8	13	18	23
4	9	14	19	24
5	10	15	20	25

Select a random number between 1 to 5, say 2. The resulting sample consists of population 2, $(2 + 5 =)$ 7, $(2 + (5 \times 2) =)$ 12, $(2 + (5 \times 3) =)$ 17, and $(2 + (5 \times 4) =)$ 22.
NOTE: All the elements are selected from a single row.

3. STRATIFIED SAMPLING

A	B	C	D	E
1	6	11	16	21
2	7	12	17	22
3	8	13	18	23
4	9	14	19	24
5	10	15	20	25

Randomly select a number from 1 to 5 for each stratum, A to E. The resulting sample consists of population elements 4, 7, 13, 19, and 21.
NOTE: One element is selected from each column.

4. CLUSTER SAMPLING (TWO-STAGE)

A	B	C	D	E
1	6	11	16	21
2	7	12	17	22
3	8	13	18	23
4	9	14	19	24
5	10	15	20	25

Randomly select 3 clusters, B, D, and E. Within each cluster, randomly select one or two elements. The resulting sample consists of population elements 7, 18, 20, 21, and 23.
NOTE: No elements are selected from clusters A and C.

identification number. Random numbers, generated using a computer routine or random number table (see Table 1 in the Appendix of Statistical Tables), are then used to determine which element to select.

In telephone surveys, the random-digit-dialing (RDD) technique often is used to generate a random sample of telephone numbers. RDD consists of randomly selecting all 10 digits of a telephone number (area code, prefix or exchange, suffix). Although this approach gives all households with telephones an approximately equal chance of being included in the sample, not all the numbers generated in this way are working telephone numbers. Several modifications have been proposed to identify and eliminate the non-working numbers. This makes the use of SRS in telephone surveys quite attractive, as illustrated in the case of P&G in the opening vignette and the following example.

Research in Action

GM Refocuses on Hybrid Technology

Lagging behind the global industry leader in hybrid technology (Toyota), American carmaker General Motors (GM, www.gm.com) funded a study examining consumers' preferences and thoughts about energy-efficient cars. The poll was conducted by Peter D. Hart Research Associates (www.hartresearch.com), a leading U.S. survey-research firm, and was carried out as a telephone survey of 1,004 adults nationwide. The respondents were selected using RDD software. The use of RDD resulted in a sample that was representative of automobile buyers. The study was conducted from June 17 to 20, 2006, and had a margin of error of 3.1 percent.

The survey found that Toyota had a 65 percent favorable rating; Honda, 64 percent; GM, 60 percent; Ford, 56 percent; and Chrysler, 47 percent. In addition, among top priorities for automakers, 36 percent of respondents wanted them to improve gas mileage and safety features, and 32 percent urged the industry to find alternatives to gas engines. Encouraged by these findings, GM introduced four new hybrid models by the end of 2007: the two-mode gas-electric systems in the Chevrolet Tahoe and GMC Yukon large sport utility vehicles and hybrid systems for the Saturn Aura and new Chevrolet Malibu sedans.[7]

SRS has many benefits. It is easily understood and produces data that are representative of a target population. Most statistical inference approaches assume that random sampling was used. However, SRS suffers from at least four significant limitations: (1) constructing a sampling frame for SRS is difficult; (2) SRS can be expensive and time-consuming because the sampling frame might be widely spread over a large geographical area; (3) SRS often results in lower precision, producing samples with large standard error; and (4) samples generated by this technique might not be representative of the target population, particularly if the sample size is small. Although samples drawn will represent the population well on average, a given simple random sample might grossly misrepresent the target population. For these reasons, SRS is not widely used in marketing research. Procedures such as systematic sampling are more popular.

Systematic Sampling

systematic sampling
A probability sampling technique in which the sample is chosen by selecting a random starting point and then picking every *i*th element in succession from the sampling frame.

In **systematic sampling**, the sample is chosen by selecting a random starting point and then picking every *i*th element in succession from the sampling frame. The frequency with which the elements are drawn, *i*, is called the *sampling interval*. It is determined by dividing the population size *N* by the sample size *n* and rounding to the nearest integer. For example, suppose there are 100,000 elements in the population and a sample of 1,000 is desired. In this case, the sampling interval, *i*, is 100. A random number between 1 and 100 is selected. If, for example, this number is 23, the sample consists of elements 23, 123, 223, 323, 423, 523, and so on.[8]

The population elements used in systematic sampling typically are organized in some fashion. If the telephone book is used as the sampling frame, the elements are organized alphabetically. In some cases, this order might be related to some characteristic of interest to the researcher. For example, credit-card customers might be listed in order of outstanding balance or firms in a given industry might be ordered according to annual sales. When the population elements are organized in a manner related to the characteristics under study, systematic sampling can produce results quite different from SRS. Systematic sampling from a list of industrial firms, organized in increasing order by sales, will produce a sample that includes small and large firms. In comparison, a simple random sample might be less representative; For example, only small firms or a disproportionate number of small firms might be drawn in SRS.

Sampling frames that are organized in a cyclical pattern tend to be less representative when systematic sampling is used. To illustrate, consider the use of systematic sampling to generate a sample of monthly department-store sales from a sampling frame containing monthly sales for the last 60 years. If a sampling interval of 12 is chosen, the resulting sample would not reflect the month-to-month variation in sales.

Systematic sampling is less costly and easier than SRS because random selection is done only once. Systematic sampling can also be applied without knowledge of the makeup of the sampling frame. For example, every *i*th person leaving a department store or mall can be intercepted. For these reasons, systematic sampling often is employed in consumer mail, telephone, and mall-intercept interviews, as illustrated by the following example.

Research in Action

Tennis Magazine's Systematic Sampling Returns a Smash

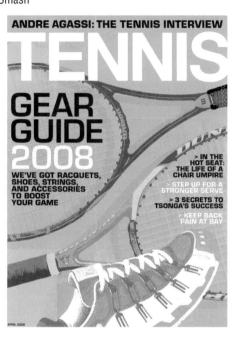

Tennis magazine conducted a mail survey of its subscribers to gain a better understanding of its market. A systematic sample was drawn from the subscription list to produce a sample of 1,472 American subscribers. The list was ordered according to the duration of subscription to ensure that recent as well as long-time subscribers would be included. If we assume that the subscriber list had 1,472,000 names, the sampling interval would be 1,000 (1,472,000/1,472). A starting point was selected between 1 and 1,000. Suppose this was 589. The sample would then be collected by selecting every 1,000th subscriber, that is, subscribers numbered 589, 1589, 2589, 3589, and so on. Systematic sampling was chosen because a convenient sampling frame was available and this procedure is easier to implement than SRS.

An incentive in the form of a brand-new dollar bill was included in the mail survey to boost participation in the study. The respondents were sent an alert postcard a week before the survey. A second, follow-up questionnaire was sent to the entire sample 10 days after the initial questionnaire. Of the 1,472 questionnaires mailed, 76 were returned with no forwarding address, so the net effective mailing was 1,396. Six weeks after the first mailing, 778 completed questionnaires were returned, yielding a response rate of 56 percent.[9]

Be an MR!

Visit www.fortune.com and find the list of *Fortune* 500 companies. A systematic random sample of 25 firms is to be selected from the list of *Fortune* 500 firms, numbered from 1 to 500. Determine the sampling interval, and specify the firms that should be selected.

Be a DM!

As the marketing director for American computer maker Dell, how would you target the *Fortune* 500 companies for computers, servers, and storage and networking equipment?

Stratified Sampling

Stratified sampling involves a two-step sampling process, producing a probability rather than a convenience or judgment sample. First, the population is divided into subgroups called *strata*. Every population element should be assigned to one and only one stratum, and no population elements should be omitted. Second, elements are then randomly selected from each stratum. Ideally, SRS should be used to select elements from each stratum. In practice, however, systematic sampling and other probability sampling procedures can be used.

A major objective of stratified sampling is to increase precision without increasing cost. The population is partitioned using stratification variables. The strata are formed based on four criteria: homogeneity, heterogeneity, relatedness, and cost. The following guidelines should be observed:

- Elements within strata must be similar or homogeneous.
- Elements between strata must differ or be heterogeneous.
- The stratification variables must be related to the characteristic of interest.

stratified sampling
A probability sampling technique that uses a two-step process to partition the population into subpopulations, or strata. Elements are selected from each stratum by a random procedure.

■ The number of strata usually varies between two and six. Beyond six strata, any gain in precision is more than offset by the increased costs.

Stratification offers two advantages. Sampling variation is reduced when the research follows these listed criteria. Sampling costs can also be reduced when the stratification variables are selected in a way that is easy to measure and apply. Variables commonly used for stratification include demographic characteristics (as illustrated in the example for quota sampling), type of customer (credit-card versus non–credit-card customer), size of firm, or type of industry. Stratified sampling improves the precision of SRS. Therefore, it is a popular sampling technique, as illustrated in the BMW 5 Series survey.

Research in Action

Stratifying the Success of BMW 5 Series

Extensive marketing research went into the design of the BMW 5 Series models (www.bmwusa.com). When a survey of American luxury car buyers was conducted to project preferences for specific luxury car features, stratified random sampling was used. This procedure was selected because it includes all the important subpopulations and results in good precision. The variables chosen for stratification were age and income, variables known to correlate with the purchase of luxury cars. The results indicated that luxury car buyers put a premium on performance, handling, engineering, and, of course, luxury.

Based on this feedback, the new 5 Series advanced the concept of a four-door sedan that embodies performance, easy handling, active and passive safety engineering, and luxury. In the U.S. models, the engine was larger, delivering greater torque for more effortless performance. For the first time, automatic climate control was standard in 5 Series models offered in the United States. Extensive innovations and new features were incorporated into virtually every part of the

vehicle (e.g., Dynamic Stability Control and Dynamic Brake Control). The results? The models were a roaring success. As of 2008, German-based BMW was marketing the new 5 Series with an extended line consisting of the 528i Sedan, the 528xi Sedan, the 535i Sedan, the 535xi Sedan, the 550i Sedan, and the 535xi Sports Wagon (www.bmwusa.com).[10]

cluster sampling
A two-step probability sampling technique. First, the target population is divided into mutually exclusive and collectively exhaustive subpopulations called clusters. Then, a random sample of clusters is selected based on a probability sampling technique, such as simple random sampling. For each selected cluster, either all the elements are included in the sample or a sample of elements is drawn probabilistically.

area sampling
A common form of cluster sampling in which the clusters consist of geographic areas, such as counties, housing tracts, blocks, and so forth.

Cluster Sampling

In **cluster sampling**, the target population is first divided into mutually exclusive and collectively exhaustive subpopulations, or *clusters*. Then a random sample of clusters is selected based on a probability sampling technique, such as SRS. For each selected cluster, either all the elements are included in the sample or a sample of elements is drawn probabilistically. If all the elements in each selected cluster are included in the sample, the procedure is called *one-stage cluster sampling*. If a sample of elements is drawn probabilistically from each selected cluster, the procedure is *two-stage cluster sampling* (Figure 12.11). Cluster sampling increases sampling efficiency by decreasing cost.

A number of key differences between cluster and stratified sampling are summarized in Table 12.3.

One common form of cluster sampling is area sampling. **Area sampling** relies on clustering based on geographic areas, such as counties, housing tracts, or blocks. Sampling can be achieved using either one or more stages. *Single-stage area sampling* involves sampling all the elements within a particular cluster. For example, if city blocks were used as the clusters, then all the households within the selected blocks would be included within a single-stage sample. In the case of *two-stage area sampling*, only a portion of the households within each block would be sampled.

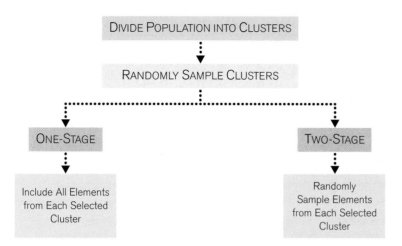

FIGURE 12.11

Types of Cluster Sampling

Cluster sampling has two major advantages: feasibility and low cost. Because sampling frames often are available in terms of clusters rather than population elements, cluster sampling might be the only feasible approach. Given the resources and constraints of the research project, it might be extremely expensive, and perhaps infeasible, to compile a list of all consumers in a population. Lists of geographical areas, telephone exchanges, and other clusters of consumers can be constructed relatively easily. Cluster sampling is the most cost-effective probability sampling technique. This advantage must be weighed against several limitations. Cluster sampling produces imprecise samples in which distinct, heterogeneous clusters are difficult to form. In the United States, for example, households in a neighborhood tend to be similar rather than dissimilar. It can be difficult to compute and interpret statistics based on clusters. The strengths and weaknesses of cluster sampling and the other basic sampling techniques are summarized in Table 12.4.

Be a DM!

As the marketing chief of Herbal Essences, a brand of hair-care products marketed by P&G, how would you determine which new shampoos should be introduced into the market?

Be an MR!

Search the Internet, as well as your library's online databases, to determine the size of the shampoo market in the United States. Herbal Essences would like to determine the demand for a new shampoo. If a survey is to be conducted using probability sampling, which sampling technique should be used and why?

TABLE 12.3 Cluster Sampling Versus Stratified Sampling

Cluster Sampling	Stratified Sampling
Only a sample of the subpopulations (clusters) is selected for sampling.	All of the subpopulations (strata) are selected for sampling.
Within a cluster, elements should be different (heterogeneous), whereas homogeneity or similarity is maintained between different clusters.	Within a strata, elements should be homogeneous with clear differences (heterogeneity) between the strata.
A sampling frame is needed only for the clusters selected for the sample.	A complete sampling frame for the entire stratified subpopulations should be drawn.
Increases sample efficiency by decreasing cost.	Increases precision.

TABLE 12.4 Strengths and Weaknesses of Basic Sampling Techniques

Technique	Strengths	Weaknesses
Nonprobability Sampling		
Convenience sampling	Least expensive, least time-consuming, most convenient	Selection bias, sample not representative, not recommended for descriptive or causal research
Judgmental sampling	Low cost, convenient, not time-consuming	Does not allow generalization, subjective
Quota sampling	Sample can be controlled for certain characteristics	Selection bias, no assurance of representativeness
Snowball sampling	Can estimate rare characteristics	Time-consuming
Probability Sampling		
Simple random sampling (SRS)	Easily understood, results projectable	Difficult to construct sampling frame, expensive, lower precision, no assurance of representativeness
Systematic sampling	Can increase representativeness, easier to implement than SRS, sampling frame not necessary	Can decrease representativeness
Stratified sampling	Includes all important subpopulations, precision	Difficult to select relevant stratification variables, not feasible to stratify on many variables, expensive
Cluster sampling	Easy to implement, cost-effective	Imprecise, difficult to compute and interpret results

Choosing Nonprobability Versus Probability Sampling

Choosing between nonprobability and probability samples is based on considerations such as the nature of the research, the error contributed by the sampling process relative to non-sampling error, variability in the population, and statistical and operational considerations such as costs and time (Table 12.5). For example, in exploratory research, the findings are treated as preliminary and the use of probability sampling might not be warranted. However, in conclusive research where the researcher wishes to generalize results to the target population, as in estimating market shares, probability sampling is favored. Probability samples allow statistical projection of the results to a target population. For these reasons, P&G decided to use probability sampling as described in the opening vignette.

When high levels of sampling accuracy are required, as is the case when estimates of population characteristics are made, probability sampling is preferred. In these situations, the researcher needs to eliminate selection bias and calculate the effect of sampling error. To do this, probability sampling is required. Even with this added sampling precision, probability sampling will not always result in more accurate results. Nonsampling error, for example, cannot be controlled with probability sampling. If nonsampling error is likely to be a problem, then nonprobability sampling techniques, such as judgment samples, might be preferable, allowing greater control over the sampling process.

When choosing between sampling techniques, the researcher must also consider the similarity or homogeneity of the population with respect to the characteristics of interest. For example, probability sampling is more appropriate in highly heterogeneous populations, in which it becomes important to draw a representative sample. Probability sampling

TABLE 12.5 **Choosing Nonprobability Versus Probability Sampling**

Factors	Conditions Favoring the Use of	
	Nonprobability Sampling	Probability Sampling
Nature of research	Exploratory	Conclusive
Relative magnitude of sampling and nonsampling errors	Nonsampling errors are larger	Sampling errors are larger
Variability in the population	Homogeneous (low)	Heterogeneous (high)
Statistical considerations	Unfavorable	Favorable
Operational considerations		
Time	Favorable	Unfavorable
Cost	Favorable	Unfavorable

also is preferable from a statistical viewpoint, because it is the basis of the most common statistical techniques.

Although probability sampling has many advantages, it is sophisticated and requires statistically trained researchers. It generally costs more and takes longer than nonprobability sampling. In many marketing research projects, it is difficult to justify the additional time and expense, and thus operational considerations favor the use of nonprobability sampling. In practice, the objectives of the study often exert a dominant influence on which sampling method will be used, as illustrated in the following example.

Research in Action

The Alluring Charm of Allure Fragrance

Chanel, Inc. (www.chanel.com), a division of the well-known French fashion and cosmetics company, wanted to launch a major new fragrance in American department and specialty stores that would reach and sustain at least the sales volume of Chanel No. 5. The target population was defined as women 18 years and older who would appreciate a unique and broadly appealing fragrance. In conducting a survey to determine women's preferences for perfumes, a nonprobability sampling scheme making use of quota sampling was adopted in conjunction with mall-intercept interviews. Quotas were assigned for age, income, and marital status. A nonprobability sampling scheme was chosen because the main objective of this exploratory research was qualitative: to understand what constituted a desirable, classic, yet contemporary, fragrance that women would choose to wear.

The results of the survey indicated a strong preference for a perfume that was fresh, clean, warm, and sexy. Moreover, women were looking for a perfume that would enable them to express themselves. Based on these findings, the company launched Allure, a unique and innovative fragrance created by Chanel perfumer Jacques Polge and packaged in a signature beige carton and sleek bottle. Diversity and individuality were successfully communicated through multi-image ads in a breakthrough print and TV campaign. The advertising portrayed many different women, because every woman expresses Allure in her own way. After its launch, Allure achieved a top-10 ranking in major retail accounts and sales volume equivalent to Chanel No. 5. The success of Allure could be attributed in no small part to the carefully designed sampling procedures that resulted in important survey findings on which the new perfume was developed and marketed. Given this success, the Allure line was extended and as of 2008 consisted of 29 items, including a wide range of cosmetics.[11]

Experiential Learning

U.S. Department of Transportation Survey

Enlightened U.S. public-policy makers seek citizen input to the development of the country's infrastructure. One example of this is the requirement for the U.S. Department of Transportation (DOT) to conduct an annual survey about citizen satisfaction with all transportation modes in the country. The Bureau of Transportation Statistics (BTS) is charged with conducting this survey in order to provide insights about citizen satisfaction with travel and transportation to members of Congress, to employees of the U.S. DOT, as well as to U.S. citizens themselves.

Go to the textbook's Web site and download the file U.S.DOT Survey from Chapter 12. This is the actual record of how the BTS and Battelle (a research organization hired to assist in the survey) designed and administered a nationally representative study called the Summer 2000 Omnibus Survey. Read the first two pages of the • Introduction and

Background (pages 3 and 4), and then Appendix F: The Final Sampling Plan (pages 124–131 or F1–F8).

1. What was the target population in this study?

2. How was the sampling frame derived in this study?

3. Was a nonprobability or probability sampling technique used?

4. What were the two variables used for stratifying the sample?

5. How many implicit strata were employed in the design of the sample?

6. The study designers wanted to secure 2,000 completed interviews. To obtain this number of completed interviews, how many phone numbers will need to be screened to determine if the phone number is a working residential phone number?

7. What do users of the survey results gain from the BTS using this sampling design instead of using a convenience sample of 2,000?

Internet Sampling

We will discuss the salient issues in online sampling as well as the commonly used online sampling techniques.

Issues in Online Sampling

As discussed in Chapter 7, Internet surveys (and sampling) offer many advantages. The respondents can complete the survey at their convenience. Internet surveys can incorporate automatic skip patterns, consistency checks, and other intelligent features, as is also true for computer-assisted surveys [computer-assisted telephone interviewing (CATI) and computer-assisted personal interviewing (CAPI)]. The data collection can be fast and inexpensive. A major issue related to Internet sampling is representativeness, because many households worldwide do not have computers with Internet access. Conversely, heavy users of the Internet might have a disproportionately higher probability of being included. Unrestricted Internet samples in which any visitor can participate are convenience samples and suffer from self-selection bias in that the respondents can initiate their own selection.

Sampling potential respondents who are surfing the Internet is meaningful if the sample that is generated is representative of the target population. More and more industries are meeting this criterion. In many technical fields, it is rapidly becoming feasible to use the Internet for sampling respondents for quantitative research, such as surveys. For internal customer surveys, where the client's employees share a corporate e-mail system, an intranet survey is practical even if workers have no access to the external Internet. Sampling on the Internet is not yet practical for many non–computer-oriented consumer products. For example, if P&G were to do a survey of Filipino housewives to determine their preferences and usage of laundry detergents, an Internet survey would not be a good choice, because an Internet sample is unlikely to be representative of the target population.

To avoid sampling errors, the researcher must be able to control the pool from which the respondents are selected. Also, steps must be taken to ensure that the respondents do not respond multiple times ("stuff the ballot box"). These requirements are met by e-mail surveys, for which the researcher selects specific respondents. Furthermore, the surveys can be encoded to match the returned surveys with their corresponding outbound e-mailings. This can also be accomplished with Web surveys by e-mailing invitations to selected respondents and asking them to visit the Web site where the survey is posted. In this case, the survey is posted in a hidden location on the Web, which is protected by a password. Hence, uninvited Web surfers are unable to access it.

Online Sampling Techniques

The sampling techniques commonly used on the Internet can be classified as online intercept (nonrandom and random), online recruited, and other techniques, as shown in Figure 12.12. Online recruited sampling can be further classified as panel (recruited or opt-in) or nonpanel (opt-in list rentals).

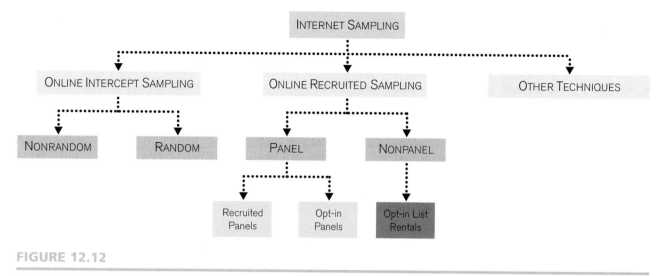

FIGURE 12.12

A Classification of Internet Sampling

In online intercept sampling, visitors to a Web site are intercepted and given an opportunity to participate in the survey. The interception can be made at one or more Web sites, including high-traffic sites such as Yahoo! In nonrandom sampling, every visitor is intercepted. This can be meaningful if the Web site traffic is low, the survey has to be completed in a short time, and no incentive is being offered. This results in a convenience sample, however. Quotas can be imposed to improve representativeness. In random intercept sampling, the software selects visitors at random and a "pop-up" window asks whether the person wants to participate in the survey. The selection can be made based on simple random or systematic random sampling. If the population is defined as Web site visitors, then this procedure results in a probability sample (simple random or systematic, as the case may be). If the population is other than Web site visitors, then the resulting sample is more similar to a nonprobability sample. Nevertheless, randomization improves representativeness and discourages multiple responses from the same respondent.

Internet panels function in ways similar to non–Internet panels discussed in Chapters 3 and 5, and they share many of the same advantages and disadvantages. In recruited panels, members can be recruited online or even by traditional means (mail, telephone). Based on the researcher's judgment, certain qualifying criteria can be introduced to prescreen the respondents. They are offered incentives for participation, such as sweepstake prizes, redeemable points, and other types of Internet currencies. Members typically provide detailed psychographic, demographic, Internet usage, and product consumption information at the time of joining. Opt-in panels operate similarly except that members choose to opt-in as opposed to being recruited. To select a sample, the online company sends an e-mail message to those panelists who qualify based on sample specifications given by the researcher. All of the sampling techniques can be implemented using both types of Internet panels. The success of probability sampling techniques depends on the extent to which the panel is representative of the target population. Highly targeted samples can be achieved (e.g., teenage girls who shop in malls more than twice a month). For example, U.S. respondents for Harris Poll Online (HPOL) surveys are drawn from the multimillion member HPOL database (www.harrisinteractive.com). E-mail addresses for respondents in the database have been obtained from a number of sources, including the HPOL registration site, HPOL banner advertisements, and Epinion registrations. To maintain the reliability and integrity in the sample, the following procedures are used:

■ **Password protection.** Each invitation contains a password that is uniquely assigned to that e-mail address. A respondent is required to enter the password at the beginning of the survey to gain access into the survey. Password protection ensures that a respondent completes the survey only one time.

- ■ *Reminder invitations.* To increase the number of respondents in the survey and to improve overall response rates, up to two additional reminder invitations are typically e-mailed at 2- to 4-day intervals to those respondents who have not yet participated in the survey.
- ■ *Summary of the survey findings.* To increase the number of respondents in the survey and to improve overall response rates, respondents often are provided with a summary of some of the survey responses via the Internet.

Nonpanel recruited sampling methods can also be used, which involves requesting potential respondents to go online to answer a survey. To illustrate, let's say that PC World (pcworld.co.uk), a chain of computer superstores based in the United Kingdom, hands customers fliers directing them to a password-protected site to respond to a questionnaire. If the population is defined as the company's customers, as in a customer satisfaction survey, and a random procedure is used to select respondents, a probability sample will be obtained. Other nonpanel approaches involve the use of e-mail lists that have been rented from suppliers. Presumably, these respondents opted in or gave permission for their e-mail addresses to be circulated. Offline techniques such as short telephone-screening interviews also are used for recruiting Internet samples. Several companies routinely collect e-mail addresses in their customer relationship databases by obtaining that information from customer telephone interactions, product registration cards, on-site registrations, special promotions, and so on.

A variety of other online sampling approaches also are possible. For example, a survey invitation might pop up every time a visitor makes a purchase. Furthermore, the Internet can be used to order and access samples generated by marketing research suppliers, such as U.S.-based Survey Sampling International (www.surveysampling.com).

Be an MR!	Be a DM!
Visit www.amazon.com and search the Internet, as well as your library's online databases, to obtain information on consumer Internet shopping behavior. Amazon wants you to conduct an Internet survey to determine customer satisfaction. How would you select the sample?	As the marketing chief for Amazon, what marketing strategies would you adopt to enhance customer satisfaction and loyalty?

Summary Illustration Using the Opening Vignette

In the Old Spice Red Zone Invisible Solid antiperspirant/deodorant survey, the target population was defined as male heads of households. Given the large size of the target population and limited time and money, P&G decided to take a sample rather than a census. The sampling unit was households, and the elements or the respondents, were male heads of households. The sampling frame consisted of telephone numbers of all U.S. households, randomly generated by computer programs. The researchers chose probability sampling because the results had to be generalizable; that is, projectable to all male heads of households. The technique of simple random sampling was selected because computer programs were available to randomly generate household telephone numbers and to minimize wastage due to nonexistent household telephone numbers. Simple random sampling was used to select 1,000 households. This sample size was selected based on qualitative considerations, such as the importance of the decision, the nature of the research, resource constraints, and the sample sizes used in similar studies conducted by P&G. Figure 12.13 provides a concept map for sampling techniques.

International Marketing Research

Implementing the sampling design process in international marketing research is seldom an easy task. Several factors should be considered in defining the target population. Identification and access to the relevant sampling elements varies widely across countries.

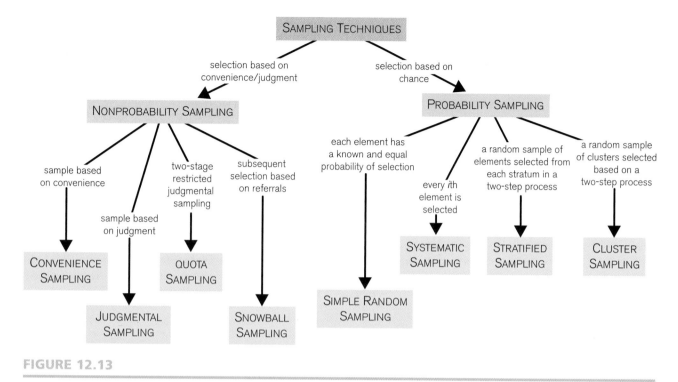

FIGURE 12.13

A Concept Map for Sampling Techniques

Additionally, a reliable sampling frame might not be available. In many studies, the researcher is interested in analyzing the attitudes and behaviors of the household decision maker. This individual responsible for making or influencing decisions also varies across countries. For example, in the United States, children play an important role in the purchase of children's cereals. In countries with authoritarian child-rearing practices, the mother might be the dominant decision maker for that purchase. For an international researcher, this means the mother, rather than the child, would be the element of interest. Identification of the decision maker and the relevant respondent might have to be done on a country-by-country basis.

Developing an appropriate sampling frame also is a difficult task. In the United States, researchers can rely on government census data or commercially available lists for their sampling frames. These types of high-quality secondary data, however, often are not available in international markets. Government data in many developing countries might be unavailable or highly biased. Population lists might not be available commercially. For example, elections are not held in Saudi Arabia, and there is no officially recognized census of population. Hence, there are no voter registration records or accurate maps of population centers. In such a case, the time and money required to compile this information might be prohibitive. Alternate sampling techniques, such as instructing the interviewers to begin at specified starting points and to sample every *n*th dwelling, could be used until the specified number of units has been sampled.

Equivalence of samples is a key issue in marketing research studies extending beyond the home country. Researchers must minimize the effects of sample differences that are not relevant to the main purposes of the study. For example, if American Express wanted to compare cultural differences in consumer attitudes toward saving in the United States and Mexico, differences in saving behavior could not be attributed to cultural differences alone if the U.S. respondents averaged 55 years of age while the Mexican respondents averaged 30 years of age. The life stage differs greatly for these two groups. The U.S. group would likely be saving for retirement years, whereas the Mexican group would be saving little in order to establish their households and to pay for the upbringing of their children. Thus, in order to compare the effects of cultural differences, it would be necessary to hold the other variables constant across the two countries.

Given the lack of suitable sampling frames; the inaccessibility of certain respondents, such as women in some cultures; and the dominance of personal interviewing over other survey methods, probability sampling techniques are uncommon in international marketing research. These constraints have led to a reliance on quota sampling for both consumer and industrial surveys.

Likewise, the use of Internet sampling in international marketing research must consider the possibility that Internet availability and use vary markedly across countries. Many countries lack servers, hardware, and software, and this lack of technical infrastructure makes Internet research difficult and expensive. In addition, there may be cultural differences in attitude toward and usage of the Internet. For example, in Latin America the attitude toward Internet research is not positive, due to the respondents missing social interaction with others while participating in the research.

Sampling techniques and procedures vary in accuracy, reliability, and cost from country to country. If the same sampling procedures are used in each country, the results might not be comparable.[12] To achieve comparability in sample composition and representativeness, it might be desirable to use different sampling techniques in different countries, as the following example illustrates.

Research in Action

Achieving Sample Comparability Through Diversity

Research in the United States found that most consumers feel that a purchase is accompanied by a degree of risk when they choose among alternative brands. A study was conducted to compare the U.S. results with those from Mexico, Thailand, and Saudi Arabia. The targeted respondent in each culture was an upper–middle-income woman residing in a major city. Reaching that target respondent presented challenges that required an adjustment in the sampling process across the countries in this study.

In the United States, random sampling from the telephone directory was used. In Mexico, judgmental sampling was used by having experts identify neighborhoods where the target respondents lived. Homes were then randomly selected for personal interviews. In Thailand, judgmental sampling also was used, but the survey took place in major urban centers, and a store-intercept technique was used to select respondents. Finally, in Saudi Arabia, convenience sampling employing the snowball procedure was used, because there were no lists from which sampling frames could be drawn and social customs prohibited spontaneous personal interviews. Comparability in sample composition and representativeness was achieved by adapting the sampling procedures to suit the social customs and information restrictions of each country.[13]

Be a DM!

As the global marketing manager for U.S.-based Intel, the computer microprocessor manufacturer, would you adopt the same or different marketing strategies in the United States and India?

Be an MR!

Search the Internet, as well as your library's online databases, to obtain information on the usage or nonusage of personal computers by households in the United States and India. Intel wants to conduct cross-cultural research to determine the similarities and differences in the usage or nonusage of personal computers by households in the United States and India. Should the same or different sampling techniques be used in the two countries, and which technique(s) should be used?

Technology and Marketing Research

Computer-based systems can make the sampling design process more effective and efficient. Computers can be used for specifying the sampling frame, because they can handle lists of population elements as well as geographical maps. Microcomputers and mainframes can be employed to select the sample needed, using either nonprobability or probability techniques. Once the sampling frame has been determined, the system generates random numbers and selects the sample directly from the database.

These systems are particularly suited for sample generation and control in telephone interviewing. In a typical application, all telephone prefixes in a geographic area (area codes and exchanges) are preprogrammed, and the system selects random numbers. The user can also exclude certain numbers or blocks of numbers. The computer can keep track of successfully completed interviews, schedule call-backs, control the interval for redialing busy numbers, and control the number of times a call is attempted by using software such as ASDE Survey Sampler (www.surveysampler.com). The software then produces lists of numbers to be included in the sample in a customized format.

Firms such as Survey Sampling International and Maritz Research (www.maritzresearch. co.uk) have developed proprietary sampling systems to generate samples using a variety of sampling techniques. For example, Survey Sampling has developed software for a range of random-digit dialing samples, clustered samples, and directory-listed samples. It has also developed software to screen and predetermine nonworking telephone numbers. This greatly increases the efficiency of the sample and saves time and money. The use of computer software to generate a random sample of household telephone numbers is illustrated in the opening vignette and in the MTV "What Would *You* Do?" decision scenario.

Ethics in Marketing Research

The researcher has the ethical responsibility to formulate a sampling design that is consistent with the objectives of the research and adequately controls the sampling error. Probability sampling techniques should be used whenever the results are to be projected to the population. Projecting findings based on nonprobability sampling to the population is misleading and therefore unethical. As the following example demonstrates, appropriate definitions of the population, sampling frame, and sampling technique are essential if the research is to be conducted and the findings are to be used ethically.

Research in Action

Systematic Sampling Reveals Systematic Gender Differences in Ethical Judgments

In an attempt to explore differences in research ethics judgments between male and female marketing professionals in the United States, data were obtained from 420 respondents. The population was defined as marketing professionals (elements), who also comprised the sampling unit. The sampling frame was the American Marketing Association directory, and the extent was the United States. The respondents were selected based on a systematic sampling plan from the directory. Systematic random sampling was chosen over simple random sampling because it was easier to implement. Respondents were asked to indicate the degree of ethicalness of various ethical scenarios and promised a copy of the results in an attempt to boost response rates.

The study revealed that female marketing professionals, in general, demonstrated higher levels of research ethical judgments than did their male counterparts. Similar findings have been obtained in other studies. Thus, the systematic random sampling plan was not only efficient, but resulted in findings that were generalizable to the target population.[14]

When conducting research with small populations, as in business-to-business marketing or employee research, researchers must be sensitive to preserving the respondents' anonymity. The results should be presented in such a way that respondents cannot be identified or linked to specific comments and findings.

What Would *You* Do?

MTV: The World's Most Widely Distributed TV Network

The Situation

As of 2008, MTV Networks included favorites such as MTV, VH1, Nickelodeon, Nick at Nite, Comedy Central, CMT: Country Music Television, Spike TV, TV Land, Logo, and more than 137 networks around the world. MTV Networks uses a free-flowing corporate culture and a group of power brands to earn big profits for parent U.S. Viacom (www.viacom.com).

Tom Freston, CEO of MTV, actually took MTV as a small start-up company and turned it into a cultural behemoth. Judy McGrath was named Chairman and CEO of

continued

MTV Networks in July 2004. Although MTV has become a global icon, with millions of viewers all over the world glued to its programming, MTV is constantly trying to keep up with what is popular and keep its viewers watching.

MTV (www.mtv.com) is always trying to find new ways to engage its target audience, which is 18- to 24-year-olds. This has not always been an easy task. For example, the channel had fading hits with shows like *Beavis & Butt-Head* and *The Real World*. Ratings began to slip as users complained that there was no longer music on MTV. Telephone surveys were conducted with the target audience. The sample was selected by choosing households based on computerized random-digit dialing. If the household had multiple 18- to 24-year-olds, one person was selected using the next-birthday method. If no person between these ages resided in the house, a new random number was selected. The results of this survey showed that MTV needed a makeover.

The Marketing Research Decision

1. As trends come and go, it is important for MTV to stay in touch with its audience members and know their wants. Judy McGrath especially wants to keep in touch with the 18- to 24-year-olds through periodic surveys. What sampling technique would you recommend?
   a. Convenience sampling
   b. Quota sampling
   c. Systematic sampling
   d. Stratified sampling
   e. Simple random sampling
2. Discuss the role of the type of sampling technique you recommend in enabling Judy McGrath to keep in touch with the 18- to 24-year-olds.

The Marketing Management Decision

1. What should Judy McGrath do to attract the 18- to 24-year-old audience group to MTV?
   a. Launch music hours shown live from popular places (e.g., New York's Times Square)
   b. Make VeeJays more authentic
   c. Feature more celebrities
   d. Focus more on music programming
   e. All of the above
2. Discuss how the marketing management decision action that you recommend to Judy McGrath is influenced by the sampling technique suggested earlier and by the findings of that research.

What Judy McGrath Did

MTV launched music hours shown live from Times Square. New shows, such as the animated *Daria,* were created, and the *Video Music Awards* were revamped. VeeJays became more authentic, and not as TV-pretty. The objective was to give MTV a cleaner, more pensive image to keep its viewers happy. The 18-to-24-year-old crowd is important to the network, because younger teens and the 25-to-35-year-old crowd looks to it for image and style ideas.

MTV is still striving to make its programming fresh and hip. TV shows such as *The Osbournes* and *Punk'd* have gotten great reviews. Also, on MTV's detailed Web site (www.mtv.com) viewers can do everything from requesting music videos to chatting with fellow MTV fans. MTV is continuing to grow and expand, and with the help of marketing research it should be able to stay hip for generations to come.[15]

Summary

Researchers can obtain information about the characteristics of a population by conducting either a sample or a census. Samples tend to be preferred because of budget and time limits, large population sizes, and small variances in the characteristics of interest. Sampling also is preferred when the cost of sampling error is low, the cost of nonsampling error is high, the nature of measurement is destructive, and attention must be focused on individual cases. The opposite conditions favor the use of a census.

Sampling design begins by defining the target population in terms of elements, sampling units, extent, and time. Then the sampling frame should be determined. A sampling frame is a list of the elements of the target population. Directions for constructing the sampling frame should also be included. Sampling techniques are applied to the sample frame to develop the eventual sample. The sample size is determined based on both quantitative and qualitative considerations. Finally, execution of the sampling process requires detailed specifications for each step in the process.

Sampling techniques can be classified as nonprobability and probability techniques. Nonprobability sampling techniques rely on the researcher's convenience and/or judgment. Consequently, they do not permit an objective evaluation of the precision of the sample results, and the estimates cannot be projected to the larger population. The commonly used nonprobability sampling techniques include convenience sampling, judgmental sampling, quota sampling, and snowball sampling.

In probability sampling techniques, sampling units are selected by chance. Each sampling unit has a nonzero chance of being selected, and the researcher can prespecify every potential sample of a given size that could be drawn from the population, as well as the probability of selecting each sample. It also is possible to determine the precision of the sample estimates and inferences and make projections to the target population. Probability sampling techniques include simple random sampling, systematic sampling, stratified sampling, and cluster sampling. The choice between probability and nonprobability sampling should be based on the nature of the research, degree of error tolerance, relative magnitude of sampling and nonsampling errors, variability in the population, and statistical and operational considerations. Nonprobability as well as probability sampling techniques can be implemented on the Internet, with the respondents being prerecruited or tapped online.

When conducting international marketing research, it is desirable to achieve comparability in sample composition and representativeness even though this might require using different sampling techniques in different countries. Several computer programs are available for implementing nonprobability and probability sampling schemes. It is unethical and misleading to treat nonprobability samples as probability samples and project the results to a target population.

Key Terms and Concepts

Suggested Cases and Video Cases

Running Case with Real Data

1.1 Hewlett-Packard

Comprehensive Critical Thinking Cases

2.1 American Idol   2.2 Baskin-Robbins   2.3 Akron Children's Hospital

Comprehensive Cases with Real Data

3.1 Bank of America   3.2 McDonald's   3.3 Boeing

Video Cases

12.1 Motorola   13.1 Subaru   14.1 Intel   19.1 Marriott

Live Research: Conducting a Marketing Research Project

1. A census might be feasible in a business-to-business project where the size of the population is small, but it is infeasible in most consumer projects.
2. Define the target population (element, sampling unit, extent, and time), and discuss a suitable sampling frame.
3. Probability sampling techniques are more difficult and time-consuming to implement, and their use might not be warranted unless the results are being projected to a population of interest.

Acronym

The sampling design process and the steps involved may be represented by the acronym SAMPLE:

    S ampling design process

    A mount: sample size determination

    M ethod: sampling technique selection

    P opulation definition

    L ist: sampling frame determination

    E xecution of the sampling process

Review Questions

1. What is the major difference between a sample and a census?
2. Under what conditions is a sample preferable to a census? When is a census preferable to a sample?
3. Describe the sampling design process.
4. How should the target population be defined?
5. What is a sampling unit? How is it different from the population element?
6. What qualitative factors should be considered in determining the sample size?
7. How do probability sampling techniques differ from nonprobability sampling techniques?
8. What is the least expensive and least time-consuming of all sampling techniques? What are the major limitations of this technique?
9. What is the major difference between judgmental and convenience sampling?
10. What is the relationship between quota sampling and judgmental sampling?
11. What are the distinguishing features of simple random sampling?
12. Describe the procedure for selecting a systematic random sample.
13. Describe stratified sampling. What are the criteria for the selection of stratification variables?
14. Describe the cluster sampling procedure. What is the key distinction between cluster sampling and stratified sampling?
15. What factors should be considered in choosing between probability and nonprobability sampling?

Applied Problems

1. Define the appropriate target population and the sampling frame in each of the following situations:
   a. The manufacturer of a new cereal brand wants to conduct in-home product usage tests in Chicago.
   b. A national chain store wants to determine the shopping behavior of customers who have its store charge card.
   c. A local TV station wants to determine households' viewing habits and programming preferences.
   d. The local chapter of the American Marketing Association wants to test the effectiveness of its new-member drive in Atlanta.
2. A manufacturer would like to survey users to determine the demand potential for a new power press. The new press has a capacity of 500 tons and costs $225,000. It is used for forming products from light- and heavyweight steel and can be used by automobile, construction equipment, and major appliance manufacturers.
   a. Identify the population and sampling frame that could be used.
   b. Describe how a simple random sample can be drawn using the identified sampling frame.
   c. Could a stratified sample be used? If so, how?
   d. Could a cluster sample be used? If so, how?
   e. Which sampling technique would you recommend? Why?
3. Ben & Jerry's Homemade Ice Cream would like to conduct a survey of consumer preferences for premium ice cream brands in Los Angeles. Stratified random sampling will be used. Visit www.census.gov to identify information that will be relevant in determining income and age strata.
4. Using a computer program, generate a set of 1,000 random numbers for selecting a simple random sample.
5. Visit the SurveySite Web site (www.surveysite.com). Examine the Internet surveys being conducted. Write a report about the sampling plans being used.

Group Discussion

1. "Given that the U.S. Bureau of the Census uses sampling to check on the accuracy of various censuses, a constitutional amendment should be passed replacing the decennial census with a sample." Discuss as a small group.
2. "Because nonsampling errors are greater in magnitude than sampling errors, it really does not matter which sampling technique is used." Discuss this statement.

Hewlett-Packard Running Case

Review the Hewlett-Packard (HP) case, Case 1.1, and questionnaire given toward the end of the book.

1. As the marketing manager of HP personal computers, what marketing programs will you design to target families?
2. Search the Internet, as well as your library's online databases, to obtain information that will assist you in targeting families.
3. HP wants to conduct a telephone survey to determine how it can attract more families to HP PCs and notebooks. Design the sampling process.

MOTOROLA: Projecting the Moto Lifestyle

Starting in 1928 as the Galvin Manufacturing Corporation, Motorola (www.motorola.com) has evolved into a worldwide company with over $36.6 billion in revenue in 2007. Today, it is a leading manufacturer and provider of wireless, semiconductor, broadband, and automotive products and services. With the wireless division, Motorola knew it needed to change. It had found through focus groups and survey research that many customers and potential customers saw Motorola's phone models as dependable, but also as dull, predictable, and boring. With the mobile phone market being flashy and consumer driven, Motorola needed answers on how to become more mainstream and popular.

To find these answers, Motorola turned to marketing research and an advertising agency named Ogilvy and Mather. Motorola and Ogilvy and Mather conducted focus groups, depth interviews, and mall-intercept surveys. Although focus groups generated some innovative ideas, depth interviews enabled the probing of emotions related to mobile phones. Mall intercepts were chosen because the respondents could be shown models of Motorola and competing brands. They found from this research that customers buying mobile phones did not buy the phone based on technical schematic selling points. Customers buy phones based on how they emotionally feel about the brand of phone and the particular style of the phone. Most customers do not understand the technical parameters of the different phone models enough to make a decision based on them. So they are choosing among cell phones based on whether the phone "fits" into their lives or by considering "Is this phone me?" This research challenged the company's management to think of cell phones not so much as engineered functional devices but as fashion accessories that help consumers make statements about who they are. It pointed Motorola into developing a marketing strategy that developed the brand name instead of pushing the features of the phone. Moreover, the brand name had to be a global one based on universal principles. Marketing research also revealed that consumers were looking for "intelligence everywhere," and therefore the brand had to be developed in that environment.

Ogilvy and Mather sought to develop the Motorola brand to represent a set of universal principles—a set of core principles that defined the brand—and then send out this idea to every country and have a localized interpretation for the idea. The result of this is that the core ethos of the brand is preserved while at the same time offering local offices the flexibility to mould the brand according to local conditions and develop the brand such that the people of that country can relate to and identify with it. For Motorola, Ogilvy developed the core idea of "intelligence everywhere." This core idea is used as the framework for all Motorola businesses around the world.

This was accomplished by creating the Moto, which is a cute name for Motorola's global-branded cell phone. The name is easy to pronounce, and it does not mean anything bad or weird anywhere in the world. It also carries a part of the Motorola name, a strong positive brand name that reminds consumers of the company's heritage. Motorola's advertising agency, Ogilvy & Mather, created a Moto lifestyle image (www.hellomoto.com). Knowing from research that customers wanted to relate to the phone and brand on a personal level, Motorola's Moto lifestyle showed the public fast, upbeat, and flashy people living and using Motorola products in an intelligent way. This created an emotional connection with customers, as they were almost saying to themselves, "That's the way I want to live." This was followed by Motodextrous ads in 2004 that projected a perfect balance between design and technology to enable people to live the Moto lifestyle with the slogan of "Intelligence Everywhere." This campaign, an obvious success, was possible due only to the marketing research conducted to find why customers buy certain brands and models of mobile phones. When marketing research indicated a big need for hands-free driving, in October 2007 the company introduced MOTOROKR T505 Bluetooth, the In-Car Speakerphone and Digital FM Transmitter, its first road-ready, music-oriented ROKR accessory and the latest addition to its portfolio of in-car solutions.

Given the high costs associated with an advertising campaign, it was well researched and backed with strong supporting evidence and data. Marketing professionals need to substantiate their spending on advertising and brand building with research data that spells out the rational for that spending. The Moto campaign, instead of inducing customers to buy Motorola phones because of their features, appealed to consumers' lifestyle choices. The campaign positioned Motorola phones as aspirational products that embodied a certain attitude. This positioning created an emotional connection with the consumers and targeted people's desires to be associated with products that stand for qualities that they consider to be "cool"; that is, fashionable and worthy of being identified with.

The key here is to identify a set of core values the brand stands for and then being able to make the brand work in all parts of the world. The success of global brand icons such as Dove, IBM, and others has shown that a brand's strengths can indeed be leveraged across countries and cultures. Identifying this set of core values, though, is no easy task and requires extensive marketing research. From finding consumer preferences to their desires and perceptions about the brand, marketing research helps to gain insight into the consumers' mindsets. For example, marketing research showed that style matters regardless of income or social status, an insight Motorola employed while developing the Motofone for developing countries.

Conclusion

Based on marketing research findings, the Moto campaign established Motorola as a chic and aspirational brand that helped it overcome its poor consumer image and branding problems. The Moto campaign projects Motorola's core values and its lifestyle appeals to consumers across the world. Possessing a Moto was no longer possessing a cell phone, but having a product whose core values represented the type of lifestyle the user of the phone desired and lived. With this dependence on marketing research in the forefront of Motorola's actions, it is certain to remain a global contender in the mobile phone market for years to come.

Questions

1. Discuss the role that marketing research can play in helping Motorola further build the Moto brand.
2. Management would like to continue rebuilding Motorola. They feel this can be best accomplished by increasing Motorola's U.S. marketing share. Define the management-decision problem.
3. Define an appropriate marketing research problem based on the management-decision problem you have identified.
4. Use the Internet to determine the market shares of the major cell phone handset manufacturers (Nokia, Motorola, Samsung, Sony/Ericsson, etc.) for the last calendar year.
5. What type of syndicate data will be useful to Motorola?
6. Discuss the role of qualitative research in helping Motorola expand its market share.
7. Do you think that the mall-intercept interviewing conducted by Motorola was the best method of administering the survey? Why or why not?

8. Discuss the role of experimentation in helping Motorola design handsets that are preferred by consumers.
9. Develop a questionnaire for assessing consumer preferences for cellular handsets.
10. What sampling plan should be adopted for the survey of question 7?
11. If Motorola were to conduct marketing research to determine consumer preferences for cellular handset manufacturers in Asia, how would the research process be different?
12. Discuss the ethical issues involved in researching consumer preferences for cellular handset manufacturers.

References

1. www.motorola.com, accessed February 15, 2008.
2. www.hellomoto.com, accessed February 15, 2008.
3. www.hoovers.com, accessed February 15, 2008.
4. www.wikipedia.org, accessed February 15, 2008.
5. www.technologyreview.com/read_article.aspx?id=17663, accessed June 4, 2007.
6. Soo Youn, "Motorola Chips Away at Nokia's Lead in Cell-Phone Market," *Knight Ridder Tribune Business News*, June 9, 2004, p. 1.

Sampling: Final and Initial Sample-Size Determination

OPENING QUESTIONS

1. What key concepts and symbols are pertinent to sampling?

2. How are the sampling distribution, statistical inference, and standard error relevant to sampling?

3. What is the statistical approach to determining sample size based on simple random sampling and the construction of confidence intervals?

4. How can formulas be derived to statistically determine the sample size for estimating means and proportions?

5. How should the sample size be adjusted to account for incidence and completion rates?

6. Why is it difficult to statistically determine the sample size in international marketing research?

7. What is the interface of technology with sample-size determination?

8. What ethical issues are related to sample-size determination, particularly the estimation of population variance?

Sizing the Sample-Size Problem

"Sample size not only is determined by statistical considerations, but also real pressures, such as time and cost."

Chris Bonbright,
Manager, Research & Market Analysis,
Tracker Marine Group.

A recent article in the *Chicago Tribune*, a leading U.S. newspaper, suggested that just as the introduction of television reduced the audiences for both theater and radio, so have online services reduced the audience for television. To support his claim, the author offered survey data about the U.S. Internet-services provider America Online, Inc. (now AOL LLC) showing that online subscribers watch less television than the average U.S. household. An executive at the research company that performed the survey said, "It doesn't matter why people watch less television. It only matters that they do."

The general reader and the general businessperson might read this piece and walk away with the notion that, indeed, increasing online use is directly related to decreasing television viewing. You can almost imagine the buzzing of such discussions at breakfast tables, water coolers, and in carpools: "Hey, I just read in the paper this morning that . . ."

A more skeptical reader would rightly question much of the study's findings and its application to everyday consumer media preferences. A closer look at the report reveals that the sample size comprised only 262 members of the online service's subscribers. Is this enough to mitigate random sampling error? Is this sample large enough to make such

bold claims about television viewing? To make decisions and set policy and strategy? The *confidence level*, which is the level of certainty, was not reported. Only the margin of error as "probably" about 5 percentage points was estimated. Was it 5 percent or not? How confident are we that this conclusion is accurate? What is the confidence level and what is the *confidence interval*; that is, the range likely to contain the true population parameter? Moreover, the completion rate was not reported. Without considering the appropriate sam-

pling specifications, it is not appropriate to draw inferences from the sample about the population. Therefore, based on this study it is not appropriate to conclude that users of online services, in general, watch less television. Such findings continue to be reported in the popular media. For example, a July 31, 2007, study reported that Canadians were switching from television and radio to the Internet. However, the findings of this study also are suspect, because the sample size and the sampling procedures were not reported.[1]

Overview

Chapter 12 discussed the role of sampling in research design formulation, described the sampling process, and presented the various nonprobability and probability sampling techniques. This chapter focuses on the determination of sample size in simple random sampling. Figure 13.1 briefly explains the focus of the chapter, the relation of this chapter to the previous ones, and the steps of the marketing research process this chapter describes.

The opening vignette illustrates the importance of statistically determining the sample size and the random sampling error before generalizing the sample findings to the population. In order to understand and appreciate these issues, the chapter presents definitions of various concepts and symbols and discusses the properties of the sampling distribution. Statistical approaches to sample-size determination based on confidence intervals are presented. In addition, formulas for calculating the sample size with these approaches will be offered and illustrated by examples.

The sample size determined statistically is the final or net sample size that represents the number of interviews or observations that need to be completed. For example, a sample size of 1,000 for a telephone survey means that the interviewers must complete 1,000 interviews. To obtain this final sample size, however, a much larger number of potential respondents must be contacted initially. Thus, to complete 1,000 interviews, it might be necessary to initially contact as many as 3,000 respondents, for example, because only some of the potential respondents might qualify to participate. That is, the incidence rate is generally less than 100 percent. Furthermore, some of those who do qualify might refuse to participate or complete the survey. The completion rate also is less than 100 percent. This chapter will describe the adjustments that need to be made to the statistically determined sample size to account for incidence and completion rates and to calculate the initial sample size. The chapter will

FIGURE 13.1

Relationship of Sample-Size Determination to the Previous Chapters and the Marketing Research Process

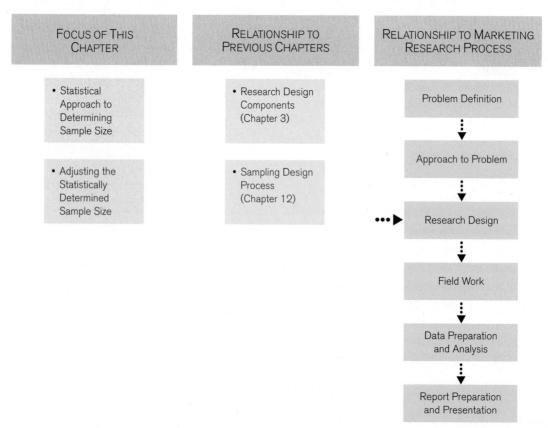

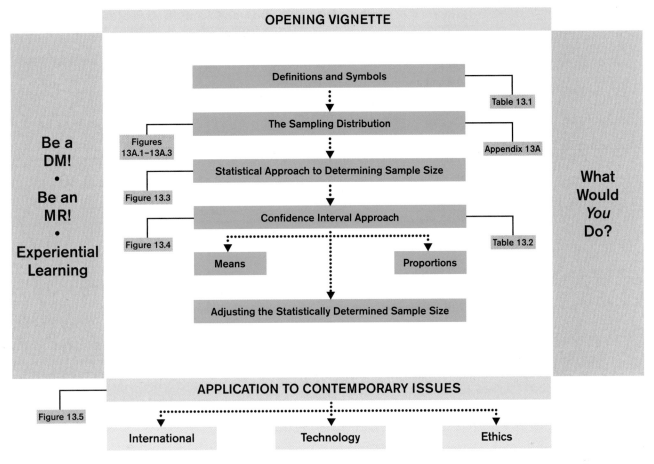

FIGURE 13.2

Final and Initial Sample-Size Determination: An Overview

also discuss the difficulty of statistically determining the sample size in international marketing research, applications of technology, and the relevant ethical issues. Figure 13.2 offers an overview of the topics discussed in this chapter and how they flow from one to the next.

Statistical determination of sample size requires knowledge of the normal distribution and the use of normal probability tables. The **normal distribution** is bell-shaped and symmetrical. Its mean, median, and mode are identical (see Chapter 16). Information on the normal distribution and the use of normal probability tables is presented in Appendix 13A. We recommend that you also review a statistics textbook.

Definitions and Symbols

The statistical concepts used in sample-size determination are defined in the following list.

- **Parameter:** A summary description of a fixed characteristic or measure of the target population. A parameter denotes the true value that would be obtained if a census (a survey of the complete population), rather than a sample, was undertaken.
- **Statistic:** A summary description of a characteristic or measure of the sample. The sample statistic is used as an estimate of the population parameter.
- **Precision level:** When estimating a population parameter by using a sample statistic, the precision level is the desired size of the estimating interval. This is the maximum permissible difference between the sample statistic and the population parameter.
- **Confidence interval:** The range into which the true population parameter will fall, assuming a given level of confidence.

normal distribution
A basis for classical statistical inference that is bell-shaped and symmetrical in appearance. Its measures of central tendency are all identical.

parameter
A summary description of a fixed characteristic or measure of the target population.

statistic
A summary description of a characteristic or measure of the sample that is used as an estimate of the population parameter.

precision level
Precision level is the desired size of the estimating interval and is the maximum permissible difference between the sample statistic and the population parameter.

confidence interval
The range into which the true population parameter will fall, assuming a given level of confidence.

TABLE 13.1 **Symbols for Population and Sample Variables**

Variable	Population	Sample
Mean	μ	$\overline{X}$
Proportion	π	p
Variance	σ^2	s^2
Standard deviation	σ	s
Size	N	n
Standard error of the mean	$\sigma_{\overline{x}}$	$s_{\overline{x}}$
Standard error of the proportion	σ_p	s_p
Standardized variate (z)	$\dfrac{X - \mu}{\sigma}$	$\dfrac{X - \overline{X}}{s}$

confidence level
The probability that a confidence interval will include the population parameter.

random sampling error
The error due to the particular sample selected being an imperfect representation of the population of interest.

■ **Confidence level:** The probability that a confidence interval will include the population parameter.
■ **Random sampling error:** The error that results when the particular sample selected is an imperfect representation of the population of interest (see Chapter 3). Note that this is different from the random error in measurement discussed in Chapter 10.

The symbols used in statistical notation for describing population and sample characteristics are summarized in Table 13.1.

The Sampling Distribution

The **sampling distribution** is the distribution of the values of a sample statistic, for example, the sample mean. These values are computed for each possible sample of a given size. Under a specified sampling plan, it is possible to draw several different samples of a given size from the target population.[2] The sampling distribution should not be confused with the distribution of the values of the elements in a sample. Suppose a simple random sample of 5 Chinese silk mills is to be drawn from a population of 20 mills. There are $(20 \times 19 \times 18 \times 17 \times 16)/(1 \times 2 \times 3 \times 4 \times 5)$, or 15,504 different samples of 5 silk mills that can be drawn from this population. If the values of the means associated with these 15,504 samples were assembled, they would form the sampling distribution of the mean.

sampling distribution
The distribution of the values of a sample statistic computed for each possible sample of a given size that could be drawn from the target population under a specified sampling plan.

An important task in marketing research is to calculate statistics, such as the sample mean and sample proportion, and to use them to estimate the corresponding true population values. This process of generalizing the sample results to the population results is referred to as **statistical inference**. In practice, a single sample of predetermined size is selected, and the sample statistics (such as means or proportions) are computed. The sample statistics become the basis for making inferences about the population values. This inferential process is possible because sampling distribution enables us to use probability theory to make inferences about the population values. Of direct relevance is the **central limit theorem**, which states that as the sample size increases, the distribution of the sample mean of a randomly selected sample approaches the normal distribution. This holds true regardless of the shape of the original population distribution from which the sample is drawn.

statistical inference
The process of generalizing the sample results to the population results.

central limit theorem
As the sample size increases, the distribution of the sample mean of a randomly selected sample approaches the normal distribution.

We now describe the important properties of the sampling distribution of the mean and the corresponding properties for the proportion for large samples (30 or more). Please refer to Table 13.1 for a definition of the symbols used in these formulas.

1. The sampling distribution of the mean is a normal distribution (see Appendix 13A). Strictly speaking, the sampling distribution of a proportion is a binomial that approximates the normal distribution in large samples ($n = 30$ or more).
2. The mean (the average) of the sampling distribution of the mean

$$\left(\overline{X} = \left(\sum_{i=1}^{n} X_i \right) \middle/ n \right)$$

or of the proportion (p) equals the corresponding population parameter value, μ or π, respectively.

3. The standard deviation of the sampling distribution is called the **standard error** of the mean or the proportion. This distinction is made to clarify the point that we are talking about a sampling distribution of the mean or the proportion, not about a distribution of elements in a sample or a population. The formula for the standard error of the mean is

standard error
The standard deviation of the sampling distribution of the mean or proportion.

$$\sigma_{\bar{x}} = \frac{\sigma}{\sqrt{n}}$$

The formula for the standard error of the proportion is

$$\sigma_p = \sqrt{\frac{\pi(1 - \pi)}{n}}$$

4. Often the population standard deviation, σ, is not known. In these cases, it can be estimated from the sample by using the following formula:

$$s = \sqrt{\frac{\sum_{i=1}^{n}(X_i - \bar{X})^2}{n - 1}}$$

or

$$s = \sqrt{\frac{\sum_{i=1}^{n} X_i^2 - \frac{\left(\sum_{i=1}^{n} X_i\right)^2}{n}}{n - 1}}$$

In cases where σ is estimated by s, the standard error of the mean becomes

$$\text{est. } \sigma_{\bar{x}} = s_{\bar{x}} = \frac{s}{\sqrt{n}}$$

The "est." denotes the fact that s has been used as an estimate of σ.

5. Likewise, the standard error of the proportion can be estimated by using the sample proportion p as an estimator of the population proportion, π, as

$$\text{est. } \sigma_p = s_p = \sqrt{\frac{p(1 - p)}{n}}$$

6. The area under the sampling distribution (normal distribution) curve between any two points can be calculated in terms of z values. The **z value** for a point is the number of standard errors that point is away from the mean. The z values may be computed as follows:

z value
The number of standard errors that a point is away from the mean.

$$z = \frac{\bar{X} - \mu}{\sigma_{\bar{x}}}$$

For example, 34.13 percent of the area under one side of the curve lies between the mean and a z value of 1.0. The area from the mean to the z values of 2.0 and 3.0 is equal to 0.4772 and 0.4986, respectively. (See Table 2 in the Appendix of Statistical Tables.) The same percentages of the area under the sampling distribution curve lie between the mean and z values of -1.0, -2.0, and -3.0. This is because the sampling distribution curve is symmetric around the mean. In the case of proportion, the computation of z values is similar.

Statistical Approach to Determining Sample Size

In addition to statistical considerations, several qualitative factors should be considered when determining the sample size (see Chapter 12). These include the importance of the decision, the nature of the research, the number of variables, the nature of the analysis, sample sizes

FIGURE 13.3

The Confidence Interval Approach to Determining Sample Size

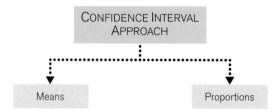

used in similar studies, incidence rates, completion rates, and resource constraints. The statistically determined sample size is the net or final sample size—the sample remaining after eliminating potential respondents who do not qualify or who do not complete the interview. Depending on incidence and completion rates, the initial sample might need to be much larger than the net or final sample requirements. In commercial marketing research, limits on time, money, and expert resources can exert an overriding influence on sample-size determination.

The statistical approach to determining sample size is based on traditional statistical inference using the formulas (equations) presented in the previous section. In this approach, the precision level is specified in advance. This approach is based on the construction of confidence intervals around sample means or proportions (Figure 13.3).

The Confidence Interval Approach

Confidence intervals around sample means or proportions are estimated using the standard error formula. As an example, suppose that a researcher has taken a simple random sample of 300 Australian households to estimate the monthly expenses on department-store shopping and has found that the mean household monthly expense for the sample is A\$182. Past studies indicate that the population standard deviation, σ, can be assumed to be A\$55.

We want to find an interval within which a fixed proportion of the sample means would fall. Suppose we want to determine an interval around the population mean that will include 95 percent of the sample means, based on samples of 300 households; that is, we choose 95 percent as the confidence level. The 95 percent could be divided into two equal parts, half below and half above the mean, as shown in Figure 13.4. Calculation of the confidence interval involves determining a distance below ($\overline{X}_L$) and above ($\overline{X}_U$) the population mean (μ), which contains a specified area of the normal curve.

The z values corresponding to $\overline{X}_L$ and $\overline{X}_U$ can be calculated as

$$z_L = \frac{\overline{X}_L - \mu}{\sigma_{\overline{x}}}$$

$$z_U = \frac{\overline{X}_U - \mu}{\sigma_{\overline{x}}}$$

FIGURE 13.4

95% Confidence Interval

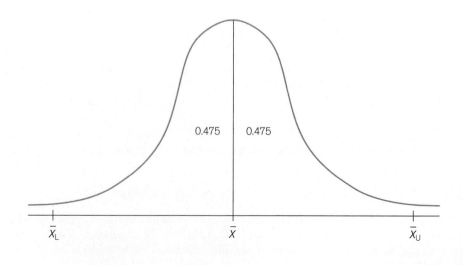

where $z_L = -z$ and $z_U = +z$. Therefore, the lower value of $\overline{X}$ is

$$\overline{X}_L = \mu - z\sigma_{\bar{x}}$$

and the upper value of $\overline{X}$ is

$$\overline{X}_U = \mu + z\sigma_{\bar{x}}$$

Note that μ is estimated by $\overline{X}$. The confidence interval is given by

$$\overline{X} \pm z\sigma_{\bar{x}}$$

We can now set a 95-percent confidence interval around the sample mean of A$182. As a first step, we compute the standard error of the mean:

$$\sigma_{\bar{x}} = \frac{\sigma}{\sqrt{n}} = 55/\sqrt{300} = 3.18$$

From Table 2 in the Appendix of Statistical Tables, we can see that the central 95 percent of the normal distribution lies within ± 1.96 z values, i.e., $z = 1.96$. The 95-percent confidence interval is given by

$$\overline{X} \pm 1.96\,\sigma_{\bar{x}}$$
$$= 182.00 \pm 1.96(3.18)$$
$$= 182.00 \pm 6.23$$

Thus, the 95-percent confidence interval ranges from A$175.77 to A$188.23. The probability of finding the true population mean to be within A$175.77 and A$188.23 is 95 percent. If the confidence interval is not reported, or cannot otherwise be calculated from the information given, we have no way of knowing how precise the sample estimates are. This was illustrated in the opening vignette, in which it was difficult to evaluate the precision of the results of the America Online survey.

Confidence intervals often are associated with scales used to measure customer satisfaction, as illustrated by the American Customer Satisfaction Index.

Research in Action

The American Customer Satisfaction Index

The American Customer Satisfaction Index (ACSI) is a national measure of satisfaction with quality that provides a resource for examining the differences in satisfaction among customers of different industries by their demographic and socioeconomic characteristics. The ACSI is based on 42,149 customer interviews and is converted to a scale of 0 to 100.

The first national measure of ACSI gave an index reading of 74.5 with a 95-percent confidence interval of 74.3 to 74.7.

This narrow confidence interval is due to the large sample size and indicates that customer satisfaction was measured with a high degree of precision. The ACSI also is broken down by economic sectors and industries. The ACSI is a useful new tool for companies to benchmark their customer satisfaction scores against those of other companies in their own and other industries.[3]

Sample-Size Determination: Means

Confidence interval estimation formulas can be used to determine the sample size that will result in a desired confidence interval. In this case, we use the same formulas but have a different unknown, namely the sample size, n. Suppose the researcher wants to estimate the monthly household expense on department-store shopping so that the estimate will be within plus or minus A$5 of the true population value. What should the size of the sample be? The following steps, summarized in Table 13.2, will lead to an answer.

1. *Specify the level of precision.* This is the maximum permissible difference (D) between the sample mean and the population mean. In our example, $D = \pm$ A$5.
2. *Specify the level of confidence.* Suppose that a 95-percent confidence level is desired.

TABLE 13.2 Sample-Size Determination for Means and Proportions

Steps	Means	Proportions
1. Specify the level of precision.	$D = \bar{X} - \mu = \pm$ A\$5.00	$D = p - \pi = \pm 0.05$
2. Specify the confidence level (CL).	CL = 95%	CL = 95%
3. Determine the z value associated with the CL.	z value = 1.96	z value = 1.96
4. Determine the standard deviation of the population.	Estimate σ	Estimate π
	$\sigma = 55$	$\pi = 0.64$
5. Determine the sample size using the formula for the standard error.	$n = \dfrac{\sigma^2 z^2}{D^2}$	$n = \dfrac{\pi(1-\pi)z^2}{D^2}$
	$n = \dfrac{55^2(1.96)^2}{5^2}$	$n = \dfrac{0.64(1-0.64)(1.96)^2}{(0.05)^2}$
	$n = 465$	$n = 355$
6. If necessary, reestimate the confidence interval by employing s to estimate σ.	$= \bar{X} \pm zs_{\bar{x}}$	$p \pm zs_p$

3. *Determine the z value associated with the confidence level using Table 2 in the Appendix of Statistical Tables.* For a 95-percent confidence level, the probability that the population mean will fall outside either end of the interval is 0.025 (0.05/2), with an associated z value of 1.96.

4. *Determine the standard deviation of the population.* The standard deviation of the population might be available from secondary sources, estimated from pilot-study data, or based on the researcher's judgment. For example, the range of a normally distributed variable is approximately equal to plus or minus three standard deviations. The standard deviation of sample data can therefore be estimated by dividing the range of that data by six. The researcher can often estimate the range based on knowledge of the phenomenon or knowledge of the scale used. For example, the traditional Likert scale has a range of four (5 through 1).

5. *Determine the sample size using the formula for the standard error of the mean.* Let us use the formula for z and derive the formula for the sample size, n. Recall that

$$z = \frac{\bar{X} - \mu}{\sigma_{\bar{x}}}$$

because $D = \bar{X} - \mu$

$$z = \frac{D}{\sigma_{\bar{x}}}$$

Solving for $\sigma_{\bar{x}}$

$$\sigma_{\bar{x}} = \frac{D}{z}$$

But

$$\sigma_{\bar{x}} = \frac{\sigma}{\sqrt{n}}$$

Therefore,

$$\frac{\sigma}{\sqrt{n}} = \frac{D}{z}$$

Solving for n

$$n = \frac{\sigma^2 z^2}{D^2}$$

In our example,

$$n = \frac{55^2 (1.96)^2}{5^2}$$

$$= 464.83$$

$$= 465 \text{ (rounded to the next higher integer)}$$

It can be seen from the preceding formulas that sample size is influenced by three factors. It increases as population variability increases, as greater confidence is required (i.e., as confidence level increases), and as the precision level required of the estimate increases (i.e., size of the estimating interval becomes smaller).

6. *If the population standard deviation, σ, is unknown and an estimate is used, it should be reestimated once the sample has been drawn.* The sample standard deviation, s, is used as an estimate of σ. A revised confidence interval should then be calculated to determine the precision level actually obtained.

Suppose that the value of 55 used for σ was an estimate because the true value was unknown. A sample size (n) of 465 is drawn, and these observations generate a mean ($\overline{X}$) of 180 and a sample standard deviation s of 50. The revised confidence interval then is

$$= \overline{X} \pm z s_{\bar{x}}$$
$$= 180 \pm 1.96(50/\sqrt{465})$$
$$= 180 \pm 4.55$$

or

$$175.45 \leq \mu \leq 184.55$$

Note that the confidence interval obtained is narrower than planned because the population standard deviation was initially overestimated to be 55, compared to the sample standard deviation of only 50.

It is very important to note that the population size, N, does not directly affect the size of the sample. An example will make this point more obvious. Suppose all the population elements are identical on a characteristic of interest. A sample size of one would then be sufficient to estimate the mean perfectly. This would be true regardless of whether there were 50, 500, 5,000, or 50,000 elements in the population. Thus, a probability sample size can be a small percentage of the population size and still be very accurate in that it has little sampling error. The sample size is directly affected by the variability of the characteristic in the population. This variability enters into the sample size calculation by way of population variance σ^2 or sample variance s^2. Also, note that the larger the sample size, the more accurate the parameter estimation (sample mean); that is, the smaller the error denoted by the precision level for a given level of confidence. This can be seen from the formula in step 5. A larger sample will also result in a narrower confidence interval. This can be seen from the formula for the confidence interval in step 6.

Be an MR!	Be a DM!
Visit the U.S. cellular and wireless provider T-Mobile at www.t-mobile.com and search the Internet, as well as your library's online databases, to obtain information on the average monthly amount U.S. households spend on cellular (cell phone) services. Assuming a confidence level of 95 percent, precision level of US$10, and a standard deviation of US$100, what should be the sample size to determine the average monthly household expenditure on cellular services?	As the vice president of marketing for T-Mobile, how would you use information on the average monthly household expenditure for cellular services to expand your revenues?

Sample-Size Determination: Proportions

Proportions are estimated when the choice is dichotomous; that is, when there are only two categories (e.g., yes or no). The researcher is examining the percentage of elements that is in one of the two categories. If the parameter of interest is a proportion, rather than a mean, the approach to sample-size determination is similar. Suppose that the researcher is interested in estimating the proportion of households possessing a department-store credit card. The researcher should follow these six steps:

1. *Specify the level of precision.* Suppose the desired precision is such that the allowable interval is set as $D = p - \pi = \pm 0.05$ (i.e., 5% expressed as a decimal equivalent).
2. *Specify the level of confidence.* Suppose that a 95-percent confidence level is desired.
3. *Determine the z value associated with the confidence level.* As explained in the case of estimating the mean, this will be $z = 1.96$.
4. *Estimate the population proportion, π.* As explained earlier, the population proportion might be estimated from secondary sources or from a pilot study or be based on the judgment of the researcher. Suppose that based on secondary data the researcher estimates that 64 percent of the households in the target population possess a department-store credit card. In this case, $\pi = 0.64$.
5. *Determine the sample size using the formula for the standard error of the proportion.* The derivation of the formula for sample size is similar to that used for means. We know that

$$\sigma_p = \frac{p - \pi}{z}$$

Substituting D for $p - \pi$ we get

$$\sigma_p = \frac{D}{z}$$

We also know that

$$\sigma_p = \sqrt{\frac{\pi(1 - \pi)}{n}}$$

Therefore, setting

$$\frac{D}{z} = \sqrt{\frac{\pi(1 - \pi)}{n}}$$

and solving for n, we get

$$n = \frac{\pi(1 - \pi)z^2}{D^2}$$

In our example,

$$n = \frac{0.64(1 - 0.64)(1.96)^2}{(0.05)^2}$$

$$= 354.04$$

$$= 355 \text{ (rounded to the next higher integer)}$$

6. *If the estimate of π turns out to be poor, the confidence interval will be more or less precise than desired.* Suppose that after the sample has been taken, the proportion p is calculated to have a value of 0.55. The confidence interval is then reestimated by employing s_p to estimate the unknown σ_p as

$$p \pm z \, s_p$$

where

$$s_p = \sqrt{\frac{p(1 - p)}{n}}$$

In our example,

$$s_p = \sqrt{\frac{0.55(1 - 0.55)}{355}}$$

$$= 0.0264$$

The confidence interval, then, is

$$= 0.55 \pm 1.96 \, (0.0264)$$

$$= 0.55 \pm .052$$

which is wider than that specified. This could be attributed to the fact that the sample standard deviation determined from our actual sample was based on $p = 0.55$. This was larger than our original estimate of the population standard deviation determined from the researcher's judgment and based on $\pi = 0.64$.

If the resulting confidence interval is too wide, the sample size can be recalculated using the maximum possible variation in the population. Maximum variation occurs when the product $\pi(1 - \pi)$ is at a maximum. This occurs when π is set at 0.5. This result can also be seen intuitively. If a population was evenly divided in terms of one value of a characteristic, more evidence would be required to obtain a valid inference than if the majority of the population possessed that characteristic. In our example, this leads to a sample size of

$$n = \frac{0.5(0.5)(1.96)^2}{(0.05)^2}$$

$$= 384.16$$

$$= 385 \text{ (rounded to the next higher integer)}$$

Thus, in our opening vignette if the proportion of online users is to be estimated with 95-percent confidence level and with a margin of error (allowable interval) not to exceed plus or minus 5 percent, the sample size should have been at least 385. The sample size was only 262, however, falling substantially short of the required size.

Research in Action

Small Businesses Have Big Technology Plans

The Hewlett-Packard (HP) Small Business Survey was conducted by Harris Interactive, Inc. among 399 small business owners or senior-level employees age 25 to 64 at American companies with fewer than 100 employees. Interviews were conducted by telephone between March 3 and 15 of 2005. The sample size was selected based on statistical considerations so that percentage estimates would not differ from the true estimates by more than 5 percent.

Survey respondents believe that technology is essential to the operations and success of their businesses, and 81 percent planned to increase technology spending in a variety of ways (e.g., company Web sites, online services, and blogs) over the next 2 to 3 years. In addition, 68 percent of those surveyed reported that they plan to adopt additional technology products in the coming year. Based on these findings, HP launched several technology initiatives aimed at small businesses, including a dedicated portion of their Web site (www.hp.com/sbso/index.html).[4]

A sample size of 400 is enough to represent China's more than 1.3 billion people or the more than 300 million American people. The sample size is independent of the population size for large populations.

Be an MR!

Visit the U.S. financial-services company Wells Fargo at www.wellsfargo.com and search the Internet, as well as your library's online databases, to obtain information on the proportion of consumers who use online banking. If about 15 percent of the people in a given area are expected to use Internet banking, what should be the sample size for a 95-percent confidence level and 5-percent precision level?

Be a DM!

As the vice president of marketing for Wells Fargo, what information would you need to determine whether the bank should expand its online services?

Experiential Learning

How the Poll Was Conducted

Credible media sources today, such as the *New York Times* (www.nytimes.com), attempt to make their research methods as transparent as possible to their readers. For example, the *New York Times* routinely runs a sidebar column explaining how a poll was conducted when an accompanying story draws heavily upon the results of such a poll. In one sidebar column entitled "How the Poll Was Conducted," the following was used as part of the details describing the research methods:

In theory, in 19 cases out of 20 the results based on such samples will differ by no more than 3 percentage points in either direction from what would have been obtained by seeking out all American adults.

In other words, "19 cases out of 20" would correspond to a 95-percent confidence level. (Remember that the value for

z associated with a 95-percent confidence interval would be 1.96.) Also, remember results showing 50 percent "for" and 50 percent "against" would have the highest amount of variance. Therefore, computations using 0.50 as the proportion (π) would account for the most challenging scenario when designing a sample.

1. Using the equations presented in this chapter, estimate the size of the sample used in this national poll if the most challenging scenario existed.

2. What would the size of the sample have to be if researchers wanted a precision level of 1 percent?

3. If the original poll had used a 90-percent confidence interval, what would the sample size have to be?

Adjusting the Statistically Determined Sample Size

The sample size specified by these statistical methods is a final, or net, sample size. It represents the number of returned mail questionnaires or the number of completed interviews. Initial oversampling, in which a much larger number of respondents are originally contacted, is required to achieve the desired net sample. This is due to two factors: the incidence rate and the completion rate.

Incidence Rate

The **incidence rate** refers to the rate of occurrence. It is influenced by the proportion of people in the population with the characteristics under study. When studying a characteristic with a low incident rate, the researcher must initially contact many more people than if the characteristic has a high incidence rate, screening out those who do not meet the study requirements. Suppose a study of jewelry in the United Kingdom calls for a sample of female heads of households aged 25 to 55 years. Of the British women between the ages of 20 and 60 years who might reasonably be approached to see if they qualify, approximately 75 percent are heads of households between age 25 and 55. That is, the incidence rate or the rate of occurrence is 0.75. This means that, on average, 1.33 (1.00/0.75) British women must be approached in order to obtain one qualified respondent.

Additional criteria for qualifying respondents (e.g., they must be using a specific product brand) will further decrease the incidence rate and therefore increase the number of contacts. Suppose it is decided that respondents must have worn jewelry in the past week in order to be eligible to participate in the study. It is estimated that 60 percent of the women contacted would meet this criterion of wearing jewelry. Then

incidence rate
The rate of occurrence of persons eligible to participate in the study expressed as a percentage.

the incidence rate drops from 75 percent to 45 percent (0.75×0.60). To deliver one qualified respondent to the sample, 2.22 individuals ($1.00/0.45$) must be contacted initially.

Completion Rate

completion rate
The percentage of qualified respondents who complete an interview. It enables researchers to take into account anticipated refusals by people who qualify.

The number of initial contacts must also be increased in anticipation of refusals coming from people qualified to participate. The **completion rate** denotes the percentage of qualified respondents who complete the interview. For example, if the researcher expects an interview completion rate of 80 percent of eligible respondents, the number of contacts should be increased by a factor of 1.25 ($1.00/0.80$).

Combined Adjustment

Combining the expected incident and completion rates results in a contacted sample that is 2.78 (2.22×1.25) times the final sample size requirement. In general,

$$\text{Initial sample size} = \frac{\text{Final sample size}}{\text{Incidence rate} \times \text{Completion rate}}$$

The number of units that must be sampled is equal to the initial sample size. These calculations assume that an attempt to contact a respondent will result in a determination as to whether the respondent is eligible. However, this might not be case. An attempt to contact the respondent might be inconclusive, because the respondent might refuse to answer, not be at home, be busy, and so on. Such instances will further increase the initial sample size. The following example illustrates a variety of variables that can be used to qualify potential respondents. It also shows that as the number of qualifying variables increases, the incidence rate will fall.

Research in Action

Targeting Women's Lips

When Lancôme (www.lancome.com), a luxury-products division of France's L'Oréal Groupe, conducted a survey to determine American women's preferences for lip color, it defined the target population very precisely. A respondent had to meet the following screening criteria to be included in the study: (1) female, (2) age 25 to 55 years, and (3) annual household income of at least $30,000. Having three qualifying factors resulted in a highly targeted sample, although it boosted the initial sample size because of a much lower incidence rate. Survey results showed that these women were looking for a lipstick that provided more moisturizing comfort, more even application and coverage, and less caking and feathering.

    Based on these findings, Lancôme developed and introduced Rouge Idole and Juicy Rouge. Rouge Idole was a lipstick with sensational effects and lasting radiance. Juicy Rouge was positioned as a "delectable treat for lips that shines on and on. The sheer pleasure of a lipstick with just-picked juicy sweetness." These lipsticks were well received in the U.S. marketplace.[5]

Another rate that is of interest in surveys is the **response rate**, which is the number of completed interviews divided by the number of eligible respondents in the sample. Thus, it is calculated as follows:

$$\text{Response rate} = \frac{\text{Number of completed interviews}}{\text{Number of eligible respondents in the sample}}$$

response rate
The number of completed interviews divided by the number of eligible respondents in the sample.

Tools such as SurveySite's (www.surveysite.com) response rate calculator are available to determine how many people are visiting a Web site and how many of those are willing participants for a pop-up Internet survey. The following is an example of the results:

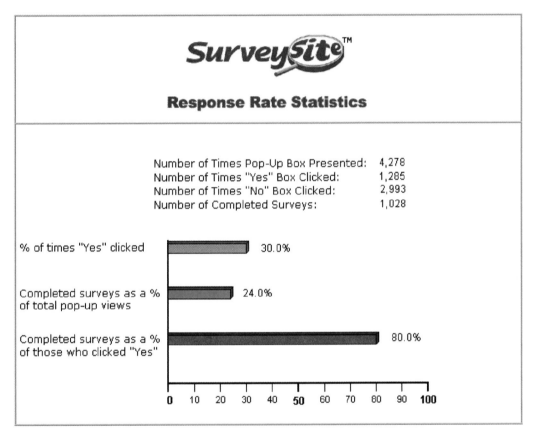

Source: www.surveysite.com

Online Sampling Adjustments

The sample size for online surveys generally exceeds that determined statistically. The reason for this is that the marginal cost of collecting and analyzing larger samples is low. Moreover, larger samples permit a more detailed level of analysis at the subgroup or segment level. Some of the biggest challenges in online research are the abilities to generate a truly random sample that is representative of the target population and to increase the response rate. This is more problematic when conducting consumer surveys as compared to business surveys.

Summary Illustration Using the Opening Vignette

The statistical approaches to determining sample size based on confidence intervals can involve estimation of the mean (e.g., mean hours spent watching TV or using online services) or proportion (e.g., proportion of respondents using online services). Statistical calculation of sample size requires specification of the precision level, the confidence level, and the population standard deviation. In the opening vignette, only the precision level (about 5%) was disclosed. Therefore, we could not determine whether the sample

Experiential Learning

The Ultimate Rocky Mountain Destination

Skiing is a popular winter sport in the United States.

1. Visit www.ski.com and search the Internet, as well as your library's online databases, to obtain information on the incidence (proportion) of people who ski every season.

2. In a survey of the general U.S. population on skiing, what should be the sample size for a 95-percent confidence level and 5-percent precision level? As an estimate of the population proportion, use the proportion you have determined in step 1.

3. Using the incidence rate you have determined and a completion rate of 50 percent, what should be the number of initial contacts to achieve a final sample size of 500 skiers?

4. As the director of marketing for Vail Cascade Resort in the western state of Colorado, "the ultimate Rocky Mountain destination," what information would you need to formulate marketing strategies to increase your sales?

size of 262 in the America Online survey was adequate and whether the conclusion reached was warranted. However, we know that the sample size required to estimate a proportion near 0.5 with a 95-percent confidence level and 5-percent precision level is 385. The sample size in the opening vignette falls substantially short of this mark. Figure 13.5 offers a concept map for determining sample size for means.

International Marketing Research

When conducting marketing research in foreign countries, statistical estimation of sample size can be difficult, because estimates of the population variance might be unavailable. Hence, the sample size often is determined by qualitative considerations, as discussed in

FIGURE 13.5

A Concept Map for Determining Sample Size for Means

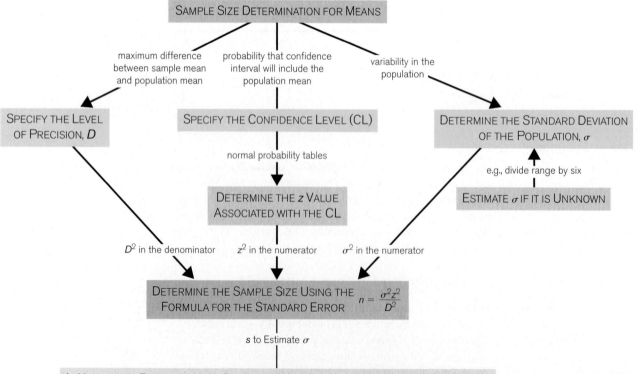

Chapter 12. When statistical estimation of sample size is attempted, the differences in esti-mates of population variance should be recognized and factored in, if possible. For exam-ple, consumer preferences for certain products might be relatively heterogeneous in markets where those products have been newly introduced. Thus, it might be a mistake to assume that the population variance is the same or to use the same sample size across countries. However, when the goal is to examine differences across countries or interna-tional markets, then it is desirable to have the same sample size across countries, as illus-trated by Nokia.

Research in Action

Nokia: Determining Inequalities with Equal Sample Sizes

With revenue at $54.292 billion and net income at $5.644 billion in 2006, the Finnish multinational communications company Nokia is the world's largest manufacturer of mobile telephones, with a global device market share of approximately 36 percent in the first quarter of 2007. But with industry disappointment in its N-Gage series, Nokia intends to revive its mobile gaming market with the new N-Series mobile phones. A survey was done by a joint effort between Nokia and the well-known U.S. marketing-research firm ACNielsen in 2007 of 1,800 mobile gamers in six nations: the United States, Germany, Spain, China, India, and Thailand. They divided the 1,800 respondents into 300 member groups from each nation and region. The sample size was kept constant across countries, because the goal was to compare the findings across nations to determine differences.

The findings revealed several differences across countries. In the U.S. market, over-the-air game distribution via the phone deck was favored by 60 percent of gamers surveyed, and only 27 percent preferred the Internet. Out of the 300 Nokia/ACNielsen surveyed in this market, 40 percent said they play games every day, as opposed to Germany, where only 21 percent do so. In time spent gaming per session, U.S. gamers (30.6 minutes) were second only to Indian players (38.9 minutes), with Chinese gamers (18.6 minutes) spending the least amount of time on games. Also, according to the sur-vey, Nokia found that 63 percent of those surveyed prefer the more sophisticated designs over older Java and 2D games once they had been trialed. Based on these findings, Nokia developed a customized strategy for penetrating each country's mobile gaming market with the new N-Series mobile phones.[6]

Technology and Marketing Research

Software is available that can be used to determine the sample size for various sampling techniques. For simple applications, appropriate sample-size formulas can be programmed using spreadsheet programs. The researcher specifies the desired precision level, confi-dence level, and population variance. The software then determines the appropriate sample size for the study. By incorporating the cost of each sampling unit, the sample size can be adjusted based on budget considerations.

Several marketing research firms supply sample design software and services, includ-ing statistical determination of sample sizes and estimation of sample statistics. Survey Sampling International (www.ssisamples.com) has a line of sampling products. Its Contact and Cooperation Rate Adjustment software statistically adjusts sample sizes by taking into account the expected contact and cooperation (completion) rates.

Ethics in Marketing Research

The sample size is one of the major determinants of cost in a marketing research project. It might seem that if the sample size is statistically determined, this procedure is free from ethical conflicts. This might not be true, however. As this chapter has emphasized, the sample size is directly proportional to the variance of the variable. Estimates of the population variance are based on small pilot studies, related research, and the researcher's judgment. Because judgment is involved, the researcher has the ethical responsibility to not use large estimates of the population variance simply to increase the cost of the project by inflating the sample size. Using the sample-size formula, we can see that increasing the standard deviation by 20 percent, for example, will increase the sample size by 44 percent. This practice is clearly unethical.

Furthermore, the researcher might be faced with ethical dilemmas when the sample standard deviation varies widely from that which is assumed. In this case, the confidence interval will be larger than required if the actual sample standard deviation turns out to be much larger than that used to estimate the sample size. If this happens, the researcher should disclose the larger confidence interval to the client and jointly arrive at a corrective action. The ethical ramifications of miscommunication of the confidence intervals of survey estimates based on statistical samples are underscored in the case of political polling.

Research in Action

Surveys Serve up Elections

In the United States, the release of political polling results during an election has been strongly criticized as manipulative and unethical. Critics have claimed that the general public is misled by these results. Polling results released before an election are thought to discourage voters from casting votes for candidates that are clearly trailing. Prediction of election results on election night has come under even harsher criticism. For example, in the Bush versus Kerry 2004 presidential election, polls by NBC and the Associated Press projected the winner in some states while polling was still open in several West Coast states. Opponents of this practice feel that this predisposes voters to vote for the projected winner or that it might even discourage voter turnout if a race appears to be decided. Not only are the effects of such projections criticized, but, frequently, the accuracy of the projections is questionable as well. Although voters might be told a candidate has a certain percentage of the votes within plus or minus 1 percent, the error denoted by the precision level might be much larger, depending on the sample size.[7]

What Would *You* Do?

Procter & Gamble: Taking a Gamble on Core Brands

The Situation

A. G. Lafley, CEO of the U.S. consumer-products company Procter & Gamble (P&G), turned around the consumer goods giant after taking the top job in 2000. He has refocused P&G on its big brands, including Tide, Pampers, and Crest. Lafley believes there is still tremendous growth in the core brands. He has made one thing clear: P&G's stodgy corporate culture is gone for good.

In May 2001, P&G acquired Moist Mates, "America's first moist bath tissue on a roll." P&G's research had found that 60 percent of consumers used some type of wet cleaning system, such as sprinkling water on dry toilet paper, using baby wipes, or wetting a washcloth. With that in mind, the purchase of Moist Mates became a strategic move in the market. P&G took the product and changed its name to Charmin Fresh Mates to go hand-in-hand with the popular Charmin dry tissue. The biggest problem consumers had experienced was that their makeshift cleaning methods were inconvenient. P&G's marketing research showed that the familiarity of brand name, convenience, and easy-to-use wet tissue on a roll appealed to the consumer. "Together, these products offer consumers a convenient way to choose dry, choose moist, or choose both," said Wayne Randall, Global Franchise Manager for Charmin. As of 2008, the Charmin line consisted of Ultra Strong, Ultra Soft, Basic, Plus, and Fresh Mates. Charmin and other P&G products are available in 180 countries around the world, and the company knows its products are "fresh." Yet some question whether Charmin and Charmin Fresh Mates are perceived as complementary or competing products.

The Marketing Research Decision

1. P&G would like to conduct periodic surveys to determine consumer perceptions and preferences for bath tissues, including Charmin and Charmin Fresh Mates. How should the sample size be determined?
   a. Using the confidence interval approach: means
   b. Using the confidence interval approach: proportions
   c. Based on sample size used in similar studies
   d. Guided by budget constraints
   e. Set at 500
2. Discuss the role of the sample size you recommend in enabling A. G. Lafley to determine consumer perceptions and preferences for bath tissues, including Charmin and Charmin Fresh Mates.

The Marketing Management Decision

1. To further increase the market share of Charmin and Charmin Fresh Mates, A. G. Lafley should do which of the following?
   a. Package Charmin and Charmin Fresh Mates together.
   b. Lower the prices of Charmin and Charmin Fresh Mates.
   c. Increase advertising expenditures on Charmin and Charmin Fresh Mates.
   d. Offer "buy one, get the other at half price" promotion.
   e. Promote Charmin products aggressively.

continued

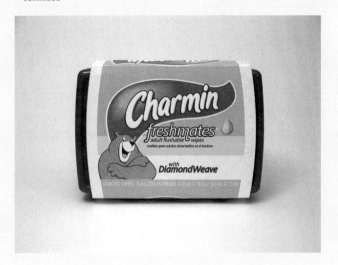

2. Discuss how the marketing management-decision action that you recommend to A. G. Lafley is influenced by the sample size that you suggested earlier and by the findings of that research.

What A. G. Lafley Did

Lafley decided to promote Charmin products aggressively. P&G introduced the Charmin Pottypalooza tour, which provided bathroom facilities with Charmin products. Charmin's in-bathroom marketing reached 30 million consumers in 2002. Research showed a 14-percent increase in Charmin sales among those consumers who used the P&G facilities, leading the company to roll out a second Pottypalooza unit for 2003. The event provided Charmin the ultimate captive audience and integrated marketing opportunity. People who lined up outside the bathrooms were entertained by a Charmin bear and once inside they saw a nonstop loop of TV ads featuring the iconic bear. The aggressive promotion of the Charmin line continued through the year 2008 with gains in sales and market share.[8]

Summary

The statistical approaches to determining sample size are based on confidence intervals. These approaches can involve the estimation of the mean or proportion. When estimating the mean or the proportion, determination of sample size using the confidence interval approach requires the specification of precision level, confidence level, and population standard deviation. The sample size determined statistically represents the final or net sample size that must be achieved. The initial sample size must be much larger to account for incidence rates and completion rates in order to deliver the final sample size.

The statistical estimation of sample size is even more complicated in international marketing research, because the population variance might differ from one country to the next. Several computer programs are available for statistically estimating the sample size and making adjustments for incidence and completion rates. The preliminary estimation of population variance for the purpose of determining the sample size also has ethical ramifications.

Key Terms and Concepts

Normal distribution, 403	Confidence level, 404	Standard error, 405
Parameter, 403	Random sampling error, 404	*z* value, 405
Statistic, 403	Sampling distribution, 404	Incidence rate, 413
Precision level, 403	Statistical inference, 404	Completion rate, 414
Confidence interval, 403	Central limit theorem, 404	Response rate, 415

Suggested Cases and Video Cases

Running Case with Real Data

1.1 Hewlett-Packard

Comprehensive Critical Thinking Cases

2.1 American Idol   2.2 Baskin-Robbins   2.3 Akron Children's Hospital

Comprehensive Cases with Real Data

3.1 Bank of America   3.2 McDonald's   3.3 Boeing

Video Cases

13.1 Subaru   19.1 Marriott

Live Research: Conducting a Marketing Research Project

1. Discuss the qualitative and statistical considerations involved in determining the sample size.
2. Illustrate the confidence interval approach (mean or proportion) to calculate the sample size of the project, even though the sample size might have been determined based on qualitative considerations.
3. Discuss the expected incidence and completion rates and the initial sample size.
4. The sampling technique and the sample size should be discussed and approved by the client.

Acronym

The statistical considerations involved in determining the sample size can be summarized by the acronym SIZE:

S ampling distribution

I nterval (confidence)

Z value

E stimation of population standard deviation

Review Questions

1. Define the sampling distribution.
2. What is the standard error of the mean?
3. What is a confidence interval?
4. What is the procedure for constructing a confidence interval around a mean?
5. How do the degree of confidence and the degree of precision differ?
6. Describe the procedure for determining the sample size necessary to estimate a population mean given the degree of precision and confidence and a known population variance. After the sample is selected, how is the confidence interval generated?
7. Describe the procedure for determining the sample size necessary to estimate a population mean when the degree of precision and confidence level are known but the population variance is unknown. After the sample is selected, how is the confidence interval generated?
8. How is the sample size affected when the absolute precision with which a population mean is estimated is doubled?
9. How is the sample size affected when the degree of confidence with which a population mean is estimated is increased from 95 percent to 99 percent?
10. Describe the procedure for determining the sample size necessary to estimate a population proportion given the degree of precision and confidence. After the sample is selected, how is the confidence interval generated?
11. How can the researcher ensure that the generated confidence interval will be no larger than the desired interval when estimating a population proportion?

Applied Problems

1. Using Table 2 of the Appendix of Statistical Tables, calculate the probability that:
   a. z is less than 1.48.
   b. z is greater than 1.90.
   c. z is between 1.48 and 1.90.
   d. z is between -1.48 and 1.90.

2. What is the value of z if:
   a. 60 percent of all values of z are larger.
   b. 10 percent of all values of z are larger.
   c. 68.26 percent of all possible z values (symmetrically distributed around the mean) are to be contained in this interval.

3. The management of a local restaurant wants to determine the average monthly amount spent by households in fancy restaurants. Management wants to be 95-percent confident of the findings and does not want the error to exceed plus or minus $5.
   a. After the survey was conducted, the average expenditure was found to be $90.30 and the standard deviation was $45. Construct a 95-percent confidence interval.
   b. What sample size would have resulted in a standard deviation of $45?
4. To determine the effectiveness of the advertising campaign for a new digital video recorder, management would like to know what percentage of the households are aware of the new brand. The advertising agency thinks that this figure is as high as 70 percent. The management would like a 95-percent confidence interval and a margin of error no greater than plus or minus 2 percent.
   a. What sample size should be used for this study?
   b. Suppose that management wanted to be 99-percent confident, but could tolerate an error of plus or minus 3 percent. How would the sample size change?
5. Assuming that $n = 100$ and $\sigma = 5$, compute the standard error of the mean.
6. Using a spreadsheet software package (e.g., Excel), program the formulas for determining the sample size under the various approaches.
7. Solve Applied Problems 3 through 5, using the programs that you have developed in Applied Problem number 6.
8. Visit the Gallup Web site (www.gallup.com). Identify some of the surveys recently completed by Gallup. What were the sample sizes, and how were they determined in these surveys?

Group Discussion

1. "Quantitative considerations are more important than qualitative considerations in determining the sample size." Discuss this statement as a small group. Alternatively, split a group into two smaller subgroups. One subgroup develops arguments for this statement, the other against.
2. Discuss the various options available for estimating incidence rates.

Hewlett-Packard Running Case

Review the Hewlett-Packard (HP) case, Case 1.1, and questionnaire given toward the end of the book.
1. Search the Internet, as well as your library's online databases, to obtain information on the proportion of U.S. households that have Internet access at home.
2. In a survey of the general population on Internet usage, what should be the sample size for a 95-percent confidence level and a 5-percent precision level? Use the estimate of the population proportion that you determined in step 1.
3. As the director of marketing for HP PCs and notebooks, what information would you need to formulate marketing strategies to increase your sales?

Appendix 13A

The Normal Distribution

In this appendix, we provide a brief overview of the normal distribution and the use of the normal distribution table. The normal distribution is used in calculating the sample size, and it serves as the basis for classical statistical inference. Many continuous phenomena follow the normal distribution or can be approximated by it. The normal distribution can, likewise, be used to approximate many discrete probability distributions.[*]

The normal distribution has some important theoretical properties. It is bell-shaped and symmetrical in appearance. Its measures of central tendency (mean, median, and mode) are all identical. Its associated random variable has an infinite range ($-\infty < x < +\infty$).

The normal distribution is defined by the population mean, μ, and the population standard deviation, σ. Because an infinite number of combinations of μ and σ exist, an infinite number of normal distributions exist and an infinite number of tables would be required. By standardizing the data, we need only one table, such as Table 2 given in the Appendix of Statistical Tables. Standardization is the process of rescaling data to have a mean of 0 and a standard deviation of 1. Any normal random variable X can be converted to a standardized normal random variable z by the formula:

$$ z = \frac{X - \mu}{\sigma} $$

Note that the random variable z is always normally distributed with a mean of 0 and a standard deviation of 1. The normal probability tables are generally used for two purposes: (1) finding probabilities corresponding to known values of X or z and (2) finding values of X or z corresponding to known probabilities. We will discuss each of these uses.

Finding Probabilities Corresponding to Known Values

Suppose Figure 13A.1 represents the distribution of the number of engineering contracts an engineering firm receives per year. Because the data span the entire history of the firm, Figure 13A.1 represents the population. Therefore, the probabilities or proportion of area under the curve must add up to 1.0. The vice president of marketing wishes to determine the probability that the number of contracts received next year will be

FIGURE 13A.1

Finding Probabilities Corresponding to Known Values

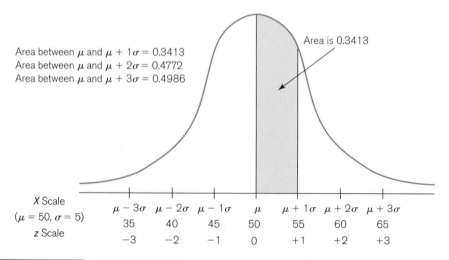

Area between μ and $\mu + 1\sigma = 0.3413$
Area between μ and $\mu + 2\sigma = 0.4772$
Area between μ and $\mu + 3\sigma = 0.4986$

Area is 0.3413

$\mu - 3\sigma$	$\mu - 2\sigma$	$\mu - 1\sigma$	μ	$\mu + 1\sigma$	$\mu + 2\sigma$	$\mu + 3\sigma$
35	40	45	50	55	60	65
-3	-2	-1	0	+1	+2	+3

X Scale ($\mu = 50$, $\sigma = 5$)

z Scale

---

[*]This material is drawn from Mark L Berenson, David M. Levine, and Timothy Krehbiel, *Basic Business Statistics: Concepts and Applications*, 11th ed. (Upper Saddle River, NJ: Prentice Hall, 2009).

between 50 and 55. The answer can be determined by using Table 2 of the Appendix of Statistical Tables.

Table 2 of the Appendix of Statistical Tables gives the probability or area under the standardized normal curve from the mean (zero) to the standardized value of interest (z). Only positive entries of z are listed in the table. For a symmetrical distribution with zero mean, the area from the mean to $+z$ (i.e., z standard deviations above the mean) is identical to the area from the mean to $-z$ (i.e., z standard deviations below the mean).

Note that the difference between 50 and 55, which is 5, corresponds to a difference in z values of 1.00 (1.00 − 0.00). Note that to use Table 2 all z values must be recorded to two decimal places. To read the probability or area under the curve from the mean to $z = +1.00$, scan down the z column of Table 2 until the z value of interest (in tenths) is located. In this case, stop in the row $z = 1.00$. Then, read across this row until you intersect the column containing the hundredth place of the z value. Thus, in Table 2, the tabulated probability for $z = 1.00$ corresponds to the intersection of the row $z = 1.0$ with the column $z = 0.00$. This probability is 0.3413. As shown in Figure 13A.1, the probability is 0.3413 that the number of contracts received by the firm next year will be between 50 and 55. It can also be concluded that the probability is 0.6826 (2 × 0.3413), or 68.26 percent, that the number of contracts received next year will be between 45 and 55.

This result could be generalized to show that for any normal distribution the probability is 0.6826 that a randomly selected item will fall within ±1 standard deviation above or below the mean. Also, it can be verified from Table 2 that there is a 0.9544 probability that any randomly selected normally distributed observation will fall within ±2 standard deviations above or below the mean and that there is a 0.9973 probability the observation will fall within ±3 standard deviations above or below the mean.

Finding Values Corresponding to Known Probabilities

Suppose the vice president of marketing wishes to determine how many contracts must come in so that this number represents 5 percent of the contracts expected for the year. If 5 percent of the contracts have come in, 95 percent of the contracts have yet to come. As shown in Figure 13A.2, this 95 percent can be broken down into two parts: contracts above the mean (i.e., 50 percent) and contracts between the mean and the desired z value (i.e., 45 percent). The desired z value can be determined from Table 2, because the area under the normal curve from the standardized mean, zero, to this z must be 0.4500. From Table 2, we search for the area or probability 0.4500. The closest value is 0.4495 or 0.4505. For 0.4495, we see that the z value corresponding to the particular z row (1.6) and z column

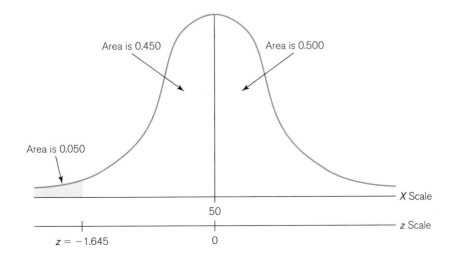

FIGURE 13A.2

Finding Values Corresponding to Known Probabilities

Finding Values Corresponding to Known Probabilities: Confidence Interval

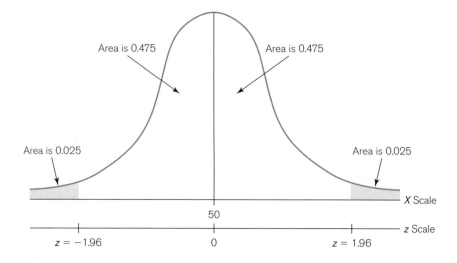

(0.04) is 1.64. However, the z value must be recorded as negative (i.e., $z = -1.64$), because it is below the standardized mean of zero. Similarly, the z value corresponding to the area of 0.4505 is -1.65. Because 0.4500 is midway between 0.4495 and 0.4505, the appropriate z value could be midway between the two z values and estimated as -1.645. The corresponding X value can then be calculated from the standardization formula as follows:

$$X = \mu + z\,\sigma$$

or

$$X = 50 + (-1.645)\,5 = 41.775$$

Suppose the vice president wanted to determine the interval in which 95 percent of the contracts for next year are expected to lie. As can be seen from Figure 13A.3, the corresponding z values are ± 1.96. This corresponds to X values of $50 \pm (1.96)\,5$, or 40.2 and 59.8. This range represents the 95-percent confidence interval.

SUBARU: "Mr. Survey" Monitors Customer Satisfaction

Subaru of America (www.subaru.com) is the automobile division of Fuji Heavy Industries (FHI). Subaru has been operating in the United States since 1968, when it began selling the 360 Minicar. Headquartered in Cherry Hill, New Jersey, the company serves nearly 600 dealers nationwide. Subaru has offered many different cars over the years, but as of 2008 it sold five different brands in the United States. These brands each have a variety of different models. The five brands are the Tribeca, the Outback, the Forester, the Legacy, and the Impreza. One of the unique things about Subaru is that 100 percent of its models come with all-wheel drive.

Subaru's strategy is apparent in one of its key players, Joe Barstys. Joe has been with Subaru for more than 20 years, and he spends his time worrying about customer satisfaction. Joe and people like him are the backbone of Subaru. These people help Subaru focus on its customers and their wants and needs by conducting marketing research. Joe has incorporated the use of customer surveys into his practice, and for this he has gained the title of "Mr. Survey." Joe's goal is to develop a customer-satisfaction level that will help build a certain level of loyalty in Subaru's customers. This loyalty is extremely important in the car business, because it has historically been much lower than in other industries. Marketing research has shown that although approximately 90 percent of customers are pleased with their automobile purchase, only 40 percent are loyal enough to buy the same brand again.

Surveys are a very valuable tool to Subaru in its quest for customer loyalty. The company mails a survey to each customer within 30 to 45 days of purchase to assess the customer's feelings toward the newly purchased vehicle, to obtain information on the nature of the interaction with the dealer, and to learn about other elements of the purchase process. Subsequent to the initial contact, more surveys follow throughout the "lifetime" of the customer (i.e., the duration of ownership of the car, on average 6 to 7 years). The latter surveys assess the long-term satisfaction with the vehicle and the dealership. The mail surveys have a high 50 percent response rate. As of 2008, about 500,000 surveys are mailed each year. Additional surveys are conducted over the Internet. Questions on the survey include: How was your service experience? How does Subaru compare to other service providers you have visited? What about the buying experience? How satisfied were you? What were the sales people like? These questions help Subaru determine how customers regard their Subaru experience and what steps Subaru should take to improve this experience further.

These surveys provide important feedback, allowing Subaru to adjust its approach based on consumer demands. An example of the importance of adjustments can be found in the case of the female consumer. Through surveys, Subaru found out that it needed to adjust its marketing to include female consumers, who are becoming an increasingly large part of the market. It was important for Subaru to understand what types of things would appeal to women in order to offer a more desirable product to them.

Another benefit of marketing and survey research is that Subaru has been able to identify the types of people who are more likely to buy its automobiles. Subaru believes that the typical Subaru owner is different from the average consumer. Its average consumer is highly intelligent, highly independent, and outside the mainstream crowd. Thus, Subaru tries to market automobiles to these types of people and attempts to distinguish itself from the larger, more mainstream competitors. Results of affinity for the company are evident as customers feel motivated to send pictures of their cars to Subaru.

Joe considers his background in philosophy and theology (he has a B.A. in Philosophy and an M.A. in Theology) to have contributed to the role of Mr. Survey he plays at Subaru. Joe explains that his theology and philosophy background allows him to look at the human experience with a product. A customer's problem could be a dysfunction with his car, his dealer, or his own ignorance about how the car works. All of these are essentially about human experience, and hence no matter whether Joe works in the automobile industry or any other he is, in effect, dealing with human experience. This human experience is just one aspect that he loves about his job, because he loves being with people and finding out what makes them tick. The other aspect that he is really excited about is the great responsibility and decision-making authority that he shoulders with the goal of maintaining customer loyalty, and every year he achieves success.

The company's goal is continued growth through 2012, and it hopes that with the help of marketing research it will be able to achieve this goal. It believes that listening to the customers and adapting its practices to meet their concerns will provide customers with a higher level of satisfaction and ultimately lead to a higher level of loyalty. Subaru's marketing research staff, like "Mr. Survey," will be critical to this endeavor.

Conclusion

The case presents an interesting overview of Joe Barstys' role at Subaru and the importance and utility of surveys in building customer loyalty. Surveys have helped Subaru get continuous feedback on key parameters that shape customer experience resulting in high brand loyalty. In sum, marketing research has helped Subaru understand its customers better and hence address their needs and expectations better.

Questions

1. Discuss the role that marketing research can play in helping Subaru understand why its customers are devoted to the brand.
2. In order to continue to grow, Subaru must foster and build customer loyalty. Define the management-decision problem.
3. Define an appropriate marketing research problem based on the management-decision problem you have identified.
4. What type of research design should be adopted to investigate the marketing research problem you have identified?
5. In what way can Subaru make use of data from the 2000 (or 2010) U.S. Census? What are the limitations of these data? How can these limitations be overcome?
6. What type of data available from syndicated marketing research firms will be useful to Subaru?
7. Discuss the role of qualitative research in understanding the devotion of consumers to a particular automobile brand. Which qualitative research technique(s) should be used and why?
8. If a survey is to be conducted to understand consumer preferences for various automobile brands, which survey method should be used and why?
9. Can Subaru make use of causal research? If yes, how?
10. Design ordinal, interval, and ratio scales for measuring consumer preferences for various automobile brands.
11. Design Likert, semantic differential, and Stapel scales for measuring consumer preferences for various automobile brands.
12. Design a questionnaire to measure consumers' evaluation of Subaru brands.
13. Develop a sampling plan for the survey of Question 8.

14. How should the sample size be determined?
15. If Subaru were to conduct marketing research to determine consumer willingness to purchase automobile brands in Germany, how would the research process be different?
16. Discuss the ethical issues involved in researching consumer willingness to purchase automobile brands.

References

1. www.subaru.com, accessed on February 20, 2008.
2. www.wikipedia.org, accessed on February 20, 2008.
3. Donald I. Hammonds, "Subaru Adds Upscale Looks to Its Durable Image," *Knight Ridder Tribune Business News,* June 16, 2004, p. 1.

Data Collection, Analysis, and Reporting

Field Work: Data Collection

OPENING QUESTIONS

1. What is meant by field work, and what is the field work process?
2. In what aspects of interviewing should field workers be trained?
3. How should the field workers be supervised to enhance their effectiveness and efficiency?
4. How should field workers be evaluated?
5. How should field work be conducted in international marketing research?
6. How does technology facilitate field work?
7. What ethical issues are involved in field work?

> "I make my living interviewing senior executives in firms. I always arrive 30 minutes early for each appointment and always write a thank-you note to anyone at the firm who helped me that day. In short, your Mom was right. Courtesy is indispensable to success."
>
> *Robert J. Berrier, Ph.D.,*
> *Founder and President, Berrier*
> *Associates.*

Gallup's Galloping Field Work

Now more than ever, Americans are hanging up on interviewers. The primary difficulty of telephone interviewing is declining response rates and, more specifically, increasing refusal rates. Many techniques and procedures have been used to combat this problem, including incentives, aggressive call designs, shorter interviews, and special introductory statements. The most critical variable, however, might be the interviewers themselves.

Refusals are largely a function of interviewing skill. Top interviewers are rarely turned down. The Gallup Organization (www.gallup.com), a prestigious American marketing research and consulting firm that specializes in survey research, has identified the following characteristics of an outstanding interviewer:

- **Work orientation.** Works hard and sees work as more than a job, but as an expression of oneself.
- **Teamwork.** Forms good team relationships with others.
- **Aptitude.** Has a natural affinity for telephone research—enjoys collecting opinions via the telephone.
- **Pride.** Is positive, quality-conscious, and likes being recognized for a job well done.

- **Discipline.** Stays focused on a task and completes it.
- **Third ear.** Empathizes with a respondent and tailors presentation accordingly.
- **Command.** "Takes charge"—can turn refusals around by conveying the purpose of the survey and its importance.
- **Woo.** Gets people to like him or her quickly; convinces people to cooperate who might not otherwise respond.
- **Ethics.** Is honest and behaves ethically at all times.

Using this theme, the hiring process for interviewers at The Gallup Organization has become very selective, hiring only 1 out of every 16 candidates. The selected interviewers are carefully trained in all aspects of interviewing, from making the initial contact to terminating the interview. The Council of American Survey Research Organizations' guidelines for effective interviewing are followed. Experienced and qualified supervisors closely monitor the interviewers' work, making sure appropriate procedures are followed and the interviews are being properly conducted.

Validation of field work and the evaluation of interviewers are continuous activities. As a result, The Gallup Organization has not only increased the retention rate of its field workers, but has significantly increased the productivity and quality of its data collection. Gallup interviews more than 3 million people every year in the United States and has built a worldwide reputation for the high quality of its data collection process. As of 2008, Gallup had operations in 40 countries around the world and employed more than 2000 professionals.[1]

Overview

Field work is the fourth step in the marketing research process. It follows problem definition and development of the approach (see Chapter 2) and formulation of the research design (see Chapters 3 through 13). Figure 14.1 briefly explains the focus of the chapter, the relationship of this chapter to the previous ones, and the steps of the marketing research process on which this chapter concentrates.

During this phase, the field workers make contact with the respondents, administer the questionnaires or observation forms, record the data, and turn in the completed forms for processing. Field workers include a personal interviewer administering questionnaires door-to-door, an interviewer intercepting shoppers in a mall, a telephone interviewer calling from a central location, a worker mailing questionnaires from an office, an observer counting customers in a particular section of a store, and others involved in data collection and supervision of the process. The opening vignette gives the characteristics of outstanding interviewers, who form the backbone of field work.

This chapter describes the nature of field work and the field work/data collection process. This process involves the selection, training, and supervision of field workers, the validation of field work, and the evaluation of field workers. Care taken at each of these stages of the field work process can pay big dividends, as illustrated by The Gallup Organization in the opening vignette. The chapter also discusses field work in the context of international marketing research and technology and identifies the relevant ethical issues. Figure 14.2 gives an overview of the topics discussed in this chapter and how they flow from one to the next.

FIGURE 14.1

Relationship of Field Work to the Previous Chapters and the Marketing Research Process

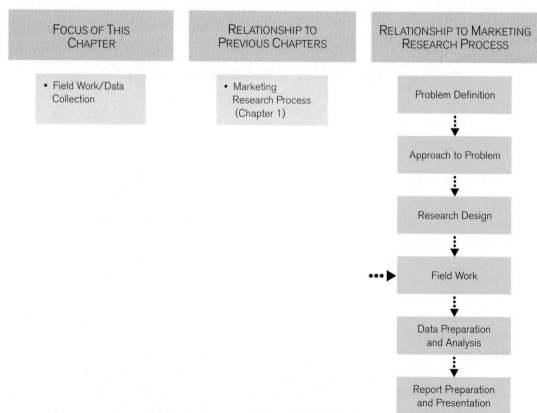

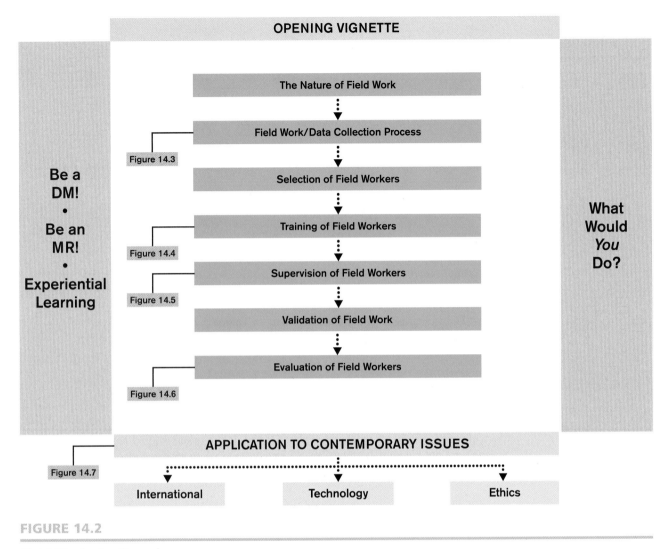

FIGURE 14.2

Field Work: An Overview

The Nature of Field Work

Those who design the research rarely collect marketing research data. Researchers have two major options for collecting their data: They can develop their own organizations, or they can contract with a field work agency. In either case, data collection involves using some kind of field force. This field force can operate either in the field (personal in-home, mall intercept, computer-assisted personal interviewing, and observation) or from an office (telephone/computer assisted telephone interviewing, mail/mail panel, and electronic surveys). The field workers who collect the data typically have little research background or training. Therefore, to ensure high quality the field work/data collection process should be streamlined and well controlled, as discussed in the following section.

Field Work/Data Collection Process

All field work involves the selection, training, and supervision of those who collect the data. The validation of field work and the evaluation of field workers also are parts of the process. All of these aspects were seen in the opening vignette, which described how

FIGURE 14.3

The Field Work/Data Collection Process

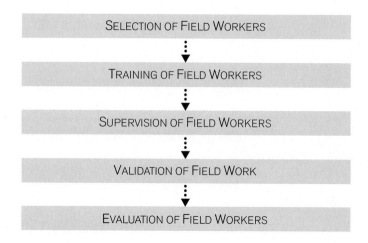

SELECTION OF FIELD WORKERS

⋮
▼

TRAINING OF FIELD WORKERS

⋮
▼

SUPERVISION OF FIELD WORKERS

⋮
▼

VALIDATION OF FIELD WORK

⋮
▼

EVALUATION OF FIELD WORKERS

Gallup selected, trained, supervised, monitored, and evaluated its field workers. Figure 14.3 represents a general framework for the field work/data collection process. Although this chapter describes a general process, it should be recognized that the nature of field work varies with the mode of data collection and that the relative emphasis on the different steps will vary for telephone, personal, mail, and electronic interviews.

Selection of Field Workers

The first step in the field work process is the selection of field workers. The researcher should (1) develop job specifications for the project, taking into account the mode of data collection; (2) decide what characteristics the field workers should have; and (3) recruit appropriate individuals. Interviewers' background characteristics, opinions, perceptions, expectations, and attitudes can affect the responses they elicit.

To the extent possible, interviewers should be selected to match respondents' demographic characteristics, because this increases the probability of a successful interview. The job requirements will also vary with the nature of the problem and the data collection method. However, some general qualifications of field workers were outlined in the opening vignette: work orientation, teamwork, aptitude, pride, discipline, third ear, command, the ability to woo, and ethics. Interviewers with these qualifications will have a high likelihood of being successful in conducting field work.

Field workers generally are paid an hourly rate or on a per-interview basis. In the United States, the typical interviewer is a married woman, age 35 to 54, with an above-average education and an above-average household income. The following example illustrates a psychographic breakdown of interviewers.

Research in Action

The Four Faces of Interviewers

Interviewers can be segmented into four psychographic groups, based on an analysis made by M/A/R/C (www.marcresearch.com) for the Marketing Research Association, a U.S. nonprofit organization that promotes global marketing research:

- **Dedicated Debbie.** To the Dedicated Debbie, interviewing is not just a job, but something much more important. She interviews because she enjoys it.

- **Independent Inez.** Independent Inez interviews because of the independence it gives her. Interviewing gives her freedom to choose when she wants to work and some freedom on the job as well.

- **Social Sara.** This interviewer enjoys interviewing almost as much as Dedicated Debbie, but she does not feel that interviewing is important. What attracts her is the chance to socialize, to meet interesting people, and to interact with others.
- **Professional Pat.** This is the career-oriented interviewer. She sees the job not only as a means to earn her living, but also as a marketing research career opportunity. Professional Pat considers the two most important attributes of an interviewer to be a detailed mind and exceptional intelligence.

Such an understanding of the psychographic profile of interviewers, along with their demographic characteristics, can greatly assist in identifying and selecting the right interviewers.[2]

Training of Field Workers

Training field workers is critical to the quality of data collected. Training can be conducted in person at a central location, or, if the interviewers are geographically dispersed, by mail, Internet, or videoconferencing. Training ensures that all interviewers administer the questionnaire in the same manner so that the data can be collected uniformly. Training should cover all phases of the interviewing process (see opening vignette): making the initial contact, asking questions, probing, recording answers, and terminating the interview (Figure 14.4).

The initial contact can result in the cooperation or the loss of potential respondents. Interviewers should be trained to make opening remarks that will convince potential respondents that their participation is important. Questions that directly ask permission, such as "May I have some of your valuable time?" or "Would you like to answer a few questions?" should be avoided, because people can answer "no." Interviewers should also be instructed on handling objections and refusals. For example, if the respondent says, "This is not a convenient time for me," the interviewer should respond, "What would be a more convenient time for you? I will call back then."

Asking questions is an art. Even a slight change in the wording, sequence, or manner in which a question is asked can distort its meaning and bias the response. Training in asking questions can yield high dividends by eliminating potential sources of bias. One method used to reduce response bias is to probe respondents. **Probing** is intended to motivate respondents to elaborate, clarify, or explain their answers. Probing also helps respondents focus on the specific content of the interview and provide only relevant information. Probing should not introduce any bias. Commonly used probes include questions such as "Any others?" "Anything else?" and "Could you tell me more about your thinking on that?" Probing can result in rich insights, as illustrated by Whirlpool.

probing
A motivational technique used when asking survey questions to induce the respondents to enlarge on, clarify, or explain their answers and to help the respondents focus on the specific content of the interview.

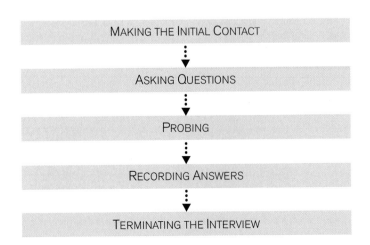

FIGURE 14.4

Training Field Workers

Research in Action

Probing Enables Whirlpool to Spin Out New Innovations

U.S.-based Whirlpool Corporation (www.whirlpool.com) is the world's leading manufacturer of major home appliances, with annual sales of more than $19.4 billion in 2007. As of 2008, the company markets its products to consumers in more than 170 countries around the world. Through in-home personal interviews, Whirlpool researched the market and the need for laundry equipment in Brazil. In-home personal interviews were used so that the interviewers could effectively probe respondents to determine their usage and underlying needs for major appliances. Great emphasis was placed on the selection and training of the interviewers.

The research concluded that there was high need for inexpensive equipment, but also showed that laundry equipment is viewed as a status symbol by many Brazilians. Moreover, the respondents expressed a strong desire to "show off" their washers to friends; they want them to be able to see how they work. These findings led Whirlpool to invest $30 million over 18 months to develop inexpensive washing machines in Brazil. These machines sell for under $200 and feature a clear plastic lid so that people can watch the washer operate.

Emphasis on the quality of field work has resulted in important findings, allowing Whirlpool to be a leader in the appliance industry and to successfully incorporate its new technologies into the marketplace.[3]

Although recording respondent answers seems simple, several mistakes are common. All interviewers should use the same format and conventions to record the interviews and edit completed interviews. Although the rules for recording answers to structured questions vary with each questionnaire, the general rule is to check the box that reflects the respondent's answer. The general rule for recording answers to unstructured questions is to record the responses verbatim.

Before terminating the interview, the interviewer should answer the respondent's questions about the project. The respondent should be left with a positive feeling about the interview. It is important to thank the respondent and express appreciation for his or her participation. The following example shows the importance of well-trained interviewers in the data collection process and the effect this has on new-product development research.

Research in Action

Brushing Interviewers Results in a Successful New Toothbrush

When Unilever USA, a division of Unilver N.V., a Dutch provider of nutritional and personal-care products, was conducting a survey to determine the market potential for a new toothbrush, the company realized that this research would be crucial to the development and introduction of a new product. To obtain high-quality data, the interviewers were carefully trained in all aspects of interviewing. Training in making the initial contact resulted in a much lower refusal rate. The interviewers were instructed to ask the questions as written, to diligently probe the respondents for open-ended questions, and to record the answers fully and accurately. Probing was crucial for questions such as, "Why are you (dis)satisfied with the brands of toothbrush currently available in the market?" Probing and recording answers to open-ended questions were particularly important, because the company was seeking to identify creative solutions to the oral-care problems consumers faced.

One innovative idea that emerged from the survey findings was a toothbrush that not only cleaned teeth, but that also offered an additional benefit of gum care. Based on this finding, Unilever developed and launched the Mentadent Oral Care toothbrush (www.mentadent.com). This was the first toothbrush to offer an additional therapeutic benefit of gum care, thereby pioneering the advanced therapeutic segment of the category. The toothbrush was designed with multilevel interior bristles to

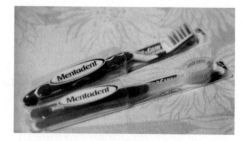

clean teeth effectively and with flared side bristles to gently massage and stimulate gums. It was positioned as the state-of-the-art choice for people who were serious about oral care.

The launch was a strong success, because the product addressed an unmet consumer need: care for both teeth and gums. In 2003, the company introduced Mentadent Inter-Sweep, the first toothbrush to integrate Flexible Picks with Micro Fiber Cleaning Bristles. The Inter-Sweep toothbrush is designed with soft flexible picks and multilevel and fan-shaped bristles to clean hard-to-reach areas between teeth, gently and effectively "sweeping" away plaque. As of 2008, Mentadent toothbrushes were available in five varieties: White & Clean, ProCare, Oral Care, Surround, and Inter-Sweep. A major factor contributing to these successes was the careful training of the interviewers that was instrumental in discovering the need for these innovative toothbrushes.[4]

Supervision of Field Workers

Supervision of field workers means making sure that they are following the procedures and techniques in which they were trained, as illustrated by The Gallup Organization in the opening vignette. Supervision involves quality control and editing, sampling control, control of cheating, and central office control (Figure 14.5).

Quality control of field workers requires checking to see if the field procedures are being properly implemented. If problems are detected, the supervisor should discuss them with the field workers and provide additional training, if necessary. To understand the interviewers' problems, the supervisors should also conduct some interviews. Supervisors should collect questionnaires and edit them daily. They should examine the questionnaires to ensure that all the appropriate questions have been completed, that unsatisfactory or incomplete answers have not been accepted, and that the writing is legible. Supervisors should also keep a record of hours worked and expenses. This will make it easy to determine the cost per completed interview, whether the job is moving on schedule, and if any interviewers are having problems.

An important aspect of supervision is **sampling control**, which attempts to ensure that the interviewers are strictly following the sampling plan rather than selecting sampling units based on convenience or accessibility. To control these problems, supervisors should keep daily records of the number of calls made, the number of not-at-homes, the number of refusals, the number of completed interviews for each interviewer, and the total for all interviewers under their control.

Cheating involves falsifying part of a question or the entire questionnaire. An interviewer might falsify part of an answer to make it acceptable or might fake answers. The most blatant form of cheating occurs when the interviewer falsifies the entire questionnaire, filling in answers without contacting a respondent. Cheating can be minimized through proper training, supervision, and validation of field work.

sampling control
An aspect of supervision that ensures that the interviewers strictly follow the sampling plan rather than select sampling units based on convenience or accessibility.

FIGURE 14.5

Supervising Field Workers

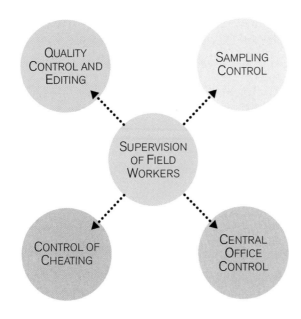

Central office control involves tabulating the responses to important demographic characteristics and key questions. It also includes checking on the quotas to make sure they are being met. Supervisors provide quality and cost-control information to the central office so that a progress report can be maintained.

The following example illustrates the importance of close supervision in collecting high-quality data.

Research in Action

Lite Bar Is from Mars

M&M Mars (www.mmmars.com), a division of the U.S. food-products company Mars, Inc. (www.mars.com), frequently conducts mall-intercept interviews to identify and test new product concepts. Shoppers are intercepted at various locations in the mall and taken to a central facility where they can taste candy bars under development and then respond to surveys. The surveys contain a fair number of open-ended or unstructured questions that require interviewers to probe respondents. Probing provides rich insights into respondents' underlying values, attitudes, and beliefs. Because all such interviews are conducted at a central location, supervision of the interviewers is greatly facilitated. Completed questionnaires are available to the supervisors immediately after the interview for editing and quality control. Sampling control is easily exercised and cheating is eliminated, so there is no need for validation. This procedure also is good for implementing quota sampling, which often is used, and also facilitates other aspects of central office control, such as tabulation of responses to key questions.

A recent mall-intercept survey indicated a strong preference for a low-fat candy bar, because such a product would

allow people to indulge without feeling guilty. Accordingly, M&M Mars introduced Milky Way Lite, a reduced-fat candy bar. This was the first nationally advertised candy bar labeled to meet regulations of the U.S. Food and Drug Administration's Nutrition Labeling and Education Act for "lite" products. It has 5 grams of fat, half the fat of the average leading chocolate brands. Close supervision of field workers, made possible by mall-intercept interviewing, facilitated the research responsible for introducing yet another winner for M&M Mars. As of 2008, Milky Way Lite is a top-selling candy bar.[5]

Experiential Learning

Feeding Interviewers Chips and Snacks

Consumption patterns for chips and snacks change often. The brand manager for Lay's chips, a division of PepsiCo specializing in snackfoods, would like to conduct a telephone survey to determine the consumption of chips and snacks.

1. Visit www.lays.com and search the Internet, as well as your library's online databases, to obtain information on the consumption of chips and snacks. Design an appropriate questionnaire.

2. Train an interviewer (a fellow student) and have her or him conduct the telephone interview with a respondent (another student).

3. How would you supervise this interviewer?

4. As the brand manager for Lay's chips, what information would help you formulate marketing strategies to increase sales?

Validation of Field Work

Validation of field work means verifying that field workers are submitting authentic interviews. To validate the study, the supervisors call 10 to 25 percent of the respondents to inquire whether the field workers actually conducted the interviews. The supervisors ask about the length and quality of the interview, reaction to the interviewer, and basic demographic data. The demographic information is cross-checked against the information reported by the interviewers on the questionnaires.

Evaluation of Field Workers

It is important to evaluate field workers to provide them with feedback on their performance. Evaluation helps identify the more effective field workers in order to build a better, higher-quality field force. As in the case of The Gallup Organization in the opening vignette, the evaluation of field workers should be an ongoing process. The evaluation criteria should be clearly communicated to the field workers during their training. The evaluation of field workers should be based on the criteria of quantity (cost and time, response rates) and quality (quality of interviewing, quality of data), as shown in Figure 14.6.

Interviewers can be compared in terms of the total cost (salary and expenses) per completed interview. Field workers should also be evaluated on how they spend their time. Time should be broken down into categories, such as actual interviewing, travel, and administration. It is important to monitor response rates on a timely basis so that corrective action can be taken if these rates are too low. Supervisors can help interviewers with an inordinate number of refusals by listening to the introductions they use and providing immediate feedback. When all the interviews are over, different field workers' percentage of refusals can be compared to identify the better workers.

To evaluate interviewers on the quality of interviewing, the supervisor must directly observe the interviewing process. The supervisor can do this in person, or the field worker can tape record the interview. The completed questionnaires of each interviewer should be evaluated for the quality of data. Some indicators of quality data are (1) the recorded data are legible; (2) all instructions, including skip patterns (discussed in Chapter 11), are followed; (3) the answers to unstructured questions are recorded verbatim; (4) the answers to unstructured questions are meaningful and complete enough to be coded (discussed in Chapter 11); and (5) for structured questions item nonresponse occurs infrequently.

Experiential Learning

Vending Field Work

What is it like to conduct field work? Go to the textbook Web site, select Chapter 14, and download the following file: Vending Machine Survey.doc. Print five copies of this survey, select a building on campus with vending machines, go there, and conduct separate survey interviews with five different people from that building.

1. How did you feel approaching these respondents?

2. What seemed to be the most challenging part of the survey for the respondents?

3. If other students were employed to collect the data for this survey project, how should they be trained?

4. If other students were employed to collect the data for this survey project, how should their field work be supervised?

5. If other students were employed to collect the data for this survey project, how should their field work be evaluated?

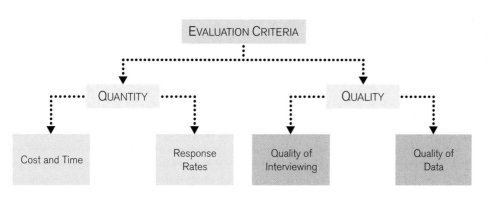

FIGURE 14.6

Evaluating Field Workers

Using the Internet in Field Work

The Internet can play a valuable role in all the phases of field work, including the selection, training, supervision, validation, and evaluation of field workers. As far as selection is concerned, interviewers can be located, interviewed, and hired via the Internet. This process can be initiated, for example, by posting notices of job vacancies for interviewers at the company Web site, bulletin boards, and other suitable locations. Although this would confine the search to only Internet-savvy interviewers, this might well be a qualification for the job.

Similarly, the Internet, with its multimedia capabilities, can be a good supplementary tool for training the field workers in all aspects of interviewing. Training in this manner can complement personal training programs and add value to the process. Facilitating communication between the supervisors and the interviewers via e-mail and secured chat rooms enhances supervision. By posting progress reports and quality and cost-control information on a secured location at a Web site, it is easily available to all the relevant parties and can strengthen central office control.

Validation of field work, especially for personal and telephone interviews, can be easily accomplished for those respondents who have an e-mail address or access to the Internet. These respondents can be sent a short verification survey by e-mail or be asked to visit a Web site where the survey is posted. The evaluation criteria can be communicated to field workers during the training stage by using the Internet, and performance feedback can also be provided to them using this medium.

Summary Illustration Using the Opening Vignette

Notice the care The Gallup Organization took in selecting its interviewers, choosing only 1 out of every 16 possible candidates. In selecting interviewers, Gallup looks for the following qualities: work orientation, teamwork, aptitude, pride, discipline, third ear, command, the ability to woo, and ethical behavior. These interviewers are thoroughly trained by following the guidelines on interviewing by the Council of American Survey Research Organizations. Experienced and qualified supervisors closely supervise the interviewers.

Research in Action

Representing 300 companies and other research organizations, the Council of American Survey Research Organizations (www.casro.org) has provided the following guidelines for effective interviewing:

1. Provide his or her full name, if asked by the respondent, as well as a phone number for the research firm.

2. Read each question exactly as written. Report any problems to the supervisor as soon as possible.

3. Read the questions in the order indicated on the questionnaire, following the proper skip sequences.

4. Clarify any question by the respondent in a neutral way.

5. Do not mislead respondents as to the length of the interview.

6. Do not reveal the identity of the ultimate client unless instructed to do so.

7. Keep a tally on each terminated interview and the reason for each termination.

8. Remain neutral in interviewing. Do not indicate agreement or disagreement with the respondent.

9. Speak slowly and distinctly so that words will be understood.

10. Record all replies verbatim, not paraphrased.

11. Avoid unnecessary conversations with the respondent.

12. Probe and clarify for additional comments on all open-end questions, unless otherwise instructed. Probe and clarify in a neutral way.

13. Write neatly and legibly.

14. Check all work for thoroughness before turning it in to the supervisor.

15. When terminating a respondent, do so in a neutral way, such as, "Thank you," or "Our quota has already been filled in this area, but thank you anyway."

16. Keep all studies, materials, and findings confidential.

17. Do not falsify any interviews or any answers to any question.

18. Thank the respondent for participating in the study.

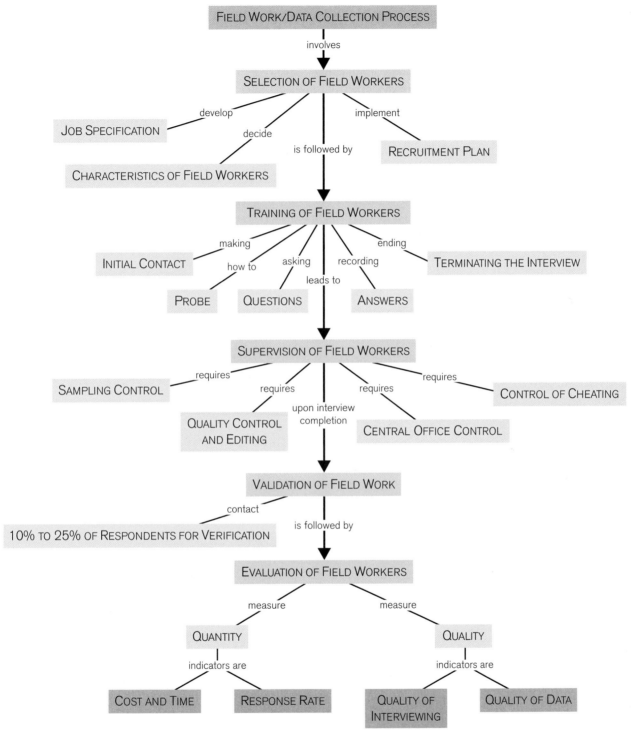

FIGURE 14.7

A Concept Map for the Field Work/Data Collection Process

The interviewers' work is validated and evaluated, and they are continuously provided with feedback on performance. As a result, Gallup has been very successful in cultivating and retaining high-quality field workers who contribute significantly to the data collection process and the reputation of the organization. Figure 14.7 provides a concept map for field work/data collection process

International Marketing Research

The selection, training, supervision, and evaluation of field workers are critical in international marketing research. Local field work agencies are unavailable in many countries; therefore, it might be necessary to recruit and train local field workers or import trained foreign workers. Using local field workers is preferable, however, because they are familiar with the local language and culture and can create an appropriate climate for the interview, being sensitive to the concerns of the respondents. In France, for example, people react negatively when they are contacted by non-native interviewers. Other interviewer characteristics might also be pertinent in some cultures. In the Middle East, the gender of the interviewer can have a strong influence on the responses to the questions.

Extensive training of field workers might be required, and close supervision might be necessary. In many countries, interviewers tend to help respondents with the answers and select households or sampling units based on personal considerations rather than the sampling plan. Also, interviewer cheating can be more of a problem in many foreign countries because of the lax ethical culture in these countries. For these reasons, validation of field work is critical. Proper application of field work procedures can greatly reduce these difficulties and result in consistent and useful findings, as the following example demonstrates.

Research in Action

Americanism Unites Europeans

An image study recently conducted by Research International (www.research-int.com), a marketing research company in the United Kingdom, showed that, despite unification of the European market, European consumers still increasingly favor U.S. products. The survey was conducted in Germany, the United Kingdom, Italy, and the Netherlands. In each country, local interviewers and supervisors were used, because it was felt they would be better able to identify with the respondents. However, the field workers were trained extensively and supervised closely to ensure that appropriate procedures were followed. The validation efforts were doubled: 20 percent, rather than the minimum 10 percent, of the interviews were validated. These procedures ensured quality results and minimized the variability in country-to-country results due to differences in field work.

A total of 6,724 personal interviews were conducted. Europeans gave U.S. products high marks for being innovative; some countries also regarded them as fashionable and of high quality. Interestingly, France, which is often considered to be anti-American, also emerged as pro-American. Among the 1,034 French consumers surveyed, 40 percent considered U.S. products fashionable and 38 percent believed they were innovative, although only 15 percent said U.S. products were of high quality. In addition, when asked what nationality they preferred for a new company in their area, a U.S. company was the first choice. These findings were comparable and consistent across the four countries. A key to the discovery of these findings was the use of local field workers and extensive training and supervision that resulted in uniformly high-quality data across the different countries.

These findings are very useful for U.S. firms marketing in Europe. "Rather than trying to hide the fact that they are American, we think companies ought to stress or try to exploit their American heritage," says Eric Salaam, director of European operations for the Henley Center, the U.K. economic forecasting consultancy. U.S. firms have, in fact, capitalized on the "made in America" equity. As a result, exports to Europe have been soaring in recent years. As of 2008, bilateral trade between the United States and European Union amounts to more than $1 billion a day, and, jointly, their global trade accounts for almost 40 percent of world trade.[6]

Be a DM!

As the international marketing manager for General Motors, what information would you like in order to formulate marketing strategies to increase your sales in China?

Be an MR!

Visit www.gm.com and search the Internet, as well as your library's online databases, to obtain information on Chinese consumers' preferences for cars. How would you select, train, and supervise field workers conducting an in-home survey in China to determine consumers' preferences for cars?

Technology and Marketing Research

A new computer technology, predictive dialing, is making it possible for marketing research companies to double their call attempts when conducting telephone surveys. A computer accesses a file of phone numbers and does the dialing. When a call is answered, it is sent to an interviewer. The interviewer's computer terminal displays the caller's name and the appropriate survey to use for the caller. If the computer dials a number that is not answered, it will recycle that number. The computer selects the telephone numbers in such a way as to maximize the probability of contact by predicting that a respondent will be at home and will participate at that time. These systems also include provisions for long, complicated questionnaires with computer-assisted quota control, telephone number management, interviewer monitoring and supervision, and management reports. Computer technology has also made personal interviewing more efficient. Many field workers now use Palmtop personal computers to collect data that are then transmitted to a central computer using a wireless system.

New technology makes it possible for companies to conduct telephone interviews without the use of a live interviewer. As discussed in Chapter 7, interviews can be conducted using completely automated telephone surveys (CATS). These systems use "interactive voice response technology." Because no human interviewer is used, CATS greatly reduces interviewer biases by conducting standardized interviews.

Ethics in Marketing Research

High ethical standards should be used when collecting data. Researchers and field workers should make the respondents feel comfortable by addressing their apprehensions and concerns. This can be done by providing respondents with adequate information about the project, addressing their questions, and clearly stating the responsibilities and expectations of both the field workers and the respondents at the beginning of the interview. Otherwise, respondents might be unsure about how their answers will be used and might not respond candidly. Researchers and field workers should respect respondents' time, feelings, privacy, and right to self-determination.

Researchers and field work agencies also are responsible to the clients for following the accepted procedures for the selection, training, supervision, validation, and evaluation of field workers. Field work procedures should be carefully documented and made available to clients. As illustrated by the following example, ethical codes are available for guiding field work/data collection.

Research in Action

An Ethical Code for Data Collection and Coding

On May 12, 2003, the Marketing Research Association (www.mra-net.org) adopted a new code of marketing research standards that clarifies expectations by delineating specific acceptable practices. Some of the salient ethical responsibilities of field work firms pertaining to respondents are as follows:

Companies Engaged in Data Collection . . .

- will treat the respondent with respect and not influence a respondent's opinion or attitude.

- will conduct themselves in a professional manner and ensure privacy and confidentiality.

- will make factually correct statements to secure cooperation and will honor promises made to respondents.

- will not use information to identify respondents without the permission of the respondent, except to those who check the data or are involved in processing the data.

- will adhere to and follow these principles when conducting online research:

    - Respondents' rights to anonymity must be safeguarded.

- Unsolicited e-mail must not be sent to those requesting not to receive any further e-mail.
- Researchers interviewing minors must adhere to the Children's Online Privacy Protection Act (COPPA).
- Data will not be used in any way contrary to the provider's published privacy statement without permission from the respondent.

- will respect the respondent's right to withdraw or to refuse to cooperate at any stage of the study.
- will obtain and document respondent consent when personally identifiable information of the respondent might be passed to a third party for legal or other purposes.

What Would *You* Do?

Nissan: Taking Xterra to the (E)Xtreme

Carlos Ghosn, president and CEO of Nissan Motor Company, is known as the "Icebreaker" for his skill at ignoring local business practices that stand in the way of making money. Ghosn is the Brazilian-born French executive charged with reviving the Japanese automaker. Ghosn is not afraid to take different paths and knows that taking risks to meet consumer demand is what business is all about.

Ghosn was faced with a new dilemma. When Nissan considered launching a new model sport utility vehicle (SUV), marketers wanted to appeal to Generation X. Hence, the Xterra was born. However, Ghosn did not want the Xterra to just be another SUV. He wanted it to fully meet the needs of drivers.

Ghosn decided to let Nissan partner with The Designory Team to determine the target audience for advertising of the new SUV. The Designory Team put together a design team for the Xterra to conduct some observational research, "trying to get to the heart of what it means to be a hardcore SUV owner." The team headed to the woods to observe how these hardcore SUV owners bungee, kayak, and mountain bike. Nissan wanted to know how to market to this younger Generation X market.

Nissan would like to conduct mall-intercept interviews with consumers to determine the type of positioning for Xterra that will appeal to Generation X consumers. The questionnaire is a mix of unstructured and structured questions. Some of the questions require substantial probing of the respondents, and the supervision of the interviewers will be critical to collecting good quality data.

The Marketing Research Decision

1. In what areas should the supervisors be trained to closely monitor the interviewers?
   a. Quality control and editing
   b. Sampling control
   c. Control of cheating
   d. Central office control
   e. All of the above
2. Discuss the role of supervisor training you recommend in enabling Carlos Ghosn to identify the needs of Generation X consumers.

The Marketing Management Decision

1. Carlos Ghosn wants to enhance the appeal of the Xterra to Generation X consumers. What changes should be made?
   a. Change the image of Xterra.
   b. Change the features of Xterra.
   c. Lower the price to make it more affordable.
   d. Promote Xterra over the Internet.
   e. All of the above.
2. Discuss how the marketing management-decision action that you recommend to Carlos Ghosn is influenced by the supervisor training that you suggested earlier and by the findings of mall intercept interviews.

What Carlos Ghosn Did

Carlos Ghosn made tremendous adaptations to Xterra in order to enhance its appeal to Generation X. It includes the availability of a supercharged V6, new front-end styling, a new hood, 17-inch wheels and off road tires, three new exterior colors, new trim colors, a radically revised interior, new dual-stage airbags, new rear child seat anchors, an optional "Enthusiast Package" for dyed-in-the-wool off roaders, and some changes to option packages in general. Nissan opted for an Eaton M62 roots-type supercharger, which is a first in a compact SUV. This is the same setup offered as part of an option package in Nissan's Frontier pickup truck. However, unlike the Frontier, Nissan offers Xterra drivers supercharger a la carte, very much in keeping with Xterra's motto, "Everything You Need, Nothing You Don't." The new model really does have more of what you need. Whether it is more power, more style, more interior, or more amenities, this Xterra builds upon an already great compact SUV. The 2008 Nissan Xterra had a starting price of $21,240.[7]

Summary

Researchers have two major options for collecting data: developing their own organizations or contracting with field work agencies. In either case, data collection involves the use of a field force. Field workers should be carefully selected and trained in important aspects of field work, including making the initial contact, asking the questions, probing, recording the answers, and terminating the interview. Supervision of field workers involves quality control and editing, sampling control, control of cheating, and central office control. Validation of field work can be accomplished by calling 10 to 25 percent of those who have been identified as respondents and inquiring whether the interviews actually took place. Field workers should be evaluated on the basis of cost and time, response rates, quality of interviewing, and quality of data collection.

Field work can contribute to, and benefit from, quality-control procedures. The selection, training, supervision, and evaluation of field workers are even more critical in international marketing research, because local field work agencies are not available in many countries. Computer technology is available to facilitate and even completely automate data collection. Ethical issues include making the respondents feel comfortable in the data collection process so that their experience is positive. Every effort must be undertaken to ensure that the data are of high quality. The Internet can greatly facilitate the field work/data collection process.

Key Terms and Concepts

Probing,   433   Sampling control,   435

Suggested Cases and Video Cases

Running Case with Real Data

1.1 Hewlett-Packard

Comprehensive Critical Thinking Cases

2.1 American Idol   2.2 Baskin-Robbins

Comprehensive Cases with Real Data

3.1 Bank of America   3.2 McDonald's   3.3 Boeing

Video Cases

14.1 Intel   19.1 Marriott

Live Research: Conducting a Marketing Research Project

1. The students conducting field work should be appropriately trained. Follow the guidelines in the chapter.
2. The team leaders can conduct fewer interviews but also act as supervisors. They should be trained in supervision.
3. The callback procedures should be specified (e.g., abandon a telephone number after three callback attempts).
4. If in-home interviews are to be conducted in the local area, each interviewer (student) can be assigned a specific part of a census track.

Acronyms

In the field work/data collection process, the organization VESTS in the field workers:

V alidation of field work

E valuation of field workers

S election of field workers

T raining of field workers

S upervision of field workers

The areas in which field workers should be trained may be summarized by the acronym TRAIN:

T erminating the interview

R ecording the answers

A sking the questions

I nitial contact development

N osy behavior: probing

Review Questions

1. What options are available to researchers for collecting data?
2. Describe the field work/data collection process.
3. What qualifications should field workers possess?
4. What are the guidelines for asking questions?
5. What is probing?
6. How should the answers to unstructured questions be recorded?
7. How should the field worker terminate the interview?
8. What aspects are involved in the supervision of field workers?
9. How can respondent selection problems be controlled?
10. What is validation of field work? How is this done?
11. Describe the criteria that should be used for evaluating field workers.

Applied Problems

1. Write interviewer instructions for in-home personal interviews to be conducted by students.
2. Comment on the following field situations, making recommendations for corrective action.
   a. One of the interviewers has an excessive rate of refusals in in-home personal interviewing.
   b. In a CATI situation, many phone numbers are giving a busy signal during the first dialing attempt.
   c. An interviewer reports that, at the end of the interviews, many respondents asked if they had answered the questions correctly.
   d. While validating the field work, a respondent reports that she cannot remember being interviewed over the telephone, but the interviewer insists that the interview was conducted.
3. Visit the Web sites of three marketing research suppliers. Make a report of all the material related to field work that is posted on these sites.
4. Visit the Marketing Research Association Web site (www.mra-net.org) and examine the ethical codes relating to data collection. Write a brief report.

Group Discussion

1. Discuss the impact of women's changing lifestyles on field work during the last decade.
2. Discuss the notion of interviewer cheating. Why do interviewers cheat? How can cheating be detected and prevented?

Hewlett-Packard Running Case

Review the Hewlett-Packard (HP) case, Case 1.1, and questionnaire given toward the end of the book.

What's it like to shop for notebook computers? Design a questionnaire to determine students' shopping behavior for notebook computers. Administer the survey to five different students on your campus.

1. How did you feel approaching these respondents?
2. What seemed to be the most challenging part of the survey for the respondents?
3. If other students were employed to collect the data for this survey project, how should they be trained?
4. If other students were employed to collect the data for this survey project, how should they be supervised?
5. If other students were employed to collect the data for this survey project, how should they be supervised?

INTEL: Building Blocks Inside Out

The Intel Corporation was founded in 1968 to build semiconductor memory products. It introduced the world's first microprocessor in 1971. Microprocessors, also referred to as central processing units (CPUs), often are described as the "brain" of a computer. Today, Intel supplies the building blocks for the computing and communications industries worldwide. These building blocks include chips, boards, systems, and software, and they are used in computers, servers, and networking/communications products.

Most of Intel's customers fall into two separate groups: the original equipment manufacturers (OEMs) and the PC and network communications products users. The OEMs manufacture computer systems, cellular handsets and handheld computing devices, telecommunications and networking communications equipment, and peripherals. The PC and network communications products users include individuals, large and small businesses, and service providers, who buy Intel's PC enhancements, networking products, and business communications products through reseller, retail, e-business, and OEM channels. Intel is an increasingly global company. Only 35 percent of its revenues are from North America, whereas Asia and Europe comprise 31 percent and 25 percent, respectively. Revenues for fiscal year 2007 amounted to $38.33 billion.

Intel has shown phenomenal growth as a company. Much of Intel's success can be attributed to innovation within its marketing department. This innovation was required to overcome several obstacles. The main problem Intel faced was trying to sell an ingredient brand, which is a component of a larger product. Thus, the difficulty is in reaching consumers that will never see your product and might not even know what it does or why it is there.

Intel began marketing research in the 1980s because it was having difficulty with its customers not upgrading from the 286 to the 386 microprocessor. Marketing research showed that this was due to a lack of customer awareness, and Intel set out to change that. It conducted a small but effective advertising campaign. In fact, in the process it realized that it had inadvertently created a brand in Intel. Because of the success of this small campaign, Intel began to realize the importance of marketing and marketing research and started to focus more effort and money on these areas.

Marketing research revealed that in order to be effective in its overall marketing campaign, Intel would have to reach the consumers and convince them that what was inside the computer was as important as what was on the outside. This became the key element of the "Intel Inside" campaign conducted during the early 1990s. This slogan helped Intel put a name with its products, and it helped it encompass several of its products under one title.

Furthermore, marketing research showed that it would be most effective to cross-market with its technology partners. This would help consumers understand the products that Intel helped make up. It did this by including the "Intel Inside" logo in its partners' ads. It also helped fund these advertisements. A problem with including its slogan in other ads is that Intel did not want to intrude on the commercials. It decided to help make the small logo sink in by accompanying it with a jingle every time it was displayed. This jingle has become extremely recognizable and synonymous with Intel's slogan. All of this helped Intel realize its goal of increased consumer awareness. Longitudinal measurement of advertising effectiveness via marketing research revealed that the "Intel Inside" campaign was very effective.

Intel's next idea was to come up with a name for its microprocessor. This would help it to avoid using the numbering scheme, which was nonpatentable, and to find a name that consumers could identify their processors with. After extensive marketing research, Intel chose the name Pentium, which it found generated positive reactions with its consumers. Intel has been marketing its processors under this name ever since.

Between 1990 and 1993, Intel invested $500 million in advertising to build its brand equity. By 1993, 80 percent of people in the United States recognized Intel and 75 percent had positive feelings about the brand. Most important, 50 percent of consumers looked for the brand when they were shopping. By 1994, Intel had captured 95 percent of the microprocessor market, due in large part to its marketing efforts.

Intel's market share for microprocessors slipped to about 80 percent in 2005, as a result of increased competition from its main competitor, AMD. On December 30, 2005, Intel announced a major overhaul of its corporate and product branding, a move designed to symbolize the chip maker's transformation into a supplier for products beyond personal computers. The changes included a new version of the company's blue logo—without the lowered "e" that had long been a part of Intel's branding—along with a new tagline, "Leap ahead." As of 2006, Intel no longer used the well-known "Intel Inside" logo.

The increased competition makes Intel's marketing research efforts more important than ever as it attempts to preserve its dominant place in the market. Intel has been able to be very successful because of its focus on technology, brand image, and brand equity. Intel still faces future challenges, including increased competition, the opening of new markets, and the development of new products. Intel will continue to rely on marketing research to meet these challenges.

Conclusion

Marketing research has played a critical role in Intel's phenomenal growth. Marketing research was instrumental in developing the Intel brand, designing the "Intel Inside" campaign, and crafting the new logo with the "Leap ahead" tag line. Continued reliance on marketing research will enable Intel to enhance its image as a preeminent building block supplier inside out.

Questions

1. Discuss the role of marketing research in helping Intel devise the "Intel Inside" and "Leap ahead" campaigns.
2. Intel would like to increase the preference for Intel chips among PC users in the individual user as well as business user segments. Define the management-decision problem.
3. Define an appropriate marketing research problem corresponding to the management-decision problem you identified in question 2.
4. Intel would like to gain a better understanding of how businesses select PC and network communications products. What type of research design should be adopted?
5. Discuss the role of the Internet in obtaining secondary data relevant to the marketing research problem you defined in question 3.
6. Discuss the role of qualitative research in understanding how businesses select PC and network communications products. Which qualitative research techniques should be used and why?
7. If a survey is to be conducted to determine businesses' selection criterion for choosing PC and network communications products, which survey method should be used and why?
8. Design a questionnaire for determining businesses' selection criterion for choosing PC and network communications products.
9. Develop a suitable sampling plan for conducting the survey identified in question 7.

10. If Intel were to conduct mall-intercept interviews to determine consumer preferences for an ultra-light notebook that uses a newly designed chip, describe the field work process that should be used.

References

1. www.intel.com, accessed January 17, 2008.
2. Don Clark, "Intel Secures Video Content for Its Viiv Multimedia Plan," *The Wall Street Journal*, January 6, 2006, p. A14.
3. Don Clark, "Intel to Overhaul Marketing in Bid to Go Beyond PCs," *The Wall Street Journal*, December 30, 2005, p. A3.
4. Olga Kharif, "Intel Is Kicking Silicon at AMD," *BusinessWeek Online* (September 24, 2002), http://www.businessweek.com/technology/content/sep2002/tc20020924_6824.htm, accessed April 10, 2008.

Data Preparation and Analysis Strategy

fifteen

CHAPTER

OPENING QUESTIONS

1. What is the nature and scope of data preparation, and how can the data preparation process be described?

2. What is involved in questionnaire checking and editing?

3. How should questionnaires be coded to prepare the data for analysis?

4. What methods are available for cleaning the data and treating missing responses?

5. How do researchers select the appropriate data analysis strategy?

6. How should data collected in international marketing research projects be prepared?

7. What is the role of technology in facilitating data preparation?

8. What ethical issues are important in data preparation and analysis?

Database Awakens a Sleeping Giant

Since its founding, the legendary U.S. retailer Sears, Roebuck and Company has been a leading department-store retailer of apparel, home products, and automobile products and services. In the late 1990s, Sears tried to lose its reputation as a "hardware and tools" store in order to create a trendier and modern store image for customers. Once held up as a textbook example of a mighty marketer failing to adapt to changing consumer demands, Sears has since become an innovator in the retail world, pulling off a comeback that has even the retailer's harshest critics gushing.

One crucial element in its success was building a high-quality database about its customers and potential customers. By 2008, Sears had built a massive database of more than 75 percent of U.S. households. The data are collected from a variety of primary and secondary sources. One hallmark is the care taken to prepare the data before they become a part of the database. In the case of primary data, completed questionnaires returned from the field are carefully checked and edited for incomplete responses (e.g., questions that are incorrectly skipped) or inconsistent responses

> "In many projects, editing, coding, cleaning, and preparing the data for analysis accounts for the majority of the time an analyst will spend with the data."
>
> *Jim McGee,*
> *Global Mapping International.*

(e.g., a respondent reports purchases made on a Sears credit card but does not have one). Any questionnaires with unsatisfactory responses are simply discarded, because the proportion of such respondents is small in relation to the total sample size. The data are coded by following appropriate procedures. To ensure uniformity in coding, Sears has prepared a codebook containing the coding instructions and the necessary information about the variables in the data set. The data are then transcribed from the questionnaires into the computer, using state-of-the-art technology.

Further checks are performed on the data to ascertain their consistency and accuracy. An effort is made to identify data that are out of range (e.g., a response of 8 on a 1-to-7 scale), logically inconsistent (e.g., sum of percentages totaling more or less than 100 percent), or have extreme values (e.g., household size of 11). Missing values are kept to a minimum by proper selection, training, and supervision of field workers and are treated by following a variety of methods to determine the impact on the results. A similar process is followed for data collected from secondary sources.

This superior database enables Sears to identify the needs of the marketplace and target its marketing efforts accordingly. Based on the findings of a survey of 3,000 randomly selected households from its database, Sears spent $4 billion renovating its stores. It markedly improved store layout, design, cleanliness, and merchandising mix. The move is clearly paying off, with Sears reporting higher sales and revenue per selling square foot than it did prior to the renovation.[1]

Overview

After the researcher has defined the research problem and developed a suitable approach (see Chapter 2), formulated an appropriate research design (see Chapters 3 to 13), and conducted field work (see Chapter 14), she or he can move on to data preparation and analysis, the fifth step of the marketing research process. Figure 15.1 briefly explains the focus of the chapter, the relationship of this chapter to the previous ones, and the steps of the marketing research process on which this chapter concentrates.

Before the raw data contained in the questionnaires can be subjected to statistical analysis, they must be converted into a suitable form. Care exercised in the data preparation phase can substantially improve the quality of the findings, resulting in better managerial decisions, as explained in the Sears opening vignette. In contrast, inadequate attention to data preparation can seriously compromise statistical results, leading to biased findings and incorrect interpretation.

This chapter describes the data preparation process, which begins with checking the questionnaires for completeness. It also discusses the editing of data and provides guidelines for handling illegible, incomplete, inconsistent, ambiguous, or otherwise unsatisfactory responses. Coding, transcribing, and data cleaning, are presented, with an emphasis on the treatment of missing responses. The chapter then discusses the selection of a data analysis strategy, the role of technology, and the ethical issues and Internet applications related to data processing. Help for running the SPSS and Excel programs used in this chapter is provided is four ways: (1) detailed step-by-step instructions are given later in the chapter, (2) you can download (from the Web site for this book) computerized

FIGURE 15.1

Relationship of Data Preparation to the Previous Chapters and the Marketing Research Process

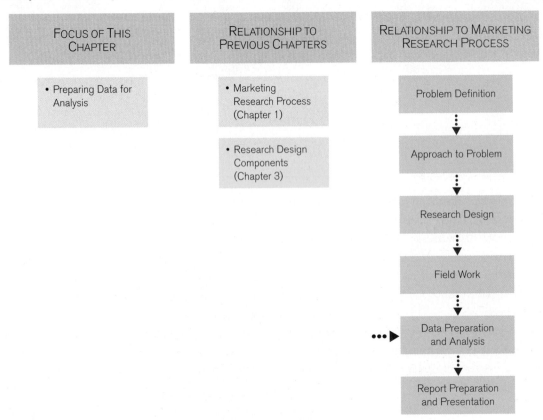

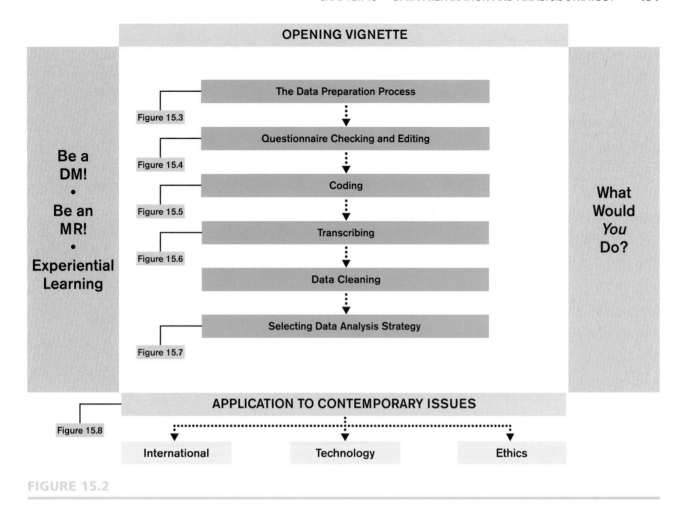

FIGURE 15.2

Data Preparation: An Overview

demonstration movies illustrating these step-by-step instructions, (3) you can download screen captures with notes illustrating these step-by-step instructions, and (4) you can refer to the Study Guide and Technology Manual, a supplement that accompanies this book, which provides more help for SPSS and Excel. Figure 15.2 provides an overview of the topics discussed in this chapter and how they flow from one to the next.

The Data Preparation Process

The data preparation process is shown in Figure 15.3. Sears followed a similar process, as explained in the opening vignette. The entire process is guided by the preliminary plan of data analysis that was formulated in the research design phase (see Chapter 3). As the first step, the field work supervisor checks for acceptable questionnaires. This is followed by editing, coding, and transcribing the data, which are all done by the data collection agency as part of field work (see Chapter 14). The researcher cleans the data, performs further checks for consistency, and then specifies how missing responses will be treated. The researcher then selects an appropriate data analysis strategy. The final data analysis strategy differs from the preliminary plan of data analysis due to the information and insights gained since the preliminary plan was formulated. Data preparation should begin as soon as the first batch of questionnaires is received from the field, while the field work is still taking place. Thus, if any problems are detected, the field work can be modified to incorporate corrective action.

FIGURE 15.3

Data Preparation Process

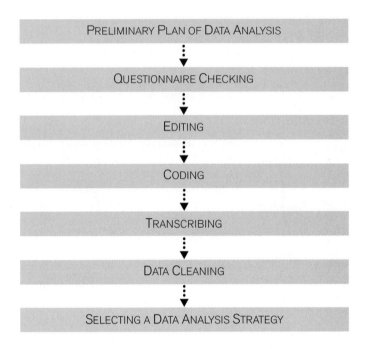

Questionnaire Checking

The initial step in questionnaire checking involves checking for completeness and interviewing quality. This is a continuous process and begins as soon as the first set of questionnaires is returned, while field work is still underway. Therefore, any problems can be detected early on and corrective action can be taken before too many surveys have been completed. A questionnaire returned from the field can be unacceptable for several reasons. For example, parts of the questionnaire might be incomplete, skip patterns might not have been followed (see Chapter 11), one or more pages might be missing, and so forth.

If quotas or cell group sizes have been imposed (see Chapter 12), the acceptable questionnaires should be classified and counted accordingly. Any problems in meeting the sampling requirements should be identified and corrective action taken, such as conducting additional interviews in the underrepresented cells.

Editing

editing
A review of the questionnaires with the objective of increasing accuracy and precision.

Editing involves reviewing questionnaires to increase accuracy and precision. It consists of screening questionnaires to identify illegible, incomplete, inconsistent, or ambiguous responses, as in the opening vignette.

Responses might be illegible if they have been poorly recorded, such as answers to unstructured or open-ended questions. Likewise, questionnaires might be incomplete to varying degrees. A few or many questions might be unanswered. At this stage, the researcher makes a preliminary check for consistency. Certain obvious inconsistencies can be easily detected; for example, a respondent in the United Kingdom who reports an annual income of less than £12,000 yet indicates frequent shopping at prestigious department stores such as Harrod's. A response is ambiguous, for example, if the respondent has circled both 4 and 5 on a 7-point scale.

Unsatisfactory responses are commonly handled by returning to the field to get better data, by assigning missing values, or by discarding unsatisfactory respondents (Figure 15.4). The questionnaires with unsatisfactory responses can be returned to the field so that the interviewers can recontact the respondents to get better/complete data. This approach is particularly attractive for business and industrial marketing surveys, where the sample sizes are small and the respondents are easily identifiable. If returning the questionnaires to the field is not feasible, the editor might assign missing values to unsatisfactory responses. This approach is desirable if (1) the number of respondents with unsatisfactory responses is small, (2) the proportion of

FIGURE 15.4

**Treatment of
Unsatisfactory
Responses**

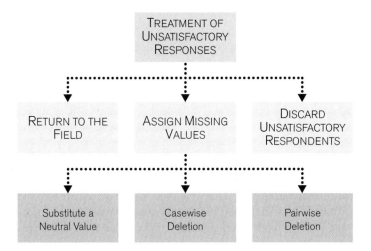

unsatisfactory responses for each of these respondents is small, or (3) the variables with unsatisfactory responses are not the key variables.

Alternatively, the respondents with unsatisfactory responses are simply discarded. This approach has merit when (1) the proportion of unsatisfactory respondents is small (less than 10 percent), (2) the sample size is large, (3) the unsatisfactory respondents do not differ from satisfactory respondents in obvious ways (e.g., demographics, product usage characteristics), (4) the proportion of unsatisfactory responses for each of these respondents is large, or (5) responses on key variables are missing (see the opening vignette). However, unsatisfactory respondents might differ from satisfactory respondents in systematic ways, and the decision to designate a respondent as unsatisfactory might be subjective. Both these factors related to unsatisfactory respondents can bias the results. If the researcher decides to discard unsatisfactory respondents, the procedure adopted to identify these respondents and the number of unsatisfactory respondents should be reported by the researcher in the project report, as in the following example.

Research in Action

A Complaint Against Consumer Complaints

In a U.S. study examining consumer complaints, 1,000 questionnaires were mailed to households in each of three service categories: automotive repair, medical care, and banking services. The numbers of responses received were automotive repair, 155; medical care, 166; and banking services, 172. The returned questionnaires were carefully checked and edited. Those respondents who did not meet the qualifying criteria (being able to recall a recent dissatisfying experience) and those with a large number of missing values or missing values on key variables were discarded. The usable samples that remained were: automotive repair, 116; medical care, 125; and banking services, 104.

The researchers complained that a large number of respondents had to be discarded because of failure to meet the qualifying criteria or a high incidence of missing values. These complaints are justified because discarding such a high proportion of returned questionnaires (25.2% for automotive repair, 24.7% for medical care, and 39.5% for banking services) is not a good research practice. According to the general guidelines, no more than 10 percent of the returned questionnaires should be discarded.[2]

Coding

coding

The assignment of a code to represent a specific response to a specific question, along with the data record and column position that code will occupy.

Coding means assigning a code, usually a number, to each possible response to each question. If the questionnaire contains only structured questions or very few unstructured questions, it is precoded. This means that codes are assigned before field work is conducted. If the questionnaire contains unstructured questions, codes are assigned after the questionnaires have been returned from the field (postcoding). Although precoding was briefly discussed in Chapter 11 on questionnaire design, the next section provides further guidelines on coding structured and open-ended questions.

Coding Structured and Open-Ended Questions

fixed field code

A code in which the number of records for each respondent are the same and the same data appear in the same columns for all respondents.

The respondent code and the record number should appear on each record in the data. The following additional codes should be included for each respondent: project code, interviewer code, date and time codes, and validation code. **Fixed field codes** are highly desirable. This means that the number of records for each respondent is the same and the same data appear in the same column(s) for all respondents. If possible, standard codes should be used for missing data. For example, a code of 9 (or –9) could be used for a single-column variable (responses coded on a 1-to-7 scale), 99 for a double-column variable (responses coded on a 1-to-11 scale), and so forth. The missing value codes should be distinct from the codes assigned to the legitimate responses.

Coding structured questions is relatively simple, because the response options are predetermined. The researcher assigns a code for each response to each question and specifies the appropriate record and columns in which the response codes are to appear. For example,

In the last month, have you bought a product or service over the Internet?
1. Yes   2. No (94)

For this question, a "yes" response is coded 1 and a "no" response receives a 2. The number in parentheses indicates that the code assigned will appear in column 94 for this respondent. Because only one response is allowed and there are only two possible responses (1 or 2), a single column is sufficient. In general, a single column is sufficient to code a structured question with a single response if there are fewer than nine possible responses.

Research in Action

Reading Magazine Readership

Which magazines have you read during the last 2 months? ("X" as many as apply.)

Time	❑	(102)
Newsweek	❑	(103)
BusinessWeek	❑	(104)
Forbes	❑	(105)
Fortune	❑	(106)
The Economist	❑	(107)
Other Magazines	❑	(108)

Suppose a respondent checked *Time, Newsweek,* and other magazines. On the record for this respondent, a 1 will be entered in the column numbers 102, 103, and 108. All the other columns (104, 105, 106, and 107) will receive a 0.

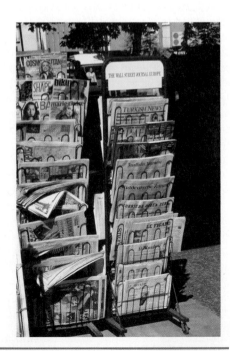

In questions that permit multiple responses, each possible response option should be assigned a separate column. Such questions include those about brand ownership or usage, television viewing, and magazine readership, as in the magazine readership example.

Coding unstructured or open-ended questions is more complex. Respondents' verbatim responses are recorded on the questionnaire. Codes are then developed and assigned to these responses by analyzing the data of a few respondents. The following guidelines are suggested for coding unstructured questions and questionnaires in general.

Category codes should be mutually exclusive and collectively exhaustive. Categories are mutually exclusive if each response fits into one, and only one, category code. Categories should not overlap. Categories are collectively exhaustive if every response fits into one of the assigned category codes. This can be achieved by adding an additional category code of "other" or "none of the above." However, only a few (10 percent or less) of the responses should fall into this category. The vast majority of the responses should be classified into meaningful categories.

Data should be coded to retain as much detail as possible. For example, if data on the exact number of trips made on commercial airlines by business travelers have been obtained, they should be coded as such, rather than grouped into two category codes of "infrequent fliers" and "frequent fliers." Obtaining information on the exact number of trips allows the researcher to later define categories of business travelers in several different ways (e.g., fewer than 3 trips per month, 4 to 6 trips per month, 7 to 10 trips per month, 11 to 15 trips per month, and more than 15 trips per month). If the categories were predefined (e.g., infrequent fliers and frequent fliers), the subsequent analysis of data would be limited by those categories. The following illustrates the coding of responses to open-ended questions.

CODING OF OPEN-ENDED QUESTION RESPONSES   Question (to respondents in India): Why do you prefer Neem to Dabur toothpaste?
Sample Responses

1. It is a better value.
2. It has a lower price.
3. Tastes better.
4. I like the packaging better.
5. Better buy for my money.
6. I don't like the taste of Dabur.
7. It prevents tooth decay.
8. It gives me fresh breath.
9. It has a better looking package.
10. I like the smell of Neem.
11. I like Neem advertising.
12. Dabur has a taste disadvantage.
13. Neem's advertising is creative.
14. Neem is more effective in fighting cavities.
15. It is better for your health.

Similar responses are grouped, and category codes are developed, as follows.

Category Descriptors	Sample	Responses Category Code
Better value/lower price/better buy	1, 2, 5	1
Tastes better/don't like taste of Dabur/Dabur's taste disadvantage	3, 6, 12	2
Better packaging/better looking package	4, 9	3
Prevents tooth decay/fights cavities/better for health	7, 14, 15	4
Fresh breath/like smell	8, 10	5
Like advertising/creative advertising	11, 13	6
Other		7

Developing a Data File

The code for a response to a question includes an indication of the column position (field) and data record it will occupy. For example, gender of respondents can be coded as 1 for females and 2 for males. A field represents a single variable value or item of data, such as the gender of a single respondent. Although numeric information is most common in marketing research, a field can also contain alphabetic or symbolic information. A record consists of related fields (i.e., variable values, such as sex, marital status, age, household size, occupation, and so forth) that all pertain to a single respondent. Thus, each record can have several columns. Generally, all the data for a respondent will be stored on a single record, although a number of records might be used for each respondent. Data files are sets of records, generally data from all the respondents in a study, which are grouped together for storage in the computer. If a single record is used for each respondent, records represent rows in a data file. In such as case, a data file can be viewed as an $n \times m$ matrix of numbers or values, where n is the number of respondents and m is the number of variables or fields. It often is helpful to prepare a **codebook** containing the coding instructions and the necessary information about the variables in the data set (see opening vignette).

codebook

A book containing coding instructions and the necessary information about variables in the data set.

Data can be entered into a spreadsheet program, such as Excel. Most analysis programs can import data from a spreadsheet. In this case, the data for each respondent for each field is a cell. Typically, each row of the (Excel) spreadsheet contains the data of one respondent or case. The columns will contain the variables, with one column for each variable or response. The use of Excel can be complicated if there are more than 256 variables. Later in this chapter, in an experiential learning situation, we show how the data from an Excel file can be converted to an SPSS file.

These concepts are illustrated in Table 15.1. This table gives the data from a pretest sample of 20 Australian respondents on preferences for restaurants. Each respondent was asked to rate his or her preference to eat in a familiar restaurant (1 = Weak Preference, 7 = Strong Preference) and to rate the restaurant in terms of quality of food, quantity of portions, value,

TABLE 15.1 Restaurant Preference

ID	Preference	Quality	Quantity	Value	Service	Income
1	2	2	3	1	3	6
2	6	5	6	5	7	2
3	4	4	3	4	5	3
4	1	2	1	1	2	5
5	7	6	6	5	4	1
6	5	4	4	5	4	3
7	2	2	3	2	3	5
8	3	3	4	2	3	4
9	7	6	7	6	5	2
10	2	3	2	2	2	5
11	2	3	2	1	3	6
12	6	6	6	6	7	2
13	4	4	3	3	4	3
14	1	1	3	1	2	4
15	7	7	5	5	4	2
16	5	5	4	5	5	3
17	2	3	1	2	3	4
18	4	4	3	3	3	3
19	7	5	5	7	5	5
20	3	2	2	3	3	3

Column Number	Variable Number	Variable Name	Question Number	Coding Instructions
1	1	ID		1 to 20 as coded
2	2	Preference	1	**Input the number circled** 1 = Weak preference 7 = Strong preference
3	3	Quality	2	**Input the number circled** 1 = Poor 7 = Excellent
4	4	Quantity	3	**Input the number circled** 1 = Poor 7 = Excellent
5	5	Value	4	**Input the number circled** 1 = Poor 7 = Excellent
6	6	Service	5	**Input the number circled** 1 = Poor 7 = Excellent
7	7	Income	6	**Input the number circled** 1 = Less than A$20,000 2 = A$20,000 to A$34,999 3 = A$35,000 to A$49,999 4 = A$50,000 to A$74,999 5 = A$75,000 to A$99,999 6 = A$100,000 or more

FIGURE 15.5

A Codebook Excerpt

and service (1 = Poor, 7 = Excellent). Annual household income was obtained and coded as: 1 = Less than A$20,000, 2 = A$20,000 to 34,999, 3 = A$35,000 to 49,999, 4 = A$50,000 to 74,999, 5 = A$75,000 to 99,999, 6 = A$100,000 or more. The codebook for coding these data is given in Figure 15.5. Note that in addition to the data of Table 15.1, the codebook also contains information on several other codes that are not shown.

If the data of Table 15.1 are entered using either Excel or SPSS, the resulting data files will resemble Table 15.1. You can verify this by downloading Excel and SPSS files for Table 15.1 from the student Web site for this book (www.prenhall.com/malhotra). Note that the SPSS data file has two views: the data view and the variable view. The data view gives a listing of the data and resembles Table 15.1. The variable view gives a listing of the variables showing the type, labels or description, values, and underlying coding for each variable, as shown in Table 15.2. Clicking on the "Values" column of the SPSS file opens a "Value Labels" dialog box. Value labels are unique labels assigned to each possible value of a variable. For example, 1 denotes weak preference and 7 denotes strong preference. If descriptors were used for the other preference values, those other preference values would also be assigned the corresponding "Value Labels." The other columns of Table 15.2 are self-explanatory.

In Table 15.1, as well as in the corresponding Excel and SPSS files, the columns represent the fields, and the rows represent the records or respondents, because there is one record per respondent. Notice that there are seven columns. The first column contains the respondent ID, and the second column contains the preference for the restaurant. Columns three to six contain the evaluations of the restaurant on quality of food, quantity of portions, value, and service, respectively. Finally, the seventh column contains the respondent's

TABLE 15.2 SPSS Variable View of the Data of Table 15.1

Name	Type	Width	Decimals	Label	Values	Missing	Columns	Align	Measure
ID	Numeric	8	0	Respondent Number	None	None	8	Right	Scale
PREFERENC	Numeric	8	0	Restaurant Preference	{1, Weak Preference} . . .	None	11	Right	Scale
QUALITY	Numeric	8	0	Quality of Food	{1, Poor} . . .	None	10	Right	Scale
QUANTITY	Numeric	8	0	Quantity of Portions	{1, Poor} . . .	None	10	Right	Scale
VALUE	Numeric	8	0	Overall Value	{1, Poor} . . .	None	10	Right	Scale
SERVICE	Numeric	8	0	Restaurant Service	{1, Poor} . . .	None	10	Right	Scale
INCOME	Numeric	8	0	Annual Household Income	{1, Less than $20,000} . . .	None	10	Right	Scale

income, coded as specified in the codebook. Each row contains all the data of a single respondent and represents a record. The table has 20 rows, or records, indicating that data for 20 respondents are stored in this data file. Note that Table 15.1 is a 20 × 7 matrix, because there are 20 respondents and 7 variables (including ID). Databases consist of one or more files that are interrelated. For example, a database might contain all the customer satisfaction surveys conducted quarterly for the last 5 years.

Be a DM!

As the marketing director for the New England Patriots of America's National Football League, what information would help you to formulate marketing strategies to increase the attendance at Patriots home games?

Be an MR!

Visit www.nfl.com and search the Internet, as well as your library's online databases, to obtain information on why people attend professional football games. A survey was administered to attendees at a Patriots home game to determine why they were attending. What guidelines will you follow in checking the questionnaire, editing, and coding?

Transcribing

Transcribing data involves transferring the coded data from the questionnaires or coding sheets onto disks or directly into computers by keypunching or other means, as in the opening vignette. If the data have been collected via CATI, CAPI, or Internet surveys, this step is unnecessary, because the data are entered directly into the computer as they are collected. Besides keypunching, the data can be transferred by using optical recognition, digital technologies, bar codes, or other technologies (Figure 15.6). Optical character recognition programs transcribe printed text into computer files. Optical scanning is a data transcribing process whereby answers recorded on computer-readable forms are scanned to form a data record. This requires responses to be recorded with a special pencil in a predesignated area coded for that response. A machine can then read the data. A more flexible process is optical mark recognition, whereby a spreadsheet-type interface is used to read and process forms created by users. These marked-sensed forms are then processed by optical scanners, and the data are stored in a computer file. Digital technology has resulted in computerized sensory analysis systems, which automate the data collection process. The questions appear on a computerized grid pad, and responses are recorded directly into the computer using a sensing device.

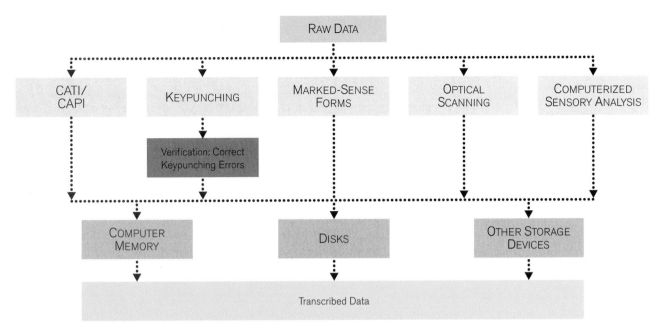

FIGURE 15.6

Data Transcription

Field interviewers use notebook computers, PDAs, and other handheld devices to record responses, which are then sent via a built-in communication modem, wireless LAN, or cellular link directly to another computer in the field or a remote location. Bar codes involve direct machine reading of the codes and simultaneous transcription. In the United States, a familiar example is the transcription of Universal Product Code (UPC) data at supermarket checkout counters. In 2000, the U.S. Census used bar codes to identify residents. Package-delivery companies such as UPS and FedEx use bar codes on labels for expedited packages shipments.

Several other technologies can also be used to transcribe the data. Voice recognition and voice response systems can translate recorded voice responses into data files. For example, Microsoft XP software includes advanced speech recognition functions that can transcribe speech into data. Newer technologies are being developed. It is now possible to integrate visual images, streaming video, and audio data that could well be used for recording a focus group or a survey interview.

When CATI, CAPI, or electronic methods are used, data are verified as they are collected. In the case of inadmissible responses, the computer will prompt the interviewer or respondent. In case of admissible responses, the interviewer or the respondent can see the recorded response on the screen and verify it before proceeding.

The selection of a data transcription method is guided by the type of interviewing method used and the availability of equipment. If CATI, CAPI, or electronic methods are used, the data are entered directly into the computer. Keypunching into a computer is most frequently used for ordinary telephone, in-home, mall-intercept, and mail interviews. However, the use of digital technology in personal interviews is growing with the increasing use of grid pads and handheld computers. Optical scanning can be used in structured and repetitive surveys, and optical mark recognition is used in special cases. Bar codes are used to collect scanner data and in a variety of other applications.

Data Cleaning

Data cleaning includes consistency checks and treatment of missing responses. Although preliminary consistency checks have been made during editing, the checks at this stage are more thorough and extensive because they are made by computer.

data cleaning
Thorough and extensive checks for consistency and treatment of missing responses.

Consistency Checks

consistency checks
A part of the data cleaning process that identifies data that are out of range, logically inconsistent, or that have extreme values. Data with values not defined by the coding scheme are inadmissible.

Consistency checks identify data that are out of range, that are logically inconsistent, or that have extreme values (see opening vignette). Out-of-range data values are inadmissible and must be corrected. For example, respondents have been asked to express their degree of agreement with a series of lifestyle statements on a 1-to-5 scale. Assuming that 9 has been designated for missing values, data values of 0, 6, 7, and 8 are out of range. These out-of-range responses can arise due to respondent or interviewer errors. Computer packages such as SPSS, SAS, Minitab, and Excel can be programmed to identify out-of-range values for each variable and print out the respondent code, variable code, variable name, record number, column number, and out-of-range value.[3] This makes it easy to check each variable systematically for out-of-range values. The correct responses can be determined by going back to the edited and coded questionnaire.

Responses can be logically inconsistent in various ways. For example, a respondent might indicate that she charges long-distance calls to a calling card, even though she does not have one. Or a respondent might report both unfamiliarity with, and frequent use of, the same product. The necessary information (respondent code, variable code, variable name, record number, column number, and inconsistent values) can be printed to locate these responses and take corrective action.

Extreme values should be closely examined. Not all extreme values result from errors; however, they might point to problems with the data. For example, an extremely low evaluation of a brand might be the result of the respondent indiscriminately circling 1s (on a 1-to-7 rating scale) on all attributes of this brand.

Research in Action

Apple's iPhone: What Does the Buzz Mean?

Despite the buzz on the new product, speculation was running wild as to whether the iPhone's sales in the mobile phone market will be able to match that of iPod's success in the digital music market. The U.S. marketing-consulting firm Markitecture conducted an online survey of a national sample of 1,300 American cell phone owners and users.

Before any analysis was done, the data were thoroughly checked for quality. Any unsatisfactory questionnaires discovered during checking or editing were resolved by recontacting the respondent. A standard coding scheme was used, and because the data were collected using an online survey subsequent transcription was unnecessary. Several procedural and logical checks were built into the online system so that inconsistencies could be identified and rectified while the data were being collected during

the course of the interview. These high-quality data provided American computer maker Apple, which markets the iPhone, with an accurate measurement of what is important to potential iPhone customers, enabling it to effectively address those issues.

Among those familiar with the iPhone, overall impressions were positive, although not overwhelming: 41 percent thought the phone was excellent or very good, based on everything they had seen or heard. On the flip side, 21 percent thought it was only fair or poor. Cost was cited as the top reason for reasons for not purchasing the iPhone: It was an issue for 77 percent of respondents. Based on these findings, Apple decided to diversify in the long term, producing iPhones of different prices, sizes, and capacities, similar to what it now offers with the iPod, in order to make an impact on the cell phone market in general.[4]

Treatment of Missing Responses

missing responses
Values of a variable that are unknown, because these respondents did not provide unambiguous answers to the question.

Missing responses represent values of a variable that are unknown, either because respondents provided ambiguous answers or their answers were not properly recorded. The former cause also is known as *item nonresponse;* it occurs because the respondent refuses, or is unable, to answer specific questions or items because of the content, form, or the effort required. The incidence of missing responses should be minimized by proper selection, training, and supervision of field workers (see Chapter 14), as illustrated by Sears in the opening vignette. Treatment of missing responses poses problems, particularly if the proportion of missing responses is more than 10 percent. The following options are available for the treatment of missing responses (see Figure 15.4):

1. *Substitute a neutral value.* A neutral value, typically the mean response to the variable, is substituted for missing responses. Thus, the mean of the variable remains unchanged and other statistics, such as correlations, might not be affected

much if the proportion of missing values is small. Although this approach has some merit, the logic of substituting a mean value (say 4) for respondents who, if they had answered, might have used either high ratings (6 or 7) or low ratings (1 or 2) is questionable.

2. *Casewise deletion.* In **casewise deletion**, cases or respondents with any missing responses are discarded from the analysis. Suppose 20 percent of the respondents do not respond to the income questions. All of these respondents will be excluded from analysis that involves the income variable, thus reducing the sample size by 20 percent. If several variables are involved in the analysis (e.g., income, education, occupation), respondents with missing values on any of those variables will be excluded. Because many respondents might have missing responses on different variables, this approach could result in a small sample. Throwing away large amounts of data is undesirable, because it is costly and time-consuming to collect data. Furthermore, respondents with missing responses could differ from respondents with complete responses in systematic ways. If so, casewise deletion could seriously bias the results.

3. *Pairwise deletion.* In **pairwise deletion**, instead of discarding all cases with any missing values, the researcher uses only the cases or respondents with complete responses for each calculation. Suppose the researcher is interested in calculating all possible correlations between a set of variables—say awareness, attitude, preference, and purchase intention—all measured on a 1-to-7 scale (see Chapter 18). Then, in calculating the correlation between attitude and preference, all respondents with legitimate responses on the two variables will be included in the analysis, even though these respondents may have missing values on the other two variables, namely awareness and purchase intentions. In contrast, in casewise deletion, respondents with missing values on any of the four variables would be excluded from the analysis.

Pairwise deletion might be appropriate when (1) the sample size is large, (2) there are few missing responses, and (3) the variables are not highly related. Yet this procedure can produce results that are unappealing, or even infeasible, because different calculations in an analysis might be based on different sample sizes. For example, statistics, such as pairwise correlations, might be based on different sample sizes, making comparisons more difficult.

The various procedures for the treatment of missing responses can yield different results, particularly when the responses are not missing at random and the variables are related. The researcher should carefully consider the implications of the various procedures before selecting a particular method for the treatment of nonresponse. It also is recommended that the data be analyzed using different options for handling missing responses to determine the impact on the results, as illustrated by Sears in the opening vignette.

Variable Respecification and Recoding

Variable respecification involves the transformation of data to create new variables or modify existing ones. The purpose of respecification is to create variables that are consistent with the objectives of the study. Respecification often involves summing the items of a Likert-type scale to create a summed score. For example, in Chapter 10 a Likert scale consisting of nine statements was used to measure attitude toward Macy's. These nine statements need to be summed, after reversing the scoring of the negative statements, to arrive at a total attitudinal score. The process of reversing the scoring for the negative statements, as well as the process of summing, involves variable respecification.

Once the data have been coded, transcribed, and cleaned, it might be necessary to redefine the categories of a categorical variable, such as income. For example, if there are too few respondents in the lowest income category, this category can be combined or merged with the next lowest category. This is referred to as recoding.

casewise deletion
A method for handling missing responses in which cases or respondents with any missing responses are discarded from the analysis.

pairwise deletion
A method of handling missing values in which for each calculation or analysis only the cases or respondents with complete responses are considered.

variable respecification
Involves the transformation of data to create new variables or modify existing ones.

Be an MR!

Visit Lexus, a division of Japan's Toyota Motor Corporation, at www.lexus.com and search the Internet, as well as your library's online databases, to obtain information on the criteria American buyers use in selecting a luxury car brand. Demographic and psychographic data were obtained in a survey designed to explain the choice of a luxury car brand. What kind of consistency checks, treatment of missing responses, and variable respecification should be conducted?

Be a DM!

As the marketing manager for Lexus, what information would you like to have in order to formulate marketing strategies to increase your market share?

Selecting a Data Analysis Strategy

Selecting a data analysis strategy should be based on the earlier steps of the marketing research process, known characteristics of the data, properties of statistical techniques, and the background and philosophy of the researcher (Figure 15.7).

When selecting a data analysis strategy, the researcher must begin by considering the earlier steps in the process: problem definition (step 1), development of an approach (step 2), and research design (step 3). The researcher should use as a springboard the preliminary plan of data analysis that was prepared as part of the research design. It might be necessary to make changes to the preliminary plan in light of additional information generated in subsequent stages of the research process.

The next step is to consider the known characteristics of the data. The measurement scales used exert a strong influence on the choice of statistical techniques (see Chapter 9). In addition, the research design might favor certain techniques. The insights into the data obtained during data preparation can be valuable in selecting a strategy for analysis.

It also is important to take into account the properties of the statistical techniques, particularly their purpose and underlying assumptions. Some statistical techniques are appropriate for examining differences in variables, others for assessing the magnitudes of the relationships between variables, and others are appropriate for making predictions (see Chapters 16, 17, and 18). The techniques also involve different assumptions, and some techniques can withstand violations of the underlying assumptions better than others. The statistical techniques can be broadly classified as univariate or multivariate. **Univariate techniques** are used for analyzing data when there is a single measurement of each element or unit in the sample, or, if there are several measurements of each element, each variable is analyzed in isolation. In contrast, **multivariate techniques** are used for analyzing data when there are two or more measurements on each element and the variables are analyzed simultaneously.

The researcher's background and philosophy affect the choice of a data analysis strategy. The experienced, statistically trained researcher will employ a range of techniques.

univariate techniques
Statistical techniques appropriate for analyzing data when there is a single measurement of each element in the sample or, if there are several measurements of each element, each variable is analyzed in isolation.

multivariate techniques
Statistical techniques suitable for analyzing data when there are two or more measurements on each element and the variables are analyzed simultaneously. Multivariate techniques are concerned with the simultaneous relationships among two or more phenomena.

FIGURE 15.7

Selecting a Data Analysis Strategy

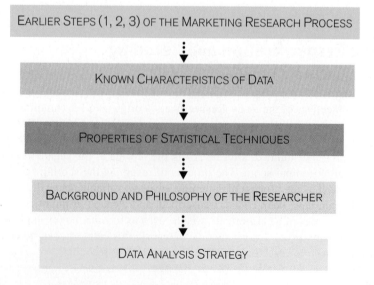

Summary Illustration Using the Opening Vignette

While collecting primary data, the completed questionnaires returned from the field are carefully checked and edited for incomplete (e.g., questions that are incorrectly skipped) or inconsistent responses (e.g., a respondent reports purchases made on a Sears credit card but does not have one). Any respondents with unsatisfactory responses are simply discarded, because the proportion of such respondents is small in relation to the total sample size and research by Sears has shown that the unsatisfactory respondents do not differ from satisfactory respondents on the key variables. The data are coded by following the standard procedures given in Sears' codebook. Then, the data are transcribed from the questionnaires into the computer using state-of-the art technology. As part of data cleaning, Sears performs further checks on the data to ascertain their consistency and accuracy. An effort is made to identify data that are out of range (e.g., a response of 8 on a 1-to-7 scale), logically inconsistent (e.g., sum of percentages adding to more or less than 100 percent), or that have extreme values (e.g., household size of 11). Missing values are kept to a minimum by proper selection, training, and supervision of field workers. In addition, Sears analyzes the data by different procedures for treating missing values, including casewise and pairwise deletion, to determine the impact on the results. A similar process is followed for data collected from secondary sources. This care taken in preparing the data has resulted in a high-quality database that enables Sears to identify the needs of the marketplace and target its marketing efforts accordingly. Figure 15.8 provides a concept map for the data preparation process.

International Marketing Research

The researcher should ensure that the data have been prepared in a comparable manner across countries or cultural units. This means that comparable procedures must be followed for checking questionnaires, editing, and coding. Note that the procedures must be comparable even though the questionnaire itself and, therefore, the coding scheme, could vary. Certain adjustments might be necessary to make the data comparable across countries. For example, the data might have to be adjusted to establish currency equivalents or metric equivalents. Furthermore, transformation of the data might be necessary to make meaningful comparisons and achieve consistent results, as shown in the following example.

Research in Action

Acer Pulls Out an Ace

As of 2008, Taiwan-based Acer (www.acer.com) has transformed itself from a no-name cloner into one of the most popular branded-PC vendors in the world. The company supports dealers and distributors in more than 100 countries. A crucial factor in Acer's success has been its knowledge of consumer preferences for PCs, which it has obtained by conducting surveys in different countries. Great pains are taken at the data-preparation stage to ensure that the data are comparable. For example, the price of PCs in each country is converted to a common unit. This transformation is necessary, because the prices are specified in different local currencies and a common basis is needed for comparison across countries. Also, in each country the premium price is defined in relation to the prices of competing brands in that country.

The care taken at the data-preparation stage has resulted in rich findings. For example, Acer found that, even though the relative importance varies from country to country, eight product attributes contribute to brand preference for desktop

PCs on a worldwide basis: price, ease of installation and use, service and support, features, performance, reliability, scope of usage, and compatibility on a network. Such findings have enabled Acer to launch global marketing strategies that are responsive to variations in local preferences.[5]

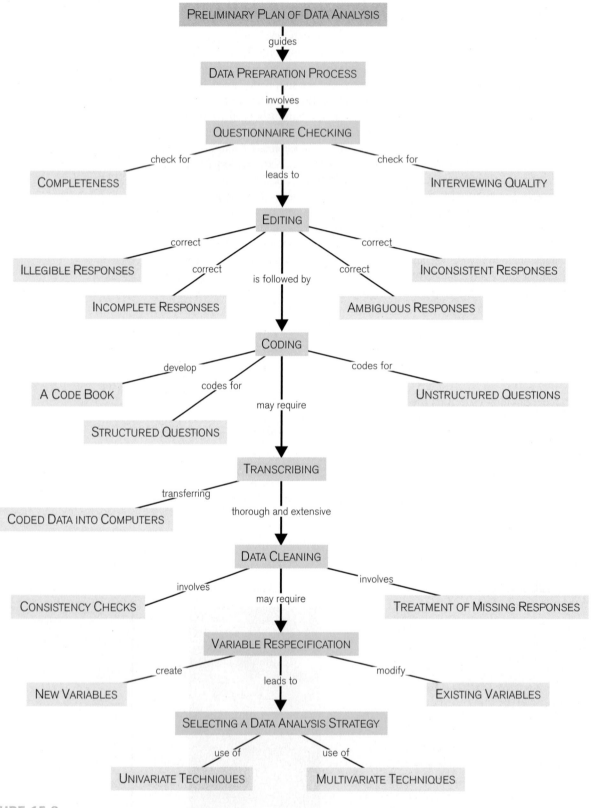

FIGURE 15.8

A Concept Map for the Data Preparation Process

Technology and Marketing Research

Advances in technology have greatly facilitated the data preparation process. When the data are collected by CATI, CAPI, or electronic surveys (e.g., Internet, e-mail), several error checks can be programmed into the questionnaire-administration process, and the data are transcribed directly into the computer.

Other advances also have been made. For example, A2iA, Artificial Intelligence and Image Analysis (www.a2ia.com), a French-based leader in handwriting-recognition software, has developed technology that is dramatically improving data recognition accuracy, reducing data entry costs, and increasing the efficiency of data preparation and analysis. The A2iA DocumentReader v3.0 automatically processes paper documents that contain both handwritten and machine-printed information. The system can read hand-printed, machine-printed, and bar-coded data, as well as optical marks, including checkmarks, Xs, and tick marks, from documents and images. Once the data have been validated and verified, the ASCII record is transferred to a database or user-application file.[6]

Ethics in Marketing Research

Ethical issues can arise during the data preparation and analysis step, particularly in areas where the researcher has to exercise judgment. While checking, editing, coding, transcribing, and cleaning, the researcher can get some idea about the quality of the data. Sometimes it is easy to identify respondents who did not take the questionnaire seriously or who otherwise provided data of questionable quality. Consider, for example, a respondent who checks the "neither agree nor disagree" response to all 30 items measuring attitude toward spectator sports. Decisions about whether such respondents should be discarded—that is, not included in the analysis—can raise ethical concerns. A good rule of thumb is to make such decisions during the data preparation phase before conducting any analysis. Discarding respondents after analyzing the data raises ethical concerns, particularly if this information is not fully disclosed in the written report. Moreover, the procedure used to identify unsatisfactory respondents and the number of respondents discarded should be clearly disclosed, as in the following example.

Research in Action

Ethical Editing of Data

In a study of American MBAs' responses to marketing ethics dilemmas, respondents were required to respond to 14 questions regarding ethically ambiguous scenarios by writing a simple sentence regarding what action they would take if they were the manager in those situations. The responses were then analyzed to determine if they were indicative of ethical behavior. However, in the data preparation phase 6 respondents out of the 561 total respondents were eliminated from further analysis because their responses indicated that they did not follow the directions that told them to clearly state their choice of action. This is an example of ethical editing of the data. The criterion for unsatisfactory responses is clearly stated, the unsatisfactory respondents are identified before the analysis, and the number of respondents eliminated is disclosed.[7]

Another ethical concern relates to interpretation of the results, drawing conclusions, and making recommendations. Although interpretations, conclusions, and recommendations necessarily involve the subjective judgment of the researcher, this judgment must be exercised honestly, free from any personal biases or agendas of the researcher or the client. Suppose a survey reveals that 31 percent of the respondents preferred the client's brand, whereas 30.8 percent preferred the closest competing brand, with all the other brands being preferred to a much lesser extent. For the researcher to state that the client's brand is the most preferred brand in the marketplace, without disclosing that a competing brand is a very close second, might be misleading if it conveys the false impression that the client's brand is the dominantly preferred brand.

What Would *You* Do?

Banana Republic: Going Bananas Over a Makeover

The Situation

For most of its time as a leading U.S. clothing retailer, Gap Inc. (www.gapinc.com) has carefully honed its image through its in-house resources, starting from the design of its clothing to the look of its ads. However, that changed as soon as Jack Calhoun took over as chief marketing officer of Gap's Banana Republic brand in 2003. Calhoun was one of the first marketing hires by former Walt Disney executive Paul Pressler, who took over as Gap Inc. president-CEO, succeeding Millard "Mickey" Drexler. One of Pressler's first acts was to hire Publias Groupe's Leo Burnett USA, Chicago, to oversee segmentation studies of the Gap brands, including Banana Republic and Old Navy. Calhoun reported to newly hired Banana Republic President Marka Hansen, most recently Gap's head of adult merchandising.

The Banana Republic makeover will be the second in the history of the chain, which started out as a travel catalog and then opened safari-themed stores with beat-up jeeps in its storefronts. After the chain was purchased by Gap Inc., Drexler, known for his ability to spot fashion trends, remade it into an upscale version of Gap.

In recent months, Banana Republic's buzz has quieted and sales have not recovered at a pace that's up to speed with siblings Old Navy, Gap, and Piperlime. "The challenge for Banana is the repetition of the fashion lines and marginal quality for the price," said Burt Flickinger, managing director, Strategic Resource Group/Flickinger Consulting, New York.

Calhoun said he and Gap management are carefully building a new positioning for Banana Republic, which traditionally had advertising echoing that of the lower-priced Gap. "We want to build an architecturally sound and beautiful house," said Calhoun of the makeover. "We don't want a Cape Cod with a lot of additions."

A telephone survey was conducted to determine American consumers' perceptions of the Banana Republic brand and how the brand could be positioned to offer more value to the consumers.

The Marketing Research Decision

1. The telephone survey resulted in a sample size of 1,008. As the data were being prepared for analysis, the researchers realized that 132 respondents had missing values. However, the variables with unsatisfactory responses were not the key variables. How should the missing values be treated?
   a. Return the questionnaires with missing values to the field.
   b. Assign missing values: substitute a neutral value.
   c. Casewise deletion.
   d. Pairwise deletion.
   e. Discard respondents with missing values.
2. Discuss how the treatment of missing values you recommend influences Jack Calhoun's decision to enhance Banana Republic's image.

The Marketing Management Decision

1. What should Jack Calhoun do to enhance the perceived value of the Banana Republic brand?
   a. Launch new product lines.
   b. Lower the price.
   c. Change advertising.
   d. Make the clothing more trendy and fashionable.
   e. Make the clothing more functional.

2. Discuss how the marketing management decision action that you recommend to Jack Calhoun is influenced by the treatment of missing values that you suggested earlier and by the findings of the telephone survey.

What Jack Calhoun Did

Jack Calhoun launched new product lines. For women, he introduced a new feminine collection with art deco-inspired details that brought a soft, romantic touch to the more structured fall looks, and the men's collection conveyed a sense of confidence. He also changed the advertising. What the change meant in terms of ads and marketing was a shift from narrowly defined, single-concept campaigns such as "work" and "suede" to those that represented a range of sensibilities in dress. The campaign was comprised of black-and-white photos, along with more vibrant color shots, all with a family album feel. The aim of the new campaign was to express the idea of diversity, age, family, and expressions of the customers. The new personality-focused approach also appealed to a more mature customer than Banana Republic has courted in the past; yet Banana Republic was not targeting a new audience, but rather refocusing on its customers. Due to his successful makeover, Jack Calhoun was promoted and as of 2008 was serving as president of Banana Republic.[8]

Software Applications

Major statistical packages, such as SPSS (www.spss.com), SAS (www.sas.com), Minitab (www.minitab.com), and Excel (www.microsoft.com/office/excel/) have Web sites that can be accessed for a variety of information. Exhibit 15.1 details how to use these packages to make consistency checks. These packages also contain options for handling missing responses and for statistically adjusting the data. In addition, a number of statistical packages can now be found on the Internet. Although some of these programs do not offer integrated data analysis and management, they can be very useful for conducting specific statistical analyses. While we discuss four statistical packages in this book, special emphasis is placed on SPSS and Excel.

SPSS and Excel Computerized Demonstration Movies

We have developed computerized demonstration movies that give step-by-step instructions for running all the SPSS and Excel programs that are discussed in this book. These demonstration movies can be downloaded from the Web site for this book. The instructions for running these demonstration movies are given in Exhibit 15.2.

SPSS and Excel Screen Captures with Notes

The step-by-step instructions for running the various SPSS and Excel programs discussed in this book are also illustrated in screen captures with appropriate notes. These screen captures can be downloaded from the Web site for this book.

SPSS Windows

Using the base module of SPSS, out-of-range values can be selected using the SELECT IF command. These cases, with the identifying information (subject ID, record number, variable name, and variable value) can then be printed using the LIST or PRINT commands. The PRINT command saves active cases to an external file. If a formatted list is required, the SUMMARIZE command can be used.

SPSS Data Entry can facilitate data preparation. You can verify that respondents have answered completely by setting rules. These rules can be used on existing data sets to validate and check the data, whether or not the questionnaire used to collect the data was constructed in Data Entry. Data Entry allows you to control and check the entry of data through three type of rules: validation, checking, and skip and fill rules.

Although the missing values can be treated within the context of the base module, SPSS Missing Values Analysis can assist in diagnosing missing values and replacing missing values with estimates. TextSmart by SPSS can help in the coding and analysis of open-ended responses.

Detailed Steps: Overview

Detailed step-by-step instructions for running the SPSS programs for the data analysis presented in this chapter can be downloaded from the Web site for this book in two forms: (1) computerized demonstration movies, and (2) screen captures. In addition, these steps are illustrated in the following sections.

Detailed Steps: Variable Respecification

We illustrate the use of the base module in creating a new variable using the data of Table 15.1 (SPSS file). We want to create a variable called overall evaluation of the restaurant (Overall) that is the sum of the ratings on quality, quantity, value, and service. Thus,

Overall = Quality + Quantity + Value + Service

These steps are as follows.

1. Select TRANSFORM.
2. Click COMPUTE.
3. Type "overall" into the TARGET VARIABLE box.
4. Click "quality" and move it to the NUMERIC EXPRESSIONS box.
5. Click the "+" sign.
6. Click "quantity" and move it to the NUMERIC EXPRESSIONS box.
7. Click the "+" sign.
8. Click "value" and move it to the NUMERIC EXPRESSIONS box.
9. Click the "+" sign.
10. Click "service" and move it to the NUMERIC EXPRESSIONS box.
11. Click TYPE & LABEL under the TARGET VARIABLE box and type "Overall Evaluation." Click CONTINUE.
12. Click OK.

Detailed Steps: Variable Recoding

We also want to illustrate the recoding of a variable to create a new variable using the data of Table 15.1. Income category 1 occurs only once and income category 6 occurs only twice. Therefore, we want to combine income categories 1 and 2 and categories 5 and 6 and create a new income variable "rincome" labeled "Recoded Income." Note that rincome has only four categories, which are coded as 1 to 4. We describe how to do this using SPSS WINDOWS.

1. Select TRANSFORM.
2. Click RECODE and select INTO DIFFERENT VARIABLES.
3. Click income and move it to the INPUT VARIABLE → OUTPUT VARIABLE box.
4. Type "rincome" into the OUTPUT VARIABLE NAME box.
5. Type "Recoded Income" into the OUTPUT VARIABLE LABEL box.
6. Click the OLD AND NEW VAULES box.
7. Under OLD VALUES, on the left click RANGE. Type 1 and 2 in the range boxes. Under NEW VALUES, on the right click VALUE and type 1 into the value box. Click ADD.
8. Under OLD VALUES, on the left click VALUE. Type 3 in the value box. Under NEW VALUES, on the right click VALUE and type 2 into the value box. Click ADD.
9. Under OLD VALUES, on the left click VALUE. Type 4 in the value box. Under NEW VALUES, on the right click VALUE and type 3 in the value box. Click ADD.
10. Under OLD VALUES, on the left click RANGE. Type 5 and 6 in the range boxes. Under NEW VALUES, on the right click VALUE and type 4 in the value box. Click ADD.
11. Click CONTINUE.
12. Click CHANGE.
13. Click OK.

Experiential Learning

Data Conversion and Preparation Using SPSS

Go to the textbook Web site and download the following comma-delimited file: Hotelsat. This is an Excel file. You will read this file into the SPSS program and then use the power of the SPSS program to (1) substitute mean values for variables into cells with missing values and (2) clean the file for out-of-range values.

Import into SPSS

Open SPSS
    FILE
        OPEN
            DATA
                OPEN FILE window

FILES OF TYPE window (All Files)

Select Hotelsat

Text Import Wizard Step 1—accept default settings—NEXT.

Text Import Wizard Step 2—variables arranged delimited—YES;

—variable names at top of file—YES.

Note: Variable names will be taken from the first row of the spreadsheet.

Text Import Wizard Step 3—accept default settings—NEXT.

Text Import Wizard Step 4—accept default settings—NEXT.

Text Import Wizard Step 5—accept default settings—NEXT.

Text Import Wizard Step 6—accept default settings—FINISH.

To view data, click the DATA VIEW tab at the bottom of the SPSS window.

Note: Variable names will be at the top of the columns. Click VARIABLE VIEW. In the DECIMALS column, set decimals for all variables to 0, one at a time.

Clean Data

1. Count how many cases have complete sets of responses.

   TRANSFORM

   COMPUTE

   COMPUTE VARIABLE window

   (TARGET VARIABLE = numval)

   (NUMERIC EXPRESSION = NVALID(Q3 to Q5)

   numval = NVALID(Q3 to Q5)

   Note: Select NVALID(variable, . . .) under FUNCTIONS. Replace the "?" with "Q3 to Q5". Click OK.

   Note: A new variable "numval" is created. Five of 200 cases have a value of "2" instead of "3," meaning 5 have one missing value.

2. Mean substitution.

   TRANSFORM

   REPLACE MISSING VALUES

   NEW VARIABLE(S) window

   Double-click Q3

   Q3_1 = SMEAN(Q3) appears as new variable.

   Double-click Q4

   Q4_1 = SMEAN(Q4) appears as new variable.

   Double-click Q5

   Q5_1 = SMEAN(Q5) appears as new variable.

   Click OK.

   Note: Output will show 5 values were replaced for variable Q4_1.

3. Check distributions of the new variables with substituted means for out-of-range values.

   ANALYZE

   DESCRIPTIVES STATISTICS

   FREQUENCIES

   FREQUENCIES window: Select (Q3_1 to Q5_1)

Note: These variables will appear as SMEAN(Q3) <Q3_1>, SMEAN(Q4)<Q4_1>, and SMEAN(Q5) <Q5_1>.

STATISTICS

Select MINIMUM, MAXIMUM, MEAN,

STD. DEVIATION

Click OK.

Note: Q4_1 has 5 cases that received the mean value of 5.8.

Q5_1 has 13 cases with the "–9" value. In some data entry plans, such an entry as "–9" is intended to represent a missing value.

4. Convert missing value entries of Q5_1 (those cases with a "–9" representing a missing value during the data-entry phase) into SYSMIS values.

   TRANSFORM

   RECODE INTO DIFFERENT VARIABLES

   RECODE INTO DIFFERENT VARIABLES window

   Select Q5_1. This appears as SMEAN(Q5) (Q5_1)

   OUTPUT VARIABLE = Q5new

   Select CHANGE

   Select OLD AND NEW VALUE

   Under OLD VALUE

   Select –9

   Under NEW VALUE

   Select SYSTEM-MISSING (SYSMIS)

   Then, select ADD

   Note: You are recoding "–9" to have a system missing value so that "–9" will now be recognized by SPSS to be "SYSMIS"—a placeholder, for all practical purposes.

   Under OLD VALUE

   Select RANGE 1 thru 7

   Under NEW VALUE

   Select COPY OLD VALUE(S)

   Then, select ADD

   Note: You are directing SPSS to copy the old values for any entries with a value of 1 through 7.

   Then select CONTINUE

   Back at the RECODE INTO DIFFERENT VARIABLES window

   Click OK.

   Check distribution for Q5new by replicating Step 3 and replacing Q5new for Q3_1, Q4_1, and Q5_1 in the FREQUENCIES window step.

   Note: You will see Q5new has no cases with "–9" now, but Q5new now has 13 cases with missing values.

5. Check work.

   ANALYZE

   DESCRIPTIVE STATISTICS

   FREQUENCIES

   FREQUENCIES window: Select Q3_1, Q4_1, and Q5new

   Note: Output for variables Q3_1, and Q5new, should now have only values of 1–7, as can be seen for SMEAN(Q3), and Q5new. Q4_1 should have five cases with 5.8, with the rest being integers from 1–7, as can be seen for SMEAN(Q4).

6. Save your new SPSS system file as follows.

FILE

SAVE AS . . .

Note: You will now select the location to save this SPSS system file.

In FILE NAME block of SAVE DATA AS window

Type in "Hotelsat New."

In SAVE AS TYPE block

Select "SPSS(*.sav)

Click on SAVE.

Note: Your new SPSS system file will be named in "Hotelsat New."

Excel

Although Excel is an effective spreadsheet program, it lacks the qualities of a relational database that SPSS offers. As a result, distributions of variables cannot be directly produced, and data recoding must be done through if-then statements.

Detailed Steps: Overview

Detailed step-by-step instructions for running the Excel programs for the data analysis presented in this chapter can be downloaded from the Web site for this book in two forms: (1) computerized demonstration movies, and (2) screen captures. In addition, these steps are illustrated in the following sections.

Detailed Steps: Variable Respecification

We illustrate the use of Excel in creating a new variable using the data of Table 15.1. We want to create a variable called overall evaluation of the restaurant (Overall) that is the sum of the ratings on quality, quantity, value, and service. Once you open Table 15.1 (Excel file), the steps are as follows.

1. Click on the cell H1.
2. Type "New Variable" in cell H1.
3. Type "=B2+C2+D2+E2" in cell H2.
4. Click on the "Accept formula value" symbol.
5. Next, right click on cell H2. An Excel pop-up menu gets displayed.
6. Select the **Copy** menu item.
7. Next, select (highlight) cells H3 through H21.
8. Right click in any one of these highlighted cells. An Excel pop-up menu gets displayed.
9. Select the **Paste** menu item.
10. The values for the new variable are now displayed in the cells.

Detailed Steps: Variable Recoding

We also want to illustrate the recoding of a variable using Excel to create a new variable using the data of Table 15.1 (Excel file). We will be recoding income into four categories (as explained earlier using SPSS).

1. Click on the cell H1.
2. Type "RINCOME" in cell H1.
3. Carefully type the formula "=IF(F2=6,4,IF(F2=5,4,IF(F2=4,3,IF(F2=3,2,IF(F2=2,1,IF(F2=1,1,1))))))" correctly in cell H2.
4. Click on the "Accept formula value" symbol.
5. Next, right click on cell H2. An Excel pop-up menu gets displayed.
6. Select the **Copy** menu item.
7. Next, select (highlight) cells H3 through H21.

8. Right click in any one of these highlighted cells. An Excel pop-up menu gets displayed.

9. Select the **Paste** menu item.

10. The recoded values for the new variable are now displayed in the cells.

Experiential Learning

Data Conversion and Preparation Using Excel

To illustrate Excel's data-recoding features, the following example is provided using the same hotelsat dataset used in Experiential Learning using SPSS. For both Q4 and Q5, the next higher digit to the mean value of each variable will be inserted into any missing or out-of-range value. In this case, the value of 6 will be inserted. The screen captures using Excel for these steps can be downloaded from the Web site for this book.

    Open Hotelsat

        In column F, type in the variable name "q4new"

           In cell F2, type in the following if-then statement:

                = IF(D2<1,6, IF(D2>7,6,D2))

This if-then statement directs Excel to evaluate the current entry in cell D2 in the following manner. If this entry in D2 is less than 1, then enter a value of 6 in cell F2; if this entry in D2 is greater than 7, then enter a value of 6 in cell F2. Otherwise, just enter the current value in D2 in F2.

Click the lower-right corner of cell F2, and drag to cell F201 in order to copy the F2 cell to all cells from F3 to F201. In this way, you have inserted the value of 6 into any cells with missing or out-of-range values, or simply copied the original values if the cell entries were okay.

    In column G, type in the variable name "q5new."

        In cell G2, type in the following if-then statement:

           = IF(E2<1,6, IF(E2>7,6,E2))

This if-then statement directs Excel to evaluate the current entry in cell E2 in the following manner. If this entry in E2 is less than 1, then enter a value of 6 in cell G2; if this entry in E2 is greater than 7, then enter a value of 6 in cell G2. Otherwise, just enter the current value of E2 in G2.

Click the lower-right corner of cell G2 and drag to cell G201 in order to copy the G2 cell to all cells from G3 to G201. In this way, you have inserted the value of 6 into any cells with missing or out-of-range values or simply copied the original values if the cell entries were okay.

Summary

Data preparation begins with a preliminary check of all questionnaires for completeness and quality. Then, more thorough editing takes place. Editing consists of screening questionnaires to identify illegible, incomplete, inconsistent, or ambiguous responses. Such responses can be handled by returning questionnaires to the field, assigning missing values, or discarding the unsatisfactory respondents.

The next step is coding. A numerical or alphanumeric code is assigned to represent a specific response to a specific question, along with the column position that code will occupy. It often is helpful to prepare a codebook containing the coding instructions and the necessary information about the variables in the data set. The coded data are transcribed onto disks or entered into computers via keypunching. Marked-sense forms, optical scanning, or computerized sensory analysis might also be used.

Cleaning the data requires consistency checks and treatment of missing responses. Options available for treating missing responses include substitution of a neutral value, such as the mean; casewise deletion; and pairwise deletion. The selection of a data analysis strategy should be based on the earlier steps of the marketing research process, known characteristics of the data, properties of statistical techniques, and the background and philosophy of the researcher.

When analyzing the data in international marketing research, the researcher should ensure that the units of measurement are comparable across countries or cultural units. Technological advances are resulting in new ways to capture, edit, code, and prepare data. Several ethical issues are related to data processing, particularly the discarding of unsatisfactory respondents, and evaluation and interpretation of results. Major statistical packages, such as SPSS, SAS, Minitab, and Excel, have Web sites that can be accessed for useful information.

Key Terms and Concepts

Suggested Cases and Video Cases

Running Case with Real Data

1.1 Hewlett-Packard

Comprehensive Cases with Real Data

3.1 Bank of America   3.2 McDonald's   3.3 Boeing

Video Cases

19.1 Marriott

Live Research: Conducting a Marketing Research Project

1. The project coordinators should number the questionnaires and keep track of any quotas.
2. The team leaders should be responsible for the initial editing of the questionnaires.
3. Each student should be responsible for coding her or his questionnaires and for data entry. It is recommended that the data be entered into an Excel spreadsheet using the coding scheme developed by the instructor or one of the teams.
4. The project coordinators should assemble all the student files into one data file, conduct the computer checks, and clean up the data.
5. The data analysis strategy should be specified by the instructor and discussed in the class.

Acronym

The data preparation process may be summarized by the acronym DATA PREP:

D ata consistency checks

A djusting the data for missing values

T ranscribing

A nalysis strategy

P ost field work questionnaire checking

R ecording numerical or alphanumerical values: Coding

E diting

P reliminary plan of data analysis

Review Questions

1. Describe the data preparation process.
2. What activities are involved in the preliminary checking of questionnaires that have been returned from the field?
3. How does one edit a questionnaire?
4. How are unsatisfactory responses discovered in the editing process treated?
5. What is the difference between precoding and post-coding?
6. Describe the guidelines for the coding of unstructured questions.
7. What does transcribing the data involve?
8. What kinds of consistency checks are made in cleaning the data?
9. What options are available for the treatment of missing data?
10. What considerations are involved in selecting a data analysis strategy?

Applied Problems

1. Shown below is part of a questionnaire used to determine consumer preferences for cameras. Set up a coding scheme for the following three questions (Q9, Q10, and Q11). Note that the first eight questions are not included.

   9. Please rate the importance of the following features you would consider when shopping for a new camera.

	Not so important			Very important	
a. DX film speed setting	1	2	3	4	5
b. Auto-film advance	1	2	3	4	5
c. Autofocus	1	2	3	4	5
d. Autoloading	1	2	3	4	5

   10. If you were to buy a new camera, which of the following outlets would you visit? Please check as many as apply.
       a. _____ Drugstore
       b. _____ Camera store
       c. _____ Discount/mass merchandiser
       d. _____ Supermarket
       e. _____ Internet stores/shopping sites
       f. _____ Other

   11. Where do you get most of your photo processing done? Please check only one option.
       a. _____ Drugstore
       b. _____ Mini labs
       c. _____ Camera stores
       d. _____ Discount/mass merchandiser
       e. _____ Supermarkets
       f. _____ Mail order
       g. _____ Kiosk/other

2. Explain how you would make consistency checks for the part of the questionnaire given in Applied Problem number 1 using SPSS, SAS, Minitab, or Excel.

3. Use an electronic questionnaire design and administration package, such as Qualtrics that is distributed with this book, to program the camera-preference questionnaire given in Applied Problem number 1. Add one or two questions of your own. Administer the questionnaire to five students and prepare the data for analysis. Does computer administration of the questionnaire facilitate data preparation?

Group Discussion

1. "Data preparation is a time-consuming process. In projects with severe time constraints, data preparation should be circumvented." Discuss this statement in a small group.

2. "The researcher should always use computer-assisted interviewing (CATI or CAPI) to collect the data, because these methods greatly facilitate data preparation." Discuss this statement in a small group.

Hewlett-Packard Running Case

Review the Hewlett-Packard (HP) case, Case 1.1, and questionnaire given toward the end of the book. Go to the Web site for this book and download the HP data file.

1. Recode the respondents based on total hours per week spent online (q1) into two groups: 5 hours or fewer (light users) and 6 hours or more (heavy users). Calculate a frequency distribution.

2. Recode the respondents based on total hours per week spent online (q1) into three groups: 5 hours or fewer (light users), 6 to 10 hours (medium users), and 11 hours or more (heavy users). Calculate a frequency distribution.

3. Form a new variable that denotes the total number of things that people have ever done online based on q2_1 to q2_7. Run a frequency distribution of the new variable and interpret the results. Note the missing values for q2_1 to q2_7 are coded as 0.

4. Recode q4 (overall satisfaction) into two groups: Very satisfied (rating of 1), and somewhat satisfied or dissatisfied (ratings of 2, 3, and 4). Calculate a frequency distribution of the new variable and interpret the results.

5. Recode q5 (would recommend) into two groups: Definitely would recommend (rating of 1), and probably would or less likely to recommend (ratings of 2, 3, 4, and 5). Calculate a frequency distribution of the new variable and interpret the results.

6. Recode q6 (likelihood of choosing HP) into two groups: Definitely would choose (rating of 1), and probably would or less likely to choose (ratings of 2, 3, 4, and 5). Calculate a frequency distribution of the new variable and interpret the results.

7. Recode q9_5per into three groups: Definitely or probably would have purchased (ratings of 1 and 2), might or might not have purchased (rating of 3), and probably or definitely would not have purchased (ratings of 4 and 5). Calculate a frequency distribution of the new variable and interpret the results.

8. Recode q9_10per into three groups: Definitely or probably would have purchased and might or might not have purchased (ratings of 1, 2, and 3), probably would not have purchased (rating of 4), and definitely would not have purchased (ratings of 5). Calculate a frequency distribution of the new variable and interpret the results.

9. Recode the demographics as follows:
   a. Combine the two lowest education (q11) categories into a single category. Thus, some high school or less and high school graduate will be combined into a single category labeled "High school graduate or less."
   b. Recode age (q12) into four new categories: 18 to 29, 30 to 39, 40 to 49, and 50 or older.
   c. Combine the two lowest income (q13) categories into a single category labeled "Under $30,000." Calculate frequency distributions of the new variable and interpret the results.

Exhibit 15.1 Computer Programs for Data Preparation

SPSS

Out-of-range values can be selected using the SELECT IF or PROCESS IF statements. These cases, with the identifying information (subject ID, record number, variable name, and variable value) can then be printed using the PRINT or WRITE commands. As a further check, the LIST command can be used to display the values of variables for each case. SPSS Data Entry II simplifies the process of entering new data files. It facilitates data cleaning and checking for logical inconsistencies.

SAS

The IF, IF-THEN, and IF-THEN/ELSE statements can be used to select cases with missing or out-of-range values. The select statement executes one of several statements or groups of statements. The LIST statement is useful for printing suspicious input lines. The LOSTCARD statement can be used to identify missing records in the data. The PRINT and PRINTTO procedures can be used to identify cases and print variable names and variable values. In addition, the OUTPUT and PUT statements can be used to write the values of variables.

Minitab

Minitab features control statements that enable the user to set the order of commands in a macro. The IF command allows implementation of different blocks of commands, including IF, ELSEIF, ELSE, and ENDIF.

Excel

In Excel, the IF statement can be used to make logical checks and check out-of-range values. The IF statement can be accessed under the INSERT <FUNCTION>ALL>IF.

Exhibit 15.2 Instructions for Running Computerized Demonstration Movies

For best results while viewing the SPSS and Excel demonstration movies, it is best to ensure that the "Display" resolution of your computer is set to 1280 by 1024 pixels. To check that, click on the "Display" icon under your computer's Control Panel. While we give instructions for running SPSS demonstration movies, those for Excel are very similar.

To initiate an SPSS demonstration, pick the folder with the appropriate name. For example, to run a variable respecification on the data of Table 15.1, use the "15_1_compute_demo" folder. Each folder will have several files. It is important you download all the files and save them in one folder. All the files are required to run the demonstration. For example, "15_1_compute_demo" has four files. However, some folders have more files, as many as 10. All the files in each folder should be downloaded and saved in a separate folder. The file that you should select to run the demonstration movie is the one that has the same name as the folder, but with the ".htm" extension appended to its name. For example, if you want to run a demonstration of variable respecification on the data of Table 15.1, using SPSS, then double click the file "15_1_compute_demo.htm", in the "15_1_compute_demo" folder. Once you double click, Internet Explorer (or, your default web browser) will be loaded, and the demonstration movie will start automatically. Note that the other three files that also need to be in the same folder are 15_1_Compute_demo_skin.swf, 15_1_Compute_demo. swf, and standard.js.

If you want to stop the demonstration movie at any specific point in the demonstration, simply click the ▮▮ button. The demonstration stops at that point. That button now changes form, and looks like ▶. To continue viewing the demonstration from that point on, simply click the ▶ button. To fast forward the demonstration, you can click the ▶ button. Click it multiple times if you need to fast forward through longer intervals. To rewind the demonstration, simply click the ◀ button. Click it multiple times if you need to rewind through longer intervals. At any time, if you want to replay the demonstration, right from the beginning, then simply click the ↺ button. Finally, you can also move the slider ▬▬▬▬ left or right to navigate through the demonstration. The slider achieves the same purpose as that of the fast forward and rewind buttons.

Data Analysis: Frequency Distribution, Hypothesis Testing, and Cross-Tabulation

OPENING QUESTIONS

1. Why is preliminary data analysis desirable, and what insights can be obtained from such an analysis?

2. What is meant by frequency counts, and what measures are associated with such an analysis?

3. What is the general procedure for hypothesis testing, and what steps are involved?

4. How should cross-tabulation analysis be conducted, and what are the associated statistics?

5. How is the chi-square statistic calculated, and for what purpose is it used?

6. What other statistics are used to test association between two variables, and when are they used?

7. What computer programs are available for conducting frequency and cross-tabulation analyses?

> "Cross-tabulation still remains the most frequently used data analysis technique for marketers. However, cross-tabulation alone leaves a lot of information unexplored and does not exploit the predictive value of research. For that, you need to go beyond cross-tabulation to much more complex and sophisticated multivariate models."
>
> *William Neal,*
> *Senior Executive Officer,*
> *SDR Consulting.*

Consumers Consume Coupons

In 2006, more than $331 billion in potential savings were distributed to American consumers through coupons in 2006, with more than $2.6 billion redeemed. This was a decline in both distribution (−12%) and redemption (−13%) from 2005. A recent Promotional Attitudes and Practices Study surveyed 682 female primary grocery shoppers who were members of the Synovate Panel (www.synovate.com). The survey data were analyzed by calculating frequency counts, percentages, and means. The survey found that 93 percent of the respondents liked coupons, 99 percent had used coupons in the last year, and 95 percent had used a coupon within the last 30 days. The survey also reported that 642 respondents (94%) said coupons were helpful in reducing the cost of groceries, 593 (87%) used coupons for brands they normally bought, and 212 (31%) used coupons to try new products. Despite the growing influence of frequent-customer clubs, frequency counts indicated that most of the respondents did not limit their shopping to a single store. Of the 44 percent who are club members, 19 percent said that their membership makes them more likely to shop at that store, whereas 51 percent shop other stores for specials. The average number of stores shopped was 2.9 per household.

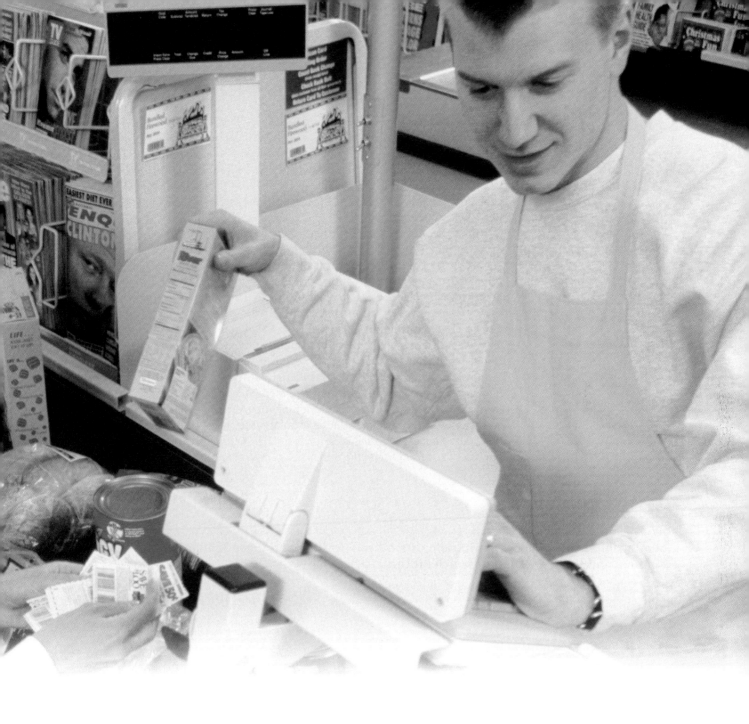

As illustrated here, survey data often are analyzed to obtain *frequency counts* (593 respondents used coupons for brands they normally bought), *percentages* (95% had used a coupon within the last 30 days), and *means* (the average number of stores shopped was 2.9 per household). A *cross-tabulation* of coupon usage with income indicated that households at all income levels were cashing coupons. Furthermore, lower-income households had higher coupon usage as compared to middle- and higher-income households, and this association was statistically significant. Supermarkets can use such findings to target their coupon and promotional strategies. It is clear that supermarkets cannot rely exclusively on frequent customer clubs; coupons and price specials also play a major role in attracting shoppers. This is why U.S. supermarkets such as Kroger make heavy use of coupons and price specials in addition to the Kroger Plus Shoppers' card.[1]

Overview

Once the data have been prepared for analysis (Chapter 15), the researcher should conduct some basic analyses. Often, this involves computing frequency counts, percentages, and averages, as in the opening vignette. This chapter describes basic data analysis techniques, including frequency distribution, hypothesis testing, and cross-tabulation. Figure 16.1 briefly explains the focus of the chapter, the relationship of this chapter to the previous ones, and the steps of the marketing research process on which this chapter concentrates.

First, the chapter describes the frequency distribution of a single variable and explains how it provides an indication of the number of out-of-range, missing, or extreme values, as well as insight into the central tendency and variability of the underlying distribution. Next, hypothesis testing is presented, and a general procedure is provided. The use of cross-tabulation for understanding the associations between variables taken two at a time is then considered. Although the nature of the association can be observed from tables, statistics are available for testing the significance and strength of the association. Help for running the SPSS and EXCEL programs used in this chapter is provided is four ways: (1) detailed step-by-step instructions are given later in the chapter, (2) you can download (from the Web site for this book) computerized demonstration movies illustrating these step-by-step instructions, (3) you can download screen captures with notes illustrating these step-by-step instructions, and (4) you can refer to the Study Guide and Technology Manual, a supplement that accompanies this book. Figure 16.2 provides an overview of the topics discussed in this chapter and how they flow from one to the next.

FIGURE 16.1

Relationship of Frequency Distribution, Hypothesis Testing, and Cross-Tabulation to the Previous Chapters and the Marketing Research Process

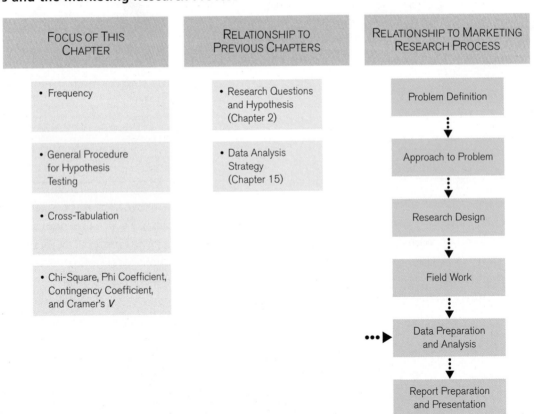

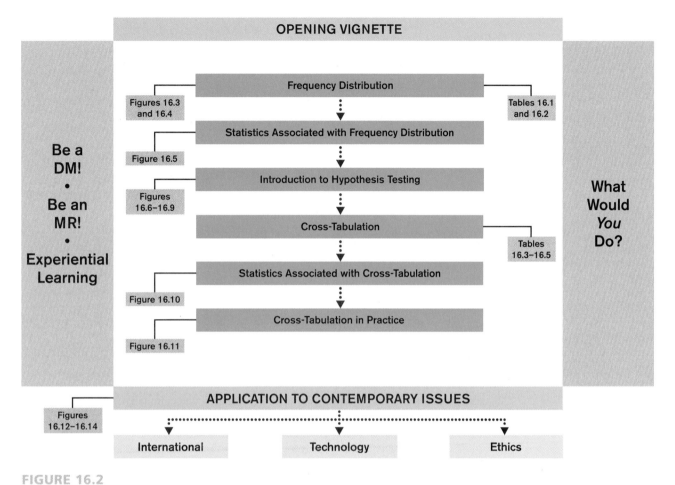

FIGURE 16.2

Frequency Distribution, Hypothesis Testing, and Cross-Tabulation: An Overview

Many commercial marketing research projects do not go beyond basic data analysis. These findings often are displayed using tables and graphs, as discussed further in Chapter 19. Although the findings of basic analysis are valuable in their own right, the insights gained from the basic analysis also are invaluable in interpreting the results obtained from more sophisticated statistical techniques. Therefore, before conducting more advanced statistical analysis, it is useful to examine the frequency distributions of the relevant variables.

Frequency Distribution

Marketing researchers often need to answer questions about a single variable. For example:

- What is the percentage of shoppers using coupons? (See opening vignette.)
- What percentage of the market consists of heavy users, medium users, light users, and nonusers?
- How many customers are very familiar with a new product offering? How many are familiar, somewhat familiar, and unfamiliar with the brand? What is the mean rating on familiarity with the brand? Is there much variance in the extent to which customers are familiar with the new product?
- What is the income distribution of brand users? Is this distribution skewed toward low-income brackets?

Conducting Frequency Analysis

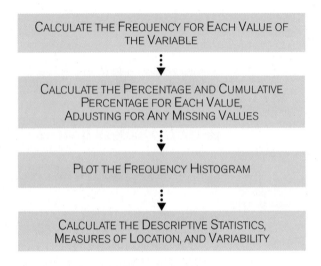

frequency distribution
A mathematical distribution with the objective of obtaining a count of the number of responses associated with different values of one variable and to express these counts in percentage terms.

The answers to these kinds of questions can be determined by examining frequency distributions. In a **frequency distribution**, one variable is considered at a time. The objective is to obtain a count of the number of responses associated with different values of the variable. The relative occurrence, or relative frequency, of different values of the variable is expressed in percentages, as in the opening vignette. A frequency distribution for a variable produces a table of frequency counts, percentages, and cumulative percentages for all the values associated with that variable.

The steps involved in conducting frequency analysis are given in Figure 16.3. The frequency procedure is illustrated using the data of Table 16.1, which gives the attitude toward Nike, the U.S. sports apparel and equipment provider, as well as usage and gender of a sample of Nike users. Attitude is measured on a 7-point Likert type scale (1 = very unfavorable, 7 = very favorable). The users have been coded as 1, 2, or 3, representing light, medium, or heavy users. Gender has been coded as 1 for females and 2 for males. This table gives the data for only 45 respondents so that that the calculations of the basic statistics by hand can be shown. These hand calculations provide the reader a better idea of the basic concepts. In practice, the sample size is much larger. The analysis of such large data sets is illustrated later in the chapter in an Experiential Learning exercise that analyzes the taste-test data for 648 respondents regarding a new reduced-fat version of Kit Kat candy bar, a product of Swiss-based Nestlé, the world's largest food company.

Table 16.2 provides the frequency distribution of attitude from Table 16.1. In the table, the first column contains the labels assigned to the different categories of the variable. The second column indicates the code or value assigned to each label or category. The third column gives the number of respondents for each value, including the missing values. For example, of the 45 respondents who participated in the Nike survey, 6 respondents have a value of 2, denoting an unfavorable attitude. One respondent did not answer and has a missing value denoted by 9. The fourth column displays the percentage of respondents checking each value. These percentages are obtained by dividing the frequencies in column 3 by 45. The next column shows percentages calculated by excluding the cases with missing values; in this example, by dividing the frequencies in column 3 by 44 (i.e., 45 − 1). As can be seen, eight respondents (18.2%) have an attitude value of 5. If there were no missing values, columns 4 and 5 would be identical. The last column represents cumulative percentages after adjusting for missing cases. The cumulative percentage for a value denotes the percentage of responses that are less than or equal to that value. The cumulative percentage corresponding to the value of 5 is 70.5 percent. In other words, 70.5 percent of the respondents have a value of 5 or less. The data of Table 16.1 as well as the SPSS and Excel outputs, along with explanatory notes, can be downloaded from the Web site for this book.

TABLE 16.1 Usage and Attitude Toward Nike Shoes

Number	User Group	Gender	Attitude
1	3.00	2.00	7.00
2	1.00	1.00	2.00
3	1.00	1.00	3.00
4	3.00	2.00	6.00
5	3.00	2.00	5.00
6	2.00	2.00	4.00
7	2.00	1.00	5.00
8	1.00	1.00	2.00
9	2.00	2.00	4.00
10	1.00	1.00	3.00
11	3.00	2.00	6.00
12	3.00	2.00	6.00
13	1.00	1.00	2.00
14	3.00	2.00	6.00
15	1.00	2.00	4.00
16	1.00	2.00	3.00
17	3.00	1.00	7.00
18	2.00	1.00	6.00
19	1.00	1.00	1.00
20	3.00	1.00	5.00
21	3.00	2.00	6.00
22	2.00	2.00	2.00
23	1.00	1.00	1.00
24	3.00	1.00	6.00
25	1.00	2.00	3.00
26	2.00	2.00	5.00
27	3.00	2.00	7.00
28	2.00	1.00	5.00
29	1.00	1.00	9.00
30	2.00	2.00	5.00
31	1.00	2.00	1.00
32	1.00	2.00	4.00
33	2.00	1.00	3.00
34	2.00	1.00	4.00
35	3.00	1.00	5.00
36	3.00	1.00	6.00
37	3.00	2.00	6.00
38	3.00	2.00	5.00
39	3.00	2.00	7.00
40	1.00	1.00	4.00
41	1.00	1.00	2.00
42	1.00	1.00	1.00
43	1.00	1.00	2.00
44	1.00	1.00	3.00
45	1.00	1.00	1.00

TABLE 16.2 Frequency Distribution of Attitude Toward Nike

Value Label	Value	Frequency	Percentage	Valid Percentage	Cumulative Percentage
Very unfavorable	1	5	11.1	11.4	11.4
	2	6	13.3	13.6	25.0
	3	6	13.3	13.6	38.6
	4	6	13.3	13.6	52.3
	5	8	17.8	18.2	70.5
	6	9	20.0	20.5	90.9
Very favorable	7	4	8.9	9.1	100.0
	9	1	2.2	Missing	____
Total		**45**	**100.0**	**100.0**	

A frequency distribution helps determine the extent of illegitimate responses. Values of 0 and 8 would be illegitimate responses, or errors. The cases with these values can be identified and corrective action taken. The presence of *outliers*, cases with extreme values, can also be detected. In the case of a frequency distribution of household size, a few isolated families with household sizes of nine or more might be considered outliers. A frequency distribution also indicates the shape of the empirical distribution of the variable. The frequency data can be used to construct a histogram, or a vertical bar chart, in which the values of the variable are portrayed along the *x*-axis and the absolute or relative frequencies of the values are placed along the *y*-axis.

Figure 16.4 is a histogram of the attitude data in Table 16.2. From the histogram, one could examine whether the observed distribution is consistent with an expected or assumed distribution. Note that in this case the observed distribution does not look like the standard normal distribution. This might be important in determining what type of statistical test is appropriate. For further illustration, consider the following example.

A frequency distribution of responses can help in understanding attitude toward Nike.

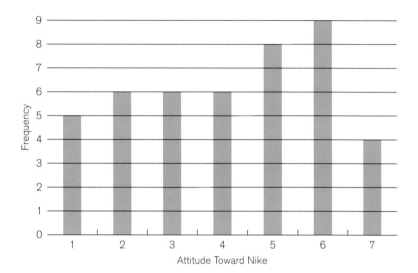

FIGURE 16.4

Frequency Histogram

Research in Action

The Signal Is Green for Yellow-Pages Advertising by Physicians

A census was conducted of every physician's Yellow Pages listing in the U.S. cities of Atlanta, Georgia; Chicago, Illinois; and Charlotte, North Carolina. The contents of these listings were analyzed to determine the types of ads. The various types of Yellow Pages ads were as follows:

Type of Yellow Pages Ad	Frequency	Percentage
Nondisplay listings: light face	5,454	46
Nondisplay listings: face	1,656	14
Display ads	4,694	40
Total advertisements	**11,804**	**100**

more appropriate for physicians with established practices who have all the patients they want. Only 40 percent were using the larger display ads that have a much higher likelihood of being seen by potential patients who consult Yellow Pages when looking for a physician. Because a majority of the physicians were looking for new patients, the study concluded that more physicians should use the display rather than nondisplay ads in the Yellow Pages.[2]

Based on the frequency counts, the study concluded that Yellow Pages listings are a widely used form of physician advertising: 11,804 ads were located in the three areas. The majority of the physicians (46% + 14% = 60%), however, were using nondisplay (light face/face) listings, which are

Note that the numbers and percentages in the preceding example indicate the extent of advertising. Because numbers are involved, a frequency distribution can be used to calculate descriptive or summary statistics. Some of the statistics associated with frequency distribution are discussed in the next section.

Statistics Associated with Frequency Distribution

As illustrated in the previous section, a frequency distribution is a convenient way of looking at the values of a variable. A frequency table is easy to read and provides basic information, but sometimes this information might be too detailed and the researcher must summarize it by the use of descriptive statistics. The most commonly used statistics associated with frequencies are measures of location (mean, mode, and median) and measures of variability (range and standard deviation).

Measures of Location

measures of location
A statistic that describes a location within a data set. Measures of central tendency describe the center of the distribution.

The **measures of location** discussed in this section are measures of central tendency, because they tend to describe the center of the distribution (see Chapter 13). If the entire sample is changed by adding a fixed constant to each observation, then the mean, mode, and median change by the same fixed amount. Suppose the number 10 was added to the attitude ratings of all the $(45-1=)$ 44 respondents who expressed their attitudes toward Nike in Table 16.1. In this case, the mean, mode, and median will all increase by 10.

mean
The average; that value obtained by summing all elements in a set and dividing by the number of elements.

MEAN The **mean**, or average value, is the most commonly used measure of central tendency or center of a distribution (see opening vignette). It is used to estimate the average when the data have been collected using an interval or ratio scale (see Chapter 9). The data should display some central tendency, with most of the responses distributed around the mean.

The mean, $\overline{X}$, is given by

$$\overline{X} = \sum_{i=1}^{n} X_i/n$$

Where

X_i = Observed values of the variable X

n = Number of observations (sample size)

Generally, the mean is a robust measure and does not change markedly as data values are added or deleted. For the frequency counts given in Table 16.2, the mean value is calculated as follows:

$$\overline{X} = (5 \times 1 + 6 \times 2 + 6 \times 3 + 6 \times 4 + 8 \times 5 + 9 \times 6 + 4 \times 7)/44$$

$$= (5 + 12 + 18 + 24 + 40 + 54 + 28)/44$$

$$= 181/44$$

$$= 4.11$$

mode
A measure of central tendency given as the value that occurs the most in a sample distribution.

MODE The **mode** is the value that occurs most frequently. It represents the highest peak of the distribution. The mode is a good measure of location when the variable is inherently categorical or has otherwise been grouped into categories. The mode in Table 16.2 is 6, because this value occurs with the highest frequency; that is, nine times (see also the histogram in Figure 16.4).

median
A measure of central tendency given as the value above which half of the values fall and below which half of the values fall.

MEDIAN The **median** of a sample is the middle value when the data are arranged in ascending or descending rank order (see Chapter 9). If the number of data points is even, the median is usually estimated as the midpoint between the two middle values—by adding the two middle values and dividing their sum by 2. The middle value is the value where 50 percent of the values are greater than that value, and 50 percent are less. Thus, the median is the 50th percentile. The median is an appropriate measure of central tendency for ordinal data. In Table 16.2, the middle value is the average of the 22nd and 23rd observations when the data are arranged in ascending or descending order. This average is 4, and so the median is 4. The median can be easily determined by using cumulative percentages in the frequency table. Note that at a value of 4, the cumulative percentage is 52.3 percent, but for a value of 5, it is 70.5 percent, and for a value of 3, it is 38.6 percent. Therefore, the 50-percent point occurs at the value of 4.

As can be seen from Table 16.2, the three measures of central tendency for this distribution are different (mean = 4.11, mode = 6, median = 4). This is not surprising, because each measure defines central tendency in a different way. The three values are equal only when the distribution is symmetric. In a symmetric distribution, the values are equally likely to plot on either side of the center of the distribution, and the mean, mode, and

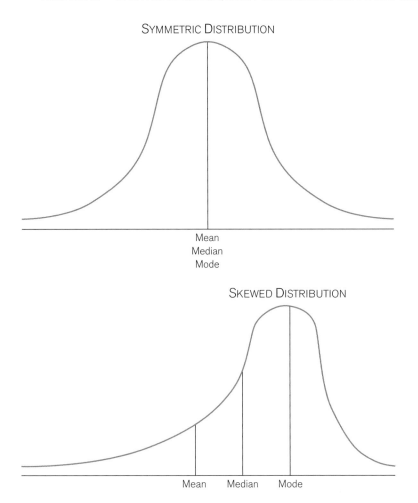

FIGURE 16.5

Skewness of a Distribution

median are equal (Figure 16.5). The normal distribution discussed earlier in Chapter 13 is a symmetric distribution, and the three measures of central tendency are equal. An advantage of calculating all three measures of central tendency is that we can determine whether the distribution is symmetric or asymmetric. The asymmetry of the distribution of Table 16.2 can also be seen from the histogram of Figure 16.4.

If the distribution is asymmetric, which measure should be used? If the variable is measured on a nominal scale, the mode should be used. If the variable is measured on an ordinal scale, the median is appropriate. If the variable is measured on an interval or ratio scale, the mode is a poor measure of central tendency. This can be seen from Table 16.2. Although the modal value of 6 has the highest frequency of nine, it represents only 20.5 percent of the sample. In general, for interval or ratio data, the median is a better measure of central tendency than the mode, although it, too, ignores available information about the variable. The actual values of the variable above and below the median are ignored. The mean is the most appropriate measure of central tendency for interval or ratio data. The mean makes use of all the information available, because all of the values are used in computing it. However, the mean is sensitive to isolated cases with outliers; that is, extremely small or extremely large values. When there are outliers in the data, the mean is not a good measure of central tendency, and it is useful to consider both the mean and the median.

Measures of Variability

The **measures of variability** indicate the dispersion of a distribution. The most common, which are calculated on interval or ratio data, are the range, variance, and standard deviation.

measures of variability
Statistics that indicate the distribution's dispersion.

range
The difference between the smallest and largest values of a distribution.

RANGE   The **range** measures the spread of the data. It is simply the difference between the largest and smallest values in the sample. As such, the range is directly affected by outliers.

$$\text{Range} = X_{\text{largest}} - X_{\text{smallest}}$$

If all the values in the data are multiplied by a constant, the range is multiplied by the same constant. The range in Table 16.2 is $7 - 1 = 6$.

VARIANCE AND STANDARD DEVIATION   The difference between the mean and an observed value is called the deviation from the mean. The **variance** is the mean squared deviation from the mean; that is, the average of the square of the deviations from the mean for all the values. The variance can never be negative. When the data points are clustered around the mean, the variance is small. When the data points are scattered, the variance is large. The variance helps us to understand how similar or different the data points are. If the data points are similar, the variance is small and their distribution is clustered tightly around the mean. If the data points are very different in value, the variance is large and their distribution is spread more widely around the mean. If all the data values are multiplied by a constant, the variance is multiplied by the square of the constant.

variance
The mean squared deviation of all the values from the mean.

standard deviation
The square root of the variance.

The **standard deviation** is the square root of the variance. Thus, the standard deviation is expressed in the same units as the data, whereas the variance is expressed in squared units. The standard deviation serves the same purpose as the variance in helping us to understand how clustered or spread the distribution is around the mean value.

The standard deviation of a sample, s_x, is calculated as

$$s_x = \sqrt{\sum_{i=1}^{n} \frac{(X_i - \overline{X})^2}{n - 1}}$$

We divide by $n - 1$ instead of n, because the sample is drawn from a population and we are trying to determine how much the responses vary from the mean of the entire population. However, the population mean is unknown; therefore, the sample mean is used instead. The use of the sample mean makes the sample seem less variable than it actually is. By dividing by $n - 1$ instead of n, we compensate for the smaller variability observed in the sample. For the data given in Table 16.2, the variance is calculated as follows:

$$\text{Variance} = s_x^2 = \{5 \times (1 - 4.11)^2 + 6 \times (2 - 4.11)^2 + 6 \times (3 - 4.11)^2$$
$$+ 6 \times (4 - 4.11)^2 + 8 \times (5 - 4.11)^2 + 9 \times (6 - 4.11)^2$$
$$+ 4 \times (7 - 4.11)^2\}/43$$
$$= (48.36 + 26.71 + 7.39 + 0.07 + 6.34 + 32.15 + 33.41)/43$$
$$= 154.43/43$$
$$= 3.59$$

The standard deviation, therefore, is calculated as

$$\text{Standard deviation} = s_x = \sqrt{3.59}$$
$$= 1.90$$

Be a DM!

Be an MR!

As the marketing director for the American fast-food chain Wendy's, how would you target heavy users of fast-food restaurants?

Visit www.wendys.com and search the Internet, as well as your library's online databases, to obtain information on the heavy users of fast-food restaurants. In a survey for Wendy's, information was obtained on the number of visits to Wendy's per month. How would you identify the heavy users of Wendy's, and what statistics would you compute to summarize the number of visits to Wendy's per month?

Introduction to Hypothesis Testing

Hypotheses were defined and illustrated in Chapter 2. Recall that hypotheses are unproven statements or propositions of interest to the researcher. Hypotheses are declarative and can be tested statistically. Often, hypotheses are possible answers to research questions. Basic analysis invariably involves some hypothesis testing. The following are examples of hypotheses generated by marketing research in the United States:

- The average number of stores shopped for groceries is 3.0 per household (see opening vignette).
- The department store is being patronized by more than 10 percent of the households.
- The heavy and light users of a brand differ in terms of psychographic characteristics.
- One hotel has a more upscale image than its close competitor.
- Familiarity with a restaurant results in greater preference for that restaurant.

Chapter 13 examined the concepts of the sampling distribution, standard error of the mean or the proportion, and the confidence interval.[3] Because all of these concepts are relevant to hypothesis testing, it would be wise to review them. The next section describes a general procedure for hypothesis testing that can be applied to test a wide range of hypotheses.

A General Procedure for Hypothesis Testing

The following steps are involved in hypothesis testing (Figure 16.6).

1. Formulate the null hypothesis H_0 and the alternative hypothesis H_1.
2. Select an appropriate statistical test and the corresponding test statistic.
3. Choose the level of significance (α).

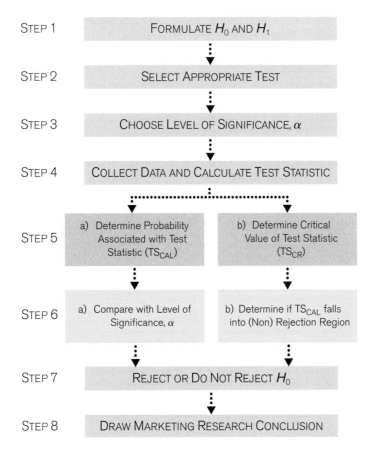

STEP 1 — FORMULATE H_0 AND H_1

STEP 2 — SELECT APPROPRIATE TEST

STEP 3 — CHOOSE LEVEL OF SIGNIFICANCE, α

STEP 4 — COLLECT DATA AND CALCULATE TEST STATISTIC

STEP 5 — a) Determine Probability Associated with Test Statistic (TS_{CAL}) — b) Determine Critical Value of Test Statistic (TS_{CR})

STEP 6 — a) Compare with Level of Significance, α — b) Determine if TS_{CAL} falls into (Non) Rejection Region

STEP 7 — REJECT OR DO NOT REJECT H_0

STEP 8 — DRAW MARKETING RESEARCH CONCLUSION

FIGURE 16.6

A General Procedure for Hypothesis Testing

4. Determine the sample size and collect the data. Calculate the value of the test statistic.
5. Determine the probability associated with the test statistic calculated from the sample data under the null hypothesis, using the sampling distribution of the test statistic. Alternatively, determine the critical value associated with test statistic that divides the rejection and nonrejection regions, given the level of significance (α).
6. Compare the probability associated with the test statistic with the level of significance specified. Alternatively, determine whether the test statistic calculated from the sample data falls into the rejection or the nonrejection region.
7. Make the statistical decision to reject or not reject the null hypothesis.
8. Arrive at a conclusion. Express the statistical decision in terms of the marketing research problem.

Step 1: Formulating the Hypothesis

null hypothesis
A statement suggesting no expected difference or effect. If the null hypothesis is not rejected, no changes will be made.

alternative hypothesis
A statement suggesting some difference or effect is expected. Accepting the alternative hypothesis will lead to changes in opinions or actions.

The first step is to formulate the null and alternative hypothesis. A **null hypothesis** is a statement of the status quo, one of no difference or no effect. If the null hypothesis is not rejected, no changes will be made. An **alternative hypothesis** is one in which some difference or effect is expected. Accepting the alternative hypothesis will lead to changes in opinions or actions. Thus, the alternative hypothesis is the opposite of the null hypothesis.

The null hypothesis is always the hypothesis that is tested. The null hypothesis refers to a specified value of the population parameter (e.g., μ, σ, π), not a sample statistic (e.g., $\overline{X}$) (See Table 13.1). A null hypothesis might be rejected, but it can never be accepted based on a single test. A statistical test can have one of two outcomes. One is that the null hypothesis is rejected and the alternative hypothesis accepted. The other outcome is that the null hypothesis is not rejected based on the evidence. However, it would be incorrect to conclude that because the null hypothesis is not rejected it can be accepted as valid. In classical hypothesis testing, there is no way to determine whether the null hypothesis is true.[4]

In marketing research, the null hypothesis is formulated in such a way that its rejection leads to the acceptance of the desired conclusion. The alternative hypothesis represents the conclusion for which evidence is sought. For example, the American cellular and wireless provider AT&T is considering the introduction of a new servicing plan. The plan will be introduced if it is preferred by more than 40 percent of customers. The appropriate way to formulate the hypotheses is as follows:

$$H_0: \pi \leq 0.40$$

$$H_1: \pi > 0.40$$

If the null hypothesis H_0 is rejected, then the alternative hypothesis H_1 will be accepted and the new service plan introduced. However, if H_0 is not rejected, the new service plan should not be introduced unless additional evidence is obtained.

one-tailed test
A test of the null hypothesis where the alternative hypothesis is expressed directionally.

two-tailed test
A test of the null hypothesis where the alternative hypothesis is not expressed directionally.

The test of the null hypothesis is a **one-tailed test** because the alternative hypothesis is expressed directionally: The proportion of customers who express a preference is greater than 0.40. However, suppose the researcher wanted to determine whether the new service plan is different (superior or inferior) from the current plan, which is preferred by 40 percent of customers. Then a **two-tailed test** would be required, and the hypotheses would be expressed as

$$H_0: \pi = 0.40$$

$$H_1: \pi \neq 0.40$$

In commercial marketing research, the one-tailed test is used more often than a two-tailed test. Typically, there is some preferred direction for the conclusion for which evidence is sought. For example, the higher the profits, sales, and product quality, the better. The one-tailed test is more powerful than the two-tailed test. The power of a statistical test is discussed further in step 3.

Step 2: Selecting an Appropriate Test

To test the null hypothesis, it is necessary to select an appropriate statistical technique. The researcher should take into consideration how the test statistic is computed and the sampling distribution that the sample statistic (e.g., the mean) follows. The **test statistic** measures how close the sample has come to the null hypothesis. The test statistic often follows a well-known distribution, such as the normal, t, or chi-square distributions. Guidelines for selecting an appropriate test or statistical technique are discussed later in this chapter, as well as in Chapter 17.

In our AT&T example, the z statistic, which follows the standard normal distribution, would be appropriate. This statistic would be computed as follows for proportions (see Chapter 13):

$$z = \frac{p - \pi}{\sigma_p}$$

Where

$$\sigma_p = \sqrt{\frac{\pi(1 - \pi)}{n}}$$

test statistic
A measure of how close the sample has come to the null hypothesis. It often follows a well-known distribution, such as the normal, t, or chi-square distribution.

Step 3: Choosing Level of Significance

Whenever an inference is made about a population, there is a risk that an incorrect conclusion will be reached. Two types of error can occur.

TYPE-I ERROR **Type-I error** occurs when the sample results lead to the rejection of the null hypothesis when it is in fact true. In our example, a type-I error would occur if we concluded, based on the sample data, that the proportion of customers preferring the new service plan was greater than 0.40, when in fact it was less than or equal to 0.40. The probability of type-I error (α) also is called the **level of significance**. The type-I error is controlled by establishing the tolerable level of risk of rejecting a true null hypothesis. The selection of a particular risk level should depend on the cost of making a type-I error. The level of significance (α), when expressed as a percentage, is equal to 100 percent minus the confidence level (see Chapter 13).

type-I error
Also known as *alpha* (α) *error*, it occurs when the sample results lead to the rejection of a null hypothesis that is in fact true.

level of significance
The probability of making a type-I error.

TYPE-II ERROR **Type-II error** occurs when, based on the sample results, the null hypothesis is not rejected when it is in fact false. In our example, the type-II error would occur if we concluded, based on sample data, that the proportion of customers preferring the new service plan was less than or equal to 0.40 when, in fact, it was greater than 0.40. The probability of type-II error is denoted by β. Unlike α, which is specified by the researcher, the magnitude of β depends on the actual value of the population parameter (i.e., mean or proportion). The probability of type-I error (α) and the probability of type-II error (β) are shown in Figure 16.7. The complement ($1 - \beta$) of the probability of a type-II error is called the *power of a statistical test.*

type-II error
Also known as *beta* (β) *error*, occurs when the sample results lead to nonrejection of a null hypothesis that is in fact false.

POWER OF A TEST The **power of a test** is the probability ($1 - \beta$) of rejecting the null hypothesis when it is false and should be rejected. Although β is unknown, it is related to α. An extremely low value of α (e.g., 0.001) will result in intolerably high β errors. Thus, it is necessary to balance the two types of errors. As a compromise, α often is set at 0.05; sometimes it is 0.01; other values of α are rare. The level of α, along with the sample size, will determine the level of β for a particular research design. The risk of both α and β can be controlled by increasing the sample size. For a given level of α, increasing the sample size will decrease β, thereby increasing the power of the test.

power of a test
The probability of rejecting the null hypothesis when it is in fact false and should be rejected.

Step 4: Data Collection

Sample size is determined after taking into account the desired α and β errors, incidence and completion rates, and other qualitative considerations, such as budget constraints (see

FIGURE 16.7

Type-I Error (Alpha) and Type-II Error (Beta)

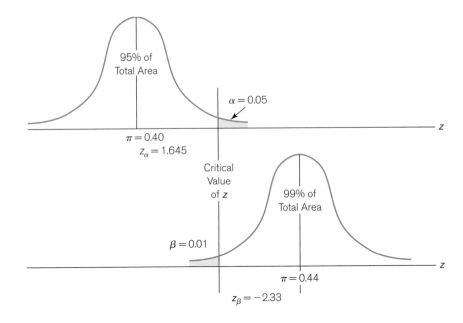

Chapter 13). Then, the required data are collected and the value of the test statistic computed. In our example, suppose 500 customers were surveyed and 220 expressed a preference for the new service plan. Thus, the value of the sample proportion is $p = 220/500 = 0.44$.

The value of σ_p can be determined as follows:

$$\sigma_p = \sqrt{\frac{\pi(1 - \pi)}{n}}$$

$$= \sqrt{\frac{(0.40)(0.6)}{500}}$$

$$= 0.0219$$

The test statistic z can be calculated as follows:

$$z = \frac{p - \pi}{\sigma_p}$$

$$= \frac{0.44 - 0.40}{0.0219}$$

$$= 1.83$$

Step 5: Determining the Probability (Critical Value)

Using standard normal tables (Table 2 of the Appendix of Statistical Tables), the probability of obtaining a z value of 1.83 can be calculated (Figure 16.8). The shaded area between $-\infty$ and 1.83 is 0.9664. Therefore, the area to the right of $z = 1.83$ is $1.0000 - 0.9664 = 0.0336$. Most computer programs automatically calculate this value. It also is called the **p value** and is the probability of observing a value of the test statistic as extreme as, or more extreme than, the value actually observed, assuming that the null hypothesis is true.

Alternatively, the critical value of z, which will give an area to the right side of the critical value of 0.05, is between 1.64 and 1.65 and equals 1.645. Note that in determining the

p value

This is the probability of observing a value of the test statistic as extreme as, or more extreme than, the value actually observed, assuming that the null hypothesis is true.

FIGURE 16.8

Probability of z Value with a One-Tailed Test

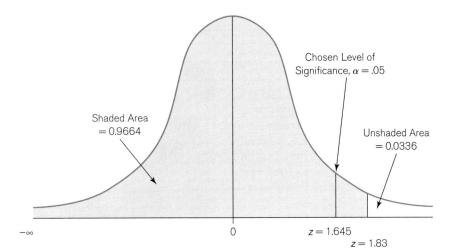

critical value of the test statistic, the area to the right of the critical value is either α or $\alpha/2$. It is α for a one-tail test and $\alpha/2$ for a two-tail test.

Steps 6 and 7: Comparing the Probability (Critical Value) and Making the Decision

a. The probability associated with the calculated or observed value of the test statistic calculated from the sample data is 0.0336. This is the probability of getting a p value of 0.44 when $\pi = 0.40$. This is less than the level of significance of 0.05. Hence, the null hypothesis is rejected.

b. Alternatively, the calculated value of the test statistic $z = 1.83$ lies in the rejection region, beyond the value of 1.645. Again, the same conclusion to reject the null hypothesis is reached.

Note that the two ways of testing the null hypothesis are equivalent but mathematically opposite in the direction of comparison. If the probability associated with the calculated or observed value of the test statistic (TS_{CAL}) is *less than* the level of significance (α), the null hypothesis is rejected. However, if the absolute value of the calculated value of the test statistic (TS_{CAL}) is *greater than* the absolute value of the critical value of the test statistic (TS_{CR}), the null hypothesis is rejected. The **critical value** is the value of the test statistic that divides the rejection and nonrejection regions. The reason for this sign shift is that the larger the absolute value of TS_{CAL}, the smaller the probability of obtaining a more extreme value of the test statistic under the null hypothesis. This sign shift can be easily illustrated as follows:

critical value
The value of the test statistic that divides the rejection and nonrejection regions. If the absolute value of the calculated value of the test statistic is greater than the absolute value of the critical value of the test statistic, the null hypothesis is rejected.

Under (a):

if probability of TS_{CAL} < significance level (α), then reject H_0

Under (b),

if $|\text{TS}_{\text{CAL}}| > |\text{TS}_{\text{CR}}|$, then reject H_0

Step 8: Marketing Research Conclusion

The conclusion reached by hypothesis testing must be expressed in terms of the marketing research problem and the managerial action that should be taken. In our example, we conclude that there is evidence that the proportion of customers preferring the new service plan is significantly greater than 0.40. Hence, the recommendation would be to introduce the new service plan. Another illustration of hypothesis testing is provided by the following example.

Research in Action

Holiday Inn: The "In" Thing

As of 2008, there were over 3,600 Holiday Inns in over 150 cities around the world. This famous hotel chain is owned by InterContinental Hotels Group (IHG), which is based in the United Kingdom. Although IHG (www.ichotelsgroup.com) has a room capacity of 18.8 million rooms, it only holds 3 percent of the market share. In an attempt to increase its market share, IHG was considering opening other hotel chains for middle-class hotel customers that would have more stylish rooms. Management analysis indicated that this would be feasible if more than 20 percent of the target customers preferred stylish rooms. The following hypotheses were formulated:

$$H_0 : \pi \le 0.20$$

$$H_1 : \pi > 0.20$$

Note that this is a one-tailed test. IHG recruited Landis Strategy & Innovation (www.landis-si.com), a U.S. provider of data-communications services, to survey 14,000 travelers on three continents. The findings of this study showed that a surprising 40 percent of middle-class hotel customers cared about style and design in their hotel rooms, leading to the rejection of the null hypothesis.

In response to this finding, IHG introduced a few different kinds of "branded" hotels, such as Holiday Indigo,

Nickelodeon Family Suites, Holiday Inn Sunspree Resorts, and Holiday Inn Garden Court. The main aim of these chains is to capitalize on mid-market customers who are willing to spend on luxury and service. Each chain is personalized and unique, fighting against the "sea of sameness" into which the hotel industry has sunk. By conducting hypothesis testing, IHG has discovered the needs of its customers in a changing market. It will be able to cater to these needs and differentiate its hotels to stand above the competition.[5]

Hypotheses testing can be related to either an examination of associations or an examination of differences (Figure 16.9). In tests of associations, the null hypothesis is that there is no association between the variables (H_0: . . . is *not* related to . . .). In tests of differences, the null hypothesis is that there is no difference (H_0: . . . is *not* different from . . .). Tests of differences could relate to means or proportions. First, we discuss hypotheses related to associations in the context of cross-tabulations.

Cross-Tabulation

Although answers to questions related to a single variable are interesting, they often raise additional questions about how to link that variable to other variables. To introduce the frequency distribution, we posed several representative marketing research questions. For each of these, a researcher might pose additional questions to relate these variables to other variables. For example:

- What percentage of coupon users have annual household incomes of more than $50,000? (See opening vignette.)

FIGURE 16.9

A Broad Classification of Hypothesis Testing Procedures

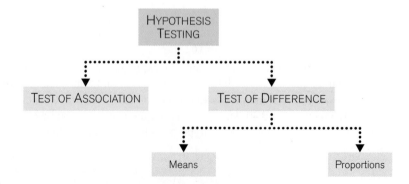

- Is product use (measured in terms of heavy users, medium users, light users, and nonusers) related to interest in outdoor activities (high, medium, and low)?
- Is familiarity with a new product (unfamiliar, familiar) related to education levels (high school or less, some college, college degree)?
- Is the income (high, medium, and low) of brand users related to the geographic region in which they live (north, south, east, and west)?

The answers to such questions can be determined by examining cross-tabulations. Whereas a frequency distribution describes one variable at a time, a **cross-tabulation** describes two or more variables simultaneously. Cross-tabulation results in tables that reflect the joint distribution of two or more variables with a limited number of categories or distinct values. The categories of one variable are cross-classified with the categories of one or more other variables. Thus, the frequency distribution of one variable is subdivided according to the values or categories of the other variables. This was illustrated in the opening vignette in which coupon usage was cross-classified with income. The analysis revealed that lower-income households had higher coupon usage as compared to middle- and higher-income households.

cross-tabulation
A statistical technique that describes two or more variables simultaneously and results in tables that reflect the joint distribution of two or more variables that have a limited number of categories or distinct values.

Suppose Nike was interested in determining whether gender was associated with the degree of usage of Nike shoes. In Table 16.1, the respondents were divided into three categories of light (denoted by 1), medium (2), or heavy users (3) based on reported wear-time per week. There were 19 light users, 10 medium users, and 16 heavy users. Although data on attitude were missing for one respondent, information on usage and gender was available for all respondents. Gender was coded as 1 for females and 2 for males. The sample included 24 females and 21 males.

The cross-tabulation is shown in Table 16.3. A cross-tabulation includes a cell for every combination of the categories of the two variables. The number in each cell shows how many respondents gave that combination of responses. In Table 16.3, 14 respondents were females and light users. The marginal totals (column totals and row totals) in this table indicate that of the 45 respondents with valid responses on both the variables 19 were light users, 10 were medium users, and 16 were heavy users, confirming the classification procedure adopted.

Furthermore, 21 respondents were males, and 24 were females. Note that this information could have been obtained from a separate frequency distribution for each variable. In general, the margins of a cross-tabulation show the same information as the frequency tables for each of the variables. Cross-tabulation tables also are called **contingency tables**.

contingency table
A cross-tabulation table. It contains a cell for every combination of categories of the two variables.

Cross-tabulation is widely used in commercial marketing research because (1) cross-tabulation analysis and results can be easily interpreted and understood by managers who are not statistically oriented; (2) the clarity of interpretation provides a stronger link between research results and managerial action; and (3) cross-tabulation analysis is simple to conduct and more appealing to less sophisticated researchers. We will discuss cross-tabulation for two variables, the most common form in which this procedure is used.

Cross-tabulation with two variables also is known as *bivariate cross-tabulation.* Consider again the cross-classification of gender and usage of Nike shoes given in Table 16.3.

TABLE 16.3 A Cross-Tabulation of Gender and Usage of Nike Shoes

Usage	Gender		Row Total
	Female	Male	
Light users	14	5	19
Medium users	5	5	10
Heavy users	5	11	16
Column total	**24**	**21**	**45**

TABLE 16.4 **Usage of Nike Shoes by Gender**

Usage	Gender	
	Female	Male
Light users	58.4%	23.8%
Medium users	20.8%	23.8%
Heavy users	20.8%	52.4%
Column total	**100.0%**	**100.0%**

Is usage of Nike shoes related to gender? It might be. We see from Table 16.3 that disproportionately more of the males are heavy users and disproportionately more of the females are light users. Computation of percentages can provide more insights.

Because two variables have been cross-classified, percentages could be computed either column-wise, based on column totals (Table 16.4), or row-wise, based on row totals (Table 16.5). Which of these tables is more useful? The answer depends on which variable will be considered as the independent variable and which as the dependent variable. The general rule is to compute the percentages in the direction of the independent variable, across the dependent variable. In our analysis, gender would be considered as the independent variable and usage as the dependent variable. Therefore, the correct way of calculating percentages is as shown in Table 16.4. Note that although 52.4 percent of the males are heavy users, only 20.8 percent of females are heavy users. This seems to indicate that compared to females, males are more likely to be heavy users of Nike shoes. The recommendation to management might be to promote more heavily to women to increase their usage rate or to promote more heavily to men to prevent brand loyalty erosion. Obviously, additional variables would need to be analyzed before management would act upon such variables. Nevertheless, this illustrates how hypotheses tests should be linked to recommended managerial actions.

Note that computing percentages in the direction of the dependent variable across the independent variable, as shown in Table 16.5, is not meaningful in this case. Table 16.5 implies that heavy usage of Nike shoes causes people to be males. This latter finding is not meaningful. The corresponding SPSS and Excel outputs for this cross-tabulation with explanatory notes can be downloaded from the Web site for this book. As another example, consider the following study.

Research in Action

Old Is Gold, but Some Marketers Treat It as Dust

A study conducted in the United States examined whether older models are depicted in a negative light in TV commercials. Television commercials emanating from the three major networks, one local station, and five cable companies were analyzed by the researchers. The results were as follows in terms of the number and percentage of models of different age groups that were depicted in a positive or negative light:

Age of the Model (yrs)	Positive Depiction		Negative Depiction		Total	
	No.	%	No.	%	No.	%
Under 45	415	83.1	85	16.9	500	100
45–64	64	66.0	33	34.0	97	100
65 and over	28	54.0	24	46.0	52	100

Note that as the age of the model increases, the percentages in the negative-depiction column increase. Therefore, the study concluded that older models do tend to be depicted in a negative manner. Thus, some marketers might be pursuing self-defeating strategies by depicting older consumers unfavorably. American marketers should note that older consumers represent a large and growing segment that controls substantial income and wealth.[6]

TABLE 16.5 Gender by Usage of Nike Shoes

Usage	Gender		Row Total
	Female	Male	
Light users	73.7%	26.3%	100.0%
Medium users	50.0%	50.0%	100.0%
Heavy users	31.2%	68.8%	100.0%

General Comments on Cross-Tabulation

Although three or more variables can be cross-tabulated, the interpretation can be quite complex. Also, because the number of cells increases multiplicatively, maintaining an adequate number of respondents or cases in each cell can be problematic. As a general rule, each cell should have at least five expected observations for the chi-square statistic used for testing cross-tabulation hypothesis to be reliable. Thus, cross-tabulation is an inefficient way of examining relationships when there are several variables. Note that cross-tabulation examines association between variables, not causation. To examine causation, the causal research design framework should be adopted (see Chapter 8).

Statistics Associated with Cross-Tabulation

This section focuses on the statistics commonly used for assessing the statistical significance and strength of association of cross-tabulated variables. The statistical significance of the observed association is commonly measured by the chi-square statistic. The strength of association, or degree of association, is important from a practical or managerial perspective. Generally, the strength of an association is of interest only if the association is statistically significant. The strength of the association can be measured by the phi correlation coefficient, the contingency coefficient, and Cramer's V.

Chi-Square

The **chi-square statistic** (χ^2) is used to test the statistical significance of the observed association in a cross-tabulation. It can be used in determining whether a systematic association exists between two variables. This is illustrated in the opening vignette where a systematic association exists between coupon usage and income, with lower-income households consuming more coupons than middle- or higher-income households. The null hypothesis, H_0, is that there is no association between the variables. The test is conducted by computing the cell frequencies that would be expected if no association was present between the variables, given the existing row and column totals. These expected cell frequencies, denoted f_e, are then compared to the actual observed frequencies, f_o, found in the cross-tabulation to calculate the chi-square statistic. The greater the discrepancies between the expected and actual frequencies, the larger the value of the statistic. Assume that a cross-tabulation has r rows and c columns and a random sample of n observations. The expected frequency for each cell, f_e, can be calculated by using a simple formula as follows:

$$f_e = \frac{n_r n_c}{n}$$

where

n_r = total number in the row

n_c = total number in the column

n = total sample size

chi-square statistic
The statistic used to test the statistical significance of the observed association in a cross-tabulation. It assists in determining whether a systematic association exists between the two variables.

For the data in Table 16.3, the total number in the row, n_r, is 19 for light users, 10 for medium users, and 16 for heavy users. The total number in each column, n_c, is 24 for females and 21 for males. Therefore, the expected cell frequencies for the six cells from left to right and top to bottom are

$$f_e = (19 \times 24)/45 = 10.1 \qquad f_e = (19 \times 21)/45 = 8.9$$

$$f_e = (10 \times 24)/45 = 5.3 \qquad f_e = (10 \times 21)/45 = 4.7$$

$$f_e = (16 \times 24)/45 = 8.5 \qquad f_e = (16 \times 21)/45 = 7.5$$

Generally, the expected cell frequency will be different for each cell, as is the case here. Only when all row totals are the same and all column totals are the same will the expected cell frequency be the same for each cell.

Once the expected cell frequencies are calculated, the value of χ^2 is calculated as follows:

$$\chi^2 = \sum_{\substack{\text{all} \\ \text{cells}}} \frac{(f_o - f_e)^2}{f_e}$$

For the data in Table 16.3, in which there are six cells, the value of χ^2 is calculated as

$$
\begin{aligned}
\chi^2 = {} & \frac{(14 - 10.1)^2}{10.1} + \frac{(5 - 8.9)^2}{8.9} \\
& + \frac{(5 - 5.3)^2}{5.3} + \frac{(5 - 4.7)^2}{4.7} \\
& + \frac{(5 - 8.5)^2}{8.5} + \frac{(11 - 7.5)^2}{7.5} \\
= {} & 1.51 + 1.71 + 0.02 + 0.02 + 1.44 + 1.63 \\
= {} & 6.33
\end{aligned}
$$

To determine whether a systematic association exists, the probability of obtaining a value of chi-square as large as or larger than the one calculated from the cross-tabulation is estimated (see Figure 16.6, step 5). An important characteristic of the chi-square statistic is the number of degrees of freedom (df) associated with it. In general, the number of degrees of freedom is equal to the number of observations less the number of constraints needed to calculate a statistical term. In the case of a chi-square statistic associated with a cross-tabulation, the number of degrees of freedom is equal to the product of number of rows (r) less one and the number of columns (c) less one. That is, df = $(r - 1) \times (c - 1)$. The null hypothesis (H_0) of no association between the two variables will be rejected only when the calculated value of the test statistic is greater than the critical value of the chi-square distribution with the appropriate degrees of freedom, as shown in Figure 16.10. (See Figure 16.6, Step 6).

chi-square distribution
A skewed distribution whose shape depends solely on the number of degrees of freedom. As the number of degrees of freedom increases, the chi-square distribution becomes more symmetrical.

Unlike the normal distribution, the **chi-square distribution** is a skewed distribution, the shape of which depends solely on the number of degrees of freedom. As the number of degrees of freedom increases, the chi-square distribution becomes more symmetrical. Table 3 in the Appendix of Statistical Tables contains upper-tail areas of the chi-square distribution for different degrees of freedom. In this table, the value at the top of each column indicates the area in the upper portion (the right side, as shown in Figure 16.10) of the chi-square distribution. To illustrate, for 2 degrees of freedom, the critical value of chi-square (χ^2_{CR}) for an upper-tail area of 0.05 is 5.991. This indicates that for 2 degrees of freedom the probability of exceeding a chi-square value of 5.991 is 0.05. In other words, at the 0.05 level of significance with 2 degrees of freedom, the critical value of the chi-square statistic is 5.991.

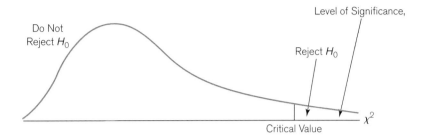

FIGURE 16.10

Chi-Square Test of Association

For the cross-tabulation given in Table 16.3, there are $(3 - 1) \times (2 - 1) = 2$ degrees of freedom. The calculated chi-square statistic had a value of 6.33. Because this is greater than the critical value of 5.991, the null hypothesis of no association is rejected, indicating that the association is statistically significant at the 0.05 level.

The chi-square statistic can also be used in *goodness-of-fit tests* to determine whether certain models fit the observed data. These tests are conducted by calculating the significance of sample deviations from assumed theoretical (expected) distributions and can be performed on cross-tabulations as well as on frequencies (one-way tabulations). The calculation of the chi-square statistic and the determination of its significance is the same as illustrated earlier.

The chi-square statistic should be estimated only on counts of data. When the data are in percentage form, they should first be converted to absolute counts or numbers. In addition, an underlying assumption of the chi-square test is that the observations are drawn independently. This means that respondents do not influence each other's responses in any way. As a general rule, chi-square analysis should not be conducted when the expected or theoretical frequencies in any of the cells is less than five. Low expected frequencies would cause the calculated value of chi-square to be higher than it should be (bias it upward) and make it more likely to commit a type-I error. The issue of cell sizes is directly related to statistical determination of sample size discussed in Chapter 13. When the frequency in any of the cells is low, it is often possible to reduce the size of the table (i.e., reduce the number of rows and/or columns) by combining categories. This was illustrated in Chapter 15 where the RECODE procedure in SPSS was employed to reduce the number of income categories from six to four. In the case of a 2×2 table, the chi-square is related to the phi coefficient.

Phi Coefficient

The **phi coefficient** (ϕ) is used as a measure of the strength of association in the special case of a table with two rows and two columns (a 2×2 table). The phi coefficient is proportional to the square root of the chi-square statistic. For a sample of size n, this statistic is calculated as

phi coefficient
A measure of the strength of association in the special case of a table with two rows and two columns (a 2×2 table).

$$\phi = \sqrt{\frac{\chi^2}{n}}$$

It takes the value of 0 when there is no association, which would be indicated by a chi-square value of 0 as well. When the variables are perfectly associated, phi assumes the value of 1, and all the observations fall just on the main or minor diagonal. (In some computer programs, phi assumes a value of -1 rather than 1 when there is perfect negative association.) In the more general case involving a table of any size, the strength of association can be assessed by using the contingency coefficient.

Contingency Coefficient

contingency coefficient
A measure of the strength of association in a table of any size.

The phi coefficient is specific to a 2×2 table; the **contingency coefficient** (C) can be used to assess the strength of association in a table of any size. This index is related to chi-square, as follows:

$$C = \sqrt{\frac{\chi^2}{\chi^2 + n}}$$

The contingency coefficient varies between 0 and 1. The 0 value occurs in the case of no association (i.e., the variables are statistically independent), but the maximum value of 1 is never achieved. Rather, the maximum value of the contingency coefficient depends on the size of the table (number of rows and number of columns). For this reason, it should be used only to compare tables of the same size.

Normally, the strength of association is not meaningful and, hence, not calculated when the null hypothesis of no association is not rejected. If there is no relationship between the two variables, there can be no strength. In our case, the null hypothesis was rejected; thus, it is meaningful to calculate the contingency coefficient. The value of the contingency coefficient for Table 16.3 is

$$C = \sqrt{\frac{6.33}{6.33 + 45}}$$

$$= \sqrt{.1235}$$

$$= 0.351$$

This value of C indicates that the association is low to moderate.

Cramer's V

Cramer's V
A measure of the strength of association used in tables larger than 2×2.

Cramer's V is a modified version of the phi correlation coefficient, ϕ, and is used in tables larger than 2×2. When phi is calculated for a table larger than 2×2, it has no upper limit. Cramer's V is obtained by adjusting phi for either the number of rows or the number of columns in the table, based on which of the two is smaller. The adjustment is such that V will range from 0 to 1. A large value of V merely indicates a high degree of association. It does not indicate how the variables are associated. As a rule of thumb, values of V below 0.3 indicate low association, values between 0.3 and 0.6 indicate low-to-moderate association, and values above 0.6 indicate strong association. For a table with r rows and c columns, the relationship between Cramer's V and the phi correlation coefficient is expressed as

$$V = \sqrt{\frac{\phi^2}{\min(r-1),(c-1)}}$$

or

$$V = \sqrt{\frac{\chi^2/n}{\min(r-1),(c-1)}}$$

The value of Cramer's V for Table 16.3 is

$$V = \sqrt{\frac{6.33/45}{1}}$$

or

$$V = \sqrt{.01409}$$

$$= 0.375$$

Thus, the association is low to moderate.

Given that the null hypothesis was rejected and we have determined the strength of association as low to moderate, we can interpret the pattern of relation by looking at the percentages in Table 16.4. There is a low-to-moderate association between gender and usage of Nike shoes. Males tend to be heavy users, whereas females tend to be light users.

Cross-Tabulation in Practice

When conducting cross-tabulation analysis in practice, it is useful to proceed following these steps (Figure 16.11):

1. Construct the cross-tabulation table.
2. Test the null hypothesis that there is no association between the variables using the chi-square statistic (see the procedure described in Figure 16.6).
3. If you fail to reject the null hypothesis, there is no relationship.
4. If H_0 is rejected, determine the strength of the association using an appropriate statistic (phi-coefficient, contingency coefficient, or Cramer's V) as discussed earlier in this chapter.
5. If H_0 is rejected, interpret the pattern of the relationship by computing the percentages in the direction of the independent variable, across the dependent variable. Draw marketing conclusions.

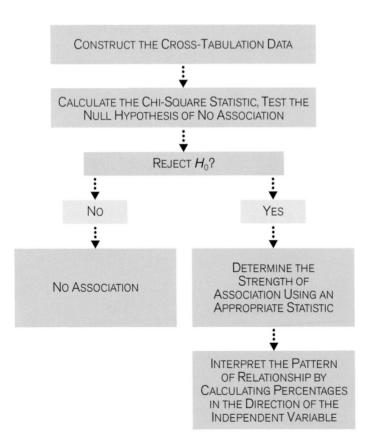

FIGURE 16.11

Conducting Cross-Tabulation Analysis

Summary Illustration Using the Opening Vignette

Basic data analysis provides valuable insights, as in the case of the coupon-usage study presented in the opening vignette. A frequency distribution produces a table of frequency counts, percentages, and cumulative percentages for all the values associated with that variable. The mean, mode, and median of a frequency distribution are measures of central tendency. Some of the important statistics and the insights they provided in the opening vignette included frequency counts (593 respondents used coupons for brands they normally bought), percentages (95% had used a coupon within the last 30 days), and means (the average number of stores shopped was 2.9 per household).

Hypotheses are declarative statements. Basic analysis invariably involves some hypothesis testing. Based on the data collected in the opening vignette, one could test the hypothesis that the average number of stores shopped for groceries is 3.0 per household. Cross-tabulations are tables that reflect the joint distribution of two or more variables. The chi-square statistic provides a test of the statistical significance of the observed association in a cross-tabulation. In the opening vignette, a cross-tabulation of coupon usage with income indicated that households at all income levels were cashing coupons. Yet, lower-income households had higher coupon usage as compared to middle- and higher-income households, and this association was statistically significant. Such findings can be used by supermarkets to target their coupon and promotional strategies. Figures 16.12, 16.13, and 16.14 provide concept maps for frequency analysis, hypothesis testing, and cross-tabulation, respectively.

FIGURE 16.12

A Concept Map for Frequency Analysis

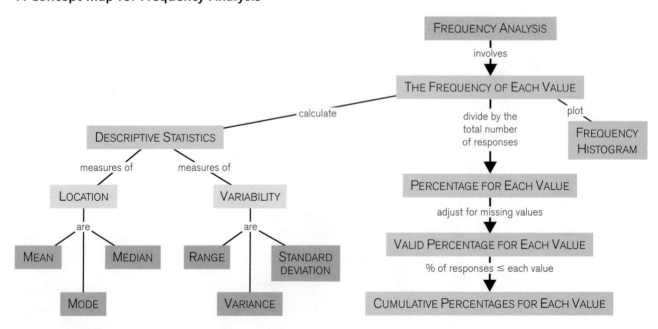

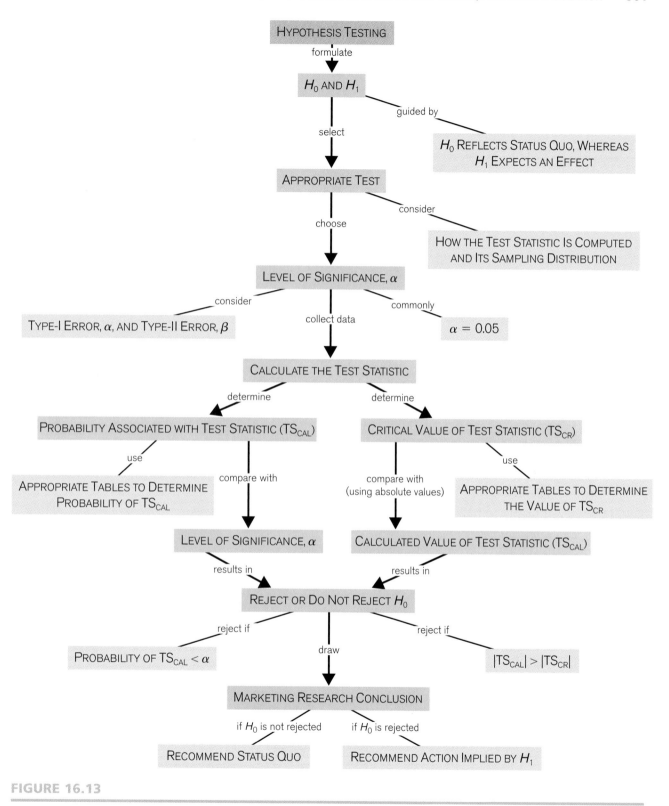

FIGURE 16.13

A Concept Map for Hypothesis Testing

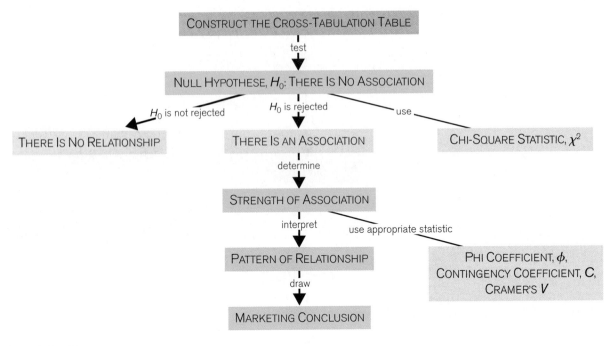

FIGURE 16.14

A Concept Map for Cross-Tabulation

What Would *You* Do?

General Mills' Curves Cereal: Helping Women Achieve Their Curves

The Situation

Stephen W. Sanger, CEO of General Mills (www.generalmills.com), is constantly faced with the challenge of how to keep up with consumers' changing tastes and preferences. General Mills, the number-two cereal maker in the United States, recently conducted thorough focus groups and survey research on the most important consumers in grocery stores today: women. It is a known fact that three out of every four grocery shoppers in the United States are women, and many of these women are focusing more on their health and the nutritious value of foods. Although there are many cereals on the market with the same amount of valuable vitamins and minerals, such as Total or Kellogg's Smart Start, General Mills decided to design a product specifically for women.

Dietitian Roberta Duyff claims that women do not get enough nutrients such as calcium or folic acid from day to day. According to Duyff, "It is great that a woman can now increase her intake of these important nutrients with a simple bowl of cereal for breakfast, and if you add milk, the vitamin D in milk makes the calcium in both the fortified cereal and milk itself more absorbable." This is one way in which General Mills saw an advantage—convenience for the woman. She can grab a bowl in the morning and start off her day with the nutrients she needs. Not only is the convenience of the product an incentive to market it, but focus group findings indicated that women like to have a product of their own. In fact, according to Megan Nightingale, Assistant Marketing Manager at General Mills, "Our research has shown that women are looking for something that's nutritious, fast, convenient, and has a good taste."

In 2007, General Mills partnered with Curves International, a U.S. franchiser of fitness centers with locations in 60 countries, to launch Curves Cereal. This new cereal of lightly sweetened toasted flakes of whole grain rice and wheat is available in two delicious flavors, Whole Grain Crunch and Honey Crunch. Both have fewer than 200 calories per serving and contain a least 33 percent of the recommended amounts of whole grains and 2 grams of fiber. They also are an excellent source of several important vitamins and minerals.

A telephone survey was conducted to determine the preference for and consumption of Curves and the relative importance that women attached to a cereal being nutritious, fast, convenient, and good tasting.

The Marketing Research Decision

1. What is the relative importance of the four variables (nutritious, fast, convenient, and good taste) in influencing women to buy Curves cereal? What type of analysis should be conducted?
   a. Frequency distribution of the importance attached to the four factors
   b. Mean levels of importance of the four variables
   c. Cross-tabulation of Curves cereal purchases with the importance of the four variables: chi-square analysis
   d. Cross-tabulation of Curves cereal purchases with the importance of the four variables: Cramer's V
   e. All of the above
2. Discuss the role of the type of data analysis you recommend in enabling Stephen W. Sanger to understand women's preference for and consumption of Curves cereal.

The Marketing Management Decision

1. Advertising for Curves cereal should stress which of the four factors?
   a. Nutrition
   b. Quick consumption

continued

    c. Convenience

    d. Good taste

    e. All of the above

2. Discuss how the management-decision action that you recommend to Stephen W. Sanger is influenced by the type of data analysis you suggested earlier and by the findings of that analysis.

What Stephen W. Sanger Did

Stephen W. Sanger decided to focus on nutrition, quick consumption, and convenience. General Mills markets Curves cereal by using the idea that women do not have the time or patience to remember all the vitamins and minerals they need each day to stay healthy. Curves cereal makes it convenient. Simply pour yourself a bowl of cereal, and you will get many of the important nutrients you need. To complement Curves cereal, in 2007 General Mills also launched Curves Chewy Granola bars in Chocolate Peanut and Strawberries and Cream varieties.[7]

Software Applications

SPSS and SAS have similar programs in their microcomputer and mainframe versions for computing frequency distributions, performing cross-tabulations, and testing hypotheses. The major programs for frequency distribution are FREQUENCIES (SPSS) and UNI-VARIATE (SAS). Other programs provide only the frequency distribution (FREQ in SAS) or only some of the associated statistics (see Exhibit 16.1). In Minitab, the main function is Stats > Descriptive Statistics. The output values include the mean, median, standard deviation, minimum, maximum, and quartiles. A histogram in the form of a bar chart or graph can be produced from the Graph > Histogram selection. Several of the spreadsheets can also be used to obtain frequencies and descriptive statistics. In Excel, the Tools > Data Analysis function computes the descriptive statistics. The output produces the mean, standard error, median, mode, standard deviation, variance, range, minimum, maximum, sum, count, and confidence level. Frequencies can be selected under the histogram function. A histogram can be produced in bar format.

    The major cross-tabulation programs are CROSSTABS (SPSS) and FREQ (SAS). These programs display the cross-classification tables and provide cell counts, row and column percentages, the chi-square test for significance, and all the measures of the strength of the association that have been discussed. In addition, the TABULATE (SAS) program can be used for obtaining cell counts and row and column percentages, although it does not provide any of the associated statistics. In Minitab, cross-tabulations and chi square are under the Stats > Tables function. Each of these features must be selected separately under the Tables function. The Data > Pivot Table function performs cross-tabulations in Excel. To do additional analysis or customize data, select a different summary function, such as maximum, minimum, average, or standard deviation. ChiTest can be assessed under the Insert > Function > Statistical > ChiTest function (see Exhibit 16.2).

SPSS Windows

The main program in SPSS is FREQUENCIES. It produces a table of frequency counts, percentages, and cumulative percentages for the values of each variable, as well as all of the associated statistics. If the data are interval scaled and only the summary statistics are desired, the DESCRIPTIVES procedure can be used. All of the

statistics computed by DESCRIPTIVES are available in FREQUENCIES. DESCRIP-TIVES is more efficient, however, because it does not sort values into a frequency table. Moreover, the DESCRIPTIVES procedure displays summary statistics for several variables in a single table and can also calculate standardized values (z scores). The EXPLORE procedure produces summary statistics and graphical displays, either for all of cases or separately for groups of cases. Mean, median, variance, standard deviation, minimum, maximum, and range are some of the statistics that can be calculated.

To select these procedures, click the following:

> Analyze > Descriptive Statistics > Frequencies . . .

or   Analyze > Descriptive Statistics > Descriptives . . .

or   Analyze > Descriptive Statistics > Explore . . .

The major cross-tabulation program is CROSSTABS. This program will display the cross-classification tables and provide cell counts, row and column percentages, the chi-square test for significance, and all the measures of the strength of the association that have been discussed.

To select this procedure, click the following:

> Analyze > Descriptive Statistics > Crosstabs . . .

Detailed Steps: Overview

Detailed step-by-step instructions for running the SPSS programs for the data analysis presented in this chapter can be downloaded from the Web site for this book in two forms: (1) computerized demonstration movies, and (2) screen captures. In addition, these steps are illustrated in the following sections.

Detailed Steps: Frequencies

Detailed steps are presented for running frequencies on attitude toward Nike (Table 16.1) and for plotting the histogram (Figure 16.4).

1. Select ANALYZE on the SPSS menu bar.
2. Click DESCRIPTIVE STATISTICS, and select FREQUENCIES.
3. Move the variable "Attitude toward Nike <attitude>" to the VARIABLE(s) box.
4. Click STATISTICS.
5. Select MEAN, MEDIAN, MODE, STD. DEVIATION, VARIANCE, and RANGE.
6. Click CONTINUE.
7. Click CHARTS.
8. Click HISTOGRAMS, then click CONTINUE.
9. Click OK.

Detailed Steps: Cross-Tabulations

We give detailed steps for running the cross-tabulation of gender and usage of Nike shoes given in Table 16.3 and calculating the chi-square, contingency coefficient, and Cramer's *V*.

1. Select ANALYZE on the SPSS menu bar.
2. Click DESCRIPTIVE STATISTICS, and select CROSSTABS.
3. Move the variable "User Group <usergr>" to the ROW(S) box.
4. Move the variable "Sex <sex>" to the COLUMN(S) box.
5. Click CELLS.
6. Select OBSERVED under COUNTS, and select COLUMN under PERCENTAGES.
7. Click CONTINUE.
8. Click STATISTICS.

9. Click CHI-SQUARE, PHI, and CRAMER'S *V.*
10. Click CONTINUE.
11. Click OK.

Experiential Learning

Categorical Data Analysis

In this experiential exercise, you will learn how to run frequencies and cross-tabulations using SPSS. Go to the textbook Web site and download the following SPSS system file: KitKat.sav. Also, download the actual taste-test instructions to customers: TasteTest.doc. These files refer to the Nestlé taste test presented in Chapter 9. Here, respondents were asked to taste three different samples of the Kit Kat candy bar. Two of the samples were the currently marketed version of Kit Kat. One of the samples was a new reduced-fat version of the Kit Kat candy bar that had not been put into the market yet. In order to minimize an effect from the presentation order (e.g., respondents might tend to prefer the first or the last one presented), the order of presentation was changed for the different respondents.

1. Read the taste-test instructions of TasteTest.doc.

2. Open KitKat.sav. Double-click the icon.

3. Check data by running frequencies.

   Check distributions for the following variables: rotation, sex, age, differen, and prefer.

   Menu Bar
      ANALYZE
         DESCRIPTIVE STATISTICS
            FREQUENCIES
               Transfer each of the five variables in the
   FREQUENCIES window.
               Click OK.
   Check the distribution of the "State" variable.

   Menu Bar
      ANALYZE
         DESCRIPTIVE STATISTICS
            FREQUENCIES
               Select "State" in the FREQUENCIES window.
               CHARTS
                  BAR CHARTS
                  CONTINUE
                  OK

4. Analyze results for the taste test using SPSS.

   Refer to the frequency distributions you just created in the preceding check data section to answer the following questions:

   a. Which of these three demographic variables (sex, age, and state) did the designers of this taste test want to have equal representation across the possible values of the demographic variables?
   b. What is the mode in the distribution of "state"?
   c. What percentage of the respondents preferred the new reduced-fat version of Kit Kat (the "different sample," in this case)? What percent preferred the currently marketed version of Kit Kat? What percent expressed no preference between the two versions?

5. Do cross-tabulation analysis to determine if a relationship exists between sex and preference for the new version of the Kit Kat candy bar. Before your analysis, write down what are the H_0 and H_1 for cross-tabbing "sex" and "prefer." Conduct the first cross-tabulation analysis as follows:

   Menu Bar
      DATA
         SELECT CASES
            ALL CASES
               Click OK.
   Menu Bar
      ANALYZE
         DESCRIPTIVE STATISTICS
            CROSSTABS
               Select "prefer" for ROW(S) and "sex" for
   COLUMN(S)
                  Click STATISTICS. Select CHI-SQUARE
                     Click CELLS. Under PERCENTAGES, check
   COLUMN
                  Click CONTINUE. Then click OK.
   After examining your results, what decision do you make regarding H_0 and H_1 now?

6. What are the H_0 and H_1 for cross-tabulating "sex" and "prefer" when only those stating a preference are considered?

   Conduct the second cross-tabulation analysis as follows:
   Menu Bar
      DATA
         SELECT CASES
            If
               Prefer <= 2
                  CONTINUE
   Menu Bar
      ANALYZE
         DESCRIPTIVE STATISTICS
            CROSSTABS
               Select "prefer" for ROWS(S) and "sex" for
   COLUMN(S).
                  Click STATISTICS. Select CHI-SQUARE.
                     Click CELLS. Under PERCENTAGES,
   check COLUMN.
                     Click CONTINUE. Then click OK.
   What decision do you make regarding H_0 and H_1 now?

Excel

This section gives the detailed steps for running the Excel programs for conducting the analysis discussed in this chapter.

Detailed Steps: Overview

Detailed step-by-step instructions for running the Excel programs for the data analysis presented in this chapter can be downloaded from the Web site for this book in two forms: (1) computerized demonstration movies, and (2) screen captures. In addition, these steps are illustrated in the following sections.

Detailed Steps: Frequencies

We give detailed steps for running frequencies on attitude toward Nike (Table 16.1) using Excel.

1. Select Tools (Alt + T).
2. Select Data Analysis under Tools.
3. The Data Analysis Window pops up.
4. Select Histogram from the Data Analysis Window.
5. Click OK.
6. The Histogram pop-up window appears on screen.
7. The Histogram window has two portions:
   a. Input
   b. Output Options
8. Input portion asks for two inputs.
   a. Click in the input range box and select (highlight) all 45 rows under ATTITUDE. $D$2: $D$46 should appear in the input range box.
   b. Do not enter anything into the Bin Range box. (Note that this input is optional; if you do not provide a reference, the system will take values based on range of the data set).
9. In the Output portion of pop-up window, select the following options:
   a. New Workbook
   b. Cumulative Percentage
   c. Chart Output
10. Click OK.
11. Note that the default chart output size is very small. Click the histogram diagram and drag it on the corners to view it better.

Detailed Steps: Cross-Tabulations

We show the detailed steps for running the cross-tabulation of sex and usage of Nike shoes given in Table 16.3.

1. Select Data (Alt + D).
2. Under Data, select Pivot Table and Pivot Chart Wizard.
3. The Pivot Table and Pivot Chart Report window pops up.
4. Step 1 of 3: Pivot Table and Pivot Chart Wizard, leave as it is.
5. Click Next.
6. Step 2 of 3: Pivot Table and Pivot Chart Wizard. In the range box, select data under the columns CASENO, USERGR, SEX, ATTITUDE. $A$1:$D$46 should appear in the range box. Click Next.
7. Step 3 of 3: Pivot Table and Pivot Chart Wizard, select New Worksheet in this window. Click Layout and drag the variables in this format.

SEX
_____

|

USERGR | CASENO (Double-click CASENO and select Count)

|

8. Click OK and then Finish.

Summary

Basic data analysis provides valuable insights and guides the rest of the data analysis as well as the interpretation of the results. A frequency distribution should be obtained for each variable in the data. This analysis produces a table of frequency counts, percentages, and cumulative percentages for all the values associated with that variable. It indicates the extent of out-of-range, missing, or extreme values. The mean, mode, and median of a frequency distribution are measures of central tendency. The variability of the distribution is described by the range and the variance or standard deviation.

The general procedure for hypothesis testing involves eight steps. Formulate the null and the alternative hypotheses, select an appropriate test statistic, choose the level of significance (α), calculate the value of the test statistic, and determine the probability associated with the test statistic calculated from the sample data under the null hypothesis. Alternatively, determine the critical value associated with the test statistic. Compare the probability associated with the test statistic with the level of significance specified or, alternatively, determine whether the calculated value of the test statistic falls into the rejection or the nonrejection region. Accordingly, make the decision to reject or not reject the null hypothesis, and arrive at a conclusion.

Cross-tabulations are tables that reflect the joint frequency distribution of two or more variables. In cross-tabulation, the cell percentages can be computed either column-wise, based on column totals, or row-wise, based on row totals. The general rule is to compute the percentages in the direction of the independent variable, across the dependent variable. The chi-square statistic provides a test of the statistical significance of the observed association in a cross-tabulation. The phi coefficient, contingency coefficient, and Cramer's V provide measures of the strength of association between the variables.

Key Terms and Concepts

Frequency distribution, 480	Null hypothesis, 488	p value, 490
Measures of location, 484	Alternative hypothesis, 488	Critical value, 491
Mean, 484	One-tailed test, 488	Cross-tabulation, 493
Mode, 484	Two-tailed test, 488	Contingency tables, 493
Median, 484	Test statistic, 489	Chi-square statistic, 495
Measures of variability, 485	Type-I error, 489	Chi-square distribution, 496
Range, 486	Level of significance, 489	Phi coefficient, 497
Variance, 486	Type-II error, 489	Contingency coefficient, 498
Standard deviation, 486	Power of a test, 489	Cramer's V, 498

Suggested Cases and Video Cases

Running Case with Real Data

1.1 Hewlett-Packard

Comprehensive Cases with Real Data

3.1 Bank of America   3.2 McDonald's   3.3 Boeing

Video Cases

19.1 Marriott

Live Research: Conducting a Marketing Research Project

1. Each team can conduct the entire analysis or the data analysis can be split between teams with different teams conducting a different type of analysis. It is helpful to run a frequency count for every variable. This gives a good feel for the data.
2. Calculate the measures of location (mean, median, and mode) and measures of variability (range and standard deviation) for each variable.
3. Relevant associations can be examined by conducting cross-tabulations. Procedures should be specified for categorizing interval or ratio-scaled variables. In this process, it is helpful to examine the frequency distributions.

Acronyms

The statistics associated with frequencies can be summarized by the acronym FREQUENCIES:

F requency histogram

R ange

E stimate of location: mean

Q uotients: percentages

U ndulation: variance

E stimate of location: mode

N umbers or counts

C umulative percentage

I ncorrect and missing values

E stimate of location: median

S hape of the distribution

The salient characteristics of cross-tabulations can be summarized by the acronym TABULATE:

T wo variables at a time

A ssociation and not causation is measured

B ased on cell count of at least five

U derstood easily by managers

L imited number of categories

A ssociated statistics

T wo ways to calculate percentages

E xpected cell frequencies

Review Questions

1. Describe the procedure for computing frequencies.
2. What measures of location are commonly computed for frequencies?
3. What measures of variability are commonly computed for frequencies?
4. What is the major difference between cross-tabulation and frequency distribution?
5. What is the general rule for computing percentages in cross-tabulation?
6. Describe the chi-square distribution.
7. What is meant by the expected cell frequency?
8. How is the chi-square statistic calculated?
9. When is it meaningful to determine the strength of association in a cross-tabulation?
10. What statistics are available for determining the strength of association in cross-tabulation.
11. Discuss the reasons for the frequent use of cross-tabulations. What are some of its limitations?

Applied Problems

1. In each of the following situations, indicate the statistical analysis you would conduct and the appropriate test or test statistic that should be used.
   a. Respondents in a survey of 1,000 households were classified as heavy, medium, light, or nonusers of ice cream. They also were classified as being in high-, medium-, or low-income categories. Is the consumption of ice cream related to income level?
   b. In a survey using a representative sample of 2,000 households from the Synovate consumer panel, the respondents were asked whether they preferred to shop at Sears. The sample was divided into small and large households based on a median split of household size. Does preference for shopping in Sears vary by household size?

2. The current advertising campaign for a major soft-drink brand would be changed if less than 30 percent of the consumers like it.
   a. Formulate the null and alternative hypotheses.
   b. Discuss the type-I and type-II errors that could occur in hypothesis testing.

3. A major department store chain is having an end-of-season sale on refrigerators. The number of refrigerators sold during this sale at a sample of 10 stores was:

   80   110   0   40   70   80   100   50   80   30

   a. Compute the mean, mode, and median. Which measure of central tendency is most appropriate in this case and why?
   b. Compute the variance and the standard deviation.
   c. Construct a histogram, and discuss whether this variable is normally distributed.

4. In a study measuring households' familiarity with downloading pictures from the Internet, the following results were obtained (1 = not at all familiar, 7 = very familiar).

Level of Familiarity	Number of Households
1	22
2	26
3	34
4	40
5	32
6	28
7	18

   a. Convert the number of household into percentages.
   b. Calculate the cumulative percentages.
   c. Construct a histogram with familiarity on the x-axis and frequency on the y-axis.
   d. Calculate the mean, median, and mode of the distribution.

5. A research project examining the impact of income on the consumption of gourmet foods was conducted. Each variable was classified into three levels of high, medium, and low. The following results were obtained.

		Income		
		Low	Medium	High
Consumption of	Low	25	15	10
Gourmet	Medium	10	25	15
Foods	High	15	10	25

   a. Is the relationship between income and consumption of gourmet food significant?
   b. Is the relationship between income and consumption of gourmet food strong?
   c. What is the pattern of the relationship between income and consumption of gourmet food?

6. A pilot survey was conducted with 30 respondents to examine Internet usage for personal (nonprofessional) reasons. The following table contains the resulting data giving each respondent's sex (1 = male, 2 = female), familiarity with the Internet (1 = very unfamiliar, 7 = very familiar), Internet usage in hours per week, attitude toward Internet and toward technology, both measured on a 7-point scale (1 = very unfavorable, 7 = very favorable), and whether the respondent shopped or banked online (1 = yes, 2 = no).
   a. Obtain the frequency distribution of familiarity with the Internet. Calculate the relevant statistics.
   b. For the purpose of cross-tabulation, classify respondents as light or heavy users. Those reporting 5 hours or less usage should be classified as light users and the remaining as heavy users. Run a cross-tabulation of sex and Internet usage. Interpret the results. Is Internet usage related to one's sex?

Internet Usage Data

Respondent Number	Sex	Familiarity	Internet Usage	Attitude Toward Internet	Attitude Toward Technology	Usage of Internet: Shopping	Usage of Internet: Banking
1	1.00	7.00	14.00	7.00	6.00	1.00	1.00
2	2.00	2.00	2.00	3.00	3.00	2.00	2.00
3	2.00	3.00	3.00	4.00	3.00	1.00	2.00
4	2.00	3.00	3.00	7.00	5.00	1.00	2.00
5	1.00	7.00	13.00	7.00	7.00	1.00	1.00
6	2.00	4.00	6.00	5.00	4.00	1.00	2.00
7	2.00	2.00	2.00	4.00	5.00	2.00	2.00
8	2.00	3.00	6.00	5.00	4.00	2.00	2.00
9	2.00	3.00	6.00	6.00	4.00	1.00	2.00
10	1.00	9.00	15.00	7.00	6.00	1.00	2.00
11	2.00	4.00	3.00	4.00	3.00	2.00	2.00
12	2.00	5.00	4.00	6.00	4.00	2.00	2.00
13	1.00	6.00	9.00	6.00	5.00	2.00	1.00
14	1.00	6.00	8.00	3.00	2.00	2.00	2.00
15	1.00	6.00	5.00	5.00	4.00	1.00	2.00
16	2.00	4.00	3.00	4.00	3.00	2.00	2.00
17	1.00	6.00	9.00	5.00	3.00	1.00	1.00
18	1.00	4.00	4.00	5.00	4.00	1.00	2.00
19	1.00	7.00	14.00	6.00	6.00	1.00	1.00
20	2.00	6.00	6.00	6.00	4.00	2.00	2.00
21	1.00	6.00	9.00	4.00	2.00	2.00	2.00
22	1.00	5.00	5.00	5.00	4.00	2.00	1.00
23	2.00	3.00	2.00	4.00	2.00	2.00	2.00
24	1.00	7.00	15.00	6.00	6.00	1.00	1.00
25	2.00	6.00	6.00	5.00	3.00	1.00	2.00
26	1.00	6.00	13.00	6.00	6.00	1.00	1.00
27	2.00	5.00	4.00	5.00	5.00	1.00	1.00
28	2.00	4.00	2.00	3.00	2.00	2.00	2.00
29	1.00	4.00	4.00	5.00	3.00	1.00	2.00
30	1.00	3.00	3.00	7.00	5.00	1.00	2.00

Group Discussion

1. "Because cross-tabulation has certain basic limitations, this technique should not be used extensively in commercial marketing research." Discuss as a small group.

2. "Why waste time doing basic data analysis? Why not just conduct sophisticated multivariate data analysis (see Chapter 15)?" Discuss.

Hewlett-Packard Running Case

Review the Hewlett-Packard (HP) case, Case 1.1, and questionnaire given toward the end of the book. Go to the Web site for this book and download the HP data file.

1. Calculate the frequency distribution for each variable in the data file. Examine the distribution to get a feel for the data.

2. Cross-tabulate the recoded questions q4 (overall satisfaction with HP), q5 (would recommend HP), and q6 (likelihood of choosing HP) with the recoded demographic characteristics. Interpret the results.

3. Cross-tabulate the recoded questions on price sensitivity (q9_5per and q9_10per) with the recoded demographic characteristics. Interpret the results.

Exhibit 16.1   Computer Programs for Frequencies

SPSS

The main program in SPSS is FREQUENCIES. It produces a table of frequency counts, percentages, and cumulative percentages for the values of each variable. It gives all of the associated statistics. If the data are interval scaled and only the summary statistics are desired, the DESCRIPTIVES procedure can be used. All of the statistics computed by DESCRIPTIVES are available in FREQUENCIES. However, DESCRIPTIVES is more efficient, because it does not sort values into a frequency table. An additional program, MEANS, computes means and standard deviations for a dependent variable over subgroups of cases defined by independent variables.

SAS

The main program in SAS is UNIVARIATE. In addition to providing a frequency table, this program provides all of the associated statistics. Another procedure available is FREQ. For one-way frequency distribution, FREQ does not provide any associated statistics. If only summary statistics are desired, procedures such as

MEANS, SUMMARY, and TABULATE can be used. It should be noted that FREQ is not available as an independent program in the microcomputer version.

Minitab

The main function is Stats > Descriptive Statistics. The output values include the mean, median, mode, standard deviation, minimum, maximum, and quartiles. A histogram in a bar chart or graph can be produced from the Graph > Histogram selection.

Excel

The Tools > Data Analysis function computes the descriptive statistics. The output produces the mean, standard error, median, mode, standard deviation, variance, range, minimum, maximum, sum, count, and confidence level. Frequencies can be selected under the histogram function. A histogram can be produced in bar format.

Exhibit 16.2   Computer Programs for Cross-Tabulation

SPSS

The major cross-tabulation program is CROSSTABS. This programs will display the cross-classification tables and provide cell counts, row and column percentages, the chi-square test for significance, and all the measures of the strength of the association that have been discussed.

SAS

Cross-tabulation can be done by using FREQ. This program will display the cross-classification tables and provide cell counts as well as row and column percentages. In addition, the TABULATE program can be used for obtaining cell counts and row and column percentages, although it does not provide any of the associated statistics.

Minitab

In Minitab, cross-tabulations and chi-square are under the Stats > Tables function. Each of these features must be selected separately under the Tables function.

Excel

The Data > Pivot Table function performs cross-tabulations in Excel. To do additional analysis or customize data, select a different summary function, such as maximum, minimum, average, or standard deviation. In addition, a custom calculation can be selected to analyze values based on other cells in the data plane. ChiTest can be assessed under the Insert > Function > Statistical > ChiTest function.

Data Analysis: Hypothesis Testing Related to Differences

OPENING QUESTIONS

1. What is the role of the *t* distribution in testing hypotheses that are related to differences?

2. How would you test the hypothesis related to one sample?

3. How does hypothesis testing change when there are two independent samples rather than one? Does the hypothesis testing procedure change when testing for difference in proportions rather than means?

4. How does hypothesis testing change for paired samples? How is it done?

5. How can the analysis of variance procedure be used for testing a hypothesis related to more than two samples?

> "While groups such as users or nonusers of a brand are similar in many ways, making statistical comparisons between such groups on their attitude toward a brand can be very revealing."
>
> *Jennifer Garvey,*
> *Director, Marketing Services,*
> *Verizon Information Services.*

Loyalty Versus Promiscuity and Convenience Versus Price

As of 2008, American grocery-store shoppers have actually been able to save money by spending more. How is this possible? Through the Internet, consumers now have access to a rewards and rebate program offered by grocery stores and other merchants. Such a program, called *microrebate investing*, moves a percentage of loyal consumers' purchases directly into an investment account. The program is designed for customers at all income levels, with no prequalifications to membership. This is only one of many ways in which supermarkets and grocery stores are attempting to build customer loyalty.

A recent study examined the differences between 138 loyal shoppers (LS) and 110 promiscuous (disloyal) shoppers (PS) of a major supermarket. Both groups of shoppers were asked to indicate the importance of 15 shopping attributes on a 7-point scale (1 = not important, 7 = very important). Based on the two-independent-samples *t*-tests, which are used to test the hypothesis of differences between means of two samples, significant differences were identified on 5 of the 15 attributes, as indicated in the following table.

Attribute	Mean Importance Rating		Significance Level
	PS	LS	
Low prices	6.30	6.14	0.044
Convenient access	6.24	6.49	0.045
Convenient parking	6.17	6.63	0.030
Convenient opening hours	5.99	6.46	0.001
Attractive displays and decor	4.67	5.14	0.026

Although the promiscuous shoppers were motivated by the low prices, the loyal shoppers gave significantly greater importance to convenience (access, parking, and opening hours) and displays and decor. Thus, even such U.S. supermarkets as Winn-Dixie (www.winn-dixie.com), with its SaveRite Grocery Warehouses that offer lower prices, albeit with a more limited product selection, cannot compete on the basis of price alone. To attract loyal shoppers, they must offer convenience, good aisle displays, and attractive internal decor.[1]

Overview

Chapter 16 described basic data analysis, including frequency distributions, cross-tabulation, and the general procedure for hypothesis testing. As was explained, hypothesis-testing procedures are classified as tests of associations or tests of differences. Statistics for examining the significance and strength of association also were considered. This chapter presents tests for examining hypotheses related to differences, as in the opening vignette. Figure 17.1 briefly explains the focus of the chapter, the relation of this chapter to the previous ones, and the steps of the marketing research process on which this chapter concentrates.

The parametric tests presented in this chapter assume that the data are at least interval scaled. We first discuss the case for difference in means for one sample followed by hypothesis testing for two samples. We then make the extension to more than two samples and also examine hypothesis testing associated with differences in proportions. Help for running the SPSS and Excel programs used in this chapter is provided is four ways: (1) detailed step-by-step instructions are given later in the chapter, (2) you can download (from the Web site for this book) computerized demonstration movies illustrating these step-by-step instructions, (3) you can download screen captures with notes illustrating these step-by-step instructions, and (4) you can refer to the Study Guide and Technology Manual, a supplement that accompanies this book. Figure 17.2 provides an overview of the topics discussed in this chapter and how they flow from one to the next.

FIGURE 17.1

Relationship of Hypothesis Testing Related to Differences to the Previous Chapters and the Marketing Research Process

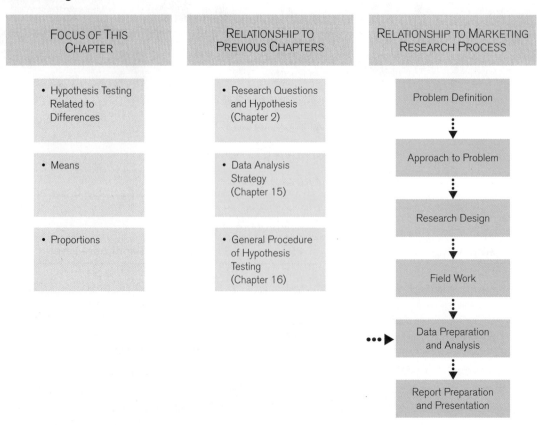

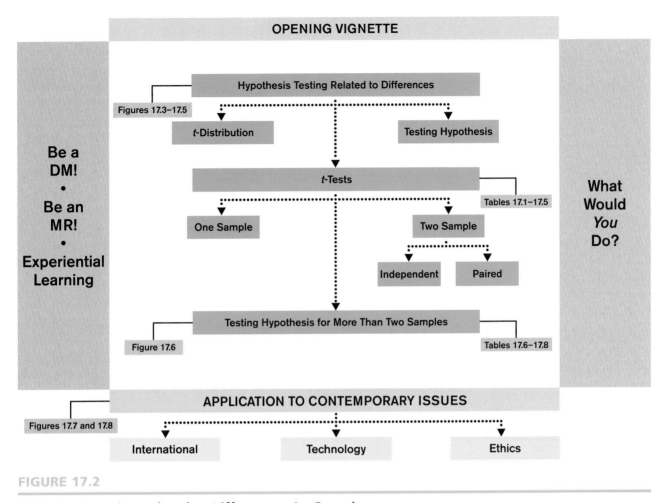

FIGURE 17.2

Hypothesis Testing Related to Differences: An Overview

Hypotheses Testing Related to Differences

Chapter 16 considered hypotheses testing related to associations. These hypotheses are of the form that two variables are associated with or related to each other. For example, the values of homes purchased are related to the buyers' incomes. Here the focus is on hypotheses testing related to differences. These hypotheses are of the form that two variables are different from each other; for example, that people living in the suburbs have higher incomes than people living in the downtown areas. A classification of hypothesis testing procedures for examining differences is presented in Figure 17.3. These procedures are related to examining differences in means or proportions. First, we focus on hypothesis testing procedures examining differences in means. These procedures also are called **parametric tests**, because they assume that the variables of interest are measured on at least an interval scale; for example, that the average household spends less than $20 per month on long-distance telephone calls. Here, the monthly expenditure on long-distance telephone calls is measured on a ratio scale. The most popular parametric test is the *t*-test conducted for examining hypotheses about means. The *t*-test can be conducted on the means of one sample or two samples of observations. In the case of two samples, the samples can be independent or paired. The opening vignette provided an application of a *t*-test for the difference in means of two independent samples—loyal shoppers and promiscuous shoppers. All *t*-tests are based on the *t* distribution.

parametric tests
Hypothesis-testing procedures that assume the variables of interest are measured on at least an interval scale.

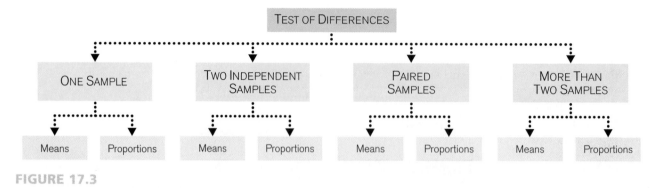

FIGURE 17.3

Hypothesis Tests Related to Differences

The *t* Distribution

t-test

A univariate hypothesis test using the *t* distribution, which is used when the standard deviation is unknown and the sample size is small.

t statistic

A statistic that assumes the variable has a symmetric bell-shaped distribution and the mean is known (or assumed to be known) and the population variance is estimated from the sample.

t distribution

A symmetric bell-shaped distribution that is useful for small-sample (*n* < 30) testing.

Parametric tests provide inferences for making statements about the means of parent populations. A ***t*-test** is commonly used for this purpose. This test is based on the *Student's t* statistic. The ***t* statistic** is calculated by assuming that the variable is normally distributed, the mean is known, and the population variance is estimated from the sample. Assume that the random variable X is normally distributed, with mean μ and unknown population variance σ^2, which is estimated by the sample variance s^2. Recall that the standard deviation of the sample mean, $\overline{X}$, is estimated as

$$s_{\overline{x}} = s/\sqrt{n}$$

Thus,

$$t = (\overline{X} - \mu)/s_{\overline{x}}$$

is t distributed with $n - 1$ degrees of freedom.

The ***t* distribution** is similar to the normal distribution in appearance. Both distributions are bell shaped and symmetric. However, the t distribution has more area in the tails and less in the center than the normal distribution. This is because population variance σ^2 is unknown and is estimated by the sample variance s^2. Given the uncertainty in the value of s^2, the observed values of t are more variable than those of z. Thus, we must go a larger number of standard deviations from zero to encompass a certain percentage of values from the t distribution than is the case with the normal distribution. As the number of degrees of freedom increases, however, the t distribution approaches the normal distribution. In fact, for large samples of 120 or more the t distribution and the normal distribution are virtually indistinguishable. Table 4 in the Appendix of Statistical Tables shows selected percentiles of the t distribution. Although normality is assumed, the t-test is quite robust to departures from normality.

Hypothesis Testing Based on the *t* Statistic

For the special case when the t statistic is used, the general procedure for hypothesis testing discussed in the previous chapter is applied as follows (Figure 17.4).

1. Formulate the null (H_0) and the alternative (H_1) hypotheses.
2. Select the appropriate formula for the t statistic.
3. Select a significance level, α, for testing H_0. Typically, the 0.05 level is selected.
4. Take one or two samples and compute the mean and standard deviation for each sample. Calculate the t statistic assuming H_0 is true. Calculate the degrees of freedom.
5. Estimate the probability of getting a more extreme value of the statistic from Table 4 in the Appendix of Statistical Tables. Alternatively, calculate the critical value of the t statistic. Note that in determining the critical value of the test statistic the area to the

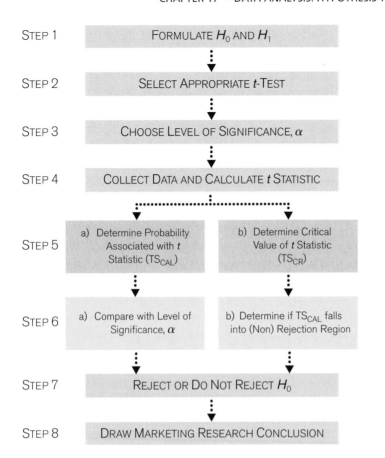

FIGURE 17.4

Conducting *t*-Tests

right of the critical value is either α or $\alpha/2$. It is α for a one-tailed test and $\alpha/2$ for a two-tailed test.

6. Compare the probability computed in Step 5 with the significance level selected in Step 3. (Alternatively, compare the calculated *t* statistic in Step 4 with the critical value determined in Step 5.)

7. Make the statistical decision to reject or not reject the null hypotheses. If the probability computed in Step 5 is smaller than the significance level selected in Step 3, reject H_0. If the probability is larger, do not reject H_0. (Alternatively, if the absolute value of the calculated *t* statistic in Step 4 is larger than the absolute value of the critical value determined in Step 5, reject H_0. If the absolute calculated value is smaller than the absolute critical value, do not reject H_0). Failure to reject H_0 does not necessarily imply that H_0 is true. It only means that the true state is not significantly different from that assumed by H_0.[2]

8. Express the conclusion reached by the *t*-test in terms of the marketing research problem.

The general procedure for conducting *t*-tests is illustrated in the following sections, beginning with the one-sample case.

One-Sample *t*-Test

In marketing research, the researcher often is interested in making statements about a single variable against a known or given standard. The following are examples of such statements:

- The market share for the new product will exceed 15 percent.
- At least 65 percent of customers will like the new package design.
- The average monthly household expenditure on groceries exceeds $500.
- The new service plan will be preferred by at least 70 percent of the customers.

These statements can be translated into null hypotheses that can be tested using a one-sample test, such as the z-test or the t-test. In the case of a t-test for a single mean, the researcher is interested in testing whether the population mean conforms to a given hypothesis (H_0). In the opening vignette, the hypothesis that the mean rating of each attribute for the overall sample (loyal shoppers and promiscuous shoppers combined) exceeded 5.0 would be tested using the one-sample t-test.

Test for a Single Mean

Suppose a new machine attachment would be introduced if it receives a mean of greater than 7 on a 10-point scale. A sample of 20 purchase engineers is shown the attachment and asked to evaluate it. The results indicate a mean rating of 7.9 with a standard deviation of 1.6. A significance level of $\alpha = 0.05$ is selected. Should the part be introduced?

$$H_0: \mu \leq 7.0$$

$$H_1: \mu > 7.0$$

$$t = (\bar{X} - \mu)/s_{\bar{x}}$$

$$s_{\bar{x}} = s/\sqrt{n}$$

$$s_{\bar{x}} = 1.6/\sqrt{20} = 1.6/4.472 = 0.358$$

$$t = (7.9 - 7.0)/0.358 = 0.9/0.358 = 2.514$$

The degrees of freedom for the t statistic to test a hypothesis about one mean are $n - 1$. In this case, $n - 1 = 20 - 1$, or 19. From Table 4 in the Appendix of Statistical Tables, the probability of getting a more extreme value than 2.514 is less than 0.05; actually it is less than 0.025. (Alternatively, the critical t value for 19 degrees of freedom and a significance level of 0.05 is 1.7291, which is less than the calculated value.) Therefore, the null hypothesis is rejected, favoring the introduction of the part.

Note that if the population standard deviation was assumed to be known as 1.5, rather than estimated from the sample, a **z-test** would be appropriate. In this case, the value of the z statistic would be:

$$z = (\bar{X} - \mu)/\sigma_{\bar{x}}$$

where

$$\sigma_{\bar{x}} = 1.5/\sqrt{20} = 1.5/4.472 = 0.335$$

and

$$z = (7.9 - 7.0)/0.335 = 0.9/0.335 = 2.687$$

From Table 2 in the Appendix of Statistical Tables, the probability of getting a more extreme value of z than 2.687 is 0.0036, which is less than 0.05. (Alternatively, the critical z value for a one-tailed test and a significance level of 0.05 is 1.645, which is less than the calculated value.) Therefore, the null hypothesis is rejected, and we can reach the same conclusion arrived at earlier by the t-test.

The one-sample t-test is further illustrated using the data of Table 17.1. This table contains data from two samples, each consisting of 10 respondents. Sample 1 consists of teenagers (ages 13 to 19), whereas sample 2 consists of adults 20 years old or older. The respondents were asked to indicate their preferences for Disney theme parks, immediately before and immediately after their visits, using a 10-point scale. This table gives the data for only 20 respondents, because we want to show the calculations of the basic statistics by hand. These hand calculations are shown to provide a better idea of the basic concepts. In practice, the sample size is much larger. The analysis of such large data sets is illustrated later in the chapter in the Experiential Learning exercise, which analyzes the data for 146 respondents in a survey for Musial University in the United States.

z-test

A univariate hypothesis test using the standard normal distribution.

TABLE 17.1 **Preference for Disney Before and After Visiting the Resort**

Respondent Number	Sample	Preference for Disney	
		Before	After
1	1.00	7.00	9.00
2	1.00	6.00	8.00
3	1.00	5.00	8.00
4	1.00	6.00	9.00
5	1.00	4.00	7.00
6	1.00	6.00	8.00
7	1.00	5.00	7.00
8	1.00	4.00	7.00
9	1.00	7.00	9.00
10	1.00	5.00	7.00
11	2.00	3.00	7.00
12	2.00	4.00	8.00
13	2.00	4.00	7.00
14	2.00	3.00	6.00
15	2.00	6.00	8.00
16	2.00	5.00	8.00
17	2.00	4.00	9.00
18	2.00	3.00	6.00
19	2.00	3.00	7.00
20	2.00	5.00	9.00

The null hypothesis for Table 17.1, based on a previous survey, is that the mean preference for sample 1 before entering the theme park (PREFERENCE 11) will be 5.0. It is possible that the preference for Disney parks could have increased or decreased since the last survey. Hence, the hypotheses are as follows:

$$H_0: \mu = 5.0$$

$$H_1: \mu \neq 5.0$$

We show the calculations for a one-sample t-test by hand. It can be seen that the mean preference of sample one before entering the park is 5.5 with a standard deviation of 1.08. These calculations are as follows:

$$\bar{X}_1 = (7 + 6 + 5 + 6 + 4 + 6 + 5 + 4 + 7 + 5)/10$$
$$= 55/10$$
$$= 5.5$$
$$\Sigma(X_i - \bar{X}_1)^2 = (7 - 5.5)^2 + (6 - 5.5)^2 + (5 - 5.5)^2 + (6 - 5.5)^2$$
$$+ (4 - 5.5)^2 + (6 - 5.5)^2 + (5 - 5.5)^2$$
$$+ (4 - 5.5)^2 + (7 - 5.5)^2 + (5 - 5.5)^2$$
$$= 2.25 + 0.25 + 0.25 + 0.25 + 2.25 + 0.25 + 0.25$$
$$+ 2.25 + 2.25 + 0.25$$
$$= 10.50$$

$$s_{x_1}^2 = 10.50/(10 - 1)$$

$$s_{x_1} = \sqrt{(10.5)/(10 - 1)}$$

$$= 1.08$$

Therefore,

$$t = (\bar{X} - \mu)/s_{\bar{x}}$$

$$s_{\bar{x}} = s/\sqrt{n}$$

$$s_{\bar{x}} = 1.08/\sqrt{10} = 1.08/3.16 = 0.342$$

$$t = (5.5 - 5.0)/0.342 = 0.5/0.342 = 1.46$$

With 9 degrees of freedom, the probability of getting a more extreme value of t exceeds 0.10 (see Table 4 in the Appendix of Statistical Tables). Hence, the null hypothesis cannot be rejected. In other words, the mean preference of sample one before entering the theme park is no different from 5.0. Thus, based on the results, the preference of teenagers has not changed since the last survey. This one-sample t-test was also conducted using a statistical program. The results are described in Table 17.2. The corresponding SPSS and Excel outputs with explanatory remarks can be downloaded from the Web site for this book.

Test for a Single Proportion

Such hypotheses relate to the proportion or percentage pertaining to a single population. Examples might be "the proportion of brand-loyal users of Coca-Cola exceeds 0.2" or "70 percent of the households eat out at least once a week." The procedure for testing a hypothesis associated with a proportion for one sample was illustrated in Chapter 16 in the section entitled "A General Procedure for Hypothesis Testing."

Two-Sample t-Test

As can be seen from Figure 17.3, the two samples can be either independent or paired. Furthermore, the hypotheses and the related tests could pertain to examining differences in means or proportions.

Two Independent Samples

independent samples
Two samples that are not experimentally related. The measurement of one sample has no effect on the values of the other sample.

Samples drawn randomly from different populations are termed **independent samples**. Several hypotheses in marketing relate to parameters from two different populations:

- The populations of users and nonusers of a brand differ in terms of their perceptions of the brand.
- The high-income consumers spend more on entertainment than low-income consumers.

TABLE 17.2 One-Sample t-Test: Teenagers' Preference Before Visiting

Variable	Number of Cases	Mean	Standard Deviation	Standard Error of Mean
Preference Before Visiting	10	5.5000	1.080	0.342

Test Value = 5

Mean Difference	95% Confidence Interval		t Value	Degrees of Freedom	Two-Tailed Significance
	Lower	Upper			
0.50	−0.273	1.273	1.46	9	0.177

- The proportion of brand-loyal users in segment I is more than the proportion in segment II.
- The proportion of households with an Internet connection in the United States exceeds that in Germany.

In each of the foregoing hypotheses, we have two different populations: users and nonusers, high-income and low-income consumers, segment I and segment II, and the United States and Germany. Samples drawn randomly from these populations will be independent samples. In the opening vignette, the loyal shoppers (LS) and the promiscuous shoppers (PS) constituted two independent samples. For the purpose of analysis, data pertaining to different groups of respondents (e.g., males and females) are generally treated as independent samples even though the data may pertain to the same survey. As in the case for one sample, the hypotheses can relate to means or proportions. The first two hypotheses in the introduction to this section relate to means, whereas the latter two relate to proportions.

MEANS   In the case of means for two independent samples, the hypotheses take the following form:

$$H_0: \mu_1 = \mu_2$$

$$H_1: \mu_1 \neq \mu_2$$

In the opening vignette, the hypotheses tested for the importance of each attribute by the loyal shoppers (LS) and the promiscuous shoppers (PS) were:

$$H_0: \mu_{LS} = \mu_{PS}$$

$$H_1: \mu_{LS} \neq \mu_{PS}$$

The two populations are sampled and the means and variances computed based on samples of sizes n_1 and n_2. If both populations are found to have the same variance, a pooled variance estimate is computed from the two sample variances as follows:

$$s^2 = \frac{\sum_{i=1}^{n_1}(X_{i_1} - \overline{X}_1)^2 + \sum_{i=1}^{n_2}(X_{i_2} - \overline{X}_2)^2}{n_1 + n_2 - 2}$$

or

$$s^2 = \frac{(n_1 - 1)s_1^2 + (n_2 - 1)s_2^2}{n_1 + n_2 - 2}$$

The standard deviation of the test statistic can be estimated as

$$s_{\bar{x}_1 - \bar{x}_2} = \sqrt{s^2\left(\frac{1}{n_1} + \frac{1}{n_2}\right)}$$

The appropriate value of t can be calculated as

$$t = \frac{(\overline{X}_1 - \overline{X}_2) - (\mu_1 - \mu_2)}{s_{\bar{x}_1 - \bar{x}_2}}$$

The degrees of freedom in this case are $(n_1 + n_1 - 2)$.

If the two populations have unequal variances, an exact t can not be computed for the difference in sample means. For example, consumers in the United States have well-developed preferences for brands, whereas such preference formation seems to be weak for consumers in developing countries. Thus, preferences for shampoo brands in the United States are expected to exhibit lower variance as compared to preferences in the developing country of Sierra Leone in West Africa. In these cases, an approximation to t is computed. The number of degrees of freedom in this case is usually not an integer, but a reasonably accurate probability can be obtained by rounding to the nearest integer.[3] In this case, the standard deviation of the test statistic can be estimated as follows:

$$s_{\bar{x}_1 - \bar{x}_2} = \sqrt{\left(\frac{s_1^2}{n_1} + \frac{s_2^2}{n_2} \right)}$$

F-test

A statistical test of the equality of the variances of two populations.

An **F-test** of sample variance can be performed if it is not known whether the two populations have equal variance. In this case, the hypotheses are

$$H_0: \sigma_1^2 = \sigma_2^2$$

$$H_1: \sigma_1^2 \neq \sigma_2^2$$

F statistic

A statistic that is calculated as the ratio of two sample variances.

The **F statistic** is computed from the sample variances as follows:

$$F_{(n_1 - 1), (n_2 - 1)} = \frac{s_1^2}{s_2^2}$$

where

n_1 = size of sample 1

n_2 = size of sample 2

$n_1 - 1$ = degrees of freedom for sample 1

$n_2 - 1$ = degrees of freedom for sample 2

s_1^2 = sample variance for sample 1

s_2^2 = sample variance for sample 2

F distribution

A frequency distribution that depends upon two sets of degrees of freedom: the degrees of freedom in the numerator and the degrees of freedom in the denominator.

As can be seen, the critical value of the **F distribution** depends on two sets of degrees of freedom—those in the numerator and those in the denominator. The critical values of F for various degrees of freedom for the numerator and denominator are given in Table 5 of the Appendix of Statistical Tables. If the probability of F is greater than the significance level α, H_0 is not rejected and t based on the pooled variance estimate can be used. However, if the probability of F is less than or equal to α, H_0 is rejected and t based on a separate variance estimate is used.

Using the data of Table 17.1, we can examine whether the teenagers have a different preference (PREFERENCE 11) than adults (PREFERENCE 21) before entering the park. A two-independent-samples t-test is conducted. Because the difference could be in either direction, a two-tailed test is used.

First, we show the calculations by hand. It can be seen that sample one has a mean of 5.5 with a standard deviation of 1.080 or a variance of $(1.080)^2 = 1.166$. These calculations were illustrated earlier for the one-sample test. Similar calculations will show that sample two has a mean of 4.0 and a standard deviation of 1.054 or a variance of 1.111.

$$\bar{X}_2 = (3 + 4 + 4 + 3 + 6 + 5 + 4 + 3 + 3 + 5)/10$$

$$= 40/10$$

$$= 4.0$$

$$\Sigma (X_i - \bar{X}_2)^2 = (3 - 4)^2 + (4 - 4)^2 + (4 - 4)^2 + (3 - 4)^2 + (6 - 4)^2$$

$$+ (5 - 4)^2 + (4 - 4)^2 + (3 - 4)^2 + (3 - 4)^2 + (5 - 4)^2$$

$$= 1 + 0 + 0 + 1 + 4 + 1 + 0 + 1 + 1 + 1$$

$$= 10$$

Therefore,

$$s_{x_2}^2 = 10/(10 - 1)$$

$$= 1.111$$

The value of the F statistic for testing the equality of variances is

$$F_{9,9} = (1.166/1.111) = 1.05$$

Note that the F-test of sample variances has a probability that exceeds 0.05. Alternatively, the critical vale of $F_{9,9}$ is 3.18 (see Table 5 in the Appendix of Statistical Tables). Accordingly, the null hypothesis of equal variances cannot be rejected, and the t-test based on the pooled variance estimate should be used.

The pooled variance estimate can be calculated as

$$s^2 = \frac{(10 - 1)1.166 + (10 - 1)1.111}{10 + 10 - 2}$$

$$= 1.139$$

Thus,

$$s_{\bar{x}_1 - \bar{x}_2} = \sqrt{1.139\left(\frac{1}{10} + \frac{1}{10}\right)}$$

$$= 0.477$$

Under the null hypothesis, the value of the t statistic is

$$t = (5.5 - 4.0)/0.477$$

$$= 3.14$$

The t value is 3.14, and with $20 - 2 = 18$ degrees of freedom this gives us a probability of 0.006, which is less than the significance level of $0.05/2 = 0.025$. Alternatively, the critical value of t is 2.1009 (see Table 4 in the Appendix of Statistical Tables). Note that in determining the critical value of the test statistic (TS_{CR}), the area to the right of the critical value is $\alpha/2$ for the two-tail test being conducted. Because the calculated value of t exceeds the critical value, the null hypothesis of equal means is rejected. Thus, the conclusion is that the teenagers and adults differ in their preferences for Disney theme parks before entering the park. This two-sample t-test also was conducted using statistical software, and the results are presented in Table 17.3; the corresponding SPSS and Excel outputs with explanatory notes can be downloaded from the Web site. Table 17.3 also shows the t-test using separate variance estimates, because most computer programs automatically conduct the t-test both ways.

TABLE 17.3 *t*-Tests for Independent Samples: Preference Before Visiting

Variable Sample	Number of Cases	Mean	Standard Deviation	Standard Error of Mean
Teenagers	10	5.5000	1.080	0.342
Adults	10	4.0000	1.054	0.333

Mean Difference = 1.5000

Test for Equality of Variances: $F = 1.05$; $P = 0.472$

t-Test for Equality of Means

Variances	t Value	Degrees of Freedom	Two-Tailed Significance	Standard Error of Difference	95% CI for Difference
Equal	3.14	18.00	0.006	0.477	(0.497, 2.503)
Unequal	3.14	17.99	0.006	0.477	(0.497, 2.503)

FIGURE 17.5

Calculating the Critical Value of the Test Statistic: TS_{CR} for Two-Tailed and One-Tailed Tests

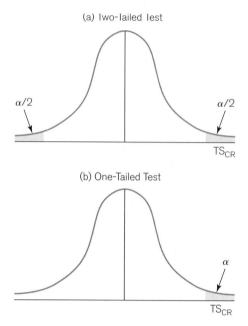

Suppose we wanted to determine whether American teenagers have a higher preference for Disney parks as compared to adults. In this case, a one-tailed rather than a two-tailed test should be used. The hypotheses are as follows:

$$H_0: \mu_1 \leq \mu_2$$

$$H_1: \mu_1 > \mu_2$$

The t statistic is calculated in exactly the same way as in the two-tailed test. In determining the critical value of the test statistic (TS_{CR}), however, the area to the right of the critical value is α for a one-tailed test (Figure 17.5). In this case, the critical value of t is 1.7341, leading to a similar conclusion as arrived at earlier. A two-tailed test is more conservative than the corresponding one-tailed test. If a hypothesis is rejected using a two-tailed test, then it will also be rejected using the corresponding one-tailed test. As explained in Chapter 16, the area to the right of the critical value is α for a one-tail test and $\alpha/2$ for a two-tail test. In other words, the absolute value of the critical value is larger for a two-tailed test than it is for a one-tailed test. As another application of the t-test, consider the following example.

Research in Action

Gen Xers Versus Baby Boomers in a Quest for Luxury

Sponsored by the U.S. issuer of credit and charge cards (and travelers checks), the American Express Platinum Luxury Survey was conducted in March 2005 among a random cross-section of 770 wealthy U.S. consumers:

- 270 consumers with a household income over $200,000 of any age group

- 250 Baby Boomers with a household income of $125,000 to $199,999 (born between 1946–1964, average age of 50 years)

- 250 Gen Xers with a household income of $125,000 to $199,999 (born between 1964–1976, average age of 34 years)

The survey was administered through several channels, including one-on-one interviews at luxury stores. The survey found that Gen Xers' annual spending far exceeds that of

Baby Boomers in a number of luxury-good categories, including:

- 60 percent more than Baby Boomers on fragrance, cosmetics, and beauty products ($3,235 vs. $2,017)

- 47 percent more on fashion accessories ($6,066 vs. $4,116)

- 36 percent more on men's and women's clothing ($23,027 vs. $16,924)

- 32 percent more on wines and liquors ($3,922 vs. $2,966)

- 33 percent more than Boomers for entertainment ($3,629 vs. $2,722)

- 17 percent more for personal/health services $3,324 vs. $2,838)

Two-sample t-tests indicated that all of these differences were statistically significant at the 0.05 level. The conclusion was that luxurious high-end products, such as those marketed by Gucci, Louis Vuitton, Hermes, Cartier, Christian Dior, and so on, should be targeted at Gen Xers, while at the same time maintaining relationships through marketing campaigns or continual quality service with the Baby Boomers.[4]

In this example, we tested the difference between means. A similar test is available for testing the difference between proportions for two independent samples.

PROPORTIONS A case involving proportions for two independent samples is illustrated in Table 17.4, which gives the number of users and nonusers of jeans in the United States and Hong Kong. Is the proportion of users the same in the United States and Hong Kong samples? The null and alternative hypotheses are

$$H_0: \pi_1 = \pi_2$$

$$H_1: \pi_1 \neq \pi_2$$

A z-test is used as in testing the proportion for one sample. This is a large-sample problem. The samples from each population must be large so that the binomial distribution of sample proportions can be approximated by the normal distribution. As a rule of thumb, both np and $n(1 - p)$ must be greater than 10 for each sample. In this case, the test statistic is given by

$$z = \frac{p_1 - p_2}{s_{p_1 - p_2}}$$

In the test statistic, the numerator is the difference between the proportions in the two samples, p_1 and p_2. The denominator is the standard error of the difference in the two proportions and is given by

$$s_{p_1 - p_2} = \sqrt{p(1 - p)\left[\frac{1}{n_1} + \frac{1}{n_2}\right]}$$

where

$$p = \frac{n_1 p_1 + n_2 p_2}{n_1 + n_2}$$

TABLE 17.4 Comparing Jeans Users for the United States and Hong Kong

Sample	Usage of Jeans		Row Totals
	Users	Nonusers	
United States	160	40	200
Hong Kong	120	80	200
Column totals	**280**	**120**	

A significance level of $\alpha = 0.05$ is selected. Given the data of Table 17.4, the test statistic can be calculated as:

$$p_1 = 160/200 = 0.8$$

$$p_2 = 120/200 = 0.6$$

$$p_1 - p_2 = 0.8 - 0.6 = 0.20$$

$$p = (200 \times 0.8 + 200 \times 0.6)/(200 + 200) = 0.7$$

$$s_{p_1 - p_2} = \sqrt{0.7 \times 0.3 \left[\frac{1}{200} + \frac{1}{200} \right]} = 0.04583$$

$$z = 0.2/0.04583 = 4.36$$

Given a two-tailed test, the area to the right of the critical value is $\alpha/2$, or 0.025. Hence, the critical value of the test statistic is 1.96. Because the calculated value exceeds the critical value, the null hypothesis is rejected. Thus, the proportion of users (0.80 for the United States and 0.60 for Hong Kong) is significantly different for the two samples.

As an alternative to the parametric z-test considered earlier, one could also use the cross-tabulation procedure to conduct a chi-square test. In this case, we will have a 2×2 table. One variable will be used to denote the sample and will assume the value 1 for sample one and the value of 2 for sample two. The other variable will be the dichotomous variable of interest. The t-test in this case is equivalent to a chi-square test for independence in a 2×2 contingency table. The relationship is

$$\chi^2_{.95(1)} = t^2_{.05(n_1 + n_2 - 2)}$$

For large samples, the t distribution approaches the normal distribution, thus the t-test and the z-test are equivalent.

Paired Samples

paired samples
In hypothesis testing, the observations are paired so that the two sets of observations relate to the same respondents.

In many marketing research applications, the observations for the two groups are not selected from independent samples. Rather, the observations relate to **paired samples** in that the two sets of observations relate to the same respondents. Examples of hypotheses related to paired samples include the following:

- In the United Kingdom, shoppers consider brand name to be more important than price when purchasing fashion clothing.
- U.K. households spend more money on pizza than on hamburgers.
- The proportion of U.K. households who subscribe to a daily newspaper exceeds the proportion subscribing to magazines.
- The proportion of U.K. bank customers who have a checking account exceeds the proportion who have a savings account.

Each of the foregoing hypotheses relates to the same set of people. Furthermore, the first two hypotheses relate to means, whereas the latter two relate to proportions.

paired-samples t-test
A test for differences in the means of paired samples.

MEANS   A sample of respondents can rate two competing brands, indicate the relative importance of two attributes of a product, or evaluate a brand at two different times. The difference in these cases is examined by a **paired-samples t-test**. In the opening vignette, the hypothesis that the loyal shoppers (LS) consider convenient parking more important than low prices would be tested by using a paired-samples t-test. To compute t for paired samples, the paired-difference variable (D) is formed and its mean and variance calculated.

Then, the t statistic is computed. The degrees of freedom are $n - 1$, where n is the number of pairs. The relevant formulas are as follows:

$$H_0: \mu_D = 0$$

$$H_1: \mu_D \neq 0$$

$$t_{n-1} = \frac{\overline{D} - \mu_D}{s_{\overline{D}}}$$

where

$$\overline{D} = \frac{\sum_{i=1}^{n} D_i}{n}$$

$$s_D = \sqrt{\frac{\sum_{i=1}^{n}(D - \overline{D})^2}{n - 1}}$$

$$s_{\overline{D}} = \frac{s_D}{\sqrt{n}}$$

For the data given in Table 17.1, a paired t-test could be used to determine if there is a difference in the preference before (PREFERENCE 11) and after visiting the Disney theme park (PREFERENCE 12) for respondents in sample one. First, the hand calculations are shown. The mean difference between the variables is 2.4, with a standard deviation of 0.516 and a standard error of 0.163. These calculations are as follows:

$$\overline{D} = ((9 - 7) + (8 - 6) + (8 - 5) + (9 - 6) + (7 - 4)$$
$$+ (8 - 6) + (7 - 5) + (7 - 4) + (9 - 7) + (7 - 5))/10$$
$$= (2 + 2 + 3 + 3 + 3 + 2 + 2 + 3 + 2 + 2)/10$$
$$= 2.4$$

$$s_D^2 = ((2 - 2.4)^2 + (2 - 2.4)^2 + (3 - 2.4)^2 + (3 - 2.4)^2$$
$$+ (3 - 2.4)^2 + (2 - 2.4)^2 + (2 - 2.4)^2 + (3 - 2.4)^2$$
$$+ (2 - 2.4)^2 + (2 - 2.4)^2)/(10 - 1)$$
$$= (0.16 + 0.16 + 0.36 + 0.36 + 0.36$$
$$+ 0.16 + 0.16 + 0.36 + 0.16 + 0.16)/9$$
$$= 0.2667$$

Thus,

$$s_D = \sqrt{0.2667}$$
$$= 0.516$$

and

$$s_{\overline{D}} = \frac{0.516}{\sqrt{10}}$$
$$= 0.516/3.162$$
$$= 0.163$$

This results in a t value of

$$2.4/0.163$$
$$= 14.7$$

TABLE 17.5 *t*-Tests for Paired Samples: Teenagers

Variable	Number of Pairs	Correlation	Two-Tailed Significance	Mean	Standard Deviation	Standard Error of Mean
Preference Before Visiting				5.5000	1.080	0.342
	10	0.881	0.001			
Preference After Visiting				7.9000	0.876	0.277

Paired Differences

Mean	Standard Deviation	Standard Error of Mean	*t* Value	Degrees of Freedom	Two-Tailed Significance	95% Confidence Interval
−2.4000	0.516	0.163	−14.70	9	0.000	(−2.769, −2.031)

With $10 - 1 = 9$ degrees of freedom, this has a probability of less than 0.001. Alternatively, the critical value of *t* for the two-tailed test is 2.2622 (see Table 4 in the Appendix of Statistical Tables), which is less than the calculated value of 14.7. Hence, the null hypothesis is rejected. Therefore, the preferences of American teenagers before and after visiting the Disney theme parks are significantly different. This paired-samples *t*-test also was conducted using statistical software, and the resulting output is shown in Table 17.5. The corresponding SPSS and Excel outputs with explanatory notes can be downloaded from the Web site for this book. A one-tailed test would have the same value for the *t*-statistic, but the level of significance will be α, rather than $\alpha/2$ (Figure 17.5). Thus, if we wanted to test whether the preferences after visiting the theme park were significantly greater than before the visit, a one-tailed test would also lead to the rejection of the null hypothesis

$$H_0: \mu_D \leq 0$$
$$H_1: \mu_D > 0$$

where

$$D = \text{preference after the visit} - \text{preference before the visit}$$

Note that the computer program tested the difference as Before − After, whereas the hand calculations were based on the difference as After − Before; hence the negative mean difference and the negative *t* value in the output given in Table 17.5. Another application is provided in the context of determining the effectiveness of advertising.

Research in Action

Rockport Rocks the Shoe Market with Comfort Appeal

In 2007, the advertising slogan of U.S. shoemaker Rockport was "The Differences Inside," touting the "lightweight comfort" and "walking comfort" of its shoes. This slogan was rendered differently for men and women, however. U.S. TV commercials, as well as print ads, were carefully tested before they were released to the media. A group of 200 men were asked to respond to a series of 10 scales designed to measure attitude toward Rockport shoes. They were then exposed to the TV commercial as part of an entertaining program. After the program, attitude toward Rockport shoes was again measured using the same 10 scales (see the one-group pretest–posttest design in Chapter 8). A paired *t*-test indicated a significant increase in attitude after exposure to the commercial. Similar testing was done for commercials and print ads geared to women. The TV commercials and the print ads not only fared well in the test, but also were successful in achieving sales growth.[5]

PROPORTIONS The difference in proportions for paired samples can be tested by the chi-square test explained in the Chapter 16.

Testing Hypothesis for More Than Two Samples

Procedures for examining differences between more than two population means are called **analysis of variance (ANOVA)**. The null hypothesis is that all means are equal. Marketing researchers often are interested in examining the differences in the mean values of more than two groups. For example:

- Do the various segments differ in terms of their volumes of product consumption?
- Do the brand evaluations of groups exposed to different commercials vary?
- Do retailers, wholesalers, and agents differ in their attitudes toward the firm's distribution policies?
- Do the users, nonusers, and former users of a brand differ in their attitudes toward the brand?

analysis of variance (ANOVA)
A statistical technique for examining the differences among means for two or more populations.

The answers to these and similar questions can be determined by conducting ANOVA, as described in Figure 17.6 and explained in this section. Suppose the researcher was interested in examining whether heavy users, medium users, light users, and nonusers of shampoo in India differed in their preferences for P&G's Rejoice shampoo, measured on a 9-point Likert. The null hypothesis that the four groups were not different in their preference for Pert could be tested using ANOVA. When conducting ANOVA, it is necessary to distinguish between dependent and independent variables.

Identify the Dependent and Independent Variables

In its simplest form, ANOVA must have a dependent variable (preference for Pert shampoo) that is metric (measured using an interval or ratio scale) and one or more independent variables (product use: heavy, medium, light, and nonusers). The independent variables must be categorical (nonmetric). The differences in preference of heavy users, medium users, light users, and nonusers would be examined by one-way analysis of variance. **One-way analysis of variance** involves only one categorical variable, or a

one-way analysis of variance
An ANOVA technique in which there is only one factor.

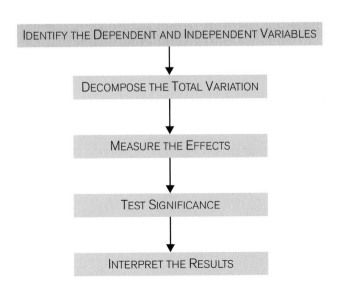

FIGURE 17.6

Conducting One-Way ANOVA

factors

Categorical independent variables. All the independent variables must be categorical (nonmetric) to use ANOVA.

treatment

In ANOVA, a particular combination of factor levels or categories.

single **factor** that defines the different samples or groups. These groups also are called **treatment** conditions. Thus, the different independent samples are treated as categories of a single independent variable. In this case, heavy users, medium users, light users, and nonusers of shampoo would constitute different samples or groups and would be treated as categories of a single independent variable called "shampoo usage."

In the opening vignette, suppose the respondents were classified into three groups: loyal shoppers (LS2—loyal to only one supermarket), multiloyal shoppers (MS2—loyal to two or three supermarkets), and promiscuous shoppers (PS2—nonloyal shoppers). The differences in the mean importance ratings attached to each attribute by the LS2, MS2, and PS2 groups would be tested using one-way ANOVA.

The dependent variable is denoted by Y and the independent variable by X. X is a categorical variable having c categories. There are n observations on Y for each category of X. Thus, the sample size in each category of X is n, and the total sample size $N = n \times c$. Although the sample sizes in the categories of X (the group sizes) are assumed to be equal for the sake of simplicity, this is not a requirement.

Decompose the Total Variation

decomposition of the total variation

In one-way ANOVA, separation of the variation observed in the dependent variable into the variation due to the independent variables plus the variation due to error.

In examining the differences among means, one-way ANOVA involves the **decomposition of the total variation** observed in the dependent variable (Figure 17.6). This variation is measured by the sums of squares corrected for the mean (SS). Analysis of variance is so-named because it examines the variability or variation in the sample (dependent variable) and, based on the variability, determines whether there is reason to believe that the population means differ.

The total variation in Y, denoted by SS_y, can be decomposed into two components:

$$SS_y = SS_{between} + SS_{within}$$

SS_y
The total variation in Y.

where the subscripts *between* and *within* refer to the categories of X. $SS_{between}$ is the variation in Y related to the variation in the means of the categories of X. It represents variation between the categories of X. In other words, $SS_{between}$ is the portion of the sum of squares in Y related to the independent variable or factor X. For this reason, $SS_{between}$ also is denoted as SS_x. SS_{within} is the variation in Y related to the variation within each category of X. SS_{within} is not accounted for by X. Therefore, it is referred to as SS_{error}. The total variation in Y can be decomposed as:

$SS_{between}$
Also denoted as SS_x, the variation in Y related to the variation in the means of the categories of X. This represents variation between the categories of X, or the portion of the sum of squares in Y related to X.

$$SS_y = SS_x + SS_{error}$$

where

SS_{within}
Also referred to as SS_{error}, the variation in Y due to the variation within each of the categories of X. This variation is not accounted for by X.

$$SS_y = \sum_{j=i}^{c} \sum_{i=1}^{n} (Y_{ij} - \bar{Y})^2$$

or

$$SS_y = \sum_{i=1}^{N} (Y_i - \bar{Y})^2$$

$$SS_x = \sum_{j=1}^{c} \sum_{i=1}^{n} (\bar{Y}_j - \bar{Y})^2$$

or

$$SS_x = \sum_{j=1}^{c} n (\bar{Y}_j - \bar{Y})^2$$

$$SS_{error} = \sum_{j=1}^{c} \sum_{i=1}^{n} (Y_{ij} - \bar{Y}_j)^2$$

where

Y_i = individual observation

$\bar{Y}_j$ = mean for category j

$\bar{Y}$ = mean over the whole sample, or grand mean

Y_{ij} = ith observation in the j th category

Measure the Effects

The effects of X on Y are measured by SS_x. Because SS_x is related to the variation in the means of the categories of X, the relative magnitude of SS_x increases as the differences among the means of Y in the categories of X increase. The relative magnitude of SS_x also increases as the variations in Y within the categories of X decrease. The strength of the effects of X on Y are measured as follows:

$$\eta^2 = SS_x/SS_y = (SS_y - SS_{error})/SS_y$$

The value of eta^2, η^2, varies between 0 and 1. It assumes a value of 0 when all the category means are equal, indicating that X has no effect on Y. The value of η^2 will be 1 when there is no variability within each category of X but there is some variability between categories. Thus, **eta^2**, η^2, is a measure of the variation in Y that is explained by the independent variable X. Not only can we measure the effects of X on Y, but we can also test for their significance.

eta^2 (η^2)
Statistic that measures the strength of the effects of X (independent variable or factor) on Y (dependent variable); value ranges between 0 and 1.

Test the Significance

In one-way ANOVA, the interest lies in testing the null hypothesis that the category means are equal in the population (Figure 17.6). In other words,

$$H_0: \mu_1 = \mu_2 = \mu_3 = ... = \mu_c$$

Under the null hypothesis, SS_x and SS_{error} come from the same source of variation. In such a case, the estimate of the population variance of Y can be based on either between-category variation or within-category variation. In other words,

the estimate of the population variance of Y
$= SS_x/(c - 1)$
$=$ **Mean square** due to X
$= MS_x$

mean square
The sum of squares divided by the appropriate degrees of freedom.

or

$= SS_{error}/(N - c)$
$=$ Mean square due to error
$= MS_{error}$

The **significance of the overall effect** in terms of the null hypothesis may be tested by the F statistic based on the ratio between these two estimates:

$$F = \frac{SS_x/(c - 1)}{SS_{error}/(N - c)} = \frac{MS_x}{MS_{error}}$$

significance of the overall effect
A test to determine whether some differences exist between some of the treatment groups.

This statistic follows the F distribution, with $(c - 1)$ and $(N - c)$ degrees of freedom (df). A table of the F distribution is given as Table 5 in the Appendix of Statistical Tables at the end of the book. As mentioned earlier, the F distribution is a probability distribution of the ratios of sample variances. It is characterized by degrees of freedom for the numerator and degrees of freedom for the denominator.[6]

Interpret the Results

If the null hypothesis of equal category means is not rejected, then the independent variable does not have a significant effect on the dependent variable. However, if the null hypothesis is rejected, then the effect of the independent variable is significant. In other words, the mean value of the dependent variable will be different for different categories of the independent variable. A comparison of the category mean values will indicate the nature of the effect of the independent variable.

Illustrative Applications of One-Way Analysis of Variance

These concepts are first illustrated with an example showing calculations done by hand followed by calculations using computer analysis. Suppose that Woolworths, Australia's largest supermarket chain, is attempting to determine the effect of in-store advertising (X) on sales (Y). In-store advertising is varied at three levels: high, medium, and low. Fifteen Woolworths

TABLE 17.6 Effect of In-Store Promotion on Sales

	Level of In-Store Promotion		
Store No.	High	Medium Normalized Sales	Low
1	10	6	5
2	9	4	6
3	10	7	5
4	8	3	2
5	8	5	2

stores are randomly selected, and five stores are randomly assigned to each treatment condition. The experiment lasts for 4 weeks. Sales are monitored, normalized to account for extraneous factors (i.e., store size, traffic, and so on) and converted to a 0-to-10 scale. The data obtained (Y_{ij}) are reported in Table 17.6. Again, the sample size ($n = 15$ stores) is limited so that the hand calculations do not become unwieldy.

The null hypothesis is that the category means are equal:

$$H_0: \mu_1 = \mu_2 = \mu_3$$

To test the null hypothesis, the various means and sums of squares are computed as follows:

$$
\begin{aligned}
\text{Category means: } \overline{Y}_j \quad & 45/5 \quad 25/5 \quad 20/5 \\
& = 9 \quad\ = 5 \quad\ = 4
\end{aligned}
$$

$$\textit{Grand mean: } \overline{Y} = (45 + 25 + 20)/15 = 6$$

$$
\begin{aligned}
SS_y &= (10 - 6)^2 + (9 - 6)^2 + (10 - 6)^2 + (8 - 6)^2 + (8 - 6)^2 \\
&\quad + (6 - 6)^2 + (4 - 6)^2 + (7 - 6)^2 + (3 - 6)^2 + (5 - 6)^2 \\
&\quad + (5 - 6)^2 + (6 - 6)^2 + (5 - 6)^2 + (2 - 6)^2 + (2 - 6)^2 \\
&= 16\ +\ 9\ +\ 16\ +\ 4\ +\ 4 \\
&\quad +\ 0\ +\ 4\ +\ 1\ +\ 9\ +\ 1 \\
&\quad +\ 1\ +\ 0\ +\ 1\ +\ 16\ +\ 16 \\
&= 98
\end{aligned}
$$

$$
\begin{aligned}
SS_x &= 5(9 - 6)^2 + 5(5 - 6)^2 + 5(4 - 6)^2 \\
&= 45\ +\ 5\ +\ 20 \\
&= 70
\end{aligned}
$$

$$
\begin{aligned}
SS_{error} &= (10 - 9)^2 + (9 - 9)^2 + (10 - 9)^2 + (8 - 9)^2 + (8 - 9)^2 \\
&\quad + (6 - 5)^2 + (4 - 5)^2 + (7 - 5)^2 + (3 - 5)^2 + (5 - 5)^2 \\
&\quad + (5 - 4)^2 + (6 - 4)^2 + (5 - 4)^2 + (2 - 4)^2 + (2 - 4) \\
&= 1\ +\ 0\ +\ 1\ +\ 1\ +\ 1\ +\ 1\ +\ 1\ +\ 4\ +\ 4\ +\ 0 \\
&\quad +\ 1\ +\ 4\ +\ 1\ +\ 4\ +\ 4 \\
&= 28
\end{aligned}
$$

It can be verified that

$$SS_y = SS_x + SS_{error}$$

as follows:

$$98 = 70 + 28$$

The strength of the effects of X on Y are measured as follows:

$$
\begin{aligned}
\eta^2 &= SS_x/SS_y \\
&= 70/98 \\
&= 0.714
\end{aligned}
$$

TABLE 17.7 One-Way Analysis of Variance

Source of Variation	Sum of Squares	Degrees of Freedom	Mean Square	F	Significance of F
Main effects	70.00	2	35.00	15.00	.001
In-store promotion	70.00	2	35.00	15.00	.001
Explained (between groups)	70.00	2	35.00	15.00	.001
Residual (within groups)	28.00	12	2.33		
Total	**98.00**	**14**	**7.00**		

In other words, 71.4 percent of the variation in sales (Y) is accounted for by in-store advertising (X), indicating a strong effect. The null hypothesis can now be tested.

$$F = \frac{SS_x / (c - 1)}{SS_{error} / (N - c)} = \frac{MS_x}{MS_{error}}$$

$$F = \frac{70/(3 - 1)}{28/(15 - 3)}$$

$$= 15.0$$

From Table 5 in the Appendix of Statistical Tables, we see that for 2 and 12 degrees of freedom and $\alpha = 0.05$, the critical value of F is 3.89. Because the calculated value of F is greater than the critical value, the null hypothesis is rejected. Therefore, we can conclude that the population means for the three levels of in-store advertising at Woolworths supermarkets are indeed different. The relative magnitudes of the means for the three categories indicate that a high level of in-store advertising leads to significantly higher sales. This one-way ANOVA was also conducted using statistical software, and the output is shown in Table 17.7. The corresponding SPSS and Excel outputs with explanatory notes can be downloaded from the Web site for this book.

Proportions for More Than Two Samples

To test differences in proportions for more than two samples, one could also use the cross-tabulation procedure to conduct a chi-square test (see Chapter 16). In this case, we will have a $2 \times c$ table. One variable will be used to denote the sample and will assume the value of 1 for sample one, the value of 2 for sample two, and the value of c for sample c. The other variable will be the dichotomous variable of interest. The various hypothesis testing procedures for examining differences in means and proportions are summarized in Table 17.8.

TABLE 17.8 A Summary of Hypothesis Testing

Sample	Test/Comments
One sample	
Means	*t*-test, if variance is unknown
	z-test, if variance is known
Proportions	*z*-test
Two independent samples	
Means	Two-group *t*-test
	F-test for equality of variances
Proportions	*z*-test
	Chi-square test
Paired samples	
Means	Paired *t*-test
Proportions	Chi-square test
More than two samples	
Means	One-way analysis of variance
Proportions	Chi-square test

Research in Action

One-Way Analysis of Variance Favors "A Style for Every Story"

The well-known U.S. jeans maker Levi Strauss & Company was battling competition from designer labels and private-label brands. Designers such as Ralph Lauren Polo, Calvin Klein, Guess?, and Tommy Hilfiger, as well as traditional competitors such as Gap, had launched substantial marketing and advertising campaigns. At the same time, major U.S. retail chains, such as JCPenney Company and Sears, Roebuck & Company, had strong national branding efforts in place for their own private-label jeans.

In response to such stiff competition, Levi Strauss developed three alternative image themes: "Levi's. They go on"; "They're not Levi's jeans until we say they are"; and "A style for every story." The three themes were tested. Three groups of 150 respondents each were recruited. Each group was asked to evaluate one theme by rating it on a 10-point scale. A one-way ANOVA was conducted to examine the differences in the ratings provided by the three groups. "A style for every story" received significantly higher

ratings than the other two alternatives. Thus, this campaign was chosen for roll-out on the national media. As of 2008, Levi Strauss is one of the largest makers of brand-name clothing globally, selling jeans and sportswear under the Levi's, Dockers, and Levi Strauss Signature names in more than 110 countries.[7]

Be a DM!

As the marketing director for U.S. computer maker Dell, how would you segment the home computer market?

Be an MR!

Visit www.dell.com and search the Internet, as well as your library's online databases, to obtain information on computer usage in U.S. households. As a marketing research analyst working for Dell, how would you determine whether the three home-computer usage segments (experts, novices, and nonusers) differ in terms of 10 psychographic characteristics, each measured on a 7-point scale?

Summary Illustration Using the Opening Vignette

Hypotheses about means of one or two populations are commonly examined by using a *t*-test. Different forms of the *t*-test are suitable for testing hypotheses based on one sample, two independent samples, or paired samples. In the opening vignette, the hypothesis that the mean rating of each attribute for the overall sample (loyal shoppers, LS, and promiscuous shoppers, PS) exceeded 5.0 would be tested using the one-sample *t*-test. The hypotheses related to differences in the mean importance ratings attached to each attribute by the LS and the PS would be tested using the two-independent-samples *t*-test. The hypothesis that the LS consider convenient parking to be more important than low prices would be tested by using a paired-samples *t*-test. Similar tests could be used for testing differences in proportions.

One-way ANOVA involves tests of differences in the means of more than two independent samples. The samples are treated as categories of a single independent variable. The null hypothesis of equal means is tested by an *F* statistic, which is the ratio of the mean square related to the independent variable to the mean square related to error. In the opening vignette, suppose the respondents were classified into three groups: loyal shoppers (LS2—loyal to only one supermarket), multiloyal shoppers (MS2—loyal to two or three supermarkets), and promiscuous shoppers (PS2—nonloyal shoppers). The differences in the mean importance ratings attached to each attribute by the LS2, MS2, and PS2 groups would be tested using one-way ANOVA. The differences in the proportion of females among the LS2, MS2, and PS2 could be tested using the cross-tabulation procedure to conduct a chi-square test (see Chapter 16). Figures 17.7 and 17.8 provide concept maps for conducting *t*-tests and one-way ANOVA, respectively.

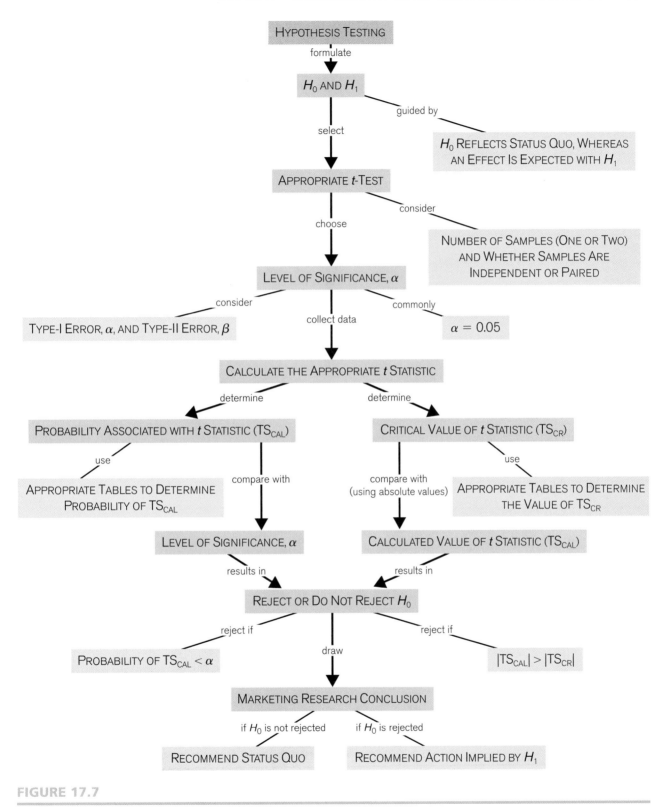

FIGURE 17.7

A Concept Map for Conducting *t*-Tests

FIGURE 17.8

A Concept Map for One-Way ANOVA

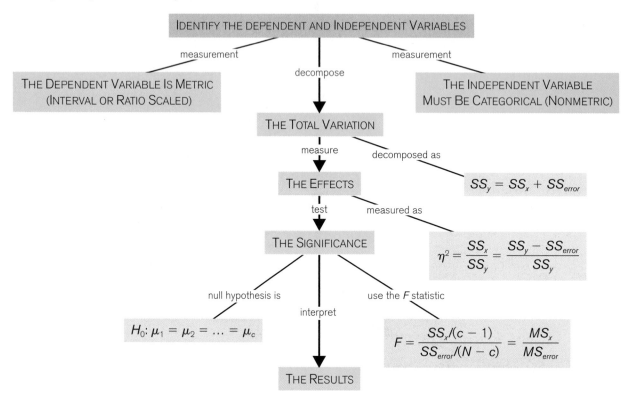

Marriott: Luring Business Travelers

The Situation

U.S.-based Marriott International, Inc. (www.marriott.com) is a leading worldwide hospitality company. Its origins can be traced to a small root beer stand opened in Washington, D.C. in 1927 by J. Willard and Alice S. Marriott. As of 2008, Marriott International has more than 3,000 lodging properties located in the United States and 68 other countries and territories. Among Marriott's most frequent visitors are its business-travel customers. For many years, business travelers have faced a fundamental problem in finding a comfortable and convenient way to accomplish their jobs in hotel rooms that lack a functional workspace. Although many of the business travelers were not very productive, they did hone important skills, such as writing legibly on top of a comforter, stretching arms beyond maximum length to reach hidden outlets behind or underneath furniture, and squinting to make documents readable by bedside lamplight.

Marriott recognized these unmet needs of its business travelers and wanted to do something about it. Susan Hodapp, brand director for Marriott Hotels, Resorts and Suites, commissioned a survey to determine business travelers' preferences for hotels and the factors that are important in their hotel selection process. Part of the questionnaire focused on the features of the hotel room. Each respondent rated the relative importance of the following factors on a 7-point scale (1 = not at all important, 7 = extremely important): Room décor, room lighting, room furniture, voice and data access in the room, and price of the room per night.

The Marketing Research Decision

1. Marriott would like to determine what features of a hotel room are most important in business travelers' choice of a hotel. What analysis should be conducted?
   a. Two-independent-samples *t*-test: Means
   b. Two-independent-samples *t*-test: Proportions

   c. Paired-samples *t*-test: Means
   d. Paired-samples *t*-test: Proportions
   e. One-way ANOVA

2. Discuss how the type of data analysis you recommend to Susan Hodapp would enable her to understand business travelers' preferences for hotel rooms.

continued

The Marketing Management Decision

1. To lure business travelers, Marriott should focus on:
   a. Room décor
   b. Room lighting
   c. Room furniture
   d. Voice and data access in the room
   e. Price of the room per night
2. Discuss how the management-decision action that you recommend to Susan Hodapp is influenced by the type of data analysis you suggested earlier and by the findings of that analysis.

What Susan Hodapp Did

The survey revealed various features business travelers wanted most in their rooms. In response, Marriott introduced its "Room That Works" program, creating a modern-day Renaissance of workspace design. Today, many guest rooms are furnished with upgraded workstations with standard features such as:

- Roomy, oversized desks with plenty of space to spread out papers
- Lighting fixtures that not only produce adequate work-area light, but also feature desk-level outlets and data ports for laptops or other productivity devices
- An ergonomic, adjustable chair that swivels
- Multiple line telephones with call-waiting feature so guests can use the Internet and receive calls simultaneously

Hodapp said she felt the company's customers wanted added flexibility in a workstation. "Our guests have a compressed time frame to get things done, so we wanted them to be able to modify the work environment for personalized comfort," she said. Therefore, Marriott's workstations feature desks on casters and an arm that swings out of the guestroom desk for additional workspace.[8]

Software Applications

The major program for conducting *t*-tests in SPSS is T TEST. This program can be used to conduct *t*-tests on independent as well as paired samples. In SAS, the program T TEST can be used. Parametric tests available in Minitab in descriptive stat function are *z*-test mean, *t*-test of the mean, and two-sample *t*-test. The available parametric tests in Excel and other spreadsheets include the *t*-test, paired two sample for means; *t*-test, two independent samples assuming equal variances; *t*-test, two independent samples assuming unequal variances; *z*-test, two samples for means; and *F*-test: two samples for variances (Exhibit 17.1).

SPSS and SAS also have programs for conducting analysis of variance. In addition to the basic analysis that we have considered, these programs can also perform more complex analysis. Minitab and Excel also offer programs. Exhibit 17.2 contains a description of the relevant programs for conducting analysis of variance. Refer to the user manuals for these packages for more details.

SPSS Windows

The major program for conducting *t*-tests in SPSS is T TEST. This program can be used to conduct *t*-tests on one sample or independent or paired samples. One-way ANOVA can be efficiently performed using the program ONEWAY. To select these procedures using SPSS for Windows, click:

    Analyze > Compare Means > Means . . .
    Analyze > Compare Means > One-Sample *T test* . . .
    Analyze > Compare Means > Independent-Samples *T test* . . .
    Analyze > Compare Means > Paired-Samples *T test* . . .
    Analyze > Compare Means > One-Way ANOVA . . .

Detailed Steps: Overview

Detailed step-by-step instructions for running the SPSS programs for the data analysis presented in this chapter can be downloaded from the Web site for this book in two forms: (1) computerized demonstration movies, and (2) screen captures. In addition, these steps are illustrated in the following sections.

Detailed Steps: One-Sample t-Test

Provided here are the detailed steps for running a one-sample test on the data of Table 17.1. The null hypothesis is that the mean preference for sample one before entering the theme park is 5.0.

1. Select DATA from the SPSS menu bar.
2. Click SELECT CASES.
3. Check IF CONDITION IS SATISFIED. Then click the IF button.
4. Move SAMPLE <sample> into the SELECT CASES: IF box. Click "=" and then click "1."
5. Click CONTINUE.
6. Check UNSELECTED CASES ARE FILTERED.
7. Click OK.
8. Select ANALYZE from the SPSS menu bar.
9. Click COMPARE MEANS and then ONE SAMPLE *T TEST*.
10. Move Preference Before Visiting <pref1> into the TEST VARIABLE(S) box.
11. Type "5" in the TEST VALUE box.
12. Click OK.

Detailed Steps: Two-Independent-Samples t-Test

Next are the detailed steps for running a two-independent-samples *t*-test on the data of Table 17.1. The null hypothesis is that the mean preference for adults and teenagers before visiting Disney theme parks is the same. First, make sure all cases will be included in the analysis.

Menu Bar
    DATA
        Select CASES.
            Choose ALL CASES.

Perform the analysis as follows:

1. Select ANALYZE from the SPSS menu bar.
2. Click COMPARE MEANS and then INDEPENDENT SAMPLES *T TEST*.
3. Move "Preference Before Visiting <pref1>" into the TEST VARIABLE(S) box.
4. Move "Sample <sample>" into the GROUPING VARIABLE box.
5. Click DEFINE GROUPS.
6. Type "1" in the GROUP 1 box and "2" in the GROUP 2 box.
7. Click CONTINUE.
8. Click OK.

Detailed Steps: Paired-Samples t-Test

Next are the detailed steps for running a paired-samples *t*-test on the data of Table 17.1. The null hypothesis is that there is no difference in the mean preference of teenagers before and after visiting Disney theme parks.

1. Select DATA from the SPSS menu bar.
2. Click SELECT CASES.
3. Check IF CONDITION IS SATISFIED. Then click the IF button.
4. Move "SAMPLE<sample>" into the SELECT CASES: IF box. Click "=" and then click "1."
5. Click CONTINUE.
6. Check "UNSELECTED CASES ARE FILTERED."
7. Click OK.
8. Select ANALYZE from the SPSS menu bar.
9. Click COMPARE MEANS and then PAIRED SAMPLES *T TEST*.

10. Select "Preference Before Visiting <pref1>" and then select "Preference After Visiting <pref2>." Move these variables into the PAIRED VARIABLE(S) box.
11. Click OK.

Detailed Steps: One-Way ANOVA

The following are the detailed steps for running a one-way ANOVA on the data of Table 17.6. The null hypothesis is that there is no difference in mean normalized sales for the three levels of in-store promotion.

1. Select ANALYZE from the SPSS menu bar.
2. Click COMPARE MEANS and then ONE-WAY ANOVA.
3. Move "Normalized Sales <sales>" into the DEPENDENT LIST box.
4. Move "In-Store Promotion <promotio>" into the FACTOR box.
5. Click OPTIONS.
6. Click Descriptive.
7. Click CONTINUE.
8. Click OK.

Experiential Learning

Testing Differences

Go to the textbook Web site and download the survey used in interviewing nonreturning students at Musial University (MU), an urban public university in the midsized American city of Musial. Although the actual name of the university has been disguised, the research project and the accompanying data are real. The administrators at MU were interested in obtaining the perspectives of "dropout" or "stopout" students so that the administrators at MU could enhance the programs, facilities, and services at MU. Download the actual survey used in this study (Musial Retention Survey.doc) as well as the relevant SPSS system file (Musial Retention Data.sav).

- Read the survey Musial Retention Survey.doc.

- Open SPSS and the SPSS system file Musial Retention Data.sav.

- At the bottom of the SPSS window, click on the tab VARIABLE VIEW.

- Enter LABELS.

  Enter abbreviated forms of the names for the questions. For example, Q1 could be "enrolled elsewhere," Q2 could be "educational plans," and so forth. Do this for Q3, Q4, and Q5a through Q5bb. Enter these names directly into each corresponding cell in the LABEL column.

- Enter VALUES for the LABELS.

  Enter labels for the possible values for each question. For example, for Q1, a value of "1" should receive a label of "Yes," a value of "2" should receive a label of "No," and so forth. Do this for all questions. For Q5a through Q5bb, the value of "1" should receive a label of "Strongly Disagree," and the value of "10" should receive a label of "Strongly Agree." Enter these names directly into each corresponding cell in the "Values" column by first clicking each cell (now with "None" entered), then clicking the gray box with three

dots that appears in the cell. In the Values window, enter the value (e.g., "1"), enter the label (e.g., "Yes"), and then click the ADD button before clicking the OK button that closes the Values window for the cell.

- Clean the data for all questions except the ID question.

As was done in the Data Prep Experiential Learning Exercise of Chapter 15, "−9" must be recoded to SYSMIS. An alternative method for doing this would be to enter "−9" into each cell in the column MISSING after clicking the VARIABLE VIEW tab at the bottom of the SPSS window. Likewise, the range "11 to highest" must be recoded to SYSMIS.

t-tests

Conduct three t-tests comparing the subgroups of Q1 (those enrolled at another institution this semester vs. those who are not) on the following dependent variables:

Q5j: MU encourages students to participate in extracurricular activities.

Q5k: MU offers good recreational facilities to students.

Q5l: The social environment at MU is great.

(What is your null hypothesis (H$_0$) and alternative hypothesis (H$_1$) for each of these t-tests?)

In SPSS, take the following steps to examine the means and standard deviations for these three variables:

ANALYZE
    COMPARE MEANS
    MEANS
       MEANS window
          DEPENDENT LIST, enter Q5j, Q5k, Q5l.
          INDEPENDENT LIST, enter Q1.
          Click OK.

In SPSS, take the following steps to conduct *t*-tests comparing the subgroups of Q1 on the three dependent variables Q5j, Q5k, and Q5l:

  ANALYZE
    COMPARE MEANS
      INDEPENDENT SAMPLES T TEST
      INDEPENDENT SAMPLES T TEST window
        TEST VARIABLE(S), enter Q5j, Q5k, and Q5l.
        GROUPING VARIABLE, enter Q1.
          DEFINE GROUPS
            GROUP 1 = 1
            GROUP 2 = 2
            Click CONTINUE.
              Click OK.

Examine your results by assuming the variance among the groups is equal, and viewing the corresponding cells for each of the three variables under the columns labeled "t" and "Sig (2-tailed)."

One-Way ANOVA

Compare the subgroups of Q2 "educational plans for the future" on the dependent variable of Q5n "I would have very much enjoyed having a football team at MU." First, collapse some of the categories to avoid splintering the subgroups for Q2 with too few cases to allow statistically meaningful comparisons. Do this in the following way:

  Recode Grouping Variable Q2:
  TRANSFORM
    RECODE INTO DIFFERENT VARIABLES
      RECODE INTO DIFFERENT VARIABLES window
        Select Q2.
          OUTPUT VARIABLE = Q2new
        Select OLD AND NEW VALUE.
          Under OLD VALUE
            RANGE
              1 through 2
          Under NEW VALUE
            COPY OLD VALUE
        Then select ADD.
          Under OLD VALUE
            VALUE
              3
          Under NEW VALUE
            NEW VALUE

              2
        Then select ADD.
          Under OLD VALUE
            RANGE
              4 through 5
          Under NEW VALUE
            NEW VALUE
              3
        Select ADD, then CONTINUE.
        Click CHANGE and then OK on the RECODE INTO DIFFERENT VARIABLES.

Check the results of this recoding in the following way:

  ANALYZE
    DESCRIPTIVE STATISTICS
      FREQUENCIES
        Q2new
          Click OK.

Note: You should have subgroups of 70 (plan to reenter MU), 46 (attending another school), and 25 (no plans).

One-Way ANOVA

Compare the sentiments for a football program (which MU does not currently have) across the three subgroups of Q2 regarding educational plans for the future. *(What are the H$_0$ and H$_1$ for your ANOVA analysis?)*

    ANALYZE
      COMPARE MEANS
        ONE-WAY ANOVA
          ONE-WAY ANOVA window
            DEPENDENT LIST
              Q5n
            FACTOR
              Q2new
                Click OK.

Epilogue

Download Musial Retention Report.ppt to get a glimpse of what was presented to the MU administrators in a PowerPoint presentation. The most illuminating finding for the MU administrators was that almost 50 percent of the nonreturning students declared an intention to return to MU before the end of the year. This was far more than any of the administrators had expected. (This result can be seen in the frequency distribution for Q2.)

Excel

We give an overview of the detailed steps involved in conducting these analyses using Excel. Then we provide detailed step-by-step instructions for conducting one-sample *t*-test, two-independent-samples *t*-test, paired-samples *t*-test, and one-way ANOVA.

Detailed Steps: Overview

Detailed step-by-step instructions for running the Excel programs for the data analysis presented in this chapter can be downloaded from the Web site for this book in two forms: (1) computerized demonstration movies, and (2) screen captures. In addition, these steps are illustrated in the following sections.

Detailed Steps: One-Sample *t*-Test

The following are detailed steps for running a one-sample test on the data of Table 17.1. The null hypothesis is that the mean preference for sample one before entering the theme park is 5.0.

1. Add a column with the name "Dummy" beside PREF2 and fill the first 10 rows with "5."
2. Select Tools (Alt + T).
3. Select Data Analysis under Tools.
4. Data Analysis Window pops up.
5. Select t-Test: Paired two Sample for Means from Data Analysis Window.
6. Click OK.
7. t-Test: Paired two Sample for Means pop-up window appears on screen.
8. t-Test: Paired two Sample for Means window has two portions:
   a. Input
   b. Output Options
9. Input portion asks for five inputs:
   a. Click in the Variable <u>1</u> Range box. Select (highlight) the first 10 rows of data under PREF1. $C$2:$C$11 should appear on Variable <u>1</u> Range.
   b. Click in the Variable <u>2</u> Range box. Select (highlight) the first 10 rows of data under DUMMY. $D$2:$D$11 should appear on Variable <u>2</u> Range.
   c. Leave Hypothesized Mean Difference and Labels as blank.
   d. Default value of Alpha 0.05 is seen on the Alpha Box. Let the Alpha value be like that.
10. In the Output portion of pop-up window, select New Workbook Options.
11. Click OK.

Detailed Steps: Two-Independent-Samples *t*-Test

The following are detailed steps for running a two independent samples *t*-test on the data of Table 17.1. The null hypothesis is that the mean preference for American adults and teenagers before visiting Disney theme parks is the same.

1. Select Tools (Alt + T).
2. Select Data Analysis under Tools.
3. Data Analysis Window pops up.
4. Select t-Test: Two-Sample Assuming Equal Variances from Data Analysis Window.
5. Click OK.
6. t-Test: Two-Sample Assuming Equal Variances pop-up window appears on screen.
7. t-Test: Two-Sample Assuming Equal Variances window has two portions:
   a. Input
   b. Output Options
8. Input portion asks for two inputs:
   a. Click in the Variable <u>1</u> Range box. Select (highlight) the first 10 rows of data under PREF1. $C$2:C$11 should appear on Variable <u>1</u> Range.
   b. Click in the Variable <u>2</u> Range box. Select (highlight) the last 10 rows of data under PREF1. $C$12:$C$21 should appear on Variable <u>2</u> Range.
   c. Leave Hypothesized Mean Difference and Labels as blank.
   d. Default value of Alpha 0.05 is seen on the Alpha Box. Let the Alpha value be like that.
9. In the Output portion of pop-up window, select New Workbook Options.
10. Click OK.

Detailed Steps: Paired-Samples *t*-Test

The following are detailed steps for running a paired samples *t*-test on the data of Table 17.1. The null hypothesis is that there is no difference in the mean preference of teenagers before and after visiting Disney theme parks.

1. Select Tools (Alt + T).
2. Select Data Analysis under Tools.

3. Data Analysis Window pops up.
4. Select t-Test: Paired two Sample for Means from Data Analysis Window.
5. Click OK.
6. t-Test: Paired two Sample for Means pop-up window appears on screen.
7. t-Test: Paired two Sample for Means window has two portions:
   a. Input
   b. Output Options
8. Input portion asks for two inputs:
   a. Click in the Variable 1 Range box. Select (highlight) the first 10 rows of data under PREF1. $C$2:$C$11 should appear on Variable 1 Range.
   b. Click in the Variable 2 Range box. Select (highlight) the first 10 rows of data under PREF2. $D$2:$D$11 should appear on Variable 2 Range.
   c. Leave Hypothesized Mean Difference and Labels as blank.
   d. Default value of Alpha 0.05 is seen on the Alpha Box. Let the Alpha value be like that.
9. In the Output portion of pop-up window, select New Workbook Options.
10. Click OK.

Detailed Steps: One-Way ANOVA

The following are the detailed steps for running a one-way ANOVA on the data of Table 17.6. The null hypothesis is that there is no difference in mean normalized sales for the three levels of in-store promotion.

1. Select Tools (Alt + T).
2. Select Data Analysis under Tools.
3. Data Analysis Window pops up.
4. Select Anova: Single Factor from Data Analysis Window.
5. Click OK.
6. Anova: Single Factor pop-up window appears on screen.
7. Anova: Single Factor window has two portions:
   a. Input
   b. Output Options
8. Input portion asks for two inputs:
   a. Click in the Input Range box. Select (highlight) all the data under the columns High, Medium, Low at the same time. $B$2:$D$6 should appear in the Input Range.
   b. Click in Columns beside Grouped by.
   c. Labels in the first row should not be checked.
   d. Leave Alpha at the default value of 0.05.
9. In the Output portion of pop-up window, select New Workbook Options.
10. Click OK.

Summary

Hypotheses related to differences in the population means and, in some cases, proportions can be tested using the *t* distribution. Different forms of the *t*-test are suitable for testing hypotheses based on one sample, two independent samples, or paired samples.

One-way ANOVA involves a single metric dependent variable and a single independent categorical variable. Interest lies in testing the null hypothesis that the category means are equal in the population. The total variation in the dependent variable is decomposed into two components: variation related to the independent variable and variation related to error. The variation is measured in terms of the sums of squares corrected for the mean (*SS*). The mean square is obtained by dividing the *SS* by the corresponding degrees of freedom. The null hypothesis of equal means is tested by an *F* statistic, which is the ratio of the mean square related to the independent variable to the mean square related to error.

Key Terms and Concepts

Parametric tests, 515
t-test, 516
t statistic, 516
t distribution, 516
z-test, 518
Independent samples, 520
F-test, 522
F statistic, 522
F distribution, 522

Paired samples, 526
Paired-samples t-test, 526
Analysis of variance
   (ANOVA), 529
One-way analysis of variance, 529
Factor, 530
Treatment, 530
Decomposition of the total
   variation, 530

SS_y, 530
$SS_{between}$ (SS_x), 530
SS_{within} (SS_{error}), 530
Eta^2 (η^2), 531
Mean square, 531
Significance of the overall
   effect, 531

Suggested Cases and Video Cases

Running Case with Real Data

1.1 Hewlett-Packard

Comprehensive Cases with Real Data

3.1 Bank of America   3.2 McDonald's   3.3 Boeing

Video Cases

19.1 Marriott

Live Research: Conducting a Marketing Research Project

1. Differences between groups are of interest in most projects. These can be examined by using an independent-samples t-test for two groups or one-way ANOVA for more than two groups.
2. Often each respondent evaluates many stimuli. For example, each respondent might evaluate different brands or provide importance ratings for different attributes. In such cases, differences between pairs of stimuli can be examined using the paired-samples t-test.

Acronym

The major characteristics of t-tests can be summarized by the acronym *T TEST*:

   T distribution is similar to the normal distribution

   T est of difference: Means or proportions

   E stimate of variance from the sample

   S ingle sample

   T wo samples: independent or paired

Review Questions

1. Present a classification of hypothesis-testing procedures.
2. Describe the general procedure for conducting a *t*-test.
3. Give the formula for the *t* statistic when examining a hypothesis related to a single mean.
4. Give the formula for the *t* statistic when examining a hypothesis related to a single proportion.
5. Give the formula for the *t* statistic when examining a hypothesis related to means of two independent samples.
6. Give the formula for the *t* statistic when examining a hypothesis related to means of paired samples.
7. What is the relationship between analysis of variance and the *t*-test?
8. What is total variation? How is it decomposed in a one-way analysis of variance?
9. What is the null hypothesis in one-way ANOVA? What basic statistic is used to test the null hypothesis in one-way ANOVA? How is this statistic computed?

Applied Problems

1. In each of the following situations, indicate the statistical analysis you would conduct and the appropriate test or test statistic that should be used.
   a. Consumer preferences for Camay soap were obtained on an 11-point Likert scale. The same consumers were then shown a commercial about Camay. After the commercial, preferences for Camay were again measured. Has the commercial been successful in inducing a change in preferences?
   b. Respondents in a survey of 1,000 households were asked to indicate their frequency of domestic air travel on an interval scale. They were also classified as being in high-, medium-, or low-income categories. Is the frequency of domestic air travel related to income level?
   c. In a telephone survey using a representative sample of 3,000 households, the respondents were asked to indicate their preference for fast-food restaurants using a 7-point Likert type scale. The sample was divided into small and large households based on a median split of the household size. Does preference for fast-food restaurants vary by household size?

2. The current advertising campaign for a major automobile brand would be changed if fewer than 70 percent of the consumers like it.
   a. Formulate the null and alternative hypotheses.
   b. Which statistical test would you use? Why?
   c. A random sample of 300 consumers was surveyed, and 204 respondents indicated that they liked the campaign. Should the campaign be changed? Why or why not?

3. A major computer manufacturer is having an end-of-season sale on computers. The number of computers sold during this sale at a sample of 10 stores was 800, 1,100, 0, 400, 700, 800, 1,000, 500, 800, and 300.
   a. Is there evidence that an average of more than 500 computers per store were sold during this sale? Use $\alpha = 0.05$.
   b. What assumption is necessary to perform this test?

4. After receiving complaints from readers, your campus newspaper decides to redesign its front page. Two new formats, B and C, are developed and tested against the current format, A. A total of 75 students are randomly selected, and 25 students are randomly assigned to each of three format conditions. The students are asked to evaluate the effectiveness of the format on an 11-point scale (1 = poor, 11 = excellent).
   a. State the null hypothesis.
   b. What statistical test should you use?
   c. What are the degrees of freedom that are associated with the test statistic?

5. A marketing researcher wants to test the hypothesis that, within the population, there is no difference in the importance attached to shopping by consumers living in the northern, southern, eastern, and western United States. A study is conducted and analysis of variance is used to analyze the data. The results obtained are presented in the following table.

Source	df	Sum of Squares	Mean Squares	F Ratio	F Probability
Between groups	3	70.212	23.404	1.12	0.3
Within groups	996	20812.416	20.896		

   a. Is there sufficient evidence to reject the null hypothesis?
   b. What conclusion can be drawn from the table?
   c. If the average importance was computed for each group, would you expect the sample means to be similar or different?
   d. What was the total sample size in this study?

6. In a pilot study examining the effectiveness of three commercials (A, B, and C), 10 consumers were assigned to view each commercial and rate it on a 9-point Likert scale. The data obtained are shown in the following table. These data should be analyzed by doing hand calculations (i.e., without using the computer).

	Commercial	
A	B	C
4	7	8
5	4	7
3	6	7
4	5	6
3	4	8
4	6	7
4	5	8
3	5	8
5	4	5
5	4	6

a. Calculate the category means and the grand mean.
b. Calculate SS_y, SS_x, and SS_{error}.
c. Calculate η^2.
d. Calculate the value of F.
e. Are the three commercials equally effective?

7. Conduct the following analyses for the Internet usage data given in Applied Problem number 6 in Chapter 16.
a. Test the hypothesis that the mean familiarity with the Internet exceeds 4.0.
b. Is the Internet usage different for males as compared to females? Formulate the null and alternative hypotheses, and conduct the test.
c. Is the proportion of respondents using the Internet for shopping the same for males and females? Formulate the null and alternative hypotheses, and conduct the test.
d. Do the respondents differ in their attitude toward the Internet and attitude toward technology? Formulate the null and alternative hypotheses, and conduct the test.

8. In a pretest, respondents were asked to express their preference for an outdoor lifestyle (V1) using a 7-point scale (1 = not at all preferred, 7 = greatly preferred). They were also asked to indicate the importance of the following variables on a 7-point scale (1 = not at all important, 7 = very important).

V2 = enjoying nature
V3 = relating to the weather
V4 = living in harmony with the environment
V5 = exercising regularly
V6 = meeting other people

The sex of the respondent (V7) was coded as 1 = female and 2 = male. The location of residence (V8) was coded as 1 = midtown/downtown, 2 = suburbs, and 3 = countryside. The data obtained are given in the following table.

V1	V2	V3	V4	V5	V6	V7	V8
7.00	3.00	6.00	4.00	5.00	2.00	1.00	1.00
1.00	1.00	1.00	2.00	1.00	2.00	1.00	1.00
6.00	2.00	5.00	4.00	4.00	5.00	1.00	1.00
4.00	3.00	4.00	6.00	3.00	2.00	1.00	1.00
1.00	2.00	2.00	3.00	1.00	2.00	1.00	1.00
6.00	3.00	5.00	4.00	6.00	2.00	1.00	1.00
5.00	3.00	4.00	3.00	4.00	5.00	1.00	1.00
6.00	4.00	5.00	4.00	5.00	1.00	1.00	1.00
3.00	3.00	2.00	2.00	2.00	2.00	1.00	1.00
2.00	4.00	2.00	6.00	2.00	2.00	1.00	1.00
6.00	4.00	5.00	3.00	5.00	5.00	1.00	2.00
2.00	3.00	1.00	4.00	2.00	1.00	1.00	2.00
7.00	2.00	6.00	4.00	5.00	6.00	1.00	2.00
4.00	6.00	4.00	5.00	3.00	3.00	1.00	2.00
1.00	3.00	1.00	2.00	1.00	4.00	1.00	2.00
6.00	6.00	6.00	3.00	4.00	5.00	2.00	2.00
5.00	5.00	6.00	4.00	4.00	6.00	2.00	2.00
7.00	7.00	4.00	4.00	7.00	7.00	2.00	2.00
2.00	6.00	3.00	7.00	4.00	3.00	2.00	2.00
3.00	7.00	3.00	6.00	4.00	4.00	2.00	2.00
1.00	5.00	2.00	6.00	3.00	3.00	2.00	3.00
5.00	6.00	4.00	7.00	5.00	6.00	2.00	3.00
2.00	4.00	1.00	5.00	4.00	4.00	2.00	3.00
4.00	7.00	4.00	7.00	4.00	6.00	2.00	3.00
6.00	7.00	4.00	2.00	1.00	7.00	2.00	3.00
3.00	6.00	4.00	6.00	4.00	4.00	2.00	3.00
4.00	7.00	7.00	4.00	2.00	5.00	2.00	3.00
3.00	7.00	2.00	6.00	4.00	3.00	2.00	3.00
4.00	6.00	3.00	7.00	2.00	7.00	2.00	3.00
5.00	6.00	2.00	6.00	7.00	2.00	2.00	3.00

Using a statistical package of your choice, answer the following questions. In each case, formulate the null and the alternative hypotheses and conduct the appropriate statistical test(s).

a. Does the mean preference for an outdoor lifestyle exceed 3.0?
b. Does the mean importance of enjoying nature exceed 3.5?
c. Does the mean preference for an outdoor lifestyle differ for males and females?
d. Does the importance attached to V2 through V6 differ for males and females?
e. Do the respondents attach more importance to enjoying nature than they do to relating to the weather?
f. Do the respondents attach more importance to relating to the weather than they do to meeting other people?
g. Do the respondents attach more importance to living in harmony with the environment than they do to exercising regularly?

Group Discussion

1. "The *t*-tests are so simple to conduct that they should be used more often in analyzing marketing research data." Discuss as a small group.

2. Which procedure is more useful in marketing research—*t*-test or analysis of variance? Discuss as a small group.

Hewlett-Packard Running Case

Review the Hewlett-Packard (HP) case, Case 1.1, and questionnaire given toward the end of the book. Go to the Web site for this book and download the HP data file.

1. The mean response on which of the evaluations of HP (q8_1 to q8_13) exceeds 5 (the midpoint of the scale)?
2. Are the two overall satisfaction groups derived based on the recoding of q4 as specified in Chapter 15 different in terms of each of the evaluations of HP (q8_1 to q8_13)?
3. Are the two likely to recommend groups derived based on the recoding of q5 as specified in Chapter 15 different in terms of each of the evaluations of HP (q8_1 to q8_13)?
4. Are the two likelihood of choosing HP groups derived based on the recoding of q6 as specified in Chapter 15 different in terms of each of the evaluations of HP (q8_1 to q8_13)?
5. Is the mean of responses to q8_1 (Make ordering a computer system easy) and q8_2 (Let customers order computer systems customized to their specifications) different?
6. Is the mean of responses to q8_9 ("Bundle" its computers with appropriate software) and q8_10 ("Bundle" its computers with Internet access) different?

7. Is the mean of responses to q8_6 (Have computers that run programs quickly) and q8_7 (Have high-quality computers with no technical problems) different?
8. Are the three price-sensitive groups based on q9_5per as derived in Chapter 15 different in terms of each of the evaluations of HP (q8_1 to q8_13)? Interpret the results.
9. Are the three price-sensitive groups based on q9_19per as derived in Chapter 15 different in terms of each of the evaluations of HP (q8_1 to q8_13)? Interpret the results.
10. Do the demographic groups as recoded in Chapter 15 (recoded q11, q12, q13) and q14 differ in terms of overall satisfaction with HP computers (q4)? Interpret the results.
11. Do the demographic groups as recoded in Chapter 15 (recoded q11, q12, q13) and q14 differ in terms of likelihood of recommending HP computers (q5)? Interpret the results.
12. Do the demographic groups as recoded in Chapter 15 (recoded q11, q12, q13) and q14 differ in terms of likelihood of choosing HP computers (q6)? Interpret the results.

Exhibit 17.1 Computer Programs for *t*-Tests

SPSS

The major program for conducting *t*-tests in SPSS is *T-TEST*. This program can be used to conduct *t*-tests on independent as well as paired samples.

SAS

In SAS, the program *T-TEST* can be used to conduct *t*-tests on independent as well as paired samples.

Minitab

Parametric tests available in MINITAB in descriptive stat function are *z*-test mean, *t*-test of the mean, and two-sample *t*-test.

Excel

The available parametric tests in EXCEL and other spreadsheets include the *t*-test paired sample for means, *t*-test: two independent samples assuming equal variances, *t*-test: two independent samples assuming unequal variances, *z*-test: two samples for means, and *F*-test: two samples for variances.

Exhibit 17.2   Computer Programs for Anova

SPSS

One-way ANOVA can be efficiently performed using the program. ONEWAY. For performing more complex analysis of variance, the program ANOVA can be used.

SAS

The main program for performing analysis of variance is ANOVA. This program can handle data from a wide variety of experimental designs.

Minitab

ANOVA can be assessed from the Stats > ANOVA function. This function performs one-way ANOVA and can also handle more complex designs. In order to compute the mean and standard deviation, the cross-tabulation function must be used. To obtain F and p values, use the balanced ANOVA.

Excel

One-way ANOVA and more complex designs can be analyzed under the Tools>Data Analysis function.

eighteen

Data Analysis: Correlation and Regression

OPENING QUESTIONS

1. What is product moment correlation, and how does it provide a foundation for regression analysis?

2. What are the nature and methods of bivariate regression analysis, and how can the general model be described?

3. How can the estimation of parameters, standardized regression coefficient, significance testing, and prediction accuracy in bivariate regression be explained?

4. How does multiple regression differ from bivariate regression?

5. What is the meaning of partial regression coefficients?

Regression Models Model the Marketing Strategy of Adidas

"As marketing research professionals, we continually examine the relationship between consumers' perceptions and ultimate purchase decisions. Consequently, correlation and regression techniques serve as the foundation for many of the most commonly used analytical tools in marketing research."

Jamie Baker-Prewitt, Ph.D.,
Vice President, Marketing and Decision
Support Sciences, Burke, Inc.

German-based Adidas AG (www.adidas.com) is the second largest sportswear manufacturer in the world. It is globally recognized by its official logo of three parallel stripes and had revenues of €10.299 billion in 2007. The company wanted to be a leader in how it brings products to market, in what its products do for the athletes, and in how it services them. Adidas is a sports-performance brand.

Adidas realized that preference for athletic shoes has strong positive correlations with sports-related variables, such as interest in sports, attitude toward sports personalities, attendance at sports events, and time spent watching sports on television. Research by the company revealed that consumers with a greater interest in sports, a more favorable attitude toward sports personalities, or higher attendance at sports events exhibited a stronger preference for brand-name athletic shoes. A multiple regression model with preference for athletic shoes as the dependent variable, and interest in sports, attitude toward sports personalities, attendance at sports events, and time spent watching sports on television as the independent variables had a very good fit. The model fit was determined by strength of association (a measure of

how strongly the dependent variable and the independent variables are related) and the accuracy of predicted values of the dependent variable. The coefficient (partial regression coefficient) associated with each independent variable was positive and significant, indicating that higher values on each independent variable were associated with stronger preference for athletic shoes. Thus, the model had the following form:

Estimated preference for athletic shoes = $a + b_1$ (interest in sports) + b_2 (attitude toward sports personalities) + b_3 (attendance at sports events) + b_4 (time spent watching sports on television)

Where a = constant, and b_1, b_2, b_3, and b_4 are positive partial regression coefficients.

Armed with such information, Adidas attempted to boost the visibility of its brand with star athletes. It featured Muhammad Ali; Ali's daughter, Laila, also a world champion boxer; European soccer icons David Beckham and Zinedine Zidane; Thai tennis star Paradorn Srichaphan; Ethiopian long-distance runner Haile Gebrselassie; and American basketball player Tracy McGrady. As of 2008, Adidas had the tag line of "Impossible is nothing." Regression models have played a key role in the development of Adidas' marketing strategy.[1]

Overview

This chapter describes regression analysis, which is widely used for explaining variation in a dependent variable in terms of a set of independent variables. In marketing, the dependent variable could be market share, sales, or brand preference, and the independent variables could be marketing management variables, such as advertising, price, distribution, product quality, and demographic and lifestyles variables. This was illustrated in the opening vignette, where the regression model had preference for athletic shoes as the dependent variable and sports-related lifestyle variables as the independent variables.

However, before discussing regression, the concept of the product moment correlation, or the correlation coefficient, which lays the conceptual foundation for regression analysis, will be described. Figure 18.1 briefly explains the focus of the chapter, the relationship of this chapter to the previous ones, and the steps of the marketing research process on which this chapter concentrates.

A simple bivariate case is presented to introduce regression analysis. The chapter describes estimation, standardization of the regression coefficients, and testing and examination of the strength and significance of association between variables, prediction accuracy, and the assumptions underlying the regression model. Next, the multiple regression model is presented, with an emphasis on the interpretation of parameters, strength of association, significance tests, and examination of residuals. Help for running the SPSS and Excel programs used in this chapter is provided is four ways: (1) detailed step-by-step instructions are given later in the chapter, (2) you can download (from the Web site for this book) computerized demonstration movies illustrating these step-by-step instructions, (3) you can download screen captures with notes illustrating these step-by-step instructions, and (4) you can refer to the Study Guide and Technology Manual, a supplement that accompanies this book. Figure 18.2 provides an overview of the different topics discussed in this chapter and how they flow from one to the next.

FIGURE 18.1

Relationship of Correlation and Regression to the Previous Chapters and the Marketing Research Process

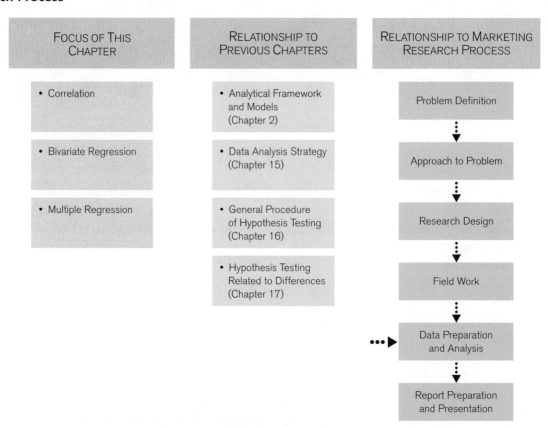

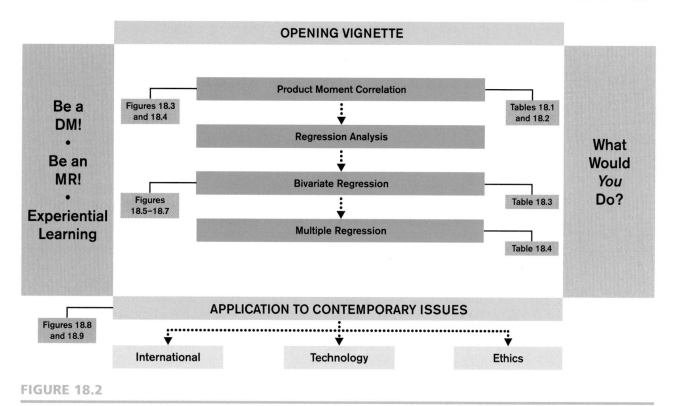

FIGURE 18.2

Correlation and Regression: An Overview

Fundamental to regression analysis is an understanding of the product moment correlation.

Product Moment Correlation

In marketing research, researchers often are interested in summarizing the strength of association between two metric variables, as in the following situations:

- How strongly are sales related to advertising expenditures?
- Is there an association between market share and size of the sales force?
- Are consumers' perceptions of quality related to their perceptions of price?

In situations like these, the **product moment correlation** is used. The product moment correlation, which is denoted by r, is the most widely used statistic that summarizes the strength and direction of association between two metric (interval- or ratio-scaled) variables, say X and Y. It is used to determine whether a linear or straight-line relationship exists between X and Y, as well as the degree to which the variation in one variable, X, is related to the variation in another variable, Y. Because it was originally proposed by British mathematician Karl Pearson, it also is known as the *Pearson correlation coefficient*. Other terms used to refer to the product moment correlation are *simple correlation*, *bivariate correlation*, or merely the *correlation coefficient*.

In the opening vignette, preference for athletic shoes showed strong positive correlations with sports-related variables, such as interest in sports, attitude toward sports personalities, attendance at sports events, and time spent watching sports on television. From a sample of n observations, X and Y, the product moment correlation, r, can be calculated as:

product moment correlation (r)
A statistic summarizing the strength of linear association between two metric variables.

$$r = \frac{\sum_{i=1}^{n}(X_i - \overline{X})(Y_i - \overline{Y})}{\sqrt{\sum_{i=1}^{n}(X_i - \overline{X})^2 \sum_{i=1}^{n}(Y_i - \overline{Y})^2}}$$

Division of the numerator and denominator by $(n - 1)$ gives

$$r = \frac{\displaystyle\sum_{i=1}^{n} \frac{(X_i - \overline{X})(Y_i - \overline{Y})}{n - 1}}{\sqrt{\displaystyle\sum_{i=1}^{n} \frac{(X_i - \overline{X})^2}{n - 1} \sum_{i=1}^{n} \frac{(Y_i - \overline{Y})^2}{n - 1}}}$$

$$= \frac{COV_{xy}}{s_x \, s_y}$$

covariance

A systematic relationship between two variables in which a change in one implies a corresponding change in the other (COV_{xy}).

In these equations, $\overline{X}$ and $\overline{Y}$ denote the sample means and s_x and s_y the standard deviations. COV_{xy}, the **covariance** between X and Y, measures the extent to which X and Y are related. The covariance can be either positive or negative. Division by $s_x s_y$ achieves standardization, so that r varies between -1.0 and $+1.0$. Note that the correlation coefficient is an absolute number and is not expressed in any unit of measurement. The correlation coefficient between two variables will be the same regardless of their underlying units of measurement.

As an example, suppose a researcher wants to explain attitudes toward sports cars (attitude) in terms of the number of years the respondent has owned a sports car (duration). The attitude is measured on an 11-point scale (1 = do not like sports cars, 11 = very much like sports cars), and the duration of car ownership is measured in terms of the number of years the respondent has owned one or more sports cars. In a pretest of 12 respondents, the data shown in Table 18.1 were obtained. This table gives the data for only 12 respondents, because we want to show the calculations of the basic statistics by hand. We think that it is important to show these hand calculations so that you can get a better idea of the basic concepts. In practice, the sample size is much larger. We illustrate the analysis of such large data sets later in the chapter in an Experiential Learning exercise that analyzes the data for 146 respondents in a survey for Musial University.

The correlation coefficient between attitude and duration based on the data of Table 18.1 is calculated as follows:

$$\overline{X} = (10 + 12 + 12 + 4 + 12 + 6 + 8 + 2 + 18 + 9 + 17 + 2)/12$$

$$= 9.333$$

$$\overline{Y} = (6 + 9 + 8 + 3 + 10 + 4 + 5 + 2 + 11 + 9 + 10 + 2)/12$$

$$= 6.583$$

TABLE 18.1 Explaining Attitude Toward Sports Cars

Respondent Number	Attitude Toward Sports Cars	Duration of Car Ownership	Importance Attached to Performance
1	6	10	3
2	9	12	11
3	8	12	4
4	3	4	1
5	10	12	11
6	4	6	1
7	5	8	7
8	2	2	4
9	11	18	8
10	9	9	10
11	10	17	8
12	2	2	5

$$\sum_{i=1}^{n}(X_i - \overline{X})(Y_i - \overline{Y}) = (10 - 9.33)(6 - 6.58) + (12 - 9.33)(9 - 6.58)$$

$$+ (12 - 9.33)(8 - 6.58) + (4 - 9.33)(3 - 6.58)$$

$$+ (12 - 9.33)(10 - 6.58) + (6 - 9.33)(4 - 6.58)$$

$$+ (8 - 9.33)(5 - 6.58) + (2 - 9.33)(2 - 6.58)$$

$$+ (18 - 9.33)(11 - 6.58) + (9 - 9.33)(9 - 6.58)$$

$$+ (17 - 9.33)(10 - 6.58) + (2 - 9.33)(2 - 6.58)$$

$$= -0.3886 + 6.4614 + 3.7914 + 19.0814$$

$$+ 9.1314 + 8.5914 + 2.1014 + 33.5714$$

$$+ 38.3214 - 0.7986 + 26.2314 + 33.5714$$

$$= 179.6668$$

$$\sum_{i=1}^{n}(X_i - \overline{X})^2 = (10 - 9.33)^2 + (12 - 9.33)^2 + (12 - 9.33)^2 + (4 - 9.33)^2$$

$$+ (12 - 9.33)^2 + (6 - 9.33)^2 + (8 - 9.33)^2 + (2 - 9.33)^2$$

$$+ (18 - 9.33)^2 + (9 - 9.33)^2 + (17 - 9.33)^2 + (2 - 9.33)^2$$

$$= 0.4489 + 7.1289 + 7.1289 + 28.4089$$

$$+ 7.1289 + 11.0889 + 1.7689 + 53.7289$$

$$+ 75.1689 + 0.1089 + 58.8289 + 53.7289$$

$$= 304.6668$$

$$\sum_{i=1}^{n}(Y_i - \overline{Y})^2 = (6 - 6.58)^2 + (9 - 6.58)^2 + (8 - 6.58)^2 + (3 - 6.58)^2$$

$$+ (10 - 6.58)^2 + (4 - 6.58)^2 + (5 - 6.58)^2 + (2 - 6.58)^2$$

$$+ (11 - 6.58)^2 + (9 - 6.58)^2 + (10 - 6.58)^2 + (2 - 6.58)^2$$

$$= 0.3364 + 5.8564 + 2.0164 + 12.8164$$

$$+ 11.6964 + 6.6564 + 2.4964 + 20.9764$$

$$+ 19.5364 + 5.8564 + 11.6964 + 20.9764$$

$$= 120.9168$$

Thus,

$$r = \frac{179.6668}{\sqrt{(304.6668)(120.9168)}}$$

or

$$r = \frac{179.6668}{(17.4547)(10.9962)}$$

$$= 0.9361$$

These calculations are summarized in Table 18.2. The product moment correlation can also be calculated using SPSS and Excel, and the corresponding outputs with explanatory notes can be downloaded from the Web site for this book. In this example, the value of r, 0.9361, is close to 1.0. This means that the number of years a respondent has owned a sports car is strongly associated with the respondent's attitude toward sports cars. Thus, the length of time a person has owned a sports car is positively related to degree of favorableness of the attitude toward sports cars. Furthermore, the positive sign of r implies a positive relationship; the longer the duration of sports car ownership, the more favorable the attitude, and vice versa. For example, if John has owned a sports car much longer than Paul, John is likely to have a much more favorable attitude toward sports cars than Paul. Over many years of ownership, John sees his sports car as a treasured possession. In contrast, Paul has only recently purchased a sports car and has yet to develop such strong feelings toward it. This can be seen from a plot of Y (attitude toward sports cars) against X (duration of sports car ownership) given in Figure 18.3. The points seem to be arranged in a band running from the bottom left to the top right.

TABLE 18.2 **Calculation of the Product Moment Correlation**

Number	Attitude (Y)	Duration (X)	$(X_i - \overline{X})$	$(X_i - \overline{X})^2$	$(Y_i - \overline{Y})$	$(Y_i - \overline{Y})^2$	$(X_i - \overline{X})(Y_i - \overline{Y})$
1	6	10	0.667	0.4489	−0.583	0.3364	−0.3886
2	9	12	2.667	7.1289	2.417	5.8564	6.4614
3	8	12	2.667	7.1289	1.417	2.0164	3.7914
4	3	4	−5.333	28.4089	−3.583	12.8164	19.0814
5	10	12	2.667	7.1289	3.417	11.6964	9.1314
6	4	6	−3.333	11.0889	−2.583	6.5664	8.5914
7	5	8	−1.333	1.7689	−1.583	2.4964	2.1014
8	2	2	−7.333	53.7289	−4.583	20.9764	3.5714
9	11	18	8.667	75.1689	7.417	19.5364	38.3214
10	9	9	−0.333	0.1089	2.417	5.8564	−0.7986
11	10	17	7.667	58.8289	3.417	11.6964	26.2314
12	2	2	−7.333	53.7289	−4.583	20.9764	33.5714
Mean	6.583	9.333					
Sum				304.6668		120.9168	179.6668

Using the above values the product moment correlation can be calculated as

$$r = \frac{\sum_{i=1}^{n}(X_i - \overline{X})(Y_i - \overline{Y})}{\sqrt{\sum_{i=1}^{n}(X_i - \overline{X})^2 \sum_{i=1}^{n}(Y_i - \overline{Y})^2}}$$

or

$$r = \frac{179.6668}{\sqrt{(304.6668)(120.9168)}} = \frac{179.6668}{(17.4547)(10.9962)} = 0.9361$$

FIGURE 18.3

Plot of Attitude with Duration of Sports Car Ownership

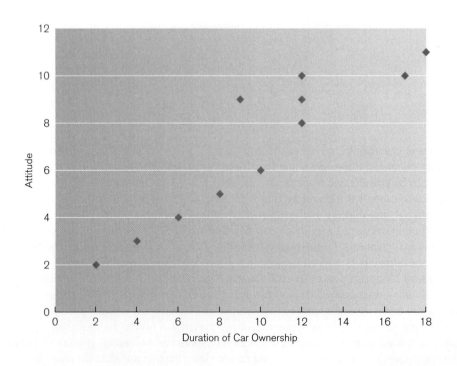

Because r indicates the degree to which variation in one variable is related to variation in another, it can also be expressed in terms of the decomposition of the total variation (see the explanation in Chapter 17). In other words,

$$r^2 = \frac{\text{Explained variation}}{\text{Total variation}}$$

$$= \frac{SS_x}{SS_y}$$

$$= \frac{\text{Total variation} - \text{Error variation}}{\text{Total variation}}$$

$$= \frac{SS_y - SS_{error}}{SS_y}$$

Therefore, r^2 measures the proportion of variation in one variable that is explained by the other. Both r and r^2 are symmetric measures of association. In other words, the correlation of X with Y is the same as the correlation of Y with X. It does not matter which variable is considered the dependent variable and which the independent. The product moment coefficient measures the strength of the linear relationship and is not designed to measure nonlinear relationships. Thus $r = 0$ merely indicates that there is no linear relationship between X and Y. It does not mean that X and Y are unrelated. A nonlinear relationship between them could exist that is not captured by r (Figure 18.4).

When it is computed for a population rather than a sample, the product moment correlation is denoted by ρ, the Greek letter rho. The coefficient r is an estimator of ρ. Note that the calculation of r assumes that X and Y are metric variables whose distributions have the same shape. If these assumptions are not met, r is deflated and underestimates ρ. In marketing research, data obtained by using rating scales with a small number of categories might not be strictly interval. This tends to deflate r, resulting in an underestimation of ρ.

The statistical significance of the relationship between two variables measured by using r can be conveniently tested. The hypotheses are:

$$H_0\text{: } \rho = 0$$

$$H_1\text{: } \rho \neq 0$$

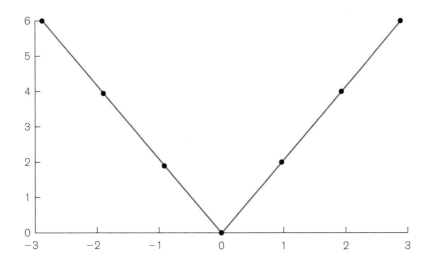

FIGURE 18.4

A Nonlinear Relationship for Which $r = 0$

The test statistic is:

$$t = r \left[\frac{n - 2}{1 - r^2} \right]^{1/2}$$

which has a t distribution with $n - 2$ degrees of freedom. For the correlation coefficient calculated based on the data given in Table 18.1,

$$t = 0.9361 \left[\frac{12 - 2}{1 - (0.9361)^2} \right]^{1/2}$$

or

$$t = 0.9361 \left[\frac{10}{0.1237} \right]^{1/2}$$

or

$$t = 0.9381 [80.8407]^{1/2}$$

$$= 0.9361 \times 8.991$$

$$= 8.414$$

and the degrees of freedom is $12 - 2 = 10$. From the t distribution table (Table 4 in the Appendix of Statistical Tables), the critical value of t for a two-tailed test and $\alpha = 0.05$ is 2.2281. Hence, the null hypothesis of no relationship between X and Y is rejected. This, along with the positive sign of r, indicates that attitude toward sports cars is positively related to the duration of sports car ownership. Moreover, the high value of r indicates that this relationship is strong. The usefulness of the product moment correlation, r, in assessing linear relationships is illustrated by the following example.

Research in Action

It's a Small World

A recent study analyzed the ratings of 186 countries on seven dimensions of quality of life (QOL): favorable cost of living (COL), culture (CUL), economy (ECON), freedom (FREE), infrastructure (INFRA), health (HEA), and environment (ENV). The simple correlations between these dimensions are as follows:

	COL	CUL	ECON	FREE	INFRA	HEA	ENV
COL	1.0						
CUL	−.03	1.0					
ECON	.27*	.66*	1.0				
FREE	−.05	.57*	.46*	1.0			
INFRA	−.26*	.76*	.85*	.55*	1.0		
HEA	−.03	.78*	.59*	.47*	.70*	1.0	
ENV	−.05	.04	−.02	.10	−.01	−.07	1.0

*Indicates correlation is statistically significant at $\alpha = .05$

The magnitude of the correlation indicates the extent to which the two QOL dimensions are interrelated. The highest correlation of .85 is observed between INFRA and ECON, indicating that infrastructure and economic development are highly interrelated. In contrast, there is no relationship between infrastructure and environment ($r = -.01$). Based on ratings on the QOL dimensions, the 186 countries were classified into 12 clusters or groups. The 10th cluster, which consisted of 19 developed countries, including the United States, Canada, the United Kingdom, Japan, France, Germany, and the Scandinavian countries, represented the highest QOL.

Country policy makers can use this information to identify possible rival countries, to direct investment, and to form alliances with countries having complementary resources, cultures, and economic development.[2]

The product moment provides a conceptual foundation for bivariate as well as multiple regression analysis.

Regression Analysis

Regression analysis is a powerful and flexible procedure for analyzing associative relationships between a metric-dependent variable and one or more independent variables. It can be used in the following ways:

1. Determine whether the independent variables explain a significant variation in the dependent variable: whether a relationship exists.
2. Determine how much of the variation in the dependent variable can be explained by the independent variables: strength of the relationship.
3. Determine the structure or form of the relationship: the mathematical equation relating the independent and dependent variables.
4. Predict the values of the dependent variable.
5. Control for other independent variables when evaluating the contributions of a specific variable or set of variables.

Although the independent variables can explain the variation in the dependent variable, this does not necessarily imply causation. The use of the terms *dependent* or *criterion* variables and *independent* or *predictor* variables in regression analysis arises from the mathematical relationship between the variables. These terms do not imply that the criterion variable is dependent on the independent variables in a causal sense, because at least two of the three criteria for causation discussed in Chapter 8 (time order of occurrence of variables and absence of other causal factors) might not be satisfied. Regression analysis is concerned with the nature and degree of association between variables and does not imply or assume any causality. We will discuss bivariate regression first, followed by multiple regression.

regression analysis
A statistical procedure for analyzing associative relationships between a dependent metric variable and one or more independent variables.

Bivariate Regression

Bivariate regression is a procedure for deriving a mathematical relationship, in the form of an equation, between a single metric dependent or criterion variable and a single metric independent or predictor variable. The analysis is similar in many ways to determining the simple correlation between two variables. However, because an equation has to be derived, one variable must be identified as the dependent variable and the other as the independent variable. For example, the economic growth rate of the European Union (EU) has a positive correlation with the level of consumer spending. Thus, a **bivariate regression model** could be constructed with the economic growth rate of the EU as the dependent variable and the level of consumer spending as the independent variable. The examples of simple correlation given earlier can be translated into the regression context:

bivariate regression
A procedure for deriving a mathematical relationship, in the form of an equation, between a single dependent metric variable and a single independent metric variable.

bivariate regression model
An equation used to explain regression analysis in which one independent variable is regressed onto a single dependent variable.

- Can variation in sales be explained in terms of variation in advertising expenditures? What is the structure and form of this relationship, and can it be modeled mathematically by an equation describing a straight line?
- Can the variation in market share be accounted for by the size of the sales force?
- Are consumers' perceptions of quality determined by their perceptions of price?

Conducting Bivariate Regression Analysis

The steps involved in conducting bivariate regression analysis are described in Figure 18.5. Suppose the researcher wants to explain attitudes toward sports cars in terms of the duration of car ownership (see Table 18.1). In deriving such relationships, it often is useful to first examine a scatter diagram.

FIGURE 18.5

**Conducting Bivariate
Regression Analysis**

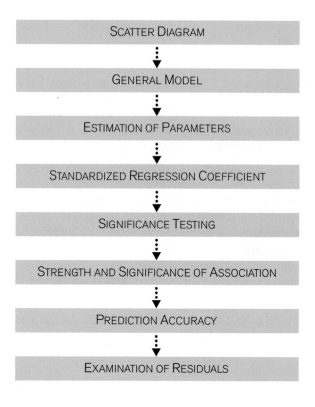

SCATTER DIAGRAM

GENERAL MODEL

ESTIMATION OF PARAMETERS

STANDARDIZED REGRESSION COEFFICIENT

SIGNIFICANCE TESTING

STRENGTH AND SIGNIFICANCE OF ASSOCIATION

PREDICTION ACCURACY

EXAMINATION OF RESIDUALS

Scatter Diagram

**scatter diagram
(scattergram)**
A plot of the values of two
variables for all the cases or
observations.

A **scatter diagram**, or *scattergram*, is a plot of the values of two variables for all the cases or observations. It is customary to plot the dependent variable on the vertical axis and the independent variable on the horizontal axis. A scatter diagram is useful for determining the form of the relationship between the variables. It also can alert the researcher to any patterns or problems in the data. Any unusual combinations of the two variables can be easily identified. A plot of Y (attitude toward sports cars) against X (duration of car owner-ship) was given in Figure 18.3. The points seem to be arranged in a band running from the bottom left to the top right.

One can see the pattern: as one variable increases, so does the other. It appears from this scattergram that the relationship between X and Y is linear and that it could be well described by a straight line. By fitting the best straight line to the data, the equation of the line gives the estimate of the underlying relationship in the data. How should the straight line be fitted to best describe the data?

least-squares procedure
A technique for fitting a straight
line to a scattergram by minimizing
the sum of square of the vertical
distances of all the points from
the line.

The most commonly used technique for fitting a straight line to a scattergram is the **least-squares procedure**. This technique determines the best-fitting line by minimizing the sum of square of the vertical distances of all the points from the line. The best fitting line is called the *regression line*. Any point that does not fall on the regression line is not fully accounted for. The vertical distance from the point to the line is the error, e_j (Figure 18.6). The distances of all the points from the line are squared and added together to arrive at the sum of the squared errors, which is a measure of total error. The equation for the total error is

$$\sum e_j^2$$

sum of squared errors
The sum of the squared vertical
differences between the actual
data point and the predicted one
on the regression line.

In fitting the line, the least-squares procedure minimizes the **sum of squared errors**. If Y is plotted on the vertical axis and X on the horizontal axis, as in Figure 18.6, the best-fitting line is called the regression of Y on X, because the square of the vertical distances is minimized. The scatter diagram indicates whether the relationship between Y and X can be modeled as a straight line, and, consequently, whether the bivariate regression model is appropriate.

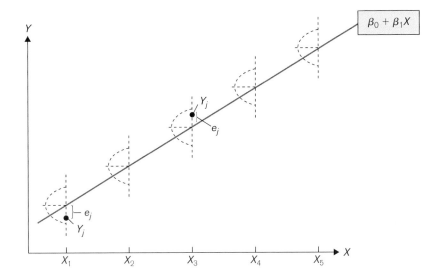

FIGURE 18.6

Bivariate Regression

Bivariate Regression Model

In the bivariate regression model, the general form of a straight line is:

$$Y = \beta_0 + \beta_1 X$$

where

Y = dependent or criterion variable

X = independent or predictor variable

β_0 = intercept of the line

β_1 = slope of the line

This equation is very similar to the equation of a straight line with which you are familiar: $y = mx + b$, with $b = \beta_0$, and $m = \beta_1$. This model implies a deterministic relationship, in that Y is completely determined by X. The value of Y can be perfectly predicted if β_0 and β_1 are known. In marketing research, however, very few relationships are deterministic. Thus, the regression procedure adds an error term to account for the probabilistic or stochastic nature of the relationship. The basic regression equation becomes:

$$Y_i = \beta_0 + \beta_1 X + e_i$$

where e_i is the error term associated with the ith observation.[3] Estimation of the regression parameters, β_0 and β_1, is relatively simple.

Estimation of Parameters

In most cases, β_0 and β_1 are unknown and are estimated from the sample observations using the equation

$$\hat{Y}_i = a + bX_i$$

Where $\hat{Y}_i$ is the **estimated or predicted value** of Y_i, and a and b are estimators of β_0 and β_1, respectively. The constant b is usually referred to as the *nonstandardized regression coefficient*. It is the slope of the regression line, and it indicates the expected change in Y when X is changed by one unit. The formulas for calculating a and b are simple.

estimated or predicted value
The value $\hat{Y}_i = a + bX_i$ where $\hat{Y}_i$ is the estimated or predicted value of Y_i, and a and b are estimators of β_0 and β_1, respectively.

The slope, b, can be computed in terms of the covariance between X and Y (COV_{xy}) and the variance of X as:

$$b = \frac{COV_{xy}}{s_x^2}$$

$$= \frac{\displaystyle\sum_{i=1}^{n}(X_i - \overline{X})(Y_i - \overline{Y})}{\displaystyle\sum_{i=1}^{n}(X_i - \overline{X})^2}$$

$$= \frac{\displaystyle\sum_{i=1}^{n}X_i Y_i - n\overline{X}\,\overline{Y}}{\displaystyle\sum_{i=1}^{n}X_i^2 - n\overline{X}^2}$$

The intercept, a, can then be calculated using:

$$a = \overline{Y} - b\overline{X}$$

For the data in Table 18.1, the estimation of parameters for the regression of attitude (Y) on duration (X) can be illustrated as follows:

$$\begin{aligned}
\sum_{i=1}^{12}X_i Y_i &= (10)(6) + (12)(9) + (12)(8) + (4)(3) + (12)(10) + (6)(4) \\
&\quad + (8)(5) + (2)(2) + (18)(11) + (9)(9) + (17)(10) + (2)(2) \\
&= 917
\end{aligned}$$

$$\begin{aligned}
\sum_{i=1}^{12}X_i^2 &= 10^2 + 12^2 + 12^2 + 4^2 + 12^2 + 6^2 \\
&\quad + 8^2 + 2^2 + 18^2 + 9^2 + 17^2 + 2^2 \\
&= 1350
\end{aligned}$$

Recall from earlier calculations of the simple correlation that

$$\overline{X} = 9.333$$
$$\overline{Y} = 6.583$$

Given $n = 12$, b can be calculated as:

$$b = \frac{917 - (12)(9.333)(6.583)}{1350 - (12)(9.333)^2}$$

or

$$\begin{aligned}
b &= \frac{917 - 737.270}{1350 - 1045.259} \\
&= \frac{179.73}{304.741} \\
&= 0.5897
\end{aligned}$$

$$\begin{aligned}
a &= \overline{Y} - b\overline{X} \\
&= 6.583 - (0.5897)(9.333) \\
&= 6.583 - 5.504 \\
&= 1.079
\end{aligned}$$

Note that these coefficients have been estimated on the raw (untransformed) data. Should standardization of the data be considered desirable, the calculation of the standardized coefficients also is straightforward.

Using software and the data shown in Table 18.1, the regression of attitude on duration of car ownership yielded the results shown in Table 18.3. The corresponding SPSS and

TABLE 18.3 Bivariate Regression

Multiple R	.9361
R^2	.8762
Adjusted R^2	.8639
Standard Error	1.2233

Analysis of Variance

	df	Sum of Squares	Mean Square
Regression	1	105.9522	105.9522
Residual	10	14.9644	1.4964
$F = 70.8027$		Significance of $F = .0000$	

Variables in the Equation

Variable	b	SE_b	Beta (B)	T	Sig. T
Duration	.5897	.0701	.9361	8.414	.0000
(Constant)	1.0793	.7434		1.452	.1772

Excel outputs with explanatory notes can be downloaded from the Web site for this book. The intercept, a, equals 1.0793, and the slope, b, equals 0.5897, as shown earlier by hand calculations. Therefore, the estimated equation is:

$$\text{Attitude}(\hat{Y}) = 1.0793 + 0.5897 \text{ (Duration of car ownership)}$$

Standardized Regression Coefficient

Standardization is the process by which the raw data are transformed into new variables that have a mean of 0 and a variance of 1. This process is similar to the calculation of z values discussed earlier (Chapters 13, 16, and 17). To standardize a variable, simply subtract the mean and divide the difference by the standard deviation. When the data (both the independent and the dependent variable) are standardized, the intercept assumes a value of 0. The term

standardization
The process by which the raw data are transformed into new variables that have a mean of 0 and a variance of 1.

Attitude toward sports cars can be explained by the duration of sports car ownership using bivariate regression.

**beta coefficient
(beta weight)**
Denotes the standardized
regression coefficient.

beta coefficient, or *beta weight*, is used to denote the standardized regression coefficient. Standardization is sometimes desirable because it is easier to compare the beta coefficients than it is to compare the raw coefficients. In this case, the slope obtained by the regression of Y on X, B_{yx}, is the same as the slope obtained by the regression of X on Y, B_{xy}. Moreover, each of these regression coefficients is equal to the simple correlation between X and Y.

$$B_{yx} = B_{xy} = r_{xy}$$

Thus, instead of running product moment correlations in the opening vignette, we could have alternatively run four separate bivariate regressions on the standardized data, with preference for athletic shoes as the dependent variable. Each of the independent variables, in turn, would serve as the independent, or predictor, variable: interest in sports, attitude toward sports personalities, attendance at sports events, and time spent watching sports on television.

A simple relationship exists between the standardized and nonstandardized regression coefficients:

$$B_{yx} = b_{yx} (s_x/s_y)$$

To illustrate the calculation of the beta coefficient by hand for the bivariate regression of Table 18.1, recall from the hand calculations for the correlation coefficient that

$$\sum_{i=1}^{n}(Y_i - \overline{Y})^2 = 120.9168$$

Therefore,

$$s_y = \sqrt{\frac{120.9168}{(12 - 1)}}$$

$$= 3.3155$$

and,

$$\sum_{i=1}^{n}(X_i - \overline{X})^2 = 304.6668$$

Therefore,

$$s_x = \sqrt{\frac{304.6668}{(12 - 1)}}$$

$$= 5.2628$$

Therefore,

$$B_{yx} = (0.5897)(5.2628)/(3.3155)$$

$$= 0.9361$$

For the regression results given in Table 18.3, the value of the beta coefficient also is estimated as 0.9361. Note that this is also the value of r calculated earlier in this chapter.

Once the parameters have been estimated, they can be tested for significance.

Significance Testing

The statistical significance of the linear relationship between X and Y can be tested by examining the hypotheses:

$$H_0: \beta_1 = 0$$

$$H_1: \beta_1 \neq 0$$

The null hypothesis implies that there is no linear relationship between X and Y. The alternative hypothesis is that there is a relationship, positive or negative, between X and Y. For example, the relationship between income and the number of times people dine out in a month can be statistically tested via bivariate regression. The null hypothesis would be that income has no relationship with the number of times people dine out in a month. The alternative hypothesis would be that income has a positive relationship with the number of times people dine out in a month. If the null hypothesis is not rejected, then it can be concluded that there is no relationship between X and Y, even though the regression coefficient might not be exactly zero. Typically, a two-tailed test is done. A t statistic with $n - 2$ degrees of freedom can be used, where

$$t = \frac{b}{SE_b}$$

SE_b denotes the standard deviation of b and is called the **standard error**.[4] The t distribution was discussed in Chapter 17.

The standard error or standard deviation of b is estimated as 0.07008, and the value of the t statistic is $t = 0.5897/0.07008 = 8.414$, with $n - 2 = 10$ degrees of freedom (see Table 18.3). From Table 4 in the Appendix of Statistical Tables, we see that the critical value of t with 10 degrees of freedom and $\alpha = 0.05$ is 2.228 for a two-tailed test. Because the calculated value of t is larger than the critical value, the null hypothesis is rejected. Hence, a significant linear relationship exists between attitude toward sports cars and duration of car ownership. The positive sign of the slope coefficient indicates that this relationship is positive. In other words, those who have owned sports cars for a longer time have more favorable attitudes toward sports cars, indicating a stronger liking for these cars.

standard error
Denotes the standard deviation of b.

Strength and Significance of Association

A related inference involves determining the strength and significance of the association between Y and X. The strength of association is measured by the **coefficient of determination**, r^2. In bivariate regression, r^2 is the square of the simple correlation coefficient obtained by correlating the two variables. The coefficient r^2 varies between 0 and 1. It signifies the proportion of the total variation in Y that is accounted for by the variation in X. The decomposition of the total variation in Y is similar to that for analysis of variance (see Chapter 17). As shown in Figure 18.7, the total variation, SS_y, can be decomposed into the variation accounted for by the regression line, SS_{reg}, and the error or residual variation, SS_{error} or SS_{res}, as follows:

coefficient of determination
The proportion of variance in one variable associated with the variability in a second variable.

$$SS_y = SS_{reg} + SS_{res}$$

where

$$SS_y = \sum_{i=1}^{n}(Y_i - \overline{Y})^2$$

$$SS_{reg} = \sum_{i=1}^{n}(\hat{Y}_i - \overline{Y})^2$$

$$SS_{res} = \sum_{i=1}^{n}(Y_i - \hat{Y}_i)^2$$

The strength of association may then be calculated as follows:

$$r^2 = \frac{SS_{reg}}{SS_y}$$

$$= \frac{SS_y - SS_{res}}{SS_y}$$

FIGURE 18.7

Decomposition of the Total Variation in Bivariate Regression

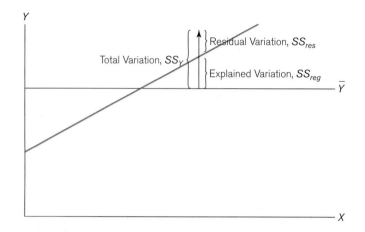

To illustrate the calculations of r^2, consider again the effect of the duration of car ownership on attitude toward sports cars. Recall from earlier hand calculations of the simple correlation coefficient that:

$$SS_y = \sum_{i=1}^{n} (Y_i - \bar{Y})^2$$

$$= 120.9168$$

The predicted values ($\hat{Y}$) can be calculated using the regression equation:

$$\text{Attitude } (\hat{Y}) = 1.0793 + 0.5897 \text{ (Duration of car ownership)}$$

For the first observation in Table 18.1, this value is:

$$(\hat{Y}) = 1.0793 + 0.5897 \times 10 = 6.9763$$

For each successive observation, the predicted values are, in order, 8.1557, 8.1557, 3.4381, 8.1557, 4.6175, 5.7969, 2.2587, 11.6939, 6.3866, 11.1042, and 2.2587. Therefore,

$$
\begin{aligned}
SS_{reg} = \sum_{i=1}^{n} (\hat{Y}_i - \bar{Y})^2 = & \ (6.9763 - 6.5833)^2 + (8.1557 - 6.5833)^2 \\
& + (8.1557 - 6.5833)^2 + (3.4381 - 6.5833)^2 \\
& + (8.1557 - 6.5833)^2 + (4.6175 - 6.5833)^2 \\
& + (5.7969 - 6.5833)^2 + (2.2587 - 6.5833)^2 \\
& + (11.6939 - 6.5833)^2 + (6.3866 - 6.5833)^2 \\
& + (11.1042 - 6.5833)^2 + (2.2587 - 6.5833)^2 \\
= & \ 0.1544 + 2.4724 + 2.4724 + 9.8922 + 2.4724 \\
& + 3.8643 + 0.6184 + 18.7021 + 26.1182 \\
& + 0.0387 + 20.4385 + 18.7021 \\
= & \ 105.9522
\end{aligned}
$$

$$
\begin{aligned}
SS_{res} = \sum_{i=1}^{n} (Y_i - \hat{Y}_i)^2 = & \ (6 - 6.9763)^2 + (9 - 8.1557)^2 + (8 - 8.1557)^2 \\
& + (3 - 3.4381)^2 + (10 - 8.1557)^2 + (4 - 4.6175)^2 \\
& + (5 - 5.7969)^2 + (2 - 2.2587)^2 + (11 - 11.6939)^2 \\
& + (9 - 6.3866)^2 + (10 - 11.1042)^2 + (2 - 2.2587)^2 \\
= & \ 14.9644
\end{aligned}
$$

It can be seen that $SS_y = SS_{reg} + SS_{res}$. Furthermore,

$$r^2 = SS_{reg}/SS_y$$
$$= 105.9524/120.9168$$
$$= 0.8762$$

Another, equivalent test for examining the significance of the linear relationship between X and Y (significance of b) is the test for the significance of the coefficient of determination. The hypotheses in this case are:

$$H_0: R^2_{pop} = 0$$
$$H_1: R^2_{pop} > 0$$

The appropriate test statistic is the F statistic:

$$F = \frac{SS_{reg}}{SS_{res}/(n-2)}$$

which has an F distribution with 1 and $n-2$ degrees of freedom. The F-test is a generalized form of the t-test (see Chapter 17). If a random variable is t distributed with n degrees of freedom, then t^2 is F distributed with 1 and n degrees of freedom. Hence, the F-test for testing the significance of the coefficient of determination is equivalent to testing the following hypotheses:

$$H_0: \beta_1 = 0$$
$$H_1: \beta_1 \neq 0$$

or

$$H_0: \rho = 0$$
$$H_1: \rho \neq 0$$

From Table 18.3, it can be seen that:

$$r^2 = 105.9522/(105.9522 + 14.9644)$$
$$= 0.8762$$

Which is the same as the value calculated earlier by hand. The value of the F statistic is:

$$F = 105.9522/(14.9644/10)$$
$$= 70.8027$$

with 1 and 10 degrees of freedom. The calculated F statistic exceeds the critical value of 4.96 determined from Table 5 in the Appendix of Statistical Tables. Therefore, the relationship is significant at $\alpha = 0.05$, corroborating the results of the t-test. If the relationship between X and Y is significant, it is meaningful to predict the values of Y based on the values of X and to estimate prediction accuracy.

Prediction Accuracy

To estimate the accuracy of predicted values, $\hat{Y}$, it is useful to calculate the **standard error of estimate** (SEE). This statistic is the standard deviation of the actual Y values from the predicted $\hat{Y}$ values. The larger the SEE is, the poorer the fit of the regression. From Table 18.3, it can be seen that SEE is 1.2233. The SEE can be used for constructing confidence intervals around predicted values of Y (see Chapter 13).

standard error of estimate (SEE)
The standard deviation of the actual $\hat{Y}$ values from the predicted $\hat{Y}$ values.

Assumptions

The regression model makes a number of assumptions in estimating the parameters and in significance testing, as shown in Figure 18.6:

1. The error term is normally distributed. For each fixed value of X, the distribution of Y is normal.

2. The means of all these normal distributions of Y, given X, lie on a straight line with slope b.
3. The mean of the error term is 0.
4. The variance of the error term is constant. This variance does not depend on the values assumed by X.
5. The error terms are uncorrelated. In other words, the observations have been drawn independently.

Insights into the extent to which these assumptions have been met can be gained by an examination of residuals, which is covered in the next section on multiple regression.

The following example illustrates how regression analysis can result in findings with great managerial relevance.

Research in Action

Avoiding Dissatisfaction to Enhance Overall Satisfaction

A large U.S. health maintenance organization (HMO) collects data regularly as part of its ongoing patient satisfaction measurement program. In a recent study, data on patient satisfaction, quality of interaction, and related variables were obtained from 4,517 patients who subscribed to 501 primary care physicians (PCPs) affiliated with the HMO. The survey was conducted by telephone. To estimate the impact of the quality of interaction with the PCP on patient satisfaction, the researchers conducted a series of regression analyses.

The dependent variable was patient satisfaction, and the independent variable was the quality of PCP interaction. Three regressions were run: for satisfied patients, for dissatisfied patients, and for all patients. The estimates of the regression coefficient for these three regressions were 1.04, 3.73, and 2.02, respectively. As can be seen, the value of the coefficient was the highest for dissatisfied patients, indicating that dissatisfied patients are differentially more sensitive to the quality of PCP interaction. The implication is that in order to enhance overall patient satisfaction health care providers should accord greater attention to those aspects of PCP interaction that lead to dissatisfaction than to those that lead to satisfaction.[5]

Be an MR!

Visit American carmaker Ford at www.ford.com and search the Internet, as well as your library's online databases, to obtain information on the relationship between advertising and sales for automobile manufacturers. Formulate a bivariate regression model explaining the relationship between advertising and sales in the automobile industry.

Be a DM!

As the marketing director for Ford Motor Company, how would you determine your advertising expenditures?

multiple regression
A statistical technique that simultaneously develops a mathematical relationship between two or more independent variables and an interval-scaled dependent variable.

Multiple Regression

Multiple regression involves a single dependent variable and two or more independent variables. Just as bivariate regression attempts to fit a best line to the data, regression with two independent variables tries to fit a best plane to the data. To extend the bivariate regression example considered earlier, the economic growth rate of the EU has a positive correlation with the level of consumer spending and a negative correlation with the level of interest rates. Thus, a **multiple regression model** could be constructed with the economic growth rate of the EU as the dependent variable and the level of consumer spending and the level of interest rates as the independent variables. The concept is similar in regression with more than two independent variables. The questions raised in the context of bivariate regression can also be answered via multiple regression by considering additional independent variables:

multiple regression model An equation used to explain the results of multiple regression analysis.

- Can variation in sales be explained in terms of variation in advertising expenditures, prices, and level of distribution?
- Can variation in market shares be accounted for by the size of the sales force, advertising expenditures, and sales promotion budgets?
- Are consumers' perceptions of quality determined by their perceptions of prices, brand image, and brand attributes?

Additional questions can also be answered by multiple regression:

- How much of the variation in sales can be explained by advertising expenditures, prices, and level of distribution?
- What is the contribution of advertising expenditures in explaining the variation in sales when the levels of prices and distribution are controlled?
- What levels of sales may be expected given the levels of advertising expenditures, prices, and level of distribution?

The general form of the multiple regression model is as follows:

$$Y = \beta_0 + \beta_1 X_1 + \beta_2 X_2 + \beta_3 X_3 + \ldots + \beta_k X_k + e$$

which is estimated by the following equation:

$$\hat{Y} = a + b_1 X_1 + b_2 X_2 + b_3 X_3 + \ldots + b_k X_k$$

As before, the coefficient a represents the intercept, but the bs are now the partial regression coefficients. The least-squares criterion estimates the parameters in such a way as to minimize the total error, SS_{res}. This process also maximizes the correlation between the actual values of Y and the predicted values $\hat{Y}$. All the assumptions made in bivariate regression also apply in multiple regression.

Conducting Multiple Regression Analysis

The steps involved in conducting multiple regression analysis are similar to those for bivariate regression analysis. The discussion focuses on partial regression coefficients, strength of association, and significance testing.

Partial Regression Coefficients

To understand the meaning of a partial regression coefficient, let us consider again the multiple regression model with the economic growth rate of the EU as the dependent variable and the level of consumer spending and the level of interest rates as the independent variables. In this case, there are two independent variables, so that:

$$\hat{Y} = a + b_1 X_1 + b_2 X_2$$

First, note that the relative magnitude of the partial regression coefficient of an independent variable is, in general, different from that of its bivariate regression coefficient. In other words, the partial regression coefficient, b_1, will be different from the regression coefficient, b, obtained by regressing Y on only X_1. This happens because X_1 and X_2 are usually correlated. In bivariate regression, X_2 was not considered, and any variation in Y that was shared by X_1 and X_2 was attributed to X_1. However, in the case of multiple independent variables, this is no longer true. Thus, in modeling the economic growth rate of the EU, the (partial) regression coefficient for the level of consumer spending in the multiple regression model will differ from that of the bivariate regression model.

partial regression coefficient
Denotes the change in the predicted value of Y when X_1 is changed by one unit but the other independent variables, X_2 to X_k, are held constant.

The interpretation of the **partial regression coefficient**, b_1, is that it represents the expected change in Y when X_1 is changed by one unit but X_2 is held constant or otherwise controlled. Thus, the partial regression coefficient for the level of consumer spending will be different in multiple regression than the coefficient in bivariate regression. Likewise, b_2 represents the expected change in Y for a unit change in X_2, when X_1 is held constant. Thus, calling b_1 and b_2 partial regression coefficients is appropriate. It can also be seen that the combined effects of X_1 and X_2 on Y are additive. In other words, if X_1 and X_2 are each changed by one unit, the expected change in Y would be $(b_1 + b_2)$.

Extension to the case of k variables is straightforward. The partial regression coefficient, b_1, represents the expected change in Y when X_1 is changed by one unit and X_2 through X_k are held constant. It can also be interpreted as the bivariate regression coefficient, b, for the regression of Y on the residuals of X_1, when the effect of X_2 through X_k has been removed from X_1.

In the opening vignette, a multiple regression model was estimated with preference for athletic shoes as the dependent variable and interest in sports, attitude toward sports personalities, attendance at sports events, and time spent watching sports on television as the independent variables. The partial regression coefficient associated with each independent variable was positive and significant, indicating that higher values on each independent variable were associated with stronger preference for athletic shoes. The partial regression coefficient for interest in sports would represent the expected change in preference for athletic shoes when interest in sports is changed by one unit and attitude toward sports personalities, attendance at sports events, and time spent watching sports on television are held constant.

The beta coefficients are the partial regression coefficients obtained when all the variables $(Y, X_1, X_2, \ldots X_k)$ have been standardized to a mean of 0 and a variance of 1 before estimating the regression equation. The relationship of the standardized to the nonstandardized coefficients remains the same as before:

$$B_1 = b_1(s_{x_1}/s_y)$$

.

.

$$B_k = b_k(s_{x_k}/s_y)$$

The intercept and the partial regression coefficients are estimated by solving a system of simultaneous equations derived by differentiating and equating the partial derivatives to 0. Because the various computer programs automatically estimate these coefficients, the details are not presented here. However, it is worth noting that the equations cannot be solved if (1) the sample size, n, is smaller than or equal to the number of independent variables, k, or (2) one independent variable is perfectly correlated with another.

Suppose that in explaining the attitude toward sports cars, we now introduce a second variable, the importance of performance. The data for the 12 pretest respondents on attitude toward sports cars, duration of sports car ownership, and importance attached to performance are given in Table 18.1. The results of multiple regression analysis are depicted in Table 18.4. The corresponding SPSS and Excel outputs with explanatory notes can be downloaded from the Web site for this book. The partial regression coefficient for duration (X_1) is now 0.4811, which is different from what it was in the bivariate case. The corresponding beta coefficient is 0.7636. The partial regression coefficient for importance attached to performance (X_2) is 0.2887, with a beta coefficient of 0.3138. The estimated regression equation is:

$$\hat{Y} = 0.3373 + 0.4811X_1 + 0.2887X_2$$

or

$$\text{Attitude} = 0.3373 + 0.4811 \text{ (Duration)} + 0.2887 \text{ (Importance)}$$

This equation can be used for a variety of purposes, including predicting attitudes toward sports cars, given knowledge of the respondents' duration of sports car ownership and the importance they attach to performance.

TABLE 18.4 Multiple Regression

Multiple R	.9721	
R^2	.9450	
Adjusted R^2	.9330	
Standard Error	.8597	

Analysis of Variance

	df	Sum of Squares	Mean Square
Regression	2	114.2643	57.1321
Residual	9	6.6524	.7392
$F = 77.2936$		Significance of F = .0000	

Variables in the Equation

Variable	b	SE_b	Beta (B)	T	Sig. T
Importance	.2887	.08608	.3138	3.353	.0085
Duration	.4811	.05895	.7636	8.160	.0000
(Constant)	.3373	.56736		.595	.5668

Strength of Association

The strength of the relationship stipulated by the regression equation can be determined by using the appropriate measures of association. The total variation is decomposed as in the bivariate case:

$$SS_y = SS_{reg} + SS_{res}$$

where

$$SS_y = \sum_{i=1}^{n}(Y_i - \bar{Y})^2$$

$$SS_{reg} = \sum_{i=1}^{n}(\hat{Y}_i - \bar{Y})^2$$

$$SS_{res} = \sum_{i=1}^{n}(Y_i - \hat{Y}_i)^2$$

The strength of association is measured by the square of the multiple correlation coefficient, R^2, which also is called the **coefficient of multiple determination**:

$$R^2 = \frac{SS_{reg}}{SS_y}$$

The multiple correlation coefficient, R, can also be viewed as the simple correlation coefficient, r, between Y and $\hat{Y}$. Several points about the characteristics of R^2 are worth noting. The coefficient of multiple determination, R^2, cannot be less than the highest bivariate, r^2, of any individual independent variable with the dependent variable. R^2 will be larger when the correlations between the independent variables are low. If the independent variables are statistically independent (uncorrelated), then R^2 will be the sum of bivariate r^2 of each independent variable with the dependent variable. R^2 cannot decrease as more independent variables are added to the regression equation. However, diminishing returns do set in, so that after the first few variables the additional independent variables do not make much of a contribution. For this reason, R^2 is adjusted for the number of independent variables and the sample size by using the following formula:

$$\textbf{Adjusted } R^2 = R^2 - \frac{k(1 - R^2)}{n - k - 1}$$

coefficient of multiple determination
In multiple regression, the strength of association is measured by the square of the multiple correlation coefficient, R^2, which is called the coefficient of multiple determination.

adjusted R^2
The value of R^2 adjusted for the number of independent variables and the sample size.

For the regression results given in Table 18.4, the value of R^2 is:

$$R^2 = 114.2643/(114.2643 + 6.6524)$$

$$= 114.2643/120.9167$$

$$= .9450$$

This is higher than the r^2 value of 0.8762 obtained in the bivariate case. The r^2 in the bivariate case is the square of the simple (product moment) correlation between attitude toward sports cars and duration of sports car ownership. The R^2 obtained in multiple regression also is higher than the square of the simple correlation between attitude and importance attached to performance (which can be estimated as 0.5379). The adjusted R^2 is estimated as:

$$\text{Adjusted } R^2 = 0.9450 - 2(1.0 - 0.9450)/(12 - 2 - 1)$$

$$= 0.9450 - 0.0120$$

$$= 0.9330$$

Note that the value of adjusted R^2 is close to R^2 and both are higher than r^2 for the bivariate case. This suggests that the addition of the second independent variable—importance attached to performance—makes a contribution in explaining the variation in attitude toward sports cars. Of course, R^2 should be significant, and higher values of R^2 are more desirable than lower values. However, in commercial marketing research, values of R^2 as high as 0.9 or higher are uncommon. Values of R^2 in the 0.5 to 0.8 range may be reasonable in many commercial marketing research projects.

Significance Testing

Significance testing involves testing the significance of the overall regression equation as well as specific partial regression coefficients. The null hypothesis for the overall test is that the coefficient of multiple determination in the population, R^2_{pop}, is zero.

$$H_0: R^2_{pop} = 0$$

This is equivalent to the following null hypothesis:

$$H_0: \beta_1 = \beta_2 = \beta_3 = \ldots = \beta_k = 0$$

The overall test can be conducted by using an F statistic:

$$F = \frac{SS_{reg}/k}{SS_{res}/(n - k - 1)}$$

$$= \frac{R^2/k}{(1 - R^2)(n - k - 1)}$$

which has an F distribution with k and $(n - k - 1)$ degrees of freedom. For the multiple regression results given in Table 18.4,

$$F = \frac{114.2643/2}{6.6524/9} = 77.2936$$

which is significant at $\alpha = 0.05$.

If the overall null hypothesis is rejected, one or more population partial regression coefficients have a value different from 0. To determine which specific coefficients (b_is) are nonzero, additional tests are necessary. Testing for the significance of the b_is can be done in a manner similar to that in the bivariate case by using t-tests. The significance of the partial coefficient for importance attached to performance can be tested by the following equation:

$$t = \frac{b}{SE_b}$$

$$= 0.2887/0.08608$$

$$= 3.353$$

which has a t distribution with $n - k - 1$ degrees of freedom. This coefficient is significant at $\alpha = 0.05$. The significance of the coefficient for duration of sports car ownership is tested in a similar way and found to be significant. Therefore, both the duration of sports car ownership and the importance attached to performance are important in explaining attitude toward sports cars. However, if any of the regression coefficients are not significant, they should be treated as zero.

Some software programs provide an equivalent F-test, often called the **partial F-test**. This involves a decomposition of the total regression sum of squares, SS_{reg}, into components related to each independent variable.

Examination of Residuals

A **residual** is the difference between the observed value of Y_i and the value predicted by the regression equation, $\hat{Y}_i$. Residuals are used in the calculation of several statistics associated with regression. Scattergrams of the residuals, in which the residuals are plotted against the predicted values, $\hat{Y}_i$; time; respondents; or predictor variables, provide useful insights in examining the appropriateness of the underlying assumptions and the regression model fitted. For example, the assumption of a normally distributed error term can be examined by constructing a histogram of the residuals. A visual check reveals whether the distribution is normal. Additionally, if the pattern of residuals is not random, then some of the underlying assumptions are being violated. In particular, we suggest the following simplified but effective procedure for examining residuals:

1. Examine the histogram of standardized residuals. Compare the frequency of residuals to the normal distribution. If the difference is small, then the normality assumption can reasonably be met.
2. Examine the normal probability plot of standardized residuals. The normal probability plot shows the observed standardized residuals compared to expected standardized residuals from a normal distribution. If the observed residuals are normally distributed, they will fall on the 45-degree line.
3. Examine the plot of standardized residuals versus standardized predicted values. This plot should be random with no discernible pattern. This will provide an indication on the assumptions of linearity and constant variance for the error term.
4. Look at the table of residual statistics and identify any standardized predicted values or standardized residuals that are more than plus or minus three standard deviations. Values larger than this might indicate the presence of outliers in the data.

The plots and the table can be requested when the regression is run, for example, when using SPSS. Go the student Web site for this book and retrieve the file named Chapter 18 Multiple Regression.spo. This is the SPSS output file for multiple regression on the data of Table 18.1, and it includes the three plots that we have recommended. From the histogram, it can be seen that five residuals are positive, whereas seven residuals are negative. By comparing the frequency distribution with the normal distribution that is plotted in the same output, we can see that the assumption of normality is probably not met but that the departure from normality might not be severe. Of course, one can do a more formal statistical test for normality if that is warranted. All the standardized residuals are within plus or minus two standard deviations. Furthermore, many of the residuals are relatively small, which means that most of the model predictions are quite good.

The normal probability plot shows that the residuals are quite close to the 45-degree line shown in the graph. When we look at the plot of the standardized residuals against the standardized predicted values, no systematic pattern can be discerned in the spread of the residuals. Finally, the table of residual statistics indicates that all the standardized predicted values and all the standardized residuals are within plus or minus two standard deviations. Hence, we can conclude that multiple regression on the data of Table 18.1 does not appear to result in gross violations of the assumptions. This suggests that the relationship we are trying to predict is linear and that the error terms are more or less normally distributed.

---

partial F-test
This is an F-test that involves a decomposition of the total regression sum of squares, SS_{reg}, into components related to each independent variable.

residual
The difference between the observed value of Y_i and the value predicted by the regression equation $\hat{Y}_i$.

Regression is a robust statistical procedure, and substantial violations of the assumptions are needed to cause serious problems. We further illustrate the application of multiple regression with an example.

Research in Action

Wendy's: Improving Likelihood of Patronage

With revenues of $2.44 billion in 2006, the American fast-food chain Wendy's has more than 6,700 restaurants worldwide. In an online survey, respondents were asked to rate their likelihood of patronizing popular fast-food restaurants and to rate those restaurants on various factors using 5-point Likert-type scales. A multiple regression analysis was conducted. Likelihood to patronize was the dependent variable. The independent variables were the evaluations of the restaurant on the various factors that influence patronage. The fit of the regression model was good, and the coefficients for the following variables were significant at the 0.05 level:

Menu selection

Quality

Service

Value

Convenience of location

Based on this analysis, Wendy's started making improvements on all the significant factors. For example,

menu selection was improved in 2007 by adding the Steakhouse Double-Melt Cheeseburger, which consists of two patties of fresh, never frozen, beef packed with a melted middle. In addition, it expanded its well-known Frosty, which is a cool, creamy chocolate or vanilla treat, by serving it with ice-cold root beer, Coca-Cola, and other drinks. Improvements were also made on the other factors.[6]

Be a DM!

As the marketing director for Dell's laptop computers, how would you improve the brand's image and competitive positioning?

Be an MR!

Visit U.S. computer maker Dell at www.dell.com and search the Internet, as well as your library's online databases, to obtain information on the factors consumer use to evaluate competing brands of laptop computers. Formulate a multiple regression model explaining consumer preferences for laptop computer brands as a function of the brand evaluations on the consumer choice criteria factors used to evaluate competing brands.

Summary Illustration Using the Opening Vignette

The product moment correlation coefficient measures the linear association between two metric variables. In the opening vignette, preference for athletic shoes showed strong positive correlations with sports-related variables, such as interest in sports, attitude toward sports personalities, attendance at sports events, and time spent watching sports on television.

Bivariate regression derives a mathematical equation in the form of a straight line between a single metric criterion variable and a single metric predictor variable. Instead of running product moment correlations, we could have alternatively run four separate bivariate regressions on the standardized data with preference for athletic shoes as the dependent variable. Each of the independent variables, in turn, would serve as the predictor variable: interest in sports, attitude toward sports personalities, attendance at sports events, and time spent watching sports on television.

Multiple regression involves a single dependent variable and two or more independent variables. The partial regression coefficient represents the expected change in the dependent variable when one of the independent variables is changed by one unit and the other independent variables are held constant. A multiple regression model—with preference for athletic shoes as the dependent variable, and interest in sports, attitude toward sports personalities, attendance at sports events, and time spent watching sports on television as the independent variables—had very good strength of association. The partial regression coefficient associated with each independent variable was positive and significant, indicating that higher values on each independent variable were associated with stronger preference for athletic shoes. The partial regression coefficient for interest in sports would represent the expected change in preference for athletic shoes when interest in sports is changed by one unit and attitude toward sports personalities, attendance at sports events, and time spent watching sports on television are held constant. Figures 18.8 and 18.9 provide concept maps for conducting product moment correlation and bivariate regression, respectively.

FIGURE 18.8

A Concept Map for Product Moment Correlation

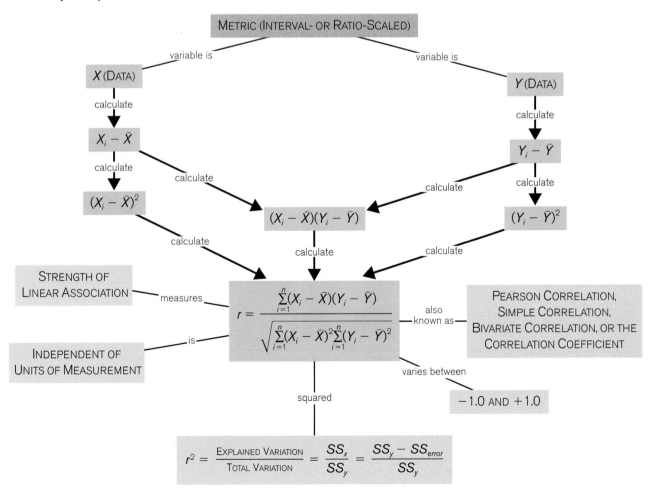

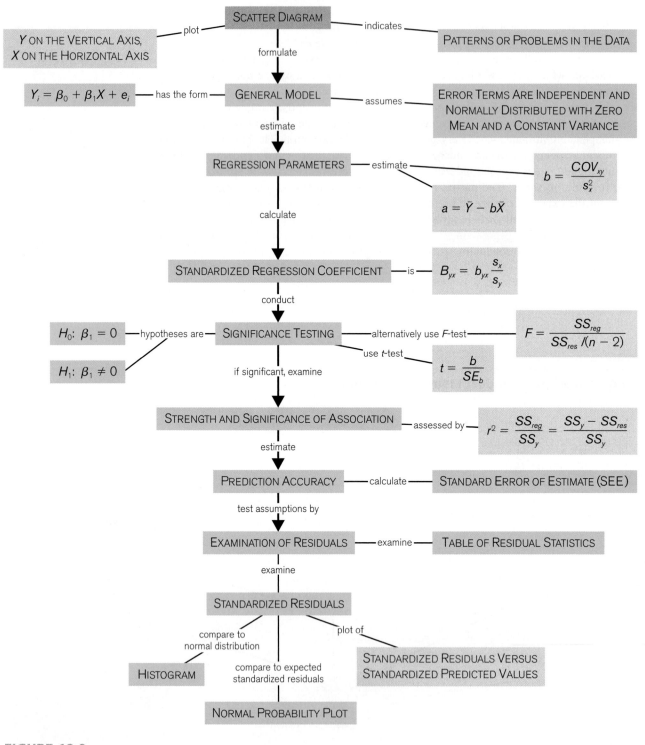

FIGURE 18.9

A Concept Map for Conducting Bivariate Regression

What Would *You* Do?

The West Michigan Whitecaps: Fanning Fan Loyalty

The Situation

The West Michigan Whitecaps (www.whitecaps-baseball.com), an American minor league baseball team, wondered what it should do to develop fan loyalty. How could the team best keep it, make it grow, and take advantage of it? In order to find out, Whitecap's president Scott Lane hired Message Factors (www.messagefactors.com), a U.S. research firm, to help the Whitecaps determine how to effectively maintain fan loyalty on a limited budget. Message Factors developed a study that used a proprietary value analysis technique that would examine the relationship between the overall perceived value and specific satisfaction attributes in order to determine loyalty drivers. The analysis technique determined four things: (1) the basics—what customers expect of the company; (2) value issues—what customers value about the company; (3) irritations—what customers do not like about the company; and (4) unimportants—what customers do not care about.

Qualitative research was conducted to identify a set of 71 attributes that influenced fan loyalty. Next, a questionnaire was designed that incorporated the 71 attributes. This questionnaire was then administered to 1,010 fans at Whitecaps games. From this, the marketing research company was able to find the information it sought. The basics were determined to be values such as stadium safety, restroom cleanliness, and variety in the food items available. The Whitecaps want to not only meet these basic expectations, but also to surpass them to guarantee that fans will return and be loyal. The value issues are the ones that can really help the team build loyalty. These included things such as helpful box office personnel, convenience of purchasing tickets, easy parking, and autograph opportunities. Some irritations were identified, such as the high price, low quality, and lack of variety of souvenirs. However, the research also showed that fans do not really expect to be pleased with these areas of sports attendance. It was also determined that there were no unimportant aspects.

The Marketing Research Decision

1. In order to determine the relative importance of value drivers, what type of data analysis should Message Factors conduct?
   a. Mean importance of helpful box office personnel, convenience of purchasing tickets, ease of parking, and autograph opportunities
   b. Cross-tabulation of overall value with helpful box office personnel, convenience of purchasing tickets, ease of parking, and autograph opportunities
   c. Product moment correlations of overall value with helpful box office personnel, convenience of purchasing tickets, ease of parking, and autograph opportunities
   d. Multiple regression with overall value as the dependent variable and helpful box office personnel, convenience of purchasing tickets, ease of parking, and autograph opportunities as the independent variables
   e. All of the above

2. Discuss the role of the type of data analysis you recommend in enabling Scott Lane to determine the relative importance of the four value drivers.

The Marketing Management Decision

1. In order to enhance the value of Whitecaps games for the fans, what should Scott Lane do?
   a. Train box office and other personnel to be helpful.
   b. Increase the convenience of purchasing tickets.
   c. Increase the convenience of parking.
   d. Provide fans with opportunities for autographs.
   e. All of the above.

2. Discuss how the marketing management decision action that you recommend to Scott Lane is influenced by the type of data analysis that you suggested earlier and by the findings of that analysis.

What Scott Lane Did

Data analysis revealed that the Whitecaps had performed well on the basics, so it was able to shift its focus to improving in the value areas. Analysis also showed that the personnel variable was a very high contributor to value perception. The Whitecaps were rated as average in this area, as were its competitors, so this is a key area that provides the Whitecaps with an opportunity to be better than and overtake the competition. Scott Lane also improved ease of ticket purchasing and provided fans with opportunities for autographs after the game. The next season, the Whitecaps raised ticket prices by 25 percent and still got a 100 percent renewal. Scott Lane had figured out how to enhance fan loyalty![7]

Software Applications

The computer programs available for conducting correlation analysis are described in Exhibit 18.1. In SPSS, CORRELATIONS can be used for computing product moment correlations; in SAS, the corresponding program is CORR. In Minitab, correlation can be computed using the STAT > BASIC STATISTICS > CORRELATION function. Correlations can be determined in Excel by using the TOOLS > DATA ANALYSIS > CORRELATION function. Use the Correlation Worksheet Function when a correlation coefficient for two cell ranges is needed.

As described in Exhibit 18.2, the statistical packages contain several programs for performing regression analysis, calculating the associated statistics, performing tests for significance, and plotting the residuals. In SPSS, the main program is REGRESSION. In SAS, the most general program is REG. Other specialized programs, such as RSREG, ORTHOREG, GLM, and NLIN also are available; however, readers who are not familiar with the intricate aspects of regression analysis are advised to stick to REG when using SAS. In Minitab, regression analysis, under the STATS > REGRESSION function, can perform simple and multiple regression analyses. In Excel, regression can be accessed from the TOOLS > DATA ANALYSIS menu.

SPSS Windows

The CORRELATIONS program computes product moment correlations with significance levels. Univariate statistics, covariance, and cross-product deviations can also be requested. Significance levels are included in the output. To select this procedures using SPSS for Windows click:

> Analyze > Correlate > Bivariate . . .

> Scatterplots can be obtained by selecting:

> Graphs > Scatter . . . > Simple > Define

> REGRESSION calculates bivariate and multiple regression equations, associated statistics, and plots. It allows for an easy examination of residuals. This procedure can be run by selecting:

> Analyze > Regression > Linear . . .

Detailed Steps: Overview

Detailed step-by-step instructions for running the SPSS programs for the data analysis presented in this chapter can be downloaded from the Web site for this book in two forms: (1) computerized demonstration movies, and (2) screen captures. In addition, these steps are illustrated in the following sections.

Detailed Steps: Correlation

The following are the detailed steps for running a correlation between attitude toward sports cars and duration of sports car ownership given in Table 18.1. A positive correlation is to be expected.

1. Select ANALYZE from the SPSS menu bar.
2. Click CORRELATE and then BIVARIATE.
3. Move "Attitude Towards Sports Cars" and "Duration of Car Ownership" into the VARIABLES box.
4. Check PEARSON under CORRELATION COEFFICIENTS.
5. Check ONE_TAILED under TEST OF SIGNIFICANCE.
6. Check FLAG SIGNIFICANT CORRELATIONS.
7. Click OK.

Detailed Steps: Bivariate and Multiple Regression

The following are the detailed steps for running a bivariate regression with attitude toward sports cars as the dependent variable and duration of sports car ownership as the independent variable using the data of Table 18.1.

1. Select ANALYZE from the SPSS menu bar.
2. Click REGRESSION and then LINEAR.
3. Move "Attitude Towards Sports Cars" into the DEPENDENT box.
4. Move "Duration of Car Ownership" into the INDEPENDENT(S) box.
5. Select ENTER in the METHOD box (default option).
6. Click STATISTICS and check ESTIMATES under REGRESSION COEFFICIENTS.
7. Check MODEL FIT.
8. Click CONTINUE.

9. Click PLOTS.

10. In the LINEAR REGRESSION:PLOTS box, move *ZRESID into the Y: box and *ZPRED into the X: box.

11. Check HISTOGRAM and NORMAL PROBABILITY PLOT in the STANDARDIZED RESIDUALS PLOTS.

12. Click CONTINUE.

13. Click OK.

The steps for running multiple regression are similar, except for Step 4. In Step 4, move "Duration of Car Ownership and "Importance Attached to Performance" into the INDEPENDENT(S) box.

Experiential Learning

Correlation and Regression

Go to the textbook Web site and download the survey used in interviewing recently nonreturning students at Musial University (MU), a public urban university in the midsized U.S. city of Musial. The administrators at MU were interested in obtaining the perspectives of "dropout" or "stopout" students so that MU could enhance its programs, facilities, and services. Although the actual name of the university has been disguised, the research project and the accompanying data are real. Download the actual survey used in this study: Musial Retention Survey.doc, as well as the SPSS system file: Musial Retention Data.sav.

1. Read Musial Retention Survey.doc.

2. Open SPSS and read-in your data from Musial Retention Data.sav.

3. Try to understand the associations for having no football program at MU.

 Focus on question Q5n ("I would have very much enjoyed having a football team at MU.") and the correlations with these variables: Q5k, good recreation facilities; Q5l, great social environment; Q5o, attended many sporting events; Q5x, rich learning environment; Q5aa, felt my progress mattered to MU administrators; and Q5bb, felt I mattered to other students.

 Create a correlation table composed of Pearson product moment correlations for the seven variables Q5n, Q5k, Q5l, Q5o, Q5x, Q5aa, and Q5bb. Review the output.
(What are the H_0 and H_1 for each of these binary relationships?)
 ANALYZE
  CORRELATE
   BIVARIATE
    BIVARIATE CORRELATIONS window
     Select Q5n, Q5k, Q5l, Q5o, Q5x, Q5aa, and Q5bb.
      Click OK.
 Using question 5x as the dependent variable ("The MU learning environment is a rich one."), conduct a multiple regression analysis composed of five independent variables: Q5k, good recreation facilities; Q5l, great social environment; Q5r, convenient location; Q5s, good advising center; and Q5bb, felt I mattered to other students.
(What are the H_0 and H_1 for your regression model?)
 ANALYZE
  REGRESSION
   LINEAR

    DEPENDENT box of the LINEAR REGRESION window
     Enter Q5x (" . . . learning environment is a rich one.").
     INDEPENDENT(S) box of the LINEAR REGRESION window
      Enter all five variables Q5k, Q5l, Q5r, Q5s, and Q5bb.
       Make sure the Method selected is ENTER.
     Click the STATISTICS button.
      Select DESCRIPTIVES in addition to the default selections.
      Click CONTINUE.
     Click the OPTIONS button.
      Under MISSING VALUES select REPLACE WITH MEAN.
       (In this way, you will make sure any missing values receive a mean value.)
        Click CONTINUE.
         Click OK.
          Review your SPSS output.
 Run the Correlation analysis for the five variables chosen for the previous regression analysis.
 ANALYZE
  CORRELATE
   BIVARIATE
    BIVARIATE CORRELATIONS window
     Select Q5x, Q5k, Q5l, Q5r, Q5s, and Q5bb.
      Click OK.
 Compare the binary correlation coefficients of Q5x with Q5k, Q5l, Q5r, Q5s, and Q5bb in the Correlations portion with the Beta values under the Standardized Coefficients column of the Coefficients table for your multiple regression analysis. What did you find? Why is this so?

Extra

As you can sense, many analyses can be conducted with this data set. Have fun doing cross-tabulations, *t*-tests, and other analyses.

Epilogue

Download Musial Retention Report.ppt to glimpse what was presented to the MU administrators in a formal presentation session.

Excel

We give an overview of the detailed steps involved in conducting these analyses using Excel. Then we provide detailed step-by-step instructions for estimating correlation, as well as bivariate and multiple regression.

Detailed Steps: Overview

Detailed step-by-step instructions for running the Excel programs for the data analysis presented in this chapter can be downloaded from the Web site for this book in two forms: (1) computerized demonstration movies, and (2) screen captures. In addition, these steps are illustrated in the following sections.

Detailed Steps: Correlation

The following are the detailed steps for running a correlation between attitude toward sports cars and duration of sports car ownership given in Table 18.1.

1. Select Tools (Alt + T).
2. Select Data Analysis under Tools.
3. The Data Analysis Window pops up.
4. Select Correlation from the Data Analysis Window.
5. Click OK.
6. The Correlation pop-up window appears on screen.
7. The Correlation window has two portions
   a. Input
   b. Output Options
8. The Input portion asks for the following inputs:
   a. Click in the Input Range box. Select (highlight) all the rows of data under ATTITUDE and DURATION. $B$2:$C$13 should appear on Input Range.
   b. Select Group by Columns.
   c. Leave Labels as blank.
9. In the Output portion of pop-up window, select New Workbook Options.
10. Click OK.

Detailed Steps: Bivariate and Multiple Regression

The following are the detailed steps for running a bivariate regression with attitude toward sports cars as the dependent variable and duration of sports car ownership as the independent variable using the data in Table 18.1.

1. Select Tools (Alt + T).
2. Select Data Analysis under Tools.
3. The Data Analysis Window pops up.
4. Select Regression from the Data Analysis Window.
5. Click OK.
6. The Regression pop-up window appears on screen.
7. The Regression window has four portions:
   a. Input
   b. Output Options
   c. Residuals
   d. Normal Probability
8. The Input portion asks for the following inputs:
   a. Click in the Input Y Range box. Select (highlight) all the rows of data under ATTITUDE. $B$2:$B$13 should appear on Input Y Range.

    b. Click in the Input X Range box. Select (highlight) all the rows of data under Duration. $C$2:$C$13 should appear on Input X Range.

    c. Leave Labels, Constant is Zero, and Confidence Level as blanks.

9. In the Output portion of pop-up window, select New Workbook Options.

10. Leave Residuals and Normal Probability as it is.

11. Click OK.

The steps for running multiple regression are similar, except for Step 8b. In Step 8b, click in the Input X Range box. Select (highlight) all the rows of data under Duration and Importance. $C$2:$D$13 should appear on Input X Range.

Summary

The product moment correlation coefficient, r, measures the linear association between two metric (interval or ratio-scaled) variables. Its square, r^2, measures the proportion of variation in one variable explained by the other.

Bivariate regression derives a mathematical equation between a single metric criterion variable and a single metric predictor variable. The equation is derived in the form of a straight line by using the least-squares procedure. When the regression is run on standardized data, the intercept assumes a value of 0, and the regression coefficients are called beta weights. The strength of association is measured by the coefficient of determination, r^2, which is obtained by computing a ratio of SS_{reg} to SS_y. Scattergrams of the residuals are useful for examining the appropriateness of the underlying assumptions and the fit of the regression model.

Multiple regression involves a single dependent variable and two or more independent variables. The partial regression coefficient, b_1, represents the expected change in Y when X_1 is changed by one unit and X_2 through X_k are held constant. The strength of association is measured by the coefficient of multiple determination, R^2. The significance of the overall regression equation may be tested by the overall F-test. Individual partial regression coefficients can be tested for significance using the t-test.

Key Terms and Concepts

Product moment correlation (r),   551
Covariance,   552
Regression analysis,   557
Bivariate regression,   557
Bivariate regression model,   557
Scatter diagram (scattergram),   558
Least-squares procedure,   558

Sum of squared errors,   558
Estimated or predicted value,   559
Standardization,   561
Beta coefficient (beta weight),   562
Standard error,   563
Coefficient of determination,   563
Standard error of estimate (SEE),   565
Multiple regression,   566

Multiple regression model,   567
Partial regression coefficient,   568
Coefficient of multiple determination,   569
Adjusted R^2,   569
Partial F-test,   571
Residual,   571

Suggested Cases and Video Cases

Running Case with Real Data

1.1 Hewlett-Packard

Comprehensive Cases with Real Data

3.1 Bank of America   3.2 McDonald's   3.3 Boeing

Video Cases

19.1 Marriott

Live Research: Conducting a Marketing Research Project

1. It is desirable to calculate product moment correlations between all interval-scaled variables. This gives an idea of the correlations between variables.
2. Students should also be encouraged to run several bivariate regressions and to compare these results with the corresponding product moment correlations.
3. Multiple regressions should be run when examining the association between a single dependent variable and several independent variables.

Acronym

The main features of regression analysis may be summarized by the acronym REGRESSION:

R esidual analysis is useful

E stimation of parameters: solution of simultaneous equations

G eneral model is linear

R^2 strength of association

E rror terms are independent and $N(0, \sigma^2)$

S tandardized regression coefficients

S tandard error of estimate: prediction accuracy

I ndividual coefficients and overall F-tests

O ptimal: minimizes total error

N onstandardized regression coefficients

Review Questions

1. What is the product moment correlation coefficient? Does a product moment correlation of zero between two variables imply that the variables are not related?
2. Give an example of a bivariate regression model and identify the dependent and the independent variables.
3. What are the main uses of regression analysis?
4. What is the least-squares procedure?
5. Explain the meaning of standardized regression coefficients.
6. How is the strength of association measured in bivariate regression? In multiple regression?
7. What is meant by prediction accuracy?
8. What is the standard error of estimate?
9. What assumptions underlie the error term?
10. What is multiple regression? How does it differ from bivariate regression?
11. Explain the meaning of a partial regression coefficient. Why is it called such?
12. State the null hypothesis in testing the significance of the overall multiple regression equation. How is this null hypothesis tested?

Applied Problems

1. A major supermarket chain wants to determine the effect of promotion on relative competitiveness. Data were obtained from 15 states on the promotional expenses relative to a major competitor (competitor expenses = 100) and on sales relative to this competitor (competitor sales = 100).

State No.	Relative Promotional Expense	Relative Sales
1	95	98
2	92	94
3	103	110
4	115	125
5	77	82
6	79	84
7	105	112
8	94	99
9	85	93
10	101	107
11	106	114
12	120	132
13	118	129
14	75	79
15	99	105

You are assigned the task of telling the manager whether there is any relationship between relative promotional expense and relative sales.
a. Plot the relative sales (y-axis) against the relative promotional expense (x-axis), and interpret this diagram.
b. Which measure would you use to determine whether there is a relationship between the two variables? Explain.
c. Run a bivariate regression analysis of relative sales on relative promotional expense.
d. Interpret the regression coefficients.
e. Is the regression relationship significant?
f. If the company matched the competitor in terms of promotional expense (if the relative promotional expense was 100), what would the company's relative sales be?
g. Interpret the resulting r^2.

2. To understand the role of quality and price in influencing the patronage of drugstores, 14 major stores in a large metropolitan area were rated in terms of preference to shop, quality of merchandise, and fair pricing. All the ratings were obtained on an 11-point scale, with higher numbers indicating more positive ratings.

Store No.	Preference	Quality	Price
1	6	5	3
2	9	6	11
3	8	6	4
4	3	2	1
5	10	6	11
6	4	3	1
7	5	4	7
8	2	1	4
9	11	9	8
10	9	5	10
11	10	8	8
12	2	1	5
13	9	8	5
14	5	3	2

a. Run a multiple regression analysis explaining store preference in terms of quality of merchandise and pricing.
b. Interpret the partial regression coefficients.
c. Determine the significance of the overall regression.
d. Determine the significance of the partial regression coefficients.

3. Imagine that you have come across a magazine article reporting the following relationship between annual expenditure on prepared dinners (PD) and annual income (INC):

$$PD = 23.4 + 0.003\ INC$$

The coefficient of the INC variable is reported as significant.
a. Does this relationship seem plausible? Is it possible to have a coefficient that is small in magnitude and yet significant?
b. From the information given, can you tell how good the estimated model is?
c. What are the expected expenditures on PDs of a family earning $30,000?
d. If a family earning $40,000 spent $130 annually on PDs, what is the residual?
e. What is the meaning of a negative residual?

4. Conduct the following analyses for the Internet usage data given in Applied Problem number 6, in Chapter 16.
a. Find the simple correlations between the following sets of variables: Internet usage and attitude toward Internet, Internet usage and attitude toward technology, and attitude toward Internet and attitude toward technology. Interpret the results.

b. Run a bivariate regression with Internet usage as the dependent variable and attitude toward Internet as the independent variable. Interpret the results.

c. Run a bivariate regression with Internet usage as the dependent variable and attitude toward technology as the independent variable. Interpret the results.

d. Run a multiple regression with Internet usage as the dependent variable and attitude toward Internet and attitude toward technology as the independent variables. Interpret the results.

5. Conduct the following analyses for the preference of the outdoor-lifestyle data given in Applied Problem number 8, of Chapter 17. Recall that:

V1 = preference for an outdoor lifestyle
V2 = enjoying nature
V3 = relating to the weather
V4 = living in harmony with the environment
V5 = exercising regularly
V6 = meeting other people

a. Calculate the simple correlations between V1 to V6 and interpret the results.

b. Run a bivariate regression with preference for an outdoor lifestyle (V1) as the dependent variable and the importance of enjoying nature (V2) as the independent variable. Interpret the results.

c. Run a multiple regression with preference for an outdoor lifestyle as the dependent variable and V2 to V6 as the independent variables. Interpret the results. Compare the coefficients for V2 obtained in the bivariate and the multiple regressions.

6. In a pretest, data were obtained from 20 respondents on preferences for sneakers on a 7-point scale where 1 = not at all preferred and 7 = greatly preferred (V1). The respondents also provided their evaluations of the sneakers on comfort (V2), style (V3), and durability (V4), also on 7-point scales where 1 = poor and 7 = excellent. The resulting data follow.

V1	V2	V3	V4
6.00	6.00	3.00	5.00
2.00	3.00	2.00	4.00
7.00	5.00	6.00	7.00
4.00	6.00	4.00	5.00
1.00	3.00	2.00	2.00
6.00	5.00	6.00	7.00
5.00	6.00	7.00	5.00
7.00	3.00	5.00	4.00
2.00	4.00	6.00	3.00
3.00	5.00	3.00	6.00
1.00	3.00	2.00	3.00
5.00	4.00	5.00	4.00
2.00	2.00	1.00	5.00
4.00	5.00	4.00	6.00
6.00	5.00	4.00	7.00
3.00	3.00	4.00	2.00
4.00	4.00	3.00	2.00
3.00	4.00	3.00	2.00
4.00	4.00	3.00	2.00
2.00	3.00	2.00	4.00

a. Calculate the simple correlations between V1 to V4 and interpret the results.

b. Run a bivariate regression with preference for sneakers (V1) as the dependent variable and evaluation on comfort (V2) as the independent variable. Interpret the results.

c. Run a bivariate regression with preference for sneakers (V1) as the dependent variable and evaluation on style (V3) as the independent variable. Interpret the results.

d. Run a bivariate regression with preference for sneakers (V1) as the dependent variable and evaluation on durability (V4) as the independent variable. Interpret the results.

e. Run a multiple regression with preference for sneakers (V1) as the dependent variable and V2 to V4 as the independent variables. Interpret the results. Compare the coefficients for V2, V3, and V4 obtained in the bivariate and the multiple regressions.

Group Discussion

1. As a small group, discuss the following statement: "Regression is such a basic technique that it should always be used in analyzing data."

2. As a small group, discuss the relationship between bivariate correlation, bivariate regression, and multiple regression.

Hewlett-Packard Running Case

Review the Hewlett-Packard (HP) case, Case 1.1, and questionnaire given toward the end of the book. Go to the Web site for this book and download the HP data file.

1. Can the overall satisfaction (q4) be explained in terms of all the 13 evaluations of HP (q8_1 to q8_13) when the independent variables are considered simultaneously? Interpret the results.

2. Can the likelihood of choosing HP (q6) be explained in terms of all the 13 evaluations of HP (q8_1 to q8_13) when the independent variables are considered simultaneously? Interpret the results.

3. Can price sensitivity of q9a (q9_5per) be explained in terms of all the 13 evaluations of HP (q8_1 to q8_13) when the independent variables are considered simultaneously? Interpret the results.

4. Can price sensitivity of q9b (q9_10 per) be explained in terms of all the 13 evaluations of HP (q8_1 to q8_13) when the independent variables are considered simultaneously? Interpret the results.

Exhibit 18.1 Computer Programs for Correlations

SPSS

The CORRELATIONS program computes product moment correlations with significance levels. Univariate statistics, covariance, and cross-product deviations may also be requested. Significance levels are included in the output.

SAS

CORR produces metric and nonmetric correlations between variables, including product moment correlation.

Minitab

Correlation can be computed using STAT > BASIC STATISTICS > CORRELATION function. It calculates product moment correlations using all the columns.

Excel

Correlations can be determined in Excel by using the TOOLS > DATA ANALYSIS > CORRELATION function. Use the Correlation Worksheet Function when a correlation coefficient for two cell ranges is needed.

Exhibit 18.2 Computer Programs for Regression

SPSS

REGRESSION calculates bivariate and multiple regression equations, associated statistics, and plots. It allows for an easy examination of residuals. Regression statistics can be requested with PLOT, which produces simple scattergrams and some other types of plots.

SAS

REG is a general-purpose regression procedure that fits bivariate and multiple regression models using the least-squares procedure. All the associated statistics are computed, and residuals can be plotted.

Minitab

Regression analysis, under the STATS > REGRESSION function can perform simple and multiple analysis. The output includes a linear regression equation, table of coefficients, R^2, R^2 adjusted, analysis of variance table, and a table of fits and residuals that provide unusual observations. Other available features include fitted line plot and residual plots.

Excel

Regression can be assessed from the TOOLS > DATA ANALYSIS menu. Depending on the features selected, the output can consist of a summary output table, including an ANOVA table, a standard error of y estimate, coefficients, standard error of coefficients, R^2 values, and the number of observations. In addition, the function computes a residual output table, residual plot, line fit plot, normal probability plot, and a two-column probability data-output table.

Report Preparation and Presentation

OPENING QUESTIONS

1. What process should be followed in preparing and presenting the final report?

2. Are any guidelines available for writing a report that includes graphs and tables?

3. How should an oral presentation be made, and what are some of the principles involved?

4. Why is the follow-up with the client important, and what assistance should be given to the client in implementing and evaluating the research project?

5. How is the report preparation and presentation process different in international marketing research?

6. How does technology facilitate report preparation and presentation?

7. What ethical issues are related to the interpretation and reporting of the research process and findings?

Research Reports Make United's Friendly Skies Even More Friendly

"In any report or presentation, get right to the point in why these results matter to the firm. The tendency for beginners is to present all the answers and all the data, whether relevant or not. The role of the analyst is to boil, filter, and distill, so the audience receives the pure distillation."

Jerry Thomas,
President/CEO, Decision Analyst, Inc.

As of 2008, United Airlines (www.united.com) operated more than 3,300 flights a day on United, United Express, and Ted to more than 200 U.S. domestic and international destinations from its U.S. hubs in Los Angeles, San Francisco, Denver, Chicago, and Washington, D.C. The airline puts a premium on customer satisfaction. For its in-flight customer satisfaction tracking program, United surveys passengers on some 900 flights per month using a four-page scanable questionnaire. It administers 192,000 questionnaires in nine languages to people traveling to 40 different countries. The survey covers passenger satisfaction with the entire air travel process: reservations, airport service, flight attendants, meal service, and the aircraft itself.

The marketing research department at United prepares a monthly report summarizing the customer satisfaction data for about 100 people worldwide, including airport, country, and regional managers; executive management; and others at United's headquarters. The report is thorough and includes all of the following: title page, table of contents, executive summary, problem definition, approach, research design, data analysis, results, and conclusions and

recommendations. Several tables and graphs are included to enhance the clarity of the findings. The report findings also are available online.

After issuing the monthly report, the marketing research department handles several requests from internal customers (i.e., various departments within United Airlines) for additional analysis. For example, the marketing department might request a breakdown of customer satisfaction rating by demographic characteristics for a specific route (city pair), such as Chicago to Los Angeles. Because the data can be linked to operational data, such as arrival and departure times and number of passengers, United's researchers can dig deep to answer questions from internal customers. Alex Maggi, United's senior staff analyst for market research, says:

We have often used the data to identify the reasons why some ratings might differ from one airport to another or one segment to another, by looking at customer mix, by linking survey data to operational data. For example, we can take ratings for a given flight and link them to the on-time performance of the flight in that market and we can show that when on-time performance went down so did the ratings in specific categories.

This monthly report on customer satisfaction and the follow-up activities that it generates has helped United Airlines to become much more customer focused, thereby improving its competitive positioning and making its friendly skies even more friendly.[1]

Overview

Report preparation and presentation constitutes the sixth and final step of the marketing research project. It follows problem definition, developing an approach, research design formulation, field work, and data preparation and analysis. This chapter describes the importance of this final step as well as a process for report preparation and presentation. Figure 19.1 briefly explains the focus of the chapter, the relation of this chapter to the previous ones, and the steps of the marketing research process on which this chapter concentrates. As illustrated in the opening vignette, well-prepared marketing research reports and associated follow-up activities add substantial value to the marketing research process.

This chapter provides guidelines for report preparation, including report writing and preparing tables and graphs. Oral presentation of the report is discussed. Research follow-up, including assisting the client and evaluating the research process, is described. The chapter also discusses special considerations for report preparation and presentation in international marketing research and identifies applications of technology and ethics. Figure 19.2 provides an overview of the topics discussed in this chapter and how they flow from one to the next.

Importance of the Report and Presentation

report
A written and/or oral presentation of the research process, results, recommendations, and/or conclusions to a specific audience.

A **report** is a written and/or oral presentation of the research process, results, recommendations, and/or conclusions to a specific audience. The written report and the oral presentation are the tangible products of the research effort, and the report serves as a historical record of the project. If inadequate attention is paid to this step, the value of the project to management

FIGURE 19.1

Relationship of Report Preparation and Presentation to the Previous Chapters and the Marketing Research Process

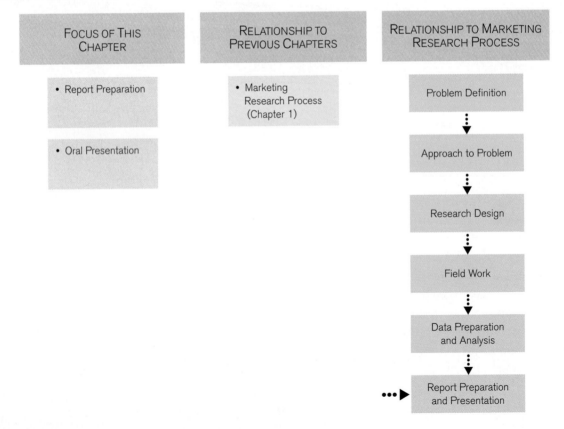

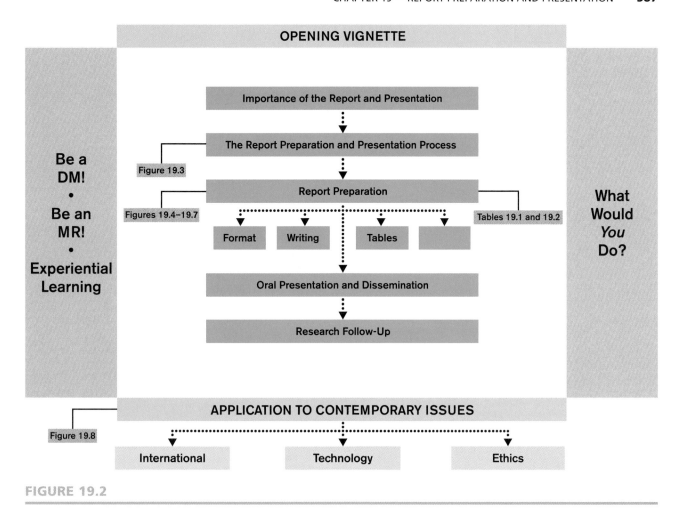

FIGURE 19.2

Report Preparation and Presentation: An Overview

will be greatly diminished. The involvement of many marketing managers in the project is limited to the written report and the oral presentation. These managers evaluate the quality of the entire project based on the quality of the report and presentation. Management's decision to undertake marketing research in the future or to use the particular research supplier again will be influenced by the perceived usefulness of the report and the presentation. For these reasons, report preparation and presentation assume great importance.

The Report Preparation and Presentation Process

Figure 19.3 illustrates the report preparation and presentation process. The process begins with interpreting the results of data analysis in light of the marketing research problem, approach, research design, and field work. Instead of merely summarizing the statistical results, the researcher should present the findings in such a way that they can be used directly as input into decision making. Wherever appropriate, conclusions should be drawn and recommendations that management can act upon should be made. Before writing the report, the researcher should discuss the major findings, conclusions, and recommendations with the client's key decision makers. These discussions play a major role in ensuring that the report meets the client's needs and is ultimately accepted. These discussions should confirm specific dates for the delivery of the written report and other data.

The entire marketing research project should be summarized in a single written report or in several reports addressed to different readers. For example, a report prepared for top management should emphasize the strategic aspects of the research project rather than the

FIGURE 19.3

The Report Preparation and Presentation Process

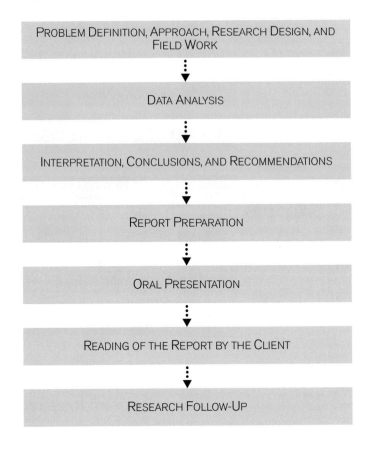

operating details. The reverse is true for a report prepared for operating managers. Generally, an oral presentation supplements these written documents. After the presentation, the client should be given an opportunity to reflect on the report and the project. After that, the researcher should take the necessary follow-up actions. Such actions are found in the opening vignette, in which United's marketing research department handles several requests for additional data analysis. The researcher should assist the client in understanding the report, implementing the findings, undertaking further research, and evaluating the research process in retrospect. The importance of the researcher being intimately involved in the report preparation and presentation process is highlighted by the following example.

Research in Action

Focus Group Moderators' Ghostwriters Can Shortchange Clients

Thomas Greenbaum, president of Groups Plus Inc. (www.groupsplus.com), a U.S. marketing research company focusing on qualitative research, notes a disturbing trend in recent years in the focus-group service sector. Greenbaum asserts that some moderators of focus groups misrepresent their work to clients because their reports are written by ghostwriters who did not participate in the focus-group sessions.

According to Greenbaum, perhaps more than half of moderators use ghostwriters to develop their reports for clients. Often, junior researchers learning the business or part-time employees write these ghostwritten reports. Greenbaum criticizes such ghostwriting because those who merely listen to audiotapes or view videotapes of focus-group sessions cannot always accurately report the nonverbal reactions of focus-group participants. Greenbaum calls upon moderators to be forthright with clients about the authorship of focus-group reports. He also calls upon clients to be more demanding of their contracted research suppliers.

"Although some people in the industry defend ghostwriting by saying they always review the reports before they are sent to the client, or perhaps even write certain key sections, this practice must be looked at carefully by clients who use focus-group research," Greenbaum says. "If the clients know in advance that their reports will be written by someone else, it is clearly less of a problem, but they still do not get the best effort from their research consultants."[2]

Report Preparation

Researchers differ in the way they prepare a research report. The personality, background, expertise, and responsibility of the researcher, along with the decision maker (DM) to whom the report is addressed, interact to give each report a unique character. In short or repetitive projects, an extensive formal written report of the type described here might not be prepared. Nonetheless, the guidelines for formatting and writing reports and designing tables and graphs generally should be followed.

Report Format

Report formats are likely to vary with the researcher or the marketing research firm conducting the project, the client for whom the project is being conducted, and the nature of the project itself. Hence, the following is intended as a guideline from which the researcher can develop a format for the research project at hand. Most formal research reports, as in the opening vignette, include most of the following elements.

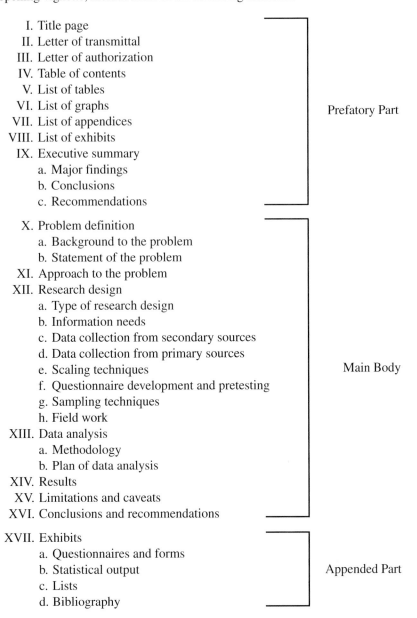

    I. Title page
    II. Letter of transmittal
    III. Letter of authorization
    IV. Table of contents
    V. List of tables
    VI. List of graphs
    VII. List of appendices
    VIII. List of exhibits
    IX. Executive summary
        a. Major findings
        b. Conclusions
        c. Recommendations

   Prefatory Part

    X. Problem definition
        a. Background to the problem
        b. Statement of the problem
    XI. Approach to the problem
    XII. Research design
        a. Type of research design
        b. Information needs
        c. Data collection from secondary sources
        d. Data collection from primary sources
        e. Scaling techniques
        f. Questionnaire development and pretesting
        g. Sampling techniques
        h. Field work
    XIII. Data analysis
        a. Methodology
        b. Plan of data analysis
    XIV. Results
    XV. Limitations and caveats
    XVI. Conclusions and recommendations

   Main Body

    XVII. Exhibits
        a. Questionnaires and forms
        b. Statistical output
        c. Lists
        d. Bibliography

   Appended Part

Sections I to IX constitute the prefatory part, sections X through XVI the main body, and section XVII the appended part of the report. This format closely follows the earlier steps of the marketing research process. The format should be flexible, however, so that it can accommodate the unique features of a specific project. For instance, the results might be presented in several chapters of the report. In Australia, for example, in a national survey data analysis might be conducted for the overall sample, and the data for the country's eight states and territories might be analyzed separately. In this case, the results can be presented in five chapters instead of one.

TITLE PAGE The title page should include the title of the report, information (name, address, and telephone numbers) about the researcher or organization conducting the research, the name of the client for whom the report was prepared, and the date of release. The title should also indicate the nature of the project.

letter of transmittal
A letter that delivers the report to the client and summarizes the researcher's overall experience with the project without mentioning the findings.

LETTER OF TRANSMITTAL A formal report generally contains a **letter of transmittal** that delivers the report to the client and summarizes the researcher's overall experience with the project. The letter should also identify the need for further action on the part of the client, such as implementation of the findings or further research that should be undertaken.

LETTER OF AUTHORIZATION The client writes a letter of authorization to the researcher before work on the project begins. It authorizes the researcher to proceed with the project and specifies its scope and the terms of the contract. Often, it is sufficient to refer to the letter of authorization in the letter of transmittal. Sometimes, however, it is necessary to include a copy of the letter of authorization in the report. The letter of transmittal and the letter of authorization may be eliminated in the case of recurring projects conducted internally by the marketing research department of the firm, as in the case of United Airlines in the opening vignette.

TABLE OF CONTENTS The table of contents should list the topics covered and the appropriate page numbers. In most reports, only the major headings and subheadings are included. A list of tables, list of graphs, list of appendices, and list of exhibits follow the table of contents.

EXECUTIVE SUMMARY The executive summary is an extremely important part of the report, because this often is the only portion of the report that executives read. The summary should concisely describe the problem, the approach, the research design, major results, conclusions, and recommendations. The executive summary should be written after the rest of the report, because it is much easier for the writer to read through the body of the report and then summarize the most important points.

PROBLEM DEFINITION This section of the report provides background on the problem, highlights discussions with the decision makers and industry experts, and discusses the secondary data analysis, the qualitative research that was conducted, and the factors that were considered. It should contain a clear statement of the management-decision problem and the marketing research problem (see Chapter 2).

APPROACH TO THE PROBLEM This section should discuss the broad approach that was adopted in addressing the problem. It should also contain a description of the theoretical foundations that guided the research, any analytical models formulated, research questions, and hypotheses and identify the information needed.

RESEARCH DESIGN The section on research design should specify the details of how the research was conducted (see Chapters 3 through 13). This should include the nature of the research design adopted, data collection from secondary and primary sources, scaling techniques, questionnaire development and pretesting, sampling techniques, and field work. These topics should be presented in a nontechnical, easy-to-understand manner. The technical details should be included in an appendix. This section of the report should justify the specific methods selected.

DATA ANALYSIS This section should describe the plan of data analysis and justify the data analysis strategy and techniques used. The techniques used for analysis should be described in simple, nontechnical terms.

RESULTS This section is normally the longest part of the report and can comprise several chapters. Often, the results are presented not only at the aggregate level, but also at the sub-group (market segment, geographical area, etc.) level. The results should be organized in a coherent and logical way. The presentation of the results should be geared directly to the components of the marketing research problem and the information needs that were identified. The details should be presented in tables and graphs and the main findings discussed in the text.

LIMITATIONS AND CAVEATS All marketing research projects have limitations caused by time, budget, and other organizational constraints. Furthermore, the research design adopted might be limited in terms of the various types of errors (see Chapter 3) that might be serious enough to warrant discussion. This section should be written with great care and a balanced perspective. On the one hand, the researcher must make sure that management does not overly rely on the results or use them for unintended purposes, such as projecting them to unintended populations. On the other hand, this section should not erode their confidence in the research or unduly minimize its importance.

CONCLUSIONS AND RECOMMENDATIONS Presenting a mere summary of the statistical results is not sufficient. The researcher should interpret the results in light of the problem being addressed to arrive at major conclusions. Based on the results and conclusions, the researcher might make recommendations to the decision makers. Sometimes marketing researchers are not asked to make recommendations because they research only one area but do not understand the bigger picture at the client firm. If recommendations are made, they should be feasible, practical, actionable, and directly usable as inputs into managerial decision making. It is very important that the report of a conclusive research project (see Chapter 3) be written in such a way that the findings can be used as input into managerial decision making. Otherwise the report is unlikely to get due attention from management, as illustrated by the following example.

Research in Action

Does Management Read Marketing Research Reports?

Every profession has its nagging doubts. Teachers sometimes wonder if their students are really learning anything; police officers occasionally question whether they are actually reducing crime. Once in a while, marketing researchers have a sneaking suspicion that no one is reading their reports.

Determined to resolve this doubt, one marketing researcher inserted a very undignified photo of himself from a recent office party in the middle of his report. Weeks went by as the report was passed through brand and category management with no response. Finally, the senior vice president of advertising called to ask if he needed a vacation. Evidently, this senior vice president was the only one who had read the report in detail.

Who is responsible when research reports are ignored—the research department or management? According to a study recently released by two U.S. industry groups, the Advertising Research Foundation and the American Marketing

Association, most marketing managers truly believe that marketing research can be valuable. They also claim that most of what they read is not delivering the kind of information they need to make business decisions. Thus, the responsibility of writing readable reports lies with marketing researchers.[3]

Report Writing

A report should be written for specific readers—the marketing managers who will use the results. The report should take into account the readers' technical sophistication and interest in the project, as well as the circumstances under which they will read the report and how they will use it.

Technical jargon should be avoided. The researcher often is required to cater to the needs of several audiences with different levels of technical sophistication and interest in the project. Such conflicting needs can be met by including different sections in the report for different readers or separate reports entirely.

The report should be easy to follow. It should be structured logically and written clearly. An excellent check on the clarity of a report is to have two or three people who are unfamiliar with the project read it and offer critical comments. Several revisions of the report might be needed before the final document emerges.

Objectivity is a virtue that should guide report writing. The report should accurately present the methodology, results, and conclusions of the project without slanting the findings to conform to management's expectations.

It is important to reinforce key information in the text with tables, graphs, pictures, maps, and other visual devices. Visual aids can greatly facilitate communication and add to the clarity and impact of the report. The appearance of a report also is important. The report should be professionally reproduced with quality paper, typing, and binding. Guidelines for tabular and graphical presentation are discussed next.

Be an MR!

Visit The Gallup Organization, the well-known U.S.-based research and consulting company, at www.gallup.com and search for recent reports posted on this Web site. What can you learn about report writing from these reports? Critically evaluate, from a researcher's perspective, the format of one of the reports posted at www.gallup.com.

Be a DM!

As the marketing manager for whom the report was meant, how useful do you find the report you considered?

Guidelines for Tables

Statistical tables are a vital part of the report and deserve special attention (see opening vignette). We illustrate the guidelines for tables using the data for sales at U.S. high-tech equipment provider Hewlett-Packard reported in Tables 19.1 and 19.2. The numbers in parentheses in the following paragraphs refer to the numbered sections of the table.

TITLE AND NUMBER Every table should have a number (1a) and title (1b). The title should be brief, yet clearly describe the information provided. Arabic numbers are used to identify tables so that they can be referred to easily in the text.

ARRANGEMENT OF DATA ITEMS Data should be arranged in a table to emphasize the most significant aspect of the data. For example, when the data pertain to time, the items should be arranged by appropriate time period. When order of magnitude is most important,

TABLE 19.1 Hewlett-Packard Revenues by Business Segment: 2006

Business Segment	Revenue in $Billions 2006
Personal Systems Group	29.166
Imaging and Printing Group	26.786
Enterprise Systems Group	17.308
HP Services	15.617
Other*	2.781
Total	91.658

*Includes all other products

Source: The 2006 Annual Report, Hewlett-Packard Company.

TABLE 19.2 Hewlett-Packard Net Revenue: 2002–2006

Year	Net Revenues (Billions of Dollars)*
2002	56.588
2003	73.061
2004	79.905
2005	86.696
2006	91.658

*Reflects HP's acquisition of Compaq on May 3, 2002

Source: The 2006 Annual Report, Hewlett-Packard Company

the data items should be arranged in that order (2a). If ease of locating items is critical, an alphabetical arrangement is most appropriate.

BASIS OF MEASUREMENT The basis or unit of measurement should be clearly stated (3a).

LEADERS, RULINGS, SPACES **Leaders**—dots or hyphens used to lead the eye horizontally— impart uniformity and improve readability (4a). Instead of horizontal or vertical rules, use white spaces (4b) to set off data items. Skipping lines after different sections of the data can also assist the eye. Horizontal rules (4c) often are used after the headings.

leaders
Dots or hyphens that are used in a table to lead the eye horizontally, impart uniformity, and improve readability.

EXPLANATIONS AND COMMENTS: HEADINGS, STUBS, AND FOOTNOTES Explanations and comments clarifying the table can be provided in the form of captions, stubs, and footnotes. Designations placed over the vertical columns are called *headings* (5a). Designations placed in the left-hand column are called **stubs** (5b). Information that cannot be incorporated into the table should be explained by footnotes (5c). Letters or symbols should be used for footnotes rather than numbers. The footnotes should come after the main table but before the source note.

stubs
Designations placed in the left-hand column of a table.

SOURCES OF THE DATA If the data contained in the table are secondary, the source of data should be cited (6a).

Guidelines for Graphs

As a general rule, graphic aids should be used whenever practical, as in the opening vignette. Graphical display of information can effectively complement the text and tables to enhance clarity of communication and impact. As the saying goes, a picture is worth a thousand words. The guidelines for preparing graphs are similar to those for tables. Therefore, this section focuses on the different types of graphical aids. Several of these are illustrated using the data from Table 19.1 and other data for Hewlett-Packard (HP) reported in Table 19.2.[4]

GEOGRAPHIC AND OTHER MAPS Geographic and other maps, such as product positioning maps, can communicate relative location and other comparative information. Geographic maps can pertain to countries, states, counties, sales territories, and other divisions. For example, suppose the researcher wanted to display the percentage of HP revenues by business segment for each state in the United States. This information could be effectively communicated in a map in which each state was divided into four areas, proportionate to the percentage sales for each of HP's major product lines: personal systems, imaging and printing, enterprise systems, and services. Each area could be displayed in a different color or pattern.

PIE CHARTS In a **pie chart**, also called a *round chart*, the area of each section, as a percentage of the total area of the circle, reflects the percentage associated with the value of a specific variable. A pie chart is not useful for displaying relationships over time or relationships among several variables. As a general guideline, a pie chart should not require

pie chart
A round chart divided into sections.

Graphs can be used to highlight the revenues of Hewlett-Packard

line chart
A chart that connects a series of data points using continuous lines.

pictograph
A graphical depiction that makes use of small pictures or symbols to display the data.

bar chart
A chart that displays data in bars positioned horizontally or vertically.

histogram
A vertical bar chart in which the height of the bars represents the relative or cumulative frequency of occurrence.

more than seven sections. Figure 19.4 shows a pie chart for HP revenues by business segment for 2006, as presented in Table 19.1.

LINE CHARTS A **line chart** connects a series of data points using continuous lines. This is an attractive way of illustrating trends and changes over time (Figure 19.5). Several series can be compared on the same chart, and forecasts, interpolations, and extrapolations can be shown. If several series are displayed simultaneously, each line should have a distinctive color or form.

PICTOGRAPHS A **pictograph** uses small pictures or symbols to display the data. As shown in Figure 19.6, pictographs do not depict results precisely. Therefore, caution should be exercised when using them.

HISTOGRAMS AND BAR CHARTS A **bar chart** displays data in various bars that can be positioned horizontally or vertically. Bar charts can be used to present absolute and relative magnitudes, differences, and changes. The **histogram** is a vertical bar chart where the height of the bars represents the relative or cumulative frequency of occurrence of a specific variable (Figure 19.7).

FIGURE 19.4

Pie Chart of 2006 HP Revenues by Business Segment

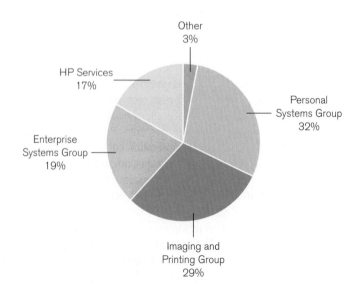

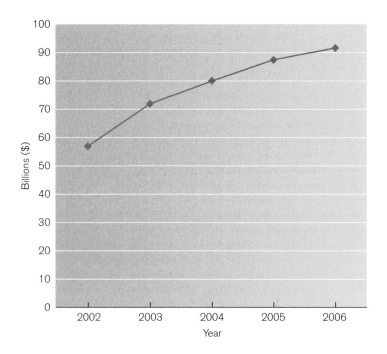

FIGURE 19.5

Line Chart of HP Revenue from 2002 to 2006

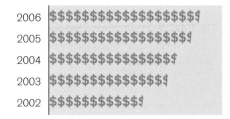

FIGURE 19.6

Pictograph of HP Revenues

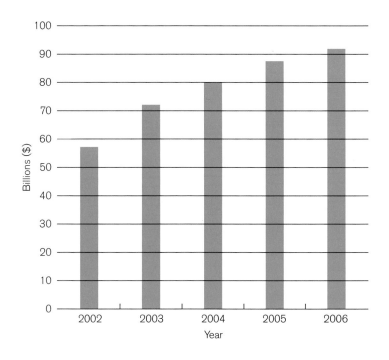

FIGURE 19.7

Histogram of HP Revenues

SCHEMATIC FIGURES AND FLOW CHARTS Schematic figures and flow charts take on a number of different forms. They can be used to display the steps or components of a process, as in Figure 19.3, or they can be used as classification diagrams. Examples of classification charts for classifying secondary data were provided in Chapter 4 (Figures 4.3 to 4.6).

Research in Action

Graphing the Impact of Ethical Brands

Growing concerns about pollution, global warming, and exploitation of workers in Third World countries have driven consumers to use their wallets to make their voices heard. A marketing research study by the German-based GfK Group (www.gfk.com) showed that companies that do not make corporate social responsibility core to their daily operations will be left behind.

The five-country study on consumer perspectives of ethical brands was conducted between January and February of 2007. It included 5,000 respondents from the United Kingdom, the United States, France, Germany, and Spain.

The study found that consumers are choosing to buy only from companies that they believe to be ethical. Companies' ethical credentials have become defining brand attributes, and many customers are willing to pay a premium for an "ethical guarantee." Nearly one-third (31%) of respondents claimed they would pay a

5- to 10-percent premium for an ethical product over a conventional one, and 43 percent stated that they thought that ethical brands made businesses more accountable for their actions. Also, 56 percent of respondents thought that ethical brands should be promoted more heavily. The study also revealed that a striking number of consumers believe that business ethics have declined in the last 5 years (ranging from 64% in Germany to 43% in Spain). To maximize the impact, several graphs were used to highlight the results, as illustrated in the accompanying figure.

Information such as this has caught the ear of several major firms, particularly the French firm L'Oréal (www.loreal.com), the world's largest provider of beauty products. To improve its image as a socially responsible company, L'Oréal bought The Body Shop (www.thebodyshop.com), a skin- and hair-care products firm voted the second "most ethical brand" in the United Kingdom.[5]

Business Ethics over the Past 5 Years—in This Country

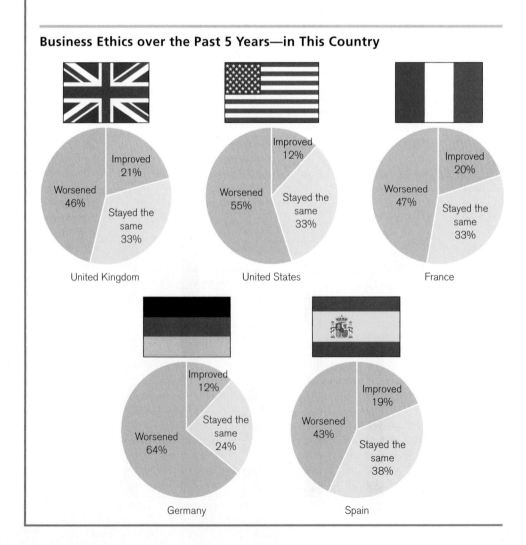

Oral Presentation and Dissemination

The researcher should present the entire marketing research project to the management of the client firm. This presentation will help management understand and accept the written report. Any preliminary questions that the management might have can be addressed in the presentation. Because many executives form their first and lasting impressions about the project based on the presentation, its importance cannot be overemphasized.

The key to an effective presentation is preparation. A written script or detailed outline should be prepared following the format of the written report. The presentation must be geared to the audience. For this purpose, the researcher should determine their backgrounds, interests, and involvement in the project, as well as the extent to which they are likely to be affected by it. For example, a presentation prepared for the advertising department should put more emphasis on advertising decisions, including budget, media, copy, and execution details. The presentation should be rehearsed several times before it is made to management.

Visual aids, such as tables and graphs, should be displayed with a variety of media. It is important to maintain eye contact and interact with the audience during the presentation. Sufficient opportunity should be provided for questions, both during and after the presentation. The presentation should be made interesting and convincing with the use of appropriate stories, examples, experiences, and quotations. Filler words such as "uh," "y'know," and "all right" should not be used.

The **"tell 'em" principle** is effective for structuring a presentation. This principle states: (1) tell 'em what you're going to tell 'em; (2) tell 'em; and (3) tell 'em what you've told 'em. Another useful guideline is the **"KISS 'em" principle**, which stands for: **K**eep **I**t **S**imple and **S**traightforward.

Body language also is important. It helps speakers to convey their ideas more emphatically. Body language can reinforce the issue or the point the speaker is trying to communicate to the audience. The speaker should vary the volume, pitch, voice quality, articulation, and rate while speaking. The presentation should terminate with a strong closing. To stress its importance, a top-level manager in the client's organization should sponsor the presentation.

TNS (www.tnsglobal.com), a U.K.-based marketing research firm, conducted a research project to measure the relative effectiveness of television, print, and radio as advertising media for a client firm. It also assessed the effectiveness of 10 TV commercials, radio commercials, and print ads. Given the nature of the project, the oral presentation of the report was particularly important in communicating the findings. In addition to a PowerPoint presentation, TNS used a DVD player (for playing TV commercials), a CD player (for playing radio commercials), and a story board (for showing print ads). The presentation was made to the client's top corporate officers, consisting of the president, all vice presidents, and all assistant vice presidents at one of their monthly meetings.[6]

The dissemination of the research results should go beyond the oral presentation. The marketing research report, or at least sections of it, should be widely distributed to key executives within the client firm and be made available on demand, as by online distribution. This was illustrated in the opening vignette in which United Airlines makes the monthly customer satisfaction report available online. After dissemination, key executives in the client firm should be given time to read the report in detail before follow-up activities are initiated.

"tell 'em" principle
An effective guideline for structuring a presentation. This principle states: (1) tell 'em what you're going to tell 'em, (2) tell 'em, and (3) tell 'em what you've told 'em.

"KISS 'em" principle
A principle of report presentation that states **K**eep **I**t **S**imple and **S**traightforward.

Research in Action

Important Presentation Realities

How many minutes should a research team that worked on a months-long consumer attitudes research project be given to brief the CEO of a *Fortune* 500 company, such as the Ford Motor Company? One hour? 30 minutes? Both of these estimates are far above what is actually done. According to Mary Klupp, a veteran researcher with the Ford Motor Company and Director of Global Consumer Insights for Ford Financial, researchers would be granted a maximum of 12 minutes. Other senior executives would give researchers a 15-minute time block.[7] The CEO's likely expectations from any research briefing are as follows:

- Remind me what this is about again.

- In our last communication, what did we agree you, the researcher, should do?

- What were the most important numbers (results) I need to know? (Give them to me in percentages, so that I will be able to make comparisons with other information I already have in that form.)

- How confident are you in making the recommendations based on this research?

- What decision should I make based on these research results?

- What will be the impact on sales/profits or our workforce?

To answer these questions effectively, the researcher needs to apply powerful thinking about how the results of extensive analysis can be linked to the issues facing the CEO. This will lead to the greatest benefit of research in that the CEO can greatly increase the likelihood of executing the right decisions or of capitalizing on valuable opportunities.

Research Follow-Up

The researcher's task does not end with the oral presentation. Two other tasks remain. First, the researcher should help the client understand and implement the findings and take any follow-up actions. Second, while it is still fresh in her or his mind, the researcher should evaluate the entire marketing research project.

Assisting the Client

After the client has read the report in detail, questions might arise. The client might not understand parts of the report, particularly those dealing with technical matters. The researcher should provide any help that is needed, as is routinely done by the marketing research department of United Airlines in the opening vignette. Sometimes the researcher helps implement the findings. Often, the client retains the researcher to help select a new product or advertising agency, to develop a pricing policy, segment the market, or take other marketing actions. An important reason for client follow-up is to discuss further research projects. For example, the researcher and management might agree to repeat the study after 2 years. Finally, the researcher should help the client firm make the information generated in the marketing research project a part of the firm's marketing (management) information system (MIS) or decision support system (DSS), as discussed in Chapter 1.

Evaluating the Research Project

Although marketing research is scientific, it also involves creativity, intuition, and expertise. Hence, every marketing research project provides an opportunity for learning, and the researcher should critically evaluate the entire project to obtain new insights and knowledge. The key question to ask is: Could this project have been conducted more effectively or efficiently? This question, of course, raises several more specific questions. Could the problem have been defined differently so as to enhance the value of the project to the client or reduce the costs? Would a different approach have yielded better results? Was the research design the best? What about the mode of data collection? Should mall intercepts have been used instead of telephone interviews? Was the sampling plan the most appropriate? Were the sources of possible design error correctly anticipated and kept under control, at least in a qualitative sense? If not, what changes could have been made? How could the selection, training, and supervision of field workers have been altered to improve data collection? Was the data analysis strategy effective in yielding information useful for decision making? Were the conclusions and recommendations appropriate and useful to the client?

Was the report adequately written and presented? Was the project completed within the time and budget allocated? If not, what went wrong? The insights gained from such an evaluation will benefit the researcher and subsequent projects.

Experiential Learning

Brevity in Report Writing and Presentation

French-based Ipsos Group SA is a leading global marketing research company. Go to www.ipsos-na.com/news/results.cfm, review the list of press releases in the archives, and choose a press release with data that can be rendered into a brief report. Use Excel to create a set of charts for your report and import the charts into PowerPoint. Some of the press releases already include PowerPoint slides; others include charts that can be readily imported into PowerPoint.

Can you make a compelling business presentation in 3 minutes? Select a topic from Ipsos' press release archive. Then, develop a 3-minute presentation using no more than five PowerPoint slides to explain (1) why this research finding matters to a firm in an industry of your choosing and (2) what this firm can do to take advantage of this finding.

Alternatively, you can create your report and presentation by using your analysis skills and the SPSS program to include a set of Excel charts from one of the following sources:

- Chapter 10's McCann Erickson Experiential Learning Exercise
- Chapter 16's Kit Kat taste test
- Chapter 17's Musial University retention study results

Share your final presentation with a group of fellow students in a formal setting.

1. What was the most challenging part of preparing, rehearsing, and making this presentation?
2. What will you do differently in your next presentation as a result of what you have learned in this experiential learning exercise?

Summary Illustration Using the Opening Vignette

Report preparation and presentation is the last, but not the least, step in the marketing research project. A formal report should be prepared and an oral presentation made. As in the case of United Airlines' customer satisfaction survey, the report should be thorough and include a table of contents, executive summary, problem definition, approach, research design, data analysis, results, and conclusions and recommendations. Several tables and graphs should be prepared to enhance the clarity of the findings. The report, or at least some portion of it, might need to be widely disseminated, for example, by making the findings available online as United Airlines did. After management has read the report, the researcher should conduct a follow-up. The researcher should provide assistance to management and conduct a thorough evaluation of the marketing research project, as illustrated by the numerous requests that the marketing research department of United Airlines handles following each report. Figure 19.8 provides a concept map for report preparation and presentation.

International Marketing Research

The guidelines presented earlier in this chapter apply to international marketing research as well, although report preparation can be complicated by the need to prepare reports for management in different countries and in different languages. In such a case, the researcher should prepare different versions of the report, each geared to specific readers. The reports should be comparable, although the formats might differ. The guidelines for oral presentation also are similar to those given earlier, with the added proviso that the presenter should be sensitive to cultural norms. For example, telling jokes, which is frequently done in the United States, is not appropriate in all cultures.

Most marketing decisions are made from facts and figures arising out of marketing research. But these figures have to pass the test and limits of logic, subjective experience, and gut feelings of decision makers. The subjective experience and gut feelings of

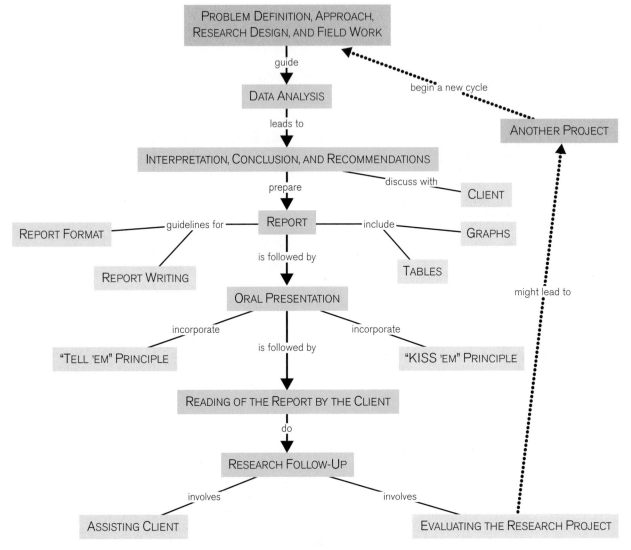

FIGURE 19.8

A Concept Map for Report Preparation and Presentation

managers vary widely across countries, thus different recommendations might be made for implementing the research findings in different countries. This is particularly important when making innovative or creative recommendations, such as advertising campaigns, as illustrated by Toyota Camry in Australia.

Research in Action

Camry Chicken Fries Ford

"Why did the chicken cross the road?" Japanese carmaker Toyota asked in a continuing series of TV commercials aired in Australia. The answer: "To sell more Toyota Camrys, of course." The spots, showing an animated chicken trying to cross the road and getting its feathers blown off by a passing Camry, were created by U.S.-based Saatchi & Saatchi Advertising. When Bob Miller, Toyota's general manager for marketing, tried to explain the ad to Toyota management in Japan, they thought he was insane.

Maybe so, but the commercials did unbelievably well. Hoary old joke that it was, the gag helped Toyota topple

American competitor Ford's dominance in Australia. As part of a continuing series, the next ad showed the featherless chicken sitting on a pile of eggs in the middle of the road and hatching chicks as the Camry sped past. Although such use of humor would not have made sense to the Japanese, it solicited a favorable response from the Australians.[8]

Technology and Marketing Research

Marketing research reports can be published or posted directly to the Web. Normally, these reports are not located in publicly accessible areas but in locations that are protected by passwords or on corporate intranets. The various word-processing, spreadsheet, and presentation packages have the capability to produce material in a format that can be posted directly to the Web, thus facilitating the process.

Publishing marketing research reports on the Web offers a number of advantages. Reports posted online can incorporate all kinds of multimedia, including graphs, pictures, animation, audio, and full-motion video. The dissemination is immediate, and an authorized person anywhere in the world can access the reports online. The reports can be searched electronically to identify material of specific interest. For example, a Coca-Cola manager in Brazil can electronically locate the portions of the report that pertain to South America. Storage and future retrieval is efficient and effortless. It is easy to integrate these reports to become a part of the decision support system. The advantages of publishing marketing research reports on the Web are illustrated by the Gallup organization.

Research in Action

Gallup Is on a Gallop

The Gallup Organization is a world leader in the measurement and analysis of people's attitudes, opinions, and behavior. Although Gallup is best known for the Gallup Poll, which dates from 1935, Gallup also provides marketing and management research, consulting, and training. Its Web site (www.gallup.com) contains several reports presenting the detailed methodology and findings of surveys it has conducted. One report posted on the Gallup Web site stated that teens considered war and terrorism to be top problems.

Most teens do not have mortgages or mouths to feed, so they are likely to tune out when they hear economy-related words that set many adults' teeth on edge, such as *runaway deficit*, *higher taxes*, and *soaring energy prices*. But teens are clearly tuning in when they hear words such as *terrorism* and *war*.

The usefulness of such reports to marketers and the general public has made the Gallup site very popular. As of 2008, Gallup had operations in 40 countries around the world.[9]

A variety of online tools and software packages are available for efficiently producing graphs, charts, tables, and indeed entire reports by largely automating the process to make it more efficient. E-Tabs (www.e-tabs.com) is one example of a system designed for reporting continuous, tracking, syndicated, and customized projects and facilitating multilevel reporting. One of its products, E-Tabs Enterprise, automates the production of charts, graphs, summary tables, and reports directly from the research data and updates them automatically for every wave, region, or brand. This can significantly boost productivity for the time-consuming task of creating charts from ongoing tracking studies.

Ethics in Marketing Research

Several ethical issues also arise during report preparation and presentation. These issues include ignoring pertinent data when drawing conclusions or making recommendations, not reporting relevant information (such as low response rates), deliberately misusing statistics, falsifying figures, altering research results, and misinterpreting the results with the objective of supporting a personal or corporate viewpoint. These issues should be addressed in a satisfactory manner, and the researchers should prepare reports that accurately and fully document the details of all the procedures and findings.

Like researchers, clients also have the responsibility for full and accurate disclosure of the research findings and are obligated to employ these findings honorably. For example, a client who distorts the research findings to make a more favorable claim in advertising can negatively affect the public. Ethical issues also arise when client firms, such as tobacco companies, use marketing research findings to formulate questionable marketing programs.

Research in Action

Tobacco Industry Is a "Smoking Gun"

It is well known that tobacco smoking is responsible for 30 percent of all cancer deaths in the United States. It also is a leading cause of heart disease and is associated with colds, gastric ulcers, chronic bronchitis, emphysema, and other diseases. Should tobacco companies be ethically responsible for this situation? Is it ethical for these companies to employ marketing research to create glamorous images for cigarettes that have a strong appeal to the target market?

Based on the findings of extensive research, it is estimated that advertising by the tobacco industry plays a part in creating more than 3,000 teenage smokers each day in the United States. Advertising for Camel cigarettes through the Old Joe cartoon advertisements increased Camel's share of the illegal children's cigarette market segment from 0.5 percent to 32.8 percent, representing sales estimated at $500 million per year.

These detrimental effects were not limited to the United States. Not only was the tobacco industry enticing children to smoke, it also targeted other less-informed populations, such as those living in Third World countries. This raises the question of whether tobacco companies employed these tactics in an effort to replace those U.S. smokers who quit or die.[10]

What Would *You* Do?

Subaru of America, Inc.: A Report on Reporting

The Situation

Tomohiko Ikeda, CEO of Japanese automaker Subaru (www.subaru.com) , knows that customer loyalty is a big part of the automotive industry today, and Subaru has long been aware of this fact. In the past, Subaru relied heavily on traditional, paper-based customer response surveys. Short, follow-up Purchase Experience Surveys and Service Experience Surveys were mailed to customers within 7 to 14 days after purchase. These surveys entailed both multiple-choice questions and open-ended questions. The response rates from the mailings ranged from 30 to 45 percent. After all the data were collected from the mailings, dealerships received a Subaru Owner Loyalty Indicator (SOLI) rating quarterly report. These reports provided valuable information to the dealer, but they received this information only four times a year. Upon receipt of the comments from their customers it was usually too late to resolve any of their problems.

The solution for Ikeda was the Internet, which would provide faster, more flexible service and information to dealers, field staff, and the management team. Subaru hired U.S.-based Data Recognition Corp. (DRC) (www.datarecognitioncorp.com) to design the program and provide ongoing service. The process begins by scanning the responses from customer survey forms using optical character recognition. Customer comments are captured and categorized. Next, all survey information is electronically added to the appropriate dealer's database using a customized program developed by DRC. The entire process is managed by DRC; this means Subaru can concentrate on selling cars.

The Web-based reports give field managers an opportunity to see what is happening at their assigned dealerships. They can access up-to-the-minute reports on a specific dealership before meeting with the dealer. This works well because the managers are able to access this information from anywhere as long as they can tap into the Internet.

Dealers are able to use the site to stay apprised of customer satisfaction. They can see their quality scores and check on a particular salesperson's performance. Dealers are able to take immediate action because of this new technology. This allows for better management and, in the long run, better performance from all employees.

As dealers became more comfortable with the Web format, they began to request more detailed and timely reports. Due to this request, Subaru has recently begun to develop a series of reports called Just in Time Reports. These reports provide immediate access to current performance rankings in addition to the quarterly rankings. This has become another tool to help Subaru boost sales and performance. This new technology and refocused goals on customer measurement and loyalty will help propel Subaru ahead of its competition.

The Marketing Research Decision

1. Although Subaru management finds the reports to be very useful, the dealers have a slightly different opinion. To improve the usefulness of the report to the dealers, the report should be modified to:
   a. Put more stress on the problem definition
   b. Describe the research design extensively
   c. Explain data analysis in more detail
   d. Emphasize the limitations and caveats
   e. Contain more graphs
2. Discuss the role of the type of report you recommend for enabling Tomohiko Ikeda to make the dealer sales effort more effective.

continued

The Marketing Management Decision

1. To make the dealer sales effort more effective, Tomohiko Ikeda should (check as many as are applicable):
   a. Build closer online relationship with consumers
   b. Build closer online relationship with dealers
   c. Boost Internet leads for dealers
   d. Make greater use of the Internet for reporting research findings to dealers
   e. Boost dealers' online presence
2. Discuss how the management-decision action that you recommend to Tomohiko Ikeda is influenced by the type of report that you suggested earlier.

What Tomohiko Ikeda Did

Subaru of America has launched an e-business program that the automaker hopes will build a closer online relationship with customers while providing Subaru dealers with enhanced e-business features for their own sites. The program, developed in partnership with The Cobalt Group (www.cobalt.com), an American firm specializing in automotive marketing services, is designed to boost Internet leads and sales for dealers and to create a consistent online presence for Subaru's 500 dealers. This collaborative effort puts dealers at the center of the sales and value equation. The system includes features that let local dealers customize their sites with

regards to online pricing flexibility to interactive hours. Since the emergence of the new Subaru dealer Internet program, dealers have seen a boost in their online traffic and are receiving better leads with more informative quote requests. As of 2008, Subaru was marketing its automobiles with the tag lines such as "Always ready. It's what makes a Subaru, a Subaru."[11]

Software Applications

The mainframe and microcomputer versions of the major statistical packages have reporting procedures. In SPSS, the program REPORT can be used to present results in the desired format. TABLE(S) is particularly suited for formatting data for a one-page presentation. In SAS, procedures such as PRINT, FORMS, CHARTS, PLOT, CALENDAR, and TIMEPLOT display information for reporting purposes. The tables and graphs produced from these packages can be directly incorporated into the report. Minitab also has the capability to create graphs and charts and to edit them for use in reports or professional presentations. Graphs can be created using GRAPH > PLOT, or GRAPH > CHART, or GRAPH > HISTOGRAM. Editing can be done using EDIT > EDIT LAST COMMAND DIALOG. Excel has extensive charting capabilities and through Microsoft Office provides a direct link to Word and PowerPoint for report preparation and presentation.

SPSS Windows

Although standard graphs can be produced using the Base module of SPSS, the DeltaGraph package can be used for more extensive graphing. This package has extensive graphing capabilities with more than 80 chart types and more than 200 chart styles.

Likewise, SPSS TABLE(s) enables the researcher to create even complicated tables. For example, the results of multiple response tables can be condensed into a single table. The researcher can create a polished look by changing column width, adding boldface, drawing lines, or aligning.

SPSS OLAP cubes are interactive tables that enable the researcher to slice the data in different ways for data exploration and presentation.

SMARTVIEWER enables the researcher to distribute reports, graphs, tables, and even pivot report cubes over the Web. Company mangers can interact with the results by putting

a report cube on the Web, intranet, or extranet. Thus, they can answer their own questions by drilling down for more detail and creating new views of the data.

Summary

Report preparation and presentation is the final step in the marketing research project. This process begins with interpretation of data analysis results and leads to conclusions and recommendations. Next, the formal report is written and an oral presentation made. After management has read the report, the researcher should conduct a follow-up, assisting management and undertaking a thorough evaluation of the marketing research project.

In international marketing research, report preparation can be complicated by the need to prepare reports for management in different countries and in different languages. Available software can greatly facilitate report preparation and presentation. Several ethical issues are pertinent, particularly those related to the interpretation and reporting of the research process and findings to the client and to the subsequent ways the client uses these results.

Key Terms and Concepts

Report, 586
Letter of transmittal, 590
Leaders, 593
Stubs, 593

Pie chart, 593
Line chart, 594
Pictograph, 594
Bar chart, 594

Histogram, 594
"Tell 'em" principle, 597
"KISS 'em" principle, 597

Suggested Cases and Video Cases

Running Case with Real Data

1.1 Hewlett-Packard

Comprehensive Critical Thinking Cases

2.1 American Idol   2.2 Baskin-Robbins   2.3 Akron Children's Hospital

Comprehensive Cases with Real Data

3.1 Bank of America   3.2 McDonald's   3.3 Boeing

Video Cases

19.1 Marriott

Live Research: Conducting a Marketing Research Project

1. The individual parts of the report can be assigned to teams, with each team writing a specific part. Each team also prepares the PowerPoint slides for that part.
2. The project coordinators should be responsible for compiling the final report and the presentation.
3. Make liberal use of graphs.
4. A presentation of the project should be made to the client, with each team presenting its portion.
5. If each team has worked on the entire report, compile the final report by combining the best parts of the various team reports. This task can be handled by the project coordinators under the supervision of the instructor. The team to make the client presentation can be selected by the instructor based on class presentations by individual teams.

Acronyms

The guidelines for constructing tables can be described by the acronym TABLES:

T itle and number

A rrangement of data items

B asis of measurement

L eaders, rulings, spaces

E xplanations and comments: headings, stubs, and footnotes

S ources of data

GRAPHS can be used as an acronym for guidelines for constructing graphs:

G eographic and other maps

R ound or pie chart

A ssembly or line charts

P ictographs

H istograms and bar charts

S chematic figures and flow charts

The guidelines for making a presentation can be summarized by the acronym PRESENTATION:

P reparation

R ehearse your presentation

E ye contact

S tories, experiences, examples, and quotations

E quipment: multimedia

N o filler words

T ell 'em principle

A udience analysis

T erminate with a strong closing

I nteract with the audience

O utline or script should be prepared

N umber-one level manager should sponsor it

Review Questions

1. Describe the process of report preparation.
2. Describe a commonly used format for writing marketing research reports.
3. Describe the following parts of a report: title page, table of contents, executive summary, problem definition, research design, data analysis, conclusions and recommendations.
4. Why is the "Limitations and Caveats" section included in the report?
5. Discuss the importance of objectivity in writing a marketing research report.
6. Describe the guidelines for report writing.
7. How should the data items be arranged in a table?
8. What is a pie chart? For what type of information is it suitable? For what type of information is it not suitable?
9. Describe a line chart. What kind of information is commonly displayed using this type of chart?
10. Describe the role of pictographs. What is the relationship between bar charts and histograms?
11. What is the purpose of an oral presentation? What guidelines should be followed in an oral presentation?
12. Describe the "tell 'em" and "KISS 'em" principles.
13. Describe the evaluation of a marketing research project in retrospect.

Applied Problems

1. The following passage is taken from a marketing research report prepared for a group of printers and lithographers without much formal business education who run a small family-owned business.

   > To measure the image of the printing industry, two different scaling techniques were employed. The first was a series of semantic differential scales. The second consisted of a set of Likert scales. The use of two different techniques for measurement could be justified based on the need to assess the convergent validity of the findings. Data obtained using both these techniques were treated as interval-scaled. Pearson product moment correlations were computed between the sets of ratings. The resulting correlations were high, indicating a high level of convergent validity.

   Rewrite this paragraph so that it is suitable for inclusion in the report for this audience.

2. Graphically illustrate the consumer decision-making process described in the following paragraph:

   > The consumer first becomes aware of the need. Then the consumer simultaneously searches for information from several sources: retailers, advertising, word of mouth, independent publications, and the Internet. Next, the consumer develops a criterion for evaluating the available brands in the marketplace. Based on this evaluation, the consumer selects the most preferred brand.

3. For the data given in Tables 19.1 and 19.2, use a graphics package or a spreadsheet, such as Excel, to construct the following graphs:
   a. Pie chart
   b. Line chart
   c. Bar chart

4. Visit www.gallup.com to identify a recent report prepared by this company. How does the format of this report compare to the one in the book?

Group Discussion

1. As a small group, discuss the following statement: "All the graphical aids are really very similar; it doesn't matter which ones you use."
2. "Writing a report that is concise yet complete is virtually impossible, because these two objectives are conflicting." Discuss.

3. "Writing, presenting, and reading reports is an acquired talent." Discuss.

Hewlett-Packard Running Case

Review the Hewlett-Packard (HP) case, Case 1.1, and questionnaire given toward the end of the book.

1. Write a report for HP management summarizing the results of your analyses. Prepare a set of charts using Excel.
2. What recommendations do you have for the management?
3. Can you make a compelling business presentation in 10 minutes? Develop a 10-minute presentation for HP management using no more than 10 PowerPoint slides.

4. Share your final presentation with a group of fellow students (representing HP management) in a formal setting.
5. What was the most challenging part of preparing, rehearsing, and making this presentation?
6. What will you do differently in your next presentation as a result of what you have learned in this experiential learning exercise?

MARRIOTT: Marketing Research Leads to Expanded Offerings

Marriott

With roots that go back to before the Great Depression, Marriott International (www.marriott.com) has come a long way from its founding by husband and wife John and Alice Marriott. As of 2008, Marriott had a presence in 68 countries with more than 2,900 properties.

This sustained vast expansion over the last several decades is due in large part to marketing research. Marriott began pioneering segmentation in the hospitality industry by expanding its product offering in the 1980s, both upward and downward in quality from its flagship Marriott brand. Marriott found from focus groups and survey research that it could have many types of hotels serving different market segments, and that these market segments, although all providing the same basic needs, would not compete with each other. Certain brands under the Marriott umbrella serve the business traveler. Courtyard by Marriott, with pricing and scaled-back service levels compared to the larger Marriott hotels, is targeted toward the price-sensitive frequent business traveler. Courtyard hotels—said to be designed for business travelers by business travelers—offer high-speed Internet access, ample workspace within the room, and other amenities that are appealing to the business traveler. Fairfield Inns are priced still more modestly to appeal to travelers who are even more price sensitive. Other brands under the Marriott flag, such as the Ramada line, serve more of a family-style vacation market, with a focus toward comfort and affordability.

However, differentiation is not based on service and pricing alone. Marketing research has revealed other attributes that are important. For example, a family or a basic business traveler on a budget might be looking for a convenient location in addition to affordability. Hence, Marriott places Fairfield Inns along interstates and highways, because these targeted groups travel by car. Convenient location becomes another attribute that adds value and enhances perception of the Marriott brand name.

When Marriott began its Fairfield Inn and Suites brand, it started simply as Fairfield Inn. Then, with marketing research (focus groups and surveys), Marriott found that its Fairfield Inn customers desired a luxury-class room within the value hotel of the Fairfield line. Responding to this, Marriott changed the name to Fairfield Inn and Suites and added high-class rooms that contain amenities such as a spa.

Analysis of internal secondary data identified a substantial number of travelers who stayed in Marriott hotels for more than a few nights. Focus groups and surveys revealed that these extended-stay travelers have different needs. They might need meeting space to conduct business, a kitchenette to dine in occasionally, or a suite space so that they do not get tired of seeing the same four walls around their beds when they come "home" in the evening after yet another day on the road. For these travelers, Marriott opened the Residence Inn line (a hotel line designed for an extended stay). Marriott found from subsequent marketing research that this segment had room to expand to a more value-priced line as well. Again, responding to this research, Marriott introduced TownePlace Suites (a value-priced extended-stay hotel line). Some of the guests at the Residence Inn or TownePlace Suites spend up to 6 months to a year at the same hotel.

At the high end, Marriott offers even fuller service and higher prices with its Hotel Resorts & Suites and its Renaissance upscale business properties. According to Marriott's research estimating potential demand, the size of this high-end segment is substantial. With all of these hotel lines, Marriott continues the commitment to quality that began with John and Alice. Knowing from research that all hotel residents desire quality, Marriott strives to provide this in all facets of the hotel service. One way in which Marriott demonstrates this is by empowering its customer service representatives to address customer problems.

Although each of the various Marriott brands has worked hard to carve out a niche for itself, they all share the Marriott brand identity—the key ingredient to their success. According to Gordon Lambourne, Vice President, Marketing and Public Relations, the Marriott brand identity is all about commitment to service excellence, a strong focus on employees that work in the hotels, taking care of the associates so that they can really focus on their jobs and provide a level of service that customers demand and expect today and that service is consistent throughout the world from Philadelphia to Hong Kong. Each of Marriott's hotels has a different personality with a distinct design and service level that make the guests feel like they are in London or Munich or Paris, but all these hotels have a common thread running through them that identifies them as Marriott hotels.

The numerous Marriott brands, rather than creating competition for each other, actually help bring in more business. According to Gordon Lambourne, each brand does an excellent job of going out to its particular segment, because each has its loyal following, each markets itself independently and as part of a group that is a portfolio of brands. There is some crossover, however, but Marriott views it as a great opportunity, to serve customers whose needs may change. So a customer looking for an extended stay might prefer the Residence Inn, but choose a full-service hotel such as the Renaissance for a shorter trip. So whatever happens, whatever that need might be, Marriott is well positioned to capture that customer and that piece of business.

Conclusion

Marriott has been highly successful in using marketing research to develop a segmentation strategy of targeting different customers with different needs by providing different products and options. The diverse offerings have helped Marriott appeal to an increasingly wide range of clients and win greater business. Continued reliance on marketing research will be critical to Marriott's success in the future.

Questions

1. Discuss the role that marketing research can play in helping Marriott formulate sound marketing strategies.
2. Marriott would like to further penetrate the non-business-travelers segment in the United States. Define the management-decision problem.
3. Define an appropriate marketing research problem based on the management decision problem you have identified.
4. What type of research design should be adopted? Justify your recommendation.
5. Use the Internet to determine the market shares of the major hotel chains for the last calendar year.
6. What type of internal secondary data will be useful to Marriott?
7. What type of syndicated data will be useful to Marriott?
8. Discuss the role of qualitative research in helping Marriott further penetrate the non-business-travelers segment in the United States.
9. Marriott has developed a new hotel package for families on a vacation. It would like to determine consumers' response to this package before introducing it in the marketplace. If a survey is to be conducted to determine consumer preferences, which survey method should be used and why?
10. In what way could Marriott make use of experimentation? What specific experimental design would you recommend?
11. Illustrate the use of the primary scales for measuring consumer preferences for hotel chains.
12. Develop Likert, semantic differential, and Stapel scales for measuring consumer preferences for hotel chains.
13. Develop a questionnaire for assessing consumer preferences for hotels when on vacation.

14. What sampling plan should be adopted for the survey of question 9?

15. How should the sample size be determined for the survey of question 9?

16. How would you conduct the training and supervision of the field workers for the survey of question 9?

17. According to Marriott's Vice President of Marketing and Public Relations, quality, price, service, amenities, comfort, and convenience are all independent variables that affect the preference for a hotel chain. Assume that in a survey of hotel chain, each of the independent variables is measured on a 7-point scale, with 1 = poor and 7 = excellent. Preference for hotel chain is also measured on a 7-point scale, with 1 = not at all preferred and 7 = greatly preferred. Each respondent rates Marriott and three competing hotel chains on all the independent variables as well as preference to stay there on a vacation. What statistical technique(s) would you use to answer the following questions:

    a. Is preference related to each of the independent variables considered individually? What is the nature of the relationship you expect?

    b. Is preference related to all the independent variables considered simultaneously?

    c. Do the respondents evaluate the hotel chains more favorable on quality than they do on price?

    d. The sample is divided into two groups: regular patrons of Marriott and patrons of other hotels. Do these two groups differ in terms of their ratings of Marriott on quality?

    e. Are the two groups of question d different in terms of income measured as high, medium, and low?

    f. The sample is divided in three groups: heavy, medium, and light users of hotels. Do the three groups differ in terms of preference for Marriott?

    g. About 13 percent of the respondents have missing values on one or more variables. How would you treat the missing values?

    h. A question asked the respondents to check as many of the seven hotels that they had stayed in the past 3 years. How should the data for this question be coded?

18. What charts and graphs would you use in preparing a report for Marriott?

19. If marketing research to determine consumer preferences for hotels was to be conducted in Latin America, how would the research process differ?

20. Discuss the ethical issues involved in researching consumer preferences for hotels.

References

1. www.marriott.com, accessed February 25, 2008.

2. www.hoovers.com, accessed February 25, 2008.

3. M. A. Baumann, "High-end Offerings the Result of In-depth Research," *Hotel and Motel Management*, 219(9) (May 17, 2004): 36.

RUNNING CASE WITH REAL DATA

CASE 1.1   HEWLETT-PACKARD (HP)

Using Marketing Research to Gain a Competitive Edge

The Hewlett-Packard Company (HP) is known worldwide for its printers, personal computers, and related services. With Headquarters in Palo Alto, California, it has a global presence in the fields of computing, printing, and digital imaging. It markets products such as printers, cameras, and ink cartridges to households and small business. It also provides software and services (www.hp.com). The company once catered primarily to engineering and medical markets but spun off that line of business as Agilent Technologies in 1999.

Founded by Stanford graduates William Hewlett and David Packard in Palo Alto in 1934, Hewlett and Packard started HP with an investment of $538. The company incorporated 15 years later and went public in 1957. Not until the 1960s and 1970s did HP recognize the market for information technology products. As a consequence of meeting this need, HP introduced the computer industry to Silicon Valley. At the time, products from Silicon Valley were limited to calculators, converters, and semiconverters. In the 1980s, HP began to develop industrial laser printers for desktops and prospered.

In the 1990s, HP expanded its computer-product line, which initially had been targeted at university, research, and business customers, to consumers. Later in the decade, HP launched hpshopping.com as an independent subsidiary to sell online, direct to consumers; the store was rebranded "HP Home & Home Office Store" in 2005. HP also grew through acquisitions, buying Apollo Computer in 1989, Convex Computer in 1995, and Compaq in 2002. Compaq itself had bought Tandem Computers in 1997 (which had been started by ex–HP employees) and Digital Equipment Corporation in

1998. Following this strategy, HP became a major player in desktops, laptops, and servers for many different markets.

HP posted $91.7 billion in annual revenue in 2006 compared to $91.4 billion for IBM, making it the world's largest technology vendor in terms of sales. In October 2006, HP gained the number one ranking in worldwide personal computer shipments, surpassing rival Dell. The gap between HP and Dell widened substantially at the end of 2006, with HP taking a near 3.5 percent market share lead. In 2007 the revenue was $104 billion, making HP the first IT company in history to report revenues exceeding $100 billion.

As of 2008, HP is a global technology company. It generates net revenue and earns its profits from the sale of products, technologies, solutions, and services to consumers, businesses, and governments. HP's portfolio includes personal computers, handheld computing devices, home and business imaging and printing devices, publishing systems, storage and servers, a wide array of information technology services, and software solutions. HP has a dynamic, powerful team of 150,000 employees with capabilities in 170 countries doing business in more than 40 currencies and more than 10 languages.

According to Computer Industry Almanac Inc., in 2005, in the first 30 years of the PC industry worldwide—from 1975 to 2004—cumulative PC sales have surpassed 1.4 billion units, reaching nearly 130 million units in 1990, and over 1.6 billion units in 2005. As seen from Table 1, the leading PC companies have changed considerably in the last 20 years. Apple and IBM were the worldwide leaders in PC unit sales until the early 1990s. Since 1994, Compaq, Dell, or HP has been the leader in PC unit sales.

TABLE 1   Worldwide Unit Sales of PCs: 1991 to 2010

Worldwide Sales	1991–1995 (Sales in Millions)	1996–2000 (Sales in Millions)	2001–2005 (Sales in Millions)	2006–2010 (Sales in Millions)*
Dell	5.4	42.1	133	246
HP and Compaq	21.3	95.0	130	205
IBM and Lenovo	18.0	43.5	64.8	107
Acer	1.7	9.5	28.8	79
NEC and PB	9.3	25.7	26.5	38
Apple	16.2	17.6	17.2	33
Toshiba	4.6	15.9	24.2	41
Gateway	3.8	18.0	16.5	32
Total PC Sales	**201**	**492**	**810**	**1,300**

*Estimated

Marketing Issue and Marketing Research

HP identified that the technical trials that customers often face crop up at the most unexpected and inconvenient times in the daily course of business. Equipment and applications are going to break down, most often right when a critical project is due or while the customer is on the road. The customer's first line of action is usually to call in to the support helpdesk or perhaps research the problem online. HP Services addresses the customer's pain points in these situations by understanding the critical role support plays and how quickly the customer needs resolution. HP's award-winning support organization is dedicated to getting the customer up and running as quickly as possible and preventing future problems so companies can continue to meet their business deliverables. In fact, HP Services customer support organization is becoming increasingly recognized as a leader, ahead of IBM and Dell.

As early as 2004, the industry acknowledged HP's commitment to customer satisfaction with more than seven honors and awards. HP earned the highest overall rating from its customers in a Computerworld/InterUnity Group Inc. survey of nearly 1,200 information technology managers and professionals. In this study, customers gave HP the top satisfaction marks in six of eight categories, including meeting customer expectations, contributing to customer profitability, product quality, product reliability, and licensing policies.

Given its commitment to customer service and satisfaction, HP conducted a survey of recent purchasers of HP PCs and notebooks. HP wants to understand how its consumers use their HP computers. It also wants to understand the level of satisfaction that consumers are deriving from HP's products. HP wants to estimate the probability that customers will be repeat buyers and whether current customers will recommend HP to their friends and family. Finally, HP wants to determine if there is any correlation on any of these identified usage factors and the underlying demographic characteristics of its customers. The questionnaire that was used is provided here; the associated data collected can be downloaded from the Web site for this book.

References

1. Wikipedia, "Hewlett-Packard Company," online at http://en.wikipedia.org/wiki/Hewlett-packard, accessed May 19, 2008.
2. B. Bergstein, "HP Extends Lead over Dell in PC Market," *International Business Times,* January 17, 2007 (Online). Available at www.ibtimes.com/articles/ 20070117 add-pc-shipments.htm, accessed May 19, 2008.
3. Computer Industry Almanac, Inc. "1.3B Cumulative PC Sales over Next 5 Years: Dell and HP Will Each Sell Over 200M PCs in Next 5 Years," June 12, 2006 (Online). Available at www.c-i-a.com/pr0606.htm, accessed June 10, 2007.
4. Hewlett-Packard, "HP Surveys Nation's Small Businesses to Learn What Fuels the Engines of Today's Economy," HP News Release, 2007. Available at www.hp.com/hpinfo/newsroom/press/2005/050427a.html, accessed June 19, 2007.

Note: This case was prepared for class discussion purposes only and does not represent the views of HP or its affiliates. The problem scenario is hypothetical and the name of the actual company has been disguised. **However, the data provided are real and were collected in an actual survey by a prominent marketing research firm, whose name is also disguised.** Some questions have been deleted, and data for other questions are not provided because of proprietary concerns.

HEWLETT-PACKARD (HP) PERSONAL COMPUTERS INTERNET INTERVIEW

Thank you for your interest in our study.

Burke is an independent marketing research firm that has been commissioned by HP Computers to get the honest opinions of recent purchasers of HP personal computer systems. You will be asked to offer your views about HP and describe your Internet usage.

This survey should only take a few minutes of your time. By completing this survey, you will be automatically entered into a drawing for $100 gift certificates that can be used at a variety of major online retailers. If you don't complete the survey, you may qualify for the drawing by writing to the address contained on the email inviting you to participate in this project.

Unless you give us your permission at the end of the survey to release your name to HP along with your responses, your individual responses will kept confidential.

INTERNET USAGE

Q1   Approximately how many total hours per week do you spend online? This would be the total from all the locations you might use.

Less than 1 hour -1
1 to 5 hours -2
6 to 10 hours -3
11 to 20 hours -4
21 to 40 hours -5
41 hours or more -6

Q2   Following is a list of things people can do online. Please indicate which of these you have ever done on the Internet. *(Rotate responses.)*

Don't Know = 0

Ask First		Yes	No
_____	Communicated with others via newsgroups or chat rooms . . . .-1	-1	-2
_____	Looked for a job . . . .-1	-1	-2
_____	Planned or booked trips . . . .-1	-1	-2
_____	Downloaded a picture or graphic . . . .-1	-1	-2
_____	Downloaded sounds or audio clips . . . .-1	-1	-2
_____	Looked up information about a TV show or movie . . . .-1	-1	-2
_____	Downloaded a video clip . . . .-1	-1	-2

Q3   What other type of things do you use the Internet for?

_____

HP SATISFACTION AND LOYALTY

Q4   Overall, how satisfied are you with your HP computer system?

Very satisfied -1
Somewhat satisfied -2
Somewhat dissatisfied -3
or Very dissatisfied -4

Q5   How likely would you be to recommend HP to a friend or relative?

Definitely would recommend -1
Probably would -2
Might or might not -3
Probably would not -4
or Definitely would not recommend -5

Q6   If you could make your computer purchase decision again, how likely would you be to choose HP?

Definitely would -1
Probably would -2
Might or might not -3
Probably would not -4
or Definitely would not -5

Q7   Deleted (Open ended)

COMPUTER MANUFACTURER IMPORTANCE/PERFORMANCE RATINGS

Q8   The following set of statements refers to personal computer manufacturers. For each statement, please first indicate to what extent you agree that **HP Computers** meets that requirement.

To do this, please use a scale from 1 to 9, where a "1" means you **do not agree at all** with the statement, and a "9" means you **agree completely**. Of course, you may use any number between 1 and 9 that best describes how much you agree or disagree with the statement. Don't Know = 0

How much do you agree that **HP Computers** does *(insert statement)*?

(Rotate statements.)

Ask First		Rating
_____	Make ordering a computer system easy	_____
_____	Let customers order computer systems customized to their specifications	_____
_____	Deliver its products quickly	_____
_____	Price its products competitively	_____
_____	Feature attractively designed computer system components	_____
_____	Have computers that run programs quickly	_____
_____	Have high-quality computers with no technical problems	_____
_____	Have high-quality peripherals (e.g., monitor, keyboard, mouse, speakers, disk drives)	_____
_____	"Bundle" its computers with appropriate software	_____
_____	"Bundle" its computers with Internet access	_____
_____	Allow users to easily assemble components	_____
_____	Have computer systems that users can readily upgrade	_____
_____	Offer easily accessible technical support	_____

Q9A   If the price of the HP computer system you purchased had been 5% higher, and all other personal computer prices had been the same, how likely would you have been to have purchased your HP computer system?

Definitely would have purchased -1
Probably would have purchased -2
Might or might not have purchased -3
Probably would not have purchased -4
or Definitely would not have purchased -5

Q9B   If the price of the HP computer system you purchased had been 10% higher, and all other personal computer prices had been the same, how likely would you have been to have purchased your HP computer system?

Definitely would have purchased -1
Probably would have purchased -2
Might or might not have purchased -3
Probably would not have purchased -4
or Definitely would not have purchased -5

EARLY ADOPTER ATTRIBUTES

Q10   Following is a series of statements that people may use to describe themselves. Please indicate how much you agree or disagree that they describe you. To do this, please use a scale of 1 to 7 where a "1" means you **disagree completely** and a "7" means you **agree completely**. Of course, you may use any number between 1 and 7.

Don't Know = 0

The first/next statement is *(insert statement)*. What number from 1 to 7 best indicates how much you agree or disagree that this statement describes you?

Ask First		Rating
	Market Maven Items	
_____	I like introducing new brands and products to my friends	_____
_____	I like helping people by providing them with information about many kinds of products	_____
_____	People ask me for information about products, places to shop, or sales	_____
_____	My friends think of me as a good source of information when it comes to new products or sales	_____
	Innovativeness	
_____	I like to take a chance	_____
_____	Buying a new product that has not yet been proven is usually a waste of time and money	_____
_____	If people would quit wasting their time experimenting, we would get a lot more accomplished	_____
_____	I like to try new and different things	_____
_____	I often try new brands before my friends and neighbors do	_____
_____	I like to experiment with new ways of doing things	_____

Opinion Leadership
_____   When it comes to computer-related products, my friends are very
likely to ask my opinion   _____
_____   I am often used as a source of advice about computer-related
products by friends and neighbors   _____
_____   I often tell my friends what I think about computer-related products   _____

DEMOGRAPHICS

Q11   These next questions are about you and your household and will just be used to divide our interviews into groups.

What was the last grade of school you completed?

Some High School or less -1
High School Graduate -2
Some College/Technical School -3
College Graduate or higher -4

Q12   Which of the following best describes your age?

18 to 19 -1
20 to 24 -2
25 to 29 -3
30 to 34 -4
35 to 39 -5
40 to 44 -6
45 to 49 -7
50 to 54 -8
55 to 59 -9
60 to 64 -10
65 to 69 -11
70 to 74 -12
75 to 79 -13
80 or older -14

Q13   Which of the following best describes your household's total yearly income before taxes?

Under $20,000 -1
$20,000 – $29,999 -2
$30,000 – $49,999 -3
$50,000 – $74,999 -4
$75,000 – $99,999 -5
$100,000 or over -6
No Answer – 0

Q14   Are you . . . ?

Male -1
Female -2

This completes all the questions.
Thank you very much for your assistance with this interview!

COMPREHENSIVE CRITICAL THINKING CASES

CASE 2.1   AMERICAN IDOL

A Big Hit for Marketing Research?

"This could be more of a challenge than we previously thought," Melissa Marcello told her business associate Julie Litzenberger. After nodding in agreement, Litzenberger put down her cup of coffee at the Vienna, Virginia, Starbucks coffee shop near her firm's headquarters.[1]

Both Marcello and Litzenberger were far along their career paths as researchers in the winter of 2006 when they met at Starbucks. Marcello was CEO of research agency Pursuant, Inc. (www.pursuantresearch.com), and Litzenberger led the public relations division at marketing communications agency Sage Communications (www.sagecommunications.com). Both were based in the Washington, D.C. area.

Litzenberger took the last bite of her cinnamon scone before sipping her latte. She nodded again to Marcello across the table for two before answering. "Research studies that are the most successful in moving the needle are the studies where the research firm uses scientific and credible methods, poses the right questions, and provides the client company with the insights needed to sufficiently reduce risk in decision making," Litzenberger said. "In short, improving decision making is what effective marketing research is about."

Over the years, Marcello and Litzenberger had witnessed prospective client companies voicing resistance to pursuing marketing research. Skeptics of professional marketing research sometimes would say said that they "already knew enough about customers to make decisions." Other times, skeptics would assail the sampling methods of studies in an attempt to dismiss the results. And in other instances, skeptics would merely claim that finding the answers to such questions about customers would be too expensive to obtain. In sum, professionally done marketing research was presented as being impractical.

Marcello and Litzenberger were attempting to overcome a challenge in client development. Specifically, they were attempting to obtain evidence to confront skeptics of professionally done marketing research without comprising the privacy of previous clients with whom they had worked. It was inappropriate for them to share the results of previous studies with anyone other than the clients who had contracted them for those studies.

While considering dozens of ideas over the past 3 weeks of project-development brainstorming sessions, Marcello and Litzenberger were now focused on one project for demonstrating the usefulness of marketing research to prospective clients. The research question was: "What still needs to be known about the viewers and voters for contestants of the popular TV show *American Idol*?"

American Idol (www.americanidol.com) is an annual televised singing competition, which began its first season in 2002. The program has always sought to discover the best young singer in the United States. Each year, a series of nationwide auditions are followed by a series of telecasts featuring the singers who advance to the next week's show based on public voting. Throughout the show's history, three judges have critiqued the singing of surviving contestants each week: record producer and bass player Randy Jackson, pop singer and dancer Paula Abdul, and the blunt-speaking music executive Simon Cowell. Good-guy Ryan Seacrest has hosted the show each year.

In the spring of 2006, *American Idol* had reached an all-time peak, garnering as many as 37 million viewers for a single episode. Despite the sizeable audience—composed of people from different demographics, from tweens to senior citizens—no third party had conducted a research study to gain more insight into who the viewers actually were or their motivations for voting for *American Idol* contestants.

"Are we kidding ourselves?" Marcello challenged Litzenberger. "Who would care about a study investigating *American Idol* viewers?"

"How about the sponsors of the show?" Litzenberger quickly countered. "Pepsi Cola passed on sponsoring the show during its development, but Coca-Cola decided to take a risk and invested $10 million to become a sponsor in *American Idol*'s first season. That's a lot of cola and that was a lot of risk to take in the volatile world of broadcast television!"

"You're right," Marcello said. "I later read in *USA Today* that Kelly Clarkson might have been voted the first American Idol, but Coke was the real winner. So maybe Pepsi was the real loser. Coke and Ford now spend tens of millions each year not only to be sponsors, but to have tie-in promotions, such as you might find at www.cokemusic.com."

"But just how durable is the show's concept?" Litzenberger asked after finishing her latte. "What if we find that voters are mostly pre-teen girls? What if we find that adults don't vote for the contestants or adults don't have confidence in the judges' opinions?"

"The news media should find such answers more delicious than that slice of pumpkin bread I am spying in that glass case over there by the cash register," Marcello said. "Journalists will almost always cover what they regard as relevant and quantifiable trends in popular culture."

Litzenberger leaned forward. "So how do you propose that we do such a study?"

"We've devoted hours to this question at my firm for better than a week. Here's our best thinking on it as of today," Marcello said. "We could place about six questions on Opinion Research Corporation's CARAVAN (www.opinionresearch.com) national omnibus telephone survey to find out more about who, among adults 18 or older living in the United States, watched and voted in the 2006 season of *American Idol*. Such an omnibus survey could be done by telephone during 3 days in April 2006."

"OK, but what about sampling?" Litzenberger said. "You know we might get attacked on this. It could be really expensive, too. Can we afford it?"

"If we do it this way, we can afford it," Marcello said. "It will run about $1,000 per question. We'll have the Opinion Research Corporation ask our questions along with those of other sponsoring companies to a randomly selected national sample of 1,045 adults comprised about evenly of men and women. With a total sample size of more than 1,000, we will be able to say with 95-percent certainty that the results would be accurate to within ±3.0 percent. This exceeds acceptable standards for a survey about media preferences."

"So if only 10 percent of our sample reported voting for *American Idol* contestants, we would be able to say with 95 percent confidence that the actual percentage of the adult population who voted was somewhere between 7 and 13 percent?" Litzenberger asked.

"You've got it", Marcello affirmed. "Of course, it could be a lower or a much higher percentage. Nobody really knows now. Anybody who says otherwise is merely speculating."

Silence now overcame these two researchers as they reflected on the future courses of action they could take. They could drop the whole idea of demonstrating the usefulness of marketing research. They could pursue this *American Idol* study. If so, what questions should be asked to respondents and why? Should they could continue to consider other ideas for such a study and pursue it later. What should they do? Why?

Critical Thinking Questions

1. Marcello and Litzenberger felt it was important to conduct this study because _____.
(State the relevant background information used to justify their work.)

2. The main purpose of Marcello and Litzenberger's study was _____.
(State as accurately as possible the purpose for doing the study.)

3. The key questions Marcello and Litzenberger are addressing are _____.
(Identify the key questions in the minds of the case's protagonists.)

4. The methods used to answer their key questions were _____.
(Describe the general approach used and include details that assist in evaluating the quality of the results; for example, sample size, etc.).

5. The most important information in this article is _____.
(Identify the facts, observations, and/or data Marcello and Litzenberger are using to support their conclusions. Be quantitative.)

6. The results can be put into context by comparing them to _____.
(Place the quantitative results into an easily understood context by expressing as percentages or by comparing them to an intuitively understood value; for example, twice the size of a football field.)

7. The main inferences/conclusions in this article are _____.
(Identify the key conclusions the case protagonists present in the article.)

8. If we take this line of reasoning seriously, the implications are _____.
(What consequences are likely to follow if people take Marcello and Litzenberger's reasoning seriously?)

Technical Questions

9. What steps of the six-step marketing research process are evident in this case?

10. What is the role of marketing research in marketing decision making suggested by this case?

11. Define the management-decision problem confronting Melissa Marcello and Julie Litzenberger and a corresponding marketing research problem and show the linkages between the two.

12. If Marcello and Litzenberger decide to conduct this study, what research design should they adopt? Relate the different phases of the research design to specific aspects of the marketing research problem.

13. What kind of secondary and syndicated data would be helpful in addressing the questions raised by Marcello and Litzenberger? What is the role played by such data?

14. Discuss the role of qualitative research in gaining a better understanding of why people view *American Idol.*

15. Is the telephone survey the most appropriate method in this case? If not, which survey method would you recommend?

16. Why did Marcello and Litzenberger not consider doing an experiment? What aspects of *American Idol* viewers should be researched by conducting an experiment?

17. Discuss the role of measurement and scaling in assessing the audience response to *American Idol.*

18. Critically evaluate the wording of the following question: "Who is your favorite American Idol?"

19. Describe the sampling process employed by Opinion Research Corporation's CARAVAN. (Hint: Visit www.opinionresearch.com).

20. Is the sample size appropriate? Why or why not?

21. If you were the supervisor in charge of the CARAVAN telephone interviewers, what challenges would you face?

22. As part of the management team at Fox that produces *American Idol,* how would you evaluate the report produced by Marcello and Litzenberger? How will the proposed study help you make decisions about the show?

Reference

1. Adapted from Melissa Marcello and Julie Litzenberger, "Fascinating Findings," *Quirk's Marketing Research Review*, Vol. 21, no. 3 (March 2007), 58–62.

Note: The contribution of Professor Mark Peterson in developing this case is gratefully acknowledged.

CASE 2.2   BASKIN-ROBBINS

Can It Bask in the Good 'Ole Days?

It was early December 2003, and Baskin-Robbins Brand Officer Ken Kimmel had just returned from lunch. To his surprise, his walk from the parking lot to the Randolph, MA headquarters building had quickly turned into a sprint. Kimmel was trying to avoid the chilly effects of a Nor'easter that was whipping most of New England with arctic winds.

Like the nasty weather Kimmel just escaped, the frozen-food retailing industry had become more hostile to Baskin-Robbins (www.baskinrobbins.com) in recent years. New entrants, such as Cold Stone Creamery founded in 1988, had popularized the in-store experience with customers watching their ice cream creations being made before their eyes on cold stone slabs. For years, Baskin-Robbins had turned their back to Cold Stone Creamery's gains, in a similar way the Baskin-Robbins counter staff turned their back on customers to make a banana split. Cold Stone Creamery's sales were now almost 75 percent of Baskin-Robbins' sales.

In response, the Baskin-Robbins executive group along with Kimmel had recently moved to redesign stores, but it was not easy convincing the thousands of franchisees who ran the Baskin-Robbins stores to change. A store redesign could run up to $50,000 and was funded mostly by the franchisees. One aspect of the redesign resulted in lowering the ice cream cases to make it easier for children to look down into the ice cream bins.

Another change being considered was changing the Baskin-Robbins logo to coincide with the redesign of store interiors. The logo appears on napkins, cone wrappers, spoons, cups, uniforms, and signs at each Baskin-Robbins store. The estimated cost for making such a change was $5 million for Baskin-Robbins headquarters. Individual franchisees would have to invest about $10,000 for the logo change to be made inside the stores.

Later that afternoon, Kimmel's brand group was deep in discussion about whether to change the brand symbol of Baskin-Robbins at the same time stores would be redesigned.

"The context has changed since the mid-1980's," visiting retailing consultant Zack Wheatly said. "Customers are more demanding about the hospitality experience. They earn more money and they can buy comparable ice creams to Baskin-Robbins in grocery stores now."

Kimmel sensed it was time to mention recent strategy decisions by the Baskin-Robbins executive group.

"While our competitors are pushing this mix-in experience—a higher-priced theater experience—Baskin-Robbins has decided to focus on delivering a great value for our consumers in an accessible kind of environment," Kimmel responded. "The executive group has decided that we are going to focus on our new products as opposed to the theater of the business. As part of this new emphasis, we have recently begun highlighting innovations such as our own frozen coffee beverage—the Cappuccino Blast—and a fruit-based beverage—Bold Breezes. Carrying frozen custard is also on the horizon."

Marsha Davis, Kimmel's research director took her turn in the conversation. "Is Baskin-Robbins such an established brand that the logo for Baskin-Robbins should not be overhauled?" Davis asked.

"I know what you are suggesting," Wheatly replied. "Conventional wisdom in this industry would say that one shouldn't tinker with an established brand."

"We have discussed this among ourselves here at headquarters with the CEO and other senior executives, and we have also invested in hearing from consultants in retailing communications," Kimmel said. "They think the decision to change the logo should be taken only after extensive deliberation and direct research with customers."

"Right," Wheatly said. "Analysts in the quick-service restaurant industry have reported in the trade journals that the new entrants have continued to grow faster than Baskin-Robbins—especially in the key metric of same-store sales compared the previous year. What did the qualitative research say about the proposed new logos?"

Davis paused, dug in her briefcase, and removed the glossy printed versions of the old logo and the leading candidate among the proposed new logo. She put them both on the table facing the others.

"We talked with four focus groups in Chicago, LA, and New York and they agreed that the Baskin-Robbins brand represented irresistible treats, smiles, and fun," Davis said. "They also liked this proposed logo that the senior executive group liked."

"So where do we go from here?" Kimmel asked.

"Because your management wants to make a change to the logo only if it is necessary, you should study your customers' attitude toward the new logo, so that you can explain whether a logo change is warranted," Wheatly said.

Everyone stopped talking to reflect on what was just said. After about 10 seconds, Kimmel raised an open hand to the group.

"Wait. This is beginning to remind me of the New Coke introduction," Kimmel said after some reflection. "Customers' subjective attachment to the old Coke was ignored, then. We need to ask about the old logo, too. Also, I know the senior executives want a clear margin of preference for the new logo. If the new logo is not preferred 2:1 in a head-to-head competition with the old one, we need to drop it."

Wheatly picked up the line of thought.

"OK, and now that you mention it, we also need to present the drawings of the new redesigned stores and have the customers respond to the old and new logos after understanding what our new stores will be like," Wheatly said.

"So restating our problem, I guess it sounds this way," Davis said. "Because management wants to make a change to the logo only if it is absolutely necessary, we should study our customers' attitudes toward the old logo and toward the new logo after showing them the drawings of the redesigned stores. Only then can we explain whether customers prefer the new logo 2:1 over the old logo."

The words seem to hang in the air in the conference room at Baskin-Robbins headquarters. The statement of the marketing research problem was sounding much improved to Kimmel. But he also had the following thoughts: (1) Given that Baskin-Robbins had moved to redesign store interiors, should the brand logo be changed to signal something new is happening at Baskin-Robbins? (2) If the logo is changed, would there be synergy between the logo change and the redesigned interiors? Synergistic results could be dramatic. A new look, a new menu, and a new strategy focused on delivering "irresistible treats, smiles, and fun" in an accessible way and at a reasonable price could check the momentum rival brands have developed by focusing on a high-end, in-store experience. Considering these elements, the strategic importance of the Baskin-Robbins' research project became more clear in Kimmel's mind.

But had they missed anything in their process of developing the statement of the research problem? Were they focused upon the right issue now? Should they continue to consider other logos for such a study? Should they just go ahead with the new logo because focus group participants had liked the new logo and the senior executives had, as well? What should they do? Why?

Critical Thinking Questions

1. Baskin-Robbins Brand Officer Ken Kimmel felt it was important to conduct this study because _____.
   (State the relevant background information used to justify their work.)

2. The main purpose of the Baskin-Robbins study was _____.
   (State as accurately as possible their reason for doing the study.)

3. The key questions the Baskin-Robbins brand team is addressing are _____.
   (Identify the key questions in the minds of the case protagonists.)

4. The methods used by Kimmel and his team to identify the marketing research problem were _____.
   (Describe the general approach used and include details that assist in evaluating the quality of the results.)

5. The most important understanding about Baskin-Robbins as an organization that led the firm to consider a new logo as part of problem definition was _____.
   (Identify the facts, observations, and/or data Kimmel and his team are using to support their conclusions. Be quantitative.)

6. The series of marketing research problem statements can be put into context by comparing each to _____.
   (Place the marketing research problem statements into other readily understood contexts.)

7. The main inferences/conclusions in this case pertaining to problem definition are _____.
   (Identify the key conclusions implied by the case.)

8. If we take this line of reasoning seriously, the implications for many other firms seeking to define the marketing research problem related to rebranding are _____.
   (What consequences are likely to follow if people take the brand team's reasoning seriously and apply them to other firms?)

Technical Questions

9. What is the role of marketing research in deciding whether to change the logo in this case?

10. Define the management-decision problem confronting the Baskin-Robbins executive group, along with Kimmel, and a corresponding marketing research problem and show the linkages between the two.

11. What specific research question and hypothesis are suggested in this case?

12. If Kimmel decides to conduct a study to address the marketing research problem, what research design should be adopted? Relate the different phases of the research design to specific aspects of the marketing research problem.

13. What kind of secondary and syndicated data would be helpful in addressing the issue of changing the brand logo? What is the role played by such data?

14. Discuss the role of qualitative research in gaining a better understanding of the influence of the brand image on consumer selection of an ice cream brand.

15. Do you think that Kimmel should commission a survey in this case? If yes, which survey method would you recommend and why?

16. Can an experiment be conducted to address the issue of changing the brand logo? If yes, what experimental design would you recommend and why?

17. Discuss the role of measurement and scaling in assessing the consumer response to the old and new logos.

18. After showing the respondent the old and the new logos, the following question is asked: "Do you like the new logo better than the old logo?" Critically evaluate the wording of this question.

19. If mall-intercept interviews are to be conducted to determine consumers' preferences for ice cream brands, design a suitable sampling process. What should be the sample size and how it should be determined?

20. If you were the supervisor in charge of mall-intercept interviewing, what challenges would you face in training the interviewers?

21. How should the executive group, along with Kimmel, evaluate the marketing research report? How will the findings of marketing research help them make decisions about changing the brand logo?

References

1. Sherri Daye Scott, "Remaining Relevant," *QSR* (February 2006): 26–30.
2. David Colker, "Ice Cream Battle Getting Hotter," *Los Angeles Times*, November 5, 2005, C1.
3. www.baskinrobbins.com/about/OurHistory.aspx, accessed February 15, 2008.

Note: The contribution of Professor Mark Peterson in developing this case is gratefully acknowledged.

CASE 2.3 KID STUFF?

Determining the Best Positioning Strategy for Akron Children's Hospital

"I'm not sure we are getting anywhere in this meeting," Aaron Powell thought to himself as he pushed his chair away from the conference room table and slowly stood up to stretch his legs after an hour had already gone past.

Powell, Akron Children's Hospital's (ACH; www.akronchildrens.org) marketing director, stood to gaze out the conference room windows onto the two ribbons of train tracks that curled near the hospital on the north side of this midsized city in Northeast Ohio. He was thinking about how rival hospitals, such as Akron City Hospital, Akron General Medical Center, and St. Thomas Hospital, had recently hired marketing directors like himself. The urgency to advance Akron Children's Hospital's marketing effort was going to intensify in the next year.

Powell's meeting was going into its second hour. In addition to Powell, the meeting's participants were Mark Norton, the hospital operations officer (Powell's boss), and Janet Jones from the Cleveland–based Marcus Thomas communications and research agency (www.marcusthomasllc.com). One staff member from finance was there, along with the soon to be retiring public relations director for the hospital. In the past, both of these staffers would support whatever Norton proposed or liked. It now looked like Powell and Jones were on the other side of a divide about how to approach positioning Akron Children's Hospital in next year's advertising campaign. To make matters worse, Powell and Jones appeared to be outnumbered, and the tension in the room was palpable.

"Let me read the research problem statement all of us revised in the first hour of our meeting," Jones said. "Akron Children's Hospital board wants the hospital to become the preferred hospital in the high-growth areas of the region. Accordingly, we are studying positioning possibilities, so that the board can select the best positioning for next year's communications campaign intended to boost the number of patient cases 10 percent in the following year."

"That's it. That's what we want," Norton said. "But I don't think we have to pursue a research project with a survey that just may lead us to reinvent the wheel—and for $60,000, too."

"What wheel is that?" Powell asked turning away from the window to face Norton.

"Aaron, you know as well as I do that this hospital is all about children. It's even in our name," Norton said. "Emphasize the kids. Whatever we do in the media should feature the kids. Just do some focus groups that will allow Marcus Thomas to get some ideas for their advertising about kids and our hospital. That should only cost about $20,000. But honestly, I am not sure we even need that."

"Mark, remember that McDonald's tends to emphasize kids, too, but adults are featured in their advertising most of the time," Powell said. "Marcus Thomas needs to cover the entire range of issues families consider when choosing a hospital for their kid. If we miss something important, one of the other hospitals in Akron might claim they are the better hospital when it comes to this."

"Aaron is making a good point," Jones said. "Right now, we don't know which positioning would help Akron Children's the most."

"So describe which paths we can pursue now," Norton said.

"Plan A—do focus groups only, as you suggested," Jones said. "Plan B—do focus groups with a follow-on survey. Plan C—do a survey with follow-on focus groups. And plan D—do no research."

"Tell me more about each of these," Norton said.

"In plan A, Marcus Thomas would conduct four focus groups, with an average of 10 respondents per group," Jones said. "We'll ask participants to discuss their experiences while at a hospital. Participants will be required to be the primary decision makers for health-care decisions within the family and have a child—newborns to 18 years old—with an acute condition and who had spent at least 3 consecutive days in a hospital. Because most health-care decision makers within a family tend to be women, most of the participants will be female between 25 and 54 years old with one or more children ranging from newborns to 18 years old."

"Cost?" Norton asked.

"About $20,000," Powell said.

Jones continued. "In plan B, we'll do plan A, plus a field survey to follow-up on the issues we identify in the focus groups. First, we'll ask about unaided and aided awareness of hospitals in the region. Then, based on what we learn in the focus groups, we will identify the concepts of three positioning strategies and ask survey respondents which one they prefer most and which one they prefer next most. We'll be able to statistically determine the degree of preference among the positioning alternatives."

"The three strategies might be, one, Akron Children's Hospital has doctors who listen to you," Powell said. "Or, two, we know how to meet the unique needs of children, or, three, we use the latest advances in treating children."

"Cost?" Norton asked again.

"About $60,000," Powell said.

"What about plan C? Why does that make sense?" Norton asked.

"We can identify the best positioning strategy by conducting a survey. The salient aspects of this positioning strategy to the consumers can then be explored via focus groups. The cost will be the same as plan B; that is, $60,000," responded Jones.

"And plan D—no research. Turn our creative staff loose and hang on for the ride," Jones said with a wry smile.

Norton returned the smile and looked around the room. "Doesn't your firm do the advertising for the Ohio Lottery?" Norton asked. "With plan D, we might do better by playing the Ohio Lottery!"

Sensing the humor, everyone in the room laughed together. Finally, tension seemed to begin dissipating.

Norton nodded slowly. Powell nodded, too. However, the questions Powell was thinking about still remained. Which of the plans would Akron Children's Hospital pursue—plan A, plan B, plan C, or plan D? If money was invested, would it be a worthwhile investment? Would the idea of research being a "cost" (with no apparent return) persist in the minds of Norton and the other staff members long after this meeting? What could be done now to help Norton and the other executives view research as an investment (with an implied return)?

Critical Thinking Questions

1. Akron Children's Hospital Marketing Director Aaron Powell felt it was important to conduct this study because _____.
   (State the relevant background information used to justify their work.)

2. The main purpose of the Akron Children's Hospital study was _____.
   (State as accurately as possible the reason for doing the study.)

3. The key questions the Akron Children's Hospital employees address in the case are _____.
   (Identify the key questions in the minds of the case protagonists.)

4. The methods used by Powell and his team to answer the marketing research problem were _____.
   (Describe the general approach used and include details that assist in evaluating the quality of the results.)

5. The most important understanding about Akron Children's Hospital as an organization that led the firm to consider the research about its positioning was _____.
   (Identify the facts, observations, and/or data Powell and his team are using to support their conclusions.)

6. The research design decision can be put into context by _____.
   (Place the research design decision into other readily understood contexts.)

7. The main inferences/conclusions in this case are _____.
   (Identify the key conclusions implied by the case.)

8. If we take this line of reasoning seriously, the implications for many other firms are _____.
   (What consequences are likely to follow if people take the brand team's reasoning seriously and apply it to other firms?)

Technical Questions

9. What is the role of marketing research in determining the best positioning strategy for Akron Children's Hospital?

10. Define the management-decision problem confronting Akron Children's Hospital and a corresponding marketing research problem and show the linkages between the two.

11. In this case, how do Norton and the finance people differ from the marketers (Powell and Jones) in their views about the roles of exploratory and conclusive designs?

12. In your opinion, what would be the best sequence for using exploratory and conclusive research in this case?

13. What kind of secondary and syndicated data would be helpful in determining a positioning strategy for Akron Children's Hospital? What is the role played by such data?

14. Discuss the role of qualitative research in gaining a better understanding of how households select a hospital for their children when in need of health care for acute cases.

15. Do you think that Norton should commission a survey in this case? If yes, which survey method would you recommend and why?

16. Can an experiment be conducted to address the issue of the best positioning strategy? If yes, what experimental design would you recommend and why?

17. Discuss the role of measurement and scaling in assessing households' preferences for hospitals for their children when in need of health care for acute cases.

18. Design a questionnaire to measure consumer preferences for children's hospitals.

19. If a mail survey is to be conducted to determine households' preferences for children's hospitals, design a suitable sampling process. What should the sample size be and how should it be determined?

20. How should Norton evaluate the marketing research report? How will the findings of marketing research help Akron Children's Hospital select an appropriate positioning strategy?

Reference

1. Adapted from Robin Segbers, "Adding a Human Touch," *Quirk's Marketing Research Review* (June 2006): 30–34.

Note: The contribution of Professor Mark Peterson in developing this case is gratefully acknowledged.

COMPREHENSIVE CASES WITH REAL DATA

CASE 3.1   BANK OF AMERICA

Leading the American Way

Bank of America, headquartered in Charlotte, North Carolina, is the largest commercial bank in the United States in terms of deposits. The bank has its roots in two former banks: NationsBank and the San Francisco–based BankAmerica. The two merged in 1998 and assumed the name Bank of America. At the time, the merger was the largest bank acquisition in history. BankAmerica began as the American Bank of Italy, which was founded in 1904 by Amadeo Giannini, and Bank of America still operates under Federal Charter 13044, which was granted to Giannini on March 1, 1927.

Bank of America caters its services to individual consumers, small and midsize businesses, and large corporations with a full range of banking, investment, asset management, and other financial products and services. As of 2008, Bank of America serves clients in 175 countries and has relationships with 98 percent of the U.S. *Fortune* 500 companies and 80 percent of the Global *Fortune* 500 companies. This publicly traded corporation provides a diversified range of financial and risk-management products and services both domestically and internationally through three market segments: Global Consumer & Small Business Banking, Global Corporate & Investment Banking, and Global Wealth & Investment Management.

Consumer and Small Business Banking
Global Consumer and Small Business Banking (GC&SBB) is the largest division in the company; it deals primarily with consumer banking and credit card issuance. The acquisition of FleetBoston and MBNA significantly expanded its size and range of services, generating about 50 percent of the company's total revenue in 2007. It competes directly with the retail banking divisions of Citigroup and JPMorgan Chase. The GC&SBB organization includes over 5,700 retail branches and over 17,000 ATMs across the United States.

Global Corporate and Investment Banking
Global Corporate and Investment Banking, also known as Banc of America Securities, provides mergers and acquisitions advisory, underwriting, as well as trading in fixed income and equities markets. Its strongest groups include Leveraged Finance, Syndicated Loans, and Mortgage Backed Securities. It has one of the largest research teams on Wall Street.

Global Wealth and Investment Management
Global Wealth and Investment Management (GWIM) manages assets of institutions and individuals. It is among the 10 largest U.S. wealth managers (ranked by private banking assets under management in accounts of $1 million or more as of June 30, 2007). GWIM has five primary lines of business: Premier Banking & Investments (including Banc of America Investment Services, Inc.), The Private Bank, Family Wealth Advisors, Columbia Management Group, and Banc of America Specialist.

Bank of America has recently spent $675 million building its U.S. investment banking business and is looking to become one of the top five investment banks worldwide. Bank of America already has excellent relationships with the corporate and financial institutions world. These relationships, as well as a balance sheet that most banks would kill for, are the foundations for a lofty ambition.

Bank of America generates 90 percent of its revenues in its domestic market and continues to buy businesses in the United States. The core of Bank of America's strategy is to be the number one bank in its domestic market. It has achieved this through key acquisitions. As a result of its mergers and acquisitions, Bank of America is now the largest issuer of credit, debit, and prepaid cards in the world based on total purchase volume, as well as the largest consumer and small business bank in the United States. It had total assets of $1715.746 billion as of the year ending December 31, 2007. On January 11, 2008 Bank of America Corporation announced a definitive agreement to purchase Countrywide Financial Corp. in an all-stock transaction worth $4.1 billion.

Competition
On a national and international level, Bank of America's main competition consists of Citigroup, Wachovia, Wells Fargo, and JP Morgan Chase & Company. However, Bank of America also encounters fierce competition from regional and local banks all over the country. Market share comparisons are given in Table 1. This was determined by total U.S. deposits.

Marketing Issue and Marketing Research
With Bank of America representing so many customers, it needed to provide a wider range of services to meet their needs. Bank of America's Innovation and Development Team (I&D Team) realized that the customers wanted different things when it came to banking other than the "traditionally designed bank branch." Therefore, Bank of America conducted a study to understand its consumers, their lifestyles, and potential for customer segmentation in terms of investment products and service needs. The questionnaire used follows and the data file is provided on the Web site for this book. The outputs and the analyses of this study should help Bank of America carve its growth plan and its successful implementation.

TABLE 1 U.S. Deposit Information According to FDIC

Bank	Total Deposits as of June 30, 2006 [in thousands ($1,000) of U.S. dollars]	Market Share
Bank of America	$590,619,659	11.10%
JP Morgan & Chase	462,295,269	8.70
Wells Fargo	308,987,142	5.80
Wachovia	308,703,702	5.80
Citigroup	224,597,260	4.20
Total U.S. deposits	5,321 billion	

Questions

Chapter 1

1. Discuss the role that marketing research can play in helping Bank of America formulate sound marketing strategies.

Chapter 2

1. Management would like to further expand Bank of America's market share in the consumer market. Define the management-decision problem.
2. Define an appropriate marketing research problem based on the management-decision problem you have identified.

Chapter 3

1. Formulate an appropriate research design for investigating the marketing research problem that you have defined in Chapter 2.

Chapter 4

1. Use the Internet to determine the market shares of the major banks for the last calendar year.

Chapter 5

1. What type of syndicated data will be useful to Bank of America?

Chapter 6

1. Discuss the role of focus groups versus depth interviews in helping Bank of America expand its market share.

Chapter 7

1. If a survey is to be conducted to determine consumer preferences for banks, which survey method should be used and why?

Chapter 8

1. Discuss the role of preexperimental versus true experimental designs in helping Bank of America expand its product offerings.

Chapter 9

1. Illustrate the use of paired comparison and constant sum scales in measuring consumer preferences for banks. Should any of these scales be used?

Chapter 10

1. Develop a multi-item scale for measuring attitudes toward Bank of America.

Chapter 11

1. Critically evaluate the questionnaire developed for the Bank of America survey.

Chapter 12

1. What sampling plan should be adopted for the survey of Chapter 7?

Chapter 13

1. How should the sample size be determined?

Chapter 14

1. How would you supervise and evaluate field workers for conducting the survey of Chapter 7?

Chapter 15

1. Many of the importance items have more than 10 percent of the values missing. Identify these items. How would you address these missing values?
2. Recode the following demographic characteristics into the categories specified:
   a. Age (Q9): 27–57 = 1, 58–68 = 2, 69–75 = 3, 76–90 = 4
   b. Marital status (Q11): now married = 1, all other, i.e., now not married = 2
   c. Number of dependent children (Q12): 3–10 = 3
   d. Education (Q14): Combine some high school, high school graduate, and vocational or technical school into a single category, and also combine law school graduate, dental/medical school graduate, and doctorate into a single category.
3. Recode the advantage of using primary provider (Q5) into two categories: 1–3 = 1 (small advantage) and 4–5 = 2 (big advantage).
4. Recode overall satisfaction with service provider (Q6_a) into three categories: 2–4 = 1, 5 = 2, 6 = 3.

Chapter 16

1. Calculate an overall rating score for the primary financial provider by summing the ratings of all the 13 items in Q6 (Q6_a through Q6_m). Obtain a frequency distribution and summary statistics. Interpret the results.
2. Are the decision-making approaches (Q8) related to any of the demographic characteristics (Q9 through Q15, as recoded in Chapter 15)?
3. Is the recoded advantage of using primary provider (recoded Q5) related to any of the recoded demographic characteristics?

Chapter 17

1. Is the recoded advantage of using primary provider (recoded Q5) related to any of the importance variables (Q1_a through Q1_l)?
2. Is the recoded advantage of using primary provider (recoded Q5) related to any of the ratings of the primary financial provider (Q6_a through Q6_m)?
3. Is "the performance of investments with this provider" (Q1_a) more important than "online services offered" (Q1_e)? Formulate the null and alternative hypotheses and conduct an appropriate test.
4. Is the likelihood of "recommend your primary provider to someone you know" (Q2) lower than the likelihood of "continue to use your primary provider at least at the same level as up to now" (Q3)? Formulate the null and alternative hypotheses and conduct an appropriate test.
5. Can the decision-making approaches (Q8) explain any of the importance variables (Q1_a through Q1_l)?

6. Is there a relationship between the importance variables considered individually (Q1_a through Q1_l) and the recoded demographic characteristics (Q9 through Q15)?

Chapter 18

1. Can the likelihood of "recommend your primary provider to someone you know" (Q2) be explained by the ratings of the primary financial provider (Q6_a through Q6_m) when these ratings are considered simultaneously?
2. Can the likelihood of "continue to use your primary provider at least at the same level as up to now" (Q3) be explained by the ratings of the primary financial provider (Q6_a through Q6_m) when these ratings are considered simultaneously?

Chapter 19

1. Write a report for Bank of America based on all the analyses that you have conducted. What you recommend Bank of America do in order to continue to grow?

References

1. http://www.bankofamerica.com, accessed February 3, 2008.
2. Associated Press, "Bank of America to acquire Countrywide Deal for country's largest mortgage lender valued at $4.1 billion" (January 11, 2008), online at http://www.msnbc.msn.com/id/22606833/, accessed May 19, 2008.
3. S. Thomke, "How Bank of America Turned Branches into Service-development Laboratories," http://hbswk.hbs.edu/item/3459.html, accessed May 31, 2007.
4. E. Spencer, "Case Study: Bank of America," *BusinessWeek* (2006), online at http://businessweek.com/magazine/content/06_25/b3989445.htm, accessed June 21, 2007.
5. Bank of America, "Building Opportunities: 2006 Annual Report," (2007), online at http://media.corporate-ir.net/media_files/irol/71/71595/reports/2006_AR.pdf, accessed May 19, 2008.

Note: This case was prepared for class discussion purposes only and does not represent the views of Bank of America or its affiliates. The problem scenario is hypothetical and the name of the actual company has been disguised. **However, the data provided are real and were collected in an actual survey by a prominent marketing research firm, whose name is also disguised.** Some questions have been deleted, while the data for other questions are not provided because of proprietary reasons.

ANNUAL FINANCIAL SERVICES SURVEY

Introduction

This survey asks some questions about financial services, i.e, about investments and banking. The **primary financial services provider** (company) is where you have the **largest** portion of your household's investments and savings/checking assets. Your cooperation in answering these questions is greatly appreciated.

Part A. Financial Services Provider

1. If you were selecting a **primary financial provider (company) today**, how important would each of the following be to you? **(X ONE box for EACH.)**

	Extremely Important	Very Important	Somewhat Important	Somewhat Unimportant	Not Important At All
a. Performance of investments with this provider	5 □	4 □	3 □	2 □	1 □
b. Fees or commissions charged	5 □	4 □	3 □	2 □	1 □

	5	4	3	2	1
c. Depth of products and services to meet the range of your investment needs	5 ☐	4 ☐	3 ☐	2 ☐	1 ☐
d. Ability to resolve problems	5 ☐	4 ☐	3 ☐	2 ☐	1 ☐
e. Online services offered	5 ☐	4 ☐	3 ☐	2 ☐	1 ☐
f. Multiple providers' products to choose from	5 ☐	4 ☐	3 ☐	2 ☐	1 ☐
g. Quality of advice	5 ☐	4 ☐	3 ☐	2 ☐	1 ☐
h. Knowledge of representatives or advisors you deal with	5 ☐	4 ☐	3 ☐	2 ☐	1 ☐
i. Representative knowing your overall situation and needs	5 ☐	4 ☐	3 ☐	2 ☐	1 ☐
j. Access to other professional resources	5 ☐	4 ☐	3 ☐	2 ☐	1 ☐
k. Degree to which my provider knows me	5 ☐	4 ☐	3 ☐	2 ☐	1 ☐
l. Quality of service	5 ☐	4 ☐	3 ☐	2 ☐	1 ☐

	Extremely Likely	Very Likely	Somewhat Likely	Somewhat Unlikely	Very Unlikely
2. How **likely** are you to recommend your primary provider to someone you know? **(X ONE box.)** . .	5 ☐	4 ☐	3 ☐	2 ☐	1 ☐
3. How **likely** is it that you will continue to use your primary provider at least at the same level as up to now? **(X ONE box.)**	5 ☐	4 ☐	3 ☐	2 ☐	1 ☐
4. How **likely** is it that you or your household will **drop** or **replace** your primary provider? **(X ONE box.)**	5 ☐	4 ☐	3 ☐	2 ☐	1 ☐
5. How would you rate the **advantage** to you of using your primary provider rather than other financial services providers? **(X ONE box.)**	5 ☐	4 ☐	3 ☐	2 ☐	1 ☐

6. How would you rate the following elements of your **primary financial provider (company)?** If it is not applicable, select "NA." **(X ONE box for EACH statement.)**

	Excellent	Very Good	Good	Fair	Poor	NA
a. Overall satisfaction with primary provider	6 ☐	5 ☐	4 ☐	3 ☐	2 ☐	1 ☐
b. Performance of investments with this provider . . .	6 ☐	5 ☐	4 ☐	3 ☐	2 ☐	1 ☐
c. Fees or commissions charged	6 ☐	5 ☐	4 ☐	3 ☐	2 ☐	1 ☐
d. Depth of products and services to meet the range of your investments needs	6 ☐	5 ☐	4 ☐	3 ☐	2 ☐	1 ☐
e. Ability to resolve problems	6 ☐	5 ☐	4 ☐	3 ☐	2 ☐	1 ☐
f. Online services offered	6 ☐	5 ☐	4 ☐	3 ☐	2 ☐	1 ☐
g. Multiple providers' products to choose from	6 ☐	5 ☐	4 ☐	3 ☐	2 ☐	1 ☐
h. Quality of advice	6 ☐	5 ☐	4 ☐	3 ☐	2 ☐	1 ☐
i. Knowledge of representatives or advisors you deal with	6 ☐	5 ☐	4 ☐	3 ☐	2 ☐	1 ☐
j. Representative knowing your overall situation and needs	6 ☐	5 ☐	4 ☐	3 ☐	2 ☐	1 ☐
k. Access to other professional resources	6 ☐	5 ☐	4 ☐	3 ☐	2 ☐	1 ☐
l. Degree to which my provider knows me	6 ☐	5 ☐	4 ☐	3 ☐	2 ☐	1 ☐
m. Quality of service	6 ☐	5 ☐	4 ☐	3 ☐	2 ☐	1 ☐

7. During the past 12 months, have you or anyone in your household switched some assets (other than checking account assets) from one investment/savings **provider** to another? (Do NOT include switching money from one individual investment such as a stock or bond to another stock or bond within the same brokerage or investment company.) Please **exclude** assets in a 401(k), 403(b), 457 or similar defined contribution retirement accounts.

    1 □ Yes   2 □ No

8. The following are some different approaches you and/or your household might take regarding advice and investment decision-making. Please read each one and then answer the question below.

   1. Using a variety of online or offline information sources, you make your own investment decisions without the assistance of an investment professional or advisor.
   2. Using a variety of online or offline information sources, you make <u>most</u> of your own investment decisions but use an investment professional or advisor for specialized needs only (e.g., alternative investments or tax advice).
   3. You regularly consult with an investment professional or advisor and you may also get additional information yourself, but <u>you</u> make most of the final decisions.
   4. You rely upon an investment professional or advisor to make <u>most</u> or <u>all</u> your investment decisions.

For the majority of your assets, which ONE of the above (1–4) BEST describes your preferred approach? **(Write in a number from 1–4.)**

Number: _____

Part B. Demographic Characteristics

Your answers to the following questions will be used to help us interpret the information you have provided.

9. What is your age?

   Age: _____ years

10. Are you . . . ?

   1 □ Male   2 □ Female

11. What is your current marital status? **(X ONE box.)**

   1 □ Now married   3 □ Divorced   5 □ Single, never married
   2 □ Widowed   4 □ Separated   6 □ Living together, not married

12. How many people in your household are dependent children? **(Write In)**

   # _____

13. How many other dependents are you supporting (e.g., parents, grandparents)? **(Write In)**

   # _____

14. For the following type of financial transaction, please indicate who is <u>primarily</u> responsible, or if the responsibilities are shared. **(X ONE box for each.)**

	Male Head of Household	Female Head of Household	Shared Equally	Other
Investment decision making	1 □	2 □	3 □	4 □

15. What is the highest level of education you have completed? **(X ONE box.)**

   01 □ Some high school   06 □ Some graduate school
   02 □ High school graduate   07 □ Master's degree
   03 □ Vocational or technical school/apprenticeship   08 □ Law school graduate
   04 □ Some college   09 □ Dental/medical school graduate
   05 □ College graduate   10 □ Doctorate

16. What is your retirement status? **(X ONE box.)**

   1 □ Retired   2 □ Semi-Retired   3 □ Not Retired

CASE 3.2 MCDONALD'S

The World's Number One Fast-Food Company!

McDonald's (www.mcdonalds.com) history began when its founder, Ray Kroc, opened the first restaurant in 1955 in Des Plaines, Illinois. The strong foundation that he built and the dedication of its talented executives has enabled McDonald's to prosper. As of 2008, McDonald's is the world's number one fast-food company by sales, with more than 31,000 flagship restaurants serving burgers and fries in more than 115 countries. The popular chain is well known for its Big Macs, Quarter Pounders, and Chicken McNuggets.

Most of its outlets are free-standing units. However, McDonald's also has many quick-service kiosk units located in airports and retail areas. Each unit gets its food and packaging from approved suppliers and uses standardized procedures to ensure that a Big Mac purchased in Pittsburgh tastes the same as one bought in Beijing. About 75 percent of its restaurants are run by franchisees. Table 1 gives the company's sales and market share in recent years.

McDonald's has always been a family restaurant. The family focus is a positioning strategy that is reflected in everything the corporation does. McDonald's knows that by targeting families, it hits one of the most attractive, loyal consumer groups available. It gets into the parents' wallets via the kids' minds. A survey of American schoolchildren found that 96 percent could recognize Ronald McDonald. Santa Claus is the only fictional character with a higher degree of popularity. The effect of McDonald's on the nation's culture, economy, and diet is hard to exaggerate.

McDonald's has not only become the number one restaurant for the children, the 1-minute service promise, the slogan "I'm lovin' it," and introducing a "forever young" brand has enabled it to gain a significant market share among youths and busy adults. McDonald's intends to add new features to its restaurants. For example, the "linger zone" would offer a place for customers to relax by offering arm chairs, sofas, and wireless connections. The "grab and go" zone would offer tall counters with bar stools for those on the go who would like to eat alone. The restaurants would also have plasma televisions televising the news and weather reports. The "flexible" zone with booths with cushions and flexible seating would target families. For each of these zones, different music would target each customer group.

In recent years, McDonald's has extended into a café-style setting, called McCafe, to compete with the popularity of Starbucks and coffee shops in general. McDonald's is now another place for the coffee lovers to get their cup of coffee. In February 2007, *Consumer Reports* magazine ranked McDonald's coffee ahead of Starbucks, saying it tastes better and costs less. McDonald's coffee has "surprisingly high" appeal, with 35 percent of consumers surveyed saying that McDonald's brew got better in the past year.

McDonald's 13,500 U.S. restaurants are uniting behind this new brand message and energy. They are focused on bringing the "I'm lovin' it" theme to life not only in its advertising, but also for every customer who visits its restaurants. This world-class marketing strategy is the latest element of McDonald's overall plan to continue stimulating customers through persuasive food choices, great service and restaurant operations, value, and exciting new restaurant decors. Still running in 2008, "I'm lovin' it" is a key part of McDonald's business strategy to connect with customers in highly pertinent, culturally important ways around the world. To quote Bill Lamar, senior vice president and chief marketing officer of McDonald's USA: "It will rekindle the emotional bond our customers have with McDonald's through a campaign that depicts how people live, what they love about life and what they love about McDonald's."

With the successful expansion of McDonald's into many international markets, the company has become a symbol of globalization and the spread of the American way of life. The business is managed as distinct geographic segments: United States; Europe; Asia/Pacific, Middle East and Africa (APMEA); Latin America; and Canada. The U.S. and Europe segments each account for approximately 35 percent of total revenues, while France, Germany, and the United Kingdom, collectively, account for approximately 60 percent of Europe's revenues. APMEA accounts for 14 percent of the total revenues, Latin America for 8 percent, and Canada for 5 percent of the total revenue. The remaining 3 percent come from other sources.

As shown in Table 2, the U.S. fast-food market has become saturated and is projected to grow at only 2.3 percent per year through 2010. This has intensified the competition. In order to maintain and fortify its leadership position in the competitive fast-food industry, McDonald's conducted a survey. McDonald's wanted to study customer demographics and awareness of different competing fast-food chains; the satisfaction responses of consumers in terms of family orientation,

TABLE 1 McDonald's Revenues and Market Share 2002–2007

	2007	2006	2005	2004	2003	2002
Revenues (USD millions)	$22,786.60	$20,896.20	$19,117.30	$18,594.00	$17,140.50	$15,405.70
Global market share (%)	22.00%*	21.56%	21.03%	20.20%	18.69%	17.21%

* Estimated

TABLE 2 U.S. Fast-Food Market Value Forecast: $ billion, 2005–2010

Year	$ Billion	% Growth
2005	$51.3	2.6%
2006	52.6	2.40
2007	53.8	2.30
2008	55.0	2.30
2009	56.4	2.40
2010	57.6	2.10
CAGR, 2005–2010		2.30

Source: Datamonitor.

comfort, price, quick service, healthy foods, cleanliness, and so on; and patronage preferences in terms of eat-in or drive-through. The questionnaire used follows and the data obtained are provided. Based on the data collected and analysis of this study, McDonald's intends to improve its service and brand orientation.

Questions

Chapter 1
1. Discuss the role that marketing research can play in helping a fast-food restaurant such as McDonald's formulate sound marketing strategies.

Chapter 2
1. McDonald's is considering further expansion in the United States. Define the management-decision problem.
2. Define an appropriate marketing research problem based on the management-decision problem you have identified.

Chapter 3
1. Formulate an appropriate research design for investigating the marketing research problem you have defined in Chapter 2.

Chapter 4
1. Use the Internet to determine the market shares of the major national fast-food chains for the last calendar year.

Chapter 5
1. What type of syndicated data will be useful to McDonald's?

Chapter 6
1. Discuss the role of qualitative research in helping McDonald's expand further in the United States.

Chapter 7
1. McDonald's has developed a new fish sandwich with a distinctive Cajun taste. It would like to determine consumers' response to this new sandwich before introducing it in the marketplace. If a survey is to be conducted to determine consumer preferences, which survey method should be used and why?

Chapter 8
1. Discuss the role of experimentation in helping McDonald's determine its optimal level of advertising expenditures.

Chapter 9
1. Illustrate the use of primary type of scales in measuring consumer preferences for fast-food restaurants.

Chapter 10
1. Illustrate the use of Likert, semantic differential, and Stapel scales in measuring consumer preferences for fast-food restaurants.

Chapter 11
1. Develop a questionnaire for assessing consumer preferences for fast-food restaurants.

Chapters 12 and 13
1. What sampling plan should be adopted for the survey of Chapter 7? How should the sample size be determined?

Chapter 14
1. How should the field workers be selected and trained to conduct the fieldwork for the survey in Chapter 7?

Chapter 15
1. How should the missing values be treated for the following demographic variables: education (D5), income (D6), employment status (D7), and marital status (D8)?
2. Recode payment method (D1) by combining Debit card, Check, and Other into one category.
3. Recode number of people living at home (D3A) as follows: for adults age 18+, four or more should be combined into one category labeled 4+; for each of the three remaining age groups (under 5, 6–11, and 12–17), two or more should be combined into a single category labeled 2+.
4. Recode education (D5) by combining the lowest two categories and labeling it completed high school or less.
5. Recode income (D6) by combining the highest three categories and labeling it $100,000 or more.
6. Recode employment status (D7) by combining homemaker, retired, and unemployed into a single category.
7. Classify respondents into light, medium, and heavy users of fast food based on a frequency distribution of S3A: In the past four weeks, approximately how many times, have you, yourself, eaten food from a fast-food restaurant? Use the following classification: 1–4 times = light, 5–8 times = medium, 9 or more times = heavy.

Chapter 16
1. Run a frequency distribution for all variables except respondent ID (responid). Why is this analysis useful?
2. Cross-tabulate fast-food consumption classification (recoded S3A, see Chapter 15 questions) with the

demographic characteristics (some recoded as specified in Chapter 15): age (S1), gender (S2), payment method (D1), number of people living at home (D3A), education (D5), income (D6), employment (D7), marital status (D8), and Region. Interpret the results.

3. Cross-tabulate payment method (recoded D1) with the remaining demographic characteristics (some recoded as specified in Chapter 14): age (S1), gender (S2), number of people living at home (D3A), education (D5), income (D6), employment (D7), marital status (D8), and Region. Interpret the results.

4. Cross-tabulate eating there more often, less often, or about the same as a year or so ago (q8_1, q8_7, q8_26, q8_36, q8_39) with the demographic characteristics (some recoded as specified in Chapter 14): age (S1), gender (S2), payment method (D1), number of people living at home (D3A), education (D5), income (D6), employment (D7), marital status (D8), and Region. Interpret the results.

Chapter 17

1. Do the ratings on the psychographic statements (q14_1, q14_2, q14_3, q14_4, q14_5, q14_6, and q14_7) differ for males and females?

2. Do the respondents agree more with "I have been making an effort to look for fast-food choices that have better

nutritional value than the foods I have chosen in the past" (q14_6) than they do with "I consider the amount of fat in the foods my kids eat at fast-food restaurants" (q14_5)?

3. Do the restaurant ratings (q9_1, q9_7, q9_26, q9_36, q9_39) differ for the various demographic characteristics (some recoded as specified in Chapter 14): age (S1), gender (S2), payment method (D1), number of people living at home (D3A), education (D5), income (D6), employment (D7), marital status (D8), and region. Interpret the results.

4. Do the four groups defined by "the extent to which you find it difficult to make up your mind about which fast-food restaurant to go to" (q13) differ in their restaurant ratings (q9_1, q9_7, q9_26, q9_36, q9_39)?

Chapter 18

1. Can each of the restaurant ratings (q9_1, q9_7, q9_26, q9_36, q9_39) be explained in terms of the ratings on the psychographic statement (q14_1, q14_2, q14_3, q14_4, q14_5, q14_6, and q14_7) when the statements are considered simultaneously?

Chapter 19

1. Write a report for McDonald's management summarizing the results of your analyses. What recommendations do you have for the management?

References

1. http://www.mcdonalds.com, accessed February 12, 2008.
2. "McDonald's Offers Ethics with Those Fries," *BusinessWeek* (2007), online at http://businessweek.com/globalbiz/ content/jan2007/gb20070109_958716.htm?link_position=link3, accessed June 18, 2007.

Note: This case was prepared for class discussion purposes only and does not represent the views of McDonald's or its affiliates. The problem scenario is hypothetical and the name of the actual company has been disguised. **However, the data provided are real and were collected in an actual survey by a prominent marketing research firm, whose name is also disguised.** Some questions have been deleted, while the data for other questions are not provided because of proprietary reasons.

Online MCDONALD'S Commitment Study Questionnaire
April 1, 2007

RID _____

Thank you for participating in our survey.

S1. To begin, which of the following categories includes your age? (CHOOSE ONE RESPONSE ONLY.)

    1 Under 18   **[TERMINATE QS1]**
    2 18–24
    3 25–29
    4 30–34
    5 35–39
    6 40–45
    7 46 or older   **[TERMINATE QS1]**
    – Refused   **[TERMINATE QS1]**

S2. Are you . . . ? (CHOOSE ONE RESPONSE ONLY.)

    1 Male
    2 Female

S3. OMITTED

S3A. In the past 4 weeks, approximately how many times, have you, yourself, eaten food from a fast-food restaurant? **[ACCEPT WHOLE NUMBERS ONLY, DO NOT ACCEPT RANGE.] [RANGE: 0–99]**

_____
& DK/refused **[TERMINATE QS3A]**
[TERMINATE QS3A IF ZERO]

1. OMITTED
2. OMITTED
3. OMITTED
3a. You have indicated that you have heard of these restaurants. When was the last time, if ever, that you, yourself, have eaten from each one. (PLEASE SELECT ONE TIMEFRAME FOR EACH RESTAURANT.) **[FORMAT AS GRID: INCLUDE RESPONSES FROM Q1].**

   1 Within the past 4 weeks
   2 More than 4 weeks to within the past 3 months
   3 More than 3 months ago
   4 Never

4. OMITTED
5. OMITTED
6. OMITTED
7. OMITTED

8. For each of the restaurants listed below, please indicate whether you, yourself, are eating from there more often, less often, or about the same frequency as a year or so ago. **[SHOW ONLY THOSE Q3a = 1 or 2]**

	More often	About the same	Less often
Insert brands	1	2	3

9. I'd like you to rate the restaurants you, yourself, have eaten from in the past 3 months using a 10-point scale, where "10" means you think it is perfect, and "1" means you think it is terrible. Now taking into account everything that you look for in a fast-food restaurant, how would you rate each of the following? **[SHOW Q3a = 1 or 2]**

Terrible (1)	2	3	4	5	6	7	8	9	Perfect (10)
○	○	○	○	○	○	○	○	○	○

10. OMITTED
11. OMITTED
12. OMITTED
13. Sometimes it is difficult for people to make up their minds about which fast-food restaurant to go to on a given visit. Think about when you go to a fast-food restaurant. In general, which of the following statements best describes the extent to which you find it difficult to make up your mind about which fast-food restaurant to go to? (CHOOSE ONE RESPONSE ONLY.)

   1 I **always know** exactly which fast-food restaurant I am going to go to
   2 I **usually know** exactly which fast-food restaurant I am going to go to
   3 I'm **usually undecided** about which fast-food restaurant I am going to go to
   4 I'm **always undecided** about which fast-food restaurant I am going to go to

14. Below is a list of statements that may or may not be used to describe you in general. Using the scale of Agree completely, Agree somewhat, Neither agree nor disagree, Disagree somewhat, and Disagree completely, please indicate how strongly you agree or disagree with each statement. (CHOOSE ONE RESPONSE FOR EACH STATEMENT.)

Disagree Completely	Disagree Somewhat	Neither Agree nor Disagree	Agree Somewhat	Agree Completely	N/A
○	○	○	○	○	○

1 I try to stay current on the latest health and nutrition information
2 I read nutritional labels on most products I buy
3 I am making more of an effort to find out about the nutritional content of the foods I eat at fast-food restaurants
4 I consider the amount of fat in the foods I eat at fast-food restaurants
5 I consider the amount of fat in the foods my kids eat at fast-food restaurants
6 I have been making an effort to look for fast-food choices that have better nutritional value than the foods I have chosen in the past
7 I am eating at fast-food restaurants less often out of concern for the high fat content in the foods at fast-food restaurants

These last few questions are for classification purposes only.

D1. Which of the following methods do you most often use when purchasing from fast-food restaurants? Do you pay . . .? CHOOSE ONE RESPONSE ONLY.)

1 Cash
2 Credit card
3 Debit card
4 Check
5 Other

D2. OMITTED

D3. OMITTED

D3A. How many people in each of the following age groups live in your home? (PLEASE ENTER A NUMBER FOR EACH AGE RANGE. ENTER "0" IF THERE IS NO ONE IN THAT RANGE IN YOUR HOUSEHOLD.)

A. Adults age 18 + **[RANGE: 1–15]**
B. Children under age 5 **[RANGE: 0–9]**
C. Children age 6–11 **[RANGE: 0–9]**
D. Children age 12–17 **[RANGE: 0–9]**

D4. OMITTED

D5. Which of the following best represents the last level of education that you, yourself, completed? (CHOOSE ONE RESPONSE ONLY)

1 Some high school or less
2 Completed high school
3 Some college
4 Completed college
5 Post graduate
– Prefer not to answer

D6. Which of the following best describes your family's annual household income before taxes? (CHOOSE ONE RESPONSE ONLY)

1 Under $25,000
2 $25,000 but under $50,000
3 $50,000 but under $75,000
4 $75,000 but under $100,000
5 $100,000 but under $150,000
6 $150,000 but under $200,000
7 $200,000 or more
– Prefer not to answer

D7. Which of the following best describes your employment status? (CHOOSE ONE RESPONSE ONLY.)

1 Full-time
2 Part-time
3 Retired
4 Student
5 Homemaker
6 Unemployed
– Prefer not to answer

D8. Are you . . . .?

1 Single, Separated, Divorced, Widowed
0 Married/Living as Married
– Prefer not to answer

Thank you for taking the time to participate in our research!

	Q1
Arby's	1
Atlanta Bread Company	2
A&W	3
Baja Fresh	4
Blimpie	5
Boston Chicken/Market	6
Burger King	7
Captain D's	8
Carl's Jr.	9
Checker's Drive In	10
Chick-Fil-A	11
Chipotle Mexican Grill	12
Church's	13
Del Taco	14
Domino's Pizza	15
El Pollo Loco	16
Grandy's	17
Green Burrito	18
Hardee's	19
In n Out Burger	20
Jack in the Box	21
KFC/Kentucky Fried Chicken	22
La Salsa	23
Little Caesars	24
Long John Silvers	25
McDonald's	26
Panda Express	27
Panera Bread	28
Papa John's	41
Pick Up Stix	29
Pizza Hut	30
Popeye's	31
Quizno's	32
Rally's	33
Rubio's	34
Sonic	35
Subway	36
Taco Bell	37
Taco Bueno	38
McDonald's	39
Whataburger	40
OMITTED—OTHER SPECIFY	
None	42

CASE 3.3   BOEING

Taking Flight

The Boeing Company (www.boeing.com), together with its subsidiaries, is an aerospace company that operates in six principal segments. The first five are collectively known as Integrated Defense Systems (IDS) and include Commercial Airplanes, Aircraft and Weapon Systems, Network Systems, Support Systems, and Launch and Orbital Systems. The sixth principal segment is Boeing Capital Corporation (BCC). The Commercial Airplanes operations principally involve development, production, and marketing of commercial jet aircraft and providing related support services, primarily to the commercial airline industry worldwide. Jim McNerney was the CEO as of 2008, and the company is a leader in the global defense and aerospace market. The company's revenues in recent years are provided in Table 1.

In April 2004, Boeing announced its first new plane in 10 years, the 787 Dreamliner, a powerful but fuel-stingy midsize aircraft. This aircraft is capable of transporting passengers on long-haul routes that now are the province of jumbo jets. With spacious interiors, large luggage cabinets, and huge windows, it promises to be a change maker. The 787 was the result of considerable marketing research, which is an ongoing process at Boeing. Nicole Piasecki, vice president of the Marketing and Business Strategy division, claimed that Boeing had researched the market for more than 40 years. It has studied passengers, airlines, airports, and the dynamics of air travel on a global scale. Internal and external secondary sources of data were analyzed first and then primary research was conducted.

To understand the needs of its customers—airlines—the company went beyond just determining the airlines' needs; it also tried to comprehend the needs of airline passengers, as well as those of the aircraft's financiers. Based on its research, Boeing concluded that the declining emphasis on hub-and-spoke travel will generate the greatest growth in smaller midmarket airplanes and lesser growth in jumbo jets. Growth in air travel has been met by an increase in new nonstop markets and by frequency growth instead of an increase in airplane capacity/size. Based on these findings, the company developed the 787 Dreamliner.

In February 2007, Boeing reiterated a 2007 delivery guidance of 440 to 445 aircraft, followed by a range of 515 to 520 in 2008. The forecast equates to a greater than 17 percent growth rate at the top end of the range, which will include the first 35 deliveries of the 787 model. Given these aggressive delivery expectations, first- and second-tier suppliers were anticipating growth of more than 10 percent in 2007, with even higher levels in 2008 as full-scale 787 production comes online.

The Dreamliner, which is expected to debut in 2008, should revive Boeing's somewhat tired product line and stem Airbus's market-share depredations. More than 3,000 midsize aircraft, including the Boeing 757 and 767 and Airbus A300, A310, and A330 models, will be reaching the end of their operating lives by 2025 or so, along with various Lockheed and Douglas models. The sales opportunity is huge. Yet, the Boeing sales force must be more effective than ever before in the company's history.

Mr. McNerney wants to put a very strong marketing and sales organization in place to take advantage of the opportunities that lie ahead for the 787 Dreamliner. His years of experience have shown him that salesperson loyalty is very important, because of the long-term nature of contracts with the major air carriers of the world. Being driven by fundamentals, McNerney wants to understand what drives a salesperson's loyalty toward the place of work. He hopes that this research effort will inform him on how to develop his business-to-business sales force in the future through improved selection, training, and leadership of Boeing salespersons. He commissioned TNS, one of the leading custom marketing research firms, to undertake the research. The research firm of TNS adopted the following methodology.

Methodology

The project began with an exploratory phase that involved a thorough analysis of secondary data. Both academic and trade sources were examined. This was followed by eight focus groups with B2B field salespersons from a variety of industries. The findings of the exploratory phase were used to design a

TABLE 1 Boeing Revenues, 2000–2007

Year	Revenue in U.S. Dollar Millions
2000	$51,321.00
2001	58,198.00
2002	53,831.00
2003	50,256.00
2004	51,400.00
2005	53,621.00
2006	61,530.00
2007	66,387.00

descriptive survey. A telephone survey was administered to a cross-section of business-to-business salespersons ages 18 to 65 in the United States and in the Canadian metropolitan areas of Toronto and Montreal using a list obtained from the Sales and Marketing Executives International (SMEI). This age qualification enabled the company to reach the population of potential adult workers in the specified regions, avoiding most retirees. The final sample size comprised 1,000 adults in the United States and Canada. This sample size ensured a sampling error of less than 3 percentage points. Expecting a cooperation rate of 33.3 percent, the sample frame consisted of 3,000 people from the SMEI list.

All U.S. telephone interviews were handled from TNS's office in Atlanta, using trained interviewers and computer-assisted telephone interviewing (CATI). Interviewing of the Montreal and Toronto metropolitan areas was conducted locally by a Canadian affiliate of the company to best facilitate regional French and English dialects.

In terms of the survey duration, TNS's experience has shown that a 30-minute telephone interview is not desirable. The completion rate suffers, because people judge it to be too long a period of time to cooperate and either refuse to participate or to complete the full interview. Therefore, the duration of the telephone interview was limited to 10 minutes. The questionnaire used is presented at the end of the case. The data obtained were analyzed. A formal report was prepared and presented to Boeing.

Building a Loyal Sales Force

As McNerney pondered the report from TNS, he still wondered what would be the best way to build the loyalty of his current sales force. He would also like to recruit a new breed of loyal salespeople. The potential for the 787 Dreamliner is high. Having a loyal sales force would be a key to realizing it.

Questions

Chapter 1

1. Discuss the role that marketing research can play in helping McNerney build a strong Boeing sales force.
2. Discuss the role that marketing research can play in enabling strong sales for the 787 Dreamliner.

Chapter 2

1. McNerney wants the 787 Dreamliner to be a strong success. Define the management-decision problem.
2. Define the corresponding marketing research problem.
3. Develop two research questions with two hypotheses corresponding to each.

Chapter 3

1. Do you think that the research design adopted by TNS was appropriate? Why or why not?

Chapters 4 and 5

1. Search the Internet to determine the demand by a major airline for new planes in the next 5 years.
2. Search the Internet to determine the total number of passengers that traveled by air in the past year.

3. What type of internal database will help Boeing in forecasting the demand for new planes by its customers?

Chapter 6

1. Discuss the role of qualitative research in helping Boeing develop and market the 787 Dreamliner.
2. Which qualitative research technique should be used to determine air passengers' attitudes and preferences for various types of aircraft?

Chapter 7

1. If a survey is to be conducted to determine air passengers' attitudes and preferences for various types of aircraft, which survey method should be used and why?
2. If a survey is to be conducted to determine commercial airlines' attitudes and preferences for various types of aircraft, which survey method should be used and why?
3. Was the telephone survey conducted by TNS the most appropriate method for determining the drivers of sales force loyalty toward the place of work? If not, which survey method would you recommend?

Chapter 8

1. Discuss the role of causal research in developing an advertising campaign for the 787 Dreamliner.

Chapter 9

1. Develop ordinal and interval scales for measuring preference of commercial airlines for Boeing 757, 767, and 787 and Airbus A300, A310, and A330 models.

Chapter 10

1. Develop Likert, semantic differential, and Stapel scales for measuring the importance that commercial airlines attach to the fuel efficiency of a plane.
2. Which type of scale would you use for measuring commercial airlines' image of Boeing? Develop such a scale.

Chapter 11

1. Critically evaluate the questionnaire given in this case. What improvements do you suggest?

Chapter 12

1. Describe the sampling plan adopted in this case. Do you think it is appropriate?

Chapter 13

1. Do you think that the sample size was appropriate in this case? Present statistical reasoning to support your answer.

Chapter 14

1. This case made use of telephone surveys. How would you customize the field work process mentioned in the book to the case of telephone interviews?

Chapter 15

1. Carry out consistency checks for the data file for this case. Do you identify any problems with the data?

2. Develop a codebook for Questions D1 to D12 of the questionnaire for this case.

Chapter 16

1. Run a frequency distribution including descriptive statistics for all the variables. Interpret the results.
2. Recode Question 3 ("How loyal would you say that you are personally to the place you work?") into a new variable with two categories (1 to 6 = 1, low loyalty; 7 = 2, high loyalty). Recode Question 4 ("How much loyalty would you say the place you work for has to you?") into a new variable with three categories (1 to 3 = 1, no loyalty; 4 to 5 = 2, some loyalty; 6 to 7 = 3, high loyalty). Are these two categorical variables associated? Interpret your results.
3. Do salespeople who exhibit low or high loyalty to a place of work (recoded Question 3) differ in terms of each of the demographic characteristics, D1 to D12? In other words, is salesperson loyalty associated with any of the 12 demographic characteristics? Note that age (D10) is recorded as the year of birth. Instead of D10, use the age variable. Divide the sample into four roughly equal age groups based on age.
4. Sum all the items (a through o) of Question 2 to form an overall satisfaction scale. Obtain a frequency distribution and summary statistics for this overall satisfaction scale. Interpret the results.

Chapter 17

1. Do salespeople who exhibit low or high loyalty to a place of work (recoded Question 3) differ in terms of each of the items of Question 1 (a through h)?

2. Do salespeople who exhibit low or high loyalty to a place of work (recoded Question 3) differ in terms of each of the satisfaction items of Question 2 (a through o)? Identify the five items that exhibit the greatest difference between the two groups.
3. Do the no-loyalty, some-loyalty, or high-loyalty groups of Question 4 (recoded Question 4) differ in terms of each of the satisfaction items of Question 2 (a through o)?

Chapter 18

1. What is the correlation between the two original loyalty measures of Questions 3 and 4? What can be said of the causal relationship between the two original measures of loyalty?
2. Conduct a multiple regression using the loyalty to the place of work (original Question 3) as the dependent variable. The five independent variables will be the five items of Question 2 that exhibited the greatest difference in the *t*-tests of Chapter 17. Interpret the results.
3. Conduct a multiple regression using the loyalty to the place of work (original Question 3) as the dependent variable and items a through f of Question 2 as the independent variables. Interpret the results.

Chapter 19

1. What do McNerney and his staff need to know about business-to-business salesperson loyalty? Create a one-page, single-spaced summary of these results.

References

1. http://www.boeing.com, accessed May 19, 2008.
2. Aerospace Industry Association, (2007), http://aia-aerospace. org/stats/charts.cfm, accessed May 29, 2007.
3. Stanley Holmes, "Boeing straightens up and flies right," *BusinessWeek* (April 27, 2008), online at http://businessweek.com/ bwdaily/dnflash/apr2006/nf20060427_0379_db016.htm?cha, accessed May 11, 2008.

Note: This case was prepared for class discussion purposes only and does not represent the views of Boeing or its affiliates. The problem scenario is hypothetical and the name of the actual company has been disguised. **However, the data provided are real and were collected in an actual survey by a prominent marketing research firm, whose name is also disguised.** Some questions have been deleted, while the data for other questions are not provided because of proprietary reasons.

SURVEY OF NORTH AMERICAN B2B SALESPERSONS

Hello, I am _____ from TNS, a national public opinion research firm. We are conducting a very important survey about job satisfaction for B2B salespersons. For your help today, we will send you an executive summary of the results of our study. This will allow you to understand how your perspectives compare with other B2B salespersons. This survey should take no more than 10 minutes.

Screener Questions

(CATI Programmer: Please note that all screener questions and responses must be included in the programming so that individual responses can be tabulated for respondents that qualify.)

S1. Are you currently employed full-time, employed part-time, or are you not employed?

a. Full-time	SKIP TO Q.1
b. Part-time	SKIP TO Q.1
c. Employed on a temporary basis	SKIP TO Q.1
d. Employed on a contract basis	SKIP TO Q.1
e. Not employed	CONTINUE
f. Retired	CONTINUE
g. Don't know/refused	DO NOT READ

S2. Do you plan to enter (or reenter) the workforce within the next year, the next 1 to 5 years, the next 5 to 10 years, longer than 10 years, or not at all?

a. Within the next year	CONTINUE
b. 1 to 5 years	CONTINUE
c. 5 to 10 years	CONTINUE
d. >10 years	CONTINUE
e. Not at all	THANK AND TERMINATE

(ASK EVERYONE)

1. I would like you to think about how work fits into your life personally, whether or not you are currently working. I am going to read you some statements about working and your career. Using a scale from 1 to 7—where 1 means *"completely disagree"* and 7 means *"completely agree,"* I'd like you to consider each statement. First (READ STATEMENT). (RANDOMIZE LIST)

   a. I am just starting out in the work world.
   b. I am moving up the ladder in my work, but I haven't reached my peak yet.
   c. I am at the peak of my working potential.
   d. I am in a holding pattern when it comes to work, not really moving ahead but not falling behind.
   e. I am now past the peak of my work life and am slowing down.
   f. I expect to retire from work in the next 5 years.
   g. I am on a break from working at the moment but expect to return to work within the next 12 months.
   h. I am not working at the moment and do not expect to return for at least a year.

   (ASKED OF THOSE WHO ANSWERED "a," "b," "c," or "d" TO S1.)

2. Please rate each of the following aspects of your work in terms of how satisfied you feel with each. Please use a scale of 1 to 7, with 1 meaning you *"disagree very much"* with that aspect and 7 meaning you *"very much agree"* with that aspect of your work. (RANDOMIZE LIST)

   a. Management really knows its job.
   b. My customers are fair.
   c. I'm really doing something worthwhile in my job.
   d. My work is challenging.
   e. I have plenty of freedom on my job to use my own judgment.
   f. I'm satisfied with the way employee benefits are handled around here.
   g. My opportunities for advancement are reasonable.
   h. I am highly paid.
   i. My job is interesting.
   j. The workspace given is adequate.
   k. Compared with other companies, employee benefits here are good.
   l. The people I work with get along well together.
   m. I'm allowed to work from home, if I desire.
   n. Management here is really interested in the welfare of employees.
   o. I have plenty of freedom on my job to use my own judgment.

   (ASKED OF THOSE WHO ANSWERED "a," "b," "c," or "d" TO S1.)

3. We hear a lot these days about company loyalty or the degree to which employees feel loyal and committed to their employer. How loyal would you say that you are personally to the place you work using a scale of 1 to 7, where 1 means *"not at all loyal"* and 7 means *"extremely loyal"*?
   1 2 3 4 5 6 7
   (ASKED OF THOSE WHO ANSWERED "a," "b," "c," or "d" TO S1.)

4. Now using the same scale where 1 means *"not at all loyal"* and 7 means *"extremely loyal,"* how much loyalty would you say the place you work for has to **you**?
   1 2 3 4 5 6 7

Demographics

D1. Gender

    a. Male
    b. Female

D2. What is the highest level of education you have completed?

    a. Some high school or less
    b. High school graduate
    c. Some college
    d. College graduate
    e. Post-graduate degree
    f. Don't know/refused   DO NOT READ

D3. What is your current marital status?

    a. Single
    b. Married
    c. Living with someone as if married
    d. Separated
    e. Divorced
    f. Widowed
    g. Don't know/refused   DO NOT READ

D4. How would you classify yourself?

    a. American Indian or Alaskan Native
    b. Asian
    c. Black or African American
    d. White
    e. Other [specify: _____]
    f. Don't know/refused   DO NOT READ

D5. Do you consider yourself to be of Hispanic origin?

    a. Yes
    b. No
    c. Don't know/refused   DO NOT READ

D6. How many children under the age of 6 are currently living at home with you?

    a. Under age 6 _____

D7. How long have you been working in your current position?

    a. Less than 1 year
    b. 1 to less than 5 years
    c. 5 to less than 10 years
    d. 10 to less than 20 years
    e. 20 to less than 30 years
    f. 30 years or more
    g. Don't know/refused   DO NOT READ

D8. Do you plan to change jobs in the next 5 years?

    a. Yes
    b. No
    c. Don't know/refused   DO NOT READ

    (ASK EVERYONE)

D9. How many jobs have you had in the past five years?
    a. 0
    b. 1
    c. 2
    d. 3
    e. 4
    f. 5

    g. 6 to 9

    h. 10 or more

    i. Don't know/refused   DO NOT READ

D10. In what year were you born?

    a. _____

    b. Refused   DO NOT READ

D11. How many people in your household contribute their income to the household?

    a. 0

    b. 1

    c. 2

    d. 3 or more

    e. Don't know/refused   DO NOT READ

D12. I'm going to read to you a list of income categories. Please stop me when I get to the category that best describes the total combined household income before taxes of all members of your household.

    a. Under $25,000

    b. $25,000 to less than $40,000

    c. $40,000 to less than $50,000

    d. $50,000 to less than $60,000

    e. $60,000 to less than $75,000

    f. $75,000 to less than $100,000

    g. $100,000 to less than $150,000

    h. $150,000 or more

    i. Don't know/refused   DO NOT READ

D13. State _____

Thank you for completing The Survey of North American B2B Salespersons. If you would like an e-mail copy of the executive summary, please provide your e-mail address now. You should receive your copy in the next 90 days from TNS.

APPENDIX

Statistical Tables

TABLE 1 Simple Random Numbers

Line/Col.	(1)	(2)	(3)	(4)	(5)	(6)	(7)	(8)	(9)	(10)	(11)	(12)	(13)	(14)
1	10480	15011	01536	02011	81647	91646	69179	14194	62590	36207	20969	99570	91291	90700
2	22368	46573	25595	85393	30995	89198	27982	53402	93965	34095	52666	19174	39615	99505
3	24130	48390	22527	97265	76393	64809	15179	24830	49340	32081	30680	19655	63348	58629
4	42167	93093	06243	61680	07856	16376	39440	53537	71341	57004	00849	74917	97758	16379
5	37570	39975	81837	16656	06121	91782	60468	81305	49684	60072	14110	06927	01263	54613
6	77921	06907	11008	42751	27756	53498	18602	70659	90655	15053	21916	81825	44394	42880
7	99562	72905	56420	69994	98872	31016	71194	18738	44013	48840	63213	21069	10634	12952
8	96301	91977	05463	07972	18876	20922	94595	56869	69014	60045	18425	84903	42508	32307
9	89579	14342	63661	10281	17453	18103	57740	84378	25331	12568	58678	44947	05585	56941
10	85475	36857	53342	53988	53060	59533	38867	62300	08158	17983	16439	11458	18593	64952
11	28918	69578	88231	33276	70997	79936	56865	05859	90106	31595	01547	85590	91610	78188
12	63553	40961	48235	03427	49626	69445	18663	72695	52180	20847	12234	90511	33703	90322
13	09429	93969	52636	92737	88974	33488	36320	17617	30015	08272	84115	27156	30613	74952
14	10365	61129	87529	85689	48237	52267	67689	93394	01511	26358	85104	20285	29975	89868
15	07119	97336	71048	08178	77233	13916	47564	81056	97735	85977	29372	74461	28551	90707
16	51085	12765	51821	51259	77452	16308	60756	92144	49442	53900	70960	63990	75601	40719
17	02368	21382	52404	60268	89368	19885	55322	44819	01188	65255	64835	44919	05944	55157
18	01011	54092	33362	94904	31273	04146	18594	29852	71685	85030	51132	01915	92747	64951
19	52162	53916	46369	58586	23216	14513	83149	98736	23495	64350	94738	17752	35156	35749
20	07056	97628	33787	09998	42698	06691	76988	13602	51851	46104	88916	19509	25625	58104
21	48663	91245	85828	14346	09172	30163	90229	04734	59193	22178	30421	61666	99904	32812
22	54164	58492	22421	74103	47070	25306	76468	26384	58151	06646	21524	15227	96909	44592
23	32639	32363	05597	24200	13363	38005	94342	28728	35806	06912	17012	64161	18296	22851
24	29334	27001	87637	87308	58731	00256	45834	15398	46557	41135	10307	07684	36188	18510
25	02488	33062	28834	07351	19731	92420	60952	61280	50001	67658	32586	86679	50720	94953
26	81525	72295	04839	96423	24878	82651	66566	14778	76797	14780	13300	87074	79666	95725
27	29676	20591	68086	26432	46901	20849	89768	81536	86645	12659	92259	57102	80428	25280
28	00742	57392	39064	66432	84673	40027	32832	61362	98947	96067	64760	64584	96096	98253
29	05366	04213	25669	26422	44407	44048	37937	63904	45766	66134	75470	66520	34693	90449
30	91921	26418	64117	94305	26766	25940	39972	22209	71500	64568	91402	42416	07844	69618
31	00582	04711	87917	77341	42206	35126	74087	99547	81817	42607	43808	76655	62028	76630
32	00725	69884	62797	56170	86324	88072	76222	36086	84637	93161	76038	65855	77919	88006
33	69011	65795	95876	55293	18988	27354	26575	08625	40801	59920	29841	80150	12777	48501
34	25976	57948	29888	88604	67917	48708	18912	82271	65424	69774	33611	54262	85963	03547
35	09763	83473	73577	12908	30883	18317	28290	35797	05998	41688	34952	37888	38917	88050
36	91567	42595	27958	30134	04024	86385	29880	99730	55536	84855	29088	09250	79656	73211
37	17955	56349	90999	49127	20044	59931	06115	20542	18059	02008	73708	83517	36103	42791
38	46503	18584	18845	49618	02304	51038	20655	58727	28168	15475	56942	53389	20562	87338

(Continued)

TABLE 1 **(Continued)**

Line/Col.	(1)	(2)	(3)	(4)	(5)	(6)	(7)	(8)	(9)	(10)	(11)	(12)	(13)	(14)
39	92157	89634	94824	78171	84610	82834	09922	25417	44137	48413	25555	21246	35509	20468
40	14577	62765	35605	81263	39667	47358	56873	56307	61607	49518	89656	20103	77490	18062
41	98427	07523	33362	64270	01638	92477	66969	98420	04880	45585	46565	04102	46880	45709
42	34914	63976	88720	82765	34476	17032	87589	40836	32427	70002	70663	88863	77775	69348
43	70060	28277	39475	46473	23219	53416	94970	25832	69975	94884	19661	72828	00102	66794
44	53976	54914	06990	67245	68350	82948	11398	42878	80287	88267	47363	46634	06541	97809
45	76072	29515	40980	07391	58745	25774	22987	80059	39911	96189	41151	14222	60697	59583
46	90725	52210	83974	29992	65831	38857	50490	83765	55657	14361	31720	57375	56228	41546
47	64364	67412	33339	31926	14883	24413	59744	92351	97473	89286	35931	04110	23726	51900
48	08962	00358	31662	25388	61642	34072	81249	35648	56891	69352	48373	45578	78547	81788
49	95012	68379	93526	70765	10592	04542	76463	54328	02349	17247	28865	14777	62730	92277
50	15664	10493	20492	38301	91132	21999	59516	81652	27195	48223	46751	22923	32261	85653
51	16408	81899	04153	53381	79401	21438	83035	92350	36693	31238	59649	91754	72772	02338
52	18629	81953	05520	91962	04739	13092	97662	24822	94730	06496	35090	04822	86774	98289
53	73115	35101	47498	87637	99016	71060	88824	71013	18735	20286	23153	72924	35165	43040
54	57491	16703	23167	49323	45021	33132	12544	41035	80780	45393	44812	12515	98931	91202
55	30405	83946	23792	14422	15059	45799	22716	19792	09983	74353	68668	30429	70735	25499
56	16631	35006	85900	98275	32388	52390	16815	69293	82732	38480	73817	32523	41961	44437
57	96773	20206	42559	78985	05300	22164	24369	54224	35083	19687	11052	91491	60383	19746
58	38935	64202	14349	82674	66523	44133	00697	35552	35970	19124	63318	29686	03387	59846
59	31624	76384	17403	53363	44167	64486	64758	75366	76554	31601	12614	33072	60332	92325
60	78919	19474	23632	27889	47914	02584	37680	20801	72152	39339	34806	08930	85001	87820
61	03931	33309	57047	74211	63445	17361	62825	39908	05607	91284	68833	25570	38818	46920
62	74426	33278	43972	10119	89917	15665	52872	73823	73144	88662	88970	74492	51805	99378
63	09066	00903	20795	95452	92648	45454	69552	88815	16553	51125	79375	97596	16296	66092
64	42238	12426	87025	14267	20979	04508	64535	31355	86064	29472	47689	05974	52468	16834
65	16153	08002	26504	41744	81959	65642	74240	56302	00033	67107	77510	70625	28725	34191
66	21457	40742	29820	96783	29400	21840	15035	34537	33310	06116	95240	15957	16572	06004
67	21581	57802	02050	89728	17937	37621	47075	42080	97403	48626	68995	43805	33386	21597
68	55612	78095	83197	33732	05810	24813	86902	60397	16489	03264	88525	42786	05269	92532
69	44657	66999	99324	51281	84463	60563	79312	93454	68876	25471	93911	25650	12682	73572
70	91340	84979	46949	81973	37949	61023	43997	15263	80644	43942	89203	71795	99533	50501
71	91227	21199	31935	27022	84067	05462	35216	14486	29891	68607	41867	14951	91696	85065
72	50001	38140	66321	19924	72163	09538	12151	06878	91903	18749	34405	56087	82790	70925
73	65390	05224	72958	28609	81406	39147	25549	48542	42627	45233	57202	94617	23772	07896
74	27504	96131	83944	41575	10573	03619	64482	73923	36152	05184	94142	25299	94387	34925
75	37169	94851	39117	89632	00959	16487	65536	49071	39782	17095	02330	74301	00275	48280
76	11508	70225	51111	38351	19444	66499	71945	05422	13442	78675	84031	66938	93654	59894
77	37449	30362	06694	54690	04052	53115	62757	95348	78662	11163	81651	50245	34971	52974
78	46515	70331	85922	38329	57015	15765	97161	17869	45349	61796	66345	81073	49106	79860
79	30986	81223	42416	58353	21532	30502	32305	86482	05174	07901	54339	58861	74818	46942
80	63798	64995	46583	09785	44160	78128	83991	42865	92520	83531	80377	35909	81250	54238

(Continued)

TABLE 1 (Continued)

Line/Col.	(1)	(2)	(3)	(4)	(5)	(6)	(7)	(8)	(9)	(10)	(11)	(12)	(13)	(14)
81	82486	84846	99254	67632	43218	50076	21361	64816	51202	88124	41870	52689	51275	83556
82	21885	32906	92431	09060	64297	51674	64126	62570	26123	05155	59194	52799	28225	85762
83	60336	98782	07408	53458	13564	59089	26445	29789	85205	41001	12535	12133	14645	23541
84	43937	46891	24010	25560	86355	33941	25786	54990	71899	15475	95434	98227	21824	19535
85	97656	63175	89303	16275	07100	92063	21942	18611	47348	20203	18534	03862	78095	50136
86	03299	01221	05418	38982	55758	92237	26759	86367	21216	98442	08303	56613	91511	75928
87	79626	06486	03574	17668	07785	76020	79924	25651	83325	88428	85076	72811	22717	50585
88	85636	68335	47539	03129	65651	11977	02510	26113	99447	68645	34327	15152	55230	93448
89	18039	14367	61337	06177	12143	46609	32989	74014	64708	00533	35398	58408	13261	47908
90	08362	15656	60627	36478	65648	16764	53412	09013	07832	41574	17639	82163	60859	75567
91	79556	29068	04142	16268	15387	12856	66227	38358	22478	73373	88732	09443	82558	05250
92	92608	82674	27072	32534	17075	27698	98204	63863	11951	34648	88022	56148	34925	57031
93	23982	25835	40055	67006	12293	02753	14827	23235	35071	99704	37543	11601	35503	85171
94	09915	96306	05908	97901	28395	14186	00821	80703	70426	75647	76310	88717	37890	40129
95	59037	33300	26695	62247	69927	76123	50842	43834	86654	70959	79725	93872	28117	19233
96	42488	78077	69882	61657	34136	79180	97526	43092	04098	73571	80799	76536	71255	64239
97	46764	86273	63003	93017	31204	36692	40202	35275	57306	55543	53203	18098	47625	88684
98	03237	45430	55417	63282	90816	17349	88298	90183	36600	78406	06216	95787	42579	90730
99	86591	81482	52667	61582	14972	90053	89534	76036	49199	43716	97548	04379	46370	28672
100	38534	01715	94964	87288	65680	43772	39560	12918	80537	62738	19636	51132	25739	56947

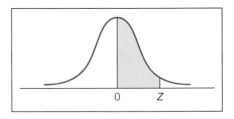

TABLE 2 Area Under the Normal Curve

Z	.00	.01	.02	.03	.04	.05	.06	.07	.08	.09
0.0	.0000	.0040	.0080	.0120	.0160	.0199	.0239	.0279	.0319	.0359
0.1	.0398	.0438	.0478	.0517	.0557	.0596	.0636	.0675	.0714	.0753
0.2	.0793	.0832	.0871	.0910	.0948	.0987	.1026	.1064	.1103	.1141
0.3	.1179	.1217	.1255	.1293	.1331	.1368	.1406	.1443	.1480	.1517
0.4	.1554	.1591	.1628	.1664	.1700	.1736	.1772	.1808	.1844	.1879
0.5	.1915	.1950	.1985	.2019	.2054	.2088	.2123	.2157	.2190	.2224
0.6	.2257	.2291	.2324	.2357	.2389	.2422	.2454	.2486	.2518	.2549
0.7	.2580	.2612	.2642	.2673	.2704	.2734	.2764	.2794	.2823	.2852
0.8	.2881	.2910	.2939	.2967	.2995	.3023	.3051	.3078	.3106	.3133
0.9	.3159	.3186	.3212	.3238	.3264	.3289	.3315	.3340	.3365	.3389
1.0	.3413	.3438	.3461	.3485	.3508	.3531	.3554	.3577	.3599	.3621
1.1	.3643	.3665	.3686	.3708	.3729	.3749	.3770	.3790	.3810	.3830
1.2	.3849	.3869	.3888	.3907	.3925	.3944	.3962	.3980	.3997	.4015
1.3	.4032	.4049	.4066	.4082	.4099	.4115	.4131	.4147	.4162	.4177
1.4	.4192	.4207	.4222	.4236	.4251	.4265	.4279	.4292	.4306	.4319
1.5	.4332	.4345	.4357	.4370	.4382	.4394	.4406	.4418	.4429	.4441
1.6	.4452	.4463	.4474	.4484	.4495	.4505	.4515	.4525	.4535	.4545
1.7	.4554	.4564	.4573	.4582	.4591	.4599	.4608	.4616	.4625	.4633
1.8	.4641	.4649	.4656	.4664	.4671	.4678	.4686	.4693	.4699	.4706
1.9	.4713	.4719	.4726	.4732	.4738	.4744	.4750	.4756	.4761	.4767
2.0	.4772	.4778	.4783	.4788	.4793	.4798	.4803	.4808	.4812	.4817
2.1	.4821	.4826	.4830	.4834	.4838	.4842	.4846	.4850	.4854	.4857
2.2	.4861	.4864	.4868	.4871	.4875	.4878	.4881	.4884	.4887	.4890
2.3	.4893	.4896	.4898	.4901	.4904	.4906	.4909	.4911	.4913	.4916
2.4	.4918	.4920	.4922	.4925	.4927	.4929	.4931	.4932	.4934	.4936
2.5	.4938	.4940	.4941	.4943	.4945	.4946	.4948	.4949	.4951	.4952
2.6	.4953	.4955	.4956	.4957	.4959	.4960	.4961	.4962	.4963	.4964
2.7	.4965	.4966	.4967	.4968	.4969	.4970	.4971	.4972	.4973	.4974
2.8	.4974	.4975	.4976	.4977	.4977	.4978	.4979	.4979	.4980	.4981
2.9	.4981	.4982	.4982	.4983	.4984	.4984	.4985	.4985	.4986	.4986
3.0	.49865	.49869	.49874	.49878	.49882	.49886	.49889	.49893	.49897	.49900
3.1	.49903	.49906	.49910	.49913	.49916	.49918	.49921	.49924	.49926	.49929
3.2	.49931	.49934	.49936	.49938	.49940	.49942	.49944	.49946	.49948	.49950
3.3	.49952	.49953	.49955	.49957	.49958	.49960	.49961	.49962	.49964	.49965
3.4	.49966	.49968	.49969	.49970	.49971	.49972	.49973	.49974	.49975	.49976
3.5	.49977	.49978	.49978	.49979	.49980	.49981	.49981	.49982	.49983	.49983
3.6	.49984	.49985	.49985	.49986	.49986	.49987	.49987	.49988	.49988	.49989
3.7	.49989	.49990	.49990	.49990	.49991	.49991	.49992	.49992	.49992	.49992
3.8	.49993	.49993	.49993	.49994	.49994	.49994	.49994	.49995	.49995	.49995
3.9	.49995	.49995	.49996	.49996	.49996	.49996	.49996	.49996	.49997	.49997

Entry represents area under the standard normal distribution from the mean to Z.

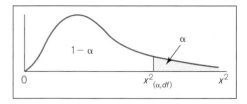

TABLE 3 Chi-Square Distribution

Degrees of Freedom	Upper-Tail Areas (α)											
	.995	.99	.975	.95	.90	.75	.25	.10	.05	.025	.01	.005
1			0.001	0.004	0.016	0.102	1.323	2.706	3.841	5.024	6.635	7.879
2	0.010	0.020	0.051	0.103	0.211	0.575	2.773	4.605	5.991	7.378	9.210	10.597
3	0.072	0.115	0.216	0.352	0.584	1.213	4.108	6.251	7.815	9.348	11.345	12.838
4	0.207	0.297	0.484	0.711	1.064	1.923	5.385	7.779	9.488	11.143	13.277	14.860
5	0.412	0.554	0.831	1.145	1.610	2.675	6.626	9.236	11.071	12.833	15.086	16.750
6	0.676	0.872	1.237	1.635	2.204	3.455	7.841	10.645	12.592	14.449	16.812	18.548
7	0.989	1.239	1.690	2.167	2.833	4.255	9.037	12.017	14.067	16.013	18.475	20.278
8	1.344	1.646	2.180	2.733	3.490	5.071	10.219	13.362	15.507	17.535	20.090	21.955
9	1.735	2.088	2.700	3.325	4.168	5.899	11.389	14.684	16.919	19.023	21.666	23.589
10	2.156	2.558	3.247	3.940	4.865	6.737	12.549	15.987	18.307	20.483	23.209	25.188
11	2.603	3.053	3.816	4.575	5.578	7.584	13.701	17.275	19.675	21.920	24.725	26.757
12	3.074	3.571	4.404	5.226	6.304	8.438	14.845	18.549	21.026	23.337	26.217	28.299
13	3.565	4.107	5.009	5.892	7.042	9.299	15.984	19.812	22.362	24.736	27.688	29.819
14	4.075	4.660	5.629	6.571	7.790	10.165	17.117	21.064	23.685	26.119	29.141	31.319
15	4.601	5.229	6.262	7.261	8.547	11.037	18.245	22.307	24.996	27.488	30.578	32.801
16	5.142	5.812	6.908	7.962	9.312	11.912	19.369	23.542	26.296	28.845	32.000	34.267
17	5.697	6.408	7.564	8.672	10.085	12.792	20.489	24.769	27.587	30.191	33.409	35.718
18	6.265	7.015	8.231	9.390	10.865	13.675	21.605	25.989	28.869	31.526	34.805	37.156
19	6.844	7.633	8.907	10.117	11.651	14.562	22.718	27.204	30.144	32.852	36.191	38.582
20	7.434	8.260	9.591	10.851	12.443	15.452	23.828	28.412	31.410	34.170	37.566	39.997
21	8.034	8.897	10.283	11.591	13.240	16.344	24.935	29.615	32.671	35.479	38.932	41.401
22	8.643	9.542	10.982	12.338	14.042	17.240	26.039	30.813	33.924	36.781	40.289	42.796
23	9.260	10.196	11.689	13.091	14.848	18.137	27.141	32.007	35.172	38.076	41.638	44.181
24	9.886	10.856	12.401	13.848	15.659	19.037	28.241	33.196	36.415	39.364	42.980	45.559
25	10.520	11.524	13.120	14.611	16.473	19.939	29.339	34.382	37.652	40.646	44.314	46.928
26	11.160	12.198	13.844	15.379	17.292	20.843	30.435	35.563	38.885	41.923	45.642	48.290
27	11.808	12.879	14.573	16.151	18.114	21.749	31.528	36.741	40.113	43.194	46.963	49.645
28	12.461	13.565	15.308	16.928	18.939	22.657	32.620	37.916	41.337	44.461	48.278	50.993
29	13.121	14.257	16.047	17.708	19.768	23.567	33.711	39.087	42.557	45.722	49.588	52.336
30	13.787	14.954	16.791	18.493	20.599	24.478	34.800	40.256	43.773	46.979	50.892	53.672
31	14.458	15.655	17.539	19.281	21.434	25.390	35.887	41.422	44.985	48.232	52.191	55.003
32	15.134	16.362	18.291	20.072	22.271	26.304	36.973	42.585	46.194	49.480	53.486	56.328
33	15.815	17.074	19.047	20.867	23.110	27.219	38.058	43.745	47.400	50.725	54.776	57.648
34	16.501	17.789	19.806	21.664	23.952	28.136	39.141	44.903	48.602	51.966	56.061	58.964
35	17.192	18.509	20.569	22.465	24.797	29.054	40.223	46.059	49.802	53.203	57.342	60.275
36	17.887	19.233	21.336	23.269	25.643	29.973	41.304	47.212	50.998	54.437	58.619	61.581
37	18.586	19.960	22.106	24.075	26.492	30.893	42.383	48.363	52.192	55.668	59.892	62.883
38	19.289	20.691	22.878	24.884	27.343	31.815	43.462	49.513	53.384	56.896	61.162	64.181

(Continued)

TABLE 3 (Continued)

Degrees of Freedom	Upper-Tail Areas (α)											
	.995	.99	.975	.95	.90	.75	.25	.10	.05	.025	.01	.005
39	19.996	21.426	23.654	25.695	28.196	32.737	44.539	50.660	54.572	58.120	62.428	65.476
40	20.707	22.164	24.433	26.509	29.051	33.660	45.616	51.805	55.758	59.342	63.691	66.766
41	21.421	22.906	25.215	27.326	29.907	34.585	46.692	52.949	56.942	60.561	64.950	68.053
42	22.138	23.650	25.999	28.144	30.765	35.510	47.766	54.090	58.124	61.777	66.206	69.336
43	22.859	24.398	26.785	28.965	31.625	36.436	48.840	55.230	59.304	62.990	67.459	70.616
44	23.584	25.148	27.575	29.787	32.487	37.363	49.913	56.369	60.481	64.201	68.710	71.893
45	24.311	25.901	28.366	30.612	33.350	38.291	50.985	57.505	61.656	65.410	69.957	73.166
46	25.041	26.657	29.160	31.439	34.215	39.220	52.056	58.641	62.830	66.617	71.201	74.437
47	25.775	27.416	29.956	32.268	35.081	40.149	53.127	59.774	64.001	67.821	72.443	75.704
48	26.511	28.177	30.755	33.098	35.949	41.079	54.196	60.907	65.171	69.023	73.683	76.969
49	27.249	28.941	31.555	33.930	36.818	42.010	55.265	62.038	66.339	70.222	74.919	78.231
50	27.991	29.707	32.357	34.764	37.689	42.942	56.334	63.167	67.505	71.420	76.154	79.490
51	28.735	30.475	33.162	35.600	38.560	43.874	57.401	64.295	68.669	72.616	77.386	80.747
52	29.481	31.246	33.968	36.437	39.433	44.808	58.468	65.422	69.832	73.810	78.616	82.001
53	30.230	32.018	34.776	37.276	40.308	45.741	59.534	66.548	70.993	75.002	79.843	83.253
54	30.981	32.793	35.586	38.116	41.183	46.676	60.600	67.673	72.153	76.192	81.069	84.502
55	31.735	33.570	36.398	38.958	42.060	47.610	61.665	68.796	73.311	77.380	82.292	85.749
56	32.490	34.350	37.212	39.801	42.937	48.546	62.729	69.919	74.468	78.567	83.513	86.994
57	33.248	35.131	38.027	40.646	43.816	49.482	63.793	71.040	75.624	79.752	84.733	88.236
58	34.008	35.913	38.844	41.492	44.696	50.419	64.857	72.160	76.778	80.936	85.950	89.477
59	34.770	36.698	39.662	42.339	45.577	51.356	65.919	73.279	77.931	82.117	87.166	90.715
60	35.534	37.485	40.482	43.188	46.459	52.294	66.981	74.397	79.082	83.298	88.379	91.952

For a particular number of degrees of freedom, entry represents the critical value of χ^2 corresponding to a specified upper-tail area, α.
For larger values of degrees of freedom (df) the expression $z = \sqrt{2\chi^2} - \sqrt{2(df) - 1}$ may be used and the resulting upper-tail area can be obtained from the table of the standardized normal distribution.

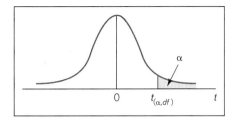

TABLE 4 *t* Distribution

Degrees of Freedom	Upper-Tail Areas (α)					
	.25	.10	.05	.025	.01	.005
1	1.0000	3.0777	6.3138	12.7062	31.8207	63.6574
2	0.8165	1.8856	2.9200	4.3027	6.9646	9.9248
3	0.7649	1.6377	2.3534	3.1824	4.5407	5.8409
4	0.7407	1.5332	2.1318	2.7764	3.7469	4.6041
5	0.7267	1.4759	2.0150	2.5706	3.3649	4.0322
6	0.7176	1.4398	1.9432	2.4469	3.1427	3.7074
7	0.7111	1.4149	1.8946	2.3646	2.9980	3.4995
8	0.7064	1.3968	1.8595	2.3060	2.8965	3.3554
9	0.7027	1.3830	1.8331	2.2622	2.8214	3.2498
10	0.6998	1.3722	1.8125	2.2281	2.7638	3.1693
11	0.6974	1.3634	1.7959	2.2010	2.7181	3.1058
12	0.6955	1.3562	1.7823	2.1788	2.6810	3.0545
13	0.6938	1.3502	1.7709	2.1604	2.6503	3.0123
14	0.6924	1.3450	1.7613	2.1448	2.6245	2.9768
15	0.6912	1.3406	1.7531	2.1315	2.6025	2.9467
16	0.6901	1.3368	1.7459	2.1199	2.5835	2.9208
17	0.6892	1.3334	1.7396	2.1098	2.5669	2.8982
18	0.6884	1.3304	1.7341	2.1009	2.5524	2.8784
19	0.6876	1.3277	1.7291	2.0930	2.5395	2.8609
20	0.6870	1.3253	1.7247	2.0860	2.5280	2.8453
21	0.6864	1.3232	1.7207	2.0796	2.5177	2.8314
22	0.6858	1.3212	1.7171	2.0739	2.5083	2.8188
23	0.6853	1.3195	1.7139	2.0687	2.4999	2.8073
24	0.6848	1.3178	1.7109	2.0639	2.4922	2.7969
25	0.6844	1.3163	1.7081	2.0595	2.4851	2.7874
26	0.6840	1.3150	1.7056	2.0555	2.4786	2.7787
27	0.6837	1.3137	1.7033	2.0518	2.4727	2.7707
28	0.6834	1.3125	1.7011	2.0484	2.4671	2.7633
29	0.6830	1.3114	1.6991	2.0452	2.4620	2.7564
30	0.6828	1.3104	1.6973	2.0423	2.4573	2.7500
31	0.6825	1.3095	1.6955	2.0395	2.4528	2.7440
32	0.6822	1.3086	1.6939	2.0369	2.4487	2.7385
33	0.6820	1.3077	1.6924	2.0345	2.4448	2.7333
34	0.6818	1.3070	1.6909	2.0322	2.4411	2.7284
35	0.6816	1.3062	1.6896	2.0301	2.4377	2.7238
36	0.6814	1.3055	1.6883	2.0281	2.4345	2.7195
37	0.6812	1.3049	1.6871	2.0262	2.4314	2.7154

(Continued)

TABLE 4 **(Continued)**

Degrees of Freedom	Upper-Tail Areas (α)					
	.25	.10	.05	.025	.01	.005
38	0.6810	1.3042	1.6860	2.0244	2.4286	2.7116
39	0.6808	1.3036	1.6849	2.0227	2.4258	2.7079
40	0.6807	1.3031	1.6839	2.0211	2.4233	2.7045
41	0.6805	1.3025	1.6829	2.0195	2.4208	2.7012
42	0.6804	1.3020	1.6820	2.0181	2.4185	2.6981
43	0.6802	1.3016	1.6811	2.0167	2.4163	2.6951
44	0.6801	1.3011	1.6802	2.0154	2.4141	2.6923
45	0.6800	1.3006	1.6794	2.0141	2.4121	2.6896
46	0.6799	1.3002	1.6787	2.0129	2.4102	2.6870
47	0.6797	1.2998	1.6779	2.0117	2.4083	2.6846
48	0.6796	1.2994	1.6772	2.0106	2.4066	2.6822
49	0.6795	1.2991	1.6766	2.0096	2.4049	2.6800
50	0.6794	1.2987	1.6759	2.0086	2.4033	2.6778
51	0.6793	1.2984	1.6753	2.0076	2.4017	2.6757
52	0.6792	1.2980	1.6747	2.0066	2.4002	2.6737
53	0.6791	1.2977	1.6741	2.0057	2.3988	2.6718
54	0.6791	1.2974	1.6736	2.0049	2.3974	2.6700
55	0.6790	1.2971	1.6730	2.0040	2.3961	2.6682
56	0.6789	1.2969	1.6725	2.0032	2.3948	2.6665
57	0.6788	1.2966	1.6720	2.0025	2.3936	2.6649
58	0.6787	1.2963	1.6716	2.0017	2.3924	2.6633
59	0.6787	1.2961	1.6711	2.0010	2.3912	2.6618
60	0.6786	1.2958	1.6706	2.0003	2.3901	2.6603
61	0.6785	1.2956	1.6702	1.9996	2.3890	2.6589
62	0.6785	1.2954	1.6698	1.9990	2.3880	2.6575
63	0.6784	1.2951	1.6694	1.9983	2.3870	2.6561
64	0.6783	1.2949	1.6690	1.9977	2.3860	2.6549
65	0.6783	1.2947	1.6686	1.9971	2.3851	2.6536
66	0.6782	1.2945	1.6683	1.9966	2.3842	2.6524
67	0.6782	1.2943	1.6679	1.9960	2.3833	2.6512
68	0.6781	1.2941	1.6676	1.9955	2.3824	2.6501
69	0.6781	1.2939	1.6672	1.9949	2.3816	2.6490
70	0.6780	1.2938	1.6669	1.9944	2.3808	2.6479
71	0.6780	1.2936	1.6666	1.9939	2.3800	2.6469
72	0.6779	1.2934	1.6663	1.9935	2.3793	2.6459
73	0.6779	1.2933	1.6660	1.9930	2.3785	2.6449
74	0.6778	1.2931	1.6657	1.9925	2.3778	2.6439
75	0.6778	1.2929	1.6654	1.9921	2.3771	2.6430
76	0.6777	1.2928	1.6652	1.9917	2.3764	2.6421
77	0.6777	1.2926	1.6649	1.9913	2.3758	2.6412
78	0.6776	1.2925	1.6646	1.9908	2.3751	2.6403
79	0.6776	1.2924	1.6644	1.9905	2.3745	2.6395
80	0.6776	1.2922	1.6641	1.9901	2.3739	2.6387

(Continued)

TABLE 4 **(Continued)**

Degrees of Freedom	Upper-Tail Areas (α)					
	.25	.10	.05	.025	.01	.005
81	0.6775	1.2921	1.6639	1.9897	2.3733	2.6379
82	0.6775	1.2920	1.6636	1.9893	2.3727	2.6371
83	0.6775	1.2918	1.6634	1.9890	2.3721	2.6364
84	0.6774	1.2917	1.6632	1.9886	2.3716	2.6356
85	0.6774	1.2916	1.6630	1.9883	2.3710	2.6349
86	0.6774	1.2915	1.6628	1.9879	2.3705	2.6342
87	0.6773	1.2914	1.6626	1.9876	2.3700	2.6335
88	0.6773	1.2912	1.6624	1.9873	2.3695	2.6329
89	0.6773	1.2911	1.6622	1.9870	2.3690	2.6322
90	0.6772	1.2910	1.6620	1.9867	2.3685	2.6316
91	0.6772	1.2909	1.6618	1.9864	2.3680	2.6309
92	0.6772	1.2908	1.6616	1.9861	2.3676	2.6303
93	0.6771	1.2907	1.6614	1.9858	2.3671	2.6297
94	0.6771	1.2906	1.6612	1.9855	2.3667	2.6291
95	0.6771	1.2905	1.6611	1.9853	2.3662	2.6286
96	0.6771	1.2904	1.6609	1.9850	2.3658	2.6280
97	0.6770	1.2903	1.6607	1.9847	2.3654	2.6275
98	0.6770	1.2902	1.6606	1.9845	2.3650	2.6269
99	0.6770	1.2902	1.6604	1.9842	2.3646	2.6264
100	0.6770	1.2901	1.6602	1.9840	2.3642	2.6259
110	0.6767	1.2893	1.6588	1.9818	2.3607	2.6213
120	0.6765	1.2886	1.6577	1.9799	2.3578	2.6174
130	0.6764	1.2881	1.6567	1.9784	2.3554	2.6142
140	0.6762	1.2876	1.6558	1.9771	2.3533	2.6114
150	0.6761	1.2872	1.6551	1.9759	2.3515	2.6090
∞	0.6745	1.2816	1.6449	1.9600	2.3263	2.5758

For a particular number of degrees of freedom, entry represents the critical value of t corresponding to a specified upper-tail area, α.

TABLE 5 F Distribution

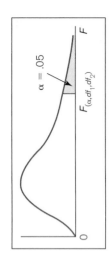

$\alpha = .05$

$F_{(\alpha, df_1, df_2)}$

Denominator df_2	Numerator df_1																		
	1	2	3	4	5	6	7	8	9	10	12	15	20	24	30	40	60	120	∞
1	161.4	199.5	215.7	224.6	230.2	234.0	236.8	238.9	240.5	241.9	243.9	245.9	248.0	249.1	250.1	251.1	252.2	253.3	254.3
2	18.51	19.00	19.16	19.25	19.30	19.33	19.35	19.37	19.38	19.40	19.41	19.43	19.45	19.45	19.46	19.47	19.48	19.49	19.50
3	10.13	9.55	9.28	9.12	9.01	8.94	8.89	8.85	8.81	8.79	8.74	8.70	8.66	8.64	8.62	8.59	8.57	8.55	8.53
4	7.71	6.94	6.59	6.39	6.26	6.16	6.09	6.04	6.00	5.96	5.91	5.86	5.80	5.77	5.75	5.72	5.69	5.66	5.63
5	6.61	5.79	5.41	5.19	5.05	4.95	4.88	4.82	4.77	4.74	4.68	4.62	4.56	4.53	4.50	4.46	4.43	4.40	4.36
6	5.99	5.14	4.76	4.53	4.39	4.28	4.21	4.15	4.10	4.06	4.00	3.94	3.87	3.84	3.81	3.77	3.74	3.70	3.67
7	5.59	4.74	4.35	4.12	3.97	3.87	3.79	3.73	3.68	3.64	3.57	3.51	3.44	3.41	3.38	3.34	3.30	3.27	3.23
8	5.32	4.46	4.07	3.84	3.69	3.58	3.50	3.44	3.39	3.35	3.28	3.22	3.15	3.12	3.08	3.04	3.01	2.97	2.93
9	5.12	4.26	3.86	3.63	3.48	3.37	3.29	3.23	3.18	3.14	3.07	3.01	2.94	2.90	2.86	2.83	2.79	2.75	2.71
10	4.96	4.10	3.71	3.48	3.33	3.22	3.14	3.07	3.02	2.98	2.91	2.85	2.77	2.74	2.70	2.66	2.62	2.58	2.54
11	4.84	3.98	3.59	3.36	3.20	3.09	3.01	2.95	2.90	2.85	2.79	2.72	2.65	2.61	2.57	2.53	2.49	2.45	2.40
12	4.75	3.89	3.49	3.26	3.11	3.00	2.91	2.85	2.80	2.75	2.69	2.62	2.54	2.51	2.47	2.43	2.38	2.34	2.30
13	4.67	3.81	3.41	3.18	3.03	2.92	2.83	2.77	2.71	2.67	2.60	2.53	2.46	2.42	2.38	2.34	2.30	2.25	2.21
14	4.60	3.74	3.34	3.11	2.96	2.85	2.76	2.70	2.65	2.60	2.53	2.46	2.39	2.35	2.31	2.27	2.22	2.18	2.13
15	4.54	3.68	3.29	3.06	2.90	2.79	2.71	2.64	2.59	2.54	2.48	2.40	2.33	2.29	2.25	2.20	2.16	2.11	2.07
16	4.49	3.63	3.24	3.01	2.85	2.74	2.66	2.59	2.54	2.49	2.42	2.35	2.28	2.24	2.19	2.15	2.11	2.06	2.01
17	4.45	3.59	3.20	2.96	2.81	2.70	2.61	2.55	2.49	2.45	2.38	2.31	2.23	2.19	2.15	2.10	2.06	2.01	1.96
18	4.41	3.55	3.16	2.93	2.77	2.66	2.58	2.51	2.46	2.41	2.34	2.27	2.19	2.15	2.11	2.06	2.02	1.97	1.92
19	4.38	3.52	3.13	2.90	2.74	2.63	2.54	2.48	2.42	2.38	2.31	2.23	2.16	2.11	2.07	2.03	1.98	1.93	1.88
20	4.35	3.49	3.10	2.87	2.71	2.60	2.51	2.45	2.39	2.35	2.28	2.20	2.12	2.08	2.04	1.99	1.95	1.90	1.84
21	4.32	3.47	3.07	2.84	2.68	2.57	2.49	2.42	2.37	2.32	2.25	2.18	2.10	2.05	2.01	1.96	1.92	1.87	1.81
22	4.30	3.44	3.05	2.82	2.66	2.55	2.46	2.40	2.34	2.30	2.23	2.15	2.07	2.03	1.98	1.94	1.89	1.84	1.78
23	4.28	3.42	3.03	2.80	2.64	2.53	2.44	2.37	2.32	2.27	2.20	2.13	2.05	2.01	1.96	1.91	1.86	1.81	1.76
24	4.26	3.40	3.01	2.78	2.62	2.51	2.42	2.36	2.30	2.25	2.18	2.11	2.03	1.98	1.94	1.89	1.84	1.79	1.73
25	4.24	3.39	2.99	2.76	2.60	2.49	2.40	2.34	2.28	2.24	2.16	2.09	2.01	1.96	1.92	1.87	1.82	1.77	1.71
26	4.23	3.37	2.98	2.74	2.59	2.47	2.39	2.32	2.27	2.22	2.15	2.07	1.99	1.95	1.90	1.85	1.80	1.75	1.69
27	4.21	3.35	2.96	2.73	2.57	2.46	2.37	2.31	2.25	2.20	2.13	2.06	1.97	1.93	1.88	1.84	1.79	1.73	1.67
28	4.20	3.34	2.95	2.71	2.56	2.45	2.36	2.29	2.24	2.19	2.12	2.04	1.96	1.91	1.87	1.82	1.77	1.71	1.65
29	4.18	3.33	2.93	2.70	2.55	2.43	2.35	2.28	2.22	2.18	2.10	2.03	1.94	1.90	1.85	1.81	1.75	1.70	1.64
30	4.17	3.32	2.92	2.69	2.53	2.42	2.33	2.27	2.21	2.16	2.09	2.01	1.93	1.89	1.84	1.79	1.74	1.68	1.62
40	4.08	3.23	2.84	2.61	2.45	2.34	2.25	2.18	2.12	2.08	2.00	1.92	1.84	1.79	1.74	1.69	1.64	1.58	1.51
60	4.00	3.15	2.76	2.53	2.37	2.25	2.17	2.10	2.04	1.99	1.92	1.84	1.75	1.70	1.65	1.59	1.53	1.47	1.39
120	3.92	3.07	2.68	2.45	2.29	2.17	2.09	2.02	1.96	1.91	1.83	1.75	1.66	1.61	1.55	1.50	1.43	1.35	1.25
∞	3.84	3.00	2.60	2.37	2.21	2.10	2.01	1.94	1.88	1.83	1.75	1.67	1.57	1.52	1.46	1.39	1.32	1.22	1.00

TABLE 5 (Continued)

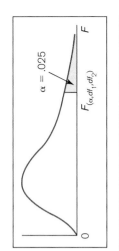

Numerator df_1

Denominator df_2	1	2	3	4	5	6	7	8	9	10	12	15	20	24	30	40	60	120	∞
1	647.8	799.5	864.2	899.6	921.8	937.1	948.2	956.7	963.3	968.6	976.7	984.9	993.1	997.2	1001	1006	1010	1014	1018
2	38.51	39.00	39.17	39.25	39.30	39.33	39.36	39.37	39.39	39.40	39.41	39.43	39.45	39.46	39.46	39.47	39.48	39.49	39.50
3	17.44	16.04	15.44	15.10	14.88	14.73	14.62	14.54	14.47	14.42	14.34	14.25	14.17	14.12	14.08	14.04	13.99	13.95	13.90
4	12.22	10.65	9.98	9.60	9.36	9.20	9.07	8.98	8.90	8.84	8.75	8.66	8.56	8.51	8.46	8.41	8.36	8.31	8.26
5	10.01	8.43	7.76	7.39	7.15	6.98	6.85	6.76	6.68	6.62	6.52	6.43	6.33	6.28	6.23	6.18	6.12	6.07	6.02
6	8.81	7.26	6.60	6.23	5.99	5.82	5.70	5.60	5.52	5.46	5.37	5.27	5.17	5.12	5.07	5.01	4.96	4.90	4.85
7	8.07	6.54	5.89	5.52	5.29	5.12	4.99	4.90	4.82	4.76	4.67	4.57	4.47	4.42	4.36	4.31	4.25	4.20	4.14
8	7.57	6.06	5.42	5.05	4.82	4.65	4.53	4.43	4.36	4.30	4.20	4.10	4.00	3.95	3.89	3.84	3.78	3.73	3.67
9	7.21	5.71	5.08	4.72	4.48	4.32	4.20	4.10	4.03	3.96	3.87	3.77	3.67	3.61	3.56	3.51	3.45	3.39	3.33
10	6.94	5.46	4.83	4.47	4.24	4.07	3.95	3.85	3.78	3.72	3.62	3.52	3.42	3.37	3.31	3.26	3.20	3.14	3.08
11	6.72	5.26	4.63	4.28	4.04	3.88	3.76	3.66	3.59	3.53	3.43	3.33	3.23	3.17	3.12	3.06	3.00	2.94	2.88
12	6.55	5.10	4.47	4.12	3.89	3.73	3.61	3.51	3.44	3.37	3.28	3.18	3.07	3.02	2.96	2.91	2.85	2.79	2.72
13	6.41	4.97	4.35	4.00	3.77	3.60	3.48	3.39	3.31	3.25	3.15	3.05	2.95	2.89	2.84	2.78	2.72	2.66	2.60
14	6.30	4.86	4.24	3.89	3.66	3.50	3.38	3.29	3.21	3.15	3.05	2.95	2.84	2.79	2.73	2.67	2.61	2.55	2.49
15	6.20	4.77	4.15	3.80	3.58	3.41	3.29	3.20	3.12	3.06	2.96	2.86	2.76	2.70	2.64	2.59	2.52	2.46	2.40
16	6.12	4.69	4.08	3.73	3.50	3.34	3.22	3.12	3.05	2.99	2.89	2.79	2.68	2.63	2.57	2.51	2.45	2.38	2.32
17	6.04	4.62	4.01	3.66	3.44	3.28	3.16	3.06	2.98	2.92	2.82	2.72	2.62	2.56	2.50	2.44	2.38	2.32	2.25
18	5.98	4.56	3.95	3.61	3.38	3.22	3.10	3.01	2.93	2.87	2.77	2.67	2.56	2.50	2.44	2.38	2.32	2.26	2.19
19	5.92	4.51	3.90	3.56	3.33	3.17	3.05	2.96	2.88	2.82	2.72	2.62	2.51	2.45	2.39	2.33	2.27	2.20	2.13
20	5.87	4.46	3.86	3.51	3.29	3.13	3.01	2.91	2.84	2.77	2.68	2.57	2.46	2.41	2.35	2.29	2.22	2.16	2.09
21	5.83	4.42	3.82	3.48	3.25	3.09	2.97	2.87	2.80	2.73	2.64	2.53	2.42	2.37	2.31	2.25	2.18	2.11	2.04
22	5.79	4.38	3.78	3.44	3.22	3.05	2.93	2.84	2.76	2.70	2.60	2.50	2.39	2.33	2.27	2.21	2.14	2.08	2.00
23	5.75	4.35	3.75	3.41	3.18	3.02	2.90	2.81	2.73	2.67	2.57	2.47	2.36	2.30	2.24	2.18	2.11	2.04	1.97
24	5.72	4.32	3.72	3.38	3.15	2.99	2.87	2.78	2.70	2.64	2.54	2.44	2.33	2.27	2.21	2.15	2.08	2.01	1.94
25	5.69	4.29	3.69	3.35	3.13	2.97	2.85	2.75	2.68	2.61	2.51	2.41	2.30	2.24	2.18	2.12	2.05	1.98	1.91
26	5.66	4.27	3.67	3.33	3.10	2.94	2.82	2.73	2.65	2.59	2.49	2.39	2.28	2.22	2.16	2.09	2.03	1.95	1.88
27	5.63	4.24	3.65	3.31	3.08	2.92	2.80	2.71	2.63	2.57	2.47	2.36	2.25	2.19	2.13	2.07	2.00	1.93	1.85
28	5.61	4.22	3.63	3.29	3.06	2.90	2.78	2.69	2.61	2.55	2.45	2.34	2.23	2.17	2.11	2.05	1.98	1.91	1.83
29	5.59	4.20	3.61	3.27	3.04	2.88	2.76	2.67	2.59	2.53	2.43	2.32	2.21	2.15	2.09	2.03	1.96	1.89	1.81
30	5.57	4.18	3.59	3.25	3.03	2.87	2.75	2.65	2.57	2.51	2.41	2.31	2.20	2.14	2.07	2.01	1.94	1.87	1.79
40	5.42	4.05	3.46	3.13	2.90	2.74	2.62	2.53	2.45	2.39	2.29	2.18	2.07	2.01	1.94	1.88	1.80	1.72	1.64
60	5.29	3.93	3.34	3.01	2.79	2.63	2.51	2.41	2.33	2.27	2.17	2.06	1.94	1.88	1.82	1.74	1.67	1.58	1.48
120	5.15	3.80	3.23	2.89	2.67	2.52	2.39	2.30	2.22	2.16	2.05	1.94	1.82	1.76	1.69	1.61	1.53	1.43	1.31
∞	5.02	3.69	3.12	2.79	2.57	2.41	2.29	2.19	2.11	2.05	1.94	1.83	1.71	1.64	1.57	1.48	1.39	1.27	1.00

(*Continued*)

TABLE 5 (Continued)

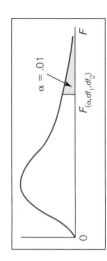

$\alpha = .01$

$F_{(\alpha, df_1, df_2)}$

Denominator df_2	\multicolumn{19}{c}{Numerator df_1}
	1	2	3	4	5	6	7	8	9	10	12	15	20	24	30	40	60	120	∞
1	4052	4999.5	5403	5625	5764	5859	5928	5982	6022	6056	6106	6157	6209	6235	6261	6287	6313	6339	6366
2	98.50	99.00	99.17	99.25	99.30	99.33	99.36	99.37	99.39	99.40	99.42	99.43	99.45	99.46	99.47	99.47	99.48	99.49	99.50
3	34.12	30.82	29.46	28.71	28.24	27.91	27.67	27.49	27.35	27.23	27.05	26.87	26.69	26.60	26.50	26.41	26.32	26.22	26.13
4	21.20	18.00	16.69	15.98	15.52	15.21	14.98	14.80	14.66	14.55	14.37	14.20	14.02	13.93	13.84	13.75	13.65	13.56	13.46
5	16.26	13.27	12.06	11.39	10.97	10.67	10.46	10.29	10.16	10.05	9.89	9.72	9.55	9.47	9.38	9.29	9.20	9.11	9.02
6	13.75	10.92	9.78	9.15	8.75	8.47	8.26	8.10	7.98	7.87	7.72	7.56	7.40	7.31	7.23	7.14	7.06	6.97	6.88
7	12.25	9.55	8.45	7.85	7.46	7.19	6.99	6.84	6.72	6.62	6.47	6.31	6.16	6.07	5.99	5.91	5.82	5.74	5.65
8	11.26	8.65	7.59	7.01	6.63	6.37	6.18	6.03	5.91	5.81	5.67	5.52	5.36	5.28	5.20	5.12	5.03	4.95	4.86
9	10.56	8.02	6.99	6.42	6.06	5.80	5.61	5.47	5.35	5.26	5.11	4.96	4.81	4.73	4.65	4.57	4.48	4.40	4.31
10	10.04	7.56	6.55	5.99	5.64	5.39	5.20	5.06	4.94	4.85	4.71	4.56	4.41	4.33	4.25	4.17	4.08	4.00	3.91
11	9.65	7.21	6.22	5.67	5.32	5.07	4.89	4.74	4.63	4.54	4.40	4.25	4.10	4.02	3.94	3.86	3.78	3.69	3.60
12	9.33	6.93	5.95	5.41	5.06	4.82	4.64	4.50	4.39	4.30	4.16	4.01	3.86	3.78	3.70	3.62	3.54	3.45	3.36
13	9.07	6.70	5.74	5.21	4.86	4.62	4.44	4.30	4.19	4.10	3.96	3.82	3.66	3.59	3.51	3.43	3.34	3.25	3.17
14	8.86	6.51	5.56	5.04	4.69	4.46	4.28	4.14	4.03	3.94	3.80	3.66	3.51	3.43	3.35	3.27	3.18	3.09	3.00
15	8.68	6.36	5.42	4.89	4.56	4.32	4.14	4.00	3.89	3.80	3.67	3.52	3.37	3.29	3.21	3.13	3.05	2.96	2.87
16	8.53	6.23	5.29	4.77	4.44	4.20	4.03	3.89	3.78	3.69	3.55	3.41	3.26	3.18	3.10	3.02	2.93	2.84	2.75
17	8.40	6.11	5.18	4.67	4.34	4.10	3.93	3.79	3.68	3.59	3.46	3.31	3.16	3.08	3.00	2.92	2.83	2.75	2.65
18	8.29	6.01	5.09	4.58	4.25	4.01	3.84	3.71	3.60	3.51	3.37	3.23	3.08	3.00	2.92	2.84	2.75	2.66	2.57
19	8.18	5.93	5.01	4.50	4.17	3.94	3.77	3.63	3.52	3.43	3.30	3.15	3.00	2.92	2.84	2.76	2.67	2.58	2.49
20	8.10	5.85	4.94	4.43	4.10	3.87	3.70	3.56	3.46	3.37	3.23	3.09	2.94	2.86	2.78	2.69	2.61	2.52	2.42
21	8.02	5.78	4.87	4.37	4.04	3.81	3.64	3.51	3.40	3.31	3.17	3.03	2.88	2.80	2.72	2.64	2.55	2.46	2.36
22	7.95	5.72	4.82	4.31	3.99	3.76	3.59	3.45	3.35	3.26	3.12	2.98	2.83	2.75	2.67	2.58	2.50	2.40	2.31
23	7.88	5.66	4.76	4.26	3.94	3.71	3.54	3.41	3.30	3.21	3.07	2.93	2.78	2.70	2.62	2.54	2.45	2.35	2.26
24	7.82	5.61	4.72	4.22	3.90	3.67	3.50	3.36	3.26	3.17	3.03	2.89	2.74	2.66	2.58	2.49	2.40	2.31	2.21
25	7.77	5.57	4.68	4.18	3.85	3.63	3.46	3.32	3.22	3.13	2.99	2.85	2.70	2.62	2.54	2.45	2.36	2.27	2.17
26	7.72	5.53	4.64	4.14	3.82	3.59	3.42	3.29	3.18	3.09	2.96	2.81	2.66	2.58	2.50	2.42	2.33	2.23	2.13
27	7.68	5.49	4.60	4.11	3.78	3.56	3.39	3.26	3.15	3.06	2.93	2.78	2.63	2.55	2.47	2.38	2.29	2.20	2.10
28	7.64	5.45	4.57	4.07	3.75	3.53	3.36	3.23	3.12	3.03	2.90	2.75	2.60	2.52	2.44	2.35	2.26	2.17	2.06
29	7.60	5.42	4.54	4.04	3.73	3.50	3.33	3.20	3.09	3.00	2.87	2.73	2.57	2.49	2.41	2.33	2.23	2.14	2.03
30	7.56	5.39	4.51	4.02	3.70	3.47	3.30	3.17	3.07	2.98	2.84	2.70	2.55	2.47	2.39	2.30	2.21	2.11	2.01
40	7.31	5.18	4.31	3.83	3.51	3.29	3.12	2.99	2.89	2.80	2.66	2.52	2.37	2.29	2.20	2.11	2.02	1.92	1.80
60	7.08	4.98	4.13	3.65	3.34	3.12	2.95	2.82	2.72	2.63	2.50	2.35	2.20	2.12	2.03	1.94	1.84	1.73	1.60
120	6.85	4.79	3.95	3.48	3.17	2.96	2.79	2.66	2.56	2.47	2.34	2.19	2.03	1.95	1.86	1.76	1.66	1.53	1.38
∞	6.63	4.61	3.78	3.32	3.02	2.80	2.64	2.51	2.41	2.32	2.18	2.04	1.88	1.79	1.70	1.59	1.47	1.32	1.00

For a particular combination of numerator and denominator degrees of freedom, entry represents the critical values of F corresponding to a specified upper-tail area, α.

Notes

Chapter 1

1. Rachael S. Davis, "Reebok: The Brand That Fits," *Textile World,* 157(6) (December 2007): 56–57; Thomas J. Ryan, "Reebok Launches Running-Focused Ad Campaign," *SGB*, 40(5) (May 2007): 14; Mei Fong, "Yao Gives Reebok an Assist in China," *The Wall Street Journal* (September 28, 2007): B1–B2.; www.reebok.com, accessed February 15, 2008.

2. Robert Swanekamp, "Southern Company Emphasizes Employee Development," *Power*, 144(6) (November–December, 2000): 25; www.southerncompany.com, accessed February 5, 2008.

3. T. L. Stanley, "Seinfeld, McD's, Brach's Help Build Bee Movie Buzz," *Brandweek,* 48(38) (October 2007): 6; Kenneth Hein, "Brisk Sales—With a Side of Trans-Fat," *Brandweek,* 48(25) (June 2007): S42–S43; About McDonald's, *McDonald's Corporation*, from www.mcdonalds.com/corp/about.html, accessed May 26, 2007; Kate MacArthur, "Fast-Food Rethinks Marketing," *Advertising Age* (Midwest region edition), 74(26) (June 30, 2003): SR2.

4. Greg Tarr, "Sony Slates $100M Ad Campaign," *TWICE: This Week in Consumer Electronics*, 22(13) (June 2007): 31–33; Normandy Madden, "Global Highlight: Sony's 'Live Color Wall,'" *Advertising Age,* 78(47) (November 2007): 22; http://news.sel.sony.com/en/press_room/corporate_news/release/26912.html.

5. John W. Huppertz, "Passion vs. Dispassion," *Marketing Research: A Magazine of Management and Applications*, 15(2) (summer 2003): 16; Naresh K. Malhotra, "Shifting Perspective on the Shifting Paradigm in Marketing Research," *Journal of the Academy of Marketing Science*, 20 (fall 1992): 379–387; William Perreault, "The Shifting Paradigm in Marketing Research," *Journal of the Academy of Marketing Science*, 20 (fall 1992): 367–375.

6. Jack Honomichl, "Top 25 Global Research Organizations," *Marketing News* (August 15, 2007): H4.

7. "Higher Education Market Research and Strategic Planning," www.forwardanalytics.com/industrial_research/Higher_Education_Market_Research.html, accessed December 16, 2007; Ralph W. Giacobbe and Madhav N. Segal, "Rethinking Marketing Research Education: A Conceptual, Analytical, and Empirical Investigation," *Journal of Marketing Education,* 16 (spring 1994): 43–58.

8. Jack Honomichl, "Top 25 Global Research Organizations," *Marketing News* (August 15, 2007): H4.

9. Anonymous, "Cracking China: In a New Book, Procter & Gamble Tells How It Brought Consumerism to an Untapped Market," http://findarticles.com/p/articles/mi_m4070/is_199/ai_n6104076, accessed December 16, 2007; Normandy Madden, "China Warms Up to P&G," *Advertising Age*, 74(14) (April 7, 2003): S5; "P&G Viewed China as a National Market and Is Conquering It," *The Wall Street Journal* (September 12, 1995): A1.

10. Steven M. Shugan, "The Impact of Advancing Technology on Marketing and Academic Research," *Marketing Science,* 23(4) (fall 2004): 469–475; Steven Landberg, "Strategic Marketing Technology," *Best's Review*, 104(6) (October 2003): 114; Marydee Ojala, "Information Role Models in Market Research," *Online*, 24(2) (March–April 2000): 69–71; Matthew W. Green, Jr. and John A. Fugel, "Third Wave Has Ups and Downs," *Rural Telecommunications*, 15(1) (January–February 1996): 10; Donald E. Schmidt, "Third Wave of Marketing Research on the Horizon," *Marketing News*, 27(5) (March 1, 1993): 6.

11. J. Garcia de Madariaga and C. Valor, "Stakeholders Management Systems: Empirical Insights from Relationship Marketing and Market Orientation Perspectives," *Journal of Business Ethics,* 71 (2007): 425–439; Anonymous, "The Market Research Industry and Research Ethics," http://media.wiley.com/product_data/excerpt/81/04717552/0471755281.pdf, accessed December 16, 2007; Scott J. Vitell, Joseph G. P. Paolillo, and James L. Thomas, "The Perceived Role of Ethics and Social Responsibility: A Study of Marketing Professionals," *Business Ethics Quarterly*, 13(1) (January 2003): 63; Diane K. Bowers, "The Strategic Role of the Telemarketing Sales Rule in the Research Industry," *Marketing Research: A Magazine of Management and Applications,* 11(1) (spring 1999): 34–35.

12. www.samsonite.com/global/history_90now.jsp, accessed January 7, 2008.

Chapter 2

1. Based on Anonymous, "Subaru Sheds Rally Car Image," *Precision Marketing (London)* (October 2007): 5; Anonymous, "Subaru Uses Smart Television Spots by DDB to Help Launch the New 2008 Model Year Lineup.—New Cars and Clever Creative Target Specific, Well-Defined Audiences," *PR Newswire* (New York) (August 2007): n/a; Karl Greenberg, "Subaru Is Driven by New Marketing, New Direction, Lance Armstrong," *Brandweek*, 44(8) (February 24, 2003): 12.

2. Hoover's, A D&B Company. (2007). "Nike Inc." http://premium.hoovers.com.gate.lib.buffalo.edu/subscribe/co/factsheet.xhtml?ID=rcthcfhfshkyjc, accessed May 31, 2007; D. Pluchino, "Coke, Pepsi, Nike, and Adidas Are Tops in Video Game Market Research Study According to Phoenix Marketing International," (November 9, 2006), www.gamesindustry.biz/content_page.php?aid=21000, accessed May 31, 2007; Decision Analyst, "Favourite Brands," www.decisionanalyst.com/publ_data/2005/FavoriteBrand.asp, accessed May 31, 2007.

3. David Eisen, "CRUISE: Holland America's Take on Freestyle," *Travel Agent*, 331(9) (November 2007): 101; Johanna Jainchill, "NCL Breaks Out a Few More Marketing Initiatives for Ad Campaign," *Travel Weekly,* 66(23) (June 2007): 34; Andrew Scott, "Norwegian Cruise Lines Rebrands with $100 Million Campaign," http://promomagazine.com/othertactics/news/norwegian_rebrands_092106/, accessed December 17, 2007; Anonymous, "Norwegian Cruise Line," *Incentive*, 177(11) (November 2003): 89; David Goetzl,

"Luxury Cruise Lines Woo Boomers to Sea," *Advertising Age*, 70(11) (March 15, 1999): 26; "It's Different Out Here—Norwegian Cruises," *Adweek* (special planning section) (August 5, 1996): 7.

4. Allison Sherry, "University of Colorado Hospital to Offer Luxury Suites Complete with Chef," *Knight Ridder Tribune Business News* (September 15, 2003): 1; Rachel Zoll, "Hospitals Offer Hotel-Style Perks to Fill Maternity Beds," *Marketing News*, 31(10) (May 12, 1997): 11; "Hospital Puttin' on the Ritz to Target High-End Market," *Marketing News* (January 17, 1986): 14.

5. Pamela Edwards, "Calendar Girl," *Essence*, 36(10) (February 2006): 45–49; Anonymous, "Vanity Fares Market Profile on: Health and Beauty Market," www.checkout.ie/MarketProfile.asp?ID=187, accessed December 17, 2007; Anonymous, "Gillette Passion for Shaving," *Retail World*, 56(15) (August 4–August 15, 2003): 30; "A Woman's Touch," *Discount Merchandiser*, 39(5) (May 1999): 104; Sean Mehegan, "Gillette Big on Body Wash," *Brandweek*, 38(5) (February 3, 1997): 5.

6. Wayne C. Booth, Gregory G. Colomb, and Joseph M. Williams, *The Craft of Research*, Chicago: University of Chicago Press, 1995.

7. Britton Manasco, "Diapers and Dollars," http://customer.corante.com/archives/2004/05/21/diapers_and_dollars.php, accessed December 17, 2007; Jennifer Pellet, "Lessons FROM Brand Leaders," *Chief Executive* 221 (October 2006): 26; Patricia Sellers, "P&G: Teaching an Old Dog New Tricks," *Fortune* (May 31, 2004): 167–180.

8. Bob Garfield, "Boring and Banal: That's a Pretty Good Fit for Lee," *Advertising Age* (Midwest region edition), 77(37) (September 2006): 45; David Lipke, "Lee Poised For New Marketing Blitz. 'Get What Fits' Campaign to Launch in August on Television, Radio and in Print," *DNR* (New York), 36(31) (July 2006): 4; Sandra O'Loughlin, "Lee Jeans Launching One True Fit in Move to Extend Market Share," *Brandweek*, 44(2) (January 13, 2003): 4; Sandra O'Loughlin, "Buddy Lee Takes Show on the Road," *Brandweek*, 44(33) (September 15, 2003): 12.

9. Pamela Accetta Smith, "GOT GAME?" *Dairy Field* (Northbrook), 190(4) (April 2007): 68; Anonymous, "On a Mission for Milk—Interactive Campaign Challenges Consumers to 'Get the Glass,'" *PR Newswire* (New York), (March 2007): n/a; Jeff Manning, "Got Milk? A Decade of Lessons Pours In," *Brandweek*, 44(22) (June 2, 2003): 24; Hillary Chura and Stephanie Thompson, "Bozell Moving Beyond Mustaches in Milk Ads," *Advertising Age*, 70(43) (October 18, 1999): 81.

10. Tania Mason, "Heinz Backs Its Best Varieties," *Marketing* (March 27, 2003): 17; Judann Dagnoli, "Why Heinz Went Sour in Brazil," *Advertising Age* (December 5, 1988): 61–62.

11. Anonymous, "Closing the Gap Between the Ethical and Profitable," *Marketing Week* (October 16, 2003): 32; Ishmael P. Akaah, "Influence of Deontological and Teleological Factors on Research Ethics Evaluations," *Journal of Business Research*, 39(2) (June 1997): 71–80; G. R. Laczniak and P. E. Murphy (1993), *Ethical Marketing Decisions, the Higher Road*, Boston: Allyn and Bacon. For hypotheses development in an ethical context see Scott J. Vitell and Encarnacion Ramos Hidalgo, "The Impact of Corporate Ethical Values and Enforcement of Ethical Codes on the Perceived Importance of Ethics in Business: A Comparison of U.S. and Spanish Managers," *Journal of Business Ethics* 64 (2006): 31–43.

12. Maja Beckstrom, "Snack Attack Battle Plan: Here Are a Few Ideas for Improving the Quality of the Between-Meal Calories Kids Consume," *Knight Ridder Tribune Business News* (March 2007): 1; Anonymous, "Kellogg's Broadens Special K Range with Oats & Honey Variant," www.talkingretail.com/products/7334/Kelloggs-broadens-Special-K-ra.ehtml, accessed December 18, 2007; www.kelloggs.com, accessed January 10, 2008.

Chapter 3

1. Anonymous, "Spiegel Brands Inc. Implements Guided Self-Service Solution from Spoken Communications, Inc. Guided Speech IVR Is Far More Effective and Efficient Than IVR Alone," *PR Newswire* (New York) (August 2007): n/a; Karyn Monget with contributions from David Moin, "Penney's, Spiegel Make Lingerie Moves," *WWD* (New York), 192(73) (October 2006): 14; Sandra O'Loughlin, "Struggling Spiegel Group Dresses Up Eddie Bauer," *Brandweek*, 44(31) (September 1, 2003): 10; Mercedes Cardona, "Eddie Bauer Banks on Basics for Season," *Advertising Age*, 74(47) (November 24, 2003): 10.

2. Valerie Bauerlein, "Bank of America CEO In Spotlight After Deal," *The Wall Street Journal*, August 27, 2007: A1, A9; and www.bankofamerica.com, accessed January 12, 2008.

3. Adapted from Anonymous, "Sara Lee Hunts Household and Body Care Marketer," *Marketing Week* (October 2007): n/a; Lisa I. Fried, "Retailers Cleaning Up with Body Washes, Gift Sets—Drugstore Chains," *Drug Store News*, http://findarticles.com/p/articles/mi_m3374/is_n17_v18/ai_18804351, accessed December 19, 2007; Don Mills, "Jergens Naturally Smooth Shave Minimizing Lotion," *Cosmetics*, 30(5) (September 2002); "Bath Boom Rah!" *Discount Merchandiser*, 39(6) (June 1999): 52; Rick Klein, "1995 Edison Best New Products Awards Winners," *Marketing News*, 30(10) (May 6, 1996): E4–E11.

4. Adapted from Rance Crain, "Hold the Love, J&J—We'd Rather Have Honesty in Our Tylenol Ads," *Advertising Age*, 78(47) (November 2007): 15; www.colorcom.com/consult.html; http://philadelphia.bizjournals.com/philadelphia/stories/2005/03/14/tidbits1.html; "Tylenol Is Different," www.tylenol.com/page.jhtml?id=tylenol/painex/subonly.inc, accessed June 21, 2007.

5. Anonymous, "Not Everyone Is Drinking Microsoft's Vista Kool-Aid," *Brandweek* (October 2007): n/a; Ina Fried, "Microsoft Readying Vista Marketing Blitz," *CNET News.com*, www.news.com/Microsoft-readying-Vista-marketing-blitz/2100–1012_3–6047217.html, accessed December 19–2007; www.windows.com, accessed January 5, 2008.

6. http://kelloggs.investoreports.com/kellogg_ar_2006/html/kellogg_ar_2006_2.php, accessed July 27, 2007; www.thetimes100.co.uk/downloads/kellogg/kellogg_9_full.pdf, accessed July 27, 2007; http://kelloggs.investoreports.com/kellogg_ar_2006/html/kellogg_ar_2006_7.php, accessed July 27, 2007.

7. Adapted from "P&G's Cell Phone Strategy in Japan: The Way to 'Double Billion-Dollar-Brand' Products," (January 29, 2007), http://business.nikkeibp.co.jp/article/eng/20070129/117847/, accessed August 27, 2007; Anonymous, "Japan Units of P&G, Unilever Seek to

Reclaim Market Share," *Nikkei Report* (July 2007): n/a; Catherine Becker, "Hair and Cosmetic Products in the Japanese Market," *Marketing and Research Today*, 25(1) (February 1997): 31–37.

8. Jeff Carlson, Glenn Fleishman, "Get in Sync," *Macworld*, 24(1) (January 2007): 64; Kami Buchholz, "GM Vehicles Talk the Talk," *Automotive Engineering International*, 114(2) (February 2006): 46; Daniel Abelow, "Networking Subsystems: Products That Talk," *Data Communications* (March 21, 1993): 90.

9. Susan Bardi Kleiser, Eugene Sivadas, James J. Kellaris, and Robert F. Dahlstrom, "Ethical Ideologies: Efficient Assessment and Influence on Ethical Judgments of Marketing Practices," *Psychology & Marketing*, 20(1) (January 2003): 1; Betsy Peterson, "Ethics Revisited," *Marketing Research: A Magazine of Management & Applications*, 8(4) (Winter 1996): 47– 48. For research design in an ethical context, see Grace T-R Lin and Jerry Lin, "Ethical Customer Value Creation: Drivers and Barriers, "*Journal of Business Ethics*, 67(2006): 93–105.

10. Barry Janoff, "Can Nascar Be Numero Uno with Hispanic Fans, Marketers?" *Brandweek*, 48(29) (August 2007): 10; Barry Janoff, "Daytona 500 Marketing on Track," *Brandweek*, 48(7) (February 2007): 14; and Leigh Somerville, "In the Driver's Seat: NASCAR Seeks Diversification," *The Business Journal*, 5(49) (August 8, 2003): 11.

Chapter 4

1. Lucia Moses, "Papers Get Bigger Piece of Ad Pie," *Editor & Publisher*, 136(44) (December 8, 2003): 5; Anonymous, "Secondary Source Materials," *Database*, 21(5) (October–November 1998): 20; Joe Nicholson, "Report for the Vindicator," *Editor & Publisher*, 132(38) (September 18, 1999): 38.

2. Marissa Fajt, "Frost Offers Video Interpretation Program for Deaf," *American Banker,* 172(175): 4; Anuradha Raghunathan, "Changes May Come for Texas Banks; Market Stunted by Savings-and-Loan Crisis," *Knight Ridder Tribune Business News* (October 30, 2003): 1; John F. Waldron, "Pat Frost Out to Build Stronger Connections South of the Border," *San Antonio Business Journal*, 16(30) (August 16, 2002): B25; Bill Stoneman, "Banking on Customers," *American Demographics*, 19(2) (February 1997): 36–41.

3. Joseph S. Rabianski, "Primary and Secondary Data: Concepts, Concerns, Errors, and Issues," *The Appraisal Journal*, 71(1) (January 2003): 43–55; John Chapman, "Cast a Critical Eye: Small Area Estimates and Projections Sometimes Can Be Dramatically Different," *American Demographics*, 9 (February 1987): 30. See also Charles Blankson and Stavros P. Kalafatis, "Positioning strategies of international and multicultural-oriented service brands," *Journal of Services Marketing*, 21(6) (2007): 435– 450.

4. Based on Beth Snyder Bulik, "Is There an Expensive Washing Machine in Your Future?" *Advertising Age,* 78(44) (November 5, 2007): 10; Gary H. Anthes, "Portal Powers GE Sales," *Computerworld*, 37(22) (June 2, 2003): 31; Pamela L. Moore, "GE Catches Online Fever," *BusinessWeek*, 3694 (August 14, 2000): 122; Andy Cohen, "General Electric," *Sales & Marketing Management* 149(11) (October 1997): 57.

5. www.news-record.com/apps/pbcs.dll/article?AID=/20060928/ NEWSREC0101/60928005/-1/NEWSREC0201, accessed January 27, 2008.

6. Martin Michalowski, Snehal Thakkar, and Craig A. Knoblock, "Automatically Utilizing Secondary Sources to Align Information Across Sources," *AI Magazine*, 26(1) (spring 2005): 33– 43. Stephen B. Castleberry, "Using Secondary Data in Marketing Research: A Project That Melds Web and Off-Web Sources," *Journal of Marketing Education*, 23(3) (December 2001): 195–203; Diane K. Bowers, "The New Research Tool," *Marketing Research: A Magazine of Management & Applications*, 10(3) (fall 1998): 34, 38.

7. www.Lexixnexis.com, accessed January 12, 2008; Helen Jezzard, "Lexis-Nexis Responds to User Demands," *Information World Review*, 173 (October 2001): 2.

8. Based on www.att.com, accessed January 14, 2008; and Society of Competitive Intelligence Professionals, "What Is Competitive Intelligence?" www.scip.org/ci, accessed July 27, 2007; Jim Underwood (2002), *Competitive Intelligence*, Oxford, UK: Capstone Publishing, pp. 56–59.

9. O. Malik, "eBay's China Syndrome" (2006), http://gigaom.com/2006/07/24/ebays-china-syndrome, accessed January 10, 2008; W. Mulligan, "Online Auction Market in China: eBay/EachNet vs. Yahoo!/Taobao" (2006), http://china.seekingalpha.com/ article/14162', accessed January 10, 2008; "EBay changes its Strategy in China: Giant eBay Loses Ground to Taobao," www.icmr.icfai.org/Business%20Updates/micro%20casestu dies/Business%20Strategy/MCBS0010.htm, accessed January 10, 2008; www.chinataiwan.org/web/webportal/W5023951/ Ushaotian/A463003.html, accessed January 10, 2008.

10. Laurence Ashworth and Clinton Free, "Marketing Dataveillance and Digital Privacy: Using Ethical Theories of Justice to Understand Consumers' Online Privacy Concerns," *Journal of Business Ethics,* 67 (spring 2006): 107–123; "Five New House Bills Highlight Privacy Concerns," http://directmag.com/news/marketing_five_ new_house/index. html, accessed August 27, 2007; California Office of Privacy Protection, "California Privacy Legislation," http://privacyprotection.ca.gov/califlegis.htm, accessed August 27, 2007.

11. Mark Ritson, "Hilfiger Has Learned the Hard Way," *Marketing* (May 17, 2006): 19; Tara Croft, "Tommy Hilfiger Seeks Targets," *The Daily Deal* (May 9, 2003): na; http://tommyhilfiger.com, accessed January 9, 2008.

Chapter 5

1. Based on Joseph Carroll, "'Business Casual' Most Common Work Attire: Women More Likely than Men to Wear Formal Business Clothing on the Job," *Gallup Poll Briefing* (October 4, 2007): 1–5; Anonymous, "Casual Monday-Through-Friday," *Adweek,* 48(40) (November 5, 2007): 60; Cyndee Miller, "A Casual Affair: Clothesmakers Respond to Dress-down Trend with New Lines, Consumer Education Programs," *Marketing News,* 29(6) (March 13, 1995): 1–2.

2. http://www.synovate.com, accessed, May 31, 2008.

3. www.gallup-robinson.com, accessed January 15, 2008; www.wzzm13.com/news/news_article.aspx?storyid=64189, accessed January 15, 2008; www.imediaconnection.com/ content/10165.asp, accessed January 15, 2008; www.daimlerchrysler.com/Projects/c2c/channel/documents/ 991609_dcx_2007_ir_releases_70214_cg_e.pdf, accessed January 15, 2008.

4. www.bigresearch.com, accessed June 22, 2007.

5. Anonymous, "Nielsen Takes First Step in Measuring Multi-format TV Audiences," *Faultline*, 179 (November 8, 2006): 7–9; Rick Wartzman, "Nielsen Ratings Spark a Battle over Just Who Speaks Spanish," *Wall Street Journal* (February 25, 2000): B1.

6. www.infores.com, accessed January 10, 2008; and Mike Duff, "Supercenters, Super-Results: Format Dominates Food-Sector," *Retailing Today,* 46(9) (June 4, 2007): 12–14.

7. www.acnielsen.com, accessed January 10, 2008.

8. www.gfkauditsandsurveys.com, accessed February 4, 2008.

9. Anonymous, "Campbell Soup," *The Wall Street Journal* (Eastern edition), 250(120) (November 20, 2007): B6; Lori Dahm, "V8 V.Fusion: A Healthy History," *Beverage Industry*, 97(10) (October 2006): 36; and Joanne Lipman, "Single-Source Ad Research Heralds Detailed Look at Household Habits," *The Wall Street Journal* (February 16, 1988): 39.

10. Paul Hannon, "European Consumers Lift Spending," *Wall Street Journal* (Eastern edition), 249(128) (June 2, 2007): A8; "Electrolux Q2 Profits Higher on Better Product Mix; Beats Market Forecasts," Update July 17, 2007, www.forbes.com/afxnewslimited/feeds/afx/2007/07/17/afx3919960.html, accessed August 28, 2007; David Smith, "A Deficit of Consumer Loyalty," *Management Today* (July 1996): 22; "Europeans More Active as Consumers," *Marketing News* (October 6, 1991): 17.

11. Anonymous, "AT&T U-Verse Launches Interactive Features in Bay Area," *RBOC Update,* 18(12) (December 2007): 8; Anonymous, "iTV: Still Finding Its Place within the New Media Mix," *New Media Age* (October 30, 2003): P16; Tim Greene, "Bell Atlantic Expands Beyond Local Data Market," *Network World*, 17(25) (June 19, 2000): 48; "Bell Atlantic TV, Mail Push Backs DirecTV," *Advertising Age*, 70(13) (March 29, 1999): 31; Richard Tedesco, "Bell Atlantic's ITV Scorecard," *Broadcasting & Cable*, 126(9) (February 26, 1996): 52; Debra Aho Williamson, "Two-Way, Interactive TV Panels," *Advertising Age* (May 1, 1995): 26.

12. Katy Bachman, "Arbitron, Nielsen Face Off In Out-of-Home TV Ratings," *MediaWeek*, 17(29) (August 6, 2007): 6; Anonymous, "Ratings Broken? Demand Better," *Advertising Age*, 74(49) (December 8, 2003): 22; Donna Petrozzello, "Arbitron Moves to Offer Audio Measuring," *Broadcasting & Cable*, 126(36) (August 26, 1996): 38; Steve McClellan, "New Nielsen System Is Turning Heads," *Broadcasting* (May 18, 1992): 8.

13. Barbara Mueller, "Just Where Does Corporate Responsibility End and Consumer Responsibility Begin? The Case of Marketing Food to Kids Around the Globe," *International Journal of Advertising*, 26(4) (2007): 561–564; Rob Gray, "Perils of Sending Brands to School," *Marketing* (April 22, 1999): 30–31; Kevin Heubusch, "Is It Ok to Sell to Kids?" *American Demographics*, 19(1) (January 1997): 55.

14. Michael Sanson, "What's It Going to Take to Fix Boston Market?" *Restaurant Hospitality*, 91(9) (September 2007):6; and www.bostonmarket.com/newsroom/index.jsp?page=pressReleases&subPage=2003/060403, accessed January 15, 2008; www.bostonmarket.com/newsroom/index.jsp?page= pressReleases&subPage=2003/012003, accessed January 15, 2008.

Chapter 6

1. http://retail.seekingalpha.com/article/43498, accessed August 7, 2007; William Symonds, "Can Gillette Regain Its Edge?" *BusinessWeek*, 3867 (January 26, 2004): 46; Charles Forelle, "Gillette to Launch Vibrating Razor," *The Wall Street Journal* (Eastern edition), 243(11) (January 16, 2004): A8; Anonymous, "RB to Launch 'Bladeless' Female Razor," *Marketing Week* (November 6, 2003): 9.

2. Rosaline Barbour, *Doing Focus Groups*, Thousand Oaks: Sage Publications, 2008; Judith Langer, "'On' and 'Offline' Focus Groups: Claims, Questions," *Marketing News*, 34(12) (June 5, 2000): H38; Richard Cook, "Focus Groups Have to Evolve if They Are to Survive," *Campaign-London* (July 9, 1999): 14; Howard Furmansky, "Debunking the Myths About Focus Groups," *Marketing News*, 31(13) (June 23, 1997): 22.

3. David Stewart, *Focus Group: Theory and Practice,* 2d ed., Thousand Oaks: Sage Publications, 2006; Elizabeth Dinan, "Focus Group Firm Uses Web for Efficiency, Size," *Mass High Tech*, 21(51) (December 22, 2003): 3; Lynn Vincent, "Seven Deadly Sins of Focus Groups," *Bank Marketing*, 31(5) (May 1999): 36–39; John M. Hess and R. L. King, eds., "Group Interviewing," *New Science of Planning*, Chicago: American Marketing Association, 1968, p. 4.

4. www.markettools.com/resources/files/CS_DelMonte.pdf, accessed July 14, 2007.

5. "'We've Picked up the Pace': Intel CEO Otellini Forecasts Profit Growth Outpacing Revenue in 2007, '08," Market Watch from DOWJONES, www.marketwatch.com/news/story/intel-ceo-sees-profit-gains/story.aspx?guid=%7B8B1D5398–2B83–49AA-94D7–33E34BFA2F6D%7D, accessed January 23, 2008; "The Times 100—Case Studies for Intel," (March 24, 2007), www.thetimes100.co.uk/case_study.php?cID=85&csID=227&pID=1, accessed June 17, 2007; Intel in Healthcare, "Intel in Healthcare Overview," http://download.intel.com/healthcare/pdf/Intel_in_Healthcare_Brochure.pdf, accessed May 30, 2007.

6. Mike Beirne, "Mars Attacks! Preps Flood of SKUs as Hershey Reels," *Brandweek*, 48(42) (November 19, 2007): 12; Mike Beirne, "Mars Gets Hot and Spicy for Hispanic Consumers," *Brandweek*, 44(21) (May 26, 2003): 10; Kennedy Carol, "The Chocolate Wars: Inside the Secret Worlds of Mars and Hershey," *Director*, 52(9) (April 1999): 80; Judann Pollack, "Mars Says Milky Way Lite Eating Up the Competition," *Advertising Age*, 67(40) (September 30, 1996): 28.

7. Kevin Wilson, "Panoply of Porsches Past," *AutoWeek*, 57(49) (December 3, 2007): 48–50, Alex Taylor, III, "Porsche Risky Recipe," *Fortune*, 147(3) (February 17, 2003): 91; Chris Reiter, "Porsche to Offer Cheaper Version of Hot SUV," *The Wall Street Journal* (Eastern edition), 242(42) (August 28, 2003): D2: Alex Taylor, III, "Porsche Slices Up Its Buyers," *Fortune*, 131(1) (January 16, 1995): 24.

8. Anonymous, "Fear of Flying," *Economist,* 383 (8542) special section (June 16, 2007): 3–5, Jill Dunning, "Fear of Flying: White-Knuckle Ride," *Director*, 57(4) (November 2003): 51; "Fear of Flying, *The Economist*, 339(7966) (May 18, 1996): 30.

9. Jens Flottau, "Bullish on Iberia," A*viation Week & Space Technology*, 167(4) (July 23, 2007): 42; Anonymous, "Airlines Brief: Iberia," *The Wall Street Journal* (February 3, 2003): C11; John Pollack, "Iberia Eyes Americas," *Advertising Age* (Midwest Region Edition) (April 27, 1992): 114.

10. Scott D. Wells and Elizabeth A. Dudash, "Wha'd'ya Know? Examining Young Voters' Political Information and Efficacy in the 2004 Election," *American Behavioral Scientist*, 50(9) (May 2007): 1280 –1289, Joan Obra, "Political Mudslinging Makes Money for Media Companies," *Knight Ridder Tribune Business News* (August 20, 2003): 1; S. Banker, "The Ethics of Political Marketing Practices, The Rhetorical Perspective," *Journal of Business Ethics*, 11 (1992): 843–848. For the role of qualitative research in ethics research, see Chong Ju Choi, Tarek I. Eldomiaty, and Sae Won Kim, "Consumer Trust, Social Marketing and Ethics of Welfare Exchange," *Journal of Business Ethics* 74 (2007): 17–23.

11. www.lotus.com, accessed January 18, 2008; www-3.ibm.com/software/swnews/swnews.nsf/n/jmae5n7sjh?OpenDocument&Site=default, accessed January 18, 2008; and J. Nicholas Hoover, "Lotus' Leap," *InformationWeek*, 1123 (January 29, 2007): 29–31.

Chapter 7

1. Based on www.pg.com and www.olay.com, accessed February 4, 2008; Louise Jack, "P&G Rebrands Laundry Products to Encourage People to Rewear Clothes," *Marketing Week,* 30(46) (November 15, 2007): 8; "1993 Edison Best New Products Awards Winners," *Marketing News* (April 25, 1994): E5.

2. Anonymous, "Pizza Hut," *Nation's Restaurant News,* 41(41) (October 15, 2007): 36; Chad Ruben, "Pizza Hut Explores Customer Satisfaction," *Marketing News*, 30(7) (March 25, 1997): 15.

3. Based on www.altamontemall.com, accessed January 12, 2008; and www.prnewswire.com/cgi-bin/stories.pl?ACCT=104&STORY=/www/story/09–14–1999/0001021344&EDATE, accessed June 21, 2007.

4. Based on Anonymous, "Soup's On," *Restaurants & Institutions*, 115(17) (September 15, 2005): 63–68; Stephanie Thompson, "Campbell Can Latest Soup Effort," *Advertising Age*, 71(32) (July 31, 2000): 1–2; "Campbell Soup's Stockpot Makes Appointments to Its Sales Teams," *Nation's Restaurant News*, 33(5) (February 1, 1999): 48; "1996 Saw Record Number of New Products," *Quirk's Marketing Research*, 11(2) (February 1997): 27–30.

5. "Accessibility Technology in Computing," www.microsoft.com/enable/research/default.aspx, accessed March 27, 2007.

6. Anonymous, "Starbucks Soars in China," *Asia Times Online Chinese Business* (June 15, 2006), www.atimes.com/atimes/China_Business/HF15Cb06.html, accessed June 20, 2007.

7. Anonymous, "Flexible Furniture for Flexible Space," *Building Design & Construction,* 48(3) (March 2007): 42–45; Anne Marie Moss, "The Office of the Future," *FDM, Furniture Design & Manufacturing*, 69(8) (August 1997): 36–42; "Ignore Your Customers," *Fortune* (May 1, 1995): 121–122, 124, 126.

8. www.porticoresearch.com, accessed January 5, 2008; Barbara Benson, "Market Researcher Wins Clients with Documentaries," *Crain's New York Business*, 17(17) (April 23, 2001): 31. See also Lorne McMillan and Brends

Ng, "Ethnography Within Consumer Research—a Critical Case Study of Consumer Film Festivals," *International Journal of Market Research*, 49(6) (2007): 707–714.

9. "Europeans Slow to Move on Obesity Concerns—New Report Reveals Data on Attitudes to Controlling Obesity," (2006), www.kraftfoods.co.uk/kraft/page?siteid=kraft-prd&locale=uken1&PagecRef=2420&Mid=2420&cache=off&Print=Yes, accessed June 18, 2007.

10. Dick Bucci, "The New Best Way to Measure Customer Satisfaction," *Call Center Magazine*, 18(11) (November 2005): 44; Nina M. Ray and Sharon W. Tabor, "Cybersurveys Come of Age," *Marketing Research*, 15(1) (Spring 2003): 32; Gordon A. Wyner, "Collaborative Filtering: Research or IT?" *Marketing Research: A Magazine of Management & Applications*, 10(3) (fall 1998): 35–37; Peter J. DePaulo and Rick Weitzer, "Interactive Phone Technology Delivers Survey Data Quickly," *Marketing News* (June 6, 1994): H33–H34.

11. Thomas R. Shaw, "The Moral Intensity of Privacy: An Empirical Study of Webmasters' Attitudes," *Journal of Business Ethics*, 46(4) (September 2003): 301; Lou E. Pelton, Jhinuk Chowdhry, and Scott J. Vitell, Jr., "A Framework for the Examination of Relational Ethics: An Interactionist Perspective," *Journal of Business Ethics*, 19(3) (Part 2) (April 1999): 241–253; Marla Royne Stafford and Thomas F. Stafford, "Participant Observation and the Pursuit of Truth: Methodological and Ethical Considerations," *Journal of the Market Research Society*, 35 (January 1993): 63–76.

12. Based on Lincoln Spector, "Block Spying Cookies, But Keep the Helpful Ones," *PC World,* 25(6) (June 2007): 134; Michael Bazeley, "Internet Users Have Ways to Reclaim Privacy," *Knight Ridder Tribune Business News* (April 17, 2003): 1; Ellen Messmer, "ISP Software Tracks Customers' Every Move," *Network World*, 14(39) (September 29, 1997): 17. For the use of surveys in ethics research see John Cherry, "The Impact of Normative Influence and Locus of Control on Ethical Judgments and Intentions: A Cross-Cultural Comparison," *Journal of Business Ethics,* 68 (2006): 113–132.

13. Anonymous, "Microsoft Enters Small-Business VoIP Market," *TelecomWeb News Break* (October 3, 2007): 2; Renee Boucher Ferguson, "Automating the Back Office: Netledger, Microsoft Aim Updates at Smaller Firms," *eWeek* (August 4, 2003): 1.

Chapter 8

1. www.muzak.com, accessed January 7, 2008; Ayala Ben-Yehuda, "Marketing via Muzak," *Billboard*, 119(32) (August 11, 2007): 16; James J. Farrell, "Merchandising Music," *Clergy Journal*, 79(4) (February 2003): 14; Colleen Bazdarich, "A Buying Mood? Maybe It's the Muzak," *Business 2.0*, 3(3) (March 2002): 100.

2. Deborah Vence, "Point of Purchase Displays," *Marketing News*, 41(18) (August 1, 2007): 8; Matthew Valentine, "And the Overall Winner Is . . . the P-O-P Sector," *In-Store Marketing* (November 2003): 15; Rachel Miller, "In-Store Impact on Impulse Shoppers," *Marketing* (November 21, 2002): 27–28; Ken Gofton, "POP Moves Up the Charts," *Marketing* (POP & Field Marketing Supplement) (April 17, 1997): XI.

3. Harper Roehm and Michelle Roehm, "The Relationship Between FSI Advertising Style and Coupon Redemption,"

Marketing Letters, 18(4) (October 2007): 237–247; Robert W. Shoemaker and Vikas Tibrewala, "Relating Coupon Redemption Rates to Past Purchasing of the Brand," *Journal of Advertising Research*, 25 (October–November 1985): 40–47.

4. Other forms of test marketing are controlled and minimarket tests, simulated test marketing, electronic test marketing, virtual test marketing, and Web-enabled test marketing. For details, see Chapter 7 of Naresh K. Malhotra, *Marketing Research: An Applied Orientation,* Fifth edition, Upper Saddle River, NJ: Prentice Hall, 2007.

5. Eric Pfanner, "Pepsi's Counterintuitive Branding Strategy," *The International Herald Tribune* (February 19, 2007), online at www.iht.com, accessed April 20, 2008; Jon Lafayette, "Life's a Virtual Beach for Pepsi; MTV Takes Steps into Online Space with Series Tie-In," *Television Week* (April 23, 2007): 29–30; "Pepsi-Cola Unveils New Global Look and Marketing Approach," PepsiCo News Release (January 12, 2007); "Pepsi Turns Over Its New Design To . . . You," PepsiCo News Release (April 4, 2007).

6. Beth Mattson-Teig, "Malls Add Virtual Shopping," *Retail Traffic*, 36(10) (October 2007): 112–113; Laurence N. Gold, "Virtual Reality Now a Research Reality," *Marketing Research* (fall 1993): 50–51; Howard Schlossberg, "Shoppers Virtually Stroll Through Store Aisles to Examine Packages," *Marketing News* (June 7, 1993): 2.

7. Anonymous, "Levi's "Copper Jeans," *Creativity,* 15(5) (May 2007): 119; Fara Warner, "Levi's Fashions a New Strategy," *Fast Company,* 64 (November 2002): 48.

Chapter 9

1. John Consoli, "Olympians Might Not Be the Idols They Once Were," *Adweek,* 47(8) (February 20, 2006): 7; James P. Sterba, "Winter Olympics 2002: Annie and Wyatt, Where Are You?—Or Why the Gun-Happy U.S. Keeps Missing the Mark in the Olympic Biathlon," *The Wall Street Journal* (February 14, 2002): A6; "Olympics Big with Teens Around the World," *Quirk's Marketing Research* (March 1996), online at www.quirks.com, accessed January 9, 2004.

2. Bruce Sylvester, "Americans Fall Prey to Weight-Loss Supplement 'Hype'," www.healthfinder.gov/news/newsstory.asp?docID=535687, accessed August 21, 2007.

3. Jackie Calmes, "Glum Mood Bodes Ill for GOP," *The Wall Street Journal* (January 25, 2008): A3.

4. Chittum Ryan and Vauhini Vara, "A Mall Grows in San Francisco," *The Wall Street Journal* (Eastern edition), 248(80) (October 4, 2006): B1, B14; "The Malling of America," *Quirk's Marketing Research Review* (May 1990): 15.

5. Tony Lewin and Hans Greimel, "Nissan Hopes for Image Boost from GT-R," *Automotive News Europe,* 12(22) (October 29, 2007): 4; Tracey Boles, "Japanese Cars Move Up a Gear in Europe," *Knight Ridder Tribune Business News* (August 12, 2003): 1; Michele Martin, "Why Nissan Cars Are Sporty in the U.S. but Sensible in Europe," *Campaign-London* (July 4, 1997): 21.

6. James R. Heichelbech, "Ethics 101 Unabridged," *Marketing Research,* 15(1) (spring 2003): 45; Cheryl MacLellan and John Dobson, "Women, Ethics, and MBAs," *Journal of Business Ethics,* 16(11) (August 1997): 1201–1209; Ishmael Akaah, "Differences in Research Ethics Judgments Between Male and Female Marketing Professionals," *Journal of Business Ethics,* 8 (1989): 375–381. For the use of primary

scales in an ethical context, see Pat Auger, Timothy M. Devinney, and Jordan J. Louviere, "Using Best-Worst Scaling Methodology to Investigate Consumer Ethical Beliefs Across Countries," *Journal of Business Ethics* 70 (2007): 299–326.

7. Judy Leand, "New Balance Targets Dedicated Runners With NBx," *SGB*, 40(3) (March 2007): 10; Hilary Cassidy, "New Balance Ages Up; IMG Skates Off with Disson," *Brandweek*, 42(2) (January 8, 2001): 8.

Chapter 10

1. http://oscar.com/oscarnight/winners/index, accessed August 8, 2007; Richard Schickel, "Martin Scorsese," *Time,* 169(20) (May 14, 2007): 132; John Lippman, "Hollywood Research Official Resigns—Rivals Seen Seeking Turf in Movie-Tracking Surveys Long Controlled by NRG," *The Wall Street Journal* (September 23, 2002): B6; Shannon Dortch, "Going to the Movies," *American Demographics*, 18(12) (December 1996): 4–7; Joe Rapolla, "Music Finds an Audience If You Know How to Look," *Marketing News*, 29(18) (August 28, 1995): 17.

2. Anonymous, "Those Who Get It—and Those Who Just Don't," *Advertising Age,* 78(24) (June 11, 2007): 21; Kate Macarthur, "McD's Taps Timberlake for 'I'm Lovin' It' Tie-In," *Advertising Age*, 74(31) (August 4, 2003): 3; William Murphy and Sidney Tang, "Continuous Likability Measurement," *Marketing Research: A Magazine of Management & Applications*, 10(2) (summer 1998): 28–35; Ian Fenwick and Marshal D. Rice, "Reliability of Continuous Measurement Copy-Testing Methods," *Journal of Advertising Research*, 31(1) (February–March 1991): 23–29.

3. www.lexus.com, accessed January 19, 2008; Jennifer Saranow, "U.S. Cars Slip in Durability Study," *The Wall Street Journal* (Eastern edition), 248(34) (August 10, 2006): D1–D2; David Kiley, "Automobile Quality Surveys Disagree," *USA Today* (June 4, 2003): B4.

4. Naresh K. Malhotra, "A Scale to Measure Self-Concepts, Person Concepts and Product Concepts," *Journal of Marketing Research*, 18 (November 1981): 456–464. See also Lawrence C. Soley, "Semantic Differential Scales in Advertising Research: A Critical Appraisal," *AddedAmerican Academy of Advertising Conference Proceedings* (2006): 10–19; Julie H. Yu, Gerald Albaum, and Michael Swenson, "Is a Central Tendency Error Inherent in the Use of Semantic Differential Scales in Different Cultures?" *International Journal of Market Research*, 45 (second quarter 2003): 213.

5. Zumbo Yan Liu and D. Bruno, "The Impact of Outliers on Cronbach's Coefficient Alpha Estimate of Reliability: Visual Analogue Scales," *Educational & Psychological Measurement*, 67(4) (August 2007): 620–634; Adam Duhachek, Anne T. Coughlan, and Dawn Iacobucci, "Results on the Standard Error of the Coefficient Alpha Index of Reliability," *Marketing Science,* 24(2) (spring 2005): 294–301; William M. Rogers, Neal Schmitt, and Morelle E. Mullins, "Correction of Unreliability of Multifactor Measures: Comparison of Alpha and Parallel Forms Approaches," *Organizational Research Methods*, 5(2) (April 2002): 184–199; Kevin E. Voss, Donald E. Stem, Jr., and Stergios Fotopoulos, "A Comment on the Relationship Between Coefficient Alpha and Scale Characteristics,"

Marketing Letters, 11(2) (May 2000): 177; Robert A. Peterson, "A Meta-Analysis of Chronbach's Coefficient Alpha," *Journal of Consumer Research*, 21 (September 1994): 381–391.

6. Mark Peterson and Naresh K. Malhotra, "Measuring the Appraisal of Ad-Based Affect with Ad Promises," *Journal of Business Research*, 42 (1998), 227–239.

7. MasterCard Worldwide, "New MasterCard Worldwide Research Explores Strategic Role of Cities in Driving Global Commerce," News Release (June 18, 2007), www.mastercard.com/us/company/en/newsroom/pr_wcoc.html, accessed July 15, 2007.

8. Naresh K. Malhotra, *Marketing Research: An Applied Orientation*, 5th ed., Upper Saddle River, NJ: Prentice Hall, Inc., 2007.

9. Joan Marie McMahon and Robert J. Harvey, "Psychometric Properties of the Reidenbach–Robin Multidimensional Ethics Scale," *Journal of Business Ethics,* 72(1) (April 2007): 27–39; Saul Klein, "Marketing Norms Measurement: An International Validation and Comparison," *Journal of Business Ethics*, 18(1) (January 1999): 65–72; Anusorn Singhapakdi, Scott J. Vitell, Kumar C. Rallapalli, and Kenneth L. Kraft, "The Perceived Role of Ethics and Social Responsibility: A Scale Development," *Journal of Business Ethics*, 15(11) (November 1996): 1131–1140; R. Eric Reidenbach and Donald P. Robin, "A Response to 'On Measuring Ethical Judgments'," *Journal of Business Ethics*, 14 (February 1995): 159–162.

10. Jemima Bokaie, "Monster Awards £77m Global Ad Task to BBDO," *Marketing* (September 12, 2007): 2; Andrea L. Stape, "Job-Search Site Monster Gets Ready to Make Noise," *Knight Ridder Tribune Business News* (August 28, 2003): 1; John R. Rossiter, "The C-OAR-SE Procedure for Scale Development in Marketing," *International Journal of Research in Marketing*, 19(4) (December 2002): 305.

Chapter 11

1. Based on www.worldvision.org, accessed January 4, 2008; Maja Pawinska, "World Vision Raises Profile Among Scots," *PR Week* (May 23, 2003): 13; Greg Gattuso, Elaine Santoro, and George R. Reis, "Notebooks Open Hearts of Sponsors," *Fund Raising Management*, 27(10) (December 1966): 10–11.

2. Based on Anonymous, "Toons' Study Finds Kids Call the Shots in Buying Decisions," *Businessline* (February 12, 2003): 1; Paul Miller, "Tapping the Teen Market," *Catalog Age*, 20(8) (July 2003): 31; www.justkidinc.com, accessed February 15, 2008.

3. Based on Timothy R. Graeff, "Reducing Uninformed Responses: The Effects of Product-Class Familiarity and Measuring Brand Knowledge on Surveys," *Psychology & Marketing*, 24(8) (August 2007): 681–702; Janet M. Kelly and David Swindell, "The Case for the Inexperienced User: Rethinking Filter Questions in Citizen Satisfaction Surveys," *American Review of Public Administration*, 33(1) (March 2003): 91–109; Kenneth C. Schneider and James C. Johnson, "Link Between Response-Inducing Strategies and Uninformed Response," *Marketing Intelligence & Planning*, 12(1) (1994): 29–36; Del I. Hawkins and Kenneth A. Coney, "Uninformed Response Error in Survey Research," *Journal of Marketing Research* (August 1981): 373.

4. Steven Gray, "ConAgra Says Healthy Choice Can Be Tasty, Too," *The Wall Street Journal* (Eastern edition), 248(44) (August 22, 2006): B2; Sonia Reyes, "Healthy Choice for Ice Cream," *Brandweek*, 44(1) (January 6, 2003): 3; "Edison, American Marketing Association, Best New Product Awards," *Marketing News*, 31(6) (March 17, 1997): E5.

5. "America Airlines Comprehensively Manages Customer and Employee Feedback with Key Survey," www.KeySurvey.com, accessed June 1, 2007.

6. Based on www.kelloggs.com, accessed January 10, 2008; Sonia R. Reyes, "Kellogg's Goes Bananas for Healthier Corn Flakes," *Brandweek*, 45(1) (January 5, 2004): 4; Judann Pollack and Beth Snyder, "Kellogg's Shifts Two JWT Brands to Burnett in Rift," *Advertising Age*, 70(5) (February 1, 1999): 3, 44; "Edison, American Marketing Association, Best New Product Awards," *Marketing News*, 31(6) (March 17, 1997): E5.

7. Rating a brand on specific attributes early in a survey can affect responses to a later overall brand evaluation. For example, see Larry M. Bartels, "Question Order and Declining Faith in Elections," *Public Opinion Quarterly*, 66(1) (spring 2002): 67–79; Barbara A. Bickart, "Carryover and Backfire Effects in Marketing Research," *Journal of Marketing Research*, 30 (February 1993): 52–62.

8. Elizabeth Dean, Rachel Caspar, Georgina McAvinchey, Leticia Reed, and Rosanna Quiroz, "Developing a Low-Cost Technique for Parallel Cross-Cultural Instrument Development: The Question Appraisal System (QAS-04)," *International Journal of Social Research Methodology*, 10(3) (July 2007): 227–241; Robert A. Peterson, *Constructing Effective Questionnaires*, Thousand Oaks, CA: Sage, 2000; Elizabeth Martin and Anne E. Polivka, "Diagnostics for Redesigning Survey Questionnaires," *Public Opinion Quarterly*, 59(4) (winter 1995): 547–567; A. Diamantopoulos, Bodo B. Schlegelmilch, and Nina Reynolds, "Pretesting in Questionnaire Design: The Impact of Respondent Characteristics on Error Detection," *Journal of the Market Research Society*, 36 (October 1994): 295–314.

9. Based on Christina Passarielo, Sarah Nassauer, and Hanting Tang, "European Jewelers Engage in Global Battle for Brides," *The Wall Street Journal* (Eastern edition), 250(28) (August 3, 2007): B1–B2; Peter Coolsen, "Opinion Surveys Uncover Cultural Preferences," *Nonprofit World* 17(2) (March–April 1999): 17–18; Edgar P. Hibbert and Jonathan Liu, *International Market Research—A Financial Perspective*, Oxford: Blackwell Publishers Inc., 1996.

10. Howard J. Gershon and Gary E. Buerstatte, "The E in Marketing: Ethics in the Age of Misbehavior," *Journal of Healthcare Management*, 48(5) (September–October 2003): 292; Thomas Donalson and Thomas Dunfee, "When Ethics Travel: The Promise and Peril of Global Business Ethics," *California Management Review*, 41(4) (summer 1999): 45–63; R. W. Armstrong, "An Empirical Investigation of International Marketing Ethics: Problems Encountered by Australian Firms," *Journal of Business Ethics*, 11 (1992): 161–171. For questionnaire design in the context of ethics research, see Ian Phau and Garick Kea, "Attitudes of University Students Toward Business Ethics: A Cross-National Investigation of Australia, Singapore and Hong Kong," *Journal of Business Ethics,* 72 (2007): 61–75.

11. Anonymous, "Survey Shows: Customers Still Must Come First," *Aviation Week & Space Technology,* 165(1) (July 3, 2006): 58; Joseph Rydholm, "A Global Perspective," *Quirks Marketing Research Review* (November 2000), www.quirks.com/articles/article.asp?arg_ArticleId=623, accessed January 18, 2008.

Chapter 12

1. Based on www.pg.com, accessed February 11, 2008; Martin Croft, "Men's Toiletries Come of Age," *Marketing Week,* 22(16) (May 20, 1999): 40–41; "Edison, American Marketing Association, Best New Product Awards," *Marketing News,* 31(6) (March 17, 1997): E5.

2. Brenda S. Farrell, "2010 Census: Planning and Testing Activities Are Making Progress," *GAO Reports* (March 1, 2006): 1–22; Anonymous, "Gearing Up for 2010," *Forecast* 23(2) (February 2003): 11; Carol O. Rogers, "Census 2000 Update," *Indiana Business Review,* 75(1) (spring 2000): 12; "Just a Traditional Census," *U.S. News & World Report* (July 29, 1991): 10.

3. For the effect of sample frame error on research results, see Gregory B. Murphy, "The Effects of Organizational Sampling Frame Selection," *Journal of Business Venturing,* 17(3) (May 2002): 237; Seymour Sudman and Edward Blair, "Sampling in the Twenty-First Century," *Journal of the Academy of Marketing Science,* 27(2) (spring 1999): 269–277.

4. Miao Wang, Jiaxin Wang, and Jinlin Zhao, "An Empirical Study of the Effect of Customer Participation on Service Quality," *Journal of Quality Assurance in Hospitality & Tourism,* 8(1) (2007): 49–73; Todd Pack, "Orlando, Fla., Survey Finds Only a Quarter of Tourists Changing Plans," *Knight Ridder Tribune Business News* (April 1, 2003): 1; "Florida Travel Habits Subject of Phone Survey," *Quirk's Marketing Research Review* (May 1987): 10, 11, 31, 56, 60.

5. Based on Anonymous, "Coffee News: An Anniversary Promo; Two Cold Coffee Concoctions," *BusinessWorld* (July 10, 2003): 1; "Edison, American Marketing Association, Best New Product Awards," *Marketing News,* 31(6) (March 17, 1997): E11.

6. Alexis A. Palmer, Patti A. Freeman, and Ramon B. Zabriskie, "Family Deepening: A Qualitative Inquiry into the Experience of Families Who Participate in Service Expeditions," *Journal of Leisure Research,* 39(3) (third quarter 2007): 438–458; Penny Maher, Peter Higgs, and Nick Crofts, "Risk Behaviours of Young Indo-Chinese Injecting Drug Users in Sydney and Melbourne," *Australian and New Zealand Journal of Public Health,* 25(1) (February 2001): 50–54; Raymond F. Barker, "A Demographic Profile of Marketing Research Interviewers," *Journal of the Market Research Society* (July 1987): 279–292.

7. Ken Thomas, "New GM Poll Shows Americans Want Energy Independence," www.detnews.com/2005/autosinsider/0506/30/0auto-233063.htm, accessed April 10, 2008; John Gartner, "GM Resurrects the Electric Car," www.wired.com/cars/futuretransport/news/2007/01/72424, accessed April 10, 2008.

8. When the sampling interval, i, is not a whole number, the easiest solution is to use as the interval the nearest whole number below or above i. If rounding has too great an effect on the sample size, add or delete the extra cases.

9. www.tennis.com, accessed January 8, 2008; Lisa Granatstein, "Tennis Moves to Net Readers," *Mediaweek,* 8(44) (November 23, 1998): 32; "Readership Survey Serves Tennis Magazine's Marketing Needs," *Quirk's Marketing Research Review* (May 1988): 75–76.

10. Based on Anonymous, "Company Spotlight: BMW," *MarketWatch: Automotive* 6(12) (December 2007): 14–20; David Chris Reiter, "BMW Reports Increase in Net, Driven by New 5 Series Sedan," *The Wall Street Journal* (November 7, 2003): B2; "Edison, American Marketing Association, Best New Product Awards," *Marketing News,* 31(6) (March 17, 1997): E4.

11. Based on http://uma.chanel.com/home.php, accessed September 4, 2007; Laurel Wentz, Emma Hall, "Kidman to Appear in Chanel No. 5 Ads," *Advertising Age,* 75(3) (January 19, 2004): 17; Barbara Busch, "The Scent of Advertising," *Global Cosmetic Industry,* 171(6) (June 2003): 24; "Edison, American Marketing Association, Best New Product Awards," *Marketing News,* 31(6) (March 17, 1997): E4.

12. For the use of different nonprobability and probability sampling techniques in cross-cultural research, see N. L. Reynolds, A. C. Simintiras, A. Diamantopoulos, "Theoretical Justification of Sampling Choices in International Marketing Research: Key Issues and Guidelines for Researchers," *Journal of International Business Studies,* 34(1) (January 2003): 80–89; Humphrey Taylor, "The Very Different Methods Used to Conduct Telephone Surveys of the Public," *Journal of the Market Research Society,* 39(3) (July 1997): 421–432; Saeed Samiee and Insik Jeong, "Cross-Cultural Research in Advertising: An Assessment of Methodologies," *Journal of the Academy of Marketing Science,* 22 (summer 1994): 205–215.

13. Julie Anne Lee, Ellen Garbarino, and Dawn Lerman, "How Cultural Differences in Uncertainty Avoidance Affect Product Perceptions," *International Marketing Review* 24(3) (2007): 330–349; B. J. Verhage, U. Yavas, R. T. Green, and E. Borak, "The Perceived Risk Brand Loyalty Relationship: An International Perspective," *Journal of Global Marketing,* 3(3) (1990): 7–22.

14. Daulatram B. Lund, "An Empirical Examination of Marketing Professional's Ethical Behavior in Differing Situations," *Journal of Business Ethics,* 24(4) (April 2000): 331–342; William A. Weeks, Carlos W. Moore, Joseph A. McKinney, and Justin G. Longenecker, "The Effects of Gender and Career Stage on Ethical Judgment," *Journal of Business Ethics,* 20(4) (Part 2) (July 1999): 301–313; Marshall Schminke and Maureen L. Ambrose, "Asymmetric Perceptions of Ethical Frameworks of Men and Women in Business and Nonbusiness Settings," *Journal of Business Ethics,* 16(7) (May 1997): 719–729; I. P. Akaah, "Differences in Research Ethics Judgments Between Male and Female Marketing Professionals," *Journal of Business Ethics,* 8 (1989): 375–381. For sampling in the context of ethics research, see William E. Shafer, Kyoko Fukukawa, and Grace M. Lee, "Values and the Perceived Importance of Ethics and Social Responsibility: The US versus China," *Journal of Business Ethics,* 70 (2007): 265–284.

15. Lars Brandle, "MTV Adopts Gold Standard," *Billboard* 119(50) (December 15, 2007): 19; Catherine Belton, Brian

Bremner, Kerry Capell, Manjeet Kripalani, Tom Lowry, Dexter Roberts, "MTV's World," *Business Week*, 3770 (February 18, 2002): 81; Gordon Masson, "MTV Availability Reaches 100 Million Mark in Europe," *Billboard*, 113(29) (July 21, 2001): 10–11.

Chapter 13

1. Based on "Study Finds Canadians Switching on to Internet, Tuning out TV and Radio" (July 31, 2007), www.cbc.ca, accessed August 9, 2007; Suzanne Vranica and Charles Goldsmith, "Nielsen Adapts Its Methods as TV Evolves," *The Wall Street Journal* (September 29, 2003): B1; Phillip E. Pfeifer, "The Economic Selection of Sample Sizes for List Testing," *Journal of Interactive Marketing*, 12(3) (summer 1998): 5–20; "The 'Infocritical' Eye," *Marketing Research: A Magazine of Management & Applications*, 9(1) (spring 1997): 37–39.

2. A discussion of the sampling distribution can be found in any basic statistics textbook. For example, see Mark L. Berenson, David M. Levine, and Timothy Krehbiel, *Basic Business Statistics: Concepts and Applications*, 10th ed., Englewood Cliffs, NJ: Prentice Hall, 2006.

3. Doug Olenick, "Customer Satisfaction Index: Majaps Brands Up, PCs Down," *TWICE: This Week in Consumer Electronics,* 22(17) (August 20, 2007): 16; Barbara Everitt Bryant and Jaesung Cha, "Crossing the Threshold: Some Customers Are Harder to Please Than Others, So Analyze Satisfaction Scores Carefully," *Marketing Research: A Magazine of Management & Applications*, 8(4) (winter 1996): 21–28.

4. www.hp.com/go/smallbusinessweek2005, accessed August 5, 2007.

5. Based on www.loreal.com and www.lancome.com, accessed January 7, 2008; Alexandra Jardine, "L'Oreal Puts Brands Under One Roof," *Marketing* (May 27, 1999): 4; "Edison, American Marketing Association, Best New Product Awards," *Marketing News*, 31(6) (March 17, 1997): E6.

6. "A First Look at 2007 Handset Sales," *Wireless Business Forecast* (May 3, 2007): 5; Hoovers, "Nokia Corporation (2007)," www.hoovers.com/nokia/—ID_41820—/free-co-factsheet.xhtml, accessed June 20, 2007; "What Mobile Gamers Say They Want," *Wireless Business Forecast* (January 12, 2007): 3.

7. Mark Halperin and Amy Sullivan, "How America Decides," *Time,* 170(25) (December 17, 2007): 38–41; Vicki G. Morwitz and Carol Pluzinski, "Do Polls Reflect Opinions or Do Opinions Reflect Polls? The Impact of Political Polling on Voters' Expectations, Preferences, and Behavior," *Journal of Consumer Research*, 23(1) (June 1996): 53–67. For sample size determination in the context of ethics research, see Sarah Steenhaut and Patrick van Kenhove, "An Empirical Investigation of the Relationship Among a Consumer's Personal Values, Ethical Ideology and Ethical Beliefs," *Journal of Business Ethics*, 64 (2006): 137–155.

8. Based on Vanessa L. Facenda, "P&G Sees Valuable Assets In $86M Charmin Relaunch," *Brandweek*, 48(37) (October 15, 2007): 5; Jack Neff, "P&G Brings Potty to Parties," *Advertising Age* (Midwest region edition), 74(7) (February 17, 2003): 22.

Chapter 14

1. Based on www.gallup.com, accessed January 4, 2008; Leah Nathans Spiro, "Gallup, the Pollster, Wants to Be Known for Its Consulting," *The New York Times* (July 21, 2003): C6; Gale D. Muller and Jane Miller, "Interviewers Make the Difference," *Marketing Research: A Magazine of Management & Applications*, 8(1) (spring 1996): 8–9.

2. Teresa Whitacre, "Behavioral Interviewing—Find Your STAR," *Quality Progress,* 40(6) (June 2007): 72–73; Ted Samson, "Interviewing 101—For Managers," *InfoWorld*, 22(13) (March 27, 2000): 101; Peggy Lawless, "Empathic Interviewing Equals Insightful Results," *Marketing News*, 33(1) (January 4, 1999): 20; Bud Phillips, "The Four Faces of Interviewers," *Journal of Data Collection*, 23 (winter 1983): 35–40.

3. "Household Appliance: Washers and Dryers—US," *MarketResearch.com* (August 1, 2006–February 24, 2007), online at www.marketresearch.com/product/display.asp?productid=1337663&SID=41184446–377143908–3365065 86&kw=whirlpool, accessed January 18, 2008; William Perreault and Jerome McCarthy, *Basic Marketing,* 15th ed., New York: McGraw-Hill, 2005.

4. Based on Christine Bittar, "Unilever Brushes Up Mentadent," *Brandweek*, 44(21) (May 26, 2003): 8; "Edison, American Marketing Association, Best New Product Awards," *Marketing News*, 31(6) (March 17, 1997): E6.

5. Based on Gemma Charles, "Mars Creates Smaller Versions of Countline Bars," Marketing (September 19, 2007): 3; Mary Carmichael, "Lite Version of Mars Launched in Australia," *Grocer*, 225(7573) (September 28, 2002): 66; "Edison, American Marketing Association, Best New Product Awards," *Marketing News*, 31(6) (March 17, 1997): E6.

6. "CalChamber Hosts European Union Ambassador John Bruton," (June 28, 2007), www.calchamber.com, accessed September 5, 2007; Janet Guyon, "Brand America," *Fortune*, 148(9) (October 27, 2003): 179; Laurel Wentz, "Poll: Europe Favors U.S. Products," *Advertising Age* (September 23, 1991): 16.

7. Jonathan Welsh, "Me and My Car," *The Wall Street Journal* (Eastern edition), 250(121) (November 21, 2007): D4; Michael McCarthy, "Nissan Xterra Discover Extra Success," *USA Today Online* (February 26, 2001), www.usatoday.com/money/index/2001–02–26-ad-track-nissan.htm#more, accessed January 28, 2008.

Chapter 15

1. Kathy Shwiff and Brian Coyle, "Sears, Vying for Restoration, Signs Confidentiality Pact," *The Wall Street Journal* (Eastern edition), 250(137) (December 11, 2007): A23; Deena M. Amato-McCoy, "Sears Combines Retail Reporting and Customer Databases on a Single Platform," *Stores*, 84(11) (November 2002): 26; Cyndee Miller, "Redux Deluxe: Sears Comeback an Event Most Marketers Would Kill for," *Marketing News*, 30(15) (July 15, 1996): 1, 14.

2. Piotr Chelminski and Robin A. Coulter, "The Effects of Cultural Individualism and Self-Confidence on Propensity to Voice: From Theory to Measurement to Practice," *Journal of International Marketing,* 15(4) (2007): 94–118; Jagdip Singh and Robert E. Wilkes, "When Consumers Complain: A Path Analysis of the Key Antecedents of Consumer

Complaint Response Estimates," *Journal of the Academy of Marketing Science*, 24 (fall 1996): 350–365.

3. See the SPSS, Excel, SAS, and Minitab manuals available for microcomputers and mainframes.

4. S. Chaudhuri, "Why Apple's iPhone Is Not the Next iPod," (2007), www.fastcompany.com/articles/2007/05/apple-iphone-not-next-ipod.html, accessed June 21, 2007.

5. Based on Carla Thornton, "Acer Gets Glossy; Lenovo Perfects Its Tablet," *PC World,* 25(10) (October 2007): 72; Geoffrey James "U.S. Computer Market: Where East Meets West," *Upside*, 8(12) (December 1996): 78–81.

6. www.a2ia.com, accessed April 10, 2008.

7. Daniel P. Lorence, "The Perils of Data Misreporting," *Association for Computing Machinery. Communications of the ACM*, 46(11) (November 2003): 85; Frederick Greenman and John Sherman, "Business School Ethics: An Overlooked Topic," *Business & Society Review* 104(2) (summer 1999): 171–177; Cheryl MacLellan and John Dobson, "Women, Ethics, and MBAs," *Journal of Business Ethics*, 16(11) (August 1997): 1201–1209; G. M. Zinkhan, M. Bisesi, and M. J. Saxton, "MBAs' Changing Attitudes Toward Marketing Dilemmas: 1981–1987," *Journal of Business Ethics*, 8(1989): 963–974. For data preparation in the context of ethics research, see Scott Vitell, Jatinder Singh, and Joseph Paolillo, "Consumers' Ethical Beliefs: The Roles of Money, Religiosity and Attitude Toward Business," *Journal of Business Ethics*, 73(4) (August 2007): 369–379.

8. Based on Vicki M. Young, "Calhoun Drops Interim Status at Banana Republic," *WWD: Women's Wear Daily,* 194(78) (October 12, 2007): 2; Alice Z. Cuneo, "Calhoun Takes Up Challenge to Revamp Banana Republic," *Advertising Age*, 74(24) (June 16, 2003): 22.

Chapter 16

1. Based on http://couponing.about.com/od/localcoupons/a/2006couponusage.htm; Susan K. Harmon and C. Jeanne Hill, "Gender and Coupon Use," *The Journal of Product and Brand Management*, 12(2/3) (2003): 166; Jack Neff, "Internet Enabling Coupon Fraud Biz," *Advertising Age*, 74(42) (October 20, 2003): 3–4; "Coupons, In-Store Promotions Motivate Consumer Purchasing," *Marketing News* (October 9, 1995): 6.

2. Anonymous, "MDs Seek PR Prescriptions," *Advertising Age,* 77(12) (March 20, 2006): 22; Daniel D. Butler and Avery M. Abernethy, "Yellow Pages Advertising by Physicians," *Journal of Health Care Marketing*, 16 (spring 1996): 45–50.

3. For our purposes, no distinction will be made between formal hypothesis testing and statistical inference by means of confidence intervals.

4. Technically, a null hypothesis cannot be accepted. It can be either rejected or not rejected. This distinction, however, is inconsequential in applied research.

5. www.ichotelsgroup.com/h/d/hi/1/en/home, accessed January 10, 2008.

6. Abbey Klaassen, "Ads for the People, by the People," *Advertising Age,* 77(9) (February 27, 2006): 1–59; Robin T. Peterson and Douglas T. Ross, "A Content Analysis of the Portrayal of Mature Individuals in Television Commercials," *Journal of Business Ethics*, 16 (1997): 425–433.

7. "General Mills and Curves International Partnership Delivers New Weight Management Food Brand," (May 8, 2007), www.midatlanticcurves.com/curves_cereal.htm, accessed September 5, 2007.

Chapter 17

1. Based on Ogenyi Omar and Sudaporn Sawmong, "Customer Satisfaction and Loyalty to British Supermarkets," *Journal of Food Products Marketing,* 13(2) (2007): 19–32; Peter J. McGoldrick and Elisabeth Andre, "Consumer Misbehavior: Promiscuity or Loyalty in Grocery Shopping," *Journal of Retailing and Consumer Services*, 4(2) (1997): 73–81.

2. Technically, a null hypothesis cannot be accepted. It can be either rejected or not rejected. This distinction, however, is inconsequential in applied research.

3. The condition when the variances cannot be assumed to be equal is known as the "Behrens–Fisher problem." Controversy exists as to the best procedure in this case.

4. American Express, "American Express Platinum Luxury Survey Shows Wealthy Gen X Consumers Are Mighty in Luxury Buying Power, Spending More Than Baby Boomer Population," http://home3.americanexpress.com/corp/pc/2005/genx_lux.asp, accessed August 1, 2007.

5. Based on Judy Leand, "Rockport Launches Torsion Comfort Footwear," *SGB*, 40(2) (February 2007): 14; Carol Krol, "Rockport Updates Image with Comfort Philosophy," *Advertising Age* (August 11, 1997): 6.

6. The F-test is a generalized form of the t-test. If a random variable is t distributed with n degrees of freedom, then t^2 is F distributed with 1 and n degrees of freedom. Where there are two factor levels or treatments, ANOVA is equivalent to the two-sided t-test.

7. Based on Anonymous, "Levi's Accelerates Comeback with 14% Increase in Profit," *Wall Street Journal* (Eastern edition), 250(8) (July 11, 2007): B5; Sandra O'Loughlin, "Levi Strauss, Sears Have It Their Way at Burger King," *Brandweek*, 45(25) (June 21, 2004): 5; Soo Youn, Soo, "Levi's New Signature Jeans Brand Seeks to Cure Company's Blues," *Knight Ridder Tribune Business News* (May 20, 2004): 1.

8. Glenn Haussman, "Desks Become Important Aspect in Laptop Culture," (June 18, 1999), www.hotelinteractive.com/news/articleView.asp?articleID=46, accessed January 8, 2008.

Chapter 18

1. Based on "The Adidas-group," www.adidas-group.com/en/News/archive/2006/default.asp, accessed July 11, 2007; Alfred Hille, "Sporting Heritage to Boost Adidas Profile," *Media* (February 27, 2004): 5; "Adidas: Earning Its Stripes in the U.S," *BusinessWeek Online* (October 13, 2003).

2. Mark Peterson and Naresh K. Malhotra, "Comparative Marketing Measures of Societal Quality of Life: Substantive Dimensions in 186 Countries," *Journal of Macromarketing*, 17(1) (spring 1997): 25–38. See also Raj Thomson, "There's No Place Like Home, Well Very Few," *Human Resources Magazine,* 12(2) (June–July 2007): 16–17.

3. In a strict sense, the regression model requires that errors of measurement be associated only with the criterion variable and that the predictor variables be measured without error.

4. Technically, the numerator is $b - \beta$. However, because it has been hypothesized that $\beta = 0.0$, it can be omitted from the formula.

5. Bryan K. Brenner, "Adopt a Marketing Model to Increase Client Satisfaction," *Journal of Financial Service Professionals,* 61(3) (May 2007): 8–10; Vikas Mittal, William T. Ross, Jr., and Patrick M. Baldasare, "The Asymmetric Impact of Negative and Positive Attribute-Level Performance on Overall Satisfaction and Repurchase Intentions," *Journal of Marketing,* 62(1) (January 1998): 33–47; Vikas Mittal and Patrick M. Baldasare, "Eliminate the Negative: Managers Should Optimize Rather Than Maximize Performance to Enhance Patient Satisfaction," *Journal of Health Care Marketing,* 16(3) (Fall 1996): 24–31.

6. "Wendy's Unveils Expansion Plans, Sports New Image," *BusinessWorld* (May 21, 2007): 1; Hoover Inc., "Sample Survey McDonald's Survey," (June 5, 2007), www.questionpro.com/akira/showSurveyLibrary.do? surveyID=189596, accessed June 7, 2007.

7. Tom Logue, "Minor League, Major Loyalty: Michigan Baseball Team Surveys Its Fans," *Quirk's Marketing Research Review* (October 2000), http://www.quirks.com/ articles/search.aspx?searchID=11015695, accessed April 22, 2008.

Chapter 19

1. www.united.com, accessed August 11, 2007; "United Airlines Enhances Easy Check-In Self-Service Units," *Airline Industry Information* (December 5, 2003): 1; Steve Raabe, "United Airlines Passengers Report Improvement in Customer Service," *Knight Ridder Tribune Business News* (December 20, 2002): 1; Joseph Rydholm, "Surveying the Friendly Skies," *Quirk's Marketing Research Review* (May 1996): 11, 33–35.

2. Michele D. Newhouse, "Writing Robust Reports," *Association Management,* 55(3) (March 2003): 83; Thomas L. Greenbaum, "Note to Clients: Hands Off Moderator Report," *Marketing News,* 31(13) (June 23, 1997): 22; Thomas L. Greenbaum, "Using 'Ghosts' to Write Reports Hurts Viability of Focus Group," *Marketing News,* 27(19) (September 13, 1993): 25.

3. Gillian Christie, "Golden Rules of Writing Well," *Chartered Accountants Journal,* 86(11) (December 2007): 60–61; Naomi R. Henderson, "In Defense of Clients," *Marketing Research: A Magazine of Management and Applications,* 15(2) (summer 2003): 38; Jeannine Bergers Everett, "Value-Added Research Begins Where the Marketplace Meets Management," *Marketing Research: A Magazine of Management and Applications,* 9(1) (spring 1997): 33–36.

4. Hewlett Packard, "HP Surveys Nation's Small Businesses to Learn What Fuels the Engines of Today's Economy," HP news release, www.hp.com/hpinfo/newsroom/press/2005/ 050427a.html, accessed June 19, 2007; Brian Bergstein, "HP extends Lead over Dell in PC Market," *International Business Times,* www.ibtimes.com/articles/20070117/ add-pc-shipments.htm, accessed July 17, 2007.

5. Gfk, "Consumers Changing the Ethical Business Agenda," (2007), www.gfk.com/imperia/md/content/businessgrafics/ pd_ethical_brands_international_efin_neu.pdf, accessed May 31, 2007.

6. Information provided by TNS.

7. Personal communication from Mary Klupp.

8. Sonja Koremans, "Auto Brands Flock to Sydney Motor Show," *B&T Weekly,* 57(2632) (October 12, 2007): 4; "Toyota Grabs Biggest Market Share in Australia in February," *Jiji Press English News Service* (March 6, 2003): 1; Lee Geoffrey, "Aussies Chicken Fries Ford," *Advertising Age* (January 18, 1993): 124.

9. Julie Ray, "Teens Zero in on War, Terrorism as Top Problems," (October 19, 2004), www.Gallup.com.

10. Anonymous, "States to Sue Reynolds American Over Cigarette Ad," *The Wall Street Journal* (Eastern edition), 250(132) (December 5, 2007): B4; Lindsey Tanner, "Tobacco Firms Put on Pressure," *Marketing News,* 36(19) (September 16, 2002): 44; Elise Truly Sautter and Nancy A. Oretskin, "Tobacco Targeting: The Ethical Complexity of Marketing to Minorities," *Journal of Business Ethics,* 16(10) (July 1997): 1011–1017; Kenman L. Wong, "Tobacco Advertising and Children: The Limits of First Amendment Protection," *Journal of Business Ethics,* 15(10) (October 1996): 1051–1064; S. Rapp, "Cigarettes: A Question of Ethics," *Marketing,* (November 5, 1992): 17. See also Waymond Rodgers and Susana Gago, "Biblical Scriptures Underlying Six Ethical Models Influencing Organizational Practices," *Journal of Business Ethics,* 64 (2006): 125–136.

11. Anonymous, "Subaru Sheds Rally Car Image," *Precision Marketing* (London) (October 2007): 5; Anonymous, "Subaru Uses Smart Television Spots by DDB to Help Launch the New 2008 Model Year Lineup—New Cars and Clever Creative Target Specific, Well-defined Audiences," *PR Newswire* (New York) (August 2007): n/a; Terry Box, "Subaru's Expansion Route Includes Solo Dealerships, Sporty Vehicles," *Knight Ridder Tribune Business News* (August 16, 2003): 1.

Photo Credits

Chapter 1, Page 28: Courtesy of Dan Galic/Alamy Images Royalty Free. Page 34: Courtesy of Chuck Nacke/Woodfin Camp & Associates, Inc. Page 38: Courtesy of Newscom. Page 49: Courtesy of Zhang Peng/OnAsia.com. Page 52: Courtesy of Samsonite Corporation.

Chapter 2, Page 58: Courtesy of PRNewsFoto/Subaru of America, Inc./Greg Jarem/Newscom. Page 72: Courtesy of Teri Stratford/Six-Cats Research Inc./© Teri Stratford. All rights reserved. Page 79: Courtesy of National Fluid Milk Processor Promotion Board. Page 83: Courtesy of Gene J. Puskar/AP Wide World Photos. Page 84: Courtesy of Frank LaBua/Pearson Education/PH College.

Chapter 3, Page 92: Courtesy of Teri Stratford/Six-Cats Research Inc./© Teri Stratford. All rights reserved. Page 105: Courtesy of David Young-Wolff/PhotoEdit Inc. Page 107: Courtesy of Teri Stratford/Six-Cats Research Inc./© Teri Stratford. All rights reserved. Page 112: Courtesy of Kyodo/Landov Media/Landov. Page 114: Courtesy of Steve Helber/AP Wide World Photos.

Chapter 4, Page 120: Courtesy of the Vidicator. Copyright 2008 the Vindicator Printing Co. Page 130: Courtesy of David Young-Wolff/PhotoEdit Inc. Page 140: Courtesy of U.S. Census Bureau. Page 145: Photo by Karl Prouse/Catwalking/Getty Images.

Chapter 5, Page 150: Courtesy of Bambu Productions/Getty Images—Creative Express. Page 158: Courtesy of Gucci America Inc. Page 168: Courtesy of Teri Stratford/Six-Cats Research Inc./© Teri Stratford. All rights reserved. Page 171: Courtesy of Boston Market Corporation. Page 174: Courtesy of eGo Vehicles, LLC.

Chapter 6, Page 176: Courtesy of Teri Stratford/Six-Cats Research Inc./© Teri Stratford. All rights reserved. Page 183: Photos, compliments of Campos Inc (Market Research and Strategic Marketing Consulting) Pittsburgh, PA, www.campos.com. Page 187: Courtesy of Billy E. Barnes/PhotoEdit Inc. Page 195: Courtesy of Teri Stratford/Six-Cats Research Inc./© Teri Stratford. All rights reserved. Page 198: Courtesy of Newscom. Page 202: Courtesy of AFP Photo/Files/Christophe Simon/Getty Images/ Newscom.

Chapter 7, Page 210: Courtesy of Teri Stratford/Six-Cats Research Inc./© Teri Stratford. All rights reserved. Page 218: Courtesy of Davis Barber/PhotoEdit Inc. Page 227: Courtesy of Teri Stratford/Six-Cats Research Inc./© Teri Stratford. All rights reserved. Page 235: Courtesy of Teri Stratford/Six-Cats Research Inc./© Teri Stratford. All

rights reserved. Page 238: Reprinted with permission from Microsoft Corporation.

Chapter 8, Page 242: Courtesy of David Young-Wolff/PhotoEdit Inc. Page 249: Courtesy of Davis Barber/PhotoEdit Inc. Page 254: Digital Photo by Adam Nemser/Photolink, www.photolink.org/Photo via Newscom. Page 264: Courtesy of Francis Dean/©Francis Dean/Dean Pictures/The Image Works. Page 266: Courtesy of Dave Gatley/Bloomberg News/Landov.

Chapter 9, Page 272: Courtesy of AP Photo/Dusan Vranic. Page 279: Courtesy of Jorge Uzon/Agence France Presse/Getty Images. Page 288: Courtesy of Joseph A. Rosen/Ambient Images. Page 291: Courtesy of Newscom. Page 293: Courtesy of New Balance Athletic Shoe, Inc.

Chapter 10, Page 300: Courtesy of the Kobal Collection/Warner Bros. Page 305: Courtesy of MSInteractive Multimedia Services/Copyright 2002 MSInteractive LLC. Page 307: Courtesy of Willie Von Recklinghausen/Toyota Motor Sales, USA, Inc./Lexus, a Division of Toyota Motor Sales, USA. Page 319: Courtesy of Joel Sartore/Getty Images. Page 321: Courtesy of Adrian Brown/Bloomberg News./Landov.

Chapter 11, Page 326: Courtesy of John Warren/World Vision USA, Inc. Page 334: Courtesy of Amy T. Zielinski/newscast/Newscom. Page 343: Courtesy of Richard Jones/Sinopix Photo/Agency Limited. Page 344: Courtesy of Lon C. Diehl/PhotoEdit Inc. Page 357: Courtesy of Jeff Greenberg/PhotoEdit Inc.

Chapter 12, Page 366: Courtesy of Teri Stratford/Six-Cats Research Inc./© Teri Stratford. All rights reserved. Page 377: Courtesy of Newscom. Page 383: Courtesy of Tennis Magazine. Page 384: Courtesy of BMW.

Chapter 13, Page 400: Courtesy of Cale Merege/Landov Media. Page 412: Courtesy of Julie Jacobson/AP Wide World Photos. Page 412: Courtesy of L.Yong/UNEP/Peter Arnold, Inc. Page 414: Courtesy of Tony Freeman Photographs. Page 417: Courtesy of Nokia. Page 419: Courtesy of Teri Stratford/Six-Cats Research Inc./© Teri Stratford. All rights reserved.

Chapter 14, Page 428: Courtesy of David Young-Wolff/PhotoEdit Inc. Page 432: Courtesy of David Young-Wolff/PhotoEdit Inc. Page 434: Courtesy of Teri Stratford/Six-Cats Research Inc./© Teri Stratford. All rights reserved. Page 436: Courtesy of Felicia Martinez/PhotoEdit Inc. Page 442: Courtesy of Newscom.

Name Index

Subject Index

Page numbers with f indicate figures; those with t indicate tables.

A

Acquiescence bias, 345
Acronyms
  DATA PREP, 472
  DEPTH, 207
  DESIGN, 116
  EXPERIMENT, 268–269
  FOCUS GROUPS, 207
  FOUR, 295
  METHODS, 240
  ORDER, 360
  PROBLEM, 88
  QUESTIONNAIRE, 359
  RATING, 323
  RESEARCH, 54
  SAMPLE, 395
  SCALES, 296
  SECOND, 147
  SIZE, 420
  TRAIN, 444
  VESTS, 444
  WORDS, 360
Adjusted R^2, 569–570
Advertising evaluation, 158–159
Advertising studies, 100–101
Aided-recall, 336
AIOs (activities, interests, and opinions), 157
All-exclusive words, 344
All-inclusive words, 344
Alternative hypothesis, 488
Analysis of variance (ANOVA), 529–534
  computer programs for, 547
  decompose the total variation, 530
  dependent and independent variables, identifying, 529–530, 529f
  effects, measuring, 531
  one-way analysis of variance, 531–533, 532t, 533t
    concept map for, 536t
  proportions, 533
  results, interpretation of, 531
  significance, testing, 531
Analytical models, 77
Analytical services, 43
Area sampling, 384
Area under the normal curve, 423
  statistical tables, 640t
Assistant project managers, 45
Association techniques, 196
Audilogs, 161
Audit, 165
Axioms, 76

B

Basic information, 346–347
Beta coefficient, 562
Beta weight, 562
Biasing questions, 344–345
Bibliographic databases, 137
Bivariate correlation, 551
Bivariate cross-tabulation, 493–494, 493–494t, 495t
Bivariate regression, 557, 561t
Bivariate regression analysis, 557–566, 558f
  assumptions, 565–566
  estimation of parameters, 559–561
  model, 557, 559f
  prediction accuracy, 565

scatter diagram, 558
  significance testing, 562–563
  standardized regression coefficients, 561–562
  strength and significance of association, 563–565
Blogs, 39
Branching questions, 348
Broad statement of the problem, 75–76
Budgeting and scheduling, 109
Buyer behavior, 70–71
Buying power index (BPI), 141

C

Calculated or observed value of the test statistic (TS$_{CAL}$), 491
Cartoon tests, 197
Case studies, 68
Casewise deletion, 461
Causal design, 104
  see also Causal research design
Causality, 245
  concept of, 244, 246
  conditions for, 246–247
  evidence and, role of, 247
Causal research, 104–105
Causal research design, 242–271
  overview of, 244, 244f, 245f
  summary illustration, 262–263
  see also Experimental designs; Experimentation
Census, 370
Central limit theorem, 404
Chi-square distribution, 496
  statistical tables, 641–642t
Chi-square statistic (χ^2), 495–497, 497f
Chi-square test of association, 497f
Classification information, 346–347
Client, 62
Clusters, 139, 384
Codebook, 456
Coding, 454–458
  data file, developing, 456–458, 456t
  of open-ended responses, 455
  SPSS variable of the data, 458t
  of structured and open-ended questions, 454–455
Coefficients
  alpha, 316
  beta, 562
  contingency coefficient *(C)*, 498
  correlation, 551–553
  of determination, 563
  of multiple determination, 569
  nonstandardized regression, 559
  partial regression, 567–569
  Pearson correlation, 551
  phi coefficient (ρ), 497
  standardized regression, 561–562
Collectively exhaustive, 279
Comparative scales, 284
Comparative scaling techniques, 285–288
  constant sum scaling, 287–288, 288f
  paired comparison scaling, 285–286, 285f
  rank order scaling, 286–287, 287f
Competitive analyses, 101
Competitive intelligence, 140
Completely automated telephone surveys (CATS), 441

Completion rate, 414
Completion techniques, 196–197
Computer-assisted personal interviewing, 219–220
  advantages and disadvantages of, 220
  telephone interviewing, 216
Computer-assisted personal interviewing (CAPI), 215, 219–220, 332, 333, 388, 465
Computer-assisted telephone interviewing (CATI), 216, 332, 333, 388, 465
Computerized databases, of secondary data, 135–138
  directories of, 138
  Internet, 136–137
  offline, 137
  online, 136
  types, categories of, 137–138
Computer mapping, 140
Conceptual map, 73
Conclusive design, 97
Conclusive research, 97
Concomitant variation, 246
Confidence intervals, 403, 406–413, 406f, 424f
  means, 407–410, 408t, 416f
  proportions, 408t, 410–413
Confidence level, 404
Confounding variables, 252
Constant sum scaling, 287–288
Construct, 314
Construction techniques, 197
Consumer perception and behavior studies, 100–101
Contingency coefficient *(C)*, 498
Contingency tables, 493
Control group (CG), 249, 255
Convergent validity, 317
Correlation coefficient, 551–553
Correlations
  computer programs for, 575–577, 583
  overview of, 550–551, 550f, 551f
  product moment correlation, 551–557, 554f, 554t, 555f
    concept map for, 573f
  SPSS Windows, 576–577, 583
  summary illustration, 572–573
Covariance, 552
Cramer's *V*, 498
Criterion variables, 316–317
Critical value, 491
  see also Probability
Critical value of the test statistic (TS$_{CR}$), 491, 524, 524f
Cronbach's alpha, 316
Cross-sectional designs, 101
Cross-tabulations, 492–499
  bivariate, 493–494, 493–494t, 495t
  categorical data analysis, 505
  computer programs for, 511
  concept map for, 502f
  contingency tables and, 493
  general comments on, 495
  in practice, 499, 499f
  software applications, 503–505
  SPSS Windows, 504–505, 511
  with two variables (bivariate cross-tabulation), 493–494, 493–494t, 495t

advantages and disadvantages of, 187–188
applications of, 191–192
characteristics of, 184t
discussion guide for pocket PCs, 185–186
interviews, 182–191
  vs. depth interviews, 194t
Focus-groups, conducting, 182–188
  discussion guide, preparing, 184–186
  environment, designing, 185
  focus-group report, preparing, 186
  group interview, conducting, 186
  moderator, selecting, 184
  participants, recruiting and selecting, 183–184
Focus-groups, online, 188–191
  advantages of, 190–191
  disadvantages of, 191
  vs. traditional focus groups, 190t
Footnotes, 593
Forced rating scale, 311
Frequency distribution analysis, 479–486
  of attitude, 480, 481–482t
  categorical data analysis, 505
  computer programs for, 511
  concept map for, 500f
  conducting, 480, 480f
  frequency histogram and, 482–483, 483t
  illegitimate responses and, 482
  measures of location, 484–485
  measures of variability, 485–486
  software applications, 503–505
  SPSS Windows, 503–504
Frugging, 237
F statistic, 522–523, 565
F-test, 522–523, 565
Full-service suppliers, 41
Full-text databases, 137
Functional magnetic resonance imaging (fMRI), 236
Funnel approach, 347–348, 347f

G

General surveys, 159
Geo-coding, 139
Geo-demographic coding, 139
Geo-visual databases, 140
Goodness-of-fit tests, 497
Graphical models, 77
Graphic rating scales, 304
Graphs, guidelines for, 593–596, 593t
  bar charts, 594
  geographic and other maps, 593
  histograms, 594, 595f
  line charts, 594, 595f
  pictographs, 594, 595f
  pie charts, 593–594, 594f
  schematic figures and flow charts, 596
Grounded theory, 195

H

Headings, 593
Histograms, 594, 595f
History *(H)*, 251
Humanistic inquiry, 228
Hypothesis (H), 78–79
Hypothesis testing, 512–547
  classification of, 492f
  concept map for, 501f
  data collection, 489–490
  Excel, 506
  formulating the hypothesis, 488
  general procedure for, 487–488, 487f
  introduction to, 487
  level of significance, choosing, 489, 490f
  marketing research conclusion, 491–492
  overview of, 514–515, 514–515f, 516f

probability, comparing and determining, 490–491, 491f
selecting an appropriate test, 489
SPSS, 503–505
summary illustration, 534
summary of, 533t
test statistic, 489
see also T-tests

I

Identification information, 346–347
Image studies, 101
Incidence rate, 413–414
Independent or predictor, 557
Independent samples, 520–526
  means, 521–525, 523t, 524f
  proportions, 525–526, 525t
Independent variables, 76, 248
Indirect approach, 182
Industry services, 166–167
Instrumentation *(I)*, 251
Interactive testing effects, 257
Interactive voice-response (IVR) technology, 236
Internal data, 128
Internal secondary data, 128–131, 129f
  combining with external, 138–141
Internal supplier, 40
Internal validity, 250
International marketing research
  causal research design, 264
  data preparation and analysis strategy, 463, 465
  descriptive research design, 233–235
  field work, 440
  marketing research problem, 82–83
  measurement, 290
  noncomparative scaling techniques, 319–320
  qualitative research, 201–202
  questionnaire and form design, 353–354
  research design, 111–112
  sample-size determination, 416–417
  sampling, 390–392
  secondary data, 141–143, 142f
  syndicated data sources, 169
Internet
  databases, 136–137
  marketing researchers and, 39
  marketing research on, 46
  project management and, 36–37
  services, 43
  syndicated services and, 161
Internet sampling, 388–390
  classification of, 389f
  issues, 388
  techniques, 388–390
Internet service provider (ISP), 67
Interviewer bias, 218
Invitation to bid (ITB), 44
Itemized rating scales, 305–310
  likert scale, 306–307
  semantic-differential scale, 307–309
  stapel scale, 309–310
  see also Noncomparitive itemized rating scale decisions
Item nonresponse, 341, 460

J

Junior-research analyst, 45

K

Key-informant technique, 66
"KISS 'em" principle, 597

L

Laboratory environment, 260
Leaders, 593

Lead-user survey, 66
Least-squares procedure, 558
Legal environment, 71
Letter of transmittal, 590
Level of significance, 489
Lifestyle, 157–158
Likert scale, 306–307
Limited-service suppliers, 43
Line charts, 594, 595f
Location, measures of, 484–485
  mean, 484
  median, 484
  mode, 484
  skewness of, 485f
Longitudinal designs, 102

M

Mail methods of survey, 220–222
  mail interviews, 220–221, 221t
  mail panels, 221–222
Mall-intercept personal interviews, 219
  advantages and disadvantages of, 219
Management-decision problem, 73–74
Market characteristic studies, 100, 101
Marketing information systems (MIS), 46–47, 46f, 47f
Marketing research, 28–57, 30
  application to contemporary issues, 49
  careers in, 44–46
  CEO's view of, 32
  classification of, 33–34, 33f
  on customer needs (case example), 631–636
  data, classification of, 180f, 182, 182f
  decision to conduct, 39–40
  defining, 30, 32f
  growth plan and implementation (case example), 620–624
  industry, overview of, 40–41, 43
  international, 49
  learning and growing through (video case), 56–57
  to maintain leadership position (case example), 625–630
  before making changes (case example), 616–617
  marketing decision making and, 37–39, 37f
  MIS and DSS and, 46–47, 46f, 47f
  overview of, 31, 31f
  positioning strategy and (case example), 618–619
  process, 35–37, 35f
    concept map for, 48f
  proposal, 109–110
  summary, 47–48
  technology and, 50
  using to gain competitive edge (case example), 609–613
Marketing research problem, 58–90
  analytical framework and models, 76–77
  buyer behavior and, 70–71
  concept map for, 82f
  development process, 63f
  economic environment and, 71–72
  information and forecasts and, past, 69–70
  information needed, specification of, 79–80
  legal environment and, 71
  management-decision problem and, 73–74, 73t, 74t
  marketing skills and, 72
  overview of, 60–61, 60f, 61f
  research questions and hypotheses, 78–79, 78f
  resource constraints and objectives and, 70
  SPSS Windows and, 85
  summary illustration of, 80–81, 82
  technological skills and, 72